Privacy and Human Rights 2005

An International Survey of Privacy Laws and Developments

Electronic Privacy Information Center
Washington, DC, USA

Privacy International
London, United Kingdom

ISBN: 1-893044-25-4

ISSN: 1559-4130

About the Electronic Privacy Information Center

The Electronic Privacy Information Center (EPIC) is a public interest research center in Washington, DC. It was established in 1994 to focus public attention on emerging civil liberties issues and to protect privacy, the First Amendment, and constitutional values. EPIC is a member of the Transatlantic Consumer Dialogue, the Global Internet Liberty Campaign, the Internet Free Expression Alliance and the Internet Privacy Coalition.

The EPIC Bookstore provides a comprehensive selection of books and reports on computer security, cryptography, the First Amendment and free speech, open government, and privacy. Visit the EPIC Bookstore at <http://www.epic.org/bookstore/>.

About Privacy International

Privacy International (PI) is a human rights group formed in 1990 as a watchdog on surveillance by governments and corporations. PI is based in London, England, and has an office in Washington, DC. PI has conducted campaigns throughout the world on issues ranging from wiretapping and national security activities to ID cards, video surveillance, data matching, police information systems, and medical privacy.

An electronic version of this report and updates are available from the EPIC web site at <http://www.epic.org> and the Privacy International web page at <http://www.privacyinternational.org/>.

EPIC Staff

Marc Rotenberg, Executive Director and President
David L. Sobel, General Counsel
Lillie Coney, Associate Director, Coordinator
    Privacy Coalition
Chris Jay Hoofnagle, Senior Counsel, Director
    EPIC West
Cédric Laurant, Policy Counsel, Director EPIC
    International Privacy Project
Marcia Hofmann, IPIOP Counsel, Director
    EPIC Open Government Project
Melissa Ngo, Staff Counsel
Sherwin Siy, IPIOP Staff Counsel
H. Kate Rears, Administrative Director
Ula Galster, International Policy Fellow
Katitza Rodríguez Pereda, International Policy Fellow
R. P. Ruiz, Technology Fellow
Harry Hammitt, Senior Fellow

Acknowledgments

This study was first undertaken by David Banisar, then EPIC Program Director, in 1997 and has been updated on an annual basis since. Sarah Andrews, Research Director at EPIC, and Gus Hosein, Senior Fellow at Privacy International, helped prepare the 2002 update. Cédric Laurant, EPIC Policy Counsel, coordinated the research for the 2003 and 2004 editions. EPIC Executive Director Marc Rotenberg was the chief editor for the 2002 through 2004 editions of the Privacy and Human Rights report. The 2005 edition of the *Privacy and Human Rights* report was produced by Marc Rotenberg (Editor in Chief), Cédric Laurant (Research Director), Ula Galster (Europe), and Katitza Rodríguez Pereda (Latin America). Melissa Ngo copy edited many sections of the report.

EPIC staff and the law students who have participated in the EPIC Public Interest Opportunities Program (IPIOP) provided substantial writing and research. The 2002 IPIOP Fellows were Nicole Anastasopoulos, Will DeVries, Marcia Hofmann, Dwayne Nelson, Carla Meninsky, Greg Pemberton, Sara Rose and Jason Young. The 2003 IPIOP Fellows were John Baggaley, Doug Barnes, Erik Blum, Eva Gutierrez, Milana Homsi, Waseem Karim, Heather Newton, Christian Schröder, Sherwin Siy, Tiffany Stedman, Liz Tockman, and Maryam Zafar. The

2004 IPIOP Fellows were Cliff Chen, Kenneth Farrell, Samantha ﹍
Mashayekhi, Patrick Mueller, Katherine Oyama, Olumide Owoo, A﹍, Dina
Tara Wheatland, and Paul Jones. The 2005 IPIOP Fellows were Mic﹍ Reid,
Charles Duan, Amina Fazlullah, Louisa Garib, Anthony Gray, Rak﹍piro,
Kristina Irion, Dhruv Kapadia, Jessica Meyers, Ibrahim Moiz, C﹍ey,
Súilleabháin, Yong Jin Park, Tori Praul, Guilherme Roschke, Kathry﹍
and Nerisha Singh.

To gather information for this study and previous editions, knowl﹍
individuals from academia, government, human rights groups and oth﹍
were asked to submit reports and information. Their reports were supple﹍
with information gathered from constitutions, laws, international and n﹍
government documents, news reports, human rights reports and other sourc﹍

EPIC and Privacy International would like to thank the following peopl﹍
providing invaluable reports, information and advice to various editions o﹍
Privacy and Human Rights survey: Reijo Aarnio, Data Protection Ombudsn﹍
Finland; Jason Abrams; Linda Ackerman, Privacy Activism, United Sta﹍
Andrzej Adamski, Nicolas Copernicus University, Poland; Ada Redonu﹍
Aguilera, www.cybernotarios.com, Guatemala; Yaman Akdeniz, University of
Leeds and Cyber-Rights & Cyber-Liberties, United Kingdom; Jair Rosales
Alegria, Guatemala; Guilherme Alberto Almeida, Kaminski, Cerdeira e Pesserl
Advogados Associados, Brazil; Ken Anderson, Information and Privacy
Commission of Ontario, Canada; Christian Hess Araya, Corte Suprema de
Justicia, Costa Rica; Fernando Argüello, El Salvador; Olesya Arkhypska,
International Renaissance Foundation, Ukraine; S. Artz, Dutch Data Protection
Authority, the Netherlands; Linda Austere, Center for Public Policy
"PROVIDUS," Republic of Latvia; Antonio M. Aveleyra Ortiz, Universidad
Iberoamericana, Mexico; Zuzana Babicová, Office for Personal Data Protection,
Slovak Republic; Maria Badeva University of Witwatersrand, South Africa;
Christoffer Badse, Danish Institute for Human Rights, Denmark; Elizabeth
Bakibinga, Ugandan Parliament, Uganda; Aiga Balode, Data State Inspection,
Republic of Latvia; Zsolt György Balogh, University of Pécs, Hungary; Andrej
D. Bartosiewicz, Association for Support of Local Democracy, Slovak Republic;
Nilgün Basalp, Istanbul Bilgi University, Turkey; Ralf Bendrath, Universität
Bremen, Germany; Colin Bennett, University of Victoria, Canada; Jacques
Berleur, Facultés Universitaires Notre-Dame de la Paix, Belgium; Mark
Berthold, Office of the Ombudsman, New Zealand; Humberto Carrasco Blanc,
Latlink.net, Chile; Diana Alonso Blas, College Bescherming Persoonsgegevens,
Netherlands; Renato Opice Blum, Opice Blum Advogados Associados, Brazil;
Joze Bogataj, Data Protection Inspectorate, Republic of Slovenia; Stefan Brands,

and McGill School of Computer Science, Canada; Ian Brown, Cre⊘n for Information Policy Research, United Kingdom; Mads Bryde Fo., University of Copenhagen, Denmark; Herbert Burkert, GMD, ⱨy; Heiner Busch, Switzerland; Beatriz Busaniche, Fundación Vía Libre, .ina; Lee Bygrave, Norwegian Research Centre for Computers and Law .utt for rettsinformatikk) and Faculty of Law, University of Oslo, Norway, ⱦr & McKenzie Cyberspace Law and Policy Centre and Faculty of Law, .versity of New South Wales, Australia; Rafael Fernández Calvo, CLI, Spain; .ine Carblanc, Organization for Economic Cooperation and Development, .rance; Alejandra Gils Carbó, Fiscal de la Cámara de Apelaciones, Argentina; Fred Carter, Privacy Commissioner's Office, Canada; David Casacuberta, Computer Professionals for Social Responsibility-Spain, Spain; Holanda Castro, Venezuela; Pavel Cerny, EPS, Czech Republic; Beng Seng Chan, Documentation for Action Groups in Asia, Hong Kong; Dmitry Chereshkin, Russian Academy of Natural Sciences, Russia; Chris Chiu, American Civil Liberties Union, United States; Kira Kolby Christensen, Legal Adviser, Datatilsynet, Denmark; Panageas Christos, City College, Greece; Tyng-Ruey Chuang, Taiwan Association of Human Rights, Taiwan; David Clancy, Information Commissioner's Office, United Kingdom; Richard Claude, United States; Julie Cohen, Georgetown University Law Center, United States; Tracy Cohen, Independent Communications Authority of South Africa; Martín Colombo, Uruguay; Carlos Vera, Corpece, Ecuador; Virgil Cristian Cristea, Institution of the Romanian People's Advocate, Romania; Bela Csiszer, Budapest University of Technology and Economics, Hungary; Iain Currie, University of Witwatersrand, South Africa; Paulo Renato Dallagnol, Brazil; Ulrich Dammann, Bundesbeauftragte für den Datenschutz, Germany; Dance Danailovska, Open Society Institute, Republic of Macedonia; Fany Davidova, Access to Information Programme, Bulgaria; Ian Deguara, Data Protection Commissioner's Office, Malta; Carlos E. Delpiazzo, Olivera & Delpiazzo, Uruguay; Ravi Dhar, Punjab Agricultural University, India; Alexander Dix, Commissioner for Data Protection and Access to Information (Brandenburg) Germany; Olena Dmytrenko, Ukraine; Ronnie Downes, Irish Data Protection Agency, Ireland; Pedro Dubie, AEDIP, Spain; Pavan Duggal, Cyberlaws.net, Cyberlaw Asia and Cyberlaw India, India; Alexandre Dulaunoy, Association Electronique Libre, Belgium; Jos Dumortier, Katholieke Universiteit of Leuven and Interdisciplinary Centre for Law and Information Technology, Belgium; Igor Dyadura, Ukrainian Internet Society, Ukraine; Kathy Eivazi, Australian National University, Australia; Bo Elkjaer, Denmark; Jón Erlendsson, Iceland; G.Erdenebat, Law School of NUM, Mongolia; Gal Eschet, University of California – Berkeley, United States; Alberto Escudero-Pascual, University of Dar es Salaam, Tanzania; Maria Farrell, International Chamber of Commerce, France; Emilio Aced Félez, Agencia de

Credentica and McGill School of Computer Science, Canada; Ian Brown, Foundation for Information Policy Research, United Kingdom; Mads Bryde Andersen, University of Copenhagen, Denmark; Herbert Burkert, GMD, Germany; Heiner Busch, Switzerland; Beatriz Busaniche, Fundación Vía Libre, Argentina; Lee Bygrave, Norwegian Research Centre for Computers and Law (Institutt for rettsinformatikk) and Faculty of Law, University of Oslo, Norway, Baker & McKenzie Cyberspace Law and Policy Centre and Faculty of Law, University of New South Wales, Australia; Rafael Fernández Calvo, CLI, Spain; Anne Carblanc, Organization for Economic Cooperation and Development, France; Alejandra Gils Carbó, Fiscal de la Cámara de Apelaciones, Argentina; Fred Carter, Privacy Commissioner's Office, Canada; David Casacuberta, Computer Professionals for Social Responsibility-Spain, Spain; Holanda Castro, Venezuela; Pavel Cerny, EPS, Czech Republic; Beng Seng Chan, Documentation for Action Groups in Asia, Hong Kong; Dmitry Chereshkin, Russian Academy of Natural Sciences, Russia; Chris Chiu, American Civil Liberties Union, United States; Kira Kolby Christensen, Legal Adviser, Datatilsynet, Denmark; Panageas Christos, City College, Greece; Tyng-Ruey Chuang, Taiwan Association of Human Rights, Taiwan; David Clancy, Information Commissioner's Office, United Kingdom; Richard Claude, United States; Julie Cohen, Georgetown University Law Center, United States; Tracy Cohen, Independent Communications Authority of South Africa; Martín Colombo, Uruguay; Carlos Vera, Corpece, Ecuador; Virgil Cristian Cristea, Institution of the Romanian People's Advocate, Romania; Bela Csiszer, Budapest University of Technology and Economics, Hungary; Iain Currie, University of Witwatersrand, South Africa; Paulo Renato Dallagnol, Brazil; Ulrich Dammann, Bundesbeauftragte für den Datenschutz, Germany; Dance Danailovska, Open Society Institute, Republic of Macedonia; Fany Davidova, Access to Information Programme, Bulgaria; Ian Deguara, Data Protection Commissioner's Office, Malta; Carlos E. Delpiazzo, Olivera & Delpiazzo, Uruguay; Ravi Dhar, Punjab Agricultural University, India; Alexander Dix, Commissioner for Data Protection and Access to Information (Brandenburg) Germany; Olena Dmytrenko, Ukraine; Ronnie Downes, Irish Data Protection Agency, Ireland; Pedro Dubie, AEDIP, Spain; Pavan Duggal, Cyberlaws.net, Cyberlaw Asia and Cyberlaw India, India; Alexandre Dulaunoy, Association Electronique Libre, Belgium; Jos Dumortier, Katholieke Universiteit of Leuven and Interdisciplinary Centre for Law and Information Technology, Belgium; Igor Dyadura, Ukrainian Internet Society, Ukraine; Kathy Eivazi, Australian National University, Australia; Bo Elkjaer, Denmark; Jón Erlendsson, Iceland; G.Erdenebat, Law School of NUM, Mongolia; Gal Eschet, University of California – Berkeley, United States; Alberto Escudero-Pascual, University of Dar es Salaam, Tanzania; Maria Farrell, International Chamber of Commerce, France; Emilio Aced Félez, Agencia de

2004 IPIOP Fellows were Cliff Chen, Kenneth Farrell, Samantha Liskow, Dina Mashayekhi, Patrick Mueller, Katherine Oyama, Olumide Owoo, Amanda Reid, Tara Wheatland, and Paul Jones. The 2005 IPIOP Fellows were Michael Capiro, Charles Duan, Amina Fazlullah, Louisa Garib, Anthony Gray, Rakeim Hadley, Kristina Irion, Dhruv Kapadia, Jessica Meyers, Ibrahim Moiz, Catherine Ó Súilleabháin, Yong Jin Park, Tori Praul, Guilherme Roschke, Kathryn Sheely, and Nerisha Singh.

To gather information for this study and previous editions, knowledgeable individuals from academia, government, human rights groups and other fields were asked to submit reports and information. Their reports were supplemented with information gathered from constitutions, laws, international and national government documents, news reports, human rights reports and other sources.

EPIC and Privacy International would like to thank the following people for providing invaluable reports, information and advice to various editions of the Privacy and Human Rights survey: Reijo Aarnio, Data Protection Ombudsman, Finland; Jason Abrams; Linda Ackerman, Privacy Activism, United States; Andrzej Adamski, Nicolas Copernicus University, Poland; Ada Redondo Aguilera, www.cybernotarios.com, Guatemala; Yaman Akdeniz, University of Leeds and Cyber-Rights & Cyber-Liberties, United Kingdom; Jair Rosales Alegria, Guatemala; Guilherme Alberto Almeida, Kaminski, Cerdeira e Pesserl Advogados Associados, Brazil; Ken Anderson, Information and Privacy Commission of Ontario, Canada; Christian Hess Araya, Corte Suprema de Justicia, Costa Rica; Fernando Argüello, El Salvador; Olesya Arkhypska, International Renaissance Foundation, Ukraine; S. Artz, Dutch Data Protection Authority, the Netherlands; Linda Austere, Center for Public Policy "PROVIDUS," Republic of Latvia; Antonio M. Aveleyra Ortiz, Universidad Iberoamericana, Mexico; Zuzana Babicová, Office for Personal Data Protection, Slovak Republic; Maria Badeva University of Witwatersrand, South Africa; Christoffer Badse, Danish Institute for Human Rights, Denmark; Elizabeth Bakibinga, Ugandan Parliament, Uganda; Aiga Balode, Data State Inspection, Republic of Latvia; Zsolt György Balogh, University of Pécs, Hungary; Andrej D. Bartosiewicz, Association for Support of Local Democracy, Slovak Republic; Nilgün Basalp, Istanbul Bilgi University, Turkey; Ralf Bendrath, Universität Bremen, Germany; Colin Bennett, University of Victoria, Canada; Jacques Berleur, Facultés Universitaires Notre-Dame de la Paix, Belgium; Mark Berthold, Office of the Ombudsman, New Zealand; Humberto Carrasco Blanc, Latlink.net, Chile; Diana Alonso Blas, College Bescherming Persoonsgegevens, Netherlands; Renato Opice Blum, Opice Blum Advogados Associados, Brazil; Joze Bogataj, Data Protection Inspectorate, Republic of Slovenia; Stefan Brands,

Protección de Datos, Spain; William G. Ferroggiard, National Security Archive, United States; Eric Fischer, Congressional Research Service, United States; Adriana Fleitas, Ferrere Abogados, Paraguay; Ádám Földes, Hungarian Civil Liberties Union, Hungary; Anne-Marije Fontein, College Bescherming Persoonsgegevens, Netherlands; Jeannine Forgues, Ferrere Abogados, Bolivia; Maurice Frankel, Campaign for Freedom of Information, United Kingdom; Gabor Freidler, Office of the Parliamentary Commissioner for Data Protection and Freedom of Information, Hungary; Tina Fugl, Danish Data Protection Agency, Denmark; Paula Jaramillo Gajardo, Derechos Digitales, Chile; Zoltan Galantai, Budapest University of Technology and Economics, Hungary; Miguel Angel Garcia, MAG (Estudios de Consumo), Spain; Robert Gellman, United States; Marie Georges, CNIL (Commission Nationale Informatique et Libertés), France; Rishab Aiyer Ghosh, India; Ann Goldsmith, Office of the Privacy Commissioner, Canada; Eric Goldstein, Human Rights Watch Middle East/North Africa, United States; Sybilla Graczyk, Association of Polish Consumers, Poland; Graham Greenleaf, University of New South Wales, Australia; Marina Gromova, Russia; Andrés Guadamuz, University of Edinburgh, Scotland; Robert Guerra, Privaterra, Canada; Valeriu Guguianu, Ministry of Public Information, Romania; Alex Hamilton, Liberty, United Kingdom; Aileen_Harrington, Office of the Data Protection Commissioner, Ireland; Edward Hasbrouck, United States; Pétur Hauksson, Mannvernd, Iceland; Bénédicte Havelange, Commission de la protection de la vie privée, Belgium; Helmut Heil, Bundesbeauftragte für den Datenschutz, Germany; Iceland; Hordur Helgi Helgason, Icelandic Data Protection Authority (Persónuvernd), Gunnel Helmers, Data Inspectorate of Norway; Dixie Ho, CIPPIC, University of Ottawa, Canada; Jan Holvast, Holvast and Partners, Netherlands; Masao Horibe, Chuo University School of Law, Japan; Axel Horns, FITUG e.V. (Förderverein Informationstechnik und Gesellschaft), Austria; Nóra Horváth, Office of the Commissioner for Data Protection and Freedom of Information, Hungary; Deborah Hurley, Harvard Information Infrastructure Project, United States; Pavol Husar, Commissioner for the Protection of Personal Data in Information Systems, Slovak Republic; Beatriz Iglesias, CPSR-Perú, Spain; Kristina Irion, EPIC Fellow; Germany Yutaka Ishikawa, Chuo University School of Law, Japan and Georgetown University School of Law, United States; Joichi Ito, Japan; Joel Jaakkola, Finland; Triinu Jaaksoo, Data Protection Inspectorate, Estonia; Ona Jakstaite, State Data Protection Inspectorate, Lithuania; Bardhyl Jashari, Foundation Metamorphosis, Republic of Macedonia; Rikke Frank Joergensen, Digital Rights, Denmark; Sigrún Jóhannesdóttir, The Icelandic Data Protection Commission, Iceland; Anna Johnston, Privacy & Information Management Consulting Salinger & Co, Australia; Barbara Jurgeleviciene, State Data Protection Inspectorate of the Republic of Lithuania, Lithuania; Neringa Kaktavičiūtė, State Data Protection

Inspectorate of the Republic of Lithuania, Lithuania; Omar Kaminski, Kaminski, Cerdeira e Pesserl Advogados Associados, Brazil; Jerry Kang, Georgetown University Law Center, United States; Myungkoo Kang, Seoul National University, South Korea; Marina Karakonova, Access to Information Programme, Bulgaria; Alexander Kashumov, Access to Information Programme, Bulgaria; Michael Kassner, Electronic Privacy Information Center, United States; Nurcan Kaya, Istanbul Bilgi University, Turkey; Yeoh Beng Keat, Ministry of Energy, Communications and Multimedia, Malaysia; Tinatin Khidasheli, Georgian Young Lawyers' Association, Georgia; Maarja Kirss, Data Protection Inspectorate, Estonia; Mindaugas Kiskis, Law University of Lithuania, Lithuania; Michalis Kitromilides, Office of the Personal Data Protection Commissioner, Cyprus; Jon Klaaren, Wits Law School, South Africa; Maija Kleemola, Office of Data Protection Ombudsman, Finland; Albert Koellner, VIBE!AT (Verein für Internet-Benutzer Österreichs), Neda Korunovska, Foundation Open Society Institute, Republic of Macedonia; Austria; Matej Kovacic, University of Ljubljana, Slovenia; Anita Kovalevska, Latvian National Human Rights Office, Republic of Latvia; Igor Kowalewski, The Bureau of the Inspector General for Personal Data Protection, Poland; Natalia Krajcovicova, Inspection Unit for the Protection of Personal Data, Slovak Republic; Artak Krakosyan, Civil Society Institute, Armenia; Andreas Krisch, VIBE!AT (Verein für Internet-Benutzer Österreichs), Austria; Dieter Kronegger, Arge Daten, Austria; Peter Kuhm, VIBE!AT (Verein für Internet-Benutzer Österreichs), Austria; Ewa Kulesza, Inspector General for Personal Data Protection, Poland; Jorma Kuopus, Office of the Parliamentary Ombudsman, Finland; Margarita Lacabe, Derechos Human Rights, United States; Anne-Christine Lacoste, Commission de la protection de la vie privée, Belgium; Gary Laden, Council of Better Business Bureaus, Inc., United States; Stephen Lau, former Hong Kong Privacy Commissioner, Hong Kong; Pierre-Emmanuel Laurant, Elsewhere Entertainment, Belgium; Pippa Lawson, Canadian Internet Policy and Public Interest Clinic (CIPPIC), Canada; Georg Lechner, Österreichische Datenschutzkommission, Austria; Anatoly Levenchuk, Russia; Vaida Linartaite, State Data Protection Inspectorate, Lithuania; Amalia Logiaki, Greek Data Protection Authority, Greece; Néstor Loizaga, Ferrere Abogados, Paraguay; Manon Lavoie, University of Ottawa, Canada; Yasha Maccanico, Statewatch, Spain; An Machtens, Commission de la protection de la vie privée, Belgium; Prathiba Mahanamahewa, University of Colombo, Sri Lanka; László Majtényi, Hungarian Information and Privacy Commissioner, Hungary; Piñar-Mañas, Agencia Española de Protección de Datos, Spain; Bogdan Manolea, Association for Technology and Internet (APTI), Romania; Romanian Information Technology Initiative, Romania; Veni Markovski, Internet Society Bulgaria, Bulgaria; Joe Meade, Data Protection Commissioner, Ireland; Arwid Mednis, partner Wierzbowski Eversheds, Poland;

Meryem Marzouki, Imaginons un Réseau Internet Solidaire, France; Viktor Mayer-Schönberger, Harvard University, United States; Robin McLeish, Hong Kong; Pedro Mendizábal Simonetti; Computer Professionals for Social Responsibility-Peru, Peru; Erich Moechel, Quintessenz, Austria; Andrea Monti, Studio Legale Monti, Italy; Christoph Mueller, University of Zurich, Switzerland; Ivonne Muñoz, Instituto Tecnológico y de Estudios Superiores de Monterrey (ITESM), México; Ioan Muraru, Avocatul Poporului, Romania; Dinesh Nair, Malaysia; Sjoera Nas, Bits of Freedom, Netherlands; Victor Naumov, Saint Petersburg Institute for Informatics RAS, Russia; Sally Neill, CPSR-Perú, Perú; Karel Neuwirt, Office for Personal Data Protection, Czech Republic; João Miguel Neves, Portugal; Detlef Nogala, Max-Planck-Institut, Germany; Bruno Nowak, Investlife, Luxembourg; Ts.Nyamkhuu, Open Society Forum, Mongolia; Mícheál O Dowd, Ireland; Nelly Ognyanova, Bulgarian Institute for Legal Development, Bulgaria; Toshimaru Ogura, Toyama University, Japan; Edetaen Ojo, Media Rights Agenda, Nigeria; Maia Okruashvili, Liberty Institute, Georgia; Ville Oksanen, Electronic Frontiers Finland, Finland; Kaidi Oone, Estonian State Chancellery, Department of State Information Systems, Estonia; Lina Ornelas, Directora General de Clasificación y Datos Personales - IFAI, México; Mercedes Ortuño, Agencia Española de Protección de Datos, Spain; Maxim Otstavnov, Computerra-Russia, Russia, Russia; Astrid Paiser Freshfields Bruckhaus Deringer,Austria; Pablo A. Palazzi, Habeas Data Forum, Argentina; Fereniki Panagopoulou, Humboldt University, Germany; Vagelis Papakonstantinou, University of Frankfurt, Germany; Iris Pappo, Eitan, Pearl, Latzer & Cohen-Zedek, Israel; Hugues Parasie, Commission de la protection de la vie privée, Belgium; Ginger Paque, Venezuela; Dragoslava Pefeva, Internet Society Bulgaria, Bulgaria; Marvin Carbajal Pérez, Costa Rica; Alberto Escudero-Pascual, Royal Institute of Technology, Sweden; Andriy Pazyuk, Privacy Ukraine, Ukraine; Marvin Carbajal Pérez, Costa Rica; Stephanie Perrin, Digital Discretion, Canada, and Electronic Privacy Information Center, United States; Charlotte Edholm Petersen, Datatilsynet, Denmark; Attila Péterfalvi, Commissioner for Data Protection and Freedom of Information, Hungary; Veronica Pinero, Ottawa University, Canada; Vladimir Pirosik, Environmental Lobbying Facility, Slovak Republic; Signe Plumina, State Data Inspection, Republic of Latvia; Erki Podra, Data Protection Inspectorate, Ukraine; Yves Poullet, Centre de Recherches Informatique et Droit, Belgium; Andrei Pribylov, Human Rights Network, Russia; Ivan Procházka, Office for Personal Data Protection, Czech Republic; Arturo Quirantes, University of Granada and Computer Professionals for Social Responsibility-Spain, Spain; Levan Ramishvili, Liberty Institute, Georgia; Felix Rauch, Swiss Internet User Group, Switzerland; Joel Reidenberg, Fordham University Law School, United States; Nelson Remolina Angarita, Universidad de Los Andes, Colombia;

Marcelo Bauzá Reilly, Uruguay; Katitza Rodríguez Pereda, Computer Professionals for Social Responsibility-Peru and Privaterra-Perú, Peru;Dorota Rowicka, Bureau of Inspector General for the Protection of Personal Data, Poland; Felipe Rodriquez, Electronic Frontiers Australia, Australia; Roman Romanov, International Renaissance Foundation, Ukraine; Anneliese Roos, University of South Africa, South Africa; Karen Rosier, Centre de Recherche Informatique et Droit, Belgium; Paul Roth, University of Otago, New Zealand; Narine Rshtuni, Civil Society Institute, Armenia; Claudio Ruiz, Derechos Digitales, Chile; Sinapan Samydorai, Think Centre, Singapore; Marina Savintseva, Transparency International-Russia, Russia; Dag Wiese Schartum, Eliane Schmid, Federal Data Protection Commissioner's Office, Switzerland; University of Oslo, Norway; Christian Schröder, Germany; Anat Scolnicov, Association for Civil Rights in Israel, Israel; Lindsay Scotton, Office of the Privacy Commissioner of Canada, Canada; Jin Wan Seo, University of Inchon, South Korea; Antonino Serra, Consumers International– Oficina para América Latina y el Caribe, Chile; Justyna Seweryoska, Bureau of the Inspector General for the Protection of Personal Data, Poland; Fumio Shimpo, University of Tsukuba, Japan; Maria U. Shkarlat, Internews-Ukraine, Ukraine; Alberto Cerda Silva, Derechos Digitales, Chile; Bernard Silva, Office of the Federal Privacy Commissioner, Australia; Pedro Mendizábal Simonetti, CPSR-Perú, Peru; Sergei Smirnov, Human Rights Network, Russia; Robert Ellis Smith, Privacy Journal, United States; Christoph Sobotta, University of Frankfurt, Germany; Daniel Soto, Amnesty International USA, Latin America; Per Helge Sørensen, Digital Rights Denmark, Denmark; Barry Steinhardt, American Civil Liberties Union, United States; Hana Stepankova, Office for Personal Data Protection, Czech Republic; Blair Stewart, New Zealand Privacy Commission, New Zealand; Filip Stojanovski, Foundation Metamorphosis, Republic of Macedonia; Bettina Stomper, Quintessenz, Austria; Laura Sukelyte, EU Phare Programme Twinning Project on Personal Data Protection, Republic of Lithuania; Helena Svatosova, Iuridicum Remedium, Czech Republic; Thordur Sveinsson, Personuvernd (Privacy and Data Protection Authority), Iceland; Iván Székely, Central European University, Hungary; Alina Szymczak, Inspector General for Personal Data Protection, Poland; Raymond Tang, Office of the Privacy Commissioner for Personal Data, Hong Kong; Gustavo Tanus, www.protecciondedatos.com.ar, Argentina; Jérôme Thorel, France; Simonas Toliu, Law University of Lithuania, Lithuania; Juan Antonio Travieso, Dirección Nacional de Protección de Datos Personales, Argentina; Kosmas Tsiraktsopulos, Swiss Data Protection Commission, Switzerland; Toivo Übi, Andmekaitse Inspektsioon, Estonia; Eduardo Ustaran, Berwin Leighton Paisner, United Kingdom; Daniel Valentovic, Office for Personal Data Protection, Slovak Republic; Mikko Valimaki, Electronic Frontiers Finland, Finland; Marie Vallée, Videotron, Canada; Shauna

Van Dongen, Privacy Journal, United States; Vasja Vehovar, University of Ljubljana, Slovenia; Ondrej Veis, Charles University, Czech Republic; Cristos Velasco, Instituto Tecnológico Autónomo de Mexico (ITAM), Mexico; Geetha Veloo, Malaysia; Maria José Viega, Estudio Viega Asociados, Uruguay; Elisabeth Wallin, The Data Inspection Board, Sweden; Nigel Waters, Pacific Privacy Consulting and Australian Privacy Charter Council, Australia; Raymond Wacks, The University of Hong Kong, Hong Kong; Elizabeth Jane Walsh, University College Cork, Ireland; Maurice Wessling, Bits of Freedom, Netherlands, and European Digital Rights; Peter Wilfling, Citizen and Democracy Association, Slovak Republic; Ingrid Wilson, Australian Privacy Commission, Australia; Niti Wirudchawong, Official Information Commission, Thailand; Bobson Wong, Digital Freedom Network, United States; Jason Young, Privaterra-Canada and Lex Informatica, Canada; Ko Youngkyoung, Social Information Networking Group, South Korea; Evhen Zakharov, Ukrainian Helsinki Human Rights Union, Ukraine.

Foreword

When EPIC and Privacy International first undertook to prepare a survey of privacy developments around the globe, we made a commitment to rigorous research, careful assessment, and a thoughtful comparison of how countries were responding to emerging challenges to civil liberties and human rights. We also sought to work closely with experts in the various regions. Our goal was not only to document significant developments concerning privacy and human rights, but also to support the development of networks among experts, government officials and human rights advocates that would make possible effective political responses.

Privacy and Human Rights began as modest project in 1997. It was inspired by the advocacy of Privacy International founder Simon Davies and the research expertise of then EPIC Policy Director David Banisar. With each edition of the report, we added new topics, new countries, and provided more in-depth analysis. EPIC Research Director Sarah Andrews and Gus Hosein, then Senior Fellow at Privacy International, took on the difficult work of assessing the response of national governments to the events of September 11, 2001. Then Cédric Laurant, Policy Counsel and Director of the EPIC International Privacy Project, undertook an ambitious and ultimately successful effort to expand the network of experts and the scope of the research, doubling in size the length of the annual report.

The 2005 edition of the *Privacy and Human Rights* report that you are now viewing is probably the most comprehensive single volume report published in the human rights field. The report covers more than 70 countries, runs almost 1,200 pages and includes about 6,000 footnotes. More than 200 experts from around the world have provided materials and commentary. The participants range from law students studying privacy to high-level officials charged with safeguarding constitutional freedoms in their countries. Academics, human rights advocates, journalists, and researchers from all across the world provided reports, insight, documents, and suggestions.

Our experts did not always agree. At times, we went back to source documents, the reports of governments, the acts of parliaments, the efforts of NGOs, to better understand privacy developments in a particular region of the world. No doubt, we made a few mistakes along the way.

Still, it is an amazing record of modern societies struggling to respond to new threats to public safety, seeking new opportunities for commerce, promoting new technologies while simultaneously safeguarding the rights of citizens, establishing new legal regimes, and responding to concerns of citizen organizations about the protection of fundamental human rights.

It would be tempting to say that the countries described in this report are seeking a "balance" among the competing claims of commerce and privacy, national security and civil liberties. However, the reality is more complex. In the best of cases, governments seek to safeguard security while preserving privacy. In the worst of cases, governments adopt measures that do little to promote security, but almost certainly erode civil liberties. In many cases, there is still not enough information to make a meaningful assessment.

If there is a message in these pages, it is that there is no simple equation that allows modern society to trade freedom for enhanced security. Each proposal must be considered on its merits. And if there is a second message, it is that citizens around the world still care deeply about the right of privacy, the right set out in the Universal Declaration of Human Rights in 1948, which is found in virtually every constitution of a modern nation state. How well governments succeed in protecting this fundamental right is the question that the annual *Privacy and Human Rights* report seeks to answer.

Financial support for the *2005 Privacy and Human Rights* report was provided by the Open Society Institute, the Ford Foundation, and the "On the Identity Trail Project" of the University of Ottawa School of Law, which is supported by Social Science and Humanities Research Council (SSHRC) of Canada. Support for the April 2006 gathering in the United States of the International Working Group on Data Protection in Telecommunicatins (IWGDPT) in Washington, DC was provided by the German Marshall Fund.

We are grateful to everyone who has helped make this report possible. As always, we welcome your suggestions.

Marc Rotenberg
EPIC Executive Director
rotenberg@epic.org
May 2006

Privacy and Human Rights 20

Executive Summary

This annual report by the Electronic Privacy Information Center International reviews the state of privacy in more than 70 countries world. It outlines legal protections for privacy, and summarizes imp the and events relating to privacy and surveillance. Each country report constitutional, legal and regulatory framework protecting privacy surveillance of communications by law enforcement, new landmark co most noteworthy advocacy work of non-governmental organizations an rights groups, various new developments, and major news stories rel privacy.

Many developments in this report have been prompted by governments' nee more security after the terrorist events of the last few years in Asia, Europe, Middle East and the United States. Many countries around the world h pursued policy and legislative efforts that aim at increasing the surveillan governments exert over individuals. They have done so by establishing c reinforcing identification schemes and monitoring individuals' communications. At the same time, governments relentlessly tried to weaken data protection regimes while intensifying the collection of information from public and private sources, and sharing it with an increasingly wider range of law enforcement and national security agencies.

1. Governmental measures against terrorism

Around the world, most governments have kept pursuing surveillance policies that the fight against terrorism legitimized. One of the most important trends has been the broader implementation of measures that ensure the identification of people crossing country borders. Many countries, following in the footsteps of the United States, released their own version of biometric machine-readable travel documents or passenger-profiling systems, relying on new technologies such as systems for fingerprints, iris scans, face recognition or radio frequency identification. In doing so, many of them are enabling the establishment of national ID schemes and biometric databases that, although they were originally conceived for foreigners, are likely to be extended to minorities, and later to all citizens.

This year, governments pursued the adoption of various new measures to respond to the threat of terrorism. Some were passed for legitimate purposes, others to provide law enforcement with new powers not in line with the original and specific objective of fighting against terrorism but were implemented and enforced later for different purposes. New laws provide for increased surveillance powers and sharing of intelligence information among government and others for the creation of new government agencies to specifically fight terrorism. However, many do not provide adequate oversight, and a recent trend is in a growing reliance by governments to delegate their tasks of collecting and storing information to the hands of private companies.

Other governmental measures

Governments have not limited themselves to deploying new surveillance measures that directly respond to the threats of terrorism. Recent areas of interest for surveillance technologies have included biometrics, smart cards, medical information databases, data mining and video surveillance. Most governments around the world increasingly relied on video surveillance technology for various public safety and law enforcement objectives, including to monitor public places and transportation means, and collect tolls.

More governments are deploying smart cards than in previous years and for a wide range of applications, from passports, driver's licenses and banking cards to patients' medical cards. Some are coupled with biometric information and may enable their holders to electronically interact with government agencies and benefit from e-government services. Such card systems seem to have been deployed first for minority populations, such as refugees and illegal foreigners, although some governments plan on rolling out the cards later for the entire population of the country. Much of the criticism they currently face has to do with the lack of adequate data protection laws in place in the country in which they are used and the higher risk of identity theft.

DNA and various medical information databases have kept growing during the last few years. Their use and scope have increased: more offenses and more individuals are likely to be included; longer retention periods are becoming more commonplace; law enforcement increasingly relies upon them to establish culpability; and some governments started creating national DNA databases. These databases are also increasingly being used for additional purposes, from social security and medical research to the monitoring of health care expenditures. They raise the highest risks to privacy when individuals have no

---

Privacy and Human Rights 2005

Executive Summary

This annual report by the Electronic Privacy Information Center and Privacy International reviews the state of privacy in more than 70 countries around the world. It outlines legal protections for privacy, and summarizes important issues and events relating to privacy and surveillance. Each country report covers the constitutional, legal and regulatory framework protecting privacy and the surveillance of communications by law enforcement, new landmark court cases, most noteworthy advocacy work of non-governmental organizations and human rights groups, various new developments, and major news stories related to privacy.

Many developments in this report have been prompted by governments' need for more security after the terrorist events of the last few years in Asia, Europe, the Middle East and the United States. Many countries around the world have pursued policy and legislative efforts that aim at increasing the surveillance governments exert over individuals. They have done so by establishing or reinforcing identification schemes and monitoring individuals' communications. At the same time, governments relentlessly tried to weaken data protection regimes while intensifying the collection of information from public and private sources, and sharing it with an increasingly wider range of law enforcement and national security agencies.

1. Governmental measures against terrorism

Around the world, most governments have kept pursuing surveillance policies that the fight against terrorism legitimized. One of the most important trends has been the broader implementation of measures that ensure the identification of people crossing country borders. Many countries, following in the footsteps of the United States, released their own version of biometric machine-readable travel documents or passenger-profiling systems, relying on new technologies such as systems for fingerprints, iris scans, face recognition or radio frequency identification. In doing so, many of them are enabling the establishment of national ID schemes and biometric databases that, although they were originally conceived for foreigners, are likely to be extended to minorities, and later to all citizens.

This year, governments pursued the adoption of various new measures to respond to the threat of terrorism. Some were passed for legitimate purposes, others to provide law enforcement with new powers not in line with the original and specific objective of fighting against terrorism but were implemented and enforced later for different purposes. New laws provide for increased surveillance powers and sharing of intelligence information among government agencies, others for the creation of new government agencies to specifically fight terrorism. However, many do not provide adequate oversight, and a recent trend has been a growing reliance by governments to delegate their tasks of collecting and storing information to the hands of private companies.

2. Other governmental measures

Governments have not limited themselves to deploying new surveillance measures that directly respond to the threats of terrorism. Recent areas of interest for surveillance technologies have included biometrics, smart cards, medical information databases, data mining and video surveillance. Most governments around the world increasingly relied on video surveillance technology for various public safety and law enforcement objectives, including to monitor public places and transportation means, and collect tolls.

More governments are deploying smart cards than in previous years and for a wide range of applications, from passports, driver's licenses and banking cards to patients' medical cards. Some are coupled with biometric information and may enable their holders to electronically interact with government agencies and benefit from e-government services. Such card systems seem to have been deployed first for minority populations, such as refugees and illegal foreigners, although some governments plan on rolling out the cards later for the entire population of the country. Much of the criticism they currently face has to do with the lack of adequate data protection laws in place in the country in which they are used and the higher risk of identity theft.

DNA and various medical information databases have kept growing during the last few years. Their use and scope have increased: more offenses and more individuals are likely to be included; longer retention periods are becoming more commonplace; law enforcement increasingly relies upon them to establish culpability; and some governments started creating national DNA databases. These databases are also increasingly being used for additional purposes, from social security and medical research to the monitoring of health care expenditures. They raise the highest risks to privacy when individuals have no control over when the genetic testing is conducted or how the results are used. Criticism has emerged on their legality or constitutionality, or the lack of public awareness about them.

Among the countries surveyed, a few have pursued drastic censorship measures as a means to control people's activities, from the monitoring of e-mails, telephone and fax communications, SMS, and Internet searching and browsing, to Internet filtering and interception of communications, and the surveillance of cybercafés.

3. Private sector surveillance

Around the world, private companies have engaged in various surveillance practices. Some of the most important technologies they have used are radio frequency identification (RFID) and video surveillance. RFID has become very popular in the private sector as a multipurpose tool for surveillance, tracking, security, product inventory, and supply chain management. Investment for the technology and the range of its potential applications are growing every day, from its use in libraries to manage book rentals to its use as a means of cashless payment. It is increasingly being promoted as a way to track individuals, starting with its use on foreign travelers, prisoners or other minority groups at borders and prisons, to recent surveillance schemes that monitor employees and government officers in the workplace or in connection with access to high-security areas. Although a useful technology in many of its applications, some of the applications of RFID raise major risks for people's privacy, especially where the technology enables extensive and surreptitious tracking of consumers and political protesters. Some legislators, government agencies and data protection authorities are now tackling its implications for people's privacy, and privacy activists groups have made the public more aware of the risks of the technology.

Although the use of video surveillance by private actors has kept increasing around the world in the last 12 months and in a wider range of settings, only a few countries have reacted by adopting safeguards to prevent abuses.

The fight against unsolicited commercial e-mails (spam) has pushed many countries to pass new laws while several bills are pending in other states. More European Union countries have transposed the Directive on Privacy and Electronic Communications, which constitutes the most important legislative effort to date that provides for a uniform legal solution to the issue of spam across jurisdictions. Other solutions are also being considered to fight the spam scourge as international organizations and governments intensified their work in the past year to foster collaboration on enforcement and prosecution, adopt technical measures and develop public awareness. At the same time, several anti-spam organizations, expert and company focus groups were created across the globe to defend their constituents' interests. Major case law further limited the intrusions of spam. Some data protection authorities also noticed that most of the complaints they had to handle concerned spam.

Many US companies that collect information from consumers and Internet users and thereafter sell it to third parties revealed, under legal obligations to disclose security breaches, that they had experienced serious data security breaches. These cases pointed to the high risk of processing data outside any data protection framework and the necessity to implement adequate security measures. They also highly increased the risk of identity theft cases in the years to come and had an impact on the trust Internet users put in e-commerce actors. Although the mismanagement of personal data was reported mostly in the United States, it has had repercussions around the world, including calls for lawmakers to strengthen data protection and security laws. Some Third World countries also experienced problems of fraud and identity theft in the sector of the business processing industry.

4. New data protection laws

Around the world, new laws have been enacted and many bills are pending to protect individuals' right to privacy and data protection. While all 25 countries of the European Union now have a harmonized set of data protection laws, most other countries that are regulating in the field of privacy are located in Asia and Latin America. They are generally following the EU data protection model. Last year, a European Directive ("on Privacy and Electronic Communications") was implemented in more EU countries compared to previous years, offering Internet and telecommunications users protections against spam and confidentiality for their communications.

5. Civil liberties groups and NGOs' successful opposition to privacy intrusions

Invasions of privacy were met in various countries with forceful reactions from human rights groups. In Australia, civil liberties advocates killed a government proposal for an extensive database using national census information. In Malaysia, the Human Rights Caucus of the Parliament and a group of citizens expressed their opposition to moral policing of behavior by state religious enforcement officials by asserting that it infringed individual privacy and personal dignity. In response to the opposition, the government told state Islamic departments that they must seek police permission before conducting raids on Muslims alleged to be committing immoral acts. In Thailand, police recently asked the government to enact a law permitting warrantless, judicially unsupervised wiretaps and searches. The opposition condemned this attempt to override civil liberties and human rights, and the idea did not develop. In the United States, after several years of opposition by civil liberties groups to government plans of passenger profiling, the "CAPPS II" air passenger profiling program was defeated.

6. Developments in open government

This year, most of the developments in open government concerned new laws or regulations (Ecuador, Macedonia, Uganda), pending laws (Germany, Guatemala, Mongolia, Nigeria, Sri Lanka), and new case law protecting the right to access to government information (e.g., Costa Rica), while the United Kingdom eventually fully implemented its Freedom of Information Act.

7. Actions of international governmental organizations

The actions of international governmental organizations, while having a definite impact on policies related to the fight against terrorism, have generally been out of the public eye. Those organizations have been very active, at a global level devoid of any democratic accountability, in developing counter-terrorism policy tools and mechanisms that have affected upcoming national policy discourse and laws aimed at combating terrorism. The Council of the European Union, for example, has been consistently pushing for new anti-terrorism measures harmonizing EU Member States' legal frameworks toward more powers for law enforcement without creating corresponding means of oversight and adequate privacy safeguards.

Summary Table of Contents

Table of Contents

Overview

Privacy is a fundamental human right. It underpins human dignity and other values such as freedom of association and freedom of speech. It has become one of the most important human rights of the modern age.[1]

Privacy is recognized around the world in diverse regions and cultures. It is protected in the Universal Declaration of Human Rights, the International Covenant on Civil and Political Rights, and in many other international and regional human rights treaties. Nearly every country in the world includes a right of privacy in its constitution. At a minimum, these provisions include rights of inviolability of the home and secrecy of communications. Most recently written constitutions include specific rights to access and control one's personal information. In many of the countries where privacy is not explicitly recognized in the constitution, the courts have found that right in other provisions. In many countries, international agreements that recognize privacy rights such as the International Covenant on Civil and Political Rights or the European Convention on Human Rights have been adopted into law.

Defining Privacy

Of all the human rights in the international catalogue, privacy is perhaps the most difficult to define.[2] Definitions of privacy vary widely according to context and environment. In many countries, the concept has been fused with data protection, which interprets privacy in terms of management of personal information.

Outside this rather strict context, privacy protection is frequently seen as a way of drawing the line at how far society can intrude into a person's affairs.[3] The lack of a single definition should not imply that the issue lacks importance. As one writer observed, "in one sense, all human rights are aspects of the right to privacy."[4]

---

[1] Marc Rotenberg, Protecting Human Dignity in the Digital Age (UNESCO 2000).

[2] James Michael, Privacy and Human Rights 1 (UNESCO 1994).

[3] Simon Davies, Big Brother: Britain's Web of Surveillance and the New Technological Order 23 (Pan 1996).

[4] Volio, Fernando, "Legal Pesonality, Privacy and the Family" in Henkin (ed), The International Bill of Rights (Columbia University Press 1981).

Some viewpoints on privacy:

In the 1890s, future United States Supreme Court Justice Louis Brandeis articulated a concept of privacy that urged that it was the individual's "right to be left alone." Brandeis argued that privacy was the most cherished of freedoms in a democracy, and he was concerned that it should be reflected in the Constitution.[5]

Robert Ellis Smith, editor of the *Privacy Journal*, defined privacy as "the desire by each of us for physical space where we can be free of interruption, intrusion, embarrassment, or accountability and the attempt to control the time and manner of disclosures of personal information about ourselves."[6]

According to Edward Bloustein, privacy is an interest of the human personality. It protects the inviolate personality, the individual's independence, dignity and integrity.[7]

According to Ruth Gavison, there are three elements in privacy: secrecy, anonymity and solitude. It is a state which can be lost, whether through the choice of the person in that state or through the action of another person.[8]

The Calcutt Committee in the United Kingdom said, "nowhere have we found a wholly satisfactory statutory definition of privacy." But the committee was satisfied that it would be possible to define it legally and adopted this definition in its first report on privacy:

> The right of the individual to be protected against intrusion into his personal life or affairs, or those of his family, by direct physical means or by publication of information.[9]

The Preamble to the Australian Privacy Charter provides, "A free and democratic society requires respect for the autonomy of individuals, and limits on the power of both state and private organizations to intrude on that autonomy . . . Privacy is a key value which underpins human dignity and other key values such as

---

[5] Samuel Warren and Louis Brandeis, The Right to Privacy, 4 Harvard Law Review 193-220 (1890).

[6] Robert Ellis Smith, Ben Franklin's Web Site 6 (Sheridan Books 2000).

[7] Privacy as an Aspect of Human Dignity, 39 New York University Law Review 971 (1964).

[8] Privacy and the Limits of Law, 89 Yale Law Journal 421, 428 (1980).

[9] Report of the Committee on Privacy and Related Matters, Chairman David Calcutt QC, 1990, Cmnd. 1102, London: HMSO, at 7.

freedom of association and freedom of speech. . . . Privacy is a basic human right and the reasonable expectation of every person."[10]

Aspects of Privacy

Privacy can be divided into the following separate but related concepts:

> **Information privacy**, which involves the establishment of rules governing the collection and handling of personal data such as credit information, and medical and government records. It is also known as "data protection";

> **Bodily privacy**, which concerns the protection of people's physical selves against invasive procedures such as genetic tests, drug testing and cavity searches;

> **Privacy of communications,** which covers the security and privacy of mail, telephones, e-mail and other forms of communication; and

> **Territorial privacy**, which concerns the setting of limits on intrusion into the domestic and other environments such as the workplace or public space. This includes searches, video surveillance and ID checks.

Models of Privacy Protection

There are four major models for privacy protection. Depending on their application, these models can be complementary or contradictory. In most countries reviewed in the survey, several models are used simultaneously. In the countries that protect privacy most effectively, all of the models are used together to ensure privacy protection.

Comprehensive Laws

In many countries around the world, there is a general law that governs the collection, use and dissemination of personal information by both the public and private sectors. An oversight body then ensures compliance. This is the preferred

---

[10] "The Australian Privacy Charter," published by the Australian Privacy Charter Group, Law School, University of New South Wales, Sydney (1994).

model for most countries adopting data protection laws and was adopted by the European Union to ensure compliance with its data protection regime. A variation of these laws, which is described as a "co-regulatory model," was adopted in Canada and Australia. Under this approach, industry develops rules for the protection of privacy that are enforced by the industry and overseen by the privacy agency.

Sectoral Laws

Some countries, such as the United States, have avoided enacting general data protection rules in favor of specific sectoral laws governing, for example, video rental records and financial privacy. In such cases, enforcement is achieved through a range of mechanisms. A major drawback with this approach is that it requires that new legislation be introduced with each new technology so protections frequently lag behind. The lack of legal protections for individual's privacy on the Internet in the United States is a striking example of its limitations. There is also the problem of a lack of an oversight agency. In many countries, sectoral laws are used to complement comprehensive legislation by providing more detailed protections for certain categories of information, such as telecommunications, police files or consumer credit records.

Self-Regulation

Data protection can also be achieved, at least in theory, through various forms of self-regulation, in which companies and industry bodies establish codes of practice and engage in self-policing. However, in many countries, especially the United States, these efforts have been disappointing, with little evidence that the aims of the codes are regularly fulfilled. Adequacy and enforcement are the major problem with these approaches. Industry codes in many countries have tended to provide only weak protections and lack enforcement.

Technologies of Privacy

With the recent development of commercially available technology-based systems, privacy protection has also moved into the hands of individual users. Users of the Internet and of some physical applications can employ a range of programs and systems that provide varying degrees of privacy and security of communications. These include encryption, anonymous remailers, proxy servers and digital cash.[11] Users should be aware that not all tools effectively protect privacy. Some are poorly designed while others may be designed to facilitate law enforcement access. (For more discussion of this subject, see the sub-section on Privacy Enhancing Technologies).

The Right to Privacy

The recognition of privacy is deeply rooted in history. There is recognition of privacy in the *Qur'an*[12] and in the sayings of Mohammed.[13] The Bible has numerous references to privacy.[14] Jewish law has long recognized the concept of being free from being watched.[15] There were also protections in classical Greece and ancient China.[16]

Legal protections have existed in Western countries for hundreds of years. In 1361, the Justices of the Peace Act in England provided for the arrest of peeping toms and eavesdroppers.[17] In 1765, British Lord Camden, striking down a warrant to enter a house and seize papers wrote, "We can safely say there is no law in this country to justify the defendants in what they have done; if there was, it would destroy all the comforts of society, for papers are often the dearest property any man can have."[18] Parliamentarian William Pitt wrote, "The poorest man may in his cottage bid defiance to all the force of the Crown. It may be frail; its roof may shake; the wind may blow through it; the storms may enter; the rain may enter – but the King of England cannot enter; all his forces dare not cross the threshold of the ruined tenement."[19]

Various countries developed specific protections for privacy in the centuries that followed. In 1776, the Swedish Parliament enacted the Access to Public Records Act that required that all government-held information be used for legitimate purposes. France prohibited the publication of private facts and set stiff fines for

---

[11] EPIC maintains a list of privacy tools at <http://www.epic.org/privacy/tools.htm>.

[12] *an-Noor* 24:27-28 (Yusufali); *al-Hujraat* 49:11-12 (*Yusufali*).

[13] Volume 1, Book 10, Number 509 (*Sahih Bukhari*); Book 020, Number 4727 (*Sahih Muslim*); Book 31, Number 4003 (*Sunan Abu Dawud*).

[14] Richard Hixson, Privacy in a Public Society: Human Rights in Conflict 3 (1987). *See also*, Barrington Moore, Privacy: Studies in Social and Cultural History (1984).

[15] *See* Jeffrey Rosen, The Unwanted Gaze (Random House 2000).

[16] *Id.* at 5.

[17] James Michael, *supra*, at 15. Justices of the Peace Act, 1361 (Eng.), 34 Edw. 3, c. 1.

[18] Entick v. Carrington, 1558-1774 All E.R. Rep. 45.

[19] Speech on the Excise Bill, 1763.

---

violators in 1858.[20] The Norwegian Criminal Code prohibited the publication of information relating to "personal or domestic affairs" in 1889.[21]

In 1890, American lawyers Samuel Warren and Louis Brandeis wrote a seminal piece on the right to privacy as a tort action, describing privacy as "the right to be left alone."[22] Following the publication, this concept of the privacy tort was gradually picked up across the United States as part of the common law.

The modern privacy benchmark at an international level can be found in the 1948 Universal Declaration of Human Rights, which specifically protects territorial and communications privacy.[23] Article 12 states:

> No one should be subjected to arbitrary interference with his privacy, family, home or correspondence, nor to attacks on his honour or reputation. Everyone has the right to the protection of the law against such interferences or attacks.

Numerous international human rights treaties specifically recognize privacy as a right.[24] The International Covenant on Civil and Political Rights (ICCPR), Article 17,[25] the United Nations (UN) Convention on Migrant Workers, Article 14,[26] and the UN Convention on Protection of the Child, Article 16[27] adopt the same language.[28]

---

[20] The Rachel *affaire*. Judgment of June 16, 1858, Trib. pr. inst. de la Seine, 1858 D.P. III 62. *See* Jeanne M. Hauch, Protecting Private Facts in France: The Warren & Brandeis Tort is Alive and Well and Flourishing in Paris, 68 Tulane Law Review 1219 (May 1994).

[21] *See* Prof. Dr. Juris Jon Bing, Data Protection in Norway, 1996, available at <http://www.jus.uio.no/iri/forskning/lib/papers/dp_norway/dp_norway.html>.

[22] Warren and Brandeis, *supra*.

[23] Universal Declaration of Human Rights, adopted and proclaimed by General Assembly resolution 217 A (III) of December 10, 1948, available at <http://www.un.org/Overview/rights.html>.

[24] *See generally*. Marc Rotenberg, ed., The Privacy Law Sourcebook: United States Law, International Law and Recent Developments (EPIC 2003).

[25] International Covenant on Civil and Political Rights, adopted and opened for signature, ratification and accession by General Assembly resolution 2200A (XXI) of December 16, 1966, entry into force March 23 1976, available at <http://www.unhchr.ch/html/menu3/b/a_ccpr.htm>.

[26] International Convention on the Protection of the Rights of All Migrant Workers and Members of Their Families, adopted by General Assembly resolution 45/158 of December 18, 1990, available at <http://www.unhchr.ch/html/menu3/b/m_mwctoc.htm>.

[27] Convention on the Rights of the Child, adopted and opened for signature, ratification and accession by General Assembly resolution 44/25 of November 20, 1989, entry into force September 2, 1990, available at <http://www.unhchr.ch/html/menu3/b/k2crc.htm>.

[28] *See generally*, Lee Bygrave, Data Protection Pursuant to the Right of Privacy in Human Rights Treaties, 6 International Journal of Law and Information Technology 247-284 (1998), available at <http://folk.uio.no/lee/publications>.

On the regional level, various treaties make these rights legally enforceable. Article 8 of the European Convention for the Protection of Human Rights and Fundamental Freedoms 1950 (ECHR) states:

> (1) Everyone has the right to respect for his private and family life, his home and his correspondence. (2) There shall be no interference by a public authority with the exercise of this right except as in accordance with the law and is necessary in a democratic society in the interests of national security, public safety or the economic well-being of the country, for the prevention of disorder or crime, for the protection of health of morals, or for the protection of the rights and freedoms of others. [29]

The Convention created the European Commission of Human Rights and the European Court of Human Rights to oversee enforcement. Both have been active in the enforcement of privacy rights and have consistently viewed Article 8's protections expansively and interpreted the restrictions narrowly.[30] The Commission found in 1976:

> For numerous Anglo-Saxon and French authors, the right to respect "private life" is the right to privacy, the right to live, as far as one wishes, protected from publicity. . . . In the opinion of the Commission, however, the right to respect for private life does not end there. It comprises also, to a certain degree, the right to establish and develop relationships with other human beings, especially in the emotional field for the development and fulfillment of one's own personality.[31]

The Court has reviewed member states' laws and imposed sanctions on numerous countries for failing to regulate wiretapping by governments and private individuals.[32] It has also reviewed cases of individuals' access to their personal information in government files to ensure that adequate procedures exist.[33] It has expanded the protections of Article 8 beyond government actions to those of

---

[29] Council of Europe, Convention for the Protection of Human Rights and Fundamental Freedoms, (ETS No: 005) open for signature November 4, 1950, entry into force September 3, 1950, available at <http://conventions.coe.int/Treaty/EN/cadreprincipal.htm>.

[30] Nadine Strossen, Recent United States and International Judicial Protection of Individual Rights: A Coparative Legal Process Analysis and Proposed Synthesis, 41 Hastings Law Journal 805 (1990).

[31] X v. Iceland, 5 Eur. Comm'n H.R. 86.87 (1976).

[32] European Court of Human Rights, Case of Klass and Others: Judgement of 6 September 1978, Series A No. 28 (1979). Malone v. Commissioner of Police, 2 All E.R. 620 (1979). *See* Note, Secret Surveillance and the European Convention on Human Rights, 33 Stanford Law Review 1113, 1122 (1981).

[33] Judgement of 26 March 1987 (Leander Case).

private persons where it appears that the government should have prohibited those actions.[34]

Other regional treaties are also beginning to be used to protect privacy. Article 11 of the American Convention on Human Rights sets out the right to privacy in terms similar to the Universal Declaration.[35] In 1965, the Organization of American States proclaimed the American Declaration of the Rights and Duties of Man, which called for the protection of numerous human rights, including privacy.[36] The Inter-American Court of Human Rights has begun to address privacy issues in its cases.

The Evolution of Data Protection

Interest in the right of privacy increased in the 1960s and 1970s with the advent of information technology. The surveillance potential of powerful computer systems prompted demands for specific rules governing the collection and handling of personal information. The genesis of modern legislation in this area can be traced to the first data protection law in the world enacted in the Land of Hesse in Germany in 1970. This was followed by national laws in Sweden (1973), the United States (1974), Germany (1977), and France (1978).[37]

Two crucial international instruments evolved from these laws. The Council of Europe's 1981 Convention for the Protection of Individuals with regard to the Automatic Processing of Personal Data[38] and the Organization for Economic Cooperation and Development (OECD) Guidelines Governing the Protection of Privacy and Transborder Data Flows of Personal Data[39] set out specific rules covering the handling of electronic data. These rules describe personal information as data that are afforded protection at every step from collection to storage and dissemination.

---

[34] *Id.* at 848-49.

[35] Signed November 22, 1969, entered into force July 18, 1978, O.A.S. Treaty Series No. 36, at 1, O.A.S. Off. Rec. OEA/Ser. L/V/II.23 dec rev. 2, available at <http://www.oas.org/juridico/english/Treaties/b-32.htm>.

[36] O.A.S. Res XXX, adopted by the Ninth Conference of American States, 1948 OEA/Ser/. L./V/I.4 Rev (1965).

[37] An excellent analysis of these laws is found in David Flaherty, Protecting Privacy in Surveillance Societies (University of North Carolina Press 1989).

[38] ETS No. 108, Strasbourg, 1981, available at <htp://conventions.coe.int/Treaty/EN/Treaties/Html/108.htm>.

[39] OECD, Guidelines Governing the Protection of Privacy and Transborder Data Flows of Personal Data" (1981), available at <http://www.oecd.org/dsti/sti/it/secur/prod/PRIV-EN.HTM>.

The expression of data protection in various declarations and laws varies. All require that personal information must be:

- obtained fairly and lawfully;
- used only for the original specified purpose;
- adequate, relevant and not excessive to purpose;
- accurate and up to date;
- accessible to the subject;
- kept secure; and
- destroyed after its purpose is completed.

These two agreements have had a profound effect on the enactment of laws around the world. Nearly thirty countries have signed the CoE convention and several others are planning to do so shortly. The OECD guidelines have also been widely used in national legislation, even outside the OECD member countries.

Rationales for Adopting Comprehensive Laws

There are three major reasons for the movement towards comprehensive privacy and data protection laws. Many countries are adopting these laws for one or more reasons.

To remedy past injustices. Many countries, especially in Central Europe, South America and South Africa, are adopting laws to remedy privacy violations that occurred under previous authoritarian regimes.

To promote electronic commerce. Many countries, especially in Asia, have developed or are currently developing laws in an effort to promote electronic commerce. These countries recognize that consumers are uneasy with the increased availability of their personal data, particularly with new means of identification and forms of transactions. These countries recognize consumers are uneasy with their personal information being sent worldwide. Privacy laws are being introduced as part of a package of laws intended to facilitate electronic commerce by setting up uniform rules.

To ensure laws are consistent with Pan-European laws. Most countries in Central and Eastern Europe are adopting new laws based on the Council of Europe Convention No. 108 and the EU Data Protection Directive. Many of these countries hope to join the European Union in the near future. Countries in other regions are adopting new laws or updating older laws to ensure that trade will not be affected by the requirements of the European Union Directive.

The European Union Data Protection Directives

In 1995, the European Union enacted the Data Protection Directive in order to harmonize member states' laws in providing consistent levels of protections for citizens and ensuring the free flow of personal data within the European Union. The directive sets a baseline common level of privacy that not only reinforces current data protection law, but also establishes a range of new rights. It applies to the processing of personal information in electronic and manual files.[40]

A key concept in the European data protection model is "enforceability." Data subjects have rights established in explicit rules. Every European Union country has a data protection commissioner or agency that enforces the rules. It is expected that the countries with which Europe does business will need to provide a similar level of oversight.

The basic principles established by the Directive are: the right to know where the data originated; the right to have inaccurate data rectified; a right of recourse in the event of unlawful processing; and the right to withhold permission to use data in some circumstances. For example, individuals have the right to opt-out free of charge from being sent direct marketing material. The Directive contains strengthened protections over the use of sensitive personal data relating, for example, to health, sex life or religious or philosophical beliefs. In the future, the commercial and government use of such information will generally require "explicit and unambiguous" consent of the data subject.

The 1995 Directive imposes an obligation on member states to ensure that the personal information relating to European citizens has the same level of protection when it is exported to, and processed in, countries outside the European Union. This requirement has resulted in growing pressure outside Europe for the passage of privacy laws. Those countries that refuse to adopt adequate privacy laws may find themselves unable to conduct certain types of information flows with Europe, particularly if they involve sensitive data.

---

[40] Directive 95/46/EC of the European Parliament and of the Council of 24 October 1995 on the Protection of Individuals with Regard to the Processing of Personal Data and on the Free Movement of such Data, available at <http://europa.eu.int/comm/internal_market/en/media/dataprot/law/index.htm>.

In 1997, the European Union supplemented the 1995 directive by introducing the Telecommunications Privacy Directive.[41] This directive established specific protections covering telephone, digital television, mobile networks and other telecommunications systems.[42] It imposed wide-ranging obligations on carriers and service providers to ensure the privacy of users' communications, including Internet-related activities. It covered areas that, until then, had fallen between the cracks of data protection laws. Access to billing data was severely restricted, as was marketing activity. Caller ID technology was required to incorporate an option for per-line blocking of number transmission. Information collected in the delivery of a communication was required to be purged once the call was completed.

In July 2000, the European Commission issued a proposal for a new directive on privacy in the electronic communications sector.[43] The proposal was introduced as a part of a larger package of telecommunications directives aimed at strengthening competition within the European electronic communications markets. As originally proposed, the new directive would have strengthened privacy rights for individuals by extending the protections that were already in place for telecommunications to a broader, more technology-neutral category of "electronic communications." During the process, however, the Council of Ministers began to push for the inclusion of data retention provisions, requiring Internet Service Providers and telecommunications operators to store logs of all telephone calls, e-mails, faxes, and Internet activity for law enforcement purposes. These proposals were strongly opposed by most members of the Parliament. In July 2001, the European Parliament's Civil Liberties Committee approved the draft directive without data retention, stating:

> The Civil Liberties Committee (LIBE Committee) expressed itself in favour of a strict regulation of law enforcement authorities' access to personal data of citizens, such as communication traffic and location data. This decision is fundamental because in this way the EP blocks European Union States' efforts underway in the Council to put their citizens under generalised and pervasive surveillance, following the Echelon model.

---

[41] Directive 97/66/EC of the European Parliament and of the Council of 15 December 1997 on the Processing of Personal Data and the Protection of Privacy in the Telecommunications Sector (Directive), available at <http://www.ispo.cec.be/legal/en/dataprot/protection.html>.

[42] European Union member countries were required to enact implementing legislation by October 1998. As of the summer 2002, however, several are still pending.

[43] European Commission, Proposal for a directive of the European Parliament and of the Council Concerning the Processing of Personal Data and the Protection of Privacy in the Electronic Communications Sector, available at <http://europa.eu.int/comm/information_society/policy/framework/pdf/com2000385_en.pdf>.

Following the events of September 11, however, the political climate changed and the Parliament came under increasing pressure from member states to adopt the Council's proposal for data retention. The United Kingdom and the Netherlands, in particular, questioned whether the proposed privacy rules still struck "the right balance between privacy and the needs of the law enforcement agencies in the light of the battle against terrorism."[44] The Parliament stood firm and up to a few weeks before the final vote on May 30, 2002, the majority of the Members of Parliament opposed any form of data retention. Finally, after much pressure by the European Council and European Union governments, and well organized lobbying by two Spanish MEPs,[45] the two main political parties (PPE and PSE, the center-left and center-right parties) reached a deal to vote in favor of the Council's position.

On June 25, 2002 the European Union Council adopted the new Privacy and Electronic Communications Directive as voted in the Parliament.[46] Under the terms of the new Directive, member states may now pass laws mandating the retention of the traffic and location data of all communications taking place over mobile phones, SMS, landline telephones, faxes, e-mails, chatrooms, the Internet, or any other electronic communication device. Such requirements can be implemented for purposes varying from national security to the prevention, investigation and prosecution of criminal offences.

In other areas, the Privacy and Electronic Communications Directive had a more favorable outcome. For example, it adds new definitions and protections for "calls," "communications," "traffic data" and "location data" in order to enhance the consumer's right to privacy and control in all kinds of data processing. These new provisions ensure the protection of all information ("traffic") transmitted across the Internet, prohibit unsolicited commercial marketing by e-mail ("spam") without consent, and protect mobile phone users from precise location tracking and surveillance. The directive also gives subscribers to all electronic communications services (such as GSM and e-mail) the right to choose whether they are listed in a public directory.

---

[44] Jelle van Buuren, "Telecommunication Council Wants New Investigation Into Privacy Rules," Heise Online, October 17, 2001.

[45] Respectively, MEPs Ana Palacio Vallelersundi and Elena Paciotti, members of the PPE (European Peoples' Party/Christian Democrats) and PSE (Social Democrats) political parties.

[46] 2439th Council meeting, Luxembourg, June 25, 2002. Transcripts of proceedings available at <http://europa.eu.int/rapid/start/cgi/guesten.ksh?p_action.gettxt=gt&doc=PRES/02/180|0|AGED&lg=EN>.

The Directive will enter into force from the date of publication in the official journal. After that time member states will have 15 months to implement its provisions.

The APEC privacy initiative

The 21 APEC economies (Asia-Pacific Economic Cooperation) commenced development in 2003 of an Asia-Pacific privacy standard, and in 2004 may develop a procedure for handling data export limitation issues.[47] This may become the most significant international privacy initiative since the European Union's Data Protection Directive of the mid-1990s. In February 2003, Australia put forward a proposal for the development of APEC Privacy Principles, using the 20-year old OECD Guidelines on the Protection of Privacy and Transborder Flows of Personal Data (1980)[48] as a starting point.[49] A Privacy Sub Group was set up comprising Australia, Canada, China, Hong Kong, Japan, Korea, Malaysia, New Zealand, Thailand and the United States. In March 2004, Version 9 of the APEC Privacy Principles was released as a public consultation draft.[50] Implementation mechanisms, including mechanisms relating to trans-border data flows are now under consideration but no drafts have yet been made public.

The positive side of the APEC privacy initiative is that it has the potential to encourage the development of stronger privacy laws in those APEC economies that at present provide little privacy protection (the majority), and to help find a regional balance between the protection of privacy and the economic benefits of trade involving personal data. The negative side is that it also presents considerable potential dangers to long-term regional privacy protection if it becomes a means by which the APEC economies accept a second-rate standard. Globally, a high APEC standard could be a means of resolving international data export issues, but low APEC standards could entrench a privacy confrontation between Europe and the Asia-Pacific. The history to date of the APEC initiative shows that the dangers are as great as the potential benefits, but a valuable outcome for privacy protection is still possible.

---

[47] For information on APEC and its 21 member economies, see the APEC Secretariat home page <http://www.apecsec.org.sg/> and
<http://www.cba.hawaii.edu/apec/home.htmhttp://www.cba.hawaii.edu/apec/home.htm>.

[48] OECD, Paris, 1980 <http://www1.oecd.org/publications/e-book/9302011E.PDF>.

[49] These documents can be obtained at <http://www.apecsec.org.sg/> in the directory Publications / Publications and Library / E-Commerce.

[50] <http://www.export.gov/apececommerce/privacy/consultation-draft.pdf>. See generally <http://www.export.gov/apececommerce/>.

Criticisms of the APEC Principles emphasize that they do not even meet the 20 year-old OECD standard, whereas they should include some significant strengthening where the OECD guidelines are now too weak.[51] The Australian Privacy Foundation (APF) and the Asia-Pacific Privacy Charter Council (APPCC)[52] have both identified[53] several key weaknesses.[54]

The Privacy Sub-group is also considering draft Implementation Mechanisms, which in the early drafts (Version 3) have major weaknesses in comparison with prior international privacy instruments.[55] These initial proposals raise doubts as to whether the APEC process will be able to adequately protect human rights across the Asia-Pacific.

Oversight and Privacy and Data Protection Commissioners

An essential aspect of any privacy protection regime is oversight. In most countries with an omnibus data protection or privacy act, there is an official or agency that oversees enforcement of the act. The powers of these officials, Commissioner, Ombudsman or Registrar, vary widely by country. Several countries, including Germany and Canada, also have officials or offices on a state or provincial level.

Under Article 28 of the EU Data Protection Directive, all European Union countries must have an independent enforcement body. Under the Directive,

---

[51] *See* the series of articles by Graham Greenleaf at <http://www.bakercyberlawcentre.org/appcc/> which trace these criticisms through successive versions of the APEC principles.

[52] The APPCC is a regional expert group formed in 2003 to develop independent standards for privacy protection in the Asia-Pacific region, in order to influence the enactment of privacy laws and international agreements in the region in accordance with those standards. *See* <http://www.bakercyberlawcentre.org/appcc/>.

[53] *See* <http://www.privacy.org.au/Papers/APEC0403.html> (APF) and <http://www.bakercyberlawcentre.org/appcc/APEC_APPCCsub.htm> (APPCC).

[54] The categories of "national exceptions" are open-ended, and should at least be identified in general terms; there are ineffective controls on the scope of any particular "national exception;"   notice is not clearly required to be given to individuals from whom information is collected; collection is not limited to the minimum information necessary for purpose; secondary uses are allowed for "compatible" purposes, a very weak test; the elevation of "choice" (or consent) to a separate Principle facilitates the commodification of privacy; "commercial proprietary" reasons should not be an exception to access and correction; "Maximising Benefits" should not become a Principle; the OECD Principles of Purpose Specification, Openness and Data Export Limitation are missing and their content should be reinstated; at least an additional Deletion Principle should be added for a minimum set of Principles.

[55] National implementation by legislation is not required, with economies allowed to choose what implementation options are sufficient to give effect to the substance of the Principles. There is no identification of the circumstances in which personal data export restrictions may be legitimate (*contra* OECD). The strongest method of assessment of national non-compliance under consideration is "self-assessment by economies coupled with peer review."

these agencies are given considerable power: governments must consult the body when the government draws up legislation relating to the processing of personal information; the bodies also have the power to conduct investigations and have a right to access information relevant to their investigations; impose remedies such as ordering the destruction of information or ban processing, and start legal proceedings, hear complaints and issue reports. The official is also generally responsible for public education and international liaison in data protection and data transfer. Many authorities also maintain the register of data controllers and databases. They must approve licensing for data controllers.

Several countries that do not have a comprehensive act still have a commissioner. A major power of these officials is to focus public attention on problem areas, even when they do not have any authority to fix the problem. They can do this by promoting codes of practice and encouraging industry associations to adopt them. They also can use their annual reports to point out problems. For example, in Canada, the Federal Privacy Commissioner announced in his 2000 report the existence of an extensive database maintained by the federal government. Once the issue became public, the Ministry disbanded the database.

In several countries, this official also serves as the enforcer of the jurisdiction's Freedom of Information Act. These include Hungary, Estonia, Thailand and the United Kingdom. On the sub-national level, many of the German Lund Commissioners have recently been given the power of information commissioner, and most of the Canadian provincial agencies handle both data protection and freedom of information.

A major problem with many agencies around the world is a lack of resources to adequately conduct oversight and enforcement. Many are burdened with licensing systems, which use much of their resources. Others have large backlogs of complaints or are unable to conduct significant number of investigations. Many that started out with adequate funding find their budgets cut a few years later.

Independence is also a problem. In many countries, the agency is under the control of the political arm of the government or part of the Ministry of Justice and lacks the power or will to advance privacy or criticize privacy invasive proposals. In Japan and Thailand, the oversight agency is under the control of the Prime Minister's Office. In Thailand, the director was transferred in 2000 after conflicts with the Prime Minister's Office. In 2001, Slovenia amended its Data Protection Act in order to establish an independent supervisory authority and thereby ensure compliance with the Data Protection Directive. This was previously the responsibility of the Ministry of Justice.

Finally, in some countries that do not have a separate office, the role of investigating and enforcing the laws is done by a human rights ombudsman or by a parliamentary official.

Transborder Data Flows and Data Havens

The ease with which electronic data flows across borders leads to a concern that data protection laws could be circumvented by simply transferring personal information to third countries, where the national law of the country of origin does not apply. This data could then be processed in those countries, frequently called "data havens," without any limitations.

For this reason, most data protection laws include restrictions on the transfer of information to third countries unless the information is protected in the destination country. For example, Article 12 of the Council of Europe's 1981 Convention places restrictions on the transborder flows of personal data.[56] Similarly, Article 25 of the European Directive imposes an obligation on member States to ensure that any personal information relating to European citizens is protected by law when it is exported to, and processed in, countries outside Europe. It states:

> The Member States shall provide that the transfer to a third country of personal data which are undergoing processing or are intended for processing after transfer may take place only if the third country in question ensures an adequate level of protection.

This requirement has resulted in growing pressure outside Europe for the passage of strong data protection laws. Those countries that refuse to adopt meaningful privacy laws may find themselves unable to conduct certain types of information flows with Europe, particularly if they involve sensitive data. Determination of a third country's system for protecting privacy is made by the European Commission. The overarching principle in this determination process is that the level of protection in the receiving country must be "adequate" rather than "equivalent." Therefore, a reasonably high standard of protection is expected

---

[56] Council of Europe, Convention for the Protection of Individuals with regard to the Automatic Processing of Personal Data 1981, available at <http://conventions.coe.int/Treaty/EN/Treaties/Html/108.htm>.

from the third party, although the precise dictates of the Directive need not be followed.

On July 26, 2000, the European Commission ruled that both Switzerland and Hungary provide "adequate" protection for personal information and therefore all transfers of personal data to these countries could continue.[57] In January 2002, the European Commission recognized that the Canadian Personal Information Protection and Electronic Documents Act (PIPEDA) provides adequate protection for certain personal data transferred from the European Union to Canada. The Commission's decision of adequacy does not cover any personal data held by federal sector or provincial bodies or information held by personal organizations and used for non-commercial purposes, such as data handled by charities or collected in the context of an employment relationship.[58] The Commission is currently looking into the privacy protection schemes in several other non-European Union countries, including New Zealand, Australia, and Hong-Kong.

Another possible way to protect the privacy of information transferred to countries that do not provide "adequate protection" is to rely on a private contract containing standard data protection contractual clauses. This kind of contract would bind the data processor to respect fair information practices such as the right to notice, consent, access and legal remedies. In the case of data transferred from the European Union, the contract would have to meet the standard "adequacy" test, in order to satisfy the Data Protection Directive.[59] Several model clauses that could be included in such a contract were outlined in a 1992 joint study by the Council of Europe, the European Commission and the International Chamber of Commerce.[60] In a June 2000 report (see below), the European Parliament accused the European Commission of a "serious omission" in failing to draft standard contractual clauses that European citizens could invoke in the courts of third countries before the Data Directive came into force.[61] It

---

[57] *See* European Commission Press Release, "Data protection: Commission adopts decisions recognising adequacy of regimes in United States, Switzerland and Hungary," July 27, 2000, available at <http://europa.eu.int/comm/internal_market/en/media/dataprot/news/safeharbor.htm>.

[58] Commission Decision of December 20, 2001, Official Journal of the European Communities L 2/13, available at <http://www.europa.eu.int/comm/internal_market/dataprot/adequacy/canada-faq_en.htm>

[59] See European Union, Internal Market Directorate, Background Information: Transfer of data to non-European Union countries – FAQ, available at <http://europa.eu.int/comm/internal_market/en/media/dataprot/backinfo/info.htm>.

[60] Joint Study of the Council of Europe and the Commission of the European Communities (1992), available at <http://www.coe.fr/dataprotection/Etudes_Rapports/ectype.htm>.

[61] European Parliament Resolution on the Draft Commission Decision on the Adequacy of the Protection Provided by the Safe Harbour Privacy Principles and related Frequently Asked Questions issued by the United

recommended that they do so before September 30, 2000.[62] In July 2001, the Commission issued a final decision approving the standard contractual clauses.[63] During the drafting process, the United States criticized the standard contacts as "unduly burdensome" and "incompatible with real world operations."[64]

European Union-United States Safe Harbor Arrangement

Although the Commission never issued a formal opinion on the adequacy of privacy protection in the United States, there were serious doubts whether the United States' sectoral and self-regulatory approach to privacy protection would pass the adequacy standard set out in the Directive. The European Union commissioned two prominent United States law professors, who wrote a detailed report on the state of United States privacy protections and pointed out the many gaps in United States protection.[65]

The United States strongly lobbied the European Union and its member countries to find the United States system adequate. In 1998, the United States began negotiating a "Safe Harbor" agreement with the European Union in order to ensure the continued transborder flows of personal data. The idea of the "Safe Harbor" was that United States companies would voluntarily self-certify to adhere to a set of privacy principles worked out by the United States Department of Commerce and the Internal Market Directorate of the European Commission. These companies would then have a presumption of adequacy and they could continue to receive personal data from the European Union. Negotiations on the drafting of the Safe Harbor principles lasted nearly two years and were the subject of bitter criticism by privacy and consumer advocates.[66] In early July, the

States Department of Commerce, available at
<http://www.epic.org/privacy/intl/EP_SH_resolution_0700.html>.

[62] For general guidance on the role of contracts see European Union Article 29 Data Protection Working Group, "Transfers of personal data to third countries: Applying Articles 25 and 26 of the European Union data protection directive," July 24, 1998, available at
<http://europa.eu.int/comm/internal_market/en/media/dataprot/wpdocs/wp12en.htm>.

[63] Commission Approves Standard Contractual Clauses For Data Transfers To Non-European Union Countries, Press Release of the Internal Market Directorate, July 18, 2001, available at
<http://europa.eu.int/comm/internal_market/en/dataprot/news/clauses2.htm>.

[64] "Bush Administration Criticizes European Union Privacy Rules," EPIC Alert 8.06, March 29, 2001
<http://www.epic.org/alert/EPIC_Alert_8.06.html>.

[65] Paul M. Schwartz and Joel R. Reidenberg, Data Privacy Law (Michie 1996).

[66] See, e.g., Public Comments Received by the United States Department of Commerce in Response to the Safe Harbor Documents April 5, 2000, available at
<http://www.ita.doc.gov/td/ecom/Comments400/publiccomments0400.html>.

European Parliament approved a forceful resolution that the agreement needed to be re-negotiated in order to provide adequate protection.[67]

On July 26, 2000, the Commission approved the agreement.[68] The Commission did, however, promise to re-open negotiations on the arrangement if the remedies available to European citizens proved inadequate. European Union member states were given 90 days to put the Commission's decision into effect and United States companies began joining Safe Harbor in November 2000. There is an open-ended grace period for United States signatory companies to implement the principles.

The principles require all signatory organizations to provide individuals with "clear and conspicuous" notice of the kind of information they collect, the purposes for which it may be used, and any third parties to whom it may be disclosed. This notice must be given at the time of the collection of any personal information or "as soon thereafter as is practicable." Individuals must be given the ability to choose (opt-out of) the collection of data where the information is either going to be disclosed to a third party or used for an incompatible purpose. In the case of sensitive information, individuals must expressly consent (opt-in) to the collection. Organizations wishing to transfer data to a third party may do so if the third party subscribes to Safe Harbor or if that third party signs an agreement to protect the data. Organizations must take reasonable precautions to protect the security of information against loss, misuse and unauthorized access, disclosure, alteration and destruction. Organizations must provide individuals with access to any personal information held about them, and with the opportunity to correct, amend, or delete that information where it is inaccurate. This right is to be granted only if the burden or expense of providing access would not be disproportionate to the risks to the individual's privacy or where the rights of persons other than the individual would not be violated. In terms of enforcement, organizations must provide access to readily available and affordable independent recourse mechanisms that may investigate complaints and award damages. They must issue follow up compliance procedures and must adhere to sanctions for failing to comply with the principles.

Privacy advocates and consumer groups both in the United States and Europe are highly critical of the European Commission's decision to approve the agreement, which they say will fail to provide European citizens with adequate protection for

---

[67] European Parliament Resolution, *supra*, n.50.

[68] Commission Decision on the adequacy of the protection provided by the Safe Harbour Privacy Principles and related Frequently Asked Questions issued by the United States Department of Commerce, available at <http://europa.eu.int/comm/internal_market/en/media/dataprot/news/decision.pdf>.

their personal data.[69] The agreement rests on a self-regulatory system whereby companies merely promise not to violate their declared privacy practices. There is little enforcement or systematic review of compliance. The Safe Harbor status is granted at the time of self-certification. There is no individual right to appeal or right to compensation for privacy infringements. There is an open-ended grace period for United States signatory companies to implement the principles. The agreement will only apply to companies overseen by the Federal Trade Commission and Department of Transportation (excluding the financial and telecommunications sectors) and there are special exceptions granted for public records information protected by European Union law.

In February 2002 the European Commission issued a report on the practical operation of the European Union-United States Safe Harbor Agreement.[70] This was the first report to evaluate the success of the agreement. It concluded that all the essential elements of the agreement are in place and that a structure exists for individuals to lodge complaints if they feel their rights have been infringed. It did find, however, that there is not sufficient transparency among the organizations that have signed up to Safe Harbor and that not all dispute resolution providers relied on to enforce Safe Harbor actually comply with the privacy principles in the agreement itself. The Commission was expeted to issue a full evaluation of the agreement in 2003, but the report has not yet been issued.

In July 2002, the Article 29 Data Protection Working Party issued a working paper on the functioning of the agreement. In it, the Working Party expressed its intention to study the agreement in further detail with particular regard to "possible gaps between the principles...and the implementing practices" and also "the transparency requirements to be met by organizations." The Working Party called on all authorities, organizations and companies concerned to enhance compliance and awareness of the Agreement.[71]

---

[69] See, e.g.the earlier Statement of the Transatlantic Consumer Protection Dialogue on United States Department of Commerce Draft International Safe Harbor Privacy Principles and FAQs March 30, 2000, available at <http://www.tacd.org/ecommercef.html#usdraft>.

[70] European Commission Staff Working Paper, February 2002, available at <http://europa.eu.int/comm/internal_market/en/dataprot/news/02-196_en.pdf>.

[71] "Working Document on the Functioning of the Safe Harbor Agreement," Article 29 Data Protection Working Party, 11194/02/EN, July 2, 2002, available at <http://europa.eu.int/comm/internal_market/en/dataprot/wpdocs/wp62_en.pdf>

Threats to Privacy

Responding to Terrorism

It may take some years to fully evaluate the effects of the terrorist attacks of the past few years on privacy and civil liberties. In the wake of each attack, earlier proposals were re-introduced, and new policies with similar objectives were drafted to extend police surveillance authority. Four years on from September 11 2001, the legal and political landscapes have shifted significantly in many, if not most, countries.

With terrorist attacks occurring around the world, including in Egypt, the United Kingdom, Spain, Bali, Russia, Morocco, and Saudi Arabia, governments have responded to these events by enhancing and creating new powers. The country reports in this survey outline, in more detail, the many legislative shifts that have taken place around the world. Terrorism politics is truly global.

The changes in anti-terrorism laws are not the only policy transformations in response to terrorism. The mere threat of terrorism has changed political discourse. In some cases, the "war on terrorism" has given new life to previously failed proposals such as national ID cards in the United Kingdom. In 2003, the UK government returned to the rhetoric of terrorism to shore up support for the cards while previously fraud and asylum seekers were used.[72] Despite more recent statements by the Home Office Minister, quietly admitting that ID cards will have no effect on combating terrorism, and would not have prevented the attacks in July 2005,[73] the policy is seen as inseparable in the minds of politicians, the media, and the general public. This is despite mounting evidence stating otherwise.[74]

In some cases, policies have been adopted from other countries with little consideration to the variances in political dynamics. Hong Kong attempted to harmonize its laws on sedition with mainland China, requiring a standardization of criminalized groups. Malaysia decided against repealing its Internal Security

---

[72] David Cracknell, "ID Cards for All to Cost £40," Sunday Times, July 6, 2003.

[73] The Today Programme, Interview with Charles Clarke, Home Secretary, July 8, 2005.

[74] Privacy International, "Mistaken Identity: Exploring the Relationship Between National Identity Cards & the Prevention of Terrorism," April 2004.

Act 1960 involving detention.[75] South Africa and Jamaica's draft anti-terrorism laws copy Canada's proposed definition of "terrorist activity," even though Canada later changed its definition because there were concerns that protesters would be confused with terrorists.

In other cases, the mere increase of state power is immediately associated with the "war on terrorism"; whether requiring the removal of veils for driver's license photos,[76] secret seizure of packages from the media,[77] clamping down on train-spotters and -photographers,[78] chasing down opposition parties,[79] and the equation of terrorism to separatism[80] and its implications,[81] or suppressing dissent,[82] amongst others. Canada created a travelers' database for anti-terrorism purposes, and *other* crimes. The United Kingdom managed to pass communications data retention laws in the legislative environment of the aftermath of September 2001; while retained data could be accessed, under another law, for practically any investigation. In the US, concerns have arisen regarding the use of counter-terrorism powers to seize funds from foreign banks that do business in the US for investigations that are unrelated to terrorism.[83]

In other situations, these laws may be passed and used to suppress dissent. In Italy, the Interior Minister warned of a growing climate of "widespread political illegality" and mixed together Islamic terrorist groups, endogenous left-wing armed groups, anarchist insurrectionaries, and right-wing groups as a common threat.[84] Moldova's bill to fight extremism coincides with the government's intention to minimize dissent as it allows the banning of political parties, public and religious associations, and media outlets if they promote violent overthrow of country's territorial integrity, undermining state power, or setting up illegal armed

---

[75] Dato' Param Cumaraswamy, "Terrorism: Meeting the Challenges/Finding the Balance," Address to the 13th Commonwealth Law Conference from the UN Special Rapporteur on the Independence of Judges and Lawyers, Melbourne, April 13-17, 2003.

[76] Mike Branom, "Judge Cites Terrorism Concerns for Ruling on Muslim Woman's Veil," Associated Press, June 7, 2003.

[77] Eric Lichtblau, "F.B.I. Opens Inquiry Into Seizure of Documents From Associated Press," New York Times, April 24, 2003.

[78] Giles Wilson, "Terrorism Fear Derails Train-Spotters," BBC News Online, May 28, 2003.

[79] Editorial, "Questions in Texas," Washington Post, May 23, 2003, at A24.

[80] Joint Declaration of the Foreign Ministers of the Russian Federation and the Association of Southeast Asian Nations on Partnership for Peace and Security, and Prosperity and Development in the Asia-Pacific Region, June 19, 2003.

[81] Jane Perlez, "Indonesia Says Drive against Separatists Will not End Soon," New York Times, July 9, 2003.

[82] Economist, "In no Mood for Dissent," February 11, 2003.

[83] Eric Lichtblau, "U.S. Cautiously Begins to Seize Millions in Foreign Banks," New York Times, May 30, 2003.

[84] Statewatch, "Interior Minister Links Terrorism and Activists' Widespread Political Illegality," February 2003.

organizations.[85] Georgia's bill, drafted in consultation with European colleagues according to a state security ministry official,[86] provides for restricting or suspending the activities of organizations that receive foreign funding and whose activities "threaten Georgia's national interests," but fails to define those interests.[87]

While the legal landscape is shifting and affecting many components of human rights, not only privacy, in many cases these policies are founded upon its curtailment.

In the Immediate Aftermath

The immediate period after September 2001 was a time of fear, flux and uncertainty. The United Nations responded with Resolution 1368 calling for increased cooperation between countries to prevent and suppress terrorism.[88] North Atlantic Treaty Organization (NATO) invoked Article 5, claiming an attack on any NATO member country is an attack on all of NATO; legislatures responded accordingly. The Council of Europe condemned the attacks, called for solidarity, and also called for increased cooperation in criminal matters.[89] Later, the Council of Europe Parliamentary Assembly called on countries to ratify conventions combating terrorism, lift any reservations in these agreements, and extend the mandate of police working groups to include "terrorist messages and the decoding thereof."[90] The European Union responded similarly, pushing for a European arrest warrant, common legislative frameworks for terrorism, increasing intelligence and police cooperation, the freezing of assets and ensuring passage of the Money Laundering Directive.[91] The Organization for Economic Cooperation and Development (OECD) furthered its support for the Financial

---

[85] RFE/RL, "Moldovan Parliament Approves Presidential Bill on Fighting Extremsism," Newsline Vol.7, No. 35, Part II, February 24, 2003.

[86] RFE/RL Newsline, Vol.7, No.34, Part I, 21 February 2003.

[87] Advocacy.ge, "Security Ministry Threatens Civil Liberties: Controversial Draft Raises Grave Concerns on Government Motivation," February 2003, available at <http://www.advocacy.ge/magazine/statia_14.shtml>.

[88] United Nations Resolution 1368 (2001), adopted by the Security Council at its 4370th meeting, September 12, 2001.

[89] Council of Europe Committee of Ministers, Declaration of the Committee of Ministers on the fight against international terrorism, adopted by the Committee of Ministers at the 763rd meeting of the Ministers' Deputies, September 12, 2001.

[90] Council of Europe Parliamentary Assembly, Recommendation 1534 (2001), Democracies Facing Terrorism, September 26, 2001 (28th Sitting), available at <http://assembly.coe.int/>.

[91] Commission of the European Communities, Brussels, Report From The Commission, Overview of European Union action in response to the events of the 11 September and assessment of their likely economic impact, 17.10.2001, COM(2001) 611 final.

Action Task Force on Money Laundering and, along with the G-7[92] and the European Commission, called for the extension of its mandate to combat terrorist financing.[93] These calls for international cooperation were perceived by many as impetus to create new laws.

The European Commission considered requiring every member state of the European Union to make cyber attacks punishable as a terrorist offense. New Zealand minimized public consultation on a proposed law to freeze the financial assets of suspected terrorists because the government felt it was bound by United Nations Security Council resolutions. France expanded police powers to search private property without warrants. Germany reduced authorization restraints on interception of communications, and increased data sharing between law enforcement and national security agencies.

Australia and Canada both introduced laws to redefine "terrorist activity" and to grant powers of surveillance to national security agencies (ASIO and CSIS respectively) for domestic purposes if terrorist activity or affiliation is suspected. India passed a law to allow authorities to detain suspects without trial, conduct increased wiretapping, and seize funds and property. The United Kingdom passed a law to permit the retention of data, which will be accessed for law enforcement purposes. The United States passed several laws that increase surveillance powers and minimize oversight and due process requirements.

As time moved on, so did many of these policies. Some changes involved the "re-balancing" or a re-assessing of state power, such as moves to restrict the USA PATRIOT Act on access to library borrowing privileges,[94] India repealed the Prevention of Terrorism Act.[95] Also, the UK's highest court found the detention powers under the Anti-Terrorism, Crime and Security Act as unlawful according to the European Convention on Human Rights.[96]

But with every subsequent terrorist incident, governments around the world saw the opportunity to enhance their powers even further. For instance, as they did after September 11, 2001, the Council of Justice and Home Affairs ministers of

---

[92] Statement of G-7 Finance Ministers and Central Bank Governors, Action Plan to Combat the Financing of Terrorism, October 6, 2001.

[93] *See generally* <http://www1.oecd.org/fatf/>.

[94] Mike Allan, "House Votes to Curb Patriot Act: FBIs Power to Seize Library Records Would Be Halted," Washington Post, June 16, 2005, at A1.

[95] BBC News, "India Withdraws Anti-Terror Law," September 17, 2004.

[96] A (FC) and others (FC) (Appellants) v. Secretary of State for the Home Department (Respondent) and X (FC) and another (FC) (Appellants) v. Secretary of State for the Home Department (Respondent), decided by the House of Lords [2004 UKHL 56], December 16, 2004.

the European Union held emergency summits after the March 2004 Madrid bombings, and again after the July 2005 London bombings, calling for greater powers of surveillance of communications and financial transactions, increased cooperation across borders, and sometimes calling for the exact same policies they sought in prior meetings. After a terrorist attack in the Philippines in February 2005, the Philippine government sought a new set of anti-terrorist measures such as requiring surveillance-enabled communications facilities at all phone providers, and a renewed push for identity cards. In the wake of terrorist attacks in Russia, a raft of new powers were introduced with little debate,[97] including harsher penalties and a ban on media coverage of terrorist attacks,[98] despite criticism from the United States.[99] As was the case after the 2001 attacks in the US, countries all around the world respond to international incidents not directly affecting them. After the July 2005 bombings in London, both France and Italy enhanced their immigration and police powers,[100] including the collection of DNA samples.[101]

Within this deluge of new policy proposals in the periods after terrorist attacks, several trends may be identified.

Increased Communications Surveillance and Search and Seizure Powers

Almost every country that changed its laws to reflect "new" terrorist threats increased the ability of law enforcement and national security agencies to perform interception of communications and the type of data that can be accessed, and transformed the powers of search and seizure. The novelty in these initiatives tends to arise in reduced authorization requirements and oversight. These included initiatives to weaken due process requirements; this occurred in Canada where the first anti-terrorism bill proposed that law enforcement agencies would no longer be required to justify the need for a wiretap.[102]

---

[97] Itar-Tass, "Duma Passes Bill on Stricter Punishment for Terrorism," February 18, 2004.

[98] Urrisa Jounral Daily, "Duma to Mull Ban on Media Coverage of Terrorism," February 20, 2004.

[99] BBC News, "Russia rejects Powell criticism," September 15, 2004.

[100] Reuters, "Italy and France boost security," July 22, 2005.

[101] Associated Press, "Italy Senate Approves Terror Laws," July 29, 2005.

[102] That is, in existing law, the judge authorizing the interception would need to be satisfied that "other investigative procedures have been tried and have failed, other investigative procedures are unlikely to succeed or the urgency of the matter is such that it would be impractical to carry out the investigation of the offence using only other investigative procedures." In the law, an exception is established for all offences that fall under the broad category of "terrorist activity." Other parts of the law allow for interception authorization by the Minister of Defense instead of requiring judicial authorization. Criminal Code of Canada, (CC 186(1b)), 2000.

There is also a general increase in the breadth of application of these powers. By incorporating and including new technologies and communications infrastructures, additional government agencies are permitted to use these powers, and formalize roving powers.[103]

Attempts to differentiate the authorization and oversight requirements based on communications technology also occurred. The Australian government created powers to intercept and read e-mail, SMS and voicemail messages without a warrant because these communications were considered access to "stored" data rather than "intercepted" in real-time.[104]

Protections against invasive searches and seizures are continually degraded. Random searches generated much public discussion after the London bombings, with some discussion of racial profiling; despite already significant rises in the stopping and searching of visible minorities since 2001.[105]

Weakening of Data Protection Regimes

In 2000, the United Kingdom proposed a policy to require the retention of communications traffic data for up to seven years by a central government authority.[106] While the proposal faced significant resistance in the public discourse at that time, in December 2001, a similar policy was introduced and passed under the United Kingdom's anti-terrorism law in response to the events of September 2001.

---

[103] The USA PATRIOT Act codified the use of Carnivore-style (data mining) Internet surveillance technology, granting access to sensitive traffic data with only a court order rather than a judicial warrant. Moreover, the reporting regime in the United States was weakened with amendments to the Foreign Intelligence Surveillance Act so that fewer warrants would have to be requested and reported because the expiration time period was increased, and "generic" orders could be requested allowing one warrant to be served on multiple service providers.

[104] This proposed act was rejected in the Senate in June 2002. (Electronic Frontiers Australia, Media Release: "Senate Rejects E-mail Snooping Law - Victory for Online Privacy," June 28, 2002.) However, the government claimed that it "remains of the view that the approach adopted in the bill with respect to stored information is appropriate. However, to avoid holding up this important package of legislation, the government has agreed to remove these provisions from the bill and to deal with the issue at a later date." (Statement of Senator Ellison, Minister of Justice and Customs, Senate Official Hansard No.6 2002, June 27, 2002, available at <http://www.aph.gov.au/hansard/senate/dailys/ds270602.pdf>.) This did not stop a significant increase in interceptions in Australia, however. According to parliamentary findings, in 2002 there were 17,000 mail investigations, 2,514 wiretaps, and access to 733,000 telephone bills, a remarkable increase from previous years. (Shelley Hodgson, "ASIO Spying on the Increase," Australian, June 29, 2003.)

[105] Daily Telegraph, "Muslims Are Told to Accept more Searches," March 1, 2005.

[106] Roger Gaspar (NCIS), "Looking to the Future: Clarity on Communications Data Retention Law," August 21, 2000, ACPO, ACPO(S), HM Customs & Excise, Security Service, Secret Intelligence Service, and GCHQ,.

The European Union Directive on Privacy and Electronic Communications also supports the creation of such data retention laws within the European community and is consistent with international pressure to weaken data protection. Such a pressure came from the US government when, in October 2001, President George W. Bush sent a letter to the president of the European Commission requesting that the European Union "[c]onsider data protection issues in the context of law enforcement and counterterrorism imperatives," and as a result, "[r]evise draft privacy directives that call for mandatory destruction to permit the retention of critical data for a reasonable period."[107]

This pressure was reiterated in May 2002, this time by the Group of 8 Justice and Interior Ministers, requesting that countries:

> Ensure data protection legislation, as implemented, takes into account public safety and other social values, in particular by allowing retention and preservation of data important for network security requirements or law enforcement investigations or prosecutions, and particularly with respect to the Internet and other emerging technologies.[108]

And again, in emergency meetings after the Madrid and London bombings, Justice ministers from EU member states called for all member states to implement mandatory data retention.[109]

At the same time, individuals and citizens are losing subject access rights under data protection and freedom of information regimes. In the interests of critical infrastructure protection, access to information is being reduced, limiting

---

[107] Letter from President George W. Bush to Mr. Romano Prodi, President, Commission of the European Communities, Brussels, October 16, 2001, forwarded by the Deputy Chief of Mission, United States Mission to the European Union, available at <http://www.statewatchchapterorg/news/2001/nov/06Ausalet.htm>. Building from previously articulated concerns that "[d]ata protection procedures in the sharing of law enforcement information must be formulated in ways that do not undercut international cooperation," (Comments of the United States Government on the European Commission Communication on Combating Computer Crime, December 2001, available at <http://www.cybercrime.gov/intl/USComments_CyberCom_final.pdf>), the United States Department of Justice submitted several recommendations to the European Commission Working Group on Cybercrime, including the recommendation that "[a]ny data protection regime should strike an appropriate balance between the protection of personal privacy, the legitimate needs of service providers to secure their networks and prevent fraud, and the promotion of public safety." (Prepared statement of the United States of America, presented at European Union Forum on Cybercrime, Brussels, November 27, 2001, available at <http://www.cybercrime.gov/intl/MMR_Nov01_Forum.doc>.)

[108] Statement of the G8 Justice and Interior Ministers: Recommendations for Tracing Networked Communications Across National Borders in Terrorist and Criminal Investigations, May 14 2002, Mont Tremblant, Quebec, available at <http://www.g8j-i.ca/english/doc2.html>.

[109] Council of the European Union, "Press Release: Extraordinary Council meeting of Justice and Home Affairs," Brussels, July 13, 2005, 11116/05 (Presse 187).

government accountability.[110] Meanwhile, in order to protect sensitive investigative and intelligence data, subject access requests are restricted as some data banks are being exempted from both data protection and freedom of information laws.[111]

Increased Data Sharing

Several policies were introduced to enable and promote increased data sharing, both within and across government agencies, and with the private sector. The sharing of data between agencies introduces mission creep, where data collected for one purpose is used for another, but also introduces highly sensitive data to arms of government that cannot be expected to protect the data adequately.

There have been significant shifts in the policies and practices in the United States, with changes to the Attorney General Guidelines regulating the actions and capabilities of the Department of Justice and Federal Bureau of Investigation (FBI); increased sharing of information between the FBI and Central Intelligence Agency supported by the USA PATRIOT Act' and proposed policies to increase sharing with local law enforcement agencies. The United States is not alone in introducing such policies. The United Kingdom continues to propose "joined-up government" within its consultation paper on modernizing government and public services[112] to create "data-sharing gateways" and provide "seamless" services.[113] It also tried unsuccessfully to allow practically any government agency to gain access to the traffic data of individuals under the Regulation of Investigatory Powers Act, including local councils and parishes.[114]

The increased flow of data is also coming from the private sector. The United Kingdom and Canada proposed laws to grant law enforcement agencies access to travelers' information. The United Kingdom Home Office has recommended that

---

[110] For instance, the US has made repeated moves to limit disclosures of government documents about cyber-security initiatives, in particular where documents from the private sector are concerned. *See* Dan Verton, "White House Rewriting Core Security Policy Document," Computerworld, November 7, 2003.

[111] In Canada, the police and intelligence are exempted from privacy laws, thus allowing government institutions to refuse individuals access to personal information about them, including refusal of access to correct erroneous personal information, or even to disclose the existence of data transfers. *See* Transport Canada, "Press Release: Government of Canada Introduces Improved Public Safety Act, 2002," October 31, 2002, No. GC004/02.

[112] Performance and Innovation Unit of the Cabinet Office, "Privacy and Data-sharing: The Way Forward for Public Services," April 2002, available at <http://www.cabinet-office.gov.uk/innovation/2002/privacy/report/>.

[113] This will all be supported by the proposed Identity Card Bill.

[114] Foundation for Information Policy Research, Press Release, "FIPR appalled by Huge Increase in Government Snooping," June 10, 2002, available at <http://www.fipr.org/press/020610snooping.html>.

---

it gain access to information from every passenger before international flights,[115] and its new "E-borders" program calls for the collection and retention of passenger data of all citizens and visitors.[116] The Canadian Public Safety Act, finally passed in May 2005, grants both the federal law enforcement and the intelligence agencies access to air passenger information, regardless of domestic or international travel, and to match this data with other personal information[117] for a wide number of purposes and investigations, not limited only to terrorism.[118]

Similarly, the European Union considered granting Europol access to the Schengen Information System, including privileges to change the information held on travelers.[119] Data sharing among financial institutions and government agencies also increased. New money-laundering agreements and regulations have been introduced to increase surveillance of transactions, and even expanded to include hedge funds and money-transfer firms.[120] Donations to charities are receiving further scrutiny as both charities and donors are monitored to investigate links with terrorist groups.[121] Some financial institutions are also sharing personal information in order to minimize risk of clients being terrorists, or "undesirables."[122]

The controversial private-run profiling system, MATRIX (Multistate Anti-TeRrorism Information eXchange) was shut down in April 2005. This system combined information from government databases and private-sector companies.[123] Although many states withdrew from the system, it was uncovered that the system, developed by Florida-based company Seisint, was used

---

[115] " 'Chaos' Warning over Airport Security Plan," BBC News Online, July 6, 2002 <http://news.bbc.co.uk/hi/english/uk/newsid_2104000/2104280.stm>.

[116] Home Office, "Partial Regulatory Impact Assessment: Data Capture and Sharing Powers for the Border Agencies," June 22, 2005.

[117] Solicitor General of Canada, RCMP and CSIS Access to Airline Passenger Information, available at <http://www.sgc.gc.ca/EPub/Pol/eAirPassInfo.htm>.

[118] Letter to Honorable David Collenette, Minister of Transport, on the subject of Bill C-55, from the Privacy Commissioner of Canada, George Radwanski, June 18, 2002, available at <http://www.privcom.gc.ca/media/nr-c/02_05_b_020618_e.asp>.

[119] "Europol to Be Given Access to the SIS, then Custody?" Statewatch, March 27, 2002.

[120] Glenn R. Simpson & Jathon Sapsford, "New Rules for Money-Laundering," Wall Street Journal, April 23, 2002.

[121] "Financial Action Task Force on Money Laundering Special Recommendations on Terrorist Financing," available at <http://www.fatf-gafi.org/SRecsTF_en.htm>.

[122] Robert O'Harrow Jr., "Financial Database To Screen Accounts: Joint Effort Targets Suspicious Activities," Washington Post, May 30, 2002; at E1.

[123] According to its promotional material, "When enough seemingly insignificant data is analyzed against billions of data elements, the invisible becomes visible." See John Schwartz, "Privacy Fears Erode Support for a Network to Fight Crime," New York Times, March 15, 2004.

extensively in the months following the 2001 attacks on the World Trade Center and Pentagon. With funding from the US departments of Justice and Homeland Security,[124] the system identified 120,000 people who showed a statistical likelihood of being terrorists.[125] This "High-Terrorism Factor" was used to conduct investigations and arrests after the information was submitted to state police, the former Immigration and Naturalization Service, FBI, and the Secret Service. Subsequent use of the system showed that it had limited use for combating terrorism, and was accessed mostly for cases involving fraud and theft.[126]

Increased Profiling and Identification

Following from data sharing, there are several proposals to create profiles or increase the existing profiles of individuals. This occurs in several stages; the most immediate appears to be the profiling of travelers. There has already been testing of a next generation computer-assisted passenger prescreening system in the United States that will bring in data from credit-reporting agencies and other companies, and even previous flights and registries, for data mining. New projects also include trusted-traveler programs involving the collection of biometrics and background checks, and are quickly becoming international standards.[127] Some airports have also installed face-recognition technologies, while similar technologies are being implemented at national monuments, and even beaches.

In the longer term there are several proposals to increase profiling of citizens and non-citizens. These proposals are typically enhanced and complemented by national identification schemes, enhanced with biometrics. There was considerable discussion in the United States in introducing such a national ID card scheme but no formal policy was introduced, though a standardization process was introduced for government-issued identity documents such as driving licenses under the REAL ID Act of 2005. Meanwhile non-citizens may already be tracked at border entry points and as they move within the United States. A system called Student and Exchange Visitor Information System (SEVIS) keeps track of foreign students to ensure that they are still registered and maintains a log of their addresses.

---

[124] Robert O'Harrow Jr., "Anti-Terror Database Got Show at White House," Washington Post, May 21, 2004.

[125] Associated Press, "Early Database Project Yielded 120,000 Suspects," May 20, 2004.

[126] "News Release: MATRIX Pilot Project Concludes," FDLE Public Information Office, April 15, 2005.

[127] Nicholas Watt, "Slip through Schipol for a Quick Trip to JFK," Guardian, January 14, 2005.

The United Kingdom proposed the adoption of entitlement cards in an effort to deal with immigration, illegal work and identity theft, but also supported by the fight against terrorism. In December 2004, it introduced the Identity Card Bill for consideration in Parliament, though it was withdrawn in April for the May 2005 elections, and again reintroduced in June 2005. Similarly, Hong Kong introduced a biometric chip identity card to verify fingerprints to authenticate travelers into China. The government of the Philippines is again proposing an identity card after a number of failed attempts.[128]

None of the above trends are necessarily new. The novelty is the speed with which these policies gained acceptance, and in many cases, became law in the periods following terrorist attacks.

The Current Landscape in the United States

New policies to combat terrorism continue to emerge. The United States continues to lead with new policies, technologies, and practices. The importance of US policies is that they tend to influence policies and citizens of other countries. By September 2002, the Office of Management and Budget counted 58 new regulations responding to terrorism.[129] In March 2003, the Government Accountability Office counted nine new National Strategies.[130] There have been innumerable laws passed at the federal and state levels,[131] and countless changes in administrative measures, including the Attorney General Investigative Guidelines. A number of technological systems have been proposed and implemented, ranging from the "Total Information Awareness" Program (TIA), to the aforementioned MATRIX systems, the Computer Assisted Passenger Prescreening System (CAPPS II) and "Secure Flight."

One of the largest such systems is implemented at the US border. On top of increased interviews of visa applicants, and requirements for machine-readable passports from other countries, in January 2004, the Department of Homeland Security introduced the US Visitor & Immigration Status Indication Technology

---

[128] Joes Fancis Guinto, "DILG Chief Pushes National ID System against Terrorism," INQ7.net, February 18, 2005.

[129] Office of Management and Budget, "Stimulating Smarter Regulation: 2002 Report to Congress on the Costs and Benefits of Regulations and Unfunded Mandates on State, Local, and Tribal Entities," March 2003.

[130] Statement of Raymond J. Decker, Director Defense Capabilities and Management, "Combating Terrorism: Observations on National Strategies Related to Terrorism," Testimony before the Subcommittee on National Security, Emerging Threats, and International Relations, Committee on Government Reform, House of Representatives, March 3, 2003.

[131] The Library of Congress stopped recording its inventory of laws and resolutions in November 2002.

System (US-VISIT). US-VISIT collects information on all visa-visitors to the US, including two fingerprints and a digital photograph. In September 2004, this procedure was extended to all visitors.[132] In July 2005, a new policy was announced to increase biometric collection to that of all ten fingerprints.

Meanwhile, US Customs officials have been meeting with EU officials regarding the transfer of, and access to, passenger personal data, as required under Aviation and Transportation Security Act 2001. The EU's Article 29 Data Protection Working Group noted several problems with the proposed data sharing, including the retention time and the excessive amount of data being requested.[133] The negotiations that followed in 2003 and the beginning of 2004 resulted in the EU's capitulation, however. The European Commission agreed in early 2004 to submit European airlines' customer information to the US Department of Homeland Security, despite numerous unresolved issues.[134]

Several other programs for data-sharing and data-mining have been developed, including the National Security Entry-Exit Registration System (NSEERS) and the Student and Exchange Visitor Information System (SEVIS). The most well-known system is the Total Information Awareness program. This program was one of many post-September 11 responses to terrorism. TIA is a now-defunct program of the Defense Advanced Research Projects Agency (DARPA); it was to scan ultra-large databases of personal information to detect the "information signature" of terrorists.[135] The program was headed by Admiral John Poindexter, and was renamed "Terrorism Information Awareness" to pacify critics.[136] Congress acted to limit the project in February 2003 by requiring DARPA to submit a detailed report on TIA and, later in the year, cut funding for Poindexter's entire Information Awareness Office.

---

[132] *See generally*, Government Accountability Office. "Data Mining: Federal Efforts Cover a Wide Range of Uses," GAO-04-548, May 2004. *See also* "US Seeks to Strengthen Border Intelligence," Financial Times, June 13, 2005.

[133] Article 29 Data Protection Working Party, Opinion 4/2003 on the Level of Protection ensured in the US for the Transfer of Passengers' Data, 11070/03/EN, adopted on June 13, 2003.

[134] Privacy International, "Transferring Privacy: The Transfer of Passenger Records and the Abdication of Privacy Protection," February 2004.
<http://www.privacyinternational.org/issues/terrorism/rpt/transferringprivacy.pdf>

[135] TIA's objectives were to "imagine, develop, apply, integrate, demonstrate and transition information technologies, components, and prototype closed-loop information systems that [would] counter asymmetric threats by achieving total information awareness useful for preemption, national security warning, and national security decision making." Report to Congress regarding the Terrorism Information Awareness Program, May 20, 2003.

[136] *See generally* EPIC's ~~Total~~ Terrorism Information Awareness Web page, available at
<http://www.epic.org/privacy/profiling/tia/>.

Further data collection measures that were controversial in 2003 included the registration and fingerprinting of immigrants. The National Security Entry-Exit Registration System (NSEERS) involved the registration of nearly 82,000 male immigrants and visitors from predominantly Muslim countries, leading to possibly 13,000 deportations.[137] The information has been stored in a secure government database along with travel data, photos, and matched against other data held on potential terrorists.[138] Officials have admitted in 2004 that only 11 individuals have been identified to have links to terrorism.[139] Another system, the Student and Exchange Visitor Information System (SEVIS), used to track the nearly one million foreign students in the US, has also been problematic due to poor technology and limited resources.[140]

There have also been several developments in surveillance law. The use of the USA PATRIOT Act continues to be questioned. There have been attempts at extending some of its contentious measures that are supposed to sunset at the end of 2005.[141] After an extensive cross-country campaign by then-Attorney General John Ashcroft, the White House exerted a great deal of pressure on Congress to prevent laws that scale back the powers[142] and to extend the more invasive provisions indefinitely.[143] One effort to water down the law was rejected in the House of Representatives by a 210-210 tie vote in July 2004, after debate was prolonged when it appeared that the law's reach would be minimized.[144] Later, in June 2005, the House voted 238-187 to restrict access to book purchases and library-borrowing records.[145] After the July 2005 terrorist bombings in London, however, both the House and the Senate moved to extend or make the USA PATRIOT Act permanent.[146]

In February 2003, a draft bill was uncovered, entitled the Domestic Security Enhancement Act of 2003, which contains several new powers including the

---

[137] Rachel L. Swarns, "More than 13,000 May Face Deportation," New York Times, June 7, 2003.

[138] Jane Black, "At Justice, NSEERS Spells Data Chaos," Business Week Online, May 2, 2003.

[139] Swarns, *supra*.

[140] Marcia Slacum Greene, "Computer Problems Slow Tracking of Foreign Students," Washington Post, March 26, 2003, Page A6.

[141] Eric Lichtblau, "Senate Deal Kills Effort to Extend Antiterror Act," New York Times, May 9, 2003.

[142] Dan Eggen, "White House Intensifies Efforts to Safeguard Patriot Act," Washington Post, January 30, 2004.

[143] Richard W. Stevenson & Eric Lichtblau, "Bush Pushes for Renewal of Antiterrorism Legislation," April 18, 2004.

[144] Dan Morgan & Charles Babington, "House GOP Defends Patriot Act Powers," July 9, 2004.

[145] Reuters, "US House Votes to Curb Patriot Act, Defies Bush," June 15, 2005.

[146] Dan Eggen, "Renewed Patriot Act Gets Boost in House, Senate Panel," Washington Post, July 22, 2005, at A12.

stripping of citizenship, wiretaps without court orders, secret detentions, limits on the challenging of secret evidence, increased use of DNA without court orders and consent, increased data sharing, and increased international cooperation in search and seizure and extradition. Though the law was never formally introduced, its components have appeared in other laws, both in the US and abroad.

In February 2005, the US House of Representatives approved H.R. 418, the REAL ID Act. It became law in May 2005 without any hearings. One aim of the law is to establish and rapidly implement regulations both for state driver's licenses and for identification document security standards. The law also requires states to deny driver's licenses to undocumented immigrants. These new regulations are seen as moving the license into the realm of a national ID card.

The general response to the REAL ID Act in the US is one of widespread concern, and there are reports of a number of plans to appeal to the courts on the matter. For instance, the National Governors Association threatened lawsuits on the grounds that it will cost states up to USD 700 million to comply with the law.[147] The Mexican government is prepared to lodge a diplomatic complaint regarding the law, referring to it as "negative, inconvenient and obstructionist."[148]

In an interesting development, the state of Georgia has prohibited the use of fingerprints in drivers' licenses. This followed concerns regarding identity theft, and acknowledgement by the law enforcement community that the fingerprints were not being used for combating crime.[149] The state assembly of Georgia responded by passing a law, by a wide majority,[150] prohibiting the collection of fingerprints for state driver's licenses.

The Extenuating Developments in the International Landscape

Other countries have found novel means of implementing invasive policies and practices. The global legal landscape is fragmented. In some countries there are no specific terrorism laws as yet, such as in Belgium. Other countries have been very active in implementing laws.

---

[147] Kim Zetter, "National ID Battle Continues," Wired News, May 12, 2005.

[148] John Authers & Edward Alden, "Mexico Furious at Tough US Law on Migrants," Financial Times, May 13, 2005.

[149] Associated Press, "Driver's License Fingerprints Debated," February 23, 2005.

[150] Bob Barr, Editorial, "Fingerprint Bill Deserves Perdue's OK," Atlanta Journal-Constitution, May 4, 2005, available at http://www.bobbarr.org/default_print.asp?pt=newsdescr&RI=624.

Recently the Philippines has been actively confronting terrorism and devising new policies. Prior identity card policies faced opposition due to their discriminatory grounds. One plan involved requiring Muslims in Manila to carry an ID card at all times, supposedly intended to detect terrorists hiding in Muslim communities. Although these measures were supported by the police and intended to be implemented very quickly, the plan disappeared after a loud and widespread outcry by Muslim groups, politicians and civil liberties groups.[151]

In August 2003, the Bureau of Immigration and Deportation presented its plans for a biometrics-enhanced smart card for all aliens residing in the Philippines, which it introduced as a counter-terrorist measure.[152] Besides the biometric data in the form of thumbprint templates and facial structure records, the "Alien Certificate of Registration Identification Card" (ACR-ICard) was to contain personal information, criminal records and ACR payment transactions, as well as the date and time of a subject's arrival/departure.[153]

After a terrorist attack in February 2005, plans were re-introduced for a national ID card. The president signed another executive order calling for its implementation and Interior Minister Angelo Reyes pushed for the system as a solution to terrorism.[154] Although the exact details of the card remain to be known, there are indications that the government of the Philippines is watching the UK process carefully.

Canada has also considered the adoption of ID Cards. The reasoning behind its introduction, according to the minister of Citizenship and Immigration, is that the US will soon require the fingerprinting of Canadians as they pass through the

---

[151] That some sections of the Muslim community supported such a plan may make sense in the light of the constant harassment Manila Muslims have had to endure from police in their hunt for members of Abu Sayyaf.

[152] The Immigration Commissioner confirmed the information by stating: "By adopting this new technology the bureau will be at par with other immigration centers around the world and, with proper coordination with international law enforcement agencies, it can now easily deter unwanted aliens from entering the country. The Philippines, being the closest ally of the United States, now becomes a tactical battlefield in war against Al Qaeda and other international terrorist cells," <http://itmatters.com.ph/news/news_08182003f.html>.

[153] Id.

[154] "With a national ID system, you cannot claim to be somebody else because there will be one number for each person. . . . If you have nothing to hide, you have nothing to fear. There will be no curtailment of civil liberties. When terrorists attack, that's when civil liberties are curtailed." Joel Francis Guinto, "DILG Chief Pushes National ID System against Terrorism," INQ7.net, February 18, 2005, http://news.inq7.net/breaking/index.php?index=1&story_id=27906.

US-Canada border.[155] The Public Safety Act 2005 grants law enforcement authorities access to travel information, even within Canada.[156]

The Public Safety Act went through a number of iterations before it became law, however. In its fourth version, the purposes for access and processing of this information had changed mildly since earlier versions. These purposes are now: transportation security purposes; national security investigations relating to terrorism; situations of immediate threat to the life or safety of a person; the enforcement of arrest warrants for offences punishable by five years or more of imprisonment and that are specified in the regulations; and arrest warrants under the Immigration and Refugee Protection Act and the Extradition Act. A record must be kept of all disclosures, the information disclosed, the reasons, and the name of the person or body to whom the information was disclosed. Information must be deleted within seven days of its receipt, unless required for security purposes. Despite these provisions, law enforcement authorities have stated clearly their intentions to interpret these provisions widely.[157]

This is a separate initiative from the Canadian Customs and Revenue Agency, a proposal to retain travel information for six years. Recently, that proposal has been altered to purge non-customs related data after it is no longer used, and to implement access controls on the database.

Australia has been actively pursuing the concept of a smart passport that includes digital photos. The government has run a trial of the SmartGate application at Sydney Airport, which was heavily criticized as involving ineffective and flawed technology.[158] At the same time, the Australian government has also been pushing for an advanced passenger processing system at the Asia-Pacific Economic Cooperation (APEC) forum.[159] In 2004, the Australian Customs agency received approval from the EU to access the passenger name records of EU citizens, because the Article 29 Working Party deemed the protections adequate.[160]

---

[155] *See* Campbell Clark, "Coderre Pushes Ottawa to Adopt National ID Cards," Globe and Mail, February 7, 2003.

[156] Canada News Wire, "Public Safety Act Receives Royal Assent," May 6, 2004.

[157] *See* Parliamentary Research Branch, "Legislative Summary of Bill C17: The Public Safety Act, 2002," Ottawa: Library of Parliament, 2004.

[158] Roger Clarke, "SmartGate: A Face Recognition Trial at Sydney Airport," February 28, 2003, available at <http://www.anu.edu.au/people/Roger.Clarke/DV/SmartGate.html>.

[159] APEC Media Release, "APEC Welcomes Australia's Support to Strengthen Regional Security," Sydney, Australia, April 30, 2003.

[160] Article 29 Data Protection Working Party, Opinion 1/2004 on the level of protection ensured in Australia for the transmission of Passenger Name Record data from airlines, January 16, 2004, 10031/03/EN WP85.

The New Zealand Customs Service began receiving advance passenger lists in 2003 from airlines under its Customs and Excise Act. The airlines would "feed data directly to the CS's computer system" before landing, and this information is checked for "people of interest." This system is seen as a first step to setting up an Advance Passenger Processing system that will identify problematic passengers prior to boarding flights.[161]

The European Union is pushing forward with a directive requiring carriers to collect and send data on all passengers at the time of boarding to law enforcement agencies in destination countries or face fines.[162]

Some legal developments pertain directly to information technology use. Cuba's law on combating terrorism includes hacking.[163] New Zealand's counter-terrorism bill could force individuals to disclose their passwords, even in non-terrorism related investigations, or face three months in jail or a fine of NZD 2,000.[164] Kenya's bill includes an offense for "collection of information for terrorist purposes," *i.e,* when someone "collects, makes or transmits a record of information of a kind likely to be useful to a person committing or preparing an act of terrorism; or possesses a document or record containing information of that kind shall be guilty of an offence' term not exceeding 10 years"; "transmit" includes by telephone, e-mail, voicemail, or other telecommunications method; and make available on the Internet. "It is a defense for a person charged with an offence under this section to satisfy the court that he had a reasonable excuse for his action or possession."

Democratic Challenges and International Policy Making

It is increasingly difficult to identify the sources of laws, however. Several countries have introduced new laws because of they feel it is imperative to model changes upon those in other countries. For example, Kenyan opposition party members accuse the United Kingdom and the United States for pressuring Kenya; they note that the definition of terrorism in the Kenyan bill is taken from

---

[161] Hon Rick Barker, "Airlines Cooperating to Provide Passenger Information," December 23, 2002, available at <http://beehive.govt.nz> (official website of the New Zealand government).

[162] Official Journal of the European Union, "Council Directive 2004/82/EC of 29 April 2004 on the Obligation of Carriers to Communicate Passenger Data," L261/24, August 6, 2004.

[163] Cuban National Assembly of People's Power, Laws Against Acts of Terrorism, Law No.92, 2002.

[164] Scott MacLeod, "Search Bill Breaks Password Barriers," New Zealand Herald, June 20, 2003.

Section 802 of the PATRIOT Act. This was denied by Justice and Constitutional Affairs Assistant Minister Robinson Njeru Githae.[165]

Another source of law includes international treaties. Romania's recently passed law on corruption includes components of the Council of Europe Convention on Cybercrime. Many countries are trying to ratify and implement into law the approximately 12 United Nations conventions on anti-terrorism. Governments report regularly to the United Nations Security Council committee on Resolution 1373 on their progress in adopting these conventions.[166] However, they are also adding to and interpreting these conventions. For example, New Zealand Justice Minister Phil Goff stated in April 2003 that the new Counter Terrorism Bill "was the final step in adopting the last of 12 United Nations conventions aimed at fighting terrorism. . . . It will give police and customs officers more powers to fight terrorism, including enabling police to use tracking devices, and will allow evidence found in the investigation of one crime to be used in the prosecution of another."[167] These additional powers are not included within the standard conventions.

It is therefore important to note not only the laws in other countries, but also the activities of international governmental organizations. These organizations have been very active in developing counter-terrorism policy tools and mechanisms.

The African Union, formerly the Organization of African Unity, released a convention in August 2002 in order to promote the criminalization of terrorist acts, and extradition and mutual legal assistance regimes.[168] While this convention contains controversial concepts with respect to civil liberties, it is far from unique considering the developments in recent years in such conventions as the Council of Europe Convention on Cybercrime.

The Asian-Pacific Economic Cooperation forum (APEC) held a summit in October 2002 in order to promote growth and fight against terrorism. An agreement emerged from the Mexico summit that aims to halt terrorist financing,

---

[165] "We have not to reinvented the wheel [sic]. What we have done is to pick the best of Suppression of Terrorism Act in the Commonwealth countries and given it a Kenyan outlook." "Suspected Terrorist, 24, Is Arrested," Nation (Nairobi), June 30, 2003, available at <http://allafrica.com/stories/200306300753.html>.

[166] For example, even Iraq under Saddam Hussein reported to the committee regarding Iraq's adherence to the conventions. *See* Mohammed A. Aldouri, Letter dated 13 August 2002 from the Permanent Representative of Iraq to the United Nations addressed to the Chairman of the Security Council committee established pursuant to resolution 1373(2001) concerning counter-terrorism.

[167] NZPA, "PM's War Stance Criticised as Parliament Debates Terrorism Bill," New Zealand Herald, April 2, 2003.

[168] Organization of African Unity Convention on the Prevention and Combating of Terrorism, August 21, 2002.

and to promote cyber-security. At the 2003 summit in Bangkok, the US tried to focus the agenda on how anti-terrorism policy can support global trade, to the concern of some APEC members who wanted to focus on economic issues.[169] The final declaration included a statement that APEC leaders will undertake measures to "dismantle, fully and without delay, transnational terrorist groups that threaten APEC economies."[170] The group will now create a fund, run by the Asian Development Bank, to finance counter-terrorism initiatives including port security and anti-money laundering.[171] It now appears that APEC is considering the creation of "financial intelligence units" to combat the diversion of money from trade to terror groups.[172] Now APEC is calling on all member states to implement biometric passports and is promoting advanced passenger information systems.[173]

The Association for Southeastern Asian Nations (ASEAN) 2003 summer summit included an agreement to obtain and share evidence amongst member countries, share bank records, cooperate in the freezing of foreign assets, and conduct searches and seizures upon request from fellow members; all in the aim to combat terrorism and cross-border crime.[174] An uncommon development, however, is the lack of agreement on extradition. Discussions have also occurred on the issue of secure identity documents. This disagreement continued, however, in the October 2003 summit when the summit statement paid little attention to anti-terrorism policy.[175] The summit did see the establishment of the ASEAN Security Community, strongly advocated by Indonesia,[176] that would not only focus on terrorism, but also on other transnational crimes.[177] This was followed up with a meeting in Bangkok of the ASEAN+3 countries (ASEAN and China, South Korea, and Japan), where ministers vowed to improve communication and enhance intelligence sharing, "especially against the growing

---

[169] Jane Macartney and Darren Schuettler, "Bush Intensifies Security Push at APEC Summit," October 20 2003.

[170] Straights Times, "US Focus on Terrorism to Be in Final Declaration," October 21, 2003.

[171] Graeme Dobell, "APEC Announces Anti-Terrorism Measures," Australian Broadcasting Corporation Online, October 21, 2003.

[172] Xinhua Online, "APEC Considers Creating Financial Intelligence Units to Fight Terrorism," March 7, 2004.

[173] Joint Statement of the Sixteenth APEC Ministerial Meeting, Santiago, Chile, 17-18 November 2004.

[174] Associated Press and Agence France Presss, "ASEAN Summit Covers Terrorism, Oil Reserves," Taipei Times, July 3, 2003, at 5.

[175] Jerry Norton, "Draft ASEAN Document Thin on Terrorism, Myanmar," Reuters, October 5, 2003.

[176] Id.

[177] Press Statement by the Chairperson of the 9th ASEAN Summit and the 7th ASEAN+3 Summit, Bali, Indonesia, October 7, 2003.

threat of terrorism in the region."[178] This would be done through the speeding up of mutual assistance and extradition treaties.

The Group of 8 industrialized countries (G8) is the primary source of discussion on secure passports. At the May 2003 summit of Justice and Home Affairs ministers in Paris, the United Kingdom reportedly promoted computerized passports.[179] The ministers unanimously stressed the importance of developing biometric technologies with the goal of developing a common framework for biometric passports, as is being discussed by the International Civil Aviation Organization (ICAO). There was some disagreement, according to reports, that the French and the US differed on which form of biometrics should be promoted (reports stated that the US supported iris scans or "other innovative technologies," while the French supported fingerprints).[180] In the end, according to ICAO, facial recognition was adopted at the end of May 2003.[181] Other issues addressed by ministers included critical infrastructure protection, child pornography, and enhancing financial investigations. In this last issue of discussion, the G8 ministers promoted the work of experts who "identified 29 best practice principles on tracing, freezing, seizing and confiscating crime-related assets," while admitting that "these principles and good practices are ambitious."[182]

The G8 Evian summit of heads of government met in June 2003. At this summit, the G8 created the Counter-Terrorism Action Group (CTAG), which would support the UN Counter-Terrorism Committee for "capacity building."[183] The proposal was led by the US, with the goal to create a group that would deal with "terrorist financing, customs and immigration controls, illegal arms trafficking, police and law enforcement"; "will identify relevant international best practices, codes, and standards in combating terrorism"; "target counterterrorism assistance to priority countries"; and "work with International Financial institutions to strengthen counterterrorism financing measures."[184]

---

[178] Nancy-Amelia Collins, "'ASEAN Plus 3' Pledge to Combat Transnational Terror," Voice of America News, January 10, 2004.

[179] Nigel Morris, "Blunkett Urges Leading Nations to Adopt Computerised Passports," Independent, May 5, 2003.

[180] John Tagliabue, "Group of 8 Finds Unity on the Threat of Terrorism," New York Times, May 6, 2003.

[181] ICAO Press Release PIO 09/2003, "Biometric Identification to Provide Enhanced Security and Speedier Border Clearance for Travelling Public," Montreal, May 28, 2003, available at <http://www.icao.int/icao/en/nr/pio200309.htm>.

[182] President's Summary, Meeting of G8 Ministers of Justice and Home Affairs, Paris, 5 May 2003.

[183] Chair's Summary, Evian, June 3, 2003, available at <http://usinfo.state.gov/topical/econ/group8/summit03/03060308.htm>.

[184] Office of the Press Secretary, "Fact Sheet: Action to Enhance Global Capacity to Combat Terror," White House, June 2, 2003.

The G8 summits for 2004, held in the US, furthered these ideas. The Justice and Home Affairs Ministers summit called for legislation to enable sharing of information among and between the intelligence community, the law enforcement community and prosecutors to the fullest degree possible, to prevent, disrupt and preempt terrorist activities; while giving due regard to civil liberties and fundamental principles of law.[185] The ministerial summit also called for "special investigative techniques" that involve undercover agents, cover filing and listening devices, and covert interception of "all forms of electronic communications," and "the use of other critical measures," but that they must take into account privacy rights; while states are encouraged to change legal procedure to allow such techniques to be used in courts.[186] The official Sea Island Summit of G8 leaders, however, did not reflect much of this. That summit included new language regarding a "Secure and Facilitated International Travel Initiative" to protect borders through the sharing of personal information and secure travel documents.[187]

At the G8 summit in Gleneagles, the world was focusing on aid and environmental issues. During the summit, a number of bombs exploded on the London transport system. This led to a number of new declarations on terrorism. Unlike past declarations, the goals gave much fewer details. Previous declarations contained specific policy initiatives, usually released with action plans. Remarkably little detail emerged regarding these new anti-terrorism initiatives. The leaders called for increased sharing of information on the movement of terrorists across borders, particularly intelligence and police information, policy expertise, and even analyses. They referred particularly to terrorist travel, and possibly document security.[188] Similarly, the G8 called for further work at the UN and other organizations to build the political will and capacity of other countries to combat terrorism.

The Commonwealth Secretariat also engaged in work to promote capacity building. In 2002 the secretariat developed "Implementation Kits for International Counter-Terrorism Conventions," a form of "do-it-yourself" manual

---

[185] Meeting of G8 Justice and Home Affairs Ministers, "Recommendations for Sharing and Protecting National Security Intelligence Information in the Investigation and Prosecution of Terrorists and Those Who Commit Associated Offenses," Washington, May 11 2004.

[186] Meeting of G8 Justice and Home Affairs Ministers, "Recommendations on Special Investigative Techniques and other Critical Measures for Combating Organized Crime and Terrorism," Washington, May 11 2004.

[187] G8 Secure and Facilitated International Travel Initiative Statement and Action Plan, Sea Island, June 10 2004.

[188] G8 Statement on Counter-Terrorism, Gleneagles, July 8, 2005.

for governments, covering all 12 multilateral treaties drawn up between 1963 and 1999 by the UN and other inter-governmental fora.[189] In September 2002, the secretariat also released "Model Legislative Provisions on Measures to Combat Terrorism," which define for specified entities a variety of offenses and their investigation, interception of communications and admissibility as evidence. The model provisions also establish procedures for trials, promotion of information sharing, ensure extradition and mutual legal assistance, empower governments to seize evidence, manage charities, outline refugee application refusals, and allow for the removal of persons.[190]

The intergovernmental policy area of financial regulations is dominated by the output of the Financial Action Task Force (FATF). In the early 1990s, FATF developed its 40 recommendations on combating money laundering. In April 2002, FATF released guidance for financial institutions for detecting terrorist financing and conducted consultation on 40 recommendations for terrorist financing, thus extending beyond money laundering. In June 2003, the new recommendations were adopted. According to FATF:

> The FATF recognises [sic] that countries have diverse legal and financial systems and so all cannot take identical measures to achieve the common objective, especially over matters of detail. The Recommendations therefore set minimum standards for action for countries to implement the detail according to their particular circumstances and constitutional frameworks. The Recommendations cover all the measures that national systems should have in place within their criminal justice and regulatory systems; the preventive measures to be taken by financial institutions and certain other businesses and professions; and international co-operation.[191]

The acknowledgement of flexibility is due to, according to reports, disagreement on regulatory procedures between American and German delegations.[192] The recommendations include the requirement that institutional secrecy laws are not used to inhibit implementation, and recommend against the keeping of anonymous accounts, with some recommendations on identification as "due

---

[189] Preface, by Anthony Aust, to the Implementation Kits for the International Counter-Terrorism Conventions, Criminal Law Section, Legal and Constitutional Affairs Division, Commonwealth Secretariat, London, United Kingdom.

[190] Commonwealth Secretariat, Model Legislative Provisions on Measures to Combat Terrorism, Criminal Law Section, Legal and Constitutional Affairs Division, September 2002.

[191] Financial Action Task Force on Money Laundering, The Forty Recommendations, June 2003.

[192] Hugh Williamson, "Tighter Rules Agreed on Money Laundering," Financial Times, June 20, 2003.

diligence." Cooperation between countries is also recommended, as is the removal of unduly restrictive conditions for this cooperation to take place. The scope of application also increases; non-financial businesses including lawyers and notaries except when under privilege.

Inter-governmental organizations in the Europe have been very active as well. The Southeastern Europe Cooperation Initiative (SECI) Regional Center for Fight Against Cross-Border Crimes had its first meeting of "Mission Force for Fight Against terrorism" [sic], in June 2003. Held in Turkey, 85 representatives attended from Albania, Bulgaria, Bosnia-Herzegovina, Croatia, Hungary, Macedonia, Moldova, Romania, Greece, Slovenia and Serbia-Montenegro. According to Turkish Security Director General Gokhan Aydiner, "Turkey has been trying for years to bring the issue of terrorism onto agenda of the world. In some countries, terrorist organizations and their members are considered fighters of freedom. Those who staged gory actions in which thousands of people lost their lives, continue their terrorism activities without any punishment."[193] According to media reports, the task force aimed to cover organized crimes and terrorism, development of common operational plans, financial sources of terrorist organizations.

The Organization for Security and Cooperation in Europe (OSCE) began a new initiative with its first annual security review conference in June 2003. A speech by US Ambassador Cofer Black, Coordinator for Counterterrorism, called on OSCE to continue fighting terrorism, to encourage FATF adherence, to implement UN conventions (noting that only 38 percent of OSCE states have become parties to all 12), and to do the utmost to prevent spread of small arms and light weapons. He also called for closer cooperation with the UN, G8, and ICAO to develop international standards and in turn to encourage regional implementation. Particularly, he called for cooperation on the issue of travel document security with G8 and ICAO.[194] This was supported by "several delegations," as it was felt that "this work could make a significant, real contribution not only to the war on terrorism, but also to the fight against organized crime and illegal immigration, all issues that many delegations had identified as threats to their security and stability."[195] The Bulgarian government, which took over the leadership of OSCE in 2004, promised to steer the

---

[193] Anadolu Agency, "Ecemis: Terrorism Is a Universal Trouble," Turkish Press, June 9, 2003.

[194] Ambassador Cofer Black, Keynote address to the Organization for Security and Cooperation in Europe; Annual Security Review Conference, Vienna, Austria, June 25, 2003.

[195] OSCE Press Release, "OSCE Security Conference Considers Fresh Options," Vienna, June 26, 2003, available at <http://www.osce.org/news/show_news.php?id=3382>.

organization towards greater international cooperation in combating terrorism and safeguarding national borders.[196]

The vast majority of these meetings of inter-governmental organizations outlined above were closed. In the coming months and years, however, their work, findings, conclusions, and conventions will affect national policy discourse.

This will be particularly the case in the European Union and primarily the output of the Council, where there is more of a binding requirement to enact policies at the national level. As accession countries to the EU begin their process of legal harmonization, interpretation and guidance on EU policies will require scrutiny. The EU has been active in all of the issues covered above. In 2001 and 2002, the Council Framework Decision on a European arrest warrant was developed and is currently being implemented into national law. A Working Party on Terrorism has been convened to develop measures to exchange information between member states and the creation of computer-aided preventative searches on the basis of offender profiles (particularly the compiling of travel patterns).[197] These profiles may include method and means of travel, "physical distinguishing features (*e.g.*, battle scars)," education, places of stay, methods of communication, psycho-sociological features, family situation, expertise in advanced technologies; with the aim to identify terrorists before an act is carried out. A proposed innovation includes searching through "relevant national databases (*e.g.*, registers of residents, registers of foreigners, universities etc.) subject to the provisions of national law, for person who need to be vetted more closely by the security authorities."[198]

The EU has also developed a "roadmap" regarding the implementation of an "EU Action Plan in the fight against terrorism." This roadmap includes the discussion of counter-terrorism in political dialogues with third countries and other multilateral fora. The EU has been particularly active in meetings with Asian countries, and in meetings with the US on mutual legal assistance.[199] The roadmap also consists of enhancing preventing of crime involving the use of

---

[196] Melanie Sully, "Combatting Terrorism to Top Agenda, Says New OSCE Chief," Voice of America News, December 30, 2003.

[197] Council of the European Union, Outcome of Proceedings of meeting of Working Party on Terrorism, November 25, 2002, released on December 12, 2002, 15147/02 LIMITE ENFOPOL 151.

[198] Council of the European Union, Note from the German Delegation to the Article 36 Committee on Computer-aided preventative searches carried out by individual Member States on the basis of coordinated offender profiles (Europe-wide electronic profile searches), Brussels, October 31, 2002, 13626/02 LIMITE ENFOPOL 130.

[199] Council of the European Union, Presidency Note – To: General Affairs and External Relations Council; Subject: European Union action plan to combat terrorism – Update of the roadmap, Brussels, November 14, 2002, 13909/1/02 REV 1.

electronic communications systems, measures to counter insider dealing, transparency criteria for legal entities, initiatives to draw up a common list of terrorist organizations, and the "systematic transmission to Europol of any piece of data relevant to terrorism," while complying with international obligations regarding protection of fundamental rights and ensuring "a balance between data protection and police efficiency," among other initiatives.

After the March 2004 bombings in Madrid, the EU rushed forward on these initiatives. Amidst calls from the UK Home Office Secretary David Blunkett to "cut the waffle" and to follow up on plans agreed to at the EU years ago, he called for EU member states to implement security measures agreed to after the September 11 attacks.[200] The UK then pushed for other countries to adopt rules on data retention and the EU-wide arrest warrant; although some resistance arose from Sweden, Germany, and Denmark.[201] The final declaration reflected these sentiments, calling for rules on the retention of communications traffic, and simplifying exchanges of information across borders, with a view to adoption by June 2005.[202]

These initiatives led to the establishment of the "Hague Programme." This is a five-year action plan, under the auspices of freedom, justice and security.[203] This program was launched in November 2004, and gained momentum in May 2005 when 10 key action areas were identified. These action plans consist of detailed proposals for EU action on terrorism, migration management, visa policies, asylum, privacy and security, the fight against organized crime and criminal justice.

Following the London bombings in July 2005, days after the UK took over the Presidency of the European Union, the data-sharing momentum increased. Topics on the UK's agenda include data retention for three years, discussion of data protection regulations in the third pillar, increased data sharing between countries under the "principle of availability,"[204] new border security measures, identity documents and fingerprinting of EU residents and citizens, and monitoring of financial transactions.

---

[200] Matthew Tempest and agencies, "Blunkett Attacks EU 'Waffle' on Security," Guardian, March 19, 2004.

[201] The Guardian newspaper reported one diplomat at the EU meeting stating that "Infringements of privacy are at most annoying. Infringements of security can be fatal." Ian Black, "Britain Urges EU to Tighten Security," Guardian, March 19, 2004.

[202] The European Council, Declaration on Combating Terrorism, Brussels, March 25, 2004.

[203] Formerly known as "Justice and Home Affairs."

[204] If one country has information that may be of use to another, then countries are obliged to make this information available for use by others.

While the anti-terrorism policy developments outlined above and later in this report have shifted the legal and technological landscape for privacy, there have been some developments in the area of civil liberties and terrorism.

In the US, opposition to the USA-PATRIOT Act has grown. In response to the law, some librarians have begun to tape warnings to computer screens that usage could be subject to scrutiny by law enforcement agencies; in some cases they are destroying records of reading habits and sign-up logs of computer use.[205] There have been successful amendments on TIA- and CAPPS II-related policies to call for studies of the privacy and civil liberties implications of these programs. Finally, in many districts and cities, there is opposition to the PATRIOT Act. Hundreds of local governments have passed laws against the act.[206] Members of Congress and Senators continue to introduce new legislation to minimize the threats to privacy and civil liberties.

Changes in proposed and existing laws are occurring for several reasons elsewhere in the world. In Hong Kong in 2003, after protests including one involving more than 400,000 demonstrators, the government appeared to have backed down on changes to the Basic Law to deal with sedition.[207] Jordan rescinded Article 150 of its penal code, which was introduced in response to the events of September 11, 2001. The article had allowed for "permanent or temporary closure" of publications that "carry false or libelous information that can undermine national unity or the country's reputation," and publications carrying articles that incite "crimes, strikes, illegal public assemblies or undermining public order."[208]

In the most severe case, Peru was forced to review sentences given out to 1,800 people when the high court handed down a decision rejecting the anti-terrorism decrees established under the Fujimori government as unconstitutional.[209] These decrees included trials for treason before hooded military judges and life sentences without review,[210] including for offenses relating to free expression.[211]

---

[205] Rene Sanchez, "Librarians Make Some Noise Over Patriot Act," Washington Post, April 10, 2003, at A20.

[206] The American Civil Liberties Union has a Web page that focuses on community resolutions, <http://www.aclu.org/SafeandFree/SafeandFree.cfm?ID=11256&c=206>.

[207] Keith Bradsher, "Hong Kong Chief Executive Faces Calls to Step Down," New York Times, July 8, 2003.

[208] Middle East Online, "Jordan Scraps Tough New Press Law Clause," April 22, 2003, available at <http://www.middle-east-online.com/english/Default.pl?id=5248>.

[209] Associated Press, "Peru to Review 1,800 Terrorism Sentences," February 21, 2003.

[210] Reuters, "Peru's Toledo Wants Power to Legislate on Terrorism," January 8, 2003.

The effectiveness of opposition may take some time to take full effect. After India's anti-terrorism bill became law, it was reported that the entire opposition to the government walked out on Parliament.[212] Since its enactment, however, and after its use to detain some politicians, the Parliament has constituted a Review Committee to ensure that the powers are not misused for non-terrorism purposes.[213]

The new government in India repealed the controversial Prevention of Terrorism Act (POTA). As stated in the President's address to Parliament in June 2004, "My government is concerned about the misuse of POTA in the recent past. While there can be no compromise on the fight against terrorism, the Government is of the view that existing laws could adequately handle the menace of terrorism. The Government, therefore, proposes to repeal POTA."[214]

Other efforts for repealing laws came close, or are in the works. In the United Kingdom House of Lords, efforts to repeal the retention of communications data almost succeeded in November 2003. A Privy Council Report emerged in December 2003 calling on data retention to be separated from anti-terror legislation and given its day in Parliament for appropriate deliberation and oversight, while also limiting retention to one year and placing that language in the primary legislation.[215] The European Commission's decision to permit the flow of passenger information from European carriers' databases to the US Department of Homeland Security has been questioned repeatedly by the European Parliament, and the Parliament has taken its case to the European Court of Justice.[216] These are merely some of the sources of change.

Non-governmental organizations around the world have questioned draft laws, bills, and court decisions and have voiced concerns, taken cases to courts, and responded to consultation processes. The arising court decisions may lead to further changes, parliamentarians may listen more, and increased attention to

---

[211] Noah Leavitt, "Peru as Our Crystal Ball? One possible Future for America's War on Terrorism, and the Lessons That Can Help Us Avoid It," Findlaw Legal Commentary, June 6, 2003, available at <http://writ.findlaw.com/commentary/20030605_leavitt.html>.

[212] CNN, "India Terror Bill Faces Upper House Test," March 21, 2002.

[213] India Express Bureau, "Allies Force Centre to Set up POTA Review Committee," March 13, 2003.

[214] Text of President Kalam's Address to the Indian Parliament, June 7, 2004.

[215] Privy Councillors Review Committee, "Anti-terrorism, Crime, and Security Act 2001 Review: Report," December 18, 2003.

[216] EGovernment News, "European Parliament Asks Court of Justice to Annul EU-US Passenger Data Deal," European Commission Interchange of Data Between Administrations eGovernment Observatory, June 25 2004.

international organizations may lead to more open policy-making, and as a result, better laws.

Identity systems

Identity (ID) cards

Identity (ID) cards are in use in one form or another in virtually all countries of the world. The type of card, its functions, and integrity vary enormously. While several countries have official, compulsory, national ID cards that are used for a variety of purposes, many countries do not. These include Australia, Canada, India, Ireland, New Zealand, the United States and the Nordic countries. Those that do have such a card include Belgium, Egypt, France, Germany, Greece, Hong Kong, Malaysia, and South Africa.

Nationwide ID systems are established for a variety of reasons. Race, politics and religion often drive the deployment of ID cards.[217] The fear of insurgence, religious differences, immigration, or political extremism have been all too common motivators for the establishment of ID systems that aim to force undesirables in a State to register with the government, or make them vulnerable in the open without proper documents.

In recent years technology has rapidly evolved to enable electronic record creation and the construction of large commercial and state databases. A national identifier contained in an ID card enables disparate information about a person that is stored in different databases to be easily linked and analyzed through data mining techniques. ID cards are also becoming "smarter" – the technology to build microprocessors the size of postage stamps and put them on wallet-sized cards has become more affordable. This technology enables multiple applications such as a credit card, library card, health care card, driver's license and government benefit program information to be all stored on the same national ID along with a password or a biometric identifier. Governments in Finland, Malaysia, and Singapore have experimented with such "Smart" ID cards. In July 2002, the Labor government in the United Kingdom launched a six-month public consultation process on whether the United Kingdom should adopt an

---

[217] Richard Sobel, The Degradation of Political Identity Under a National Identification System, 8 B.U. J. Sci. & Techapter L. 37, 48 (2002). *See also* National Research Council, "IDs - Not that Easy: Questions about Nationwide Identity Systems," 2002, available at <http://www.nap.edu/catalog/10346.html?opi_newsdoc041102>.

"entitlement card" with similar features.[218] Critics contend that such cards, especially when combined with information contained in databases, enable intrusive profiling of individuals and create a misplaced reliance on a single document, which enables precisely the type of fraud the cards are meant to eliminate.[219] In April 2004 the UK Government announced its draft bill on the identity card and a back-end database of all residents.

In several countries, these systems have been successfully challenged on constitutional privacy grounds. In 1998, the Philippine Supreme Court ruled that a national ID system violated the constitutional right to privacy.[220] In 1991, the Hungarian Constitutional Court ruled that a law creating a multi-use personal identification number violated the constitutional right of privacy.[221] The 1997 Portuguese Constitution states "Citizens shall not be given an all-purpose national identity number."[222]

In other countries, opposition to the cards combined with the high economic cost and other logistical difficulties of implementing the systems has led to their withdrawal. Massive protests against the Australia Card in 1987 resulted in the near collapse of the government. Card projects in South Korea and Taiwan were also stopped after widespread protests. In the United States plans to convert the state driver's license into a nationwide system of identification have stalled because of the stiff resistance from a broad coalition of civil society groups.[223]

Biometrics

Biometrics is the identification or verification of someone's identity on the basis of physiological or behavioral characteristics. Biometrics involves comparing a previously captured unique characteristic of a person to a new sample provided by the person. This information is used to authenticate or verify that a person is who they said they were (a one-to-one match) by comparing the previously

---

[218] "Entitlement Cards and Identity Fraud: A Consultation Paper," Presented to the Parliament by the Secretary of State for the Home Department, July 2002, available at <http://www.homeoffice.gov.uk/cpd/entitlement_cards.pdf>.

[219] Simon Davies. "The Id Card Is the Fraudster's Friend," The Sunday Telegraph, July 7, 2002. *See also*, Oscar H. Gandy, Jr., The Panoptic Sort: A Political Economy of Personal Information (Westview Press 1993).

[220] Philippine Supreme Court Decision of the National ID System, July 23, 1998, G.R. 127685, available at <http://bknet.org/laws/national*Id.*html>.

[221] Constitutional Court Decision No. 15-AB of 13 April 1991, available at <http://www.privacy.org/pi/countries/hungary/hungarian_id_decision_1991.html>.

[222] Article 35 (5), Constitution Of The Portuguese Republic 1976 (as amended), available at <http://www.parlamento.pt/leis/constituicao_ingles/crp_uk.htm#article_35>.

[223] *See generally* EPIC's National ID Pages <http://www.epic.org/privacy/id_cards/>.

stored characteristic to the fresh characteristic provided. It can also be used for identification purposes where the fresh characteristic is compared against all the stored characteristics (a one-to-many match). New biometric technology attempts to automate the identification or verification process by converting the provided biometric into an algorithm, which is then used for matching purposes. The computer matching technique necessarily produces either false positives, where a person is incorrectly identified as someone else, or false negatives, where a person who is meant to be identified by the system is not correctly identified. The two error rates are dependent, so for example reducing the number of false positives increases the number of false negatives. The tolerance level is adjusted depending on the need for security in the application.

The most popular forms of biometric ID are fingerprints, retina/iris scans, hand geometry, voice recognition, and digitized (electronically stored) images. The technology is gaining interest from governments and companies because, unlike other forms of ID such as cards or papers, it can be more difficult to alter or tamper with one's own physical or behavior characteristics. Important questions remain, however, about the effectiveness of the automated biometric matching techniques, particularly for large-scale applications.[224] Critics also argue that widespread deployment of biometric identification technology could remove the veil of anonymity or pseudo-anonymity in most daily transactions through the creation an electronic trail of people's movements and habits.[225]

Biometrics schemes are being implemented across the world. The technology is widely used in small settings for access control to secure locations such a nuclear facility or bank vault. It is increasingly being used for broader applications such as retail outlets, government agencies, childcare centers, police forces and automated-teller machines. Spain has commenced a national fingerprint system for unemployment benefits and healthcare entitlements. Russia has announced plans for a national electronic fingerprint system for banks. Jamaicans are required to scan their thumbs into a database before qualifying to vote in elections. In France and Germany, tests are under way with equipment that puts fingerprint information onto credit cards. Many computer manufacturers are considering including biometric readers on their systems for security purposes.

The most controversial form of biometrics – DNA identification – is benefiting from new scanning technology that can automatically match DNA samples

[224] Deutsche Bank Research, "Biometrics – Hype and Reality," May 22, 2002, available at <http://www.dbresearchaptercom/PROD/999/PROD0000000000043270.pdf>

[225] Roger Clarke, "Biometrics and Privacy," April 15, 2001, available at <http://www.anu.edu.au/people/Roger.Clarke/DV/Biometrics.html>.

against a large database in minutes. Police forces in several countries including Canada, Germany, and the United States have created national DNA databases. Samples are being routinely taken from a larger group of people. Initially, it was only individuals convicted of sexual crimes. Then it was expanded to people convicted of other violent crimes and then to arrests. Now, many jurisdictions are collecting samples from all individuals arrested, even for the most minor offenses. Former New York City Mayor Rudolf Giuliani even proposed that all children have a DNA sample collected at birth. In Australia, the United Kingdom, and the United States, police have been demanding that all individuals in a particular area voluntarily provide samples or face being considered a suspect. United States Attorney General Ashcroft has testified that he has asked the FBI to increase the capacity of its database from 1.5 million to 50 million profiles.[226]

At the same time, DNA data has been used as exculpatory evidence in many criminal trials.

Biometric Passports

The USA-PATRIOT Act, passed by the US Congress after the events of September 11, 2001 included the requirement that the President certify a biometric technology standard for use in identifying aliens seeking admission into the US, within two years. The schedule for its implementation was accelerated by another piece of legislation, the little known Enhanced Border Security and Visa Entry Reform Act 2002. Part of this second law included seeking international co-operation with this standard. The incentive to international co-operation was made clear: "By October 26, 2004, in order for a country to remain eligible for participation in the visa waiver program its government must certify that it has a program to issue to its nationals machine-readable passports that are tamper-resistant and which incorporate biometric and authentication identifiers that satisfy the standards of the International Civil Aviation Organization (ICAO).

These laws gave momentum to the standards that were being considered at the ICAO by requiring visa waiver countries (which include many EU countries, Australia, Brunei, Iceland, Japan, Monaco, New Zealand, Norway, Singapore, and Slovenia) to implement biometrics into their Machine-Readable Travel

---

[226] Attorney General Transcript, News Conference - DNA Initiatives, Monday, March 4, 2002, DOJ Conference Center.

Documents (MRTDs), *i.e.* passports. Failure to do so, presumably, means a removal from the program.

Moving the decision to the ICAO pushes the policy well beyond the Visa Waiver Program countries. The ICAO is the international standard-setter for passports already and the ICAO has been researching biometric passports since 1995. Since then the technologies have changed sufficiently to allow for facial recognition, fingerprints and iris scans to be considered for implementation in passports standards.

The primary purposes of biometric use, according to the ICAO, is to allow for verification ("confirming identity by comparing identity details of the person claiming to be a specific living individual against details previously recorded on that individual") and identification ("determining possible identity by comparing identity details of the presenting person against details previously recorded on a number of living individuals"). Beneficial side effects include advanced passenger information to ports of entry, and electronic tracking of passport use.

In May 2003, the facial recognition emerged as the primary candidate. Intellectual Property issues prevented iris scans from being accepted; while it was felt that the facial recognition is more socially acceptable. Multiple applications of biometrics are also considered, and permitted. Although the use of a single biometric technology by all States is preferred by the ICAO to ensure interoperability, "[h]owever, it is also recognized that some States may conclude it desirable to deploy two biometrics on the same document." Already the EU is discussing requiring fingerprints in passports.

The ICAO is aware, however, that there are contentious legal issues involved with the infrastructure for these passports, including the collisions between the goals of centralizing citizens' biometrics and protecting privacy laws, and with "cultural practices." Not only does this involve a central data store of fingerprints and photos (and face scans) that can be scanned against other databases for other purposes, but this sensitive information may be transferred to other countries when verification is required at border controls. The ICAO foresees that this information may be retained by these other countries. In essence, this may turn into a global distributed database of personal information.

Something that may be important to remember at the time of national implementation is that there is some flexibility permitted by the ICAO. Some states may interpret the ICAO standards to require centralised databases.[227]

The ICAO calls for central databases that allow for additional security confirmation checks, but does not go so far as to require such systems. It may be interesting to see if national governments recall this option, or if they rather change their national laws to allow for centralized storage, as allowed in other ICAO documents. Already the EU is moving towards a centralized registry of biometrics from the passport enrolment process.

Surveillance of Communications

Most countries around the world regulate the interception of communications by governments and private individuals and organizations. These controls typically take the form of constitutional provisions protecting the privacy of communications and laws and regulations that implement those requirements.

There has been great pressure on countries to adopt wiretapping laws to address new technologies. These laws are also in response to law enforcement and intelligence agencies pressure to increase surveillance capabilities. In Japan, wiretapping was only approved as a legal method of investigation in 1999. Other countries such as Australia, Belgium, Germany, New Zealand, South Africa and the United Kingdom have all updated their laws to facilitate surveillance of new technologies.

The United States government has been at the forefront of promoting greater use of electronic surveillance. Former FBI Director Louis Freeh traveled extensively around the world, promoting the use of wiretapping in newly democratic countries such as Hungary and the Czech Republic. At the same time, the United States has led world efforts to ensure that all communications technologies have built-in surveillance capabilities and to prohibit the manufacture and use of equipment that cannot be eavesdropped upon. The United States has also been working through international organizations such as the OECD, G-8 and the Council of Europe to promote surveillance.

---

[227] *See generally* ICAO. Biometrics Deployment of Machine Readable Travel Documents ICAO TAG MRTD/NTWG Technical Report: Development and Specification of Globally Interoperable Biometric Standards for Machine Assisted Identity Confirmation using Machine Readable Travel Documents, Montreal: ICAO, May 12 2003.

It is recognized worldwide that wiretapping and electronic surveillance are a highly intrusive form of investigation that should only be used in limited and unusual circumstances. Nearly all major international agreements on human rights protect the right of individuals from unwarranted invasive surveillance.

Nearly every country in the world has enacted laws on the interception of oral, telephone, fax and telex communications. In most democratic countries, intercepts are initiated by law enforcement or intelligence agencies only after it has been approved by an judge or some other kind of independent magistrate or high level official and generally only for serious crimes. Frequently, it must be shown that other types of investigation were attempted and were not successful. There is some divergence on what constitutes a "serious crime," and appropriate approval.

Several countries including France and the United Kingdom have created special commissions that review wiretap usage and monitor for abuses. These bodies have developed an expertise in the area that most judges who authorize surveillance do not have, while they also have the ability to conduct follow up investigations once a case is complete. In other countries, the privacy commissioner or data protection authority has some ability to conduct oversight of electronic surveillance.

An important oversight measure that many countries employ is the requiring of annual public reporting of information about the use of electronic surveillance by government departments. These reports typically provide summary details about the number of uses of electronic surveillance, the types of crimes that they are authorized for, their duration and other information. This is a common feature of wiretap laws in English-speaking countries and many others in Europe. Countries that issue annual reports on the use of surveillance include Australia, Canada, France, New Zealand, Sweden, the United Kingdom, and the United States. Meanwhile in the Netherlands, the Minister of Justice in April 2003 announced that he saw no additional value in maintaining a log of the frequency of wiretaps, or installing a special functionary to oversee the warranty process.[228][229]

---

[228] Joe Figueiredo, "Dutch Authorities Decline Request for Wiretapping Details," Europemedia.net, April 4, 2003, available at <http://www.europemedia.net/shownews.asp?ArticleID=15745>.

[229] It is therefore not surprising to notice that the Netherlands have one of the highest rates of wiretaps in the European Union. *See* Hans-Jorg Albrecht, Claudia Dorsch, Christiane Krupe, *Rechtswirklichkeit und Effizienz der Überwachung der Telekommunikation*, Max Planck Institute for Foreign and International Criminal Law. June 2003. Italy actually has the highest number (76 taps per 100.000 inhabitants), the Netherlands comes

These countries recognize that it is necessary to allow for people outside governments to know about its uses to limit abuses. They are widely used in many countries by the Parliaments for oversight and also by journalists, NGOs and others to examine the activities of law enforcement. The reports have shown an increase in the use of surveillance in many countries including Australia,[230] the United States, and the United Kingdom while others such as Canada have remained steady. Most recently, however, Canada has reduced the amount of reporting; despite statutory requirements, annual reports from the Solicitor General on surveillance activities have not been released since 1999.[231]

These laws are designed to ensure that legitimate and normal activities in a democracy such as journalism, civic protests, trade union organizing or political opposition are free from being subjected to unwarranted surveillance because they have different interests and goals than those in power. It also ensures that relatively minor crimes, especially those that would not generally involve telecommunications for facilitation, are not used as a pretext to conduct intrusive surveillance for political or other reasons.

However, wiretapping abuses have been revealed in most countries, sometimes occurring on a vast scale involving thousands of illegal taps. The abuses invariably affect anyone "of interest" to a government. Targets include political opponents, student leaders and human rights workers.[232] This can occur even in the most democratic of countries such as Denmark and Sweden, where it was recently disclosed that intelligence agencies were conducting surveillance of thousands of left-leaning activists for nearly 40 years.

The United Nations Commissioner on Human Rights in 1988 made clear that human rights protections on the secrecy of communications broadly covers all forms of communications:

> Compliance with Article 17 requires that the integrity and confidentiality of correspondence should be guaranteed *de jure* and *de facto*. Correspondence should be delivered to the addressee without interception and without being opened or otherwise read. Surveillance, whether electronic or otherwise, interceptions of telephonic, telegraphic

---

second with 62 and Switzerland is number three with 32. *See*
<http://www.iuscrim.mpg.de/verlag/online/Band_115.pdf>.

[230] Reuters News Agency, "In Australia, Chances Are that Your Phone Is Tapped," September 16, 2002.

[231] Tyler Hamilton, "Powers Snoop More, Explain Why Less," Toronto Star, March 24, 2003.

[232] United States Department of State, Country Report on Human Rights Practices 1997, January 30, 1998.

and other forms of communication, wire-tapping and recording of conversations should be prohibited.[233]

The need for greater protection is recognized by many democratic countries around the world. Most recently, the German Federal Constitutional Court has considered whether the interception laws passed in 1998 are constitutional.[234] In March 2004, the German Federal Constitutional Court ruled[235] that significant portions of the 1998 Grosser Lauschangriff[236] wiretapping laws infringed upon the guarantees of human dignity and the inviobility of the home under Articles 1 and 13 of the constitution, or Basic Law.[237] The court held that certain communications are protected by an absolute area of intimacy where citizens can communicate privately without fear of government surveillance.[238] This includes conversations with close family members, priests, doctors and defense attorneys, but excludes conversations about crimes that have already been committed or the planning of future crimes. However, to justify surveillance between the target and such persons of trust, the government must show "there is strong reason to believe that the content of conversation does not fall in the area of intimacy,"[239] and that the crime is "particularly serious".[240] Once a specially protected conversation begins the eavesdropping must stop immediately and any recordings of that portion of the conversation must be erased. The German legislature has until June 2005 to amend Grosser Lauschangriff to comply with the court's decision.

---

[233] United Nations Human Rights Commissioner, The right to respect of privacy, family, home and correspondence, and protection of honour and reputation (Article 17), CCPR General Comment 16, April 8, 1988.

[234] The Associated Press, "Top German Court Hears a Challenge to Eavesdropping," in New York Times, July 2, 2003.

[235] BVerfG, 1 BvR 2378/98 vom 3.3.2004, Absatz-Nr. (1 - 373), available at http://www.bverfg.de/entscheidungen/rs20040303_1bvr237898.html (in German).

[236] "Grosser Laushcangriff: Definition, Bedeutung, Erklärung im Lexikon", Net Lexicon, available at http://www.lexikon-definition.de/Grosser-Lauschangriff.html (in German).

[237] Basic Law for the Federal Republic of Germany, I. Basic Rights, Articles 1, 13, available at http://www.bundesregierung.de/en/Federal-Government/Function-and-constitutional-ba-,10222/I.-Basic-rights.htm.

[238] C. Schröder, "Wiretap in Germany", German American Law Journal: American Edition (March 11, 2004), available at http://www.recht.us/amlaw/2004/03/11.

[239] Schröder, Id.

[240] "German Legal News - Constitutional Law", University College of London, Faculty of Laws, Institute of Global Law, available at http://www.ucl.ac.uk/laws/global_law/legal-news/german/index.shtml?constitution.

In the past 15 years, the United States government has led a worldwide effort to limit individual privacy and enhance the capability of its police and intelligence services to eavesdrop on personal conversations. This campaign had two strategies. The first is to promote laws that make it mandatory for all companies that develop digital telephone switches, cellular and satellite phones and all developing communication technologies to build in surveillance capabilities; the second is to seek limits on the development and dissemination of products, both in hardware and software, that provide encryption, a technique that allows people to scramble their communications and files to prevent others from reading them.[241]

Law enforcement agencies have traditionally worked closely with telecommunications companies to formulate arrangements that would make phone systems "wiretap friendly." These agreements range from allowing police physical access to telephone exchanges, to installing equipment to automate the interception. Because most telecommunications operators were either monopolies or operated by government telecommunications agencies, this process was generally hidden from public view.

Following deregulation and new entries into telecommunications in the United States in the early 1990s, law enforcement agencies, led by the FBI, began demanding that all current and future telecommunications systems be designed to ensure that they would be able to conduct wiretaps. After several years of lobbying, the United States Congress approved the Communications Assistance for Law Enforcement Act (CALEA) in 1994.[242] The act sets out legal requirements for telecommunications providers and equipment manufacturers on the surveillance capabilities that must be built into all telephone systems used in the United States. In 1999, at the request of the Federal Bureau of Investigation, an order was issued under CALEA requiring carriers to make available the physical location of the antenna tower that a mobile phone uses to connect at the beginning and end of a call.[243]

---

[241] *See* David Banisar & Simon Davies, "The Code War," Index on Censorship, January 1998.

[242] *See* EPIC's Wiretap web page <http://www.epic.org/privacy/wiretap/>.

[243] Third Report and Order adopted by the Federal Communications Commission, In the Matter of Communications Assistance for Law Enforcement Act, CC Docket No. 97-213, FCC 99-230 (1999) (the "Order"). The Order was released on August 31, 1999. A summary of the Order was published in the Federal Register on September 24, 1999. *See* 64 Fed. Reg. 51710.

Due to heavy lobbying, the Internet Service Providers (ISPs) in the United States were exempted from implementing these technical requirements under CALEA. Changes are in the wind, however as the FBI is calling for the Federal Communications Commission to expand the law to reconsider Voice Over IP, *i.e.*, phone calls over the Internet and providers as telecommunications carriers under CALEA.[244] If these providers are reclassified as carriers, then the requirements for intercept capability under CALEA will also apply to them. The Senate is currently reviewing legislation on regulating VOIP.[245]

Intercepting content over digital services is a common legal practice in other countries. In Australia the Telecommunications Act 1997 places obligations on telecommunications operators to positively assist law enforcement in the performance of their duties and to provide an interception capability. The costs of these obligations are borne by the operators themselves.[246][247]

In the United Kingdom the Regulation of Investigatory Powers Act 2000 requires that telecommunications operators maintain a "reasonable interception capability" in their systems and be able to provide on notice certain "traffic data."[248] It also imposes on obligation on third parties to hand over encryption keys. These requirements were further clarified in the Regulation of Investigatory Powers (Maintenance of Interception Capability) Order 2002. In the Netherlands, a new Telecommunications Act was approved in December 1998 that required that ISPs have the capability by August 2000 to intercept all traffic with a court order and maintain users logs for three months.[249] The law was enacted after XS4ALL, a Dutch ISP, refused to conduct a broad wiretap of electronic communications of one of its subscribers. In New Zealand, the Telecommunications (Residual Powers) Act 1987 requires network operators to assist in the operation of a call data warrant (equivalent to the United States trap and trace or pen register warrant).[250] An obligation to assist in the operation of a

---

[244] EPIC Letter to the Honourable Michael K. Powell, Chairman of the Federal Communications Commission, December 15, 2003, available at <http://www.epic.org/privacy/voip/fccltr12.15.03.html>.

[245] The VOIP Regulatory Freedom Act, S.2281, Senate Commerce Committee Hearings, June 16 2004.

[246] Telecommunications Act 1997, Parts 14 and 15.

[247] Furthermore, the 2001 Cybercrime Act allows executing officers to require a "specified person" with "knowledge of a computer or a computer system" to provide assistance in accessing, copying or converting data held on or accessible from that computer. Failing to provide this assistance is an offence punishable by six months imprisonment. Cybercrime Act 2001, No. 161, 2001, inserting Sections 3LA and 201A in the Crimes Act 1914, available at <http://scaleplus.law.gov.au/html/pasteact/3/3486/pdf/161of2001.pdf>.

[248] Regulation of Investigatory Powers Act 2000, Sections 12 (1) and 22 (4) respectively, available at <http://www.hmso.gov.uk/acts/acts2000/20000023.htm>.

[249] Telecommunications Act 1998. Rules pertaining to Telecommunications (Telecommunications Act), December 1998.

[250] Telecommunications (Residual Powers) Act 1987, Section 10D.

full interception warrant is now also being considered in New Zealand. The Telecommunications (Interception Capabilities) Bill currently being drafted by the Government would require all ISPs and telephone companies to upgrade their systems so that they are able to assist the police and intelligence agencies intercept communications. It would also require a telecommunications operator to decrypt the communications of a customer if that operator had provided the encryption facility.[251] In January 2002, a new Law on the surveillance of mail and telecommunications entered into force in Switzerland, requiring ISPs to take all necessary measures to allow for interception.[252] In contrast, the Austrian Federal Constitutional Court held, in a decision[253] in February 2003, that the law compelling telecommunications service providers to implement wiretapping measures at their own expense is unconstitutional.[254] Most recently, Poland and New Zealand have been reported as proposing and adopting new laws requiring ISPs to monitor and record communications transactions.

International cooperation played a significant role in the development of these standards. In 1993, the FBI began hosting meetings at its research facility in Quantico, Virginia called the "International Law Enforcement Telecommunications Seminar" (ILETS) . The meetings included representatives from Canada, Hong Kong, Australia and the European Union. At these meetings, an international technical standard for surveillance, based on the FBI's CALEA demands, was adopted as the "International Requirements for Interception." In January 1995, the Council of the European Union approved a secret resolution adopting the ILETS standards.[255] Following this, many countries adopted the resolution into their domestic laws without revealing the role of the FBI in developing the standard. Following the adoption, the European Union and the United States offered a Memorandum of Understanding (MOU) for other countries to sign to commit to the standards. Several countries including Canada and Australia immediately signed the MOU. Others were encouraged to adopt the standards to ensure trade. International standards organizations, including the International Telecommunications Union (ITU) and the European Telecommunication Standardisation Institute (ETSI), were then successfully approached to adopt the standards.

[251] "Interception Capability – Government Decisions," New Zealand Government Executive Press Release, March 21, 2002, available at <http://www.executive.govt.nz/speechaptercfm?speechralph=37658&SR=0>.

[252] *Loi fédérale sur la surveillance de la correspondance postale et des télécommunications,* (www.admin.ch/ch/f/rs/c780_1.html) and the respective new decree (www.admin.ch/ch/f/rs/c780_11.html)

[253] <http://www.vfgh.gv.at/vfgh/presse/G37-16-02.pdf>.

[254] *See* for more details <http://www.epic.org/privacy/intl/austrian_vfgh-022703.html>.

[255] Council Resolution of 17 January 1995 on the lawful interception of telecommunications, Official Journal of the European Communities, November 4, 1996, available at <http://europa.eu.int/eur-lex/en/lif/dat/1996/en_496Y1104_01.html>.

The ILETS group continued to meet. Several committees were formed and developed a more detailed standard extending the scope of the interception standards. The new standards were designed to apply to a wide range of communications technologies, including the Internet and satellite communications. It also set more detailed criteria for surveillance across all technologies. The result was a document called ENFOPOL 98, the European Union designation for documents created by the European Union Police Cooperation Working Group.[256]

In 1998, the document became public and generated considerable criticism. The committees responded by removing most of the controversial details and putting them into a secret operations manual that has not been made publicly available. The new document, now called ENFOPOL 19, expanded the type of surveillance to include "IP address (electronic address assigned to a party connected to the Internet), credit card number and E-mail address."[257] In April 1999, the Council proposed the new draft council resolution to adopt the ENFOPOL 19 standards into law in the European Union. The Council of Ministers revised the document and, in June 2000, approved a resolution calling for countries:

> to ensure that, in the development and implementation – in cooperation with communication service providers – of any measures which may have a bearing on the carrying out of legally authorised forms of interception of telecommunications, the law enforcement operational needs . . . are duly taken into account.[258]

The annex for the document sets out detailed guidelines for interception requirements for "all telecommunications services, circuit and packet-switched, fixed and mobile networks and services." It expands the coverage of the original International User Requirements (IURs) to now include networking technologies, without acknowledging that technologies such as computer networking generate more and greater details of information including web browsing and mobile location information and thus applying traditional surveillance analogies result in more intrusive surveillance.

---

[256] ENFOPOL 98, September 1998, available at <http://www.heise.de/tp/deutsch/special/enfo/6326/1.html> (in German). *See also* Duncan Campbell, "Special Investigation: ILETS and the ENFOPOL 98 Affair," Heise Online, April 29, 1999, available at <http://www.heise.de/tp/english/special/enfo/6398/1.html>.

[257] Draft Council Resolution on the Lawful Interception of Telecommunications in Relation to New Technologies ENFOPOL 19, March 15, 1999.

[258] Council of the European Union, Council Resolution on law enforcement operational needs with respect to public telecommunication networks and services, 9194/01, ENFOPOL 55, June 20, 2001.

A related development has been the use of "black boxes" on ISP networks to monitor user traffic. The actual workings of these black boxes are unknown to the public. What little information has been made public reveals that many of the systems are based on "packet sniffers" typically employed by computer network operators for security and maintenance purposes. These are specialized software programs running in a computer that is hooked into the network at a location where they can monitor traffic flowing in and out of systems. These sniffers can monitor the entire data stream searching for keywords, phrases or strings such as net addresses or e-mail accounts. It can then record or retransmit for further review anything that fits its search criteria. In many of the systems, the boxes are connected to government agencies by high-speed connections.

In April 2000, it was publicly revealed that the FBI had developed and was using an Internet monitoring system called "Carnivore" (now called "DCS 1000").[259] The system places a PC running Windows NT at an ISP's offices and can monitor all traffic about a user, including e-mail and browsing. Carnivore "can scan millions of e-mails a second" and "would give the government, at least theoretically, the ability to eavesdrop on all customers' digital communications, from e-mail to online banking and Web surfing."[260] In response to the public uproar over Carnivore, Attorney General Janet Reno announced that the technical specifications of the system would be disclosed to a "group of experts" to allay public concerns.[261] In the fall of 2000, the Justice Department commissioned a team of experts at the IIT Research Institute and the Illinois Institute of Technology Chicago-Kent College of Law (IITRI) to undertake an independent review of the carnivore system. The IITRI group issued its final report on Carnivore in December 2000 and made several recommendations for changes to the system.[262]

In some countries, there have been laws or decrees enacted to require the systems to build in these boxes. Russia was the first country where this requirement was made public, and according to Russian computer experts, the United States government advised them on implementation. In 1998, the Russian Federal

---

[259] Testimony of Robert Corn-Revere, before the Subcommittee on the Constitution of the Committee on the Judiciary, United States House of Representatives, The Fourth Amendment and the Internet, April 6, 2000, available at <http://www.house.gov/judiciary/corn0406.htm>.

[260] "FBI's System to Covertly Search E-Mail Raises Privacy," Wall Street Journal, July 11, 2000.

[261] "Reno to Double-Check Carnivore's Bite," Reuters, July 13, 2000.

[262] IITRI, Independent Technical Review of the Carnivore System, Final Report, December 8, 2000, available at <http://www.epic.org/privacy/carnivore/carniv_final.pdf>.

Security Service (FSB) issued a decree on the System for Operational Research Actions on the Documentary Telecommunication Networks (SORM-2) that would require ISPs to install surveillance devices and high-speed links to the FSB which would allow the FSB direct access to the communications of Internet users without a warrant.[263] ISPs are required to pay for the costs of installing and maintaining the devices. When an ISP based in Volgograd challenged FSB's demand to install the system, the local FSB and Ministry of Communication attempted to have its license revoked. The agencies were forced to back off after the ISP challenged the decision in court. In a separate case, the Supreme Court ruled in May 2000 that SORM-2 was not a valid ministerial act because it failed several procedural requirements. Following the Russian lead, in September 1999, Ukrainian President Leonid Kuchma proposed requiring that ISPs install surveillance devices on their systems based on the Russian SORM system. The rules and a subsequent bill were attacked by the Parliament and withdrawn. However, in August 1999, the security service visited several of the large ISPs who were reported to have installed the boxes.

In the Netherlands, following the passage of the 1998 Telecommunications Act (see above), the Dutch Forensics Institute[264] developed a "black-box" for ISPs to install on their networks. The black box would be under control of the ISP and turned on after receiving a court order. The box would look at authentication traffic of the person to wiretap and divert the person's traffic to law enforcement if the person is online. Due to the inability of ISPs to adopt the requirements of the law, however, its implementation has been delayed.

In China, a system know as the "Great Firewall" routes all international connections through proxy servers at official gateways, where Ministry for Public Security (MPS) officials identify individual users and content, define rights, and carefully monitor network traffic into and out of the country. At a 2001 security industry conference, the government announced an ambitious successor project known as "Golden Shield." Rather than relying solely on a national Intranet, separated from the global Internet by a massive firewall, China will now build surveillance intelligence into the network, allowing it to "see," "hear" and "think." [265] Content-filtration will shift from the national level to millions of digital information and communications devices in public places and

---

[263] "Russia Prepares to Police Internet," The Moscow Times, July 29, 1998. More information in English and Russian is available from the Moscow Libertarium Forum <http://www.libertarium.ru/libertarium/sorm/>.

[264] See Dutch Forensics Institute Homepage <http://www.holmes.nl/>.

[265] G. Walton, China's Golden Shield: Corporations and the Development of Surveillance Technology in the People's Republic of China 9 (Rights and Democracy, 2001) available at <http://serveur.ichrdd.ca/english/commdoc/publications/globalization/goldenShieldEng.html>.

people's homes.[266] The technology behind Golden Shield is incredibly complex and is based on research developed largely by Western technology firms, including Nortel Networks, Sun Microsystems and others. The Golden Shield efforts do not signal an abandonment of other avenues of access and content control. For example, details are only beginning to emerge about a new "black box" device, derived from technology previously used in airline cockpit data recorders, and broadly similar to the Carnivore system. Chinese Internet police would use the black box technology to monitor dissidents and collect evidence on illegal activities.[267]

New methods of surveillance, and in particular those capable of circumventing encryption, are also being developed. One such technological device is a "key logger" system. A key logger system records the keystrokes an individual enters on a computer's keyboard. Keystroke loggers can be employed to capture every key pressed on a computer keyboard, including information that is typed and then deleted. Such devices can be manually placed by law enforcement agents on a suspect's computer, or installed "remotely" by placing a virus on the suspect's computer that will disclose private encryption keys.

The question of such surreptitious police decryption methods arose in the case of *United States v Scarfo*.[268] There, the FBI manually installed a key logger device on the defendant's computer in order to capture his PGP encryption password. Once they discovered the password, the files were decrypted, and incriminatory evidence was found. In December 2001, the United States FBI confirmed the existence of a similar technique called "Magic Lantern."[269] This device would reportedly allow the agency to plant a Trojan horse keystroke logger on a target's computer by sending a computer virus over the Internet; rather than require physical access to the computer as is now the case. The new Danish Anti-Terrorism law, enacted in June 2002, appears to give law enforcement the power to secretly install this kind of snooping software on the computers of criminal suspects.[270]

---

[266] B. Rappert, "Assessing the Technologies of Political Control" (1999) 36(6) J. of Peace Research 741. The Golden Shield Project contemplates automated voice recognition through digital signal processing, distributed, network video surveillance, and content-filtration of the Internet.

[267] *See, e.g.,* L. Weijun, "China Plans to Build Internet Monitoring System," China News Daily, March 20, 2001, available at <http://www.cnd.org/Global/01/03/20/010320-3.html>.

[268] United States v. Scarfo, 180 F. Supp. 2d 572 (D.N.J. 2001). *See generally* EPIC's Scarfo web page <http://www.epic.org/crypto/scarfo.html>.

[269] Elinor Mills Abreu, "FBI Confirms 'Magic Lantern' Project Exists," Reuters, December 12, 2001.

[270] Law No. 378, June 6, 2002.

Transactional and Location Data: Surveillance and New Communications Technologies

As new telecommunications technologies emerge, many countries are adapting existing surveillance laws to address the interception of networked and mobile communications. These updated laws pose new threats to privacy in many countries because the governments often simply apply old standards to new technologies without analyzing how the technology has changed the nature and sensitivity of the information. It is crucial for the protection of privacy and human rights that transactional data created by new technologies is given greater protection under law than traditional telephone calling records and other transactional information found in older systems.

In the traditional telephone system, transactional data usually takes the form of telephone numbers or telephone identifiers, the call metrics (*e.g.*, length of call, time and date), countries involved, and types of services used. This data is usually collected and processed by telephone companies for billing and network efficiency (*e.g.*, fault correction) purposes. While this data is stored by telephone companies, it is available to law enforcement authorities. Communications content, *i.e.*, conversations, are not stored routinely. As a result, the obstacles to law enforcement access to this data were minimal: traffic data was available, legally less sensitive, and so accessible with lower authorization and oversight requirements. The content of communications was treated as more sensitive, and more invasive, and more difficult to collect, thus typically requiring greater authorization and oversight mechanisms.

Different communications infrastructures give rise to different forms of transactional data, however. When surfing the net, a user can visit dozens of sites in just a few minutes and reveal a great deal about their personal situation and interests. This can include medical, financial, social interests and other highly sensitive personal information. As the Council of Europe acknowledges in the Explanatory Report of the Convention on Cybercrime:

> The collection of this data may, in some situations, permit the compilation of a profile of a person's interests, associates and social context. Accordingly Parties should bear such considerations in mind when establishing the appropriate safeguards and legal prerequisites for undertaking such measures.[271]

---

[271] Council of Europe Convention on Cybercrime (ETS no: 185), opened for signature on November 8, 2001.

The detailed and potentially sensitive nature of the data makes it more similar to content of communications than telephone records.

Similarly, location information generated by mobile communications infrastructure, such as mobile phones and mobile IP, is more sensitive than the mere location of a fixed telephony communication. The location information of mobile communications can provide details of an individual's movements and activities and whom they have met with. This location information may be combined with other transactional information such as websites visited using the mobile device, individuals called, search engine requests; all used to create a considerable profile. This affects a wide variety of human rights beyond the right of privacy including the rights of free speech and assembly.

Moreover, newer mobile communications protocols are becoming increasingly specific about location data, and the availability of this information is becoming part of the actual communications protocol. That is, the means of identifying the location of a device is becoming more precision-based, and this location information is communicated to several parties, not necessarily only between the device and the mobile communications operator. As a result, the location of the device can be more easily discerned, not necessarily requiring access to the data held by the operator.

In addition to this data that naturally arises from the functioning of a wireless network, there are other initiatives driving the development of technologies that build in location-tracking capabilities. For example, in the United States, the Federal Communications Commission (FCC) directed wireless telephone service providers to begin implementing Automatic Location Identification (ALI) for emergency (911) calls by October 1, 2001. The ALI "accuracy standards" require providers to develop capabilities that will permit the location of users with the following degrees of precision: for handset-based solutions – 50 meters for 67 percent of calls, 150 meters for 95 percent of calls; for network-based solutions – 100 meters for 67 percent of calls, 300 meters for 95 percent of calls.[272] Other wireless devices and services increasingly are coming into use, including wireless personal digital assistants, wireless Internet access, and automotive navigation and assistance services (telematics), which when combined with Global Positioning Satellite capabilities, can determine the physical locations of users very precisely.

---

[272] *See generally* <http://www.fcc.gov/e911/>.

While there is likely to be strong commercial and law enforcement demand for the collection and use of the location data generated by these services, a legal framework to protect privacy specifically with respect to location information has not yet been implemented. In the absence of legal clarity, some operators have been keeping this kind of data indefinitely. In October 2001, British mobile operator Virgin Mobile revealed that that it had retained all call records since it was created in 1999. Similarly, in November 2001, it was reported that Irish operators, Eircell and Digifone, were holding customer records for more than six years. In both cases, the operators, stated that they believed they were required to keep these records under the law. [273]

The level of legal protection afforded to other traffic data is similarly unclear. Policies generally treat all of this transactional data as "traffic data;" this data then bears the protections afforded under the traditional telephone system. The United Kingdom in its Regulation of Investigatory Powers Act 2000 accepted, after an extensive debate, that there are varying levels of sensitivity to this data, and separates "traffic data" (source and destination of a transaction used for routing within a network) from the more sensitive "communications data" that includes URLs, domain names, etc. The latter requires greater authorization and oversight procedures. Not all countries have pursued this line of reasoning.

Previous United States policy differentiated between traffic data on cable and telephone communications. The Cable Act traditionally protected traffic data to a greater degree than telephone traffic data. Now that cable infrastructure is used for Internet communications (which were previously used over telephone lines, and thus traditional laws applied), successive White House administrations worked to erase this distinction, finally succeeding with the USA-PATRIOT Act. Rather than deal with the specifics of digital communications media and services, the changes in United States law reduces the protections of traffic data for all communications to what had previously existed for telephone communications data. This was clearly intended, under the guise of technological neutrality. According to Attorney General Ashcroft:

> Agents will be directed to take advantage of new, technologically neutral standards for intelligence gathering . . . Investigators will be directed to pursue aggressively terrorists on the internet. New authority in the

---

[273] "Telecom Companies Stored Information for Over Six Years," BNA World Data Protection Report, Volume 1, Issue 12, December 2001.

legislation permits the use of devices that capture senders and receivers addresses associated with communications on the Internet.[274]

Retention of Traffic and Location Data[275]

On May 30, 2002, the European Parliament voted on the European Union Electronic Communications and Privacy Directive.[276] In a remarkable reversal of their original opposition to data retention, the members voted to allow each EU government to enact laws to retain the traffic and location data of all people using mobile phones, SMS, landline telephones, faxes, e-mails, chatrooms, the Internet, or any other electronic communication devices, to communicate. The new Directive reverses the 1997 Telecommunications Privacy Directive by explicitly allowing European Union countries to compel Internet service providers and telecommunications companies to record, index, and store their subscribers' communications data.[277] The data that can be retained includes all data generated by the conveyance of communications on an electronic communications network ("traffic data") as well as the data indicating the geographic position of a mobile phone user ("location data").[278] The contents of communications are not covered by the data retention measures. These requirements can be implemented for purposes varying from national security to criminal investigations and prevention, and prosecution of criminal offences, all without specific judicial authorization.

Although this data retention provision is supposed to constitute an exception to the general regime of data protection established by the directive, the ability of governments to compel ISPs and telecommunications companies to store all data about all of their subscribers can hardly be construed as an exception to be narrowly interpreted. The practical result is that all users of new communications technologies are now considered worthy of scrutiny and surveillance in a generalized and preventive fashion for periods of time that States' legislatures or governments have the discretion to determine. Furthermore, because of the cross-border nature of Internet communications, this Directive is likely to have negative repercussions for citizens of other countries. There is a significant risk

---

[274] Testimony of the Attorney General to the Senate Committee on the Judiciary, Washington DC, September 25, 2001.

[275] *See* EPIC's International Data Retention Page <http://www.epic.org/privacy/intl/data_retention.html>.

[276] Directive 2002/58/EC of the European Parliament and of the Council concerning the processing of personal data and the protection of privacy in the electronic communications sector <http://register.consilium.eu.int/pdf/en/02/st03/03636en2.pdf>.

[277] Article 15 (1), *id.*

[278] Article 2 (b) and (c), *id.*

that non-European Union law enforcement agencies will seek data held in Europe that it can not obtain at home, either because it was not retained or because their national law would not permit this kind of access.

During the debates on the Directive, many members of the European Parliament, and the European Union privacy commissioners consistently opposed data retention, arguing that, these policies are in contravention of data protection practices of deletion of data once it is no longer required for the purpose for which it was collected; and also in contravention of proportionality principles in accordance with constitutional laws and jurisprudence. Similarly, the Global Internet Liberty Campaign, a coalition of 60 civil liberties groups organized a campaign and drafted an open letter to oppose data retention. The letter was sent to all European Parliament members and heads of European Union institutions after more than 16,000 individuals from 73 countries endorsed it in less than a week.[279] The letter asserted that data retention (for reasons other than billing purposes) is contrary to well-established international human rights conventions and case law.

While a few other countries have already established data retention schemes (*e.g.*, Belgium, Denmark, France, the Netherlands, Spain, Switzerland and the United Kingdom) the implementation phase of the Directive's data retention provision may be bumpy in other Member States. The German Parliament has repeatedly refused to allow for retention, finally settling on a new Telecommunications Act, passed in May 2004 that allows telecommunications providers to retain data, but does not require them to do so. In the United Kingdom, after a review by a parliamentary committee, significant questions were raised regarding the legality, invasiveness, and the financial burdens involved in data retention.[280] This did not prevent the UK Government from upholding the practice in secondary legislation, however. The Directive may be seen as being in conflict with the constitutions of some European Union countries, with respect to fundamental rights such as the presumption of innocence, the right to privacy, the secrecy of communications, or freedom of expression.[281] In Finland, because of concerns regarding freedom of speech and

---

[280] All Party Parliamentary Internet Group, Communications Data: Report of an Inquiry by the All Party Internet Group, January 2003 <http://www.apig.org.uk/APIGreport.pdf>.

[281] This is, *e.g.*, the case in Spain where the recent law allowing data retention for a year (the "LSSICE") has been challenged as being in direct opposition to the Spanish Constitution. *See generally*, EPIC's LSSI web page <http://www.epic.org/privacy/intl/lssi.html>.

privacy, content retention requirements have been reduced to three weeks at most, and for Internet traffic data no retention is required.[282]

Meanwhile, the situation is uncertain in Austria, Germany, Greece, Luxembourg, Portugal, and Sweden as they consider or question the means through which they can establish retention policies.[283] In Ireland, proposals from the Department of Justice have been poorly received from the industry, the Data Protection Commissioner, the Department of Communications, and the Marine and Natural Resources.[284] Industry associations in several countries[285] and the International Chamber of Commerce have all announced their concerns with general retention laws.[286] In all, nine states have established laws so far; while 10 out of 15 EU governments favor a "harmonizing" EU measure.[287] In October 2003 Privacy International released guidance that the practice of retention violates Article 8 of the European Convention on Human Rights.[288] This is likely to become the key battleground as the EU moves forward on a harmonizing measure for a deadline of June 2005, which is a direct response to the Madrid bombing of February 2004.

Europe is not alone, however. Australia has proposed a code of practice for ISPs to retain traffic data on a voluntary basis.[289] Argentina also passed a law calling for the retention of traffic data for 10 years.[290] Other countries are also calling for the retention of subscriber details, and are preventing anonymous access to the Internet through ID card requirements at cybercafés,[291] while others are banning the use of anonymous mobile telephony.

---

[282] EFFi, "Finland Rewrote the Internet Censorship Law," Press Release, February 16, 2003.

[283] Council of the European Union, "Answers to a questionnaire on traffic data retention," November, 20, 2002 <http://servizi.radicalparty.org/data_retention/>.

[284] Karlin Lillington, "Departments at Odds on Data Retention Bill," The Irish Times, June 27, 2003.

[285] European Competitive Telecommunications Association (ECTA"), "ECTA Statement on Data Retention in the EU," Update June 2003; see generally <http://www.epic.org/privacy/intl/data_retention.html#industry>.

[286] EICTA, ETNO, EuroISPA, ICC, Intug, and UNICE, "Common Industry Statement on Storage of Traffic Data for Law Enforcement Purposes," June 4, 2003 <http://www.iccwbo.org/home/statements_rules/statements/2003/Common%20Industry%20Position%20on%20data%20retention%20final%20june%202003%20logos.pdf>.

[287] Statewatch, "Majority of Governments Introducing Data Retention of Communications," January 2003, available at <http://www.statewatch.org/news/2003/jan/12eudatret.htm>.

[288] Privacy International, Memorandum of Laws Concerning the Legality of Data Retention with Regard to the Rights Guaranteed by the European Convention on Human Rights, October 10, 2003, available at <http://www.privacyinternational.org/countries/uk/surveillance/pi_data_retention_memo.pdf>.

[289] Electronic Frontiers Australia, "Big Brother ISP Code Condemned," August 19 2003.

[290] Pablo Palazzi, Terrorism Laws in Latin America, Privacy International, September 2004.

[291] Privacy International & the GreenNet Educational Trust, Silenced: An International Report on Censorship and Control on the Internet, September 2003.

A related effort for enhancing government control of the Internet and promoting surveillance is also being conducted in the name of preventing "cyber-crime," "information warfare" or protecting "critical infrastructures." Under these efforts, proposals to increase surveillance of the communications and activities of Internet users are being introduced as a way to prevent computer intruders from attacking systems and to stop other crimes such as intellectual property violations.

The international lead bodies are the Council of Europe and the G-8, while there has also been some activity within the European Union.[292] The United States has been active behind the scenes in developing and promoting these efforts.[293] After meeting behind closed doors for years, these organizations finally, in 2000, made public proposals that would place restrictions on online privacy and anonymity in the name of preventing cyber-crime.

Council of Europe

The Council of Europe (CoE) is an intergovernmental organization formed in 1949 by West European countries. There are now 45 member countries. Its main role is "to strengthen democracy, human rights and the rule of law throughout its member states." Its description also notes that "it acts as a forum for examining a whole range of social problems, such as social exclusion, intolerance, the integration of migrants, the threat to private life posed by new technology, bioethical issues, terrorism, drug trafficking and criminal activities."

On September 8, 1995, the CoE approved a recommendation[294] to enhance law enforcement access to computers in member states. In 1997, the CoE formed a Committee of Experts on Crime in Cyber-space (PC-CY). The group met in

---

[292] Dr Paul Norman, "Policing 'High Tech Crime' in the Global Context: the Role of Transnational Policy Networks," available at <http://www.bileta.ac.uk/99papers/norman.htm>.

[293] For details *see* <http://www.privacyinternational.org/issues/cybercrime/>.

[294] The Recommendation of the Committee of Ministers to Member States Concerning Problems of Criminal Procedure Law Connected with Information states: "Subject to legal privileges or protection, investigating authorities should have the power to order persons who have data in a computer system under their control to provide all necessary information to enable access to a computer system and the data therein. Criminal procedure law should ensure that a similar order can be given to other persons who have knowledge about the functioning of the computer system or measures applied to secure the data therein. Specific obligations should be imposed on operators of public and private networks that offer telecommunications services to the public to avail themselves of all necessary technical measures that enable the interception of telecommunications by the investigating authorities. Measures should be considered to minimize the negative effects of the use of cryptography on the investigation of criminal offenses, without affecting its legitimate use more than is strictly necessary."

secret for several years drafting an international treaty, and in April 2000, released the "Draft Convention on Cyber-crime, version 19." Several subsequent versions were released until version 27 was released in June 2001.

The convention has three parts. Part I proposes the criminalization of on-line activities such as data and system interference, the circumvention of copyright, the distribution of child pornography, and computer fraud. Part II requires ratifying states to pass laws to increase their domestic surveillance capabilities to cater for new technologies. This includes the power to intercept internet communications, gain access to traffic data in real-time or through preservation orders to ISPs, and access to secured or "protected" data. The final part of the treaty requires all states to cooperate in criminal investigations. So, for example, country A can request country B to utilize any of the aforementioned investigative powers within country B for a crime that is being investigated in country A. There is no requirement for the crime in country A to actually qualify as a crime in country B, *i.e.*, no requirement for dual-criminality. In this sense, the convention is the largest mutual legal assistance regime in criminal matters ever created.

The draft convention text was strongly criticized by a wide variety of interested parties including privacy and civil liberties groups for its promotion of surveillance and lack of controls such as authorization requirements and dual criminality;[295] prominent security experts for previously articulated limitations on security software;[296] and industry for the costs of implementing the requirements, and the challenges involved in responding to requests from 43 different countries. The Article 29 Data Protection Working Group has expressed concern regarding the convention's implications upon privacy and human rights, concluding that:

> The Working Party therefore sees a need for clarification of the text of the articles of the draft convention because their wording is often too vague and confusing and may not qualify as a sufficient basis for relevant laws and mandatory measures that are intended to lawfully limit fundamental rights and freedoms.[297]

---

[295] *See, e.g.*, Global Internet Liberty Campaign (GILC) Member Letter on Council of Europe Convention on Cyber-Crime, October 18, 2000 <http://www.gilc.org/privacy/coe-letter-1000.html>; GILC Member Letter on Council of Europe Convention on Cyber-Crime Version 24.2, December 12, 2000 <http://www.gilc.org/privacy/coe-letter-1200.html>.

[296] Statement of Concerns, July 20, 2000. <http://www.cerias.purdue.edu/homes/spaf/coe/index.html>.

[297] European Union Article 29 Data Protection Working Group, Opinion 4/2001 on the Council of Europe's Draft Convention on Cyber-crime, March 22, 2001 <http://www.europa.eu.int/comm/internal_market/privacy/docs/wpdocs/2001/wp41en.pdf>.

The convention text was finalized in September 2001. After the terrorist attacks on the United States, the convention was positioned as a means of combating terrorism. A signing ceremony took place in November 2001 where it was signed by 30 countries, and later signed by another eight.

The convention came into force on January 7, 2004, once it was ratified by five signatory states, all members of the Council of Europe.[298] The Convention was originally open to the members of the CoE and to countries that were involved in its development, which includes Canada, Japan, South Africa and the United States. Now that it is in force, other non-COE countries like China and Singapore can also ask to join. The Australian government announced in July 2001 that its bill on computer crime, which requires users to provide encryption keys, is based on the Convention.[299] So far only Albania, Croatia, Estonia, Hungary, Lithuania, and Romania have ratified the convention. Romania has incorporated some of the language of the convention into its law on transparency and corruption.[300]In December the Bush Administration signaled its intention to ratify the convention. In June, the Senate Committee on Foreign Relations began its review of the convention

A protocol on Racism and Xenophobia was released in November 2002. This protocol will require the criminalization of certain forms of Internet speech that some might find offensive.[301] The Bush Administration has already stated that it will not support the protocol.[302] There was some discussion of a second protocol on "terrorist messages and the decoding thereof," however discussion on this matter has not advanced publicly.[303]

G-8

The G-8 is made up of the heads of state of eight industrialized countries in the world (Canada, France, Germany, Italy, Japan, Russia, the United Kingdom, and

---

[298] Council of Europe, Convention on Cybercrime, Status as of: 18/06/2004, available at <http://conventions.coe.int/Treaty/Commun/ChercheSig.asp?NT=185&CM=8&DF=&CL=ENG>.

[299] Cybercrime Bill 2001 Second Reading Speech by the Attorney General, The Parliament of the Commonwealth of Australia.

[300] The Romanian Parliament, A Law on Certain Steps for Assuring Transparency in Performing High Officials Positions, Public and Business Positions, for Prevention and Sanctioning the Corruption.

[301] See, e.g., GILC, Member Letter to Council of Europe Secretary-General Walter Schwimmer, February 6, 2002, available at <http://www.gilc.org/speech/coe_hatespeech_letter.html>.

[302] Declan McCullagh, "U.S. Won't Support Net 'Hate Speech' Ban," CNET News.com, November 15, 2002.

[303] See, e.g., GILC, Member Letter to Council of Europe Secretary-General Walter Schwimmer, February 28, 2002, available at <http://www.gilc.org/speech/coe_hatespeech_2.html>.

the United States. The European Commission participates as an observer). The leaders have been meeting annually since 1975 to discuss issues of importance, including economics and finance, transnational organized crime, terrorism, and the information society.

Since 1995, the G-8 has become increasing more involved in the issue of high-tech crime, and has created working groups and issued a series of communiqués from the leaders and actions plans from justice ministers. Much of this work has been coordinated by the Lyon Group, established formally in 1997.

At the Birmingham, England summit in May 1998, the G-8 adopted a recommendation on ten principles and a ten-point action plan on high-tech crime. The ministers announced:

> We call for close cooperation with industry to reach agreement on a legal framework for obtaining, presenting and preserving electronic data as evidence, while maintaining appropriate privacy protection, and agreements on sharing evidence of those crimes with international partners. This will help us combat a wide range of crime, including abuse of the Internet and other new technologies.

The G-8 has met several times with industry and is actively promoting requirements that ISPs maintain records of all of their users' activities in case there is a future need to investigate a crime that might have occurred. These requirements were strongly criticized at a meeting held by the G-8 in Japan in 2001 where industry and a civil liberties group were invited and a draft press release and guidelines that promoted data retention had to be withdrawn after they had already been made public.

The G-8 has continued its activity in the area of law enforcement and combating terrorism, however. Throughout 2002 several summits involving Finance Ministers, Justice and Interior Ministers, and heads of state have released several statements regarding increased surveillance, traceability of communications,[304] and data retention.[305] Increased cooperation across borders was discussed at length; and as with the Council of Europe convention, no requirements of dual-criminality are necessary.

---

[304] Recommendations for Tracing Networked Communications Across National Borders in Terrorist and Criminal Investigations, published at the G8 Justice and Interior Ministers' Meeting in Mont-Tremblant, Quebec, May 2002 <http://www.g8j-i.ca/english/doc2.html>.

[305] Principles on the Availability of Data Essential to Protecting Public Safety, published at the G8 Justice and Interior Ministers' Meeting in Mont-Tremblant, Quebec, May 2002 <http://www.g8j-i.ca/english/doc3.html>.

The European Union

In July 2000, the Commission announced plans for a new directive for fighting cyber-crime.[306] A communication was released in January 2001.[307] While similar to the Council of Europe convention in many ways, the Commission's proposal also included proposals regarding data retention and the reduction of anonymity. These policies were sought within "public forums" (only with limited invited speaking slots) in the fall of 2001, with unclear and unpublished results.

The retention proposal was sought in the alternative forum of the Directive on Privacy and Electronic Commerce in the European Parliament. The substantive law measures of criminalizing data and systems interference and defining other such offences are being pursued as a Council Framework Decision, which was in draft mode for almost a year and nearly forgotten,[308] until the Madrid bombings of 2004 when it was placed back upon the agenda with an expected implementation date of June 2005. This initiative is designed to be consistent with the CoE and G-8 activities.

The Organization for Economic Co-Operation and Development

In contrast to many of these law enforcement-driven initiatives, the Organisation for Economic Cooperation and Development (OECD) has tended to take a broader view of security issues. In 1992, the OECD issued Guidelines for the Security of Information Systems.[309] Containing nine principles, the Guidelines stress the importance of ensuring transparency, proportionality and other democratic values when establishing measures, practices and procedures for the security of information systems. In the fall of 2001, the OECD Working Party on Information Security and Privacy (WPISP) established a group of experts to conduct a review of these guidelines (such a review must take place every five years). The group of experts met four times between December 2001 and June 2002 and recommended several changes. The OECD Council adopted the 2002

---

[306] "European Union Ministers Vow Cyber Crime Crackdown," Reuters, July 29, 2000.

[307] Communication from the Commission to the Council, the European Parliament, the Economic and Social Committee and the Committee of the Regions, Creating a Safer Information Society by Improving the Security of Information Infrastructures and Combating Computer-related Crime, COM(2000) 890 final, January 26, 2001, available at <http://www.privacyinternational.org/issues/cybercrime/eu/>.

[308] Commission Proposal for a Council Framework Decision on Attacks against Information Systems (COM (2002) 173 final), April 19, 2002.

[308] OECD Guidelines for the Security of Information Systems, adopted November 1992, available at <http://www.oecd.org/EN/document/0,EN-document-29-nodirectorate-no-24-10249-29,00.html>.

Security Guidelines[310] on July 25, 2002 and they remain in effect.[311] Although the guidelines have been substantially revised, the need to ensure key democratic values, such as openness, transparency and the protection of personal information, is nonetheless reiterated in the principles. The OECD also developed a "Culture of Security" web site[312] launched after the "OECD Global Forum on Information Systems and Network Security: Towards a Global Culture of Security" held in Oslo, Norway in October 2003. The site provides member and non-member governments with an international information-exchange tool on initiatives to implement the Guidelines and serves as a portal to relevant Web sites as a first step towards creating a global culture of security. OECD member countries adopted an implementation plan[313] and released it to the public in January 2003. The OECD also took a survey of OECD member countries in July 2003, analyzing measures taken since the adoption of the Security Guidelines in July 2002 as consistent with the OECD Implementation Plan. The survey results[314] were released on June 7, 2004.

National Security, Intelligence Agencies and the "Echelon system"

In the past several years, there has been considerable attention given to mass surveillance by intelligence agencies of international and national communications. Investigations have been opened and hearings held in parliaments around the world about the "Echelon" system coordinated by the United States.

Immediately following the Second World War, in 1947, the governments of the United States, the United Kingdom, Canada, Australia and New Zealand signed a National Security pact known as the "Quadripartite," or "United Kingdom–United States" (UKUSA) agreement. Its intention was to seal an intelligence bond in which a common national security objective was created. Under the terms of the agreement, the five nations carved up the earth into five spheres of

---

[310] OECD Guidelines for the Security of Information Systems and Networks: Towards a Culture of Security, adopted July 2002, available at
<http://www.oecd.org/document/42/0,2340,en_2649_34255_15582250_1_1_1_1,00.html>.

[311] OECD Guidelines for the Security of Information Systems and Networks: Towards a Culture of Security, Questions and Answers, available at <http://www.oecd.org/dataoecd/27/6/2494779.pdf>.

[312] Culture of Security web site, available at
<http://webdomino1.oecd.org/COMNET/STI/IccpSecu.nsf?OpenDatabase>.

[313] "Implementation Plan for the OECD Guidelines for the Security of Information Systems and Networks: Towards a Culture of Security," adopted October 2003, available at
<http://webdomino1.oecd.org/COMNET/STI/IccpSecu.nsf?OpenDatabase>.

[314] "Summary of Responses to the Survey on the Implementation of the OECD Guidelines for the Security of Information Systems and Networks: Towards A Culture of Security," June 2004, available at
<http://webdomino1.oecd.org/COMNET/STI/IccpSecu.nsf?OpenDatabase>.

influence, and each country was assigned particular signals intelligence (SIGINT) targets.

The UKUSA Agreement standardized terminology, code words, intercept handling procedures, arrangements for cooperation, sharing of information, Sensitive Compartmented Information (SCI) clearances, and access to facilities. One important component of the agreement was the exchange of data and personnel.

The strongest alliance within the UKUSA relationship is the one between the United States National Security Agency (NSA), and Britain's Government Communications Headquarters (GCHQ). The NSA operates under a 1952 presidential mandate, National Security Council Intelligence Directive (NSCID) Number 6, to eavesdrop on the world's communications networks for intelligence and military purposes. In doing so, it has built a vast spying operation that can reach into the telecommunications systems of every country on earth. Its operations are so secret that this activity, outside the United States, occurs with little or no legislative or judicial oversight. The most important facility in the alliance is Menwith Hill, a Royal Air Force base in the north of England. With over two dozen domes and a vast computer operations facility, the base has the capacity to eavesdrop on vast chunks of the communications spectrum. With the creation of Intelsat and digital telecommunications, Menwith Hill and other stations developed the capability to eavesdrop on an extensive scale on satellite-borne fax, telex and voice messages.

The current debate over NSA activities has focused on the existence of a signals intelligence system known as "Echelon." United States officials have refused to confirm the existence of this or any other surveillance systems. In May 2001, the European Parliament's Temporary Committee on the Echelon Interception System (established in July 2000) issued a report concluding that "the existence of a global system for intercepting communications . . . is no longer in doubt."[315] According to the committee, the Echelon system (reportedly run by the United States in cooperation with Britain, Canada, Australia and New Zealand) was set up at the beginning of the Cold War for intelligence gathering and has developed into a network of intercept stations around the world. Its primary purpose, according to the report, is to intercept private and commercial communications, not military intelligence.

---

[315] European Parliament, Temporary Committee on the Echelon Interception System, Report on the Existence of a Global System for the Interception of Private and Commercial Communications (ECHELON interception system) (2001/2098(INI)), May 18, 2001 (adopted July 11, 2001), available at <http://www.europarl.eu.int/tempcom/echelon/pdf/prechelon_en.pdf>.

The report recommended "self-protection" by EU citizens and companies, and encouraged further development and use of encryption technology within Europe to protect communications against surveillance. The report also recommended actions to be taken by the European Parliament during its September 2001 session in Strasbourg. These included provisions for the United States to (1) negotiate and sign an agreement with the European Union (European Union) requiring both parties to "observe, *vis-à-vis* the other, the provisions governing the protection of the privacy of citizens and the confidentiality of business communications applicable to its own citizens and firms;" (2) sign the International Covenant on Civil and Political Rights so complaints by individuals could be submitted to the Human Rights Committee created by the covenant; (3) negotiate with Member States a code of conduct akin to that of the European Union; and (4) begin a dialog with the European Union on economic intelligence gathering. On this point the Committee did not find widespread evidence of Echelon being used primarily for economic intelligence gathering. The Committee also recommended that Germany and the United Kingdom condition further authorization of United States communications interception operations within their territories on United States compliance with the European Convention on Human Rights. No further action on these recommendations has been taken.

Prior to issuing its report, the Temporary Committee traveled to Washington, DC to meet with senior Bush administration government and intelligence officials to discuss Echelon. When they arrived, however, their meetings with these officials at the Departments of State, Commerce and Defense, the CIA and the NSA were cancelled at the last minute. The European Parliament subsequently issued a Resolution protesting this move.[316]

The work of the recent Temporary Committee was based on two earlier reports of the European Parliament. The first, "An Appraisal of the Technologies of Political Control,"[317] was published in 1997 and stated that the NSA had established an integrated communications surveillance capability in Europe. It described Echelon as a communications intelligence sharing sub-system capable of scanning particular communications to detect information of interest. In 1999, the second European Parliament report, "Interception Capabilities 2000" set out

---

[316] Steve Kettmann, "U.S. Echelon Snub Angers Europe," Wired News, May 18, 2001, available at <http://www.wired.com/news/privacy/0,1848,43921,00.html>.

[317] Published by STOA (Science and Technology Options Assessment). Reference Project No. IV/STOA/RSCH/LP/politicon.1

the technical specifications of the interception system.[318] The report described the merger of Echelon and the (ILETS) stating that in time, the two vast systems – one designed for national security and one for law enforcement – would merge, and in the process will compromise national control over surveillance activities.

These recent events have left observers contemplating two profound conclusions. First, as long as the UK-USA SIGINT partners police and govern their own operations outside of actual effective parliamentary and judicial oversight, there is good reason to believe that SIGINT can be turned against individuals and groups exercising civil and political rights. There is ample evidence that the activities of Greenpeace, Christian Aid, Amnesty International, the International Committee to Ban Landmines, the Tibetan government-in-exile, various anti-globalization movements like the Independent Media Center, and the International Committee of the Red Cross have been targeted by UKUSA agencies. Second, there is an increasing blurring between the activities of intelligence agencies and law enforcement. The creation of a seamless international intelligence and law enforcement surveillance system has resulted in the potential for a huge international network that may, in practice, negate current rules and regulations prohibiting domestic communications surveillance by national intelligence agencies.

Second, there is an increasing blurring between the activities of intelligence agencies and law enforcement. The creation of a seamless international intelligence and law enforcement surveillance system has resulted in the potential for a huge international network that may, in practice, negate current rules and regulations prohibiting domestic communications surveillance by national intelligence agencies.

The use of Echelon to target diplomatic communications was highlighted as a result of disclosures made in 2003 by a British intelligence employee, former United Nations officials, and a former British Cabinet Minister concerning eavesdropping by the US NSA and the British GCHQ over UN Secretary General Kofi Annan's telephone communications and private conversations.[319]

---

[318] Report to the Director General for Research of the European Parliament (Scientific and Technical Options Assessment programme office) on the development of surveillance technology and risk of abuse of economic information, available at <http://jya.com/echelon-dc.htm>.

[319] The controversy began when the British government suddenly dropped its Official Secrets Act case against Katharine Gun, a Chinese linguist working for GCHQ in Cheltenham, UK. Gun was accused of leaking to the British media a TOP SECRET/COMINT memorandum from NSA to GCHQ asking for its help in eavesdropping the communications of non-permanent members of the UN Security Council to determine their intentions on the Security Council resolution authorizing the war on Iraq. After the case against Gun was dropped, former British International Development Minister Clare Short revealed that she was shown a transcript of a confidential conversation of UN Secretary General Kofi Annan. It was reported that Annan's

The issue of eavesdropping on the diplomatic communications of the UN and its member nations' missions is covered by four international conventions: the Universal Declaration of Human Rights (Article 12),[320] the 1961 Vienna Convention on Diplomatic Relations (Article 27),[321] the 1947 Headquarters Agreement between the UN and the United States,[322] and the 1946 Convention on the Privileges and Immunities of the UN (Article 2).[323]

Travel Privacy

Since the terrorist attacks of September 11, 2001, one of the greatest fears of security officials in the world has been that would-be terrorists would board commercial airline flights without their malicious intentions being detected in advance. As a result, the US and many of its international allies have placed a high priority on identifying, tracking, and profiling travelers, especially air travelers.

Travelers and workers at transportation facilities such as airports have come to be regarded as objects of suspicion, potential terrorists, and targets of surveillance. Security agencies have sought access to reservations and other travel data collected for commercial purposes; compulsory identification of travelers and

---

telephone communications and private conversations were bugged by NSA and GCHQ. Accordig to Andrew Wilkie, a former Australian intelligence official, the spying against the UN was supported by Australia, through the "five eyes agreement," a reference to Echelon and the UKUSA Agreement. (Mark Forbes, "Australia 'Party to Bugging of UN,'" The Age (Melbourne), June 19, 2004.) Since Short's revelations, several other former UN officials have come forward to describe similar eavesdropping by the British and Americans, which share a decades-old signals intelligence relationship known as the UK-USA Agreement, along with Canada, Australia, and New Zealand. Former UN Secretary General Boutros Boutros Ghali, UN weapons inspectors Hans Blix, Rolf Ekeus, and Richard Butler, UN Human Rights Commissioner Mary Robinson, former Mexican UN ambassador Aguilar Zinser, current Mexican UN ambassador Enrique Berruga, Chilean Foreign Minister Soledad Alvear, Chilean ambassador to Britain Mariano Fernandez, and former Chilean UN ambassador Juan Gabriel Valdes, have all spoken about eavesdropping against them and their countries by the Americans and British. See generally <http://www.epic.org/privacy/wiretap/diplomatic.html>.

[320] "No one shall be subjected to arbitrary interference with his privacy, family, home or correspondence, nor to attacks upon his honour and reputation. Everyone has the right to the protection of the law against such interference or attacks."

[321] "1. The receiving State shall permit and protect free communication on the part of the mission for all official purposes. In communicating with the Government and the other missions and consulates of the sending State, wherever situated, the mission may employ all appropriate means, including diplomatic couriers and messages in code or cipher. However, the mission may install and use a wireless transmitter only with the consent of the receiving State; 2. The official correspondence of the mission shall be inviolable. Official correspondence means all correspondence relating to the mission and its functions."

[322] Section 9 provides: "The headquarters district shall be inviolable."

[323] "The premises of the United Nations shall be inviolable. The property and assets of the United Nations, wherever located and by whomsoever held, shall be immune from search, requisition, confiscation, expropriation and any other form of interference, whether by executive, administrative, judicial or legislative action."

travel and transportation workers; mandatory collection of additional traveler data and compilation of personal travel dossiers; and deployment of new technologies for real-time tracking and logging of travelers' movements.

Fear is not necessarily proportional to actual danger,[324] and it is not clear that these policy and procedural changes are the outcome of a considered evaluation of risks, benefits, and trade-offs.[325] But whatever the motivation or effectiveness for their declared purposes, these aviation and transportation "security" measures create substantial potential for both commercial and government misuse of personal travel data. Taken together, they could – if successful – lead to the creation of a global infrastructure of surveillance of the movements of persons, incorporating both the travel industry and government agencies.

Privacy Protection for Commercial Travel Records

The privacy of travel records has been less well protected than that of any comparably sensitive category of commercial data. Existing travel industry norms for personal data handling fail to provide the level of protection provided for other categories of data, and required by generally accepted norms of data protection. Even in jurisdictions where data protection laws include travel data, enforcement against violations by the travel industry has been lax.

Reservation and transaction records created by travel companies for commercial purposes contain intimate personal information about airline (and sometimes intercity train and bus) travelers and their movements, as well as personally identifiable information about third-party ticket purchasers, travel industry personnel involved in making and changing reservations, and other business and personal associates of travelers.[326]

Reservation data or one or more people traveling on the same itinerary is stored in a Passenger Name Record (PNR), which typically contains names of travelers and details of flights, hotels, car rentals, and other travel services. PNRs can also contain residential and business postal and e-mail addresses and phone numbers, credit card details, and names and personal information of emergency contacts. Through billing, meeting, and discount eligibility codes, PNRs contain information about memberships and organizational affiliations. Since a single

---

[324] Edward Hasbrouck, "Travel Safety and Civil Liberties: Fear vs. Danger" (last updated May 2003) <http://hasbrouck.org/articles/fear.html>.

[325] Bruce Schneier, Beyond Fear: Thinking Sensibly about Security in an Uncertain World (New York 2003).

[326] Hasbrouck, "What's in A Passenger Name Record (PNR)?," <http://hasbrouck.org/articles/PNR.html>.

PNR typically is used for an entire travel party, PNRs contain detailed information on patterns of association between travelers. PNRs can contain religious meal preferences and special service requests that describe intimate details of physical and medical conditions (*e.g.*, "Uses wheelchair, can control bowels and bladder") – categories of information that have special protected status in the European Union and some other countries as "sensitive" personal data.

Airlines and travel agencies around the world, even those that compete with each other, have long been part of an integrated global network of reservation systems. Most of these systems predate current norms of data protection. While PNR formats vary, "interline" agreements between airlines, joint industry ticketing and financial clearinghouses, and industry-standard protocols[327] facilitate easy global sharing of PNR data.

Most of the world's airlines and travel agencies outsource hosting of their PNR databases to one of four companies: Sabre, Galileo (a division of the Cendant Corp.), Worldspan, and Amadeus. These Computerized Reservation System (CRS) or Global Distribution System (GDS) companies function both as data warehouses and data aggregators, and have a relationship to travel data analogous to that of credit bureaus to financial data. After the completion of a trip, copies of PNRs are "purged" from live to archival storage systems, and can be retained indefinitely by CRSs, airlines, and travel agencies.

Unlike medical and financial data, travel data has not generally been legally recognized as posing special privacy issues, or afforded any special protection. PNRs and ticketing records had been regarded as simply another category of commercial transaction data.

In many countries airlines and travel agents are overseen by different government agencies than other businesses, and few if any aviation regulatory agencies include data protection divisions or enforcement staff. In the US, for example, most consumer privacy policies are enforced by state and local consumer protection authorities and the Federal Trade Commission (FTC). But

---

[327] Such as the ATA/IATA Reservations Interline Message Procedures - Passenger (AIRIMP). Published annually by the International Air Transportation Association (IATA), Montreal and Geneva; available from IATA at
<https://www.iataonline.com/Store/Products/Product+Detail.htm?cs_id=9098%2D28&cs_catalog=Publications>; *see also* <http://www.iata.org/idfs/ps/passenger_standards/reservations_standards_rescom.htm>. The 28th edition of the AIRIMP, effective June 1, 2004, for the first time added standard formats for transmission between travel agencies, airlines, and CRSs of personal data collected solely for government purposes (*see* Section 3.14).

enforcement of privacy policies by airlines and travel agencies, and of compliance by airlines and travel agencies with the EU-US Safe Harbor arrangement,[328] is under the exclusive jurisdiction of the Department of Transportation (DOT). The DOT has no staff dedicated to consumer privacy or data protection, and has never brought an enforcement action for violation of a privacy policy or of the Safe Harbor arrangement.

The International Civil Aviation Organization (ICAO) has adopted a model Code of Conduct on the Regulation and Operation of Computer Reservation Systems (CRS) that aims at safeguarding privacy.[329] However, the ICAO Code of Conduct on the Regulation and Operation of Computer Reservation Systems has not been widely adopted by ICAO member states. CRSs operate under government regulations in the US[330] and Canada,[331] but those regulations include no provisions related to privacy or data protection.

The European Union Code of Conduct for Computerized Reservation Systems, Article 5(d), provides that, "personal information concerning a consumer and generated by a travel agent shall be made available to others not involved in the transaction only with the consent of the consumer."[332] But there is no record of any enforcement action ever having been taken under this section, despite a history of widespread and systematic violations by all four major CRSs.

National data protection authorities in Belgium (on the complaint of data subjects, including a Member of the European Parliament)[333] and France[334] have

---

[328] <http://www.export.gov/safeharbor/>.

[329] *See* Article 11: Safeguarding the Privacy of Personal Data: a) States shall take appropriate measures to ensure that all parties involved in CRS operations safeguard the privacy of personal data; b) Air carriers, system vendors, subscribers and other parties involved in air transportation are responsible for safeguarding the privacy of personal data included in CRSs to which they have access, and may not release such data without the consent of the passenger. ICAO Code of Conduct on the Regulation and Operation of Computer Reservation Systems (CRS), adopted by the Council of ICAO June 25, 1996, effective November 1, 1996, available at <http://www.icao.int/icao/en/atb/ecp/CodeOfConduct.htm>; *see also* Notes on the Application of the Code of Conduct, available at <http://www.icao.int/icao/en/atb/ecp/notes.htm>.

[330] Computer Reservations System (CRS) Regulations, 14 CFR Part 255, 69 FR 975, January 7, 2004, available at <http://www.dot.gov/affairs/Computer%20Reservations%20System.htm>.

[331] Canadian Computer Reservation Systems (CRS) Regulations, SOR/95-275, June 6, 1995, available at <http://laws.justice.gc.ca/en/A-2/SOR-95-275/>, as amended by Regulations Amending the Canadian Computer Reservation Systems (CRS) Regulations, October 23, 2003), available at <http://canadagazette.gc.ca/partI/2003/20031025/html/regle15-e.html>.

[332] Council Regulation (EEC) No 2299/89 of July 24, 1989 on a Code of Conduct for Computerized Reservation Systems, Official Journal L 220 of July 29, 1989, as amended by Council Regulation (EEC) No 3089/93 of 29 October 1993, Official Journal L 278 of November 11, 1993, and Council Regulation (EC) No 323/1999 of 8 February 1999, Official Journal L 40 of February 13, 1999.

[333] Letter from P. Thomas, Président, *Commission de la Protection de la Vie Privée, Royaume de Belgique*, to Marco Cappato, MEP; January 19, 2004, available at <http://www.radicalparty.org/privacy/etats_un.pdf>.

ruled that transfers of PNR data by airlines to US government agencies without passengers' consent are illegal. Additional citizen complaints against airlines for violations of national data protection laws have been made in Spain[335] and the Netherlands.[336] However, no corrective action or change in data sharing practices has been ordered as a result of any of these enforcement proceedings.

Like the ICAO standards, the recommendations of the Passenger Services Conference of the International Air Transportation Association (IATA) are only advisory. In addition, they relate only to the conduct of IATA member airlines and not to travel agencies or CRSs. Even if followed, the IATA recommendations serve more to legitimate than to limit airlines' transfers of passenger data to government agencies.[337]

Privacy of Travel Records Since September 11, 2001

Almost immediately after September 11, 2001, airlines and the US government – often in collaboration, and of necessity involving the CRSs in their work – began accessing and using archived PNRs to investigate the hijackings and to test the possibility of identifying "suspicious" travelers through PNR profiling. Most of the major US-based airlines and CRSs, and a variety of US government agencies and contractors, were involved in these investigations and experiments over the next two years.[338] All of these tests were conducted at the time in secret, without

---

[334] *Commission Nationale de l'Informatique et des Libertés*, "PNR: la position de la CNIL sur le transfert de ces informations nominatives," February 24, 2004, available at <http://www.cnil.fr/index.php?id=1017>.

[335] Arturo Quirantes, "Don't Fly My Data," <http://www.ugr.es/~aquiran/cripto/nofly.htm>.

[336] Letter from Ulco van de Pol, Vice-President, *College bescherming persoonsgegevens*, to Northwest Airlines, April 6, 2004, available at <http://www.cbpweb.nl/downloads_uit/z2004-0310.pdf>.

[337] *See* IATA Recommended Practice 1774, Protection of Privacy and Processing of Personal Data Used In International Air Transport of Passengers and Cargo, defines the purposes for which personal data is presumed to have been provided as including "facilitating immigration and customs procedures, and providing such facilitating data to government agencies." The standard contract terms in IATA Recommended Practice 1724, General Conditions of Carriage (Passenger and Baggage), Article 5.3, Personal Data, grant even broader permission for airlines to transfer reservation data to government agencies: "You recognise that personal data has been given to us for the purposes of . . . making available such data to government agencies, in connection with your travel. For these purposes, you authorise us to retain and use such data and to transmit it to . . . government agencies."

[338] John Schwartz and Micheline Maynard, "F.B.I. Got Records on Air Travelers", New York Times, May 1st, 2004, available at <http://www.nytimes.com/2004/05/01/politics/01AIRL.html>; American Airlines, "American Airlines Passenger Data Released In June 2002," press release, April 9, 2004, available at <http://www.amrcorp.com/news/april04/09_aai.htm>; Electronic Privacy Information Center (EPIC), Northwest Airlines' Disclosure of Passenger Data to Federal Agencies <http://www.epic.org/privacy/airtravel/nasa/>; US Senate Committee on Governmental Affairs, Pre-hearing Questionnaire for the Nomination of Admiral David Stone to be Assistant Secretary of Homeland Security, Transportation Security Administration, June 24, 2004, answer to question 16 available at <http://govt-aff.senate.gov/_files/062304stone_q16.pdf>; *see also* responses to additional questions http://www.epic.org/privacy/airtravel/stone_answers.pdf; Hasbrouck, "Total Travel Information Awareness" (last updated 25 June 2004), http://hasbrouck.org/articles/travelprivacy.html#testing.

---

notice to, or consent of, the data subjects, and in most cases – except the initial investigation of the events leading up to September 11 – without warrants or subpoenas. They were gradually revealed to the public as a result of US Freedom of Information Act (FOIA) requests and lawsuits, Congressional questioning, investigative journalism, and admissions by airlines. Governments, airlines, and CRSs in other countries were pressured by the US to cooperate in providing reservation data for these programs, irrespective of national data protection laws against such use without travelers' prior consent.

These profiling systems and tests have not been shown to be effective in identifying would-be terrorists from reservation data, either alone or in conjunction with other databases.[339] It's impossible to identify from a PNR in what country (or countries) the data it contains was collected, so each of these tests probably included data subject to many international jurisdictions. The US government proceeded with these tests without waiting for any of the legal changes needed to harmonize them with any other countries' laws. Nonetheless, the US and some other governments have, after the fact, sought to modify existing data protection rules and industry standards to mandate – or failing that, at least to permit – government access to PNR data in order to attempt to identify "suspicious" travelers.

Currently, only the United States, Canada, Australia and New Zealand have legislation in place that makes government access to airline reservation data mandatory. A number of other States are exploring this process.[340]

In Canada, the Personal Information Protection and Electronic Documents Act (PIPEDA) was amended in 2001 by Bill C-44 to allow Canadian airlines to provide foreign governments with "any information . . . relating to persons on board or expected to be on board the aircraft and that is required by the laws of the foreign state."[341] The PIPEDA was further amended in 2004 by Bill C-7 to expand the exemption of travel data.[342] Bill C-7 in particular provoked considerable criticism, including opposition from the Canadian Bar

---

[339] General Accounting Office, Aviation Security: Computer-Assisted Passenger Prescreening System Faces Significant Implementation Challenges, GAO-04-385, February 12, 2004, available at <http://www.gao.gov/cgi-bin/getrpt?GAO-04-385.pdf>.

[340] Airline Reservation System and Passenger Name Record (PNR) Access by States, Working Paper FAL/12-WP/74, presented by IATA to the 12th Session of the ICAO Facilitation (FAL) Division, Cairo, March 15, 2004, available at <http://www.icao.int/icao/en/atb/fal/fal12/documentation/fal12wp074_en.pdf>.

[341] An Act to Amend the Aeronautics Act, S.C. 2001, c.38, enacted December 18, 2001, available at <http://laws.justice.gc.ca/en/2001/38>.
342. Public Safety Act, 2002 (enacted 6 May 2004), available at <http://www.parl.gc.ca/37/3/parlbus/chambus/house/bills/government/C-7/C-7_3/C-7TOCE.html>.

Association.[343] Both bills were widely characterized as Canada's counterparts to the USA PATRIOT Act. In May 2004, the European Commission approved a conditional finding that the level of protection afforded to PNR data transferred to the US Department of Homeland Security (DHS) Bureau of Customs and Border Protection (CBP) satisfies the standard of "adequacy" required by the EU Data Protection Directive,[344] on the basis of which the Council of the European Community signed an agreement purporting to authorize PNR transfers to the US, if certain conditions were met.[345]

The finding of adequacy was contrary to the formal opinion of the working party of EU national data protection officers.[346] Both the agreement and the finding of adequacy of protection of PNR data in the US prompted extraordinary public controversy within the EU and conflict between EU institutions. Both were denounced by privacy advocates on both sides of the Atlantic.[347] In June 2004, the President of the European Parliament moved the Court of Justice of the

---

343. F. William Johnson, President, Canadian Bar Association, Letter to the Senate Committee on Transport and Communications, March 17, 2003 <http://www.cba.org/CBA/submissions/pdf/04-09-eng.pdf>; *also see generally* Office of the Privacy Commissioner of Canada, Key Issues – Advance Passenger Information/Passenger Name Record <http://www.privcom.gc.ca/keyIssues/ki-qc/mc-ki-api_e.asp>.

344 Commission Decision of 14 May 2004 on the Adequate Protection of Personal Data Contained in the Passenger Name Record of Air Passengers Transferred to the United States' Bureau of Customs and Border Protection, available at <http://europa.eu.int/comm/internal_market/privacy/docs/adequacy/pnr/c-2004-1914/c-2004-1914_en.pdf>.

345 Council Decision of 17 May 2004 on the Conclusion of an Agreement Between the European Community and the United States of America on the Processing and Transfer of PNR Data by Air Carriers to the United States Department of Homeland Security, Bureau of Customs and Border Protection, 2004/496/EC, Official Journal L/2004/183/83, May 20, 2004, available at <http://europa.eu.int/cgi-bin/eur-lex/udl.pl?REQUEST=Seek-Deliver&LANGUAGE=en&SERVICE=eurlex&COLLECTION=oj&DOCID=2004l183p00830083>; Agreement Between the European Community and the United States of America on the Processing and Transfer of PNR Data by Air Carriers to the United States Department of Homeland Security, Bureau of Customs and Border Protection, Official Journal L/2004/183/84, May 20, 2004, available at <http://europa.eu.int/cgi-bin/eur-lex/udl.pl?REQUEST=Seek-Deliver&LANGUAGE=en&SERVICE=eurlex&COLLECTION=oj&DOCID=2004l183p00840085>.

346 Article 29 Data Protection Working Party, Opinion 2/2004 on the Adequate Protection of Personal Data Contained in the PNR of Air Passengers to Be Transferred to the United States' Bureau of Customs and Border Protection (US CBP), January 29, 2004, available at <http://europa.eu.int/comm/internal_market/privacy/docs/wpdocs/2004/wp87_en.pdf>.

347 Privacy International, *et al.*, Transferring Privacy: The Transfer of Passenger Records and the Abdication of Privacy Protection; The First Report on "Towards an International Infrastructure for Surveillance of Movement", with a Commentary from the American Civil Liberties Union on "A Perspective from America", February 2004 <http://www.privacyinternational.org/issues/terrorism/rpt/transferringprivacy.pdf>; Trans Atlantic Consumer Dialogue (TACD), Resolution on Passenger Name Records, Doc No. Internet-30-04, June 2004 <http://www.tacd.org/docs/?id=254>, also available with list of endorsers and supporting references at <http://www.thepublicvoice.org/take_action/pnr-resol-action.html>; *also see generally* Statewatch, Observatory on the Exchange of Data on Passengers (PNR) with USA <http://www.statewatch.org/pnrobservatory.htm>; EPIC, EU-US Airline Passenger Data Disclosure <http://www.epic.org/privacy/intl/passenger_data.html>; Hasbrouck, "Privacy and Travel", The Practical Nomad blog <http://hasbrouck.org/blog/archives/cat_privacy_and_travel.html>.

European Communities, on behalf of the Parliament, to annul both the agreement and the adequacy finding.[348]

The stated goal of the US government is the adoption of permanent international standards overriding existing national data protection laws, and mandating access to PNR data by all governments worldwide.[349]

New Measures for Tracking and Monitoring of Travelers

In addition to seeking access to existing PNRs, some governments have sought to require data in PNRs beyond that which would otherwise be entered for commercial purposes; to modify PNR formats to facilitate desired government uses of PNR data; and/or to require airlines to transmit additional Advance Passenger Information (API) data collected solely to satisfy government demands.[350] While API data is typically described as corresponding to the information that could already be gleaned from travelers' tickets and passports, the majority of the categories of PNR and API data sought by the US cannot be obtained from current travel documents.[351]

These governmental initiatives have been led primarily by the US and, within the EU, by Spain.[352] In April 2004, a Spanish proposal that all airlines operating to, or within, the EU be required to collect and transmit to the governments of destination countries information concerning all passengers, was adopted by the

---

[348] "European Parliament Asks Court of Justice to Annul EU-US Passenger Data Deal," June 25, 2004) <http://europa.eu.int/ISPO/ida/jsps/index.jsp?fuseAction=showDocument&documentID=2655&parent=chapter &preChapterID=0-140-194>.

[349] For fiscal year 2004, the goal is "to negotiate an agreement with the EU that gives CBP and TSA permanent access to PNR data," and for fiscal year 2005 to "[e]nsure access to PNR data for border and passenger screening on a global basis" as, "Opinions by the public and political leadership in Europe and Eurasia soften on US government] use of PNR." US Department of State, "FY 2005 Performance Summary, Strategic Goal 3: Secure the Homeland by Strengthening Arrangements that Govern the Flows of People, Goods, and Services Between the United States and the Rest of the World," February 2004 <http://www.state.gov/m/rm/rls/perfplan/2005/html/29302.htm>.

[350] Advance Passenger Information (API) – A Statement of Principles, Working Paper FAL/12-WP/60, presented by IATA to the 12th Session of the ICAO FAL Division, Cairo, March 10, 2004), available at <http://www.icao.int/icao/en/atb/fal/fal12/documentation/fal12wp060_en.pdf>.

[351] Hasbrouck, "'Undertakings' by the USA on Use of Reservation Data", February 2, 2004 <http://hasbrouck.org/blog/archives/000131.html>.

[352] Council of the European Union, Initiative of the Kingdom of Spain with a View to Adopting a Council Directive on the Obligation of Carriers to Communicate Passenger Data, January 9, 2004, available at <http://register.consilium.eu.int/pdf/en/04/st05/st05183.en04.pdf>; *also see generally* <http://www.statewatch.org/eu-pnrobservatory.htm>.

Council of the European Union over the objections of the European Parliament committees that had considered it.[353]

Canadian customs and immigration agencies have developed and deployed their own airline reservation profiling software and algorithms, but use "risk management criteria that are common to both countries" to determine what travel data to share with the US.[354]

Australia has mandated that all airlines provide the government with continuous real-time access to their reservations systems, and has implemented an automated profiling system, based on certain elements of PNR and API data, which selects certain reservations for review and possible action by customs officers.[355]

In New Zealand, government access to PNR and API data has been limited to international flights, and law enforcement authorities have used the advance passenger processing system developed by Australia. The New Zealand government has sought, but has not yet obtained, legal authority to issue "do not board" orders to airlines on the basis of automated analysis of PNR and API data.[356]

The US has imposed a requirement for collection and automated transmission of API data on all international flights to the US, and has pursued multilateral agreements on API data transfers with the EU (as part of the PNR agreement), the G-8[357] and, globally, through ICAO.

The US has also proposed to use secret security directives to impose both the requirement for travelers to display evidence of their identity and the requirement for airlines and travel agents to create a PNR containing specified identifying information for each traveler, concealing the details of the requirements from the public and frustrating judicial review. A federal court has found that such

---

[353] Council Directive on the obligation of carriers to communicate passenger data, April 27, 2004, available at <http://www.statewatch.org/news/2004/apr/8078pnr.pdf>.

[354] Canadian Advance Passenger Information Program, Working Paper FAL/12-WP/38, presented by Canada to the 12th Session of the ICAO FAL Division, Cairo, December 11, 2003, available at <http://www.icao.int/icao/en/atb/fal/fal12/documentation/fal12wp038_en.pdf>.

[355] Article 29 Data Protection Working Party, Opinion 1/2004 on the level of protection ensured in Australia for the transmission of Passenger Name Record data from airlines, January 16, 2004, available at <http://europa.eu.int/comm/internal_market/privacy/docs/wpdocs/2004/wp85_en.pdf>.

[356] Introduction of Advance Passenger Screening (APS) in New Zealand, Working Paper FAL/12-WP/81, presented by Canada to the 12th Session of the ICAO FAL Division, Cairo, March 20, 2004, available at <http://www.icao.int/icao/en/atb/fal/fal12/documentation/fal12wp081_en.pdf>.

[357] "G-8 Secure and Facilitated International Travel Initiative (SAFTI)," White House press release, June 9, 2004 <http://www.whitehouse.gov/news/releases/2004/06/20040609-51.html>.

---

identification requirements do not violate constitutional guarantees against unreasonable search and seizure.[358]

Registered Traveler

In 2004, the US government began testing the Registered Traveler Pilot Program at Minneapolis-St. Paul International Airport.[359] The program allows certain passengers to volunteer personal and biometric information to the government for prescreening.[360] In exchange, program participants go through special security lines for physical screening.[361] The pilot program has been expanded to five airports throughout the US.[362] A privatized version of the program is being developed at Orlando International Airport.[363]

Computer Assisted Passenger Prescreening System II (CAPPS II)

The model for the global travel data regime sought by the US was the second generation Computer Assisted Passenger Screening System (CAPPS II), which was proposed by the US government in January 2003 for flights to, from, and within the US.[364] In 2004, the US government announced its decision to abandon the program.[365] Department of Homeland Security Secretary Tom Ridge said that privacy concerns surrounding the pilot program coupled with ongoing Congressional doubts about the effectiveness of the program contributed to the decision. When asked whether the program could be considered "dead," Ridge answered "yes."[366]

However, civil liberties organizations and air travel experts expressed skepticism about the announcement. Some said that CAPPS II was simply being renamed or

---

[358] Gilmore v. Ashcroft, 2004 U.S. Dist. 4869 (N.D. Ca. March 24, 2004), appeal docketed, No. 04-15736 (9th Cir. April 19, 2004), case documents available at <http://www.freetotravel.org/legal.html>; see also Frontier Travel v. TSA, (D. Alaska, filed May 24, 2004), case documents available at <http://www.alaskafreedom.com/akn/case.html>.

[359] Press Release, Transportation Security Administration, TSA Announces Start of Registered Traveler Pilot Program (July 7, 2004), available at <http://www.tsa.gov/public/display?content=09000519800b5e9e>.

[360] Transportation Security Administration, Registered Traveler Pilot Program Fact Sheet, available at <http://www.tsa.gov/public/interweb/assetlibrary/Factsheet.pdf>.

[361] Id.

[362] Id.

[363] See Clear Registered Traveler, <http://www.flyclear.com>.

[364] System of Records Notice, 68 Fed. Reg. 2101 (January 15, 2003).

[365] Press Release, Transportation Security Administration, TSA to Test New Passenger Pre-Screening System (August 26, 2005), available at <http://www.tsa.gov/public/display?theme=44&content=09000519800c6c77>.

[366] Mimi Hall & Barbara DeLolli, "Plan to Collect Flier Data Canceled," USA Today, July 14, 2004, available at http://www.usatoday.com/news/washington/2004-07-14-fly-plan_x.htm.

merged into other programs, and that the US government would continue to pursue its essential functionality: mandatory identification of all air travelers, entry of identifying data into reservations, and government access to those reservations.[367] These goals were also endorsed by the "9/11 Commission" in the US, whose first recommendation for how to "protect against terrorist attacks" was "targeting travel" and expanding "travel intelligence collection," *i.e.* surveillance of travelers.[368]

CAPPS II or its successor would be a system of automated identity- and reservation-based profiling unlike any other airline passenger screening or security system in the world.[369] CAPPS II would have profiled each passenger and assign them a risk or "suspiciousness" score on the basis of their identity as determined from their PNR. That would not be possible unless each passenger (a) is identified, (b) has a reservation, and (c) has sufficient information entered in their reservation to identify them uniquely. CAPPS II would therefore have the had effect of prohibiting anonymous or unreserved travel, and mandating entry of specified identifying information about each passenger in his or her PNR.[370]

The US had sought permission from other countries, including the EU and Canada, to use data collected in those countries for CAPPS II.[371] The "Undertakings" by the US, which were a condition for the European Commission's finding of adequacy of passenger data protection in the US, specifically declare that the US may use data from the EU in CAPPS II tests,[372] although that authorization refers specifically to "CAPPS II," and thus may be invalidated by the change of the program's name (see below).

As the US Communications Assistance to Law Enforcement Act (CALEA) did with the infrastructure of transport of information, government travel security initiatives would require the embedding of "intelligence gathering" capabilities into the infrastructure of transportation of people, imposing as an unfunded mandate on the travel industry whatever changes, at whatever cost, are required

---

[367] Hasbrouck, "CAPPS-II Is Dead. Long Live CAPPS-II!" <http://hasbrouck.org/blog/archives/000282.html>.

[368] Final Report of the National Commission on Terrorist Attacks Upon the United States, Chapter 12: What to do? A Global Strategy, July 22, 2004, available at <http://www.9-11commission.gov/report/911Report_Ch12.pdf>. (The 9/11 Commission also endorsed the proposed ICAO standard for RFID/biometric passports and the US-VISIT program, among other travel surveillance schemes).

[369] Hasbrouck, "What's Wrong With CAPPS-II? (And What Should Be Done about It?)" (last updated June 25, 2004) <http://hasbrouck.org/articles/CAPPS-II.html>.

[370] Hasbrouck, "CAPPS-II Will Require 3 New Directives," December 10, 2003) <http://hasbrouck.org/blog/archives/000084.html>.

[371] Chris Strohm, "US, Canada Launch Talks on Sharing Citizen Data," GovExec.com, January 30, 2004 <http://www.govexec.com/dailyfed/0104/013004c1.htm>.

[372] Commission Decision of 14 May 2004, *supra.*

to provide that surveillance functionality. Even airlines that supported CAPPS II were concerned about the cost of the changes it would require to reservation data structures, messaging formats and protocols, and business procedures worldwide, especially if those costs are not reimbursed by governments.[373] While the US government has suggested that it might cut back on the use of other, non-travel commercial databases in the profiling component of its revised and/or renamed successor to CAPPS II, the intelligence gathering component and its required changes to airline databases would remain as extensive and costly as ever.

CAPPS II would have incorporated existing US "no-fly" and other airline passenger "watch lists." As part of its international initiatives for government access to, and trans-border sharing of, PNR and API data, the US government has sought to establish a global system for exchanges of traveler watch list information, and to exempt it from requirements of disclosure, due process, and judicial review.[374] PNR data obtained through CAPPS II would have also been included in the lifetime "biographic and biometric travel history" created and maintained on each foreign visitor to the US under the US-VISIT system.[375]

The information required by CAPPS II would have been, by design, the information needed to ensure that all passengers could be uniquely identified from reservations, and, as a result, that reservations for separate trips could be indexed into lifetime travel histories. Under CAPPS II, travel companies in the US, including the CRSs, which host most airline reservations, would have been permitted to retain all of this information indefinitely after passing it on to governments, and use it to construct their own permanent files on travelers. These records could be accessed by government agencies at any time, even if the government itself did not retain the CAPPS II data.

---

[373] IATA, Airline Reservation System and Passenger Name Record (PNR) Access by States, *supra*; Advance Passenger Information (API) – A Statement of Principles, Working Paper FAL/12-WP/60, *supra*; James C. May, President and CEO, Air Transport Association (ATA), Testimony Before the US Senate Committee on Commerce, Science, and Transportation at a Hearing on Aviation Security, June 22, 2004, available at <http://commerce.senate.gov/hearings/testimony.cfm?id=1245&wit_id=1923>; May, Status of the Computer Assisted Passenger Prescreening System ("CAPPS II"), Testimony Before the Aviation Subcommittee of the House Committee on Transportation and Infrastructure, March 17, 2004, available at <http://www.house.gov/transportation/aviation/03-17-04/may.html>; Hasbrouck, "Why CAPPS-II Would Cost a Billion Dollars", February 13, 2004 <http://hasbrouck.org/blog/archives/000149.html>; Hasbrouck, Comments Re: Docket Number DHS/TSA-2003-1, "Passenger and Aviation Security Screening Records" (PASSR), September 30, 2003, available at <http://hasbrouck.org/articles/Hasbrouck_TSA_comments-30SEP2003.pdf>.

[374] EPIC, "Documents Show Errors in TSA's 'No-Fly' Watchlist", April 2003 <http://www.epic.org/privacy/airtravel/foia/watchlist_foia_analysis.html>; ACLU, "ACLU Challenges Government No-Fly List" <http://www.aclu.org/SafeandFree/SafeandFree.cfm?ID=15422&c=206>; ACLU, "ACLU Seeks Government Accountability For No-Fly List" <http://www.aclu.org/SafeandFree/SafeandFree.cfm?ID=15422&c=206>.

[375] Hasbrouck, "USA Will Keep Visitor Travel Histories for 100 Years" <http://hasbrouck.org/blog/archives/000103.html>.

Secure Flight

On August 26, 2004, The Department of Homeland Security Transportation Security Administration announced that the government would begin testing Secure Flight, a new passenger prescreening system, in November.[376] Secure Flight will compare PNRs against information maintained by the FBI's Terrorist Screening Center, which includes expanded "selectee" and "no fly" lists. TSA will also seek to identify "suspicious indicators associated with travel behavior" in passengers' itinerary PNR data. Furthermore, the agency is testing the use of commercial databases to verify the accuracy of information provided by travelers.[377] TSA will administer the program, removing all passenger screening responsibility from the airlines. The agency also ordered 72 airlines to turn over their passenger records from June 2004 for Secure Flight testing.[378]

Though TSA plans to implement a redress process for travelers improperly flagged by Secure Flight, it is unclear how this process will work. The government has long used "selectee" and "no fly" lists for aviation security purposes, but passengers have experienced great difficulty clearing their names when improperly flagged. In 2002, EPIC obtained through the Freedom of Information Act dozens of complaint letters sent to TSA by irate passengers who felt they had been incorrectly identified for additional security or were denied boarding because of the watch lists. The complaints describe the bureaucratic maze passengers encounter if they happen to be mistaken for individuals on the list, as well as the difficulty they encounter trying to exonerate themselves.[379]

Secure Flight will be tested live with two airlines beginning in August 2005.

---

[376] Press Release, Transportation Security Administration, TSA to Test New Passenger Pre-Screening System, August 26, 2005, available at <http://www.tsa.gov/public/display?theme=44&content=09000519800c6c77>.

[377] System of Records Notice, 69 Fed. Reg. 57345, 57346 (September 24, 2004), available at <http://a257.g.akamaitech.net/7/257/2422/06jun20041800/edocket.access.gpo.gov/2004/04-21479.htm>.

[378] Notice of Final Order for Secure Flight Test Phase, 69 Fed. Reg. 65619 (November 15, 2004), available at <http://a257.g.akamaitech.net/7/257/2422/06jun20041800/edocket.access.gpo.gov/2004/04-25396.htm>.

[379] See EPIC FOIA documents on "selectee" and "no fly" watch lists, available at <http://www.epic.org/redirect/watchlist_foia.html>. See generally, EPIC, "Passenger Profiling Page," available at <http://www.epic.org/privacy/airtravel/profiling>.

Biometric Passports

Foreign visitors will be required to identify themselves with passports satisfying ICAO machine-readable travel document (MRTD) standards,[380] which may also include secretly and remotely readable RFID chips containing digitally encoded biometric data.[381] US travelers will be allowed to obtain "registered travel" tokens or credentials only by having biometric data recorded, and by submitting to a background check of government and commercial databases.[382] The motivation to register can only be that unregistered travelers will be subjected to longer delays and/or more intrusive searches and screening.[383]

Although the overwhelming emphasis has been on air travel, some of these measures and others are now being extended to other transportation modes, starting with trains and buses. Already intercity train and bus passengers in the US are required to display "valid photo identification" to purchase tickets and on boarding.[384]

A government-required RFID/biometric Transportation Worker Identification Credential (TWIC) is being tested for eventual issuance to more than 10 million workers in transportation facilities in the US, including airports, seaports, rail and

---

[380] Enhanced Border Security and Visa Entry Reform Act of 2002, Pub. L. No. 107-173, Sec. 303(b)(1); Machine Readable Travel Documents, ICAO Doc. 9303 (Montreal, 5th ed. 2003); *also see generally* ICAO New Technologies Working Group, Technical Reports <http://www.icao.int/mrtd/download/technical.cfm>.
381. ICAO, Report of the Twelfth Session of the Facilitation (FAL) Division (Cairo, Egypt, 22 March – 1 April 2004) <http://www.icao.int/icao/en/atb/fal/fal12/documentation/fal12Report_en.pdf>; Privacy International, ACLU, *et al.*, An Open Letter to the ICAO: A Second Report on "Towards an International Infrastructure for Surveillance of Movement," March 30, 2004
<http://www.privacyinternational.org/issues/terrorism/rpt/icaoletter.pdf>; Barry Steinhardt, Witness Testimony at the hearing on "Radio Frequency Identification (RFID) Technology: What the Future Holds for Commerce, Security, and the Consumer," Subcommittee on Commerce, Trade, and Consumer Protection, Committee on Energy and Commerce, US House of Representatives, July 14, 2004, available at
<http://energycommerce.house.gov/108/Hearings/07142004hearing1337/Steinhardt2150.htm>; *also see generally* Privacy International, About the Open Letter to the ICAO, March 2004
<http://www.privacyinternational.org/issues/terrorism/rpt/icaobackground.html>; ICAO, Twelfth Meeting of the Facilitation Division (Cairo, 22 March 2004 - 1 April 2004) <http://www.icao.int/icao/en/atb/fal/fal12/>; ICAO Technical Advisory Group on Machine Readable Travel Documents (TAG/MRTD)
<http://www.icao.int/mrtd/>.

[382] TSA, Registered Traveler Pilot Combined Synopsis Solicitation, HSTS02-04-R-RET002, posted April 5, 2004, available at <http://www.eps.gov/EPSData/DHS-BT/Synopses/35287/HSTS02-04-R-RET002/RTCSSFinal.doc>.

[383] The travel industry "Simplifying Passenger Travel" initiative has been developing and testing, in several countries, schemes for biometric/RFID credentials that could be used for both commercial and government functions. These combine elements of the functionality of electronic tickets, boarding passes, ticket payment credit or debit cards, frequent flyer cards, and registered traveler identification credentials. Simplifying Passenger Travel Interest Group <http://www.simplifying-travel.org>.

[384] *E.g.*, Amtrak, Important Information About Amtrak Passenger Security available at <http://www.amtrak.com/idrequire.html>.

---

truck terminals, etc.[385] The TWIC was, however, intended in the future to identify all users of transportation systems, *i.e.* travelers.[386] Eventually, all persons on transportation vehicles or in transportation facilities may be required to carry government-issued RFID/biometric identification credentials.

The Case of US-VISIT: a New Tool for Monitoring Travelers

The Department of Homeland Security deployed the United States Visitor and Immigrant Status Indicator Technology (US-VISIT) at 115 airports and 15 major seaports on January 5, 2004.[387] When this practice began, the general response was one of shock and alarm. Brazil, China, Greece[388] and Switzerland[389] were among countries that protested against their citizens being fingerprinted by the Department of Homeland Security. Brazil even threatened reciprocity.[390]

This border security program is intended to improve the United States' capability to collect information about foreign nationals who travel to the US, as well as control the pre-entry, entry, status, and exit of these travelers. US-VISIT is expected to be operational at every US air and seaport and the 50 busiest land ports of entry by the end of 2005.[391] Some information in US-VISIT will be kept for 100 years,[392] and all information may be disclosed to any law enforcement agency in the US and any other country.[393]

When a visitor subject to US-VISIT applies for a visa to travel to the US, he is fingerprinted and photographed at an overseas US consular office.[394] This biometric information is then checked against more than 20 interfacing

---

[385] TSA TWIC Program <http://www.tsa.gov/public/display?theme=68>; Hasbrouck, Transportation Worker Identification Credential (TWIC), April 6, 2004 <http://hasbrouck.org/blog/archives/000189.html>.

[386] US Dept. of Transportation, Credentialing Direct Action Group, National Transportation Worker ID Card (TWIC) Functional Requirements Draft, January 23, 2002, available at <http://www.apta.com/government_affairs/regulations/documents/workerid.pdf>.

[387] Department of Homeland Security, Travel & Transportation: US-VISIT <http://www.dhs.gov/dhspublic/interapp/content_multi_image/content_multi_image_0006.xml/>; *see also* EPIC's US-VISIT web page <http://www.epic.org/privacy/us-visit/>.

[388] Kathiminerini English Edition, "New Twist in US Visa Process," May 6, 2004.

[389] Swissinfo, "Swiss Criticize Tougher US Border Checks," April 5, 2004.

[390] Raymond Colitt, "Brazil Stands Firm on Fingerprinting of US Visitors," Financial Times, January 12, 2004.

[391] Department of Homeland Security, Travel & Transportation: US-VISIT Frequently Asked Questions <http://www.dhs.gov/dhspublic/interapp/editorial/editorial_0440.xml>.

[392] Notice of Privacy Act System of Records, 68 Fed. Reg. 69412 (December 12, 2003).

[393] Interim Final Rule and Notice, 69 Fed. Reg. 467 (January 5, 2004). *See also* US-VISIT Program, Increment 1, Privacy Impact Assessment, December 18, 2003, at 6, 13, available at <http://www.dhs.gov/interweb/assetlibrary/VISITPIAfinal3.pdf>.

[394] Department of Homeland Security, Travel & Transportation: US-VISIT, *supra.*

government databases to determine the likelihood that the visitor is a criminal or terrorist.[395] When the visitor arrives at a US port of entry, he is again fingerprinted and photographed to verify that he is the same person who was issued the visa.[396] A pilot program has been launched to fingerprint visitors when they exit the US, as well.[397]

US-VISIT did not apply to visitors to the US traveling through the Visa Waiver Program until September 20, 2004 when the program was expanded to include Visa Waiver travelers arriving at air and seaports.[398] The general response to this expansion of US-VISIT was very quiet, possibly because the enlargement of the program was a result of the proposed extension of the biometric passport deadline.[399] If any Visa Waiver program countries do not present acceptable plans by October 2005 for launching biometric e-passports by 2006, US law requires that these countries be removed from the Visa Waiver program, resulting in all nationals being forced to get visas.[400] Earlier, the Department of Homeland Security indicated that it intended to link CAPPS II and US-VISIT when both programs were fully operational to ensure that "the processes at both border and airport points of entry and exit are consistent."[401]

Other countries are considering similar systems now that the US has expanded US-VISIT. The EU has proposed a similar system involving fingerprints, enhanced by the fact that EU countries will also have fingerprint-based biometric passports, creating a database of biometrics on over 450 million people.

Key Developments Threatening Travel Privacy

- Lack of enforceable legal protection for travel data comparable to that for financial, medical, or other sensitive categories of personal information

---

[395] Interim Final Rule and Notice, 69 Fed. Reg. 476 (January 5, 2004).

[396] Department of Homeland Security, Travel & Transportation: US-VISIT <http://www.dhs.gov/dhspublic/interapp/content_multi_image/content_multi_image_0006.xml/>.

[397] Department of Homeland Security, Travel & Transportation: US-VISIT Frequently Asked Questions <http://www.dhs.gov/dhspublic/interapp/editorial/editorial_0440.xml>.

[398] *Id.*

[399] Press Office, "Departments of Homeland Security and State Request Extension for Biometric Passport Requirement, Visa Waiver Program Travelers to Be Enrolled in US-VISIT," Department of Homeland Security, April 2, 2004.

[400] Press Release, Department of State, DHS to Require Digital Photos in Passports for Visa Waiver Travelers (June 15, 2005), available at <http://www.state.gov/r/pa/prs/ps/2005/47984.htm>.

[401] Interim Final Privacy Act Notice, 68 Fed. Reg. 45265 (August 1, 2003).

- Government demands for access to reservations and other commercial travel data and exemption of travel-related data from existing privacy and data protection regulations
- Compulsory identification of travelers (through biometrics, compulsory carrying or display of credentials, etc.) and compulsory entry of identifying data into reservations
- Indexing of reservations and travel transactions into lifetime personal travel dossiers
- Inclusion of secretly and remotely readable RFID chips in passports, tickets, "registered traveler" credentials, or other travel documents
- Profiling of travelers, denial of freedom of travel, slower or more intrusive searches, or other differential treatment of travelers on the basis of watch lists, profiles, or as a "registered traveler" status
- Integration of commercial and government databases about travelers; integration and conversion of travel industry infrastructure into an infrastructure of surveillance

Audio Bugging

Advances in technology are also making it easier and cheaper to conduct covert audio surveillance. Bugs come in many shapes and sizes. They range from micro engineered transmitters the size of an office staple to devices no bigger than a cigarette packet that are capable of transmitting video and sound signals for miles. Many of the bugs are cleverly camouflaged. They are hidden in everything from umbrella stands to light shades. Sometimes, the infiltrator will hide them in a business or sports trophy where they will stay indefinitely. The latest bugs remain active with their own power supply for around ten years.

Laws restricting the use of covert audio devices vary widely across the world. Many countries have provisions in their general wiretap laws that also cover the use of bugs. The European Court of Human Rights has ruled several times that all signatories of the Convention must enact laws governing their use. While it is illegal in most circumstances in the United States to use or sell such devices, the British market had no restrictions whatever until recently. As one private investigator told the London Daily Telegraph, "It's a game anyone can play." Millions of bugs are sold every year in Asian countries such as Hong Kong and Japan.

The devices are used for a variety of reasons. In many Asian countries, use of the devices for industrial espionage is widespread. They are also frequently used in the workplace or in homes. Law enforcement and intelligence agencies also use the devices but according to government records in the United States, Canada and other countries, they are used much less frequently than traditional wiretaps for law enforcement purposes.

Video Surveillance

Surveillance cameras (also called Closed-Circuit Television or CCTV[402] are increasingly being used to monitor public and private spaces throughout the world. The leader is the United Kingdom, where between GBP 150 and 300 million per year is spent on expanding a surveillance industry that has an estimated one and a half million cameras watching public spaces.[403] Many central business districts in Britain are now covered by surveillance camera systems involving a linked system of cameras with full pan, tilt, zoom and night vision or infrared capability. CCTV systems are also in wide use in several other European countries where they are closely regulated. Surveillance of public spaces has grown markedly in the United States and Australia. In New York City, the NYCLU Surveillance Camera Project identified 2,397 cameras in Manhattan, an admittedly incomplete list.[404] The Mayor of Washington, DC had proposed a "London style" blanket surveillance of public areas to cover the several public protests that takes place in the capital, but public opposition has prevented the adoption of the plan.[405] In Singapore, cameras are widely deployed for traffic enforcement and to prevent littering. Several governments are now considering using surveillance systems as an anti-terrorism tool. Some observers believe the surveillance camera phenomenon is dramatically changing the nature of cities. The technology has been described as the "fifth utility,"[406] where CCTV is being integrated into the urban environment in much the same way as the electricity supply and the telephone network in the first half of the century.[407]

---

[402] CCTV is a visual surveillance technology, either analog or digital, designed for monitoring various environments and activities. CCTV systems typically involve a dedicated communications link between cameras and monitors, and involve a linked system of cameras able to be viewed and operated from a control room.

[403] Jeffrey Rosen, "A Cautionary Tale for a New Age of Surveillance," New York Times Magazine, October 7, 2001.

[404] NYCLU Surveillance Camera Project <http://www.nyclu.org/surveillance.html>. *See also*, New York Surveillance Camera Players <http://www.notbored.org/the-scp.html>.

[405] "Eyes in the Sky: DC Police Are Building a Network of Cameras to Keep Tabs on the Public," Wall Street Journal Classroom Edition, April 2002.

[406] Stephen Graham, The Fifth Utility, Index on Censorship, Issue 3, 2000, available at <http://www.indexoncensorship.org/300/gra.htm>.

[407] *See generally* EPIC's Video Surveillance web page <http://www.epic.org/privacy/surveillance/>.

Governments and law enforcement authorities have used video surveillance in various circumstances ranging from the prevention of crimes,[408] the safety of urban environments and government buildings, traffic control,[409] the monitoring of demonstrators,[410] and in the context of criminal investigations. In the United States, several cities have started implementing sophisticated systems of surveillance. In Washington, DC, surveillance cameras have been placed on national monuments, such as the Lincoln Memorial. New York, Tampa, Virginia Beach,[411] Baltimore,[412] and Chicago have also started installing cameras.[413] In the United Kingdom, the government and police authorities have covered the country with more than one and a half million cameras, some of them being used to check the license plates of cars entering cities, and even the face of drivers,[414] making CCTV the single most heavily funded non-criminal justice crime

---

[408] In 2002, the city of Garden Grove, California, enacted an ordinance requiring cybercafés (providing Internet access for a fee) to maintain a video surveillance system. The goal of this and other regulatory measures was to control gang activity in cybercafés. In 2004, the California Court of Appeal overturned a lower court's restraining order against implementation of the law. The appeals court found that the surveillance requirement did not violate constitutional privacy or free speech rights. Vo v. City of Garden Grove <http://www.courtinfo.ca.gov/opinions/documents/G032058.PDF>.

[409] See Marcia Biederman, "Automobiles: Are Red-Light Cameras Aimed at Safety or Fines?," New York Times, October 23, 2002, available at <http://www.nytimes.com/2002/10/23/automobiles/23BIED.html> (on the use of red-light cameras by law enforcement); John Tierney, "Traffic Cameras Could Help Solve Crimes," New York Times, October 15, 2002, available at <http://www.nytimes.com/2002/10/15/national/15CAME.html>.

[410] See Kristen Lombardi, "Candid Cameras. Activists, Unions, and the ACLU Question Worcester Cops' Practice of Photographing Peaceful Demonstrators," Boston Phoenix, March 28, 2002 <http://www.www.bostonphoenix.com/boston/news_features/top/features/documents/02212398.htm>; Dorothy Korber, "Protesters Cry Foul over Police Videotaping," Sacramento Bee, June 5, 2003, available at <http://www.sacbee.com/content/news/crime/story/6218889p-7173447c.html>; Ian Austen, "For the Spy in the Sky, New Eyes," New York Times, June 20, 2002, available at <http://www.nytimes.com/2002/06/20/technology/circuits/20SPYY.html?8ict=&pagewanted=print&position=bottom> (on the use of helicopter cameras).

[411] See David McGuire, "Virginia Beach Installs Face-Recognition Cameras," Washington Post, July 3, 2002, available at <http://www.washingtonpost.com/ac2/wp-dyn/A19946-2002Jul3?language=printer>.

[412] "24-hour Surveillance Cameras Planned for Baltimore," Mercury News, June 10, 2004 <http://www.siliconvalley.com/mld/siliconvalley/8890312.htm>, "24-hour Camera Surveillance in City Is Part of Bigger Plan," Baltimore Sun, June 10, 2004 <http://www.reclaimdemocracy.org/articles_2004/baltimore_surveillance_cameras.html>.

[413] For an overview of surveillance use in the United States, see California Research Bureau, Public and Private Applications of Video Surveillance and Biometric Technologies (2002) (CRB 02-006), available at <http://www.library.ca.gov/crb/02/06/02-006.pdf>. See also Letter from Marc Rotenberg, Executive Director, Electronic Privacy Information Center, to Councilperson Kathy Patterson, District of Columbia City Council (December 17, 2003) <http://www.epic.org/privacy/protest/dccouncil_letter12_03.html>.

[414] See Mark Towsend & Paul Harris, "Security Role for Traffic Cameras," The Observer, February 9, 2003, available at <http://www.observer.co.uk/politics/story/0,6903,892001,00.html>.

prevention measure.[415] A 2003 survey conducted by the Dutch data protection authority found that one municipality in five uses camera surveillance.[416]

In Europe, because the encompassing data protection legal framework of the European Union Data Protection Directive applies to video surveillance records, privacy authorities have started drawing up guidelines aimed at implementing the Directive's data protection principles to the field of video surveillance.[417] The European Commission, in a recent consultation aimed at evaluating how the Directive had been implemented in practice as regards the processing of sound and image data, concluded that no change was required to the current rules for it to be applicable to the processing of personal data in the context of video surveillance, although more practical guidance was definitely needed.[418] The Article 29 Working Party (established under the EU Data Protection Directive) has issued several documents on video surveillance. One includes a summary of guidance issued by national data protection authorities.[419]

In July 2000, the United Kingdom Data Protection Commissioner issued a code of practice on the use of CCTV. The code sets out guidelines for the operators of

---

[415] Over the three-year period of 1999 through 2001, the British government has made available GBP 170 million (~USD 272.5 million) for CCTV schemes in town and city centres, car parks, crime hot-spots and residential areas. *See* Brandon C. Welsh & David P. Farrington, Crime Prevention Effects of Closed Circuit Television: A Systematic Review, Home Office Research Study 252, August 2002, available at <http://www.homeoffice.gov.uk/rds/pdfs2/hors252.pdf>.

[416] *College Bescherming Persoonsgegevens*, "*Cameratoezicht in de openbare ruimte*," November 2003 <http://www.cbpweb.nl/documenten/rap_2003_cameratoezicht_in_de_openbare_ruimte.htm>.

[417] In May 2004, the *Deutsches Institut für Normung* (German Institute for Standardization), published a draft standard for a graphic symbol to indicate surveillance by electronic means. DIN 33450 "Graphic Symbol to Indicate Surveillance by Electronic Means (video symbol)." The uniform symbol, a pictograph, is intended to provide a simple way of fulfilling any legal requirement of making video surveillance known to the public. *See* <http://www2.din.de/sixcms/detail.php?id=16327>.

[418] The consultation shows that there has been so far insufficient public debate about the limits to be placed on the use of video surveillance in order to safeguard data subjects' rights and freedoms, and that a number of legal and practical issues resulting from the implementation of the Directive in the Member States with respect to sound and image data is creating some uncertainty for operators called on to comply with the legislation and for individuals entitled to exercise their data protection rights. European Commission, First report on the implementation of the Data Protection Directive (95/46/EC), COM (2003) 265(01), available at <http://europa.eu.int/eur-lex/en/com/rpt/2003/com2003_0265en01.pdf>; *see also* European Commission's Report on the transposition of Directive 95/46/EC homepage <http://europa.eu.int/comm/internal_market/privacy/lawreport_en.htm>. *See also* British Institute of International & Comparative Law, Report on the Implementation of Directive 95/46/EC to the Processing of Sound and Image Data, May 16, 2003, available at <http://europa.eu.int/comm/internal_market/privacy/docs/lawreport/consultation/biiclstudy-soundimage_en.pdf> (expert report that substantiates the European Commission's report).

[419] *See* Article 29 Data Protection Working Party (WP29), Opinion 4/2004 on the Processing of Personal Data by means of Video Surveillance (February 2004) (WP 89) <http://europa.eu.int/comm/internal_market/privacy/docs/wpdocs/2004/wp89_en.pdf>. The WP29's opinion also discusses the consequences of processing of image and sound data under the standards of the European Data Protection directive. *See also* WP29, Working Document on the Processing of Personal Data by means of Video Surveillance (November 2002) (WP 67) <http://europa.eu.int/comm/internal_market/privacy/docs/wpdocs/2002/wp67_en.pdf>.

CCTV systems and makes clear their obligations under the recently implemented Data Protection Act 1998.[420] Also in 2000, the Greek Data Protection Commissioner issued a directive prohibiting the use of CCTV, except in certain circumstances.[421] In Sweden, the 1998 Law on Secret Camera Surveillance restricts the use of video surveillance. Norway's Personal Data Registers Act of 2000 also provides specific rules for video surveillance. In Italy, the data protection authority issued guidelines in May 2004 for the installation of surveillance cameras, requiring, among other things, an assessment of whether the surveillance is proportional to the objectives and whether alternative measures would be possible.[422] In 2003, the European Court of Human Rights issued a judgment holding that the disclosure of CCTV pictures by a public authority may constitute a violation of an individual's right to privacy under Article 8 of the European Convention on Human Rights.[423] In Canada, various provinces' privacy commissioners have established video surveillance guidelines,[424] while Canada's Privacy Commissioner was active in limiting surveillance cameras[425] by, *e.g.*, launching a lawsuit against the Royal Canadian Mounted Police, calling their use of the system an unconstitutional breach of privacy.[426] In Washington, DC, after the District of Columbia (DC) City Council and the US Congress conducted several hearings on video surveillance,[427] the

---

[420] United Kingdom Data Protection Commission, CCTV Code of Practice, July 2000, available at <http://www.dataprotection.gov.uk/dpr/dpdoc.nsf/ed1e7ff5aa6def30802566360045bf4d/db76232b37b5bb6480 25691900413c9d?OpenDocument>.

[421] Hellenic Republic Data Protection Authority, Directive on Closed Circuit Television Systems, September 29, 2000.

[422] Garante per la protezione dei dati personali, "Le regole di privacy per installare telecamere" <http://www.cittadinolex.kataweb.it/Article/0,1519,28643|4,00.html>. *See also* <http://www.statewatch.org/news/2004/may/19italy-surveillance.htm>.

[423] European Court of Human Rights, Fourth Section, Peck v. The United Kingdom, Application No. 44647/98, Strasbourg, January 28, 2003, FINAL 28/04/2003 <http://hudoc.echr.coe.int/hudoc/ViewRoot.asp?Item=0&Action=Html&X=701174921&Notice=0&Noticemod e=&RelatedMode=0>.

[424] *See* Commission d'accès à l'information du Québec, Rules for Use of Surveillance Cameras with Recording in Public Places by Public Bodies (June 2004) <http://www.cai.gouv.qc.ca/06_documentation/01_pdf/new_rules_2004.pdf>. Other Québec video surveillance documents are available at <http://www.cai.gouv.qc.ca/index-en.html>.

425 Charles Mandel, "Security Cams not OK in Canada?," Wired News, April 16, 2002 <http://www.wired.com/news/politics/0,1283,51821,00.html>.

426 A British Columbia court dismissed the suit in June 2003, ruling that the Commissioner had exceeded his authority in bringing the action. See "Privacy Challenge Tossed out by Courts," Canada.com <http://www.canada.com/vancouver/news/story.asp?id=1AA08491-0B8A-4C02-AFB2-D26B6401950A> (Decision available at <http://www.courts.gov.bc.ca/jdb%2Dtxt/sc/03/08/2003bcsc0862.htm>. The Privacy Commissioner subsequently withdrew his appeal <http://www.privcom.gc.ca/media/nr-c/ma_am/ma_030704_e.asp>. In another video surveillance case, the Commissioner upheld a complaint against a railroad for installation of a surveillance camera in a company yard <http://www.privcom.gc.ca/cf-dc/2003/cf-dc_030123_e.asp>. The Commissioner's finding was overturned by a court. Eastmond v. CP Railway, 2004 FC 852 (2004) at <http://decisions.fct-cf.gc.ca/fct/2004/2004fc852.shtml>.

427 The US House of Representatives' Committee on Government Reform, Subcommittee on the District of Columbia, held a hearing on "Privacy vs. Security: Electronic Surveillance in the Nation's Capital" on March

DC City Council enacted legislation directing the Chief of Police of the Metropolitan Police Department (MPD) to issue regulations on the use of video surveillance cameras and technology.[428] The MPD subsequently issued formal rules on the use of CCTV in 2002.[429] Some other police departments and at least one federal government agency have also established video surveillance guidelines.[430]

In the United States, video surveillance is not regulated by federal legislation, although some States have adopted statutes prohibiting the use of video surveillance for peeping purposes,[431] and video voyeurism legislation is under active consideration by the US Congress.[432]

As surveillance systems are becoming a routine part of the urban landscape, scholars, data protection commissioners, legislators, and the public are beginning to grapple with the implications and purposes of this new technology, and to ask questions about its assumed effectiveness.[433] Broader questions about the social consequences of video surveillance activities are also being asked.[434]

Proponents contend that video surveillance is a deterrent to crime and gathers evidence of crimes. Generally, camera systems have been rolled out with little

---

22, 2002. See <http://www.dcwatch.com/issues/privacy.htm>. The DC City Council held hearings on video surveillance in June and November 2002: hearing by the District of Columbia City Council Committee on the Judiciary and the Committee on Public Works and the Environment on the Use of Video Technology in Police Surveillance and Traffic Control, June 13, 2002 <http://www.dcwatch.com/issues/privacy.htm>; see also Adam Clymer, "Big Brother vs. Terrorist in Spy Camera Debate," New York Times, June 19, 2002, available at <http://www.nytimes.com/2002/06/19/national/19PRIV.html> (on the DC Council hearing of June 2003).
428 Metropolitan Police Department Video Surveillance Regulations Emergency Act of 2002, Act 14-302 (March 25, 2002) <http://www.dccouncil.washington.dc.us/images/00001/20020314161451.pdf>.
429 District of Columbia, Metropolitan Police Department, Metropolitan Police Department Use of Closed Circuit Television Cameras, 49 D.C. Reg. 11443 (December 20, 2002) (to be codified at D.C. Mun. Regs. tit. 24, ch. 25).
430 *See* Associated Press, "Police Set Policy on Photos, Taping," Boston Herald, May 19, 2002, available at <http://www2.bostonherald.com/news/local_regional/ap_photo05192002.htm> (Worcester, Massachusetts). The federal agency of the National Park Service has recently released guidelines in response to a March 2002 United States Congress hearing on video surveillance. *See* "Controversy Grows over Police Video Surveillance," CNSNews.com, March 22, 2002, available at <http://www.townhall.com/news/politics/200203/CUL20020322b.shtml>; National Park Service guidelines available at <http://www.epic.org/privacy/surveillance/uspp-cctv_policy-070903.pdf>
431 *See, e.g.*, Mo. Rev. Stat. §565.253, Wash. Rev. Code §9A-44-115. *See also* State of Washington v. Glas at <http://www.courts.wa.gov/opinions/opindisp.cfm?docid=715149MAJ> (Wash. 2002).
432 See, e.g., S.1301, Video Voyeurism Prevention Act of 2003, 108th Congress (2003) <http://thomas.loc.gov>.
433 *See* On the Threshold to Urban Panopticon? Analysing the Employment of CCTV in European Cities and Assessing its Social and Political Impacts, a four-year European Commission funded project, available at <http://www.urbaneye.net>. *See also* Christopher Slobogin, Camera Surveillance of Public Places and the Right to Anonymity, 72 Mississippi Law Journal 213, 233 (2002).
434 *See, e.g.*, papers presented at Sheffield University (UK) Centre for Criminological Research, Conference on CCTV and Social Control: The Politics and Practice of Video Surveillance (2004) <http://www.sheffield.ac.uk/ccr/publicity/conference>.

prior research into the effectiveness or appropriateness of the technology, as in most cases the deployment is driven by a public relations need to create the impression of heightened security.[435] The evidence supporting the effectiveness of the camera system has been inconclusive. The most important and comprehensive research to date is the United Kingdom Home Office meta-study that has systematically reviewed the best studies done in the past that have analyzed the effectiveness of CCTV systems.[436] Other studies, released earlier, found that in many areas with CCTV crime increased and street lighting was a more effective deterrent.[437] In March 2002, a report issued by researchers at the University of Hull in United Kingdom, found that cameras do not have a major impact on most criminal activity, and even where they appear to have an effect it is because that crime is often just displaced elsewhere.[438] Recent studies conducted by the Scottish Center for Criminology have yielded similar results.[439] Questions are now surfacing about the use of cameras in Australia.[440] In 2003, the United States General Accounting Office (GAO) released a report on the use of CCTV by law enforcement in Washington, DC, evaluating how law enforcement agencies have responded to civil liberties risks flowing from CCTV surveillance systems.[441] A 2003 study released by the Australian Institute of Criminology reached equivocal conclusions about effectiveness of cameras in Australia.[442]

---

[435] *See* Michael McCahill & Clive Norris, Literature Review, Urbaneye Working Paper No. 2, March 2002, available at <http://www.urbaneye.net>.

[436] The Home Office study assesses the effectiveness of CCTV in three settings, center city areas and public housing, public transportation, and parking lots and garages. The report concludes that CCTV generally reduces crime to a small degree and has had no beneficial effect on crime in the US. However, it categorizes the findings depending on the settings, with a "very small" or "negligible beneficial effect on crime" in center city areas and public housing; "conflicting evidence of effectiveness" in public transportation; and "statistically significant reduction in crime of about forty-one percent" in parking lots and garages. The study also notes that other measures (improved lighting, painting, fencing, payment schemes, notices about CCTV, and security personnel) were in operation at the same time as CCTV. The report has also found out that CCTV had no effect on violent crimes, but had a significant desirable effect on vehicle crimes. Brandon C. Welsh & David P. Farrington, Crime Prevention Effects of Closed Circuit Television: A Systematic Review, *supra*.

[437] NACRO, "CCTV not a Crime Prevention Cure-All, Says Report," June 28 2002, available at <http://www.nacro.org.uk/templates/news/newsItem.cfm/2002062800.htm>.

[438] Michael McCahill & Clive Norris, CCTV in Britain, Working Paper No. 3, Urbaneye Project, Centre for Criminology and Criminal Justice, University of Hull, March 2002, available at <http://www.urbaneye.net>.

[439] The Scottish Centre for Criminology, Crime Prevention Publications, available at <http://www.scotcrim.u-net.com/researchc.htm>; and, Al Webb, "'Spy' Cameras vs Villains in Britain," UPI. March 8, 2002.

[440] Bruce Andrews, "Here's Looking at You," Australian Center for Independent Journalism, April 2002 <http://www.reportage.uts.edu.au/stories/2002/social/cctv_24042002.html>.

[441] Video Surveillance – Information on Law Enforcement's Use of Closed-Circuit Television to Monitor Selected Federal Property in Washington, DC, GAO 03-748, June 2003, available at <http://www.gao.gov/new.items/d03748.pdf>.

[442] Dean Wilson & Adam Sutton, Open-street CCTV in Australia, November 2003 (Australian Institute of Criminology, No. 271) <http://www.aic.gov.au/publications/tandi2/tandi271.pdf>.

Campaigns have begun in several countries to stop the spread of surveillance camera systems,[443] and to monitor the deployment of cameras in several cities.[444] In Washington, DC, EPIC has launched Observing Surveillance[445] to document the presence of surveillance cameras in the nation's capital. For several years, an international coalition composed of artists, scientists, engineers, scholars, and others have declared December 24 to be "World Sousveillance" day, and have staged several public protests to draw attention to the use of surveillance cameras.[446]

The debate over the appropriateness of surveillance technology is likely to become sharper as the technology becomes increasingly sophisticated. New systems can digitally record images, which facilitate easy archiving, recovery, and sharing of information. Features include night vision, computer-assisted operation, thermal imaging,[447] and motion detection facilities that help improve the operator's attentiveness by sounding an alert if suspicious activity is taking place.[448] The clarity of the pictures is usually excellent, with many systems being able to read a newspaper at a hundred meters. Technology is also being developed to spot patterns in the surveillance data such as recognizing faces, analyzing crowd behavior, and scanning the intimate area between skin surface and clothes using "passive millimeter wave technology" to search for contraband

---

[443] *See generally* Privacy International, CCTV Pages, <http://www.privacyinternational.org/issues/cctv/index.html>; "Watching Them, Watching Us," United Kingdom CCTV Surveillance Regulation Campaign <http://www.spy.org.uk/>; EPIC's Video Surveillance web page <http://www.epic.org/privacy/surveillance>.

[444] In Washington, DC (*see* EPIC, Observing Surveillance Project homepage <http://www.observingsurveillance.org>); Vilnius (the Surveillance Camera Players Lithuania homepage <http://www.cameraplayers.tk/>; New York City (the Surveillance Camera Players homepage <http://www.notbored.org/the-scp.html>); Stockholm (<http://sot.smufsa.nu/index.html>); Amsterdam (<http://www.spotthecam.nl>); Bologna (<http://www.notbored.org/bologna-scp.html>); Munich (<http://www.dergrossebruder.net/main.php?id=30000>); Budapest (<http://hu.bigbrotherawards.org/camera/megfigyeles.htm>).

[445] EPIC, Observing Surveillance <http://www.observingsurveillance.org>.

[446] World Sousveillance Day's homepage <http://wearcam.org/wsd.htm>.

[447] In Kyllo v. United States, 533 U.S. 27 (2001), the US Supreme Court considered the police use of a thermal imager that detected infrared radiation (heat) emanating from a private home onto a public street. The Court worried that advancing technology would leave the homeowner at the mercy of "imaging technology that could discern all human activity in the home." The decision turned in part on use by the government of "a device that is not in general public use, to explore the details of the home that would previously have been unknowable without physical intrusion." The Court overturned a criminal conviction for growing marijuana that involved the warrantless use of a thermal imager.

[448] See John Markoff, "Technology Gives Sight to Machines, Inexpensively," New York Times, June 17, 2002 <http://www.nytimes.com/2002/06/17/technology/17VISI.html>.

---

or weapons.[449] Research into these technologies is receiving significant government funding for crime fighting and anti-terrorism purposes.[450]

Tremendous progress in video surveillance technologies have led to the miniaturization of cameras and enabled wireless connectivity and access through the Internet. These developments, together with the fact that more and more people use them in a private setting and for private purposes, either to protect their property (security cameras), look after their children and nannies ("nanny cams")[451], monitor nursing home residents,[452] conduct virtual child visitation by divorced parents,[453] or send pictures to each other by mobile phone,[454] raise questions about the extent to which people are ready to be observed everywhere they go in public places, or even, in private areas. Private bans on cell phone cameras have been imposed by health clubs, schools, and employers.[455]

Video surveillance is also being increasingly used by private actors for law enforcement type purposes: to monitor their properties, business and commercial areas;[456] to watch for thieves and pickpockets in shopping malls[457] and

---

[449] Ivan Amato, "Beyond X-ray Vision: Can Big Brother see right through your clothes?" Discover Volume 23 No. 7 (July 2002) <http://www.discover.com/july_02/feattechapterhtml>.

[450] *See* United States Defense Department's Human ID at a Distance Project <http://www.darpa.mil/iao/HID.htm>; Kari L. Dean, "Smartcams Take Aim at Terrorists," Wired, June 4, 2003, <http://www.wired.com/news/technology/0,1282,59092,00.html>; Seth Schiesel, "Security Cameras Now Learn to React," New York Times, March 6, 2003, available at <http://www.nytimes.com/2003/03/06/technology/circuits/06secu.html>.

[451] *See* Dennis K. Berman, "Will Cameras-Phones Be Used to Humiliate Ordinary People?," The Wall Street Journal, June 2, 2003. Tapes made by so-called *nanny cams* have been used in criminal prosecutions. In a 1998 New Jersey case, a nanny being prosecuted for mistreatment of a child in her care was convicted using evidence from a nanny cam installed in the home by the parents. New Jersey v. Diaz, 308 N.J. Super. 504 (N.J. Super. Ct. App. Div 1998) <http://lawlibrary.rutgers.edu/decisions/appellate/a6400-96.opn.html>.

[452] *See* 2003 Md. Laws ch. 409 (requiring the Department of Health and Mental Hygiene to develop guidelines for nursing homes that elect to use electronic monitoring with specified consent); Tex. Health & Safety Code §242.501(a)(5) (authorizing a resident of a nursing home "to place in the resident's room an electronic monitoring device that is owned and operated by the resident or provided by the resident's guardian or legal representative.").

[453] Jim Buie, "Visitation Rights Are Becoming High-Tech," Washington Post, June 15, 2004, at C10.

[454] *See* Elisa Batista, "New Privacy Menace: Cell Phones?," Wired News, February 17, 2003 <http://www.wired.com/news/business/0,1367,57692,00.html>; Sarah Marcisz, "Digital Advances Bring Privacy Concerns," The Washington Times, February 10, 2003, available at <http://www.washtimes.com/culture/20030210-99696823.htm>.

[455] Carolyn Said, "Are Camera Phones too Revealing? Locker Room Snooping, School Cheating Prompt Bans, High-Tech Protection Plans," San Francisco Chronicle, May 16, 2004 <http://sfgate.com/cgi-bin/article.cgi?file=/c/a/2004/05/16/SPYPHONE.TMP>.

[456] *See* Dean E. Murphy, "As Security Cameras Sprout, Someone's Always Watching," New York Times, September 29, 2002, available at <http://www.nytimes.com/2002/09/29/technology/29TAPE.html>; Jane Prendergast, "They Log On, Look Out with Web Crime Cams. Citizens on Cyber Patrol," The Cincinnati Enquirer, June 17, 2003, available at <http://www.enquirer.com/editions/2003/06/17/loc_wwwloc1bcyber17.html>; Liza Porteus, "Cincinnati Residents Try High-Tech Crime Stopping," Fox News, July 15, 2003, <http://www.foxnews.com/story/0,2933,91885,00.html>.

casins;[458] to keep an eye on private gated communities and passengers in aircraft;[459] or to detect drug dealing activities at schools.[460] Cameras are also used to monitor some police activities.[461] In countries without rules regulating video surveillance, it is relevant to question whether those private actors' monitoring activities should be limited, or at least be subject to the same constraints as government agents are.

Face Recognition

Face recognition technology[462] uses computerized pattern matching technology to automatically identify peoples' faces. While it is still very much in its infancy, it raises significant public policy questions because it enables the covert identification and classification of people in public. The borough of Newham in the United Kingdom first deployed a face recognition system to scan faces against a database to identify people "of interest." The Reykjavik airport in Iceland was among the first airports to use the technology. In the United States, this same kind of face recognition technology was used at the 2001 Super Bowl in Tampa, Florida to compare the faces of attendees to faces in a database of mug shots. There was widespread public outcry, prompting some to call the event the "Snooper Bowl."[463]

The reliability of face recognition technology remains in dispute. For instance, it was not accurate enough for use in the Salt Lake Winter Olympic games where

---

[457] *See* Bill Clements, "Brother's Corporate Sponsor," CityPages, June 18, 2003, available at <http://www.citypages.com/databank/24/1176/article11318.asp>.

[458] *See* Jeffrey Selingo, "Online, All the Time, An All-Seeing Surveillance System," New York Times, April 24, 2003, available at <http://www.nytimes.com/2003/04/24/technology/circuits/24howw.html?tntemail1=&pagewanted=print&position=>.

[459] *See* Elisa Batista, "Videocams Record Airline Flights," Wired News, <http://www.wired.com/news/business/0,1367,59652,00.html>; Lisa Stark, "Airline to Be First to Install Cameras on Planes," ABC News, March 30, 2002, available at <http://abcnews.go.com/sections/wnt/DailyNews/jetblue_cameras020330.html>.

[460] *See* Katie Hafner, "Where the Hall Monitor Is a Webcam," New York Times, February 27, 2003 <http://www.nytimes.com/2003/02/27/technology/circuits/27scho.html>.

[461] In 2001, Texas passed a law encouraging the use of cameras by law enforcement agencies for traffic and pedestrian stops. 2001 Tex. Crim. Proc. Code §§ 2.131-2.138. The tapes are useful in measuring the extent of racial profiling in traffic stops.

[462] *See generally* General Accounting Office, Technology assessment: Using Biometrics for Border Security, November 2002) (GAO-03-174) available at <www.gao.gov>.

[463] For more information, *see* EPIC's Face Recognition web page <http://www.epic.org/privacy/facerecognition/>. For more on Tampa's experience with face recognition technology, *see* Jay Stanley & Barry Steinhardt, "Drawing a Blank: The Failure of Facial Recognition Technology in Tampa, Florida (2002)" (American Civil Liberties Union) <http://archive.aclu.org/issues/privacy/drawing_blank.pdf>.

---

the security chief said, "it's just not proven technology yet."[464] Studies sponsored by the United States Defense Department showed the system is right only 54 percent of the time and can be significantly compromised by changes in lighting, weight, hair, sunglasses, subject cooperation, and other factors.[465] Tests on the face recognition systems in operation at Palm Beach Airport in Florida,[466] and Boston Logan Airport also showed the technology to be ineffective and error-ridden.[467]

As the power and capabilities of surveillance technology increases while the cost and size of systems decreases, there will be further incentives to use the technology. For example, the US Government plans to require other countries to use biometric passports using face recognition technology in the near future, although immediate implementation of the requirement is likely to be postponed until 2006 because of "challenging technical reasons."[468] These and other developments may create new pressures for appropriate regulations to safeguard privacy and to prevent the misuse of the technology.[469]

Satellite Surveillance

Developments in satellite surveillance (also called "remote sensing") during the last decade have embraced features similar to those of more conventional visual surveillance. Satellite resolution has constantly improved since the end of the Cold War, largely due to efforts by companies such as EarthWatch, Motorola and Boeing. These companies have invested billions of dollars to create satellites capable of mapping even the most minute detail on the face of the earth.

---

[464] "Games Notebook," The Ottawa Citizen, February 10, 2002.

[465] Declan McCullagh & Robert Zarate, "Scanning Tech a Blurry Picture", Wired News, February 16, 2002, available at <http://www.wired.com/news/print/0,1294,50470,00.html>. *See also* Barnaby J. Feder, "Face-Recognition Systems Looking Better," TechNewsWorld, June 3, 2004 <http://www.technewsworld.com/story/34206.html> (reporting that the technology's performance is improving but requires nearly perfect lighting and cooperative subjects).

[466] American Civil Liberties Union Press Release, "Data on Face-Recognition Test at Palm Beach Airport further Demonstrates Systems' Fatal Flaws," May 14, 2002, available at <http://www.aclu.org/news/2002/n051402b.html>.

[467] Hiawatha Bray, "'Face Testing' at Logan Is Found Lacking," Boston Globe, July 17, 2002, available at <http://www.boston.com/dailyglobe2/198/metro/_Face_testing_at_Logan_is_found_lacking+.shtml>.

[468] US Senate Committee on the Judiciary, Hearing on Biometric Passports, Testimony of Asa Hutchinson, Undersecretary for Border and Transportation Security Directorate, Department of Homeland Security, June 15, 2004 <http://judiciary.senate.gov/testimony.cfm?id=1226&wit_id=2961>.

[469] *See* Testimony of EPIC Executive Director Marc Rotenberg before DC City Council, June 2002 <http://www.epic.org/privacy/surveillance/testimony_061302.html>.

The use of commercial satellite imagery by governments has increased substantially in recent years. Images obtained through commercial satellites were key in aiding US military forces carrying out Operation Iraqi Freedom.[470] The US Commercial Remote Sensing Space Policy, signed in 2003, ordered all federal government agencies to utilize commercial satellite imagery and encouraged development of a strong US remote sensing industry.[471] Space Imaging and DigitalGlobe are the two major players in the commercial satellite industry, collecting thousands of square kilometers of imagery each day. Both companies are the recipients of substantial contracts with the US government for images from their satellites.

Space Imaging was the first to launch one of the new generation high-resolution satellites, the IKONOS, in September 1999.[472] Its parabolic lens can recognize objects as small as one meter (3.28 feet) anywhere on earth and, according to the company, viewers can see individual trees, automobiles, road networks, and houses. Collecting data at a rate of over 2,000 square kilometers (772 square miles) per minute, the volume of imagery provided by this satellite is staggering. Considered the grandfather of commercial satellites, IKONOS is used by a number of industries in addition to government.[473] Public interest groups are also using the information to show images of nuclear testing by countries and even images of secret United States bases such as Area 51 in Nevada.[474]

The most powerful commercial imaging satellite to date was launched by DigitalGlobe in 2001. The satellite, QuickBird, provides images as small as two feet (0.61 meters). DigitalGlobe is currently working on improving resolution and collection capacity with their new system, called the WorldView Imaging system. The company anticipates that the satellite will be capable of achieving a half-meter resolution.[475]

While governments are increasingly relying on commercial satellite technology, private companies are raising public awareness by providing access to images

---

[470] Patrick Clarke, "Commercial Satellite Imagery Matures as an Asset," Military Geospatial Technology, April 23, 2004, Vol. 1, Issue 1 <http://www.military-geospatial-technology.com/article.cfm?DocID=461>.

[471] See "Fact Sheet: US Commercial Remote Sensing Space Policy," May 13, 2003 <http://www.whitehouse.gov/news/releases/2003/05/20030513-8.html>.

[472] See <http://www.spaceimaging.com/>.

[473] Id.

[474] See, e.g, Federation of American Scientists, Dimona Photographic Interpretation Report <http://www.fas.org/nuke/guide/israel/nuke/>.

[475] See Patrick Clarke, "Commercial Satellite Imagery Matures as an Asset," Military Geospatial Technology, April 23, 2004, Vol. 1, Issue 1, available at <http://www.military-geospatial-technology.com/article.cfm?DocID=461>.

through the Internet. Upon acquisition of the satellite image firm, Keyhole, in October 2004, Google Inc. combined satellite imagery, maps and its popular search engine to create Google Earth.[476] Google Earth is a free download that allows users to view a map in satellite form by simply entering an address or executing a search. The service is still in the early stages, and the level of resolution varies from distant aerial photographs to street level, depending on the area. For an additional fee, the company offers two upgraded versions of Google Earth, incorporating Global Positioning System (GPS) technology and data import capability for more advanced application. The satellite option was initially offered through Google's Internet mapping service, Google Maps, but in a more limited form. Other companies, such as Microsoft, also offer satellite imagery through various Web sites.[477]

Satellite images have long been offered for sale to consumers by companies such as Terraserver and ImageAtlas but the widespread use of the Google search engine and the ability to link searches to the mapping service raised awareness, pushing discussions of privacy to the forefront.[478] Currently, the photographs are six to 18 months old, but critics have voiced concern over the possibility that Google may begin offering real-time images and the potential invasions of privacy that could result. Privacy advocates have suggested that Google offer an opt-out policy for this service, allowing individuals to enter their address and blank out their home from the public image database.[479]

Integration of existing satellite images with ground-based Geographic Information System (GIS) databases have produced interactive maps available for widespread use. GIS technology allows users to link detailed data on human activity to mapping software. Information ranging from census data to crime statistics may be incorporated into these maps.[480] Because there is no limit to the types of information that can be linked to satellite imagery, the implications of this technology are far-reaching. Were personal information integrated into such a map, simply double-clicking on a satellite image of an urban area could reveal

---

[476] *See* <http://earth.google.com>.

[477] *See generally* <http://terraserver.microsoft.com/> and <http://www.globexplorer.com/>.

[478] For example, by entering a publicly listed telephone number into Google's search engine, a user is able to acquire the customer's name and address, then directly link to a map showing an aerial image of the residence. Although this information is public record, the ease by which a visual of a person's home can be obtained alarms critics.

[479] Leslie Walker, "Google Service Homes in on the Street where You Live," The Washington Post, April 10, 2005, at F7.

[480] *See generally* <http://www.gis.com>. For example, a Web site provides access to a database of crimes in the area of the city of Chicago in the United States, allowing users to search by type of crime or geographic area to obtain a record of offenses during a given period. *See* <http://www.chicagocrime.org>.

precise details about the occupants of a particular house. The "Open Skies"[481] policy accepted worldwide means that there are few restrictions of the use of the technology.[482]

Despite these advances, private companies have a distance to go before they catch up with governments. Experts estimate that the current generation of secret spy satellites, such as the Ikon/Keyhole-12, can recognize objects as small as ten centimeters (approximately four inches) across and some analysts say that it can image a license plate.[483] The airplane manufacturer Boeing is currently fulfilling a 10-year contract with the United States government for a Future Imagery Architecture (FIA) to replace the KH satellites and the ground infrastructure.[484] The FIA is based on a constellation of new satellites that are smaller, less expensive, and placed in orbit to allow for real-time surveillance of battlefields and other targets.

Government use of satellites is extensive, ranging from homeland security operations to agricultural analysis. For example, the United Nations (UN) Office on Drugs and Crime uses IKONOS imagery to assess the illegal drug trade in Afghanistan, Laos, Myanmar, and Bolivia.[485] By analyzing satellite images, the UN is able to assess the level of production of illicit crops such as heroin and cocaine, and estimate the portion of the drug trade attributable to these nations.

Following the September 11, 2001 terrorist attacks on the United States, the US National Geospatial Intelligence Agency (NGA) began focusing its observation internally rather than abroad. Prior to the attacks, domestic US satellite surveillance most often involved natural disaster relief. Although laws limit the use of intelligence resources to issues of national security, the NGA admits to the existence of gray areas in which aiding the FBI in criminal investigations is common practice.[486]

---

[481] The Open Skies Treaty allows one signatory country to fly over another for the purpose of collecting imagery. 31 countries currently participate in the treaty. *See generally* <http://www.nawcwpns.navy.mil/~treaty/OS.html>.

[482] *See* Federation of American Scientists, Open Skies Treaty Guide, available at <http://www.fas.org/nuke/control/os/>.

[483] "Spy Satellites: the Next Leap Forward," International Defense Review, January 1, 1997.

[484] "Boeing to Build New United States Satellites," Jane's Defense Weekly, September 15, 1999.

[485] *See* "The Satellite Wars" <http://www.spacetoday.org/Satellites/YugoWarSats.html>.

[486] Associated Press, "Spy Imagery Agency Watching Inside US," September 26, 2004, available at <http://www.usatoday.com/tech/news/surveillance/2004-09-26-civilian-spying_x.htm>.

Satellite utilization is not limited to visual surveillance, but also involves location tracking. The Global Positioning System (GPS)[487] is a satellite navigation system comprised of 24 satellites transmitting signals that enable mobile ground receivers to pinpoint their exact location. The system was created by the US Department of Defense[488] and is used primarily for military purposes. Initially, the US government relied on a "selective availability" feature that degraded the signal for civilian devices, allowing minimal accuracy. However, in 2000, the US Air Force discontinued use of this software, upgrading the accuracy of civilian devices from 100 meters to roughly 10 meters.[489]

Development of the European satellite system, Galileo,[490] will likely enhance surveillance technology. The system will consist of 30 satellites to be launched in 2006 and 2007 and is expected to be operational as early as 2008.[491] Galileo will be fully interoperable with GPS and, when used in conjunction, will offer much greater reliability and an expected accuracy of close to one meter.

Use of GPS is becoming increasingly common, as the technology finds its way into consumer wireless devices such as cellular phones, personal data assistants, and car navigation systems.[492] Although GPS provides convenient navigational assistance, the ability for others to track users raises serious concerns.[493] A number of relatively inexpensive devices, advertising the ability to covertly monitor the movements of individuals, are currently on the market.

Employer use of GPS to monitor their workforce is also on the rise.[494] The number of trackers installed on fleet vehicles in the US is expected to exceed 1.3

---

[487] The term "GPS" refers specifically to the satellite navigation system run by the United States.

[488] Although controlled by the US military, GPS is an open system that offers freely accessible signals throughout the world. However, the DOD maintains the capability to "jam" units in certain areas or limit functionality to military units if necessary.

[489] See "USAF Upgrades Accuracy of GPS Signal for Civilian Use," Space and Tech Digest, May 8, 2000 <http://www.spaceandtech.com/digest/sd2000-09/sd2000-09-005.shtml>.

[490] Galileo is largely an attempt to decrease dependence on the US system. The system is civilian-controlled and therefore, unlike GPS, may not be shut down for military purposes.

[491] See generally "Q&A: What Is Galileo?," BBC News, March 23, 2002 <http://news.bbc.co.uk/1/hi/sci/tech/1883358.stm>; European Commission (Directorate-General Energy and Transport), "Galileo: European Satellite Navigation System" <http://europa.eu.int/comm/dgs/energy_transport/galileo/programme/phases_en.htm> (last updated September 30, 2004).

[492] See generally Wikipedia, "Global Positioning System" <http://en.wikipedia.org/wiki/Global_Positioning_System> (last modified July 18, 2005).

[493] See Richard C. Balough, "Global Positioning System and The Internet: A Combination with Privacy Risks," CBA Record (Chicago Bar Association), October 2001 <http://www.isoc.org/internet/issues/privacy/balough.shtml>.

[494] See Diane Cadrain, "GPS on Rise; Workers' Complaints May Follow," HR Magazine, April 2005 <http://www.findarticles.com/p/articles/mi_m3495/is_4_50/ai_n13629523>.

million by 2005.[495] Some companies require employees to carry GPS-enabled cell phones to allow for tracking on the job.[496] Employers cite legitimate purposes for such monitoring but the lack of clear standards governing this practice leaves the potential for abuse wide open.

Electronic Commerce

Surveillance by law enforcement is not the only online privacy risk. The growth of the Internet and electronic commerce has dramatically increased the amount of personal information that is collected about individuals by corporations. As consumers engage in routine online transactions, they leave behind a trail of personal details, often without any idea that they are doing so. Much of this information is routinely captured in computer logs.

Most on-line companies keep track of users' purchases. This information ranges from the trivial to the most sensitive and, unless adequately protected, can be used for purposes that seriously harm the interests of the consumer. Other companies gather personal information from visitors by offering personalized services such as news searches, free e-mail and stock portfolios. They then sell, trade, or share that information among third party companies without the consumer's expressed knowledge or consent. The perceived value of this kind of information is behind the stock-market valuations of many dotcom companies.

Spam

Many on-line companies, for example, provide lists of their customers' e-mail addresses to companies that specialize in sending unsolicited commercial e-mail (spam). Other companies mine e-mail address from sources such as messages posted on mailing lists, newsgroups, or domain name registration data. In one test by the US Federal Trade Commission, an e-mail address posted in a chat room began receiving spam within eight minutes of submitting a post.[497] Mining or harvesting e-mail addresses produces a barrage of online advertisements. Studies show that consumers resent spam both for the time it takes to process and for the loss of privacy resulting from their e-mail address circulating freely on countless

---

[495] Charles Forelle, "GPS Units Keep Tabs on Employee Loafing," CareerJournal.com, June 3, 2004 <http://www.careerjournal.com/hrcenter/articles/20040603-forelle.html>.

[496] *Id.*

[497] *See* the Federal Trade Commission Spam Workshop <http://www.ftc.gov/bcp/workshops/spam/index.html>.

directories.[498] Furthermore, spam can result in significant economic loss to the consumer. A 2001 report by the European Commission found that "Internet subscribers worldwide are paying an estimated EUR10 billion (~USD 9 billion) a year in connection costs to receive junk e-mails."[499] The European Union's Privacy and Electronic Communications Directive prohibits unsolicited commercial marketing by e-mail without "opt-in" consent.[500] In Japan two new anti-spam laws were passed in 2002. The laws allow users of the Internet and text-enabled mobile phones to opt-out of spammers' contact lists, and require that all unsolicited commercial e-mail be clearly identified.[501] In concert with a February 2004 conference in Brussels, the OECD's Directorate for Science, Technology and Industry released a background paper on spam.[502] The report summarizes challenges to effective enforcement of regulation, which includes, very low compliance with labeling regulations, the possibility that do-not-e-mail registries may only punish "reputable marketers" who comply with them, and some consumers' mistrust of opt-out frameworks. The report surveyed industry responses to spam, cross-border issues, and enforcement, and ultimately concluded that a multi-dimensional approach and international co-operation was necessary. The International Telecommunications Union has begun a new project on Countering Spam.

According to the ITU, "Unsolicited commercial communications or spam, as it is more usually known, has grown into one of the major plagues affecting today's digital world . . . . A multi-pronged approach, including technical solutions, consumer education, industry partnership, appropriate laws and enforcement mechanisms and international cooperation is therefore needed."[503] At the ITU WSIS Thematic meeting on Countering Spam, held in Geneva in July 2004, a wide range of topics were addressed.[504]

---

[498] For more information on spam generally and how to reduce it see <http://www.junkbusters.com> and <http://www.cauce.org/>.

[499] European Commission, Unsolicited Commercial Communications and Data Protection, January 2001 available at <http://europa.eu.int/comm/internal_market/en/dataprot/studies/spam.htm>.

[500] <http://register.consilium.eu.int/pdf/en/02/st03/03636en2.pdf>.

[502] Organization for Economic Co-operation and Development's Directorate for Science, Technology and Industry, "Background Paper for the OECD Workshop on Spam," January 22, 2004. (Originally presented to the Working Parties on Telecommunications and Information Services Policy and on Information Security and Privacy, and the Committee on Consumer Policy, during their meetings in 2003. Declassified in January 2004.)

[503] http://www.itu.int/osg/spu/spam/

[504] http://www.itu.int/osg/spu/spam/meeting7-9-04/index.html

Profiling

Many companies, including Internet Service Providers (ISPs), search engine firms, and web-based businesses, monitor users as they travel across the Internet, collecting information on what sites they visit, the time and length of these visits, search terms they enter, purchases they make, or even "click-through" responses to banner ads. In the off-line world this would be comparable to, for example, having someone follow you through a shopping mall, scanning each page of every magazine you browse though, every pair of shoes that you looked at and every menu entry you read at the restaurant. When collected and combined with other data such as demographic or "psychographic" data, these diffuse pieces of information create highly detailed profiles of individuals. These profiles have become a major currency in electronic commerce where they are used by advertisers and marketers to predict a user's preferences, interests, needs and possible future purchases. Most of these profiles are currently stored in anonymous form. However, there is a distinct likelihood that they will soon be linked with information, such as names and addresses, gathered from other sources, making them personally identifiable.

The most pervasive tracking technology is the cookie. The cookie is a small file containing an ID number that is placed on a user's hard drive by a website. Cookies were developed to improve websites' ability to track users over a session. The cookie can also notify the site that the user has returned and can allow the site to track the user's activities across many different visits. The use of cookies expanded greatly when it was realized that a single cookie could be used across many different sites. This led to the development of advertising network companies that can track users across thousands of sites. The largest ad service, DoubleClick, has agreements with thousands of web sites and maintains cookies on over 100 million unique users; each linking to hundreds of pieces of information about the user's browsing habits. It is possible to configure the dominant Internet browsers to reject or send a warning notice before cookies are set. This does not provide much protection, however, as websites will often condition access on acceptance of cookies or send floods of requests to set new cookies, thereby frustrating the browsing experience.

A more secretive manner of monitoring online users takes place through the use of web bugs. Web bugs are invisible graphics that are placed on Web sites or in e-mails in order to track visitors to that Web site or the recipients of e-mails (often spam). A Web bug on a Web site collects information such as the IP address of the visiting computer, the browser being used, the time of the "hit," and also a previously set cookie value. In an e-mail a Web bug is used to discover if and when the e-mail message was read, how many times it was forwarded, and the IP address of the recipient. A marketing e-mail directing users to Web sites can also be used to link the e-mail addresses of those that later visit the site to their cookie data. Web bugs can also be used in newsgroup messages to track readers.[505]

In April 2004, Google announced a new, free webmail service called "Gmail." Under Google's system, Gmail subscribers would receive an entire gigabyte of storage space on the condition that the company could extract content from incoming and outgoing messages for ad targeting.[506] Gmail's in-depth analysis of subscriber and non-subscriber e-mail raises serious privacy issues ranging from new commercial intrusions into communications to the possibility that the content capture system could be employed for law enforcement purposes similar to the FBI's Carnivore system. There are also risks that ad tracking could create data files related to the content of e-mail communication that would not enjoy strong legal protection against law enforcement subpoenas. A coalition of privacy and civil liberties groups urged Google to suspend the Gmail system,[507] and a subset of the coalition requested that the Attorney General of California investigate the company for violations of the state's strict wiretapping laws.[508] Privacy International filed a complaint on Gmail with over a dozen countries, the European Commission, and the Article 29 Data Protection Working Group.[509] Legislation to address Gmail has been introduced in California, and the system's introduction sparked the Massachusetts legislature to strengthen the State's privacy act.

Individuals are also tracked online through "spyware," invasive software that transmits browsing habits or personal information to others. Some spyware is motivated by commercial profiling, and is primarily designed for ad targeting. Other spyware is specifically advertised as a method for spying on individuals. Spyware is generally difficult to define, and in comments to US regulators, EPIC has argued that even "legitimate" software can possess "indicia of invasiveness" that typically appear in unsavory spyware programs.[510] Spyware is sometimes bundled with other programs, so that users download and install it without fully

---

[505] Computerbytesman, "Web Bug Search Page," available at
<http://www.computerbytesman.com/privacy/wbfind,htm>.

[506] <http://gmail.google.com/gmail/help/about.html>.

[507] <http://privacyrights.org/ar/GmailLetter.htm>.

[508] <http://www.epic.org/privacy/gmail/agltr5.3.04.html>.

[509] <http://www.privacyinternational.org/issues/internet/gmail-complaint.pdf>.

[510] <http://www.ftc.gov/os/comments/spyware/040419epic.pdf>.

understanding the tracking capabilities. Spyware can also be installed by "drive by downloads," situations where individuals are tricked into accepting a program for installation, and through vulnerabilities in Internet browsers.

The European Commission's Working Party on the Protection of Individuals with Regard to the Processing of Personal Data, in its January 1999 report entitled "Recommendation 1/99 on Invisible and Automatic Processing of Personal Data on the Internet Performed by Software and Hardware," addressed the issue of governmental response to spyware.[511] Recommendations of the Working Party include giving the data subject notice of the data processing and collection, a user right of access to the data, prevention of the creation of client persistent information, and technical protections against spyware. In April 2004, the US Federal Trade Commission held a forum on spyware.[512]

In the offline world, profiling has been thriving for decades.[513] Profiling companies build personally identifiable databases based on a plethora of sources including supermarket purchases, product warranty cards, public records, census records, magazine and catalog subscriptions, and surveys. This is done in the absence of legislation that would prevent dossier building. Companies also "enhance" dossiers that they already own by combining or "overlaying" information from other databases. For instance, a business may request a name and phone number directly from the customer, and then use this information to purchase other personal details. These dossiers may link individual's identities to any number of facts deemed private by advanced societies including medical conditions, physical characteristics, and lifestyle preferences.

The line between online and offline profiling has become more and more blurred. In 1999, DoubleClick announced that it was buying Abacus, owner of the largest direct marketing lists in the country, with information on the purchasing habits of 90 percent of all United States households, and that DoubleClick was going to merge information from the purchasing databases with information from online browsing. Following a public outcry, the company suspended its plan to merge personal data with profiles. However, in July 2000 the Federal Trade Commission reached an agreement with the Network Advertisers Initiative, a group consisting of the largest online advertisers including DoubleClick, which

---

[511] <http://europa.eu.int/comm/internal_market/privacy/workinggroup/wp1999/wpdocs99_en.htm>.

[512] <http://www.ftc.gov/bcp/workshops/spyware/index.htm>.

[513] *See* EPIC's Profiling page <http://www.epic.org/privacy/profiling/>.

will allow for online profiling and any future merger of such databases to occur with only "opt-out" consent.[514]

Another important player in this move towards complete identification of Internet users is the Microsoft Corporation. In 2001 Microsoft began aggressively promoting the Passport and Hailstorm services in preparation for the launch of Microsoft XP, the newest version of the Windows operating system. Passport is an online identification and authentication system, which employs a single sign-on system to facilitate e-commerce and browsing among different web sites that require a user to identify oneself. Once a user signs on to Passport, other affiliated sites visited by the user receive information about the user. Passport stores user information in a central database. The Passport service is intended to give Microsoft and Passport affiliates the ability to send unsolicited commercial e-mail to Internet users and to profile their activities. To register for Passport, a user must submit an e-mail address. Users can also submit their real name, city/locale, gender, age, occupation, marital status, personal statement, hobbies and interest, favorite quote, favorite things, a personal photo, and a home page. Hailstorm was a group of services[515] that Microsoft intended to provide from central servers. In theory it would have collected an extraordinary range of consumer information. Privacy and consumer groups in the United States filed a series of complaints against Passport and Hailstorm with the Federal Trade Commission in 2001, detailing the risks to privacy and security in these systems. In July 2002, European Union (European Union) officials confirmed publicly that they were pursuing an investigation into Passport for breach of European privacy laws.[516] In January 2003, the EU Working Party on Data Protection – Article 29 issued an opinion requiring substantial changes to Microsoft Passport.[517] Among other things, the opinion requires Microsoft to allow users to restrict the use and sharing of information for commercial and marketing purposes.

---

[514] Electronic Privacy Information Center (EPIC) and Junkbusters. "Network Advertising Initiative: Principles not Privacy," July 28, 2000, available at <http://www.epic.org/privacy/internet/NAI_analysis.html>.

[515] Including MyAddress, MyProfile, MyContacts, MyNotifications, MyInbox, MyCalendar, MyDocuments, MyApplicationSettings, MyWallet, MyUsage, and MyLocation.

[516] European Union Article 29 Data Protection Working Group, "First orientations of the Article 29 Working Party Concerning Online Authentication Services," July 2, 2002, available at <http://www.epic.org/redirect/eu_redirect.html>.

[517] European Union Working Group Document - Article 29, "On-line Authentication Services," (WP 68) January 29, 2003, available at <http://europa.eu.int/comm/internal_market/privacy/docs/wpdocs/2003/wp68_en.pdf>.

A competitor to Microsoft's Passport, Project Liberty, is being developed by a coalition of companies.[518] This identification system is similar to Microsoft's single sign-on. However, it allows users to choose what companies will be able to authenticate the user.[519]

Attempts at developing more permanent methods of identifying users have been underway for years. In 1999, Intel announced that it was including a serial number in each new Pentium III chip that could be accessed by websites and internal corporate networks. Most of the manufacturers suppressed the number after a consumer boycott was announced, and Intel announced in 2000 that it is dropping the serial number in future chips. Microsoft and RealAudio were discovered using the internal networking number found in most computers as another identifier for online users. Microsoft's Windows Media Player contains a globally-unique identifier (GUID) that can be tracked by website operators. Finally, the Media Access Control (MAC) address embedded in many network cards are unique and can be used to identify many computers.

Security Breaches

The privacy of online consumers can also be seriously compromised by security breaches. Many web sites are poorly secured against both physical and electronic attacks.[520] In December 2002, thieves stole hard drives containing the unencrypted personal information of over 500,000 United States servicemen from the Triwest Corporation.[521] In March 2000, following a security breach, De Beers lost 35,000 names, addresses, phone numbers and e-mail addresses of people inquiring about buying diamonds. In April 2000, it was revealed that an unknown Microsoft engineer had included a backdoor into its web server software. If someone typed, "Netscape engineers are weenies!" backwards, they would have access to the websites and associated data. In August 2000, Kaiser Permanente, a top United States health insurer, admitted that it had compromised the confidentiality and privacy of its members when it sent over 800 e-mail messages, many containing sensitive information, to the wrong members.[522] Similarly in July 2001, Eli Lilly, the makers of the anti-depressant drug Prozac, revealed the names and e-mail addresses of over 700 patients that subscribed to

---

[518] *See* Project Liberty Homepage <http://www.projectliberty.org/>.

[519] *See* EPIC's Project Liberty web page <http://www.epic.org/privacy/authentication/projectliberty.html>.

[520] *See, e.g.,* Eric Murray, "SSL Server Security Survey," July 31, 2000 showing that encryption on most e-commerce sites is inadequate, available at <http://www.meer.net/~ericm/papers/ssl_servers.html>.

[521] "Lawsuit accuses TriWest Healthcare of negligence," Arizona Republic, January 30, 2002.

[522] "Sensitive Kaiser E-Mails Go Astray," Washington Post, August 10, 2000.

the company's e-mail service for information on the drug and other issues.[523] In 2003, a security breach notice law took affect in California that requires entities to notify individuals when their personal information may have been accessed with authorization.[524] Since implementation of that law, every month brings a new series of notices of major security breaches.

Seal Programs

A common practice among online companies is to sign on to a "seal" program in order to provide consumers with a sense of security that their personal information is being protected. These programs follow the traditional seal programs in laying down certain eligibility standards which participant companies must respect in order to get a compliance seal. The better seal programs conduct monitoring and compliance checks, provide educational information, offer consumer dispute resolution, and enforce sanctions against errant companies. There are many disadvantages of seal programs operating within a self-regulatory system. All too often, seal program operators have been shown to be ineffective and reluctant to take enforcement measures against their members including companies such as Microsoft.[525] A 1999 Forrester research report found that, "because independent privacy groups like TRUSTe and BBBOnline earn their money from e-commerce organizations, they become more of a privacy advocate for the industry – rather than for consumers."[526]

Privacy Enhancing Technologies

There are tools available that can be used to protect the privacy of users in many cases. These technologies are known as "Privacy Enhancing Technologies" (PET) and are aimed at eliminating or minimizing the collection of personally identifiable information. Encryption is an important tool for protection against certain forms of communications surveillance. When properly implemented, a message is scrambled (*i.e.*, encrypted) so that only the intended recipient will be able to unscramble (*i.e.*, decrypt), and subsequently read, the contents. Pretty Good Privacy (PGP) is the best-known encryption program and has hundreds of thousands of users. An alternative is the open source program called GNU

---

[523] "Prozac Maker Reveals Patient E-Mail Addresses," Washington Post, July 4, 2001, at E01.

[524] Senate Bill 1386, available at <http://leginfo.ca.gov/pub/01-02/bill/sen/sb_1351-1400/sb_1386_bill_20020926_chaptered.html>.

[525] "Just How Trusty is Truste," Wired, April 9, 2002 <http://www.wired.com/news/exec/0,1370,51624,00.html>.

[526] Forrester Research Inc, "Privacy Wake-Up Call," September 1, 1999.

Privacy Guard (GPG) that allows anyone to view the full source of the system to ensure that it does not allow for secret surveillance.[527] Cryptographic modules are also implemented in applications; for example web browsers, in order to maintain some confidentiality in electronic commerce transactions, include Secure Sockets Layer (SSL) to encrypt sessions between users and servers.

It is important to note that encryption of content alone does not prevent the disclosure of traffic data; that is, it is still clear that person A is e-mailing person B, or that person A is visiting web site W. Other applications are available to maintain the privacy of these transactions. "Anonymous remailers" strip identifying information from e-mails and can deter traffic analysis.[528] Services such as Anonymizer provide anonymous websurfing, anonymous e-mail messaging, banner ad and pop-up blocking, and automated deletion of cookies and web bugs after Internet sessions.[529]

There have been significant setbacks in the effort to develop commercially viable privacy enhancing techniques. In October 2001, Zero Knowledge Systems ceased to operate the Freedom Network, which used to provide a fully encrypted and pseudonymous link between the user and secure servers, and replaced it with a simpler proxy-based service. In February 2002, several flaws were discovered in SafeWeb, an anonymous-surfing technology originally funded by the Central Intelligence Agency.[530] In March 2002, Network Associates, the company that provided the commercial version of PGP, discontinued support for the application.[531] The international (free) version continues to be available from PGP International.[532]

At the same time, human rights groups and even large corporations explored new techniques to protect online privacy. The Canadian-based Privaterra worked with NGOs to encourage the use of strong encryption techniques and other methods for online privacy.[533] Hacktivism efforts continued with new efforts to empower dissident political organizations operating over the Internet. In July 2002, the

---

[527] *See* <http://www.gnupg.org/>.

[528] *See generally* André Bacard, "Anonymous Remailer FAQ" <http://www.andrebacard.com/remail.html>.

[529] *See* <http://www.anonymizer.com>.

[530] Declan McCullagh, "SafeWeb's Holes Contradict Claims," Wired News, February 12, 2002, available at <http://www.wired.com/news/politics/0,1283,50371,00.html>.

[531] Sam Costello, "Network Associates Abandons Search for PGP Buyer, Axes 18," IDG News Service, March 6, 2002 <http://www.nwfusion.com/news/2002/0306naipgp.html>.

[532] Homepage <http:/www.pgpi.com/>.

[533] Homepage <http://www.privaterra.com>.

international hacker group, Hacktivismo,[534] announced a new free service called "Camera Shy" to allow users to conceal messages in ordinary image files on the Internet. The browser-based steganography[535] application automatically scans and decrypts content straight from the Internet and leaves no traces on the user's system.[536] The same group released a developer version of a free secure and anonymous web tool called "Six/Four" in February 2003. The CryptoRights Foundation is on the cusp of releasing a suite of programs to help human rights and other advocates communicate securely.[537]

It is important to distinguish between genuine privacy enhancing techniques and data security technologies that seek to render processing safe but not to reduce the disclosure and processing of identifiable data.[538] Moreover, there are many products offered by industry that are not privacy protective. Many of these systems, such as Microsoft's Passport and the World Wide Web Consortium's Platform for Privacy Preferences (P3P), are designed to facilitate data sharing rather than to limit disclosure of personal information.[539]

Electronic Numbering

Electronic Numbering (ENUM) is an Internet infrastructure that will allow a single number to reference contact or other information in a public database.[540] Individuals or businesses holding an ENUM account will be able to store information, including phone numbers, e-mail addresses, voicemail numbers, fax numbers, or any other type of data in the ENUM database. Persons wishing to contact the entity would use the ENUM to query a public database for the stored information.

ENUM raises a host of privacy issues that are yet to be resolved. Most importantly, because of the different ways in which ENUM can provide means to

---

[534] Homepage <http://www.hacktivismo.com>.

[535] The word steganography literally means "covered writing" as derived from Greek. It includes a vast array of methods of secret communications that conceal the very existence of the message such as invisible inks, microdots, character arrangement, and digital signatures.

[536] Eric Auchard, "Hacker Group Targets Countries that Censor Internet," Reuters, July 14, 2002.

[537] Homepage <http://www.cryptorights.org/>.

[538] Herbert Burkert, "Privacy-Enhancing Technologies: Typology, Critique, Vision" in Philip Agre and Marc Rotenberg, eds, Technology and Privacy: The New Landscape 125 (MIT Press 1997).

[539] *See* EPIC and Junkbusters, "Pretty Poor Privacy: An Assessment of P3P and Internet Privacy," June 2000 <http://www.epic.org/reports/prettypoorprivacy.html>; EPIC, "Why is P3P Not a PET?" November 2002 <http://www.epic.org/reports/p3pnotpet.pdf>.

[540] For current information on the development of ENUM, *see, e.g.*, <http://www.enum-forum.org/> and EPIC's ENUM page <http://www.epic.org/privacy/enum/>.

contact a person, ENUM has the potential to become a Globally Unique Identifier (GUID). At a more fundamental level, issues of notice and individual participation have yet to be resolved. Since the ENUM database is public, one can assume that it will be mined for commercial and government surveillance purposes. This may lead to an unprecedented amount of spam, as a single ENUM can reveal multiple methods of contacting a person.

Radio-Frequency Identification (RFID)

Radio Frequency Identification (RFID) is a type of automatic identification system that enables data to be wirelessly transmitted by portable tags to readers that process the data according to the needs of a particular application. Tags in use today are small enough to be invisibly embedded in products, product packaging, and even printing inks. They can be read from a distance and through a variety of substances such as snow, fog, ice, or paint, where barcodes have proved useless.[541] The data transmitted by the tag may provide identification or location information, or specifics about the product tagged, such as price, color, or date of purchase. RFID readers are often connected to computer networks, facilitating the transfer of data from the physical object to databases and software applications thousands of miles away and allowing objects to be continually located and tracked through space. RFID may also be used to identify documents and currency. RFID may even be deployed to identify individuals.[542] Today, major uses of RFID include supply chain management, animal tracking, and electronic roadway toll collection.

While barcodes have historically been the primary means of tracking products, RFID systems are rapidly becoming the preferred technology for monitoring pets, products, vehicles and even people.[543] RFID systems enable tagged objects to speak to electronic readers over the course of a product's lifetime – from production to disposal – which could provide retailers with an unblinking, voyeuristic view of consumer attitudes and purchase behavior.[544] RFID systems of all kinds are capable of generating a volume of consumer data several orders

---

541 *See* "What is Radio Frequency Identification (RFID)?," AIM Global, Association for Automatic Identification and Mobility <http://www.aimglobal.org/technologies/rfid/what_is_rfid.asp>; Savi Technology and EPCglobal, "Learn About RFID" <http://www.savi.com/rfid.shtml>; and John Stermer, "Radio Frequency ID: A New Era for Marketers?," Consumer Insight magazine, Winter 2001 <http://www.acnielsen.com/pubs/ci/2001/q4/features/radio.htm>.

542 Ellen Mesner, "RFID Is Really Getting under People's Skin," NetWorld Magazine, April 4, 2005 <http://www.networkworld.com/news/2005/040405widernetchip.html>.

543 Even the most basic form of RFID tag, the passive, "class 0" tag with no independent source and no rewriting capability, enables the real-time tracking of objects, and, by association, the individuals that carry them.
544 *Id.*

of magnitude greater than has been possible before. With in-store deployment, it is predicted that Wal-Mart will generate more than seven terabytes of RFID data a day.[545] All of this data will reap a bonanza of high-resolution consumer information to be aggregated for further data mining or sold to third parties.[546] Industry experts estimate that the market for RFID technology will top USD 6 billion by 2010.[547]

The debate over RFID technology touches upon many controversial policy issues.[548] At its most fundamental, widespread use of RFID tags could enable corporations to track every move consumers make. Corporations that compile the data transmitted by the tags could determine which products a consumer purchases, how often products are used, and even where the product – and, by extension, the consumer – travels. By aggregating data to form consumer profiles, corporations could make assumptions about a consumer's income, health, lifestyle, travel and buying habits. This information could be sold to governments to create dossiers of individual citizens or simply sold to other corporations for marketing purposes. The potential to track spending habits and share RFID data for marketing is the highest cause for concern among consumers.[549] While the ability of RFID readers to collect data from tags once a consumer has left a store or moved beyond the readers' range is currently limited, many consumer groups and privacy advocates note that RFID technology is quickly advancing, while measures to protect individual privacy by limiting the amount and type of information corporations can collect is lacking.[550]

In the widely adopted EPCGlobal RFID standard, the data imprinted on a tag, the Electronic Product Code (EPC), provides a unique link to individual product data. The data is stored in a globally distributed, centrally managed electronic database, known as the Object Name Service (ONS). Tag readers in remote physical locations can connect to ONS via the Internet and then read and modify the item's ONS "dossier" throughout its lifecycle.[551] In January 2004, EPCGlobal

---

545 Mark Palmer, "Overcoming the Challenges of RFID," ZDNET.com, February 27, 2004 <http://zdnet.com.com/2100-1107_2-5165705.html>.

546 Hadley Sharpe, "Marketing Benefits Tops in RFID Adoption, Says Study," RFID Product News, May/June 2005 <http://www.rfidproductnews.com/issues/2005.05/feature/marketingbenefits.php>.

547 "RFID Market to Exceed $6 billion Worldwide by 2010," Supply & Demand Chain Executive, May 27, 2005, <http://www.sdcexec.com/article_arch.asp?article_id=7199>.

548 Rich McIver, "How RFID Will Impact Consumer Privacy," RFIDGazette.org, March 22, 2005 <http://www.rfidgazette.org/2005/03/rfid_privacy_is.html>.

549 Mary K. O'Conner, "Surveys Reveal Dubious Consumers," RFID Journal, February 17, 2005 <http://www.rfidjournal.com/article/articleview/1409/1/132/>.

550 See generally EPIC's RFID Systems Web page <http://www.epic.org/privacy/rfid/>.

551 EPCGlobal, "How the EPC Network Will Automate the Supply Chain," <http://riccistreet.net/port80/charthouse/future/rfid.htm>.

chose Verisign, Inc. to manage the root directory of ONS because of similarities between the name service and Domain Name Service (DNS), which Verisign manages for the .COM and .NET top-level domains.[552] This choice has raised alarm bells with privacy advocates, who note Verisign's poor track record in electronic privacy.[553] Recognizing that new innovative uses will drive RFID's profit potential, Verisign labeled 2005 as "The Year of the [RFID] Pilot" and sponsored a number of conferences aimed at EPC developers.[554]

Opponents of RFID tags have proposed measures to sidestep the chips' relentless information-gathering, ranging from disabling the tags by crushing or puncturing them, boycotting the products of companies that use or plan to implement RFID technology,[555] or finding ways to block the reading of a tag using special mylar bags or other technological means. The RFID industry has moved to meet this consumer demand with its own solutions, most notably the EPCGlobal standard for "killing tags," which allows for tags to be physically disabled at point of sale by the merchant.[556] Another industry-level solution has been proposed by RSA Security, Inc., which would provide a system for tag reading to be blocked in specified "privacy zones" of varying scope.[557] Both "tag killing" and tag blocking are problematic solutions that have yet to be proven in the field.[558] The "Blocker

---

[552] Paul Roberts, "VeriSign to Manage RFID 'Root' Server," Industry Standard, January 13, 2004, available at <http://www.thestandard.com/article.php?story=20040113174055565>.

[553] In September 2003, Verisign was criticized for using its control over DNS root servers for .COM and .NET top-level domains to promote its own commercial services and potentially put consumer privacy at risk. Domain names that were mistyped during web browsing or e-mail writing were redirected to Verisign servers instead of responding with standard error messages. Redirection of mistyped e-mail addresses to Verisign servers made it possible for Verisign to intercept and store private personal e-mail messages. SecurityFocus, "Verisign's SiteFinder Finds Privacy Hullabaloo," The Register, September 19, 2003, available at <http://www.theregister.co.uk/2003/09/19/verisigns_sitefinder_finds_privacy_hullabaloo/>. Verisign stopped the practice in October 2003 after a demand from Internet regulatory body ICANN. Robert Lemos, "VeriSign Calls Halt to .com Detours," CNET.com, October 3, 2003 <http://news.com.com/2100-1032_3-5086101.html>.

[554] DataMonitor, Inc., "2005 Year of the RFID Pilot Says VeriSign," January 24, 2005 <http://www.datamonitor.com/~688e2e78ed2046e8a3ecfba341d342b5~/industries/news/article/?pid=2134C8A F-3C7C-4F06-B244-34E4F51254FD&type=NewsWire>.

[555] Andrew Donohue, "Privacy Activists Demand Tesco Boycott over RFID," ZDNet UK.com, January 26, 2005 <http://news.zdnet.co.uk/communications/wireless/0,39020348,39185481,00.htm>.

[556] Junko Yoshida, "RFID Backlash Prompts 'Kill' Feature," EETimes. April 28, 2003, <http://www.eetimes.com/article/printableArticle.jhtml?articleID=12803964&url_prefix=story&sub_taxonomy ID=2251>.

[557] RSA's blocker tags, using a technique to confuse tag readers into thinking they are scanning a large number of tags, would work in conjunction with a "privacy bit" stored in the individual tag's EPC code. Using such a system, a merchant would "flip" the privacy bit on an item (from 0 to 1) at the point of sale. The consumer could then keep one of their blocker tags in the proximity of the item whenever they want to prevent the tag from being read. If, at a later date, the consumer needed to have the tag read for some reason, they could remove the blocker tag from the presence of the RFID reader so that data could be read normally. A. Juels, R. L. Rivest, and M. Szydlo, "The Blocker Tag: Selective Blocking of RFID Tags for Consumer Privacy," in V. Atluri, ed. 8th ACM Conference on Computer and Communications Security, pp. 103-111, ACM Press, 2003 <http://www.rsasecurity.com/rsalabs/node.asp?id=2060>.

[558] The EPC protocol "kill command" leaves the final step of the process, physically disabling the chip, to the individual chip manufacturer. Many technologists have admitted that real world implementations of the kill

Tag" remains an unproven solution for many reasons. Technologists appear to disagree as to the ease with which such a system might be circumvented,[559] and it places a significant burden on consumers to make sure they protect their privacy through the duration of their ownership of a product.

Currently, RFID tags are not widely used in consumer products because the price of the tags is still prohibitively expensive.[560] However, developments in RFID technology are yielding lower-cost systems with larger memory capacities, wider reading ranges, and faster processing.[561] Over the next few years, industry experts expect to see a broad range of RFID pilots, and even several fully integrated systems, launched. Companies, such as IBM, Sun, and Microsoft, are racing to develop the leading software that will enable retailers, manufacturers, and distributors to use RFID tags to track goods within stores and factories, as well as programs specifically designed to use the new retail tagging technology.[562]

Many large organizations have begun implementing RFID technology. Gillette, Wal-Mart, and Levi Strauss are among the early pioneers, using RFID for real-time tracking of inventory levels.[563] RFID systems have provided immediate benefits such as accurate replenishment of out-of-stock items and precise product sales performance statistics.[564] Other companies are developing "smart" shopping cart technology that makes use of RFID.[565] Using the Internet or a swipe card, the cart will guide consumers to their desired items and make suggestions for

---

command have been shown to have bugs and don't always work. *See e.g.*, Miyako Ohkubo, Koutarou Suzuki and Shingo Kinoshita (NTT Laboratories), "Cryptographic Approach to 'Privacy-Friendly' Tags," available at <http://www.rfidprivacy.org/papers/ohkubo.pdf> and Kim Zetter, "Jamming Tags Block RFID Scanners," Wired News, March 1, 2004 <http://www.wired.com/news/business/0,1367,62468-2,00.html?tw=wn_story_page_next1>. Furthermore, some industry "kill" solutions involve erasing the data but not destroying the circuitry, enabling the chip to be "recycled" at a later date. In fact, some RFID proponents have publicly attested to the value of a sleep command, where a chip will be publicly unresponsive (appear to be killed) until sent an encoded "revitalize" command. *See* Joe Best, "Zombie RFID Tags May never Die," Silicon.com, May 18, 2004 <http://zdnet.com.com/2100-1103_2-5214648.html>.

[559] *See* Scott Mace, "RFID Blocker Tag Concerns," Information Manager Journal, March 5, 2004 <http://scottmace.typepad.com/imanager/2004/03/rfid_blocker_ta.html>.

560 Diane M. Ward, "5-Cent Tag Unlikely in 4 Years," RFID Journal, August 26, 2004 <http://www.rfidjournal.com/article/articleview/1098/1/1/>.

561 Junko Yoshida, TI, "Phillips to Collaborate on Next-Gen RFID Standard," Embedded.com, June 17, 2005 <http://www.embedded.com/showArticle.jhtml?articleID=164901180>.

562 Paula Rooney, "Microsoft Develops Own RFID Framework," InformationWeek.com, July 8, 2005, <http://informationweek.com/story/showArticle.jhtml?articleID=165700509>.

563 Chris Murphy, "Real-World RFID: Wal-Mart, Gillette, and Others Share What They're Learning," InformationWeek.com, May 25, 2005 <http://informationweek.com/story/showArticle.jhtml?articleID=163700955>.

564 *Id.*

565 Sun Microsystems, Inc., "Smart Carts Promise to Take the Drudgery out of Shopping," July 4, 2005 <http://www.sun.com/br/1004_ezine/ret_cart.html>.

other products.[566] Hospitals are also beginning to use RFID to monitor medical supplies and track patients.[567]

Public organizations are also making use of the technology. For example, public libraries have embraced RFID.[568] A growing number of libraries in the United States[569] have already tagged every book, tape, CD, or other item in their collections.[570] Thirteen US government agencies plan to implement RFID within their operations in 2006.[571] The Energy Department wants to track hazardous waste materials.[572] The Labor Department plans to implement an RFID system to monitor and locate its tremendous volumes of case files.[573] These uses are not problematic, as RFID tags are not being used to identify and locate people. However, the Homeland Security and State departments want to use the technology to aid in border control and immigration management without taking travelers' privacy sufficiently into account.[574] The State Department's proposal[575] to roll out RFID-enabled passports with biometric data by Spring 2005[576] raised serious privacy and security issues that the agency disregarded. After more than two thousand critical comments[577] were filed,[578] the State Department backed off

---

566 Evan Schuman, "A Smarter Smart Cart?," eWeek.com, February 16, 2005
<http://www.eweek.com/article2/0,1759,1765474,00.asp>.
567 Sandy Kendall, "RFID Tagging for Hospital Patients," CIO Magazine, March 1, 2005, available at
<http://www.cio.com/archive/030105/tl_tracking.html>.
568 Katharine Mieszkowski, "The Checkout Line -- or the Check-you-out Line?" Salon.com, July 26, 2004
<http://www.salon.com/tech/feature/2004/07/26/rfid_library/index_np.html>.
569 Eric Ipsen, "Librarians Focus on RFID," RFID Journal, March 15, 2004
<http://www.rfidjournal.com/article/articleview/829/1/82/>.
570 David Molnar & David Wagner, "Privacy and Security in Library RFID Issues, Practices, and
Architectures," paper draft, available at <http://www.cs.berkeley.edu/~dmolnar/library.pdf>.
571 Florence Olsen, "Feds Find RFID Uses," Federal Computer Week, May 31, 2005, available at
<http://www.fcw.com/article89026-05-31-05-Web>.
572 Id.
573 Id.
574 US Dep't of Homeland Security, Press Release, "Homeland Security Announces Plans to Test Radio
Frequency Technology at Land Borders," January 25, 2005, available at
<http://www.dhs.gov/dhspublic/display?content=4308>.
575 US Dep't of State, "Proposal to Issue Enhanced Passports that Use Radio-frequency Identification
Technology," February 18, 2005, 70 Fed.Reg. 8305-8309, available at <http://frwebgate5.access.gpo.gov/cgi-
bin/waisgate.cgi?WAISdocID=648011101812+0+0+0&WAISaction=retrieve>. See also Testimony of
Secretary of State Colin Powell before the House Judiciary Committee, "Passports and Visas with Embedded
Biometrics and the October Deadline," April 21, 2004, available at
<http://www.state.gov/secretary/former/powell/remarks/31639.htm>.
576 Erin Biba, "Biometric Passports Set to Take Flight," PCWorld.com, March 21, 2005
<http://www.pcworld.com/news/article/0,aid,120112,00.asp>.
577 See, e.g., Electronic Frontier Foundation, Electronic Privacy Information Center, PrivacyActivism et al.,
Comments on the State Department's Notice for Public Rulemaking on RFID Passports, April 4, 2005, available
at <http://www.epic.org/privacy/rfid/rfid_passports-0405.pdf>.
578 Ryan Singel, "Passport Chip Criticism Grows," Wired.com, March 31, 2005
<http://www.wired.com/news/privacy/0,1848,67066,00.html>.

its original rollout date[579] and agreed to modify some of the RFID passport features to address some privacy and security problems. The State Department has decided to go forward with RFID-enabled passports, arguing that the technology can be secured.[580]

Corporations in Europe and Asia have moved forward with plans to tag consumer products. The German retail conglomerate Metro is planning to have 300 suppliers use RFID tags on their cases and pallets by 2006.[581] Marks & Spencer, one of the largest retailers in the United Kingdom, will have RFID systems in 53 of its 433 stores by Spring 2006.[582] The project is a follow-up to the company's implementation of RFID tags into 4 million produce delivery trays in 2002.[583] In South Korea, a company introduced a system to track freight at one of Asia's largest shipping ports.[584]

In Singapore, plans have been unveiled to create an RFID electronic passport that stores biometric data.[585] Singapore expects its citizens to begin registering for the new passports in October 2005.[586] China has been developing an RFID standard since 2004 and is partnering with Korea and Japan on joint RFID projects.[587]

Europe's largest amusement park, Legoland in Denmark, uses active RFID tags contained in bracelets and Wi-Fi networks to help parents track their children through the park.[588] The PRISM system, developed by Alanco Technologies, Inc. for use in correctional facilities, uses tamper-proof RFID-enabled wrist bracelets to monitor the location of prison inmates in real-time, reducing instances of prison vandalism and other unruly behavior. "A host of management reporting tools are available that include medicine and meal distribution, adherence to pre-determined time schedules, restricted area management, and specific location,

---

[579] Chris Gonsalves, "An RFID Passport to Trouble," eWeek.com, May 9, 2005
<http://www.eweek.com/article2/0,1759,1812731,00.asp>.

[580] Mary Mosquera, "State Bolsters Passport Security," Government Computer News, May 2, 2005
<http://appserv.gcn.com/24_10/news/35692-1.html>.

581 "Metro to Extend RFID Roll-out to Cases and Cartons," Food Production Daily.com, February 4, 2005
<http://www.foodproductiondaily.com/news/news-ng.asp?n=57851-metro-to-extend>.

582 Miya Knights, "Marks & Spencer Extends RFID Trial," Computeractive.co.uk, February 23, 2005
<http://www.computeractive.co.uk/computing/news/2071527/marks-spencer-extends-rfid-trial>.

583 Id.

584 Mike Clendenin, "South Korea Rolls out RFID for Cargo Port," EETimes.com, March 8, 2005
<http://www.eetimes.com/news/semi/showArticle.jhtml;jsessionid=30EACERIOSRPSQSNDBCCKH0CJUME
KJVN?articleID=60407369&_requestid=452269>.

585 W. David Gardner, "E-Passport Program Rolls Out In Singapore," InformationWeek.com, April 11, 2005
<http://informationweek.com/story/showArticle.jhtml?articleID=160700741>.

586 Id.

587 Laurie Sullivan, "China Works Out RFID Standards," InformationWeek.com, March 3, 2005
<http://www.informationweek.com/story/showArticle.jhtml?articleID=60405010&tid=5978>.

[588] Laurie Sullivan, "Legoland Uses Wireless And RFID For Child Security," InformationWeek, April 28, 2004 <http://www.informationweek.com/story/showArticle.jhtml?articleID=19202099>.

arrival and departure information."[589] The United States Transportation Security Administration (TSA) is considering the use of RFID-tagged airline boarding passes.[590] In Spring 2005, TSA awarded grant monies for companies to develop tracking technologies for airport ground vehicles and baggage using RFID.[591]

Applications that are not initially designed to track individuals, such as the US RFID-based electronic highway toll collection system EZ Pass, might nonetheless make human tracking possible. One of the more offbeat proposals is to use RFID chips to track human corpses as a way to prevent the black-market sale of organs.[592] In California, a school board attempted to track all of its children with cards containing RFID tags, but the proposal was quickly rejected by parents and privacy advocates.[593] This incident led California Senator Joe Simitian to introduce a bill banning the use of RFID technology in most state-issued ID cards.[594] The proposed Identity Information Protection Act would further require government IDs to use the highest level of RFID encryption.[595] A school in Japan experimented with tracking children in a short-term trial in 2004.[596] RFID manufacturer Applied Digital Solutions (ADSX) has developed a passive chip the size of a pen point that can be implanted in the human body. The VeriChip Personal Identification System is designed for use in a variety of applications including financial and transportation security, residential and commercial building access, military and government security.[597] A nightclub in Spain began using the VeriChip system in March 2004, to improve access for

---

[589] *See* Alanco Technologies, Inc., "TSI Technology: Unique, Proprietary and Patented," <http://www.alanco.com/corporate.asp>.

[590] Communications security technology chief at the agency, Anthony Cerino, stated that RFID boarding passes would let security personnel "know people's whereabouts." Bob Brewin, "TSA Eyes RFID Boarding Passes to Track Airline Passengers," Computerworld, April 1, 2004, <http://www.computerworld.com/securitytopics/security/privacy/story/0,10801,91830,00.html>.

[591] Claire Swedborg, "TSA Funds Tracking System for Seaport," RFID Journal, April 20, 2005 <http://www.rfidjournal.com/article/articleview/1519/1/1/definitions_off>.

[592] Associated Press, "Body ID: Barcodes for Cadavers," February 5, 2005, available at <http://www.wired.com/news/medtech/0,1286,66519,00.html>.

[593] *See* EPIC's Children & RFID Systems Web page <http://www.epic.org/privacy/rfid/children.html>. *See also* Alorie Gilbert, "Elementary School Nixes Electronic IDs," CNet News.com, February 17, 2005 <http://news.com.com/Elementary+school+nixes+electronic+IDs/2100-1029_3-5581275.html>; Jane Wakefield, "Hi-tech Answers to Pupil Problems," BBC News, February 16, 2005, available at <http://news.bbc.co.uk/1/hi/technology/4268203.stm>.

[594] Alorie Gilbert, "California Bill Would Ban Tracking Chips in IDs," CNet News.com, April 28, 2005 <http://news.com.com/California+bill+would+ban+tracking+chips+in+IDs/2100-1039_3-5689358.html>.

[595] Mark Robert, "A Compromise on the California RFID Bill," RFID Journal, July 4, 2005 <http://www.rfidjournal.com/article/articleview/1702/1/128/>.

[596] "RFID in Japan: Report on School RFID Project Released," March 17, 2005 <http://ubiks.net/local/blog/jmt/archives3/003535.html>.

[597] *See* EPIC's VeriChip Web page <http://www.epic.org/privacy/rfid/verichip.html>; VeriChip FAQ, <http://www.adsx.com/faq/verichipfaq.html>.

VIPs and allow them to pay for drinks without cash or credit cards.[598] ADSX has begun a campaign to promote the technology with the slogan "Get Chipped," and a mobile van called the "ChipMobile" can perform the chip insertion procedure in towns that it visits.[599]

Many individuals and non-government organizations have voiced strong opposition to widespread implementation of RFID tags without proper privacy protections.[600] One US organization opposing the use of RFID tags is Consumers Against Supermarket Privacy Invasion and Numbering (CASPIAN). CASPIAN organized a worldwide boycott of global retailer Tesco in opposition to its plan to expand item-level RFID tagging.[601] CASPIAN's main objection to Tesco is that its RFID tags are not deactivated at checkout to prevent possible tracking of consumers after the sale.[602] CASPIAN has proposed US federal legislation known as "RFID Right to Know Act of 2003," which calls for mandatory labels on RFID-equipped products so that consumers can identify and make informed choices about purchasing products installed with tracking chips.[603] EPIC has testified before Congress[604] and the Federal Trade Commission[605] to discuss privacy and security concerns raised by RFID and has called for the adoption of strong privacy guidelines for RFID technology[606] to protect consumers against potential abuses of the tracking technology. EPIC also advocated for stronger oversight of RFID use in the medical and health sectors.[607]

---

[598] Chetna Purohit, "Technology Gets under Clubbers' Skin," CNN, June 9, 2004, available at <http://www.cnn.com/2004/WORLD/europe/06/09/spain.club/>.

[599] *See* VeriChip information at ADSX Web site, <http://www.adsx.com/prodservpart/verichippreregistration.html> and <http://www.adsx.com/prodservpart/verichip.html>.

[600] Alorie Gilbert, "Privacy Questions Arise as RFID Hits Stores," CNet News.com, September 30, 2004 <http://news.com.com/Privacy+questions+arise+as+RFID+hits+stores/2100-1012_3-5390446.html>.

[601] Andrew Donohue, "Privacy Activists Demand Tesco Boycott over RFID," ZDNet UK.com, January 26, 2005 <http://news.zdnet.co.uk/0,39020330,39185481,00.htm>.

[602] *Id.*

[603] CASPIAN, "RFID Right to Know Act of 2003," <http://www.nocards.org/rfid/rfidbill.shtml>. *See also* CASPIAN, "Consumer Group Unveils RFID Labeling Legislation," June 11, 2003 <http://www.nocards.org/press/pressrelease06-11-03.shtml>.

[604] *See* Cédric Laurant, Testimony and Statement for the Record before the Subcommittee on Commerce, Trade, and Consumer Protection, House Committee on Energy and Commerce, July 14, 2004, available at <http://energycommerce.house.gov/108/Hearings/07142004hearing1337/Laurant2152.htm> and *see generally*, "Radio Frequency Identification (RFID) Technology: What the Future Holds for Commerce, Security, and the Consumer," Hearing before the US House of Representatives, Subcommittee on Commerce, Trade, and Consumer Protection, July 14, 2004, available at <http://energycommerce.house.gov/108/Hearings/07142004hearing1337/hearing.htm>.

[605] Cédric Laurant and Kenneth Farrall, Comments to the Federal Trade Commission Workshop on "Radio Frequency Identification: Applications and Implications for Consumers," July 9, 2004, available at <http://www.epic.org/privacy/rfid/ftc-comts-070904.pdf>.

[606] EPIC's Privacy Guidelines for RFID Technology <http://www.epic.org/privacy/rfid/rfid_gdlnes-070904.pdf>.

[607] *See* Marc Rotenberg, "Privacy Implications of RFID Technology in Health Care Settings," EPIC, January 11, 2005, available at <http://www.epic.org/privacy/rfid/rfid_ncvhs1_05.ppt>.

During the past year, there has been widespread activity on the part of governments and NGOs to begin the process of regulating the use of RFID to protect individual privacy. US Government Accountability Office, in June 2005, issued a report highlighting key RFID security and privacy issues.[608] US Department of Commerce held workshops and issued a comprehensive report in 2005 discussing the privacy challenges raised by RFID.[609] Federal Trade Commission issued a report[610] in March 2005 from an earlier workshop[611] that examines consumer privacy implications of RFID. Amidst the attention placed on RFID and privacy, there were reports[612] that the Department of Homeland Security - who firmly denied these reports[613] - planned to implement RFID in its new employee ID cards. Bills have been drafted and debated in state legislatures of the United States, and several other countries, including Canada, Italy, Australia and Japan, have outlined guidelines for domestic industry to follow in their use of RFID.

In its 2005 RFID Resolution, the Trans-Atlantic Consumer Dialogue (TACD), a consortium of US and EU consumer groups, called for urgent attention to the risks to consumers associated with RIFD.[614] The approach of regulatory movements worldwide varies considerably. RFID bills drafted in the US, all share a "notice" clause. This clause requires any consumer products bearing RFID tags to be conspicuously labeled. There is no legislation currently being considered in the US at the federal level.[615]

Although it does not explicitly call for labeling, a joint resolution on RFID, proposed by data protection authorities in Germany, Spain and Switzerland and adopted at the International Conference of Data Protection and Privacy

---

[608] US Government Accountability Office, "Key Considerations Related to Federal Implementation of Radio Frequency Identification Technology," June 22, 2005, available at <http://www.gao.gov/new.items/d05849t.pdf>.

[609] US Department of Commerce, "Radio Frequency Identification: Opportunities and Challenges in Implementation," April 2005, available at <http://www.technology.gov/reports/2005/RFID_April.pdf>.

[610] US Federal Trade Commission, "RFID: Applications and Implications for Consumers," March 8, 2005, available at <http://www.ftc.gov/os/2005/03/050308rfidrpt.pdf>.

[611] US Federal Trade Commission, Workshop: "RFID: Applications and Implications for Consumers," June 11, 2004, <http://www.ftc.gov/bcp/workshops/rfid/index.htm>.

[612] See Mark Baard, "RFID Invades the Capital," Wired.com, March 7, 2005 <http://www.wired.com/news/privacy/0,1848,66801,00.html>.

[613] Jacqueline Emigh, "Homeland Security Officials Refute RFID Reports," Ziff Davis Internet, March 17, 2005 <http://www.cioinsight.com/article2/0,1397,1777399,00.asp>.

[614] Trans-Atlantic Consumer Dialogue, Resolution on RFID, May 5, 2005 <http://www.tacd.org/cgi-bin/db.cgi?page=view&config=admin/docs.cfg&id=274>.

[615] Federal Trade Commission, Workshop on Radio Frequency Identification: Applications and Implications for Consumers, June 21, 2004, available at <http://www.ftc.gov/bcp/workshops/rfid/>.

Commissioners in Sydney, Australia on November 20, 2003, requires consumers to be able to delete data and destroy or disable tags on consumer items. Further, the resolution asserts "all the basic principles of data protection and privacy law have to be observed when designing, implementing and using RFID technology." The European Union published RFID privacy guidelines outlining the consumer's right to control and access information gathered through RFID technology[616] Joint guidelines released by Japan's Ministry of Public Management, Home Affairs, Posts and Telecommunications (MPT) and the Ministry of Economy, Trade and Industry (METI) on June 8, 2004, call for consumers to be given options on how they might interfere with the reading of tags, but appear to say nothing about rights to have the tag removed or destroyed.[617]

At the World Summit on the Information Society (WSIS) in Geneva, Switzerland, in the fall of 2003, three international researchers from the United Kingdom, Switzerland and Sweden discovered that the security system used to control access to the United Nations Summit included hidden RFID tags embedded in the official summit badges. The researchers issued a press release detailing the manner in which individual attendees could be identified and tracked as they moved through the conference and argued that the processing of the personal data by WSIS violates "the principles of the Swiss Federal Law on Data Protection of June 1992, the European Union Data Protection Directive (1995/46/EC), and the 1990 United Nation Guidelines concerning Computerized personal data files."[618]

There is continuing debate over how existing laws and regulations in the US and Europe might apply to the use of RFID technology. In the United States, there is little in the way of omnibus legislation that might apply to RFID practice. In Europe, however, existing data protection directives apply to both the issue of individual tracking and the association of data with personal identification. As a result, any use of RFID tags that involves processing of personal data is likely to be subject to a number of data protection obligations.[619]

---

[616] *See* International Conference of Data Protection & Privacy Commissioners, "Resolution on Radio-frequency Identification," Final Version, November 20, 2003, available at
<http://www.privacyconference2003.org/resolutions/res5.DOC>. Laura Rohde, "EU Offers Privacy Guidelines for RFID," Industry Standard, April 4, 2005<http://www.thestandard.com/internetnews/000996.php>.

[617] "Japanese RFID Privacy Guideline Released," June 8, 2004, RFIDBuzz.com, available at
<http://www.rfidbuzz.com/news/2004/japanese_rfid_privacy_guideline_released.html>; *see also* Nikkei BP,
June 8, 2004, available at <http://nikkeibp.jp/wcs/leaf/CID/onair/jp/flash/312386> (in Japanese).

[618] Alberto Escudero-Pascual, Stephane Koch and George Danezis, press release, "The Physical Access Security to WSIS:
a Privacy Threat for the Participants," December 12, 2003 <http://www.nodo50.org/wsis/>.

[619] Article 8 of the EU Data Protection Directive of 1995, for example, prohibits the processing "personal data revealing racial or ethnic origin, political opinions, religious or philosophical beliefs, trade-union membership,

Public Records

Public records present some of the most difficult privacy challenges. On one hand, public records may assist individuals in ensuring that a government remains transparent and accountable. On the other, public records may be converted from this tool of citizen empowerment to one that empowers governments and businesses to track citizens.[620] Increasingly, personal information is being harvested from public records to create detailed profiles on individuals. Public records may contain many types of personal information that are commercially valuable. These include: Social Security numbers, birth records, arrest information, civil case history, criminal case history, addresses, drivers license information, land sales transactions, records of asset holdings, ownership of corporations, marital status, presence of children, employment status, and health information. Often, individuals are compelled by law to provide truthful and complete personal information to government authorities that is then placed in the public record. For instance, in order to exercise the right of marriage, in some states a publicly available license must be filed at a courthouse containing the individuals' Social Security Numbers.

The advent of remote electronic access to public records systems has raised the specter of vastly increased data mining and profiling. Mining a public records database soon will no longer require the time and expense involved in traveling to the physical location of the records. Data miners will be able to remotely access public records systems and use widely available software to harvest personal information. This harvesting of personal information already has had a substantial impact on individuals. In 2002, the Wall Street Journal reported that drug maker Eli Lilly had terminated employees for decade-old convictions discovered in dossiers aggregated from public records.[621]

Unrestricted commercial harvesting of public records has enabled the American government to obtain detailed dossiers on citizens with ease.[622] Through private-

---

and the processing of data concerning health or sex life." Further, the more recent Directive on Privacy and Electronic Communications states that "location data may only be processed when it is made anonymous or with the consent of the individual." *See* Eduardo Ustaran, "Data Protection and RFID Systems," 3/6 Privacy & Data Protection 6 <http://www.berwinleighton.com/download/PDP-RFIDtagsimplications.pdf>.

[620] Daniel J. Solove, Access and Aggregation: Public Records, Privacy, and the Constitution, 86 Minnesota Law Review 6 (2002).

[621] "Firms Dig Deep Into Workers' Pasts Amid Post-Sept. 11 Security Anxiety," Wall Street Journal, March 12, 2002.

[622] Chris J. Hoofnagle, Big Brother's Little Helpers: How ChoicePoint and Other Commercial Data Brokers Collect, Process, and Package Your Data for Law Enforcement, University of North Carolina Journal of International Law & Commercial Regulation (Spring 2004).

public partnerships, several profiling companies make consumer dossiers available to the government. One company in particular, ChoicePoint,[623] has emerged as the leading provider for law enforcement and other government agencies.[624] ChoicePoint maintains web pages customized for individual federal agencies to facilitate the sale of public record information to police.[625] As a result of FOIA requests initiated by EPIC, it was discovered that ChoicePoint was selling the national ID databases of several Latin American countries to the American immigration law enforcement agency.[626] Since that revelation, several Central and South American countries have initiated investigations into the legality of the information transfer.

Census

The counting of citizens can be traced back to the Biblical recordings of Moses. In the Book of Numbers, Moses counted people in areas surrounding his kingdom in order to strengthen the count of the population under his control. Scholars discuss that the list of names was used as an original census, creating a legal identity of, and control over, a group of people.[627]

The US Census has been administered every 10 years since the Revolutionary War, and it was intended to be used primarily for the apportionment of Representatives for the nation's Congress. The complexity of the census has grown with the expansion of the United States; the country's government has found extensive uses for census related statistics. The census has also been crucial in tracking the population needs of various regions and understanding the structural composition of the nation's population.

The census raises important privacy issues. The risks that accompany the electronic compilation of personal information include re-identification,[628] which is the practice of linking individuals' identities to anonymous census records; the

---

[623] *See* ChoicePoint, available at <http://www.epic.org/privacy/choicepoint/>.

[624] "If the FBI Hopes to Get the Goods on You, It May Ask ChoicePoint," Wall Street Journal, April 13, 2001.

[625] *See* ChoicePoint FBI <http://www.cpfbi.com>; ChoicePoint DEA <http://www.cpdea.com>; ChoicePoint Government <http://www.cpgov.com>.

[626] Documents available at <http://www.epic.org/privacy/publicrecords/inschoicepoint.pdf>.

[627] In the United States, the census dates back to pre-Revolutionary times. It is thought that the census was developed to establish an equitable way to distribute the burden of the Revolutionary War, both economically and in manpower. *See generally* EPIC Census Privacy Page, available at <http://www.epic.org/privacy/census/>.

[628] Latanya Sweeney, "Uniqueness of Simple Demographics in the U.S. Population," LIDAP-WP4. Carnegie Mellon University, Laboratory for International Data Privacy (Pittsburgh, PA 2000).

use of personal information for marketing solicitations; and even more serious consequences of political abuse.

In the United States, census data is protected statutorily.[629] The US Code requires that information gathered by authorities be kept confidential and be used exclusively for statistical purposes. The statute provides penalties for employees who willfully disclose such information illegally. Authorities are restricted from using the information for any purpose other than statistics, making any publication allowing any individual to be identified, or permitting any unauthorized person to examine the census reports.

Internationally, data protection norms apply to census data. Article 6(1)(b) of the European Union Data Protection Directive provides that "appropriate safeguards" must be established for "processing of data for historical, statistical or scientific purposes."

A specific example of the privacy risks of the US census can also be found in the 1940s. It has been recorded that even before the Japanese attack on Pearl Harbor, President Franklin Delano Roosevelt ordered the Census Bureau to collect information on "American-born and foreign-born Japanese" from the Census data lists. Information was gathered from the 1930 and 1940 censuses on all Japanese-Americans and then given to the Federal Bureau of Investigation (FBI) and top military officials. These sources point directly to the census information as one of the reasons that led to the internment of almost 110,000 Japanese-Americans on the West Coast, two-thirds of whom were US citizens.

In July 2004, a Freedom of Information Act request pursued by the Electronic Privacy Information Center revealed that the Census Bureau provided specially tabulated population statistics on Arab Americans to the Department of Homeland Security, including detailed information on how many people of Arab backgrounds live in certain ZIP codes. The tabulations were produced in August 2002 and December 2003 in response to requests from what is now the Customs and Border Protection division of the Department of Homeland Security. One set listed cities with more than 1,000 Arab Americans. The second, far more detailed, provided ZIP-code-level breakdowns of Arab American populations, sorted by country of origin. The categories provided were Egyptian, Iraqi, Jordanian, Lebanese, Moroccan, Palestinian, Syrian and two general categories,

---

[629] 13 USC § 9.

"Arab/Arabic" and "Other Arab."[630] Following the efforts of a coalition of ethnic advocacy groups, privacy watchdogs and civil rights and civil liberties organizations.[631] the Census Bureau subsequently announced that it would no longer assist law enforcement or intelligence agencies with special tabulations on ethnic groups and other "sensitive populations" without the approval of senior bureau officials.[632]

In the United Kingdom, it was determined that compulsory transfers were considered in Northern Ireland in 1972.[633] A UK government top-secret memo has surfaced describing a plan to relocate Irish Catholics; the plan was written with census data. Although never implemented, the use of census data for non-statistical purposes has caused great concern in Europe.

The Census continues to be controversial in Germany.[634] Since the Census was instrumental in identifying individuals persecuted by the Nazi regime, Germans have been sensitive to the administration and planned expansions of the Census.[635] In the 1980s, the German Government instituted a law requiring more information to be provided on the national census. After a public outcry, the law was challenged in court. The issue was brought before the German Federal Constitutional Court by representatives who had been instrumental in the passage of the first German Data Protection Act during the 1970s. The court found the census law unconstitutional based upon what the court termed a fundamental right to informational self-determination implicit in the German Constitution.

---

[630] Lynette Clemetson, "Homeland Security given data on Arab-Americans," The New York Times, July 30, 2004 at A14.

[631] Lynette Clemetson, "Threats and Responses: Privacy; Coalition Seeks Action on Shared Data on Arab-Americans," The New York Times, August 13, 2004 at A11.

[632] Lynette Clemetson, "Census Policy On Providing Sensitive Data Is Revised," The New York Times, August 31, 2004 at A14.

[633] Kathleen Cahill, "When Catholics Were 'to Be Removed,'" Washington Post, January 12, 2003.

[634] For discussions on census privacy issues, *see generally*, Kent Walker, "Where Everybody Knows Your Name: A Pragmatic Look at the Costs of Privacy and the Benefits of Information Exchange," 1 Stan. Tech. L. Rev. 106 (2000) (citing Jerry M. Rosenberg, The Death of Privacy 1 (1969)); Thomas S. Mayer, "Privacy and Confidentiality Research and the US Census Bureau: Recommendations Based on a Review of the Literature" Research Report Series (Survey Methodology #2002-01);
Viktor Mayer-Schonberger, Privacy and the Law: A Symposium, No Choice: Trans-Atlantic Information Privacy Legislation and Rational Choice Theory, 67 Geo. Wash. L. Rev. 1309 (1999).

[635] *See* Edwin Black, "IBM and the Holocaust: The Strategic Alliance Between Nazi Germany and America's Most Powerful Corporation" (New York, Random House 2001; Richard Sobel, "The Demeaning of Identity and Personhood in the National Identification Systems," 15 Harv. J.L. & Tech. 319 (2002).

Digital Rights Management

Several companies have developed Digital Rights Management (DRM) systems to prevent the unauthorized use of digital files.[636] DRM technologies can control file access (number of views, length of views), altering, sharing, copying, printing, and saving. These technologies may be contained within the operating system, program software, or in the actual hardware of a device. Some DRM technology can disable users' machines for unauthorized access to files. InTether Point-to-Point, for instance, imposes "penalties" for those who attempt an "illegal use" of a digital file.[637] Penalties include automatic rebooting of the users' machine, or destruction of the file the user is attempting to access.

DRM systems take two approaches to securing content. The first is "containment," an approach where the content is encrypted in a shell so that it can only be accessed by authorized users.[638] The second is "marking," the practice of placing a watermark, flag, or a XrML tag on content as a signal to a device that the media is copy protected. Some systems combine the two approaches. Nevertheless, according to an authority in the field,[639] DRMs are vulnerable to cracking by individuals with moderate programming skills.[640]

These technologies have been developed with little regard for privacy protection. DRM technology usually requires the user to reveal his or her identity and rights to access the file. Upon authentication of identity and rights to the file, the user can access the content. Under the Digital Millennium Copyright Act, tampering with or producing "circumvention" tools for copyright control technologies is illegal.

These systems can prevent anonymous consumption of content, and could be employed to profile users' preferences or to limit access to digital books, music, or programs. DRM technologies may "...enable an unprecedented degree of intrusion into and oversight of individual decisions about what to read, hear and view."[641] For instance, a DRM technology called Copyright Agent quietly scans

---

[636] *See* EPIC's DRM web page <http://www.epic.org/privacy/drm/>.

[637] InTether Point to Point Product Page <http://www.infraworks.com/p2p.html>.

[638] Professor Edward Felten, Address at the Boalt Hall Copyright Workshop (March 22, 2002).

[639] Princeton University Computer Science Professor Ed Felten.

[640] *Id.*

[641] Julie Cohen, A Right to Read Anonymously: A Closer Look at "Copyright Management" in Cyberspace, 28 Connecticut Law Review 981 (1996); *see also* Chris J. Hoofnagle, Digital Rights Management: Many Technical Controls on Digital Content Distribution Can Create A Surveillance Society, 5 Columbia Science and Technology Law Review (Spring 2004).

peer-to-peer networks to discover whether users possess illegal content. If a copyright violation is found, the program automatically informs the users' Internet Service Provider that his or her service should be severed.[642]

In February 2002, the European Commission Information Society Directorate held a workshop on DRM technologies to examine, among other issues, their effects on privacy.[643] Similar workshops have also been held at the US Department of Commerce Technology Administration[644] and the Berkeley Center for Law and Technology.[645]

In February 2002, Sunncomm, Inc., a DRM systems developer, and Music City Records settled a lawsuit brought by a California woman who objected to their practice of tracking and disclosing personal information to third-parties with no opt-out scheme.[646] The settlement agreement required the companies to provide notice to consumers of their information collection practices and to refrain from requiring consumers to disclose their personal information as a condition of downloading, playing, or listening to a CD.[647]

In June 2002, Microsoft released information regarding its new "Palladium" initiative, which was renamed in 2003 to "Next-Generation Secure Computing Base."[648] Through software and hardware controls, Palladium could place Microsoft as the architect of computer identification and authentication. Additionally, systems embedded in both software and hardware would control access to content, thereby creating ubiquitous DRM schemes that can track users and control their use of media and even access to websites. Microsoft has experienced a delay in its implementation of Palladium, and now expects to have elements of the system in by 2006.

---

[642] Dawn C. Chmielewski, "Stealth Software Robot Puts Bootleggers on Notice," San Jose Mercury News, March 19, 2001, available at
<http://web.archive.org/web/20010626223307/http://www.chicagotribune.com/business/printedition/article/0,2669,SAV-0103190188,FF.html>.

[643] More information and the final report of the workshop are available at
<http://europa.eu.int/information_society/topics/multi/digital_rights/events/index_en.htm>.

[644] See EPIC's Comments to the Department of Commerce
<http://www.epic.org/privacy/drm/tadrmcomments7.17.02.html>.

[645] See <http://www.law.berkeley.edu/institutes/bclt/>.

[646] DeLise v. Fahrenheit, No. CV-014297 (Cal. Sup. Ct. Sept. 6, 2001)(Pl. Comp. at ¶ 1), available at
<http://www.techfirm.com/mccomp.pdf>.

[647] Press Release, SunnComm, Inc., "Sunncomm and Music City Records Agree to Resolve Consumer Music Cloqueing Law Suit by Providing Better Notice and Enhancing Consumer Privacy," February 22, 2002
<http://www.xenoclast.org/free-sklyarov-uk/2002-February/001580.html>.

[648] See EPIC's Palladium web page <http://www.epic.org/privacy/consumer/microsoft/palladium.html>.

In November 2003, the US Federal Communications Commission voted unanimously to create a requirement that consumer products be able to recognize a Digital Broadcast Flag by July 2005. Such a flag will mark digital content as "protected" and direct devices to limit individuals' use of the content. EPIC recommended against the adoption of a Digital Television Broadcast Flag mandate unless it incorporates privacy protections for viewer data.[649]

In April 2004, the European Commission (the Commission) advocated passing legislation to unify content licensing, arguing that the market for digital content will be ineffective without a single standard for Europe.[650] Specifically, the Commission called for Community-level regulation of collecting societies, the companies that administer royalties and license fees for content owners. DRM systems, too, would have to be interoperable under the plan. The balance struck among rights holders, media players owners, and users will have great effect on users' ability to access digital content and to shield themselves from monitoring.

Authentication and Identity Disclosure

Authentication is the process of verifying a claim that is being made regarding an identity, an attribute pertaining to an identity (*e.g.*, "this person is a citizen of the United States"), or a set of attributes. Traditionally, the greatest demand for secure authentication solutions has come from enterprises looking to meet their own intra-organizational security needs, as well as from government organizations in contexts where national security interests are believed to be at stake. In recent years, the demand for (and the adoption of) secure authentication solutions has been sharply on the rise in all kinds of other contexts that directly affect the privacy of individuals on a scale unimaginable two decades ago. Much of this is driven by the growing popularity of the Internet and mobile communication networks, as well as by the rapid increase in PCs and information appliances such as Web-enabled mobile phones and handheld computers.

As new authentication architectures are being developed (through *de jure*, *de facto*, and technical standards) and adopted for an ever-growing number of applications, the privacy of individuals is being eroded at an unprecedented pace, often with little or no justification at all. New electronic communication and transaction mechanisms automatically capture and record identities in central

---

[649] EPIC comments in the Matter of Digital Broadcast Copy Protection, MB Docket No. 02-230, December 6, 2002 <http://www.epic.org/privacy/drm/broadcastflagcomments.html>.

[650] "Europe Demands Open-to-All DRM Tech," The Register, April 20, 2004 <http://www.theregister.co.uk/2004/04/20/european_union_drm/>.

computer systems without individuals even being aware of it. As more and more personal information is collected and recorded on central systems, policies and traditional security safeguards to prevent against leakage and abuse are rapidly becoming ineffective.

Much of this explosive tension between the (perceived or real) need for authentication on the one hand and privacy demands on the other can be attributed to a widespread misbelief: namely, that identification is the same as authentication, and that privacy and authentication are opposite goals. This misbelief is perpetuated by all kinds of influential standards organizations. The International Standard Organization[651] (ISO), for example, defines authentication as "the provision of assurance of the claimed identity of an entity," and the Internet Engineering Task Force[652] (IETF) defines authentication as "[t]he process of verifying an identity claimed by or for a system entity." Likewise, at the political level, authentication and identity are often mistakenly equated.

The actual fact of the matter is that authentication is a much broader notion than identification. In many contexts, authentication does not require identification. Indeed, organizations are often not interested in the identity *per se* of the person they are dealing with, but only in the confirmation of previous contacts of that person, the affiliation of the person to a group, the authenticity of personal data of the person, the entitlements or privileges of the person, and so on. For example, to authenticate whether a user is permitted to purchase alcohol, all that needs to be authenticated is that the user is at least 21 years of age. In this example, identification of the person would only serve as an indirect means to accomplish the authentication that is of actual interest ("over 21 years of age").

In the "old" world, individuals could easily gain access to services without disclosing their identity, either by showing the right privileges or entitlements or by providing service providers with "context-specific" identifiers, such as employee numbers or a health insurance number. While such identifiers serve to identify users, they only do so within specific spheres of activity; organizations cannot use them to cross-profile users across spheres of activity.

Unfortunately, today's most widespread authentication technologies (such as passwords, biometrics, Kerberos, and PKI) all fundamentally cause inescapable identification through identifiers that are globally unique. These identity-based

---

[651] Glossary of IT Security Terminology, SC 27 Standing Document 6 (SC 27 N 2776), March 31, 2002.

[652] Internet Security Glossary, RFC 2828, IETF Network Working Group, May 2000. *See* <http://www.ietf.org/rfc/rfc2828.txt>.

authentication technologies were invented many decades ago, when open networks were hardly existent, let alone organizations seeking to securely share personal information over such networks. Consequently, the only privacy protection that the designers of traditional authentication techniques had in mind was protection against wire-tappers and other unauthorized outsiders. Traditional authentication technologies are not appropriate to address the growing authentication needs in today's day and age, however, since they enable organizations to track and cross-profile users on the basis of globally unique identifiers (such as cryptographic keys) that are inescapably assigned to them.

An equally worrisome trend is the centralization of authentication powers from different organizations into a single trusted organization that acts on behalf of all its constituent organizations. In its original Passport architecture[653] for example, Microsoft relied on the centralization of all data collected from Web site visitors in order to provide authentication services on behalf of a rapidly increasing number of Web sites. Microsoft abandoned this architecture following privacy complaints from consumer groups and EU officials,[654]] as well as a lack of adoption from service providers who were highly reluctant to entrust Microsoft with their customer data.

The "federated" authentication architecture promoted by the Liberty Alliance[655] (an industry alliance of some 160 key industry players in a wide range of sectors, led by a number of major companies who were unwilling to delegate their autonomy to Microsoft in the original Passport initiative) leaves personal data at the organizations that collect it, and allows for multiple "circles of trust" to co-exist. However, even this architecture does nothing to improve the privacy of users: the authentication power (and therefore the access control power) remains centralized. Specifically, whenever a service provider deals with a user, it queries in real time the central "identity provider" in its circle of trust; the identity provider simply returns an authentication assertion as to the validity of the identity claim of the access requestor, which the service provider then uses in its own authorization process. Even though users may be "pseudonymous" towards service providers (in Liberty Alliance the identity provider assigns different user names to the same user, one per service provider), they are certainly not *vis-à-vis* the most powerful parties in this architecture: the identity providers. Within each circle of trust, the identity provider can track, trace and link in real time all

---

[653] More information available at <http://www.epic.org/privacy/consumer/microsoft/passport.html>.

[654] *Id.*

[655] More information available at <http://www.epic.org/privacy/authentication/projectliberty.html>.

interactions between users and organizations. The identity provider can even impersonate users and falsely deny them access everywhere.

While such centralized authentication approaches may meet the needs of large enterprises that want to do employee-related and supplier-related identity management across their own internal branches, beyond this restricted context the approach rapidly becomes highly problematic with regard to privacy. It may even be in conflict with privacy legislation. If adopted on a government-wide scale, the implications of these privacy-invasive architectures would certainly be unprecedented.

In an electronic world, if at the technical level (by analyzing the electronic data flow) everything is inescapably identifiable through globally unique identifiers, privacy legislation becomes virtually meaningless; how can one force organizations not to collect identifiable information when they cannot prevent it from being delivered to them? The only way out of the seeming conflict between authentication and privacy is to resort to authentication technologies that technically separate the notion of authentication from that of identification. Two decades of research in cryptography have demonstrated that secure authentication and privacy are not trade-offs, but that they are in fact mutually reinforcing when implemented properly. Using techniques that are rooted in modern cryptography, such as Digital Credentials,[656] it is entirely feasible to do secure authentication without necessarily requiring identification. For instance, role-based authentication can be implemented in such a manner that the access requestor cannot be identified.

More generally, privacy-preserving authentication techniques allow each party involved in the electronic processing and forwarding of privacy-sensitive information to securely retain fine-grained control over the information, even as the information is electronically transmitted beyond corporate firewalls and across arbitrary organizational domains. At no point in the chain of electronic information transfer from one party to the next will any party be able to learn more than precisely that which its sender expressly allows.

Each time when implementing a new authentication measure for an existing or new transaction mechanism, it is imperative that designers and adopters analyze how much personally identifiable information really needs to be disclosed for the purposes of authentication. Assuming the information disclosure is found to be

---

[656] Stefan Brands, "Rethinking Public Key Infrastructures and Digital Certificates; Building in Privacy," MIT Press, August 2000, with a foreword by Prof. Ronald L. Rivest. *See* <http://www.credentica.com/technology/book.html>.

necessary and proportionate with respect to the nature of the transaction, they should then seek to implement security needs using authentication technologies that protect privacy, instead of resorting to approaches based on inescapable identification.

WHOIS

In the first quarter of 2004, more than 4.7 million new domain names were registered. This brings the total number of registrations to an all time high of 63 million domain names.[657] Registrants include large and small businesses, individuals, media organizations, non-profit groups, public interest organizations, political, and religious organizations, and support groups. These domain name registrants share their services, ideas, views, activities, and more by way of websites, e-mail, newsgroups, and other Internet media. Registrants are required to provide information in the registration process, which is then made publicly available.

The Internet Corporation for Assigned Names and Numbers (ICANN), a private-sector corporation that coordinates policy for the Internet,[658] has established contractual arrangements with the registries that manage the top-level domains and the registrars that sell the domain names to the registrants. ICANN requires public disclosure on the Internet of domain name registrants' contact information (such as mailing address, phone number and e-mail address), administrative contact information, technical contact information, domain name and servers, and other information.[659] This information is referred to as "WHOIS" data. Its public availability has generated concerns over privacy protection.

Under ICANN's WHOIS policy, Internet users are unable to register for a domain anonymously. The WHOIS database broadly exposes domain name registrants' personal information to a global audience, including criminals and spammers.[660] Anyone with Internet access has access to WHOIS data, including stalkers, corrupt governments cracking down on dissidents, spammers, aggressive

---

[657] VeriSign Domain Name Industry Brief, "The Domain Name Registrant Profile," June 2004
<http://www.verisign.com/nds/naming/domainbrief/2004/report_200406.pdf>.

[658] *See generally* The Internet Corporation for Assigned Names and Numbers homepage
<http://www.icann.org/>.

[659] The Internet Corporation for Assigned Names and Numbers, Registrar Accreditation Agreement
<http://www.icann.org/registrars/ra-agreement-17may01.htm>.

[660] Milton Mueller, Ruling the Root 235 (MIT Press 2002).

intellectual property lawyers, and police agents without legal authority.[661] Even those speaking out for human rights cannot conceal their identity. While it is true that some registrants use the Internet to conduct fraud, most domain name registrants do not, and many have legitimate reasons to conceal their identities and to register domain names anonymously. For example, political, artistic and religious groups around the world rely on the Internet to provide information and express views while avoiding persecution. Concealing actual identity may be critical for political, artistic, and religious expression.[662]

WHOIS data lends itself to both good faith and bad faith uses, and investigating fraud is only one of many uses of WHOIS data.[663] There now exist various automated data mining procedures that provide bad-faith users with access to large amounts of personal data at a time, rather than just individual queries. Web-based WHOIS services now have to complicate their access procedures, for example, requiring users to enter number codes before they can retrieve information. The WHOIS database was not originally intended to allow access for such a variety of purposes. The original purpose of WHOIS was instead to allow network administrators to find and fix technical problems with minimal hassle in order to maintain the stability of the Internet.

ICANN's WHOIS policy requires that registrants provide accurate WHOIS information, or otherwise forgo a domain name.[664] If a domain registration is assumed to have inaccurate information, registrants are contacted and given a very limited amount of time to address the problem. Data entered at registration may change in the real world and registrant may forget to update it. They may lose their domain if they are unable to respond quickly to any attempts to contact them. Privacy experts have noted that a policy requiring accurate WHOIS data and then publicly disclosing the data creates serious implications for free speech.[665]

---

[661] Comments of the Public Interest Registry (PIR) on the Final Report on WHOIS Accuracy and Bulk Access of the Whois Task Force of the Generic Names Supporting Organization (hereinafter "PIR Comments on WHOIS"), available at <http://gnso.icann.org/dnso/dnsocomments/comments-whois/Arc03/pdf00000.pdf>.

[662] PIR Comments on WHOIS, *supra*.

[663] EPIC, Privacy Issues Report: The Creation of A New Task Force Is Necessary for an Adequate Resolution of the Privacy Issues Associated with WHOIS, March 10, 2003 <http://www.epic.org/privacy/whois/privacy_issues_report.pdf>.

[664] The Internet Corporation for Assigned Names and Numbers, Registrar Accreditation Agreement <http://www.icann.org/registrars/ra-agreement-17may01.htm> and The Internet Corporation for Assigned Names and Numbers, WHOIS Data Reminder Policy, Advisory on June 16, 2003, <http://www.icann.org/announcements/advisory-16jun03.htm>.

[665] EPIC Privacy Issues Report, *supra*, and PIR Comments on WHOIS, *supra*.

The ICANN WHOIS policies conflict with national privacy laws, including the EU Data Protection Directive, which require the establishment of a legal framework to ensure that when personal information is collected, it is used only for its intended purpose. At a recent ICANN meeting, George Papapavlou, a representative from the European Commission stated that if the original purpose of the WHOIS database is purely technical, the rights of access to and collection of that information pertain solely to that original purpose.[666] Speaking at the "Freedom 2.0" conference held by EPIC in May 2004, Vinton G. Cerf, the President of ICANN, confirmed directly that the original purpose of WHOIS was indeed purely technical.[667] As personal information in the directory is used for other purposes and ICANN's policy keeps the information public and anonymously accessible, the database could be found illegal according to many data protection laws including the European Data Protection Directive.[668]

Under European law, technical users would be the only ones with a legitimate claim to the information. While intellectual property lawyers and law enforcement officials claim the WHOIS database must retain all its current data in its public form as a resource for investigations, the fact that the WHOIS database was originally created for technical purposes makes it clear that such claims to the database would be inconsistent with its original purpose.

In 2003, ICANN's Generic Names Supporting Organization (GNSO) began a policy development process identifying three issues, access, data and accuracy, and creating task forces to study and make recommendations on each. EPIC is serving on one of the WHOIS task forces. The outcome of the WHOIS Policy Development Process will have a significant impact on privacy, civil liberties, and freedom of expression for Internet users.[669] Civil liberties groups and the Non-Commercial Users Constituency[670] of ICANN have urged ICANN to limit the use and scope of the WHOIS database to its original purpose, which is the resolution of technical network issues, and to establish strong privacy protections based on internationally accepted privacy standards. This limitation would entail restricting access to the data, minimizing data required to only that needed for technical matters, and not penalizing registrants for protecting their personal information by entering inaccurate personal data elements.

---

[666] "WHOIS data: The EU Legal Principles," March 2, 2004, available at
http://www.icann.org/presentations/papapavlou-whois-rome-03mar04.pdf .

[667] "Vint Cerf Discusses Privacy and the Internet," EPIC Alert, May 29, 2004, available at
http://www.epic.org/alert/EPIC_Alert_11.10.html.

[668] Available at<http://europa.eu.int/comm/internal_market/privacy/law_en.htm>.

[669] *See generally* EPIC's WHOIS web page <http://www.epic.org/privacy/whois/>.

[670] *See generally* the Non-Commercial Users Constituency's homepage <http://www.ncdnhc.org>.

The task forces have drafted reports[671] on WHOIS policy in these three areas, yet it is unclear whether the recommendations will improve privacy protections. Some of the recommendations entail more privacy risks than safeguards. At the same time, some of the better recommendations, including some restrictions on access and data required, may not be accepted by the GNSO Council and the ICANN Board should they decide to rule on the policy development. After three years, this policy development process, including the establishement of previous task forces, has not made any strides in the protection of privacy and the current problematic policy remains.

While ICANN has considerable authority over the development of WHOIS policies for the generic top-level domains (gTLDs), such as .com, .org, and .net, it is unclear whether ICANN will be able to exercise similar control over the country-code top-level domains (ccTLDs), such as .uk and .de, which may choose to follow national policies. Significantly, country code Top Level Domains are moving to provide more privacy protection in accordance with national law. For example, regarding Australia's TLD, .au, the WHOIS policy of the .au Domain Administration Ltd (AUDA) states in section 4.2, "In order to comply with Australian privacy legislation, registrant telephone and facsimile numbers will not be disclosed. In the case of id.au domain names (for individual registrants, rather than corporate registrants), the registrant contact name and address details also will not be disclosed." In addition, auDA does not allow bulk access to WHOIS data, which ICANN's gTLDs do.[672] It is unclear what, if any, indirect effect the GNSO WHOIS policy development will have on the policies of ccTLDs.

The ICANN WHOIS policy process has continued for several years, yet has failed to resolve the privacy risks faced by Internet users that result directly from ICANN's own data practices.

UN WSIS and Privacy

The World Summit on the Information Society (WSIS) is the first in the series of United Nations (UN) summits that deals with issues of the information

---

[671] WHOIS Task Force Preliminary Reports <http://www.gnso.icann.org/issues/whois-privacy/index.shtml>.
672 The .au Domain Administration Ltd, WHOIS Policy (2002-2004) <http://www.auda.org.au/policies/auda-2002-04/>.

society.[673] The Summit was split into two phases, the first which concluded in Geneva in December 2003, and the second in Tunis in November 2005. The Summit process was first initiated by the UN General Assembly in 2001. The task of the Summit is not a small one: to develop a "common vision of the information society." Because of the general feeling that this could not be done by governments alone, the summit process allowed limited participation of observers in a multi-stakeholder process.

At the Geneva summit meeting governments adopted a Declaration[674] and Plan of Action,[675] and established a UN Working Group on Internet Governance. How big the Summit's impact will be in the end will depend more on the momentum and networks created by the summit process, not by the two texts it adopted. In the end this is actually beneficial in the interest of privacy and human rights development, as the texts themselves fell short in these areas. Civil society worked to improve these documents, to center them around human rights, but was forced to issue separate documents: "Shaping Information Societies for Human Needs: Civil Society Declaration to the World Summit on the Information Society,"[676] and "Civil Society Essential Benchmarks for WSIS."[677]

As the idea for the summit had developed first in the International Telecommunications Union (ITU), the telecommunications body of the UN, the initial focus was very technology-centered. Mainly because of the efforts of a global coalition of activists and academics from civil society groups, the general discussion moved from "information" to "society" over the course of the summit preparations. One outcome was that human rights gained a prominent place in the Geneva Summit Declaration and Plan of Action.[678] The Universal Declaration of Human Rights is underlined in the first paragraph of the Summit Declaration, and

---

[673] It is also the first summit that takes place in two parts: The first summit meeting was held in Geneva in December 2003, the second one will be in Tunis in November 2005. Official web site <http://www.wsis.org>. For an extensive overview of WSIS, *see* EPIC, The Public Voice WSIS Sourcebook: Perspectives on the World Summit on the Information Society (Washington DC 2004). WSIS Civil Society news and documents are available at <http://www.worldsummit2005.org>.
674 WSIS Declaration of Principles: Building the Information Society: a Global Challenge in the New Millennium, Document WSIS-03/GENEVA/DOC/4-E, December 12, 2003, available at <http://www.itu.int/wsis/documents/doc_multi.asp?lang=en&id=1161|1160>.
675 WSIS Plan of Action, Document WSIS-03/GENEVA/DOC/5-E, December 12, 2003, available at <http://www.itu.int/wsis/documents/doc_multi.asp?lang=en&id=1161|1160>.
[676] Shaping Information Societies for Human Needs: Civil Society Declaration to the World Summit on the Information Society, December 8, 2003 <http://www.wsis-cs.org>.
677 Civil Society Essential Benchmarks for WSIS, November 3, 2003 <http://www.prepcom.net/wsis/1069062981246>.
678 WSIS Declaration of Principles: Building the Information Society: a Global Challenge in the New Millennium, *supra*; WSIS Plan of Action, *supra*.

---

its Article 19 on freedom of speech is quoted as "central to the Information Society."

Because the summit preparations took place in the context of the global "war on terrorism," one of the most discussed topics was security.[679] The United States and the Russian Federation placed particular emphasis on this matter. This was enforced by developments in other international organizations, like the Council of Europe,[680] the OECD[681] or even the UN General Assembly,[682] where cyber-security or similar topics have moved up the agenda in recent years. The respective paragraph of the WSIS summit declaration ends with an explicit reference to the war on terrorism: "It is necessary to prevent the use of information resources and technologies for criminal and terrorist purposes, while respecting human rights."

In this context, the protection of privacy was not a popular goal. The first drafts of the summit declaration made no reference to privacy at all. Civil society groups were concerned about the strong focus on security in the whole text. In their view, security is a vague political goal that can be higher or lower on the agenda depending on day-to-day politics. Privacy and other human rights and civil liberties, on the other hand, are constitutional fundamentals of every democracy that must not be violated for the sake – or, as often is the case, under the guise – of security.

The international NGO network active in the WSIS-process, mainly the Privacy and Security Working Group and the Human Rights Caucus, advocated for the insertion of a new paragraph specifically on privacy and for placing it at the beginning of the "Security" section of the Summit Declaration.[683] However, the

---

679 For a more comprehensive analysis of the security and privacy discussions before the summit, see Ralf Bendrath, National Security or Civil Liberties? WSIS Debate on Security Issues in Deadlock, in Heinrich Boell Foundation (Ed.): Visions in Process. World Summit on the Information Society. Geneva 2003 - Tunis 2005 (Berlin 2003) <http://www.worldsummit2003.de/download_de/Vision_in_process.pdf>.
680 Council of Europe, Convention on Cybercrime, November 2001
<http://conventions.coe.int/Treaty/en/Treaties/Html/185.htm>.
681 Organization for Economic Cooperation and Development (OECD): Guidelines for the Security of Information Systems and Networks: Towards a Culture of Security, June 2002
<http://www.oecd.org/dataoecd/59/0/1946946.pdf>.
682 UN General Assembly: Resolution 57/239,Creation of a Global Culture of Cybersecurity, 78th plenary meeting, December 2002 <http://ods-dds-ny.un.org/doc/UNDOC/GEN/N02/555/22/PDF/N0255522.pdf>.
683 The paragraph would have read "The right to privacy is a human right and is essential for self-determined human development in regard to civic, political, social, economic, and cultural activities. It must be protected online, offline, in public spaces, at home and in the workplace. Every person must have the right to decide freely whether and in what manner he or she wants to receive information and communicate with others. The possibility of communicating anonymously must be ensured for everyone. The collection, retention, use and

whole debate in the Intergovernmental Drafting Group on Security was overly centered around the security language, so that no delegation wanted to insist strongly on privacy. Privacy was only later mentioned in the Summit Declaration due to the efforts of a few countries and political entities, including the European Union, Switzerland, Brazil, and Australia. It now calls for a "global culture of cyber-security," in particular for strengthening a "trust framework, including information security and network security, authentication, privacy and consumer protection." Here, privacy and security as well as authentication and consumer protection are seen as parts of a holistic strategy. Only "within this global culture of cyber-security, is [it] important to enhance security and to ensure the protection of data and privacy, while enhancing access and trade," the summit declaration continues. Privacy did not gain nearly such a prominent role as freedom of speech or other human rights.

Even the private sector itself had suggested more specific privacy language in the summit declaration. For example, the Coordinating Committee of Business Interlocutors, a committee that had been set up for the WSIS by the International Chamber of Commerce, had asked for "*effective* privacy protection of personal data."[684]

The Plan of Action that was also adopted by the Summit is generally vague. It was intended to facilitate the implementation of the principles espoused in the Declaration and provides concrete measurements of progression in the vision of the Information Society. Besides some initiatives like linking every school and library in the world to the Internet by 2015, there are no clearly defined benchmarks or schedules for implementation. The second phase of the Summit that ends in Tunis in November 2005 has not brought substantial progress here.

The paragraph of the Action Plan that deals with security and privacy does not mention the "war on terrorism," but is still mainly focused on security and makes an implicit reference to the Council of Europe's Cybercrime Convention. Of the 10 initiatives suggested by the action plan in the context of security and privacy, only one specifically mentions privacy, but only calls for "user education and awareness," specifically about "online privacy and the means of protecting

---

disclosure of personal data, no matter by whom, should remain under the control of and determined by the individual concerned." Crucial Issues for Privacy and Security Working Group, Geneva, September 22, 2003.

[684] Paragraph for the Declaration of Principles suggested by the Coordinating Committee of Business Interlocutors, August 27, 2003. Italics added.

privacy."[685] There is no reference to specific measures or initiatives governments or private corporations should take as the major users of personal information.

The second Summit phase mainly involves discussions on implementation and follow-up, financing, and Internet governance. The Working Group on Internet Governance (WGIG),[686] an independent body set up by the UN Secretary-General in November 2004 with a mandate from the Geneva WSIS Summit, was tasked with developing a report that defines "Internet governance," identifies related public policy issues, and develops a common understanding of the respective roles and responsibilities of the different stakeholders. The WGIG had a balanced membership from governments, the private sector, civil society, and international organizations. The group conducted regular open online and offline consultations and produced a number of draft "issue papers." One of these dealt with "consumer protection and privacy."[687] Its content included language like "while privacy is recognized as a human right, it is a right that balances the competing and legitimate interests of government and business to intrude upon privacy under law."[688]

The WSIS NGO coalition suggested including privacy as a key element of the WGIG's deliberations, because "in an 'Information Society,' where almost all attributes of an individual can be known, interactions mapped, and intentions assumed based on records, the need for protection of privacy is more crucial than ever."[689] Like many other stakeholders, the International Working Group on Data Protection in Telecommunications (IWGDPT)[690] also submitted input to the WGIG and referred to its "Ten Commandments to protect Privacy in the Internet World."[691]

---

685 "Governments, and other stakeholders, should actively promote user education and awareness about online privacy and the means of protecting privacy," WSIS Plan of Action, Para. 12 c).

686 <http://www.wgig.org>.

687 <http://www.wgig.org/docs/WP-Consumer.pdf>.

688 WGIG, Draft Issues Paper on Consumer, User Protection and Privacy, February 2005 <http://www.wgig.org/docs/WP-Consumer.pdf>.

689 Statement of the Civil Society Privacy and Security Working Group (PSWG) at PrepCom2, February 24, 2005 <http://www.itu.int/wsis/docs2/pc2/plenary/24feb-privacy.doc>. It should be noted that this was the first ever civil society intervention in the WSIS process that was read in Arabic. *See also* the PSWG comment to the WGIG issue paper on Cybersecurity and Cybercrime <http://www.wgig.org/docs/CommentWSIS-CS3.doc> and the two PSWG comments on Consumer Protection and Privacy <http://www.wgig.org/docs/CommentWSIS-CS1.doc> and <http://www.wgig.org/docs/CommentWSIS-CS2.doc>. All comments to the WGIG are available at <http://www.wgig.org>.

690 Home page <http://www.datenschutz-berlin.de/doc/int/iwgdpt/tc_en.htm>.

691 International Working Group on Data Protection in Telecommunications, Comments on WGIG Draft Issues Paper on Consumer, User Protection and Privacy, April 12, 2005, available at <http://www.wgig.org/docs/Letter-IWGDPT.pdf>.

The report of the WGIG was published on July 15, 2005.[692] While the centre of discussions had been around the unilateral control of core Internet resources by the US government, the report also deals with other Internet governance issues like interconnection costs, multilingual domain names, spam, and intellectual property rights. It contains a paragraph on data protection and privacy rights. The WGIG states that there is "a lack of national legislation and enforceable global standards for privacy and data-protection rights over the Internet," and recommends to the Summit to "encourage countries that lack privacy and/or personal data-protection legislation to develop clear rules and legal frameworks, with the participation of all stakeholders, to protect citizens against the misuse of personal data, particularly countries with no legal tradition in these fields." It also suggests a revision of the privacy policies for the WHOIS databases according to privacy legislation in the country of the registrar and the registrant, and the development of open technical proposals for privacy requirements for global electronic authentication systems. The WGIG recommends that "arrangements and procedures between national law enforcement agencies" should be "consistent with the appropriate protection of privacy, personal data and other human rights," and to "ensure that all measures taken in relation to the Internet, in particular those on grounds of security or to fight crime, do not lead to violations of human rights principles." The WGIG background report includes a lengthy paragraph on privacy that begins by stating that privacy "becomes even more important over the Internet, where the intrinsic nature of the Internet makes it possible to effectively track an individual in cyberspace and use information about him/her illegally or without authorization. Threats to personal privacy increase the mistrust towards the Internet."[693]

The outcomes of the WGIG will provide the basis for negotiations and decisions among governments for the second WSIS Summit meeting in Tunis in November 2005. The strong emphasis on privacy protection in the Working Group's report is an improvement compared to the Geneva Summit documents from 2003. However, the WGIG was not a negotiating body, and its report only makes recommendations to governments. The privacy and other human rights emphasis from this report might easily get lost before the Summit concludes, as the main focus, and the reason the Working Group was set up in the first place, is the international struggle around unilateral US government control over the Internet names and numbers authorities.

---

[692] <http://www.wgig.org/docs/WGIGREPORT.pdf>. Translations into all UN working languages are available at <http://www.wgig.org>.

[693] The Working Group on Internet Governance, Background Report, June 2005, Para 141 <http://www.wgig.org/docs/Background-Report.htm>.

Spy TV: Interactive Television & "T-Commerce"

The convergence of communications networks, computers and mass media into an interactive network combining television and the Internet is the next progression of the technology currently being developed. New boxes are replacing the traditional cable TV set-top box with an interactive device that also includes the functions of a limited personal computer and video recorder. At the same time, personal computers are regularly equipped with TV tuner cards to handle advanced video operations.

The designers of these new appliances paint a pleasant picture of the conveniences that will be available with these new systems. They anticipate that viewers will be able to make spur of the moment purchases through their boxes, based on what their favorite star is wearing or on an individually tailored ad that appears between shows. Communities will be formed as people chat live about the plots of their favorite shows or sporting events. Vast libraries of movies and shows will be available for renting on demand by simply pressing a button on the remote control. The industry calls this "T-Commerce" for Television Commerce.

Interactivity has been the dream of the television industry since the invention of the TV. For several decades, there have been a series of expensive tests that have failed because the technology has been crude and expensive.[694] The change that now makes Interactive Television (ITV) possible is the evolution of the Internet and the advancement of digital television. The protocols underlying the Internet are now being used to allow for interactive high-speed access over existing cable lines. More and more, intelligent cable TV boxes, which connect to broadband and interactive cable systems, are being deployed. Although efforts to attract sizable numbers of subscribers to ITV services have yet to yield outstanding results, experts expect the industry to boom in the near future. Recently, the major cable operators have shifted focus from advanced interactive services, such as access to stock quotes or viewer control of camera angles, to providing video-on-demand and digital video recording (DVR) services.[695]

Popular use of enhanced digital television services is currently limited to the United States and the United Kingdom, but experts expect other countries to join

---

[694] L. J. Davis, The Billionaire Shell Game: How Cable Baron John Malone and Assorted Corporate Titans Invented a Future Nobody Wanted (1998).

[695] *See* Jane Weaver, "Interactive TV Struggles to Connect," February 25, 2004) <http://www.msnbc.msn.com/id/3073178/>.

the growing tide in coming years.[696] Researchers predict that 20 percent of US households will own a DVR by 2006.[697] DVR devices allow users to peruse and rewind live television shows, while they automatically record television shows for viewers and make recommendations for new shows based on viewers' previous behavior. The new systems are being designed, like their Internet predecessors, to track every activity of users as they surf the net through the boxes. They also are being designed to track the shows and commercials users watch and to use that information to tailor advertising for the greatest effect.[698] CEO Rupert Murdoch said in the NewsCorp annual report, "It will tell us not only who our customers are, but what they buy, what they watch, what they read and what they want."[699] George Orwell's vision of the television that watches you will soon be a standard consumer appliance.

Microsoft inched one step closer to this vision in 2001 when it teamed with Predictive Networks to bring Microsoft TV to the mainstream. Microsoft TV is a software platform that can be used to run devices such as DVRs, set-top boxes, and gaming consoles, providing various interactive TV services. Predictive Networks specializes in personalization software – the collection of user behavior and viewing habits to create what they call "digital silhouettes" of users.[700] The combination of these technologies raises questions about the implications for privacy. Although Predictive Networks attempted to assuage these fears by insisting that the information gathered indicates little about a given user and that anonymous IDs can be kept separate from personal data by not retaining demographic information on the devices, the potential for invasions remains significant.[701]

Digital video recording company TiVo encountered a wave of criticism over its data-gathering practices after reporting that a certain Super Bowl clip was the most-watched moment since the inception of the service. Even though this particular report was based on aggregate information gathered according to postal zip codes, consumers voiced concern that personal information may be linked to

---

[696] Australian Market & Social Research Society, "The Future of Audience Measurement," June 2005 <http://www.mrsa.com.au/index.cfm?a=detail&id=1794&eid=112>.

[697] Id.

[698] See David Burke, Spy TV (Slab-O-Concrete Press 1999), available at <http://www.spyinteractive.com/spyinteractive/>.

[699] Cited in Privacy Journal, October 1999.

[700] <http://www.wbrtv.com/underwriters/predictive/>.

[701] See Michelle Delio, "MS TV: It'll Be Watching You," Wired News, December 11, 2001 <http://wired-vig.wired.com/news/privacy/0,1848,49028,00.html>.

the viewing habits of particular boxes or somehow leaked during transmission.[702] TiVo boxes collect information about user viewing habits, which is then transmitted to TiVo headquarters via phone lines. Although the data collected and transmitted by TiVo is stripped of any identifying information, the company could conceivably track individual habits if it chose to do so.

Even where systems are designed to not report this kind of information, there is increasing pressure from the content industries to build systems this way so that they can monitor viewer's habits and protect against copyright infringement. In 2001, SONICBlue Inc., the maker of Replay TV, a personal video recorder, was sued by the entertainment studios who argued that features allowing users to pause, fast forward, and skip commercials violated their copyrights. As part of the lawsuit, the studios requested all data that the company had on its customers viewing habits, including what shows were recorded, watched, and forwarded to friends. Because the ReplayTV 4000 product did not transmit this type of data back to the company, SONICBlue had no data to provide to the studios. It was, therefore, ordered by a court to re-engineer its product and install software to record TV usage data and transmit that data back to SONICBlue so that it could then be turned over to the studios. This order was overturned in May 2002, but the issue is likely to resurface.[703]

Unlike personal computers that give users control over their actions and choices, the new ITV systems are generally based on a sealed "black box" controlled by the company that gives the user little or no control. In the MSNTV (formerly WebTV) box, users are not able to refuse cookies and must request a special tool to view and delete cookies. The systems are closed and it is difficult for even advanced users to identify what the system is doing. It will also prevent users from being able to use their own software.

There are other significant differences in that the media is more top-down, and corporatized than the Internet, which is decentralized and allows nearly any user to set up his own Web site and become a content producer. In the past, many ITV providers described their systems as "closed gardens" that will only show content in which the providers have a financial interest. Moving away from this concept, UK satellite broadcaster Sky recently announced plans to introduce a new interactive TV portal that will allow greater access to interactive TV. The new portal lowers the barriers to entry by allowing publishers of sites to register and

---

[702] Ben Charney, "TiVo Watchers Uneasy after Post-Super Bowl Reports," CNet News.com, February 5, 2004) <http://news.com.com/2100-1041_3-5154219.html>.

[703] Paramount Pictures Corp., et al. v. ReplayTV, Inc. and SONICblue, Inc., United States District Court, Central District of California, Case No. 01-09358 FMC (Ex).

launch a site for no charge, opening up the possibilities for a wide range of online providers. For a fee, publishers will be able to promote their site on the portal and register a code to allow easy access to their site.[704]

Some video game consoles provide an Internet access functionality[705] that requires subscribers to register much of their personal information (name, address, telephone number, e-mail address, credit card number, etc.). The game console's hard disk also records all the games played and their patterns, names of all the players involved in a game, scores obtained, and other similar information, and transmits the data to the console manufacturer the next time the player connects. The next generation consoles (Xbox 360, PlayStation 3 and Nintendo Revolution) threaten to oust interactive TV set-top boxes from the center of home entertainment by offering, in addition to games, the same services as set-top boxes: personal video recorders (such as Tivo and ReplayTV), e-commerce, e-mail, web access, photo albums, DVDs, home movies and music.

In response to the growing popularity of digital television, the US Federal Communications Commission (FCC) attempted to regulate the use of digital content by adopting a broadcast flag mandate. The flag works by sending a set of status bits, or "flags," in a data stream of digital programming to compatible digital receivers that define the uses of the content. The flag may indicate that certain programming is not recordable, prevent skipping of commercials, or prohibit the program from being saved on digital video recorders.[706] The broadcast flag was set to go into effect by July 2005 but the District of Columbia Circuit Court struck it down, stating that the FCC exceeded its authority by creating this rule.[707]

Civil liberties advocates are critical of the broadcast flag because it creates strong incentives to use privacy-invasive copy protection to enforce the interests of the content industry. By tracking the viewing habits of a consumer, content providers may overstep the boundaries established by the Cable Communications Policy Act and the Video Privacy Protection Act. To address these concerns, advocates

---

[704] "Sky Opens Platform to Internet on Interactive TV," June 16, 2005
<http://informitv.com/articles/2005/06/16/skyopensplatform/>.

[705] *E.g.*, Microsoft Xbox Live system and Sony PlayStation 2 online access module.

[706] *See generally* Declan McCullagh, "Court Yanks Down FCC's Broadcast Flag," CNet News, May 6, 2005 <http://news.com.com/Court+says+FCCs+broadcast+flag+is+toast/2100-1030_3-5697719.html> (discussing the broadcast flag and the recent court decision).

[707] American Library Assoc'n v. FCC, 406 F.3d 689 (D.C. Cir. 2005).

called for incorporation of privacy requirements into the mandate.[708] Because the FCC's rule was ultimately struck down, the repercussions on personal privacy have yet to surface. However, most digital receivers are currently outfitted with this technology and the possibility remains that Congress will grant the FCC the authority to create this regulation or that a higher court will overturn the ruling.

Genetic Privacy

Genetic data poses unique privacy issues because it can serve as an identifier and can also convey sensitive personal information. Not only does genetic information provide something like a fingerprint through variations in genetic sequences; it also provides a growing amount of information about genetic diseases and predispositions.

Errors in the genetic code are responsible for an estimated 3,000 to 4,000 hereditary diseases, including Huntington's disease, cystic fibrosis, neurofibromatosis, and Duchenne muscular dystrophy. Furthermore, altered genes are now known to play a role in cancer, heart disease, diabetes, and many other common diseases. In these more common and complex disorders, genetic alterations increase a person's risk of developing that disorder. The disease itself results from the interaction of such genetic predispositions and environmental factors, including diet and lifestyle.[709]

In addition to indicating predisposition to disease, "genes do appear to influence behavior."[710] Although the findings are controversial and far from conclusive, genes have been found to influence homosexuality, thrill-seeking and tendencies towards violent criminal behavior.[711] Twin and adoption studies have shown that "nearly all behaviors that have been studied show moderate to high inheritability – usually to a somewhat greater degree than do many common physical diseases."[712]

---

[708] *See* Comments of the Electronic Privacy Information Center, *In re* Digital Broadcast Copy Protection before the Federal Communications Commission, December 6, 2002 (No. 02-230), available at <http://www.epic.org/privacy/drm/broadcastflagcomments.html>.

[709] "Understanding Our Genetic Inheritance," National Human Genome Research Institute, <http://www.genome.gov/10001477>.

[710] Leroy Hood and Lee Rowen, "Genes, Genomes, and Society," Genetic Secrets: Protecting Privacy and Confidentiality in the Genetic Era, Edited by Mark A. Rothstein 27 (Yale University Press 1997).

[711] *Id.*

[712] Peter McGuffin, Brien Riley, Robert Plomin, "Genomics and Behavior: Toward Behaviorial Genomics," Science 291 (5507): 1232, available at <http://www.sciencemag.org/cgi/content/full/291/5507/1232>.

The prevailing scientific opinion is that most behavior and human diseases are not the result of a single mutation or gene. Rather, most facets of human development "represent the culmination of lifelong interactions between our genome and the environment."[713] Currently, available scientific knowledge does not seem to provide a strong link between an individual's genetic sequence and that person's eventual development of disease or personality traits; such conclusions are matters of probability and must be interpreted accordingly.

However, it is an area of scientific development that is undergoing rapid change and the body of knowledge about the human genome is increasing rapidly. The human genome sequence was published in February 2001, immediately kicking off a debate of the future of genetic technology and its impact on society – including privacy.[714] For example, United States Senators James M. Jeffords and Tom Daschle have commented, "[o]ne of the most difficult issues is determining the proper balance between privacy concerns and fair use of genetic information."[715]

Both the general public and scientific researchers have recognized that safeguards for genetic information are needed. For example, polls have found that 86 percent of adults believe that doctors should ask permission before conducting any genetic testing and 93 percent believe that researchers should do the same before any analysis.[716] Dr. Francis S. Collins, Director of the National Human Genome Research Institute, has observed that "in genetics research studies, we are seeing individuals who opt not to participate in research because of their fear that this information could fall into the wrong hands and be used to deny them a job or a promotion."[717] Privacy concerns about genetic testing are heightened by the potential that test results may be inaccurate because of quality control problems in testing laboratories. A 1999 survey of genetic testing

---

[713] Leena Peltonen and Victor A. McKusick, "Genomics and Medicine: Dissecting Human Disease in the Postgenomic Era," Science 291 (5507): 1224, available at <http://www.sciencemag.org/cgi/content/full/291/5507/1224>.

[714] Genome Landmark, Science <http://www.sciencemag.org/feature/plus/sfg/special/index.shtml>.

[715] James M. Jeffords and Tom Daschle, "Policy Issues: Political Issues in the Genome Era," Science 291 (5507): 1249, available at <http://www.sciencemag.org/cgi/content/full/291/5507/1249>.

[716] "Public Attitudes Toward Medical Privacy," conducted by the Gallup Poll for the Institute for Health Freedom, September 2000 <http://www.forhealthfreedom.org/Gallupsurvey/IHF-Gallup.html>.

[717] Testimony of Francis S. Collins, M.D., Ph.D., Director, National Human Genome Research Institute, National Institutes of Health, Testimony Before the Health, Education, Labor, and Pensions Committee, United States Senate, Hearing on Genetic Information in the Workplace, July 20, 2000 <http://www.genome.gov/10001380>.

facilities found that of the 245 laboratories examined, 36 failed to meet high quality assurance standards.[718]

Genetic Identification

Each person's DNA, with the exception of identical twins, is different from that of every other human being.[719] DNA identification, therefore, works by comparing particular regions of two sequences and looking for differences rather than similarities. Identification is actually a process of combining several such comparisons and calculating the probability that the two sequences are a false match.

Reliable identification requires that samples be handled carefully to prevent contamination, that a sufficient number of segments be compared, and that laboratory technicians meet an appropriately high threshold for acceptable probability of a chance match. "Provided that tests are actually looking at different regions of the genome, and provided that the genetic patterns aren't 'structured' within a community by inbreeding, using multiple tests can reduce the chance of a false match from one in a hundred to one in a million or even one in 500 million. But they can't entirely eliminate the chance of a false match."[720] In the United States, the standard for forensic identification requires a comparison of 13 DNA segments.[721] According to an FBI spokesman, "[t]here's a greater chance that you'll find a close match as the databases get bigger."[722] Besides false matches, some criminals have reportedly become savvier at manipulating results of DNA identification by wearing gloves, masks, and condoms in an attempt to avoid leaving behind any bodily fluids or other evidence at crime scenes.[723] In England, a police union has stopped officers from

---

[718] Margaret M. McGovern, MD, PhD; Marta O. Benach; Sylvan Wallenstein; Robert J. Desnick, PhD, MD; Richard Keenlyside, MD, MS, "Quality Assurance in Molecular Genetic Testing Laboratories," Journal of the American Medical Association, Volume 281 No. 9, March 3, 1999, at 835-40, available at <http://jama.ama-assn.org/cgi/content/full/281/9/835>.

[719] "Commission on DNA Technology in Forensic Science," National Research Council, DNA Technology in Forensic Science 9 (1992), available at <http://books.nap.edu/books/0309045878/html/>; Simson Garfinkel, Database Nation: The Death of Privacy in the 21st Century, 49 (O'Reilly 2000).

[720] Simson Garfinkel, Database Nation: The Death of Privacy in the 21st Century, 49 (O'Reilly 2000).

[721] "DNA Forensics," US Department of Energy, Human Genome Project Information <http://www.ornl.gov/sci/techresources/Human_Genome/elsi/forensics.shtml>.

[722] Rebecca Pollard, "Crime Genes: A DNA Mismatch Raises Fears," ABCNews.com, June 19, 2000 <http://www.techreview.com/articles/00/05/benchmarks60500.asp?p=0>; Richard Willing, "Mismatch Calls DNA Tests into Question," USA Today, February 8, 2000.

[723] Richard Willing, "Criminals Try to Outwit DNA," USA Today, August 28, 2000, available at <http://www.fairfaxidlab.com/html/news.html>.

giving voluntary DNA samples in a sweep to catch a rapist, although policemen's fingerprints are routinely included in forensic fingerprint databases.[724]

Law enforcement agencies worldwide are increasingly relying upon DNA evidence. According to the 2002 global survey by Interpol, 77 of its 179 member countries perform DNA analysis and 41 member countries have forensic DNA databanks, which include both physical samples and databases of DNA profiles.[725] As of 2003, 36 of 46 European Interpol members perform forensic DNA testing, and 26 of them allow international exchange of information.[726] The percentage of members having DNA databanks is predicted to double in the next few years.

To facilitate the exchange of DNA information between member states, Interpol set up a DNA database pilot project in July 2003. Profiles are sent to Interpol in standardized numeric format and additional information such as name of the individual or the crime to which the individual is connected, is not required. If a match is found when searches are performed, police forces of the two countries communicate directly. The first "hit" on the Interpol database was recorded in 2004 when one of the DNA profiles submitted by the Slovenian authorities was matched against a profile sent to Interpol by the Croatian police.[727]

The United Kingdom has the largest forensic DNA databank in the world, which has expanded from 750,000 records in 2000 to more than 2.9 million records in 2005.[728] Since April 4, 2004, those who have been arrested but not charged are also included in the databank, as are those arrested for drunk driving, even if not convicted.[729] In fact, a 13-year old schoolgirl was arrested in early 2005 for throwing a snowball at a police car, and as part of the arrest the girl's DNA profile was recorded, and it will remain in the National DNA Database for the rest of her life.[730] In a recent decision, the House of Lords ruled that the law permitting retention of DNA samples taken from individuals, who are later

---

[724] DNA Resource Report, May 21, 2004.

[725] Interpol, "Global DNA Inquiry Results 2002"
<http://www.interpol.int/Public/Forensic/dna/inquiry/default.asp>.

[726] Christopher H. Asplen, "International Perspectives on Forensic DNA Databases," ISRCL Conference, The Hague, August 24-28, 2003.

[727] Interpol, "First Hit From Interpol DNA Database"
<http://www.interpol.int/Public/News/dna20040505.asp>.

[728] Tom Wall, "A Simple Prank by a 13-year-old. Now Her Genetic Records Are on the National DNA Database for ever: Britain Commands Greater Powers than any Other State to Obtain, Use and Store Genetic Information," New Statesman, April 25, 2005.

[729] <http://www.thepublican.com/cgi-bin/item.cgi?id=12959&d=32&h=24&f=23&dateformat=%25o%20%25B%20%25Y>.

[730] Tom Wall, *supra.*

acquitted or against whom charges are dropped, does not violate the European Convention on Human Rights.[731] A pilot project is also underway in the British city of Bristol to collect DNA samples from 25,000 babies and their parents as part of a national DNA database that could be used for law enforcement.[732] Several Australian states have been considering laws that would permit the creation of a national DNA database.[733] Israel has also been considering such a database.[734]

The rules for inclusion in forensic DNA databanks and the rules that govern access to data, physical specimen retention, and privacy protections differ from country to country. In countries that operate under federal systems, such as the United States and Australia, rules for forensic DNA databanks can vary from jurisdiction to jurisdiction. Several European nations have expanded their databanks by including new categories of offenses (*e.g.*, burglaries) or classes of offenders (*e.g.*, violent offenders). Additionally, some nations include profiles of suspects or arrestees, either based on the crime for which they are arrested or based on the length of expected sentence if convicted. Some nations, however, remove or expunge these profiles or underlying samples, but there are nations that do not. For example, UK maintains all samples and profiles indefinitely.[735] In contrast to UK, some European countries have taken steps to further protect and limit the use of any genetic data they collect. In Sweden, the state only maintains genetic data for criminals who have spent more than two years in prison, while Norway only maintains data on serious offenders and requires a court order for such retention.[736] Germany also requires that the government obtain a court order and limits their genetic data to individuals convicted of certain specific offenses and are deemed likely to re-offend.[737]

In 2005, the Japanese National Police Agency also began using DNA data obtained from blood samples and bodily fluids collected at crime scenes to help

---

[731] Regina v. Chief Constable of South Yorkshire Police (Respondent) *ex parte* LS (by his mother and litigation friend JB) (FC) (Appellant) and Regina v. Chief Constable of South Yorkshire Police (Respondent) *ex parte* Marper (FC)(Appellant) Consolidated Appeals, [2004] UKHL 39, July 22, 2004, available at <http://www.publications.parliament.uk/pa/ld200304/ldjudgmt/jd040722/york-1.htm>.

[732] Alfred Lee, "Britain Compiles National DNA Database," May 17, 2004 <http://straitstimes.asia1.com.sg/techscience/story/0,4386,251325,00.html>.

[733] "Concern over Proposed DNA Databases," Australian Broadcasting Corporation (ABC) Online, January 24, 2000 <http://web.archive.org/web/20040205071008/http://www.abc.net.au/worldtoday/s95485.htm>; Stewart Taggart, "DNA Testing Furor in Wee Waa," Wired News, April 18, 2000 <http://www.wired.com/news/print/0,1294,35727,00.html>.

[734] "Cabinet Favors DNA Database," IsraelINN.com, June 28, 2004.

[735] Asplen, *supra*.

[736] Tom Wall, *supra*.

[737] *Id.*

in the identification of criminal suspects.[738] Prior to the system's implementation, DNA taken from suspects was considered to be personal information and all samples were destroyed at the completion of criminal investigations. With this new database, however, the government has stated the importance of this new technology as a possible replacement to fingerprints in identifying criminal suspects.[739]

In the United States, trends are also toward the expansion of forensic DNA databases. As of January 2005, each of the 50 states has a DNA database of some kind, and each collects and enters information regarding all persons convicted of sex crimes, and 38 states also collect the genetic profiles of all felons.[740] In the US, judges and courts have issued warrants,[741] indictments[742] and even convictions[743] based solely on DNA identification. In the UK, a man was found and charged on the basis of a family member's DNA found in the country's DNA databank.[744]

Along with the expanded use of DNA evidence around the world, there has also been an expanded amount of criticism for some of the methods used to collect samples. The University of Nebraska, in September 2004, released a report examining the use and effectiveness of DNA "dragnets" or "sweeps" in the US.[745] The report focused on 18 instances where police asked individuals to give voluntary DNA samples in order to identify the perpetrator of a crime or series of crimes. The report found that of the 18 instances where "sweeps" were employed, in only one case was the DNA evidence used to identify the perpetrator of the crime. Therefore, the report concluded that DNA "sweeps," although becoming increasingly common, are extremely unproductive in identifying criminal suspects.[746]

---

[738] "NPA brings DNA database online," Daily Yomiuri (Tokyo), December 17, 2004.

[739] "DNA Resource Report January 14, 2005," DNAresource.com, January 14, 2005.

[740] State DNA Databases Laws: Qualifying Offenses, available at <http://www.dnaresource.com/Table%20of%20State%%202004.pdf>; see also Applied Biosystems, Violent Crime Requirements, available at http://www.dnaresource.com/Murder,%20Assault%20&%20Battery%20Map.pdf; see also Applied Biosystems, All Felons Requirements, available at <http://www.dnaresource.com/All-Felons%20Map.pdf>.

[741] Richard Willing, "Police Expand DNA Use: Charge Man with Rape Using only Genetic Profile," USA Today, October 25, 2000.

[742] Michael Luo, "Unnamed Man Indicted by DNA: Suffolk DA Charges Suspect in 6 South Shore Rapes," Newsday, August 9, 2000.

[743] Bruce Hight, "DNA Can Carry Conviction," Austin-American Statesman, April 14, 2000.

[744] Shaoni Bhattacharya, "Killer Convicted thanks to Relative's DNA," New Scientist, April 20, 2004, <http://www.newscientist.com/news/news.jsp?id=ns99994908>.

[745] "A National Survey of DNA 'Sweeps,' " University of Nebraska at Omaha, Department of Criminal Justice, September 2004, available at <http://www.policeaccountability.org/dnareport.pdf>.

[746] Id.

DNA identification is also used in order to exonerate persons where post-conviction DNA testing of evidence can yield conclusive proof of innocence. One of the best-known efforts in this field is the Innocence Project. This clinical law program provides legal assistance to persons who are challenging their convictions based on DNA evidence. As of June 2005, 159 individuals have been exonerated as a result of the work by the Innocence Project.[747] Based on the proportion of cases that have been overturned and related FBI data, the Innocence Project estimates that thousands of individuals who have been wrongly convicted could be freed if provided with easier access to DNA testing.[748] Due to the success of the Innocence Project, similar programs have now been established in 43 states.[749]

Despite the recognition of limitations in DNA-based identification, there is a push for more and larger DNA databases. Forensic DNA databases, originally created for tracking violent sex offenders, have expanded in purpose and scope. "In less than a decade, we have gone from collecting DNA from convicted sex offenders – on the theory that they are likely to be recidivists and that they frequently leave biological evidence – to data banks of all violent offenders; to juvenile offenders in 29 states; to testing of persons who have been arrested, but not convicted of a crime," according to Barry Steinhardt, Associate Director of the American Civil Liberties Union.[750] In the United States, local, state and federal law enforcement agencies contribute DNA profiles from crime scenes and from those convicted of violent crimes into a national database in order to look for potential matches.[751] In April 2003, the Bush Administration also proposed adding DNA profiles from juvenile offenders and from adults who had been arrested but not convicted to the FBI's national DNA database.[752] The White House also indicated it would spend about USD 1 billion over five years to promote the use of DNA for law enforcement purposes.[753]

---

[747] Data from the Innocence Project <http://www.innocenceproject.org/>.

[748] *Id.*

[749] "The Innocence Project: Other Projects by States" <http://www.innocenceproject.org/about/other_projects.php>.

[750] Testimony of Barry Steinhardt, Associate Director of the American Civil Liberties Union, Before the House Judiciary Committee, Subcommittee on Crime, March 23, 2000, available at <http://web.archive.org/web/20030905040952/archive.aclu.org/congress/l032300a.html>.

[751] FBI Press Room, Press Release, October 13, 1998, DNA Index, available at <http://www.fbi.gov/pressrel/pressrel02/ndis061402.htm>.

[752] Richard Willing, "White House Seeks to Expand DNA Database," USA Today, April 15, 2003.

[753] *Id.*

Other, non-law enforcement related DNA databases have also emerged for use in identification. Since the early 1990s, all personnel serving in the United States Armed Forces have been required to submit DNA samples to possibly be used for later identification. As of May 2003, the United States military's DNA depository contained 3.8 million samples, including samples from active duty and reserve personnel and some military contractors.[754] Pursuant to a 1996 Department of Defense Directive,[755] individuals also have the right to request their samples be destroyed at the end of their term of service.[756] However, the overall program has faced resistance within the military's own ranks. In 1996, two United States Marines faced court-martials when they refused to provide DNA samples for the identification program.[757]

In addition to government-related DNA identification, a new industry – paternity testing – has emerged, and is placing large amounts of genetic data wholly under private sector control. Despite the controversy surrounding law enforcement collection of DNA, a larger proportion of genetic identification is performed to establish paternity. In the United States, part of the reason for the rise in paternity DNA testing has been the introduction of federal laws requiring the identification of fathers in order to receive child support.[758] Additionally, although paternity testing previously required blood samples and was difficult to perform, tests currently in use require only a few strands of hair.[759]

Detection and Treatment of Disease

Advances in technology have also made genetic testing easier and faster. According to genetic testing companies, kits costing USD 100 to USD 2,000 are available for more than 400 diseases with hundreds more on the way.[760] The easy

---

[754] Armed Forces Institute of Pathology, "Armed Forces Repository of Specimen Samples for the Identification of Remains" <http://www.afip.org/Departments/oafme/dna/afrssir/>.

[755] Department of Defense Directive 5154.30 of October 28, 1996, superseded by Department of Defense Directive 5154.30 of March 18, 2003.

[756] Armed Forces Institute of Pathology, "Request for Specimen Destruction" <http://www.afip.org/Departments/oafme/dna/afrssir/destruction.html>. "Will DNA Identification End Unknown Soldier Tradition?" Associated Press, May 29, 1998, available at <http://www.onlineathens.com/1998/052998/0529.a3soldier.html>.

[757] Neil A. Lewis, "2 Marines who Refused to Comply with Genetic-testing Order Face a Court-Martial," New York Times, April 13, 1996.

[758] Genelex: The Paternity DNA Testing Site, "Chapter 4: DNA in Parentage Testing, Updated for the Web Edition," April 2000 <http://www.genelex.com/paternitytesting/paternitybook4.html>.

[759] DNAnow.com, "Frequently Asked Questions," <http://www.dnanow.com/faq.html>.

[760] Lisa M. Krieger, "Genetic Testing Leaps ahead of Social Implications," San Jose Mercury News, July 3, 2001, available at

---

availability of these tests vastly increases the amount of information at an individual's disposal. However, it is important to remember that for disorders that involve the interaction between multiple genes and various environmental and lifestyle factors, the links between genes and their corresponding disease are not well understood. Genetic information may provide some indication of vulnerability, but it is not possible to say whether a specific individual will develop the disease, when the disease might develop, or how severe it may become. For example, the Washington Post reported in 2003 that researchers identified a gene responsible for the development of depression after exposure to extreme stress. People with a variation in the identified gene are more than twice as likely as people with the normal version of the gene to react to a traumatic event by becoming depressed. Nevertheless, 57 percent of people with the mutated gene never became depressed and 17 percent of people without the mutation developed depression in response to similar events.[761]

Several countries, such as Iceland and Estonia are building nationwide DNA databases for medical research. Many of these undertakings are encouraged by pharmaceutical companies and other business enterprises hoping to profit from new medical procedures and services. Some efforts have been made to establish legal frameworks for these databanks.[762] Nevertheless, Iceland's Supreme Court ruled in the spring of 2004 that the Health Database Act of 1998, which created the national DNA databank, does not comply with the country's constitutional privacy protections.[763]

In March 2005, the UK Human Genetics Commission released its report on profiling of newborns, after receiving a reference from the UK government to look into including every newborn's genome in a national health database.[764] The commission found that although genetic profiling is feasible and likely to become available commercially in less than 20 years, some steps must be taken in order to prevent any possible misuse of the information derived from it.[765]

<http://web.archive.org/web/20011118081116/http://www.siliconvalley.com/docs/news/depth/gene070301.htm>.

[761] Shankar Vedantam, "Variation in One Gene Linked to Depression," Washington Post, July 18, 2003, Page A1 <http://www.washingtonpost.com/ac2/wp-dyn?pagename=article&contentId=A8672-2003Jul17&notFound=true>.

[762] See, e.g., Iceland Act on Bio Banks.

763 Icelandic Supreme Court, Case No. 151/2003, Ragnhildur Gudmundsdóttir v. The State of Iceland, November 27, 2003, <http://www.mannvernd.is/english/lawsuits/Icelandic_Supreme_Court_Verdict_151_2003.pdf>.

[764] "Profiling the Newborn: A Prospective Gene Technology?" UK Human Genetics Commission, March 2005 <http://www.hgc.gov.uk/UploadDocs/Contents/Documents/Final%20Draft%20of%20Profiling%20Newborn%20Report%2003%2005.pdf>.

[765] Id.

Additionally, although the commission also expressed the need to develop a program of research to identify the full costs and potential benefits of genetic profiling, they also indicated that the program was not ready to be implemented as part of a national health screening program.[766]

While genetic screening has become easier and cheaper, treatment of genetic disease lags behind. Thus, while someone may have the ability to determine if they are at high-risk of disease, many people may choose not to find out due to the inability to take any precautionary measures. The concept of a "right not to know" would apply in these situations, allowing a person to control the knowledge about whether she has a certain genetic predisposition.

For example, Huntington's disease is an inherited neurological disease that results in death by a person's in their late 30s or early 40s after a period of extended deterioration of both mental and physical control. Although there is no treatment for the condition, a reliable test for Huntington's does exist. The inheritability of the disease is straightforward, as demonstrated by the fact that children of a person with Huntington's will have a 50 percent chance of also being affected. The resistance to knowing one's propensity for Huntington's is evident in surveys finding that only 66 percent of those at risk of developing the disease would test themselves, with 15 percent of that group indicating they would contemplate suicide if they tested positive. Of those indicating that they would not want to test themselves, 30 percent indicated they would consider suicide if they did find out that they would manifest the disease.[767] Due to the emotional and psychological impact that such information would have, many people in these situations exercise their "right not to know" by refusing to test themselves.

In practice, maintaining a "right not to know" can be difficult. Due to the simple inheritability of Huntington's, one family member's decision to test herself for the disease will reveal information about other family members. For example, if a daughter decides to test herself for Huntington's due to a history of the disease through her mother's side of the family, the test results would indicate whether or not her mother also has the disease – thus compromising the mother's desire not to know.[768]

---

[766] *Id.*

[767] Office of Technology Assessment (OTA): Genetic monitoring and screening in the workplace, OTA-BA-455 (Washington, United States Government Printing Office, October 1990), p. 13. (As cited in Conditions of Work Digest, "Workers' privacy III: Testing in the workplace," (International Labour Office 1993), at 66.)

[768] *See* Margaret R. McLean, "When What We Know Outstrips What We Can Do," Markkula Center for Applied Ethics, Issues in Ethics - V. 9, N. 2, available at
<http://www.scu.edu/SCU/Centers/Ethics/publications/iie/v9n2/outstrips.html>; Sally Lehrman, "Predictive

More problematic than the inability to properly interpret genetic test results is the possibility that individuals will not be able to control when genetic testing is conducted or how the results are used. The two most controversial areas of genetic testing are in the workplace and in the provision of medical and life insurance.

In the Workplace

As genetic databases become more common worldwide, there has been a concurrent rise in the use of testing by employers. Although there are legitimate uses of genetic testing, such as the prevention of occupational diseases, there is also concern that employers will use these tests to discriminate against current or potential employees. Without legal intervention, information indicating, for example, whether someone is prone to a debilitating illness or even an "undesirable" condition (such as laziness or depression) may be used by employers to discriminate against employees.

Genetic screening in the workplace has been conducted for decades but, based on limited polling of employers, still seems relatively rare when compared to general medical information accessed by employers. Some of the earliest genetic screening took place as early as the 1960s. Dow Chemical conducted genetic monitoring (genetic tests conducted over time to detect possible mutagenic effects of the workplace environment) from 1964-1977.[769] In 1982, a United States federal government survey found that 1.6 percent of companies were using genetic testing for employment purposes.[770]

Despite the uncertainty about how commonly workplace genetic testing takes place, it has happened. In 1994, employees at the Lawrence Berkeley National Laboratory at the University of California at Berkeley discovered the laboratory's surreptitious practice of testing its employee blood and urine samples for syphilis, sickle cell anemia and pregnancy.[771] The laboratory, funded by the

---

Genetic Testing: Do You Really Want to Know Your Future?" DNA Files, November 1998, available at <http://www.dnafiles.org/about/pgm4/topic.html>.

[769] United States Congress, Office of Technology Assessment, "Genetic Monitoring and Screening in the Workplace" 44-45 (1990); "Are Your Genes Right for Your Job?" 3 Cal Law 25, 27 (May 1983). (As cited in Employee Privacy Law, ed. L. Camille Hébert, (West Group 2000) § 12:03.)

[770] United States Congress, Office of Technology Assessment, "The Role of Genetic Testing in the Prevention of Occupational Diseases" 33-35 (1983); United States Congress, Office of Technology Assessment, "Genetic Monitoring and Screening in the Workplace" 173-177 (1990).

[771] Dana Hawkins, "A Bloody Mess at One Federal Lab: Officials May Have Secretly Checked Staff for Syphilis, Pregnancy, and Sickle Cell," United States News and World Report, June 23, 1997.

United States Department of Energy, conducted non-classified research and had been testing its employees for decades.[772] In subsequent litigation, the government argued that since its employees had agreed to a general medical examination, they had no reason to expect that genetic testing would not be conducted. The government also argued that notice was provided via a list of tests to be conducted that was posted on an examining room wall. Although the government won in the federal district court, the US Court of Appeals for the Ninth Circuit reversed and concluded the conditions being tested for raised "the highest expectations of privacy."[773] In 2000, the laboratory settled with employees for USD 2.2 million, ceased conducting the tests and allowed earlier test results to be reviewed and deleted.

More recently, in February 2001, an employee of the Burlington Northern Santa Fe Railroad in the United States sued the company for conducting tests for a genetic predisposition associated with carpal tunnel syndrome. The company had allegedly collected blood samples from 125 employees and tested 18 of those samples without employee consent. The employee filing the suit had refused to contribute a blood sample and was told he would be investigated. The lawsuit alleged violation of disability law and existing legal prohibitions on genetic testing by employers.[774]

The European Group on Ethics in Science and New Technologies (EGE) published an opinion in 2003, detailing the ethical aspects of workplace genetic testing.[775] As a general rule, the report recommends that employers consider a potential employee's current health situation and not on attempts to predict future health. Additionally, the report does recognize certain "exceptional cases" where the health and safety of third parties must be protected, and prescribes a set of "stringent conditions" for such screening. Among the conditions set forth in the report is the need for documented validity of the test used, informed consent of the individual, and protection of the confidentiality of the genetic information

---

[772] Even more shocking was the practice of the research facility to test certain minority employees for particular traits. For example, while all new hires were tested for syphilis, only African-American and Latino employees were re-tested during subsequent medical examinations. Only one Caucasian employee was repeatedly tested for syphilis; he was married to an African-American woman. African-American employees were also repeatedly tested for sickle cell anemia although one test is normally sufficient.

[773] Norman-Bloodsaw v. Lawrence Berkeley Laboratory, 135 F.3d 1260, 1269-70 (9th Cir. 1996). See also L. Camille Hébert, Employee Privacy Law § 12.07 (West Group 2000); "Court Declares Right to Genetic Privacy," United States News and World Report, February 16, 1998 <http://www.usnews.com/usnews/letters/articles/980216/archive_003212.htm>.

[774] Dana Hawkins, "The Dark Side of Genetic Testing: Railroad Workers Allege Secret Sampling," United States News, February 19, 2001.

[775] European Group on Ethics in Science and New Technologies, "Ethical Aspects of Genetic Testing in the Workplace," July 28, 2003 <http://europa.eu.int/comm/european_group_ethics/docs/avis18EN.pdf>.

itself, which should be provided only to an independent health professional and not to the employer.[776]

Insurance

While often tied to workplace genetic testing in the US, where employers often provide and pay for health insurance, genetic testing has also been directly used in the underwriting of life and medical insurance. In February 2001, Norwich Union Life, one of Britain's largest insurers, admitted using genetic tests for breast and ovarian cancer and Alzheimer's disease to evaluate applicants. Moreover, Norwich Union Life was violating the industry's code of conduct since the genetic tests had not been approved by the government's Human Genetics Commission.[777] The controversial practice resulted in some individuals paying higher insurance premiums based on genetic predispositions, creating political pressure to outlaw the use of genetic data by insurers in the United Kingdom altogether.[778]

While representatives of Norwich Union Life claimed that the genetic tests were not compulsory, simply providing lower premiums for people that do not test positive for genetic tests can lead to rampant genetic testing. An "assessment spiral" will result when one company offers discounts for those with a particular genetic profile, creating pressure on competitors to offer similar discounts in order to keep "low-risk" policy holders and resulting in higher premiums for those that are not tested or do not possess the correct genetic make-up.[779] Thus, non-compulsory genetic testing can easily lead to genetic discrimination.

Some insurance companies, however, have taken steps to embrace the science of genetic testing while ensuring a patient's privacy. Aetna, one of the largest insurance companies in the US, recommended in 2002 that the health care industry "support legislation and consider adopting guidelines for access to genetic counseling, genetic testing and the appropriate use of test results."[780] As part of his recommendations, Dr. Rowe, Chairman and CEO of Aetna, encouraged health plans to support legislation that would prohibit the

---

[776] *Id.*

[777] Melissa Kite, "Insurance Firm Admits Using Genetic Screening," Times, February 8, 2001.

[778] T. R. Reid, "Britain Moves to Ban Insurance Gene Tests," Washington Post, April 30, 2001.

[779] *See* Mark A. Rothstein, "Genetic Secrets: A Policy Framework," Genetic Secrets: Protecting Privacy and Confidentiality in the Genetic Era, Edited by Mark A. Rothstein (Yale University Press 1997), at 469-70.

[780] "Aetna Recommends Guidelines for Access to Genetic Testing," June 17, 2002
<http://www.aetna.com/news/2002/pr_20020617.htm>

establishment of rules for health coverage eligibility based on genetic testing, prohibit requesting genetic testing results as a condition to providing health insurance coverage, prohibit the use of genetic testing for risk selection or risk classification purposes in providing health coverage, and prohibit the disclosure of genetic testing results that may come into an insurance company's possession without member authorization.[781]

In Canada, however, recent articles have brought to light the issue that privacy and human rights legislations offer only limited protection to insurance applicants.[782] Many insurance companies have begun to request that individuals consent to having their health information verified and possibly even shared with other insurers through the Medical Information Bureau (MIB). The Canadian Genetics and Life Insurance Task Force recently convened, however, in an attempt to create a voluntary moratorium or voluntary agreement on the use of genetic information by insurers.[783]

Legal Safeguards

Recognizing the issues implicated in widespread genetic testing, several international bodies have recommended that genetic testing be carefully circumscribed by law. In 1989, the European Parliament issued a resolution recommending legislation to prohibit genetic testing for the purposes of selecting workers or examining employees without their consent. It advised that employees must be informed of any analysis and implications of genetic data before tests are carried out and allowed to withdraw from testing at any time.[784] The Council of Europe has also recommended that "the admission to, or the continued exercise of . . . employment, should not be made dependent on the undergoing of tests or screening."[785] Similarly, the World Medical Association (WMA) has issued statements to this effect. In 1992, issuing a Declaration on the Human Genome Project, it recommended the adoption of laws similar to those that prohibit "the use of race discrimination in employment or insurance."[786] In October 2002, it

---

[781] *Id.*

[782] Yann Joly, "Focus on Privacy Law," Lawyers Weekly, July 1, 2005.

[783] *Id.*

[784] European Parliament, "Resolution on the Ethical and Legal Problems of Genetic Engineering," O.J., No. C.96, April 17, 1989.

[785] Council of Europe, Committee of Ministers: Recommendation No. R(92)3 on Genetic Testing and Screening for Heath Care Purposes, Principle 6 (a)
<http://web.archive.org/web/20040229042552/http://cm.coe.int/ta/rec/1992/92r3.htm>.

[786] *See* International Labour Office, Conditions of Work Digest: Worker's Privacy Part II: Monitoring and Surveillance in the Workplace (1993) 12(1).

announced that it had adopted guidelines on the development of centralized health storage databases that addressed "the issues of privacy, consent, individual access and accountability."[787] In 1997, the United Nations Educational, Scientific and Cultural Organization (UNESCO) adopted a Universal Declaration on the Human Genome and Human Rights, outlining the rights of individuals to control the collection and use of genetic information.[788] More recently, the Article 29 Data Protection Working Party of the European Commission has further defined the appropriate safeguards that should be implemented with regard to the processing of genetic data.[789] The European Commission recognized the importance of genetic data in safeguarding a person's health and in pursuing scientific research, but also stressed the need for the creation of national rules in accordance with data protection principles established by the EU Data Protection Directive. These principles should "render the blanket implementation of mass genetic screening unlawful," and would attach special importance to the management, destruction, and anonymization of a person's sample after the information is obtained.[790]

In many cases, existing labor codes may indirectly prohibit genetic testing.[791] It is also possible that the use of genetic data by employers to discriminate against workers may violate equal opportunity or anti-discrimination laws. In the United States, for example, genetic testing may violate the 1964 Civil Rights Act that prohibits discrimination in employment on the basis of "race, sex, national origin, and religion," or the Americans with Disabilities Act of 1990, which prohibits discrimination in employment against a "qualified individual with a disability."[792]

Local and national governments are also beginning to address genetic privacy issues directly. In the United States, most laws applying to genetic discrimination, testing or identification have been passed by states rather than the federal government. Some states have passed laws that prohibit employment

---

[787] "The World Medical Association Declaration on Ethical Considerations Regarding Health Databases," WMA Policy, October 2002 <http://www.wma.net/e/policy/d1.htm>.

[788] United Nations Educational, Scientific and Cultural Organization (UNESCO), "Universal Declaration on the Human Genome and Human Rights," November 11, 1997 <http://unesdoc.unesco.org/images/0010/001096/109687eb.pdf>. Also see "Implementation of the Universal Declaration on the Human Genome and Human Rights: Report by the Director-General," September 22, 1999 <http://unesdoc.unesco.org/images/0011/001173/117335e.pdf>.

[789] "Working Document on Genetic Data: 12178/03/EN," Article 29 Data Protection Working Party, March 17, 2004 <http://europa.eu.int/comm/justice_home/fsj/privacy/docs/wpdocs/2004/wp91_en.pdf>.

[790] *Id.*

[791] *See generally*, International Labour Office, Conditions of Work Digest: Worker's Privacy Part III: Testing in the Workplace, (1993) 12(2).

[792] Pub. L. No. 101-335 (1990), codified at 42 USC §§ 1201.

discrimination on the basis of genetic information.[793] In 2000, President Bill Clinton issued an executive order prohibiting the use of genetic information in federal agency hiring and promotion decisions.[794]

In contrast to the US, most European countries have had broad data protection statutes in effect for many years. In February 1997, the Council of Europe's Committee of Ministers adopted the Recommendation on the Protection of Medical Data. This document, which applies to genetic data, protects personally identifiable information, limits the circle allowed to process health data, and sets standards for the use of medical data in scientific research.[795] In Australia, the application of the country's Privacy Act to genetic samples collected by authorities remains unclear. The law, however, has been determined to protect genetic data collected as part of a newborns screening card.[796]

Workplace Privacy

Workers around the world are frequently subject to some kind of monitoring by their employers.[797] Employers supervise work processes for quality control and performance purposes. They collect personal information from employees for a variety of reasons, such as health care, tax, and background checks.

Traditionally, this monitoring and information gathering in the workplace involved some form of human intervention and either the consent, or at least the knowledge, of employees. The changing structure and nature of the workplace, however, has led to more invasive and often covert monitoring practices which call into question employees' most basic right to privacy and dignity within the workplace. Progress in technology has facilitated an increasing level of automated surveillance. Now the supervision of employee performance, behavior, and communications can be carried out by technological means, with

---

[793] National Conference of State Legislatures, "State Genetics Employment Laws," <http://www.ncsl.org/programs/health/genetics/ndiscrim.htm>.

[794] Executive Order 13145 - To Prohibit Discrimination in Federal Employment Based on Genetic Information, February 10, 2000 <http://frwebgate.access.gpo.gov/cgi-bin/getdoc.cgi?dbname=2000_register&docid=fr10fe00-165.pdf>.

[795] Council of Europe, Recommendation of the Committee of Ministers to Member States on the Protection of Medical Data: No. R (97) 5, February 13, 1997.

[796] Australian Law Reform Commission, Essentially Yours: The Protection of Human Genetic Information in Australia, March 14, 2003 <http://www.austlii.edu.au/au/other/alrc/publications/reports/96/>.

[797] For a helpful overview of workplace privacy issues, mainly in the United States, see generally the Electronic Privacy Information Center (EPIC)'s Workplace Privacy Page <http://www.epic.org/privacy/workplace/>; and Daniel J. Solove & Marc Rotenberg, Information Privacy Law (Aspen 2003).

---

increased ease and efficiency. The technology currently being developed is extremely powerful and can extend to every aspect of a worker's life. Software programs can record keystrokes on computers and monitor exact screen images, telephone management systems can analyze the pattern of telephone use and the destination of calls, and miniature cameras and "Smart" ID badges can monitor an employee's behavior, movements, and even physical orientation.

Advances in science have also pushed the boundaries of what personal details and information an employer can acquire from an employee. Psychological tests, general intelligence tests, performance tests, personality tests, honesty and background checks, drug tests, and medical tests are routinely used in workplace recruitment and evaluation methods. Since the discovery of DNA, there has also been an increased use of genetic testing, allowing employers to access the most intimate details of a person's body in order to predict susceptibility to diseases, medical, or even behavioral conditions. The success of the Human Genome Project will likely make this kind of testing more prevalent. Currently, genetic testing is prohibitively expensive for many employers, and not used as frequently as other forms of medical or drug testing. Article 21 of the European Union Charter of Fundamental Rights provides explicitly that "any discrimination based on . . . genetic features . . . shall be prohibited."[798]

Employers' collection of personal information and use of surveillance technology is often justified on the grounds of health and safety, customer relations, or legal obligation. However, according to a recent study by the Privacy Foundation, it is actually the low cost of surveillance technologies more than anything else that contributes to the increased monitoring.[799] In many cases, workplace monitoring can seriously compromise the privacy and dignity of employees. Surveillance techniques can be used to harass, to discriminate, and to create unhealthy dynamics in the workplace.

Legal Background

Privacy advocates have long maintained that providing notice of a monitoring or surveillance policy should, at a bare minimum, be required before employers can engage in such invasive activities. Advocates support strong privacy principles in the workplace such as the International Labor Office's "Code of Practice on the

---

[798] Article 21, Charter of Fundamental Rights of the European Union
<http://ue.eu.int/df/docs/en/CharteEN.pdf>.

[799] The Privacy Foundation, The Extent of Systematic Monitoring of Employee E-mail and Internet Use, July 9, 2001 <http://www.sonic.net/~undoc/extent.htm>.

Protection of Workers' Personal Data," which protects employees' personal data and fundamental right to privacy in the technological era.[800] These guidelines were issued by the International Labor Office in 1997, following three comprehensive studies on international workers' privacy laws.[801] The general principles of the code are:

- personal data should be used lawfully and fairly; only for reasons directly relevant to the employment of the worker and only for the purposes for which they were originally collected;
- employers should not collect sensitive personal data (*e.g.,* concerning a worker's sex life; political, religious, or other beliefs; or trade union membership or criminal convictions) unless that information is directly relevant to an employment decision and is collected in conformity with national legislation;
- polygraphs, truth-verification equipment or any other similar testing procedure should not be used;
- medical data should only be collected in conformity with national legislation and principles of medical confidentiality; genetic screening should be prohibited or limited to cases explicitly authorized by national legislation; and drug testing should only be undertaken in conformity with national law and practice or international standards;
- workers should be informed in advance of any monitoring, and any data collected by such monitoring should not be the only factors in evaluating performance;
- employers should ensure the security of personal data against loss, unauthorized access, use, alteration or disclosure; and
- employees should be informed regularly of any data held about them and be given access to that data.

The code does not form international law and is not of binding effect. It was intended to be used "in the development of legislation, regulations, collective agreements, work rules, policies and practical measures." Unfortunately, however, the laws differ greatly from country to country, and in some countries there are few legal constraints on workplace surveillance.

---

[800] "Protection of workers' personal data," An ILO Code of Practice, Geneva, International Labour Office (1997).

[801] International Labour Office, Conditions of Work Digest: Worker's Privacy Part I: Protection of Personal Data 10 (2) (1991); Worker's Privacy Part II: Monitoring and Surveillance in the Workplace (1993) 12(1); and Worker's Privacy Part III: Testing in the Workplace, 12(2) (1993).

In the United States, for example, the courts have typically been slow to recognize employees' rights to privacy. There has not yet been any satisfactory and uniform determination of what level of privacy employees are entitled to and how that privacy should be protected. Many believe that since employers have ownership or "control" over the working premises, and its contents and facilities, that employees give up all rights and expectations to privacy and freedom from invasion. Others simply avoid the question by making employees consent to surveillance, monitoring, and testing as a condition of employment. Legislation has recently been introduced, however, which would prevent employers from secretly monitoring the communications and computer use of their employees.[802]

US public sector employees are protected by several laws. The Fourth Amendment applies not only to law enforcement officers, but to government officials and employers as well. A constitutional right to information privacy, recognized in *Whalen v. Roe*,[803] can protect against employer disclosures of employees' personal information. Other laws which may protect the privacy of public employees include relevant state constitutional provisions, federal and state wiretap laws, the Americans with Disabilities Act (ADA), the federal Privacy Act, and the common law privacy torts. In addition, depending on the type of employment contract governing the work agreement, public employees may have recourse under contractual remedies. However, most employment agreements are considered "at will," which means that employees may be dismissed for any or no reason, provided sufficient notice is given. One exception to this general rule is that employees may not be dismissed for a reason that violates public policy, such as for not complying with a privacy-invasive procedure. Should this occur, employees can sue for wrongful termination in violation of public policy.

US private sector employees have some, but not all, of the protections afforded public sector employees. The Fourth Amendment and many state constitutions do not apply to private employers. However, the federal wiretap law applies to both public and private sector employers. Private sector employees may also establish recourse for invasions of privacy under the ADA, breach of contract theories, and privacy torts.

Internationally, regulations governing the compilation and use of employees' personal data vary significantly. In European countries, the collection and processing of personal information is protected by the EU Data Protection and

---

[802] The "Notice of Electronic Monitoring Act" (S.2898 and H.R.4908), introduced July 20, 2000.
[803] 429 U.S. 589 (1977).

the Telecommunication Privacy Directives.[804] That last Directive, however, provides for the confidentiality of communications for "public" systems and therefore would not cover privately owned systems in the workplace.[805] However, the principles laid out in these directives are general in scope and their application to workplace privacy issues is not always clear.

Nonetheless, many European countries, such as Austria, Germany, Norway and Sweden, have strong labor codes and privacy laws that directly or indirectly prohibit or restrict this kind of surveillance. In Finland, a new law on Data Protection in Working Life entered into force in October 2001. In October 2000, the United Kingdom Privacy Commissioner issued "The Employment Practices Data Protection Code," a draft code of guidance for employer/employee relationships.[806] In March 2002, the first part of this code, regarding data protection in recruitment and selection of employees, was issued.[807] In October 2002, the Information Commission released part two of the code, which covers employment records. One significant provision requires that any sickness and accident records, detailing the medical cause of any absence be maintained separately from medical records that do not reveal medical conditions.[808] Two further parts on monitoring at work and medical information and testing will be issued over the next few months. In 1999, the Swedish government established a Committee to study workplace privacy issues. In March 2002, the Committee issued a proposal recommending specific legislation to protect the personal information of current employees, former employees and employment applicants in both the private and public sectors.[809] In May 2002, the European Union Article 29 Data Protection Working Party issued a working paper on monitoring and surveillance of electronic communications in the workplace. The document set out a list of questions to be asked before any monitoring measure is put in place. For example: Is the monitoring activity transparent to the workers? Is it necessary? Could not the employer obtain the same result with traditional

---

[804] *See* "Data Protection at Work: Commission Proposes New EU framework to European Social Partners," European Commission (2002) <http://europa.eu.int/comm/employment_social/news/2002/nov/181_en.html>.

[805] Directive Concerning the Processing of Personal Data and the Protection of Privacy in the Telecommunications Sector (Directive 97/66/EC of the European Parliament and of the Council of 15 December 1997), available at <http://www2.echo.lu/legal/en/dataprot/protection.html>.

[806] Data Protection Commissioner, Employment: (Draft COP), October 2000, available at <http://www.dataprotection.gov.uk/dpr/dpdoc.nsf>.

[807] Data Protection Commissioner, Employment: Part 1: Recruitment & Selection, Employment Practices, Data Protection Code, March 2002, available at <http://wood.ccta.gov.uk/dpr/dpdoc.nsf - 25/02/99>.

[808] "Data Protection: Employment Practices Data Protection Code on Employment Records," published, Freshfields Bruckhaus Deringer, October 2003, available at <http://www.icclaw.com/devs/uk/ep/ukep_373.htm>.

[809] The proposal (in Swedish with a summary in English) is available at <http://naring.regeringen.se/propositioner_mm/sou/pdf/sou2002_18a.pdf>.

methods of supervision? Is the processing of personal data proposed fair to the workers? Is it proportionate to the concerns that it tries to allay? The working paper also set out principles employers should bear in mind when processing workers' personal data. These principles include: finality (data must be collected for a specific and legitimate purpose); transparency (workers should know which data the employer is collecting about them); and security (the employer must implement security measures at the workplace to ensure the safety of the personal data of workers).[810]

In October 2002, the European Commissioner for Employment and Social Affairs launched a formal consultation initiative to improve the protection of workers' personal data throughout the EU.[811] The substance of the consultation addressed issues such as the effectiveness of employee consent in safeguarding personal data, access to, and the processing of medical data within the employment context, identifying the permissible scope of drug and genetic testing, and employer monitoring and surveillance of employees. Currently, both the International Labor Organization (ILO) and the Council of Europe have established specific guidelines establishing data protection in the employment relationship.[812] In addition, Article 8 of the EU Charter of Fundamental Rights refers to the protection of personal data, and Articles 21, 26, and 31 contain provisions relevant to the protection of employees' private data.[813]

There have also been developments outside of Europe on this issue. In June 2002, the Hong Kong Data Protection Commission issued a draft code of practice on workplace for public consultation. The draft code covers telephone, closed-circuit television, e-mail and computer usage and possibly location monitoring.[814] In Australia, the Privacy Amendment (Private Sector) Act 2000 put in place limited restrictions on employers' monitoring of communications by requiring the establishment of formal e-mail use policies that must be made clear to all employees. It also requires employers to prove that the monitoring of e-mails is justifiable–for instance, on grounds of employees' excessive use of e-mail, distributing offensive material, suspected criminal activities, or passing on

---

[810] Data Protection Working Party - Article 29, Working Document on The Surveillance of Electronic Communications in the Workplace, 5401/01/EN/Final WP 55, May 29, 2002, available at <http://europa.eu.int/comm/internal_market/privacy/docs/wpdocs/2002/wp55_en.pdf>.

[811] "Data Protection at Work: Commission Proposes New EU framework to European Social Partners," European Commission (2002) <http://europa.eu.int/comm/employment_social/news/2002/nov/181_en.html>.
[812] Id.
[813] Id.

[814] Privacy Commissioner for Personal Data, Draft Code of Practice on Monitoring and Personal Data Privacy at Work, (Hong Kong, PCO, 2002), available at <http://www.pco.org.hk/english/ordinance/codes.html>.

of sensitive information.[815] However, the legislation grants exemptions to small businesses and the media and also exempts all employee records in any industry sector.

Workplace Searches

Employer searches of an employee's workspace raises important privacy issues. In the public sector, the US Supreme Court has held that whether an employee has a reasonable expectation of privacy in a workspace is to be decided on a case-by-case basis because of the great variety of workplace settings.[816] The Court also held that a public employer's intrusions, even into constitutionally protected privacy interests of government employees for either non-investigatory, work-related purposes or for investigations of work-related misconduct, should be judged under a standard of reasonableness. The Court noted that requiring an employer to obtain a warrant whenever he or she wished to enter an employee's workspace for work-related purpose would seriously disrupt business routine and be unduly burdensome. In terms of workplace computer searches, a federal court has held that an employee has a reasonable expectation of privacy in the contents of an office computer, but an investigatory search for evidence of work-related employee misconduct is constitutionally reasonable if the search is justified at its inception and is of appropriate scope (*i.e.*, reasonably related to the objectives of the search and not excessively intrusive in light of the nature of the misconduct).[817] In addition, government employers cannot require employees to undergo unreasonable searches under the Fourth Amendment as a condition of employment, but the search is permissible if the employee consents to the search.

In the private sector, employees may have a reasonable expectation of privacy in certain areas and personal items. One court has held that an employee who is under no suspicion of wrongdoing and secures a locker with her own lock and with the employer's consent has a reasonable expectation of privacy in the locker and its contents.[818] In addition, employers may be liable if they reveal confidential information about their employees.[819] Public sector employees have an additional course of redress for the disclosure of personal information by an

---

[815] Helene Zampetakis, "Email snooping almost banned," Information Technology News Service, June 26, 2001 <http://it.mycareer.com.au/news/2001/06/26/FFXDJRS4DOC.html>.

[816] O'Connor v. Ortega, 480 U.S. 709 (1987).

[817] Leventhal v. Knapek, 266 F.3d 64 (2d Cir. 2001).

[818] K-Mart Corp. v. Trotti, 677 S.W.2d 632 (Tex. Ct. App. 1984).

[819] Miller v. Motorola, Inc., 560 N.E.2d 900 (Ill. App. 1990).

employer by means of a civil action under the constitutional right to information privacy.[820]

Workplace Surveillance

Employers are increasingly turning to video surveillance to monitor the activities of employees. In answering the question of whether an employer's use of video surveillance is permissible, US courts have examined an employee's expectation of privacy in the area being monitored, as well as considered any applicable laws or regulations governing such a search. Federal courts have held almost unanimously that silent video surveillance is not prohibited by Title I of the Electronic Communications Privacy Act (ECPA) of 1986.[821] But video surveillance that includes the ability to record conversations would violate Title I. Silent video surveillance is subject to the Fourth Amendment's protections against unreasonable searches, but at least one court has held that the Fourth Amendment is only implicated if an employee has a reasonable expectation of privacy in the area being surveilled.[822] If employees have no reasonable expectation of privacy in an area under observation–such as in a locker area that can be viewed by anyone who enters–the Fourth Amendment is not violated, regardless of the nature of the search.

Internationally, video surveillance is used extensively for many different reasons. Australia spent substantially more money per capita than any other industrialized nation on video surveillance equipment.[823] Video cameras are now one of the most commonly used surveillance devices in the Australian workplace, and their use is regulated by The Workplace Video Surveillance Act of 1998.[824] Video surveillance is justified as a security measure to deter theft, vandalism, or other unauthorized intrusions, and to monitor employee conformance with occupational health and safety procedures, as well as general performance.

Workplace surveillance in New Zealand is prevalent, and often occurs beyond the reach of the law given the deregulated labor market, according to a report issued by the Office of the Privacy Commissioner.[825] The current policy in New

---

[820] *See* 42 U.S.C. § 1983.

[821] 18 U.S.C. §§ 2510-2522.

[822] Thompson v. Johnson County Community College, 930 F. Supp. 501 (D. Kan. 1996).

[823] "Report 98, Surveillance: an interim report," Law Reform Commission Publications (2001) <http://www.lawlink.nsw.gov.au/lrc.nsf/pages/r98chp07>.

[824] *Id.*

[825] "Workplace Monitoring, Surveillance "Common,"" News From the Office of The Privacy Commissioner, Issue No. 30, Jan-Feb 1999 <http://www.knowledge-basket.co.nz/privacy/semployf.html>.

Zealand is to leave negations involving workplace surveillance to employment agreements between employers and employees rather than establishing legislation regulating such activities, although employment law and contractual implied terms of fair dealing offer employees some protections. New Zealand employers are entitled to take reasonable steps to monitor employee performance, to safeguard working conditions, and to secure the place of business. Employees, in turn, are generally granted protections to safeguard their person, property, and private conversations and beliefs, and are provided with avenues to amend irrelevant, inaccurate, or incomplete facts that are considered in employment decisions.

Performance Monitoring

Automated workplace monitoring has become increasingly common in recent years. Even in workplaces staffed by highly skilled information technology specialists, employers demand the right to spy on every detail of a worker's performance. Modern networked systems can interrogate computers to determine which software is being run, how often, and in what manner. A comprehensive audit trail gives managers a profile of each user, and a panorama of how the workers are interacting with their machines. Software programs can also give managers total central control of individual PCs. A manager can now remotely modify or suspend programs on any machine, while at the same time reading and analyzing e-mail traffic and Internet activity. A recent report by the American Management Association found that nearly eighty percent of major US companies monitor employees at work by checking communications such as telephone conversations, computer files, e-mails and Internet connections or by using video surveillance for performance evaluation and security purposes.[826]

An employer can monitor the level of use of a computer by surveilling the number of keystrokes an employee enters into a word processing program in a specified period of time or the amount of time a computer is idle during the workday. Numerous technologies are available which monitor and analyze the performance of IT workers. Some allow network administrators to observe an employee's screen in real time, scan data files and e-mail, analyze keystroke performance, and even overwrite passwords. Once this information is collected, it can be analyzed by standard processing programs to determine a worker's performance profile. These monitoring products are sold at very low prices and have infiltrated the market. These snooping programs have also become popular

---

[826] American Management Association, Annual Survey on Workplace Monitoring and Surveillance 2001, April 18, 2001.

not just among employers but also law enforcement agencies, private attorneys, investigators, and suspicious lovers.

The use of video cameras and closed circuit televisions (CCTV) is another common way of monitoring employees within the workplace. Even areas where employees would previously have enjoyed high expectations of privacy, such as bathrooms or locker rooms, have come under increasing surveillance. Postal workers in New York City found hidden cameras in restroom stalls and waiters in the Boston Sheraton were secretly videotaped in the hotel locker room.[827] Where staff are more mobile, companies are now using a range of technologies to track geographic movements.[828] Some hospitals now require nurses to wear badges on their uniforms so they can be located constantly.[829] Advances in this area now allow carrier companies to place an electronic mechanism (described as a geostationary satellite-based mobile communications system)[830] on trucks that then sends back to a main terminal the exact position of the vehicle at all times. In this way, carrier companies can ensure that no side trips nor other deviations are taken from the prescribed route.[831] Wide area systems such as Trackback are in use throughout the United Kingdom.

Telephone Monitoring

Telephone surveillance has become endemic throughout the private and public sector. In the United States, employers have broad discretion to monitor employees' calls for "business purposes." Companies are extensively using telephone analysis technology. Call center workers for British Telecom are regularly presented with a comprehensive analysis sheet, showing their performance relative to other workers. Airline reservations clerks in the United States and elsewhere wear telephonic headsets that monitor the length and content of all telephone calls, as well as the duration of their bathroom and lunch breaks.[832] In one instance, telephone calls received by airline reservation agents were electronically monitored on a second-by-second basis: agents were allowed

[827] ACLU, Workplace Rights, Electronic Monitoring <http://www.aclu.org/library/pbr2.html>.

828 Laura Pincus Hartman, "The Economic and Ethical Implications of New Technology onPrivacy in the Workplace," Business and Society Review, March 22, 1999.

[829] "Monitoring Shrinks Worker Privacy Sphere," Eric Auchard, Reuters, May 29, 2001.

830 "Bulkmatic Equips Fleet with OmniTRACS System," Qualcomm Press release, December 19, 1996. <http://www.qualcomm.com/Press/pr961219c.html>.

831 Qualcomm Press release, December 19, 1996.

832 Laura Pincus Hartman, "The Economic and Ethical Implications of New Technology on Privacy in the Workplace," Business and Society Review, March 22, 1999.

only 11 seconds between each call and 12 minutes of break time each day.[833] Other airline agents have complained that they are evaluated based on how many times they use a customer's name during a call or how often they try to overcome a customer's initial objections to buying a ticket.

The level of sophistication of telephone surveillance systems can be astonishing. Some systems can record all transactional activity on a phone, together with destination numbers and times. Other technology can then process and analyze this data. A British program called "Watcall," produced by the Harlequin company, can analyze telephone calls and group them into "friendship networks" to determine patterns of use.[834] Voice mail systems are also subject to systematic or random monitoring by managers. Most new systems have default pass codes for administrators, and these can open all message boxes.

Email and Internet Use Monitoring

Computers and networks are particularly conducive to surveillance. The Privacy Foundation study[835] found that fourteen million employees in the United States are subject to this kind of surveillance on a continuous basis. This number obviously increases dramatically when random surveillance checks are included. Employers can monitor e-mail by randomly reviewing e-mail transmissions, by specifically reviewing transmissions of certain employees, or by selecting key terms to flag e-mail. In the latter case, software analyzes a company's entire e-mail traffic phrase by phrase, and draws conclusions about whether a message is legitimate company business. It can be instructed to search for specific keywords and "damaging" phrases. Some programs can even use algorithms to analyze communications patterns and turn them into images. Monitors can then look at these images to follow traffic patterns and detect whether sensitive data is at risk.

Many employers rely on software for remote monitoring of e-mail messages. With a few clicks they can see every e-mail message that employees send or receive and determine whether they are "legitimate" or not. Managers give a variety of reasons for installing such software. Some say it is to protect trade secrets or preventing sexual harassment incidents. Others want to prevent oversized-mails clogging networks and using too much bandwidth. Still others simply don't want employees "wasting" company time by using the systems for

---

833 Charles Pillar, "Bosses with X-Ray Eyes," MacWorld., July 1993.

834 Simon Davies, "Watch out for the Old Bill," Daily Telegraph, April 29, 1997.

835 *See* Privacy Foundation, The Extent of Systematic Monitoring of Employee E-mail and Internet Use, July 9, 2001 <http://www.sonic.net/~undoc/extent.htm>.

personal activities. In an ideal world, this monitoring should follow the conventional format, *i.e.*, identical to the quality check that has applied to correspondence sent out on company letterhead. However, the speed and efficiency of e-mail means that digital communication involves a vast intersection with personal correspondence. It also has features more in common with an internal memo, for which there has always been less monitoring and management.

According to the American Management Study,[836] nearly two thirds of all companies discipline employees for abuse of e-mail or Internet connections and twenty-seven percent dismiss employees for those reasons. In 2000, Dow Chemical Company fired fifty US employees and threatened two hundred others with suspension after they found "offensive" material in their e-mail. The company opened the personal e-mail of more than 7,000 employees.[837] Similarly, the New York Times fired twenty-three employees in 1999 for sending "obscene" messages. Internationally, employer monitoring of e-mail and Internet usage varies from country to country. The Swiss Federal Data Protection Commissioner issued a statement in its annual report explaining the circumstances under which use of Internet and e-mail at the workplace may be monitored.[838] According to the report, surveillance activities by employers are primarily focused on preventing technical malfunctions. Records of an individual's e-mail and Internet use may be evaluated only once an abuse has been identified and the individual is notified of the evaluation.[839] In Hong Kong, the Office of the Privacy Commissioner for Personal Data in 2000 commissioned a survey to examine employer surveillance in the workplace.[840] According to the survey, sixty-four percent of employers had installed at least one type of employee monitoring equipment, but only eighteen percent of the employers had a written policy on employee monitoring. Further, thirty-five percent of respondents did not even know whether such a policy existed.[841] In contrast, France has established stringent policies that protect the privacy of employees' e-mail usage. The French Supreme Court held recently that employers do not have the right to open any of their employees' messages. The Court ruled in a case between Nikon and a

---

[836] *See* American Management Association, *supra.*

837 'Dow Chemical Fires Employees Over Inappropriate E-mails', ABCNEWS.com, July 27, 2000.

[838] "E-mail and Internet surveillance at the workplace," Extract from the 8th Annual Report, Swiss Federal Data Protection Commissioner (2001).

[839] *Id.*

[840] "A Draft Code of Practice on Monitoring and Personal Data Privacy at Work," Office of the Privacy Commissioner for Personal Data, June 1, 2002
<http://www.pco.org.hk/textonly/english/ordinance/files/consult_paper.doc>.

[841] *Id.*

former employee that the company had no automatic right to search through an e-mail inbox.[842]

Courts in the United States have taken various positions in cases involving an employee's use of e-mail and the Internet at work. One court has found that an at-will employee has no reasonable expectation of privacy in the contents of an e-mail voluntarily sent on an employer's e-mail system, even though the employer had assured its employees that e-mail communications would remain confidential and privileged.[843] The court reasoned that once an employee communicated comments to a second person over an e-mail system utilized by the entire company, any reasonable expectation of privacy is lost. And even if an employee had a reasonable expectation of privacy in the contents of an e-mail, a reasonable person would not consider an employer's interception of such communications to be substantial or highly offensive. Another court has held that an employer that has a "business use only" policy for Internet usage may conduct audits of its computer network to identify, terminate, and prosecute unauthorized activity.[844] The court found that while employees may have a legitimate expectation of privacy in their computer equipment, some office practices, regulations, or procedures may reduce such an expectation.[845]

These cases raise complex legal and ethical questions concerning an employee's fundamental right to privacy and due process, such as: what if an employee is sent an "offensive" e-mail, accidentally or maliciously? The e-mail cannot simply be deleted. It remains logged on the company server, threatening the relationship of trust between employee and management. Or what if an employee is dismissed on the grounds of sensitive personal information (for example, issues relating to sexual preferences, medical conditions, etc.) gathered through a system? This problem also arises when companies monitor all Internet activity looking for visits to "inappropriate" sites. Such surveillance has elements in common with traditional surveillance for hard copy pornography, but there are significant dangers to workers in the realm of electronic surveillance. An employee may accidentally visit a pornographic site upon opening a spam e-mail that links to such a site. Or websites may be accidentally visited when displayed as a "hit" in response to a perfectly innocent search query. The surveillance technology does not, however, distinguish between an innocent mistake and an intentional visit.

---

[842] Nikon v. Onof, Decision No. 4164, October 2, 2001 (99-42.942).

[843] Smyth v. Pillsbury Co., 914 F. Supp. 97 (E.D. Pa. 1996).

[844] United States v. Simons, 206 F.3d 392 (4th Cir. 2000).

[845] Id.

The monitoring of chat room visits has also created some distress in the workplace. There is an increasing trend among companies to dismiss or sue employees for divulging company "trade secrets" or defaming the company in chat rooms. These have become known as "John Doe" cases. Because most people log on to chat rooms anonymously or use an alias, once a company observes a certain party in a chat room engaging in "illegitimate" speech, they must subpoena the message-board services such as Yahoo! or America Online, it obtain the identity of the specific author. The service providers often turn over identifying information when presented with a subpoena without any notice to the individual. The number of these cases is rapidly increasing and threatens not only the privacy of employees but also their rights to anonymity and free speech.

Drug Testing

There is also an increasing amount of drug testing in many countries. The number of companies using these tests has risen in proportion to the decreasing costs of the tests. For many employees, drug testing is now a standard part of working life. Companies routinely administer tests in the recruitment stage or at intermittent periods during employment, even where there is no evidence of misconduct, poor performance, or any other reason to suspect drug use. There are thousands of easy-to-use kits, which can detect traces of drugs within minutes and without the need for a laboratory, available on the market today. Most of these tests analyze hair or urine samples to detect traces of drugs such as amphetamines, marijuana, cocaine, opiates, and methamphetamines.

Internationally, the use of and justifications for workplace drug testing varies from country to country. In European countries, one of the most frequently used arguments for workplace drug testing and one of the least controversial is that the test is a means of ensuring the safety of employees. In France, Norway, and the Netherlands, only workers in traditional safety-sensitive positions, or those positions which include access to dangerous materials or classified information, are subjected to testing in any form.[846] Accordingly there is less testing and there are more legal restrictions in these countries. In the Netherlands, pre-employment testing is illegal, and in France only the occupational physician may decide to conduct drug tests, not the employer.[847] On the other hand, workplace drug

---

[846] Behrouz Shahandeh & Joannah Caborn, "Ethical Issues in Workplace Drug Testing in Europe," SafeWork: ILO Geneva (February, 2003) <http://www.ilo.org/public/english/protection/safework/drug/wdt.pdf>.
[847] *Id.*

testing is more commonplace in British and Swedish companies, where workers in all types of jobs are tested in order to ensure "business-safety."[848]

A major ethical issue implicated by drug testing is that the process amounts to an unwarranted invasion of privacy. Most guidelines for workplace drug testing, such as the ILO Guiding Principles on Drug and Alcohol Testing of 1996, require that informed consent be obtained before testing. Opponents of testing, such as the German Federal Data Protection Commission and the Swiss Data Protection Commissioner, argue that because workers are dependent on their employers, meaningful consent to workplace drug testing is not possible.[849] This policy is not followed in some countries. In the United Kingdom, failure to comply with a requirement for drug testing that is included in an employment agreement can be interpreted as a disciplinary offence.[850]

Some European constitutions, for example in Belgium and Finland, hold that fundamental rights such as the right to privacy are indivisible and that the individual cannot consent to waive these rights.[851] Privacy issues are often implicated in the realm of workplace drug testing within the larger concerns for data protection. The testing process involves collecting sensitive data both on use of drugs and on medication taken which might influence the test result. The collecting and storage of such information is therefore not only subject to strict controls in many European countries, but also the subject of European rules such as the EU Data Protection and Telecommunications Privacy Directives and the ILO Code of Practice on the Protection of Workers' Personal Data of 1996.[852] In some European countries, the tension between the need for workplace security and the protection of personal information is resolved by strengthening the role of the occupational physician. In Finland, France, Belgium, Germany, and Austria, the drug test results are communicated to the occupational doctor, not to the employer. The doctor is only allowed to inform the employer whether the person is fit for work or not; not what results were revealed from the drug test.

In the United States, courts have upheld the legality of workplace drug testing in many different circumstances. The US Supreme Court upheld regulations mandating blood and urine tests of railroad employees to ensure workplace

---

[848] *Id.*

[849] *Id.*

[850] *Id.*

[851] *Id.*

[852] *Id.*

safety.[853] Courts have also upheld drug testing by schools of all students involved in athletics and extracurricular activities.[854] However, the US Supreme Court recently struck down a policy of performing drug tests on pregnant women in a public hospital, finding that the employees of the hospital are government actors subject to Fourth Amendment limitations.[855]

US courts have also considered the issues of notice and consent in relation to workplace drug testing. Providing notice of future drug tests shields employers from liability for intrusion upon seclusion because the employee has provided explicit consent to take the test. In addition, employers may lawfully condition employment upon successfully passing a drug test. The issue of wide scale preventative drug testing raises a host of other questions concerning privacy, bodily integrity, individual freedom, and the presumption of innocence. The process of testing itself can be hugely invasive. Observers are often present to prevent employees from tampering with samples. In the case of urine testing, the monitor's observation of the drug testing process can be particularly offensive. Consider the case of one employee who felt humiliated while undergoing a urine drug test:

> I waited for the attendant to turn her back before pulling down my pants, but she told me she had to watch everything I did. I am a 40-year-old mother of three: nothing I have ever done in my life equals or deserves the humiliation, degradation and mortification I felt.[856]

This type of test can quickly turn from a necessary evil needed to protect lives and reputations into a process of intimidation and harassment. It raises questions about whether the benefits to employers really outweigh the rights and dignity of workers. Companies which manufacture drug testing equipment extol the advantages of drug tests, claiming the tests can save employers thousands of dollars by reducing incidences of absenteeism, low productivity, accidents, injuries, compensation, and health care claims stemming from employees' drug usage. Governments generally have also encouraged testing as part of a larger war on drugs. What employers are not told, however, is that there are also numerous ethical and economic disadvantages to drug testing.

---

[853] Skinner v. Railway Labor Executives' Association, 489 U.S. 602 (1989).

[854] Vernonia School District v. Acton, 515 U.S. 646 (1995).

[855] Ferguson v. City of Charleston, 532 U.S. 67 (2001).

856 ACLU, "Drug Testing: A Bad Investment," September 1999, available at http://www.aclu.org/issues/worker/drugtesting1999.pdf.

Drug testing fosters a climate of negativity based on suspicion and secrecy rather than trust, openness, and respect. Low morale or resentment among workers may consequently lead to low productivity or profits. In addition, even though individual tests may no longer be expensive because they are so sweepingly administered among employees, the negative costs may be costing employers far more than they are saving them. Catching one or two light drug users for every few thousand people tested is hardly an economical justification for the initial outlay. Even if tests do reveal traces of drugs there is no clear evidence to suggest that mild drug use has a greater effect on productivity than, for example, alcohol. Dismissing workers on grounds of policy and suspicion rather than performance and proof, may result in the loss of valuable employees to the employer. Evidence has not shown that drug testing can deter future use, and it is in no way a substitute for proper guidance, support and counseling. In fact, in an ironic twist, routine testing may even encourage more serious drug usage among employees. As one commentator says:

> If one wants to get inebriated on a Friday night and still pass a urine test Monday, smoking a joint would be foolish. Cocaine and alcohol would represent the "safer" choices of intoxicants because alcohol is "legal" and cocaine cannot be detected in the body as long.[857]

Finally, drug testing is inaccurate and can often lead to false and misleading results. A report by the Ontario Information and Privacy Commissioners' Office says up to 40 percent of tests are inaccurate.[858] Highly sensitive tests can be positive even when the drug sought is not present. Some say positive reactions may result from a carry-over following a strong positive earlier or from human error, such as contamination due to failure to cleanse equipment.[859] Others note that certain legal substances can also result in positive tests for illegal drugs. For example, there have been reports of Vicks inhalers resulting in positive tests for amphetamines and methamphetamines, standard anti-inflammatory drugs like Ibuprofen showing up positive on marijuana tests, and even traces of morphine being detected from poppy seeds.[860]

---

857 Ethan A. Nadelmann, "Drawing the Line on Drug Testing," IntellectualCapital.Com, October 14, 1999.

858 Information and Privacy Commissioner/Ontario, Workplace Privacy: The Need for a Safety-Net, November 1993. <http://www.ipc.on.ca/english/pubpres/sum_pap/papers/safnet-e.htm>.

859 John P. Morgan, "Problems of Mass Urine Screening for Misused Drugs," Journal of Psychoactive Drugs. Volume 16(4) 305-317 (1984) available at The Lindesmith Center - Drug Policy Foundation <http://www.lindesmith.org/library/grmorg2.html>.

860 National Academy of Sciences, "Under the Influence? Drugs and the American Work Force," 1994. See also ACLU, "Drug Testing: A Bad Investment," September 1999, available at <http://www.aclu.org/issues/worker/drugtesting1999.pdf>.

Other issues that raise workplace privacy concerns are employer requirements that employees complete medical tests, questionnaires, and polygraph tests. In the United States, employer use of polygraph testing has been limited by federal statute. Congress passed the Employee Polygraph Protection Act (EPPA),[861] which makes it unlawful for private sector employers to require current or prospective employees to take a lie detector test. The statute exempts public employers at the federal, state, and local levels. However, there are a few exceptions to the EPPA. For example, employers may use polygraphs as part of an ongoing investigation involving economic loss or injury to the employer's business, and employers who provide security services are exempt. One court has held that an employer who performed unauthorized tests using blood and urine samples provided by a job applicant violated the individual's privacy.[862] The court looked to the constitutional right to information privacy recognized in *Whalen*, and held that unauthorized tests were unconstitutional searches under the Fourth Amendment. In another case, a court found that questionnaires that collected health information about employees were permissible.[863] The court reasoned that an individual's interest in protecting his or her privacy is not as great when the information is sought by the government, is not publicly disseminated, and when measures are in place to protect the privacy of information that is collected. Some states have statutes which restrict the degree to which employers may require potential employees to undergo testing or complete mandatory questionnaires.

Internationally, there are fewer workplace privacy laws that specifically address the use of polygraphs in the employment context. In Europe, honesty testing through mechanical devices, such as polygraphs or voice stress analyzers, or through questionnaires that strive to evaluate workers' attitudes to honesty, are not expressly regulated.[864] Elsewhere, mechanical honesty testing is prohibited by statute in the Canadian territories of New Brunswick and Ontario, and is also prohibited in the Australian State of New South Wales.[865]

---

[861] 29 U.S.C. §§ 2001-2009.

[862] Norman-Bloodsaw v. Lawrence Berkeley Laboratory, 135 F.3d 1260 (9th Cir. 1998).

[863] American Federation of Government Employees v. HUD, 118 F.3d 786 (D.C. Cir. 1997).

[864] Proposals for the agenda of the 87th Session (1999) of the Conference, before the ILO Governing Body, GB.267/2, 267th Session, Geneva, November 1996
<http://www.ilo.org/public/english/standards/relm/gb/docs/gb267/gb-2.htm>.

[865] Id.

E-Voting Privacy

Technology that facilitates the right of citizens to participate in the public discourse may threaten privacy, especially when it is associated with the administration of elections and, under certain conditions, the very act of voting.[866] The use of technology in the online[867] and offline[868] voting process is growing in popularity around the world[869]. The Charter of Fundamental Rights of the European Union[870] and the United Nations Universal Declaration of Human Rights'[871] support the right of citizens to both privacy and self-governance. Democracies are universally defined as the most efficient means of supporting self-governance through citizen participation in the form of voting. The secret ballot has long been considered an integral requirement of democractic governance, In 1983, the Strasbourg Conference on Parliamentary Democracy said that genuine democract is protected by "the citizen's right to choose and change government in elections conducted under universal suffrage and by secret ballot.[872]

E-voting technology allows for the first time independent voting in public elections for millions of disabled and language minority voters through the benefit of a secret ballot.[873] Efforts existed prior to the introduction of electronic voting to facilitate independent voting for the blind.[874]

Direct Recording Electronic (DRE) Voting Machines

DRE voting machines produce no tangible evidence of the ballot, but instead save the voters choice to a memory card or disk stored in the voting device.[875] However a hybrid DRE voting machine that uses the technology as a paper

---

[866] Associated Press, "Widow with Visible Vote Gets No Help," Los Angeles Times, March 12, 1992, Part A, at 15.

[867] Parliamentary Office of Science and Technology Post Notes, May 2001 Number 155 Online Voting, available at <http://www.parliament.uk/post/pn155.pdf>.

[868] European Commission Cybervote Project Report, Chapter 2: The History of the Internet, available at <http://www.eucybervote.org/Reports/KUL-WP2-D4V1-v1.0-01.htm>.

[869] See generally EPIC's Voting Page web page <http://www.epic.org/privacy/voting/>.

[870] Charter of Fundamental Rights of the European Union Article 39, available at <http://www.europarl.eu.int/comparl/libe/elsj/charter/art39/default_en.htm>.

[871] UN Declaration of Human Rights General Assembly resolution 217 A (III). 10 December 1948, available at <http://www.un.org/Overview/rights.html>.

[873] ACE Project, Focus on Elections and Disabilities, <http://www.aceproject.org/focuson/disability/>.

[874] ACE Project, Best Practices, Ballot Templates, <http://www.electionaccess.org/Bp/Ballot_Templates.htm>.

[875] Roy G. Saltman, National Institute of Standards and Technology, "Accuracy, Integrity, and Security in Computerized Vote-Tallying," NBS Special Publication 500-158, August 1988, at 112.

---

ballot-marking device is now available for use in public elections.[876] These DRE paper and paperless voting machines are applicable to online and offline voting systems. They each may use one of two dominant forms of voter interface: push buttons or a touch screen display.[877] DRE voting machines provide privacy to voters through the application of cryptography[878] and assistive technology.[879] The use of smart cards, tokens or the registration of the order in which voters use the machines could each compromise users' privacy.[880]

Automated Tabulation of Paper Ballots

Technology may be used to expedite the counting of paper punch card ballots or optical scan ballots used in public elections.[881] Ballots are collected at polling locations and in most cases transported to a central location for counting.[882] Ballot reading technology may be present in voting locations to allow voters to verify their ballots before leaving them and for counting purposes.[883] This may present privacy problems should the ballot choices be visible to others. Some voting administration procedures if not clear may be interpreted to allow voters to give their ballots to poll workers to place ballots through ballot readers, which threatens ballot secrecy.[884]

Internet Voting

In October 2000, the Internet Corporation held the first binding global Internet Election for Assigned Names and Numbers (ICANN), the technical coordinating entity for the Internet. The election selected Directors for the ICANN Board.[885]

---

[876] Accupoll on a Voter Verified Paper DRE Voting Machine, press release, available at <http://www.accupoll.com/News/NewsReleases/releases/2004-06-11.html>.

[877] ACE Project, The Administration and Cost of Elections <http://www.aceproject.org/main/english/em/emf02.htm>.

[878] *See generally* EPIC's Cryptography web page <http://www.epic.org/crypto/>.

[879] *See generally* National Committee for Voting Integrity (NCVI)'s Voting Accessibility web page <http://www.votingintegrity.org/Issues/Access.html>.

[880] *See generally* ACE Project, Elections and Technology, Guiding Principles <http://www.aceproject.org/main/english/et/et20.htm>.

[881] NCVI's Optical Scan web page <http://www.votingintegrity.org/Issues/OpticalScan.html>.

[882] Douglas Jones, Counting Mark-Sense Ballots Relating Technology, the Law and Common Sense, <http://www.cs.uiowa.edu/~jones/voting/optical/>.

[883] *See generally* ACE Project, Electoral Management. Election Automation – Types of Computerized Voting Systems <http://www.aceproject.org/main/english/em/emf02.htm>.

[884] Letter from the Chinese for Affirmative Action to John Arntz, Department of Elections California, November 22, 2002, available at <http://www.caasf.org/PDFs/pollletter112202.pdf>.

[885] European Commission, Cybervote Project Report, Chapter 2, *supra*.

Internet or online voting is still in its infancy with a small number of countries attempting public elections using this method.[886] Most of the public elections attempted involve low-level political contest or decisions. Internet voting may take one of two forms: a polling place Internet voting system and/or a remote Internet voting system. In 1999, an Internet voting project by the European Union (EU) was launched to conduct three years of remote election pilot projects.[887] The EU Commission's Information Society Technologies (IST) 1999 Program for Research, Technology Development and Demonstration[888] funded a three-year Internet voting project that began in 2000. The use of cryptography in three pilot voting projects to protect voter privacy was reported as successful.[889] Trial Internet elections were held in Kistaand, Stockholm, Sweden, Issy-les-Moulineaux, France, and Bremen, Germany.[890]

An Internet voting paradigm raises several privacy questions: are Internet votes cast in secret? Are Internet voters free of intimidation or undue influence by others? How can adequate private space around personal computers acting as voting machines be maintained, and how can data in transit be secure from disclosure or tampering? The answers to these questions will indicate how much Internet voting will help to ensure privacy and voting in the future.

Electronic Voter Registration and Centralized Registration Databases

Electronic voter registration and centralized registration databases present challenges to privacy.[891] To participate in most public elections some form of voter registration is required.[892] Electronic voter registration that establishes centralized databases of personally identifiable information on voters for a region or nation would be a target for identity thieves, manipulation, and tampering.[893] There is also a concern that national voter registration requirements could be

---

[886] European Commission, CyberVote Report by Voto Electronico, April 5, 2004, available at <http://www.euskadi.net/botoelek/otros_paises/sim0_i.htm>.

[887] European Commission, "CyberVote Project - Vote in Total Confidence Via the Internet!," press release, October 13, 2000, available at <http://www.eucybervote.org/press_release.html>.

[888] European Commission, CyberVote: An Innovative Cyber Voting System for Internet Terminals and Mobile Phones, July 3, 2003, available at <http://www.eucybervote.org/MSI-WP6-D21-v1.0.pdf>.

[889] European Commission CyberVote Project Brochure, available at December 2002-January 2003 <http://www.eucybervote.org/CyberAnglais.pdf>.

[890] European Commission CyberVote Trial Elections December 2003-January 2003, available at <http://www.eucybervote.org/trials.html>.

[891] ACE Project Voter Registration Web Page <http://www.aceproject.org/main/english/ei/eie05.htm>.

[892] *Id.*

[893] National Committee for Voting Integrity (NCVI) Centralized Voter Registration Databases Web Page, available at <http://www.votingintegrity.org/Issues/CenteralizedData.html>.

used in ways that were not initially disclosed by governments.[894] Some proposals for centralized voter registration would allow governments to check voter registration information against other government-managed databases.[895] In the United States, the Help America Vote Act allows states to check voter registration list with other state databases like those kept for driver's licenses or public assistance, to verify the identity of potential voters.

Absentee Voting or Voting by Mail

Absentee voting or voting by mail exposes voters to the threat that their votes may not be kept secret. Absentee voting systems must ensure that only qualified voters and those who have not participated in the regular election are the only absented ballots counted. These conditions over time have lead to a system of absentee voting that associates each absentee ballot to the voter, which could threaten ballot secrecy.[896]

Nanotechnology

Nanotechnology is an emerging science in which developers create devices and systems that have novel properties and functions because of their small size.[897] This new technology is believed to have the potential to fundamentally transform the way in which common products are produced by manipulating their component parts on the atomic level.[898] This manipulation is hoped to result in the manufacturing of products that are smaller, stronger, and lighter than those available today.[899]

Nanotechnology will likely raise new challenges to the protection of individual privacy. As nanotechnology makes computing devices smaller and more efficient, collecting, storing, sharing and processing large amounts of information

---

894 ACE Project, Voter Registration Information Collection: Situation Assessment, January 15, 2002, available at <http://www.aceproject.org/main/english/vr/vrd02b.htm>.

895 Id.

896 Rokita, Todd, "It's Important for Hoosiers to Understand Absentee Ballot Procedure," South Bend Tribune (Indiana), October 21, 2003, at A7.

897 Eva Gutierrez, "Privacy Implications of Nanotechnology," EPIC (Spring 2004), available at <http://www.epic.org/privacy/nano/>.

898 Mike Treder, "The Meaning of Nanotechnology," Center for Responsible Nanotechnolgy, January 14, 2005 <http://crnano.typepad.com/crnblog/2005/01/the_meaning_of_.html>.

899 Jennifer Bails, "Nanotechnology Is Next Big Thing in Electronics and Manufacturing," PittsburghLive.com, January 2, 2005 <http://www.pittsburghlive.com/x/search/s_295352.html>.

will become easier and cheaper.[900] Nanotechnology has the capability of dramatically expanding surveillance devices and producing new weapons.[901]

Nanotechnology is considered to be in its "pre-competitive" stage, which the federal government defines as having limited application for commercial use. However, the potential is great for both commercial and non-commercial applications. For this reason, US federal resources are being made available for work in several key areas of nanotechnology: biology, materials research, medical, and defense applications.

In 2005, funding for nanotechnology research is to begin under the 21st Century Nanotechnology Research and Development Act of 2003.[902] The National Nanotechnology Advisory Panel, created by the Act, issued a report on nanotechnology in May 2005.[903] According to the report, USD 82 million will be budgeted to examine, among other things, the impact of nanotechnology on personal privacy.[904] Legislation is being developed to spur innovation and place the United States in a leading position with this early stage technology.[905]

The European Union issued its strategy for nanotechnology in 2005 and called for a responsible approach that would examine the "implications for the protection of privacy and personal data."[906]

---

[900] Ricardo Ochoa, "Tiny Devices Offer Tremendous Potential," News from the States, National Conference of State Legislatures, Summer 2005
<http://www.ncsl.org/programs/lis/CIP/CIPCOMM/summer05.htm#INTERNET>.

[901] Charles Choi, "Nano World: Nano could lead to new WMDs," UPI, May 23, 2005, available at <http://washingtontimes.com/upi-breaking/20050520-114429-1570r.htm>.

[902] US White House, "President Bush Signs Nanotechnology Research and Development Act," (press release), December 3, 2003, available at <http://www.whitehouse.gov/news/releases/2003/12/20031203-7.html>.

[903] National Nanotechnology Advisory Panel, The National Nanotechnology Initiative at Five Years (2005)<http://nano.gov/FINAL_PCAST_NANO_REPORT.pdf>.

[904] Id., at 35.

[905] Johan Bostrom, "Senators Will Propose Legislation to Spur Innovation," Infoworld.com, July 20, 2005 <http://www.infoworld.com/article/05/07/20/HNgovinnovation_1.html?source=NLC-TB2005-07-21>.

[906] Nanotechnology Service of the European Commission, Nanosciences and Nanotechnologies: An Action Plan for Europe 2005-2009 (2005), available at
<ftp://ftp.cordis.lu/pub/nanotechnology/docs/nano_action_plan2005_en.pdf>.

Country Reports

Highlights

ARGENTINA

- Launch of the National Database Registry: anyone creating files with personal data is now legally mandated to register them.
- Under strong pressure from ISPs and the public, the 10-year data retention law was suspended and held unconstitutional.
- To fight against kidnapping, a new law has eliminated mobile phone users' anonymity.

ARMENIA

- A new Freedom of Information Law was enacted.
- A mandatory referendum on constitutional amendments took place about the right to privacy.

AUSTRALIA

- The Australian Capital Territory became the first jurisdiction to incorporate a bill of rights that includes a right of "privacy and reputation."
- New amended legislation has eliminated the warrant requirement for accessing stored communications (email, SMS, and voice mail), allowing non-law enforcement government agencies to access this information without a court order.
- The government is considering launching biometric RFID passports at the end of 2005.
- A new law allowed the motor vehicle and driver licensing agency to issue photo ID cards to non-drivers and retain personal information about them. A privacy group campaigned against the law, likening it to a State-based universal ID card.
- National census administrators proposed to alter the nature of the national census to make it the most extensive data collection tool on any person. An immediate outcry from civil liberties groups caused the proposal to be dropped.

AUSTRIA

- A smart card is set to replace current health insurance certificate and serve as a European health insurance card.
- An Amendment to the Police Law now allows police to keep public places under audio and video surveillance, and store the data collected up to 48 hours, or longer in case of suspicion of a criminal offence.
- A new amendment to the Data Protection Act introduced clarifications regarding the use of personal data by call centers that airlines and other organizations established to deal with catastrophes.

BELGIUM

- The Council of Ministers is considering the creation of a new entity to coordinate the evaluation of terrorist and extremist threats, and collect information from intelligence and security agencies.
- A new electronic ID card is being rolled out to the entire population, through late 2009. The Privacy Commission and civil liberties organizations have been very critical of the project.
- Belgium is the second country in the world after Malaysia to have issued RFID passports, with the ability to store biometrics at a later stage.

BOLIVIA

- There is no comprehensive data protection act. However, several regulations protect privacy.
- The Constitution was recently modified to introduce the action of *habeas data*.

BRAZIL

- Several bills have been introduced in Congress on data retention, spam and the establishment of a do-not-call list.
- A new bilateral cooperation agreement with the US establishes sharing of information about air travelers.

BULGARIA

- The Ministry of Interior's Public Register of Declassified Archival Documents was made available to the public.
- The Parliament adopted the Ombudsman Act, which sets up a formal system of advocacy in cases where state or municipal authorities violate the rights and freedoms of individuals by their action or failure to act. Parliament later appointed the first Bulgarian Ombudsman.

CANADA

- A government proposal relating to the interception of communications by law enforcement agencies now includes a requirement for telecommunications service providers to have interception capability in place, and warrantless access by police to "subscriber data" upon request.
- The agreement on the transfer of passenger data between Canada and the European Union is scheduled to be signed late 2005.
- The controversial Bill C-17, the Public Safety Act, eventually entered into force after two and a half years of discussions. The Bill amends approximately 23 existing Acts.
- Under a recent case, plaintiffs may compel ISP's to reveal the identities of the subscribers among them who have infringed copyright law by sharing music online. The Court set out a test that plaintiffs must meet in order to obtain disclosure of individuals' identities.
- A Spam Task Force completed its work and presented a report to the government. It is comprised of experts from various fields.

CHILE

- Law 19.423 added new provisions to the Penal Code related to the protection of privacy. It stresses that the collection of information by recording, wiretapping, or other secretive means is prohibited.
- Two bills are also pending on reforming the Penal Code with respect to cyber-crimes.
- New anti-spam legislation was enacted.
- A statute on child pornography created new powers for the Public Prosecutor, judges and police officers.

CHINA

- 8 million of the new second-generation smart ID cards, launched in March 2004, have been distributed nationwide in 2005. All citizens over 16 should receive the new cards by 2008.
- The government started to require all China-based Web sites to register by March 2006, and will close down all non-officially registered Web sites and blogs. The initiative gives even more power to authorities to control online news more effectively. Two American companies, Google and Yahoo!, have been cooperating with Chinese authorities in their censorship efforts.
- The draft of the first personal privacy protection law of the country is being reviewed.
- The Central Bank is expected to build a national database by the end of 2005, which will link seven cities and collect personal data such as occupation, address, and financial credit.
- In late 2004, government officials and representatives of Chinese Internet companies issued anti-spam guidelines for China and put in place an anti-spam center to deal with consultations and complaints.

COLOMBIA

- Anti-terrorism laws were held unconstitutional by the Constitutional Court because they allow the surveillance of communications without judicial authorization.

COSTA RICA

- Three data protection bills are pending.
- Although *habeas data* is not yet regulated, there is case law by the Supreme Court of Justice that provides data protection principles and procedural rules.
- The Supreme Court of Justice has recognized the right to access public information, even though this right is not regulated.

CYPRUS

- The European Directive on Privacy and Electronic Communications was transposed.

- The government will take part in the "Operation Spam Zombies" of the US Federal Trade Commission that aims at combating spam sent through hijacked computers.
- Cyprus will participate in the cooperation procedure concerning the transmission of complaint and intelligence information relevant for the enforcement of applicable laws regulating the use of spam.

CZECH REPUBLIC

- A government report recommends strengthening police and security services' investigative powers.
- The Data Protection Commissioner's Office became a member of the Article 29 Working Party and Europol.

DENMARK

- The Act on Central DNA Register was amended to expand its use in investigative matters.
- Legal framework on spam is modified with more relaxed rules for spammers.

ECUADOR

- A new open government law was enacted.

EL SALVADOR

- A company was involved in a scandal for selling a database containing personal data of millions of Salvadorans to the US government.
- The Regulation of the Penitentiary Law establishes rules protecting the privacy of inmates by adopting many of the principles and rights of the European Data Protection Directive.
- The Constitutional Chamber of the Supreme Court of Justice recognized the right to informational self-determination.

ESTONIA

- Every Estonian citizen will have an electronic ID card by the end of 2006. The cards will be used to identify voters in local elections.

EUROPEAN UNION

- Late 2004, all Member States and three of the candidate Member States signed the Treaty establishing a Constitution for Europe, which provides that everybody has the right to the protection of personal data concerning him or her. If the Constitution is ratified by all signatory countries, data protection will make a significant leap forward to a fundamental right with direct effect throughout the EU.
- The European Network and Information Security Agency, a new agency of the European Union, came into being early 2004. The agency assists the European Commission, the Member States and, consequently, the private sector in meeting the requirements of network and information security, including present and future Community legislation.

FINLAND

- The mobile "Citizen Certificate," a government-issued electronic ID card, will be made available to every Finnish resident before the end of 2005, and used for e-government services.
- RFID Lab Finland, a Finnish application center for RFID technology opened in early 2005. It will partner with universities, research centers and government agencies to provide information, consulting, training services and a testing room.

FRANCE

- Government has plans to introduce biometrics on passports by 2006, and on ID cards by 2007. The ID card will include a contactless chip.
- The national airline company, Air France, has started a campaign of voluntary biometric (fingerprint) identification at one of Paris's airports, in co-operation with the borders police.

GEORGIA

- The Parliament prepared a draft law on counter-surveillance based on the United States Foreign Intelligence Surveillance Act.
- The Parliament and the Council of Europe approved a draft law on freedom of speech and expression.

GERMANY

- The EU Directive on Privacy and Electronic Communications was transposed into national law. The new law does not impose any obligation on providers of electronic services to retain traffic data for law enforcement purposes.
- A new open government law is in draft and is likely to be enacted and enter into force early 2006. *Länder* open government commissioners criticized the scope of the restrictions to the right of access.
- A new criminal law protects against the invasion of privacy by the taking of pictures of persons in their apartments or other protected areas.
- Biometric travel documents will be issued starting in the fall of 2005, while biometric ID cards are planned for 2007. There will be no centralized database containing biometric identifiers.

GREECE

- Video surveillance cameras, originally installed to ensure security of the Olympic games, have stayed in place, but with a new objective: improve traffic.
- Greece developed its first Digital City, an e-government functionality, to simplify public transactions, and deliver new electronic services and methods for citizens to participate to policy-making.

GUATEMALA

- A new open government bill is pending.

HONG KONG

- The UN (Anti-Terrorism Measures) Ordinance, which seeks to implement international conventions against terrorism, was enacted. Its measures against terrorist acts, associates and property, as well as its new powers, may have implications on the rights guaranteed under the Basic Law on privacy.
- The Office of the Privacy Commissioner released non-binding workplace privacy guidelines to standardize best practice among employers.
- All ID card holders had to apply for smart ID cards at the beginning of 2005. The multi-function smart ID card contains basic identity details, a photograph and fingerprint information. A Code of Practice will regulate the processing of smart ID card data.
- The government has developed an anti-spam initiative to strengthen existing regulation, introduce new statutory measures, promote technical solutions and educate people. It also promoted cooperation with neighboring states in order to reduce spam coming from abroad.

HUNGARY

- The Data Protection Act was amended three times in order to fulfill the requirements of the EU Data Protection Directive. The last amendment regarding transborder data flows was enacted in 2005.
- On May 1, 2004 Hungary became a full member of the Article 29 Working Party.

ICELAND

- The Telecommunications Law was recently amended. It provides police with critical communications data, as needed for investigation purposes, without the need for a court order.
- The State Health Insurance Institution intends to increase surveillance of the recipients of disability payments, and of their doctors.

INDIA

- There is increasing pressure on the government to enact a data protection law or a Safe Harbor-type agreement that complies with US and European standards. This push comes in the wake of fraud and identity theft in the business process outsourcing industry.

- The Prevention Of Terrorism Act (POTA) was repealed following heavy criticism that its provisions were frequently misused against Muslims. Critics argued that the Act had often been misused by authorities for political ends, and that POTA had done little to curb those excesses.

IRELAND

- The Criminal Justice (Terrorist Offences) Act of 2005 introduced a 3-year period of data retention.

- The National Database Directory, which lists the individuals unwilling to receive unsolicited telephone calls, started to operate in July 2005.
- Recently landlords compelled tenants to divulge their Personal Public Service Number (PPSN) in order to register with the Private Residential Tenancies Board. The PPSN is used as a unique personal identifier in communications between the individual and specified State agencies such as government departments, hospitals, local authorities, and educational institutions.

ISRAEL

- The Criminal Procedure Law was amended to authorize Israeli police to collect DNA samples from suspects and convicts in custody.
- As part of the disengagement process, the Defense Ministry installed new high-tech border crossing surveillance technologies north of the Gaza Strip. Security guards will use video surveillance cameras and biometrics to identify individuals.

ITALY

- In February 2005, an Italian mobile operator warned that they could not answer law enforcement demands for wiretaps anymore because of over-stretched interception equipment.
- Human sub-dermal RFID implants are one of the most recent deployments of RFID technology. They have already been tested in order to store and make available, where necessary, information on a patient's health, or to check access to high-security areas, or even to ensure quick payments in various commercial transactions.

JAPAN

- Ministries have drawn up 30 privacy guidelines in various industry areas, including in the field of genetic research.
- New legislation was enacted in the medical, financial and telecommunications sectors.
- The police are creating a DNA database for crime suspects.
- Several lawsuits have examined whether the Resident Registry Network System infringes on individuals' constitutionally protected right to privacy when it places individuals' information in the system without their consent.
- A company developed a monitoring security system to track the whereabouts of children to protect them against a growing trend of kidnapping among school children.

JORDAN

- A recent study on e-commerce found that Jordan was one of the leading countries in adjusting its laws to conform to technological evolution. Another study showed that would-be e-commerce users feel their privacy is not adequately protected by the law.
- 15 new laws deal with labor, telecommunications, private shareholding and IP, education sector reform and private-public partnerships. But privacy and data protection legislation are noticeably absent from the legislative agenda.

LATVIA

- A new law establishes a national database of DNA information to be used for the investigation of crimes.
- ID cards, which deployment was originally scheduled for 2005, will be compulsory for all residents in 2007.

LITHUANIA

- A new government resolution requires Internet service providers to retain traffic data and content, and make it available to law enforcement.
- An important EU assistance program was launched, and finalized a year later, between Lithuania and Austria in order to strengthen administrative

and technical capacity of the country to ensure the protection of personal data.

LUXEMBOURG

- A new law implemented the Directive on Privacy and Electronic Communications. The law adopts a 12-month traffic data retention regime and an "opt-in" system for spam.
- The Privacy Commission launched a national information and advertising campaign about the data protection legislation to raise awareness.

MACEDONIA

- The National Strategy for Information Society was created. Its objective is to strengthen and expand e-governance-based democratic practices, and support integration into the European Union.

- A draft open government law will take effect on January 1, 2006.

MALAYSIA

- The government, which has been gradually phasing in a multi-purpose national ID smart card ("MyKad"), intends for its remaining 3 million citizens to adopt MyKad by the end of 2005. So far, its value-added applications have seen little usage, because of perception, privacy concerns, or lack of awareness.

- The Parliament opposed moral policing of private behavior by religious enforcement officials. Civil society also strongly objected to it, arguing it infringes individual privacy.

- Police introduced a plan to fingerprint all newborn babies to combat crime. The plan met opposition from lawyers, human rights activists, and others, who argued that the proposal is unconstitutional.

- The government began to implement a biometric system to keep a record of foreigners in the country.

MALTA

- The European Directive on Electronic Communications and Privacy was transposed into the national legislation.

- The government has initiated a program aimed at switching all voice communications between central departments to Voice over Internet Protocol.

MEXICO

- Three different data protection bills were reviewed in the last few years. They are still pending.

- The Federal Consumer Protection Law places restrictions on direct marketing and credit reporting agencies.

MONGOLIA

- A national program was adopted to improve the status of the right to privacy.

- An open government law is in the drafting stage.

- The government drafted a law on information and communications technologies. The draft law was later submitted to the Parliament for discussion.

NETHERLANDS

- In February 2005, the DNA Testing of Convicted Persons Act came into force. It mandates selected convicts to provide DNA samples.
- Early 2005, the government intends to store its citizens' biometric data in a central database, enabling the identification of persons that do not carry a passport with fingerprints or face recognition.
- Compulsory identification for all persons from the age of 14 started in 2005 with the enactment of the Extended Compulsory Identification Act. The legislation is intended to increase general public safety but has been subject to much criticism.

NEW ZEALAND

- Anti-terrorism legislation was amended to make the country comply with international conventions to criminalize those who provide financial support to terrorist organizations. Further anti-terrorist and anti-money-laundering measures are being considered.

- A new bill creates new offenses that prohibit the making, possession and publication of intimate visual recordings in circumstances that a person expects to be private and without her knowledge.

NIGERIA

- The government is producing ID cards throughout the country to provide data for planning, investigate and control crimes, assist in identification of illegal immigrants, and enhance national security.
- A Freedom of Access to Information Bill is pending. It seeks to provide access to public records to facilitate greater access to federal, state, and local government information.
- A new electronic passport that will contain biometrics is set to replace the previous one by the end of 2005. The country ratified an international convention that implements a biometric identity verification system for seafarers.

NORWAY

- Legislation was recently amended to comply with the Cybercrime Convention.
- A new draft bill would compel Internet service providers to retain their customers' traffic data for one year for law enforcement purposes.

PARAGUAY

- A new bill on terrorism-related crimes aims at achieving a balance between the right to privacy and the investigation of potential terrorist actions.

PERU

- A pending data protection bill is based on the EU Data Protection Directive.

- The new Code of Criminal Procedure allows police to require identification and surveillance of individuals under relaxed standards.

- A new anti-spam law provides victims with redress rights.

PHILIPPINES

- An anti-terrorism bill, prompted by recent terrorist bombings, establishes a national identification system and gives authorities broad new powers, including arresting subjects without warrants and detaining them for longer periods of time. There is opposition from human rights organizations and within the government.

- A new airport identification computer system ("PISCES") screens for potential terrorists who attempt to travel to the US. PISCES processes facial images, fingerprints, and biographical information, and allows for exchange of passenger information.

POLAND

- The Computerization Act, recently enacted, aims at modernizing public administration and the coordination of computerization.
- Poland ratified the Protocol amending the European Convention on the Suppression of Terrorism.
- The Inspector General became a member of the Article 29 Working Party and Poland has become a party to the Europol Convention and a member of the Europol Joint Supervisory Body.

PORTUGAL

- The project of citizen card has been brought to full speed, with a view to deliver its multi-purpose features by 2006. The card will hold ID, tax, social security, health insurance and elector information.

- New regulation added AIDS to the list of diseases that have to be notified by any doctor to the Health Ministry.

ROMANIA

- The new Data Protection Law No. 506/2004 transposed the Directive on Electronic Communications and Privacy.
- A law that establishes the first data protection authority of the country was enacted.

RUSSIA

- The Public Chamber was created after a major terrorist attack. It will serve as a collective ombudsman, and analyze draft legislation and the government's expertise when making decisions involving the public interest.

- The government established a special office to investigate crimes in the field of information technologies.

- A new counter-terrorism bill introduced the concept of "state of terrorist emergency." Such state may last up to 60 days and cover the territory of the whole country.

- A newly created expert group is working to establish the legal, technical and financial conditions for using new biometric passports before the beginning of 2006.

SAN MARINO

- San Marino becomes a party to the Second Optional Protocol to the International Covenant on Civil and Political Rights.

SINGAPORE

- Authorities have recently called for increased use of video surveillance cameras in the streets in order to beef up security against terrorism.

- RFID has increasingly attracted the attention of the major technology players because it could be a huge revenue generator in years to come in several areas, such as airports, seaports and retail logistics applications. However, major concerns remain such as cost, lack of common standards and privacy.
- Late 2004, the government launched a giant e-government portal and a national electronic payment hub. According to the government, its data privacy protection code will apply. However, there are still critical concerns about the potential information security risks these projects raise.
- The Bioethics Advisory Committee drew up guidelines to ensure that individuals undertake genetic testing voluntarily and protect their privacy and the confidentiality of their information.

SLOVAK REPUBLIC

- The Data Protection Act was amended.
- The Slovak government announced plans to start issuing biometric passports by September 1, 2006.
- The new law on terrorism will be drafted in the fall of 2005.

SLOVENIA

- The Electronic Central Registry started to operate. The Register is a reference electronic population registry enabling authorized administrators' access to the population registry.
- A major bank published information about its customers' accounts on the Internet, which made it easy for everyone to access account holders' names, addresses, tax numbers and account numbers.

SOUTH AFRICA

- The Interception Act of 2002, which has yet to come into force, aims at regulating the interception and monitoring of certain communications. Several problems have begun to emerge, such as impractical operational requirements and high costs.
- Plans to issue a multi-purpose smart card are in the works. The card would be used to provide access to all government departments with banking facilities. In the long term, the card could function as a passport,

driver's license, identity document and bankcard, linked to fingerprint information.

- The Post Office is planning a joint venture with a private company to launch a National Address Database, which would contain personal information on millions of South Africans, including sensitive data such as income segmentation, date of birth, gender, and ethnic group.

SOUTH KOREA

- In February 2005, the government proposed to develop a new online identification system to replace the use of resident registration numbers.
- Unauthorized phone taps have been increasing at an alarming rate.
- Despite rising public awareness about violations of privacy, the Ministry of Justice has been pushing a controversial new law that grants government authorities greater freedom to gather evidence through phone-taps, by requiring landline and wireless telephone companies to implement new surveillance technologies. The law is expected to be completed by August 2005.
- The MIC purchased private information of fingerprints and facial skeletal features without legal basis. The Korea Information Security Agency, has carried out the collection of 3,600 fingerprints and 2,020 facial skeletal features, but denied any wrongdoing.

SPAIN

- The terrorist attack in Madrid was followed by a set of measures to address Islamist terrorism.

SRI LANKA

- The government is working on a regulatory and policy framework for the development of information and communication technologies in the country. It would include a code of practice for data protection, to be drafted in consultation with the private sector.
- The Prevention of Computer Crime Bill of 2003 has been approved by the Cabinet of Ministers and recently presented to the Sri Lanka Parliament. This act aims at combating computer crime.
- The Freedom of Access to Official Information Bill 2003 is pending, waiting for cabinet approval.

SWEDEN

- New biometric passports, based on ICAO specifications to be introduced on October 1, 2005.
- Sweden and a few other EU Member States came forward with a proposal for new EU Framework rules on mandatory retention of traffic data. The proposal aims at harmonizing retention rules throughout the EU in order to facilitate judicial cooperation in criminal matters.
- Following the tsunami disaster in December 2004, the Parliament authorized a database of children's blood samples to be used for identification of victims.

SWITZERLAND

- Biometric passports will be available around September 2006.
- The government agreed with its US counterpart to disclose the data of its air travelers to US authorities in transatlantic flights.

TAIWAN

- The Household Registration Law requires citizens over age 14 to submit all 10 fingerprints upon receipt of their renewed national ID cards in late 2005, which the government plans to use to establish a national fingerprint bank.
- Originally intended to store only enough information to make patient registration easier, the health insurance integrated circuit (IC) card now includes a record of every major illness, injury, organ donation, prescription and results of diagnostic tests. This data-processing system is heavily criticized because it arguably violates data protection legislation.
- The amended Sexual Violation Prevention Law now requires "high risk" sex offenders to wear electronic RFID tags after their release from jail to enable police to monitor their movements.

THAILAND

- Wiretapping is prevalent throughout the country. Police recently asked the government to enact a law permitting warrantless, judicially unsupervised wiretaps and searches. The opposition condemned this attempt to override civil liberties and human rights, and the idea did not develop.

- Political bugging is no less common. Politicians and human rights activists accused a political party of wiretapping political opponents and journalists.
- The government is currently implementing a system of national ID smart cards. It plans to integrate them into an e-government campaign, which would provide access to most of its services through the Internet. Several human rights and privacy advocates criticized the government for pushing an intrusive identification system while the country still lacks a data protection law.

TURKEY

- The Telecommunications Authority adopted a new data security regulation which follows the EU Telecommunications Data Protection Directive (97/66/EC).
- A draft of Data Protection Act is being reviewed at the government level.

UGANDA

- Although Uganda does not have a data protection authority *per se*, its Human Rights Commission handles complaints that deal with intrusion into privacy.
- The Suppression of Terrorism Act permits an authorized officer to intercept the communications of, and conduct surveillance on, individuals. The Act allows interception of letters, telephone calls, facsimile messages, e-mails, and bank records. It also allows rigorous security checks and surveillance of persons or premises.
- The new Access to Information Act provides that the right of access should not interfere with the right to privacy.

UKRAINE

- In March 2003, the Law on Combating Terrorism severely restricted the guarantees of secrecy in banking, access to information, and increased telecommunications monitoring powers of the Security Service.
- Six cases where the Ukrainian government is a defendant are pending before the European Court of Human Rights. They deal with the

infringement of convicts' right to private life in their correspondence, the receipt of parcels, postal packets, the limitation of meetings with relatives.

UNITED KINGDOM

- The government reintroduced its National ID Proposal. It requires the creation of a central National Identity Register and the issuing of "voluntary" ID cards with biometric identifiers.
- The Freedom of Information Act was eventually fully implemented after its adoption in 2000.

UNITED STATES

- Several major consumer information security breaches occurred in the private sector, triggering serious scrutiny from Congress and state legislatures. Many bills are pending that would better protect consumers by limiting the collection and use of their sensitive information, informing them when security breaches occur, and strengthening industry data-processing security rules.
- The controversial REAL ID Act of 2005 was enacted as a response to the 9/11 Commission's recommendations to prevent would-be terrorists from obtaining identity documents. The law requires all states to comply with federal standards when issuing driver's licenses by May 2008, and creates a de facto national identity card.
- Congress has considered renewal of a few USA PATRIOT Act provisions, set to expire at the end of 2005, and the passage of additional provisions that would expand law enforcement powers while reducing accountability.
- The government abandoned a passenger profiling program ("CAPPS II") in late 2004, to quickly replace it with another slightly different program. An independent report questioned the efficacy of its privacy protections and the adequacy of its traveler redress measures. The government and the private sector are also working on "Registered Traveler" programs, aimed at speeding up airport security checks. Such programs raise considerable privacy concerns over the way passenger information is collected and used, and how likely they are to cause inequity in treatment among travelers.
- Through its US-VISIT program, the government has expanded its surveillance to include almost all foreign visitors at immigration border

controls. An independent report concluded that the government had failed to fully address privacy issues when developing the program.

- Although several federal agencies are already using or planning to use RFID tags, an independent investigation reported a general failure to address privacy issues raised by the use of the new technology. In one case, the planned implementation of RFID passports was designed in utter disregard for fundamental security and privacy risks, but later modified for improved security because of heavy criticism by privacy advocates.

URUGUAY

- A new data protection law regulates data banks containing commercial information and establishes the institution of *habeas data*.
- A new data protection authority was established that functions under the Ministry of Economy

VENEZUELA

- A new law establishes censorship and restrictions on the type of information that can be published.
- The names of petition signers for the presidential recall referendum were made available to the public on the Internet, thereby endangering voting secrecy.
- The first draft of the project of Law for the Protection of Data and Habeas Data has been archived.
- A new law on identification promotes the adoption of biometrics to ensure better identification and to incorporate them in new ID cards.

Argentine Republic

Articles 18 and 19 of the Argentine Constitution provide (in part), "The home is inviolable as is personal correspondence and private papers; the law will determine what cases and what justifications may be relevant to their search or confiscation. The private actions of men that in no way offend order nor public morals, nor prejudice a third party, are reserved only to God's judgment, and are free from judicial authority. No inhabitant of the Nation will be obligated to do that which is not required by law, nor be deprived of what is not prohibited." Article 43, enacted in 1994, provides a right of "*habeas data*"[907]: "Every person may file an action to obtain knowledge of the content and purpose of all the data pertaining to him or her contained in public records or databanks, or in private ones whose purpose is to provide reports; and in the case of falsehood of information or its use for discriminatory purposes, a person will be able to demand the deletion, correction, confidentiality or update of the data contained in the above records. The secrecy of journalistic information sources may not be affected."[908] *Habeas data* remedy is also included in the constitutions of many provinces of Argentina[909] but only a few of them have local data protection legislation. Argentine jurisprudence has recognised this remedy as a fundamental and directly applicable right. Up to now most *habeas data* cases have dealt with correction of commercial and credit information.

In 1999, the Supreme Court of Argentina ruled in two important cases on the scope of *habeas data*. The leading case is *Urteaga v. Estado Nacional*.[910] There, the Supreme Court allowed an individual access to personal information about his brother, who had disappeared during the military government, presumably in an armed conflict.[911] The lower courts dismissed the action of *habeas data* for

---

[907] *Habeas data* is a subcategory of the procedure enshrined in the Constitution for the protection of constitutional rights, therefore making the protection of personal data a fundamental, as well as directly applicable, right. *See* European Commission Decision pursuant to Directive 95/46/EC of the European Parliament and of the Council on the Adequate Protection of Personal Data in Argentina, June 30, 2003, available at <http://europa.eu.int/comm/internal_market/privacy/docs/adequacy/decision-c2003-1731/decision-argentine_en.pdf>.

[908] *Constitución de la Nación Argentina* (1994), available at <http://www.oefre.unibe.ch/law/icl/ar00000_.html>, *see also* <http://www.constitution.org/cons/argentin.htm> (in Spanish).

[909] List available at <http://www.protecciondedatos.com.ar/legislacion.htm#legis4>.

[910] Urteaga c. Estado Nacional, Supreme Court of Argentina, October 15, 1998, 1-2 Derecho y Nuevas Tecnologías 193 (2000).

[911] This case was decided one month after a case where the Supreme Court denied a mother the right to access to information about her daughter, who had also disappeared during the military regime. In "Aguiar de Lapaco," the Court based its opinion in the principle of *non bis in idem* or guarantee against double prosecution (double

lack of standing. The Court of Appeals reasoned that *habeas data* grants access only to personal information, and the claimant was trying to access data related to a third person. However, the Supreme Court reversed the ruling. The core of the judgment indicated an expanding approach to the interpretation of *habeas data*, granting a wide right of access to personal information.

The other case is *Ganora v. Estado Nacional*,[912] where the Supreme Court of Argentina established that *habeas data* can be used against any kind of public database. The claim was initiated by two lawyers who were defending Adolfo Scilingo, an ex-navy official who confessed his participation in crimes during the military regime. Arguing investigation and surveillance from the Government, the lawyers requested access to data in official databases about them. The district court judge and the Court of Appeals refused access, even without hearing the government's arguments based on a national security exception. The Supreme Court of Argentina restated its holding in *Urteaga* and the need to interpret *habeas data* in light of the international and foreign legislation. They cited the European Human Rights case *Leander*[913] and also made a reference to *Nixon v. United States*,[914] where the United States Supreme Court rejected the arguments of President Nixon, who alleged a confidential privilege over information. Finally they concluded that *habeas data* allowed access to government databases, and that an exception based on public interest should be subject to judicial review. This case shows the expanding interpretation of *habeas data* by the Supreme Court of Argentina.

The Law for Protection of Personal Data

In November 2000, Argentina passed the Law for the Protection of Personal Data (LPDP).[915] It is in conformance with Article 43 of the Constitution and based on the European Union Data Protection Directive and the Spanish Data Protection Acts of 1992 and 1999. It contains provisions relating to general data protection principles, the rights of data subjects, the obligations of data controllers and data users, the supervisory authority, sanctions, and rules of procedure in seeking

---

jeopardy) because the right of access was used in criminal proceedings and the defendants were granted a presidential pardon. But the Court opinion was the object of strong political and scholarly criticism, and the high tribunal distinguished "Aguiar de Lapaco" from "Urteaga" since the last one was a civil case. Justice Boggiano's dissidence in "Aguiar de Lapaco" stated that *habeas data* could be used in the case to access to any kind of information held by government.

[912] Ganora, Mario c/ Estado Nacional y otros /habeas corpus y habeas data, Supreme Court of Argentina, September 16, 1999, 1-2 Derecho y Nuevas Tecnologías 229 (2000).

[913] Leander Case, 116 Eur. Ct. H.R. (ser. A) at 9 (1987).

[914] 418 United States 683 (1974).

[915] Law No. 25.326, available at <http://www.ulpiano.com/Dataprotection_argentina.htm> (in Spanish).

habeas data as a judicial remedy. *Habeas data* is a special, simplified and quick judicial remedy for the protection of personal data. International transfer of personal information is prohibited to countries without adequate protection. The European Union decided that Argentina could be considered as providing an adequate level of protection for personal data meeting the requirements of the EU Data Protection Directive.[916] The adequacy finding implies that all transborder data flows between Argentina and the European Union are presumptively considered in compliance with the EU Directive. Argentina is the first country in Latin America to obtain such adequacy approval.

In addition to the LPDP, data protection provisions are also contained in several legal instruments regulating different sectors, such as credit card transactions, statistics, banking, telecommunications or health.[917] On November 2001 the Government enacted the Regulation of the Data Protection Act,[918] which lays down rules for the enactment of the Act, supplements its provisions, and clarifies diverging interpretations of the LPDP. Argentine data protection rules cover the protection of personal data recorded in data files, registers, databanks or other technical means, which are public; and the protection of personal data recorded in data files, registers, databanks or other technical means which are private, whose purpose is to provide reports. This includes those whose purpose is more than exclusively personal, and those that are intended for the assignment or transfer of personal data. Collection of sensitive data is given additional protections and is prohibited unless authorized by law.[919]

The LPDP has established a data protection authority within the Ministry of Justice, the *Dirección Nacional de Protección de Datos Personales* (DNPDP) (Nation Directorate for the Protection of Personal Data),[920] which has a staff of 12 persons,[921] and is charged with receiving and processing complaints, enforcing the LPDP and endowed with powers of investigation and intervention (*e.g.*, through sanctions of an administrative and a criminal nature). On June 25,

---

[916] European Commission Decision pursuant to Directive 95/46/EC of the European Parliament and of the Council on the Adequate Protection of Personal Data in Argentina, *supra*. *See also* the Data Protection Working Party - Article 29, Opinion 4/2002 on Adequate Level of Protection of Personal Data in Argentina (WP 63). October 3, 2002, available at
<http://europa.eu.int/comm/internal_market/privacy/docs/wpdocs/2002/wp63_en.pdf>, which the European Commission took into account to make its decision.

[917] <www.protecciondedatos.com.ar/legislacion.htm#legis3>.

[918] Approved by Decree No. 1558/2001.

[919] *See* Data Protection Working Party - Article 29, Opinion 4/2002 on Adequate Level of Protection of Personal Data in Argentina (WP 63). October 3, 2002, *supra*.

[920] DNPDP web site available at <http://www.jus.gov.ar/minjus/DPDP/Guia.htm> (in Spanish).

[921] E-mail from Prof. Dr. Juan Antonio Travieso, Director of the DNPDP, to Cédric Laurant, Policy Counsel, Electronic Privacy Information Center, July 13, 2004 (on file with EPIC).

2003, the DNPDP issued it first disposition (see disposition 1/2003, describing different kind of infringements and providing administrative sanctions for breach of the law, consisting in warnings, suspensions, fines, and cancellation of databases. Fines range from ARS 1,000 to 100,000 (between USD 335 and 33,500).[922] In 2003, the DNPDP has received complaints regarding the financial system (62 percent), the army and security agencies (22 percent), and commercial services (nine percent).[923]

Meanwhile, courts have started to interpret the LPDP. A civil court held in 2000 that information about marriage is not within the kind of personal data requiring consent from the data subject. The Commercial Court of Appeals ruled in March 2002 that the term "private databases whose purpose is to provide reports" encompasses all kind of databanks, including banks and financial companies, even if their database was not intended initially to provide reports,[924] and also that the data protection law applies to bank and financial entities in general.[925] Also, courts are applying the prohibition to provide information about credit card transactions and correcting information that is not kept up to date. In an interesting case that applied the data protection act, another trial Court ordered Equifax/Veraz to provide personal data without any kind of codification and in an intelligible way.

The Federal Police also applied the LPDP to a case of surveillance of a political party. The president of this political party, Gustavo Beliz, sued the police under the data protection law and *habeas data* clause of the Constitution requesting all the information that the police had obtained from his party. The Administrative Court of Appeals held that the plaintiff had the right to access the personal information that the police had collected about him without any suspicions of criminal activity. It also held unconstitutional the secret regulation opposed by the defendant for the collection of this data. Finally, in February 2002, the Civil Court of Appeals of Buenos Aires decided a leading case. The Court held that companies trading personal information are to be held strictly liable for damages produced by them.

In February 2004, a Court of Appeals of the Province of Tucumán ruled that judges could not impose fines in the LPDP because the only authority authorized

---

[922] Available at <http://www.proteecciondedatos.com.ar/law12003.htm> (in Spanish).

[923] E-mail from Prof. Dr. Juan Antonio Travieso, *supra*.

[924] Halabi, Ernesto c/ Citibank NA s/amparo, CNCom, Sala C, 26/3/2002.

[925] Becker, José c/Banco de la Provincia de Buenos Aires s/amparo, CNCom, Sala E, 15/5/2002, with a sounded opinion of the Attorney General (*Fiscal de Cámara*).

by law is the DNPDP.[926] Up to June 2004, no penalty has yet been imposed by DNPDP for law infringements. Also, in February 2004 the DNPDP enacted a regulation[927] calling for a mandatory national census of private databases in order to appraise the amount and characteristics of databases existing in the country. The census has to be carried out by June 30, 2004. Census results will be used to determine the final registration requirements of the National Database Registry.

Among many other duties, the LPDP requires that any private or public database containing personal information, either in electronic or hard-copy format, must be registered with the National Database Registry (the Registry) of the DNPDP. Although created in November 2003,[928] the National Database Registry was launched on August 1, 2005.[929] Any person or entity creating files of personal data must register his database and provide detailed information on the kind of data it contains, what its purpose is, where it is stored, how the information was obtained, and the security safeguards in place. The Registry will affect both Argentine and foreign companies doing business in Argentina. Only databases intended for exclusive personal use and not shared with others are excluded.[930] Every holder of a private database containing personal information on private citizens, corporate officials, or an organization's members had to fill out an online form by August 1.

The Registry is an organ integrated in the DNPDP. Its purpose is to enable every individual to exercise the right to know about the existence of data processing, its purpose and the identity of the data controller in order to be able to exercise the right of access, rectification, deletion and opposition. This Register is free and available to the public for consultation.

In May 2003, government documents obtained by the Electronic Privacy Information Center revealed that ChoicePoint, a United States company, had entered into a contract with the United States Government to provide international data from public registries obtained from Argentina, Brazil, Colombia, Costa Rica and Mexico. The transfer of personal information abroad is a matter of much concern for the governments of those countries, as these

---

[926] Moisa, Benjamín c/ Banco Río de la Plata S.A. s/ amparo informativo, Cámara de Apelaciones en lo Civil y Comercial común de Tucumán, Sala I, available at <http://www.diariojudicial.com/nota.asp?IDNoticia=21427> (in Spanish).

[927] Regulation 1/2004, available at <http://infoleg.mecon.gov.ar/txtnorma/93025.htm> (in Spanish).

[928] Regulation 2/2003, available at <http://infoleg.mecon.gov.ar/txtnorma/90557.htm> (in Spanish).

[929] Regulation 2/2005, available at <http://infoleg.mecon.gov.ar/txtnorma/103921.htm> (in Spanish), modify in part by Regulation 4/2005, available at <http://infoleg.mecon.gov.ar/txtnorma/106280.htm> (in Spanish).

[930] Databases created before the launch of the Registry, must be registered between August 2005 and January 31, 2006, while new databases, created after the launch of the Registry, should be registered before its creation.

countries have strict data protection laws (*e.g.*, Argentina) or are about to enact data protection bills (*e.g.*, Colombia, Costa Rica and Mexico). The Argentine data protection authority launched a criminal investigation and the prosecutor has asked for evidentiary measures.

The Civil Code prohibits "that which arbitrarily interferes in another person's life: publishing photos, divulging correspondence, mortifying another's customs or sentiments or disturbing his privacy by whatever means."[931] This article has been applied widely to protect the privacy of the home, private letters and several situations involving intrusive telephone calls, and neighbor's intrusions into one's private life. This provision has been applied widely to private and public plaintiffs.

In 1998, the Argentine Congress enacted the Credit Card Act.[932] The object of this bill is to regulate credit card contracts between consumers and financial institutions and specifically the interest rates that banks charge to consumer credit cards. Article 53 restricts the possibility of transferring information from banks or credit card companies to credit reporting agencies.[933] There is also a specific right of access to personal data of a financial character. The Central Bank of Argentina, whose jurisdiction includes the overview of the monetary policy in the Argentine financial market, has authority to regulate banks. Under that authority it created a public debtor's database,[934] requiring financial entities and banks to collect and classify debtors within a range of risk and to send the information to the database. Under Article 8.1 of the regulation,[935] the data subject (a client of a bank) has a right of access to his information and to know the reason why he or she was included in the database.[936]

Under the Criminal Code the illegal sale of personal data and data trafficking over the Internet may be prosecuted. The Attorney General and the Ministry of Justice have drafted a bill to specifically deal with computer crimes. The bill will prohibit violation of privacy by any means and illegal access to computer

---

[931] *Código Civil* (Civil Code), Article 1071bis, incorporated by Law No. 21.173.

[932] Law No. 25.065 of December 7, 1998 (Official Bulletin of January 14, 1999).

[933] Credit Card Act, Article 53 ("Bar to inform. Credit Card entities, companies and banks and other financial entities shall not transfer information about credit card debts to credit report agencies when the data subject has not paid its debts or is having financial problems, without prejudice of personal data that must be transferred to the Central Bank under current regulations. Those who transfer this information to third parties shall be liable for the damages produced by the release of the personal data.")

[934] *See* Financial System Debtors Database "Central de Deudores del Sistema Financiero," regulated by the Central Bank Circular A 2729 (consolidated version by Circular 2930).

[935] Article 8.1, Central Bank Circular A 2729 (consolidated version by Circular 2930).

[936] Available at <http://www.bcra.gov.ar> (in Spanish) and on CD-ROMs. The last CD-ROM contained a list with 1,950,000 individuals including data on their financial status.

systems and networks. Government is pursuing the enactment of this bill due to a case of hacking of the web site of the Supreme Court. The federal judge investigating the case concluded that the 1921 Criminal Code had no crimes related to computer damage or illegal access. After this decision, the Supreme Court asked the Ministry of Justice to draft a bill to cover this new kind of crime. The bill is currently pending.

Recent Developments

In 2004, a massive pressure came from the Argentine society to deal with the issue of kidnapping which has been increasing in recent years.[937] In May 2004, the Law of Mobile Communication Services was enacted[938] to strengthen security measures to fight against kidnapping by eliminating the anonymity of purchasers of mobile phones.[939] The law compels companies that sell mobile equipment or terminals, to collect their customers' identity. These provisions will also be applicable in the case of prepaid card users. The law also establishes that commercialization of mobile communication services should be made through legally authorized companies, thereby prohibiting the activity of resellers, wholesalers and any other unauthorized person.

In January 2004 the Congress approved a controversial Data Retention Law that amended the National Telecommunications Law of 2003.[940] The new law compels all telecommunications companies and Internet service providers to record, index and store traffic data for a 10-year period, in order to give information to the Judicial Power and the Attorney General's Office (*Ministerio Público*) when required.[941][942]

---

[937] "Por Axel, por Nuestros Hijos," La Nación, August 4, 2005, available at <http://www.reforma-politica.com.ar/rp/noticias.php?page=noticia-407> (in Spanish).

[938] Law No. 25.891 of Mobile Communication Services (*Ley No. 25.891 de servicios de comunicaciones móviles*), enacted on May 21, 2004, available at <http://www1.hcdn.gov.ar/dependencias/cceinformatica/Sanciones/Ley_25891.html> (in Spanish).

[939] "Todo Lo que Blumberg ya Logró,", Página 12, August 27, 2004, available at <http://www.pagina12web.com.ar/diario/imprimir/40254-2004-08-27.html> (in Spanish).

[940] Law No. 25.873 of December 17, 2003, available at <http://infoleg.mecon.gov.ar/txtnorma/92549.htm> (in Spanish).

[941] Article 45 *ter* of the National Telecommunications Law No. 19.798 (*Ley Nacional de Telecomunicaciones*).

[942] Law No. 19.798, National Telecommunications Law (*Ley Nacional de Telecomunicaciones*), approved on August 1972, modified by Law No. 25873, Official Journal, February 9, 2004, available at <http://infoleg.mecon.gov.ar/txtnorma/texactley19798.htm> and <http://infoleg.mecon.gov.ar/scripts1/busquedas/norma.asp?num=92549> (in Spanish).

On November 8, 2004, a new decree (No. 1563/2004) was enacted to implement the Data Retention Law.[943] It requires that companies develop an infrastructure that allows authorities to obtain, store and forward traffic data.[36] In addition, it compels companies to acquire the appropriate technology to be able to immediately intercept and forward intercepted communications to the authorities when required to do so by a court order, as provided for by the National Intelligence Law No. 25520.[944] The same Decree requires telecommunications service providers and ISPs to decrypt their customers' encrypted communications if they have offered encryption tools to their customers as part of their services. It mandates them not to disclose the technical and administrative methods used to comply with their disclosure obligations to law enforcement.

There was a strong pressure from ISPs and the public opinion against this decree.[945] In April 2005, the mainstream media soon reported on the controversial measure.[946] On April 25, the President suspended the decree to allow some time for its evaluation.[947]

The Argentinean Chamber of Databases and Online Services (Camara Argentina de Base de Datos y Servicios en Línea)[948] introduced an Acción de Amparo[949]

---

[943] Decree No. 1563/2004 (*Decreto* 1563/2004) of November 8, 2004, available at <http://infoleg.mecon.gov.ar/txtnorma/100806.htm> (in Spanish).

944 Article 5 of National Intelligence Law No. 25520 (*Ley de Inteligencia Nacional No. 25520*), approved on December 3, 2001 states' "Communication by telephone, post, telegraph, fax or any other means of sending objects or transmitting images, voice or packages of data as well as any other type of information, files, records and/or private documents or reading material not intended for public audience are inviolable throughout the Republic of Argentina unless otherwise exempted by a court order". The Law is available at <http://infoleg.mecon.gov.ar/txtnorma/70496.htm> (in Spanish).

[945] *See* Beatriz Busaniche web log's at <http://www.d-sur.net/bbusaniche/index.php?cat=4> (in Spanish) and Digital Journalism web log at <http://dialogica.com.ar/periodismo/archives/2005/03/captacion_conse.html> (in Spanish).

[946] *See* Mariana Carvajal, "Hay Un Espía en Mi PC," available at <http://pagina12web.com.ar/diario/elpais/1-49541.html> (in Spanish), "Vigilancia Electrónica," available at <http://pagina12web.com.ar/diario/elpais/subnotas/49541-16767.html> and "Invasión a la Privacidad," *Página 12*, April 10, 2004, available at <http://pagina12web.com.ar/diario/elpais/subnotas/49541-16768.html> (in Spanish); "Frenan la Polémica Ley para Controlar a Usuarios de Internet," Clarín, April 12, 2005, available at <http://www.clarin.com/diario/2005/04/12/um/m-955963.htm>. *See also* "Los Datos de Tráfico Gozan de la Misma Protección que los Datos de Contenido," Interview of Pablo Palazzi, Diario Judicial, April 12, 2005, available at <http://www.diariojudicial.com/nota.asp?IDNoticia=25196> (in Spanish).

[947] Decree No. 357/2005 that suspends the application of the Decree No. 1563 of November 8, 2004. (Decreto 357/2005 Suspéndase la aplicación del Decreto No. 1563 del 8 de noviembre de 2004, available at <http://infoleg.mecon.gov.ar/txtnorma/105679.htm> (in Spanish). See also Carvajal, Mariana. "Marcha atrás con el Espionaje por Computadora", available at <http://www.clarin.com/diario/2005/04/12/um/m-955963.htm>.

948 Cámara Argentina de Base de Datos y Servicios en Línea (CABASE) is the Argentinean chamber that groups the Internet Service Providers in that country.

949 The "*acción de amparo*" is an individual constitutional complaint mechanism that has the purpose of protecting all constitutional rights, with the exception of *habeas corpus*, the action of *habeas data* and the *acción de cumplimiento* against the violation, or threats of violation, from an individual or an institution.

---

against the National State (Estado Nacional) in relation to Law No. 25873 and Decree No. 1563/2004. In May 13, 2005, the court ruled that the Law was unconstitutional.[950] This resolution was recently appealed by the National State (Estado Nacional).[951]

Communications PrivacyUnder the Code of Penal Procedure, "A judge may arrange, for the purposes of building a case, the intervention of telephone communications or whatever other means of communication." The Penal Code provides penalties for publishing private communications.[952] The National Defense Law prohibits domestic surveillance by military personnel.

In April 1999, the Criminal Court of Appeals in Buenos Aires recognized a right to privacy in electronic mail communications applying a section of the Penal Code related to the protection of secrets. Although the criminal provision was drafted in 1921, the Court had an open approach to the interpretation of the statute.[953] Under this case, data such as stored files and e-mail is not to be examined by anyone else without the user's permission.

In 1995, the United Nations Human Rights Committee expressed concern that the judicial authorization for wiretaps was too broad.[954] In December 2001, a new intelligence law was enacted with implementing regulations to be issued 180 days later. The law provides for legislative oversight of government intelligence activities. It also prohibits the unauthorized interception of telephone, postal, facsimile, and other communications and private documents. The Penal Code, dating from 1921, did not previously punish wiretapping. There have been numerous scandals relating to unauthorized wiretapping over the years and several cases of wiretapping were dismissed because of the lack of a criminal statute.

In 1996, the national government began a new crackdown on tax evaders. Measures included reviewing citizens' credit cards, insurance, and tax records.

---

[950] *See* <http://www.cpsr-peru.org/bdatos/argentina/privacidad/sentencia2.pdf> (in Spanish).

951 See "Kirchner Insiste en Revisar Corresponencia Ajena: Los Abogados del Gobierno Defendieron la Ley Espía," Urgente 24, June 2, 2005, available at

<http://www.urgente24.com/columnas/index.php?IDTEMA=154&IDDOCUMENTO=38096&IDPUBLICACI
ON=88141&SEC> (in Spanish).

[952] *Código Penal de la República Argentina*, Articles 153-157, available at <http://www.codigos.com.ar/penal/indice.htm> (in Spanish).

[953] Criminal Court of Appeals in Buenos Aires (Sixth chamber), 4.3.99 "Lanata c. Dufau," in El Derecho, (E.D.), May 17, 1999.

[954] United Nations, 19th Annual Report of the Human Rights Committee, A/50/40, October 3, 1995.

One bill allowed citizens whose credit card records had been obtained to sue for invasion of privacy.[955] The same year, the Argentina Passport and Federal Police Identification System, developed by Raytheon E-Systems, was inaugurated at the Buenos Aires airport. The system combines personal data, color photos and fingerprints.[956]

In 2003, two labor courts issued decisions on workplace privacy. In the first case,[957] an employee was dismissed because he was using computer resources for his personal use. Because the computer was shared with other employees, there was only one Internet connection on the office premises, and there was no privacy policy in place, the court ruled that the employee had not used the computer resources in an inappropriate manner, and that he had no expectation of privacy in its use. In another case, which involved an employee dismissed for distributing e-mail with obscene contents to her co-workers during working hours, the Court found in favor of the employee because the company had not implemented a written policy regarding e-mail use and monitoring.[958] On July 13, 2003, one of the most important Argentinean newspapers, *Diario Clarin*, reported that the government was planning to gather in a database all the information available in several public databases of the administration. At the same time the government was planning to issue new and enhanced IDs for all citizens and homologue the database with the Federal Bureau of Investigation.[959] The government was also planning to sell commercial information like a credit bureau to individuals and companies. The proposal was criticized by the privacy community, but was finally adopted on December 2003.[960] No opposition was heard from the DNPDP.

In November 1998, the City of Buenos Aires approved a law on access to information. The law gives all persons the right to ask for and to receive information held by the local authorities and creates a right of judicial review. Individuals have the right under *habeas data* to update, rectify, maintain the

---

[955] New York Times, June 10, 1996.

[956] Business Wire, September 12, 1996.

[957] Pereyra, Leandro R. v. Servicios de Almacén Fiscal Zona Franca y Mandatos SA., C. NAC. TRAB., sala 7ª, 27/3/2003.

[958] V.R.I. c/ Vestiditos SA s/ despido, C.NAC.TRAB. sala 10º, November 17, 2003.

[959] *See* Lucas Guagnini & Jorgelina Vidal, "El Tema del Domingo – Control y Privacidad: Un Proyecto de 1.500 Millones de Pesos," Diario Clarin, July 13, 2003, available at <http://www.ulpiano.com/dataprotection_clarin.pdf> (in Spanish).

[960] Decree 1187/2003, available at <http://infoleg.mecon.gov.ar/txtnorma/90867.htm> (in Spanish).

---

confidentiality of, or suppress their information.[961] But critics say that government agencies jealously keep public records and that it is very difficult to obtain information.[962] While the national Congress stalled any legislative proposals in this matter, on December 2003 a Presidential decree[963] established freedom of information in the Executive Power.[964] In 1984, Argentina adopted the American Convention on Human Rights into domestic law. The Convention was incorporated into the Constitution in 1994 and has since been used by the Argentine Supreme Court to determine domestic cases.[965] In a recent case the Court decided that a famous sportsman had the right to forbid the media to broadcast the existence of a lawsuit related to his natural child base under the right to privacy provided in the American Convention on Human Rights and section 19 of the Federal Constitution.[966] In September 2001, the Court ruled that a weekly news magazine had violated the privacy of former president Carlos Menem when it reported, in 1994 and 1995, that he had used his office to advance the career of Congresswoman with whom he was having an affair.[967]

In March 2004, in a search made at the Police Investigation Department of the Province of Santiago del Estero, a judge found and seized 40,000 illegal folders and two computers that contained personal data about local politicians, lawyers, journalists, judges, monks, professionals and representatives of human rights organizations, most of whom were known as political opponents to the provincial government.[968] The DNPDP could not intervene due to its lack of jurisdiction over Province public databases, despite the flagrant violation of the LPDP.

On April 16, 2004, Consumers International,[969] the *Instituto de Derecho del Consumidor del Colegio Público de Abogados de la Capital Federal*, the *Foro de*

---

[961] *See* Pablo Andrés Palazzi, El Derecho de Acceso a la Información Pública en la Ley No. 104 de la Ciudad Autónoma de Buenos Aires, 11 REDI– (June 1999), available at <http://publicaciones.derecho.org/redi/index.cgi?/N%FAmero_11_-_Junio_de_1999> (in Spanish).

[962] *See* La Nación, "Es de Difícil Cumplimiento la Ley de Acceso a la Información," July 11, 2000.

[963] Decree 1172/2003, available at <http://infoleg.mecon.gov.ar/txtnorma/90763.htm> (in Spanish).

[964] *See* María Baron, "The Transparency Labyrinth in Argentina", April 13, 2004 <http://www.freedominfo.org/case/argentina.htm> (in Spanish).

[965] *See* Janet Koven Levit, The Constitutionalization of Human Rights in Argentina: Problem or Promise? 37 Columbia Journal of Transnational Law 281. *See also* Néstor Pedro Sagues, Judicial Censorship of the Press in Argentina, 4 Sw. J. of L. & Trade Am 45 (1997) (explaining the importance of understanding the make-up of both the Inter-American Court and the Inter-American Commission on Human Rights because the Argentine Supreme Court relies on their opinions as a guide for interpreting personal rights issues).

[966] *See* Supreme Court, Fallos 324:975.

[967] *See* Menem v. Noticias, Supreme Court, Fallos 324:2895.

[968] *See* "Espiaban a 40 mil santiagueños", *La voz del Interior* On Line, March 7, 2004, available at <http://www.lavoz.com.ar/2004/0307/politica/nota226431_1.htm> (in Spanish).

[969] Consumers International – *Oficina para América Latina y el Caribe*'s web site <http://www.consumidoresint.cl>.

Habeas Data[970] and the Electronic Privacy Information Center organized a roundtable on emerging privacy issues in South America.[971] The objective of this meeting was to promote the dialogue between South American consumer protection organizations, government agencies and experts in consumer and privacy law, and help make South American consumer protection groups more aware of the issue of privacy.

On November 11, 2003 a federal judge from the City of Buenos Aires ordered halt to spamming in Argentina's first spam case.[972] The decision was very welcome because spam was previously not under control in the country.[973] The plaintiffs argued that the LPDP gives them a right to opt out from receiving spam, which the defendant, a well-known Argentine spammer, did not comply with when the plaintiffs asked to be removed from his database.[974] The case was stalled for almost one year on jurisdictional grounds. The Federal Court of Appeals eventually decided that federal courts had jurisdiction to hear the case because the Internet was used to send spam.[975]

At the same time, iCAUCE.ar,[976] the Argentinean Committee of the International Coalition Against Unsolicited Commercial Email was created. In 2004 several anti-spam bills have been introduced in Congress, most of them proposing opt-out systems. In June 2004, The Argentine Chamber of Databases and Online Services (CABASE) and the Argentine Direct and Interactive Marketing Association (AMDIA) organized the first AntiSpam Conference in Argentina.[977] As a result both associations signed a letter of intent in order to work together against spam. The most interesting and complete anti-spam law proposal came from iCAUCE.ar.[978] The bill[979] will be introduced in Parliament soon but will first be shared with AMDIA and CABASE members, which are the two major

---

[970] <http://ar.groups.yahoo.com/group/habeasdata/>.

[971] <http://www.thepublicvoice.org/events/buenosaires04/default.html>.

[972] Gustavo Daniel Tanús and Pablo Andrés Palazzi, c. Cosa, Carlos Alberto y Magraner, Ana Carolina s. Habeas Data, Federal Civil and Commercial Court No. 3, Secretariat No. 6.

[973] David Haskel, "Judge in Argentina Orders Halt to Spamming in First E-mail Junk Case," BNA Privacy & Security Law Report, Vol. 2, No. 47, p. 1344, November 24, 2003.

[974] *See* <http://www.protecciondedatos.com.ar/resolucionspam.htm>.

[975] *See* <http://dataprotection.blogspot.com/2003_08_01_dataprotection_archive.html#106191745168612252>.
976 iCAUCE is an international organisation formed by organisations around the world engaged in pressing for laws against e-mail spam, which includes both unsolicited commercial email and unsolicited bulk email . iCAUCE's mission is to provide a support mechanism for volunteers who wish to undertake these activities in countries that do not have an independent lobbying organization

977*See* <http://www.antispamforum2004.org.ar>.

978 *See* <http://www.cauce.org.ar>.

979 *See* <http://wiki.cauce.org.ar/cgi-bin/moin.cgi/PropuestaDeLeyDeIcauceAr>.

associations dealing with spam in Argentina, and whose members are marketing and ISP companies which aim is to submit a bill together with iCAUCE.

Republic of Armenia

Constitutional Privacy Framework

The Constitution of the Republic of Armenia (RA) was adopted on July 5, 2005. According to the article 20 of the Constitution of RA:

> Everyone is entitled to defend his or her private and family life from unlawful interference and defend his or her honor and reputation from attack. The gathering, maintenance, use and dissemination of illegally obtained information about a person's private and family life are prohibited. Everyone has the right to confidentiality in his or her correspondence, telephone conversations, mail, telegraph and other communications, which may only be restricted by court order.

The grounds for carrying out searches are determined by the Constitution of the Republic of Armenia:

> Everyone is entitled to privacy in his or her own dwelling. It is prohibited to enter a person's dwelling against his or her own will except under cases prescribed by law. A dwelling may be searched only by court order and in accordance with legal procedures.[980]

In 2005, a mandatory referendum on constitutional amendments is scheduled to take place in Armenia that will consider changes to Article 20. The new proposal includes the following statements: "Everyone has the right that his or her personal and family life is being respected." "State authorities cannot collect, store, use or give information regarding a person other than it is prescribed by law." "Everyone, except the cases prescribed by law, has right to have an access to official personal data concerning himself/herself and to require correction or extermination of that data if it is not reliable or was received illegally." "Everyone has the right to confidentiality in his or her correspondence, telephone

---

[980] Consitution of the Republic of Armenia, article 21, English version available at <http://www.arminco.com/hayknet/laws/conarm-e.htm>.

conversations, mail, telegraph and other communications, which may only be restricted by the way, prescribed by law, by court order."

Statutory Rules on Privacy

On October 8, 2002, the "Law of the Republic of Armenia on Personal Data" was adopted and since January 2003, it has been in force. This Law regulates relationships that arise during the processing of personal data by state or local self-governance bodies, state or municipal institutions, as well as natural persons and legal entities.

The Law does not regulate relationships related to the processing of personal data published in public sources and not considered to be of special importance, as well as related to the processing of personal data by natural persons for their personal, family or other matters.

According to the Law, personal data is any data on facts, cases, circumstances with regard to a natural person, contained on a physical carrier and in a form that allows or may allow someone to identify the individual.[981] Personal data are collected for strictly defined and announced legal purposes and cannot be used for other purposes except in cases prescribed by the law. It is prohibited to collect and process personal data that are not required for the purpose for which the data are processed.[982]

Personal data processing is legal: When the data subject consents to personal data processing; When data processing is required for the protection of the data subject's vital interests, if there is no ground to presume that the data subject would not consent to their processing; In cases prescribed by the law or directly following from the provisions of the law or when data processing required for the law implementation; When it is required for state or public safety. Data subject may withdraw his/her consent at any time in a written form. Consent cancellation shall not have a retroactive effect.[983]

---

[981] Law of the Republic of Armenia on Personal Data, article 2.
[982] *Id.* at article 4.
[983] *Id.* at article 6.

The grounds and procedure for conducting searches are also determined by the Criminal Procedure Code. Pursuant to article 225 of the Code the investigator, having sufficient grounds to suspect that in some premises or in possession of a person, there are instruments of crime, articles and valuables acquired by criminal activity, as well as other items or documents, which can be significant for the case, conducts a search. The search can also be conducted to find missing or presumed dead persons. The search is conducted only by a court decree.[984]

Article 6 of the Criminal Procedure Code, is also of great importance. According to the article "residence" means a building or structure, temporarily or permanently used for inhabitation of a definite person or several persons, including: private or rented apartment, garden house, hotel room, cabin, and train compartment, as well as any verandah, terrace, gallery, staircase, balcony, and other immediate attachments thereto, along with other spaces of common use and other constituent parts of the above residences, used for rest, storage of property, or other needs of a definite person or several persons; the basement and the attic of a residential building. The notion of "residence" shall also mean: private vehicle, river or sea vessel, as well as personal office and service car, or studio. Aforementioned notion is in compliance with the comments of the European Court of Justice regarding the notion of "dwelling," provided by the European Convention on Human Rights and Fundamental Freedoms.[985]

The examination of correspondence, post, telegraph and other transmissions may be implemented only by the order, determined by law. When there are sufficient grounds to believe that there is valuable data in the mail or other correspondence, telegrams and other communications (referred to below as correspondence) sent by the suspect or the accused, or to them by other persons, the investigator can make a grounded decision to impose monitoring on the correspondence of these people.

The decision must indicate the name of the post office, which is responsible for withholding of the correspondence, the name(s), surname(s) of the person(s) whose correspondence will be withheld, the accurate address of these persons, type of correspondence that will be monitored and the period of monitoring. The correspondence, which can be withheld by the post office, concerns in particular

---

[984] Criminal Procedure Code, article 225.
[985] *Id.* at article 6 point 46.

the following items: letters, telegrams, radiograms, parcels (printed matter), cases, post containers, transmissions, fax and e-mail messages.

Decision on the monitoring of correspondence is sent to the appropriate post office director who is bound by it. The director of the post office withholds the correspondence indicated in the decision of the investigator and advises the latter with regard to that. The monitoring of correspondence is lifted by the investigator, prosecutor or court that took the decision.[986]

According to article 240 of the Code, the investigator familiarizes the director of the post office and, when necessary, other employees of the given office, with the seizure decree, with subscription, and with participation of selected attested witnesses from the employees of the office. The investigator then opens and examines the correspondence.

When revealing documents and items that can be significant for the case, the investigator seizes the appropriate articles or confines himself to copying them. In case of absence of data that can be significant for the case, the investigator instructs whether to hand the examined correspondence to the addressee or to withhold it within the established period.[987]

On the basis of a court decree supervision may be conducted over the telephone conversation. If there are sufficient grounds to suspect that the telephone conversations of the suspect or the accused or the conversations conducted by other means of communication can contain significant information for the case, the court decides to permit the supervision and recording of these conversations.

The investigator makes a grounded decision on initiating an application to the court, which indicates the criminal case and grounds on which the appropriate investigatory actions must be taken, the surnames and names of the persons whose conversations are subject to the supervision, the supervision period, institution which is instructed to conduct the technical implementation of supervision and recording. The decree is forwarded to the court.

In case of approval by the judge, the conversation supervision and recording decision is forwarded by the investigator to the appropriate institution for implementation. Conversation supervision and recording can be conducted for no longer than six months. They are canceled when the necessity for them expires,

---

[986] Code of Criminal Procedure, article 239.
[987] Code of Criminal Procedure, article 240.

but in any case, are canceled no later than the end of the preliminary investigation.

The investigator is entitled to demand the record at any time for examination within the established period. The record is handed to the investigator in the sealed form with an accompanying letter that must indicate the beginning and the end of the recorded conversations, and necessary technical description the devices used during the interception. Examination of records by the investigator is done in the presence of attesting witnesses, and when necessary, experts. There is a protocol made about the examination, which must literally reproduce the part of the conversation concerning the case.[988]

Open Government

On September 23, 2003, the law on Freedom of Information was adopted in the Republic of Armenia. The main principles of securing freedom of information are: a) definition of unified procedures to record, classify and maintain information; b) insurance of freedom to seek and get information; c) insurance of information access; d) publicity However, the law provides also some limitations of freedom of information.

Information holder refuses to provide information if: it infringes the privacy of a person and his family, including the privacy of correspondence, telephone conversations, post, telegraph and other transmissions; With the exception of cases if the decline of the information request will have a negative influence on the implementation of state programs of the Republic of Armenia directed to socio-economic, scientific, spiritual and cultural development.

Activity concerning the use of archives is also regulated by law. Relevant law was adopted on of June 8, 2004. In the archives may be kept the documents that are considered to be state or communal property. Moreover, by owner's agreement, documents that are considered to be property of legal entity or natural person may also be kept in the archives.

A person who uses archival documents has a right to a free search and to receive archival documents from state and municipal archives for research purposes. However, accessibility of archival documents may be limited to a person who uses archival documents by a decision of owners of archival documents that are

---

[988] *Id.* at article 241.

considered to be a property of legal entity or natural person. Accessibility of archival documents that contain information on personal or family secrets is limited for the 100-year period since their creation, provided the law does not state otherwise. Archival documents that contain information on personal or family secrets may be available earlier than 100 years since their creation by a written permission of a person or after his/her death by a written permission of his/her heir.[989]

According to the "Law on National Security Agencies of the Republic of Armenia," which was adopted on December 28 2001, national security bodies cannot collect, store or disseminate data on personal and family life of a citizen, which was received during the activity of national security bodies without consent of the citizen, except in cases prescribed by the law.

During the implementation of the activity of the national security bodies the protection of rights and freedoms of a citizen are guaranteed. Each person has a right to appeal the actions of the national security bodies or officials that have violated his/her rights and freedoms in the way prescribed by the legislation of the Republic of Armenia. Data on national security bodies officials, or persons who confidentially cooperate or cooperated with those agencies, documents on methods and ways of their activity are stored in the authorized archive.

Information Card Index of the information center of the police of the Republic of Armenia is operating under the Government of RA. The activity of the card index is regulated by the Decree of Government of RA No. 933, adopted on May 20' 2004.

In the information card index[990] the following categories of people are registered: Citizens of the Republic of Armenia, foreign countries citizens`, persons without citizenship accused of committing a crime on the territory of the Republic of Armenia regardless of the nature of crime, punishment measure, term of the punishment; Persons, who served a sentence in other countries and were returned to the Republic of Armenia; Persons who are in the criminal investigation inquiry; Persons who were accused and the cases were ceased by not justifying bases, prescribed by the Criminal Procedure Code of the Republic of Armenia; Those juveniles who were excused from the criminal liability and to whom were applied compulsory measures of a pedagogical nature; Persons, who committed

---

[989] Law on Archives, article 22.

[990] A department/division that operates within the structure of information center of the police of the Republic of Armenia, where data on the following category of persons are collected, processed, coordinated and stored.

an act prescribed by law and to whom were applied compulsory measure of a medical nature;Those convicts who were granted pardon or amnesty before court decision came into force; Those persons whose criminal proceeding were not terminated on the justified basis; Persons who are released from detention on the basis, prescribed by Criminal Procedure Code, Article 132, part 1, point 1.[991]

First copies of cards of registration and fingerprints are stored in the information center of the police of the Republic of Armenia and second copies are sent to the information center of the Ministry of Interior of Russian Federation, according to the intergovernmental agreement about the exchange of the information, signed by the ministries of interior of CIS countries, on August 3, 1992.

The following structures are eligible for direct use of the Information Card Index: Administration of President of RA, Administration of Government of RA, Police of RA, National Security Service of Government of RA, Ministry of Defense of RA, Ministry of Foreign Affairs of RA, Ministry of Justice of RA, Public Prosecutor's Office of RA, Courts, State Tax Service of Government of RA, State Custom Committee of Government of RA, as well as Civic Servant Council of RA and structures mentioned in 1st part of 4th article in a law "About Civic Service" (Administration of President, Administration of Government, Administration of Republican Executive Bodies, Administration of Marzpetarans (city administration of Yerevan), and relevant bodies of standing commissions created by law.

Other State structures, natural persons are eligible to use Information Card Index through local Police stations of RA. Information Card Index is directly available to police representatives of those CIS countries, that have signed relevant intergovernmental agreements.

Information on persons who are checked in the Information Card Index is available for: Administration of President of the Republic of Armenia, administration of Government of RA, Police of RA, National Security Service of Government of RA, General Prosecutor's Office of RA, courts, Criminal–executive department of Ministry of Justice of RA, Ministry of Defense of RA. Listed structures are eligible to obtain the information on accused persons, detainees, arrestees, convicts, revised court decisions, place and time of imprisonment, place of deprivation of liberty, fact of escape, inquiry, death in the

---

[991] Criminal Procedure Code, article 132, part 1, point 1 states: "The detained shall be released on the basis of the decision of the body which carries out criminal proceeding if the suspicion about his committing an action forbidden by criminal law has not been proven correct."

place of deprivation of liberty, application of amnesty or pardon, place where archival criminal cases are stored

Other state bodies are eligible to obtain the information on conviction or inquiry of those persons who applied for a position or who hold the position but are ineligible to hold these positions because of the conviction.
Natural persons are eligible to obtain the information on the facts of their conviction or inquiry as well as registered and stored information.

Australia

Constitutional Privacy Framework

While privacy issues are now featured prominently in the daily news in Australia, the legal safeguards for personal information remain limited. Neither the Australian Federal Constitution nor the Constitutions of the six States and two Territories contain any express provisions relating to privacy.

However, in 2004 the Australian Capital Territory (ACT) became the first jurisdiction to incorporate a bill of rights. Section 12 of the Human Rights Act 2004 (ACT) creates a right of "privacy and reputation."[992] The Human Rights Act incorporates international human rights standards into local ACT law by requiring all ACT laws to be interpreted consistently with human rights "as far as possible." From July 1, 2004, the ACT Human Rights and Discrimination Commissioner has functions including reviewing the effect of ACT laws on human rights, reporting to the Attorney General. The Commissioner's reports must later be tabled in the Legislative Assembly. However, the Commissioner does not have power to handle complaints.

There is continued debate about the value of a Bill of Rights in other jurisdictions, but only one current proposal, in the State of Victoria.[993]

The Australian Constitution limits the legislative power of the Australian (federal) government, with areas not expressly authorized being reserved for the

---

[992] Section 12 states: Everyone has the right - (a) not to have his or her privacy, family, home or correspondence interfered with unlawfully or arbitrarily; and (b) not to have his or her reputation unlawfully attacked. *See* <http://www.austlii.edu.au/au/legis/act/consol_act/hra2004148/>

[993] Angela Ward, "Australia Stands Alone on Human Rights," The Australian Financial Review, May 6, 2005, at 58.

States.[994] The constitutionality of federal laws imposing privacy rules on the private sector has been questioned, but not so far challenged. Most commentators believe that the Commonwealth could base any private sector privacy law on a "cocktail" of constitutional powers including those giving authority over telecommunications, corporations and foreign affairs (*e.g.*, treaties).

Data Protection Framework

Privacy Law in Australia comprises several federal statutes covering particular sectors and activities, some State or Territory laws with limited effect, and the residual common law protections.

In Australia there has until recently been no recognition of a general tort of protection of privacy. Very occasionally the common law been used in support of privacy rights through actions for breach of confidence, defamation, trespass or nuisance.

In the 2001 *Lenah v ABC* decision,[995] the High Court discussed the issue and effectively issued an invitation that a tort might be found if the right case came forward involving an individual (the *Lenah* case involved allegations of breach of corporate privacy). In June 2003, a Queensland District Court judge took up the invitation and in *Grosse v Purvis*[996] awarded the plaintiff AUD 178,000 for breach of privacy occasioned by intrusion and harassment over a sustained period. It remains to be seen if this affirmation of a common law right is followed in other cases.

The principal federal statute is the Privacy Act of 1988,[997] which has four main areas of application and which gives partial effect to Australia's commitment to the Organization for Economic Cooperation and Development (OECD) Guidelines and to the International Covenant on Civil and Political Rights (ICCPR), Article 17. It creates a set of 11 Information Privacy Principles (IPPs), based on those in the OECD Guidelines that apply to the activities of most federal government agencies. A separate set of rules about the handling of consumer credit information, added to the law in 1989, applies to all private and public sector organizations. The third area of coverage is the use of the government issued Tax File Number (TFN), where the entire community is

---

[994] The Commonwealth of Australia Constitution Act <http://www.aph.gov.au/senate/general/constitution/>.

[995] *See* <http://www.austlii.edu.au/au/cases/cth/high_ct/2001/63.html>.

[996] *See* <http://www.austlii.edu.au/au/cases/qld/QDC/2003/151.html>.

[997] Privacy Act 1988 (Cwth) <http://www.austlii.edu.au/au/legis/cth/consol_act/pa1988108/longtitle.html>.

subject to Guidelines issued by the Privacy Commissioner, which take effect as subordinate legislation. The fourth area of coverage, which only commenced in December 2001, is widespread private sector organizations regulated by the National Privacy Principles (NPPs).

The origins of the Privacy Act derived from protests in the mid-1980s against the Australia Card scheme – a proposal for a universal national identity card and number. That controversial proposal was dropped, but use of the TFN was enhanced to match income from different sources with the Privacy Act providing some safeguards. The use of the TFN has been further extended to include benefits administration as well as taxation. Some controls over this matching activity were introduced in 1990.[998] In June 2004, the outgoing Federal Privacy Commissioner called for a renewed debate on identity management – though not a debate on the possibility of another Australia Card proposal – because "identity management is the big next push in response to fraud and theft."[999]

After several policy reversals, the conservative federal government introduced legislation in April 2000 to extend privacy protection to the private sector. The Privacy Amendment (Private Sector) Act 2000 was passed in December 2000 and took effect in December 2001 (but another year later for some small businesses). The NPPs were based on the National Principles for Fair Handling of Personal Information originally developed by the Federal Privacy Commissioner in 1998 as a self-regulatory substitute for legislation. Private companies are now required to observe these principles although they can apply to the Privacy Commissioner for approval of a self-developed Code of Practice containing principles that are an "overall equivalent" to the NPPs.

The Act has been widely criticized as failing to meet international standards of privacy protection. A review of privacy protection for employee records was announced with the release of a discussion paper in February 2004 by the Australian Attorney General's Department,[1000] with submissions called by April 2004, but no resulting report to date. Likewise a promised inter-departmental committee to look into the need for specific privacy protection for children's' personal information has yielded nothing to date.

---

[998] The Data-matching program (Assistance and Tax) Act 1990.
<http://www.austlii.edu.au/au/legis/cth/consol_act/dpata1990349/>.
[999] Siobhan Chapman, "Privacy Chief Calls for Identity Management Debate," iTnews, June 12, 2004
<http://www.itnews.com.au/storycontent.asp?ID=12&Art_ID=18953>.
[1000] See
<http://www.ag.gov.au/agd/WWW/agdHome.nsf/Page/Publications_2004_Employee_Records_Privacy>

The then Attorney General indicated in 2000 that the Privacy Act would undergo a full review within two years, but the Government only settled the terms of reference for the review in August 2004, after a new Privacy Commissioner had been appointed. The terms of reference required the Privacy Commissioner to conduct the review, but only examine the newer private sector provisions of the Act. The Commissioner, Karen Curtis, finalized her report, "Getting in on the Act," in March 2005, and it was released by the Government in May 2005.[1001]

The limited terms of reference prompted the Senate Legal and Constitutional Committee to launch its own review of the whole Act, looking at the Act's overall effectiveness and appropriateness "as a means by which to protect the privacy of Australians". The Senate Committee is due to report on its review by June 30, 2005.[1002]

However, the power of the Senate committee to effect change is minimal. On July 1, 2005, the conservative Government (comprising a Coalition of the Liberal and National parties) will gain control of the Senate through an outright majority of seats, the first time since the 1970s that a federal Government has had an upper house majority. Some commentators are suggesting the Government is waiting until it has its Senate majority before proposing changes to possibly water down the Privacy Act.[1003] The NPPs impose a lower standard of protection in several areas than the EU Data Protection Directive. For example, organizations are required to obtain consent from customers for secondary use of their personal information for marketing purposes where it is "practicable"; otherwise, they can initiate direct marketing contact, providing they give the individual the choice to opt out of further communications. Controls on the transfer of personal information overseas are also limited, requiring only that organizations take "reasonable steps" to ensure personal information will be protected, or "reasonably believe" that the information will be subject to similar protection as applied in the Australian law.

In addition, the Act provides for several broad exemptions for employee records (defined as a record of personal information relating to the employment of the employee including, for example, health information, contact details, salary or wages, performance and conduct, trade union membership, recreation and sick

---

[1001] *See* the Commissioner's report at <http://www.privacy.gov.au/act/review/review2005.htm> and an analysis of that report by the Australian Privacy Foundation at <http://www.privacy.org.au/Papers/OFPC_GetIinOnAct_APF050606.pdf>

[1002] *See* <http://www.aph.gov.au/senate/committee/legcon_ctte/privacy/>

[1003] Fred Brenchley, "Ruddock wants 'fix' for privacy laws," The Australian Financial Review, February 22, 2005, at 3.

leaves, banking affairs, etc.); media organizations (defined very broadly); political parties; and small businesses (defined as having less than AUD 3 million (~USD 2,3 million) annual turnover and not disclosing personal information for a benefit).

According to the Federal Government the small business exemption will exempt about 94 percent of all Australian businesses but only 30 percent of total business sales, an exception that includes many Internet companies.[1004] The breadth of the exemption for political parties was demonstrated in March 2005 when the Privacy Commissioner had to decline a request to investigate complaints regarding telemarketing activities during the campaign period for the October 2004 federal election, including the use of spam,[1005] and allegations that the Liberal Party had accessed silent telephone numbers to make political canvassing calls.[1006] The exemption also excludes from view the increasing use of databases by political parties to track voter preferences and create customized marketing material for voters.[1007]

There are also weaknesses in the enforcement regime including, for example, allowing privacy complaints to be handled initially by an industry-appointed code authority, although a right of appeal to the Privacy Commissioner was inserted by Opposition parties. The Act does, however, include an innovative principle of anonymity. Principle 8 states that: "Wherever it is lawful and practicable, individuals must have the option of not identifying themselves when entering into transactions with an organization." However, the mere existence of the anonymity principle has not prevented the development of electronic road tolling systems that identify every vehicle, and the impact of this principle on the development of electronic health records, for example, remains to be seen.

In March 2001, the Article 29 Data Protection Working Party of the European Commission expressed many reservations about the Act, suggesting that it would not, as currently written, satisfy the adequacy test in Articles 25 and 26 of the EU Data Protection Directive for data to flow to third countries.[1008] The group recommended the introduction of additional safeguards to address these

---

[1004] *See* Patrick Gunning, Central Features of Australia's Private Sector Privacy Law, Privacy Law and Reporter, Vol. 7, No. 10 1 (2001). Back issues available at <www.austlii.edu.au/au/other/plpr>; Global Privacy Law Update, The Computer Lawyer Vol. 20 No. 6 (Privacy), June 2003, at 1.

[1005] Mike Seccombe, "PM pays his son to dish up spam," Sydney Morning Herald, August 27, 2004.

[1006] *See* <http://www.privacy.gov.au/news/03_05.html>

[1007] Max Suich, "2004: Big Brother is watching you," The Age, September 24, 2004; and Peter van Onselen and Wayne Errington, "Cheap way to pitch the budget," Sydney Morning Herald, May 23, 2005, at 11.

[1008] Opinion 3/2001 on the level of protection of the Australian Privacy Amendment (Private Sector) Act 2000 <http://europa.eu.int/comm/internal_market/en/media/dataprot/wpdocs/index.htm>.

concerns. In response, the Attorney General issued a press release stating that the Committee's comments "display an ignorance about Australia's law and practice and do not go to the substance of whether our law is fundamentally "adequate" from a trading point of view." He acknowledged that officials from Australia and Europe would "obviously" continue to talk but that "Australia will only look at options that do not impose unnecessary burdens on business."

The Privacy Amendment Act 2004,[1009] which commenced on April 21, 2004, introduced amendments to meet some of the criticisms by the EU. The amendments included extending correction rights to non-Australians, extending the scope of the transborder data flow control (Principle 9) to data about non-Australians, and ensuring that the Privacy Commissioner could approve Codes of Practice that voluntarily covered otherwise exempt acts and practices.[1010]

However, some of the key EU objections remain and may prevent an "adequacy" assessment. As of March 2005, although Australia is non-compliant with the EU Data Protection Directive, the Privacy Commissioner found that trade between the countries has not been impacted,[1011] nor have any EU companies refused to deal with Australian partners.[1012]

There are two other federal privacy-related laws for which the federal Privacy Commissioner is also the supervisory and complaint handling agency. The first one is Part VIIC of the Crimes Act,[1013] enacted in 1989, which provides some protection to individuals who have had criminal convictions in relation to so-called "spent" convictions (i.e., convictions for relatively minor offenses which they are allowed to "deny" or have discounted after a set period of time). The second one is the Data-Matching Program (Assistance and Tax) Act 1990[1014] that provides detailed procedural controls over the operation of a major program of information matching between federal tax and benefit agencies.

[1009] *See* <http://scaleplus.law.gov.au/html/comact/11/6805/top.htm>.

[1010] Letter from Timothy Pilgrim, Acting Federal Privacy Commissioner for Australia, to Patrick Mueller, Law Clerk, Electronic Privacy Information Center, June 18, 2004 (on file with EPIC).

[1011] *See* <http://www.privacy.gov.au/act/review/review2005.htm> under "International concerns."

[1012] Simon Hayes, "EU Renews Attack on Privacy," The Australian, September 16, 2003.

[1013] <http://www.austlii.edu.au/au/legis/cth/consol_act/ca191482/s85zl.html>.

[1014] <http://www.austlii.edu.au/au/legis/cth/consol_act/dpata1990349/>.

Data Protection Authority

The Office of the Federal Privacy Commissioner,[1015] which enforces the Privacy Act, was initially established as a member of the Human Rights and Equal Opportunity Commission but has been operating as a separate statutory agency since July 1, 2000. The Office has wide range of functions, including handling complaints, auditing compliance, promoting community awareness, and advising the government and others on privacy matters. The outgoing Privacy Commissioner in April 2004 urged a move away from the initial strategy of facilitative cooperation with the business sector towards greater enforcement, a transition that will likely be hampered by limited funding.[1016]

The Commissioner has so far approved three Codes of Practice under the private sector regime: for the General Insurance Industry, which has its own adjudicator for complaints, the Licensed Clubs in the state of Queensland, which defaults to the Privacy Commissioner for complaints, and the "Market and Social Research and Privacy Code" for the Association of Market Research Organisations.[1017] As of June 2004, no complaints or enquiries have been made under the Market Research Code.[1018] The Code provides some standards that are higher than the NPPs, including giving the data subject the right to choose whether to destroy or de-identify their information after use.[1019]

The Commissioner's office, which had received cut backs in the late 90's, received additional resources to accompany its jurisdiction over the private sector, which has become one of its main focuses since 2001. However, these resources have proved inadequate to cope with a major increase in inquiries and complaints, leading to a growing backlog. Outgoing Privacy Commissioner Malcolm Crompton in March 2004 indicated that his office was forced to drastically scale back services, including auditing, in order to accommodate the rising level of complaints.[1020] In fact, the auditing function ceased to exist as of June 2004, except when the Office received dedicated funding for such

---

[1015] *See* <http://www.privacy.gov.au>.

[1016] *Id.*

[1017] *See* <http://www.privacy.gov.au/business/codes/index.html#1>.

[1018] Letter from Timothy Pilgrim, Acting Federal Privacy Commissioner for Australia, to Patrick Mueller, Law Clerk, Electronic Privacy Information Center, June 18, 2004 (on file with EPIC).

[1019] Press Release, Office of the Federal Privacy Commissioner, Privacy Commissioner Approves Market Research Code (August 3, 2003) <http://www.privacy.gov.au/news/media/03_11.html>.

[1020] Karen Dearne, "Little Progress on New Privacy Boss," AustralianIT, March 9, 2004 <http://australianit.news.com.au/articles/0,7204,8906964%5e15441%5e%5enbv%5e15306-15319,00.html>.

purposes.[1021] The office was forced to employ a "triage approach," dealing with only the most serious issues first.[1022] As of 2004, the Office has 36 full time staff divided into four sections: Compliance, Policy, Corporate and Public Affairs, and the Executive.[1023]

The number of complaints received in the period from July 2003 to June 2004 totaled 1,158 with 1,183 matters raised (some complaints contained more than one matter), presenting a more than five-fold increase since 2000-01, just before the private sector provisions commenced.[1024] The Compliance section of the Office handles complaints.[1025] The majority of matters raised – a total of 766 – concern application of the NPPs to the private sector; 207 matters concern credit reporting; and 173 matters concern information privacy principles.[1026] Of the 766 matters concerning private sector NPP compliance, the largest category of matters concerned the financial industry (144); followed by health service providers (114); telecommunications and Internet service providers (69); landlords and real estate agents (51); insurance organizations (48); tenancy databases, credit reporting agencies and debt collectors (41); retail (36); and legal, accounting and management services (34).[1027] Out of the 1,158 complaints received since July 1, 2003, 826 had been finalized by June 11, 2004. The time to resolve these complaints varied; 47 percent within 10 days; 28 percent within 30 days; 19 percent within 90 days; five percent within 180 days; and one percent within nine months.[1028] Of those taking less than 10 days to resolve, the majority was declined investigation by the Office.[1029] Section 40(2) allows the Commissioner to investigate privacy violations on its own in the absence of a complaint; as of June 11 2004, the Office has opened 45 matters under this provision.[1030] As of June 2004, the Office has 450 open complaints, half of which have been allocated to an investigations officer.[1031]

[1021] Letter from Timothy Pilgrim, Acting Federal Privacy Commissioner for Australia, to Patrick Mueller, Law Clerk, Electronic Privacy Information Center, June 18, 2004 (on file with EPIC).

[1022] Dearne, *supra*.

[1023] Letter from Timothy Pilgrim, *Acting Federal Privacy Commissioner for Australia, to Patrick Mueller, Law Clerk, Electronic Privacy Information Center, June 18, 2004 (on file with EPIC)*.

[1024] *Letter from Timothy Pilgrim, Acting Federal Privacy Commissioner for Australia, to Patrick Mueller, Law Clerk, Electronic Privacy Information Center, June 18, 2004 (on file with EPIC)*.

[1025] *Id.*

[1026] *Id.*

[1027] *Id.*

[1028] *Id.*

[1029] *Id.*

[1030] *Id.*

[1031] *Id.*

For the 11 months from July 2004 to May 2005, the Commissioner's office received 1160 new complaints, 19,166 telephone enquiries, and 1,893 written enquiries.[1032]

The total of all complaints made against private sector organizations under the NPPs, from December 2001 to June 2004, when categorized by privacy principle at issue, are broken down as: use and disclosure 41 percent, collection 19 percent, access 14 percent, quality 12 percent, security eight percent, direct marketing three percent, and "other" three percent.[1033]

Section 52 of the Privacy Act provides that the Commissioner may make formal determinations in relation to complaints investigated. The determination by the Commissioner may dismiss the complaint, or may find the complaint substantiated and declare that the respondent should cease to breach the Act, take any reasonable steps to redress damage suffered by the complainant, or pay compensation to the complainant. Importantly, Section 52 determinations are not legally binding on the respondent. The Commissioner, the complainant, or the adjudicator for an approved privacy code can commence proceedings in the Federal Court or Federal Magistrates Court for an order to enforce a determination. As of June 2004, no parties have sought such enforcements of determinations made by the Commissioner.[1034] Recently, the Commissioner has reviewed several complaints regarding the sharing of information among government agencies. One complaint in particular dealt with the disclosure of sensitive personal information by a Commonwealth agency, where the complainant was employed, to another Commonwealth agency where the complainant had applied for a position.[1035] Of inquiries outside the Commissioner's jurisdiction, some of the most common concerns were workplace privacy, video surveillance, and disclosure of information from public registers.

The first class action brought under the Privacy Act was successful. A tenant class sued the largest Residential Tenancy Database provider – a database used to identity "problem" renters – claiming that the data held on them was erroneous and that they were charged excessive fees to access their files, among other

---

[1032] See <http://www.privacy.gov.au/about/complaints/index.html>

[1033] See <http://www.privacy.gov.au/about/complaints/index.html>

[1034] Letter from Timothy Pilgrim, *Acting Federal Privacy Commissioner for Australia, to Patrick Mueller, Law Clerk, Electronic Privacy Information Center, June 18, 2004 (on file with EPIC).*

[1035] Office of the Privacy Commissioner, Case Note Number 1, available at <http://www.privacy.gov.au/act/casenotes/ccn2_03.html>.

claims stemming from the service.[1036] The database contains files on about 300,000 people.[1037] The Privacy Commissioner determined that the defendant company violated NPP 3 "by failing to take reasonable steps to make sure the personal information it collects, uses and discloses is up-to-date"; and NPP 4.2 by "by failing to take reasonable steps to destroy or de-identify personal information that is no longer needed for any purpose."[1038] The commissioner ordered the defendant to cease the violative practices.[1039]

In May 2004, the first case successfully invoked Section 98 of the Privacy Act, allowing anyone, not necessarily the victims of the alleged breach of privacy, to bring suit seeking an injunction against a party violating the NPPs.[1040] The federal court in *Seven Network Limited v. Media Entertainment and Arts Alliance* case granted the injunction after finding that the defendant trade Union engaged in collection of personal data via telephone surveys in violation of the NPPs.[1041]

In August 2005 the Privacy Commissioner announced that following an investigation into the accuracy of consumer credit reports generated by OneTel, a failed telecommunications company, the credit reporting organization Baycorp Advantage agreed to the Commissioner's request to remove all 65,000 records relating to former OneTel customers.[1042]

In 2001, the Privacy Commissioner released the results of a comprehensive research project into public attitudes towards privacy issues that was commissioned earlier in the year.[1043] The research findings were incorporated into three separate reports: Privacy and the Community; Privacy and Business; and Privacy and Government. The results indicated overwhelming support for privacy protection. For example, 91 percent of the public said that they would like businesses to seek permission before engaging in direct marketing; 89 percent would like organizations to advise them who would have access to their

---

[1036] Office of the Privacy Commissioner, Case Note Number 3 of 2004, available at <http://www.privacy.gov.au/act/casenotes/comdeter0403.html>.

[1037] Tenant Checking Company Breach Privacy Law; Australian Class Action Prevails, Privacy and Security Law Report, Vol. 3 No. 17, at 501 (2004).

[1038] Office of the Privacy Commissioner, Case Note Number 3 of 2004, *available at* .

[1039] *Id.*

[1040] Letter from Timothy Pilgrim, *Acting Federal Privacy Commissioner for Australia, to Patrick Mueller, Law Clerk, Electronic Privacy Information Center, June 18, 2004 (on file with EPIC).*

[1041] *See* <http://www.austlii.edu.au/au/cases/cth/federal_ct/2004/637.html>.

[1042] <http://www.privacy.gov.au/news/media/04_16.html>.

[1043] Office of the Federal Privacy Commissioner, "The results of Research into Community, Business and Government attitudes towards Privacy in Australia." July 31, 2001 <http://www.privacy.gov.au/research/index.html#1.1>.

personal information and 92 percent would like to be told how it would be used; 42 percent have refused to deal with organizations they felt did not adequately protect their privacy. When asked what kind of data they considered most sensitive 40 percent identified financial details, 11 percent identified income, seven percent identified medical or health information, four percent identified home address, three percent identified phone number and three percent identified genetic information.[1044]

In 2004, the Privacy Commissioner repeated the community attitudes survey.[1045] The survey looked at issues including health privacy and privacy in the workplace.

Telecommunications

A complex mix of privacy standards applies to the telecommunications sector. The Telecommunications Act 1997[1046] contains a detailed list of exceptions from a basic presumption of confidentiality of customer records.[1047] These exceptions are similar to those in the Use and Disclosure Principles of the federal Privacy Act. An Industry Forum prepares detailed codes and guidelines, some of which are binding.[1048] A Code of Practice on the Protection of Customer Personal Information that was binding on all telecommunications carriers and service providers was de-registered once the private sector amendments took effect. The enforcement position remains confusing, with the Australian Communications Authority (ACA); the Telecommunications Industry Ombudsman and the Privacy Commissioner all having overlapping jurisdictions. There is also a binding Code of Practice on Calling Number Display (CND),[1049] which requires carriers to offer free per call and per line blocking (but only on an opt-out basis) and attempts to impose guidelines on telephone users' use of CND information. Other Codes deal incidentally with privacy issues such as directories, numbering and emergency calls. The ACA investigated the sale and marketing use of customer proprietary network information (CPNI) – data about incoming and outgoing

---

[1044] "Privacy and the Community: Main Findings"
<http://www.privacy.gov.au/publications/rcommunity.html#4>.

[1045] <http://www.privacy.gov.au/publications/rcommunity/index.html>.

[1046] <http://www.austlii.edu.au/au/legis/cth/consol_act/ta1997214/>.

[1047] Id. Part 13.

[1048] See <http://www.acif.org.au>.

[1049] Code C 522. See <http://www.acif.org.au>.

calls – of customers by phone companies.[1050] It found that industry practices probably violated current legislation, and proposed new industry standards to be instituted in 2004.[1051]

Complaints were made in 2003 to both the ACA and the Privacy Commissioner about the use by ISPs of "blocked" CND information (including on silent lines).[1052] The ACA investigation found unlawful conduct, but declined to take action. Findings by the Privacy Commissioner, and by the Ombudsman in relation to the ACA's failure to act, are awaited. The ACA has also investigated the use of telephone directory data and in May 2005 issued a draft Standard.[1053]

The Telecommunications (Interception) Act of 1979[1054] regulates the interception of telecommunications. A warrant is required under the Act and it also provides for detailed monitoring and reporting. However, the Interception Act safeguards need to be read alongside Part 15 of the Telecommunications Act 1997 that places obligations on telecommunications providers to provide an interception capability and positively assist law enforcement agencies in relation to interception. There have been several changes to the interception regime in recent years, including broadening the range of offenses for which warrants can be obtained; allowing more law enforcement agencies to apply for warrants and more of them to execute warrants themselves; and transferring the warrant issuing authority from federal court judges to designated members of the Administrative Appeals Tribunal (who are on term appointments rather than tenured and are arguably less independent). Significant loopholes exist within the legislation, and uncertainty in relation to allowable "participant monitoring."[1055]

There also remains considerable uncertainty as to the position of e-mail and other stored communications, under the telecommunications laws – it is not clear which communications are subject to the strict Interception Act safeguards and which only to the lesser controls of the Telecommunications Act. In April 2004,

---

[1050] Australian Communications Authority, "Who's Got Your Number? Regulating the Use of Telecommunications Customer Information," available at
<http://www.aca.gov.au/telcomm/industry_standards/regulating_use_of_customer_information.htm>.

[1051] Id.; see also Electronic Frontiers Australia, "Regulating the Use of Telecommunications Customer Information" (May 14, 2004), available at <http://www.efa.org.au/Publish/efasubm-aca-ipnd.html> (Comments submitted to ACA public comment invitation).

[1052] <http://www.efa.org.au/Issues/Privacy/cni-complaints/>.

[1053] Telecommunications (Use of Integrated Public Number Database) Industry Standard 2005 at <www.aca.gov.au>.

[1054] Telecommunications (Interception) Act 1979
<http://www.austlii.edu.au/au/legis/cth/consol_act/ta1979350/>.

[1055] Section 6 (2) of the Act is very unclear. An industry working party is currently reviewing Guidelines on 'participant monitoring'. See ACIF Guideline G516 <http://www.acif.org.au>.

anti-terrorism legislation was proposed in Queensland that would grant law enforcement covert search warrant capabilities but would not extend wiretap capabilities to Queensland law enforcement organizations, as Opposition leaders wanted.[1056] Changes to the federal law are also sought; in May 2004, legislation to amend the Telecommunications (Interception) Act was introduced.[1057] The amendments would eliminate the warrant requirement for accessing stored communications – email, SMS, and voice mail – allowing non-law enforcement government organizations and even private investigators to access these communications without a court order.[1058] Additional proposed federal legislation would further weaken surveillance protections. The Surveillance Devices Bill 2004[1059] seeks to increase the number of offenses for which surveillance may be initiated by law enforcement.[1060]

In late 2004, legislation to amend the federal Telecommunications (Interception) Act was[1061] amended to eliminate the warrant requirement for accessing stored communications – email, SMS, and voice mail – allowing non-law enforcement government organizations and even private investigators to access these communications without a court order.[1062] A 12 month sunset clause applies to these changes, and a review of the Interception Act was conducted in April-May 2005. Several submissions argued against renewal of the stored communication provisions.[1063] The findings of the Review are awaited.

Additional federal legislation has further weakened surveillance protections. The Surveillance Devices Bill Act 2004[1064] seeks to increase the number of offenses for which surveillance may be initiated by law enforcement agencies.[1065] In April 2004, anti-terrorism legislation was proposed in Queensland that would grant law

[1056] Johanna Leggatt, "QLD 'Needs Phone Tapping,'" AustralianIT, April 19, 2004
<http://australianit.news.com.au/articles/0,7204,9323562%5e15306%5e%5enbv%5e,00.html>.

[1057] See <http://www.efa.org.au/Issues/Privacy/tia-bill2004-sc.html>.

[1058] Electronic Frontiers Australia, "Briefings Paper:
Telecommunications (Interception) Amendment (Stored Communications) Bill 2004" (June 3, 2004), available at <http://www.efa.org.au/Issues/Privacy/tia-bill2004-sc.html>.

[1059] See <http://www.aph.gov.au/library/pubs/bd/2003-04/04bd147.htm>.

[1060] See Electronic Frontiers Australia, "Surveillance Devices Bill 2004" (June 4, 2004), available at <http://www.efa.org.au/Issues/Privacy/sd_bill2004.html>.

[1061] See <http://www.efa.org.au/Issues/Privacy/tia-bill2004-sc.html>.

[1062] Electronic Frontiers Australia, "Briefings Paper:
Telecommunications (Interception) Amendment (Stored Communications) Bill 2004" (June 3, 2004), available at .

[1063] See <http://www.privacy.org.au/Papers/SubmTelecomIntercept050520.pdf> and <http://www.efa.org.au/Publish/efasubm-agd-tiactreview2005.html>.

[1064] See <http://www.aph.gov.au/library/pubs/bd/2003-04/04bd147.htm>.

[1065] See <http://www.efa.org.au/Issues/Privacy/sd_bill2004.html>.

enforcement covert search warrant capabilities but would not extend wiretap capabilities to Queensland law enforcement organizations, as Opposition leaders wanted.[1066]

Interception activity continues to increase. In 2002/2003, the number of warrants issued increased to 2,514, with only four applications refused.[1067] This excludes an undisclosed number of interception warrants issued to the Australian Security Intelligence Organisation (ASIO) by the Attorney General. In 2002-2003, warrants increased by 22 percent with 3,058 issued and nine refused.[1068]

In 2003/2004, the number of warrants dropped slightly, with 3,059 requests made, 3,028 successfully.[1069] However, the total number of applications for telecommunications interception warrants made by telephone increased, from 56 (in 2002/2003) to 90; none of these emergency requests have been refused in the past three years. Of the 31 unsuccessful normal applications, by 11 different federal and state agencies, the report does not distinguish how many were actually refused by a judge, as opposed to being withdrawn by the requesting agency.

In late 2004, the Inspector-General of Intelligence and Security revealed that ASIO had undertaken unauthorized telephone taps in three instances during 2003/2004.[1070] The Inspector-General also criticized ASIO's lack of detail in post-operation reports about privacy protection.

In April 2003, the National Office for the Information Economy (NOIE) released a final report of its review of the spam problem and how it can be countered.[1071] The NOIE report makes several recommendations, largely endorsing proposals by the Privacy Commissioner, including outlawing spam, urging ISPs and consumers to use anti-spam software, and committing to working internationally on this issue. One recommendation of the NOIE Report proposed that the Australian Competition and Consumer Commission, the Australian Securities

---

[1066] Johanna Leggatt, "QLD 'Needs Phone Tapping,'" AustralianIT, April 19, 2004
<http://australianit.news.com.au/articles/0,7204,9323562%5e15306%5e%5enbv%5e,00.html>.

[1067] See Telecommunications (Interception) Act 1979 Annual Report for Year Ending 30 June 2002
<http://law.gov.au/www/agdhome.nsf/Web+Pages/696D22E493C27350CA256D480027BCE7?OpenDocument>.

[1068] See Telecommunications (Interception) Act of 1979 Annual Report for Year Ending 30 June 2003
<http://law.gov.au/www/agdHome.nsf/AllDocs/6EDC9CC0FC414ED6CA256E45000023F7?OpenDocument>.

[1069] <http://www.ag.gov.au/agd/WWW/agdhome.nsf/Page/RWP3BD452E345D42468CA256FD5001672B8>.

[1070] "ASIO Makes Unauthorised Phone Taps," The Age, 31 October 2004 <www.theage.com.au>.

[1071] Office of the Federal Privacy Commissioner, "Privacy and the NOIE Spam Report," April 16, 2003
<http://www.privacy.gov.au/news/03_01.html>.

and Investment Commission and the Office of the Federal Privacy Commissioner should ensure that relevant legislation is fully applied to spam. Spam legislation (Spam Act 2003) became effective April 2004, outlawing unsolicited marketing messages on electronic mediums including email, SMS (short message service), MMS (multimedia messaging service), and instant messaging; requiring opt-out facilities and an accurate sender address.[1072] Penalties range up to AUD 1.1 million (~USD 832,000) for businesses that repeatedly violate the law. The complex law confused affected organizations, prompting the Australian Computer Society to release simplified guidelines for compliance.[1073] Emailers must have prior consent of the recipient, although consent can be inferred from prior conduct and relationships.[1074] The Australian Communications Authority will enforce the law, which has begun establishing enforcement capabilities, although early goals target compliance rather than prosecution.[1075] Civil liberties organizations have criticized the Spam Act because the search and seizure provisions allow some government employees and police to seize an individual's computer without a search warrant.[1076]

The first prosecution under the Spam Act resulted in a car sales company paying a AUD 6,600 (~USD 5,000) fine for unwanted SMS text messages that were sent to the mobile telephones of people who had listed their numbers in classified advertisements to sell their cars.[1077]

As of early 2004, legislation regulating spyware and "adware" (that tracks users' web visits to target advertising via pop-up ads) was expected to be introduced.[1078] The Privacy Commissioner commented that the methods employed by both types of software violate the NPPs.[1079]

[1072] Spam Act 2003 (2003) (Cwth) <http://scaleplus.law.gov.au/html/pasteact/3/3628/top.htm>.

[1073] David Frith, "Five Basic Rules for Complying with Spam Act," Canberra Times, April 12, 2004, at A15.

[1074] Edward Manda, "Act Won't Slam the Door on Spam, but It Will Help," The Australian, April 20, 2004, at 35.

[1075] Australia Readies for New Spam Act as Official Releases Guide for Businesses, Privacy and Security Law Report, Vol. 3, No. 10 at 270 (2004); "Australia Spam Authorities Target Repeat Offenders," Precision Marketing, February 27, 2004, at 9.

[1076] Electronic Frontiers Australia, "Analysis of Spam Bills 2003" (November 1, 2003) available at <http://www.efa.org.au/Publish/spambills2003.html>.

[1077] Kirsty Needham, "SMS campaign backfires as car firm is fined for sending spam," The Sydney Morning Herald, April 6, 2005, at <www.smh.com.au>

[1078] Mike Barton, "Security Fears Over 'Spyware,'" The Age, December 23, 2003 <http://www.theage.com.au/articles/2003/12/22/1071941668618.html>.

[1079] Id.

Electronic Frontiers Australia[1080] and the Australian Privacy Foundation[1081] have both criticized the international proposal for ENUM (or "electronic numbering"), a protocol for translating telephone numbers into Internet domain names and mapping telephone numbers to other means of communication such as e-mail, fax and mobile numbers. ENUM poses serious risks to privacy due to its creation of a unique individual identifier. There is also concern about how the proposed system will protect contact information about individuals, who have an ENUM address that is made publicly accessible in an Internet database. It is possible that if the database contains too much information, marketers, spammers, and malicious actors will mine the database for personal contact information.[1082] Since there are no statutory protections in place regulating the use of ENUM contact information, marketers and spammers may use the contact information for junk mail, unsolicited commercial e-mail, and other forms of commercial solicitations. The system could facilitate an unprecedented amount of spam because programs could be designed to send solicitations to all of the registrant's communications devices if the ENUM holder is not sufficiently aware of the potential for doing so and reveals too much information in the public directory. The ACA created a working group in September 2003 to study the privacy and security implications of ENUM.[1083] ENUM trials will commence in 2005, although the ACA proposed mandatory requirements including opt-in user consent, NPP compliance as a minimum, and full disclosure of privacy risks.[1084]

The Crimes Act[1085] also contains a range of other privacy related measures, such as offenses relating to unauthorized access to computers, unauthorized interception of mail and telecommunications and the unauthorized disclosure of Commonwealth government information.[1086] In late June 2001, the Government introduced draft legislation targeting online crime. A recent Federal Court of Australia decision marks one of the first Australian cases to deal with a clear case of cyber squatting. In *CSR Limited v. Resource Capital Australia*, the court ordered the transfer of the domain and ordered Melbourne IT to set conditions on

---

[1080] Homepage <http://www.efa.org.au/>.

[1081] Homepage <http://www.privacy.org.au/>.

[1082] This is still an outstanding issue at the time of the proposed trial. Privacy is not mentioned in the FAQ accompanying the project, merely reliance on existing "rights" provided telephone subscribers. *See* <http://www.enum.com.au/faqs.htm>.

[1083] James Pearce, "Privacy, Security on Aust Single-Identifier Group's List," ZDNet Australia, September 26, 2003 <http://tinyurl.com/32j52>.

[1084] *Id.*

[1085] Crimes Act 1914 (as amended) available at: <http://www.austlii.edu.au/au/legis/cth/consol_act/ca191482/index.html#s85m>.Act, 1989 <http://www.austlii.edu.au/au/legis/cth/consol_act/ca191482/s85zl.html>.

[1086] *See* <http://www.austlii.edu.au/au/legis/cth/consol_act/ca191482/index.html#s85m>.

any future registrations by the defendant.[1087] The court relied on the Trade Practices Act to find that the registration was misleading.

In September 2003, an online censorship bill was passed, allowing the Australian Broadcasting Authority and the Office of Film and Classic Literature to withhold information regarding what online information is being restricted.[1088] The amendments to the Freedom of Information (FOI) Act prevent public scrutiny (and potential criticism) of the operation of the Federal Internet censorship regime that became operative on January 1, 2000. The Act restricts the details regarding the net blocking system that restricts access to material that is "objectionable" or "unsuitable for minors."[1089] Under Australia's FOI law, the agencies may withhold information regarding their practices and the details of their agency operations. Earlier in 2003, Electronic Frontier Australia (EFA) and other civil liberties groups had opposed the Internet content regime put in place under the Broadcasting Services Act, and had tracked the operation of the laws through FOI applications.[1090]

Health privacy

During 2000, the Australian federal and State governments announced plans to move towards unique patient identifiers in the health sector, likely to be centered on a health smart card. Health services are primarily delivered by the public sector in Australia, with only around a third of the population having private health insurance. The responsibility for delivery of health services is shared between the Australian Government, which is responsible for much of the funding of the health system, and the States and Territories, which operate hospitals and community health services. The Australian Government's proposal, HealthConnect, is intended as a voluntary national health information network under which health-related information about an individual would be collected in a standard, electronic format at the point of care.[1091] As a first phase of this system the Department of Health and Aged Care drafted the Better Management System Bill that would establish individual electronic medication records in order to improve access to information about drugs for doctors and patients. The

---

[1087] <http://www.austlii.edu.au/au/cases/cth/federal_ct/2003/279.html>.

[1088] <http://www.efa.org.au/FOI/clabill2002/index.html>.

[1089] Electronic Frontiers Australia, "Internet Censorship in Australia" (December 20, 2002), available at <http://www.efa.org.au/Issues/Censor/cens1.html>.

[1090] Simon Hayes, "Net Anti-FOI Bill Set to Fail," Australian IT, April 15, 2003 <http://australianit.news.com.au/articles/0,7204,6283083%5E15319%5E%5Enbv%5E15306,00.html>.

[1091] <http://www.health.gov.au/healthconnect/index.html>.

system was widely criticized by consumers and doctors groups concerned about patient confidentiality and professional liability.[1092] On July 30, 2001, the Department of Health announced that all negotiations on the implementation of this system and the introduction of the enabling legislation had been postponed due to "technical difficulties."[1093] However, the plan was moving forward and as of September 2003, with the federal government expecting national deployment of HealthConnect "within about five years." [1094] It noted that technology – not privacy – presents the major hurdles, at least from the government health organization's perspective.[1095] A pilot project is now underway in the State of Tasmania.[1096]

Meanwhile the New South Wales State Government has been working on its own electronic health records project, Healthelink.[1097] Despite the NSW health privacy law requiring express consent before a patient is placed on a system to link electronic health records across organizations, it was revealed in June 2005 that pilots planned for late 2005 were being developed instead on the basis of a compulsory record, with only an "opt out" choice as to the sharing of the record with other health service providers.[1098]

A national registration scheme for doctors was introduced in April 2004 whereby doctors wanting to practice in more than one state or territory would only have to pay one national registration fee rather than face multiple fees per state.[1099] Doctors' professional associations opposed the system – citing privacy concerns – because the system would provide a centralized and possibly Internet-accessible repository containing personal and professional details of all doctors.[1100]

An emerging health privacy issue is the use of software in General Practitioners' offices, which automatically extract patient data, for sale to pharmaceuticals companies. The Federal Privacy Commissioner dismissed a complaint because

[1092] Karen Dearne, "Medicos Oppose Data Bill," Australian IT, July 24, 2001
<http://australianit.news.com.au/common/storyPage/0,3811,2414429%5E442,00.html>.
[1093] John Kerin, "Medical E-Files 'Delayed For Poll," Australian IT, July 30, 2001
<http://australianit.news.com.au/common/storyPage/0,3811,2460860%255E1286,00.html>.
[1094] Mark Metherell, "Privacy Fear Rejected for Health Data," Sydney Morning Herald, September 27, 2003.
[1095] Id.
[1096] <http://www.hic.gov.au/yourhealth/our_services/medicare_smartcard.htm>.
[1097] <http://www.health.nsw.gov.au/im/ibs/ehr/index.html>.
[1098] Ruth Pollard, "Privacy alert: every patient on database", Sydney Morning Herald, June 1, 2005, at 1.
[1099] Stephanie Kennedy, "National Registration Scheme for Doctors Gives Rise to Privacy Concerns," ABC Online, April 23, 2004 <http://www.abc.net.au/am/indexes/2004/am_archive_2004_Friday23April2004.htm>.
[1100] Id.

the patient data was being de-identified.[1101] However, the political reaction to the Commissioner's decision was strong enough that she made a clarifying media statement.[1102] The federal Minister for Health, the Opposition's Shadow Minister, and minor parties, all criticized the practice based on the risk of de-identification.[1103]

A major report on genetic privacy was issued in March 2003 by the Australian Law Reform Commission and the Australian Health Ethics Committee of the National Health and Medical Research Council. "Essentially Yours" makes 144 recommendations about the ethical, legal and social implications of genetic privacy.[1104] The report recommends that privacy laws be harmonized and tailored to address the particular challenges of human genetic information, including extending protection to genetic samples, and acknowledging the familial dimension of genetic information. Employers should not be permitted to collect or use genetic information – except in those rare circumstances where this is necessary to protect the health and safety of workers or third parties, and the action complies with stringent standards set by a new Human Genetics Commission of Australia (HGCA). The insurance industry should be required to adopt a range of improved consumer protection policies and practices with respect to its use of genetic information (including family history) for underwriting purposes. A new criminal offense should be created to prohibit someone submitting another person's sample for genetic testing knowing that this is done without consent or other lawful authority. DNA parentage testing should be conducted only with the consent of each person sampled (or both parents in the case of young children), or pursuant to a court order.

Law Enforcement & Security

In 2001 the Prime Minister announced the establishment of a national digital database of DNA and fingerprint samples in order to facilitate law enforcement.[1105] CrimTrac, a Commonwealth agency, coordinates the national DNA database system. The system when fully operational will enable the comparison of DNA profiles across all Australia's jurisdictions for law

---

[1101] <http://www.privacy.gov.au/news/media/05_02.html>.

[1102] <http://www.privacy.gov.au/news/05_05.html>.

[1103] See <http://www.democrats.org.au/news/index.htm?press_id=4607&display=1>;
<http://www.labor.com.au/media/0505/dsiagrhea250.php>.

[1104] Essentially Yours: The Protection of Human Genetic Information in Australia, available at
<http://www.alrc.gov.au/media/2003/mr2905.htm>.

[1105] "Australia Launches DNA Database to Fight Crime," Reuters, June 20, 2001.

enforcement purposes. Commonwealth, State and Territory legislation underpin the system. A Report of a Review of Part 1D of the Crimes Act 1914 (the relevant federal law) was tabled in Parliament on 15 May 2003. The Review found that the national system is not yet operational and only one jurisdiction (New South Wales) has loaded profiles onto the relevant CrimTrac database known as the National Criminal Investigation DNA Database (NCIDD). While there has been relatively little experience of the operation of Part 1D, the Review has recommended improved accountability arrangements both within and across Australia's jurisdictions. The Review sees effective accountability mechanisms as crucial to maintaining public confidence in the use of DNA analysis for law enforcement purposes. The Review recommends that the external scrutiny mechanisms be based upon existing cooperation between Australian Ombudsmen with involvement of Privacy Commissioners and other monitoring bodies. Under legislation proposed by the Victoria Law Reform Committee, suspected thieves would be required – if compelled by police via a court order – to submit DNA samples.[1106] Currently only suspects of more serious crimes, such as rape and murder, can be required to submit DNA.[1107]

Legislative amendments in 2002 and 2003 have given the Australian Security Intelligence Organization (ASIO) significant and highly controversial new powers, including the ability to detain and question individuals suspected of having information relevant to terrorism. Despite extracting many concessions and additional safeguards from the government, the Opposition allowed the final changes through in June 2003 without ruling out the possibility of indefinite detention without charges under repeated warrants. The amendments allow ASIO to detain and question a journalist who may have information regarding suspected terrorists gained through her interviews and contacts; refusing to cooperate could result in a five-year imprisonment.[1108] However, the amendments included a sunset clause, due to lapse in July 2006. The Parliamentary Joint Committee on Australian Security and Intelligence Organization[1109] (ASIO), Australian Secret Intelligence Service (ASIS)[1110] and Defence Signals Directorate[1111] (DSD) is reviewing the questioning and detention powers. The Committee is due to report in January 2006.[1112]

[1106] Misha Ketchell, "Plan to Take DNA From Theft Suspects," The Age, March 4, 2004.

[1107] Id.

[1108] Simeon Beckett, "New Terrorism Law Raises Spectre of Agency Abuse," Sydney Morning Herald, June 26, 2003, at 13.

[1109] Australia's national security service.

[1110] Australia's overseas intelligence collection agency.

[1111] Australia's national authority for signals intelligence and information security.

[1112] <http://www.aph.gov.au/house/committee/pjcaad/asio_ques_detention/index.htm>.

The budget for ASIO has doubled since September 11, 2001, after receiving a AUS 131 million boost in 2004.[1113]

Identity Management and Biometrics

In November 2003, Australia introduced the "M-Series" tamper resistant passports.[1114] In order to meet the requirements of the United States Visa Waiver Program, the Australian government fast-tracked proposed legislation amending the Australian Passports Act in order to provide facial biometric features in passports.[1115] A Passports Legislation Consultation Group was established, including members from privacy and human rights groups as well as travel, financial and biometrics industries.[1116]

The federal Department of Foreign Affairs and Trade is working on a biometric passport, incorporating an unencrypted RFID chip, to meet the demands of the US Government of countries wishing to keep their visa-waiver status for travelers to the US. However, privacy advocates have warned of the dangers of "skimming" and "eavesdropping."[1117] The Department finally acknowledged these concerns,[1118] although as at mid-2005 the Department was still working towards a launch by October 2005.[1119]

In 2005 the federal government agency administering social security, Centrelink, released a tender for fingerprint scanners for their 31,000 staff.[1120]

In April 2005, the NSW Government introduced a new law, to allow the motor vehicle and driver licensing agency, the Roads and Traffic Authority, to start issuing photographic identity cards to non-drivers. The Photo Card Act 2005

[1113] Mark Forbes, Michelle Grattan, "PM Gives $232m For The 'Fight of Our Lives,'" The Age, May 6, 2004 <http://www.theage.com.au/articles/2004/05/05/1083635204653.html?oneclick=true>.

[1114] James Pearce, "New AU High Security Passport Omits Biometrics," ZDNet Australia, November 28, 2003 <http://www.privacy.gov.au/news/media/03_17.html>.

[1115] Karen Dearne, "Canberra Faces up to Security," AustralianIT, February 24, 2004 <http://australianit.news.com.au/articles/0,7204,8767093%5e15841%5e%5enbv%5e,00.html>.

[1116] "New Law to Step up Australian Passport Security, Increase Penalties," BBC Monitoring International Reports, February 17, 2004.

[1117] See <http://www.privacy.org.au/Campaigns/E_passport/>.

[1118] Rachel Lebihan, "Two Steps forward, One back in e-Passport Saga," The Australian Financial Review, May 17, 2005, at 34.

[1119] Jeanne-Vida Douglas, "ePassports on Course for October Launch," The Australian Financial Review, June 14, 2005, at 39.

[1120] "Centrelink to move from passwords to fingerprints," The Age, March 16, 2005, at <www.theage.com.au>

---

allows the Authority to hold personal information about non-drivers on the same database as for all drivers in the State, and to issue cards using the same unique numbering system.[1121] The Australian Privacy Foundation campaigned against the proposal, seeing it as introducing a State-based universal identity card by stealth.[1122]

Location-tracking

At least one major retailer in Australia – a food and liquor chain – is planning RFID trials.[1123] The Australian Privacy Commissioner cautioned against privacy invasive RFID plans, but no specific guidelines or legislative efforts are underway.[1124]

In 2005 the NSW Police sought tenders for automated number plate recognition to enable instant transmission of vehicle ownership details to a roadside police officer.[1125]

In early 2004, mobile phone operators were considering adding location-tracking features to their phones and networks.[1126] The proposal was driven in part by an ACA report finding that over 80 percent of the more than five million calls to emergency services in 2002-2003 were hoaxes.[1127] A concept car introduced at the 2004 Melbourne Motor Show unveiled another possible location-based service. Toyota's Sportivo Coupe – a prototype – featured a system whereby the driver inserts a smart card as a replacement for a key.[1128] The car would communicate with traffic cameras designed to catch speeders, linking the citation to the driver instead of just the car.[1129] Additionally, the car displays the driver's

---

[1121] <http://www.austlii.edu.au/au/legis/nsw/consol_act/pca2005112/>

[1122] <http://www.privacy.org.au/Campaigns/ID_cards/NSWPhotoID05.html>

[1123] "Privacy Fears Could Stymie Tracking Chips," The Australian, May 4, 2004, at C05.

[1124] Press Release, Office of the Federal Privacy Commissioner, World's Privacy Regulators Call for Privacy Friendly RFID Tags, September 12, 2003 <http://www.privacy.gov.au/news/media/03_17.html>.

[1125] Christopher Jay, "Big brother on a road near you," The Australian Financial Review, March 4, 2005, at 75.

[1126] Sue Lowe, "Mobiles May Blow Whistle On Fake Sickies – Or Save Your Life," Sydney Morning Herald, January 23, 2004 <http://reg.smh.com.au/splash.do?site=SMH&server=http:%2f%2fwww.smh.com.au&retn=%2farticles%2f2004%2f01%2f22%2f1074732543954.html>.

[1127] Id.

[1128] Joshua Dowling, "Strange Concept: This Car Dobs You in to the Speed Camera," Sydney Morning Herald, February 27, 2004 <http://www.smh.com.au/articles/2004/02/26/1077676900598.html>.

[1129] Id.

license number – instead of the license plate – on the front and back of the car.[1130]

In February 2004, an Australian court granted an order giving the music industry – the copyright owners – rights of search and seizure against the makers of a popular peer-to-peer application, Kazaa.[1131] The offices of the vendor of the application were raided, along with those of the chief executive, several universities, and other businesses.[1132]

Census

The Australian Bureau of Statistics (ABS) conducts the Australian Census of every household in the country every five years in August. Until 1996, the Census was always collected in an identified manner, but the identifying information, including name and address, was retained only as long as necessary to enable administration of the collection process. After capture and checking, the forms on which the data was collected were also destroyed.

In 2001, people were offered the option of having their record, including name and address, passed to the National Archives of Australia, to be released to the public in 99 years. The ABS did not retain name and address information. 54 percent opted in to this arrangement.

In March 2005 the ABS announced a proposal to radically alter the nature of the Census, by both keeping identified information, and using it to link to data from multiple other sources, including disease registers, immigration data, and births and deaths registries. Although an immediate outcry from privacy and civil liberties advocates caused the ABS to drop its original proposal,[1133] the proposal resurfaced in a Discussion Paper published in April 2005, with few changes.[1134]

The Australian Privacy Foundation has described the proposal as being to replace the anonymous "snapshot" of the five-yearly Census with instead a permanent

---

[1130] *Id.*

[1131] *See* <http://www.austlii.edu.au/au/cases/cth/federal_ct/2004/183.html>.

[1132] Patrick Gray, "Kazaa Tripped up in Aussie Court," Wired, March 4, 2004 <http://wired.com/news/print/0,1294,62532,00.html>.

[1133] <http://www.privacy.org.au/Campaigns/Census/Census0503.html>
[1134] <http://www.abs.gov.au/Ausstats/abs@.nsf/525a1b9402141235ca25682000146abc/b623ba52d01116f0ca256fee 007a5adf!OpenDocument>

"movie" of every Australian's life.[1135] The Foundation argues that the result will be a centralized, national population database, holding the most extensive collection of data on every person, in an identifiable form. Submissions on the proposal were due to the ABS in June 2005. A promise by the ABS to publish its Privacy Impact Assessment on the proposal before the due date for submissions was not honored.

In the same week submissions were due to the ABS on the Census proposal, it was revealed that a senior officer within the ABS had abused his high-level computer access within the Bureau, to alter his office football tips in an internal tipping competition.[1136]

Miscellaneous issues

Public sector privacy issues continue to raise concerns. As part of reforms to the Australian tax system from July 2000, the Australian Taxation Office (ATO) required all enterprises to obtain an Australian Business Number. The ATO collected registration details including address and e-mail contact, and planned to make this available to the public through the Australian Business Register (ABR) and through selling it to database companies. A storm of protest occurred in June 2000 when it was realized that the register would include the home address and other details of almost two million individuals who were sole traders, contractors or even had just a minor income from a hobby or some other activity. The Government agreed to amend the legislation, limit the content of the Australian Business Register and allow individuals to suppress their details. At the same time, the Government was forced into another back-down after receiving legal advice that the Australian Electoral Commission had illegally disclosed information on around 10 million registered Australian voters, after the Prime Minister had asked for this information in order to conduct a targeted direct mailing campaign outlining the benefits of the tax reform package.

[1135] <http://www.privacy.org.au/Campaigns/Census/index.html>

[1136] Leonie Lamont, "Sacked office footy tipster gets a good result, again," Sydney Morning Herald, June 7, 2005, at <www.smh.com.au>

Open Government

The federal Freedom of Information Act of 1982[1137] provides for access to government records, requiring agencies to respond within 30 days to requests.[1138] The FOI Act is the mechanism through which the access right in the Privacy Act is implemented for public sector agencies. The Commonwealth Ombudsman promotes the FOI Act and handles complaints about procedural failures. Merits review (appeal) of adverse FOI decisions is provided by the Administrative Appeals Tribunal, with the possibility of further appeals on points of law to the Federal Court. Budget cuts have severely restricted the capacity of the Attorney General Department and Ombudsman to support the Act and there is now little central direction, guidance or monitoring. In 2002-2003, there were 41,481 requests, an 11 percent increase over the previous year; of those finalized, 71 percent were granted in full, 23 percent granted in part, and 6 percent refused.[1139] Nearly 92 percent of the requests were for personal information, mostly to the Department of Veterans' Affairs, the Department of Immigration and Multicultural and Indigenous Affairs (DIMIA), and Centrelink (a government agency delivering a range of Commonwealth services).[1140] In 2001, the Senate held an inquiry into whether to adopt changes recommended by a 1995 report critical of the FOI law, but no substantive changes have since been made to the law.[1141]

State and Territory Laws

The Australian States and Territories have varying privacy laws. New South Wales (NSW), the most populous State, passed the Privacy and Personal Information Protection Act 1998 (PPIP Act) which applies (since July 2000) to most state government agencies and all local councils, although there are

---

[1137] Freedom of Information Act 1982 <http://www.austlii.edu.au/au/legis/cth/consol_act/foia1982222/>, Freedom of Information (Fees and Charges) Regulations 1982
<http://www.austlii.edu.au/au/legis/cth/consol_reg/foiacr432/index.html>, Freedom of Information (Miscellaneous Provisions) regulations 1982
<http://www.austlii.edu.au/au/legis/cth/consol_reg/foipr612/index.html>.

[1138] David Banisar, The Freedominfo.org Global Survey: Freedom of Information and Access to Government Records Around the World (May 2004) at 11-12 <http://freedominfo.org/survey.htm>.

[1139] Australia Attorney-General's Department, Freedom of Information Act 1982 Annual Report 2002-2003, October 24, 2003, available at
<http://www.ag.gov.au/www/securitylawHome.nsf/AllDocs/RWPC99101F32A5A081CCA256DEE00760ED3?OpenDocument>.

[1140] *Id.*

[1141] Banisar, *supra* at 11.

numerous and generous exemptions, and agencies can apply for temporary directions, regulations or Codes of Practice that can weaken the principles.

The former Privacy Committee (which acted as an Ombudsman since 1975 and also issued several reports and guidelines on matters such as video surveillance and smart cards) was replaced in 1999 by a part time Privacy Commissioner with a very small staff.[1142] Although funding and staffing levels were lifted in 2003, they were cut again in 2004. The Privacy Commissioner's position has been vacant since May 2003, when the inaugural Commissioner resigned. A series of temporary, acting, part-time officers have been in the role since then, mostly on short-term contracts that can be terminated at the discretion of the NSW Attorney General. In November 2003, the NSW Government moved to abolish the Office of the Privacy Commissioner, but withdrew the Bill when faced with united opposition from the various parties controlling the upper house of Parliament.[1143]

The PPIP Act is based on a set of OECD-style Information Protection Principles and requires all government departments and agencies to develop a Privacy Management Plan demonstrating their compliance plans. It also allows for the development of Codes of Practice that weaken the Information Protection Principles, and several such Codes have already been made.[1144]

A statutory five-year review of the PPIP Act is now underway. Privacy NSW, the Office of the NSW Privacy Commissioner, commented on the legislation in a comprehensive submission in June 2004.[1145] The Government is yet to report on the review, which is being undertaken by the NSW Attorney General's Department.[1146]

In 2002, a new health-specific law, Health Records and Information Privacy Act 2002 (HRIP Act), took health information out of the scope of the PPIP Act. Instead, health information is regulated by 15 Health Privacy Principles, which apply to the private sector as well as State and local government agencies.[1147] The HRIP Act commenced on September 1, 2004.

[1142] *See* <http://www.lawlink.nsw.gov.au/pc.nsf/pages/index>.
[1143]
<http://www.parliament.nsw.gov.au/prod/parlment/NSWBills.nsf/0/161AB955397555D0CA256DBF0021B5E
6>.
[1144] *See* <http://www.lawlink.nsw.gov.au/lawlink/privacynsw/ll_pnsw.nsf/pages/PNSW_03_ppipexemptions>
[1145] <http://www.lawlink.nsw.gov.au/lawlink/privacynsw/ll_pnsw.nsf/pages/PNSW_publications#13>
[1146] <http://www.lawlink.nsw.gov.au/lawlink/legislation_policy/ll_lpd.nsf/pages/lp_aboutus>
[1147] <http://www.lawlink.nsw.gov.au/lawlink/privacynsw/ll_pnsw.nsf/pages/PNSW_03_hripact>

NSW enacted a Workplace Video Surveillance Act[1148] in 1998 (partly in response to a Privacy Committee report). In a report issued publicly in early 2002,[1149] the NSW Law Reform Commission reviewed the laws governing surveillance more generally, including the operation of the existing Listening Devices Act 1984.[1150] The NSW government indicated in 2001 that it was disposed to legislate on e-mail monitoring in the workplace. A new Workplace Surveillance Bill was tabled for public submissions in mid 2004, with a revised version passing through the lower house of Parliament in May 2005. The Bill now awaits debate in the upper house. The Bill would replace the existing Workplace Video Surveillance Act with much the same provisions, but extend its reach to also cover e-mail, Internet monitoring and location tracking in the workplace. The Australian Privacy Foundation has criticized the Bill as weak in its level of actual privacy protection, and difficult in terms of implementation for employers.[1151]

In July 2002, the Office of Information Technology (OIT), an agency of the state government of NSW, issued guidelines pursuant to the Privacy and Personal Information Protection Act of 1998. The guideline states that as a matter of good practice, each agency should have a designated privacy contact officer. It adds that the obligations of the chief information officer in each agency include ensuring there is a privacy management plan. The responsibilities of other staff, including librarians, web managers, human resources managers and records managers, are also described.[1152]

The State of Victoria has enacted the Information Privacy Act 2000, which applies privacy principles (an almost exact copy of the NPPs in the federal Act) to most state government agencies and local councils. There are relatively few exemptions and while there is provision for Codes of Practice, they cannot weaken the principles. The Act created an office of Privacy Commissioner,[1153] very active so far, with a monitoring, enforcement and education role, and to conciliate complaints.

[1148] Workplace Video Surveillance Act 1998
<http://www.austlii.edu.au/au/legis/nsw/consol_act/lda1984181/index.html#s20>.

[1149] Law Reform Commission, Report 98 (2001) - Surveillance: an interim report
<http://www.lawlink.nsw.gov.au/lrc.nsf/pages/r98toc>.

[1150] Listening Devices Act 1984 <http://www.austlii.edu.au/au/legis/nsw/consol_act/lda1984181/index.html>.

[1151] <http://www.privacy.org.au/Campaigns/Workplace/>.

[1152] "Data Protection: Australian State Issues New Guidelines To Help Government Manage Private Data," Privacy Law Watch, August 6, 2002. The OIT Guidelines are available at
<http://www.oit.nsw.gov.au/pages/4.3.20.S-IM-Privacy.htm>.

[1153] Homepage <http://www.privacy.vic.gov.au/>.

The Victorian Civil and Administrative Tribunal can determine unresolved complaints. Victoria has also passed the Health Records Act 2001 to complement the information privacy legislation by requiring Victorian health service providers to handle health information responsibly. The Health Records Act also gives patients a right of access to their records held by private practitioners. The Victorian Law Reform Commission[1154] received a reference in April 2001 to review the coverage of privacy law in Victoria. It published an Issues Paper in 2002 on workplace privacy, and an Options Paper in September 2004, which called for submissions on workplace privacy by November 2004.[1155]

The government of the Australian Capital Territory (ACT), which used to be a local authority under Commonwealth (federal) law, and was consequently covered by the federal Privacy Act, achieved self-government as a separate Territory in 1989. The Privacy Act was amended to continue coverage, intended as an interim measure, but this remains the position, with the Federal Privacy Commissioner in effect serving also as the ACT's Commissioner, responsible to its own government. However, in 1997 the ACT government passed its own Health Records (Access and Privacy) Act,[1156] which applies to personal health information held by anyone in the public or private sector. Its provisions are similar to those of the IPPs in the Privacy Act, and supersedes them for ACT government agencies in this area of data handling.

The self-governing Northern Territory has enacted a combined privacy and FOI law – the Information Act 2002,[1157] which took effect in July 2003. The Office of the Information Commissioner was established in 2004.[1158]

Queensland had a purely advisory Privacy Committee from 1984 to 1991[1159] and has a limited privacy statute[1160] covering the use of listening devices, credit reporting (operating alongside the 1989 amendments to the federal Privacy Act) and physical intrusions into private property. In April 1998, after a yearlong review, a Parliamentary Committee recommended comprehensive privacy

---

[1154] Homepage <http://www.lawreform.vic.gov.au/>.

[1155] <http://www.lawreform.vic.gov.au/CA256A25002C7735/OrigDoc/~0456DDC1026247E4CA256A7900217AA4?OpenDocument&1=30-Current+projects~&2=30-Privacy~&3=~>.

[1156] <http://www.austlii.edu.au/au/legis/act/consol_act/hraaa1997291/>.

[1157] <http://notes.nt.gov.au/dcm/legislat/legislat.nsf/d989974724db65b1482561cf0017cbd2/33ef7122365a039e69256d55000a938c?OpenDocument>.

[1158] See <http://www.privacy.nt.gov.au>.

[1159] Privacy Committee Act 1984 (Qld).

[1160] Invasion of Privacy Act 1971 (Qld).

legislation for the public sector.[1161] The government indicated that it intended to legislate but no timetable has been set, and in 2001 the government adopted privacy principles on a hopefully interim non-statutory basis.[1162]

The other states, Tasmania, South Australia and Western Australia, also operate administrative schemes based on variations of the standard sets of privacy principles.[1163] In May 2003, the Western Australian government released a discussion paper[1164] proposing a public sector privacy law. In late 2004, the Personal Information Protection Bill was passed in Tasmania's Parliament, but does not yet appear to have commenced.[1165]

All of the States and Territories also have FOI laws that include rights for individuals to access and correct personal information about themselves.[1166]

Republic of Austria

Constitutional Privacy Framework

The Austrian Federal Constitutional Law (*Bundes-Verfassungsgesetz*[1167]) does not explicitly recognize the right of privacy but several civil rights are contained in special laws. Data protection is a civil right in Austria.[1168] Some sections of the data protection law (*Datenschutzgesetz*, or DSG) have constitutional status and may only be restricted under the conditions of Article 8 of the European Convention of Human Rights (ECHR). The entire ECHR has constitutional status and the constitutional court in privacy matters often cites Article 8.

[1161] Privacy in Queensland, Report No 9, Legal Constitutional and Administrative Review Committee, April 1998, available at <http://www.parliament.qld.gov.au/comdocs/legalrev/lcarc9.PDF>.

[1162] <http://www.justice.qld.gov.au/dept/privacy.htm>.

[1163] <http://www.justice.tas.gov.au/legpol/privacy/index.htm> (Tasmania);
<http://www.archives.sa.gov.au/services/public/privacy_index.html> (South Australia); and
<http://www.ecc.online.wa.gov.au/matrix/priv-wa.htm> (Western Australia).

[1164] <http://www.ministers.wa.gov.au/main.cfm?MinId=06&Section=0607>.

[1165] <http://www.parliament.tas.gov.au/bills/pdf/52_of_2004.pdf>

[1166] For an overview of FOI laws in Australia and links to relevant government sites, *see generally* the University of Tasmania's FOI Review web page <http://www.comlaw.utas.edu.au/law/foi/>.

[1167] B-VG, Federal Law Gazette No. 1/1930.

[1168] Austrian law permits the adoption of regulations which are "constitutional provisions" (*Verfassungsbestimmungen*), even though they appear in a regular law. These provisions are part of the constitution, the core of which is the federal constitutional law (*Bundes-Verfassungsgesetz*). Federal Law Gazette No. 1/1930, available at <http://www.ris.bka.gv.at/hilfe/erv/law_list.html>.

Data Protection Framework

A new data protection law (*Datenschutzgesetz* 2000, DSG 2000) was approved in December 1999 and went into force in January 2000.[1169] The Act replaces a 1978 law[1170] of the same name and incorporates the EU Data Protection Directive (1995/46/EC). It protects the right of individuals in relation to the processing of their personal data. The civil right to secrecy protects data contained in paper files, but most of the other rights (access, rectification, and deletion) only cover data that are automatically processed. The Austrian law also protects organizations, such as companies, religious or political organizations. Individuals have the right to access, correct, delete personal data, or keep them confidential.[1171] Data controllers are required to provide information to the data subject who has the right to access the data, its origin, and the identity of any recipients. Disclosure to third parties is only allowed when the data subject gives express written permission; if it is in the legitimate objective of the data controller to disclose the information; if it concerns legitimate published data or only indirectly personal data, or if it is necessary for the protection and interests of a third party.[1172]

Following the tsunami disaster in early 2005, the DSG 2000 was amended, introducing clarifications regarding the use of personal data by call centers established by airlines and other organizations in case of catastrophes.[1173]

Data Protection Authority

All claims against public-sector controllers must be brought before the Data Protection Commission (DPC).[1174] Claims against private sector data controllers must be brought before the courts, with the exception of claims about the refusal to give information pursuant to Section 26 DSG 2000, which are brought before the DPC. An individual data subject can bring claims before the DPC. The DPC

[1169] *Datenschutzgesetz* 2000 (DSG 2000), Austrian Federal Law Gazette part I No. 165/1999 <http://www.dsk.gv.at/legal.htm>.

[1170] *Datenschutzgesetz* (Data Protection Act), Federal Law Gazette No. 565/1978, available at <http://www.dsk.gv.at/legal.htm>.

[1171] Christopher Millard & Mark Ford, Data Protection Laws of the World, Austria Report (Clifford Chance 2001).

[1172] Section 7-9 *Datenschutzgesetz. See also* Christopher Millard & Mark Ford, *supra.*

[1173] Amendment to the DGS 2000 available at Federal Law Gazette I, Nr. 13/2005 <http://ris1.bka.gv.at/authentic/findbgbl.aspx?name=entwurf&format=html&docid=BR_DOKV-BR_1109>.

[1174] Organs of legislation or jurisdiction may not be examined by the data protection commission pursuant to Section 31 DSG 2000. One cannot appeal a law before the DPC nor bring a complaint against a parliamentary control committee (similar to a senate subcommittee). The DPC cannot overturn a court decision, either.

decides with a ruling that can be enforced. Civil and criminal provisions apply.[1175] The Austrian member states (*Länder*) have adopted their own legislation. Experts have criticized the new law as inadequate because it retains the cumbersome structure of the original 1978 Act rather than replacing it.[1176]

Under the 2000 Act, a DPC and a Data Protection Council (the Council) are established. The DPC has powers of investigation and enforcement to ensure compliance with the Act. The Council (*Datenschutzrat*) is a political advisory body.[1177] The Commission (*Datenschutzkommission*) is currently staffed with six permanent members, six deputies, and four full-time employees; another eight employees work in the Data Processing Register (*Datenverarbeitungsregister,* or DVR).[1178] The DPC is responsible for investigating public sector data processing and reporting bi-annually to the federal government on public sector data processing. It oversees private sector activity including the authorization of international data transmissions and applications for data processing registration, but excluding claims that must be brought before the courts. The DPC will only deny the export of data if such transport conflicts with public interests, violates international legal obligations, disregards data disclosure requirements, damages the interests of the person warranting protection or has inadequate safeguards. The DPC can act as an ombudsman and make recommendations to private and public sector data controllers, which are not binding.[1179]

The DPC handles complaints concerning infractions of the rights to secrecy, access to data, right to information and right to rectification and erasure against public-sector data controllers, or the right of access to data against private-sector data controllers.[1180] Bi-annually the DPC handles 80-100 formal complaints. From January 1, 2005, to April 30, 2005, the DPC handled 26 formal complaints about processing of personal data. In the same period the DPC also dealt with: 12 applications for data export (about 10 per year and rising sharply); 27 Ombudsman's cases requiring an administrative decision (about 80 annually); and over 700 notification cases throughout the year 2004 because of large-scale

---

[1175] *Id.*

[1176] *See* Viktor Mayer-Schoenberger & Ernst Brandl, *Datenschutzgesetz* 2000 (Line Publishing Vienna 1999).

[1177] *See* Section 41-44 DSG 2000 <http://www.dsk.gv.at/dsg2000e.htm#E41>. English version available at <http://www.ris.bka.gv.at/erv/erv_1999_1_165.pdf>.

[1178] The DVR is the register where data controllers have to declare their activities if they are not included in the list of standard data processing activities that do not require a declaration. *Datenschutzbericht* 2001, at 8 (Official Report of the Data Protection Commission), available at <http://www.dsk.gv.at/ds2001.pdf>.

[1179] Section 30 DSG 2000.

[1180] E-mail from Mag. Georg Lechner, Austrian Data Protection Authority, to Ula Galster, International Policy Fellow, Electronic Privacy Information Center (EPIC), June 3, 2005 (on file with EPIC).

notification in the banking sector.[1181] All of these cases are complex. A complaint case ends with a formal ruling (*Bescheid*) that can be appealed. The rulings are legally binding, and can be enforced where appropriate. All the decisions of the DPC are available for public access through the DPC's decision database.[1182]

The Ombudsman's function is often used to resolve private sector disputes that do not require a lawsuit. Instead Ombudsman's cases require an administrative decision. The DPC can act on a complaint by a citizen pursuant to Section 30 DSG 2000. These are called "ombudsman" cases because the DPC acts as a privacy ombudsman, and makes recommendations. These cases vary widely in terms of complexity. Some can be resolved by simply contacting a data controller and asking him to fix some mistake or oversight; others require much work and can involve several companies.[1183]

The DPC has investigated many issues that were not rated as "complaints," but have a similar impact. Moreover, the office of the DPC routinely answers informal help requests by e-mail or telephone. While most of these are just requests for information, some can involve elements of a complaint, or can help prevent an unnecessary complaint.[1184]

The DPC uses different enforcement tools for Ombudsman's cases.[1185] To establish the rightful state, the DPC can issue recommendations; an appropriate period for compliance shall be set if required. If a recommendation is not obeyed within the set period, the DPC shall, depending on the kind of transgression and *ex officio*: 1) initiate an administrative inquiry to check the registration pursuant to Section 22 para. 4 DSG 2000; or 2) bring a criminal charge pursuant to Sections 51 or 52 DSG 2000; or 3) in case of severe transgressions by a private sector controller file a lawsuit before the competent court of law pursuant to Section 32 para. 5 DSG 2000; or 4) in case of a transgression by an organ of a territorial corporate body (*Gebietskörperschaft*), involve the highest competent authority. This authority shall within an appropriate period, not exceeding 12 weeks, take measures to ensure that the DPC's recommendation is complied with, or inform the DPC why the recommendation is not complied with. The reason for

---

[1181] The DPC makes their statistics on a yearly basis, from January 1 to December 31. For the purposes of this report, the numbers have been estimated for the period of January 1 to April 30.

[1182] *See* <http://www.ris.bka.gv.at/dsk/>.

[1183] E-mail from Mag. Georg Lechner, *supra*.

[1184] *Id.*

[1185] *See* Section 30, Paragraph 6, DSG 2000

non-compliance may be publicized by the DPC in an appropriate manner, as long as it is not contrary to official secrecy.

As of April 2005, there were between 70,000 and 71,000 registered data controllers who can be roughly defined as the natural or legal person ordering the collection, processing, or disclosure of data.[1186] It must be noted that one data controller may notify multiple data processing. 2,300 changes were recorded in 2004 (new registrations, corrections and deletions). The DSG 2000[1187] contains many exceptions from notification, which should make notification unnecessary for most normal businesses that run typical bookkeeping, inventory, and staff management software. Moreover, many controllers who go out of business or who do not need to register anymore do not have to formally withdraw their notification. The number of data controllers has to be estimated for this reason.[1188] Data controllers are required to notify the data subject who has right to access the data, its origin, and the identity of any recipients. Disclosure to third parties is only allowed when the data subject gives express written permission; it is in the legitimate objective of the data controller to disclose the information; if an explicit legal authorization or obligation exists to use the data, the data subject has given his consent; or if it is necessary for the protection and interests of a third party.[1189] Claims against private sector data controllers can be brought under DSG 2000 by an individual data subject, or by the DPC on behalf of data subjects. Civil and criminal provisions both apply.

Due to a severe reduction of personnel from 2001 to 2003, the DPC has complained that it is no longer able to actively pursue investigations and file claims.[1190]

Statutory Rules Related to Privacy

Since 2004, the Austrian Civil Code contains a provision[1191] offering individuals a right to obtain damages caused by any illegal privacy intrusions where individuals are granted a right to claim for a minimum of EUR 1,000 for pain and suffering or other immaterial loss.

[1186] Section 4 No. 4, DSG 2000.

[1187] Austrian Federal Law Gazette part I No. 165/1999.

[1188] E-mail from Mag. Georg Lechner, *supra.*

[1189] *See* DSG 2000 s. 8.

[1190] *Id. at* 8.

[1191] § 1328a ABGB, available at <http://www.dsk.gv.at/abgb.htm>.

There are also several sectoral privacy laws. The telecommunications law contains special data protection provisions for telecommunications systems, particularly problems like phone directories, unsolicited calls, spamming or calling line identification.[1192] The Genetic Engineering Act of 1994 requires prior written consent for information to be used for purposes other than the original purpose and the use of genetic data by insurance companies and employers is explicitly prohibited. The Data Protection Act (DSG 2000) deals with medical data in a very general way, by considering them sensitive data, with benefit of special protection, as well as by providing some provisions on research in Sections 46 and 47. There are provisions in other statutes dealing with the use of medical or health data. As in most countries, Austria has laws requiring that carriers of dangerous diseases be reported to health authorities.[1193] The normal rules for medical confidentiality apply, although with exceptions, as doctors must report serious injuries that were obviously caused by criminal activity or cruelty to children.

The Banking Act of 1993 deals with special requirements in relation to credit data. Section 18 of the DSG 2000 states that a data application containing information regarding a person's creditworthiness requires prior registration and authorization by the DVR. In their regular business relations, all financial institutions must comply with DPA provisions stating that they cannot use personal data obtained through client accounts for other purposes. Austria adopted a new anti-money laundering law according to the requirements of the Organization for Economic Cooperation and Development (OECD).[1194] Banks must establish the identity of customers who wish to open an account, or in case of money transfers exceeding EUR 15,000.[1195]

In 2000, the Austrian Provinces (*Länder*) adopted various laws relating to data protection. Some have passed legislation regarding notification about suspicions of neglect, mistreatment or sexual abuse, and the collection of personal data related to these notifications. There are also additional federal laws regarding military authorities' standards in their use of personal data for military affairs.[1196]

[1192] §§ 92-107, *Telekommunikationsgesetz 2003* (Telecommunications Law) ("*TKG2003*," *BGBl* I 70/2003).

[1193] A complete list can be obtained at <http://www.infektionsnetz.at/TextExtMeldepflicht.phtml>.

[1194] Financial Action Task Force, FATF Welcomes Proposed Austrian Legislation to Eliminate Anonymous Passbooks, June 22, 2000 <http://www1.oecd.org/fatf/Ctry-orgpages/ctry-at_en.htm#Follow%20up%20(2000)>.

[1195] Section 40 *Bankwesengesetz*, Federal Law Gazette No. 532/1993.

[1196] Data Protection Working Party - Article 29, Fifth Annual Report of the Situation Regarding the Protection of Individuals with Regard to the Processing of Personal Data and Privacy in the European Union and in Third Countries Covering the Year 2000, March 6, 2002, available at

In June 2002, the Parliament adopted a law that allows the Austrian military to request from Internet Service Providers (ISPs) or other telecommunications service providers the name, address and telephone number of every telecommunications user.[1197] The draft was strongly opposed by Austrian privacy organizations since the military would simply have to pretend that it necessarily needs this information for intelligence purposes or for the fulfillment of its own duties.[1198]

In January 2003, the *Bildungsdokumentationsgesetz* (Law on the Documentation of Education)[1199] went into force. It regulates the use of data on pupils and students for purposes of long-term documentation. It mandates schools, universities, and other professional academies to collect a large set of data including social security numbers, religious affiliation, need for special educational assistance, grades and degrees, and transmit that information to the Federal Ministry of Education, Science, and Culture and the Austrian Agency for Statistics where the data will be stored for up to 60 years. During all these years, all data on individuals can be identified by social security numbers.[1200]

Identity Cards

Over the past few years, Austria has been working on introducing a smart card for social security. This smart card, which will replace the present health insurance certificate in 2005, will be given to every person who benefits from social security.[1201] It will contain a digital signature. Currently, only the name, the social security number and the date of birth will be stored. The card will also serve as a European health insurance card. Earlier discussions on the inclusion of health data for emergency cases did not lead to storage of such data on the card. The previous project to introduce a mandatory "citizen card" with tax number and other information has been abandoned. Today, many privately issued smart

---

<http://europa.eu.int/comm/justice_home/fsj/privacy/docs/wpdocs/2002/wp54en_1.pdf> and
<http://europa.eu.int/comm/justice_home/fsj/privacy/docs/wpdocs/2002/wp54en_2.pdf>.

[1197] § 22 (2a) *Militärbefugnisgesetz* (Federal Law Gazette I, Nr. 86/2000).

[1198] Arge Daten Privacy Service, "Militärs - Lauschgeil durchs Land," June 17, 2002, available at <http://www.ad.or.at/news/pw20020624.html>; VIBE, "Willkürlicher militärischer Zugriff auf Benutzerdaten," June 18, 2002, available at <http://www.vibe.at/aktionen/200206/mil_18jun2002.html>.

[1199] Federal Law Gazette I, Nr. 2002/12, available at
<http://www.bmbwk.gv.at/medienpool/9076/Bundesgesetz-2002.pdf>.

[1200] The data types that are stored have been formulated as a standard application "SA025" in this ordinance: Standard- und Muster-Verordnung 2004 (StMV 2004), Federal Law Gazette II Nr. 312/2004.

[1201] "Daten auf der E-Card," available at
<http://www.chipkarte.at/esvapps/page/page.jsp?p_pageid=220&p_menuid=51909&p_id=4>.

---

cards, such as private member organization cards or bank debit cards that fulfill special technical requirements, can be equipped with the functionality of an electronic citizen authentication card if so desired. The card can therefore be used for several kinds of interaction with private businesses or government agencies.[1202] The Austrian Computer Society issued the first examples of these citizen cards in December 2002.[1203] The social security card satisfies these technical requirements as well.

In March 2004 the E-Government-Act[1204] went into force. It introduces in an identity card (*Bürgerkarte*, or citizen's card) a variant of the citizen's number (*Stammzahl*) known in other countries to enable citizens to electronically interact with state agencies and certain private entities. The "*Bürgerkarte*" is defined as a functionality (electronic signature combined with certified identification of the signer (*Personenbindung*), not as a certain type of physical object.[1205] The citizen's number stored on the citizen's card is based on the unique number of a citizen's residence-registration file. Starting from this citizen's number, each administrative body will derive an identification number that is unique for its administrative area (*bereichsspezifisches Personenkennzeichen*, or bPK[1206]) and that – under certain circumstances – can be used to reveal the citizen's number again. The *Bürgerkarte* functionality can be implemented in various forms, without any card. One of its forms is, for example, being used with mobile phones or ATM cash cards. The DPC will administer the citizen's number. Austrian privacy organizations have strongly criticized the DPC's role because it will be its own control board and no independent control will be established at the heart of this national identification system.

[1202] Chief Information Office (*Bundeskanzleramt Österreich*), Konzept Bürgerkarte <http://www.cio.gv.at/identity/>.

[1203] *Oesterreichische Computer Gesellschaft* (Austrian Computer Society), "OCG-Mitgliedskarte mit Bürgerkarten-Funktion," available at <http://www.members.ocg.at/>.

[1204] E-GovG, Federal Law Gazette I, Nr. 2004/10.

[1205] The name "*Bürgerkarte*" has been kept for historical reasons, although it no longer defines the card itself.

[1206] The bPK is the result of a mathematical one-way (hash) function, based on the individual citizen's number and the code of the specific administrative body. This function cannot be reversed, which means that the original citizen's number cannot be revealed via the bPK. However, in certain cases it will be possible to find out whether bPKs in different administrative areas refer to the same person. This is regulated in §10 E-GovG and is done as follows: The DPC receives the bPK and the person's name, and then calculates all bPKs of persons with the same name. Via "trial and error" the resulting bPKs will be compared until a match is found. Based on this the DPC will calculate the bPK of this person for the area of the applying administrative body and communicate the bPK to the applicant. At no time is the citizen's number of a natural person known to anybody outside the DPC. Neither is there a way to reveal the number via the bPK alone, without already "knowing" the citizen's number, i.e. the DPC's "trial and error" method.

The Code of Criminal Procedure regulates wiretapping, electronic eavesdropping and computer searches.[1207] A judge can permit telephone wiretapping if it is needed for investigating a crime punishable by more than one year in prison. Electronic eavesdropping and computer searches[1208] can be allowed by a judge if they are needed to investigate criminal organizations or crimes punishable by more than 10 years in prison. The provisions concerning electronic eavesdropping and computer searches became effective between October 1, 1997, and July 1, 1998. The law previously contained sunset clauses that were later repealed in the fall of 2001.[1209] Criticism of the drafts of this law has led to several restrictions, but whether or not these provisions can effectively prevent eavesdropping on innocent persons remains unresolved. In February 2001, the Federal Minister of Transport, Innovation and Technology issued a draft ordinance that would require all telecommunications operators to install technical equipment to facilitate the surveillance of telecommunications traffic in accordance with the Code of Criminal Procedure.[1210] One of the high points of the discussion on eavesdropping was the controversy over who had to bear the cost of surveillance measures. The Federal Constitutional Court declared unconstitutional an ordinance that would have placed most of the cost on the telecommunication operators.[1211] In August 2003 a new telecommunications law (TKG 2003) came into force that still requires telecommunications providers to provide the necessary surveillance equipment. This equipment is specified in an ordinance issued by the Federal Minister of Transport, Innovation and Technology in December 2001.[1212] A separate ordinance issued by the Federal Minister of Justice in September 2004 specifies the reimbursement of costs to telecommunications providers on a case-by-case basis for their assistance in surveillance measures.[1213] Costs for staff and installation, maintenance and monitoring of surveillance equipment are subject to reimbursement.

[1207] § 149a to § 149p *Strafprozeßordnung* – StPO 1975, BGBl. Nr. 631/1975.

[1208] *"Automationsunterstützter Datenabgleich,"* regulated by Section 149i of the Code of Penal Procedure.

[1209] "Österreich übernimmt Lauschangriff und Rasterfahndung ins Dauerrecht," Heise, October 13, 2001, available at <http://www.heise.de/tp/deutsch/inhalt/te/9806/1.html>.

[1210] Draft Ordinance of the Federal Minister of Transport, Innovation and Technology over the Surveillance of Telecommunications, February 7, 2001 <http://www.vibe.at/misc/uevo.en.html>.

[1211] *See* for more details <http://www.epic.org/privacy/intl/austrian_vfgh-022703.html>.

[1212] Ordinance of the Federal Minister of Transport, Innovation and Technology over the Surveillance of Telecommunication (Überwachungsverordnung – ÜVO), Federal Law Gazette II, Nr. 418/2001.

[1213] Ordinance of the Federal Minister of Justice over the reimbursement of costs for the assistance in the Surveillance of Telecommunication (*Überwachungskostenverordnung* – ÜKVO) Federal Law Gazette II, Nr. 322/2004, available at <http://ris1.bka.gv.at/authentic/findbgbl.aspx?name=entwurf&format=html&docid=COO_2026_100_2_117197>.

In January 2005, an Amendment to the *Sicherheitspolizeigesetz* (SPG, Police Law) went into force. It allows police to keep public places under audio and video surveillance and to store the data collected up to 48 hours, or longer in case there is a suspicion that a criminal offence was conducted (§ 54 (6) SPG).[1214]

Anti-terrorism Measures

On October 15, 2001, in response to the terrorist attacks in the United States, the federal government announced a package of measures to fight money laundering and terrorism. Police forces increased surveillance on diplomatic missions, airports, and other sensitive sites.[1215] A week later the government passed legislation increasing punishment for those found guilty of terrorist hoaxes, increased spending on additional security personnel and equipment, and voted on an extension of police permission to carry out electronic surveillance.[1216]

Voting Privacy

Voting in Austria is compulsory for those 18 years or older. Although the law is not strictly enforced, non-voting could result in a request for the reason for non-compliance and a fine.[1217] In 1990, following a ruling by the Austrian Constitutional Court, postal voting or Internet voting was introduced for the first time, to allow those living abroad to exercise their right to vote in elections.[1218] Since that time, Austria has engaged in ongoing discussions regarding the application of Internet voting as an alternative to the ballot box.[1219] As of today, there are no laws that govern Internet voting at the national, regional, or local level. In two Länder, Lower Austria and Upper Austria, members of the public

---

[1214]Amendment to the Police Law (*Sicherheitspolizeigesetz, SPG*) Federal Law Gazette I, Nr. 151/2004, available at
<http://ris1.bka.gv.at/authentic/findbgbl.aspx?name=entwurf&format=html&docid=COO_2026_100_2_137404>.

[1215] Republic of Austria News Report. "Austrian Federal Government Supports US Actions," October 21, 2001, available at <http://www.austria.gv.at/cgi-bin/search_show.pl.cgi?page=/aktuell/database/informationen/english/single/20011015_5812.html> .

[1216] Republic of Austria News Report. "Stronger Sentences for Terror-Hoaxes," October 24, 2001, available at <http://www.austria.gv.at/cgi-bin/search_show.pl.cgi?page=/aktuell/database/informationen/english/single/20011024_2814.html>.

[1217] International Institute for Democracy and Electoral Assistance (IDEA), Web page on Compulsory Voting, available at <http://www.idea.int/vt/compulsory_voting.cfm>.

[1218] Strengthening regional and local democracy in the European Union, Volume I, Austria page 71, available at <http://www.cor.eu.int/document/documents/cdr171_2004_vol1_etu_en.pdf>.

[1219] *Id.*

may vote by e-mail on non-legally binding consultations on measures being considered by the assembly and the regional council.[1220]

Open Government

The *Auskunftspflichtgesetz* is a Freedom of Information law that compels federal authorities to answer questions regarding their areas of responsibility.[1221] However, it does not permit citizens to access documents, just to receive answers from the government on the content of information. The nine Austrian Provinces have laws that place similar obligations on their authorities.

In April 2001, the Ministry of Justice presented draft amendments of the Code of Criminal Procedure, which aimed at bringing about important changes to the Austrian judicial system. According to the draft Law on the Security of Information (*Informationssicherheitsgesetz*), authorities, journalists and other persons who disclose classified information could have faced sanctions if the disclosure impaired Austria's public security, national defense, foreign relations, or economic interests.[1222] It therefore would have been possible to imprison journalists who publicly disclose secret documents from public officials even if the publication had been of public interest. While sanctions against journalists and other persons did not find their way into the law, violations committed by public officials can lead to up to one year in prison. While the main aim of the draft law was to protect military secrets, critics claimed that since the law was so poorly formulated, it could have potentially adversely affected the free flow of information. Moreover it seemed that since any official could have declared their files classified, they could also have restricted public scrutiny of their actions and limited freedom of information access.[1223] The purpose of the law, as well as its scope, was modified before it was adopted. The aim of the adopted *Informationssicherheitsgesetz* (Law on the Security of Information (*Informationssicherheitsgesetz* - InfoSiG)[1224]) is to fulfill requirements of international law to protect classified information that is provided to Austria by international organizations.

[1220] *Id.*, at 72.

[1221] *BGBl*, 1987/287 (May 15, 1987), available at <http://www.rz.uni-frankfurt.de/~sobotta/Austria.htm>.

[1222] International Helsinki Federation for Human Rights. 2002 Report on Austria (Events of 2001), May 28, 2002, available at <http://www.ihf-hr.org/viewbinary/viewdocument.php?download=1&doc_id=145>.

[1223] *Id.*

[1224] Federal Law Gazette I, Nr. 23/2002. *See*, for more details, the Parliament's Web site <http://www.parlament.gv.at/portal/page?_pageid=908,308521&_dad=portal&_schema=PORTAL>.

International Obligations

Austria is a member of the Council of Europe (CoE) and has signed and ratified the Convention for the Protection of Individuals with Regard to Automatic Processing of Personal Data (ETS No. 108).[1225] It has signed and ratified the ECHR.[1226] In November 2001, it signed, but has not ratified, the CoE Convention on Cybercrime.[1227] It is a member of the OECD and has adopted the OECD Guidelines on the Protection of Privacy and Transborder Flows of Personal Data.

Kingdom of Belgium

Constitutional Privacy Framework

The Belgian Constitution recognizes the right of privacy and private communications.[1228] Article 22 states, "Everyone has the right to the respect of his private and family life, except in the cases and conditions determined by law. . . . The laws, decrees, and rulings alluded to in Article 134 guarantee the protection of this right." Article 29 states, "The confidentiality of letters is inviolable. ... The law determines which nominated representatives can violate the confidentiality of letters entrusted to the postal service." Article 22 was added to the Belgian Constitution in 1994. Prior to the constitutional amendment, the Supreme Court (*Cour de cassation*) ruled that Article 8 of the European Convention applied directly to the law and prohibited government infringement on the private life of individuals.[1229]

Data Protection Framework

The Law on Protection of Personal Data of 1992 governs the processing and use of personal information in Belgium. Amending legislation to update the 1992 Act and make it consistent with the European Union (EU) Data Protection Directive

---

[1225] Signed January 28, 1981, ratified March 30, 1988, entered into force July 1, 1988, available at <http://conventions.coe.int/>.

[1226] Signed December 13, 1957, ratified September 3, 1958, entered into force September 3, 1958, available at <http://conventions.coe.int/>.

[1227] Signed November 11, 2001.

[1228] Constitution of Belgium, available at <http://www.fed-parl.be/constitution_uk.html>.

[1229] *Cour de cassation*, September 26, 1978.

was approved by the Parliament in December 1998.[1230] A Royal Decree (*Arrêté royal*) to implement the Act was approved in July 2000. The decree, as a whole, broadens the scope of application of the law by extending the definition of "processing," determines how special categories of data may be processed, and reinforces data subjects' rights. The decree was finally adopted in February 2001, and the law came into effect in September 2001.

Two months after the entry into force of the new data protection regime, the government announced that it had put in place an Internet Rights Observatory (*Observatoire des droits de l'Internet*)[1231] in order to better assess and analyze the impact of the Internet on the economy and consumer protection. The Observatory aims, through its composition, at being an open forum for all Internet stakeholders, and will issue advisory opinions and annual reports, organize a dialogue between economic actors, and inform the public.[1232] The Observatory has released reports on the protection of minors on the Internet,[1233] e-commerce,[1234] e-government[1235] and Voice over IP.[1236] A recent survey found that, while 90 percent of Belgian web sites collect personal data, 55 percent of them display a privacy policy, although some of those policies are unclear, incomplete and hard to find on the site.[1237]

[1230] Act concerning the Protection of Privacy with regard to the Treatment of Personal Data Files, December 8, 1992 (*Loi relative à la protection des données à caractère personnel du 8 décembre 1992*) as amended by the Act of December 11, 1998 transposing EU Directive 95/46/EC of October 24, 1995, available at <http://www.law.kuleuven.ac.be/icri/papers/legislation/privacy/tabel/index.html>. An unofficial English translation is available at <http://www.law.kuleuven.ac.be/icri/papers/legislation/privacy/engels/>.

[1231] <http://www.internet-observatory.be/>.

[1232] Alain Jennotte, "Un Observatoire au chevet du Net," Le Soir, December 1, 2001, available at <http://www.lesoir.be>.

[1233] Observatoire des Droits de l'Internet, The Protection of Minors on the Internet, Opinion No. 1, February 2003, available at <http://www.internet-observatory.be/internet_observatory/pdf/advices/advice_en_001.pdf>.

[1234] Observatoire des Droits de l'Internet, Pistes pour renforcer la confiance dans le commerce électronique, Opinion No. 3 submitted to the Federal Minister of Economy, June 1, 2004, available at <http://www.droit-technologie.org/redirect.asp?type=legislation&legis_id=185&url=legislations/Observatoire_2_avis__01062004.pdf>, <http://www.internet-observatory.be/internet_observatory/pdf/advices/advice_en_003.pdf>.

[1235] Observatoire des Droits de l'Internet, Facteurs de succès de l'e-gouvernement, Opinion No. 2, December 2003, available at <http://www.droit-technologie.org/redirect.asp?type=legislation&legis_id=173&url=legislations/avis_observ_egov.pdf>, <http://www.internet-observatory.be/internet_observatory/pdf/advices/advice_en_002.pdf>.

[1236] In its opinion, the Observatory examines the opportunities and challenges related to the development of VoIP services. It concludes that it is important right now to make clear choices about VoIP services and determine the applicable legislation, while avoiding the creation of too many regulatory obstacles to their development, in order to protect consumers and provide legal security. Observatoire des Droits de l'Internet, Opportunités et défis liés au développement des services *Voice over IP*, Opinion No. 4, May 2005, available at <http://www.internet-observatory.be/internet_observatory/pdf/advices/advice_fr_004.pdf>.

[1237] Michel Walrave, e-Privacy.be, Protection des donnés en ligne: amelioration de la protection des données dans les sites Web belges, un an après l'entrée en vigueur de la "nouvelle" Loi Vie Privée?, Katholieke Universiteit Leuven, January 2003, available at <http://www.droit-technologie.org/redirect.asp?type=dossier&dossier_id=92&url=dossiers/privacy_etude_walrave.pdf>.

The Council of Ministers is currently working on the second version of a bill (*avant-projet de loi relatif aux communications électroniques*)[1238] that aims at transposing into Belgian law the EU "telecom package," a set of six directives that establish a new legal framework for electronic communications in the EU. This package includes the EU Directive on Privacy and Electronic Communications. The Commission for the Protection of Private Life (see below) issued a positive opinion on the part of the bill covering the protection of personal data in which it discussed the security of networks and telecommunications services, the confidentiality of communications, the retention of traffic data, the surveillance of communications, and cookies and spyware.[1239] The State Council (*Conseil d'Etat*) and the Belgian Institute for Postal Services and Telecommunications (*Institut belge des services postaux et telecommunications*, or IBPT) were also consulted.

Data Protection Authority

The Commission for the Protection of Private Life (*Commission de la protection de la vie privée*, or Commission) oversees the law.[1240] The statute of the Commission has changed since 2004 to make it directly depend on the Parliament instead of the Ministry of Justice.[1241] The Commission investigates complaints, issues opinions and maintains the registry of personal files.[1242] In 2004, the Commission answered 678 complaints and requests for

---

[1238] Available at <http://www.droit-technologie.org/redirect.asp?type=legislation&legis_id=188&url=legislations/projet_be-paquetelecom.pdf>. The *exposé des motifs* is available at <http://www.droit-technologie.org/redirect.asp?type=legislation&legis_id=188&url=legislations/paquettelecom_be_%20exposem otifs.pdf>.

[1239] Commission de la protection de la vie privée, Avis No. 08/2004 du 14 juin 2004 sur l'avant projet de loi relatif aux communications électroniques, June 14, 2004, available at <http://www.droit-technologie.org/redirect.asp?type=legislation&legis_id=195&url=legislations/avis_paquet_telecoms_vieprivee. pdf>. *See also* Janice Dervaux & Thibault Verbiest, *Projet de loi sur les communications électroniques: avis du Conseil d'Etat et de la Commission vie privée*, August 5, 2004 <http://www.droit-technologie.org/1_2.asp?actu_id=968>.

[1240] *Commission de la protection de la vie privée* homepage <http://www.privacy.fgov.be/>.

[1241] Law of February 26, 2003 amending the Law on Protection of Personal Data of 1992. The new law creates sector committees to control the compliance with data protection in some sectors, such as public administration, social security, and national registry. The committees will work under the supervision of the Commission. Belgian report to the International working group on data protection in telecommunications – 34th meeting – Berlin, September 1 and 2, 2003, Ref.: 10/TM/2003/002/004/ACL. Its new president and new members of the Commission were elected on October 2004. The mandate of a president lasts six years.

[1242] As of June 30, 2004, there were 23,883 records in the Commission's registry. E-mail from An Machtens, Conseiller POMIS, Commission de la protection de la vie privée, to Cédric Laurant, Policy Counsel, Electronic Privacy Information Center (EPIC), July 12, 2004 (on file with EPIC).

information.[1243] The number of public requests also increased from about 6,200 in 1999 to about 7,400 in 2001. As of November 2004, there are 34 permanent staff members,[1244] compared to 19 in 2001 and 28 in 2000.[1245]

The Commission has issued in the last five years a number of recommendations relating to workplace privacy,[1246] video surveillance,[1247] the compatibility of the census survey (conducted ever 10 year) with Belgian privacy regulations,[1248] the protection of privacy in the context of electronic commerce,[1249] the regulation of direct marketing under the data protection legal framework,[1250] the recording by banks of their customers' telephone communications,[1251] the use of electronic communications for electoral advertising purposes,[1252] the project of Royal Decree regarding the model-contract on matrimonial brokerage,[1253] etc.

Since 1998, the Commission has had to determine the legality of specific "black lists," from casinos' lists of cheaters to insurance companies' lists of bad debtors and risks. In 2002, the Commission was asked to assess whether the upload on the Internet of a "black list" of renters[1254] by the National Association of Property Owners (*Syndicat National des Propriétaires*) was legal. In its opinion,

---

[1243] E-mail from Anne-Christine Lacoste, Conseiller, Commission de la protection de la vie privée, to María Verónica Pérez Asinari, researcher at the Centre de Recherches Informatique et Droit (CRID), February 1, 2004 (on file with EPIC).

[1244] E-mail from An Machtens, *supra*.

[1245] E-mail from Anne-Christine Lacoste, *supra*.

[1246] Avis d'initiative n° 10/2000 du 3 avril 2000 relatif à la surveillance par l'employeur de l'utilisation du système informatique sur le lieu de travail, available at <http://www.privacy.fgov.be>.

[1247] Avis d'initiative n° 34/99 relatif aux traitements d'images effectués en particulier par le biais de systèmes de vidéo-surveillance, December 13, 1999, available at <http://193.191.208.6/juris/jurfv.htm>; avis d'initiative n° 3/2000 relatif à l'utilisation de systèmes de vidéo-surveillance dans les halls d'immeubles à appartements, January 10, 2000, available at <http://193.191.208.6/juris/jurfv.htm>; avis n° 10/2005 sur le projet d'arrêté royal relatif à l'installation et au fonctionnement de caméras de surveillance dans les stades de football, June 15, 2005, available at <http://193.191.208.6/juris/jurfv.htm>.

[1248] Avis d'initiative n° 37/2001 of October 8, 2001 concernant l'enquête socio-économique 2001, available at <http://www.privacy.fgov.be>.

[1249] Avis d'initiative n° 34/2000 of November 22, 2000 relatif à la protection de la vie privée dans le cadre du commerce électronique, available at <http://www.privacy.fgov.be>.

[1250] Commission de la protection de la vie privée, "Marketing direct et protection des données personnelles," March 24, 2003, available at <http://www.privacy.fgov.be/publications/note_marketing.pdf>; *see also* Commission de la protection de la vie privée, Les droits des utilisateurs face aux courriers électroniques non-sollicités, <http://www.privacy.fgov.be/publications/note_spam.htm>.

[1251] Recommandation n° 01/2002 du 22 août 2002 sur l'enregistrement des télécommunications effectuées dans le cadre des services bancaires, available at <http://www.privacy.fgov.be>.

[1252] Avis n° 07/2003 du 27 février 2003 sur l'utilisation des moyens de communications électroniques à des fins de propagande électorale, available at <http://www.privacy.fgov.be>.

[1253] Avis n° 06/2005 concernant le projet d'arrêté royal relatif au contrat-type de courtage matrimonial, May 4, 2005, available at <http://193.191.208.6/juris/jurfv.htm>.

[1254] The list was available at <http://www.check4rent.com>.

the data protection authority found the database illegal under the Law on Protection of Personal Data of 1992, and that it required prior legislative action to authorize it – if it were to be authorized – and determine the conditions of access.[1255] In 2005, the Commission was asked to deliver an opinion concerning the legality of "black lists" in the private sector. The Commission recommended that they be regulated by a law, especially where they are likely to violate a fundamental right or restrain access to an "essential service." In this latter case, the establishment of black lists should be authorized only upon prior approval by the Commission. Where the lists process sensitive data (*e.g.*, medical data), they should be regulated by a specific law and strictly follow the provisions of the Law on Protection of Personal Data.[1256]

In 2005 also, the Commission issued an opinion about a project of bill (*avant-projet de loi*) regarding the Analysis of Threat.[1257] The purpose of the bill is to improve the gathering, use and analysis of information useful to assess terrorist and extremist threats likely to harm national security, Belgian assets and the safety of Belgian citizens abroad. To this end, the bill creates a new institution, the Coordination Agency for the Analysis of Threat (*Organe de coordination pour l'analyse de la menace*, or OCAM); its task will be to coordinate the collection of that information from various security and intelligence government agencies, and evaluate it. The privacy authority emphasizes that this new type of data collection and analysis by law enforcement is highly sensitive due to the grounds on which it is justified (likelihood and probability) and because it operates unbeknownst to the persons concerned. Although it welcomes the government's project because it provides at least a legal basis to its new processing of data, the Commission has reservations about how the project of bill complies with the provisions of the Law on Protection of Personal Data. In this regard, it recommends that the language of the bill be modified in order to specify the purposes (more than only for "threat analysis" purposes) for which personal data will be transferred between partner security and police agencies and the OCAM, and determine the criteria to be used to appreciate whether to proceed with this transfer; better implement the security safeguards surrounding

---

[1255] Avis n° 52/2002 du 19 décembre 2002 relatif à la constitution d'un fichier externe des locataires défaillants, available at <http://193.191.208.6/juris/jurfv.htm>. *See also* Actualité en détail - « Liste noire » des locataires et avis de la Commission pour la protection de la vie privée, DroitBelge.Net, January 16, 2003 <http://www.droitbelge.be/actualites.asp?display=detail&id=86>.

[1256] Avis n° 09/2005 concernant la demande d'avis sur un encadrement des listes noires, June 15, 2005, available at <http://193.191.208.6/juris/jurfv.htm>.

[1257] Avis n° 08/2005 concernant l'avant-projet de loi relatif à l'analyse de la menace, May 25, 2005, available at <http://193.191.208.6/juris/jurfv.htm>. *See also* Conseil des Ministres, "Organe de coordination pour l'analyse de la menace," press release, March 25, 2005 <http://www.belgium.be/eportal/application?languageParameter=fr&pageid=contentPage&docId=38242>.

the processing of data; and establish the guarantees to protect international data transfers among foreign authorities.[1258]

Statutory Rules Related to Privacy

In November 2000, the Belgian Parliament enacted a Computer Crime Law.[1259] The law creates four new crimes: computer forgery ("*faux en informatique*"), computer fraud ("*fraude informatique*"), hacking, and sabotage of computer data ("*sabotage de données informatiques*"). Recent case law tends to temper the harshness of some provisions of the new law.[1260]

In December 1999, the Commission issued an opinion on the Computer Crime Bill, in which it raised serious concerns about its potential negative impact on the protection of privacy. It recommended certain amendments to the Bill including the establishment of a "police monitoring system," which would report back to the Commission, and a three-year review provision.[1261] These suggestions were not included in the law, and the data retention provision even goes against the Commission's official opinion. However, the law provides that the Privacy Commission's opinion is mandatory before any royal decree is enacted on the issue of data retention.

After almost a year of negotiations, a national collective labor organization of employers and employees' representatives (the *Conseil national du travail*) eventually agreed on common rules regulating the electronic surveillance of workers' computers in the workplace. The common agreement (called *convention collective de travail* or CCT) entered into force on June 29, 2002 through a royal decree[1262] and applies to all employers and employees in the country. It provides for rules implementing to the specific setting of the workplace the already existing and enforceable European and Belgian general data protection regulations, by ensuring the workers of fairness, information, and compliance

---

[1258] *Id.*

[1259] Loi du 28 novembre 2000 relative à la criminalité informatique, Moniteur belge, February 3, 2001, available at <http://www.cass.be/cgi_loi/legislation.pl>.

[1260] *See* Jeoffrey Vigneron, Pour la première fois, un juge belge applique la "nouvelle" loi sur la cybercriminalité, January 26, 2004 <http://www.droit-technologie.org/1_2.asp?actu_id=881>.

[1261] Opinion n° 33/99 de la Commission de la protection de la vie privée, available at <http://www.privacy.fgov.be/>.

[1262] Arrêté royal rendant obligatoire la Convention Collective de Travail No. 81 du 26 avril 2002, conclue au sein du Conseil National du travail, relative à la protection de la vie privée des travailleurs à l'égard du contrôle des données de communication électroniques en réseau, Moniteur belge, 29489-29501, available at <http://www.droit-technologie.org/redirect.asp?type=legislation&legis_id=120&url=legislations/AR_120602_rendant_obligatoire_CCT_81_cybersurveillance_travailleurs.pdf>.

with the basic data processing principles of proportionality, purpose specification, and transparency.[1263] The data protection authority had released earlier an opinion[1264] on the same topic in which it refers to the general principles applicable: a general prohibition of the interception of telecommunications, proportionality and transparency, balance of the interests and limited storage of personal data. Also in the field of workplace privacy, another CCT was released in 1998 to regulate the surveillance of workers by video surveillance cameras.[1265]

In August 2002, a new law was enacted that better protects patients' privacy rights by giving them, *e.g.*, the right to be clearly informed about their health state, to consent to any medical interventions, and to have access to their medical files.[1266] There are also laws relating to consumer credit,[1267] social security,[1268] electoral rolls,[1269] the national ID number,[1270] professional secrets,[1271] and employee rights.[1272]

[1263] *See* Bertrand Géradin, La convention collective de travail relative à la protection de la vie privée des travailleurs à l'égard du contrôle des données des communications électroniques en réseau du 26 avril 2002, June 14, 2002 <http://www.droit-technologie.org/redirect.asp?type=dossier&dossier_id=77&url=dossiers/analyse_CCT81_260402.pdf>.

[1264] Commission de la protection de la vie privée, Avis d'initiative relatif à la surveillance par l'employeur de l'utilisation du système informatique sur le lieu de travail, opinion No. 10, April 3, 2000, available at <http://www.privacy.fgov.be>.

[1265] Convention Collective de Travail n° 68 relative à la protection de la vie privée des travailleurs à l'égard de la surveillance par cameras sur le lieu de travail, June 16, 1998, available at <http://www.privacy.fgov.be/textes_normatifs/cct-68_FR.pdf>. *See generally* on recent developments in workplace privacy, Olivier Rijckaert, Surveillance des travailleurs: nouveaux procédés, multiples contraintes, in Orientations, "L'employeur et la vie privée du travailleur," n° spécial 35 ans, 41 *et seq.* (2005), available at <http://www.droit-technologie.org/redirect.asp?type=dossier&dossier_id=144&url=dossiers/Surveillance_Travailleurs_nouvelles_contraintes.pdf>.

[1266] *See* Loi du 22 août 2002 relative aux droits du patient (Law on Patient's Rights of August 22, 2002), available at <http://www.cass.be/cgi_loi/legislation.pl>; *see also* Dominique Mayerus & Pascal Staquet, Actualité en détail: La loi du 22 août 2002 relative aux droits du patient, DroitBelge.Net, October 8, 2002 <http://www.droitbelge.be/actualites.asp?display=detail&id=81>.

[1267] Loi du 12 juin 1991 relative au crédit à la consommation, available at <http://www.privacy.fgov.be/textes_normatifs/loicrdit.PDF>; l'arrêté royal du 11 janvier 1993 modifiant l'arrêté royal du 20 novembre 1992 relatif à l'enregistrement par la Banque Nationale de Belgique des défauts de paiement en matière de crédit à la consommation, available at <http://www.cass.be/cgi_loi/legislation.pl>.

[1268] Loi du 15 janvier 1990 relative à l'institution et à l'organisation d'une banque-carrefour de la sécurité sociale. Modified by the loi du 29 avril 1996, available at <http://www.privacy.fgov.be/textes_normatifs/loicarrefour.PDF>.

[1269] Loi du 30 juillet 1991, available at <http://www.users.skynet.be/psetranger/moniteur.htm>.

[1270] Loi du 8 août 1993: le registre national, available at <http://www.privacy.fgov.be/textes_normatifs/loiregistre.PDF>.

[1271] Article 458 of the Penal Code.

[1272] *See* Roger Blanpain, Employee Privacy Issues: Belgian Report, 17 Comp. Lab. L. 38, Fall 1995. The employer generally has no right to obtain medical information from his employee, unless the information is absolutely necessary for the appropriate fulfillment of the employee's obligations under the employment contract.

Surveillance of communications is regulated under a 1994 law.[1273] Prior to its enactment, there was no specific law. The law requires permission of a *juge d'instruction* before wiretapping can take place. Orders are limited to a period of one month. There were 114 orders issued in 1996,[1274] and, reportedly, around 1,000 in 2002.[1275] The law was amended in 1997 to remove restrictions on encryption.[1276] The Parliament also amended the law in 1998[1277] to require greater assistance from telecommunications carriers and to give the *juge d'instruction* and the Attorney General (*Procureur du Roi*) more powers. The *juge d'instruction* now has the authority to request the cooperation of experts or network managers to help decrypt telecommunications messages that have been intercepted. The experts, network managers, etc., cannot refuse to cooperate; criminal sanctions are possible in cases of refusal. The law also provides that telecommunications network operators and telecommunications service providers have to record and store calling data (*données d'appel*) and telecommunications services subscribers' identification data for future law enforcement authorities' needs during a minimum period of 12 months. The law is very vague as to the duration of data retention ("a certain time") and would not prevent an implementing decree from increasing this period for much longer. The Belgian police are officially in favor of a three-year general retention policy.[1278] In 2003,

---

[1273] Loi du 30 juin 1994 relative à la protection de la vie privée contre les écoutes, la prise de connaissance et l'enregistrement de communications et de télécommunications privées, available at <http://www.cass.be/cgi_loi/legislation.pl>.

[1274] "Ecoutes: une pratique décevante et flamande ! Le résultat judiciaire des écoutes téléphoniques est médiocre. La Chambre va modifier la donne," Le Soir, December 12, 1997, available at <http://www.lesoir.be>.

[1275] The increase in wiretaps is partly due to the higher number of types of communications that the police is now able to intercept, from regular landline telephones, to mobile phones, SMS messages, facsimiles, satellite communications, e-mails, chat sessions, etc. Filip Verhoest, "'Meest geavanceerde' telefoontapkamer van Europa in gebruik genomen. Boeven afluisteren in stereo," May 13, 2003, De Standaard; *see also* Ricardo Gutiérrez, "La Belgique se dote de grandes oreilles," Le Soir, May 12, 2003, available at <http://www.lesoir.be/articles/a_03E4C3.asp>.

[1276] Chapitre 17, Loi modifiant la loi du 21 mars 1991 portant réforme de certaines entreprises publiques économiques afin d'adapter le cadre réglementaire aux obligations en matière de libre concurrence et d'harmonisation sur le marché des télécommunications découlant des décisions de l'Union européenne, December 19, 1997, available at <http://www.cass.be/cgi_loi/legislation.pl>.

[1277] Loi du 10 juin 1998 (adding Art. 88*bis*, 90*ter et seq.* to the Code of Criminal Procedure (*Code d'instruction criminelle*)), modifiant la loi du 30 juin 1994 relative à la protection de la vie privée contre les écoutes, la prise de connaissance et l'enregistrement de communications et de télécommunications privées, June 10, 1998, available at <http://www.cass.be/cgi_loi/legislation.pl>; *see* "Le GSM en toute sécurité ? Pas sûr," Le Soir, February 20, 1998, available at <http://www.lesoir.be>.

[1278] The European Commission made strong critiques of the law before its enactment. However, most of its critiques were not addressed, and most of them rejected without adequate motivation. Some of the European Commission's critiques mentioned that the law was too vague and could not be considered a "law" pursuant to current case law of the European Court of Human Rights (ECtHR). The European institution also specified that the law, by not restricting the strictures within which the government has to implement data retention measures, is too vague and gives the government *carte blanche* to act in a discretionary fashion. According to the

---

a new royal decree was enacted to implement the June 10, 1998 Law to provide more details about the practical and technical measures that telecommunications network and service providers have to comply with to cooperate with law enforcement authorities.[1279]

Almost unnoticed, a law enacted in December 2001 bans anonymity for subscribers and users of telecommunications network operators and services providers, while the application of the law is, however, subject to a proportionality requirement. A royal decree may prohibit the exploitation of telecommunications services if they render the identification of the caller impossible, or otherwise make it difficult to track, monitor, wiretap, or record communications. With this new rule, the government can now prohibit any telecommunications service that hinders the application of the wiretapping laws.[1280]

In March 2005, the Council of Ministers (*Conseil des Ministres*) adopted a new Pre-Project of Law (*avant-projet de loi*) creating a new entity, OCAM, to coordinate the evaluation of the threats of terrorism and extremism. The project of law assigns this task to the OCAM and provides it with the authority to coordinate the collection of such information from security and intelligence entities, as well as other government agencies, such as the Customs Bureau and the Ministry of Foreign Affairs, and assess and analyze it.[1281]

European Commission, the data retention provision of the Belgian law is also disproportionate with respect to the Court of Justice of the European Community's case law. One has to note that, even though the new EU Directive on Privacy and Electronic Communications allows EU Member States to allow data retention for a reasonable period, the Belgian law, as it is now written, could be considered in violation of current ECtHR's case law. For more information, *see* European Commission, Opinion regarding Belgian bill on computer crime ("Notification 2000/151/B – Projet de loi relatif à la criminalité informatique – Emission d'un avis circonstancié au sens de l'article 9, paragraphe 2 de la Directive 98/34/CE du 22 juin 1998 – Emission d'observations au sens de l'article 8, paragraphe 2 de la directive 98/34/CE"), June 2000, appended to the Parliamentary report of the Justice Commission, Chamber of Representatives of the Belgian Parliament, October 19, 2000, DOC 50 0213/011.

[1279] Arrêté royal du 9 janvier 2003 portant exécution des articles 46bis, § 2, alinéa 1er, 88bis, § 2, alinéas 1er et 3, et 90quater, § 2, alinéa 3, du Code d'instruction criminelle ainsi que de l'article 109ter, E, § 2, de la loi du 21 mars 1991 portant réforme de certaines entreprises publiques économiques, available at <http://www.just.fgov.be/cgi/article_body.pl?language=fr&caller=summary&pub_date=2003-02-10&numac=2003009111>. For more information, *see generally* P. Van Eecke & J. Dumortier, Elektronische Handel (Die Keure, Brugge 2003).

[1280] The wording of the law is so vague that a decree might prohibit any kind of anonymization software, the use of proxies by ISPs, since they all make the identification or tracking of communications "difficult," Etienne Wéry, "Surfer anonymement devient illégal en Belgique," March 18, 2002 <www.droit-technologie.org/fr/1_2.asp?actu_id=553>.

[1281] Question from Mr. Tony Van Parys to the vice-Prime Minister and Minister of Justice about the "fight against terrorism following the terror attacks in London," July 12, 2005, at 6-8 (Question de M. Tony Van Parys à la vice-première et ministre de la Justice sur "la lutte contre le terrorisme à la suite des actes de terreur commis à Londres" (n° 7871), *C.R.I.*, Ch. Repr., Comm. Justice, sess. ord. 2004-2005, séance du 12 juillet 2005, pp. 6-8), available at <http://www.dekamer.be/doc/CCRI/pdf/51/ic683.pdf>. *See also* Permanent Committee for the

---

The Constitutional Court (*Cour d'Arbitrage*) ruled that the personal details of sportsmen suspended on the basis of a violation of the Flemish doping regulations may not be published on an official publicly available Web site. The court held that publishing personal data in such a general way involves an interference[1282] with the right to privacy that Article 22 of the Constitution guarantees, as well as Article 8 of the European Convention on Human Rights and Article 17 of the International Covenant on Civil and Political Rights.[1283]

National ID, Travel Documents and Smart Cards

Belgium is the first country in Europe to embed a digital signature in an ID card and to massively roll out ID smart cards at a national level.[1284] The "e-ID" (which stands for "electronic ID") embeds a digital certificate that will, according to the government, allow Belgians to communicate online and conduct secure transactions with government agencies, access e-government applications, and perform e-banking, or other future private applications.[1285] Under the plan, every Belgian citizen (as young as 12 years old)[1286] gets an identification card with his or her name and other identifiers,[1287] photograph and two digital certificates. One is to be used for authentication, the other as a digital signature to sign documents

---

Control of Intelligence Services, Report of Activities 2004 (Comité permanent de contrôle des services de renseignements, Rapport d'activités 2004), available at <http://www.comiteri.be/rapports/rapport2004_fr.pdf>.

[1282] For such an interference to be allowed, it has to be necessary to achieve a certain legitimate goal, which implies, *i.a.*, that there be a reasonable connection of proportionality between the measure's consequences for the concerned person and the interests of society.

[1283] As a result, the court declared void part of an article of the Flemish Decree of March 27, 1991 on the Medically Justified Practice of Sport. *See* Cour d'arbitrage, recours en annulation de l'article 40, § 6, alinéa 2, du décret flamand du 27 mars 1991 relatif à la pratique du sport dans le respect des impératifs de santé, tel qu'il a été inséré par le décret du 19 mars 2004, arrêt 16/2005 du 19 janvier 2005, available at <http://www.droit-technologie.org/redirect.asp?type=jurisprudence&juris_id=182&url=jurisprudences/cour_arbitrage_190105.pdf>. *See, for more details,* Thierry Léonard & Wim Germonpré, "The Publication of Suspended Sportsmen's Personal Details Is Nullified by the Court of Arbitration," March 23, 2005 <http://www.droit-technologie.org/1_2.asp?actu_id=1057>.

[1284] "Belgium Plans Digital ID Cards," "Belgium Plans Digital ID Cards," BBC News Online, October 4, 2003 <http://news.bbc.co.uk/hi/technology/2295433.stm> and TB6/SINCE Interoperability Group, Open Smart Cards Infrastructure for Europe, eESC Common Specifications v2; Volume - Part 3, February 18, 2004 <http://www.eurosmart.com/Update/Download/February04/SINCE_survey.pdf>.

[1285] TB6/SINCE Interoperability Group, *supra.*

[1286] Including every foreigner holding an identity card.

[1287] Including the sex, nationality, date of birth, address, card number, identification number in the National Registry and signature.

---

such as declarations or application forms, which will have the same legal value as documents signed by hand.[1288]

The e-ID project, which was originally called "BELPIC" (or Belgian Personal Identity Card) started in July 2001, when the Council of Ministers (*Conseil des ministres*) approved the idea of introducing an electronic identity card for all Belgians.[1289] In February 2003, the Parliament approved the introduction of BELPIC[1290] and the new chipcards were tested in 11 municipalities (*communes*) until September 2003. After the government considered the test satisfactory, it decided to roll out the cards to the rest of the Belgian population[1291] – about nine million individuals – on a schedule that would end in late 2009.[1292]

The Commission and civil liberties organizations criticized the new ID card as presenting a serious threat to individuals' privacy. The data protection authority noted that it was still unclear how the government answers several important privacy concerns due to the uncertainty of many aspects of the project, and the information that the Commission has so far been provided with from the

---

[1288] The signature file on the card would ostensibly be required when conducting transactions with the government, banks, and other public or private entities, including the payment of taxes and electronic voting. BELPIC contains several digital keys to enable remote identification via the Internet, and personal data on the chip are secured via a public key infrastructure (PKI). Children `would also receive their own cards although without the signature feature. *See* "Belgium Plans Digital ID Cards," *supra*; EDRI-gram, No. 3, February 26, 2003. *See also* TB6/SINCE Interoperability Group, *supra*.

[1289] Région wallonne, Le projet BELPIC, July 20, 2004 <http://egov.wallonie.be/pa030401.htm>. *See also* Hervé Feuillien, E-Government en Région de Bruxelles-Capitale, December 4-5, 2003 <http://www.cities-lyon.org/fr/articles/227>.

[1290] *See* Arrêté royal portant des mesures transitoires relatives à la carte d'identité électronique, 25 mars 2003, M.B., 28 mars 2003, p. 15.942, available at <http://www.droit-technologie.org/redirect.asp?type=legislation&legis_id=201&url=legislations/AR_mesures_transitoires_CI_ele ctronique_250303.pdf>. *See also* Arrêté ministériel déterminant le modèle du document de base en vue de la réalisation de la carte d'identité électronique, 26 mars 2003, M.B., 28 mars 2003, p. 15.946, available at <http://www.droit-technologie.org/redirect.asp?type=legislation&legis_id=202&url=legislations/AM_modele_CI_electronique_26 0303.pdf>.

[1291] Arrêté royal du 1er septembre 2004 portant la décision de procéder à l'introduction généralisée de la carte d'identité électronique, M.B., 15 septembre 2004, p. 67.527, available at <http://www.droit-technologie.org/redirect.asp?type=legislation&legis_id=199&url=legislations/AR_usage_generalise_CI_electro nique_010904.pdf>. *See also* "La Belgique adopte la carte d'identité électronique," NetEconomie.com, September 7, 2004 <http://www.neteconomie.com/perl/navig.pl/neteconomie/infos/article/20040907185201>; Etienne Wéry & Sébastien Mélardy, "La Belgique généralise la carte d'identité pour l'ensemble de la population," September 21, 2004 <http://www.droit-technologie.org/1_2.asp?actu_id= 988, 21 Septembre 2004>.

[1292] Corinne De Permentier, Rapport d'évaluation de l'introduction de la carte d'identité électronique fait au nom de la Commission de l'Intérieur, des Affaires Générales et de la Fonction Publique, Chambre des Représentants de Belgique, No. 51K1094, May 5, 2004, available at <http://www.lachambre.be/FLWB/pdf/51/1094/51K1094001.pdf>. *See also* "Belgium Extends e-ID Applications," eGovernment News, February 7, 2005 <http://europa.eu.int/idabc/en/document/3854/332>.

government.[1293] Other critics say that the e-commerce identity of Internet users should not be linked to day-to-day authentication, that integration of data damages the integrity and rights of users, and that the fact that the Belgian government handed the project to a private company (security firm Ubizen) jeopardizes citizens' privacy rights.[1294] While it does not appear such concerns have been thus far addressed, both the public and private sectors have already developed several new applications and services compatible with e-ID, including online tax returns, certified e-mail, online request of official documents, Internet banking services and electronic library services.[1295]

Belgium began a test program in May 2004 that made it the second country in the world (after Malaysia) to issue passports with an imbedded computer chip for personal information.[1296] The government began producing the RFID[1297] passports in November 2004, and issuing them to the public on January 30, 2005, in full compliance with the current European, US and ICAO[1298] standards and deadlines for biometric based e-passports.[1299] Initially, the chip will be used only for basic information, such as name, date and place of birth, passport number, issuing date and place, digital photo and signature. However, it has the ability to store fingerprints, an iris scan and other biometrics.[1300] Although the Belgian passport received "the world's most secure passport" award from Interpol in

---

[1293] Avis n° 08/2003 du 27 février 2003 sur deux projets d'arrêté royal en exécution de la loi du … modifiant la loi du 8 août 1983 organisant un Registre National des personnes physiques et la loi du 19 juillet 1991 relative aux registres de population et aux cartes d'identité, available at <http://193.191.208.6/juris/jurfv.htm>; *see also* avis n° 19/2002 du 10 juin 2002 sur le projet de loi modifiant la loi du 8 août 1983 organisant un Registre national des personnes physiques et la loi du 19 juillet 1991 relative aux registres de la population et modifiant la loi du 8 août 1983 organisant un Registre national des personnes physiques, le projet d'arrêté royal relatif aux cartes d'identité et le projet d'arrêté royal portant mesures transitoires en ce qui concerne la carte d'identité électronique en Belgique, available at <http://193.191.208.6/juris/jurfv.htm>.

[1294] "Belgium Plans Digital ID Cards," *supra.*

[1295] "Belgium Extends e-ID Applications," *supra.* There is also a plan to use BELPIC for online identification in conjunction with the Microsoft Corp.'s MSN Messenger service. Proponents of the plan point to the security benefits that an online age verification system would have for individuals who want to log on to children-only chat rooms. *Id. See also* "MSN Belgium to Use eID Cards for Online Checking," February 1, 2005, The Register <http://www.theregister.co.uk/2005/02/01/msn_belgium_id_cards/> and "Belgian Government Presents e-ID Toolkits for Citizens and Developers," eGovernment News, May 19, 2004 <http://europa.eu.int/idabc/en/document/2557/332>.

[1296] BBC Worldwide Monitoring, "Passport Acquires Chip," May 19, 2004.

[1297] Radio frequency identification passports. *See* Section on "RFID" in the "Threats to Privacy" Chapter.

[1298] International Civil Association Organization. *See*, for more details about biometric passports, the Sections on "Identity Systems" and "Travel Privacy" in the "Threats to Privacy" Chapter.

[1299] Rudi Veestraeten, Oversight Hearing on "October 2005 Statutory Deadline for Visa Waiver Program Countries to Produce Security Passports: Why It Matters to Homeland Security," Committee on the Judiciary, US House of Representatives, April 20, 2005, available at <http://judiciary.house.gov/OversightTestimony.aspx?ID=352>.

[1300] *Id.*

2003,[1301] now that it is equipped with a RFID chip, it may present new privacy and security risks, including the unauthorized reading of its data.[1302]

Miscellaneous Developments

After opening a spam mailbox (*boîte à spam*) for three months at the end of 2002 to store the unsolicited commercial e-mails spontaneously forwarded by Belgian Internet users, the Commission released a study on "spam" in July 2003 that assesses the phenomenon of spam in Belgium. The Commission found out that most of the e-mails come from abroad – mainly from the United States – and details the measures it has taken to combat illegal spam. The report also outlines spammers' obligations under the 1998 amendment of the Law on Protection of Personal Data of 1992 and provides legal and practical advice for data subjects receiving unsolicited commercial e-mails.[1303] Since 2003, the use of e-mails for marketing purposes is prohibited without the prior, free, specific and informed consent of the recipients, in compliance with the EU Directive on Electronic Commerce,[1304] transposed by the Law of March 11, 2003,[1305] and with the EU Electronic Communications and Privacy Directive.[1306] [1307]

In 2004, the Commission ruled that disclosures of passenger name records (PNR) by airline companies to the US government without passengers' consent are

---

[1301] *Id.*

[1302] As of April 30, 2005, no reliable public information was available about the.security features (encryption and measures against clandestine scanning and tracking, skimming and eavesdropping) used in the Belgian e-passport. *See* "Ari Juels, David Molnar and David Wagner, "Security and Privacy Issues in E-Passports," to appear, IEEE SecureComm 2005, available at <http://www.cs.berkeley.edu/~dmolnar/papers/RFID-passports.pdf>.

[1303] Commission de la protection de la vie privée, Le spam en Belgique – Etat des lieux en juillet 2003, July 4, 2003, available at <http://www.privacy.fgov.be/publications/spam_4-7-03_fr.pdf>.

[1304] Directive 2000/31/EC of the European Parliament and of the Council of 8 June 2000 on Certain Legal Aspects of Information Society Services, in particular Electronic Commerce, in the Internal Market, available at <http://europa.eu.int/cgi-bin/eur-lex/udl.pl?REQUEST=Seek-Deliver&COLLECTION=oj&SERVICE=eurlex&LANGUAGE=en&DOCID=2000l178p0001>.

[1305] Loi du 11 mars 2003 sur certains aspects juridiques des services de la société de l'information, Moniteur belge, March 17, 2003, at 12960-12970, available at <http://www.droit-technologie.org/3_1.asp?legislation_id=142>.

[1306] *See* for more details Thibault Verbiest & Etienne Wéry, "Courriers électroniques non sollicités: le débat juridique n'est pas clos," Droit et Nouvelles Technologies, February 5, 2004 <http://www.droit-technologie.org/1_2.asp?actu_id=896>.

[1307] For more information, *see generally* Thibault Verbiest, "La loi belge enfin adoptée !," Droit et Nouvelles Technologies, April 22, 2003 <http://www.droit-technologie.org/1_2.asp?actu_id=747>; and Jos Dumortier & Mieke Loncke, Ongevraagde reclame langs elektronische post, 21 Mediarecht, Telecommunicatie en telematica 43-74 (Mechelen 2003)

illegal (on the complaint of data subjects, including a Member of the European Parliament).[1308]

From the end of 2000, IFPI Belgium, the recording industry trade association, started tracking people downloading and uploading music files from MP3 audio file-sharing web sites such as Napster, Gnutella or KaZaa. In a move that left many Belgian music fans outraged, IFPI collaborated by simple "gentlemen's agreements,"[1309] outside any legal framework, with Internet service providers (ISPs) to get the names and addresses of high-speed Internet connection subscribers in order to send them personalized letters threatening them with legal action if they did not stop their file-sharing practices. In November 2001, the Privacy Commission released an initiative opinion[1310] severely condemning the way IFPI had behaved with respect to the protection of people's privacy and stating that IFPI had violated several Belgian and European telecommunications privacy and data protection laws.[1311]

In April 2005, a new law was enacted that protects journalists' right not to disclose the names of their sources,[1312] complying in this with the constraining jurisprudence of the European Court of Human Rights in its 1996 *Goodwin* decision.[1313] Before 2005, journalists had often had to reveal their sources due to the lack of legal rules, and because the Constitution, and the case law interpreting it, did not offer more than unclear and low standards of protection. It will from now on be very difficult to compel journalists to disclose the names of their informants considering the very strict exceptions the law provides.[1314]

[1308] Commission de la protection de la vie privée, Avis 48/2003, Plaintes relatives à la transmission de données à caractère personnel par certaines compagnies aériennes vers les Etats-Unis, December 18, 2003, available at <http://193.191.208.6/jurispdf/J/Z/03/C/JZ03CI4.pdf#Page1>.

[1309] Olivier Van Vaerenbergh, "L'IFPI poursuit, mais la justice renâcle – Napster: plaintes en Belgique," Le Soir, February 16, 2000, available at <http://www.lesoir.be>.

[1310] Avis No. 44/2001 of November 12, 2001, Avis d'initiative concernant la compatibilité de la recherché d'infractions au droit d'auteur commises sur Internet avec les dispositions juridiques protégeant les données à caractère personnel et les télécommunications, available at <http://www.privacy.fgov.be>. For comments: Etienne Wéry, "La Commision vie privée n'aime pas les manières de l'IFPI de traquer les pirates sur l'internet" (December 17, 2001) <http://www.droit-technologie.org/1_2_1.asp?actu_id=497>.

[1311] The Commission de protection de la vie privée found that IFPI had violated Belgian data protection law of December 8, 1992, Belgian telecommunications privacy laws, and EU Directive 2000/31/EC on electronic commerce. *See* Avis No. 44/2001, *supra*.

[1312] Law on the Protection of Journalists' Sources of April 7, 2005 (*Loi relative à la protection des sources des journalistes*), Moniteur belge, April 27, 2005, at 19522, available at <http://www.ejustice.just.fgov.be/doc/rech_f.htm>.

[1313] E.Ct.H.R., Goodwin v. United Kingdom, March 27, 1996, available at <http://www.ius-software.si/EUII/EUCHR/dokumenti%5C1996%5C03%5CCASE_OF_GOODWIN_v._THE_UNITED_KINGDOM_27_03_1996.html>.

[1314] *See generally* Dirk Voorhoof, The Protection of Journalistic Sources under Fire?, 1 Auteurs & Media 9-23 (2003), available at <http://www.ifj-europe.org/docs/POS-Voorhoof2005.doc>.

A Law of December 19, 2003[1315] implemented a framework decision of the Council of the European Union on the European arrest warrant.1316 Some of its provisions specifically cover cyber-crimes and pedopornography offenses.1317

Voting Privacy

Voting is mandatory for those 18 years and older.[1318] The laws regarding voting, enacted in 1919 and amended to include women in 1949, are strictly enforced.[1319] Non-voting requires an acceptable explanation and may result in a fine, imprisonment, infringement of civil rights, disenfranchisement, or prevent employment in the public sector.[1320] Voter registration lists are publicly posted in polling locations on Election Day and may also be obtained for political campaign purposes.[1321] Election administrators take an oath to maintain the secrecy of votes cast. Voters are guaranteed the right of secrecy of their vote.[1322] In 1989, Belgium became one of the first countries to use electronic means of casting ballots in public elections.[1323] In 1991, experiments began with the use of electronic voting machines at polling locations.[1324] The Election Law was amended by the Act of April 11, 1994 to allow a "system of electronic voters" and was amended again on December 18, 1998 to allow "automated" voting.[1325]

[1315] Loi du 19 décembre 2003 relative au mandat d'arrêt européen, Moniteur belge, December 22, 2003, at 60075, available at <http://www.droit-technologie.org/redirect.asp?type=legislation&legis_id=172&url=legislations/loi_191203_mandat_arret_europe en_belgique.pdf>.

[1316] Council Framework Decision of June 13, 2002 on the European arrest warrant and the surrender procedures between Member States (2002/584/JHA), OJEC, 18.7.2002, L 190/1, at 0001 – 0020, available at <http://europa.eu.int/eur-lex/pri/en/oj/dat/2002/l_190/l_19020020718en00010018.pdf>. The Framework Decision's objective has been for the EU to abolish the formal extradition procedure between Member States and replace it by a system of surrender between judicial authorities. This new legal framework aims at replacing traditional cooperation relations between Member States by a system of free movement of judicial decisions in criminal matters, covering both pre-sentence and final decisions.

[1317] *See* Etienne Wéry, La Belgique adopte le mandat d'arrêt européen: cybercriminalité et pédopornographie sont en point de mire," January 9, 2004 <http://www.droit-technologie.org/1_2.asp?actu_id=874>.

1318 CIA Country Fact Book Online, available at <http://www.cia.gov/cia/publications/factbook/geos/af.html#Govt>.

[1319] International Institute for Democracy and Electoral Assistance, Report: Compulsory Voting, Feburary 11, 2005, available at <http://www.idea.int/vt/compulsory_voting.cfm>.

[1320] *Id.*

1321 European Commission, CyberVote Report Contract number IST-1999-20338, Project: Cybervote, June 1, 2001 available at <http://www.eucybervote.org/MSI-WP6-D21-v1.0.pdf>.

1322 Belgian Constitution, Article 55, available at <http://www.oefre.unibe.ch/law/icl/be00000_.html>.

[1323] Basque Government, Home Office Department, Management of Electoral Processes and Documentation, Voto Electrónico, April 5, 2004, available at <http://www.euskadi.net/botoelek/otros_paises/sim0_i.htm>.

[1324] Strengthening Regional and Local Democracy in the European Union, Volume I, Belgium, at 148, available at http://www.cor.eu.int/document/documents/cdr171_2004_vol1_etu_en.pdf, February 2004

[1325] *Id.*

The Federal Council of Ministers Rulings of June 20 and July 18, 1997 formally endorsed the adoption of electronic voting. By 1999, 40 percent of voters participating in Belgium's public elections used electronic voting machines.[1326] The direct recording electronic (DRE) system identified was used by 44 percent of voters in 2000. By 2003, an estimated three million votes were cast using electronic voting technology.[1327]

Open Government

The Constitution recognizes that "everyone has the right to consult any administrative document and to have a copy made, except in the cases and conditions stipulated by the laws, decrees, or regional council decrees (*i.e.*, the "rulings referred to in Article 134").[1328] There are freedom of information laws, implementing this constitutional right, on the right of access to administrative documents on the federal,[1329] regional,[1330] community,[1331] provincial and municipal levels.[1332] The basic exemptions to the general rule of access are public security, the protection of fundamental rights, international interests, public order, security or defense, confidentiality, and privacy. Each jurisdiction has a Commission of Access to Administrative Documents (*Commission d'Accès aux Documents Administratifs*, or CADA) that oversees the act. Citizens can appeal denials of information requests to the administrative agency, which in turn asks for advice from the CADA. The CADA issues advisory opinions both on request and on its own initiative. Requestors can then pursue a limited judicial

---

[1326] *Id.*

[1327] "Belgian National Elections on May 18, 2003 - Over 3.2 Million Belgians Voted Electronically," M2 Presswire, May 23, 2003.

[1328] Article 32, Constitution of Belgium, 1994 <http://www.fed-parl.be/constitution_uk.html>.

[1329] Loi du 11 avril 1994 relative à la publicité de l'administration des actes des autorités administratives fédérales, Moniteur Belge, 30 juin 1994, modifiée par la loi du 25 juin 1998 et la loi du 26 juin 2000. The Law allows individuals to request in writing for access to any document government authorities hold, including documents in judicial files. The Law also includes a right to have the document explained. Government agencies must respond immediately, or within 30 days if the request is delayed or rejected.

[1330] Région flamande (Flemish Region), Décret relatif à la publicité de l'administration, May 18, 1999), Moniteur belge, June 15, 1999; Région wallonne (Walloon Region), Décret relatif à la publicité de l'administration dans les intercommunales wallonne, March 7, 2001, Moniteur belge, March 20, 2001; Région wallonne (Walloon Region), Décret relatif à la publicité de l'Administration, March 30, 1995, Moniteur belge, June 28, 1995; available at <http://www.cass.be/cgi_loi/legislation.pl>.

[1331] Commission Communautaire Commune de Bruxelles-Capitale, Ordonnance relative à la publicité de l'administration, June 26, 1997; Commission communautaire française, Décret relatif à la publicité de l'administration, July 11, 1996, Moniteur belge, August 27, 1996.

[1332] Loi du 12 novembre 1997 relative à la publicité de l'administration dans les provinces et les communes, available at <http://www.cass.be/cgi_loi/legislation.pl>.

---

appeal to the Counsel of State (*Conseil d'Etat*).[1333] At the federal level, each federal public authority is required to provide a description of their functions and organization, and must have an information officer.[1334] The Law on Protection of Personal Data gives individuals the right to access and correct files about themselves that public and private entities hold, and is enforced by the Commission for the Protection of Private Life. As to the administrative documents that contain personal information, access is regulated by the Law of April 11, 1994.

International Obligations

Belgium is a member of the Council of Europe (CoE) and has signed and ratified the Convention for the Protection of Individuals with Regard to Automatic Processing of Personal Data (Convention No. 108).[1335] It has signed and ratified the European Convention for the Protection of Human Rights and Fundamental Freedoms.[1336] It is a member of the Organization for Economic Cooperation and Development (OECD) and has adopted the OECD Guidelines on the Protection of Privacy and Transborder Flows of Personal Data. The government signed, but has not ratified, the CoE Convention on Cybercrime in November 2001.

Republic of Bolivia

Constitutional Privacy Framework

Article 20 of the Constitution of the Republic of Bolivia1337 recognizes the inviolability of any kind of communications and private documents, and establishes that private documents that are violated or seized will not produce legal effect. The Constitution also provides that neither a public authority, nor a person or a public or private entity will be able to intercept conversations and private communications, nor will they be able to install equipment that controls

---

[1333] David Banisar, The Freedominfo.org Global Survey: Freedom of Information and Access to Government Records around the World, May 2004, at 14, available at
<http://www.freedominfo.org/survey/global_survey2004.pdf>.

[1334] *Id.*

[1335] Signed May 7, 1982; ratified May 28, 1993; entered into force September 1, 1993, available at
<http://conventions.coe.int/>.

[1336] <http://conventions.coe.int/>.

1337 Constitution of Bolivia of 1967 with amended text of 1995 and reforms of 2002, [Constitución de 1967, texto reformado de 1995 y reformas de 2002], available at
<http://www.georgetown.edu/pdba/Constitutions/Bolivia/consboliv1615.html> (in Spanish).

or centralizes private conversations or communications.Article 21 of the Constitution recognizes the inviolability of the home.[1338]

In 2004, the Constitution was modified1339 and the action of *Habeas Data* was introduced.1340 The *Habeas Data* action can be filed by any person who believes he is unduly or illegally restrained from knowing, objecting or obtaining the rectification or deletion of personal data registered by any physical, electronic or magnetic means in computer files or public or private databases. The *Habeas Data* action is processed pursuant to a summary procedure (*proceso sumarísimo*) as provided for by Article 19 of the Constitution.

Any citizen can introduce a *Habeas Data* action in front of the Superior Court of the district (*Corte Superior del Distrito*) or in front of any Judge (*Juez de Partido*). If the tribunal or competent judge declares the *habeas data* action reasonable, he will order the disclosure, deletion or rectification of the personal data registered in the database that is challenged. The sentence can be appealed before the Constitutional Tribunal, within the next 24 hours. However, the execution of the sentence will not be suspended. The action of *Habeas Data* cannot compel journalists to reveal their sources.

Statutory Rules on Privacy

Bolivia does not have a comprehensive data protection act. However, several regulations protect privacy. The Bolivian Tax Code[1341] and Banking Law,[1342] regulate privacy and confidentiality: the Resolutions of the Superintendence of Banks[1343] held that the Banking and Financial Information Bureaus (*Buros de información crediticia*) are covered by the banking secrecy provisions, and

---

1338 "At night it will not be possible to enter into a home without the consent of its owner, and during the day, a person could not enter to a house unless it has a previous written order from a competent authority, except in the case of a flagrant crime."

1339 Law that modifies the Constitution, Law No. 2650 of April 13, 2004, available at <http://www.constitution.org/cons/bolivia/texto.htm> (in Spanish).

1340 Luis Huerta Guerrero, Bolivia: Reforma constitucional y derechos fundamentales, Comisión Andina de Juristas, March, 2004, available at <http://www.cajpe.org.pe/NUEVODDHH/articuloreformabolivia.htm> (in Spanish).

1341 Article 67 of the Tax Code (*Código Tributario*) 2492, available at <http//:www.cainco.org.bo/es/doc/Cod%20Trib%20Ultimo.pdf> (in Spanish).

1342 Banking Law 1488 (*Ley de Bancos y Entidades Financieras No. 1488 de 14 de abril de 1993*), available at <http://www.cgap.org/regsup/docs/law_Bolivia_01_spa.pdf> (in Spanish); Text of the Law on Banks and Financial Entities. Supreme Ordinance No. 26851 (*Texto Ordenado de la Ley de Bancos y Entidades Financieras Decreto Supremo No. 26851*), March, 2002. *See also* Law of Economic Reactivation Law No. 2064 of 2000 (*Ley de Reactivación Económica Ley 2064 del 2000*).

1343 Central Bank Resolution No. 108, November 29, 2000 and Central Bank Resolution No. 113/2003.

---

therefore must not provide any information to third parties, except in special cases. Liability for damages may arise from the breach of bank secrecy.

The Criminal Code (*Código Penal*) sets forth as a crime any disclosure of information obtained without authorization. It establishes several offences related to the violation of privacy. Article 296 of the Penal Code guarantees the privacy of correspondence, establishing that whoever opens an envelope containing a letter that is not directed to himself, with the intent of learning about its content, is guilty of a felony. Article 298 of the Code also punishes the disclosure of information obtained by any means similar to those referred to in Article 296. Article 297 punishes the interception of telephone or telegraphic communications.[1344]

International Obligations

Bolivia is a signatory of the 1948 Universal Declaration of Human Rights, the 1966 International Covenant on Civil and Political Rights, and the American Convention on Human Rights, which all recognize the right of a person not to be subjected to arbitrary or unlawful interference with his privacy, home or correspondence, nor to unlawful attacks to his honour and reputation.

Federative Republic of Brazil

Constitutional Privacy Framework

Article 5 of the 1988 Constitution of Brazil[1345] provides that "the privacy, private life, honor and image of people are inviolable, and the right to compensation for property or moral damages resulting from their violation is ensured."[1346] The Constitution also holds the home as "inviolable," and "no one may enter therein without the consent of the dweller, except in the event of *flagrante delicto* or disaster, or to give help, or, during the day, by court order."[1347] Correspondence and electronic communication are also protected, except by court order "for purposes of criminal investigation or criminal procedural finding of facts."[1348]

[1344] Penal Code of 1768 modified by a law of March 10, 1997. (*Modificación al Código Penal 10 de marzo de 1997*), available at <http://www.cajpe.org.pe/RIJ/bases/legisla/bolivia/1768.HTM> (in Spanish).

[1345] Brazilian Constitution, available at <http://webthes.senado.gov.br/web/const/const88.pdf>.

[1346] Brazilian Constitution, Title 2, Chapter 1, Article 5, X.

[1347] *Id.* at XI.

[1348] *Id.* at XII.

"Access to information is ensured to everyone and the confidentiality of the source shall be safeguarded, whenever necessary to the professional activity."[1349] Finally, the Constitution provides for *habeas data*, which guarantees the rights: a) to ensure the knowledge of information related to the person of the petitioner, contained in records or databanks of government agencies or of agencies of a public character; and, b) for the correction of data, when the petitioner does not prefer to do so through a confidential process, either judicial or administrative.[1350]

Statutory Rules on Privacy

These constitutional guarantees to privacy and data protection have since been augmented with additional statutory protections. The scope of the constitutional right to *habeas data* was clarified with the passage of additional procedures and definitions in 1997.[1351] Under the Habeas Data Law, an individual has a right to petition for rectification of incorrect data.[1352] However, if the maintaining organization disputes or chooses not to make the correction, the petitioner only has the right to annotate the data with an explanation, rather than force a correction.[1353]

The Brazilian Civil Code, effective since January 2003, provides protection by declaring, "the private life of an individual is natural and inviolable" and evinces that the judiciary, at the request of an individual, must adopt measures to protect against actions to the contrary.[1354] In particular, the Civil Code states that the non-authorized disclosure of writings, transmission of words, publication, exhibition or use of a person's image may be hindered, at his/her request and without prejudice to any potential indemnifications, in case such acts may cause harm to the honor, good fame or respectability of said individual, or in case such use is made for commercial purposes. Exception is made in cases where such disclosure, transmission or use is required to ensure the administration of justice and/or the maintenance of public order.

In 1990, Brazilian law provided protection for the privacy of children, outlawing the total or partial unauthorized divulgence of a child or adolescent's name, or

---

[1349] *Id.* at XIV.

[1350] *Id.* at LXXII.

[1351] Federal Law No. 9,507, November 12, 1997.

[1352] *Id.* at Article 4 § 1.

[1353] *Id.* at Article 4 § 2.

[1354] Federal Law No. 10,406, January 12, 2002.

their police, agency or judicial documents.[1355] This law was amended in November 2003,[1356] expressly including the Internet as a way of perpetrating the crime of publishing or disclosing pornography involving children or teenagers.

The Information Technology Law,[1357] which establishes the guidelines for a national policy concerning technology development, determines as a principle the creation of legal and technical mechanisms in order to protect the secrecy of stored, processed and disclosed data, in the interest of the privacy and security of natural persons and legal entities. The Telecommunications Act of 1997 states as one of its operating principles that users of telecommunications services have the right to have their privacy respected in the usage of their personal data.[1358]

Consumer Protection

Broad consumer rights in data were created under the 1990 Consumer Protection Law,[1359] which provides that consumers have access to personal data, consumer files and other information stored in files, and databases about themselves, as well as about the sources of this data. The law further requires that consumer files and data be objective, clear, true, easily comprehensible, and shall not contain derogatory information regarding periods prior to five years ago. In addition, the opening of a consumer file, archive, registry, or database should be communicated in writing to the consumer, if not opened at the behest of the consumer. Also, whenever consumers find that data and files about them are incorrect, they can demand immediate correction, and the archivist shall communicate the corrections within five days. Finally, once the consumer has settled his or her debts, Credit Protection Services shall not provide any information that may prevent or hinder further access to credit for that consumer.

It is worth mentioning that there is currently neither a public data agency nor private entities specifically acting in the defense of privacy rights. Courts have recognized that infringement upon any of these rights is subject to costly settlements, based on consumers' affected moral rights.[1360] Also, a recent ruling

---

[1355] Federal Law No. 8,069, July 13, 1990.

[1356] Federal Law No. 10,764, November 12, 2003.

[1357] Federal Law No. 7,232, October 29, 1984.

[1358] Federal Law No. 9,472, July 16, 1997, Book 1, Art. 3, IX. (Telecommunications Act).

[1359] Federal Law No. 8,078, Article 43, September 11, 1990.

[1360] Superior Tribunal de Justiça, RESP No. 653568-MG (12/14/2004), RESP No. 595170-SC (11/16/2004), RESP No. 612619-MG (10/21/2004), RESP No. 540944-RS (08/17/2004), RESP 602401-RS (03/18/2004), RESP No. 511921-MT (03/09/2004), RESP No. 556745-SC (10/14/2003), RESP No. 471091-RJ (05/22/2003), RESP No. 448010-SP (02/06/2003), RESP No. 419365-MT (11/11/2002), RESP No. 442051-RS (11/07/2002),

by the 2nd Regional Labor Court determined that no worker may be fired solely based on the fact that they have an open file in a Credit Protection Service.[1361]

National Registry

A 1997 law provided for the creation of a National Register for Civil Identification.[1362] The law stated that each Brazilian citizen should have a unique identification number, which would be linked to further data on the citizen and should be used in every relationship with public and private entities. The law also said that all then current ID documents would not be valid after a 5-year term beginning from the enactment of the law. However, more than eight years after its issuance, no further norms have been issued, nor has the National Register for Civil Identification been implemented.

Financial Privacy

The Financial Institutions Secrecy Law provides that "financial institutions will preserve secrecy in their active and passive operations and services."[1363] However, broad exemptions to this secrecy exist, including information exchanged between financial institutions,[1364] reporting of information requested by the *Secretaria da Receita Federal* (Federal Revenue and Customs Secretariat),[1365] or to report illegal activity to the appropriate authorities.[1366] In addition, confidentiality can be breached when necessary to confirm suspicion of any illegal activity in any phase of an inquiry or action at law.[1367] As a rule, such a confidentiality breach shall depend upon a court order.

The Brazilian Supreme Court has declared that bank records are private,[1368] and are covered by the constitutional right to privacy. This entails that bank records

---

RESP No. 402958-DF (08/30/2002), RESP No. 373219-RJ (05/28/2002), RESP No. 292045-RJ (08/27/2001), RESP No. 285401-SP (04/19/2001), RESP No. 165727-DF (06/16/1998).

[1361] TRT 2ª Região, Recurso Ordinário n° 02831.2002.037.02.00-1, 6ª Turma, Rel. Juiz Valdir Florindo, j. September 09, 2004.

[1362] Federal Law No. 9,454, April 7, 1997.

[1363] Federal Supplementary Law No. 105, January 10, 2001.

[1364] *Id.* at § 3, I.

[1365] *Id.* at § 3, III.

[1366] *Id.* at § 3, IV.

[1367] *Id.* at § 4.

[1368] Supremo Tribunal Federal, Recurso Extraordinário No. 219.780 – PE.; Supremo Tribunal Federal, Mandado de Segurança No. 21.729-4.

---

may only be used as exhibits in judicial proceedings if previously authorized by a judge.

In addition, a recent ruling issued by the *Rio Grande do Sul* State Court of Justice[1369] determined that the breach of secrecy concerning banking accounts constitutes an intrusion into an individual's privacy, and that, as long as such privacy rights are protected by the Brazilian Constitution, any breach to such rights may only be justified by a clear determination of the need for the intrusion based on a plausible argument. Based on that reasoning, the Court denied a company's request for information regarding the defendant's banking records.

On the other hand, since 2002 the Brazilian Central Bank has been implementing an electronic system named "Bacen-Jud,"[1370] which allows judges to determine, through a judicial order sent via electronic means, whether to freeze accounts held by individuals in any financial institution in Brazil.

On January 9, 2004, the City of São Paulo regulated the activity of computer games in "Lan Houses,"[1371] by mandating those establishments to register patrons under 18 years old, or to face civil penalties of up to BRL 6,000 and business license revocations.[1372]

New Privacy Bills

In addition to the enactment of the Financial Institutions Secrecy Law, there are several bills under consideration that will affect individual privacy interests. A bill promoting the privacy of personal data in conformance with the OECD Guidelines on the Protection of Privacy and Transborder Flows of Personal Data (OECD Guidelines), to affect both public and private sector databases, was originally proposed in the Senate in 1996. The bill provided that: "No personal data nor information shall be disclosed, communicated, or transmitted for purposes different than those that led to structuring such data registry or database, without express authorization of the owner, except in case of a court order, and for purposes of a criminal investigation or legal proceedings. . . . It is forbidden to gather, register, archive, process, and transmit personal data referring to: ethnic origin, political or religious beliefs, physical or mental health,

---

1369 TJRS - 12ª Câmara Cível, Agravo Interno n° 70009729112, Rel. Des. Orlando Heemann Junior, j. October 14, 2004.

1370 <http://www.bcb.gov.br/?BCJUDINTRO>.

1371 Cybercafes specialized in multiplayer online games.

1372 São Paulo City Municipal Law No. 13,720, January 9, 2004.

sexual life, police or penal records, family issues, except family relationship, civil status, and marriage system. . . . Every citizen is entitled to, without any charge, access to his/her personal data, stored in data registries or databases, and correct, supplement, or eliminate such data, and be informed by data registry or database managers of the existence of data regarding his/her person."[1373] This proposed law was shelved on January 29, 1999, and Brazilian legislation is still not in conformity with the OECD Guidelines.[1374]

Since then, several bills[1375] have been introduced in Congress, especially in the House of Representatives, a few of them protecting, most of them infringing upon, individual privacy. Some require Internet Service Providers (ISPs) and Web Host Providers to maintain personally identifiable information such as name, ID number, address and telephone number, for a minimum of two to five years. Technical details of an individual's Internet connections and activities, including IP addresses of recipients and senders, login and logout time, and the quantity of data sent and received should also be recorded and kept for a minimum of six months to five years. One of these bills[1376] also determines that refusal to disclose such information to police officers, at their sole request, even without a judicial mandate, is considered a crime. Other bills assert that disclosure of the information could be made only in accordance with the law, with a penalty for unauthorized disclosure. A few bills[1377] establish mandatory identification before participation in public online chat rooms, supposedly in an effort to reduce child pornography, or restrict the publication and exchange of images with sexual content. Another bill[1378] establishes special regulations on the use of Internet through educational and government organizations, while others[1379] additionally mandate that ISPs should keep a record of the date, time and recipients of all e-mails sent by their users for a minimum of one year, allegedly for the purpose of reducing spam. According to an additional bill,

---

[1373] Senate Proposed Law No. 61, 1996, available at
<http://legis.senado.gov.br/pls/prodasen/PRODASEN.LAYOUT_MATE_DETALHE.SHOW_MATERIA?P_C OD_MAT=26236>.

[1374] Senate Official Bulletin No. 22-A, 2002, page 3276 (published in supplement).

[1375] Senate Proposed Law No. 151, 2000; House of Representatives Proposed Law No. 3,016, 2000; House of Representatives Proposed Law No. 3,891, 2000; House of Representatives Proposed Law No. 6,557, 2002; House of Representatives Proposed Law No. 3,303, 2000; House of Representatives Proposed Law No. 3,301, 2004; House of Representatives Proposed Law No. 4,972, 2001; House of Representatives Proposed Law No. 5977, 2001; House of Representatives Proposed Law No. 7,461, 2002; House of Representatives Proposed Law No. 408, 2003; House of Representatives Proposed Law No. 1,256, 2003; House of Representatives Proposed Law No. 4,562, 2004.

[1376] House of Representatives Proposed Law No. 408, 2003.

[1377] House of Representatives Proposed Law No. 6,557, 2002; House of Representatives Proposed Law No. 1,256, 2003.

[1378] House of Representatives Proposed Law No. 5,977, 2001.

[1379] House of Representatives Proposed Law No. 4,562, 2004.

Internet usage and access would depend on prior user registration in the ISP of, at least, his legal name, his legal address and his CPF or CNPJ identification number.[1380]

All of these bills have been appended onto another,[1381] which is still pending in a committee. In April 2003, the House of Representatives approved a motion of urgency for these matters and on April 12, 2005, a Special Commission in the Senate was designated to analyze them.[1382]

A general law was proposed in 1999[1383] delineating information crimes, including restrictions on the collection, processing and distribution of information. In addition, it would outlaw computer crimes such as unauthorized access to, or alteration of, data or computer programs. After its approval at the House of Representatives, the bill was sent to the Senate for further discussions, where it still was under deliberation as of November 2004.

Finally, in 2000, evincing a concern with data profiling practices, a law[1384] was proposed to restrict the collection of personal data and data residing on an individual's computer. The proposal states that such data can only be collected with prior notice, under the express permission of the subject, and used only for the purpose for which it was collected, under penalty of a statutory fine. In February 2003, a privacy bill[1385] was introduced, which would make illegal the transmission to a third party of information provided by a person or organization. An amendment was made in June 2003, establishing that this prohibition would not apply to public organizations, registries or notaries. In April 2003, an Internet privacy law was proposed[1386] to establish criminal sanctions referring to the unauthorized disclosure of protected information and harvesting of personal information. As of December 2004, all of these bills were still under deliberation.

[1380] The CPF (Cadastro de Pessoas Físicas) and CNPJ (Cadastro Nacional de Pessoas Jurídicas) are mandatory registrations under the Secretaria da Receita Federal (Federal Revenue Secretary) for the purpose of taxpayer identification.

[1381] House of Representatives Proposed Law No. 5,403, 2001.

[1382] "Internet Segura: Projeto prevê registro de acessos à internet por um ano," Consultor Jurídico, April 13th, 2005, <http://64.207.161.190/novo/static/text/34147,1>.

[1383] House of Representatives Proposed Law No. 84, 1999, altered to Senate Proposed Law No. 89, 2003.

[1384] House of Representatives Proposed Law No. 3,360, 2000.

[1385] House of Representatives Proposed Law No. 123, 2003.

[1386] Senate Proposed Law No. 95, 2003.

Anti-spam legislation has been introduced in several separate bills,[1387] none of which has yet reached a final vote. Another bill, proposed in 2002, would create criminal penalties for disseminating or selling personal data without the data subject's permission.[1388] Brazil Anti-Spam Group[1389] (a committee composed of the main marketing, software and advertising trade groups)[1390] issued in November 2003 an "Anti-Spam Code of Ethics and Best Practices for the Use of Electronic Messages."[1391] This market-oriented self-regulation initiative legitimizes the sending of "commercially ethical" e-mails in which e-mail advertisers commit to provide accurate information about themselves to recipients, to observe truth-in-advertising norms, and to let recipients opt-out of future mailings, thus aiming at promoting consumer confidence in the use of e-mails.[1392] However, the effectiveness of the Anti-Spam Code of Ethics has been questioned, because there are no proposed sanctions for the breach of its terms other than the listing of the spammers on the Brazil Anti-Spam Group's website and because the Code of Ethics allows the sending of unsolicited e-mails as long as some conditions have been met.[1393]

In 2003, three separate bills were introduced to regulate the telemarketing activities, and two in 2004[1394] – mainly, a reflection of the US "do-not-call list."

[1387] House of Representatives Proposed Law No. 1589, 1999; House of Representatives Proposed Law No. 2,358, 2000; House of Representatives Proposed Law No. 7,093, 2002, Senate Proposed Law No. 367, 2003; House of Representatives Proposed Law No. 2,186, 2003; House of Representatives Proposed Law No. 2,423, 2003; Senate Proposed Law No. 21, 2004; Senate Proposed Law No. 36, 2004; House of Representatives Proposed Law No. 3,731, 2004; House of Representatives Proposed Law No. 3,872, 2004.

[1388] House of Representatives Proposed Law No. 6,541, 2002.

[1389] <http://www.brasilantispam.org>.

[1390] The Associação Brasileira de Anunciantes (ABA) (Brazilian Association of Advertisers), the Associação Brasileira de Agências de Publicidade (ABAP) (Brazilian Association of Advertising Agencies), the Associação Brasileira de Marketing Direto (ABEMD) (Brazilian Association of Direct Marketing), the Associação Brasileira das Empresas de Software (ABES) (Brazilian Association of Software Companies, the Associação Brasileira dos Provedores de Acesso, Serviços e Informações da Rede Internet (ABRANET) (Brazilian Association of Internet Access, Service and Information Providers), the Associação de Mídia Interativa (AMI) (Association of Interactive Mass Communication), the Business Software Alliance (BSA), Câmara-e.net – Câmara Brasileira de Comércio Eletrônico (Brazilian Chamber of Electronic Commerce), and the Federação do Comércio do Estado de São Paulo – Fecomércio-SP (Federation of Commerce of the State of São Paulo).

[1391] Available at <http://www.brasilantispam.org/main/codigo.htm>.

[1392] The Anti-Spam Code is based on the provisions of the "Code of Ethics" of the National Auto Regulation Advertising Council (CONAR) and on the "Code of Ethics" of the Brazilian Association of Direct Marketing (ABEMD), as well as on current legislation and international rules; "Brazil Group Launches Anti-Spam Campaign," The Miami Herald, November 20, 2003, available at <http://www.miami.com/mld/miamiherald/business/7309579.htm>.

[1393] Amaro Morais e Silva Neto, "Código de Ética Antispam Representa um Passo para Trás," (Antispam Ethics Code Represents a Step backwards), Consultor Jurídico, November 24, 2003, available at <http://conjur.uol.com.br/textos/23041/>.

[1394] House of Representatives Proposed Law No. 2,130, 2003; House of Representatives Proposed Law No. 2,387, 2003; House of Representatives Proposed Law No. 2,404, 2003, Senate Proposed Law No. 243, 2004; House of Representatives Proposed Law No. 4,412, 2004.

In general, the intent is to create such lists under the control of either telemarketing companies or the Brazilian Ministry of Communications.

Wiretapping and Other Government Surveillance

In 1996, a law regulating wiretapping was enacted.[1395] Official wiretaps are permitted for 15 days, renewable on a judge's order for another 15 days, and can only be resorted to in cases where police suspect serious crimes punishable by imprisonment, such as drug smuggling, corruption, contraband smuggling, murder, and kidnapping. The granting of judicial eavesdropping permits by judges was previously an *ad hoc* process without any legal basis.[1396] By now, procedures involving legal wiretapping are treated in confidentiality, which means that access to recordings and transcripts is restricted to the judge and the parties involved in the procedure.

Illegal wiretapping by police and intelligence agencies is still common. In 1992, amid a scandal that toppled President Fernando Collor de Mello, it was discovered that Vice President Itamar Franco's phones at his official residence in Brasilia and in a Rio de Janeiro hotel room had been tapped.[1397] Several ministers resigned in 1998 after tapes of wiretapped conversations involving the Brazilian Development Bank were disclosed in what was called the "Telegate scandal." The Brazilian Information Agency (*Agência Brasileira de Informações* – ABIN) was suspected of wiretapping President Cardoso after tapes of his conversations were leaked to the press in May 1999.[1398] In 2000, a news magazine released information obtained through wiretaps, implicating a powerful former presidential aide, a member of the economic cabinet, a senator and several congressional deputies in an illegal patronage and influence-trafficking network. In June 2004, President Luis Inácio Lula da Silva nominated Mauro Marcelo Lima e Silva as the head of ABIN.[1399] Lima e Silva, a former Police Chief, is known for his expertise in the investigation of cybercrimes and his academic experience at the Federal Bureau of Investigation in the United States.

[1395] Federal Law No. 9,296, July 24, 1996.

[1396] "Brazil Makes Police Phone-Taps Legal," Reuters World Service, July 24, 1996.

[1397] "Brazil Vice-President Claims His Phone Was Tapped," Reuters North American Wire, September 9, 1992.

[1398] "Is Abin behind Telegate?" Latin America Weekly Report, June 8, 1999.

[1399] "Delegado É Indicado Para Assumir a Abin," (Police Chief Is Nominated to Head Abin), Agência Brasil, June 9, 2004, available at <http://www.radiobras.gov.br/materia.phtml?materia=188975&editoria=/>.

Illegal wiretapping by private investigation companies, as well as recording of private conversations, are also common. By 2004, as a result of some scandals involving federal government individuals, the Minister of Justice expressed his intent to present a new bill aimed at prohibiting illegal wiretapping and use of the collected data, as well as punishing with imprisonment any journalists who use any information obtained through such means.[1400]

In principle, investigative powers to instruct criminal procedures are restricted to the judiciary police, which is an auxiliary body of the Judiciary Branch. The Attorney General's Office (*Ministério Público*) is the entity officially competent to propose criminal actions of a public nature. There is still a controversy, based on different interpretations of the Brazilian Constitution, on whether the Attorney General's Office should be entitled to initiate criminal investigations. Such controversy is under review before the Supreme Court. A decision that would allow prosecution attorneys to promote criminal investigations could weaken privacy rights by allowing privacy violations within the investigations conducted by prosecution attorneys, as long as the judicial control over such investigations is bypassed. On the other hand, a decision denying such investigative powers to prosecution attorneys would certainly nullify several criminal procedures currently initiated and in which such powers have been employed, such as corruption cases involving judges, police chiefs and politicians.

The Federal Penal Code was altered in 2000 to criminalize certain information crimes.[1401] The insertion of false data into an information system is punishable by a prison sentence of two to 12 years.[1402] Unauthorized alteration of an information system is punishable by detention from three months to two years.[1403] The Federal Penal Code and Federal Procedural Penal Code were also altered in July 2003[1404] in order to strengthen sanctions corresponding to the violation of copyrights, and to criminalize the unauthorized distribution of copyrighted works through cable, fiber optics, satellite, radio waves or any other means. Changes in Federal Procedural Penal Code facilitated search and seizure procedures, thereby minimizing the defendant's rights. As a consequence, criminal actions have been initiated by the Brazilian Association of Record Producers (ABPD) against suspects of online music distribution. According to

---

[1400] "Governo Quer Punir Jornalistas que Divulgarem Grampos" (Government wants to punish journalists who divulge wiretappings), Consultor Jurídico, July 28, 2004, available at
<http://conjur.uol.com.br/textos/246232/>.

[1401] Federal Law No. 9,983, July 14, 2000.

[1402] *Id.* at Article 313-a.

[1403] *Id.* at Article 313-b.

[1404] Federal Law No. 10,695, July 1, 2003.

the ABPD's Web site,[1405] they have been monitoring the Brazilian Internet since 1999 – even before the alterations to Federal Penal Code were enacted – and such practices could represent potential privacy violations, since the intercept of Internet communications is allowed only with a judge's order.[1406]

US-VISIT

As a response to United States anti-terrorism policies that created a registration system for foreign citizens (the US-VISIT system), including Brazilian citizens, which records their photographs and fingerprints before they can enter the United States, a Brazilian court decided on reciprocity grounds, at the beginning of 2004, that US citizens must submit to similar identification procedures before being allowed to enter Brazil.[1407] Although the court order was later revoked, a similar identification mechanism has been established through a federal government order. Such measures have caused significant inconvenience to US tourists and even some diplomatic incidents.[1408]

By means of a bilateral cooperation agreement, the Brazilian government has agreed, by the end of 2004, to share with the US government information on travelers who make reservations to go to the United States but have not yet traveled.[1409] Such information will be used by US authorities to prescreen terrorism threats. The agreement also provides for reciprocity, thus mandating US airline companies to provide information concerning travelers to Brazil.

Consumer & Internet Privacy

In the beginning of 2003, São Paulo State Attorney's General Office (*Ministério Público do Estado de São Paulo*) investigated and questioned the data collection and processing practices of a major supermarket chain (CBD) that tracked its

---

[1405] <http://www.abpd.org.br/noticias/noticias_det.asp?cdg=100>.

[1406] Brazilian Constitution, Title 2, Chapter 1, Article 5, XII.

[1407] "Brazil Judge Orders US Citizens Fingerprinted," CNN, December 30, 2003, available at <http://www.cnn.com/2003/WORLD/americas/12/30/brazil.usa.immigration.reut/index.html>.

[1408] "Angry Reax to Airport Screening," CBS, January 5, 2004, available at <http://www.cbsnews.com/stories/2004/03/04/terror/main604015.shtml>; "US Tourists Spend Hours Waiting to Get into Brazil," CNN, January 5, 2004, available at <http://www.cnn.com/2004/WORLD/americas/01/05/brazil.us.fingerprinting.ap>; "N. J. Man Pays 'Finger' Fine," CBS News, February 8, 2004, available at <http://www.cbsnews.com/stories/2004/01/12/world/main592699.shtml>.

[1409] "Brazil Will Share Air Passenger Data," Miami Herald, February 25, 2005, available at <http://article.wn.com/link/WNAT6A9FFCE1F17C9FB527992808EB24C915?source=templategenerator&template=limapost/headlines1.txt>; *see also* <http://www.miami.com/mld/miamiherald/10991443.htm?1c>.

---

customers' purchases thanks to a loyalty card marketing scheme.[1410] As a consequence, on June 2003, São Paulo State Attorney's General Office and CBD executed an Undertaking of Performance (*Termo de Ajustamento de Conduta*)[1411] in which CBD committed itself to clearly informing its clients about the scope and intended use of the data it collected from customers, as well as to obtain their express consent before any future data collection. CBD further promised to delete customers' names from its current database if they did not expressly authorize the processing of their data.

An internal regulation of the House of Representatives determined specific rules for the use of e-mail by their deputies and staff.[1412] The fact that the Information Technology Center of the House is competent to regulate and supervise e-mail systems, and is entitled to gather evidence on potential unauthorized uses, has raised some concerns on potential privacy violations of deputies' e-mails.

The social relationship network called "Orkut," affiliated with Google, recently became a craze in Brazil. As of June 2004, Brazil surpassed the United States in the number of active users. Brazilians represent more than one-third of Orkut's members. Potential negative privacy impacts concerning the disclosure of personal information and preferences within such services have been mostly neglected by Brazilians in general. By the end of 2004, a group hijacked several communities in Orkut, by using an social engineering attack against community owners exploiting flaws both in Orkut and Microsoft Internet Explorer.[1413] More than 30 communities, which are areas for internal discussion of various subjects, each of them including more than 1,000 members, were hijacked. Communities were returned to their original owners some time later. Orkut later implemented better security measures to prevent similar problems from happening again. In April 2005, the Brazilian Information Agency (*Agência Brasileira de Informações* – ABIN) took down two allegedly false profiles from the Orkut network, one for the Chief Ministry of the Communication and Strategic Management Secretary, Luiz Gushiken, and the other for the President's wife.[1414]

[1410] *See* "Pão de Açúcar Pode Perder Base de Dados" (Pão de Açúcar may lose its databases), Rádio Bandeirantes, April 23, 2003, available at
<http://www.radiobandeirantes.com.br/reporteronline/interna.asp?id_not=27144>.

[1411] Available at <http://www.mp.sp.gov.br/caoconsumidor/atua%E7%E3opr%E1tica/termos/TA563-03.doc>.

[1412] Câmara dos Deputados, Portaria No. 96, August 20, 2004.

[1413] "O Grande Roubo das Comunidades do Orkut" (The great theft of Orkut communities), Giordani Rodrigues, Infoguerra, January 9, 2005, available at
<http://www.infoguerra.com.br/infonews/viewnews.cgi?newsid1105149979,29493,>.

[1414] "Governo tira da Internet falso orkut do ministro Luiz Gushiken," Consultor Jurídico, April 1st, 2005, available at <http://64.207.161.190/novo/static/text/33899,1>.

Privacy Case Law

On December 2003, the Supreme Court issued a decision mitigating the scope of privacy rights.[1415] According to the decision, the seizure of e-mails stored in computers upon a court order is an issue referring to privacy rights instead of the protection of electronic communications. The Supreme Court recognized that such privacy rights are not absolute, and may therefore be mitigated in view of social and public interests, as well as in view of the interest of justice.

A decision issued by the 9th Regional Labor Court[1416] determined that auditing or monitoring an employee's computer is illegal as it is considered to be a violation of the principle of secrecy of electronic communications. Any employer's labor agreement allowing such monitoring practices is therefore considered illegal. Any monitoring shall be authorized only upon a prior court order. Another decision, issued by the 10th Regional Labor Court,[1417] held that the intimacy right and the right to the secrecy of correspondence and electronic communications are inviolable. As a consequence, evidence obtained by infringing these rights will not be admissible.

Medical Privacy

Medical record-keeping is regulated by the Federal Council of Medicine (*Conselho Federal de Medicina* – CFM).[1418] Recent regulations authorize the use of electronic means for the storage of such documents, not only for documents originally in the electronic format, but also for digitized documents originally created as paper documents. Specific procedures in order to ensure the confidentiality, privacy and integrity of the data have been established, and the secure transmission of data shall use ICP-Brasil's digital certificates in order to ensure its confidentiality.

Under the scope of the Federal Decree on the Safeguard of Confidential Data,[1419] the Brazilian National Health Surveillance Agency (*Agência Nacional de Vigilância Sanitária* – ANVISA) issued a regulation concerning the secrecy, security and access to its own information.[1420] According to its terms, each

---

[1415] Supremo Tribunal Federal, Agravo Regimental no Recurso Extraordinário No. 373.058-4 – RS.

[1416] TRT9 – 5ª T., RO 5568/2002, Rel. Juíza Janete do Amarante, j. 20.02.2003, DJ 04.04.2003.

[1417] TRT 10 – 13.000613/2000, issued on October 9, 2001.

[1418] Federal Council of Medicine, Resolution No. 1,639, July 10, 2002.

[1419] Federal Decree 5,301, December 9, 2004.

1420 Resolução da Diretoria Colegiada- RDC No. 5, January 20, 2005.

ANVISA employee shall execute non-disclosure agreements concerning the information obtained during his or her working hours. Non-authorized disclosure, use or grant of access to confidential information within ANVISA is now punished by administrative, civil and criminal sanctions.

Digital Certification

The use of digital certification in Brazil is regulated by specific norms.[1421] Current regulation foresees two different levels of digital certificates: those issued under the structure of ICP-Brasil (Brazilian Public Key Infrastructure), which are considered presumptively valid, and those issued by certification authorities outside the structure of ICP-Brasil, which may be considered valid if such validity has been granted or accepted by the parties or persons, and/or entities to which such documents have been presented. Technical regulation of the digital certification system is issued by ICP-Brasil's Steering Committee. ICP-Brasil stands as a hierarchical public-key infrastructure, in which the Root Certification Authority plays a fundamental role, certifying further certification authorities in the structure. The *Instituto Nacional de Tecnologia de Informação* (ITI) (the Brazilian Information Technology Institute), an entity directly connected to the Presidential Cabinet, is the Root Certification Authority of ICP-Brasil. ITI also stands as the entity officially entitled to promote the popularization of digital certificates in Brazil.

Use of ICP-Brasil's digital certificates is already compulsory in some spheres. In particular, its use is required in certified electronic communications between entities of the federal administration, such as ministries. Recently, the Federal Revenue and Customs Secretariat determined that the use of ICP-Brasil's digital certificates should be compulsory for the delivery of tax statements for companies whose income surpasses BRL 30 million per year (about USD 10 million per year).[1422] As of now, tax statements for individuals and companies with lower yearly income may also be performed by electronic means, without the use of digital certificates. Nevertheless, the Federal Revenue and Customs Secretariat has shown its express intent to compel all electronic statement deliveries to be performed with the use of digital certificates in the coming years. However, a recent preliminary ruling by a federal court has determined that no law firm in the state of São Paulo is required to acquire a digital certificate in order to fulfill their tax obligations based on the fact that such a requisite violates

---

[1421] In particular, Federal Provisional Measure 2200-02, August 24, 2001.

[1422] Secretaria da Receita Federal, Normative Instruction 482, December 21, 2004.

basic constitutional principles, such as legality and the public administration morality.[1423]

Video Surveillance

Due to security concerns, the number of surveillance cameras in public and private places has increased significantly in Brazil. Some regulations have been implemented in this regard. The City of São Paulo, for instance, passed a Municipal Law[1424] mandating the installation of signs informing the public of the existence of surveillance cameras, both in public and private areas. Recorded images are meant to be confidential and protected under law. Failure to comply with the installation of warning signs may subject infringers to statutory fines.

Voting Privacy

Voting is mandatory in Brazil[1425] for citizens between the ages of 18 and 70 and voluntary for those 16-18 and over 70. After two periods of suspended democratic rule public elections returned once again to Brazil in 1982.[1426] In 1989, Brazil introduced computer voting in the Santa Catarina State. By 1996, almost a third of Brazil's[1427] 100 million voters cast ballots on direct recording electronic (DRE) voting machines. In 1998, 57 percent of the country's voters cast ballots on DREs. In 2002, Brazil held the first fully electronic election in the world with more than 115 million participants voting.[1428] Chapter 4, Article 14 of the Constitution guarantees the secrecy of the ballot in public elections to its citizens.[1429]

Open Government

In addition to laws specifically addressing individual privacy rights and data protection, Brazil has apparently unrelated laws and treaties that have privacy

---

[1423] 3ª Vara Federal de São Paulo, Mandado de Segurança No. 2005.61.00.004736-2, Juíza Maria Lúcia Lencastre Ursaia, j. April 6th, 2005.

[1424] São Paulo City Municipal Law No. 13,541, March 24, 2003.

1425 Brazil Electoral Law, available at <http://www.aceproject.org/main/samples/lf/lfx_l005.pdf>.

1426 "The History of Brazil," available at <http://www.ccc.commnet.edu/stuweb/~quiterio5816/History.htm>.

29 Brazilian National Elections, available at <http://lists.virus.org/isn-9902/msg00059.html>.

[1428] Center for Digital Government, "Brazil Holds National Electronic Election," available at <http://www.centerdigitalgov.com/international/story.php?docid=29221>.

[1429] Brazilian Constitution, Chapter IV, Article 14, available at <http://www.oefre.unibe.ch/law/icl/br00000_.html>.

---

implications. The Brazilian national policy on access to government information[1430] grants individuals the right to receive information of general or individual concern. However, the right is self-limited by individual privacy: "the inviolable intimacy, private life, and honor and image of people."[1431] According to the Brazilian Constitution, "every citizen is granted the right to receive, from public entities, information of his/her personal interest, or of general or collective interest, which shall be provided on the terms established in the law."[1432] The Brazilian Constitution also determines that access to such information may be denied where secrecy is required to ensure the security of society or the Brazilian State. The law provides for such exceptions[1433] and has established a new specific body, the Commission for the Verification and Analysis of Secret Information, composed of ministers, in order to verify the adequacy, necessity, and possibility of disclosure concerning personal data of a top secret nature.

Further, Brazilian national administrative policy on the safeguarding of confidential data, information, documents and materials[1434] considers as "secret documents" not only any data whose unrestricted access could constitute a risk for the security of Brazilian society or its government, but also any data whose secrecy may be required in order to preserve an individual's privacy, intimacy, honor or image. Access to this kind of information is restricted, classified according to specific rules, and provided only on a "need-to-know" basis. Access may also be made available to citizens, as regards their own personal information, or information of their particular interest, or of collective or general interest, by means of a request to the competent governmental agency. Decisions denying such requests shall be based on a reasonable justification.

International Obligations

The Constitution holds that the Federative Republic of Brazil will act internationally according to the "prevalence of human rights"[1435] and that "no one will be subject to torture, nor to inhuman or demeaning treatment."[1436] Brazil signed the United Nations Convention on Torture (1984) on September 23, 1985,

---

[1430] Federal Law No. 8,159, January 8, 1991, Chapter 1, Article 4.

[1431] Id.

[1432] Brazilian Constitution, Title 2, Chapter 1, Article 5, XXXIII.

[1433] Federal Provisional Measure 229, December 9, 2004 and Federal Decree 5,301, December 9, 2004.

[1434] Federal Decree No. 4,553, December 27, 2002.

[1435] Brazilian Constitution, Title 1, Article 4, II.

[1436] Brazilian Constitution, Title 2, Chapter 1, Article 5, III.

and the American Convention on Human Rights[1437] on September 25, 1992. The latter provides that every person has "the right to have his honor respected and his dignity recognized." Additionally, "no one may be the object of arbitrary or abusive interference with his private life, his family, his home, or his correspondence, or of unlawful attacks on his honor or reputation." According to the convention, "everyone has the right to the protection of the law against such interference or attacks." Also, Brazil recognizes the competence of the American Court of Human Rights[1438] for interpretation and judgment of human rights cases, subject to international reciprocity.

Since May 2003, President Luis Inácio Lula da Silva has been promoting several reforms, including the creation of the *Secretaria Especial dos Direitos Humanos* (Special Secretariat for Human Rights).[1439] He has also promoted reforms in the judicial system[1440] that supposedly target backlogs in the judicial system, and that were eventually approved by Congress in December 2004, through a constitutional amendment.[1441] The reforms included provisions such as: 1) the creation of the *Conselho Nacional de Justiça* (National Council of Justice) and the *Conselho Nacional do Ministério Público* (National Council of Public Prosecution), independent institutions dedicated to controlling the Judicial Branch by civil society; 2) the independence of the *defensorias públicas* (public defenders free of charge for poor citizens); 3) the turning of human rights crimes into federal crimes, which could avoid local influence suffered by state courts; 4) the harmonization of criteria for admission of new judges; 5) the creation of the *súmula vinculante*, which would make Supreme Court decisions binding on lower courts; and 6) the submission of Brazil to the International Criminal Court. This reform, along with others, has received the 2004 UNESCO Award in the Human Rights and Peace Culture category.

Republic of Bulgaria

Constitutional Privacy Framework

The Bulgarian Constitution of 1991 recognizes rights of privacy, secrecy of communications and access to information. Article 32 states, "(1) The private life

---

[1437] American Convention on Human Rights, Art. 11, July 18, 1978, available at <http://www1.umn.edu/humanrts/oasinstr/zoas3con.htm>.

[1438] Legislative Decree No. 89, December 3, 1998; Decree No. 4,463, November 8, 2002.

[1439] Federal Law No. 10,683, May 28, 2003.

[1440] More information is available at the Ministry of Justice at <http://www.mj.gov.br/reforma/index.htm>.

[1441] Constitutional Amendment No. 45, 2004.

of citizens shall be inviolable. Everyone shall be entitled to protection against any illegal interference in his private or family affairs and against encroachments on his honor, dignity and reputation. (2) No one shall be followed, photographed, filmed, recorded or subjected to any other similar activity without his knowledge or despite his express disapproval, except when such actions are permitted by law." Article 33 states, "(1) The home shall be inviolable. No one shall enter or stay inside a home without its occupant's consent, except in the cases expressly stipulated by law. (2) Entry into, or staying inside, a home without the consent of its occupant or without the judicial authorities' permission shall be allowed only for the purposes of preventing an immediately impending crime or a crime in progress, for the capture of a criminal, or in extreme necessity." Article 34 states, "(1) The freedom and confidentiality of correspondence and all other communications shall be inviolable. (2) Exceptions to this provision shall be allowed only with the permission of the judicial authorities for the purpose of discovering or preventing a grave crime." The right to freedom of expression is also protected by Article 39 of the Bulgarian Constitution, which states, "(1) Everyone shall be entitled to express an opinion or to publicize it through words, written and oral, sound or image, or in any other way. (2) This right shall not be used to the detriment of the rights and reputation of others, or for the incitement of a forcible change of the constitutionally established order, the perpetration of a crime, or the incitement of enmity or violence against anyone." Article 41 states, "(1) Everyone shall be entitled to seek, obtain and disseminate information. This right shall not be exercised to the detriment of the rights and reputation of others, or to the detriment of national security, public order, public health and morality. (2) Citizens shall be entitled to obtain information from state bodies and agencies on any matter of legitimate interest to them which is not a state or other secret prescribed by law and does not affect the rights of others."[1442] The Constitution provides equality and protection against discrimination for the rights of the citizens.[1443] However, discrimination still exists, particularly against women and Roma.

Statutory Rules on Privacy

The Personal Data Protection Act (PDPA) was adopted by the National Assembly in December 2001 and came into effect in January 2002. Adoption of the law was a key part of the administrative reforms being undertaken in preparation for accession to the European Union (EU). The law closely follows

---

[1442] Constitution of the Republic of Bulgaria of July 13, 1991, available at <http://www.uni-wuerzburg.de/law/bu00t___.html>.

[1443] Id. at article 6(2).

the EU Data Protection Directive. It sets out rules for the fair and responsible handling of personal information by the public and private sector. Personal information is defined as "any information relating to a natural person, legal entity or group of individuals revealing physical, psychological, mental, economic, cultural or public identity, regardless of the form or method used for its recording."[1444] Entities collecting personal information must inform people why their personal information is being collected and what it is to be used for; allow people reasonable access to information about themselves and the right to correct it if it is wrong; ensure that the information is securely held and cannot be tampered with, stolen or improperly used; and limit the use of personal information, for purposes other than the original purpose, without the consent of the person affected, or in certain other circumstances. Sensitive information, including information concerning racial or ethic origin, political or religious affiliation, health, sexual life, and beliefs, is given special protection and can only be processed with the express written consent of an individual.[1445] Some concerns have been raised that the law has too broad a scope. The Bulgarian Access to Information Programme notes that the definition of "personal data" includes information relating to the performance of government officials and management or supervisory bodies of legal entities and as such may have a negative impact on access to information rights and government accountability.[1446]

In April 2005, the Council of Ministers adopted a new draft amendment to the PDPA. The Personal Data Protection Commission and the Access to Information Programme[1447] stated they were surprised by such an action, as they are parties interested in the process, but no experts from either the commission or the program were invited to participate in drafting of the amendment.[1448] The changes made by the amendment in the article 5 have been widely discussed and named by the journalists as "censorship," and "death sentence to the free speech." The clause in question forbids processing of personal data with regard to crimes, violations, sentences, etc., without the control of the respective

---

[1444] "Bulgarian Assembly Passes Personal Data Protection Bill on First Reading," BBC Worldwide Monitoring, November 13, 2001.

[1445] The Current Situation of the Access to Public Information in Bulgaria in 2001, Access to Information Program 2002, available at <http://www.aip-bg.org>.

[1446] Id. Access to Information Programme Foundation, Opinion of the Access to Information Programme on the Personal Data Protection Bill, October 24, 2001, available at <http://www.aip-bg.org/documents/zld_aip_eng.htm>.

[1447] Access to information Programme (AIP) Bulgarian NGO aiming to promote the right to information and initiate a public debate on relevant issues.

[1448] Article at the website of the Personal Data Protection Commission – an interview with Alexander Kashumov, expert from AIP, available at <http://xdata.gateway.bg/htmls/read_news.htm?id=6148> (in Bulgarian only).

authority.[1449] The proposed abolishment of the existing article 35, para. 1, gives priority to the access to information, over the personal data protection, as far as the documents, containing public information or public registries are concerned. The clause allows access to the information without any restraints. The proposed change bears the risk of unjustified protection of the public data concerning public persons.[1450] Moreover, the access to such information has been protected by the same article 35 in the first place; however, with the amendments, this data shall be fully controllable by the persons whom it concerns.[1451]

Supervisory Authority

The law creates a Commission on Protection of Personal Data (the Commission) to supervise compliance and implementation, maintain a national register of data controllers, examine complaints and take legal action for violations. The members of the Commission and the Chairperson serve a five-year term and may be re-elected once. They are nominated by the President and approved by the National Assembly. The first Commission was established by a parliamentary decision in May 2002 and started work in June 2002. Under the PDPA the Commission must adopt internal rules regulating its activities, describing the structure of its administration, the procedures for registering data controllers and considering appeals, issuing orders and imposing sanctions. The rules initially adopted for the work and organization of the Commission provide for an administration of 76 officials, including its members. Until now most of the positions have not been filled.[1452] Two years after the adoption of the Act only 1/7 of the provided officials have been appointed, while all the stipulated departments exist only on paper.

The PDPA mandates registration for all data controllers that hold information about more than two people. It also has broadened the categories of protected personal data. The Commission adopted in its new internal rules a broad interpretation of the PDPA that construes it to mandate all data controllers, regardless of their size, to register. In practice, it has compelled thousands of

---

[1449] Proposed amendment to PDPA article 5a.

[1450] Articles with comment on the topic made by Alexander Kashumov from AIP – available at <http://xdata.gateway.bg/htmls/news.htm>(in Bulgarian only).

[1451] As an example, the public persons' public data could be related to education, declarations of the government officials for conflict of interests, property issues, etc.

[1452] In comparison to the Bulgarian Commission, the Personal Data Commissioner of Ireland has an administration of 16 officials, while 40 people work for the Commissioner of Sweden.

small-size employers, such as lawyers, doctors, and tradesmen, to submit registration forms.[1453]

In May 2003, the Parliament adopted the Ombudsman Act (effective January 1, 2004), which sets up a formal system of advocacy in cases when actions as well as inactions of state or municipal authorities violate the rights and freedoms of individuals. The Act stipulates that the Ombudsman has no right to publicize any circumstances that came into his knowledge during the execution of his specific functions, and are state, official or trade secrets, or have a personal nature.[1454] In April 2005, almost 2 years from the adoption of the Ombudsman Act, the Parliament appointed Mr. Ginjo Ganev (77, MP of Coalition for Bulgaria, led by the Socialist Party) as the first Ombudsman.

In September 2003, the National Assembly passed the Protection Against Discrimination Act (PADA), scheduled to take effect on January 1, 2004. The Act aims to prohibit discrimination on the grounds of race, sex, religion, disability, age, and sexual orientation. It provides for the establishment of a nine-member anti-discrimination commission with powers to receive and investigate complaints, issue rulings, and impose sanctions.[1455] It sets up an administrative body with effective powers to investigate and punish discriminatory acts and shifts the onus from the victim to the perpetrator. Each direct or indirect instance of discrimination, based on gender, race, nationality, ethnics, recognition, origin, religion and faith, education, convictions, political affiliation, personal or public status, disability, age, sexual orientation, family status, property, or any other indications, stated in acts or in an international treaty under which Bulgaria is a party, is prohibited by the law.[1456]

Wiretapping and Surveillance Rules

In August 2004, the Appeal Prosecution of the city of Plovdiv issued an order, stating that all Internet clubs and cafes in Plovdiv should require and keep records of customers' social security numbers and personal data, as well as the

---

[1453]Currently, about 1,025,000 entities are recorded in the BULSTAT register, from which about 850,000 are registered under the Trade Act. If five minutes are needed for registering a single data controller – which would be practically impossible – the five members of the Commission would have to work eight hours a day for 365 days a year for five years in order to register half of the administrators (around 876 000).

[1454] The Ombudsman Act, Article 20, para. (2).

[1455] Country Reports on Human Rights Practices 2003. For more information *see* <http://www.state.gov/g/drl/rls/hrrpt/2003/27830.htm>.

[1456] PADA Article 4 para. 1.

time for which visitors accessed the Internet.[1457] On March 24, 2005, the National Service for combating organized crime to the Ministry of Interior delivered a "Direction for action" to Bulgarian web site hosting companies. It was issued and signed by the Chief of the Department of Intellectual Property, Trademark, Computer Crimes and Gambling. The document imposed an obligation on the ISP executives, stating: "in seven days term from the date of issuing this order you must terminate free hosting web space with quota bigger than 100 MB to anonymous users. More than 100 MB of web space should be given only to customers with signed user contract, accompanied with a copy of their ID card or other relevant document for identification. Until undersigning of such contracts with the already existing users, operating with the according quota, the access to the relevant directories must be terminated. In case of technical difficulties in order to provide the above mentioned restrictions, the access to the server should be terminated. All free hosting servers content which contains works, audio records, entertaining or business software, images, pictures, books, graphical logos, etc., must be removed. All websites, images, pictures and texts, containing racial hatred propaganda, pornography, pedophilia, Nazism, and websites for gambling and etc., violating the Bulgarian legislation must be removed."[1458]

Under the Bulgarian Penal Law, sanctions can only be imposed on individuals, not companies. This "Direction for action" is considered by the Internet community as an attempt to make the ISP liable for content. Such actions may result in legal suits, where content that the ISPs have mistakenly considered illegal has been removed. ISPs cannot be liable, unless the individual in question has been properly informed by the police about illegal content, and the individual refuses to remove it. This warning should be in a written form, so that the interests of all users are protected. The case was largely reviewed in Bulgarian and foreign media.[1459]

One month later, The National television announced that a similar order had been issued for the small local Internet providers, and the restrictions for users' quota were increased – no files exceeding 3MB should be hosted on the local servers. Many observers noted that this move by the police aims at ensuring better business opportunities for the local representatives of the Motion Picture Association of America (MPAA), Recording Industry Association of America (RIAA), Business Software Alliance (BSA).

[1457] Order No 30/27.07.2004 issued by Plovdiv Appeal Prosecution.

[1458] This order has been issued and sent personally to the ISP executives. Not available online.

[1459] See German Edition of "Heise.de" available at <http://www.heise.de/newsticker/meldung/58114>.

The PDPA provides that special rules could be introduced to regulate the processing of personal data for the purposes of defense, national security, law enforcement and criminal justice. Electronic surveillance used in criminal investigations is regulated by the Code of Criminal Procedure and requires a court order.1460 Failure to follow this procedure resulting in unlawful wiretapping is a crime.1461 The Telecommunications Law also requires that agencies must ensure the secrecy of communications.1462 Unlawful opening of e-mail correspondence is a criminal offense.1463 The 1997 Special Surveillance Means Act regulates the use of surveillance techniques by the Interior Ministry for investigating crime but also for loosely defined national security reasons. A court order is generally required but the Ministry of the Interior has a discretionary power to authorize wiretaps without judicial review. The full extent of this power is not well known but there are regular complaints of abusive and illegal bugging of individuals.

In January 2001, it was announced that approximately 10,000 wiretaps were authorized during the year 2000. According to the Bulgarian Helsinki Federation, only two to three percent of the intercepts were ever used in criminal proceedings.1464 No reasons for this surveillance were given.1465 These statistics have not been updated since then, as the Prosecutor General denied public access to his 2001 report on the surveillance used. The case is still pending. In another case, the Supreme administrative court decided that the denial by the president of a district court to disclose the annual statistic of orders for intercepts was lawful. In December 2002, the media reported information about possibly unlawful telephone-tapings of public figures including the former National Security Service director and the Minister of Justice, and about the investigation of a person dubbed "Gnom."1466 The Interior Minister partly confirmed the information. A Parliamentary Commission held hearings in 2001 on the activities of "public order" agencies, which include the National Intelligence Service, the National Bodyguard Service and the National Security Service.1467 In October 2001, the Interior Ministry reported that they had found illegal wiretapping

---

1460 Article 111a - 111c (as amended SG, Nos 64/1997, 70/1999).

1461 Article 171 (3) of the Criminal Code.

1462 Telecommunications Law, Article 5.

1463 Article 171 (1) item 3 (as amended SG No 92/2002) of the Criminal Code.

1464 Annual Report of the Bulgarian Helsinki Committee, Human Rights in Bulgaria in 2000, March 2001, available at <http://www.bghelsinki.org/frames-reports.htm>.

1465 Id.

1466 "Bulgarian Government Faces New Bugging Scandal," RFE/RL, December 23, 2002, available at <http://www.rferl.org/newsline/2002/12/4-See/see-231202.asp>.

1467 United States Department of State, Country Reports on Human Rights Practices 2001, March 4, 2002, available at <http://www.state.gov/g/drl/rls/hrrpt/2001/eur/8238.htm>.

devices, in recording mode, in the Central Telephone Exchange in Sofia and preparations for such devices in several of the city's other exchanges. The bugging of telephone subscribers has been taking place since 1994 and was said to be economically motivated.[1468] In November 2001, the director of the NSS resigned from his position. Several allegations were made that he wiretapped politicians, but they were never substantiated.[1469] Earlier, in August 2000, listening devices were found in the apartment of the Prosecutor General Nikola Filchev and several politicians. Filchev blamed the bugs on the Interior Ministry's Criminal Intelligence Service (CIS). A parliamentary session was held after 53 Democratic Left Parliamentarians demanded a hearing.[1470] Following the debate, members of the opposition Bulgarian Socialist Party (BSP) submitted draft amendments to put in place a system of judicial oversight for the use of surveillance.[1471] In November 2000, the Movement for Rights and Freedoms (DPS), a party of ethnic Turks, reported that its leaders were being monitored by the security services.[1472]

In December 1998, the Bulgarian Committee for Post and Telecommunications issued an executive decree to licensed Internet Service Providers (ISPs). The decree gave governmental employees the authorization to enter ISPs' offices at any time and obtain any documentation, including user names and passwords, as well as other private information.[1473] The decision was extensively criticized by Internet users, service providers and others, including German Chancellor Gerhard Schroeder, who said that licensing was not appropriate. The Bulgarian Internet Society (ISOC) chapter filed a case at the Supreme Administrative Court to stop the decree in January 1999. The Court ordered a temporary restraint of the decree on June 17, 1999. In November 1999, the Bulgarian Prime Minister ordered the Minister of Telecommunications to negotiate an out of court agreement with ISOC. A few weeks later, the decree was changed, and the ISPs were removed from the licensing requirements and placed in the "free regime" category.

[1468] "Bugging Affair 'Economically Motivated', Interior Ministry Says," BBC Worldwide Monitoring, October 4, 2001.

[1469] "Security Chief Says 'Low Confidence' in Office Led to Resignation," BBC Worldwide Monitoring, November 28, 2001.

[1470] "Buggate Scandalizes Bulgaria," Transitions online, July 31 - August 6, 2000.

[1471] "Courts Should Be Involved in Controlling Bugging Devices," BBC, August 09, 2000.

[1472] "Security Services Bugged Ethnic Turk's Leaders," BBC Worldwide Monitoring, November 26, 2000.

[1473] Committee for Post and Telecommunications, List of Telecommunication Services, December 18, 1998, State Gazette, December 29, 1998.

During 2003 significant changes have been made in various laws in order to bring them in accordance with the new data protection standards laid down by the PDPA and the Council of Europe (CoE) Convention for the Protection of Individuals with Regard to Automatic Processing of Personal Data (ETS No. 108) (Convention No. 108).[1474]

Recent Developments Related to Privacy

At the beginning of 2003, the Ministry of Interior Act (MIA) was amended[1475] to regulate the powers of police officers to collect, process and keep biometrics identification data about individuals, such as fingerprints, photographs, and DNA profile samples. Another amendment explicitly bans the collection of sensitive information revealing racial or ethnical origin, political opinions, or religious or other beliefs, as well as concerning health or sexual life. The MIA was also amended to provide an opportunity for every individual to access his/her own personal data collected or processed by the Ministry of Interior, even in cases when the collection or processing has been done without his/her knowledge or consent.[1476]

The MIA also authorizes the Ministry of Interior to fully or partially withhold personal data from data subjects' access in case their disclosure could jeopardize national security or public order, or when information classified as a state or official secret might be revealed.[1477] Access could also be restricted under the discretion of Ministry of Interior officials, when there is a danger of revealing information sources, or exposing the secret methods and procedures of information collection, or when disclosure of personal data to the data subject would hamper the implementation of the Ministry's activities. The formulation of Art. 182 has left an unduly broad opportunity for Ministry officials to withhold information from the data subjects.

A new regulation on adoption procedures, amending the Family Code, provides adequate protection of personal data for birth parents, adopted children and

---

[1474]The source for the 2003 changes in PDP law and practice in Bulgaria is the Access to Information Programme Foundation report: Access to Public Information in Bulgaria 2003, pp.23 – 29. Available at <http://www.aip-bg.org/pdf/aip-report2003.pdf>.

[1475] Ministry of Interior Act – Promulgated SG issue 122/19.12.1997; amended in issue 17/21.02.2003; Amending act in issue 26/21.03.2003, in force from 01.01.2003, SG issue 95/28.10.2003; amended issue 103/25.11.2003; amended issue 112/23.12.2003 in force from 1.01.2004; issue 114/30.12.2003.

[1476] Article 182, para. 4 of MIA.

[1477]Article 182, para. 7 of MIA. In practice this question was brought before the court in the case Yonchev v. the Ministry of Interior. See<http://www.aip-bg.org/library/dela/case25.htm>.

adoptive parents. The regulation creates two new registers, one containing information about children subject to adoption, the other one about the parents wishing to adopt children. Both registers contain information about their health and family status, property, as well as various details about the personal and family life of the concerned individuals.

In accordance with the requirements of CoE's Convention No. 108, amendments were adopted in the Health Insurance Act.[1478] They require health insurance companies to protect information concerning persons' health insurance contracts and related information.

On April 30, 2003, the Parliament adopted the Human Cells, Tissues, and Organs Transplantation Act, which entered into force on January 1, 2004. The Act regulates the donation, processing of personal data related to transplantations. The Act provides for the creation of a public and "official-use-only" register for keeping information about transplantations.

A public Register of Declassified Archival Documents of the Ministry of Interior will be available to the public. The announcement was made in January 2005 by the Deputy Minister of Interior Bojko Kotsev, who explained that the register is located in the reading room of the Archival Information Department and is accessible to everyone.[1479]

In February 2005, an article was published by AIP stating: "the Supreme Administrative Council Closed its Sessions after the Chief Prosecutor's Intervention. The European Commission has still to wait for the implementation of transparency principles in the activity of the Prosecutor's Office." During the last week of November 2004, the members of the Supreme Judicial Council (SJC) allowed the media to be present for the first time during their sessions. The opportunity was given after the National Assembly had passed the amendments to the Judiciary Act, which prescribed the sessions of the Council to be public. It came as a surprise then, that the same Chief Prosecutor proposed that the SJC discussed "in darkness" the report of the chief of the National Investigation Services on serious offences in the work of the Sofia Investigation Services. The grounds on which Mr. Filchev closed the session on February 23, 2005, was: "The report contained too much official information…" This statement, thus, is in conflict with the provisions of the Judiciary Act, under which all sessions of

---

[1478]Health Insurance Act, promulgated in SG, issue 70/19.06.1998.

[1479]Available at <http://www.aip-bg.org/bulletin/13_eng/07.htm>.

the Council should be open, with the exemption of discussions on immunity withdrawal or punishment of a magistrate.[1480]

As of March 2005, the criminality reports of the Prosecutor's Office are still inaccessible. The journalist Hristo Hristov from "Dnevnik" newspaper has been fighting for his right of access to the reports of the Prosecutor's Office for the last three years. During the autumn of 2004, the journalist asked the Supreme Judicial Council to give him copies of the reports. The supreme magistrates decided that the information could not be disclosed to the society since the documents had no significance of their own. The case is expected to soon be decided by a five-member panel of the Supreme Administrative Court judges.

Anti-terrorism Measures

In the sphere of the terrorism prevention and combating, Bulgaria has adopted the European Convention on the Suppression of Terrorism,[1481] the Measures Against the Financing of Terrorism Act,[1482] which was amended two times – in 2003 and 2005. Bulgaria also ratified the International Convention for Combating Against Bomb Terrorism in 2001.[1483]

In 2004, the PDPA endured two major amendments. The first one complemented the "personal data" concept,[1484] adopting the human gene data that are now also protected personal data. This amendment was adopted according to a new Health Act. The second change affected article 34 para. 3 (new) and it gives full freedom to personal data administrators to refuse access to personal data, motivating their decision with possible danger to the national security.[1485] Moreover, this decree releases data administrators from the obligation to provide a reason for a potential refusal.[1486] This change was made in order to synchronize the PDPA with the Armed Forces and Defense Act and aimed at achieving correlation between "national security" and "personal data" concepts.

[1480] The full article is available at <http://www.aip-bg.org/bulletin/14_eng/01.htm>.

[1481] Adopted on January 27, 1977. Ratified by Bulgaria on January 14, 1998. Date of coming into force May 18,.1998.

[1482] Promulgated in the State Gazette No. 16/18.02.2003.

[1483] Promulgated in the State Gazette No. 36/09.04.2002.

[1484] Personal data protection act Article 2, para. 1, amended issue 70/2004.

[1485] Personal data protection act Article 34, para 3 (new), amended issue 93/2004.

[1486] Access to information report 2004, available at <www.aip-bg.org>.

A new Telecommunications Act was adopted at the end of 2003.[1487] The purpose of the Act is to create conditions for the development of new technologies in the telecommunications market, while at the same time, guarantee the freedom and confidentiality of communications, as well as the protection of end users' personal data. Specifically, the Act introduces an obligation for telecommunications service providers to take technical measures guaranteeing the confidentiality of the communications. These measures cover the kind of service, its content and all information related to its provision. Besides technical coverage, service providers are prohibited from disclosing the content of the communications and related data that come to their knowledge when providing their services.[1488]

Recently, in Bulgaria the need for personal data protection over the Internet has significantly increased. A growing number of people are using the global network as part of their everyday work. As e-business is entering Bulgarians' homes, it is becoming essential to guarantee that electronic commerce is secure and end users' personal data is adequately protected. This is especially important because of the wide variety of online services that commercial companies have launched, such as online dating, marketing surveys and shopping web sites. Bulgarian legislation still provides inadequate guarantees to ensure the protection of personal data over the Internet, since only the DPDA and the Electronic Document and Electronic Signature Act provide some – although insufficient – level of protection.[1489]

At the end of 2003, the Penal Code was amended to make criminal the publication or distribution of system or user passwords with subsequent disclosure of personal data. The penalty can be as high as one year of imprisonment, while in cases of malicious usage or where substantial harm is caused, lawbreakers can serve up to three years in prison.

There are additional provisions relating to privacy in laws such as the Statistics Law, Tax Administration Law, Insurance Law,[1490] and Social Assistance

---

[1487] Telecommunications Act, promulgated in SG, issue 88/7.10.2003; entered into force on October 7, 2003.

[1488] A problem in the implementation of the Act could arise from the obligation of universal telecommunication services providers to publish a directory of their customers' telephone numbers. The Telecommunications Act contains no provisions requiring the telecommunications service providers to request their clients' consent before including their telephone numbers.

[1489] Electronic Document and Electronic Signature Act – promulgated in SG issue 34 from 6.04.2001 in force from 7.10.2001 amended in issue 112 from 29.12.2001, in force from 5.02.2002.

[1490] Insurance Law, Article 7 para. 1.

Law.[1491] The Radio and Television Act sets limits[1492] on broadcasting of personal information.

With regard to the draft of the Radio and Television Act, and also regarding the draft on Telecommunications Act, a declaration has been issued by the Free Information Society Federation and published at the public Media Watch Society Forum. The declaration states: "The draft-laws of telecommunications and radio and television restrict the freedom of information and place its flow under the control of the ruling party and state bureaucracy. These drafts introduce undemocratic and unrepresentative partisan-bureaucratic bodies for the management of the media and telecommunications. The citizens' needs are absent in these laws which place the full information power in the hands of partisan and state bureaucracy - no matter of what color. The citizens are eliminated from participation in the management and the work of the media. The concentration and bureaucratization of media power does not promise anything good for democracy in Bulgaria. The National Council of Radio and Television and the Program Council of the national TV and radio should consist of at least 25 members. 15 members representing civil society (universities, trade unions, consumers, churches, listeners, workers in the media etc.) and not the majority in the Parliament. Special rules should be designed guaranteeing transparency and accessibility of media to citizens. The citizens should be consulted when media power is designed and should not be silently excluded from it. Accordingly we insist that the laws are passed after a public discussion."[1493]

Open Government

The Law for Access to Information to provide access to government records was enacted in June 2000 and went into force in July 2000.[1494] The law allows for access to records except in cases of state security or personal privacy. The Parliamentary Commission for Security and Public Order issued an opinion and a set of recommendations about the Freedom of Information in the Memorandum on The Bulgarian Law on the Protection of Classified Information by Article 19.[1495]

[1491] Social Assistance Law, Article 32 para. 2.

[1492] Radio and Television Act, Articles 10, 15.

[1493] Available at <http://www.mediator.online.bg/moderold.htm>.

[1494] Access to Public Information Act (draft), available at <http://www.aip-bg.org/documents/access.htm>.

[1495] Available at<http://www1.parliament.bg/kns/39NS/Zakdein/KlasInf/KlInf-Article19.htm>.

One of the concerns raised by the Commission was that the law could be largely undermined by an excessively broad classification thereof, particularly given the climate of secrecy that is still present in Bulgaria. Indeed, the Commission questioned the fact that a secrecy law has been developed separately from the freedom of information law when it would have been more logical and more transparent to develop these systems together, as has been done in other democratic countries. In these countries, secrecy is established as part of the regime of exceptions to the right to obtain information, rather than as an independent system. The document has also given the following recommendations: 1) An authorized information security officer should be able to amend classifications originally assigned to ensure appropriate and consistent classification; 2) Classification should be subject to a full judicial review, *in camera* if necessary; 3) There should be a presumption that even secret and top secret material is subject to declassification within a relatively short time period, say 10 years, although this may be overridden where necessary; and 4) The law should provide protection for whistleblowers.

Alexander Kashumov, Coordinator of Legal Projects, AIP, for the Open Society Justice Initiative, commented on the Right to Information in Bulgaria by saying: "The main challenge for a country like Bulgaria in relation with the conflict between freedom of information (FOI) and national security law and practices is to practically promote the principle that FOI takes precedence. Like other Central and East European states, Bulgaria has a serious background of uncontrolled secrecy and only a slight law and practice of FOI."[1496] Amendment of the Act is currently underway in order to implement Council of Europe Recommendation R2 (2000) on Access to Official Documents, adopted in February 2001.[1497]

During 2004, the public interest toward Access to Public Information Act (APIA) cases increased. Refusals to grant access to information on topics of public debate were disputed in court.[1498] The following lawsuits are examples: electronic newspaper "Vseki Den" against the Foreign Ministry's refusal to make public correspondence between Bulgaria and Spain from 1970, regarding the status of the current prime minister, who was living in Spain at that time, under exile; journalists from four media organizations against the Supreme Judicial Council's refusal to provide access required by law to its public sessions; a reporter from "Dnevnik" (daily newspaper) against the Interior Minister's refusal

---

[1496]Available at <http://www.justiceinitiative.org/activities/foifoe/foi/opengov>.

[1497] The Current Situation of the Access to Public Information in Bulgaria in 2001, Access to Information Programme report 2002, available at <http://www.aip-bg.org>.

[1498] Human Rights Report 2004, available at <http://bghelsinki.org/frames-reports.htm>.

to provide access to archival material related to Georgi Markov, the writer murdered in London in 1978; a reporter from "Monitor" against the refusal of the President's administration to provide a security services report on the business deals of Bulgarian firms in Iraq; a reporter from "24 Chassa" against the government's refusal to provide information about the financing of its ministers' official travel; and two members of the Parliament have won a case against minister of State Administration, who denied them the right to review the contract between the Bulgarian Government and Microsoft, signed in 2002, and discussed largely in Bulgarian and Foreign Media for lack of transparency and possible corruption because of the lack of public bid.[1499] The Minister still has not revealed the contract. The case was also under investigation by the Chief Prosecution's Office in 2005.

The number of journalists from nationwide and local media outlets seeking protection in court from infringements on their right to information also increased. As a rule, these cases receive widespread public attention.[1500]

Chairman of the Center of Nongovernmental Organizations in Razgrad -- Georgy Milkov has recently criticized APIA stating: "The authorities turn APIA in a hurdle race. Public Officials aim to discourage the citizens in their search for information." Center of Nongovernmental Organizations (CNGO), unites seven civil associations in Razgrad. Chairman Milkov is a founder of the Bulgarian Association for Fair Elections and Civil Rights in the town. Since September 2004, the Center presided by Milkov has submitted 24 requests for access to public information to the mayor of Razgrad, Venelin Uzunov. None of the requested information was provided in the legally prescribed time frames. As a result of the information refusals, CNGO filed an appeal in the court. Currently, the Razgrad District Court is to hear 24 cases under the APIA.[1501]

The press release of the Sofia City Court on March 16, 2005, shows that the President's administration is also being sued under APIA. An administrative panel of the Sofia City Court delivered a decision on the appeal of Zoya Dimitrova against a refusal of the head of the President's administration. The journalist had been refused access, following an information request for a report by the National Security Services and the National Investigation Services by demand of the President. The refusal refers to the APIA, and the report contains

---

[1499] Portal.bg, Dec. 9, 2004, available at <http://portal.bg/news.php?cat=main&read=20040912002>.

[1500] Human Rights Report 2004, available at <http://bghelsinki.org/frames-reports.htm>.

[1501] The full interview is available at <http://www.aip-bg.org/bulletin/13_eng/02.htm>.

data about Bulgarian citizens and companies who were involved in oil trade with Iraqi companies or their representatives during the Saddam regime.[1502]

In June 2005, AIP released the final version of the report "Access to Information in Bulgaria 2004." The purpose of this report is to summarize the developments in terms of the freedom of information legislation and its implementation. The problems of the implementation of the right to information outlined by the reporting team allowed AIP to make certain conclusions, as well as policy recommendations, in an attempt to improve the practices of providing access to information.[1503]

The amended State Archives Act[1504] states that besides the regular acts, directions, regulations, etc., it also keeps records of personal correspondence, including those in a digital form.[1505]

The Protection of Classified Information Act was passed in April 2002 and went into force in May 2002. It regulates state and official secrets and establishes a Commission on the Security of Information. The general provisions in Article 1 state: "(1) This Act governs the public relations arising in connection with the generation, the processing, and the storing of classified information, and lays down the conditions and procedure for the release thereof and the access thereto. (2) The purpose of this Act is to protect classified information from unauthorized access. (3) Within the meaning of this Act, "classified information" is any information which is a State secret or an official secret, and any foreign classified information." The law abolished the 1997 Access to Documents of the Former State Security Service Act regulating the access, proceedings of disclosure and use of information kept in the documents of the former State Security Service. The Constitutional court rejected the claim of a group of Members of Parliament that the abolition and some other provisions of the new law are unconstitutional.[1506]

On February 9, 2005, the Council of Ministers proposed to the Parliament amendments to the Protection of Classified Information Act. This happened after the Cabinet officially informed AIP that it would put off sending the text of the amendments to the Parliament in order to coordinate the work on the Act with

---

[1502] Press release is available at <http://www.aip-bg.org/bulletin/15_eng/05.htm>.

[1503] The Report is available at <http://www.aip-bg.org/all.htm>.

[1504] In force since January 1, 2002.

[1505] State Archives Act, Article 3, para. (1).

[1506] The Current Situation of the Access to Public Information in Bulgaria in 2002," Access to Information 2002, available at <http://www.aip-bg.org>.

different ministries. In spite of the serious public criticism, including the one expressed by AIP, the Council of Ministers insisted on legalizing the destruction of classified documents. The amendments were discussed in the leading Committee of Internal Security and Public Order. The suggestion that caused most heated debate was one saying that access to classified information should only be guaranteed to the President, the Prime Minister and the Speaker of the Parliament, although he has a status of *primus inter pares* (first among equals) in the Parliament. The sponsors of the amendments suggested that the rest of the 239 MPs would have to go through an investigation before being able to access the classified documents.

Major Privacy Case Law

In 2004, the Supreme Administrative Court (SAC) provided interpretations of important limitations in the sphere of information law: those regarding so-called "state secrets" and "trade secrets" respectively. In its interpretation of the term "trade secret," the SAC imposed the limitation that access to a municipal public procurement contract could not be refused on the grounds of protecting the interests of a third party.[1507] Furthermore, the court issued the opinion[1508] that even when there is a trade secret, the information must still be provided, after the clause in question has been excised.[1509]

An international scandal arose on November 16, 2004, when the journalist George Buhnici of the privately owned Romanian TV station "Pro TV," was arrested by the Bulgarian authorities for using a concealed camera to film in a duty-free shop on the Romanian-Bulgarian border. Pro TV said Buhnici used a hidden camera to film cigarette trafficking in the duty-free shop. Bulgarian customs officials seized the camera and the video recording. The Sofia prosecutor's office examined the confiscated material in order to decide what charge would be brought against him. Article 339(a) of Bulgaria's Criminal Code[1510] provides that anyone using "tools of espionage to acquire secret

---

[1507] Before this reform, all procurement contracts with the municipality as the Contractor, fell outside of the freedom of information law scope and were not accessible to public.

[1508] Opinion of the Supreme Administrative Court of the Republic of Bulgaria, quoted in a publication by AIP, regarding the "Crown Agents" case, publication available at <http://www.aip-bg.org/bulletin/12/01.htm>(in Bulgarian only).

[1509] Human Rights Report 2004 page 14 – Bulgarian Helsinki Committee, available at <http://bghelsinki.org/frames-reports.htm>.

[1510] Criminal Procedure Code, Article 339(a).

information" without specific authorization is liable to up to 3 years in prison. A concealed camera is regarded as such a tool.[1511]

The journalist was released on bail of about 2,500EUR three days later. Buhnici had to stay in Bulgaria until the prosecutor's office decided if he is to be tried for using a concealed camera without permission, for which he could be jailed for up to 3 years. In December 2003, Buhnici was sentenced to pay a fine of BGN 1000. He appealed, and on April 07, 2005, the Rousse Regional Court repealed the sentence.[1512]

A couple of days after the Buhnici scandal, the Chief Prosecutor started an investigation against BBC journalists who created a movie called "Buying The Games," about the alleged bribery for the 2012 Olympic Games city selection, in which the Chairman of the Bulgarian Olympic committee Ivan Slavkov was accused of agreeing to lobby members of the IOC. According to the prosecution, Articles 307[1513] and 339(a) [1514] from the Penal Act were violated. The prosecutor considered the journalists exposing facts about corruption to be guilty, rather than the person who participated in a corruption scheme. This incident gave U.S. Ambassador James Pardew occasion to state that the actions of the Bulgarian magistrates reminded him of the repression at the time of the Cold War. After the broadcast of the movie, the Executive Bureau of the International Olympic Committee (IOC) suspended his membership at the Committee and declared him *persona non grata*.[1515]

The Law on Combating Anti-Social Behaviour of Juveniles[1516] underwent two major reforms – in 1996 and in 2004. The first reform introduced minor changes in the procedure for placement of children in educational boarding schools. It introduced a very formal court review (without hearing) of the decisions of the commissions by the district courts. The second reform introduced more due process standards – court hearings, a possibility to appeal and a possibility to be represented by a lawyer. It too, however, preserved the vagueness of the concept of an "anti-social behaviour" without spelling out specific offences and with all the improvements offered lower due process standards than the Juvenile Penal

---

[1511] Reporters without borders, available at <http://www.rsf.org/article.php3?id_article=11873>.

[1512] *Id.*

[1513] Related to bribery instigation.

[1514] For usage of special technical devices in order to collect information without special permission.

[1515] "What the Papers Say- Buying the Games," BBC News, August 4, 2004. For more information on this issue, *see*, <http://news.bbc.co.uk/1/hi/programmes/panorama/3534718.stm>.

[1516] Law on Combating Anti-Social Behaviour of Juveniles amended in issue 28 / 1.04.2005, in force since April 1, 2005.

Procedure (e.g., unlike the latter, it does not provide for an obligatory participation of a lawyer).[1517] Article 16 para. 4 point 2 assigns to a member of the local commission a duty to prepare a written report concerning the personal idiosyncrasies of the perpetrator and other personal information as age, health condition, physical and psychical state, family environment, relations in the family, education and intelligence, etc.[1518]

International Obligations

Bulgaria is a member of the Council of Europe and has signed and ratified the European Convention for the Protection of Human Rights and Fundamental Freedoms.[1519] It has adopted the CoE's Convention No. 108.[1520] Both conventions are part of the domestic legislation under Article 5, para. 4 of the Constitution and take precedence before contravening statutes. In November 2001, Bulgaria signed but still has not ratified the Council of Europe Cybercrime Convention (ETS No. 185).[1521] In 2003, Bulgaria signed a cooperation agreement with the European Police Office (Europol)[1522] that regulates the transfer of information, including personal data, between the Bulgaria and Europol. The agreement provides guarantees for data protection and integrity. Bulgaria takes whole responsibility for damages incurred by an individual as a result of factual or legal errors in any information exchanged as part of the data transfers between Bulgaria and Europol. On April 2, 2004, Bulgaria became a member of NATO. The ratification document was adopted by the National Assembly on March 18, 2004.

On April 25, 2005, Bulgarian President Georgi Parvanov and the Prime Minister Simeon Saxe-Coburg Gotha signed the European Union Accession Treaty of Bulgaria.[1523] Bulgaria is to become a member state of the EU in 2007, which will result in a wide adoption of the European legislation. On April 28, the Cabinet proposed to the National Assembly ratification of the Accession Treaty of Bulgaria and Romania to the European Union together with the Protocol on the conditions and negotiations for the accession of these countries. The Cabinet

---

[1517] Report from the visit of the delegation of human rights NGOs to places of detention in Bulgaria on September 27 and 28 of 2004, available at <http://www.ihf-hr.org>.

[1518] Law on Combating Anti-Social Behaviour of Juveniles, amended in issue 66, 2004.

[1519] Signed May 10, 1992; ratified September 7, 1992; entered into force September 7, 1992.

[1520] Signed June 2, 1998; ratified on May 20, 2002; entered into force January 1, 2003.

[1521] Signed November 23, 2001.

[1522] Agreement on Cooperation between Bulgaria and the European Police Office (Europol), ratified on July, 31, 2003; entered into force on August 25, 2003; State Gazette issue 92/17.10.2003.

[1523] Available at<http://www.government.bg/English/2524.html>.

also recommended ratification of the following: the Act of Accession concerning the conditions for their accession and the adjustments to the Treaties on which the European Union is founded and the Final Act on Bulgaria's accession to the EU. Under the Constitution of Bulgaria, the documents are to be ratified.[1524]

Canada

Constitutional Privacy Framework

Canada's Charter of Rights and Freedoms (the Charter)[1525] does not provide a guaranteed right to privacy. Despite the lack of an explicit constitutional right to privacy, Canada's courts have recognized an individual's right to a reasonable expectation of privacy as part of the Charter right to be secure against unreasonable search or seizure (Section 8).[1526] The degree of privacy protection under Section 8 depends on the reasonable expectations of the individual in the circumstances.[1527] In *R. v. Edwards*, the Supreme Court of Canada identified several factors that define "reasonable expectations" in this context.[1528]

Courts have also suggested that the individual has a right to privacy as part of the right to "life, liberty and security of the person" under Section 7 of the Charter. The Supreme Court of Canada has suggested that there may be a Section 7 right to privacy when dealing with medical records,[1529] the physical integrity of the person[1530] and decisions that are intensely personal.[1531] The Federal Court of Appeal has also noted the emerging view that Section 7's liberty interest includes

---

[1524] Available at<http://www.government.bg/English/2539.html>.

[1525] Canadian Charter of Rights and Freedoms, Part I of the Constitution Act, 1982, being Schedule B to the Canada Act 1982 (United Kingdom), 1982, c. 11, s. 8, available at <http://laws.justice.gc.ca/en/charter/>.

[1526] Hunter v. Southam, 2 S.C.R. 145, 159-60 (1984), available at <http://www.lexum.umontreal.ca/csc-scc/en/pub/1984/vol2/html/1984scr2_0145.html>.

[1527] R. v. Wise, [1992] 1 S.C.R. 527, R.v. M. (M.R.), [1998] 3 S.C.R. 393, available at <http://www.lexum.umontreal.ca/csc-scc/en/pub/2003/vol1/html/2003scr1_0003.html>.

[1528] [1996] 1 S.C.R. 128, available at <http://www.lexum.umontreal.ca/csc-scc/en/pub/1996/vol1/html/1996scr1_0128.html>.

[1529] L'Heureux-Dubé, in dissenting judgment but with agreement of the Court on her views of privacy, R.v. O'Connor, [1995] 4 S.C.R. 411, 1995 CarswellBC 1098, 1995 CarswellBC 1151; Canadian AIDS Society v. Ontario (1995), 25, O.R. (3d) 388 (Gen. Div); affirmed (1996), 31 O.R. (3d) 798 (C.A.), leave to appeal refused (1997), 216 N.R. 159 (note) (S.C.C.); M, (A.) v. Ryan, [1997] 1 S.C.R. 157.

[1530] Rodriguez v. British Columbia (Attorney General), [1993] 3 S.C.R. 519, available at <http://www.lexum.umontreal.ca/csc-scc/en/pub/1993/vol3/html/1993scr3_0519.html>.

[1531] R. v. Morgentaler (No. 2), [1988] 1 S.C.R. 30, available at <http://www.lexum.umontreal.ca/csc-scc/en/pub/1988/vol1/html/1988scr1_0030.html>.

---

a right to privacy, based again on reasonable expectations and the degree of potential infringement.[1532]

Statutory Rules on Privacy

Privacy is regulated in both the public and private sectors in Canada, and at both federal and provincial levels. The Privacy Act[1533] regulates the federal public sector, while provincial and territorial statutes offer public sector privacy protection in those jurisdictions. The Personal Information Protection and Electronic Documents Act (PIPEDA)[1534] applies to private sector commercial activities throughout the country, with the exception of three provinces (Alberta, British Columbia and Quebec) that have enacted "substantially similar" provincial legislation of their own. Four provinces have passed legislation for the protection of information in the health sector.[1535]

Public Sector Privacy Protection

The federal Privacy Act has been in force in Canada since 1983, protecting the personal information of individuals held by federal government institutions. It governs the collection, use and disclosure of personal information held by most federal public agencies and provides individuals with a right of access to personal information held by those agencies, subject to some exceptions.[1536] The Act also sets out the mandate and duties of the federal Privacy Commissioner, who is responsible for investigating and resolving complaints under the Act, conducting audits of federal agencies, making recommendations for changes in governmental data management practices, and reporting annually to Parliament. The Commissioner does not have order-making powers under this Act.

In 1999, the Privacy Commissioner completed an extensive review of the Act and recommended over 100 changes to the law in order to improve and update it. Some of the changes included giving the Office of the Privacy Commissioner primary authority over all information collected by the federal government,

---

[1532] Ruby v. Canada (Attorney General), [2000] 3 F.C. 589 (Fed. C.A.), available at <http://www.canlii.org/ca/cas/fca/2000/2000fca10500.html>.

[1533] Privacy Act, R.S. 1985, c. P-2, available at <http://laws.justice.gc.ca/en/P-21/index.html>.

[1534] Personal Information Protection and Electronic Documents Act, 2000, c.5, available at <http://laws.justice.gc.ca/en/P-8.6/93196.html>.

[1535] Ontario (Personal Health Information Protection Act, 2004), Manitoba (Personal Health Information Act), Saskatchewan (Health Information Protection Act) and Alberta (Health Information Act).

[1536] Privacy Act at c. P-21, *supra*, available at <http://canada.justice.gc.ca/stable/EN/Laws/Chap/P/P-21.html>.

extending its coverage beyond "recorded" information, increasing notice of disclosures, expanding court reviews, creating rules on data matching, controlling "publicly available" information and expanding the mandate of the Privacy Commissioner.[1537] As of May 2005, these recommendations have not been acted upon.

Data protection legislation covering government bodies also exists in all 10 provinces and three territories.[1538] In most cases, provincial legislation covers access to information rights (i.e., rights to access government information) as well as data protection in the public sector. In two cases, (Quebec and New Brunswick), data protection and access to information are covered in separate statutes.

Federal Private Sector Privacy Protection

The Personal Information Protection and Electronic Documents Act (PIPEDA) was approved by the federal Parliament in April 2000, and parts of the Act came into force on January 1, 2001.[1539] The Act deals with protection of data that is collected, used or disclosed in the course of commercial activity. Since January 1, 2004, the Act applies to every private sector organization (federally regulated and most provincially regulated organizations) that collect, use or disclose personal information, as well as to federally regulated employers with respect to their employees. The purpose clause of the Act[1540] recognizes not only individual rights to data protection, but also "the needs of organizations to collect, use and disclose personal information for purposes that a reasonable person would consider appropriate in the circumstances." The Act incorporates a private sector Code for the Protection of Personal Information[1541] that was developed by a multi-stakeholder committee of the Canadian Standards Association (CSA).

Now the core of the Act, the CSA Code sets out 10 privacy principles that organizations must comply with when dealing with personal information:

[1537] Privacy Commissioner, 1999-2000 Annual Report, May 2000, available at <http://www.privcom.gc.ca/english/02_04_08_e.htm>.
1538 A list of provincial and territory privacy laws and commissions is available at <http://canada.justice.gc.ca/en/ps/atip/provte.html>.

[1539] PIPEDA, *supra*. The province of Quebec has launched a constitutional challenge to PIPEDA, arguing that the federal government exceeded its jurisdiction in enacting such legislation. This case is expected to be heard by the Quebec courts in late 2005 or early 2006. Tyler Hamilton, "Privacy Law Faces Legal Challenge," The Toronto Star, December 30, 2003, available at <http://www.torontostar.com/NASApp/cs/ContentServer?pagename=thestar/Layout/Article_Type1&c=Article &cid=1072739408672&call_pageid=968332188492&col=968793972154>.
[1540] PIPEDA at s.3, *supra*.
[1541] A national standard: CAN/CSA-Q830-96.

accountability, purpose, openness, consent, limiting use and collection, disclosure, retention, individual access, safeguards, accuracy, and challenging compliance. Specific exceptions to the general requirement for knowledge and consent to any collection, use or disclosure are set out in Section 7 of the Act. These exceptions include collection of personal information for journalistic, artistic, and literary purposes. The use and disclosure of personal information for an emergency that threatens the life, health or security of an individual or for research are other examples of exceptions in the Act.

Section 29 of PIPEDA mandates that a review of Part One of the Act will be done every five years after its coming into force. Having come into force on January 1, 2001, a parliamentary committee will be responsible for providing the House of Commons with a report, including any recommendations, within one year of the review date of January 1, 2006. Privacy advocates, experts, and courts have already noted a number of deficiencies with the Act: vague language (especially in the CSA Code/Schedule 1), unclear scope, and a weak oversight and redress regime.[1542]

While the Act applies to provincially regulated private organizations, it does not apply to provincially regulated organizations in provinces that have enacted their own privacy legislation deemed to be "substantially similar" by the federal government. As of May 2005, the only provinces to have enacted "substantially similar" private sector privacy legislation are Alberta,[1543] British Columbia[1544] and Quebec.[1545]

Provincial Private Sector Privacy Protection

Quebec's Act Respecting the Protection of Personal Information in the Private Sector came into effect in 1994, long before PIPEDA. It regulates the collection, confidentiality, correction, disclosure, retention and use of personal information by businesses in that province. It also provides individuals with a right of access and correction. The British Columbia and Alberta Acts both came into effect on

---

[1542] *E.g.*, John Lawford, *Consumer Privacy under PIPEDA: How are we doing?* (PIAC, 2004); Christopher Berzins, "Three years under the PIPEDA: a disappointing beginning," Canadian Journal of Law and Technology, vol. 3 no.3 (November 2004) pp.113-126.

[1543] Personal Information Protection Act, S.A. 2003, c. P-6.5, available at <http://www.qp.gov.ab.ca/documents/Acts/P06P5.cfm?frm_isbn=0779726316>.

[1544] Personal Information Protection Act, S.B.C. 2003, c. 63, available at <http://www.oipc.bc.ca/legislation/PIPA2003%20(2004).pdf>.

[1545] Act respecting the protection of personal information in the private sector, R.S.Q., c. P-39.1 available at <http://www2.publicationsduquebec.gouv.qc.ca/dynamicSearch/telecharge.php?type=2&file=/P_39_1/P39_1_A.html>.

January 1, 2004. They apply to personal information collected, used and disclosed by all businesses and non-profit organizations in those provinces that are not covered by public sector statutes.

Although considered "substantially similar" by the federal government, there are significant differences between PIPEDA and the provincial Acts. First, PIPEDA's rules are based on a general principle of consent; the provincial acts go one step further to carve out consent obligations in specific areas such as employee information and business transactions. Unlike PIPEDA, the British Columbia and Alberta Acts contain a grandfathering provision, which provides that information collected by the private sector before the Act comes into force does not need consent. The British Columbia and Alberta Acts also allow the collection, use and disclosure of an employee's personal information without consent as long it is done for "reasonable" purposes, while PIPEDA makes no distinction between personal information collected for employment or commercial activities. The provincial acts also allow the provincial Privacy Commissioners to issue binding orders to settle disputes; the federal Privacy Commissioner is restricted to making recommendations.

Although the privacy law framework in Canada has received much media attention, a 2003 study from the Alberta Office of the Information and Privacy Commissioner found that there is a low level of awareness of current privacy laws: 60 percent of respondents were unaware of Canadian laws that protected their personal information. Out of 1,004 Canadians surveyed, only six could cite PIPEDA.[1546] There was also a low level of awareness about Alberta's Health Information Act – only 53 percent of Albertans had heard of it.

In addition to statutes cited above, four provinces (British Columbia, Saskatchewan, Manitoba, and Newfoundland) have legislation creating a statutory tort of invasion of privacy of a person. Quebec's Civil Code includes several provisions that create causes of action based on invasion of an individual's privacy.

Sector-Specific Privacy Legislation

A number of other federal statutes address the privacy of personal information in specific sectors. For example, the Bank Act,[1547] Insurance Companies Act,[1548]

[1546] Alberta OIPC Stakeholder Survey, 2003, Highlights Report, March 2003, available at <http://www.oipc.ab.ca/ims/client/upload/survey_2003.pdf>.

[1547] Bank Act, c. 46, ss. 242, 244, 459, available at <http://www.canlii.org/ca/sta/b-1.01/>.

and Trust and Loan Companies Act[1549] permit regulations regarding the use of information provided by customers. Under the Telecommunications Act,[1550] the Canadian Radio-Television and Telecommunications Commission (CRTC) is mandated to regulate telecommunications companies so as "to protect the privacy of persons," among other policy objectives. It has done so through regulations governing the confidentiality of customer records, the maximum rate that can be charged for unlisted service (per month, CAD 2 (~USD 1.65)), and the ability of customers to block the display of their names and numbers on the telephone sets of people whom they are calling. Section 41 of the Act specifically authorizes the CRTC to regulate unsolicited communications, which it has done through rules governing telemarketing (but not spam).

Additional privacy protections are built into the Young Offenders Act [1551] and the Corrections and Conditional Release Act.[1552] The Young Offenders Act regulates the information that can be disclosed about offenders under the age of 18, while the Corrections and Conditional Release Act speaks to the information that can be disclosed to victims and their families.

Some provinces also have sector-specific laws to protect personal information, including health-specific privacy laws, consumer credit reporting laws, laws regulating information from credit unions, and legislation imposing restrictions on the disclosure of personal information held by private investigators and other professionals. Ontario,[1553] Alberta,[1554] Manitoba,[1555] and Saskatchewan[1556] have all passed health privacy legislation, which sets rules for the collection, use, and disclosure of personal health information. These laws apply to personal health information held by hospitals, government ministries, regulated health professionals, and other health care facilities or information custodians.

[1548] Insurance Companies Act, s. 489, s. 607, available at <http://www.canlii.org/ca/sta/i-11.8/>.

[1549] Trust and Loan Companies Act, s. 444, available at <http://www.canlii.org/ca/sta/t-19.8/>.

[1550] Telecommunications Act, 1993, c. 38, s. 39, s. 41, available at <http://www.canlii.org/ca/sta/t-3.4/>.

[1551] Young Offenders Act, C. Y-1, s. 38.

[1552] Corrections and Conditional Release Act, 1992, c. 20, s. 26, 142, available at <http://www.canlii.org/ca/sta/c-44.6/>.

[1553] Personal Health Information Protection Act, S.O. 2004, c. 3, Sched. 1, available at <http://www.canlii.org/on/laws/sta/2004c.3sch.a/20050511/whole.html>.

[1554] Health Information Act, H-5 RSA 2000, available at <http://www.qp.gov.ab.ca/Documents/acts/H05.CFM>.

[1555] Personal Health Information Act, S.M. 1997, c. 51 [C.C.S.M., c. P33.5] as am. S.M. 1998, c. 45, s. 14 (Fr.); 2001, c. 18, s. 18; 2004, c. 36, available at <http://web2.gov.mb.ca/laws/statutes/ccsm/p033-5e.php>.

[1556] Health Information Protection Act, S.S. 1999, c. H-0.021 [ss. 17(1), 18(2), (4), 69 not in force at date of publication.] as am. S.S. 2002, c. R-8.2, s. 77 [s. 77(2)(f), 77(4) not in force as date of publication; s. 77(4) repealed 2003, c. 25, s. 19.]; 2003, c. 25, ss.1-18; 2004, c. A-26.1, s.37; 2004, c. 65, s. 11, available at <http://www.qp.gov.sk.ca/documents/english/chapters/1999/H0-021.pdf>.

Both the Privacy Act and PIPEDA are overseen by the independent federal Privacy Commissioner of Canada, an officer of Parliament who is appointed by, and reports directly to, the Parliament of Canada.[1557] As of May 2005, the federal Office of the Privacy Commissioner (OPC) has a full-time staff of 86 people.[1558] The OPC is charged with investigating complaints, promoting public awareness of privacy issues and researching privacy issues. Provincial and Territorial privacy legislation is overseen by provincial oversight bodies. In most cases, the relevant authority is an Information and Privacy Commissioner, responsible for the administration of both privacy laws and access to information laws. In a few cases (Manitoba, New Brunswick, and Yukon Territory), an Ombudsman has powers to investigate matters relating to privacy as well as other matters.[1559] These oversight bodies vary significantly in their powers and scope of regulation.

The federal Privacy Commissioner ("the Commissioner") receives complaints, conducts investigations and issues findings on matters related to both the public sector (Privacy Act) and the private sector (PIPEDA). Under both of these Acts, the Commissioner has the power to make recommendations; however, she cannot issue orders or impose penalties. Also under both statutes, the Commissioner has broad investigatory powers, including the power to subpoena witnesses and compel testimony, to enter premises in order to obtain documents and to conduct interviews. The Commissioner is also charged with conducting periodic audits of both federal institutions and private organizations to determine their compliance with the Privacy Act and PIPEDA, respectively.

While not binding, the Privacy Commissioner's decisions are considered to be of national importance. In a 2004 Federal Court decision involving a Privacy Commissioner finding, the court did not hesitate to classify PIPEDA as a fundamental law of Canada.[1560] It was also determined that the Privacy Commissioner could be granted a degree of deference with regards to his or her expertise, but not to findings of fact.[1561]

[1557] Privacy Commissioner of Canada Homepage <http://www.privcom.gc.ca>.

[1558] Telephone call with Maureen Munhall, Human Resources, Office of the Privacy Commission of Canada, May 30, 2005.

[1559] Privacy Commissioner of Canada website <http://www.privcom.gc.ca/information/comms_e.asp#013>.

[1560] Eastmond v. Canadian Pacific Railway, 2004 F.T.R. 169, 2004 CF 852. 33 C.P.R. (4th) 1, 16 Admin. L.R. (4th) 275, 2004 F.C. 852 (F.C.), available at <http://www.canlii.org/ca/cas/fct/2004/2004fc852.html>.

[1561] *Id.*

As of April 6, 2005, the OPC had made 294 findings on PIPEDA compliance since PIPEDA came into force.[1562] The OPC also responded to 13,422 telephone and written inquiries about PIPEDA and 4,728 telephone and written inquiries about the Privacy Act.[1563] The increase can be attributed to a number of major privacy conflicts, primarily related to the Privacy Act.

In 2003 and 2004, several groups of complaints arose under the Privacy Act. One series of complaints related to broadly worded health care consent forms that were required from members of Canada's aboriginal community. Correctional Services Canada (CSC) also received a series of complaints by employees and inmates. CSC employees made denial-of-access complaints as well as complaints of the CSC's protection of the employees' contact information. Offenders in a federal institution also made complaints against the CSC, in particular that they had not received timely responses to their requests for the personal information held in personal information banks.[1564] Of the 30 incidents of mismanagement of personal information that the OPC reviewed, seven cases related to government management of personal information contrary to the Privacy Act.[1565]

In 2003, the OPC received 302 complaints under PIPEDA, approximately the same number as the year before. However, an additional 324 complaints were received between January and June 2004. This illustrates a trend in increased complaints arising from full implementation of the Act in the private sector on January 1, 2004.[1566] Of the 184 well-founded complaints, partially well-founded and resolved complaints, Principle 4.3 (knowledge and consent of collection) and Principle 4.9 (individual access upon request) of Schedule One of PIPEDA were the most often violated principles.[1567]

Anyone can complain to the Commissioner about an alleged violation of PIPEDA. If the Commissioner is satisfied that there are reasonable grounds to

---

[1562] Murray Long, "Key Statistics on Privacy Commissioner Findings under PIPEDA," PrivacyScan, April 2005. This includes well-founded, partially well-founded, resolved, not well-founded, discontinued and no jurisdiction complaints.

[1563] For the 2003-2004 period, the OPC received a record 4,206 complaints under both the Privacy Act and PIPEDA, which is a 250 percent increase from the 2002-2003 period. For more information, *see generally*, Privacy Commissioner of Canada, 2003-2004 Annual Report, November 2004, p. 38, 83, available at <http://www.privcom.gc.ca/information/ar/200304/200304_e.asp>.

[1564] *Id.*

[1565] *Id.* at p. 35.

[1566] The number of cases finalized in 2003 rose to 278, a 58 percent increase from the previous year. Business categories that faced the most number of complaints were banks (44 percent) and telephone companies (20 percent). *See*, Murray Long, "Key Statistics on Privacy Commissioner Findings under PIPEDA," *supra*. This includes early resolution and complaints settled in the course of investigation.

[1567] Murray Long, "Key Statistics on Privacy Commissioner Findings under PIPEDA," *supra*.

investigate a matter under the Act, she may initiate her own complaint.[1568] Once a complaint is received, the Commissioner assigns an investigator to look into the matter. The investigator then submits his findings to the Commissioner, who considers the case and issues a report with recommendations. Reports must be issued within one year of the complaint. The Commissioner can also request the organization in question to submit, within a specified period of time, notice of any action taken, or proposal to be taken, to implement her recommendations.[1569]

Under PIPEDA, the Commissioner is also authorized to conduct broad research into privacy issues and promote awareness and understanding of privacy issues among Canadians. Under these powers, federal commissioners have engaged in significant public advocacy and some public education. For example, they have spoken out forcefully and repeatedly against unnecessary privacy incursions in the fight against terror. Most recently, the current federal Commissioner publicly called for greater transparency, accountability, and oversight of agencies involved in national security.[1570] In May 2005, she also launched the first-ever audit of cross-border flows of Canadians' personal information to the United States via the Canadian Border Services Agency. In 2004, the federal Commissioner also launched a funding program for research into privacy issues. Several organizations obtained grants totaling more than CAD 370,000 (~USD 304,000) to engage in privacy research in 2004 and 2005.[1571]

Some provincial Privacy Commissioners also engage in significant research, advocacy and public education. The Privacy Commissioners of British Columbia,[1572] Ontario,[1573] and Quebec[1574] all provide extensive information on privacy issues on their websites and have been active on a number of current privacy issues. For example, in 2004, British Columbia's Privacy Commissioner launched an investigation to determine if the USA Patriot Act applies to the personal information of Canadians that has been outsourced for processing to US

[1568] Stephanie Perrin, Heather Black, David Flaherty & T. Murray Rankin, The Personal Information Protection and Electronic Documents Act: An Annotated Guide (Toronto, 2001).

[1569] *See generally*, "Your Privacy Responsibilities: A Guide for Business and Organizations," Office of the Privacy Commissioner of Canada, December 2000.

[1570] News Release, May 9, 2005, "Contained surveillance and increased oversight needed in Anti-terrorism Act to protect against loss of privacy rights," available at <http://www.privcom.gc.ca/media/nr-c/2005/nr-c_050509_e.asp>.

[1571] Privacy Commissioner of Canada website, *supra.*

[1572] Office of the Information and Privacy Commissioner for British Columbia, available at <http://www.oipc.bc.ca/>.

[1573] Office of the Information and Privacy Commissioner of Ontario, available at <http://www.ipc.on.ca/>.

[1574] Commission d'accès à l'information du Québec, available at <http://www.cai.gouv.qc.ca/index-en.html>.

companies.[1575] This investigation was sparked by public concerns about the British Columbia's government's proposal for contracting the administration of the provincial medical services plan to a Canadian subsidiary of an American company. The federal Privacy Commissioner was among many individuals and organizations who contributed a submission to the investigation.[1576]

In May 2002, Canada became the first national government to make privacy assessments by federal departments and agencies mandatory. The Privacy Impact Assessment Policy means that all new and existing federal programs and services with potential privacy risks will undergo a Privacy Impact Assessment (PIA). The goal is to produce a comprehensive report that ensures that privacy protection is a core consideration in the initial framing of program or service objectives and in all subsequent activities. According to the policy, the OPC will review all PIAs and offer comments to departments at an early stage.[1577] Since it came into effect, the OPC has conducted more than 100 PIAs and PPIAs (pre-privacy impact assessments). This has been effective in identifying potential risks; however, many PIAs fail to include an action plan to resolve the potential privacy problems.[1578]

Surveillance

Municipal police forces in a number of Canadian cities have indicated an interest in installing public video surveillance systems, and have moved forward with such systems in some cases. In 2001, the federal Privacy Commissioner sought to challenge the right of the Royal Canadian Mounted Police (RCMP) to engage in video surveillance of public spaces. According to the Commissioner, such monitoring and recording violated the legal requirement to collect only the minimal amount of personal information required for the intended purpose.[1579] The Commissioner relied upon an opinion by former Supreme Court Justice

---

1575 Information & Privacy Commissioner for British Columbia, available at <www.oipcbc.org/sector_public/usa_patriot_act/pdfs/report/privacy-final.pdf>.

1576 Office of Privacy Commissioner of Canada, "Transferring Personal Information about Canadians across Borders- Implications of the USA Patriot Act,: submitted to the Office of the Information and BC Privacy Commissioner for British Columbia, available at <http://www.privcom.gc.ca/media/nr-c/2004/sub_usapa_040818_e.pdf>.

1577 *See* Treasury Board of Canada Secretariat, "Privacy Impact Assessment Report," available at <http://www.tbs-sct.gc.ca/pubs_pol/ciopubs/pia-pefr/paip-pefr_e.asp>.

1578 Privacy Commissioner of Canada, 2003-2004 Annual Report, at 53, *supra.*

1579 News Release, Office of the Privacy Commissioner, October 4, 2001, available at <http://privomc.goc.ca/media/nr-c/02_05_b_011004_e.asp>.

Gerard La Forest who argued that the practice was unconstitutional.[1580] The Commissioner was concerned that there was no guarantee that the cameras are not recording at all times and that this case would lead to the proliferation of video surveillance cameras in public spaces as well as citizen profiling.[1581] The case became mired in procedural issues and was ultimately withdrawn by a subsequent Privacy Commissioner, who has focused instead on developing guidelines for the use of video surveillance by public authorities.[1582]

In June 2001, the federal Privacy Commissioner issued a finding on the commercial use of video cameras, stating that both live video pictures and recorded video pictures of individuals qualify as "personal information" under the Act and that where such surveillance takes place in a commercial context, it falls under PIPEDA.1583 In such circumstances, video images can only be collected with consent of the individuals. The Commissioner also stated that public places should only be monitored for public safety reasons where a demonstrated need is shown.

The Quebec government is also involved in surveillance issues. Quebec's Privacy Commission held public hearings on this issue in the fall of 2003. A summary of the report from the public consultation was released in June 2004.[1584] The Commission is active in advocating privacy standards for the use of surveillance cameras. In 2004, it released "Rules for use of surveillance cameras with recording in public places by public bodies," which intend to protect privacy by controlling the purposes and length of time for which video cameras can be used.[1585]

[1580] Charles Mandel, "Security Cameras not OK in Canada?" Wired News, April 6, 2002, available at <http://www.wired.com/news/politics/0,1283,51821,00.html>.

[1581] News Release, Office of the Privacy Commissioner, June 21, 2001, available at <http://www.privcom.gc.ca/media/nr_c/02_05_b_020621>.

[1582] Privacy Commissioner of Canada, 2003-2004 Annual Report, at 16, *supra*.

[1583] News Release, Office of the Privacy Commissioner, June 20, 2001, available at <http://www.privcom.gc.ca/media/nr-c/nt_010620_e.asp>, and the finding is available at <http://www.privcom.gc.ca/cf-dc/cf-dc_010615_e.asp>. The case concerned the installation of security cameras in the town of Yellowknife by a local security company, Centurion Security Services. The company had installed surveillance cameras on the main street to monitor crimes as a marketing demonstration intended to generate business.

[1584] Commission d'accès à l'information, Summary of the Report on the public consultation: Use of Surveillance Cameras by Public Bodies in Public Places, June 2004, available at <http://www.cai.gouv.qc.ca/06_documentation/01_pdf/summary_report.pdf>.

[1585] Commission d'accès à l'information, Minimum Rules for Use of Surveillance Cameras with Recording in Public Places by Public Bodies, June 2004, available at <http://www.cai.gouv.qc.ca/06_documentation/01_pdf/new_rules_2004.pdf>.

Surveillance cameras in schools are also becoming the subject of greater debate and attention. School boards in Ontario that plan to use video surveillance in their schools must abide by strict guidelines in order to ensure that the privacy of their students and employees is not violated. Surveillance is to be conducted under the controls set forth in the new "Guidelines for Using Video Surveillance Cameras in Schools."[1586] Ontario's Privacy Commissioner commented on the guidelines, remarking that they "provide step-by-step guidance to help ensure that if cameras are used, the surveillance system is operated in a manner that serves security needs but doesn't needlessly infringe on the rights of students and staff."[1587]

The use of video surveillance by employers is another current issue in Canada. In a 2003 finding, the federal Privacy Commissioner determined that a complaint by a railway employee about digital video recording cameras installed on company premises was well-founded, insofar as the cameras would collect the personal information of employees without consent. Following the Commissioner's recommendations in 2003 that an employer refrain from video surveillance of his employees because the purpose of reducing theft did not justify the extra intrusion into employee privacy,[1588] the complainant sought to have the decision confirmed by the Federal Court. The court ruled that the video surveillance in this case was reasonable and not a violation of PIPEDA.[1589]

The use of infrared technology to gather evidence of potential criminal activity was addressed by the Supreme Court of Canada in a 2004 case called *R. v. Tessling*.[1590] The Court concluded that the use of FLIR (Forward Looking Infra-Red) aerial cameras did not violate the individual's Section 8 Charter right against unreasonable search or seizure by the state, because the individual has no reasonable expectation of privacy with regards to the external surfaces of his or her home. The Court further reasoned that FLIR does not offer insight into an

---

[1586] "Ontario Official Issues School Surveillance Code," BNA World Data Protection Report Vol. 3, Issue 1, January 2004, at 20.

[1587] *Id.* Some of the main elements of the guidelines include the use of video cameras in areas only where they have been identified as necessary for detection or deterrence, drafting by the school board of a formal policy governing the use of surveillance, no cameras in areas where there is a reasonable expectation of privacy, notification of the cameras and no hidden cameras. A retention period of no longer than 30 days has also been recommended. See Ann Cavoukian, Guidelines for Using Video Surveillance in Schools, December 2003, available at <http://www.ipc.on.ca/docs/vidsch-e.pdf>.

[1588] Andrea York, "Video Surveillance and Workplace Privacy: The Privacy Commissioner Recommends Removal of Video Cameras," 13 Employment and Labour Law Reporter 5-7 (April 2003); *see also,* Great Library Employment/Labour Law Digest, May 2003, "Federal Privacy Commissioner Finds Video Surveillance Unreasonable," available at <http://library.lsuc.on.ca/GL/whats_employment.htm#Federal%20Privacy%20Commissioner%20finds%20video%20surveillance%20unreasonable>.

[1589] *Id.*

[1590] R. v. Tessling, [2004] S.C.J. No. 63, 244 D.L.R. (4th) 541, 2004 S.C.C. 67, 189 C.C.C. (3d) 129, 23 C.R. (6th) 207, available at <http://www.canlii.org/ca/cas/scc/2004/2004scc67.html>.

individual's private life, nor does it reveal anything about the individual's "biographical core of personal information." While this decision is consistent with some previous lower court decisions,[1591] it reversed the Ontario Court of Appeal ruling from which it was appealed.

FLIR technology detects patterns of heat emitted by buildings, which may be used to investigate potential marijuana-growing operations. In this case, FLIR was used by police to obtain a warrant to search the defendant's house. The court did state that a person's "reasonable expectation of privacy" is not solely determined by technological developments, but rather that it is "a normative rather than a descriptive standard." It noted: "Suggestions that a diminished subjective expectation of privacy should automatically result in a lowering of constitutional protection should therefore be opposed."[1592]

Part VI of Canada's Criminal Code makes the interception of private communications a criminal offense.[1593] Police are required to obtain a court order and interception is only authorized in cases "where other investigative procedures are unlikely to succeed." In December 2000, the Supreme Court of Canada clarified this requirement, stating that in order to obtain a wiretapping warrant police must submit documents showing that "there is no other reasonable alternative method of investigation." The Court stressed that it is not enough to show that wiretaps are simply the most efficient way to investigate a crime, because this standard could threaten civil liberties.[1594] Amendments to the Radiocommunication Act[1595] also forbid the divulgence of intercepted radio-based telephone communications. The Canadian Security Intelligence Service Act[1596] authorizes the interception of communications for national security reasons. The federal court ruled in 1997 that the Canadian Security Intelligence Service was required to obtain a warrant in all cases.[1597]

[1591] R. v. Hutchings, 111 C.C.C. (3rd) 215, 39 C.R.R. (2d) 309 (B.C.C.A.), leave to appeal refused [1977] 2 S.C.R. x (S.C.C.). 44 C.R.R. (2d) 188 (note), available at <http://www.canlii.org/bc/cas/bcca/1996/1996bcca527.html>.

[1592] Id.

[1593] Criminal Code, c. C-46. ss. 184, 184.5, 193, 193.1 available at <http://www.canlii.org/ca/sta/c-46/>.

[1594] Janice Tibbetts, "Top Court Sets Ground Rules For Wiretaps," The Ottawa Citizen, December 15, 2000.

[1595] Radiocommunication Act, R.S.C. 1985, c. R-2, s. 9, available at <http://www.canlii.org/ca/sta/r-2/>.

[1596] Canadian Security Intelligence Service Act, Chapter C-23, available at <http://canada.justice.gc.ca/STABLE/EN/Laws/Chap/C/C-23.html>.

[1597] "CSIS Has Wiretap Green light," The Hamilton Spectator, October 1, 1997.

Canada's Response to the Cybercrime Convention: "Lawful Access"

In 2002, the Canadian government announced plans to modernize its criminal law and establish new rules regarding "lawful access" in light of the challenges posed by new technologies to law enforcement. These plans, which originated in the 1990s, became more important in light of the September 11, 2001 attacks in the United States and the perceived heightened threat of terrorism. They are Canada's domestic implementation of its obligations under the Council of Europe's Cybercrime Convention, which Canada has signed but not yet ratified. The proposals, which would amend the Criminal Code and related statutes, are expected to be introduced as legislation in late 2005.

"Lawful Access" refers to the lawful interception of communications as well as search and seizure of information by law enforcement agencies. In order to be lawful in Canada, such interception or searches must be authorized by judicial order and conducted in a manner consistent with the Canadian Charter of Rights and Freedoms. The proposals are designed to provide law enforcement agencies with more effective tools to investigate criminal acts in the digital age.

In 2002, the government consulted with stakeholder groups, including civil society, on its proposals.[1598] Over 300 submissions were received, many from individuals and organizations concerned about the potential impact of the proposed changes on privacy and civil liberties. Federal and provincial Privacy Commissioners commented on the proposed amendments, alleging that they lacked adequate privacy safeguards and grant law enforcement agencies excessive powers to intercept communications during investigations.[1599] The law enforcement community, in contrast, strongly supported the proposals and urged swift action. During the subsequent two years, the government developed and refined its proposals in light of input received. In the fall of 2004, the Minister of Public Safety announced that legislation to facilitate lawful access would be introduced shortly. In early 2005, government officials initiated targeted, closed consultations with stakeholders, including industry and civil society, on its revised proposals.

[1598] Justice Canada "Lawful Access" webpage <http://www.canada.justice.gc.ca/en/cons/la_al/>.
[1599] Tyler Hamilton, "Watchdog Denounces Cyber-Snooping Plan" November 26, 2002, Toronto Star, available at
<http://www.thestar.ca/NASApp/cs/ContentServer?pagename=thestar%2FLayout%2FArticle_Type1&c=Articl
e&cid=1035774825744&call_pageid=968332188492&col=968705899037>.

Meanwhile, in 2004, the Criminal Code was amended to provide for "production orders" – one of the Cybercrime Convention requirements. Sections 487.012 and 487.013 now allow law enforcement authorities to obtain, with judicial authorization on "reasonable grounds to suspect" threshold, production orders compelling a person (e.g., an Internet service provider) to produce the relevant information required by the police. The concept of a production order as an investigative tool already exists under Canadian law through the Competition Act,[1600] although it is a new addition to the Criminal Code.[1601] Such orders are time-sensitive and can be made to third parties or to the individuals themselves and failure to comply can result in the party being forced to report to the court with reasons as to why they have not complied.

The 2005 lawful access proposals include new production orders and preservation orders, as required by the Cybercrime Convention. They also include a requirement for telecommunications service providers (TSPs) to have interception capability in place, and warrantless access by police to "subscriber data" (name, IP address, telephone number, e-mail address) upon request. TSPs have expressed serious concerns about the cost of such mandated measures. Civil society groups have objected to a number of aspects of the proposals, including warrantless access to subscriber data, a lower judicial threshold for issuing production orders and preservation orders, and the lack of privacy safeguards and oversight mechanisms to protect civilians from abuse of these new powers.[1602] The Ontario Assistant Privacy Commissioner made a number of proposals for improved safeguards.[1603] It should be noted that the Canadian government is not proposing mandatory data collection or retention, nor would the proposals permit broad "fishing expeditions" as under the USA Patriot Act. In response to civil society concerns, the government is also no longer proposing to establish a national database of subscriber information; instead, all requests must be individual-specific.

Legislative and Policy Responses to Terrorism

The events of September 11, 2001, caused much concern in Canada about the need for government policy to protect against future terrorist activity. In response to public safety concerns, the government hastily introduced legislation, the Anti-

---

[1600] Competition Act, R.S.C., Ch. C-34 (1985), available at <http://www.canlii.org/ca/sta/c-34/>.

[1601] Criminal Code, *supra*.

[1602] BCCLA News Release <http://www.bccla.org/pressreleases/05lawfulaccess2.htm>.

[1603] *See* <http://www.ipc.on.ca/scripts/index_.asp?action=31&P_ID=16087&N_ID=1&PT_ID=11457&U_ID=0>.

Terrorism Act (Bill C-36), designed to institute the necessary procedures and mechanisms to deter terrorism at home and cooperate with other states abroad.[1604]

As originally introduced, the Bill ambiguously defined terrorist groups and terrorist activity; made it an offense to knowingly participate or facilitate, harbor, or fund terrorist activity; increased police electronic surveillance tools; limited disclosure of information and increased exemptions on access to subject data for national security reasons; required individuals with knowledge of a terrorist activity to be detained "preventively" and appear before a judge to offer information under the pretense of "investigative hearings"; amended the Official Secrets Act to permit increased numbers of high level security clearances for private sector technical personnel, to perform operations for national security purposes; and substantially enhanced the interception capabilities and investigative powers of security services. The Bill would have also given the Attorney General of Canada the power to issue blanket certificates that prohibit the disclosure of any information for the purpose of protecting international relations, national defense, or security. Critics were concerned with the Bill's limited oversight applications and sunset clauses, and with the possibility that the government, by issuing certificates, could render federal privacy law powerless, especially against the power of Canadian Security Intelligence Services (CSIS) and other security departments or agencies.

Due to widespread protest,[1605] the Bill was amended with provisions that preventative arrest and investigative hearing powers would sunset after five years unless the government extended them.[1606] The Bill also stated that ministers responsible for policing would be required to report annually to Parliament on the use of preventative arrest and investigative hearing powers.[1607] Provisions

---

[1604] Department of Justice Press Release, "Government of Canada introduces Anti-Terrorist Act," October 15, 2001, available at <http://canada.justice.gc.ca/en/news/nr/2001/doc_27785.html>.

[1605] This was the general consensus at the University of Toronto Law School's conference "The Security of Freedom," in November 2001, where law faculty and leading experts in criminology and political science analyzed Bill C-36 and questioned the government's efforts to expand its powers at the expense of civil rights and liberties. The presenters called for increased "democratic deliberation" and were skeptical not only of the transfer of emergency powers to the state, but were also concerned whether these new criminal laws and tougher penalties would prevent such crimes in the future. There were concerns regarding the Bill's expansion of information gathering and information suppressing powers, which could threaten citizens' privacy and lead to information warehousing, profiling, or the monitoring of legitimate political protests and the stifling of legitimate speech. Finally there were concerns with the Bill's excessive preventative arrest provisions and limited safeguards, sunset clauses, and oversight measures. Ronald Daniels, Patrick Macklem, & Kent Roach (Eds.), The Security of Freedom: Essays on Canada's Anti-Terrorism Bill (Toronto 2001).

[1606] News Release, Department of Justice. Amendments to Bill C-36. available at <http://canada.justice.gc.ca/en/news/nr/2001/doc_27902.html>.

[1607] See Annual Report on the Use of Arrest Without Warrant Pursuant to the Anti-Terrorism Act, available at <http://www.psepcsppcc.gc.ca/publications/national_security/ARC36_2002_e.asp>.

dealing with Attorney General certificates would be amended so that the certificate could no longer be issued at any time, but only after an order or decision for disclosure has been made in a proceeding. The certificates would also be subject to review by a judge of the Federal Court of Appeal. A new interpretive clause was set that clarified that any political, religious, or ideological beliefs would not be considered a terrorist activity unless they specifically met the definition of "terrorist activity." Finally, some of the Bill's measures would be subject to parliamentary review in three years. While former federal Privacy Commissioner George Radwanski was satisfied that these amendments would safeguard privacy rights, the Information Commissioner John Reid, among others, expressed concern that the amendments to the Bill did not go far enough.[1608] The Bill passed into law in December 2001.

Civil liberties groups have been highly critical of the legislation.[1609] The Canadian-based International Civil Liberties Monitoring Group, for example, stated in a 2004 report that:

> Bill C-36 has given police extraordinary powers of preventative arrests that are now being used to threaten and coerce members of visible minorities to "cooperate" with them. This new omnibus law extends and institutionalizes the practice of "secret evidence" to be used in "secret trials" already permitted under provisions of the Immigration and Refugee Protection Act. It grants a sole cabinet minister the power to issue "security certificates" which can be used to detain non-citizens indefinitely or deport them.

As of May 2005, six men had been imprisoned without charges under Anti-Terrorism Act security certificates.

In a highly publicized case, a Canadian named Maher Arar brought the dangers of excessive security measures to Canadians' attention. In September 2002, Mr. Arar was detained, interrogated and imprisoned for 12 days in the US while en route home from a family holiday in Tunisia. He was then handcuffed and shackled, put on a private jet, and flown to Syria where he was subjected to intense interrogation and locked in a tiny, grave-like cell for more than 10 months. In October 2003, he was finally released and sent back to Canada. After

---

1608 News Release, Office of the Information Commissioner of Canada, "Open Letter from the Information Commissioner of Canada to the Special Senate Committee on the Subject-Matter of Bill C-36: Anti-Terrorism," November 28, 2001, available at <http://www.infocom.gc.ca/pressreleases/preleaseview-e.asp?intPreleaseId=4>.
1609 See this law firm website for a list of submissions and publications on Anti-Terrorism law in Canada: <http://www.antiterrorismlaw.ca/cdnterr.htm>.

extensive public pressure, the Canadian government agreed in January 2004 to an inquiry into the Arar affair.[1610] The Commission of Inquiry into the Actions of Canadian Officials in Relation to Maher Arar began its work in the spring of 2004,[1611] and continues to investigate as of May 2005. Much of the proceedings are confidential due to national security concerns. A number of civil society groups, including the British Columbia Civil Liberties Association, the Muslim Lawyers' Association, and the International Civil Liberties Monitoring Group are intervening in the proceedings and calling for greater transparency and accountability of police actions related to national security.

In December 2004, the House of Commons Subcommittee on Public Safety and National Security began the statutorily mandated three-year review of the Anti-Terrorism Act. This committee has been hearing from witnesses since February 2005.[1612] They are expected to release a report in the fall of 2005, which will likely also include findings on the use of security certificates. There is a concurrent Special Senate Committee on the Anti-Terrorism Act. They met in March 2005 to undertake a review of the provisions and operations of the Act.[1613] As of May 2005, the Committee has met with government ministers, the CSIS Director, and international and domestic experts on the current status of the threat environment.

Bill C-7, the Public Safety Act, received Royal Assent in May 2004. It is a controversial piece of legislation that took two and a half years and four attempts to pass. It amends approximately 23 existing Acts and creates a new statute to implement the Biological and Toxin Weapons Convention. The federal Privacy Commissioner raised objections to two aspects of the Bill: clauses requiring air carriers and reservation system operators to provide detailed passenger information to law enforcement agencies without the consent of the passenger; and the provision amending PIPEDA to allow organizations to collect personal information without consent for the purposes of disclosing it to government, law enforcement, and national security agencies.[1614] As the Commissioner pointed out, this latter provision effectively permits private sector organizations to act as

---

[1610] British Columbia Civil Liberties Association website <http://www.bccla.org/pressreleases/04arar.htm>.

[1611] Commission of Inquiry into the Actions of Canadian Officials in Relation to Maher Arar <http://www.ararcommission.ca/eng/>.

[1612] <http://www.parl.gc.ca./committee/CommitteeList.aspx?Lang=1&PARLSES=381&JNT=0&SELID=e21_&COM=9242>.

[1613] <http://www.parl.gc.ca/38/1/parlbus/commbus/senate/Com-e/anti-e/05evb-e.htm?Language=E&Parl=38&Ses=1&comm_id=597>.

[1614] Jennifer Stoddart, Privacy Commissioner, Senate Standing Committee on Transport and Communications, Bill C-7, the Public Safety Act, 2002, March 18, 2004, available at <http://www.privcom.gc.ca/speech/2004/sp-d_040318_e.asp>. See also Privacy Commission of Canada's Annual Report, *supra* at 10-11.

agents of the state. It applies to all organizations subject to PIPEDA, not just airline carriers, and does not limit the amount of information that can be collected and disclosed without knowledge or consent.

In response to pressure for improved national security, Canada established a new Department of Public Safety and Emergency Preparedness (PSEPC) in December 2003. PSEPC is responsible for six agencies - the Royal Canadian Mounted Police (RCMP), CSIS, the Correctional Service of Canada, the National Parole Board, the Canada Firearms Centre, and Canada Border Services Agency, all of whom are focused on crime prevention, policing and enforcement, security and intelligence, corrections, border services and integrity, as well as emergency preparedness, management, and response.

In April 2004, the federal government announced its first ever National Security Policy.[1615] The government described the policy as "a strategic framework and action plan designed to ensure that Canada is prepared for and can respond to current and future threats."[1616] This policy included, among other things, the establishment of an "Integrated Threat Assessment Centre" to collect and analyze intelligence regarding national security, a Cyber-Security Task Force; and a Real Time Identification (RTID) Project for the RCMP that will allow fingerprints to be electronically recorded, transmitted and instantly verified against broader databases. The policy also calls for biometric passports and "smart borders." It also includes a cross-cultural Roundtable on Security, composed of persons from ethnic and religious minorities in Canada.

The April 2005 Progress Report on Canada's National Security Policy notes, among other things, that "improvements have been made to Canada's watch list system, to ensure that watch lists are better integrated and updated on a real time basis and that appropriate safeguards are in place to respect the privacy rights of Canadians." It also notes that the cross-cultural Roundtable is serving "to better inform policy makers by providing insights into how national security measures may impact Canada's diverse communities and promoting the protection of civil order, mutual respect and common understanding."[1617]

As part of its response to the events of September 1, 2001, Canada now operates an Advance Passenger Information/Passenger Name Record (API/PNR)

[1615] Securing an Open Society: Canada's National Security Policy, April 2004, available at <http://www.pco-bcp.gc.ca/default.asp?Language=E&Page=publications&Sub=natsecurnat&Doc=natsecurnat_e.htm>.

[1616] Id.

[1617] Government of Canada, Securing an Open Society: One Year Later, April 2005, available at <http://www.pco-bcp.gc.ca/docs/ministers/deputypm/secure_e.pdf>.

database, through the Canada Border Services Agency (CBSA). Personal information about all airline passengers arriving in Canada is collected and stored in this database, and is used in the NEXUS and FAST border-crossing programs to allow pre-approved low-risk travelers and commercial shipments to move back and forth between Canada and the US. CBSA phased in the requirement to provide PNR data relating to persons on board flights bound for Canada between March 2003 and September 2004, and from February 2005 introduced a system of monetary penalties for non-compliance. As of July 2005, airlines will face potential sanctions for non-compliance. However the penalties were suspended for European airlines during the negotiation of the EU-Canada API/PNR agreement on the use of personal data provided by airlines to the border authorities of Canada. This agreement provides that airlines flying from the EU to Canada will have to transfer selected passenger data to the Canadian authorities to help identify passengers who could be a security, and in particular, a terrorist threat.

In July 2005, the European Parliament rejected the EU-Canada API/PNR agreement.[1618] The Members of Parliament (MEPs), although they agreed in principle with the content of the Canada agreement, argued that the signature of such an agreement should be postponed until the Court of Justice of the European Communities makes a final decision on the validity and legality of the EU-US PNR Agreement of May 2004,[1619] a case that is currently pending before the court.

The MEPs also argued that for this kind of agreement, the assent procedure should be used, as opposed to the consultation procedure, as it is the case now. Even if the MEPs decided to reject the Council's initial proposal for these procedural reasons, they consider the content of the agreement with Canada to be an "acceptable balance" between ensuring security and protecting personal data. They argued that the agreement to transfer personal information from citizens who travel into Canada would be acceptable, since Canada has a good legislative

---

[1618] Council decision on the conclusion of an Agreement between the European Community and the Government of Canada on the processing of Advance Passenger Information (API)/Passenger Name Record (PNR) data</Titre>
<DocRef>(COM(2005)0200 – C6-0184/2005 – 2005/0095(CNS) not yet published in OJ. Report from the Parliaments' consultation procedure, available at
<http://www2.europarl.eu.int/omk/sipade2?L=EN&OBJID=97771&LEVEL=4&MODE=SIP&NAV=X&LSTDOC=N>.
[1619] See <http://europa.eu.int/eur-lex/lex/LexUriServ/site/en/com/2005/com2005_0200en01.pdf>.

system on data protection and because the use of such data would be strictly limited.[1620]

The rejection of the agreement by MEPs is not binding for the Council.[1621] On July 18, 2005, the Council signed the EU-Canada API/PNR agreement with Canada Signature and entry into force of the Agreement will follow in early autumn 2005.[1622]

The current API/PNR database is substantially different from that originally proposed in 2002, as a result of criticism from the federal Privacy Commissioner and privacy advocates.[1623] Changes to the original proposal include purging information not required for customs purposes, such as what people order to eat and health information. All information will be accessible to customs officers in the first 72 hours after it is collected and then become more restricted over time. Only a limited number of intelligence officers will have full access to the database. Law enforcement agencies will also need a warrant to access information except when dealing with an immediate situation at the border or where a "real or apprehended threat" to Canadian security exists.

National and Biometric ID Cards

As of May 2005, there is no active initiative to adopt a national identification card in Canada. In 2003, the Minister of Immigration called for a public debate on the issues, and a parliamentary committee studied the matter. Although his primary reasons for the national ID card proposal are motivated by security concerns, the Minister noted other benefits from the cards such as combating identity theft, facilitating Canadian travel abroad, preventing racial profiling, and providing a reliable proof of identity at the border.[1624] The federal Privacy Commissioner appeared before the Committee and urged it to reject the proposal on the grounds of substantial privacy risks and lack of evidence of significant

---

[1620] *See,* "MEPs Reject the EU-Canada Agreement on Transfer of Personal Data," EP Press Release, July 7, 2005, available at <http://www.statewatch.org/news/2005/jul/ep-canada-pnr.pdf>.

[1621] *Id.*

[1622] "Commission Welcomes Council's Decision to Sign Agreement on the Transfer of Air Passenger Data to Canada"" Europa-Rapid- Press Releases, July 18, 2005, available at <http://europa.eu.int/rapid/pressReleasesAction.do?reference=IP/05/965&format=HTML&aged=0&language=EN&guiLanguage=en.

[1623] "Big Brother Travel Database Restricted," CBC News, April 9, 2003, available at <http://www.cbc.ca/stories/2003/04/09/privacy_030409>.

[1624] *Id.*

benefits to the Canadian public from such a card.[1625] More than 60 witnesses appeared before the Committee and almost all opposed the introduction of a national ID card. The Commissioner's office therefore urged Parliament to reject the proposal. Despite the privacy concerns associated with a national ID card, however, the possibility of implementation still exists.[1626]

While it has been less controversial than the national ID card debate, the implementation of biometrics in Canadian passports has been a matter of concern for Canadian privacy advocates. Biometrics[1627] are a "means of identifying a person or verifying the claimed identity of a person using unique physical or behavioral characteristics. Fingerprints, facial recognition, and iris scans are some of the biometrics commonly found in biometrics applications."[1628] Canada is an active member of the International Civil Aviation Organization (ICAO), which is developing international standards for biometric passports.[1629] Although biometrics have not yet been included in Canadian passports, several pilot projects have been launched since 2002,[1630] and the federal government has announced that it will start issuing passports with facial recognition biometric technology in 2005.[1631] According to the Canadian Passport Office, the need for biometric passports is increasing as the need for precise and efficient identification becomes more important for security reasons. No doubt, Canadian policy is influenced by the US requirement for electronic passports by October 2005 (for citizens wishing to enter the US without a visa).

[1625] Robert Marleau, "Why We Should Resist a National ID Card for Canada," Office of the Privacy Commissioner of Canada, September 18, 2003, available at <http://www.privcom.gc.ca/media/nr-c/2003/submission_nid_030918_e.asp>.

[1626] *See* Maria McClintock, "National ID Card on Its Way: Coderre," July 13, 2003, available at <http://www.canoe.ca/NewsStand/TorontoSun/News/2003/07/13/134409.html>.

[1627] *See generally,* Canada Internet Policy and Public Interest Clinic, Biometrics <http://www.cippic.ca/biometrics>.

[1628] Passport Office, Frequently Asked Questions – Biometrics <http://www.ppt.gc.ca/faq/index_e.asp#700>.

[1629] *See* Privacy International's webpage on biometric passports: <http://www.privacyinternational.org/article.shtml?cmd[347]=x-347-61327&als[theme]=Border%20and%20Travel%20Surveillance>.

[1630] As of the summer of 2003, Canadians are no longer permitted to smile in their passport photographs as the facial expression purportedly makes it more difficult for the face to be identified security screeners. Shawn McCarthy, "No Smiling! We're Canadian", The Globe and Mail, August 23 2003, available at <http://www.globetechnology.com/servlet/story/RTGAM.20030827.wsmile0827/BNStory/National/>.

[1631] Privacy Commissioner of Canada, 2003-2004 Annual Report, at 7, *supra*; Government of Canada Releases Comprehensive National Security Policy, April 27, 2004 <http://pm.gc.ca/eng/news.asp?id=186> (implementing the Passport Security Strategy, including facial recognition biometric technology on the Canadian Passport, in-line with international standards (USD 10.31 million)).

Public Opinion

In a speech in April 2005, the federal Privacy Commissioner presented public opinion research done in March 2005 by EKOS Research.[1632] The study revealed that Canadians were concerned about the use of their personal information by private sector companies and about the disclosure of their personal information to other countries, in particular, to the US The study also revealed that 70 percent of respondents believed that there is less protection of their personal information now than there was 10 years ago. "As Canadians become more aware of privacy concerns, they are increasingly challenging the flows of their personal information," the survey concluded.[1633]

Unsolicited E-mail

Until the spring of 2004, Canada had taken no action against the growing problem of spam, despite a number of private members' bills proposing various measures to combat this problem. In 2004, the federal government finally announced "An Anti-Spam Action Plan for Canada."[1634] This "action plan" included the creation of a SPAM Task Force comprised of experts from legal, business, government, and technical fields. The Task Force completed its work and presented a report to the Minister of Industry Canada on May 7, 2005. Its findings confirmed that a multi-pronged effort at both national and international levels is required in order to combat spam. The Task Force made numerous recommendations including the introduction of anti-spam legislation, the creation of a center of expertise, the development of industry best practices, a public education campaign and continued support of global anti-spam initiatives. The federal government is expected to act on this report in the fall of 2005.

Online Privacy

In May 2005, the Federal Court of Appeal ruled on the Canadian Recording Industry Association's (CRIA's) request to have Internet Service Providers (ISPs) reveal the identities of subscribers who had allegedly infringed copyright law by

---

[1632] Privacy Commissioner of Canada, Speech "Privacy and Technology: More Action Needed," April 20, 2005, available at <http://www.privcom.gc.ca/speech/2005/sp-d_050420_e.asp>.

[1633] *Id.*

[1634] Industry Canada, SPAM Task Force <http://e-com.ic.gc.ca/epic/internet/inecic-ceac.nsf/en/h_gv00248e.html>.

sharing music online.[1635] In BMG Canada Inc. v. John Doe,1636 the Court recognized the importance of online privacy, and set out a test that plaintiffs must meet in order to obtain court orders for the disclosure of subscriber identities.[1637]

Voting Privacy

In Canada, those 18 years or older may vote, but it is not mandatory.[1638] In 1997, Canada moved to create a centralized national voter registration database.[1639] The proposed centralization of voter registration into a national database raised privacy concerns.[1640] Canadians who are outside of the country and wish to vote must attach copies of government identity documents, which expose them to the possibility of identity theft and threatening the secrecy of their ballot.[1641]

Different direct recording electronic (DRE) voting methods have been used in a number of municipalities in Canada, including Montreal, Ottawa, Toronto, Winnipeg and Edmonton. The machines, which allow electors to indicate the candidate of their choice on an electronic screen, were used for the first time in Canada in 1996, during the municipal elections in Barrie (Ontario). Since then, the municipalities of Rivière-du-Loup, Rock Forest and La Plaine in Quebec have also experimented with them. There is an interest to be sure that information collected will be used only as intended. The consideration of publicly available

---

1635 CRIA argued for documents to be disclosed but they were relying on a rule that did not compel the creation of documents that did not already exist. Several of the ISPs noted that it would be too costly for them to keep the type of records that CRIA sought. Furthermore, there was no foolproof way for CRIA to demonstrate that the filesharers' Kazaa usernames would not be linked to an innocent subscribers' identity.

1636 BMG Canada Inc. v. John Doe, 2005 FCA 193, available at <http://decisions.fca-caf.gc.ca/fca/2005/2005fca193.shtml>.

1637 Noting that the need of plaintiffs to be able to sue those who are harming them through illegal activities must be balanced against the private rights of individuals, the court set out a test that requires a *bona fide* claim of illegal behavior, admissible and timely evidence linking the IP address in question to the impugned behavior, clear evidence that the information cannot be obtained from another source, and the collection of no more information than necessary for the purposes of the civil suit. In order to make out a *bona fide* claim, plaintiffs must show that they intend to bring an action for copyright protection based on the personal information that they obtain and that there is no other improper purpose for seeking the identity of these persons. As well, the court stated that, "caution must be exercised by the courts in ordering such disclosure, to make sure that privacy rights are invaded in the most minimal way". In particular, if a disclosure order is granted, specific directions should be given as to the type of information disclosed and the manner in which it can be used. In addition, courts should consider making a confidentiality order or identifying the defendant by initials only.

1638 CIA Country Fact Book, available at <http://www.cia.gov/cia/publications/factbook/geos/af.html#Govt>.

1639 SAIC Canada, press release, available at <http://www.saic.com/news/apr97/news04-03c-97.html>.

1640 Jean-Pierre Kingsley, Chief Electoral Officer, Canada, Statement before the House of Commons on Bill C-63, available at <http://www.elections.ca/content.asp?section=med&dir=spe&document=oct3096&lang=e&textonly=false>.

1641 Canada's Absentee Voting website <http://www.elections.ca/content.asp?section=ele&document=register&dir=38e/svr&lang=e&textonly=false#reg1>.

networks was rejected because of many issues associated with security and privacy.[1642]

The first municipal experiments with Internet voting took place on November 2003, in Markham, Ontario, voters were given a choice of voting online or by traditional ballot at advanced polls, while on election day, voting was done exclusively online. Eleven other Ontario municipalities in the counties of Prescott-Russell, Stormont, Dundas and Glengarry experimented with Internet and telephone voting at the same time, in an attempt to increase voter turnout by providing greater convenience in voting. Privacy concerns with Internet voting exist in the link between the voter's computer and the ISP. Once the computer is linked to the ISP, "hackers" could access and manipulate election results.[1643]

Some 36 percent of votes in the municipalities were cast online. The overall turnout rate was 51 percent. In Stormont, Dundas and Glengarry voter turnout rose five percent from 2000. Despite the apparent lack of immediate knowledge of privacy legislation, Canadians are increasingly concerned about their civil liberties and the protection of their privacy in response to the threat of terrorism. 75 percent of Canadians surveyed were not prepared to see law enforcement agencies afforded more power in order to fight terrorism, if it meant that their privacy and personal information would be compromised.[1644]

Access to Information

Access to information (both general information and personal information) held by government is governed by statutes at both the federal and provincial levels in Canada. The federal Access to Information Act is administered by a full time Information Commissioner. Each province has its own freedom of information law, administered by an Information Commissioner or other public official.[1645]

The federal Access to Information Act[1646] provides individuals with a right of access to information held by the federal public sector. The Act gives Canadians and other individuals and corporations present in Canada the right to apply for

---

[1642] "Technology and the Voting Process: Final Report," Elections Canada, Prepared by KPMG/Sussex Circle, June 15, 1998, available at <http://www.elections.ca/loi/vot/votingprocess_e.pdf>.

[1643] *Id.*

[1644] Ipsos-Reid Survey, Almost Half (45%) Believe Police Have Gone too far in Using Anti-Terrorism Powers, available at <http://www.ipsos-na.com/news/pressrelease.cfm?id=2043&content=full>.

[1645] *See* Alasdair Roberts, Limited Access: Assessing the Health of Canada's Freedom of Information Laws, April 1998, available at <http://qsilver.queensu.ca/~foi/foi.pdf>.

[1646] Access to Information Act, C. A-1, available at <http://www.canlii.org/ca/sta/a-1/>.

and obtain copies of federal government records. "Records" include letters, memos, reports, photographs, films, microforms, plans, drawings, diagrams, maps, sound and video recordings, and machine-readable or computer files. The Federal Court ruled that the government has an obligation to answer all access requests regardless of the perceived motives of the requesters. About 23,000 access requests for government records were received in 2002-2003.[1647] For the 2003-2004 period, government agencies received less than half the number of requests that they expected to receive in 1983, the Access to Information Act's first year of existence (50,000).

The Office of the Information Commissioner of Canada (OICC) can initiate a Federal Court review in limited circumstances relating to denial of access to records. The Information Commissioner can also investigate and issue recommendations, but does not have the power to issue binding orders. The Commissioner must investigate all complaints even if the government seeks to block him or her from so doing on the grounds that the complaints are made for an improper purpose. After numerous legal challenges brought by the federal government, it is now established that the Commissioner has authority to compel records from the Prime Minister's and ministers' offices.

In four cases completed in 2005, the OICC issued reports on the Minister of Transport, the Royal Canadian Mounted Police, the Prime Minister and Privy Council's Offices and the Minister of National Defence. All complaints in these four cases were determined to be well-founded, leading to recommendations for further disclosure, better records management and better education of officials.[1648]

For the 2004-2005 period, 1,506 complaints were lodged with the OICC (an increase from 1,331 the previous year). During the same period, 1,140 complaints were investigated, of which more than 99 percent were resolved without the intervention of the courts. The highest percentage of complaints was based on a refusal to disclose information (720 complaints for 2004-2005). The OICC also noticed a significant increase in the number of complaints relating to untimely delay in giving information, from 191 to 318 complaints, representing an increase from 14.4 percent to 21.1 percent. As of 1996, the Commissioner implemented measures to hold government departments accountable for the number of delay-related complaints that they received. This resulted in a steady decrease in these types of complaints, reaching an all-time low last year of 14.4

[1647] Office of the Information Commissioner of Canada, 2003-2004 Annual Report, p. 6.

[1648] Office of the Information Commissioner of Canada, 2004-2005 Annual Report, p. 35.

percent. The Commission warned that this year's increase may signal a recurrence of these types of complaints, thus close monitoring of government delays to access requests is necessary.[1649]

According to the OICC, the top five "complained against" institutions for which the Information Commissioner found the complaints to have merit include National Defence (132 complaints, 73 with merit), Royal Canadian Mounted Police (67 complaints, 96 with merit), Statistics Canada (96 complaints, 96 with merit) and Public Works and Government Services Canada (84 complaints, 57 with merit).[1650] The overall average turnaround time for a complaint in the 2004-2005 reporting period was 7.45 months, an increase from the average of 5.57 months in 2003-2004.[1651] The OICC has raised concerns about the increasing difficulty of meeting their objectives with limited resources.

In 2004-2005, the majority of well-founded complaints were resolved (61.1 percent) while 21.4 percent of complaints were found to be without merit. Of the 1,331 complaints that were closed, 32.8 percent of complaints related to institutions' refusal to disclose, 21.1 percent related to untimely delay in giving information. Other categories of complaints including time extensions, Section 69 exclusion, fees and miscellaneous complaints accounted for the remaining complaints. The number of complaints opened by the OICC increased to 1,506 in the 2004-2005 period from 1331 in the 2003-2004 period.[1652]

Under the tenure of the new Prime Minister Paul Martin in 2004, several initiatives were set in place to fulfill the Prime Minister's promise to promote public accountability of government officials. In response to the Attorney General's report on the mismanagement of the Federal sponsorship program, the Prime Minister proposed changes that made Crown Corporations and certain Officers of Parliament including both the Information Commissioner and the Privacy Commissioner, subject to the Access to Information Act. Not all changes were consistent in advancing the policies of transparency. In particular, the replacement of the Ethics Counsellor with Office of the Ethics Commissioner made the new office less transparent since the Commissioner will not be subject to the Access to Information Act, as the previous Counsellor was.[1653]

[1649] *Id.,* at 25, 28-29.

[1650] *Id.* at 26.

[1651] *Supra,* note 119, at 30.

[1652] *Id.* at 28.

[1653] Office of the Information Commissioner of Canada, 2003-2004 Annual Report, p. 3-4.

Another example of the government's distrust of the Access to Information Act is the proposed whistleblower legislation. The bill has faced significant criticism from the Commissioner based on its proposal to protect all information collected and compiled as a result of a whistleblower report, for a period of 20 years. The Commissioner has described this overbroad power as a means for "the government legal means to engage in cover-up and damage control."[1654] The criticism is rooted in the bill's disregard for a long-standing rule against anonymous accusations. The bill also makes amendments to the Privacy Act, removing a whistleblower's right to access their own personal information related to the report.[1655]

Canadians' access to information rights have been restricted by the Anti-Terrorism Act, which gives the Minister of Justice the authority to issue a secrecy certificate concealing information related to terrorism, and terminating any ongoing investigations by the Information Commissioner related to such information. An example of a post-September 11, 2001 restriction to access of information was the refusal of Transport Canada to disclose information about tests of airport baggage and passenger screening. Partly in response, the Senate Committee released a report entitled "The Myth of Security at Canada's Airports," where it found that the government's refusal to release security-related information: "acts against national security[18]. . . [because] [i]t shields incompetence and inaction, at a time that competence and action are both badly needed."[1656]

According to the Access to Information Review Task Force's June 2002 report, "Canadians are making relatively modest use of the Access to Information Act. After 20 years, the Act is still not well-understood by the public."[1657] The report goes on to state that the events of September 11, 2001 require one to balance the government's need to protect sensitive information with the public's right to access information and suggests 139 recommendations for modernizing access to information.[1658]

[1654] *Supra*, note 121, p. 10.

[1655] *Id.* at p. 11.

[1656] "The Myth of Security at Canada's Airports," Report of the Standing Senate Committee on National Security and Defense, January 2003, available at <http://www.parl.gc.ca/37/2/parlbus/commbus/senate/Com-e/defe-e/rep-e/rep05jan03-e.pdf>.

[1657] Report of the Access to Information Review Task Force. "June 2002 Report Access to Information: Making it Work for Canadians," June 2002, available at <http: www.atirtf-geai-gc.ca/accessreport-e.pdf>.

[1658] *Id.*

In May 2005, the results of a national access-to-information audit were released.[1659] The audit was conducted by 89 reporters from 45 newspapers across Canada, under the umbrella of the Canadian Newspaper Association. Reporters made access requests of several government offices to determine how well government officials are obeying access-to-information laws. The results indicated a wide range of disclosure practices, from poor compliance in Prince Edward Island to a compliance score of 93 percent in Alberta. The federal government scored only 25 percent. The report cites problems of red tape, poor disclosure, prohibitive fees, and incompliance with statutory time limits for responses across all levels of government. Information that is free of charge in some provinces and municipalities, and can cost thousands of dollars in others.

International Obligations Pertaining to Privacy

Canada is a member of the Organization for Economic Cooperation and Development (OECD) and relied on the OECD's 1980 Guidelines on the Protection of Privacy and Transborder Flows of Personal Data in the drafting of the federal Privacy Act of 1982.[1660] Canada also has observer status at the Council of Europe and although it was not a member, it was a key player in the negotiations on the Cybercrime Convention. It has signed, but not yet ratified the Convention.[1661]

Canada is preparing for closer cooperation with the European Police Office (EUROPOL), the EU agency whose mandate is to improve police cooperation and move criminal intelligence between the EU Member States. In September 2002, the Council of the European Union released a data protection report on Canada, where it concluded that no obstacle exists for the Council to start negotiations in preparation of an agreement on the transmission of data from the European Police Office to Canada that would meet the EU's data protection standards.[1662] The report noted that any agreement should bind both federal and provincial authorities in Canada.

[1659] Canadian Newspaper Association, News Release, May 28, 2005, available at <http://www.cna-acj.ca/client/CNA/cna.nsf/web/Public's+right+to+know+in+failing+health>.

[1660] Stephanie Perrin *et al.*, The Personal Information Protection and Electronic Documents Act: An Annotated Guide (Toronto 2001).

[1661] Council of Europe Cybercrime Convention, available at <conventions.coe.int/Treaty/EN/CadreListeTraites.htm>.

[1662] Data Protection Report: Canada, EUROPOL, 11647/02 (June 9, 2002).

Republic of Chile

Constitutional Privacy Framework

The Constitution of the Republic of Chile of 1980 recognizes the right to privacy. Article 19 secures for all persons: "Respect and protection for public and private life, the honor of a person and his family, as well as the inviolability of the home and of all forms of private communications. The home may be invaded and private communications and documents intercepted, opened, or inspected only in cases and manners determined by law."[1663]

Statutory Rules on Privacy

Chile is the first Latin American country to enact a data protection law. The Law for the Protection of Private Life came into force on October 28, 1999.[1664] It covers the processing and use of personal data in the public and private sectors, and the rights of individuals (of access, correction, and judicial control). The law contains a chapter dedicated to the use of financial, commercial and banking data, and specific rules addressing the use of information by government agencies. It also includes fines and damages for the unlawful denial of access and correction rights. Only databanks in the government must be registered. The law was slightly amended in 2002[1665] and modifies the Labor Code by providing that employers cannot condition hiring an employee to the lack of personal or economic debts.[1666]

The law has been criticized for certain ambiguities in its language, such as for the concept of "public access source" and "sensitive personal data." It has also been criticized for the weak protection measures for some categories of personal data. For example, no difference is made between "personal" and "sensitive" data, such as data revealing political opinions, religious beliefs, or health or sex life; and the

---

[1663] Article 19 (4) and (5) of the Chilean Constitution of 1980, available at
<http://www.georgetown.edu/LatAmerPolitical/Constitutions/Chile/chile97.html> (in Spanish).

[1664] Law for the Protection of Private Life (Ley sobre protección de la vida privada), Law No.19628 of August 30, 1999, Official Journal, August 28, 1999, available at http://www.cpsr-peru.org/bdatos/chile/privacidad/Ley%2019.628sobreProteccionVida%20Privada.rtf (in Spanish).

[1665] Law No. 19.812 that modifies the Law for the Protection of Private Life (Ley No. 19.812, que modifica la ley sobre protección de la vida privada), available at <http://www.cpsr-peru.org/bdatos/chile/privacidad/Ley%2019.812MODIFICA%20LEY19628Chile.rtf> (in Spanish).

[1666] The only exception will be if the employee will be administering money of the company or the employer. The new law also provides that the ""right to forget"" (the duration personal data can be stored) is reduced to five years for commercial debts and to zero years if the debt has been paid.

law lacks control mechanisms aimed at sanctioning illegitimate data processing by data controllers.[1667] The EU expressed concerns about the data protection law[1668], as this law does not contain restrictions for transfers of personal data to third countries, nor does it have a data protection authority.

In August 1996, the head of the *Dirección de Inteligencia Policial* (Dipolcar), the police intelligence service, was charged with authorizing a surveillance operation against the defense ministry official responsible for *Carabineros*, the militarized national police force. His resignation in disgrace allowed a greater role for the *Investigaciones*, the civilian security police, in anti-drug operations.[1669] In 1992, a surveillance center with 24-hour scanning devices was uncovered in downtown Santiago. It was run by an active army intelligence unit (DINE) incorporating former members of the secret police (the CNI) and, among other incidents, was found to have tapped into presidential candidate Sebastian Pinera's cellular phone[1670] and taped the calls of President Patricio Aylwin.[1671] The Army admitted to tapping telephones in order to comply with its mission, but reaffirmed that it "does not tap phones in an attempt to interfere with peoples' privacy."[1672] The scandal provoked the retirement of General Ricardo Contreras, head of the Army Telecommunications Command.[1673]

Chile's transition to democratic rule in 1990 did not eliminate personal privacy violations by government agencies. The Investigations Police – a plainclothes civilian agency that functions in close collaboration with the International Criminal Police Organization (Interpol) and with the intelligence services of the army, navy, and air force – keeps records of all adult citizens and foreign residents and issues identification cards that must be carried at all times.[1674] The

---

1667 Alberto Cerda, "La Autoridad de Control en la Legislación Sobre Protección De Datos Personales," tesis para optar al grado de Magister en Derecho Público, Universidad de Chile, Noviembre, 2003; Paula Jervis, Comentario Jurisprudencial: Intimidad y Tratamiento de Datos Personales en el Portal del Poder Judicial, Revista Chilena de Derecho Informático de la Universidad de Chile 1 (2002); Paula Jervis, Derechos del Titular De Datos y Habeas Data en la Ley 19.628, Revista Chilena de Derecho Informático de la Universidad de Chile 2 (2003).

1668 Political, Economical and Cooperation Pact of Association between Chile and the European Union, subscribed in Bruselas in November, 18, 2002, available in
<http://www.direcon.cl/frame/acuerdos_internacionales/f_bilaterales.html> (in Spanish).

1669 "Rows Grow over Security Services," Southern Cone Report, September 12, 1996.

1670 "Television Nacional de Chile," BBC Summary of World Broadcasts, September 26, 1992.

1671 "Army"s Bugging Centre Uncovered," Latin America Weekly Report, October 8, 1992.

1672 "Navy, Air Force Deny Allegations of Telephone Tapping," BBC Summary of World Broadcasts, September 28, 1992.

1673 "Chile Army to Take Action against Servicemen Involved in Telephone-Tapping Case," BBC Summary of World Broadcasts, November 27, 1992.

1674 Chile: A Country Report, 1994: United States Library of Congress.

personal data compiled during military rule was never destroyed. In January 1998, former dictator General Augusto Pinochet threatened to use "compromising information" from secret military intelligence files against those who were trying to keep him from becoming a Senator for Life, a position that would provide immunity from civil suits and public accountability for crimes that took place during his dictatorship.[1675] Under current law, the voter registration list is publicly disclosed and used for direct marketing purposes. In 1999, the United Nations Human Rights Committee criticized the requirement that hospitals report all women who receive abortions.[1676]

A 1996 privacy law sets penalties for those who infringe on the private and public life of individuals and their families. The privacy law has never been applied to the media.[1677]

On May 28, 1993, Law 19.223 that protects the right of privacy was enacted.[1678] This law, which modifies the Penal code, protects the right to privacy by sanctioning the person who, without authorization, illegally seeks to know information contained in a database or alters, destroys or discloses that information.

In November 2005, Law 19.423 added new provisions to the Penal Code related to the protection of the private life. Under this law, the collection of information by recording, wiretapping, or other secretive means, is prohibited. Such surveillance may be conducted in narcotics-related cases upon the issuance of a judicial order.[1679]

Two pending bills aim at reforming the Penal Code with respect to cyber crimes. The first one modifies Law No. 19.223 about cybercrimes and criminalizes the improper access to information included in a database and its destruction or

---

[1675] "Chile"s Ex-Dictator Tries to Dictate His Future Role," The New York Times, February 1, 1998.

[1676] Human Rights Committee Consideration of Chile"s Fourth Periodic report, March 25, 1999.

[1677] United States Department of State, Country Reports on Human Rights Practices 2002, March 31, 2003, available at <http://www.state.gov/g/drl/rls/hrrpt/2002/18324.htm>.

1678 Articles 161-A and 161-B of the Penal Code, introduced by Law No. 19.423, November 20, 1995, available at <http://www.cpsr-peru.org/bdatos/chile/privacidad/19423> (in Spanish); 36 B General Law of Telecommunications, available at <http://www.cpsr-peru.org/bdatos/chile/privacidad/36b> (in Spanish).

[1679] Ley No. 19.423, "Agrega disposiciones que indica en el Código Penal, en lo relativo a delitos contra el respecto y protección a la vida privada y pública de la persona y su familia," November 20, 2005, available at <http://www.cpsr-peru.org/bdatos/chile/privacidad/delitosinformaticos> (in Spanish).

alteration, and damage to computer data.1680 The second bill introduces new crimes, such as the falsification of electronic documents and credit cards.1681

In August 2000, Decree No. 779 that regulates the registration of public sector-controlled databases was enacted.1682 The registration will have the responsibility of the Civil Registration and Identification Services.

In April 2002, a Law on Electronic Documents, Electronic Signature and Electronic Signature Certification Services (the Law) was enacted. The law establishes that contracts and agreements entered into through the use of electronic signatures shall be equally valid and effective as those executed on paper.[1683]

In January 2004, Law No. 19.927 was enacted.[1684] It establishes sanctions for the distribution, disclosure, importation and exportation of child pornography materials; it also increases the penalties and creates new powers for the Public Prosecutor (*Fiscal del Ministerio Público*), justices and police officers to enable them to intercept or wiretap all kinds of telecommunications and pursuant to a judicial order.

On June 29, 2004, the new Consumer Protection Law (No. 19.955) was enacted.[1685] This law is the first regulation that addresses some of the problems related to unsolicited commercial communications, also known as "spam." Article 28B establishes an opt-out system and provides that any electronic commercial email must indicate the name of the sender, the precise description of what is advertised, and a valid address where the consumer can send a message to avoid any future email. The same provisions are applicable to advertisements

---

1680 Project of Law that modifies the Law 19.223, and typifies criminal figures about the informatics - Bulletin 2.974-19 (Proyecto de ley que modifica la Ley 19.223 y tipifica figuras penales relativas a la informática - Boletín 2.974-19), available at <http://sil.congreso.cl/pags/index.html>.

1681 Project of Law who modifies the Criminal Code, with the object to receive the traditional criminal types, new criminal manners arisen from the informatics development - Bulletin 3083-07 (Proyecto de ley que modifica el Código penal con el objeto de recepcionar, en los tipos penales tradicionales, nuevas formas delictivas surgidas a partir del desarrollo de la informática – Boletín 3083-07). See generally <http://sil.congreso.cl/pags/index.html> (in Spanish).

1682 Supreme Decree No. 779 that approves the regulation of the registration of databases of personal data in charge of public organisms (Decreto Supremo No. 779, que aprueba el reglamento del registro de bancos de datos personales a cargo de organismos públicos), available at <http://www.cpsr-peru.org/bdatos/chile/privacidad/> (in Spanish).

1683 BNA World Data Protection Report, Vol. 2, Issue 7, July 2002, at 5.

1684 Law 19.927, January 12, 2004, modifies the Penal Code, the Code of Penal Procedure (*Código Procesal Penal*) and the Code of Criminal Procedure (*Código de Procedimientos Penales*).

1685 Ley 19.955, July 14, 2004, modifies the Law 19.496 about the protection of consumer's rights (Ley 19.955, 14 de Julio de 2004, que modifica la Ley 19.496 sobre protección de los derechos del consumidor), available at <http://www.sernac.cl/docs/texto_ley_del_consumidor.pdf> (in Spanish).

coming via regular mail, fax or telephone. These communications must indicate an easy mechanism to avoid future similar distribution.

In December 2004, a regulatory order[1686] provided that ministries that use electronic communications must keep records of all their communications for at least six years.[1687] The order does not give details about the meaning of "records." The regulatory order is not clear whether it mandates that public entities keep records only about traffic data or electronic communication content, too.

International Obligations

Chile signed the American Convention on Human Rights on August 20, 1990. Chile entered in October 2002 into a bilateral association agreement with the European Union (EU), by which the two parties agree on cooperating in the increase of the level of data protection on each other's sides.[1688]

People's Republic of China

Constitutional Privacy Framework

There are limited rights to privacy in the Chinese Constitution. Article 38 states that the personal dignity of citizens of the People's Republic of China (PRC) is inviolable and that insult, libel, false accusation or false incrimination directed against citizens by any means is prohibited.[1689] Articles 37 and 39 define,

---

[1686] A regulatory order is an administrative order given by the Minister General Secretary of the President.

[1687] Regulatory Order 77, January 13, 2005, approves the technical norm about the efficiency of the communications between State Administration organs and between those and the citizen. Available at <http://www.modernizacion.cl/1350/articles-70677_decreto_77.pdf> (in Spanish) (Decreto Supremo 77, de 13 de Enero de 2005, que aprueba norma técnica sobre eficiencia de las comunicaciones electrónicas entre órganos de la Administración del Estado y entre éstos y los ciudadanos).

[1688] Article 30 of the European Union-Chile Association Agreement, October 3, 2002, available at <http://europa.eu.int/comm/trade/issues/bilateral/countries/chile/euchlagr_en.htm>; *see also* Ministerio de Relaciones Exteriores – Dirección General de Relaciones Económicas Internacioles (Ministry of Foreign Affairs, General Directorate of International Economic Relations), Acuerdo de Asociación entre Chile y Unión Europea (Association Agreement between Chile and the European Union), available at <http://www.direcon.cl/frame/acuerdos_internacionales/f_bilaterales.html> (in Spanish).

[1689] People's Republic of China Constitution (Constitution Act, 1993) Chapter II (Fundamental Rights and Duties of Citizens), Article 38, translation available at <http://www.helplinelaw.com/law/china/constitution/china02.php>.

respectively, the protection of freedom of the person and the residence. Article 40 provides for the freedom and privacy of correspondence of the citizen.[1690]

Despite these provisions and those set out in more detailed laws, the Chinese government itself admits that it has room for improvement in applying *any* laws fairly and systematically. "The Chinese society is now in the process of transition from too much emphasis on the rule of person and insufficient emphasis on the rule of law to establishing concept of the rule of law, from supremacy of the power to supremacy of the law."[1691] The annual report of the US Congressional-Executive Commission on China for 2002 described the problem more bluntly: "An evaluation of human rights and the rule of law in China reveal a complex picture of contradictory trends and isolated improvements, overshadowed by the Chinese government's persistent violations of fundamental, internationally recognized human rights."[1692] In 2003, the Commission found that although some human rights developments are underway in China, "these changes have been incremental, and their overall impact has been limited."[1693] In March 2004, China included a promise to ensure human rights in the amendment of its Constitution.[1694] The amendment reflects a growing awareness of human rights concerns. However, the legal system, with its vague protections and the questionable independence of its judiciary, remains a source of human rights violations.[1695] Once again, in 2004, the Commission found that China had made limited progress in human rights related-issues.[1696]

Statutory Rules on Privacy

China's General Principles of Criminal Law include Article 252, which states that "[t]hose infringing upon the citizen's right of communication freedom by hiding, destroying, or illegally opening others' letters, if the case is serious, are to be sentenced to one year or less in prison or put under criminal detention."[1697]

[1690] Id. at Articles 37, 39-40

[1691] Human Rights Achievements in China, April 9, 2000
<http://swedenembassy.fmprc.gov.cn/eng/7068.html>.

[1692] Congressional-Executive Commission on China, Annual Report (2002), available at
<http://www.cecc.gov/pages/annualRpt/annRptCombo2.php>.

[1693] Congressional-Executive Commission on China, Annual Report (2003), available at
<www.cecc.gov/pages/annualRpt/2003annRpt.pdf>.

[1694] Human Rights Watch World Report: China, 2005; Congressional-Executive Commission on China, Annual Report (2004), available at <http://www.cecc.gov/pages/annualRpt/annualRpt04/index.php>.

[1695] Human Right Watch World Report: China, 2005, *supra*.

[1696] Congressional-Executive Commission on China, Annual Report (2004), *supra*.

[1697] Criminal Law of China, Part I, Chapter IV, Article 252 (October 1, 1997), available at
<http://www.eastlaw.net/service/datacnlaw/code/criminal/criminal.htm>.

Article 245 also provides that "[t]hose illegally physically searching others or illegally searching others' residences, or those illegally intruding into others' residences, are to be sentenced to three years or fewer in prison, or put under criminal detention."[1698]

However, law enforcement officials can issue search warrants on their own authority or else simply ignore legal requirements for independent oversight.[1699] "During the year, authorities monitored telephone conversations, facsimile transmissions, e-mail, text-messaging, and Internet communications. Authorities also opened and censored domestic and international mail. The security services routinely monitored and entered residences and offices to gain access to computers, telephones, and fax machines. All major hotels had a sizable internal security presence, and hotel guestrooms were sometimes searched for sensitive materials."[1700] The growing number of Chinese Internet sites accelerated the government's effort to tighten control on topics of discussion that are subject to monitoring.[1701]

Article 101 of the General Principles of Civil Law (1986) provides a "right of reputation" to citizens and corporations, stating "[t]he personality of citizens shall be protected by law, and the use of insults, libel or other means to damage the reputation of citizens or legal persons shall be prohibited."[1702] Article 246 of the provides a further basis for the protection of the right, stating "[t]hose openly insulting others using force or other methods or those fabricating stories to slander others, if the case is serious, are to be sentenced to three years or fewer in prison, put under criminal detention or surveillance, or deprived of their political rights."[1703]

In 1988 and 1992, as the result of "invasion of privacy" litigation, many journalists were imprisoned. This stimulated much academic and public debate on such issues as the role of journalism in matters of public interest, the proper balance between the right to privacy and the right to know, the appropriate

---

[1698] *Id.* at Part I, Chapter IV, Article 245.

[1699] US Department of State, China Country Reports on Human Rights Practices for 2002 (March 2003), available at <http://www.state.gov/g/drl/rls/hrrpt/2002/18239.htm>.

[1700] U.S. Department of State, China Country Report on Human Rights Practices for 2003 (February 2004), available at <http://www.state.gov/g/drl/rls/hrrpt/2003/27768.htm>.

[1701] Human Rights Watch World Report: China, 2005, *supra*.

[1702] General Principles of Civil Law, Article 101, available at <http://www.abailaw.com/mingshang/mingfa-english.htm>. This right would seem to roughly correspond with the American tort of invasion of privacy, as defined by Prosser, of placing a person in a false light in the public eye, see W. Prosser, The Law of Torts 863-866 (St. Paul: West Group, 5th ed. 1984).

[1703] General Principles of Criminal Law, Article 246, available at <http://www.cecc.gov/pages/virtualAcad/exp/explaws.php>.

ethical norms that should govern the conduct of journalists, and the freedom of the press. Some judicial decisions during this period emphasized these debates; for example, *Two Art Models v. The Organizers of the Exhibition* and *The Rock 'n' Roll Star Cui Jian v. The Writer Zhao Jianwei and his Publisher*.[1704] In 2004, the Chinese government continued to put its citizens in prison for exercising their freedom of expression, despite efforts to improve public relations after some law enforcement abuse cases.[1705]

The Law on the Protection of Minors (1991) provides that "no organization or individual may disclose the personal secrets of minors" and "with regard to cases involving crimes committed by minors, the names, home addresses and photos of such minors as well as other information which can be used to deduce who they are, may not be disclosed, before the judgment, in news reports, films, television programs and in any other openly circulated publications."[1706] The Law on the Protection of Rights and Interests of Women (1992) provides that "women's right of reputation and personal dignity shall be protected by law. Damage to women's right of reputation and personal dignity by such means as insult, libel or giving publicity to private affairs shall be prohibited."[1707] The Law on Lawyers (1996) requires lawyers to protect the personal secrets of their clients;[1708] the Law on Statistics (1983) provides that data collected from investigations shall not be disclosed without the consent of data subjects;[1709] and, the Provisional Regulations Relating to Bank Management (1986) provide that all information concerning the savings of clients shall not be disclosed.[1710]

These provisions taken together provide a minimum level of protection for the privacy of the citizen. However, in practice there has been a degree of confusion in applying these provisions cases concerning privacy. Consequently, the Supreme People's Court has issued two general judicial interpretations regarding the application of The General Principles of Civil Law to privacy. In *Opinions on Several Questions concerning the Implementation of the "General Principles of Civil Law of the PRC"* (1998) the Court held:

> The cases in which a person discloses personal secrets in written or oral way, or fabricates facts to publicly vilify the personal dignity, or

---

[1704] G. Zhu, The Right to Privacy: An Emerging Right in Chinese Law 18(3) Statute L. Rev. 208, 211 (1997).

[1705] Congressional-Executive Commission on China Annual Report (2004), *supra*.

[1706] Law on the Protection of Minors, Article 30; Zhu, *supra*.

[1707] Law on the Protection of Rights and Interests of Women, Article 39; Zhu, *supra*.

[1708] Law on Lawyers, Article 23; Zhu, *supra*.

[1709] Law on Statistics, Article 14; G. Zhu, The Right to Privacy: An Emerging Right in Chinese Law, *supra*.

[1710] Provisional Regulations Relating to Bank Management, Article 47; Zhu, *supra*.

damages the reputation by such means as insults and defamation of the others, and these acts have caused a certain negative impact on the persons concerned, shall be treated as an invasion of the right of reputation.[1711]

In the case *Yu Meifang* v. *Xinzhou Prefectural People's Hospital,* the Xinzhou Intermediate People's Court of Shanxi Province ordered the defendant hospital to pay Yu CNY 20,000 (~USD 2,400) in compensation for the anguish and humiliation she experienced when the hospital released false information about her medical condition.[1712] In February 2000, Yu had gone to the orthopedics section of the hospital for treatment. A doctor from the hospital tested her blood and suspected her of being HIV-positive. The hospital separated her from other patients immediately and informed both the Xinzhou Epidemic Prevention Station and the shopping center where Yu worked that she was infected with HIV. The shopping center subsequently refused to rent her retail space, and her business partner severed their partnership.

The Practicing Physician Law requires that doctors not reveal health information obtained during treatment. Doctors who violate the law face criminal penalties. In May 1999, the Ministry of Health, with the approval of the State Council, published an administrative order declaring that personal information about HIV/AIDS sufferers be kept secret and that the legal rights and interests of those people and their relatives should not be infringed. The Ministry of Health order asked all units and individuals in charge of diagnosis, treatment, and management work not to publish any personal information about HIV/AIDS sufferers such as the name and the family address. In 2001, Ministry of Health officials again called for more attention to the protection of the right to privacy of HIV/AIDS patients, following a court ruling that a hospital damaged a patient's reputation by releasing false HIV-related information about her.[1713]

The Maternal and Child Health Care Law requires premarital and prenatal examinations to determine whether couples have acute infectious diseases or certain mental illnesses (not including mental retardation) or are at risk for passing on debilitating genetic diseases. Based on medical advice, the Ministry of Health can recommend sterilization or abortion. At least five provincial governments have implemented local regulations seeking to prevent persons with

---

[1711] Opinions on Several Questions concerning the Implementation of the ""General Principles of Civil Law of the PRC" at para. 140; Zhu, *supra*.

[1712] "Patient's Privacy Rights Become an Issue in China," China Daily, July 17, 2001.

[1713] *Id.*

severe mental disabilities from having children.[1714] In August 1998, the government issued an "explanation" to provincial governments clarifying that no sterilization of persons with genetic conditions could be performed without their signed consent. In practice, most areas still do not have the capacity to determine accurately the likelihood of passing on debilitating genetic diseases.

In 2002, the China Psychiatric Association ceased listing homosexuality as a mental illness. Many gays and lesbians saw the move as a sign of increased government tolerance. Nonetheless, most gatherings of gays and lesbians still take place clandestinely.[1715]

There is no general data protection law in China and very few laws that limit government interference with collection, use and disclosure of personal information. Furthermore, there are no laws or regulations that limit the ability of Internet Service Providers (ISPs) in using and distributing personal data gathered through the Internet.

Article 6 of the Postal Law prohibits postal enterprises and staff from providing information to any organization or individual about users' dealings with postal services except as otherwise provided for by law.[1716] However, Article 21 permits postal staff to examine on the spot the contents of "non-letter postal materials." Mail handed in or posted by users must be in accordance with the stipulations concerning the content allowed to be posted; postal authorities have the right to examine mail, when necessary.[1717] However, in an age when e-mail is replacing letters as the preferred mode of written communication, China continues to ramp up massive and systematic surveillance of electronic communications.

Business travelers in China carrying laptops with "ordinary business software" are no longer required to register with the government, even if their computers have software with encryption capabilities, as they would have been under an unpopular regulation that the government reversed.[1718] Chinese law now only requires that certain special hardware and software products, primarily used for encryption, be registered with the government. Beijing, under pressure from the

---

[1714] 2002 US State Dept. Report, *supra.*

[1715] *Id.*

[1716] Postal Law of the People's Republic of China. (December 2, 1986) § 6.

[1717] *Id.* at § 21.

[1718] M. Forney, "China Relaxes Strong Rules on Net Encryption Programs," Wall Street Journal, March 13, 2000.

international community, also reversed a law requiring foreign businesses to register the keys to their encryption software or devices.

China has had a long-standing policy – dating back to the 4th Century B.C. – of keeping close track of its citizens. Even in those early times, many Chinese provinces were often successful in keeping records of their whole populations, so that they could be taxed and conscripted: "The state had the surname, personal name, age and home place of every subject and was also able to ensure that nobody could move far from home without proper authorization."[1719]

Freedom of association remains tightly controlled. All social organizations – from book clubs to congregations and visiting relatives – must be reported and registered with the Ministry of Civil Affairs. Any group that operates without registering risks prosecution.[1720] Failure to notify local authorities concerning visiting guests is also punishable by fine.[1721] Labor unions remain illegal.[1722] Government authorities systematically monitor[1723] some individuals and groups more closely than others, including advocates of democratic reform,[1724] human rights activists,[1725] minorities,[1726] and members of Falun Gong.[1727]

[1719] W.J.F Jenner, "China and Freedom" in D. Kelly and A. Reid, Asian Freedoms: The Idea of Freedom in East and Southeast Asia (Cambridge University Press, 1998).

[1720] M. Jendrzejczyk, "China: Human Rights and US Policy," Statement to Congressional Human Rights Caucus, May 15, 2001, available at <http://www.hrw.org/press/2001/05/chinastatement.htm>, eight members of a book club were arrested in May 2001 for failing to register with local authorities.

[1721] Regulations of the People's Republic of China on Administrative Penalties for Public Security, September 5, 1986.

[1722] China ratified the International Covenant on Economic, Social and Cultural Rights in February 2002, but reserved the right to freely organize and join trade unions.

[1723] For a discussion of possible modalities of class-based surveillance see J. Young, On the Fringe: State Surveillance and Differential Privacy Rights in Canada," Lex Informatica, April 2000, available at <http://www.lexinformatica.org/dox/panopticsort.pdf>.

[1724] In June 2000, authorities arrested Huang Qi, operator of a website on missing children at <http://www.6-4tianwang.com> for posting an article critical of the PRC leadership's handling of Tiananmen Square. On May 9, 2003, a Sichuan court sentenced Huang Qi to a five-year prison term on charges of subversion. See "Human Rights Defenders: Internet Dissenters," Human Rights Watch, 2003, available at <http://www.hrw.org/advocacy/internet/dissidents/7.htm>; see e.g. V. Pik-Kwan Chan, "Amnesty Says 200 in Prison over June 4," South China Morning Post, May 31, 2002.

[1725] No independent watchdog organizations were permitted in China, see Human Rights Watch World Report 2003 at "Defending Human Rights," available at <http://www.hrw.org/wr2k3/asia4.html#defending>.

[1726] Authorities monitor and regularly detain "splittist" activists in Tibet and Xianjiang, see Human Rights Watch World Report 2003, supra, at "Tibet," "Xinjiang."

[1727] T. Ee Lyn, "HK Bars More Falun Gong Members before Anniversary" Reuters, June 29, 2002, quoting one Australian Falun Gong member: "As soon as the authorities punched my name into the computer, [the Customs Officer] sent for guards right away and I was taken to a waiting room." R. Callick, "Out of China to Outer Melbourne" Australian Financial Review, June 21, 2002, documenting the story of Zeng Zheng, a Falun Gong supporter, who was arrested when she tried to explain the movement to her parents in an email, which authorities intercepted.

The Constitution provides for freedom of religious belief and the freedom not to believe; however, the government seeks to restrict religious practice to government-sanctioned organizations and registered places of worship, and to control the growth and scope of the activity of religious groups.[1728] It is the government's belief that religion should be tightly controlled in order to stop it from becoming a major source of political dissents.[1729] There are five officially recognized religions: Buddhism, Taoism, Islam, Protestantism, and Catholicism. For each faith, there is a government-affiliated association to monitor and supervise its activities.[1730] In 2003, a significant number of Christian, Muslim, and Tibetan Buddhist worshippers were arrested or detained.[1731] In June 2004, after the arrest of three bishops, the Vatican accused China of violating the right to religious freedom.[1732] In 2004, government repression of free religious belief and practice worsened, as many unauthorized places of worship were demolished and hundreds of unregistered believers suffered from continued government intimidation and harassment.[1733]

In late 2000, six million census takers attempted an accurate count of the number of Chinese citizens in the fifth national census, but privacy and economic concerns made citizens less cooperative than in the past. Zhang Weimin, a statistician at China's National Statistics Bureau, noted that "under the planned economy, people had no privacy. Everybody's income was the same across the country. But now [China has] a market economy, and people want to protect their secrets," adding that cooperation "will not be as good as before."[1734]

An estimated five million children go unreported because of China's "one-child policy," under which authorities heavily fine parents who have more than one child, subject to some exceptions. In the recent census, enumerators were so concerned with accuracy that they promised not to divulge census results to the police, the family planning commission or any other state organization. They also promised to burn the paper results once computer data entry was complete, in order to ease the fears that these records would be used for other purposes.[1735]

[1728] People's Republic of China Constitution at § 36, *supra.*

[1729] Human Rights Watch World Report: China: 2004, available at <http://hrw.org/english/docs/2005/01/13/china9809.htm>.

[1730] 2002 US State Department Report, *supra.*

[1731] Congressional-Executive Commission on China, Annual Report (2003), *supra.*

[1732] P. Pullella, "Vatican Accuses China of Religious Repression," Reuters, June 24, 2004, at A20.

[1733] Congressional-Executive Commission on China, Annual Report (2004), *supra.*

[1734] M. Cernetig, "Census Takers in China Can Count on Mistrust," The Globe & Mail, November 16, 2000.

[1735] "Massive Liscount Looms as Privacy Issues,"'One Child' Policies Hinder China Census," China Online, October 31, 2000.

Smart ID Card

Since 1985, all Chinese citizens over the age of 16 have been required to carry identification cards issued by the Ministry for Public Security. Identification cards include name, sex, nationality, date of birth, address and expiration date, which varies depending on the age of the cardholder. A new law regulating the use of ID cards, the Law of Citizen Identification Cards, went into effect on January 1, 2004.[1736] The law stipulates that no organization or individual has the right to check or hold a citizen's ID card except for the police, who are required to keep confidential any personal data obtained from the ID cards. However, public security agencies have the right to demand the production of identification at any time.[1737] Failure to register for an ID card, forging or otherwise altering a residence registration, or assuming another person's registration are all prohibited by law and punishable by fines. The law also mandates that citizens use the cards for such events as opening a bank account, purchasing flight tickets, and registering a marriage.[1738]

Smart-card development is well underway in China. Eight million of the new second-generation ID cards that were launched in March 2004 have been distributed nationwide in 2005.[1739] All citizens over 16 years old should receive the new cards by 2008.[1740]

In 2001, the city of Shanghai adopted a smart social security card designed to hold driving licenses, passports and even marriage registration. The information on the card comes from, and can be verified by, social security, police, medical insurers, public housing and other local authorities.[1741] Critics fear that government-issued smart cards can be used by the police to monitor citizen's activities, such as with the new Shanghai regulations that require Internet cybercafé customers to use swipe cards that allow administrators or others to record their national identity numbers and track their Internet use.[1742]

[1736] "Civil Rights Protected in New Chinese Laws, Regulations," Xinhua News Agency, January 1, 2004, available at <http://www.china.org.cn/english/2004/Jan/83740.htm>.

[1737] "Regulations of the People's Republic of China Concerning Resident Identity Cards" Xinhua News Agency, May 7, 1984.

[1738] "One Million Beijingers to Face Problems as ID Cards Expire," Xinhua General News Agency, December 24, 2004.

[1739] "New Chinese National ID Card Creates a Demand for Terminals," American Banker-Bond, May 2005.

[1740] "New ID Cards for All Citizens by 2008: Official." Xinhua News Agency, April 28, 2005.

[1741] "Electronic Social Security Card in Shanghai," BNA World Data Protection Report, September 2001, at 6.

[1742] H. French, "Despite an Act of Leniency, China Has Its Eye on the Web," The New York Times, June 26, 2004.

The US State Department reports that China's national identification system is being liberalized and the ability of most citizens to move around the country to live and work continues to improve.[1743] However, authorities have retained the ability to restrict freedom of movement through other mechanisms, and increased restrictions on movement during the year, particularly during politically sensitive anniversaries and to forestall Falun Gong demonstrations.[1744]

Censorship

It is well documented that the Chinese government is committed to monitoring media – online and in more traditional channels – for information that might harm unification of the country, endanger national security, or subvert government authority.[1745] In February 1999, the government announced the creation of the State Information Security Appraisal and Identification Management Committee that "will be responsible for protecting government and commercial confidential files on the Internet, identifying any net user, and defining rights and responsibilities. . . . [t]he move is intended to guard both individual and government users, protect information by monitoring and keep them from being used without proper authorization."[1746] In 2004, the Chinese government continued to impose restrictions on news reporting and publishing[1747] by censoring publishers and punishing unauthorized publishers. Authorities continuously oppressed the expression of opinions that the Party deemed objectionable.[1748]

In addition to Internet filters, which are dynamically updated and block sites on topics ranging from politics to religion to entertainment, the government monitors discussion forums in real time.[1749] A recent study documented in detail

---

[1743] 2002 US State Dept. Report, *supra.*

[1744] *Id.*

[1745] *See, e.g.,* Human Rights Watch, Freedom of Expression and the Internet in China: A Human Rights Watch Backgrounder (2001), available at <http://www.hrw.org/backgrounder/asia/china-bck-0701.htm>. *See also* Revised Provisional Regulations Governing the Management of Chinese Computer Information Networks Connected to International Networks § 6, May 20, 1997, which prohibits connection to international networks except through approved "access channels," available at <http://web.archive.org/web/20020613133506/http://msnhomepages.talkcity.com/NonProfitBlvd/cnlawyer/netregu0.htm>.

[1746] "China Forms Information Security Oversight Committee," Xinhua News Agency, February 12, 1999.

[1747] Congressional-Executive Commission on China 2004 report. *Supra.*

[1748] *Id.*

[1749] J. Zittrain and B. Edelman, "Empirical Analysis of Internet Filtering in China," available at <http://cyber.law.harvard.edu/filtering/china/>. See also J. Zittrain and B. Edelman, "Internet Filtering in China," IEEE Internet Computing, March 1, 2003.

government monitoring and censorship of discussion forums, where controversial postings are removed within minutes or hours.[1750] Both the study and other commentators question how long it will be possible to maintain such labor-intensive controls as Internet use increases in China,[1751] especially since people are reportedly successful in circumventing Internet censorship mechanisms to access foreign news sources.[1752]

In October 2000, the Ministry of Information Industry (MII) promulgated the Internet Information Services Regulations aimed at controlling Internet usage. Promoting "evil cults" was prohibited, as was providing information that "disturbs social order or undermines social stability." One regulation, covering chat rooms, requires all service providers to monitor content and restrict controversial topics. Content providers must keep files of what they post and who reads it, for 60 days. Other regulations make it illegal to store, process, or retrieve information deemed to be "state secrets" from international computer networks. Authorities do not consider persons who receive dissident e-mail publications responsible, but forwarding those messages to others is illegal.[1753]

Another provision of the regulations requires Internet café patrons to register with "software managers" and produce a valid ID card to log on.[1754] The English chat room of sohu.com, partly owned by Dow Jones & Company, Inc., posted a list of prohibited topics including criticism of China's Constitution, topics which damage China's reputation, discussion that undermines China's religious policy, and "any discussion and promotion of content which PRC laws prohibit." The posting continues: "If you are a Chinese national and willingly choose to break these laws, sohu.com is legally obligated to report you to the Public Security Bureau."

In June 2005, the Chinese government announced a new initiative that closes down all non-officially registered websites and blogs.[1755] The new initiative was announced in a decree by the Ministry for the Information Industry (MII). The

---

[1750] A Stroehlein, "Internet Censors in China Loosening Their Grip," May 23, 2003, available at <http://web.archive.org/web/20041010021247/http://www.ojr.org/ojr/world_reports/1053660077.php>.

[1751] Rand Center for Asia-Pacific Policy, "China and the Internet: A Game of Cat and Mouse?" available at <http://www.rand.org/nsrd/capp/newsletter/03/mar.html>.

[1752] Congressional-Executive Commission on China, Annual Report (2004), *supra*.

1753 "China Enacts Sweeping Rules on Internet Firms," Reuters, October 2, 2000.

[1754] "US Embassy Beijing, Kids, Cadres and "Cultists" All Love It: Growing Influence of the Internet in China" (Beijing 2001), available at <http://web.archive.org/web/20030405111759/www.usembassy-china.org.cn/english/sandt/netoverview.html>.

[1755] Reporters Without Borders, "Authorities Declare War on Unregistered Websites and Blogs" The Internet Under Surveillance, Internet Freedom Desk, available at <http://www.rsf.org/rubrique.php3?id_rubrique=433>.

initiative requires all China-based websites to register by March 20, 2006. According to Reporters without Borders, the requirement is designed to identify those who are responsible for site contents and to control information that "endanger[s] the country."[1756] The initiative gives even more power to authorities to control online news more effectively.[1757]

The People's Bank of China (PBOC), China's Central Bank, is expected to build a national database by the end of 2005. The nationwide database system will collect personal data such as occupation, address, and financial credit, and link seven cities.[1758] The Central Bank is to compile a blacklist for those with bad credits. The regulation draft stipulates how citizens apply to correct information,[1759]

As signatories to the "Internet News Information Service Self-Discipline Pledge" of December 2003, major Chinese online news and information providers, including the largest websites sohu.com and sina.com.cn, agreed to cooperate with the authorities to regulate the Internet and "resist firmly the transmission of information that violates the fine cultural traditions and moral codes of the Chinese nation."[1760] A similar statement was signed in March 2002 by more than 300 companies offering Internet-related services in China. International signatories of the pledge ("not to produce or disseminate news . . . likely to jeopardize national security or social stability") include Yahoo, which provides e-mail services to many of China's estimated 87 million Internet users.[1761]

Article 7 of the Computer Information Network and Internet Security, Protection and Management Regulations states "the freedom and privacy of network users is protected by law. No unit or individual may, in violation of these regulations, use the Internet to violate the freedom and privacy of network users."[1762] However, Articles 8, 10 and 13 stipulate that individuals must be registered, that

---

[1756] Id.

[1757] Id.

[1758] "China to Build National Database for Personal Credit Information," Xinhua News Agency, March 17, 2005.

[1759] Id.

[1760] G. Kim and N. Tim, "Freedom vs. Regulation: You May Think You Can Do Whatever You Want Online, but Are You Really as Free as You'd Like to Believe?," Internet Magazine, July 1, 2004.

1761 Id.

88 "China's Internet Users Exceed 87 Million, People's Daily Online," August 11, 2004, available at <http://english1.people.com.cn/200408/11/eng20040811_152529.html>.

1762 Computer Information Network and Internet Security, Protection and Management Regulations, Article 7 (December 11, 1997), available at

<http://web.archive.org/web/20041015045802/http://www.qis.net/chinalaw/prclaw54.htm>.

transferring accounts is prohibited and all those engaged in Internet business are subject to security supervision, inspection, and guidance, including assisting in incidents involving law violations and criminal activities involving computer information networks."[1763] Articles 285 to 287 of the Criminal Code make unauthorized intrusions into computer systems illegal.[1764]

Monitoring of Cybercafés

By law, all Internet cafés must be licensed. However, due to the labyrinthine licensing requirements and registration – for both the operator and the user – and high demand, it is estimated that more than 60 percent of China's 200,000 plus Internet cafés remain unlicensed. Licensed cybercafés require patrons to provide identification and register each time they visit. It is unsurprising that a significant percentage of China's Internet users log on – using prepaid, anonymous phone cards – through unlicensed cybercafés.[1765] These cafés offer inexpensive access and an unregulated degree of freedom that might not otherwise be possible.[1766]

In 2001, more than 1,700 Internet cafés in Chongqing began operating "security management" software distributed by the local bureau of public security. The program filters materials deemed to be objectionable by the government and is capable of "capturing" computer screens and "casting" them onto screens at local public security bureaus.[1767] The program was designed in part to keep "unhealthy" information, such as cults, sex, and violence, off the Internet. Local police departments stated that strengthening the administration and control over the Internet cafés would benefit the healthy development of this fledgling industry.

In April 2001, the State Council ordered a three-month investigation into all public Internet service providers and announced that no new Internet cafés could be opened during that time. By June 2001, the *Shenzhen Legal Daily* reported that Chinese police had inspected more than 56,800 cafés. More than 6,000 of

---

1763 *Id.* at Articles 8, 10, 13.

1764 General Principles of Criminal Law, Articles 285-287, available at

<http://web.archive.org/web/20041009190241/http://www.qis.net/chinalaw/prclaw60.htm>.

1765 "China Launches Crackdown on 'Harmful' Internet Content," Yahoo News Singapore, May 1, 2002, available at <http://web.archive.org/web/20020807225418/http://sg.news.yahoo.com/020501/1/2otr6.html>.

1766 The anonymity provided by Internet cafés hearkens to the use of "big-character posters" of an earlier era and provides a unique opportunity for Chinese citizens – particularly students – to express personal opinions.

1767 Human Rights Watch, A Human Rights Watch Backgrounder (2001), *supra*. Called "Internet Police 100," the software comes in versions designed for home, cafés and schools.

these were disconnected and 2,300 shut down completely.[1768] The *Shanghai Daily* said the move was China's second major clampdown in a little more than a year. In May 2002, a devastating fire in an unlicensed café killed 25 people and prompted another nationwide crackdown.[1769]

In June 2003, China began to license Internet café "chains" that would serve as an alternative to the privately held cafés that were the target of previous crackdowns.[1770] This has been widely viewed as an attempt to promote consolidation in to the hands of fewer, larger, easier-to-control organizations. The Xinhua News Agency, the Chinese state news agency, reported that the government shut down 8,600 "illegal" Internet cafés between March and April 2004.[1771] In Fall 2004, the government announced that it was implementing an "Internet cafe technology management system" to cover the entire nation by 2005.[1772]

As the latest move to control online browsing in 2005, the Beijing Internet Safety Service Centre of the Beijing Public Security Bureau recruited 4,000 web watchdogs to put cybercafés and Internet service providers in Beijing under surveillance.[1773] Human rights groups estimated that in 2002 alone the Chinese government employed 30,000 people to monitor Internet traffic.[1774] More than 50 Internet users are serving prison terms for posting opinions online in 2004.[1775]

The monitoring of Internet activity has led to numerous arrests and long jail sentences for online activists. According to Reporters Without Borders, roughly 30,000 Chinese are employed maintaining China's Internet monitoring services and more than 36 individuals are in prison for expressing their views on the Internet.[1776] However, despite near-constant government monitoring and

---

[1768] "Chinese Man Sentenced for Posting Articles on Net," Digital Freedom Network, June 19, 2000, available at <http://web.archive.org/web/20030706075308/http://dfn.org/focus/china/liuweifang.htm>.

[1769] "Mass Shutdown of Chinese Internet Cafes," The Guardian, July 10, 2002, available at <http://www.guardian.co.uk/internetnews/story/0,7369,752802,00.html>.

[1770] "China Seen Tightening Control over Internet Cafes," Reuters, June 10, 2003, available at <http://web.archive.org/web/20041023102724/http://www.reuters.com/newsArticle.jhtml?storyID=2905528>

[1771] G. Kim and N. Tim, *supra*.

1772 US Department of State, China Country Report on Human Rights Practices for 2003, *supra*.

[1773] Shi Ting. "Search on for 4,000 Web Police for Beijing." South China Morning Post, June 17, 2005.

[1774] Neil Taylor. "Great Firewall Has Little Chance of Stopping Messages." South China Morning Post, July 6, 2004.

[1775] *Id.*; Amnesty International Report, China/Hong Kong, 2004.

[1776] "Living Dangerously on the Net," Reporters Without Borders, May 12, 2003, available at <http://www.rsf.fr/article.php3?id_article=6793>.

filtering, China's Internet usage continues to surge. As of 2004, more than 84 million regular Internet users were estimated, up 24 million from 2002.[1777]

The crackdown on Internet dissidents has gained speed recently. In 2003, China saw a 60 percent increase in the number of people detained or sentenced for Internet-related offences.[1778] In February 2003, an Internet critic of the government, Tao Haidong, was sentenced to seven years in prison.[1779] Sichuan website manager Huang Qi, founder of a site for missing persons from the 1989 Tiananmen crackdown, was sentenced to five years in prison.[1780] In May 2003, four student activists who posted essays critical of the government were given prison sentences of up to 10 years for subversion.[1781] Internet essayist Luo Yongzhong was sentenced to three years in prison after publishing articles on overseas websites calling for democracy and human rights.[1782] Reporters Without Borders named China "the biggest jail in the world for cyber dissidents," stating that the country has jailed 48 persons for their Internet writing in recent years.

In 2004, surveillance of electronic communications, and detentions for Internet-related offenses continued to rise, partly in anticipation of the fifteenth anniversary of the Tiananmen Square protests on June 4, 2004. In March 2004, Chinese dissident Ma Yalian was sentenced to 18 months in a "Re-education Through Labor" camp for posting an article to two Chinese websites reporting police harassment and abuse of several Chinese petitioners.[1783] Reporters Without Borders described the May 2004 trial of Chinese dissident Du Daobin, who was arrested for posting pro-democracy articles to the Internet, as "shocking," noting that he was denied access to his attorney and forced to plead guilty. In June 2004, after the case drew sharp criticism from human rights groups and served as a rallying cry for China's growing number of online commentators, a Chinese court announced that Du Daobin would get a suspended sentence instead of a long prison term.[1784] In China and abroad, some commentators quickly applauded what seemed like an official show of leniency

---

[1777] "China's Internet Users Exceed 87 Million," People's Daily Online, August 11, 2004, available at <http://english1.people.com.cn/200408/11/eng20040811_152529.html>.

[1778] M. Honan, *supra*.

[1779] "China Sentences Internet Writer," Baku Today, February 26, 2003, available at <http://www.bakutoday.net/view.php?d=2941>.

[1780] US Department of State, China Country Report on Human Rights Practices for 2003 (February 2004), *supra*.

[1781] "China Jails Four Internet Activists for Subversion," Reuters, May 29, 2002.

1782 US Department of State, China Country Report on Human Rights Practices for 2003, *supra*.

[1783] G. Kim and N. Tim, "Freedom vs. Regulation: You May Think You Can Do Whatever You Want Online, But Are You Really As Free As You'd Like To Believe?" Internet Magazine, July 1, 2004.

[1784] H. French, "Despite an Act of Leniency, China Has Its Eye on the Web," The New York Times, June 26, 2004.

toward Du Daobin, a prolific author of online essays on issues of democracy and free speech.[1785]

Human Rights Violations & NGO Activities

Online activists have continued using the Internet to express political opposition in 2005 with the same level of government censorship. Reporters Without Borders reported that Shi Tao, who worked for the daily Dangdai Shang Bao, in the southern province of Hunan, China, has been detained by Chinese authorities since November 2004 for posting a document related to the 1989 Tiananmen Square protests on a foreign website.[1786] The charge against him, according to Reporters Without Borders, needs international attention because the EU is considering lifting the arms embargo imposed on China after the 1989 massacre of pro-democracy demonstrators.[1787]

In 2005, other incidents included the sentencing of two cyber-dissidents: Kong Youping and Ning Xianhua. They were sentenced to 15 and 12 years in prison for posting articles online in support of the Chinese Democratic Party (CDP), an underground opposition group.[1788] He Depu, a member of CDP, continues to serve eight years imprisonment for signing an open online letter that appealed for political reform in November 2002.[1789] The Chinese government also arrested Zhang Lin, a cyber-dissident, for posting lyrics of a punk song.[1790] Human Rights in China (HRIC) questioned whether song lyrics constitute a serious threat to national security.[1791]

[1785] Reporters Without Borders, "Cyberdissident Zhang Lin to Go on Trial for Posting Articles Including Lyrics to a Punk Song Online," The Internet Under Surveillance, June 16, 2001. According to Xiao Qiang, director of the China Internet Project at the University of California at Berkeley, in the Du case the government is saying "Look, our actions may be nicer than in the past, but fundamentally, the judgment of the crime is unchanged, so don't be fooled, we are also willing to be harsh." Xia Qiang concludes "No matter how hard they try, though, it is a fact that the volume of online information is increasing vastly, and there's nothing the government can do about that. You can monitor hundreds of bulletin boards, but controlling hundreds of thousands of bloggers is very different."

[1786] Reporters Without Borders, "China: Journalist Faces Possible Life Sentences for Posting Tiananmen Document on Website," press release, February 4, 2005, available at <http://www.internet.rsf.org>.
[1787] Id.

[1788] Reporters Without Borders, "Two Cyberdissidents Handed down Harsh Prison Sentences," The Internet Under Surveillance, September 17, 2004, available at <http://www.rsf.org/rubrique.php3?id_rubrique=432>.
[1789] Reporters Without Borders, "Cyber-dissident He Depu Begins Third Year in Prison," The Internet Under Surveillance, October 4, 2004, available at <http://www.rsf.org/rubrique.php3?id_rubrique=432>.
[1790] Reporters Without Borders, "Cyberdissident Zhang Lin to Go on Trial for Posting Articles Including Lyrics to a Punk Song Online," supra.
[1791] Id.

The number of bloggers in China has grown from a few thousand in 2002 to anywhere from 100,000 to half a million in 2004. In March 2004, the government temporarily shut down four leading blogging sites – Blogbus.com, Blogcn.com, Blogdriver.com and Typepad – for allowing politically sensitive content to be posted.

In November 2004, Chinese authorities blocked access to Google's news website for about 10 days. The Chinese government, by blocking the site, has forced Internet users to use the Chinese-language version of the Google and Yahoo search engines that, unlike their non-Chinese versions, do not contain politically sensitive information. Reporters Without Borders has criticized the two American companies for cooperating with Chinese authorities in their censorship efforts.[1792] A similar cooperation also involved Microsoft with its Chinese government-compliant version of its blog tool MSN Spaces.[1793] According to Reporters Without Borders, the system automatically blocks certain words or phrases that contain "democracy," "June 4" (the date of the Tiananmen Square protests), "China + corruption," and "Dalai Lama."

Regulation of the Internet

China's Internet regulations and legislation are guided by the principle of "guarded openness" – seeking to preserve the economic benefits of new information and communication technologies, while guarding against foreign economic domination and the use of technology to coordinate anti-government activity.[1794] According to Human Rights Watch, China has enacted at least 60 sets of regulations aimed at controlling Internet content – or access to content outside of China – since commercial Internet accounts were first authorized in 1994.[1795]

Using technological assistance and equipment from Western companies such as Nortel Networks and IBM, China's Ministry for Public Security (MPS) passes all international connections through proxy servers at official gateways, where MPS

[1792] Reporters Without Borders, "Google Urged to React after Chinese Authorities Block Google News," The Internet Under Surveillance, November 29, 2004, available at <http://www.internet.rsf.org>; Reporters Without Borders, "Google-Yahoo Market Battle Threatens Freedom of Expression," The Internet Under Surveillance, July 26, 2004, available at <http://www.internet.rsf.org>.

[1793] Reports Without Borders, "Microsoft Censors Chinese Version of Its Blog Tool," June 15, 2005, available at <http://www.internet.rsf.org>.

[1794] G. Walton, China's Golden Shield: Corporations and the Development of Surveillance Technology in the People's Republic of China 9, (Rights and Democracy, 2001), available at <http://serveur.ichrdd.ca/english/commdoc/publications/globalization/goldenShieldEng.html>.

[1795] Human Rights Watch, A Human Rights Watch Backgrounder (2001), *supra*.

officials identify individual users and content, define rights, and carefully monitor network traffic into and out of the country.[1796] Derisively termed the "Great Firewall" by activists and journalists worldwide, the Ministry of Information Industry (MII) also uses the firewall to periodically filter access to Western websites, particularly media organizations, such as the Washington Post and Voice of America;[1797] human rights organizations, such as Amnesty International; or any other website deemed subversive.[1798] Recently, the government has taken public steps to relax filtering on a case-by-case basis.[1799]

The pace and scale of the development of the Internet has reduced the significance of the Great Firewall. Economic modernization is leading to exponential growth in the demand for international bandwidth and the sheer volume of Internet traffic today poses a serious challenge to state control at the network level. China observers hold out the existence of many anti-government postings on the Internet as evidence that censorship regulations are inconsistently enforced. Further, data from a 2001 Chinese Academy of Social Sciences (CASS) survey on Internet use shows that 10 percent of users admit to regularly using, and 25 percent occasionally using, proxy servers to defeat censorship measures.[1800] However, heavy restrictions on international connectivity remain a key principle in China's nascent Internet security strategy and penalties for Internet-related offences include life imprisonment or the death penalty.

At a recent security industry conference, the PRC government announced an ambitious successor to its Great Firewall strategy. Rather than relying solely on a national intranet, separated from the global Internet by a massive firewall, China will now build surveillance intelligence into the network, allowing it to "see," "hear" and "think."[1801] Content-filtration will shift from the national level to

---

[1796] Walton, *supra* at 9.

[1797] *See, e.g.,* J. Lee, "United States Backs Plan to Help Chinese Evade Government Censorship of Web," The New York Times, August 30, 2001, at A10. At other times, the Australian Broadcasting Corporation, The New York Times and the BBC have been blocked.

[1798] M. Cohn, "China Seeks to Build the Great Firewall; Controlled Modernization the Mantra," Toronto Star, July 21, 2001, at A01.

[1799] The Australian Broadcasting Corporation and The New York Times were separately removed from the "blacklist" after complaints to the PRC government. *See, e.g.,* D. Miklovic *et al.,* "Internet Shutdown: 200,000 China Cybercafes Shut in a Day," Gartner Group, June 25, 2002, available at <http://www3.gartner.com/resources/107700/107751/107751.pdf>.

[1800] See China Academy of Social Sciences, Survey of Internet Use 2001, May 2001, available at <http://web.archive.org/web/20040716031655rn_2/www.cass.net.cn/webnew/index.asp>; see also US Embassy Beijing, China's Internet Information Skirmish (Beijing 2000), available at <http://web.archive.org/web/20030212205449/http://www.usembassy-china.org.cn/english/sandt/webwar.htm>.

[1801] Walton, *supra.*

millions of digital information and communications devices in public places and people's homes.[1802] This project is dubbed the "Golden Shield."

The technology behind Golden Shield is complex and is based on research developed largely by Western technology firms, including Nortel Networks, Sun Microsystems and others. The Golden Shield efforts do not signal an abandonment of other avenues of access and content control. For example, details are only beginning to emerge about a new "black box" device, derived from technology previously used in airline cockpit data recorders, and broadly similar to the Carnivore system developed by the US government.[1803] Once attached to a server at the ISP, Carnivore works by intercepting all incoming transmissions and then parsing out pertinent material, based on keywords provided by the administrator. Chinese Internet police would use the black box technology to monitor dissidents and collect evidence on illegal activities.[1804] Human rights advocates express concern that the Golden Shield project combines Internet filtering with others forms of surveillance technology, such as cameras with face-recognition software, fingerprint databases, and speech-recognition software to monitor telephone conversations, and may be used to create a computerized national network of citizens in the future.[1805]

Chinese authorities are increasingly making use of technology to control the circulation of news and information. After text messages helped to expose the national cover-up of the SARS health crisis in May 2003, the Public Security Ministry granted permission to a technology firm, Venus Info Tech, to market surveillance software for text messages to service providers.[1806] The technology, based on filtering algorithms created by the Chinese Academy of Sciences, enables service providers to monitor and block messages that contain keywords that authorities consider suspicious.[1807]

[1802] B. Rappert, "Assessing the Technologies of Political Control," 36(6) J. of Peace Research 741 (1999). The Golden Shield Project contemplates automated voice recognition through digital signal processing, distributed network video surveillance, and content-filtration of the Internet.

[1803] EPIC Carnivore FOIA Litigation page <http://www.epic.org/privacy/carnivore/>.

[1804] See, e.g., L. Weijun, "China Plans to Build Internet Monitoring System," China News Daily, March 20, 2001, available at <http://www.cnd.org/Global/01/03/20/010320-3.html>. For more on current discussions of Carnivore, see B. Krebs, "Groups Urge Ashcroft to Act On Carnivore, Privacy Issues," Newsbytes, May 3, 2001.

[1805] F. Guterl, "Surveillance," Newsweek, March 8, 2004.

[1806] Reporters Without Borders, 'Bware, SMS Unda Ctrl: [sic] Chinese Government Gets a New SMS Messaging Surveillance System," July 1, 2004, available at <http://www.rsf.org/article.php3?id_article=10870>.

[1807] Id.

New Mobile Technologies

According to China Telecom, China's nearly 300 million mobile phone users sent 220 billion text messages in 2003. In May 2004, the government announced that it would begin screening all mobile phone messages in order to protect the morality of the country's youth. In June 2004, China began filtering billions of mobile phone messages to ensure that people do not use text communications tools to undermine the one-party rule.[1808] During the first week of government inspections in June 2004, the government fined 10 text-message service providers and forced 20 others to shut down for not properly policing messages passing through their communications systems. Reporters Without Borders criticized the new surveillance system stating, "the Chinese authorities are making ever greater use of new technology to control the circulation of news and information. In the past months we have been witnessing a real downturn in press freedom particularly on the Internet."[1809] Human rights organizations have also expressed concern that the surveillance tool could be exported at a low cost to additional countries. In 2004, the Chinese government established a set of guidelines, the "Self-Discipline Standards on Content in Mobile Short Messaging Services," that allows mobile phone service providers to filter text messages on their networks.[1810] The system filters keywords or phrases, identifying text messages for pornography, spam, political rumors and opinions. Experts point out that such filtering will be ineffective due to the ever-increasing number of users.[1811] About 260 million Chinese mobile users sent 240 billion text messages in 2004 alone.

Unsolicited Electronic Messages ("Spam")

The Internet Society of China, a Beijing trade association, reported in March that China received 46 billion junk e-mails – 30 percent of all e-mail – in 2003, making it second to the US in spam receipt. Also, six percent of the Chinese population is reportedly online. China has no spam laws.[1812] Another group, the China Internet Network Information Center, also reported that 6.2 percent of the country was online – 80 million Chinese – which is up 35 percent from 2002.

[1808] "China is Filtering Phone Text Messages to Regulate Criticism," The New York Times, July 3, 2004, at A3.

[1809] Reporters Without Borders, "Bware, SMS Unda Ctrl: [sic] Chinese Government Gets a New SMS Messaging Surveillance System," *supra*.

[1810] Neil Taylor. "Great Firewall Has Little Chance of Stopping Messages," *supra*.

[1811] *Id.*

[1812] Andrew Yeh, "China Now World's Number Two Spam Recipient, After United States," Privacy and Security Law Report, Vol. 3, No. 13, March 29, 2004, at 361.

The group noted that there were just 620,000 Chinese Web users six years ago. About 70 percent of Chinese Web users are under 30.[1813]

In February 2004, the Chinese Ministries of Public Security, Education and Information Industry announced an effort to combat servers that send "junk e-mail that is reactionary, pornographic, involves gambling, or spreads computer viruses or other damaging content," and that the government was also considering anti-spam legislation.[1814] Early in March of that same year, National People's Congress deputies proposed anti-spam laws, but no legislation was passed.

In September 2004, government officials and representatives of Chinese Internet companies joined US online companies to issue anti-spam guidelines for China.[1815] An anti-spam center was also set up the same month, which has generated wide public support since its foundation, and has received about 10,000 consultations and complaints about e-mail, phone, or online forums.[1816]

In March 2005, Chinese and Australian Internet industry associations agreed on an anti-spam action plan. The plan, that the Internet Society of China (ISC) and Australia's Internet Industry Association (IIA) developed, prevents the indiscriminate blacklisting of ISPs by anti-spam groups.[1817] Other measures include an early warning system, a resource for information sharing, and training of network administrators in China.[1818] China is increasingly concerned about unsolicited e-mails.

New Developments

In 2005, the government's efforts to adopt privacy-related legislation has been ongoing. The draft of China's first personal privacy protection law was under review in January 2005. The effort is driven by the State Council Information Office to promote electronic commerce as well as to protect privacy. In March

---

[1813] Andrew Yeh, "Closely Monitoring Citizens' Internet Use, China Eyes Political E-Mail in Anti-Spam Plan," Privacy and Security Law Report, Vol. 3, No. 6, February 9, 2004, at 145.

[1814] Andrew Yeh, *supra*.

[1815] "Chinese Government, Internet Firms Issue Anti-spam Declaration." Kyodo News Service: Japan Economic Newswire, September 3, 2004.

[1816] "China Prohibits Accessing to over 60 IP Sections." Comtex News Network, November 17, 2004.

[1817] Murray Griffin, "China and Australia Agree to Measures to Tackle Spam, Develop 'Whiltelist' of ISPS." Vol. 4, No. 10, Privacy & Security Law, March 7, 2005, available at <http://subscript.bna.com/SAMPLES/pvl.nsf/0/e654d42ab874b92e85256fbb0004563b?OpenDocument>.

[1818] *Id.*

2005, the China's State Council also issued a document that urged the implementation of a series of laws in order to accelerate the development of e-commerce. Laws and regulations under consideration concern electronic signatures, privacy protection, security certification, and technical and regulatory standards for online payments.[1819]

In April 2005, a law on electronic signatures eventually came into effect; this is China's first e-commerce law. It enables contracting parties to use electronic signatures in legally binding documents with the same legal standing as the traditional handwritten signatures.[1820] Despite its benefits for the promotion of e-commerce, experts have commented that the law has limitations because it does not have provisions that cover the liability of service providers and the protection of consumers in the electronic commerce market.[1821] At present, there is no certification authority set up by the Chinese government.[1822]

On January 20, 2004, Shanghai, home to 16 million people, adopted "The Provisions of Shanghai Municipality on Open Government Information." This is China's first provincial-level open information legislation, and it could "represent the most comprehensive framework to date in China for accessing government-held information."[1823] The Shanghai provisions provide that citizens, legal persons and other organizations have the right to request "government information" from government agencies, including information about individuals themselves.[1824] Furthermore, the law imposes a legal obligation on government agencies to disclose information that is not covered by six exemptions for information.[1825] Although it remains to be seen how widely the exemptions will be interpreted, the new legislation is significant not only for advancing the

---

[1819] Shi, Ting. "Landmark Privacy Law Submitted for Review; Draft Legislation Sets out the Emerging Concept of Personal Data Protection," South China Morning Post, January 20, 2005.

[1820] "Ecommerce Legislation Comes into Effect," China Daily, April 1, 2005, available at <http://www.china.org.cn/english/BAT/124412.htm>.

[1821] Id. "Telecom Carriers Give Cold Shoulder to Digital Signature Act," Financial Times: Asia Africa Intelligence Wire, January 27, 2005.

[1822] Id.

[1823] J. Horsley, "Shanghai Advances the Cause of Open Government Information in China," April 20, 2004, available at <www.freedominfo.org/news/shanghai/shanghai_print.htm>.

[1824] The Shanghai Provisions define "government information" as information held in physical form by government agencies that is related to economic and social management and public services. The "right to know" does not appear in China's Constitution or any national law to date. However, the concept was recently cited in China's report "Progress in China's Human Rights Cause in 2003." See J. Horsley, supra. See also State Council Information Office, Progress on China's Human Rights Cause in 2003, March 31, 2003, available at <http://chineseculture.about.com/library/china/whitepaper/hr/blshr2003.htm>.

[1825] The six exemptions are: (1) a state secret, (2) a commercial secret, (3) an individual's private information, (4) related to a matter that is in the course of being investigated, discussed, or processed, (5) related to an administrative enforcement action that might influence the enforcement activity or endanger an individual's life or safety, or (6) otherwise exempted from disclosure by law or regulation.

---

concept of open government information in China, but also because of the inclusive process – that included posting a draft for public comment – by which the Shanghai provisions were formulated.

APEC Privacy Framework

China has participated in the Asia-Pacific Economic Cooperation's (APEC) privacy initiative. In February 2003, the APEC Privacy Subgroup was established with the mandate to develop privacy guidelines for all APEC Member Economies.[1826] China, as a member of this subgroup, was involved in the negotiations about the Privacy Framework in 2004. The participation in the subgroup signals the recognition by the Chinese government of the significance of international privacy regime. However, although Chinese government officials are aware of the development of the APEC Privacy Framework, the weak standard of the framework means that is unlikely to have any direct impact on Chinese legislation.

Open Government

In the wake of criticism over the Chinese government's handling of the 2003 SARS crisis, the Chinese State Council recently began work on a draft of China's first freedom of information legislation. The drafting of a national law on open government information has been placed on the National People's Congress legislative agenda for the current session running through 2007.

International Obligations

On February 28, 2002, China ratified the International Covenant on Economic, Social and Cultural Rights but took a reservation on the right to freely organize and join trade unions. China still has not ratified the International Covenant on Civil and Political Rights, which its government signed in 1998.[1827]

[1826] Symposium, "APEC Symposium on Data Privacy Implementation Mechanisms: Developing The APEC Privacy Framework," Santiago (Chile), March 2004. *See also* R. Tang, Privacy Commissioner for Personal Data, Hong Kong, "Asian Privacy at the Crossroads," IAPP Truste Symposium: Privacy Futures, June 10, 2004.
[1827] Its first review by the Committee on Economic, Social, and Cultural Rights was planned for April-May 2005. Human Rights Watch, 2004, *supra*.

Colombia

Constitutional Privacy Framework

The Colombian Constitution protects the right to privacy as a fundamental human right.[1828] Article 15 provides that:

- Every individual has the right to personal and family privacy, and to his or her good name *(buen nombre)*, while the State will respect them and must ensure they are respected. Similarly, individuals have the right to know, update, and rectify information gathered about them in data banks and in the records of public and private entities. Freedom and the other guarantees established by the Constitution will be respected in the collection, processing, and transfer of data.
- Correspondence and other forms of private communications are inviolable. They may only be intercepted or recorded pursuant to a court order and to formalities established by law.
- For tax or legal purposes, and for cases of inspection, supervision, and state intervention, the disclosure of accounting records and other private documents may be required within the limits provided by law.

Article 28 provides that "No one may be bothered in his person or family, sent to jail or arrested, nor may his home be searched, except pursuant to a written judicial order and to the law, and for reasons previously established by law."

The Court has recognized the right to privacy as a fundamental human right. It interprets this right as "protective of the private sphere of an individual and his family information that should not be transmitted to third parties, nor disclosed or published."[1829] The Constitutional Court has identified, on general terms, certain acts that are considered as part of private life by most people, by describing a wide range of facts, situations and phenomenons that an individual can usually protect from the knowledge of other people.[1830]

[1828] Constitution of Colombia, available at
<http://www.presidencia.gov.co/constitu/actoslegis/02del2003.htm> (in Spanish).

[1829] Constitutional Court. Ruling C-872, September 30 2003.

[1830] "When Article 15 of the Constitution establishes the right to personal and family privacy, it is obvious that it protects, in the first place, that which concerns the individual alone, such as his health, his sexual habits or preferences, his racial or family origin, his religious and political views. In addition, it protects the family orbit, what takes place within the family core and does not transcend the domestic sphere. Only under abnormal circumstances, and in order to return the situation back to normal, could the State, for instance, intervene, and

The Legislative Act No. 2 of 2003 modified certain articles of the Constitution in order to grant authorities powers to fight and prevent terrorism.1831 The Act allows authorities:

- to intercept or register mail and other forms of private communications without a court warrant, but on serious grounds only, and upon immediate notification to the *Procuraduría General de la Nación*,1832 and to be reviewed by a judge within the following 36 hours;
- to keep a register of the residence of every inhabitant on the Colombian territory;
- to conduct, without previous court order, arrests, raids and residence inspections, where there are serious motives related to the prevention of terrorist acts, but only upon immediate notification to the *Procuraduría General de la Nación*; and subject to a later review by a judge within the following 36 hours.

On September 9, 2003, the Prosecutor General's Office charged five members of Medellin's anti-kidnapping unit with illegally wiretapping the telephone lines of 2,000 individuals and NGOs between 1997 and 2000. "Paramilitaries and guerrillas routinely interfered arbitrarily with the right to privacy. They forcibly entered private homes, monitored private communications, engaged in forced displacement and conscription, and punished family members for the alleged violations of individuals."1833

On December 10, 2003, the Senate passed a constitutional reform named "Anti-terrorism Act" containing provisions that would authorize government authorities to intercept private communications without judicial authorization in cases related to terrorism. This Constitutional reform provides that: "In order to prevent terrorist acts, a law will regulate the form and conditions in which the authorities it indicates can, based on serious reasons, intercept or examine the

---

the right to privacy must yield, temporarily, before a higher right." Constitutional Court, Ruling T-623, November 19, 1996.

1831 Legislative Act N° 2 of 2003 of December 18, 2003 (Acto Legislativo 02 de 2003 que modifica los artículos 15, 24, 28 y 250 de la Constitución Política de Colombia para enfrentar el terrorismo), available at <http://www.cpsr-peru.org/bdatos/colombia/privacidad/> (in Spanish).

1832 An internal affairs agency, responsible for investigating reports of crimes or unlawful actions by government employees and recommending administrative sanctions such as suspensions, fines, and dismissals.

1833 See Bureau of Democracy, Human Rights, and Labor, Country Reports on Human Rights Practices 2003, Colombia, February 25, 2004, available at <http://www.nationbynation.com/Columbia/Human.html>.

correspondence and other forms of private communication, without previous judicial order."[1834] According to Amnesty International, this constitutional reform undermines human rights.[1835]

In June 2004, the House of Representatives enacted legislation implementing the new constitutional reform. Article 4 of the anti-terrorism law allows the army, the police and the Administrative Department of Security (DAS) to carry out searches, tap telephones and intercept private correspondence without a judicial authorization in the case of persons suspected of terrorist links. Because the "anti-terrorism statute" involves a constitutional reform and the "anti-terrorism law" involves fundamental human rights, they must receive the endorsement of the Constitutional Court before becoming law. On August 30, 2004, the Constitutional Court declared this reform unconstitutional due to procedural irregularities during the approval of the law in Congress.[1836]

Statutory Rules Related to Privacy

There is no comprehensive data protection legal framework for the private sector despite some congressional activity on data protection since 1986 with a view to having a full range of legislation that is compatible with constitutional and international data protection principles. Sectoral laws include protections for medical records[1837] and the inviolability of correspondence and other forms of private communications.[1838] The Criminal Code[1839] establishes penalties for the

---

[1834] Constitutional Reform No. 2 of December 18, 2003.

[1835] "This measure is not only flouting the government's repeated commitments to the international community to act within the rule of law and respect human rights, but also failing Colombia's obligation to guarantee basic human rights standards." See Amnesty International, "Colombia - Constitutional Reform Undermines Human Rights," December 11, 2003. AI Index: AMR 23/077/2003 (Public). News Service No: 281, available at <http://www.amnesty.org or http://news.amnesty.org> and at <http://www.nationbynation.com/Columbia/Human.html>.

[1836] Sentence C-818-04 sobre inexequibilidad del Acto Legislativo No. 02 de 2003, available at <http://www.cpsr-peru.org/bdatos/colombia/privacidad/> (in Spanish).

[1837] Law No. 23 of 1981, available at <http://www.cpsr-peru.org/bdatos/colombia/privacidad/> (in Spanish).

[1838] Decree No. 229 of 1995, available at <http://www.cpsr-peru.org/bdatos/colombia/privacidad/> (in Spanish).

[1839] Law No. 599 of 2000, available at <http://www.secretariasenado.gov.co/leyes/L0599000.HTM>.

following offenses: the illicit violation of communications[1840] and the offer, sale or purchase of suitable instrument to intercept private communications.[1841]

The State must guarantee the inviolability, privacy and secrecy of communications.[1842] Additionally, it must ensure "individual and family privacy as a fundamental right of the individual, against any interference of telecommunications activities."[1843] Secrecy of communications, particularly regarding postal, telegraphic, and telephone communications, is guaranteed,[1844] except in cases provided by the law or the Constitution and after the issuance of a judicial order. Telecommunications operators, on the other hand, must adopt all security measures required to guarantee the inviolability of communications and of users' personal data. Secrecy of telecommunications extends to voice and data communications, as well as sound and image documents, and the publication, or unauthorized use, of the existence or content of communications.[1845]

Privacy Case Law

Habeas data[1846] is also included in the Constitution. From 1992, the Constitutional Court, through more than 120 rulings, has defined the characteristics and the scope of *habeas data*, as well as the conditions under which the processing of data must be carried out. It has ruled that personal data (any information relating to an identifiable person) collected from individuals must be processed fairly and lawfully; collected and processed for specified, explicit and legitimate purposes; adequate, relevant and not excessive in relation to the purposes for which they are collected or further processed; and individual consent must be obtained before, or at the time of collection, and whenever a new use is identified for the personal information. The data controller must not

---

[1840] Article 192 of the Criminal Code provides that a person "who unlawfully removes, hides, misleads, destroys, intercepts, controls or cuts a private communication directed to another person, orillegally discover its contents, shall be punished with imprisonment of one to three years. If the author of that conduct reveals the content of the communication, or uses it for his own, or other people's benefi, or to cause damage to another, he or she shall be punished with imprisonment of two to four years." Law 599 issued in 2000, available at <http://www.cpsr-peru.org/bdatos/colombia/privacidad/> (in Spanish).

[1841] Article 193 of the Criminal Code provides that a person who, without permission of competent authority, offers, sells, or purchases suitable instruments to intercept private communications, shall be punished with a fine.

[1842] Article 8 of the Decree 1900 of 1990, available at <http://www.crt.gov.co/documentos/normatividad/decretos/DEC_1900_90.doc> (in Spanish).

1843 See Article 9, Decree 1900 issued in 1990.

[1844] See Article 10, Decree 1900 issued in 1990.

[1845] See Article. 7.1.2 of Resolution 575 of 2002, of the Commission of Regulation of Telecommunications (Comisión de Regulación de Telecomunicaciones) (CRT).

[1846] "Habeas data" is the right to know, update, and rectify information gathered about individuals in data banks and the records of public and private entities.

process any personal information in a way that has not been previously authorized; only collected to the extent necessary for the purposes identified; accurate and updated permanently; and kept in a form that permits identification of individuals for no longer that is necessary.[1847] In addition the data controller must provide customers with the right of access to such information, and the right to correct any inaccuracies in the data. Once collected, personal data may not be processed unless the customer has unambiguously given his or her consent.

About 85 percent of the Constitutional Court cases are related to complaints about the processing of data by financial companies (breach of contract cases). The other 15 percent are related to situations concerning, *inter alia*, the processing of health and social security data, as well as criminal records. In its rulings, the Court has incorporated guidelines contained in international documents issued by the United Nations and the European Union. A brief overview of some of the constitutional principles that must be observed throughout the processing of personal data follows:

> a. *Duties of the controller of personal data*: Given the risks involved with the inadequate use of personal data, the Court has established that controllers of data banks have a constitutional duty to correctly manage the databases, and protect them and the personal data, or other socially relevant information, they hold,[1848] with the objective of preventing their alteration, loss, or unauthorized processing and access.[1849]

The Court has also prescribed those controllers to:

> 1. Abide by the constitutional rights of individuals during the collection, processing and transmission of data. As a result, data obtained, for instance through illegal means, shall not be incorporated into databases nor be transmitted. Likewise, the controller cannot include data pertaining to the individual's sphere of intimacy (*esfera íntima*);[1850]
> 2. Obtain consent from the data subject whose information is to be included in the database;[1851]
> 3. Inform the data subject of the insertion of his data in the bank;[1852]

[1847] For more information about data protection in Colombia, *see generally* Nelson Remolina, Central of Information, Habeas Data and Data Protection: Advances, Challenges and Elements for its Regulation, in Internet and Telecommunications Law 358-437 (Legis 2003).

[1848] See Constitutional Court, Ruling T-227 (March 17, 2003).

[1849] See Constitutional Court, Rulings T-049 of 2004 and T-846 of 2004.

[1850] See the following rulings by the Constitutional Court: SU 082/95 and 089/95.

[1851] See Constitutional Court, Ruling No. T-615 of 1995.

[1852] See Constitutional Court, Ruling No. SU-089 of 95.

4. Permanently keep the personal information up-to-date, without a request from the data subject, so as to ensure its integrity and accuracy;[1853]

5. Oversee that the information on the individual is complete, and that details or circumstances that could alter his good reputation are not disregarded;[1854]

6. Eliminate, without needing a request from the data subject, negative information that has expired;[1855]

7. Register true, unbiased, complete and sufficient information. In order to do so, extreme caution must be observed when inserting in a database that will be available to third parties, value judgments or personal appreciations about the data subject;[1856] and,

8. Compensate the damages caused by negligence or possible flaws in the processing and management of personal data.[1857]

b. The individual is considered as a *title holder of his personal data*: from its first ruling on the subject,[1858] the Court has made it clear that the individual, and not the controller of the database, owns his personal data. The citizen, as a titleholder of his personal data, is the bearer of legal rights and actions to claim from the controller, the loyal, legal and adequate processing of the information concerning him.

c. *Principle of usefulness*: This principle is established in order to restrict the possibility that personal data be recorded and stored without a legal purpose. This is why the Court has declared that "the collection, processing and transmission of personal data must be directed towards the accomplishment of a specific function, which is related to the satisfaction of a legitimate interest determined by the importance and utility of the information."[1859]

d. *Consent*: As a fundamental principle of the processing of personal data, the controller of the data bank must obtain consent from the data subject prior to the inclusion of the data in the database. If he fails to do so, the information must be immediately deleted.[1860]

1853 See, e.g., Constitutional Court, Rulings No. T-615 of 1995; T-096ª of 1995 and T-303 of 1998.

1854 See Constitutional Court, Ruling No. T-086 of 1996 and T-199 of 1995.

1855 See Constitutional Court, Ruling T-097 of 1995.

1856 See Constitutional Court, Ruling No. T-307 of 1999.

1857 See Constitutional Court, Ruling No. T-729 of 2002 and T-310 of 2003.

1858 See Constitutional Court, Ruling No. T.414 of June 1992.

1859 See Constitutional Court, Ruling No.C-185 of 2003.

1860 See Constitutional Court, Ruling No. T-002 of 1993.

e. *Right of access, correction and update*: The individual has the right to know the information relating to him that is stored in databases. The controller must guarantee that right. If the information is erroneous or incomplete, the individual can demand its amendment. According to the Constitutional Court, these rights comprise the citizen's ability to learn, immediately and completely, how, where and why there is information concerning him and, if the information is erroneous or incomplete, the individual can demand that the entity responsible for the system make the necessary amendments, clarifications or deletions, so as to preserve the fundamental rights that have been compromised.1861

f. *Accuracy*: Article 20 of the Constitution recognizes the right to inform and to receive "true and unbiased information." These conditions must be fulfilled in the processing of personal data. The information contained in a data bank must be permanently updated, and all the actions and circumstances related to the data must be included in the archive.1862 The amendment to and updating of information must be primarily carried out by the controller.1863

g. *Relevance and Purpose*: The Court considers that data must be collected for a "constitutionally legitimate purpose."1864 The Court has held that the principle of relevance implies that: "(i) the sole information that can be disclosed and solicited is that which is related to the functions, as attributed by law, of the soliciting institution . . . and that (ii) there must be a direct correlation between the required data and the subject matter that accounts for its collection."1865 The principle of purpose, on the other hand, calls for the information solicited and disclosed to be "(i) strictly necessary to accomplish the purposes . . . and (ii) used solely for the purposes authorized by law."1866

h. *Non-discrimination and sensitive data*: As a complement to the principle of legality of data, the Court has declared that every piece of information must be collected with a constitutionally legitimate purpose, which means that

---

1861 See, e.g., Constitutional Court, Rulings No. T-110 of 1993; T-303 of 1998 and T-321 of 2000. In Ruling T-309 of 1999, the Court stated that "the right to habeas data includes the right for every person to solicit and obtain, within a reasonable period of time, the amendment, insertion, limitation, cancellation, update or completion of the information that concerns him."
1862 See the following rulings by the Constitutional Court: T-615 of 1995; T-176 of 1995; T-443 of 1994; T-094 of 1995; T-094 of 1995; SU-089 of 1995; T-443 of 1994; T-552/97; T-096 of 1995; T-086 of 1996; T-097 of 1995; T-414 of 191992; T-008 of 1993, T-022 of 1993 and T-060 of 1903.
1863 See Constitutional Court's rulings No. SU 082 of 1995, SU-089 of 1995 and T-310 of 2003.
1864 Constitutional Court, Ruling No. T-307 of 1999.
1865 Constitutional Court, Ruling No. T-440 (May 29, 2003).
1866 The same argument is contained in Ruling T-307 of 1999.

"information on 'sensitive data' such as, sexual orientation, political views or religious dogma should not be collected, when such collection can lead, directly or indirectly, to a policy of discrimination and marginalization."[1867]

i. *Inappropriate and illegitimate practices*: The Court has held that the following acts and operations when processing personal data are inappropriate or illegitimate: the interconnection and indiscriminate disclosure of secret information or databases,[1868] the manipulation of information, the inclusion of incomplete data and the failure to update data.[1869]

j. *Notification to the data subject of negative information, prior to its dissemination or disclosure to third parties*: Whenever erroneous information is transmitted, the data subject will suffer damages and several of his human rights will be violated (for example, good reputation). The subsequent rectification of inaccurate information will not suffice to fully repair the damage caused with respect to the violated right. This is why the Court has stated that the individual has the right to amend erroneous information before it is published or transmitted.[1870]

k. *Expiration of negative information*: Ever since its first ruling on the subject,[1871] the Court has held that due to the data's own nature and relation to fundamental rights and liberties, they expire, they "cannot have the character of unmodified in nature,"[1872] and adverse data are not going to be perpetual[1873] or be kept indefinitely.[1874]

Unfortunately, there have been cases in which, despite the fact that the aforementioned period had passed, individuals remained registered in databases as defaulters.[1875]

1867 See Constitutional Court, Ruling No T-307/99.

1868 Constitutional Court, T-729 of 2002.

1869 Constitutional Court, T-814 of 2002.

1870 See Constitutional Court, Ruling T-592 of 1903.

1871 See Constitutional Court, T-414 of 1992.

1872 Constitutional Court, Ruling T-303/98.

1873 Constitutional Court, Rulings T-527 of 2000; T-856 of 2000 y T-268 of 2002, among others.

1874 Constitutional Court, Rulings T-414 of 1992; T-110 of 1993, T-303 of 1998; T-729 of 2002, T-814 of 202 y T-060 of 2003, among others.

1875 In one case, the fact that a woman had been late in her payments for seven months should have been kept only for 14 months according to the Court guidelines. She decided to file a complaint because the information was kept for longer than 48 months and the negative data had not been removed from the data bank. The Court found that the Banco de Occidente (Bank of the West) did not give Computec S.A. accurate information regarding the date when the citizen had paid her debt. Accordingly, the Court established that "such institutions are mandated to provide data banks with exact, complete and timely information, as well as any new

Even with the adoption of legal rules and case law on data protection, violations of privacy remain a concern. Colombian legislation has not kept up with the technology, leaving big gaps in protection. Unlike some other countries, Colombia does not have law that directly tackles Internet privacy.

Despite the constitutional recognition of *habeas data* in Article 15 of the 1991 Constitution, there is no law that further regulates *habeas data*. Since 1986, several projects have been proposed to Congress but none of them has resulted in the enactment of a law. In the absence of legislation, the *acción de tutela* (the possibility of requesting in court the protection of a fundamental right) and the right of petition are the only tools a citizen can use to demand the respect of *habeas data*.[1876]

Miscellaneous Developments

In April 2003, the press revealed that a US company, ChoicePoint, had allegedly collected personal data from Colombian government agencies or private companies and sold them to US government agencies and law enforcement. ChoicePoint sold the following information about Colombian people: "national registry files of all adult Colombians, including date and place of birth, gender, parentage, physical description, marital status, registration data, registration and passport numbers, as well as registered profession."[1877]

Law No. 527 of 1999 defines and regulates the access and use of data messages, electronic commerce and digital signatures, and establishes certification entities. The certification entities must, among other things, guarantee the protection, confidentiality and proper use of the information provided by the subscriber.[1878]

---

circumstances concerning the data subject so as to allow data banks to register the individual's complete history in their records and transmit true and complete information. Overlooking such duties will affect the clients as well as the data banks " Sentence T- 814 (September 3, 2002.

1876 In Colombia, if a person wishes to protect his fundamental rights with respect to the processing of personal data, she must first address the controller of the data bank and solicit the elimination, correction or amendment of the data. If the controller does not act upon the request, the citizen can turn to the judges and present an acción de tutela The judge must adjudicate within 10 days.

1877 El Tiempo, May 12, 2003; Portafolio, May 8, 2003 and Revista Semana, No. 1099, May 2003.

1878 Article 32 of Law No. 527 of 1999, available at <http://www.sic.gov.co/general.php?modulo=Normatividad/Leyes/Lista%20leyes> (in Spanish).

Open Government

Article 74 of the Constitution states that "Every person has a right to access public documents except in cases established by law." The main law regulating the access to public documents is Law No. 57 of July 5, 1985. Its Article 12, for example, grants every person the right to access and consult the documents that are held by the government, and to get a copy of them. However, people cannot consult or take a copy of documents that by law are considered exempted from disclosure (confidential information, medical records or documents that could have an impact on national security). The legal exemption is not effective 30 years after a document has been expedited. After that, the document acquires historical character and can be consulted by any citizen.[1879]

A key principle of the recent General Law of Public Archives[1880] is entitled "Administration and access." According to this law, the administration of public files is a duty of the State and a right of the citizens to get access to them.

International Obligations

Colombia signed the American Convention on Human Rights (the Pact of San Jose, Costa Rica) and the United Nations International Covenant on Civil and Political Rights. Colombia also ratified the Rome Statute of the International Criminal Court (ICC).

Costa Rica

Constitutional Privacy Framework

The Constitution of the Republic of Costa Rica[1881] does not protect privacy as such, but it allows for the protection of intimacy and the right to secret communications. Article 24 reads: "The right to intimacy, freedom and secret of communications is guaranteed."

[1879] Articles 13 and 28 of Law No. 594 of July 4, 2000, available at <http://www.cpsr-peru.org/bdatos/colombia/privacidad/> (in Spanish).
[1880] Law No. 594 of July 4, 2000, available at <http://www.cpsr-peru.org/bdatos/colombia/privacidad/> (in Spanish).
[1881] *Constitución de la República de Costa Rica de 1949*, available at <http://www.costaricalaw.com/legalnet/constitutional_law/constitenglish.html>

Besides setting out the right to intimacy, Article 24 of the Constitution has been recently amended[1882] to provide a thorough and strict framework for wiretapping, other invasions of the personal space, and violations of the basic right to private communications. Article 24 reads:

> Private documents and written, verbal or other communications of the inhabitants of the Republic are inviolable. However, a law, which enactment and amendment shall require the vote of at least two thirds of the entire membership of the Legislative Assembly, shall determine those cases in which courts of justice may order the seizure, search, or examination of private documents, whenever this is absolutely necessary to clarify matters submitted to their cognizance.

> Likewise, this law shall determine the cases in which courts of justice can order the interception of any communication and indicate the investigation of offences in which the use of this exceptional investigatory power can be authorized; and the period of time during which such an intervention shall be permitted. The law shall also determine the responsibilities and penalties of any officials who illegally apply this exception. Any judicial resolution under this provision shall be duly motivated and can be immediately enforced. Its application and control shall be the responsibility of judicial authorities and cannot be delegated . . .

> A special law, passed by two thirds of the entire membership of the Legislative Assembly, shall determine which other bodies of the Public Administration shall be authorized to examine the documents established by said law in the performance of their duties of regulation and control for public ends. This law shall also provide the cases when such an examination is appropriate.

> Any correspondence seized or information obtained as a result of the illegal interception of any communication shall have no legal effect.

Data Protection Bills

There is no statutory protection of privacy in Costa Rica. However, there are currently three different bills under discussion that attempt to regulate the automated processing of personal data and ensure the protection of information self-determination.

[1882] Law No. 7607, May 29, 1996, available at <http://www.pgr.go.cr/scij/>.

The first bill (No. 14778[1883]) amends the existing Law of Constitutional Jurisdiction.[1884] This law regulates the individual complaints to the Costa Rican Constitutional Court. At this time, the law recognizes three actions, *habeas corpus*, *amparo* and the unconstitutionality action.[1885] The new bill would create another individual complaint called *habeas data*, meaning "you should have the data."[1886] This type of complaint can be brought up by any citizen against any register to find out what information is held about him or her. That person can request the rectification, update or even the destruction of the personal data held, most of the time, regardless of whether the register is private or public. The legal nature of the individual complaint of *habeas data* is that of voluntary jurisdiction, which means that the person whose privacy is being compromised can be the only one to present it. The courts do not have any power to initiate the process by themselves.[1887]

The second bill (No. 14785[1888]) has a similar structure to the first one, as it attempts to reform the Law of Constitutional Jurisdiction to add the *habeas data* procedure to the list of individual constitutional complaints accepted by the Constitutional Court. In both projects, the *habeas data* complaint does not require the creation of supervisory bodies, as it uses the existing rights enforced by the Constitutional Court.

The third bill (No. 15178[1889]) is not a *habeas data* project, but rather an attempt to implement a European-style data protection regime in Costa Rica. The intellectual precursor of this project seems to emanate from a close reading of the European Union Data Protection Directive,[1890] as it follows closely its structure, and of several Latin American versions of data protection legislation based on the European model, such as legislation from Argentina and Chile.[1891] The

---

[1883] Proyecto de Ley, Adición de un capítulo IV a la Ley de Jurisdicción Constitucional (Recurso de Hábeas Data). Expediente N° 14.778, June 12, 2002.

[1884] Ley No. 7128.

[1885] A Mavcic, The Constitutional Review and its Development in the Modern World: A Comparative Constitutional Analysis (1999), available at <http://www.concourt.am/Books/harutunyan/monogr3/ogl.htm>.

[1886] See generally A Guadamuz, Habeas Data vs the European Data Protection Directive, 3 The Journal of Information, Law and Technology (2001), available at <http://elj.warwick.ac.uk/jilt/01-3/guadamuz.html>.

[1887] Id.

[1888] Adición de un nuevo capítulo IV, denominado del recurso de habeas data, al título III de la Ley de Jurisdicción Constitucional, Ley 7135, de 11 de octubre de 1989, Expediente N° 14785, June 18, 2002.

[1889] Ley de Protección de la Persona Frente al Tratamiento de Sus Datos Personales, Expediente No. 15178, March 17, 2003.

[1890] Directive 1995/46/EC of the European Parliament and of the Council of 24 October 1995 on the Protection of Individuals with Regard to the Processing of Personal Data and on the Free Movement of Such Data, OJEC L281/31 (1995), available at <http://europa.eu.int/comm./internal_market/privacy/law_en.htm>.

[1891] In Chile, see Ley sobre protección de la vida privada No. 19628, August 30, 1999.

definitions and principles of the bill are very similar to the EU directive and the Argentine data protection law.[1892] The bill also contains an export restriction principle and creates a new governmental supervisory authority, the *Agencia para la Protección de Datos Personales* (PRODAT), which will have very similar functions to that of European data protection authorities. The PRODAT will report to the Parliament, having the highest level of an agency has ever obtained by statutory law in Costa Rica. It will be empowered to create administrative rulemakings against individuals and corporations who violate data protection rules, including the power to fine and prohibit commercial activities for a limited time, and through a procedure respectful of due process.

It is unfortunate that all legislative efforts in Costa Rica are being spent on these three bills. The bills are assigned to the parliamentary Commission of Juridical Affairs and can only be examined after the discussion about the new Criminal Code.[1893] While the first two are very similar and can be implemented almost immediately after approval from the Costa Rican Parliament, the third bill is simply a parroting of the EU Data Protection Directive, with very little regard to the effectiveness of the European data protection model. This could have been an opportunity to marry both the *habeas data* style of data protection and the European style into a hybrid law that could have brought together the best of both regimes. However, some experts believe that it is not necessary to create a statute on *habeas data* in Costa Rica since the Constitutional Chamber of the Supreme Court of Justice has already created by case law a special kind of *amparo*, by regulating both material and procedural rules related to data protection.[1894] In any case, the h*abeas data* in other Latin American countries has been unable to prevent violations of privacy.[1895] It is very possible that the three bills will simply cancel each other out, and that privacy in Costa Rica will remain protected only by the case law of the Constitutional Chamber.

Wiretapping and Surveillance

Wiretapping can only be performed under special circumstances, as specified by Article 24 of the Constitution. Unauthorized violation of personal privacy by the

---

[1892] *Ley de protección de datos*, September 14, 2000, available at
<http://www.ulpiano.com/habeadata_diputados.htm>.

[1893] <http://www. asamblea.go.cr/cjuri.htm>.

[1894] Sala Constitucional, sentencias números 4154-97, 7175-97, 4347-99, 5802-99, 1345-98, 1119-00, 00754-02, 08996-02, 12698-03, etc., available at <http://www.poder-judicial.go.cr/scij/>.

[1895] Alfredo Chirino and Marvin Carvajal, El camino hacia la regulación normativa del tratamiento de datos personales en Costa Rica, Revista de Derecho Constitucional 4, 91 (2004). *See also* Cristina Sansoneti, Protección de datos personales en Costa Rica, available at <http://www.bufetenassar.com/boletin.htm>.

police or any official authorities is considered a criminal offense. Title VI, Sections I and II of the Criminal Code[1896] creates a number of offenses related to individual privacy. For example, Article 198 of the Criminal Code establishes prison sentences from one to three years for any person who intercepts or listens to verbal communications by any medium, or implants a listening device to intercept or listen to a private conversation. If the person committing the offense is a public official, the imprisonment will range between two and six years. In 2001, the Criminal Code was amended to make computer-related crimes illegal. Articles 196 bis, 217 bis and 229 bis[1897] punish the interception of electronic communications, computer fraud and hacking.

Wiretapping and surveillance can only be performed with a court order via the Public Prosecution Office, pursuant to the Code of Criminal Procedure.[1898] Similarly, entering into a home for a search and seizure must be ordered by a court, and any public officer who enters into a home without authorization will be subject to a suspension from work for a period between six months and three years.[1899] Article 196 of the Criminal Code specifies that any person who opens or intercepts a written communication destined to a third party will be subject to one to three years' imprisonment, regardless of the medium of the communication.

Open Government

Article 30 of the Constitution provides limited freedom of information rights. The article states, "Free access to administrative departments for purposes of information on matters of public interest is guaranteed. State secrets are excluded from this provision."

The right to access public information is not regulated in any statute. However, the Constitutional Chamber of the Supreme Court of Justice has recognized this right in its case law. It has held that access to public files is unlimited, except in those cases classified as "top secret," where information concerning individuals,

---

[1896] *Código Penal de la República de Costa Rica. Ley No. 4573*, March 4, 1970.

[1897] *Ley No. 8148 de 24 de octubre del 2001*, available at <http://www.pgr.go.cr/scij/index_pgr.asp?url=busqueda/normativa/normas/nrm_articulo.asp?nBaseDato=1&nNorma=47430&nVersion=1&nArticulo=2>.

[1898] *Código de Procedimientos Penales*, October 19, 1973.

[1899] *Código Penal, supra* at Article 205,.

groups or corporations is considered confidential, or when the information can seriously affect public security, public order or public health.[1900]

International Obligations

Costa Rica and Canada signed the "Joint Statement of Global Electronic Commerce Costa Rica – Canada."[1901] Both countries committed themselves to cooperate bilaterally to create a positive international environment by "ensuring safeguards to provide protection and increase confidence in the digital marketplace by addressing such issues as privacy, security, and consumer protection."[1902] These goals will be achieved by two means. First, both countries recognize that they will encourage the enactment of legislation protecting consumers' privacy. Second, both countries "agree to share information on the functioning of their respective data protection regimes."[1903] Although encouraging, the statement is only a declaration of principles without implementation or enforcement mechanisms of any kind. Costa Rican government officials and experts also signed "The Minimum Rules for the Diffusion of Information on the Internet," known as the "Rules of Heredia," which seek to protect the user of judicial services.[1904]

Republic of Cyprus

Constitutional Privacy Framework

The Constitution of the Republic of Cyprus[1905] was established in July 1960 and has the following two provisions regarding privacy:

> Article 15: (1) Every person has the right to respect for his private and family life; (2) There shall be no interference with the exercise of this right, except such as is in accordance with the law and is necessary in the

---

[1900] Sentencias de la Sala Constitucional números2002-03074, 2003-03489, 2004-09705, etc., available at <http://www.poder-judicial.go.cr/scij/>.

[1901] Joint Statement of Global Electronic Commerce Costa Rica - Canada, March 21, 2001, available at <http://www.comex.go.cr/acuerdos/comerciales/TLC%20Canada/ingles/e-commerce.pdf>.

[1902] *Id.*

[1903] *Id.*

[1904] <http://www.iijusticia.edu.ar/Reglas_de_Heredia.htm> and <https://www.agpd.es/index.php?idSeccion=349>.

[1905] Constitution of the Republic of Cyprus, of July 1960, non-official English version available at <http://kypros.org/Constitution/English/>.

interests of the security of the Republic, constitutional order, public safety, public order, public health, public morals or the protection of the rights and liberties guaranteed by this Constitution to any person.

Article 17: Every person has the right to respect for, and to the secrecy of, his correspondence and other communication, if such other communication is made through means not prohibited by law.

Statutory Rules on Privacy

The Processing of Personal Data (Protection of Individuals) Law of 2001[1906] came into force on November 23, 2001. The Law was introduced in the context of the harmonization process with the European Data Protection.[1907]

The Law applies to natural persons and covers automated, partially automated, and in some cases, non-automated processing operations, both in the public and the private sectors. It defines rights and obligations of controllers and data subjects, and sets the parameters for lawful processing of data. In order for the Law to be applicable, a data controller resident in the Republic must carry out the processing of personal data. The Law also applies at a place where Cyprus law is applied by virtue of public international law or by a data controller who is not resident in the Republic, who, for the purpose of processing personal data, has recourse to automated or other means existing in the Republic, unless they were used only for the purpose of transmitting the data through the Republic. The Law does not apply to the processing of personal data that is carried out by a natural person for the exercise of exclusively personal or domestic activities.

In April 2004, the Regulation of Electronic Communications and Postal Services Law of 2004,[1908] was enacted. Part 14 of the Law transposing the provisions of the Directive on Privacy and Electronic Communications (2002/58/EC),[1909] regulates the secrecy of communications and the use of traffic and location data, telephone directories and unsolicited communications. It particularizes and

---

[1906] Law No. 138(I)/2001.

[1907] Directive 1995/46/EC of the European Parliament and of the Council of 24 October 1995 on the protection of individuals with regard to the processing of personal data and on the free movement of such data, OJ L 281/31, available at <http://europa.eu.int/eur-lex/lex/LexUriServ/LexUriServ.do?uri=CELEX:31995L0046:EN:HTML>.

[1908] Law No. 112(I)/2004.

[1909] Directive 2002/58/EC of the European Parliament and of the Council of 12 July 2002 concerning the Processing of Personal Data and the Protection of Privacy in the Electronic Communications Sector (Directive on Privacy and Electronic Communications), available at <http://europa.eu.int/comm/justice_home/fsj/privacy/law/index_en.htm>.

complements the provisions of the Law for the Processing of Personal Data and provides for the protection of the legitimate interests of subscribers of electronic communications networks and services who are legal persons.

Section 98 of the Law provides for the appropriate technical and organizational measures to be taken by providers of publicly available electronic communications services and networks to safeguard the security of their services and networks. Section 99 provides for the confidentiality of the communications and related traffic data. With regards to traffic data, Section 100 provides that such data relating to subscribers and users processed and stored by the provider of a public communications network or publicly available electronic communications service must be erased or made anonymous when it is no longer needed for the purpose of the transmission of a communication.

However, the necessary secondary legislation for the Law on Electronic Communications has not yet been adopted. In 2004, Cyprus adopted the modification of the 2002 Law on Radio communications in order to transpose the new EU regulatory framework and introduced four pieces of secondary legislation in the field of radio communications.

To regulate the field of electronic commerce, Cyprus adopted in 2004 the Law on Certain Aspects of Information Society, and specifically Electronic Commerce, and Relevant Matters (the Electronic Commerce Law),[1910] as well as the Law on the Conclusion of Distance Contracts of 2000.[1911] The Electronic Commerce Law implements Directive 2000/31/EC of the European Parliament and of the Council of 8 June 2000 on certain legal aspects of information society services, in particular electronic commerce, in the Internal Market (Directive on Electronic Commerce). The Law aims at ensuring the free movement of information society services between the Republic and the Member States of the European Union relating to the establishment of service providers, commercial communications, the conclusion of electronic contracts, the liability of intermediaries, codes of conduct, out-of-court dispute settlements, means of legal protection and the cooperation between Member States.

Also in 2004, Cyprus adopted a Law on a Legal Framework for Electronic Signatures and Relevant Matters.[1912] It establishes the legal framework governing electronic signatures and certain certification-services for the purpose

---

[1910] Law No. 156(I)/2004.
[1911] Law No. 14(I)/2000).
[1912] Law No. 188(I)/2004.

of facilitating the use of electronic signatures and their legal recognition. It does not, however, cover aspects related to the conclusion and validity of contracts or other legal obligations that are governed by requirements as regards their form. Moreover, it does not affect rules and limitations in relation to the use of documents provided by other applicable legislation in force. The Law grants power to the Minister of Commerce, Industry and Tourism (the Competent Authority) to exercise control over and ensure the effective application of this Law.[1913]

Furthermore, the Cyprus Government intends to introduce "e-ID," or "electronic identity" smart cards to be used for electronic identification and authentication in public services. This project will be done in cooperation with other EU Member States in order to achieve a seamless access to public services across national borders. E-ID standardization or interoperability is essential in order to put in place key pan-European services such as cross-border company registration, electronic public procurement, job search, e-voting and e-health.[1914]

Data Protection Authority

The Commissioner for Personal Data Protection was appointed by the Council of Ministers in January 2002 for a four-year term. The Commissioner's Office was established in Nicosia on May 1, 2002.[1915]

The Commissioner is an Independent Administrative Authority. The Commissioner deals with the protection of personal information relating to an individual, against its unauthorized and illegal collection, recording and further use. The Commissioner also grants the individual certain rights, *i.e.* the right of information and access.[1916] The Commissioner is responsible for monitoring the application of the Processing of Personal Data Law.[1917]

Section 23 of the Law sets out the functions of the Commissioner. These include: the assistance to the drawing up of codes of conduct; the reporting of any contraventions to the law to the relevant authorities; the conduct of inquiries

---

[1913] *See* <http://www.ldlaw.com.cy/services/it_ecommerce.htm>.

[1914] EGovernment Fact Sheet Cyprus, available at <http://europa.eu.int/idabc/servlets/Doc?id=21004>.

[1915] E-mail from Michalis Kitromilides, Office of the Personal Data Protection Commissioner, Cyprus, to Ula Galster, International Policy Fellow, Electronic Privacy Information Center (EPIC), June 23, 2005 (on file with EPIC).

[1916] Commissioner's homepage
<http://www.dataprotection.gov.cy/dataprotection/dataprotection.nsf/index_en/index_en?opendocument>.

[1917] Processing of Personal Data Law, Section 18 (1).

following complaints or on his own initiative. The Commissioner is also competent to keep the Registers and grant the Licenses provided by the Law, issue directions, rules and recommendations, conduct administrative inquiries and impose sanctions for breaches of the Law. In 2004, with the enactment of Law 112(I)/2004, the responsibilities of the Commissioner were extended to cover the regulation of the use of traffic data, location data, telephone directories and unsolicited communications.[1918] Moreover, the Commissioner maintains cooperation with the data protection authorities of European Union and Council of Europe Member States.[1919]

Between June 1, 2004 and April 30, 2005, the Office of the Commissioner received about 60 complaints. Most of them refer to unlawful disclosure of personal information by the Public Sector and to the sending of unsolicited commercial communications by private companies.[1920]

At this early stage in the creation of the office of the Commissioner, its aim is to comply with the Law. A great number of complaints were resolved in favor of the complainants, while controllers voluntarily complied with the Commissioner's instructions for lawful processing of data, with no necessity to impose any sanctions.

In addition, the Commissioner's Office has issued two booklets with guidelines for the public. One educates the public about how to protect their personal data on the Internet and recommends data controllers create Web sites that comply with data protection rules. The other includes guidelines about the lawful use of video surveillance cameras.[1921]

Wiretapping and Surveillance Rules

The Protection of Secrecy of Private Communications (Call Interception) Law of 1996[1922] mandates that the Attorney General file for a court order before using wiretaps.

[1918] *Id.*

[1919] E-mail from Michalis Kitromilides, *supra.*

[1920] *Id.*

[1921] *See* Commissioner's homepage, *supra.*

[1922] Law No. 92(I)/1996.

Recent Developments

Cyprus transposed in April 2004 the European Directive on Privacy and Electronic Communications. As a result, the Commissioner's Office is the appropriate authority for enforcing anti-spam provisions.[1923] The Commissioner is discussing with Internet Service Providers about ways to cooperate in the fight against spam.

Cyprus has recently agreed to participate in the cooperation procedure concerning the transmission of complaint and intelligence information relevant for the enforcement of Article 13 of the Privacy and Electronic Communication Directive, or any other applicable national law pertaining to the use of unsolicited electronic communications. A Contact Network of spam authorities has put in place a cooperation procedure by which an authority will forward complaints to the authority of the country from which the e-mails originate for it to lead the investigations.[1924] Cyprus has also agreed to take part in the "Operation Spam Zombies" initiative of the United States Federal Trade Commission. The Operation is a new global effort to combat spam e-mail sent through hijacked computers, known as "zombies."[1925]

In 2001, the Government of Cyprus established an *ad hoc* Ministerial Committee for the development of the Information Society, comprising representatives of several Ministries and the Planning Bureau, the Telecommunication Authority and the Department of Computer Science at the University of Cyprus.[1926] The Committee has delegated authority to the Planning Bureau of the Republic to deal with e-commerce in Cyprus. The Bureau, which is the authority responsible for development policies in Cyprus, has taken the initiative to prepare a national strategy for the development of electronic commerce, including the introduction of the appropriate legal framework.[1927]

[1923] E-mail from Michalis Kitromilides, *supra.*

[1924] *Id.*

[1925] *See* <http://www.ftc.gov/bcp/conline/edcams/spam/zombie/partners.htm>.

[1926] Available at <http://europa.eu.int/idabc/en/document/1601/593>.

[1927] *See* Report on the Implementation in Cyprus of the Recommendations of the Charter for Small Businesses. Ministry of Commerce, Industry and Tourism, September 2002, available at <http://europa.eu.int/comm/enterprise/enlargement/charter/report_2003/cyprus20902.pdf>.

International Obligations

The Republic of Cyprus is a member of the Council of Europe and has signed and ratified the Convention for the Protection of Individuals with Regard to Automatic Processing of Personal Data No. 108.[1928] Cyprus has also signed and ratified the Additional Protocol to the Convention, regarding supervisory authorities and transborder data flows[1929] and the Council of Europe's Convention on Cybercrime.[1930] The Law ratifying the Cybercrime Convention provides for the establishment of criminal offences of the acts described in Chapter II of the Convention, such as illegal access, illegal interception, data interference, system interference, etc. and their respective penalties.

Czech Republic

Constitutional Privacy Framework

The 1993 Charter of Fundamental Rights and Freedoms provides for extensive privacy rights. Article 7(1) states, "Inviolability of the person and of privacy is guaranteed. It may be limited only in cases specified by law." Article 10 states, "(1) Everybody is entitled to protection of his or her human dignity, personal integrity, good reputation, and his or her name. (2) Everybody is entitled to protection against unauthorized interference in his or her personal and family life. (3) Everybody is entitled to protection against unauthorized gathering, publication or other misuse of his or her personal data." Article 13 states, "Nobody may violate secrecy of letters and other papers and records whether privately kept or sent by post or in another manner, except in cases and in a manner specified by law. Similar protection is extended to messages communicated by telephone, telegraph or other such facilities."[1931]

[1928] Convention for the Protection of Individuals with Regard to Automatic Processing of Personal Data No. 108, signed: July 25, 1986, ratified: February 21, 2002, entered into force on June 1, 2002, available at <http://conventions.coe.int/Treaty/Commun/ListeTraites.asp?PO=CYP&MA=10&SI=2&DF=22%2F08%2F2005&CM=3&CL=ENG>.

[1929] Additional Protocol to the Convention for the Protection of Individuals with regard to Automatic Processing of Personal Data, regarding supervisory authorities and transborder data flows, signed on October 3, 2002; ratified on March 17, 2004; entered into force July 1, 2004.

[1930] Signed on November 23, 2001; ratified on January 19, 2005; entered into force on May 1, 2005. Ratification Law No. 22(III)/2004.

[1931] Charter of Fundamental Rights and Freedoms, 1993, <http://www.psp.cz/cgi-bin/eng/docs/laws/charter.html>.

Statutory Rules on Privacy

On May 1, 2004, the Czech Republic joined nine other countries in entering the European Union (EU), formally linking itself to the EU and to the EU regulatory framework for data protection.[1932] In preparation for accession, the Czech Republic enacted a new act "On Personal Data Protection," which went into effect on June 1, 2000.[1933] The act replaced the 1992 Act on Protection of Personal Data in Information Systems.[1934] The act implements the requirements of the EU Data Protection Directive, granting exceptions from several key provisions to the police and intelligence services in matters of public and national security in accordance with the directive. Data controllers were required to register their systems and fully comply with the act by June 1, 2001. A May 2001 amendment exempted political parties, churches, sports clubs, and other civic organizations engaged in standard and legitimate activities from some of the act's requirements, such as registering their data processing activity or obtaining consent of individuals before collecting personal information.

Data Protection Authority

The act also established an Office for Personal Data Protection (the Office) as an independent oversight body.[1935] The Office is responsible for supervising the implementation of the act; maintaining a register of databases; investigating complaints; imposing fines for violations; conducting audits and providing consultations on data protection; and commenting on legislative proposals. Dr. Karel Neuwirt is the President of the Office, appointed to a five-year term that began September 1, 2000. The President of the Czech Republic also appointed seven independent inspectors, each position carrying a 10-year term.

A 2004 amendment to an act on records of inhabitants and birth certificate numbers granted the Office greater authority over cases involving unauthorized use of birth certificate numbers.[1936] The Office has gained new authority over

---

[1932] *See generally* <http://europa.eu.int/comm/enlargement/index_en.html>.

[1933] Act No. 101 of 2000 "On Personal Data Protection."

[1934] Act of April 29, 1992 on Protection of Personal Data in Information Systems (No. 256/92).

[1935] Office for Personal Data Protection homepage <http://www.uoou.cz/>.

[1936] Office for Personal Data Protection, Annual Report 2003, available at <http://www.uoou.cz/eng/vyroc_zprava.php3>.

spam and related issues by the Act No. 480/2004,[1937] which implements provisions of the EU Directive on Privacy and Electronic Communications.[1938]

Amendment of Banking Act[1939] exempted banks from some obligations set by Data Protection Act. As these obligations are set by Convention 108 and EU Data Protection Directive, the new law was found unconstitutional. But it was rectified by the next amendment in June 2004.[1940] This amendment also completes harmonization with EU Data Protection Directive (1995/46/EC). The amendment refines certain terms, as well as, introduces new terms in accordance with the EU directive. The amendment includes terms regulating the granting of consent for personal data processing, the relationship between data controllers and data subjects, the notification duty of controllers, and indemnification of data subjects for breaches of duty committed by data controllers or data processors.[1941]

During 2004, the Office for Personal Data Protection processed 1,972 registrations by data controllers, maintaining 2,4588 registration notices in total. The Control Department of the Office received 641 complaints and petitions. Office imposed 35 fees for breaches of the data protection act, totaling more than CZK 500,000 (EUR 51,000). The Office authorized 35 of the 52 requests for the transfer of personal data abroad. The Office also conducted 79 investigations.[1942] Inspections were aimed at police, financial institutions such as banks, city and municipality bodies, Internet business, schools, social and health care facilities, services connected with housing, land registry and other publicly accessible registers, as well as, self-government and public sector.[1943]

A number of complaints referred to excessive utilization of birth numbers based on an incorrect opinion that a birth number is an absolute identifier of a natural person and thus a natural supplement to the name and the surname. However, a fundamental change in this area was brought about by the adoption of an amendment to Act No. 133/2000 Coll., on Register of Population and Birth Numbers, through Act No. 53/2004 Coll., which came into effect on April 1,

---

[1937] Act of April 12, on records of inhabitants and birth certificate numbers (No. 133/2000).

[1938] E-mail from Ivan Procházka, Head of Department of Foreign Relations for the Office for Personal Data Protection, Czech Republic, to Clifford Chen, Law Clerk, Electronic Privacy Information Center, June 11, 2004 (on file with EPIC).

[1939] Act of March 13, amending Banking Act and some other laws (No. 126/2002).

[1940] Act of June 24, amending Data Protection Act and some other laws (No. 439/2004).

[1941] Office for Personal Data Protection, Annual Report 2004, available at <htto://www.uoou.cz/vz_2004.pdf>.

[1942] E-mail from Karel Neuwirt the President of the Office for Personal Data Protection, to Ula Galster, International Policy Fellow, Electronic Privacy Information Center, May 18, 2005, (on file with EPIC).
[1943] Id.

2004. The Amendment to the Act on Register of Population and Birth Numbers imposed supervisory duties on the DPA's Office in the area of management of birth numbers.[1944]

Complaints also followed similar patterns as in the past, including lack of awareness by controllers of their notification duties under the Personal Data Protection Act, unclear sources of data used to address clients in direct marketing, excessive use of birth certificate numbers, inappropriate copying and retention of personal documents, and publishing of lists of debtors as a method of exacting debts. One new issue that gained prominence was the installation of security equipment in dwellings (including monitoring of premises and recordings of arrivals and departures) and handling of personal data of sport matches spectators.

The Office for Personal Data Protection consists of 79 persons. From January 1 to November 31, 2004, when a change was made in processing of complaints in the framework of reorganization, the Control Department petitions were made through: (1)   written or electronic petitions, mainly of citizens and legal persons; (2) petitions by governmental authorities; (3) on the basis of personal visits by complainants; and (4) monitoring of the media;[1945]

The first task of the Control Department is to thoroughly review the complaints and establish the degree of their justification, by means of further enquiries aimed at obtaining objective information on the described state of affairs. This could be done either by monitoring of publicly accessible sources or by requesting further information or documents from the person submitting the complaint.[1946]

Due to the potential for frustration of evidence, which could occur in these cases, in 2004, the Control Department, as a rule, no longer addressed the entity against which the petition was aimed. Where the circumstances indicate that a criminal offense was committed, the matter is promptly submitted to the bodies actively engaged in criminal proceedings, and then the Control Department further cooperates with these bodies. The department continues to fully engage in resolving of these issues within its responsibility until the criminal proceedings are closed.[1947]

[1944] Id.

[1945] Id.

[1946] E-mail from Karel Neuwirt, *supra.*

[1947] Id.

In the course of supervision, the Office followed the principle that, as a rule, the identity of the complainant is not disclosed to third persons in the framework of the relevant enquiries; his or her identity is revealed only when necessary and after obtaining his consent. The Control Department also does not refuse to handle anonymous complaints.

In 2004, the Office used administrative punishment as a standard instrument in the framework of its supervisory activities, i.e. imposing fines for breach of the duties stipulated by the Personal Data Protection Act. No penalties have been imposed from the date of effect of the Personal Data Protection Act based on a statutory exemption, as the controllers and processors of personal data had the benefit of a transition period for bringing their processing of personal data into accord with the requirements of the new Act.[1948]

Financial penalty for proven misconduct usually accompanies remedial and indemnification measures and it facilitates remediation of the defective state of affairs in the course of the Office's supervisory activities. The Personal Data Protection Act still distinguishes between misconduct of controllers and processors, who are liable to a fine of up to CZK 10 million (CZK 20 million for repeated torts), and misdemeanors of natural persons, which are subject to a fine of up to CZK 25,000, or, as the case may be, CZK 50,000. The act does not stipulate the amounts of fine applicable for individual torts; however, consideration must always be taken of the general criteria stipulated by the act, including the nature, seriousness and manner of conduct, degree of fault, duration and consequences of the misconduct.[1949]

Certain Information Society Services Act [1950] introduced new duties in the sphere of dissemination of commercial communications. The aforementioned new competence, not only results in a substantial increase in the workload, but also imposes new requirements on human resources.[1951]

The Office for Personal Data Protection is responsible for ensuring that commercial communications sent by electronic means meet the set requirements and ensure that the opt-in principle is strictly complied with, i.e. that commercial communications are sent only to entities that express their prior consent thereto.

[1948] Id.

[1949] Id.

[1950] Act No. 480/2004 Coll.

[1951] E-mail from Karel Neuwirt, *supra*.

An entity sending a commercial communication must be able to demonstrate this consent at any time.[1952]

The Office actively engages in making the relevant information about its activities public. The Office holds regular press conferences. It also publishes two journals: the official one (five issues per year including the positions of the Office and European documents relevant for personal data protection. A quarterly is designed for the public at large. It provides information on the Office's activities, as well as the world wide news concerning personal data protection.[1953]

At the end of 2004, a campaign for citizens was launched. It involved publication of leaflets related to the Act on Personal Data Protection, rights and responsibilities of data subjects and risks that they ought to prevent. About 300,000 issues have been distributed (to the regional and local administrative bodies and high schools – with the cooperation of the Ministry of Education). The campaign has been supported by TV, radio stations and newspapers. The Office is also cooperating with media (354 publications and broadcasting items through the year 2004).[1954]

The Czech Republic's accession to the European Union on May 1, 2004 did not cause any radical changes in the activities of the Office. This was possible because of the Office efforts during the pre-accession period to cope with most of the EU/EC law harmonization and law application requirements. The accession nevertheless brought along some new challenges, tasks and opportunities.[1955]

In fundamental pre-accession documents of the European Commission, namely the 2003 Comprehensive Monitoring Report, the level of preparatory efforts of the Czech Republic for the EU membership in the area of personal data protection was highly appreciated. However, it was also stated that some fine-tuning of general Data Protection Act No. 101/2000 Coll., as well as several changes of the special data protection provisions of Act on Banks No. 21/1992 Coll. are still needed to be fully harmonized with Directive 95/46/EC on the protection of individuals with regard to the processing of personal data and on the free movement of such data. The Office prepared the draft amending both acts in September 2003 but, due to quite complicated legislative procedure when

---

[1952] *Id.*
[1953] *Id.*
[1954] *Id.*
[1955] E-mail from Karel Neuwirt, *supra.*

passing through the Czech Republic's Government and the Parliament, the amended acts came into force on July 26, 2004. There have been many more difficulties accompanying the transposition of Directive 2002/58/EC concerning the processing of personal data and the protection of privacy in the electronic communications sector. Only a few provisions concerning unsolicited commercial communications were included into the new Act No. 480/2004 Coll. (Certain Information Society Services Act) that took effect on September 7, 2004. Directive 2002/58/EC, together with several other directives of the "telecommunications packet," should be transposed into Czech law by the Act on Electronic Communications that has been drafted by the Ministry of Informatics of the Czech Republic. The new act is supposed to enter into force in June 2005.[1956]

The accession to the EU changed the position of the Office in the Article 29 Data Protection Working Party ("WP 29"), which is an independent EU advisory body. WP 29 is the main platform of the Office for cooperation with both the partner bodies from the EU member states and the European Commission. Before the date of the accession the representative of the Office had been invited only as observer to the WP 29 meetings; since then he has shared become a regular member.[1957]

Soon after the accession, the Czech Republic signed the Europol Convention and became member of Europol, which was followed by the membership of a representative of the Office in the independent Joint Supervisory Body of Europol. At the 31st meeting of JSB Europol held on December 20, 2004 the Office's representative (Inspector of the Office Mrs. Miroslava Matoušová) was elected Deputy President of this body. The same shift in the position from observer to full membership is awaited from May 2005 as regarded the Joint Supervisory Authority acting under the regime of the Convention on the Use of Information Technology for Customs Purposes.[1958]

The application of new supervisory competence of the Office in the field of unsolicited commercial communications under the new Act No. 480/2004 Coll. brought considerable enlargement of the agenda of handled complaints. At the end of 2004 authorities endowed with anti-spam enforcement powers from 13 European countries including the Czech Republic (represented by the Office) established CNSA – Contact Network of Spam Enforcement Authorities - as a

---

[1956] Id.
[1957] Id.
[1958] Id.

common platform for cooperation in investigating complaints about cross-border spam within the EU.[1959]

In mid-March 2001, the Office asked the Czech Statistical Office (CSO) to stop processing the results of the national census (carried out earlier that month) because of doubts as to the ability of the CSO to safeguard the data and because of the involvement of a private company, DELTAX Systems, in the processing.[1960] The Constitutional Court recently returned a verdict in favor of the Office, confirming the Office's power to intervene in and decide the disputed matters.[1961]

A privacy issue of recent importance is the status of medical registries in the Czech Republic The Czech Republic maintains a number of medical registries that consolidate information from groups such as oncological patients, expectant mothers, women who undergo abortions, people with professional diseases, and drug addicts.[1962] The legal status of these registries was uncertain, as they had existed on the basis of lower-level legal regulations that could not be maintained after January 2004. The Czech Medical Association advised doctors in February 2004 to refrain from providing data to the national registers to reduce the risk of liability for infringement of privacy laws.[1963] A bill allowing for continued operation of the registries and use of birth identification numbers passed the Chamber of Deputies but was vetoed by President Vaclav Klaus who preferred that registry data be entirely anonymous, citing privacy concerns echoed by the Data Protection Office. The Chamber of Deputies overrode President Klaus's veto in March 2004, however, creating the necessary legal basis for the medical registries.[1964]

Amendment of Prison Service Act[1965] proposed by the government at the end of 2003, contained new powers for prison officials to collect DNA samples from prisoners to be stored in the national DNA database. The bill did not contain clear specification of the offenses that would qualify the offender to be filed in

---

[1959] E-,mail from Karel Neuwirt, *supra*.

[1960] E-mail from Ivan Procházka, Head of Department of Foreign Relations for the Office for Personal Data Protection, Czech Republic, to John Baggaley, Law Clerk, Electronic Privacy Information Center, June 10, 2003 (on file with EPIC).

[1961] *See id.*

[1962] "Chamber Approves Medical Registers, Overriding Klaus's Veto," CTK National News Wire, March 24, 2004.

[1963] "CLK Appeals to Doctors not to Send Data Statements to Register," CTK National News Wire, February 20, 2004.

[1964] Act of February 20 amending Act on Public Health Care (No. 156/2004)

[1965] Act of December 13 amending Prison Service Act (No. 436/2003).

DNA database. This and some other controversial provisions triggered public debate that resulted in omitting these provisions from the amendment.

Bill of law on Protection of Classified Information[1966] also contains a provision of a different matter: it grants powers to secret services to require personal data from various public and even private databases (social security system, health insurance institutions, private insurance companies, banks etc.) for purposes of "security proceedings."[1967] Although, objections against this provision were raised by Coalition of NGOs (Iuridicum remedium, Transparency Intl ČR and Open Society) during the whole 2004 (in the phase of pre-parliamentary proceedings), in February 2005 the unchanged bill was submitted to the Parliament. However, coalition of above named NGOs prepared proposal to omit these provisions and asked several MPs to raise these proposals in legislative procedure. They were partially successful in Defense and Security Committee and rest of proposal changes are promised to be raised on the second reading on the plenary session. The bill also allows for some technical activities (certification of cryptographic or technical facility or electromagnetic rays measuring in order to qualify equipment to classified information disposal) to be done by private companies and sole entrepreneurs.

Law amending Act on Measures against Money Laundering (implementation of *acquis*[1968]), proposed by the government in March 2003, aimed to limit lawyer-client privilege and obliged solicitors to report their client´s "suspicious" financial transactions to the Ministry of Finance. Resistance and lobbying by Czech Bar Association led to less intrusive text of the Act. Suspicious activities are reported via Czech Bar Association serving as control body. This wording appears in the final text of the Act, which was approved in April 2004.[1969]

New Act on Electronic Communications[1970] was adopted by the Parliament in February 2005, implementing the "packet" of EU directives on telecommunications. The law contains an obligation for telecommunications providers to retain telecommunications data for a 12-month period, referring details to an ordinance issued by the Ministry of Informatics.

[1966] Documents of January 27, 2005, No. 880 and 881 of Chamber of Deputies, IV. election period.

[1967] Proceedings according to Law on Protection of Classified Information, which include screening of person who applied for certificate allowing access classified information.

[1968] Directive No. 91/308/EEC, as amended.

[1969] Act of May 7 amending Act on Measures Against Money Laundering and other laws (No. 284/2004).

[1970] Act of February 22 on Electronic Communications .

Wiretapping and Surveillance Rules

Electronic surveillance, wiretapping, and the interception of mail by the police are regulated under the criminal process law and require a court order.[1971] A judge can approve an initial wiretap order for up to six months. There are special rules for intelligence services. However, legal grounds for secret services' wiretapping do not guarantee that it is used only in necessary cases, as they rely on the discretion of secret service to decide whether the wiretapping violates fundamental rights and freedoms. In case it does not constitute such a violation, according to the secret service's judgment, no court permission is needed. The right to demand data on telecommunications traffic is granted to secret services by laws on secret services, and no court permission is needed.[1972]

Electronic surveillance, the tapping of telephones, and the interception of mail require a court order, in case when wiretapping is ordered by the Custom Administration[1973] and the Prison Service. Law on wiretapping, as a whole, lacks remedies, in case of wiretapping being illegal or when the court permission is void. Absence of proper public control of wiretapping (especially conducted by intelligence services) is often discussed as a concerning issue by politicians and media. In practice, the special commission of the Chamber of Deputies[1974] has almost no oversight power to deal with this issue. In addition, there are insufficient safeguards for interception of spaces outside individual's home (e.g. car), as no court permission is necessary.

While there have been past reports of illegal wiretaps, significant violations have not been reported in recent years. However, wiretapping became a hot topic in October 2004, when information leaked from police files that even the communications of the president of the republic were intercepted – when he engaged into telephone conversation with a man whose criminal proceedings were pending. Although this interception was founded on the court permission, bitter debate was stirred as a reaction to the police chief's public allegation asserting that "innocent people have no reason to oppose wiretapping, so they could stand for."[1975] In May 2001, the Foreign Ministry confirmed that bugging

---

[1971] Article 88 of Criminal Process Law.

[1972] Act of July 24 on Security and Information Service (No. 154/1994); Act of January 29 on Military Defense Intelligence Agency (No. 67/1992).

[1973] Act of December 15 on Customs (No. 13/1993); Act of November 17 on Prison Service and Justice Guard (No. 555/1992).

[1974] Commission for Intelligence Technics´ Control (Komise pro kontrolu zpravodajské techniky).

[1975] Zdeňka Kuchařová, "President Deems that Jiří Koláč Shouldn't Hold Post of Police President after His Statement on Wiretapping," BBC Radio October, 10, 2004, available at<http://www.radio.cz/cz/zpravy/59499>.

devices had been found in the Stirin conference center, which was used by the Ministry to host major negotiations during January 2000.[1976] In December 1999, former Health Minister Ivan David alleged that a bugging device was installed in his office a few months before his resignation.[1977] Also in 1999, following a letter Romani activists sent to the mayor protesting racial discrimination, there were complaints that the police conducted several searches without warrants of Romani homes.[1978] In 1996, the Security and Information Service (BIS) was accused of monitoring politicians and civic and environmental groups such as Greenpeace.[1979] In 1993, Justice Minister Jiri Novak's telephone was reportedly tapped.

There have been continuous attempts to legalize and to expand secret services' wiretaps. In 2001, there were attempts to grant powers to require information on telecommunications traffic and some other information from public bodies to the police and BIS by adding such provisions to a bill that dealt with a different subject matter (asylum law).[1980] This was prepared by members of the Lower Chamber's Security and Defense Committee and apparently coordinated by secret services. The Senate did not approve this part of the proposed law.

In April 2003, the government proposed an amendment to the Act on BIS,[1981] which would entitle BIS to require information on telecommunications traffic, and impose a duty on telecommunications service providers to have wiretapping equipment. The Chamber of Deputies rejected this bill.

In 2004, a debate about cameras and interceptions of space in children asylums and in young offenders institutions, which involved the Ministry of Education, had arisen. The Czech Ombudsman investigated the case. The Ministry of Education sustained its opinion that its earlier permission for audiovisual recording from canteens, corridors, health isolation rooms, leisure rooms and even bedroom (in one case) complied with the Czech Bill of Fundamental Rights[1982] as well as with the international human rights conventions. The majority of chiefs of the children asylums and young offenders institutions,

---

[1976] "Bugging Device Found in Czech Foreign Ministry Conference Centre," BBC Worldwide Monitoring, May 22, 2001.

[1977] US State Department, Human Rights Report, 1999, available at <http://www.state.gov/g/drl/rls/hrrpt/1999/index.cfm?docid=325>.

[1978] *Id.*

[1979] CTK National News Wire, November 8, 1996.

[1980] Document of April 30, 2001,No. 921 of Chamber of Deputies, III election period.

[1981] Document of April, 29, 2003, No. 308 of Chamber of Deputies, IV. election period.

[1982] Czech Bill of Fundamental Rights, Constitutional Law No. 23/1991 Coll.

however have removed the devices because of the Ombudsman's opinion that this practice is illegal and unconstitutional.

There is an increase in video surveillance; closed circuit television (CCTV) systems are being used both by private institutions and local governments. Although using CCTV and other camera systems for recording is considered to be processing personal data, almost no organization using such systems registered with the Office for Personal Data Protection, which is a legal duty imposed by the Personal Data Protection Act. The Office has no capacity for oversight and cannot penalize those routine breaches of law. Moreover, no legal duties concerning video surveillance conditions are embodied in any law (e.g. duty of notice, maximum period of storage of records, ban of data attachments, no discrimination on the basis of record) and no legal initiative is currently being prepared.

The Penal Code covers the infringement of the right to privacy in the definitions of criminal acts of infringement of the home,[1983] slander,[1984] and infringement of the confidentiality of mail.[1985] There are also sectoral acts concerning statistics, medical personal data, banking law, taxation, social security and police data. Unauthorized use of personal data systems is considered a crime.[1986] The new draft Penal Code Bill[1987] contains higher protection from privacy infringements. Unauthorized wiretapping and recording of private conversation is considered crime as well as unauthorized use of private documents, records or electronics data files.[1988]

Employer monitoring employees' e-mail is an important issue as well. The Data Protection Office issued a legal opinion finding employers' reading of the content of employee's e-mail to be illegal. However, the Office allowed monitoring the titles of employees' e-mail correspondence. Scholars and practitioners broadly discussed this issue.

Act No. 480/2004 on Several Services of Information Society was approved at the end of 2004. It addresses spam and limits liability of the providers as far the content of communicated information is concerned.

[1983] Penal Code, section 238.

[1984] Id. at Section 206.

[1985] Id. at Section 239.

[1986] Centre de Recherches Informatique et Droit, Legal Aspects of Information Services and Intellectual Property Rights in Central and Eastern Europe, February 1995.

[1987] Document of July 27,2004, No. 744 of Chamber of Deputies, IV. election period.

[1988] Penal Code Bill, *supra* at Sections 158, 161 and 162.

Open Government

The Parliament approved the Freedom of Information Law in May 1999.[1989] The law provides for citizens' access to all government records held by State bodies, local self-governing authorities, and certain other institutions, except for classified information, trade secrets, or personal data.[1990] In 2002, the government rejected a Senate-sponsored amendment to the law that would have required applicants to pay only for material costs rather than having to pay for the costs associated with searching.[1991] A 1998 act governs access to environmental information.[1992]

In April 1996, the Parliament approved a law that allows any Czech citizen to obtain his or her file created by the Communist-era secret police (StB). Non-citizens are not allowed to access their records. The Interior Ministry holds 60,000 records, but it is estimated that many were destroyed in 1989.

In 2003, the Interior Ministry decided to publish a list of Communist StB secret service collaborators. The Office for the Protection of Personal Data, which offered comments on the original legislation that allowed for the release of the information, stated that such a release would not be in conflict with the law on the protection of personal data.[1993]

Anti-terrorism Measures

Security interests clashed strongly with privacy interests as the United States began to demand that the Czech air carrier CSA provide data on all its passengers. Terrorism was cited as the rationale for this demand, as well as, threats of fines and denial of U.S. landing rights in case of non-compliance. CSA agreed to provide the requested data, but the release of data was likely to infringe the existing privacy laws. CSA had been granted permission from the Data Protection Office to transfer the data, but its validity was limited by the Czech Republic's accession to the European Union in May 2004. On May 28, 2004, the U.S. Department of Homeland Security and the Council of the European Union

---

[1989] Act No. 106/1999 Coll., on free access to information.

[1990] "Freedom of Info Clears Last Hurdle," The Prague Post, May 19, 1999.

[1991] "Czech Cabinet Rejects Legislation Facilitating Access to Information," CTK News Agency, August 5, 2002.

[1992] Act No. 123/1998 Coll., on the right to information about the environment.

[1993] "Internet publication of Czech communist era agents' names legal," CTK news agency, March 17, 2003, available at <http://www.mvcr.cz>.

came to an agreement for a legal framework governing the transfer of passenger data and providing guarantees of the privacy protections. The Office of Personal Data Protection has strongly criticized the data transfers, warning of privacy abuses by CSA and insufficient notice given to passengers traveling to the U.S.[1994]

The Office also expects an emphasis on data mining by police and customs groups. The data processing of greatest interest is related to Europol, Eurodac, technology development work for customs systems, and eventually, to accession to an enlarged Schengen system.[1995] Other issues that will likely be addressed include, prevention of identity theft stemming from unauthorized collection of personal data or inadequate protection of personal data, processing of biometric data, and regulation of consent given to financial institutions.

A document called Analysis of Security System of the Czech Republic (the Analysis)[1996] prepared by the Ministry of Interior based on National Anti-terrorist Plan[1997] drafted by the Lower Chamber Defense and Security Committee, recommends to extend powers of police and security services. In particular, it calls for obligation of individuals and companies to provide their personal data to security services. This program document is to be implemented by legislative proposals. The document also plans for public-private partnership in investments into security projects. Terrorism threat is stated as the main reason for creating the Analysis. The United Kingdom's "Anti-terrorism, Crime and Security Bill" and the U.S. "Patriot Act" are quoted in the Analysis, as examples of desirable strengthening of investigation powers.

Other privacy-invasive legislation is intended to be launched by the Ministry of Informatics. It calls for linking up different personal data databases run by different government agencies and to concentrate it on the central level (it will enable linking data about certain individual from different databases). Proponents of this initiative argue that this would make the public administration more efficient; however, the Data Protection Office opposes this plan. The government

---

[1994] "Data Protection Office Warns About Misuse of U.S. Visitor Info," CTK National News Wire, April 20, 2004.

[1995] *See* E-mail from Ivan Procházka, *supra.*

[1996] Analýza bezpečnostního systému ČR, available at <http://www.mvcr.cz/2003/odbor/obp/dokumenty_odbor_info.html>.

[1997] Governmental resolution of April 10, No. 385, available at <http://wtd.vlada.cz/vlada/cinnostvlady_usneseni.htm>.

agreed that the Ministry on Informatics could prepare the first draft of the Act on Public Administrations Data Sharing.[1998]

International Obligations

The Czech Republic is a member of the Council of Europe and has signed and ratified the European Convention for the Protection of Human Rights and Fundamental Freedoms. In September 2000, the Czech Republic signed the Council of Europe Convention No. 108[1999]; it was ratified on July 9, 2001. The Czech Republic is also a member of the Organization for Economic Cooperation and Development (OECD). It has adopted the OECD Guidelines on the Protection of Privacy and Transborder Flows of Personal Data.

Kingdom of Denmark

Constitutional Privacy Framework

The Danish Constitution of 1953 contains two provisions relating to privacy and data protection. Section 71 provides for the inviolability of personal liberty. Section 72 states, "The dwelling shall be inviolable. House searching, seizure, and examination of letters and other papers as well as any breach of the secrecy to be observed in postal, telegraph, and telephone matters shall take place only under a judicial order unless particular exception is warranted by Statute."[2000] Section 72 also applies to all kinds of telecommunication and electronic data. The European Convention on Human Rights[2001] (ECHR) was ratified in 1953 and was formally incorporated into Danish law in 1992.[2002]

[1998] Government resolution of November 3, 2004, No. 1064, available at
<http://wtd.vlada.cz/vlada/cinnostvlady_usneseni.htm>.

[1999] *See* Council of Europe—Treaty Office, Convention for the Protection of Individuals with regard to Automatic Processing of Personal Data, available at
<http://conventions.coe.int/Treaty/EN/Treaties/Html/108.htm>.

[2000] Constitution of Denmark 1953, available at <http://www.uni-wuerzburg.de/law/da00t___.html>.

[2001] Convention for the Protection of Human Rights and Fundamental Freedoms CETS No.: 005.

[2002] Act No. 285 of April 29 1992.

Statutory Rules on Privacy

The Act on Processing of Personal Data (the Act) entered into force on July 1, 2000.[2003] The Act implements the European Union (EU) Data Protection Directive (1995/46/EC) into Danish law. It replaces the Private Registers Act of 1978, which governed the private sector,[2004] and the Public Authorities' Registers Act of 1978, which governed the public sector.[2005] The law divides personal information into three categories: ordinary, sensitive and semi-sensitive and provides different conditions for the processing of each.[2006] According to Section 2 (2), the Act should not be applied if this is contradictory to the freedom of expression and information as stipulated in Article 10 of the European Convention on Human Rights. An exemption from the Act is provided for the Danish Security Intelligence Service (PET) and the Danish Defence Intelligence Service (FE).

Data Protection Authority

The Danish Data Protection Agency (*Datatilsynet* or DPA) enforces the Act. The DPA is a public body consisting of a council and a secretariat. The Minister of Justice appoints the members of the council. Neither the Ministry of Justice nor any other public body has instructive authority over the agency, but the agency is attached to the Ministry of Justice regarding recruitment of staff and budgetary issues.[2007] The DPA supervises registries established by public authorities and private enterprises in Denmark. It ensures that the conditions for registration, disclosure and storage of data on individuals are complied with. It mainly deals with specific cases based on inquiries from public authorities or private individuals, or cases taken up by the agency on its own initiative. Staff of the DPA is allowed to enter any premise where a file is operated without a court order. Decisions made by the DPA are final and may not be appealed by any

---

[2003] Act on Processing of Personal Data, Act No. 429 of May 31, 2000 (*Lov om behandling af personoplysninger*), available at <http://147.29.40.90/_GETDOC_/ACCN/A20000042930-REGL>.

[2004] Private Registers Act of 1978 (*Lov nr 293 af 8 juni 1978 om private registre mv*), in force January 1,1979.

[2005] Public Authorities' Registers Act of 1978 (*Lov nr 294 af 8 juni 1978 om offentlige myndigheders registre*), in force January 1, 1979.

[2006] Peter Blume *et al.*, Nordic Data Protection 19-20 (DJOEF Publishing Copenhagen 2001).

[2007] The DPA consists of a Counsel and an independent Secretariat who is only answerable to the Counsel. The Counsel, which is set up by the Minister of Justice, is composed of a chairman, who is a legally qualified judge, and of six other members. The Council decides in leading cases. The day-to-day business is attended by the Secretariat, which currently counts 30 employees distributed as: one director, one head of department, one head of the technical department, three consultants, 13 legal advisors, one technician/engineer, six clerical workers and four students (part-time employees). E-mail from Tina Fugl, Head of Section of the Danish Data Protection Agency, to Ula Galster, International Policy Fellow, Electronic Privacy Information Center, May 1, 2005 (on file with EPIC).

other administrative body. They may, however, be brought before the courts. According to the Act, the DPA is required to give an opinion before any new laws or regulations that have an impact on privacy are issued.[2008] The DPA has recently examined the Act on Prohibition of Video Surveillance and assessed whether this type of surveillance complies with the Act.[2009]

In 2004, the DPA received 965 inquiries and complaints, 80 inspections, 226 cases of preparatory work, 2,616 notifications.[2010] Of the 965 complaints and inquiries, 571 concerned private entities and 394 concerned public bodies) and 110 were initiated on DPA's own initiative.[2011] Private entities filed 1,425 notifications for registrations of personal information; public bodies filed 1,191. Of the 4,441 cases in total, other topics of interest are: issues of security (26), legislative preparation (226) and international cases (168). The issues of digital surveillance as a crime preventive measure and security in relation to the transfer of personal information on the Internet have been central in many of the inquiries and statements.

According to the DPA, the Act on Processing of Personal Data covers information published on the Internet and provides that it is mandatory to have explicit consent before publishing any personal information about an individual. In two decisions, however, the DPA did allow personal information to be available on a website without the individual's consent. The DPA ruled that freedom of speech and information, as provided for in Article 10 of the ECHR as well as the DPA's interest, outweighed the respect for the individual's privacy.[2012]

Open Government

Other laws regulating the processing of personal information by the public sector include the Public Administration Act of 1985,[2013] the Publicity and Freedom of

---

[2008] Homepage <http://www.datatilsynet.dk/>English version available at <http://www.datatilsynet.dk/eng/index.html>.

[2009] Memorandum on Prohibition of Video Surveillance, September 13, 2004, available at <http://www.datatilsynet.dk/attachments/2003724125353/tv.pdf> (in Danish only).

[2010] E-mail from Tina Fugl, *supra*.

[2011] In 2003, the DPA received 910 inquiries and complaints (415 concerning private entities and 495 concerning public bodies) and initiated 114 inquiries on its own initiative. Private entities filed 1,227 notifications for registrations of personal information, public bodies 743. The majority of the rest of the 3,521 cases cover issues of security, legislative preparation and international cases.

[2012] Individual complaints filed at the Danish Data Protection Agency the 10 January 2004 and the 20 May 2003. Summary of decisions, available in the Danish Institute for Human Rights Annual Status Report (2004), at 117-118 <http://www.humanrights.dk/upload/application/5a4e82ff/status_2004web.pdf> (in Danish only).

[2013] Lov 1985-12-19 nr. 571 *Forvaltningslov*.

Information Act of 1985,[2014] and the Act on Public Records of 2002.[2015] These laws set out basic data protection principles and determine which data and governmental records are accessible to the public and which should be kept confidential.[2016] Sectoral laws also provide special protections for medical information[2017] and credit card details[2018] and lay down restrictions on direct marketing (including spam).[2019] If they are in accordance with Denmark's international obligations, these sectoral laws take priority over the general Data Protection Act.[2020]

Danish citizens do not have an identification card but all citizens are provided with a Central Personal Registration (CPR)[2021] number, which is used to identify them in public registers. The information in the CPR register includes: name, address, municipality, prior addresses, place and date of birth, gender, nationality, membership information regarding the Danish National Church, information on family ties, guardians, information on marriage and information on job positions. The Ministry of Interior can hand over information for purposes of statistics or research. According to Section 38 of the Act, private entities can gain access to information[2022] on a larger group of persons identified individually.[2023] A condition for the access is that the private entity has a legitimate purpose. According to the Act an individual can upon request be granted a name and address protection lasting one year in relation to private entities.[2024]

Anti-terrorism Measures

In October 2001, the Minister of Justice and the Ministry of the Interior issued a package of "anti-terrorism" proposals in order to implement the United Nations (UN) Security Council's Resolution 1373 (2001) on Combating Terrorism and to

---

[2014] Lov 1985-12-19 nr. 572 *om offentlighed i forvaltningen.*

[2015] Lov 2002-12-17 nr. 1050 *Arkivlov* .

[2016] Peter Blume *et al.*, *supra* at 13.

[2017] Patients' Rights Act of 1998.

[2018] Credit Cards Act of 2000.

[2019] Consolidated Act on Marketing Practices No. 699, 17 July 2000, *Lovbekendtgørelse 2000-07-17 nr. 699 om markedsføring.*

[2020] Peter Blume *et al.*, *supra* at 14.

[2021] As regulated in Consolidated Act on Central Personal Registration, No. 140, March 3, 2004. *Lovbekendtgørelse 2004-03-03 nr. 140 om Det Centrale Personregister.*

[2022] The information accessible include primarily: name, address, job position, death and disappearance.

[2023] Identified by either CPR number, date of birth and name or address and name.

[2024] The Consolidated Act on Central Personal Registration, Section 28.

prepare for the UN's International Convention for the Suppression of the Financing of Terrorism.[2025] These proposals were postponed because of the general election but were re-introduced, with minor changes, by the new government in January 2002. In May 2002, the Parliament approved the anti-terrorism bill despite vocal opposition from non-governmental organizations and industry groups. The bill became law in June 2002.[2026] Among other things, the legislation establishes mandatory retention of traffic data for one year by telecommunications and Internet providers. It also gives law enforcement the power to secretly install snooping software on the computers of criminal suspects. The software will record keystroke data and transmit it electronically to the law enforcement agency. This power may only be used for serious crimes and will require an interception warrant. Serious crimes are defined as those punishable by jail for six years or more, including narcotics offenses, homicide, assault and battery, causing danger to other people's lives and health, theft, computer crimes, trafficking of refugees, child pornography, and crimes against national security and the public order. During the adoption of the act, there was considerable debate about what kind of traffic data would have to be retained by service providers and, also, what constitutes a service provider for the purposes of the retention requirement.

The creation of administrative order from the Ministry of Justice has, since 2002, been underway as a follow-up to the "anti-terrorism package," which extended the scope of Section 786 of the Administration of Justice Act (Act No. 378 of June 6, 2002). The administrative order aims to regulate in detail the obligations of the Danish telecommunications providers (small-size private Internet Service Providers (ISPs) included), specify how they must assist the Danish police interfering with the secrecy of communication, what data should be retained, and how it should be done. When a first draft of the administrative order was circulated for comments in May 2004, it was heavily criticized by ISPs, cooperative housing associations and non-governmental organizations for being disproportionate and inconsistent, *e.g.*, letting private entities store huge amounts of personal information, while at the same time being easy to evade, because libraries and universities, for example, are not included. Following this criticism, the Ministry of Justice established a working group, with participation of the industry, but has not presented a new draft. The Ministry of Justice is likely

---

[2025] "The Danish 'Anti-Terror' Package," Danish Center for Human Rights, available at <http://www.humanrights.dk>.

[2026] Act No. 378, June 6, 2002, Concerning the Change of Criminal Code, Administration of Justice Act, Act on Competition and Consumer Regulation of the Telecommunications Market, Act on Small Arms, Act on Extradition and Act on Extradition of Criminals to Finland, Iceland, Norway and Sweden.

awaiting the pending EU regulation[2027] on data retention before presenting a new Danish proposal.

On June 4, 2003, the Parliament enacted a bill to combat organized crime. The act amends the Administration of Justice Act and Criminal Code and expands crimes for which the police can secretly install snooping software on criminal suspects' computers.[2028] This is an extension of the anti terrorism package, and expands the area in which the police can use snooping software to also cover all crimes carrying a maximum penalty of six years or more, grave theft, serious tax fraud and smuggling.

A new act amending the Criminal Code, the Administration of Justice Act and the Marketing Practices Act[2029] was adopted in May 2004, in order to ratify the Council of Europe's Convention on Cybercrime and adopt the (EU) Council Framework Decision on Attacks against Information Systems.[2030] According to the act the police may, without a court order, require telecommunication and Internet service providers to retain electronic data for up to 90 days in all cases where such electronic evidence may be essential; however, access to the data by the police requires a court order. The retention will involve identification, freezing and possible copying the contents of a user's electronic communication, including the content of the communication. The amendments were criticized by several organizations for not being proportionate and for not ensuring basic procedural guarantees.

On July 4, 2003, the Committee on Citizens IT [Information Technology] Rights under the Danish Ministry of Science, Technology and Innovation published a list of recommendations[2031] on digital rights related to privacy, freedom of expression and access to public information. With regard to data retention, the committee advised the government to inform both citizens and ISPs about the rules and procedures following from anti-terrorism legislation, and to ensure that privacy standards are met. Among the recommendations for freedom of information is a call to ensure that filters or other means of protecting minors in public libraries do not hinder adults' rights to freely seek information. The

---

[2027] Council of the European Union Draft Framework Decision on the retention of data (8958/2004 – C6-0198/2004 – 2004/0813(CNS)).

[2028] Section 791 b. *Retsplejeloven* (Administration of Justice Act), available at <http://www.retsinfo.dk>.

[2029] Act amending the Criminal Code, the Administration of Justice Act, the Marketing Practices Act and the Copy Right Act No. 352 of May 19, 2004 (Lov 2004-05-19 om ændring af straffeloven, retsplejeloven, markedsføringsloven og ophavsretsloven (It-kriminalitet m.v.)).

[2030] COM/2002/0173 final.

[2031] The recommendations are available at the website of the Ministry of Science, Technology and Innovation, <http://www.videnskabsministeriet.dk/fsk/div/itsoejlen/rettigheder_pdf.pdf> (in Danish).

committee included representatives from various ministries, consumer organizations, the IT business sector and civil society, and was set up in 2002.[2032] Lastly it should be noted that Denmark will chair the UN Counter Terrorism Committee (CTC) from April 2005 through the next two years.

Recent Developments in Privacy

A new act on the activities of the police was adopted in 2004,[2033] establishing a common foundation for the work of the police. The act regulates the procedures for the use of force, and for police interference and investigations, which are not regulated by other legislation. One issue, which has been criticized in relation to this recently adopted act, is the lack of regulation regarding the use of electronic tracking devices on vehicles as a means of police surveillance.[2034]

In October 2004, the Minister of Justice proposed an amendment to the Act on the Central DNA Register,[2035] expanding the possibilities of the use of the DNA register in investigative matters. By the adoption of the proposal the requirements for dealing with fingerprints and DNA profiles will be identical, i.e. the DNA profiles will be kept in the register until the person is 80 years of age, regardless of whether the person is acquitted for the alleged crime. Furthermore the minimum requirement for collecting the DNA profiles in relation to the character of the crime is lowered to a maximum penalty of one year and six months. The bill is currently pending.

Spamming has, since June 2000, been forbidden under the Marketing Practices Act (*Markedsfoeringsloven*).[2036] Article 13 of the EU Privacy and Electronic Communications Directive[2037] was implemented into Danish legislation on June 10, 2003.[2038] It changed Denmark's legal data protection framework on spam. According to the directive, people who have already given their address to

---

[2032] *See* <http://www.videnskabsministeriet.dk/cgi-bin/doc-show.cgi?doc_id=55207&doc_type=26>.

[2033] Act on Police Activities No. 444 of June 9, 2004 (Lov 2004-06-09 nr. 444 om politiets virksomhed).

[2034] Christoffer Badse, The Use of Electronic Tracking Devices Should Be Regulated, (*Pejling bør reguleres*) Lov og Ret No. 8, December 2004, (27-32).

[2035] L 24. Bill proposed October 7, 2004.

[2036] Section 6a(1).

[2037] Danish version of the directive available at:
<http://europa.eu.int/information_society/topics/telecoms/regulatory/new_rf/documents/l_20120020731da0037 0047.pdf>.

[2038] Act No. 450, June 10, 2003. Law concerning the change of Law of Competition and Consumer Regulation of the Telecommunication Market etc.

---

companies can now be spammed with advertisements for "similar services" ("soft opt-in"), which the Marketing Practices Act had not previously allowed.[2039]

Major Privacy Case Law

In March 2005, the Danish Maritime and Commercial court convicted the mobile phone company Debitel Denmark for spamming.[2040] The company paid a fine of DKK 2,000,000 (EUR 269,000) for sending out unsolicited advertising material. In Denmark, this is the largest fine ordered for spamming. Debitel Denmark had sent 12,000 text messages and 36,000 e-mails advertising for products. The size of the fine was also based on other violations of the Marketing Practices Act[2041]

The Danish Consumer Ombudsman has published guidelines for industry regarding spamming and Section 6a of the Marketing Practices Act. Also, the Danish Consumer Ombudsman has established e-mail addresses where consumers can file complaints regarding spam.[2042]

On November 11, 2004, a Danish district court found a person guilty of violating the Act on Prohibition of TV Surveillance and imposed a fine of DKK 3,000 EUR 400. The individual had set up webcams to record movements in a public place and published the recordings on a website. The webcams provided an overview of a public area, and individuals could not be identified in the recordings.[2043] The Act on Prohibition of TV Surveillance[2044] generally prohibits private entities from placing video cameras in public places. However, the Act

---

[2039] According to an amendment to Section 6a of the Marketing Practices Act, there will be an exception to the prohibition of advertising via e-mails to consumers without prior consent. If the consumer has, in connection with a purchase on the Internet, forwarded his or her e-mail address to a company, the company is allowed to mail or spam the consumer's e-mail address. According to Section 6a § 2, it is a precondition for the spamming that the consumer be informed of the possibility to say "no" to any form of electronic advertising material. This means that the consumer must express dissent to avoid getting spammed, which is a change compared to the former regulation where the consumer had to positively express his or her wish to receive advertising material. The amendment entered into force on July 25, 2003.

[2040] Judgment No.: M-0001-04 available at (in Danish) <http://www.domstol.dk/ref.aspx?s=-300011&id=8906&pageid=16692>

[2041] Consolidated Act on Marketing Practices (No. 699 of 17 July 2000 (Lovbekendtgørelse 2000-07-17 nr. 699
om markedsføring)

[2042] The Guidelines can be downloaded (in Danish) from <http://www.forbrug.dk> and complaints can be filed at spamdk@fs.dk and spam@fs.dk.

[2043] The judgment is available at <http://www.el-fix.com/SCN_20041118100922.pdf> (in Danish).

[2044] Consolidated Act on Prohibition of TV Surveillance No. 76 of February 1, 2000 (Lovbekendtgørelse 2000-02-01 nr. 76
om forbud mod tv-overvågning mv.)

allows video surveillance of shopping centers, stores and ATM machines, but requires notices to be posted informing the public of the ongoing surveillance.

Wiretapping and Surveillance Rules

The Criminal Code regulates wiretapping.[2045] In 2001, the Danish parliament adopted an amendment to the Act on Administration of Justice increasing the police surveillance mandate by allowing access to a list of all active mobile phones near the scene of a crime at the time the crime was committed. This law was approved by the Parliament in June 2001. Statistical data on the interference of communications by the police in 2004 show that the courts approved 2,624 of 2,667 requests. The majority of requests were related to drug-related crimes (1,484); 24 related to computer crimes; 1,361 requests involved telephone tapping; and 1,484 dealt with the "requiring of information[2046] from telecommunication providers."[2047]

According to the Aliens Act,[2048] immigration authorities may require DNA samples from applicants for residency or persons with whom the applicant claims family ties for the purposes of residency. In its October 2001 report, the United Nations Human Rights Committee expressed concern about the privacy implications of this practice and called on Denmark to ensure that such testing is used only when "necessary and appropriate to the determination of the family tie on which a residence permit is based."[2049]

Also in 2001, Denmark amended its laws on search and seizure in accordance with its obligations under the Agreement on Trade-Related Aspects of Intellectual Property Rights (TRIPs) and under pressure from the US software industry. The Administration of Justice Act now authorizes physical searches for copyright infringements without "prior notification of the defendant if it is assumed that the notification would cause a risk of removal, destruction or modification of objects, documents, information in computer systems or anything

---

[2045] Criminal Code at Section 263.

[2046] The telecommunication provider must hand over stored information when telephones or similar communication devices have been in connection with a specific telephone or the case where a telecommunication provider must hand over stored information concerning all telephones or similar communication devices, which have been in connection with other telephones or similar communication devices within a specified area as set out in Section 780 (iii) and (iiii) of the Administration of Justice Act.

[2047] Annual statistics on secret surveillance measures initiated by the Danish Police 2004 provided by Rene Holleufer, *Rigspolitiet, Administrationsafdelingen.*

[2048] Consolidated Aliens Act No. 808 of 14 July 2004 (Lovbekendtgørelse 2004-07-14 nr. 808 Udlændingelov).

[2049] Report of the Human Rights Committee, A/56/40, Volume 1, October 26, 2001.

else that are comprised by the petition for investigation." The law took effect on April 1, 2001.[2050]

International Obligations

On January 6, 1972, Denmark ratified the UN International Covenant on Civil and Political Rights and the Optional Protocol allowing the UN Human Rights Committee to receive and consider communications from individuals. Denmark is a member of the Council of Europe and has ratified the European Convention for the Protection of Human Rights and Fundamental Freedoms and the Convention for the Protection of Individuals with Regard to Automatic Processing of Personal Data.[2051] Denmark signed the Convention on Cybercrime on April 22, 2003, but has not ratified it. The Additional Protocol to the Convention on Cybercrime, concerning the criminalization of acts of a racist and xenophobic nature committed through computer systems[2052] was signed on February 11, 2004, but has not been ratified. Denmark is a member of the Organization for Economic Cooperation and Development (OECD) and has adopted the OECD Guidelines on the Protection of Privacy and Transborder Flows of Personal Data.

Greenland

The original (un-amended) Danish Public and Private Registers Acts of 1978 and Guidelines regarding Notification of Data Processing Bureaus of 1979 continue to apply within Greenland, a self-governing territory. The Danish Data Protection Agency oversees compliance with the law. The 1988 amendments that brought Denmark into compliance with the Council of Europe Convention for the Protection of Individuals with Regard to Automatic Processing of Personal Data do not apply to Greenland. Furthermore, Greenland is not part of the European Union and therefore has not adopted the EU Data Protection Directive. Greenland's data protection requirements are much less stringent than those of Denmark and the other member states of the European Union.

[2050] "Denmark Enacts Anti-Piracy Search and Seizure Law," Cluebot, July 20, 2001, available at <http://www.cluebot.com/article.pl?sid=01/06/26/042210>.
[2051] Signed January 28, 1981; ratified October 23, 1989; entered into force February 1, 1990.
[2052] CETS No.: 189.

Republic of Ecuador

Constitutional Privacy Framework

Different articles of the Constitution of Ecuador[2053] protect the personal and family intimacy, the inviolability and confidentiality of correspondence, the inviolability of the home, freedom of the press, and the freedom of opinion and expression regardless of the medium of communication.[2054] Article 23 of the Constitution specifically recognizes and guarantees the following rights to individuals:

- The right to honor, good reputation, personal and family privacy (*intimidad personal y familiar*);[2055]
- The protection of the name, image and voice of the individual;[2056]
- The freedom of conscience and religion, individually or as a member of a group, in public or private. Individuals can freely practice their religion;[2057]
- The inviolability and confidentiality of correspondence. Correspondence can only be withheld, opened and examined in cases stipulated by law. Confidentiality will be maintained for related matters that may lead to the examination of personal information. The same principle will be observed with any other type or form of communication;[2058] and,
- The inviolability of the home. No one can enter or inspect an individual's home without either authorization from the person concerned or a judicial order, as established by law.[2059]

The Law of Constitutional Control creates *habeas data*. *Habeas Data* can be used by anyone – citizens and foreigners, public and private entities – wishing to access documents, databases or reports about themselves or about the properties

---

[2053] Constitution of 1998, available at
<http://www.georgetown.edu/pdba/Constitutions/Ecuador/ecuador98.html> (in Spanish).
2054 Id. at Article 23, Subsections 9 and 10.
[2055] *Id.* at Article 23, Subsection 8.
[2056] *Id.* at Article 23, Subsection 8.
[2057] *Id.* at Article 23, Subsection 11.
2058 Id. at Article 23, Subsection 13.
[2059] *Id.* at Article 23, Subsection 12.

they hold. Citizens who want to know the use and purpose given to their data, are able to use *habeas data* to request information about them.2060

The purpose of *habeas data* is to ensure that the data controller provides the data subject with complete, clear, and truthful information; that the data subject be able to obtain direct access to their information; that the data controller correct, delete and not disclose information to third parties; and that the data subject obtain certifications or verifications that the data controller has rectified, eliminated, or not disclosed, the information.[2061]

Habeas data does not apply where it infringes upon professional confidentiality, where it could obstruct justice, or where the documents solicited are secret for reasons of national security. It is not possible to delete data when the law requires that public or private records be maintained.[2062]

The Law of Constitutional Control (*Ley del Control Constitucional*)2063 was enacted on July 2, 1997, before the new Constitution of 1998 came into force.2064 On July 9, 2001, the Constitutional Court proposed to the National Congress a new Project of Organic Law of the Constitutional Court (*Proyecto de Ley Orgánica del Tribunal Constitucional*) that should be in accordance with the new Constitution and will replace the Law of Constitutional Control. The National Congress has not approved the bill yet.

Statutory Rules on Privacy

Ecuador does not have a comprehensive data protection act. However, numerous specific legal regulations protect the right to privacy. Article 14 of the Telecommunications Law (*Ley de Telecomunicaciones*) recognizes the right to

---

2060 Article 34 of the Law of Constitutional Control (*Ley del Control Constitucional*), available at <http://www.uc3m.es/uc3m/inst/MGP/JCI/02-ecuador-leycontrolconstitucionalidad.htm#II.II> (in Spanish).

2061 Constitution of Ecuador, Article 38.

2062 *Id.* at Article 36.

2063 This law indicates the activities of the Constitutional Court *(Tribunal Constitucional)* like an organ that controls whether the laws that are approved are in agreement with the Constitution, available at <http://www.viviendolademocracia.org/download/l_control_constitucional.doc> (in Spanish).

2064 This law has not been substituted, nor updated, and can only be applied where there is no conflict between the old Constitution and the new one. This unusual situation has given rise to countless problems for the Constitutional Court that applies the Constitutional Control Law. *See* Constitutional Court Law (*Ley de control constitucional*), available at <http://www.tribunalconstitucional.gov.ec/normativas.asp?ss=7> (in Spanish).

secrecy and privacy of the telecommunications. This article prohibits third persons from interceptng, interfering with, publishing or disclosing without the parties' consent, information transmitted by any means of telecommunications services.[2065]

In March 2001, a Law on Persons with Disabilities (*Ley sobre Discapacidades del Ecuador*) was enacted.[2066] This law creates a National Registry of Persons with Disabilities. The registry will be administered by the Center of Information of the National Council of Persons with Disabilities (*Centro de Información del Consejo Nacional de Discapacidades*).[2067]

A Law of Transparency and Access to Public Information was adopted in May 10, 2004.[2068] The law provides citizens and foreigners with the right to know and obtain information about acts, contracts with public institutions and projects financed by public resources. The law requires that public institutions or institutions that work with public resources publish information of their activities on an Internet portal, except the information classified as "secret" for reasons of national security.[2069] All information older than 15 years should be declassified. Public officials who deny access to information shall be sanctioned with a fine or the suspension of their position.

A law on e-commerce and electronic signatures,[2070] enacted in 2000, establishes that contracts and agreements entered into through the use of electronic signatures shall be equally valid and effective as those executed on paper. Though there are various human rights organizations in Ecuador,[2071] not one works for the protection of privacy.

[2065] Special Telecommunications Law (*Ley Especial de Telecomunicaciones*), Law No. 184 Official Register No. 996, August 10, 1992, available at
<http://www.supertel.gov.ec/PDF/Ley_Teleco_reforma.pdf> (in Spanish).
[2066] Available at http://www.conadis.gov.ec/legislacion/ley.html (in Spanish).
[2067] Article 14 of the *Reglamento General de la Ley Reformatoria de la Ley de Discapacidades* (General Ruling of the Law Reforming the Law on Persons with Disabilities), available at
<http://www.conadis.gov.ec/legislacion/reglamento.html> (in Spanish).
[2068] Law of Transparency and Access to Public Information, (*Ley Orgánica de Transparencia y Acceso a la Información Pública*), May 10, 2004, available at
<http://probidad.org/regional/legislacion/2004/LeydetransparenciaEcuador.pdf> (in Spanish).
[2069] The law establishes that public institutions should implement Internet portals within a year.
[2070] *Ley de Comercio Electrónico, Firmas Y Mensajes de Datos*, available at
<http://www.corpece.org.ec/documentos/ley/ley_ce.doc> (in Spanish).
[2071] For a comprehensive list of NGOs working in Ecuador, *see*
<http://www.ecuadorexplorer.com/html/ngo_list.html> (in Spanish).

Voting Privacy

Voting is compulsory for those between the ages of 18 to 65; for those older than 65 voting is optional.[2072] October 2, 2004, marks Ecuador's first attempt at electronic voting. A pilot election project was done in the capital, Quito, under the direction of the Electoral Supreme Tribunal. The project selected a group of qualified voters by means of a random process using computer matching to ensure randomness. Only the election results, which include no personally identifiable information, were transferred to the Electoral Supreme Tribunal for processing.

International Obligations

Ecuador signed the American Convention on Human Rights on November 22, 1969.[2073] The Convention provides that every person has "the right to have his honor respected and his dignity recognized." Additionally, "no one may be the object of arbitrary or abusive interference with his private life, his family, his home, or his correspondence, or of unlawful attacks on his honor or reputation. And everyone has the right to the protection of the law against such interference or attacks."

El Salvador

Constitutional Privacy Framework

Several articles of the Constitution of El Salvador[2074] protect the right to privacy, which includes the inviolability of the home, the right to honor, personal and family intimacy, and the right to one's own image.[2075] The Constitution also protects the inviolability of any kind of communications by expressly prohibiting wiretapping[2076] and provides that any intercepted communication cannot be used

---

[2072] The World Fact Book, available at
http://www.cia.gov/cia/publications/factbook/geos/ec.html#Govt.

[2073] *Convención Americana sobre Derechos Humanos* "Pacto de San José de Costa Rica,"
available at <http://www.oas.org/juridico/spanish/firmas/b-32.html> (in Spanish).

2074 Political Constitution of the Republic El Salvador 1983, updated as of July 2000. (Constitución Política de la República de El Salvador de 1983, actualizada hasta reforma introducida por el DL No. 56, del 06.07.2000), available at <http://www.georgetown.edu/pdba/Constitutions/ElSal/ElSal83.html> (in Spanish).

2075 Article 2 of the Constitution guarantees the right to honor, personal and family intimacy, and the respect of one's own image.

2076 Article 24 of the Constitution.

in any proceeding, except in insolvency and bankruptcy proceedings.2077 Every individual can express his thoughts freely whenever and in whatever way he chooses, unless it is against the public order, offends the morals, the honor or intrudes upon the private life of other persons (Article 6).

The Constitution does not contain any specific remedy against infringement to the right of privacy, unlike constitutions of other Latin American countries.2078 However, the Constitution offers with the "*Acción de Amparo*" a general remedy that comes before any type of actions or omissions of any authority and before final decisions, pronounced by administrative dispute courts, that violate a fundamental right or impede its exercise.2079

According to the Law of Constitutional Proceedings (*Ley de Procedimientos Constitucionales*), every person has the right to request an "*Acción de Amparo*" before the Constitutional Chamber of the Supreme Court of Justice, for violations of constitutional rights.

Statutory Rules on Privacy

El Salvador does not have a comprehensive law that establishes general data protection principles for the processing of personal data. The Regulation of the Penitentiary Law2080 establishes rules protecting the privacy of inmates by adopting many of the principles and rights of the European Data Protection Directive. It provides that the penitentiary administration can only give the inmate's personal data to governmental institutions and public entities after getting the inmate's written consent, and with adequate justification of the usefulness of the data, the Attorney General's Office and judges being

---

2077 *Id.*

2078 *Habeas data* has different meanings in different countries in Latin America. In some Constitutions, like the Peruvian one, *habeas data* is used to refer to the "constitutional guarantee process," which protects not only the right of an individual to access information about himself (right to informational self-determination) but also the right to access whatever information an individual may require from any public body (freedom of information and access to government records). However, in Argentina, *habeas data* is "a right" by which every person may file an action to obtain knowledge of the content and purpose of collection of all the data pertaining to him contained in public records or databanks, or in private databanks whose purpose is to provide reports. In the case of false information or its use for discriminatory purposes, a person will be able to demand the deletion, correction, confidentiality or update of the data contained in the above records.

2079 Article 247 of the Constitution; *see also* Article 12 of the Law of Constitutional Proceedings (Ley de Procedimientos Constitucionales) that provides that "[a]ll persons can request an *acción de amparo* before the Constitutional Court of the Supreme Court of Justice, for violation of the rights granted in the Constitution," available at <http://www.uc3m.es/uc3m/inst/MGP/JCI/02-elsalvador-leydeprocedimientosconstitucionalesl.htm> (in Spanish).

2080 Regulation of the Penitentiary Law (Reglamento General de la Ley Penitenciaria), November 14, 2000, available at <http://www.oas.org/juridico/spanish/gapeca_sp_docs_slv2.pdf> (in Spanish).

exempted.2081 International transfers of personal data can only be carried out when they are needed for cooperation or assistance in law enforcement or judicial matters, pursuant to applicable international agreements. Inmates' political opinions, religious or philosophical beliefs, and health records, can only be disclosed or made public to persons, public or private institutions, national or international organizations, with the inmate's written consent, except for public interest reasons covered by law.2082 The same Regulation contains data access and correction provisions.2083 The penitentiary administration must adopt security measures to protect the integrity of the data and keep it confidential, even after the inmate has left the prison.2084

The Telecommunications Law protects the right to the secrecy of communications. It makes the act of intentionally interfering with and intercepting phone communications a serious offense sanctioned with heavy fines.2085

The Penal Code identifies as a crime the invasion of other people's privacy by taking possession (*tomar posesión*) of their confidential data of a personal or familial character that is contained in public or private databases, as well as the possession of written communications or any other document directed to them. The Code slightly sanctions the disclosure of data to third parties, and sanctions more severely if the data controller or data processor of the filing system commits the offense.2086 The Code also sanctions with an imprisonment between six months and one year, the person who, with the purpose of intruding upon the privacy of others, intercepts, impedes or interrupts a telegraphic or telephone communication, or uses instruments or wiretapping devices to listen, transmit or record sounds, images or any other communication signs.2087

In 2003, the company *Informes en Red Sociedad Anónima* (Infornet) was involved in a scandal for allegedly selling databases to the United States

---

2081 *Id.* at Article 19.

2082 *Id.* at Article 20.

2083 *Id.* at Article 21.

2084 *I* Regulation of the Penitentiary Law, *supra* at Article 22.

2085 *See* Articles 29, 31 and 36 (a) of the Telecommunications Law (Ley de Telecomunicaciones), available at <http://www.asamblea.gob.sv/leyes/19960807.htm> (in Spanish).

2086 Articles 184 and 185 of the Penal Code (Código Penal), approved by Legislative Decree No. 883 (aprobado mediante Decreto Legislativo No. 1030 y modificado mediante Decreto Legislativo No. 883), June 27, 2002, available at <http://www.oas.org/juridico/MLA/sp/slv/sp_slv-int-textes-cp.html> (in Spanish).

2087 Salvadoran Penal Code, Article 186 (about the interception of communications).

government that contained personal data of millions of Salvadorans.2088 The Attorney General's office started investigating but has not found any evidence of liability. Since there is no law that regulates the way personal data is processed by public and private entities, no restrictions exist to the handling and use of personal data, as long as the information is obtained through public sources, including the gathering of information from public registries and telephone directories.

Privacy Case Law

In *Boris Rubén Solorzano v. Dicom, CentroAmerica, S.A. de C.V.*2089 *and General Automotriz, S.A. de C.V.*,2090 the Constitutional Chamber of the Supreme Court of Justice (*Sala Constitucional de la Corte Suprema de Justicia*) established an important precedent for privacy in El Salvador. It was the first time the Constitutional Court made a reference to the so called "right to informational self-determination" *(derecho a la autodeterminación informativa)* as a manifestation of the right to privacy and which purpose is to protect the individual's information contained in public or private records, as well as, the right of access to one's own information to ask for the correction, update, modification and elimination of data. The Court reaffirms that the right to privacy in the field of computer science (*en el ámbito informático*) implies that: (a) every data subject has the right to access his personal information, especially the information stored in computer databases; (b) every data subject must have the possibility and the right to control, in a reasonable way, the distribution and transmission of any information that concerns him; and (c) the judicial system must have a procedure that provides effective means of redress. In the same case, the court also explained the right to be forgotten *(derecho al olvido)*: every data subject's credit information stored in a public or private database should be eliminated from it a certain time after the information was created; and the use and handling of personal information must be justified.

2088 "Crece Escándalo: Todos Espiados," El Nuevo Diario, 2003, available at
<http://www.onpe.gob.pe/prensa/prensa02A.php?id=1758>; *see also* "¿Quién Vendió Informes? Privacidad en Venta Pública," April 30, 2003, available at
<http://www.elsalvador.com/noticias/2003/04/30/nacional/nacio1.html>; "Daños a Los Salvadoreños Son Irreversible," May 14, 2003, available at
<http://www.elsalvador.com/noticias/2003/05/14/nacional/nacio2.html> (in Spanish).
2089 Dicom/Equifax is a multinational company with offices in several countries around the world and is dedicated to provide information services and products. In 1996, Dicom/Equifax started its operations in El Salvador in order to obtain credit information and credit rating of potential customers with the purpose of analyzing their credit behavior, available at <http://www.equifax.com.sv/informativo/index.html> (in Spanish).
2090 Sentencia de la Sala Constitucional de la Corte Suprema de Justicia, M 118-2002, (El Salvador, March 2, 2004), available at
<http://www.jurisprudencia.gob.sv/exploiis/indice.asp?nBD=1&nDoc=32047&nItem=33366&nModo=1>.

International Obligations

In December 2003, El Salvador and others countries from Central America, signed a Political Dialogue and Cooperation Agreement with the European Union and its member States.[2091] The Agreement provides that its signatories agree to cooperate to protect the processing of personal data and other data, with a view to promoting the highest international standards. The signatories also agree to work towards the free movement of personal data between their jurisdictions, with due regard to their respective domestic legislation.

El Salvador is a signatory of the 1948 Universal Declaration of Human Rights, the 1966 International Covenant on Civil and Political Rights, and the American Convention on Human Rights on November 22, 1969.[2092] The Convention provides that every person has "the right to have his honor respected and his dignity recognized." Additionally, "no one may be the object of arbitrary or abusive interference with his private life, his family, his home, or his correspondence, or of unlawful attacks on his honor or reputation. And everyone has the right to the protection of the law against such interference or attacks."[2093]

Republic of Estonia

Constitutional Privacy Framework

The 1992 Estonia Constitution recognizes the right of privacy, secrecy of communications, and data protection. Article 42 states, "No state or local government authority or their officials may collect or store information on the persuasions of any Estonian citizen against his or her free will." Article 43 states, "Everyone shall be entitled to secrecy of messages transmitted by him or to him by post, telegram, telephone or other generally used means. Exceptions may be made on authorization by a court, in cases and in accordance with procedures determined by law in order to prevent a criminal act or for the purpose of

---

[2091] Acuerdo de Cooperación y Diálogo Político entre Europa y América Central (EU-Central America Political Dialogue and Cooperation Agreement), available at
<http://europa.eu.int/comm/external_relations/ca/pol/comments.htm>, and at
<http://europa.eu.int/comm/external_relations/ca/pol/pdca_12_03_es.pdf> (in Spanish).

[2092] *See* Convención Americana sobre Derechos Humanos Pacto de San José de Costa Rica, available at
<http://www.oas.org/juridico/spanish/firmas/b-32.html> (in Spanish).

2093 According to the Salvadoran Constitution, international treaties are hierarchically superior to the law but are below the Constitution. In case of conflict between the Constitution and the Treaty, the Constitution prevails.

establishing facts in a criminal investigation." Police must obtain a warrant in order to intercept communications. Illegally obtained evidence is not admissible in court.[2094] Article 44 (3) of the Constitution states, "Estonian citizens shall have the right to become acquainted with information about themselves held by state and local government authorities and in state and local government archives, in accordance with procedures determined by law. This right may be restricted by law in order to protect the rights and liberties of other persons, and the secrecy of children's ancestry, as well as to prevent a crime, or in the interests of apprehending a criminal or to clarify the truth for a court case."[2095]

Statutory Rules on Privacy

The *Riigikogu*, Estonia's Parliament, enacted the Personal Data Protection Act (PDPA) in June 1996.[2096] The Act protects the fundamental rights and freedoms of persons with respect to the processing of personal data and in accordance with the right of individuals to obtain freely any information that is disseminated for public use. The PDPA divides personal data into two groups – non-sensitive and sensitive personal data. Sensitive personal data reveal political opinions, religious or philosophical beliefs, ethnic or racial origin, health, sexual life, criminal convictions, legal punishments and involvement in criminal proceedings. Processing of non-sensitive personal data is permitted without the consent of the respective individual if it occurs under the terms set out in the PDPA. Processed personal data are protected by organizational and technical measures that must be documented. Chief processors[2097] must register the processing of sensitive personal data with the data protection supervision authority. Between 1999 and April 2005, 1,494 data processors of sensitive data have registered with the Data Protection Inspectorate.

In April 1997, the *Riigikogu* passed the Databases Act.[2098] The Databases Act is a procedural law for the establishment of national databases. The law sets out the general principles for the maintenance of databases, prescribes requirements and

---

[2094] The Human Rights Report submitted to the United States Congress by the United States Department of State, Section 1f <http://www.ncbuy.com/reference/country/humanrights.html?code=en&sec=1f>.

[2095] Constitution of Estonia, available at <http://www.uni-wuerzburg.de/law/en00t___.html>.

[2096] Law on the Protection of Personal Data (RT I 1996, 48, 944), available at <http://www.dp.gov.ee/eng/Personal_Data_Protection_Act.html>.

[2097] Based on the definition in the 2003 version of the Personal Data Protection Act, "chief processors" are equivalent to "controllers" as it is defined by Art. 2 (d) of the European Union Data Protection Directive (1995/46/EC). The Estonian term "authorized processor" is the equivalent of the term "processor" as it is defined by Art. 2 (e) of the EU Directive 1995/46/EC.

[2098] Databases Act (RT* I 1997, 28, 423), available at <http://www.dp.gov.ee/eng/Databases_Act.html>.

---

protection measures for data processing, and unifies the terminology to be used in the maintenance of databases. Pursuant to the Databases Act, the statutes of state registers or databases that were created before the law took effect must be brought into line with the Act within two years. The Act also mandates the establishment of a state register of databases for state and local government databases, as well as databases containing sensitive personal data maintained by persons in private law. The chief processor of the register has the right to make proposals to the government, to the chief processors of various databases, and to the state information systems. He or she would also be responsible for coordinating authority with respect to the expansion, merger or liquidation of databases, database cross-usage, or the organization of data processing or data acquisition in a manner aimed at avoiding duplication of effort or substantially repetitive databases.

There have been several amendments to both of these acts over the last number of years but most have been of technical importance with no principal changes. The Government worked on an amendment bill to the PDPA to bring it into full compliance with the 1995 EU Data Protection Directive. The bill passed in February 2003 and entered into force on October 1, 2003.[2099] This new version of the PDPA includes changes in registration procedures becoming effective on July 1, 2004. After that date, registration applications are accepted only via the Internet, through the home page of the Data Protection Inspectorate.[2100] In 2002, the Databases Act was amended. The changes related to support systems for state and local registers.[2101] On January 1, 2001, a significant amendment was made to the list of sensitive data in the PDPA. According to the amendment, information relating to criminal charges is now treated as sensitive only if it is announced prior to the trial or before the judgment. Such data is deemed sensitive if it is necessary to protect morality or individual's private or family life, or necessary in the interests of a minor, a victim, a witness or a fair trial. The amendment also added information about heredity to the list of sensitive data.

[2099] RT I 2003, 26, 158 (State Gazette).
<http://www.legaltext.ee/en/andmebaas/ava.asp?tyyp=SITE_ALL&ptyyp=I&m=000&query=data+protection&nups.x=38&nups.y=12>.

[2100] E-mail from Triinu Jaaksoo, Public Relations Officer, Estonian Data Protection Inspectorate to Cédric Laurant, Policy Counsel, Electronic Privacy Information Center (EPIC), July 4, 2003 (on file with EPIC),

[2101] RT I 2002, 63, 387 available at
<http://www.legaltext.ee/en/andmebaas/ava.asp?tyyp=SITE_ALL&ptyyp=I&m=000&query=databases&nups.x=45&nups.y=8>.

Data Protection Authority

The Data Protection Inspectorate (DPI) is the supervisory authority for the PDPA and the Databases Act. The DPI, a national supervisory authority under the area of government of the Ministry of Internal Affairs, monitors compliance, issues licenses, takes complaints, and settles disputes. The Legal Committee of Parliament exercises supervision over the Data Protection Inspectorate.

Supervision regarding data protection is regulated by Personal Data Protection Act (PDPA) and Databases Act (DA) the processing of data and liability are also regulated by Public Information Act (PIA), Health Protection Act, Archives Act, State Secrets Act, Statistics Act, Code of Administrative Offenses.

The agency can conduct investigations and demand documents, impose fines and administrative sanctions.[2102] The DPI has three departments and 15 employees.[2103] The Administrative Department supports all the major activities and is responsible for EU integration issues. The Control Department is divided into two divisions; the Division of Registration is responsible for issuing permits while the Division of Supervisory is responsible for monitoring compliance with laws and other legislation related to managing data files of the state and local governments, compliance with the personal data processing requirements provided by law, and for resolving petitions and complaints submitted with regard to the processing of personal data. The Development and Analysis Department is responsible for preparing opinions on legislation, preparing analysis documents, and providing long-term planning and strategies with respect to the progress of technology.[2104]

During the period from July 2004 to April 2005, the DPI received 22 complaints on the violation of PDPA and 29 challenges on the breaches of PIA. For the violation of the PDPA, the DPI issued five precepts to personal data processors and carried out three misdemeanor proceedings. During the period from July 2004 to April 2005, the DPI registered 258 processors of sensitive data.[2105] The organizational and technical measures for the protection of data were supervised

---

[2102] Homepage <http://www.dp.gov.ee/>.

[2103] E-mail from Maarja Kirss Estonian Data Protection Inspectorate, to Ula Galster, International Policy Fellow, Electronic Privacy Information Center, May 1, 2005 (on file with EPIC).

[2104] E-mail from Triinu Jaaksoo, *supra*, and e-mail from Toivo Übi.

[2105] E-mail from Maarja Kirss, *supra*.

15 times at data processors' location of data processing. The DPI also held 15 training sessions on personal data protection in various locations.[2106]

The main goal for DPI for the 2005 is to prepare joining with Schengen, Europol and Custom Information Systems. This implies preliminary work – professional training, acquaintance with relevant laws and complementing of supervision methodology in case of need.[2107]

The DPI maintains close relations with the data protection authorities (DPAs) in other central and eastern European countries. In December 2001, the data protection commissioners from the Czech Republic, Hungary, Lithuania, Slovakia, Estonia, Latvia and Poland signed a joint declaration agreeing to closer cooperation and assistance. The commissioners agreed to meet twice a year in the future, to provide each other with regular updates and overviews of developments in their countries, and to establish a common website for more effective communication.[2108] The DPI participates in the e-PRODAT project, which includes Data Protection Authorities, Universities and Regional/City Governments from Spain, Italy, Greece and Estonia. The main goals of e-PRODAT are: The exchange of knowledge and experiences related to personal data protection in public bodies of different European countries; the creation of an Internet based "European e-Government data protection observatory"; identification of best data protection practices already in use for e-Government and other public services and making recommendations to improve data protection standards in the public sector.[2109]

Health Privacy

On December 13, 2000, the Estonian Parliament approved the Human Genes Research Act.[2110] The Act created a national genetic database to be used for research into disease. The database is owned and controlled by the Estonian

---

[2106] E-mail from Toivo Übi, *supra*. From November 2001 to November 2002, the DPI received 807 registration applications from different processors for permission to process sensitive personal data. Of these applications received, 380 requests were granted. E-mail from Triinu Jaaksoo, *supra*. In 2001, the DPI received a total of 103 complaints under the PDPA and the Public Information Act. It issued 57 orders and referred eight cases of criminal violations to relevant authorities. It received 88 registration applications for processing of sensitive data. As of July 2002, there were 17 staff members, up from eight in 1999. E-mail from Erki Podra,.

[2107] The Yearbook of EDPI, available at <http://www.dp.gov.ee>.

[2108] E-mail from Karel Neuwirt, President, Office for Personal Data Protection, Czech Republic, to Sarah Andrews, Research Director, Electronic Privacy Information Center, May 15, 2002 (on file with EPIC).

[2109] Homepage <http://www.dp.gov.ee>

[2110] <http://cmgm.stanford.edu/biochem118/Papers/Genome%20Papers/Estonian%20Genome%20Res%20Act.pdf>
.

Genome Project Foundation.[2111] However, the Estonian government provides only 20 percent of the funding for the project. A United States registered company, EGeen International Corporation, has agreed to provide the remaining financing.[2112] Since 2001, approximately EUR 3.8 million have been expanded on the project, 3.5 million of which was received from international venture capital funds and private investors.[2113] In April 2004, EGeen agreed to provide an additional EUR 1.6 million to the project for the collection and processing of samples from 5,000 donors.[2114] The focus of the Estonian database is different than that of the Icelandic database. Rather than looking for genes that cause disease, as in Iceland, the Estonian project is focusing on how genes influence individual responses to medicines.[2115] The main project is underway after successful completion of pilots in three regions.[2116]

Privacy protection for donors is included in the project design. Doctors who collect samples and medical histories for the project must register their databases with the DPAs before they can participate in the project. Individual data is stored in coded form on computers that are not connected to networks. The rights of donors and the consent form they have to sign before donating their samples are publicly available on the Estonian Genome Project Foundation website. The rights include voluntary nature of the consent, the right not to know the nature of one's genetic profile, the right to obtain one's own information or to give one's doctor the ability to obtain the information, and the right to have all data removed and deleted from the database.[2117]

Recent Developments

A new Law on Personal Identity Documents, requiring mandatory identity (ID) cards for all Estonian citizens and resident aliens, took effect on January 1, 2002. The first Estonian ID Card was issued on January 28, 2002. A total of 100,000

[2111] <http://www.geenivaramu.ee>.

[2112] "Estonian Genome Foundation Signs Pilot Project Financing Accords," Baltic News Service, January 2, 2002.

[2113] "The Estonian Government Decided to Allocate Funds for the Estonian Genome Project," January 23, 2004,
<http://www.geenivaramu.ee/index.php?lang=eng&show=uudised&id=142&PHPSESSID=4ea0bb01a2c4bbb9 28a2b709878a1b6f>.

[2114] "The Estonian Genome Project Foundation and EGeen Agreed upon Year 2004 Financing," April 5, 2004,
<http://www.geenivaramu.ee/index.php?lang=eng&show=uudised&id=156>.

[2115] <http://www.genomics.ee/index.php?lang=eng&nid=125>.

[2116] A. Metspalu et al., "The Estonian Genome Project in the Context of European Genome Research,"
<http://www.genomics.ee/index.php?lang=eng&show=16&nid=272>.

[2117] <http://www.geenivaramu.ee/index.php?lang=eng&sub=74>.

cards were issued in 2002 and 250,000 in 2003. By 2007, one million cards are planned to be issued.[2118]

On its face, the card contains standard personal information including name, sex, date of birth, citizenship, personal identification code (ID code), date of expiration and signature, and a photograph of the holder.[2119] The card also incorporates a microchip storing an electronic identification certificate and an asymmetric key pair allowing for digital identification and digital signatures. The usage of digital signature is mandatory for public sector institutions. Digital signatures are being used throughout the Estonian court system in communication between proceedings parties and in the Estonian Tax Board to receive any tax documents from individuals or businesses, and in order to conclude loan agreements in online banks.[2120]

For resident aliens with valid papers, the ID card also contains residence and work permit data.[2121] Under the Digital Signatures Act of 2000,[2122] electronic signatures are given the same legal status as handwritten signatures. A personal identification number (PIN) is currently used to activate the card but this may eventually be replaced by a biometric identifier.[2123] In May 2002, it was discovered that the sealed security envelopes containing the secret PIN and PUK (public key) codes issued with the cards were see-through when placed under an ordinary light bulb. The Citizen and Migration Board stated that it would immediately change the printing practices.[2124] In June 2001 members of the Reform Party introduced a bill seeking to reform the law and make the cards voluntary rather than compulsory. The bill was defeated in Parliament in December 2001. In December 2004, a problem came up with using the ID codes. All the ID codes of issued certificates of ID cards are in the certificate database, and access is provided through the homepage of the Certificate Center. Some telephone services in Estonia afford authentication using only names and ID

[2118] Estonian Citizenship and Migration Board, press release: "350 000 Estonian ID Cards Issued by the End of 2003," January 4, 2004, <http://www.id.ee/pages.php/030307,517>.

[2119] Regulation No. 370 of December 4, 2001 on the Establishment of Format and Technical Description of Identity Card and List of Data Entered on Identity Card and Determination of Period of Validity of Digital Data Entered on Identity Card.

[2120] Estonian Citizenship and Migration Board, *supra.*

[2121] *See* <http://www.pass.ee/63.html>.

[2122] Digital Signatures Act, (RT I 2000, 26, 150), passed March 8, 2000, entered into force December 15, 2000, available at<http://www.riik.ee/riso/digiallkiri/digsignact.rtf>.

[2123] "European States Roll out EID Cards," Cards International, February 22, 2002.

[2124] "Estonian ID-Card Security Envelopes Shine Through," Baltic News Service, May 3, 2002.

codes, thus this may lead to the identity-theft, because of the availability of the ID codes at the homepage of the Certificate Center.[2125]

The Estonian Data Protection Inspectorate notified the Ministry of Economic Affairs and Communication and the Ministry of Internal Affairs about the problem. The ID codes are still available at the homepage of the Certificate Center. The authentication problem still exists.

In 2000, a government-backed proposal to amend the tax laws and provide for publication of income tax paid by individuals sparked controversy among the public and opposition parties. Responding to this criticism, the government told the Parliament in October to discuss the bill but not to enact it as law.[2126]

On June 28, 2005, the Estonian Parliament decided to allow Internet voting for local elections despite the continued opposition of President Arnold Ruutel. The President has already refused to sign the bill twice since May 2005, arguing that one of the provisions of the law – which would allow voters to change their vote several times – violates the principle of "uniformity" as voters using paper ballots cannot change their choice. Because this principle is enshrined in the Estonian Constitution, the President believes the proposed legislation cannot be passed in its present form. In addition, President Ruutel has also indicated that additional work was needed in the field of voter identification and authentication in order to prevent fraud.[2127]

The proposed bill, which would amend the Local Elections Act in order to allow for the use of Internet voting in the local elections of October 2005, was approved by a very narrow margin during its third reading, with only 52 of the 101 representatives voting in favor. According to press reports, the bill is now likely to be referred to the Constitutional Court by President Ruutel.[2128]

The Estonian e-voting system, which uses the Estonian electronic ID card[2129] to identify voters, was developed by IT services company Cybernetica[2130] for the

---

[2125] Valdo Praust, "ID Code is not suitable for authentication" Äripäev, December 9, 2004, available at <http://www.aripaev.ee/2768/rubr_artiklid_276406.html>.

[2126] "Estonian Government Advises Parliament not to Pass Income Tax Publication Bill," Baltic News Service, October 3, 2000.

[2127] "Controversy over Internet voting goes on in Estonia," eGoverment news, June 28, 2005 available at <http://europa.eu.int/idabc/en/document/4431/591>.

[2128] Id.

[2129] See <http://www.pass.ee/>.

[2130] Homepage <http://www.cyber.ee>.

Estonian National Electoral Committee. In order to vote online, voters need to access the election website and place their electronic ID cards in a card reader connected to a PC. Users then identify themselves with a PIN code and, after voting, confirm their choice with a second code. More than 50% of citizens today hold such a card and, according to the government, every Estonian citizen will have an electronic ID card by the end of 2006.[2131]

Major Privacy Case Law

In 2004 the DPI was involved in two cases, which found their way to the Supreme Court. Both of them were with regard to access to public information. The first one concerned the DPI and the Estonian Tax and Customs Board.[2132] The case involved the Board's register of documents and the restriction on access.[2133] The Supreme Court upheld the previous decisions made by administrative court and circuit court. According to them, the complaint made by the Board is not within the sphere of competence of the administrative court. Thus the decision made by DPI (that the restriction is illegal) was not proceeded by the courts. In November 2004, the restriction on access was made legal with the alteration of Taxation Act.[2134]

Another case involved the DPI and a private individual.[2135] The case was about the complaint made by the private person on the DPI's decision on appeal. According to the DPI's challenge, the private person (who was a member of city council) had no right to ask information about the wages and salaries of the employees of the institutions administrated by the city, because these employees are not officials. The Supreme Court's decision was that the private individual wanted to get information as a member of the city council and because of that, this was not even a request of information for the purposes of Public Information Act.[2136] The Supreme Court repealed previous decisions made by the administrative court and circuit court and concluded the proceeding b[2137]ecause the employees of the institutions administrated by the city are not officials and their salaries and wages are not public. The DPI's decision was sustained.

[2131] "Estonian President vetoes Internet voting plans," eGoverment news, May 26, 2005, available at <http://europa.eu.int/idabc/en/document/4325/591>.

[2132] Available at http://www.nc.ee/klr/lahendid/tekst/RK/3-3-1-38-04.html.

[2133] Supreme Court case nr. 3-3-1-38-04, available at <http://www.nc.ee/klr/lahendid/tekst/RK/3-3-1-38-04.html>.

[2134] Amendment of the Taxation Act, available at <https://www.riigiteataja.ee/ert/act.jsp?id=901885>.

[2135] Available at <http://www.nc.ee/klr/lahendid/tekst/RK/3-3-1-55-04.htm>l

[2136] Public Information Act, available at <http://www.legaltext.ee/text/en/X40095K2.htm>.

[2137]

Wiretapping and Surveillance Rules

The 1994 Surveillance Act regulates the interception of communications, covert surveillance, undercover informants, and police and intelligence databases.[2138] Surveillance can be approved by a "reasoned decision made by the head of a surveillance agency." "Exceptional surveillance" requires the permission of a judge in the Tallinn Administrative Court for serious crimes. The punishment for illegal surveillance is a fine and three years imprisonment for general surveillance activity, and five years imprisonment for special measures like opening correspondence or telephone bugging.[2139] Illegally obtained evidence is not admissible in court. Citizens have a right under the Surveillance Act to obtain access to information held about them by surveillance agencies. Agencies must respond within three months if the agency maintains information about them.[2140] In October 1999, the Estonian Police Department refused to grant the Tallinn City Police authority the right to plant eavesdropping devices in apartments, offices and telephones to combat organized crime.[2141] The law was amended in May 2000 to allow the tax police to conduct surveillance.[2142] Under the Telecommunications Act approved in February 2000, surveillance agencies can obtain information on the sender and receiver of messages by written or oral request.[2143] Telecommunications providers are also prevented to disclose users' information without proper authorization. Amendments in 2003 to the Estonian Telecommunications Act (which entered into force on June 28, 2004) mandate telecommunications providers to keep traffic data for three years. Previously, data was kept only a few months.[2144]

On January 1 2005 the new Electronic Communications Act [2145]came in force. The act replaced the Telecommunication Act and is in accordance with the EU legislation.

[2138] Surveillance Act (RT* I 1994, 16, 290, February 22, 1994), available at
<http://vlf.juridicum.su.se/master99/library2/teste/Surv.htm>.

[2139] Criminal Code Art. 134.

[2140] Surveillance Act (RT* I 1994, 16, 290, February 22, 1994)
<http://vlf.juridicum.su.se/master99/library2/teste/Surv.htm>.

[2141] Baltic News Service, October 8, 1999.

[2142] "Estonian Government Approves Plans for Tax Police," BBC Worldwide Monitoring, May 16, 2000.

[2143] Telecommunications Act passed February 9, 2000 (RT I 2000, 18, 116), entered into force March 19, 2000. <http://www.legaltext.ee/tekstid/X/en/X30063.HTM>.

[2144] E-mail from Toivo Übi, *supra.*

[2145] Electronic Communication Act, in English available at
<http://sa.riik.ee/atp/failid/Elektroonilise_side_seadus_eng.htm>.

In May 1996, the Estonian Intelligence Service started an inquiry on the involvement of former Vice Prime Minister Edgar Savisaar in a politically motivated wiretapping scandal. It eventually led to a change of government.[2146] Swedish papers reported in January 2000 that the Estonian secret services had spied on Swedish diplomats.[2147] In March 2002, the Estonian United People's Party issued a statement alleging that the National Security Police (NSP) engaged in secret surveillance of politicians and members of Parliament. The NSP denied these allegations.[2148]

Open Government

The Public Information Act was approved by the Parliament and entered into force in January 1, 2001. Supervision and enforcement of the Act will be conducted by the DPI. The law includes significant provisions on electronic access. Government departments and other holders of public information will have a duty to post information on the web, and e-mail requests must be treated as official requests for information. There were no significant developments in 2002, although several projects were conducted in preparation for the 2003 legislative session.[2149] From July 2004 to April 2005), the DPI conducted 29 challenges about the infringement of the Public Information Act.[2150]

The Government of Republic enacted on August 12, 2004, new security measures for information systems. The regulation enacts usable information systems and related security measures systems in the maintenance of state and local governments' databases. The security measures system consists of the regulation of specifying security requirements and the description of data's organizational, physical and infotechnological security measures. The regulation comprises the description of security classes and levels. Security classes are divided into four components: time criticality, severity of consequences of delay, integrity and confidentiality.[2151]

[2146] "Estonian Intelligence Begins Probe into Former Premier Saavisar," Deutsche Presse-Agentur, May 16, 1996.

[2147] "Estonian MP Rejects Reports that Estonian Secret Services Spied on Swedes," BBC Worldwide Monitoring, January 13, 2000.

[2148] "Estonian Security Police is not Involved in Politics," Baltic News Service, March 14, 2002.

[2149] IT in Public Administration of Estonia, Yearbook 2002, Section 1.4, <http://www.ria.ee/english/2002/p14_t.htm>.

[2150] E-mail from Maarja Kirss, *supra.*

[2151] RT I 26.08.2004.63.443, available at <http://riigiteataja.ee/ert/act.jsp?id=791875> (in Estonian).

Estonia is a member of the Council of Europe and has signed and ratified the European Convention for the Protection of Human Rights and Fundamental Freedoms.2152 In November 2001, Estonia ratified the Convention for the Protection of Individuals with Regard to Automatic Processing of Personal Data (ETS No. 108) (Convention No. 108).2153 Also in November, Estonia signed and ratified the CoE Convention on Cybercrime.2154

European Union

The European Union (EU) unites under one roof the three pillars of European cooperation, with the European Community (EC) serving as the "First Pillar," the Common Foreign and Security Policy as the "Second Pillar," and the Cooperation in Justice and Home Affairs as the "Third Pillar," The EU and its three pillars have been established by the two major treaties between the 25 Member States.[2155]

The Council of Europe, which adopted the European Convention on Human Rights (ECHR) in 1950, is distinct from the EU and EC. Article 8 of the ECHR declares that everyone has the right to respect for his private and family life, his home and his correspondence. Article 6 (2) of the Treaty on European Union makes the European Union comply with the ECHR's fundamental rights.[2156] All EU Member States have ratified this convention and are bound by its guarantees.

Following the advancements of information technologies, the Council of Europe issued a separate Convention on Data Protection in 1981.[2157] Parties to this convention, which include EU Member States, are required to implement the convention into their national laws. An additional protocol regarding supervisory

---

[2152] Signed May 14, 1993; ratified April 16, 1996; entered into force April 16, 1996.

[2153] Signed January 24, 2000; ratified November 14, 2001; entered into force March 01, 2002.

[2154] Signed November 23, 2001; ratified December 5, 2003; entry into force July 1, 2004.

[2155] Treaty on the European Union (in the consolidated version of Nice), [2002] OJ C 325/1, available at <http://www.europa.eu.int/eur-lex/pri/en/oj/dat/2002/c_325/c_32520021224en00010184.pdf>; first pillar: The Treaty Establishing the European Community (as amended by the Treaty of Amsterdam), [2002] OJ C 325, available at <http://www.europa.eu.int/eur-lex/en/treaties/dat/C_2002325EN.003301.html>; the second and third pillar are integrated in Titles V and VI of the Treaty on the European Union, *id.*

[2156] Treaty on the European Union (in the consolidated version of Nice), *supra.*

[2157] Convention for the Protection of Individuals with Regard to Automatic Processing of Personal Data, adopted by the Council of Europe in Strasbourg, January 28, 1981, available at <http://conventions.coe.int/Treaty/en/Treaties/Html/108.htm>.

authorities and transborder data flows, that entered into force on July 1, 2004, now complements the convention.[2158] The EU sought accession to this convention to help create a stronger international forum on data protection, particularly *vis-à-vis* third countries.[2159] The convention was amended in 1999, and once this amendment has entered into force the EU will be able to accede.[2160]

Article 286 of the EC Treaty was adopted in 1997 as part of the Treaty of Amsterdam. The treaty provides that EC institutions are required to adhere to European Community acts on the protection of individuals with regard to the processing of personal data and the free movement of such data from January 1, 1999.[2161]

Since 2000, the EU is committed to protect personal data pursuant to Article 8 of the Charter of Fundamental Rights of the European Union (CFREU). According to the CFREU, it is imperative that personal data be processed fairly for specified purposes, and based on the person's consent, or some other legitimate basis laid down by law.[2162]

On October 29, 2004, all Member States and three of the candidate Member States signed the Treaty Establishing a Constitution for Europe.[2163] In order for the European Constitution to enter into force on November 1, 2006, it has to be ratified in all signatory countries. EU data protection would then make a significant leap forward to a fundamental right with direct effect throughout the

---

[2158] Additional Protocol to the Convention for the Protection of Individuals with regard to Automatic Processing of Personal Data, regarding supervisory authorities and transborder data flows (CETS No. 181), adopted by the Committee of Ministers of the Council of Europe in Strasbourg, November 8, 2001, available at <http://conventions.coe.int/treaty/en/Treaties/Html/181.htm>.

[2159] Explanatory Memorandum on the amendments to Convention 108 allowing the accession of the European Communities, at No 4, available at
<http://www.coe.int/T/E/Legal%5Faffairs/Legal%5Fco%2Doperation/Data%5Fprotection/Documents/Internati onal_legal_instruments/Explanatory%20Memorandum%20on%20the%20amendments%20to%20Convention%20108.asp#TopOfPage>.

[2160] Amendments to the Convention for the Protection of Individuals With Regard to Automatic Processing of Personal Data (ETS No. 108) allowing the European Communities to Accede, adopted by the Committee of Ministers, in Strasbourg, June 15, 1999, available at <http://www.coe.int/T/E/Legal_affairs/Legal_co-operation/Data_protection/Documents/International_legal_instruments/Amendements%20to%20the%20Convention%20108.asp#TopOfPage>.

[2161] Treaty Establishing the European Community (as amended by the Treaty of Amsterdam), [2002] OJ C 325, available at <http://www.europa.eu.int/eur-lex/en/treaties/dat/C_2002325EN.003301.html>.

[2162] Charter of Fundamental Rights of the European Union of the European Parliament, December 7, 2000, [2000] OJ C 364/1, available at <http://www.europarl.eu.int/charter/pdf/text_en.pdf>.

[2163] Treaty Establishing a Constitution for Europe, [2004] OJ C 310, available at <http://europa.eu.int/constitution/download/print_en.pdf>.

EU.[2164] Article I-51(1) provides that everybody has the right to the protection of personal data concerning him or her. According to Section (2), European legislation shall spell out data protection rules with which administrative bodies of the European Union and the Member States have to comply. A second reference to the right to data protection can be found in Article II-68 of the Constitutional Treaty, which is part of the incorporated Charter of Fundamental Rights (CFREU) referred to above.

All points of reference to data protection mentioned above require an independent authority to be in charge with supervision of compliance with data protection rules, in order to ensure the effective protection of individuals. European Data Protection is therefore institutionalized contrary to the American approach. (For more discussion of this subject, see the subsection on Oversight and Privacy and Data Protection Commissioners.)

European Data Protection Supervisor

At the EC level, the European Data Protection Supervisor was established by Article 41(f) of Regulation (EC) No 45/2001.[2165] This measure applies to EC institutions and activities, which derive their competences from the EC Treaty, which is the "First Pillar" in the EU. The obligations in the regulation are similar to the EC Data Protection Directive 95/46/EC.[2166] Also, the European Data Protection Supervisor has the influential task of advising the commission and other EC institutions on proposals for new legislation that might have an impact on the protection of personal data.

The "Third Pillar" of the EU covers cooperation in the fields of justice and home affairs. There are separate data protection responsibilities in each principal field of activities, which are set up by the Europol Convention, the Council Decision setting up Eurojust, the Convention implementing the Schengen Agreement, and the Convention on the use of Information Technology for Customs Purposes. For Europol, which is a cooperative effort of EU Member States to combat serious forms of international organized crime, data protection supervision is in the

---

[2164] It should be noted that the right to data protection is the only fundamental right that entered the European Constitutional Treaty twice.

[2165] Regulation (EC) No 45/2001 of the European Parliament and of the Council of 18 December 2000 on the protection of individuals with regard to the processing of personal data by the Community institutions and bodies and on the free movement of such data, [2001] OJ L 8/1, available at <http://europa.eu.int/eur-lex/pri/en/oj/dat/2001/l_008/l_00820010112en00010022.pdf>.

[2166] *Id.*

hands of the Europol Joint Supervisory Body.[2167] The objective of Eurojust is to improve EU-wide investigations and prosecutions, thereby conferring data protection authority to the Eurojust Joint Supervisory Body.[2168] The Schengen Information System (SIS) is a database that has been established in the conjunction of the abolition of international border controls in much of the EU (Schengen territory). The SIS records personal information required in the context of cross-border applications, *e.g.*, missing or wanted persons. The Schengen Joint Supervisory Authority is responsible for data protection issues surrounding SIS.[2169] The same construction applies to the Customs Information Systems (CIS).

In 2004, the Council of the European Union, which represents the Member States, determined that, as of 2008, the exchange of law enforcement information should be governed by the principle of availability.[2170] This means that throughout the EU, a law enforcement officer in one Member State who needs information in order to perform his duties can obtain it from the law enforcement agencies of another Member State.

The European Network and Information Security Agency, ENISA, is a new agency of the European Union, which formally came into being in March 2004.[2171] The agency assists the European Commission, the Member States and the private sector in meeting the requirements of network and information security, including present and future European Community legislation. ENISA also follows the development of standards, promotes risk assessment activities and interoperable risk management routines, and produces studies on those issues that impact public and private sector organizations.

Data Protection Directive

The Data Protection Directive (95/46/EC) defines the basics of data protection that Member States have to transpose into national law where the actual

---

[2167] Homepage of the Europol Joint Supervisory Body <http://europoljsb.ue.eu.int>.

[2168] Compare Rules of Procedure on the Processing and Protection of Personal Data at Eurojust, [2005] OJ C 68/1, available at <http://www.eurojust.eu.int/PDF/ropdp/c_06820050319en00010010.pdf>.

[2169] Homepage of the Joint Supervisory Authority of Schengen <http://escher.drt.garanteprivacy.it/garante/navig/schengen/jsp/index.jsp?language=english>.

[2170] *See* Presidency Conclusion of the Council of Europe in Brussels, November 4/5, 2004, reference No 14292/04, available at <http://europa.eu.int/comm/external_relations/gac/pres_concl/nov2004.pdf>, at page 28f; Compare Statewatch Bulletin, "The 'Principle of Availability' Takes over from the 'Notion of Privacy': What Price Data Protection?," Vol. 14, No. 6, November-December 2004, available at <http://database.statewatch.org/unprotected/article.asp?aid=26245>.

[2171] ENISA's homepage <http://www.enisa.eu.int/>.

regulation of data protection and its enforcement are taking place.[2172] As a secondary EC measure, the directive does not have immediate effect, though its provisions can be invoked in the national courts against Member States' data protection rules in order to oust the application of rules of national law that are contrary to those provisions.[2173] In 2003, the European Commission issued a report on the status of the implementation of the Data Protection Directive.[2174] The report, which identified the shortcomings of harmonization, set out a work plan to narrow divergences of national legislation. It did not propose amendments to the directive itself, which will be examined during the second evaluation scheduled for 2005.

As an EC measure aiming at harmonization of Member States laws and the integration of the Internal Market, the Data Protection Directive is limited to EC activities ("First Pillar" of the EU).[2175] This directive applies to any automated processing of personal data and any other handling of personal data that forms part of a filing system.[2176] Personal data is defined as any information that relates to an "identified or identifiable natural person."[2177] Processing operations concerning public security, defense, state security and activities of a Member State in areas of criminal law fall outside the scope of the directive.[2178] Data processing by a natural person in the course of purely private and household activities are exempted as well.[2179]

The directive mandates that the data controller ensure compliance with the principles relating to data quality[2180] and provides a list of legitimate reasons for data processing.[2181] The data controller has information duties toward the data subject whenever personal data is collected directly from the person concerned or

---

[2172] Directive 1995/46/EC of the European Parliament and of the Council of 24 October 1995 on the protection of individuals with regard to the processing of personal data and on the free movement of such data, OJ L 281/31, available at <http://europa.eu.int/eur-lex/lex/LexUriServ/LexUriServ.do?uri=CELEX:31995L0046:EN:HTML>.

[2173] CJEC, judgment of May 20, 2003, joint cases C-465/00, 138/01, 139/01 ("*Rechnungshof*").

[2174] First Report from the Commission on the Implementation of the Data Protection Directive, COM(2003)265, available at <http://europa.eu.int/eur-lex/en/com/rpt/2003/com2003_0265en01.pdf>.
2175 Directive 95/46/EC, Article 3 (2).

[2176] *Id.* at Article 3 (1).

[2177] *Id.* at Article 2 (a).

[2178] *Id.* at Article 3 (2).

[2179] *Id.* at Article 3 (2).

[2180] Directive 95/46/EC, *supra* at Article 6 (1).

[2181] *Id.* at Article 7.

obtained otherwise.[2182] The data controller is also mandated to implement appropriate technical and organizational measures against unlawful destruction, accidental loss or unauthorized alteration, disclosure or access.[2183]

Data subjects' individual rights, as established by the directive, are: the right to know who the data controller is, the recipient of the data and the purpose of the processing;[2184] the right to have inaccurate data rectified;[2185] a right of recourse in the event of unlawful processing;[2186] and the right to withhold permission to use data in some circumstances.[2187] For example, individuals have the right to opt-out free of charge from being sent direct marketing material. The directive contains strengthened protections concerning the use of sensitive personal data relating, for example, to health, sex life or religious or philosophical beliefs.[2188]

Enforcement of the regulatory framework on the processing of personal data can either be through administrative proceedings of the supervisory authority or judicial remedies.[2189] Member States' supervisory authorities are endowed with investigative powers and effective powers of intervention, such as powers to order blocking, erasure and destruction of data or to impose a temporary or definite ban on processing. In the event of the infringement of individual rights, the person concerned can lodge a complaint with the regulator or seek judicial remedies in front of the national courts.[2190] Any person who has suffered damage as a result of an unlawful processing operation is entitled to receive compensation from the liable controller.[2191]

The Data Protection Directive transfers some competences directly to EC institutions. It sets up a body called the Working Party on the Protection of Individuals with regard to the Processing of Personal Data, or "Article 29 Working Party" (WP29).[2192] This body is made up of representatives of Member States' data protection authorities (DPAs) and the European Data Protection

---

[2182] This information must reveal the identity of the data controller and the purpose of the data processing, as well as further information on recipients of data, available options with corresponding legal consequences, and the right to access and rectify data if necessary. *Id.* at Article 10.

[2183] *Id.* at Article 17.

[2184] *Id.* at Article 11.

[2185] Directive 95/46/EC, *supra* at Article 12.

[2186] *Id.* at Articles 22 and 23.

[2187] *Id.* at Article 14.

[2188] *Id.* at Article 8.

[2189] *Id.* at Articles 22 and 28.

[2190] Directive 95/46/EC, *supra* at Article 28.

[2191] *Id.* at Article 23.

[2192] *Id.* at Article 29.

Commissioner. As an independent body, it has advisory status and can issue opinions and recommendations.[2193] The WP29 can determine European Community codes of conduct that are submitted for approval by trade associations and other bodies. It also serves as a platform for exchange and coordination between EU Member States, addresses upcoming developments related to data protection policy, and conducts public consultations. Resulting working documents are a common point of reference for interpretation of the Data Protection Directive.[2194]

The Data Protection Directive provides a mechanism by which transfers of personal data outside the territory of the EU have to meet a level of processing "adequate" to the one prescribed by the directive's provisions. A finding by the European Commission of an adequate level of protection in a country outside the EU effectively clears the transfer of personal data to that third country. European Commission's decisions on the adequacy of the protection of personal data in third countries presently cover Argentina, Canada, Guernsey, the Isle of Man and Switzerland.[2195] Commercial transfers of EU-originated data to the US is provided for under the Safe Harbor Agreement and its implementing decision.[2196] (For more discussion of this subject, see the section on Transborder Data Flows and Data Havens.)

The Court of Justice of the European Communities (CJEC) gives precedents on the interpretation of EC law that Member States' court have to take into account when applying national law in order to stay in line with EC law. The CJEC has ruled on the Data Protection Directive in two instances that national courts conferred with questions on the interpretation of EC law. First, in an Austrian case (*Rechnungshof*), the CJEC held that the processing of personal data within the public sector is covered by the Data Protection Directive.[2197] The plaintiff can invoke specific provisions of the directive that grant individual rights before national courts if the national data protection law contradicts these rights. Second, in another case from Sweden (*Bodil Lindqvist*), the CJEC decided that the main principles of the directive also apply to Web sites, and that the uploading of personal information for Internet access does not trigger the

---

[2193] Homepage of the Article 29 Data Protection Working Party
<http://europa.eu.int/comm/justice_home/fsj/privacy/workinggroup/index_en.htm>.
[2194] A comprehensive list of working documents is available at
<http://europa.eu.int/comm/justice_home/fsj/privacy/workinggroup/wpdocs/2005_en.htm>.
[2195] Updated decisions on adequacy findings are published at
<http://europa.eu.int/comm/justice_home/fsj/privacy/thridcountries/index_en.htm>.
[2196] *Id.*
[2197] CJEC, judgment of May 20, 2003, joint cases C-465/00, 138/01, 139/01 ("*Rechnungshof*").

provision for transfers of personal data to third countries even though the Web page is universally accessible.[2198]

Telecommunications Privacy Directive

The EC took specific measures to ensure the protection of privacy in the field of telecommunications. First, in 1997, with the Telecommunications Privacy Directive (1997/66/EC),[2199] which is no longer in force.[2200] Then, in 2002, with the Directive on Privacy and Electronic Communications that had to be transposed into Member States' law by February 2004.[2201] The directive authorizes Member States to pass laws mandating the retention of the traffic and location data of all communications taking place over mobile phones, SMS, landline telephones, faxes, e-mails, chatrooms, the Internet, or any other electronic communication device. Such requirements can be implemented for purposes varying from national security to the prevention, investigation and prosecution of criminal offences. The directive also adds to the protections of the now-defunct Telecommunications Privacy Directive (1997/66/EC) new definitions and protections for "calls," "communications," "traffic data" and "location data" in order to enhance the consumer's right to privacy and control in all kinds of data processing. These new provisions ensure the protection of all information ("traffic") transmitted across the Internet, prohibit unsolicited commercial marketing by e-mail ("spam") without consent, and protect mobile phone users from precise location tracking and surveillance. The directive also gives subscribers to all electronic communications services (such as GSM and e-mail) the right to choose whether they are listed in a public directory.

[2198] CJEC, judgment of November 6, 2003, case C-101/01 ("*Bodil Lindqvist*").

[2199] Directive 1997/66/EC of the European Parliament and of the Council of 15 December 1997 on the Processing of Personal Data and the Protection of Privacy in the Telecommunications Sector (Directive), available at <http://www.ispo.cec.be/legal/en/dataprot/protection.html>.

[2200] This directive established specific protections covering telephone, digital television, mobile networks and other telecommunications systems. It imposed wide-ranging obligations on carriers and service providers to ensure the privacy of users' communications, including Internet-related activities. It covered areas that, until then, had fallen between the cracks of data protection laws. Access to billing data was severely restricted, as was marketing activity. Caller ID technology was required to incorporate an option for per-line blocking of number transmission. Information collected in the delivery of a communication was required to be purged once the call was completed.

[2201] Directive 2002/58/EC of the European Parliament and of the Council of 12 July 2002 concerning the Processing of Personal Data and the Protection of Privacy in the Electronic Communications Sector (Directive on Privacy and Electronic Communications), available at <http://europa.eu.int/comm/justice_home/fsj/privacy/law/index_en.htm>.

Republic of Finland

Constitutional Privacy Framework

Section 10 of the Constitution of Finland, entitled "The right to privacy," states: "Everyone's private life, honour and the sanctity of the home are guaranteed. More detailed provisions on the protection of personal data are laid down by an Act. The secrecy of correspondence, telephony and other confidential communications is inviolable. Measures encroaching on the sanctity of the home, and which are necessary for the purpose of guaranteeing basic rights and liberties or for the investigation of crime, may be laid down by an Act. In addition, provisions concerning limitations of the secrecy of communications which are necessary in the investigation of crimes that jeopardise the security of the individual, society or the sanctity of the home, at trials and security checks, as well as during the deprivation of liberty may be laid down by an Act."[2202] Also, Section 12 of the Constitution, titled "Freedom of expression and right of access to information," provides that "documents and recordings in the possession of the authorities are public, unless their publication has for compelling reasons been specifically restricted by an Act. Everyone has the right of access to public documents and recordings."[2203] Information in the public domain includes each Finland resident's name, birth year, municipality of residence, state taxable income, state property taxes, and total taxes paid.

Statutory Rules on Privacy

The Personal Data Act of 1999 (PDA)[2204] went into effect on June 1, 1999. The PDA replaced the 1987 Personal Data File Act[2205] to make Finnish law consistent with the EU Data Protection Directive.[2206] The PDA was amended by the Act on the Amendment of the Personal Data Act, effective December 1, 2000, to incorporate provisions on policy and effects of the European

---

[2202] Constitution of Finland (unofficial translation), available at <http://www.finlex.fi/pdf/saadkaan?E9990731.PDF>.

[2203] *Id.*

[2204] Personal Data Act (523/99), available at <http://www.tietosuoja.fi/uploads/hopxtvf.HTM>.

[2205] Personal Data Files Act (Law No. 471/87).

[2206] *See* Directive 95/46/EC of the European Parliament and of the Council of October 24, 1995, on the Protection of Individuals with Regard to the Processing of Personal Data and on the Free Movement of Such Data, available at <http://europa.eu.int/comm/justice_home/fsj/privacy/docs/95-46-ce/dir1995-46_part1_en.pdf>.

Commission's decision-making.[2207] Under the PDA, everyone has the right of access to the data files on him or her or to notice that the file contains no such data. If a data controller refuses to rectify an error at the request of a data subject, the data subject may inform the Data Protection Ombudsman (DPO) of the matter. The DPO may order a data controller to recognize the data subject's right of access or to rectify an error. The PDA does not apply to processing of personal data for a private or purely personal use. Activities of "the media, the arts and literary expression" are also excluded from its scope. Exemptions for defense and public security are included in separate legislation.

The PDA introduces the concept of informed consent and self-determination into Finnish law, giving data subjects the rights to access or correct their data, or to prohibit their use for stated purposes. The previous act regulated the use and disclosure of information in a personal data file but did not generally require the individual's consent or provide for the same level of notice and access.[2208] Processing without consent may still occur under the new system -- for example, if there is "assumed consent," or the Data Protection Board (DPB) has granted permission, or if the matter concerns publicly available data on the "status, duties or performance" of a public figure.[2209] The PDA lays down civil and criminal sanctions (including imprisonment of up to one year)[2210] for unlawful processing.[2211]

Data Protection Authority

The Data Protection Ombudsman (DPO) enforces the Personal Data Act (PDA) and receives complaints. The DPO's primary tools for compliance with legislation are direction and guidance. Under the PDA, the DPO provides direction and guidance on the processing of personal data and supervises the processing to achieve the objectives of the statute. Before bringing charges of a violation of the DPA, the public prosecutor must hear from the DPO. In such cases, the court affords the DPO an opportunity to be heard. In 2004, there were 50 cases of hearings by the prosecutor and courts.[2212]

[2207] Amendment of the Personal Data Act (986/2000), available at
<http://www.tietosuoja.fi/uploads/p9qzq7zr3xxmm9j.rtf>.

[2208] Peter Blume *et al.*, Nordic Data Protection 49 (DJOF Publishing 2000).

[2209] *Id.*

[2210] *See* Finland Penal Code 1389/99, Chapter 38, § 9, available at
<http://www.finlex.fi/pdf/saadkaan/E8890039.PDF>,

[2211] Personal Data Act (523/1999), *supra.*

[2212] E-mail from Reijo Aarnio, Data Protection Ombudsman, Finland, to Kate Ó Súilleabháin, Law Clerk, Electronic Privacy Information Center (EPIC), June 13, 2005 (on file with EPIC).

In 2000, the number of new cases brought before the DPO increased by nearly one-third.[2213] The DPO attributed this increase in part to the switching from telephone to electronic customer service. The DPO usually receives 5,000 to 8,000 requests for advice each year.[2214] In 2004, the office conducted 2,012 cases, which included 828 requests for action made by citizens. During the same period, the DPO made 58 decisions concerning right of access and 46 decisions concerning the rectification of an error. Most of these decisions were made in the areas of health care and police investigation. In 2004, there were 178 registrations with the DPO's office. As of December 2004, there were 23 persons working at the Data Ombudsman's office.[2215] Each DPO inspector specializes in a certain field of problems, including education, social services, working life and credit issues.[2216]

The DPB resolves disputes and hears appeals of decisions rendered by the DPO and, under the PDA, grants permissions for the processing of personal data.[2217] The DPB consists of a chair, a deputy chair and five members, and they are required to be familiar with register operations. The Board is appointed by the Council of State for a term of three years.[2218] At the DPO's direction, the DPB drafts regulations for the processing of personal data. The DPO must be heard during the preparation of legislative or administrative reforms that may affect individual privacy rights, including the estimated 650 legislative provisions regulating the processing of personal data in Finland.[2219] During 2004, the DPO issued 38 statements on legislative reforms related to the protection of personal rights or freedoms in the processing of personal data. In the statements related to crime prevention, the DPO emphasized the principle of proportionality.[2220]

[2213] The Data Protection Ombudsman's Year in Review 2000, available at <http://www.tietosuoja.fi/10993.htm>.

[2214] *Tietosuojaviranomaiset* (Data protection in Finland) <http://www.tietosuoja.fi/>.

[2215] E-mail from Reijo Aarnio, Data Protection Ombudsman, Finland, to Kate Ó Súilleabháin, *supra*. Permanent staff included 12 inspectors (lawyers), two information technology experts, and four secretaries. Temporary staff included one senior inspector and one inspector.

[2216] E-mail from Reijo Aarnio, Data Protection Ombudsman, Finland, to Kenneth Farrall, Law Clerk, Electronic Privacy Information Center (EPIC), June 30, 2004 (on file with EPIC).

[2217] Personal Data Act (523/1999), *supra*.

[2218] Privacy International, Privacy, Technology, and Europe: A Report for Japan's Ministry of Public Management, Home Affairs, Postal, and Telecommunication, March 2003.

[2219] European Union Article 29 Data Protection Working Party ("WP29"), Sixth Annual Report on the Situation Regarding the Protection of Individuals with Regard to the Processing of Personal Data and Privacy in the European Union and in Third Countries Covering the Year 2001, December 16, 2003, available at <http://europa.eu.int/comm/justice_home/fsj/privacy/docs/wpdocs/2003/2003-6th-annualreport_en.pdf>.

[2220] E-mail from Reijo Aarnio, *supra*.

The DPO also issues guidance and consultation documents, and assists in the compilation and review of Codes of Conduct by the private sector. In January 2005, the DPO issued a guidance paper on the transfer of personal data to other EU nations and to third countries.2221 In response to a European Commission survey showing that Europeans have a relatively low level of awareness of data protection,2222 the DPO recently published an article to raise public awareness of data protection rights in Finland.2223

The enlargement of the EU has affected to the responsibilities of the DPO's office – for example, by decreasing the number of cases related to the transfer of personal data to third countries. Before the EU expansion, some Finnish industrial and commercial activities had already begun to be moved to the new member states. These moves were considered transfers of data to third countries, which required notification of the DPO. In 2006, the evaluation of the new member states that will begin to apply the Schengen agenda falls onto the Finnish Presidency. Evaluation related to data protection will significantly increase the workload of the DPO office.

On December 14, 2001, the Article 29 Data Protection Working Party made the following statement, which the DPO advocates as the best approach to the threat:2224

> Measures against terrorism should not and need not reduce standards of protection of fundamental rights which characterize democratic societies. A key element of the fight against terrorism involves ensuring that we preserve the fundamental values which are the basis of our democratic societies and the very values that those advocating the use of violence seek to destroy.2225

In November 2002, in an answer to a questionnaire by the Council of the European Union, Finland responded that data traffic retention is covered by the

---

2221 Data Protection Ombudsman, Issues about Data Protection 15.1.2005, Transfer of Personal Data to a Foreign Country According to the Personal Data Act, available at<http://www.tietosuoja.fi/uploads/afcmo1bdksojyoj.rtf>.

2222 European Commission, Special Eurobarometer: Data Protection, December 2003, available at <http://europa.eu.int/comm/public_opinion/archives/ebs/ebs_196_data_protection.pdf>.

2223 The Individual's Awareness of the Right to Privacy, efinland, April 1, 2005, at <http://www.e.finland.fi/netcomm/news/showarticle.asp?intNWSAID=34385>.

2224 E-mail from Reijo Aarnio, *supra*.

2225 Article 29–Data Protection Working Party, Opinion 10/2001: On the Need for a Balanced Approach in the Fight Against Terrorism, Adopted on 14 December 2001, available at <http://europa.eu.int/comm/justice_home/fsj/privacy/docs/wpdocs/2001/wp53en.pdf>.

Finnish Data Protection Law, and that, by default a communications service provider (CSP) must either destroy or alter retained traffic data in such a way that communicating individuals cannot be identified afterwards.2226

The publicizing of Finland's policy on data retention in 2002, coupled with the news that the head of Finland's largest telecommunications company was arrested in connection with his company's suspected "serious traffic data misuses," led to outrage among privacy advocates.2227 (He received a six-month suspended sentence for illegal use of mobile-telephone records, and five other executives were also convicted.2228) At the same time, Finland's Parliament was considering a proposed law that would have imposed far-reaching data retention obligations and liability for Internet providers, for the posted content of their members, while extending the coverage of the law to include Internet-based discussion groups in Finland.2229

This proposal received tremendous opposition, including from Electronic Frontier Finland (EFFI),2230 and resulted in "substantial revisions" by the Constitutional Committee of the Finnish Parliament.2231 The final draft. proposed on February 11, 2003 and passed by the Finnish Parliament on February 17, 2003, contained all of the Constitutional Committee's revisions.2232 These included: "Section 1.2 of the law now explicitly states that the freedom of expression principle should always have a priority when interpreting the law." The definitions were clarified so that the regulation essentially applies only to material produced by or codified by the publisher. The law is no longer a threat to the discussion groups: everyone will be responsible for his or her own writing. Web portals or typical homepages were also excluded from the definition.[2233]

2226 A CSP may retain logs for a maximum period of three years, should it be necessary for either business (invoicing, marketing) or data security-related tasks. If a CSP is selling services, it must keep the traffic data for a minimum of three months for invoicing purposes. Other than that, there is no obligation to retain any data traffic. Council of the European Union: Answers to questionnaire on traffic data retention - Electronic Frontier Finland ("EFFI"), available at <http://www.effi.org/sananvapaus/eu-2002-11-20.html>.

2227 Electronic Frontier Finland, "Finland Proposes Extensive Data Retention while the Country's Largest Telco Executives Are Arrested for Data Misuse," available at <http://www.effi.org/julkaisut/tiedotteet/pressrelease-2002-11-25.html>.

2228 "Five Get Suspended Sentences in Sonera Telephone Record Case," Helsingin Sanomat International Edition, May 31, 2005, available at <http://www.helsinginsanomat.fi/english/article/1101979719153>.

2229 Id.

2230 Homepage <http://www.effi.org/>.

2231 EFFI, "Finland Rewrote the Internet Censorship Law," available at <http://www.effi.org/julkaisut/tiedotteet/pressrelease-2003-02-16.html>.

2232 EFFI, "Freedom of Expression: The law on Liabilities in Public Communications," available at <http://www.effi.org/sananvapaus/index.en.html>.

2233 Id.

The law also protects similarly the sources for traditional newspapers and web publication (including blogs).

Moreover, the time period publishers are required to store the web publications or programs was reduced from two or three months, to three weeks. However, it remains unclear whether the three weeks begins the moment of first publication or from the time the publication was last available to the public. Mandatory storing of traffic data was completely removed from the law.[2234]

Anti-terrorism Measures

On April 28, 2005, four EU nations proposed an antiterrorism initiative that would compel all Internet service providers and telephone companies to retain traffic data, including personal information, for 12 to 36 months.[2235] On June 7, 2005, the European Parliament rejected the initiative.[2236]

On July 2005, the Finnish government took a tentatively positive position on the Council of Europe Draft Framework decision. The matter was sent to the Parliament in autumn. It was first put on fast track but EFFI and the Green Party intervened and forced the matter into full discussion.[2237]

After extensive hearings in three different parliamentary committees, the Parliament finally ended up voting on the Finnish position, which is highly uncommon in EU matters. The Green Party and the leftist party argued against retention but the government's position prevailed.[2238] In the summer of 2005, the Finnish Minister of Interior, Kari Rajamäki, requested additional research on the cost of the proposed data retention system.[2239]

[2234] *Id.*

[2235] Council of the European Union, Draft Framework Decision on the Retention of Data Processed and Stored in Connection with the Provision of Publicly Available Electronic Communications Services or Data on Public Communications Networks for the Purpose of Prevention, Investigation, Detection and Prosecution of Crime and Criminal Offences Including Terrorism, April 28, 2004, available at <http://register.consilium.eu.int/pdf/en/04/st08/st08958.en04.pdf>.

[2236] EU Parliament Rejects Controversial Data-Retention Plan, European Tech Wire, June 10, 2005, available at http://www.europeantechwire.com/etw/; *See also* European Digital Rights, To the President of the Political Groups in the European Parliament, June 6, 2005 (open letter from European Digital Rights, whose members include Electronic Frontier Finland, opposing the initiative), at <http://www.edri.org/docs/open_letter_alvaro_report.pdf>.

[2237] *See* <http://www.effi.org/effiemail/4_2004.html> (in Finish).

[2238] *Id.*

[2239] *See* <http://www.intermin.fi/intermin/bulletin.nsf/PFS/2E85EC27695BD02BC2257019003CDACE> (in Finish).

On September 4, 2003, the Finnish government submitted a resolution on the National Information Security Strategy. The Strategy aims to increase citizens' and companies' trust in the information society and formulates the efforts of the government, trade and industry organizations, and private citizens into common information security objectives. The Strategy, one of the first proposals in the world that concern the development of information security in the whole society, was praised as the best European security guidelines at the International RSA Information Security Conference held in Amsterdam in November, 2003.[2240]

In October 2003, the Finnish Ministry of Transport and Communications appointed the National Information Security Advisory Board to oversee implementation of the National Information Security Strategy.[2241] The Board began its work in spring 2004 and will continue through May 2007. On December 14, 2004, the Board submitted to the government a progress report that provided an overview of the state of information security in Finland. The report also outlined four primary projects for 2005: adoption of a program on information-secure electronic services, analysis of national information security risks, assessing and remedying cybercrime, and organizing the nation's second annual National Information Security Day, which was held on February 8, 2005.[2242]

Telecommunications Privacy

Telecommunications privacy is regulated by the Act on the Protection of Privacy in Electronic Communications, which was approved by the President on June 16, 2004, and came into force on September 1, 2004.[2243] The law, which replaces the Protection of Privacy and Data Security Act of 2000, is broad in scope, covering all telecommunications, including e-mails and communications on the Internet.[2244] The new Act clarifies rules for processing confidential identification and location data: except in an emergency, telecommunications users aged 15 years or older may not be located without their prior consent.[2245] However,

---

[2240] E-mail from Reijo Aarnio, *supra,* and Timo Poropudas, "Finnish Information Security Strategy Receives an Award," Mobile Monday, November 5, 2003, available at
<http://www.mobilemonday.net/mm/story.php?story_id=3394>.

[2241] National Information Security Advisory Board Report Submitted to the Government on December 14, 2004, available at <http://www.mintc.fi/oliver/upl501-NISAB%20report%20(lowres).pdf>.

[2242] *Id.*

[2243] Act on the Protection of Privacy in Electronic Telecommunications, 516/2004, available at
<http://www.finlex.fi/en/laki/kaannokset/2004/en20040516.pdf>.

[2244] *Id.*

[2245] Finland Ministry of Transport and Communication, "New Means to Improve Data Protection and Information Security—Act on Data Protection in Electronic Communications to Enter into Force on 1

parents or guardians of children under 15 years old may decide on the use of location services, a change in the law that was made in response to a 2003 proposal to allow parents track the whereabouts of their young children through the use of mobile phones.[2246] Finland's leading mobile operators TeliaSonera and Elisa, offer such positioning services, which are based on user proximity to base stations.[2247]

The Act on the Protection of Privacy in Electronic Communications also provides new means to prevent spam and viruses. Previous legislation banning the sending of spam failed to protect against messages sent from outside Finland; thus, the Act permits telecommunications operators and corporate and association subscribers to block e-mail and to remove malicious content in order to protect against security infringement or to ensure communications access.[2248] The Act prohibits direct marketing through e-mail or mobile telephone except with the user's prior consent.[2249] The Act also broadens police access to telecommunications information in criminal cases: in addition to permanent Internet protocol (IP) addresses and telephone numbers, police now have the right to obtain dynamic IP addresses and international mobile equipment identity (IMEI) codes of mobile telephones. The Finnish Communications Regulatory Authority (FICORA) is responsible for ensuring compliance with the Act and regulations issued under it, while the DPO monitors the processing of location data and provisions on direct marketing.[2250] The Act transposed the EU Privacy and Electronic Communications Directive nearly a year after the European Commission deadline of October 31, 2003.[2251]

The Ministry of Finance broadly oversees the coordination of information security for the Finnish Government and for this purpose created the Government Information Security Board (Steering Committee for Data Security in State Administration), or VAHTI.[2252] On June 15, 2004, VAHTI appointed a working group to develop and prepare propositions to privacy in administration and

---

September," Press release, June 16, 2004, available at
<http://www.valtioneuvosto.fi/vn/liston/base.lsp?r=86388&k=en&old=754>.

[2246] Associated Press, "Finns Ready Cellphone Tracking Law"" MSNBC, October 17, 2003, available at <http://msnbc.msn.com/id/3226848/>.

[2247] Id.

[2248] Id.

[2249] Id.

[2250] Id.

[2251] Paul Meller, "EU Pressures Member States to Implement Spam Law," IDG News Service, April 1, 2004, available at <http://www.infoworld.com/article/04/04/01/HNeuspamlaw_1.html>.

[2252] Ministry of Finance, Information Security and Management by Results, January 2005, available at http://www.vm.fi/tiedostot/pdf/en/94247.pdf.

---

electronic surveillance. The issues that the working group is dealing with include biometrics, electronic identification, and electronic surveillance. The working group will further consider privacy when dealing with data security and develop cooperation in administration which is related to privacy issues.[2253]

Recent Developments Related to Privacy

On February 1, 2003, the Act on Electronic Signatures[2254] went into effect. The purpose of the Act is to promote the use of electronic signatures and the provision of products and services related to them, as well as to promote data protection and data security of electronic commerce and electronic communication. The Finnish Communications Regulatory Authority (FICORA) has authority to ensure, through monitoring and auditing, that certification service providers that issue qualified certificates comply with the Act.[2255] FICORA also issues regulations governing information supplied by certification service providers and handles customer complaints.[2256]

In late 2002, VTT Technologies, a government research center, developed a new type of high-frequency (900 MHz) Radio Frequency Identification (RFID) tag that can be read with a transceiver up to four meters away. The signal can also penetrate obstacles. In 2004, the city library of Kauhajoli was the first in Finland to implement RFID technology, which was introduced to help manage collections, cut losses, speed up customer service, and increase self-service.[2257] Other libraries have already implemented RFID technology for theft prevention.[2258]

In the Helsinki region, the most familiar application of RFID technology is the travel cards, which replaced paper tickets in the area's public transport system by the end of 2002. The partners in the project are Helsinki Metropolitan Area Council (YTV), Helsinki City Transport, and the railway company VR. The use of travel cards is recorded in a database. This information can be accessed to aid

---

[2253] E-mail from Reijo Aarnio, *supra.*

[2254] Act on Electronic Signatures (14/2003), available at
<http://www.finlex.fi/en/laki/kaannokset/2003/en20030014.pdf>.

[2255] *Id.*

[2256] Finnish Communications Regulatory Authority, Electronic Signature and Certification Services,
<http://www.ficora.fi/englanti/tietoturva/allekirjoitus.htm>.

[2257] "Library Introduces RFID Technology," eFinland, June 9, 2004, at
<http://www.e.finland.fi/netcomm/news/showarticle.asp?intNWSAID=24842>.

[2258] "Finland: RFID To Be Used in Libraries," eFinland, April 20, 2005, at
<http://e.finland.fi/netcomm/news/showarticle.asp?intNWSAID=35683>.

transport capacity planning. The movements of travel card users are saved and can be accessed for later retrieval. The data from the transport system has been used for crime investigations in serious cases.[2259] YTV records the customer information it needs for customer service and consumer protection in the Travel Card System. Then, YTV municipal service points' employees, and the people in charge of the system, have the right to browse and update the customer data recorded in the system, as well as the data stored in the central processing unit, concerning travel periods and the amount of money a passenger has loaded into his/her card and where the card was last used. It is not possible to browse the travel data at the point of service.[2260]

The travel card received heavy public criticism after its introduction since it was theoretically possible to connect a specific traveler's identity with travel route information. After the DPO made the issue public, YTV changed its policy.[2261]

RFID Lab Finland, a Finnish application center for RFID technology that is partly publicly funded, opened in early 2005.[2262] Partnering with universities, research centers, and government programs in Finland, the center will provide information, consulting, and training services and will include a showroom and a test room for Finnish RFID applications. Nokia Corporation and UPM Rafsec are among 11 companies that agreed to provide equipment and demonstrations.[2263]

On October 1, 2004, the Act on the Protection of Privacy in Working Life took effect.[2264] The new Act replaces the Act on Data Protection in Working Life,[2265] which had been in force since October 2001. Like its predecessor, the new Act determines the legality of several issues in the workplace, such as psychological, genetic, and drug tests; the processing of medical histories; and the use of video and audio surveillance devices. The Act also delineates procedures by which employers may, in their employees' absence, open e-mail messages sent to or

---

[2259] Privacy International, Privacy, Technology, and Europe: A report for Japan's Ministry of Public Management, Home Affairs Postal and Telecommunications, March 2003, available at <http://is.lse.ac.uk/staff/hosein/pets/japan_pets.pdf>.

[2260] Id.

[2261] Id.

[2262] "RFID Lab Finland Is a Newly Opened Finnish Application Center for RFID Technology," eFinland, February 11, 2005, at <http://e.finland.fi/netcomm/news/showarticle.asp?intNWSAID=33122>.

[2263] Id.

[2264] Act on the Protection of Privacy in Working Life (759/2004), available at <http://www.finlex.fi/en/laki/kaannokset/2004/en20040759.pdf>.

[2265] The Act on Data Protection in Working Life (477/2001), available at <http://www.mol.fi/english/working/dataprotection.html>.

from employees' work e-mail addresses. [2266] Previously, the Telecommunications Privacy Act prevented Finnish employers from monitoring the contents of employee's e-mail messages.[2267] The statute also contains new regulations on camera surveillance (allowed as long as no employee is singled out and employees are informed how and when such monitoring is to be conducted) and drug testing (widely allowed at work, provided such testing is legally justified, as when the job requires accuracy or ability to react quickly).[2268]

The Finnish government has enacted special ordinances that apply to particular personal data systems. These include those operated by the police such as criminal information systems,[2269] the National Health Service, passport systems, population registers,[2270] farm registers, and motor vehicle registers.[2271] In January 2001, a new law on the status and rights of social welfare clients came into force and includes data protection provisions relating to the use of social services.[2272] In October 1999, the government amended the laws and granted the police a new high-tech means of enforcing traffic fines, which in Finland are based on the driver's income. Whereas before the police would simply ask violators for their income and calculate the fine manually based on that income, they now use cellular phones to access the official tax records. Within seconds the drivers reported income appears up on the screen along with the corresponding fine.[2273]

The Act on the Openness of Government Activities, most of which came into force in December 1999, also contains provisions on privacy.[2274] Chapter 6 of the Act exempts from public disclosure government documents containing data on the annual income or net worth of a person, documents containing information on a secret telephone number or information on the location of a mobile communications device, and documents revealing a person's place of residence, telephone number, or other contact information if the person has asked that the

---

[2266] Act on the Protection of Privacy in Working Life, *supra.*

[2267] Peter Blume *et al.*, *supra* at 71.

[2268] *Id.*

[2269] Criminal Records Act (770/93).

[2270] Act on Population Information (1993/507).

[2271] Jorma Kuopus, Data Protection Regulatory System - Data Transmission and Privacy (D. Campbell & J. Fisher, eds., Martinus Nijhoff Publishers 1994).

[2272] Act on Experiments with Seamless Service Chains in Social Welfare and Health Care Services and with a Social Security Card (811/2000), available at <http://www.finlex.fi/pdf/saadkaan/E0000811.PDF>.

[2273] Steve Stecklow, "Finnish Drivers Don't Mind Sliding Scale, but Instant Calculation Gets Low Marks," Wall Street Journal, January 2, 2001.

[2274] Act on the Openness of Government Activities, available at <http://www.finlex.fi/en/laki/kaannokset/1999/en19990621.pdf>.

information be kept secret and is justified in believing that disclosure would endanger himself or his family.[2275]

Wiretapping and Surveillance Rules

Electronic surveillance and telephone tapping by the government are authorized by the criminal law. A judge can give permission to tap the telephone lines of a suspect if the suspect is liable for a jail sentence for crimes that are exhaustively listed in the Coercive Criminal Investigations Means Act. Transactional data of a suspect's telecommunications activity can be obtained if the suspect faces at least four months of jail. Electronic surveillance is possible, with the permission of the judge, if the suspect is accused of a drug-related crime or a crime that can be punished with more than four years in jail. There were 12 orders for wiretapping in 1997. Although cases of political telecommunications eavesdropping are rare in Finland, there have been published reports that the Finnish military has either supported Western signals intelligence operations (via its large base at Santahamina on the outskirts of Helsinki), or acquiesced to a Swedish/United States eavesdropping collaborative effort from the Swedish embassy in downtown Helsinki.[2276] In 1996, the PENET anonymous re-mailer was forced to shut down after Scientologists demanded that the identity of users posting critical messages be revealed to the Church. The court order was later enjoined by the Court of Appeals.[2277]

National identification numbers have long been in use in Finland. Since the 1970s, all citizens have been issued a national identification number consisting of their date of birth and four other characters. The number is used extensively in the public and private sectors. It is included on passports, driving licenses, and other personal data files held by the public administration.[2278] The Finnish government in December 1999 began issuing new national ID cards (FINEID) based on smart card technology.[2279] The cards include digital signatures to communicate online with government agencies and companies. The Finnish Population Register Centre operates as the digital signature certificate authority. The cards can be used in smart card readers in personal computers. Beginning in June 2004, medical insurance data could be put into identification cards, thus

---

[2275] *Id.*

[2276] *See* <http://www.qainfo.se/~lb>.

[2277] *See* Philip Giordano, "Invoking Law as a Basis for Identity in Cyberspace," note 38, 1998 Stanford Technology Law Review 1, at <http://stlr.stanford.edu/stlr/articles/98_stlr_1/article.htm>.

[2278] Peter Blume *et al., supra* .

[2279] *See,* Finnish Population Register Centre's homepage <http://www.vaestorekisterikeskus.fi/>.

replacing social security (KELA) cards issued by the Social Security Institution of Finland.[2280] As of the end of 2004, the Mobile Citizen Certificate, enabling mobile commerce and communication, has also been available in Subscriber Identity Module (SIM) cards in mobile phones,[2281] and there are plans to put them in interactive television systems.

The Electronic Services in Administration Act was passed in early 2000 to encourage the use of digital ID cards but, so far, they have not proved very popular among the public.[2282] There are about 51,000 valid Finnish electronic ID cards. Each card is valid for five years and contains a citizen certificate issued by the Population Register Centre. As of June 2003, cardholders have been able to have their cards imprinted with their social security data. The card can be used as a travel document in EU member states, and about 50 services use the card. The citizen certificate can also be used on different platforms and is channel-independent. Since October 2003, it has been available for the Visa Electron cards issued by the OP Bank Group. The first mobile citizen certificate started to be used in November. The mobile phone service based on the use of the mobile citizen certificate that allows the electronic identification of users became available for consumers in early 2005.[2283]

E-Voting Privacy

The Population Register Centre is also working with mobile operators to design a smart card suitable for remote electronic voting. Electronic voting is scheduled for testing in the advance voting phase of the 2007 Parliamentary election. An electronic ID card or other certification will be used to protect voter identity.[2284]

The Finnish Ministry of Interior had planned to introduce biometric identification in passports as early as May 2005, making Finland a pioneer in biometric passports. However, the introduction of biometrics has been stalled by a Market Court hearing of a claim brought by Finnish passport manufacturer, Setec, which is challenging the award of the contract for manufacture of the passports to its

---

[2280] "Social Security Data on Electronic ID Cards," eFinland, June 2, 2004, at
<http://e.finland.fi/netcomm/news/showarticle.asp?intNWSAID=24579>.

[2281] "Mobile Citizen Certificate Launched," eFinland, November 26, 2004, at
<http://e.finland.fi/http://e.finland.fi/netcomm/news/showarticle.asp?intNWSAID=30340>.

[2282] Peter Blume *et al.*, *supra*.

[2283] "Pan-European Electronic Identity Being Developed in Wide Cooperation," eFinland, December 22, 2004, at <http://e.finland.fi/netcomm/news/showarticle.asp?intNWSAID=30901>.

[2284] "Electronic Voting To Be Tested in 2007," eFinland, April 15, 2005, at
<http://e.finland.fi/netcomm/news/showarticle.asp?intNWSAID=35478>.

Swedish and Dutch competitors.[2285] According to the Ministry, biometrics will improve efficiency of identification and help fight illegal immigration and terrorism.[2286]

Health Privacy

Privacy in health care is protected by the Act on the Status and Rights of Patients, which became effective in 1993. Under the Act, health care must be administered in a way that does not violate human dignity and that protects the patient's convictions and privacy. In general, medical records may not be released without the patient's written consent except when otherwise provided by law.[2287] In addition, the Medical Research Act, in force since November 1, 1999, prohibits disclosure of patient information including, health status, personal circumstances, or financial situation, by medical research workers and ethics committee members.[2288]

Open Government

The Act on the Openness of Government Activities (mentioned above) replaced the Publicity of Official Documents Act of 1951.[2289] It provides for a general right to access any document created by a government agency, or sent or received by a government agency, including electronic records. Finland is a country that has traditionally adhered to the Nordic tradition of open access to government files. In fact, the world's first Freedom of Information act dates back as far as the *Riksdag's* (Swedish Parliament's) 1766 Access to Public Records Act. This Act also applied to Finland, then a Swedish-governed territory.[2290]

[2285] R. A. Hettinga, "Finland's Issuing of Biometric Passports Delayed," Helsingin Sanomat International Edition, March 31, 2005, available at <http://www.helsinginsanomat.fi/english/article/print/1101978984487>.

[2286] "Biometric Passports Possibly in May 2005," eFinland, March 9, 2004, at <http://www.e.finland.fi/netcomm/news/showrticle.asp?intNWSAID=21813>.

[2287] Act on the Status and Rights of Patients (785/1992), August 17, 1992, available at <http://www.finlex.fi/fi/laki/kaannokset/1992/en19920785.pdf>.

[2288] Medical Research Act (488/1999), issued April 9, 1999, available at <http://www.finlex.fi/en/laki/kaannokset/1999/en19990488.pdf>.

[2289] Act 83/9/2/1951.

[2290] Wayne Madsen, Handbook of Personal Data Protection (Stockton Press 1992).

International Obligations

Finland is a member of the Council of Europe (CoE) and has signed and ratified the Convention for the Protection of Individuals with Regard to Automatic Processing of Personal Data (Convention No. 108).[2291] Finland has signed and ratified the European Convention for the Protection of Human Rights and Fundamental Freedoms.[2292] Finland signed the CoE Convention on Cybercrime in November 2001 but has not ratified it yet.[2293] Finland is a member of the Organization for Economic Cooperation and Development (OECD) and has adopted the OECD Guidelines on the Protection of Privacy and Transborder Flows of Personal Data.

Åland Islands

The Parliament of the self-governing Åland Islands (*Landsting*) passed its own Data Protection Act in 1991 and independently ratified the CoE's Convention No. 108.[2294] If an international treaty entered into by Finland contains a provision that is in conflict with the Autonomy Act[2295] or that falls within the authority of Åland, the Parliament must approve such a provision for it to be valid in Åland.[2296] Although the Åland Data Protection Act makes reference to the Finnish Data Protection Act, there has always been some resistance by the Åland Swedish-speaking majority to follow orders from Helsinki. Constitutionally, the Åland Parliament may nullify Finnish laws on its territory.[2297]

French Republic

Constitutional Privacy Framework

The right of privacy is not explicitly included in the French Constitution of 1958. The Constitutional Court ruled in 1995 that the right of privacy was implicit in

---

[2291] Signed April 10, 1991; ratified December 2, 1991; entered into force April 1, 1992.

[2292] Signed May 5, 1989; ratified May 10, 1990; entered into force May 10, 1990; *See also* Finland Ministry of Foreign Affairs, Government Report to Parliament on the Human Rights Policy of Finland 2004, May, 2004, available at <http://formin.finland.fi/doc/eng/policies/human-rights04.pdf>.

[2293] Signed November 23, 2001.

[2294] Kuopus, *supra.*

[2295] Act on the Autonomy of Åland, available at <http://www.lagtinget.Aland.fi/eng/act.html>.

[2296] Åland and the European Union, available at <http://www.lagtinget.Aland.fi/eng/eu.html#anchor360419>.

[2297] Madsen, *supra.*

the Constitution,[2298] and confirmed this in 1999, by stating that the freedom proclaimed in Article 2 of the 1789 Declaration of the Rights of Man and the Citizen ("Déclaration des droits de l'homme et du citoyen de 1789") implies the respect of privacy.[2299]

Statutory Rules on Privacy

The Data Protection Act was enacted in 1978 and covers personal information held by government agencies and private entities.[2300] This acts provides that anyone wishing to process personal data must register and obtain permission in many cases relating to processing by public bodies and for medical research. Individuals must be informed of the reasons for collection of information and may object to its processing either before or after it is collected. Individuals have rights to access information being kept about them and to demand the correction and, in some cases, the deletion of this data. Fines and imprisonment can be imposed for violations.

France has just adopted a revision of its Data Protection Act on July 15, 2004. As a member of the European Union (EU), France should have amended its data protection regime to make it consistent with the EU Data Protection Directive (1995/46/EC) by October 1, 1998.[2301] The legislative process started in July 2000, with a pre-draft legislation to update the law sent to the data protection authority for review and consultation.[2302] It took four readings by both the National Assembly and the Senate, with a change of political majority in the meantime, to have the new bill[2303] adopted, four years after the start of the process. Since the bill was submitted on July 20, 2004, by the Parliamentary opposition to the French Constitutional Council (*Conseil constitutionnel*), it will be promulgated only after the decision of the Council, which may result in some modifications of the text.

[2298] Décision 94-352DC du Conseil constitutionnel du 18 Janvier 1995, available at <http://www.conseil-constitutionnel.fr/decision/1994/94352dc.htm>.

[2299] Décision 99-416DC du Conseil constitutionnel du 23 juillet 1999, available at <http://www.conseil-constitutionnel.fr/decision/1999/99416/index.htm>.

[2300] Loi n° 78-17 du 6 janvier 1978, Loi relative à l'informatique, aux fichiers et aux libertés, available at <http://www.cnil.fr/index.php?id=301>.

[2301] Arrêt de la Cour (deuxième chambre) du 14 février 2001. Commission des Communautés européennes contre République française. Manquement d'Etat - Manquement non contesté - Directive 95/16/CE, Affaire C-219/99.

[2302] Avis de la Commission nationale de l'informatique et des libertés sur le projet de loi modifiant la loi du 6 janvier 1978 relative à l'informatique, aux fichiers et aux libertés, September 26, 2000, available at <http://www.cnil.fr/fileadmin/documents/approfondir/textes/aviscnildonneesperso.pdf>.

[2303] Successive versions of the bill are available at <http://www.senat.fr/dossierleg/pjl01-203.html>.

This recently adopted bill has faced strong criticisms by a French coalition of organizations named DELIS, which gathers some 40 French non-governmental organizations (NGOs) and trade unions, among them the French Human Rights League (LDH) and Imaginons un Réseau Internet Solidaire (IRIS), a civil liberties organization. The three organizations issued a press release after the adoption of the bill, which summarizes their criticisms since the beginning of the legislative process.[2304] These criticisms, most of them being the basis of the submission to the Constitutional Council, include: the non-inclusion of genetic and biometric data in the list of sensitive data; the file declaration exemption for private companies having appointed a "data correspondent," without ensuring this correspondent with a protected status, necessary to his/her independence with respect to his/her employer; the possibility for any non-public entity (including NGOs, professional associations, religious organizations, intellectual property rights trade organizations, etc.) to set up and maintain records and databases which are normally only maintained by public authorities for the purpose of fighting and/or preventing these infringements. This last measure would *de facto* limit the exercise for filed persons of their rights of access and rectification. When these private entities are royalty collection organizations that represent authors, performers, phonogram and videogram producers' interests, the right to create private records of intellectual property rights infringers may be likened to the creation of suspects' files without providing appropriate access rights for data subjects.

Data Protection Authority

The data protection authority is the *Commission nationale de l'informatique et des libertés* (CNIL), an independent agency that enforces the Data Protection Act and other related laws.[2305] The Commission takes complaints, issues rulings, sets rules, conducts audits, makes reports, and ensures the public access to information by being a registrar of all data controllers' processing activities. The new law gives the CNIL more authority over commercial data processing files by allowing it to investigate, issue warnings, and impose sanctions (by fines of up to EUR 150,000). However, at the same time, it weakens the commission's control over large government information systems by creating a new data system category, known as "sovereignty files" over which the CNIL looses key

---

2304 DELIS, LDH, IRIS, "French Data Protection Act Revision: the Accomplished Regression," July 16, 2004, available at <http://www.iris.sgdg.org/info-debat/comm-infolib0704-en.html>.

2305 Homepage <http://www.cnil.fr>.

powers.[2306] Whereas before the approval of the commission was needed prior any government processing system could be established, this would no longer be necessary for these sovereignty files. They are defined to include files relating to the safety of the State, defense, public security or penal repression, or those that use the NIR (social security number). It is thought that this revision is a response to the difficulties experienced by the government in implementing the STIC (*Système de Traitement des Infractions Constatées*). This system was first envisioned in 1995 but was not implemented until July 2000 following the reluctant approval of the CNIL.

In early 2004, the CNIL composition has been partly renewed. Its former president, Michel Gentot, has not been nominated again by the government, and is not a commissioner anymore. This decision is reportedly explained by Mr. Gentot's strong position against what are currently called sovereignty files, and, more generally speaking, by a global trend of the current conservative majority, and especially of President Jacques Chirac, to nominate politically trustworthy people at key positions.[2307] It should be noted that new CNIL President, Alex Türk, has at the same time been the rapporteur of the new bill at the Senate.

The CNIL carried out 31 inspections in 2003, the most important of which concerned local authorities, credit reference agencies and debt collectors, cancer registers, controls over "cybersurveillance" activities, and controls pursuant to Article 96 of the Schengen Convention. Four inspections were initiated upon specific complaints. Other important enforcement activities: Fight against unsolicited faxes for advertising purposes, the CNIL having taken judicial action against eight companies in such cases; efforts vis-à-vis credit reference agencies to correct unlawful processing, with the cooperation of the supervisory authorities of the banking sector; and, efforts vis-à-vis the "fichier PREVENTEL," a database put in place to fight against unpaid bills by the telecommunication sector.[2308]

The CNIL also engaged in a range of proactive enforcement strategies. Internal reflection is currently ongoing at the CNIL to reformulate the enforcement

---

[2306] Stéphane Foucart, "Les pouvoirs de la CNIL devraient être considérablement amoindris," Le Monde, July 14, 2004, available at <http://www.lemonde.fr/web/recherche_articleweb/1,13-0,36-372444,0.html> and "La nouvelle loi Informatique et libertés autorise le fichage des internaures," Le Monde, July 17, 2004, <http://www.lemonde.fr/web/recherche_articleweb/1,13-0,36-372827,0.html>.

[2307] Hervé Gattegno and Philippe Le Coeur, "L'Etat-Chirac impose les siens aux sommets du pouvoir," Le Monde, July 13, 2004.

[2308] "Recent examples of enforcement actions carried out by data protection authorities" Article 29-Data Protection Working Party, (Article 29 WP Report) January 2005, available at <http://europa.eu.int/comm/justice_home/fsj/privacy/docs/wpdocs/2004/wp101a_en.pdf>.

strategy and activities of this authority, in particular in the context of the adoption of the new Data Protection Law in France. Upon the assessment of its past enforcement activities (324 specific actions have been taken to date since the creation of the authority in 1978), the CNIL is reflecting on a new policy that would differentiate between controls and inspections on the spot, with appropriate follow-up of complaints received, putting in place of appropriate security measures, enforcement on the Internet and even sector-based investigations, in agreement with other data protection authorities notably within the framework of the Article 29 Working Party activities.[2309]

Since 1978 the CNIL has received over 13,700 requests for advice and 44,830 complaints. While it reported in its 2002 annual report that the number of inquiries received annually had more than doubled since 1995,[2310] with a total of 7,909 inquiries[2311] in 2002 (up 38 percent from 2001 to 2002), the 2003[2312] report notes a 22 percent drop of the total number of inquiries (6,136 inquiries[2313] received in 2003). According to the CNIL, this important drop mainly reflects the decline of complaints due to the Commission's warning to junk fax companies of the new legislation banning them.

The CNIL's 2003 report addresses access to police files, biometrics and genetic data, Passenger Name Record (PNR), unsolicited commercial faxes, spam fighting, people movement traceability, e-government, etc. It shows that the use of biometrics and genetic data has increased in France.

On genetic data, the Internal Safety Law[2314] ("Loi pour la sécurité intérieure") promulgated on March 18, 2003, has extended the list of infractions leading to a record in the National Computerized File of Genetic Data (*Fichier national automatisé des empreintes génétiques* or FNAEG), as well as the list of persons whose genetic data may be kept in the FNAEG or compared to its content. At its

---

[2309] *Id.*

[2310] CNIL, 23e rapport d'activité 2002, June 26, 2002, available at <http://www.ladocumentationfrancaise.fr/brp/notices/034000366.shtml>.

[2311] Of these 5,076 (+ 42 percent compared to 2001) were complaints, 1,126 (+ 16 percent) were requests for advice, 1,264 (+ 51 percent) were access requests, 333 (+ 32 percent) were requests for the registration lists maintained by the CNIL and 110 (+ 17 percent) were requests to be removed from commercial files. In particular, the number of requests by private individuals for checking files held on them by police forces rose by 51 percent. In response to complaints, the CNIL also carried out about 52 on-the-spot checks at commercial companies, two of which were sued by the CNIL.

[2312] CNIL, 24e rapport d'activité 2003, June 22, 2004, available at <http://www.ladocumentationfrancaise.fr/brp/notices/044000252.shtml>.

[2313] Of these 3,567 were complaints (-31% compared to 2002), 1,102 were requests for advice (-2%), 1163 were access requests (-7%), 304 were requests for the registration lists maintained by the CNIL (-8%).

[2314] Loi n° 2003-239 du 18 mars 2003, Loi pour la sécurité intérieure, available at <http://www.legifrance.gouv.fr/WAspad/UnTexteDeJorf?numjo=INTX0200145L>.

creation in 1998, the FNAEG was restricted to genetic data of persons who were condemned for serious sexual crimes, like rape and child abuse. After successive extensions of its use, it may now contain genetic data of persons simply suspected (but not yet condemned) of almost all infractions related to prejudice against property or people. While the CNIL has obtained a few minor improvements to this regime (*e.g.*, the maximum duration of data retention limited to 25 years instead of 40), the FNAEG remains a strong concern in France. In April 2004, the FNAEG was recently used to record the genetic data of a trade-unionist, Charles Hoareau, who had been condemned in 2000 to a five-month suspended sentence for "voluntary violence" against the police during a protest action in Marseille. This has been denounced by the CGT trade-union as a "criminalization of trade-union activity."[2315]

On biometrics, France is taking its part in the EU trend to extend the use of biometrics in passports, visas, and other travel and immigration documents. On November 26, 2003, the Immigration Law[2316] has generalized the use of biometric techniques for visa delivery and border controls, and stores all visa requesters' fingerprints and biometric pictures in databases for further processing. Biometrics is not only used by the government, but also by companies such as national air carrier Air France.[2317]

Furthermore, a new national file has been added to the many files already in place, with the adoption on March 2004 of the "Perben II Law"[2318] (*Loi portant adaptation de la justice aux évolutions de la criminalité*).[2319] It creates the National judicial computerized record system of sexual offenders (*Fichier judiciaire national automatisé des auteurs d'infractions sexuelles* or FNAIS). This file records, for up to 30 years, the identity and addresses of persons (including minors) who have committed all kinds of sexual offenses, except

---

[2315] UD-CGT 13, "Le syndicalisme n'est pas une activité criminelle," petition available at
<http://marseille.naros.info/article.php3?id_article=462>.

[2316] Loi n°2003-1119 du 26 novembre 2003. Loi relative à la maîtrise de l'immigration, au séjour des étrangers en France et à la nationalité. Available at
<http://www.legifrance.gouv.fr/WAspad/UnTexteDeJorf?numjo=INTX0300040L>.

[2317] Air France has been testing a biometrics-based technique that uses fingerprints to confirm passenger identities on selected flights leaving from the Orly and Charles de Gaulle Airports in Paris. The CNIL authorized the biometrics experiment. It accepted the air security and anti-terrorism arguments behind Air France's experiment, but issued confidentiality recommendations aimed at ensuring respect for passenger privacy. These conditions include strict rules against any future use of stored information and tight standards on controlling access to data. Pascal de Izaguirre, Air France's senior vice-president for ground operations, said that the company is "already working with the authorities to extend use of biometrics." "Biometrics: French Privacy Watchdog Approves Plan For Airline Biometric Security System," Privacy Law Watch, December 18, 2002.

[2318] Called "Perben II" after the name of the French Minister of Justice, Dominique Perben.

2319 Loi n° 2004-204 du 9 mars 2004, Loi portant adaptation de la justice aux évolutions de la criminalité, available at <http://www.legifrance.gouv.fr/citoyen/jorf_nor.ow?numjo=JUSX0300028L>.

exhibitionism and sexual harassment. This record system can only be consulted by judicial authorities and specific government agencies.

In the future, major problems are expected to arise with the new Computerized Patient Record (CPR) that is being currently introduced by law in France, in the context of the reform of the social security legislation. The DELIS coalition and the French Human Rights League, together with major doctors' associations, have started a campaign against the CPR, as it would seriously undermine individual freedoms and the right to privacy, and discriminate between categories of the population, since the use of the CPR would be mandatory to obtain the reimbursement of medical expenses.[2320]

Wiretaps and Surveillance Rules

Electronic surveillance is regulated by a 1991 law that requires permission of an investigating judge before a wiretap is installed. The duration of the tap is limited to four months and can be renewed.[2321] The law created the *Commission nationale de contrôle des interceptions de sécurité* (CNCIS), which sets rules and reviews wiretaps each year. From 1995 to 1999 the number of wiretaps granted annually was between 4,500 and 4,700. This number decreased slightly in 2000. In 2004, there were 5,651[2322] requests for wiretaps (3,733 new and 1,918 renewals).[2323] This represents a 13 percent increase in comparison with 2003 when there were 4,994 interceptions (3,317 new requests and 1677 renewals). This number, however, must also be interpreted in conjunction with the evolution of the phone infrastructure (44.5 million mobile phones and 33 million land lines). The interceptions of communication, however, should remain the exceptional measure required by the law.[2324]

[2320] LDH and DELIS, "Réactions au projet actuel de dossier médical partagé," June 28, 2004, available at <http://www.delis.sgdg.org/>.

[2321] Loi n° 91-646 du 10 juillet 1991 relative au secret des correspondances émises par la voie des communications électroniques. available at <http://www.legifrance.gouv.fr/WAspad/Visu?cid=20655&indice=1&table=CONSOLIDE&ligneDeb=1>.

[2322] Among the new requests, 50% (idem in 2003) were motivated by organized crime matters, 34% by terrorism, 16% by national security protection, while among renewals, 36.5% were motivated by organized crime matters, 40% by national security protection and 41% by prevention of terrorism. This total inversion of respective rates is motivated, according to CNCIS, by the fact that wiretaps for organized crime matters do not need to be renewed, since one year is enough for investigation.

[2323] 13e rapport d'activité 2005, Commission nationale de contrôle des interceptions de sécurité, May 2005, available at <http://www.ladocumentationfrancaise.fr/informations/presse/2005/interceptions-securite.shtml>.(in French).

[2324] *Id.*

On May 17, 2005, the highest court in France, the Cour de Cassation, has struck down an appeals court verdict from November 2002 that allowed companies to search the computers of their employees for undesired Internet behavior. The medical supplies company Nycomed Amersham Medical System (later renamed Cathnet-Science) searched the computer of an employee after somebody had found erotic pictures in his drawer (during his absence). At the very least, the employee must be warned before and be present if a search is conducted, the high court has ruled. The Cour de Cassation also found the employee's subsequent dismissal unacceptable and has referred the case back to the appeals court of Versailles, to decide on the fate of the employee and a possible reimbursement for damages.[2325]

It is the second instance where the Cour de Cassation has upheld the privacy of employees. In an earlier case, an employee of Nikon was dismissed after having used his work computer for private activities.[2326] On October 2, 2001, the Cour de Cassation struck down the decision validating this dismissal as well. The judgment was based on the court's condemnation of the computer search pursuant to the article 8 of the ECHR, article 9 of the French Civil Code and articles 120-122 of the Working Code.[2327]

Major Privacy Case Law

The European Court of Human Rights has ruled against France several times for violations of Article 8 of the Convention. The Court's 1990 decision in *Kruslin v. France* resulted in the enactment of the 1991 law.[2328] In 1998, the Court fined France FRF 25,000 (EUR 3,800) for wiretap law violations.[2329] There have been many cases of illegal wiretapping, including most notably a long-running scandal over an anti-terrorist group in the office of former President Francois Mitterand monitoring the calls of journalists and opposition politicians.[2330] The CNCIS estimated that there were over 100,000 illegal taps conducted by private companies and individuals in 1996, many on behalf of government agencies. A

[2325] "Highest court France defends workfloor privacy once more," Edri-gram newsletter, number 3.11, June 2, 2005 available at <http://www.edri.org/edrigram/number3.11/privacy>. See also, Cour de Cassation, Mr K. vs. Sté Cathnet-Science, May 17 2005, available at <http://www.juritel.com/Ldj_html-1095.html> (in French).
2326 See, Cour de Cassation, Société Nikon France vs. Monsieur 0, October, 2 2001, available at<http://www.foruminternet.org/documents/jurisprudence/lire.phtml?id=171> (in French).
[2327] *Id.*

[2328] Kruslin v. France, 176-A, Eur. Ct. H.R. (ser. A) (1990).

[2329] "La France condamnée par la Cour européenne des droits de l'homme," Le Monde, August 27, 1998.

[2330] *See* Capitaine Paul Barril, Guerres Secrètes à L'Élysée (Albin Michel, 1996); Francis Zamponi, Les RG à l'écoute de la France: Police et politique de 1981 à 1997 (La Découverte, 1998).

decree was issued in 1997 to limit the dissemination of tapping equipment.[2331] Only government requests for interception are under review by the CNCIS. There is a separate control scheme for wiretap requests by the judiciary. In May 21, 2003, the Cour de Cassation ruled that wiretapping a lawyer at a judge's request was fair and legal because the lawyer had not yet been in charge of the case at stake at the time of the wiretap and his client had been prosecuted regardless of the wiretap result. A subsequent ruling by the same court in October 1, 2003, has also restricted the circumstances of unfair wiretaps of lawyers at a judge's request. In addition, the "Perben II" law extends the circumstances where judicial interceptions of electronic communications are authorized (Article 1).

The tort of privacy was first recognized in France as far back as 1858[2332] and was added to the Civil Code in 1970.[2333] There are additional specific laws on administrative documents,[2334] archives,[2335] video surveillance,[2336] correspondence,[2337] and employment.[2338] There are also protections incorporated in the Penal Code.[2339]

Data retention is ruled by the Daily Safety Law (*Loi sur la Sécurité Quotidienne*, or LSQ)[2340], enacted on November 15, 2003, and by the Digital Economy Law

---

[2331] 5e rapport d'activité 1997, Commission nationale de contrôle des interceptions de sécurité, May 1998.

[2332] The *Rachel* affaire. Judgment of June 16, 1858, Trib. pr. inst. de la Seine, 1858 D.P. III 62. *See* Jeanne M. Hauch, Protecting Private Facts in France: The Warren & Brandeis Tort is Alive and Well and Flourishing in Paris, 68 Tul. L. Rev. 1219 (May 1994).

[2333] Civil Code, Article 9, Statute No. 70-643 of July 17, 1970.

[2334] Loi n° 78-753 du 17 juillet 1978 portant diverses mesures d'amélioration des relations entre l'administration et le public et diverses dispositions d'ordre administratif, social et fiscal (Journal officiel, July 18, 1978, at 2851), available at <http://www.cnil.fr/textes/text05.htm>.

[2335] Loi n° 79-18 du 3 janvier 1979 sur les archives (Journal officiel, January 5, 1979, at 43, *erratum* at Journal officiel, January 6, 1979, at 55).

[2336] Loi d'orientation et de programmation n° 95-73 du 21 janvier 1995 relative à la sécurité (Journal officiel, January 24, 1995, at 1249), available at <http://www.cnil.fr/textes/text054.htm>; *see also* Décret n° 96-926 du 17 octobre 1996 relatif à la vidéo-surveillance pris pour l'application de l'article 10 de la loi n° 95-73 du 21 janvier 1995 d'orientation et de programmation relative à la sécurité (Journal officiel, October 20, 1996, at 15432), available at <http://www.cnil.fr/textes/text055.htm>, and Circulaire du 22 octobre 1996 relative à l'application de l'article 10 de la loi n° 95-73 du 21 janvier 1995 d'orientation et de programmation relative à la sécurité (décret sur la vidéosurveillance) (Journal officiel, December 7, 1996, at 17835), available at <http://www.cnil.fr/textes/text056.htm>.

[2337] Code of Post and Telecommunications, L. 41.

[2338] Loi n° 92-1446 du 31 décembre 1992 relative à l'emploi, au développement du travail à temps partiel et à l'assurance chômage. (Journal officiel, January 1, 1993, at 19).

[2339] Penal Code, Article 368.

[2340] Loi n° 2001-1062 du 15 novembre 2001 relative à la sécurité quotidienne, available at <http://www.legifrance.gouv.fr/WAspad/UnTexteDeJorf?numjo=INTX0100032L>.

(*Loi pour la confiance dans l'économie numérique*, or LEN), promulgated on June 21, 2004.[2341]

On February 4, 2005, the appeal court of Paris extended the general obligations for data retention to companies. According to the verdict, like Internet providers all companies are obliged to store traffic data originating from their employees, to allow identification of e-mails with illegal contents sent from company machines.

The court decision follows proceedings from the company World Press Online (WPO) against the bank BNP Paribas. Two commercial partners from WPO received a litigious e-mail about the company at the end of 2003, sent from a Yahoo e-mail address. WPO tracked the IP-address back to a branch from the bank in France and demanded to know which employee had used the specific computer. BNP didn't reply at first. WPO instigated a case and BNP was ordered on October 12, 2004, by the commercial court of Paris to hand over the requested information. BNP appealed, but lost again and was forced to hand over data about their employees. The court also said that the obligation to retain identification data and provide these data upon judicial request does not imply that the company has to do any investigations on the raw material to identify the possible sender of the e-mail.[2342]

On March 10, 2005, the Court of Appeals in Versailles, France, ruled that search engine Google has lost an appeal against a French court order to change its advertisement practices. The case about the advertisement practice was instigated by the travel companies Luteciel SARL and Viaticum SA. Competitors bought the search terms 'bourse des vols' and 'bourse des voyages' (flight exchange and trip exchange) so that their advertisements would show next to the search results. The two companies successfully claimed they had exclusive trademark rights on these terms, and accused Google of something akin to counterfeiting. Google was ordered to pay EUR 75,000 (US 100,000) in fines and legal costs in first instance. In February 2005 Google lost a similar case against the French luxury goods company Moët Hennessy Louis Vuitton. Another search engine, Yahoo,

---

[2341] Loi n°2004-575 du 21 juin 2004, Loi pour la confiance dans l'économie numérique, available at <http://www.legifrance.gouv.fr/WAspad/UnTexteDeJorf?numjo=ECOX0200175L>.

[2342] "French court decision on traffic data retention,"EDRi-gram newsletter number 3.5 March 10, 2005, available at <http://www.edri.org/edrigram/number3.5/France.>. See also, Verdict of the Paris appeal court, February 4, 2005, available at
<http://www.foruminternet.org/telechargement/documents/ca-par20050204.pdf.> (in French).

lost a similar case in January 2005 as well, when the French hotel chain Accor complained about advertisements from competitors using its hotel names.[2343]

Anti-terrorism Measures

The LSQ is a law in which new anti-terrorism provisions were added, in direct response to the September 11, 2001 terrorist attacks. It includes provisions on data retention and provides for a government access to cryptography keys. These provisions have been extracted from the draft Law on the Information Society (LSI),[2344] introduced on June 13, 2001, *i.e.* prior to September 11, 2001, by the government and purporting to implement the EU E-Commerce Directive (2000/31/EC). In submitting comments to the government on this proposal in May 2001, the CNIL recommended that a distinction be drawn between information necessary for invoicing purposes and information kept solely for law enforcement purposes and that there should be a three-month limitation for retention of the latter.[2345] With the LSQ, Internet Service Providers (ISPs) are required to store log files on all their customers' activities for up to one year. Moreover, the government has access to private encryption keys, import and export of encryption software are restricted, and strict sanctions are imposed for using cryptographic techniques to commit a crime. Many civil liberties groups opposed the LSQ because it heavily curtails human rights, was adopted hurriedly in defiance of regular legislative procedure, and under the pretense of the fight against terrorism. Civil liberties watchdog IRIS launched a campaign[2346] against this law (following its previous campaign against the LSI draft law), arguing that the data retention provisions of the LSQ violate the EU Telecommunications Privacy Directive (1997/66/EC), which was still applicable at that time. IRIS even filed a complaint with the European Commission (the Commission) against France for violation European legislation. After six months, the case was dropped by the Commission because the LSQ provisions on data retention had not yet entered into force.

In addition to the LSQ, the LEN also provides for data retention provisions. The concerned data are personally identifying information (including name, address, and log data). These provisions are extracted from the Liberty of Communication

---

[2343] "French jurisprudence about Google and cybersquatting," EDRi-gram newsletter number 3.6 March 24, 2005, available at <http://www.edri.org/edrigram/number3.6/google>

[2344] *See* <http://www.iris.sgdg.org/actions/lsi>.

[2345] CNIL. Délibération portant avis sur le projet de loi sur la société de l'information, May 3, 2001, available at <http://www.legifrance.gouv.fr/WAspad/Visu?cid=4564&indice=1&table=CNIL&ligneDeb=1>.

[2346] *See* <http://www.iris.sgdg.org/actions/loi-sec/>.

Act[2347] (*Loi sur la liberté de communication*) promulgated on August 1, 2000, and modifying the former audio-visual law.[2348] ISPs (host and access providers) are required to collect and keep identification and log data of their subscribers. These data are covered by the "professional secret," so that they may only be disclosed upon judicial request. The law also requires all persons wishing to post content on the Internet to identify themselves, either to the public, by publishing their name and address on their website (in the case of a business), or to their host provider (in the case of a private individual). The LEN has added a penalty of one year of imprisonment and a EUR 75,000 fine for any infringement of these provisions, either by the ISP of its subscribers. These provisions will enter into force when their implementing decrees (*décret d'application*) are published. In addition, the LEN now includes the LSQ provisions on cryptography, with the following two additions: first, a lower penalty is applicable (jail and fine) in cases where cryptography has been used to commit or prepare an infraction, where the suspect herself provided decryption keys to the police, thus allowing for self-incrimination; second, some uses of cryptography for research or professional purposes are not specifically mentioned anymore, therefore assimilating these categories of people to cybercriminals, when they conduct such activities.[2349]

On February 13, 2003, the Internal Safety Law (*Loi sur la sécurité intérieure*) has also authorized the immediate access by law enforcement authorities to the computer data of telecommunications operators, including Internet access providers, as well as of almost any public or private institution, organization or company. The second important measure authorizes the warrantless search of any information system, provided that the data is accessible through a network to which the computer being searched with a warrant is connected. If the data is stored in a computer located in a foreign country, its access remains subject to applicable international agreements.[2350] Finally, the Internal Safety law has perpetuated[2351] the so-called anti-terrorism provisions of the LSQ, which were initially valid only until December 2003.[2352]

[2347] Loi n° 2000-719 du 1er août 2000, modifiant la loi n° 86-1067 du 30 septembre 1986 relative à la liberté de communication.

[2348] A full history of the developments since the law was first introduced in May 1999 is available at <http://www.iris.sgdg.org/actions/loi-comm> (in French).

[2349] The LEN has also added a definition of electronic mail, as part of the transposition of the EU Directive on Privacy and Electronic Communications (2002/58/EC). This definition does not provide that e-mail is a correspondence, notwithstanding the fact that all the legislation on privacy (including the already cited 1991 law) refers to correspondence.

[2350] *See* <http://www.iris.sgdg.org/actions/loi-si>.

[2351] Article 31 of the Internal Safety law.

[2352] Article 22 of the Daily Safety law.

ISP liability for hosted content is now governed by the LEN. Before the LEN was enacted, the law held ISPs liable only for failing to delete content once ordered to do so by a judge. This liability regime, respectful of freedom of expression, the right to a fair trial and the principle of the presumption of innocence, was the result of widespread criticism from civil liberties groups.[2353] An additional provision that would have also held ISPs liable for failing to "take appropriate actions" once informed by a third party that they were hosting illegal or harmful content was later struck down by the Constitutional Council.[2354]The Council ruled that the "appropriate actions" to be taken by ISPs should have been specified in the law.

After the LEN enactment, the current French regime for ISP liability is exactly the one provided by the EU Directive on Electronic Commerce (2000/31/CE), transposed by the LEN. This means in particular that a notice and take down procedure has been introduced in the French legislation to rule ISP civil and penal liability.

The LEN has been the subject of a strong campaign by French civil liberties groups, from the very beginning of the legislative process. IRIS has a comprehensive dossier on its website, where all the steps of its campaign, run together with other organizations, among them the French Human Rights League (LDH), are extensively reported, with all documents provided.[2355] After the final adoption of the law by the Parliament, IRIS and LDH called the Parliamentary opposition to challenge the LEN before the Constitutional Council, providing them with all the necessary arguments.[2356]

[2353] Loi sur la liberté de communication, Déclaration des acteurs d'Internet, available at <http://www.iris.sgdg.org/actions/loi-comm/declaration.html>.

[2354] Conseil Constitutionnel, Décision n° 2000-433 DC, July 27, 2000.

[2355] *See* <http://www.iris.sgdg.org/actions/len>.

[2356] The recourse submitted by the socio-democrats challenged only three provisions: the one on the electronic mail definition (found constitutional), the one on ISP liability (found constitutional, with a reservation restricting the interpretation of this provision to cases where the content is 'manifestly illegal'), and a third one that introduced different time bars for online and off-line content when exercising the right of reply or when filing judicial complaints against offences identified in the press law (found unconstitutional, and the time bar is now the same in both cases). (Socialist Parliamentarians, recourse submitted to the Constitutional Council challenging the LEN, May 18, 2004, available at <http://www.conseil-constitutionnel.fr/decision/2004/2004496/saisine1.htm>.) IRIS and LDH submitted in addition their own brief to the Constitutional Council (IRIS and LDH, brief to the Constitutional Council challenging the LEN, May 24, 2004, available at <http://www.iris.sgdg.org/actions/len/LEN-memoireCC-IRIS-LDH.pdf>), complementing the analysis of the Parliamentary opposition recourse. The points addressed in this brief are: limitation of freedom of online communication for the needs of "national defense, public service necessity, technical constraints" (Article 1 of the LEN); limitation of freedom of online communication for the need "of audiovisual services, to develop and audiovisual production" (Article 1); definition of audiovisual services (Article 1); censorship of online content by access providers, as a consequence of the censorship by host providers (Article 9); limitation of freedom of online communication for the need of "protecting young audience" (Article 13); definition of online information providing as an e-commerce service (Article 14); and lower penalty (jail and

Case law in the field of surveillance at the workplace significantly progressed in clarity with a landmark decision by the *Cour de Cassation* in 2001. The French Supreme Court established that an employee has the right to privacy even at the workplace and during working hours, and that, as a result, deserves respect of the secrecy of his correspondence by his employer. The employer is now prohibited from getting access to his employee's e-mails if they are labeled private, even if the employer were to prove that the e-mail is limited to professional matters.[2357] A report published in March 2004 by the French Data Protection Authority summarizes the situation with regards to surveillance at the workplace.[2358] Finally, a recent law has modified the Labor Code, introducing explicitly for the first time the possibility for trade-union organizations to use the company Intranets and mail for their activities, including their communications to the company employees. This possibility is subject to an internal agreement between the employer and the trade-union organizations.[2359]

NGOs' Advocacy Work

On April 11, 2005, the French government outlined its plan to introduce biometrics on passports by 2006 and on ID cards by 2007. The French minister of the Interior, Dominique de Villepin, has announced plans to force every Frenchman to buy a new electronic ID card with a chip containing a photograph and fingerprints.[2360]

---

fine) in case cryptography has been used to commit or prepare an infraction, when decryption keys have been provided to police/justice by the person (Article 37). The status of such briefs in France is not official, thus the Constitutional Council does not have to examine them, although they can influence the decision of the Council. In the case of the LEN challenge, the Council disregarded the brief. It should also be mentioned that for the first time ever, the French Constitutional Council explicitly stated in its decision on the LEN that, since the transposition of European Directives is a constitutional obligation of the State, the Council could only oppose the resulting transposition law when it infringes an explicit provision of the French Constitution. Otherwise, only the community judge may control the respect of a European Directive. (Constitutional Council. Decision n°2004-496, June 10, 2004, available at <http://www.conseil-constitutionnel.fr/decision/2004/2004496/2004496dc.htm>.) This jurisprudence of the Constitutional Council can be interpreted as a step back in the democratic process in France.

[2357] Cass. fr. October 2, 2001, S.A. Nikon France v. Frédérick Onof; *see also* Christophe Guillemin, "L'entreprise n'a aucun droit de regard sur les couriers personnels," ZDNet France, available at <http://news.zdnet.fr/cgi-bin/fr/printer_friendly.cgi?id=2096632>.

[2358] CNIL, "La cybersurveillance sur les lieux de travail," La Documentation française, Mars 2004, available at <http://www.cnil.fr/ fileadmin/documents/approfondir/rapports/Rcybersurveillance-2004-VD.pdf>.

[2359] Loi n°2004-391 du 4 mai 2004, Loi relative à la formation professionnelle tout au long de la vie et au dialogue social, article 52 modifying article L 412-8 of the Labor Code. Available at <http://www.legifrance.gouv.fr/WAspad/UnTexteDeJorf?numjo=SOCX0300159L>.

[2360] "French minister demands compulsory biometric ID card," EDRi-gram newsletter number 3.8 April 20, 2005, available at <http://www.edri.org/edrigram/number3.8/ID>.

In a press conference held on May 26, 2005 in Paris, six organizations have launched a campaign against the French project of mandatory biometric ID cards.[2361] The French Human Rights League (LDH), the union of magistrates, the union of French barristers, EDRI-member IRIS, DELIS (a coalition of more than 60 French NGOs and trade unions for the defense of privacy and personal data protection) and the French Association of Democrat Lawyers have published a joint position statement and have started a petition demanding the withdrawal of the project of the French Ministry of the Interior to introduce a mandatory biometric ID card.[2362]

The ministry aims to provide the whole population by 2007 with an ID card with a contactless chip containing not only the civil status of the citizen but also two biometric identifiers: digital photograph and fingerprints. The data would be filed in centralized databases. The card will be mandatory and would also include the address of the holder.[2363]

"The government recognises that the ultimate goal of the project is to set up a universal card which integrates the identity, the benefit of social rights and the ability to make private transactions; the idea is to make the individual totally transparent to both public authorities and commercial actors," they added. Moreover, the six organizations question the motivations of the French government, especially with regards to the fight against terrorism. They also insist that the French government has been unable to provide any statistics regarding identity fraud.[2364]

On June 1, 2005, Air France started a campaign of voluntary biometric (fingerprint) identification at Roissy-Charles de Gaulle Airport in Paris (terminal 2F), in cooperation with the borders police. This experiment was approved by the CNIL, even though it implies the constitution of a centralized database, "because the program is voluntary." This program, called "Pegasus," allows for quicker and easier border control for travelers who register with it. These travelers may be EU or Swiss citizens. The six organizations against the mandatory biometric ID card project say that one fear is that the use of biometrics becomes

---

[2361] Joint position statement and petition of the six organizations, May 26, 2005, available at <http://www.ldh-france.org/actu_derniereheure.cfm?idactu=1059 (in French)>.

[2362] "French campaign against biometric ID card," EDRi-gram newsletter number 3.11 June 2, 2005, available at <http://www.edri.org/edrigram/number3.11/biometrics>.

[2363] Id.

[2364] Id.

commonplace for daily activities. This new experiment shows that the danger is already there.[2365]

On January 22, 2005, the jury of the French Big Brother Awards needed no less than seven of the famous negative Big Brother Awards to name and shame projects, people, institutions and companies for destroying privacy and promoting control. The minister of Health, Mr. Douste-Blazy received a special Jury Award for promoting a new law that created the "Dossier Medical Partagé," renamed "Dossier Medical Personnel (DMP)"[2366] (from "shared medical record" to "personal medical record"), that puts the entire medical records of every citizen on the Internet, in order to spend less money and "optimize" French medical care.[2367]

The Lifetime Menace Award was presented to the three French "homeland security" ministers Vaillant (left wing), Sarkozy & Perben (right wing), who introduced new DNA-sampling powers, not just for those convicted of sexual & violent crimes, but for every kind of suspect and for minor offences.[2368]

A new Award was invented by the French organizers to honor the creative use of language to hide the real meaning, accurately described in George Orwell's novel *1984* as "newspeak." The first Novlang Award was presented to Gixel, a trade association of manufacturers of electronic interconnect systems, components and subsystems. They propose to "educate" children under 6 (and their parents) about the usefulness of biometric products, helping the government to spread "security values."[2369]

Freedom of Information

As far as access to information is concerned, two laws in France provide for a right to access administrative documents held by public bodies.[2370] The

---

[2365] *Id.*

[2366] See <http://www.assurancemaladie.sante.gouv.fr/comprendre/pointparpoint_1.htm>, see also Opinion of the Commission Nationale de l'Informatique et des Libertés (CNIL) on the DMP, available at<http://www.cnil.fr/index.php?id=1613>(in French).

[2367] "French Big Brother Awards," Edri-gram newsletter number 3.2, January 26, 2005, available at <http://www.edri.org/edrigram/number3.2/BBA>.

[2368] *Id.*

[2369] *Id.*

[2370] Loi n° 78-753 du 17 juillet 1978 sur la liberté d'accès au documents administratifs; Loi N° 79-587 du juillet 1979 relative à la motivation des actes administratifs et à l'amélioration des relations entre l'administration et le public. Amended by Loi N° 2000-321 du 12 avril 2000 relative aux droits des citoyens dans leurs relations avec les administrations (Journal officiel, April 13, 2000).

Commission d'accès aux documents administratifs (CADA)[2371] is charged with enforcing the acts.[2372] It can mediate and issue recommendations but its decisions are not binding. According to the CADA, it handled 4,000 inquiries per year between 1996 and 1999, and 4,900 in 2000.[2373] The law was amended in April 2000 to clarify access to legal documents and also identify the civil servant processing the request.[2374]

Voting Privacy

Voting is open to those 18 years or older, but is not mandatory. Although the right to privacy is not enumerated in the French Constitution, the French Constitutional Court ruled in 1994 that it is implied.[2375] The French Electoral Code requires voters to cast their vote in total confidentiality.[2376] A decree dated December 27, 1972, allowed those areas of 30,000 citizens or more to use electronic voting machines. In 1988, that figure was cut to 3,500 inhabitants. A recent reform of the French electoral legislation leaves the regulation of electronic elections to the High Council for French Expatriates (CSFE). In 1993, the CNIL adopted new recommendations on electronic voting systems.[2377] The recommendations warn about the need to maintain rigorous measures for the separation of the voter's identity and his vote.[2378] In September 2000, France allowed for the first time Internet voting on a five-year term referendum in the City of Brest. The referendum had no legal significance.[2379] There are concerns regarding Internet voting and about voters not being intimidated or denied privacy in casting their ballots.[2380] On December 11, 2002, 860 volunteers participated in an Internet voting project conducted by the EU in the city of Issy-les-Moulineaux.

[2371] Homepage <http://www.cada.fr>.

[2372] 12e rapport d'activité 2002. Commission d'accès aux documents administratifs, July 2003, available at <http://www.ladocumentationfrancaise.fr/brp/notices/034000645.shtml>.

[2373] For more details, *see* David Banisar, Freedom of Information and Access to Government Records Around the World, available at <http://www.freedominfo.org/survey.htm>.

[2374] Loi n° 2000-321 du 12 avril 2000 relative aux droits des citoyens dans leurs relations avec les administrations (J.O. April 13, 2000).

[2375] Décision 94-352 du Conseil Constitutionnel du 18 Janvier 1995, available at <http://www.conseil-constitutionnel.fr/decision/1994/94352dc.htm>.

[2376] European Commission, CyberVote Report Chapter 3: "The Election regulations today," July 1, 2001, available at <http://www.eucybervote.org/Reports/KUL-WP2-D4V2-v1.0-02.htm>.

2377 Commission Nationale de l'informatique et des libertés (CNIL), Vote électronique, July 1, 2003, available at <http://www.cnil.fr/index.php?id=1009>.

[2378] *Id.*

[2379] European Commission, Cybervote Report, An Innovative Cyber Voting System, *supra*.

[2380] "What is the Future of Electronic Voting in France, Recommendations," September 26, 2003 available at <http://www.foruminternet.org/telechargement/documents/reco-evote-en-20030926.htm>.

International Obligations

France is a member of the Council of Europe (CoE) and has signed and ratified the Convention for the Protection of Individuals with Regard to Automatic Processing of Personal Data (ETS No. 108)[2381] and the European Convention for the Protection of Human Rights and Fundamental Freedoms.[2382] On November 23, 2001, the French government signed, but has not ratified yet, the CoE Cybercrime Convention, which entered into force on July 1, 2004.[2383] France is a member of the Organization for Economic Cooperation and Development (OECD) and has adopted the OECD Guidelines on the Protection of Privacy and Transborder Flows of Personal Data.

Federal Republic of Germany

Constitutional Privacy Framework

Article 10 of the Basic Law (or *Grundgesetz*, the German Constitution) states: "(1) Privacy of letters, posts, and telecommunications shall be inviolable. (2) Restrictions may only be ordered pursuant to a statute.[2384] Where a restriction serves to protect the free democratic basic order or the existence or security of the Federation, the statute may stipulate that the person affected shall not be informed of such restriction and that recourse to the courts shall be replaced by a review of the case by bodies and auxiliary bodies appointed by Parliament."

In a 1983 case against a government census law, the Federal Constitutional Court formally acknowledged an individual's "right of informational self-determination," which is only limited by the "predominant public interest." The central part of the verdict stated, "Who can not certainly overlook which information related to him or her is known to certain segments of his social environment, and who is not able to assess to a certain degree the knowledge of his potential communication partners, can be essentially hindered in his capability to plan and to decide. The right of informational self-determination stands against a societal order and its underlying legal order in which citizens could not know any longer who what and when in what situations knows about

---

[2381] Signed January 28, 1981; ratified March 24, 1983; entered into force October 1, 1985.

[2382] Signed November 11, 1950; ratified May 3, 1974; entered into force May 3, 1974.

[2383] Council of Europe. Convention on Cybercrime, CETS N°185 available at <http://conventions.coe.int/Treaty/Commun/ListeTraites.asp?CM=1&CL=ENG&NT=185>.

[2384] Available at <http://www.bundesregierung.de/en/Federal-Government/Function-and-constitutional-ba-,10222/I.-Basic-rights.htm>.

them."[2385] This landmark court decision derived the "right of informational self-determination" directly from Articles 1(1) and 2(1) of the Basic Law, which declare personal rights (*Persönlichkeitsrecht*) to freedom are inviolable. Attempts to amend the Basic Law to include a right to data protection were discussed after reunification, when the Constitution was revised, and were successfully opposed by the then-conservative political majority.

Data Protection Framework

Germany has one of the strictest data protection laws in the European Union. The world's first data protection law was passed in the German Land of Hessen in 1970. In 1977, a Federal Data Protection Act (*Bundesdatenschutzgesetz* or BDSG) followed, which was reviewed in 1990, amended in 1994[2386] and 1997. The final revision took place in 2002 to be in line with the EU Data Protection Directive.[2387] The general purpose of this Act is to protect the individual against his right to privacy being impaired through the handling of his personal data. The Act covers collection, processing and use of personal data by public federal authorities and state administrations (as long as there is no state regulation and insofar as they apply federal laws), and by private bodies, if they rely on data-processing systems or non-automated filing systems for commercial or professional use. The majority of federal statutes that have an impact on personal information and privacy contain references to the Federal Data Protection Act if they do not carry special sections on the handling of personal data themselves.

The 2001 revisions to the BDSG include regulations on personal data transfers abroad, video surveillance, anonymization and pseudonymization, smart cards, and sensitive data collection (relating to race or ethnic origin, political opinions, religious or philosophical convictions, union membership, health, and sexual orientation). It grants data subjects greater rights of objection. It also states that, apart from public bodies, private companies are now also required to appoint a data protection officer if they collect, process, or use personal information. Without this responsible person, each introduction of automated data processing must be registered with the Federal Commissioner for Data Protection (BfD). The BDSG also provides that consent from the individual whose data is collected is required after full disclosure of data collection and its consequences. The

---

[2385] Federal Constitutional Court (*Bundesverfassungsgericht*) decision of December 15, 1983, reference number: 1 BvR 209, 269, 362, 420, 440, 484/83.

[2386] Federal Act on Data Protection ("BDSG") January 27, 1977 (*Bundesgesetzblatt*, Part I, No 7, February 1, 1977), amended in 1990, available at <http://www.datenschutz-berlin.de/gesetze/bdsg/bdsgeng.htm>.

[2387] Federal Act on Data Protection ("BDSG"), January 14, 2003 (Bundesgesetzblatt, Part I, No 3, January 16, 2003), available at <http://www.bfd.bund.de/information/bdsg_eng.pdf>.

German Parliament renewed its request for secondary legislation on auditing requirements.[2388]

A general revision of the BDSG has been considered for 2005.[2389] Albeit an expert report on the modernization of the data protection law was published in 2001,[2390] there has been no visible legislative progress. This reputable report recommends reducing the number of laws governing specific details of privacy protections and creating one general statute, which would only refer to more detailed regulations where necessary.[2391] An ideal statute would provide general rules about the use of privacy-friendly techniques, data security, privacy standards, control of data processing, and self-regulation tools.[2392] On February 17, 2005, the German Parliament (*Bundestag*) called upon the government to swiftly submit a draft for a Federal Data Protection Act incorporating these recommendations.[2393]

Data Protection Authority

The Federal Data Protection Commissioner (*Bundesbeauftragter für den Datenschutz*, or BfD) is an independent federal agency that supervises the Federal Data Protection Act.[2394] Its chief duties include monitoring the compliance with the provisions of the BDSG by public bodies of the Federation, receiving and investigating complaints, as well as submitting recommendations to parliament and other governmental bodies. The BfD publishes a biannual activity report.[2395] However, the number of controllers is steadily decreasing as federal agencies, in compliance with the 2001 changes to the Act, appoint in-

---

[2388] German Parliament (*Bundestag*) decision of February 17, 2005, available at <http://dip.bundestag.de/btd/15/045/1504597.pdf>; Response of the Federal Government from January 26, 2005 to the questionnaire of the Parliament, available at <http://dip.bundestag.de/btd/15/047/1504725.pdf> (in German).

[2389] *See* Overview of upcoming legislation of the Federal Data Protection Commission (October 27, 2004), available at <http://www.bfd.bund.de/information/aktbuges271004.pdf>.

[2390] English summary available at <http://www.datenschutz-berlin.de/recht/de/bdsg/summary-gutachten.pdf>; Full version available at <http://www.bmi.bund.de/cln_012/nn_174154/Internet/Content/Common/Anlagen/Broschueren/2001/Modernis ierung__des__Datenschutzrechts__Id__11659__de,templateId=raw,property=publicationFile.pdf/Modernisieru ng_des_Datenschutzrechts_Id_11659_de> (in German).

[2391] *Id.*

[2392] *Id.*

[2393] German Parliament (*Bundestag*) decision of February 17, 2005, available at <http://dip.bundestag.de/btd/15/045/1504597.pdf>.

[2394] Homepage http://www.bfd.bund.de/; English description of the duties of the Federal Data Protection Commissioner available at <http://www.bfd.bund.de/information/datprotec_en.html>.

[2395] "20. Taetigkeitsbericht 2003/ 2004," available at <http://www.bfd.bund.de/information/20tb_broschuere.pdf>.

house data protection officers, as an alternative to registration under the Act.[2396] The BfD, which has 70 people on staff, handles about 4,500 written and oral complaints and carries out approximately 45 investigations each year.[2397] In 2004, the BfD received 477 complaints relating to data protection in the field of telecommunications that is assigned to his authority.[2398]

All of the sixteen *Länder* have their own specific data protection regulations that cover the public sector of the *Länder* administrations. All *Länder* have adopted new data protection laws pursuant to the EU Data Protection Directive.[2399] Each *Land* also has a data protection commissioner to enforce the *Länder* data protection acts.[2400] Moreover, it falls within the competence of the *Länder* DPAs to supervise the compliance of the private sector with the Federal Data Protection Act. The federal and *Länder* data protection officers hold conferences on a regular basis to exchange information and issue common statements.[2401]

Another important federal law in Germany is the G-10 Law, which imposes limitations on the secrecy of certain communications as provided in Article 10 of the Basic Law (*Grundgesetz*).[2402] Under the G-10 Law, parliamentary control commissions, established on federal and *Länder*'s level, supervise the surveillance powers of intelligence agencies. As amended in 1994 by the Crime Fighting Law (*Verbrechensbekämpfungsgesetz*), the G-10 Law allows warrantless automated wiretaps of international communications by the Intelligence Service (BND) for purposes of preventing terrorism and illegal trade in drugs and weapons. In July 1999, the Federal Constitutional Court upheld the screening method authorized under the G-10 Law.[2403] The Law was amended in 2001 to require that electronic communications service providers give

---

[2396] E-mail from Ulrich Dammann, *Bundesbeauftragte für den Datenschutz*, to Christian Schröder, Law Clerk, Electronic Privacy Information Center, April 4, 2003 (on file with EPIC).

[2397] *Id.*

[2398] Germany, Country Report to the International Working Group on Data Protection in Telecommunications, 36th meeting, Berlin, November 18-19, 2004 (on file with EPIC).

[2399] Complete text in German available <http://europa.eu.int/comm/internal_market/privacy/law/implementation_en.htm#germany>; <http://www.datenschutz-bremen.de/gesetze/datenschutzgesetz/inhalt.htm>; <http://www.saxonia-verlag.de/recht-sachsen/212_2bs.pdf>.

[2400] *Landesbeauftragte für den Datenschutz* (the Representatives of the Länder's data protection authorities), available at <http://www.datenschutz-berlin.de/sonstige/behoerde/ldbauf.htm>.

[2401] *See* for a complete list of documents <http://www.bfd.bund.de/information/DS-Konferenzen/index.html> (in German).

[2402] Available at <http://bundesrecht.juris.de/bundesrecht/g10_2001/gesamt.pdf> (in German).

[2403] Federal Constitutional Court (*Bundesverfassungsgericht*), decision of July 14, 1999, reference numbers: 1 BvR 2226/94, 1 BvR 2420/95, 1 BvR 2437/95.

intelligence agencies the means to monitor data as well as voice lines.[2404] DPAs complain that after a G-10 measure any notification of the person concerned is dispensable if the data is ready for deletion.[2405]

In May 2002, the European Parliament voted to adopt a series of amendments that modifed current telecommunications privacy law and took effect in October 2003.[2406] Germany transposed the EC Directive on Privacy and Electronic Communications into national law.[2407] Part 7 of the Telecommunications Act 2004 (TKG) now comprises all provisions on telecommunications secrecy, data protection and its limitations.[2408] Apart from content, all positive and negative (*e.g.* the unsuccessful attempt to call) circumstances of telecommunications are protected as telecommunications privacy. Service providers are required to protect their users' personal data and telecommunications privacy. The collection and use of traffic data is strictly limited to: (1) the purposes of charging and billing, (2) remedy malfunctions in telecommunications systems, and (3) detect telecommunications service fraud and, *with the consent of the data subject*, (4) to market and customize services to service providers' subscribers, as well as to provide value-added services.

The federal government and many *Länder* had been especially keen on the inclusion of traffic data retention. However, the TKG does not impose any obligation on providers of electronic services to retain traffic data for the purpose of law enforcement An introduction through the backdoor would come with the adoption of the framework decision by the European Council on the retention of traffic data for the purpose of criminal investigations (including terrorism).[2409] Already a 2002 questionnaire circulated by the EU working party on cooperation in criminal matters indicated a proposal to mandate retention of such data for law enforcement purposes for a period of 12-36 months.[2410] This proposal and others

---

[2404] "Germany: New Law Allows More Extensive Government Monitoring of Phone Calls and Email," World Socialist Web Site, February 20, 2001.

[2405] *61. Konferenz der Datenschutzbeauftragten des Bundes und der Länder*, Düsseldorf, 8.-9.05.2001." available at <http://www.bfd.bund.de/information/DS-Konferenzen/61dsk_ent8.html> in German.

[2406] Tamsin McMahon, "European Parliament Accepts Privacy Law," EuropeMedia.net, May 30, 2002, available at <http://www.europemedia.net/shownews.asp?ArticleID=10749>.

[2407] Directive 2002/58/EC of the European Parliament and the European Council of 12 July 2002 concerning the processing of personal data and the protection of privacy in the electronic communications sector, available at <http://europa.eu.int/eur-lex/pri/en/oj/dat/2002/l_201/l_20120020731en00370047.pdf>.

[2408] Telecommunications Act (TKG) of 22 June 2004, available at <http://www.bmwa.bund.de/Redaktion/Inhalte/Pdf/telekommunkationsgesetz-en,property=pdf.pdf>.

[2410] "Answers to a Questionnaire on Traffic Data Retention," Council of the European Union, November, 20, 2002, available at <http://blubb.at/kuhm/temp/20112002tidy.html>; John Leyden, "Germany, Austria Take Stand against EU ISP Data Retention Laws," The Register, November 21, 2002, available at <http://www.theregister.co.uk/content/6/28228.html>.

continue to be strongly opposed by the German Parliament (*Bundestag*) and the data protection authorities because of the implications for the hindrance of freedom of speech, access to information, and privacy of communications[2411]

As prescribed by EC Directive on Privacy and Electronic Communications, the TKG 2004 sets out the requirements of the processing of location data, either anonymously or with the subscriber's consent, for the provision of location based services. It is upon the subscriber to inform any co-users of all such consent given. In the case of "Track your Kid" services parents consent to give up their child's data protection because they are the subscribers, whereas the child is the user of the mobile phone.[2412]

Communications Surveillance

Service providers are now legally compelled to request the name and address of new customers to which they allocate a telephone number, even though they only use prepaid services. Telecommunications operators providing publicly available services are also mandated to provide – at their own expense – the technical facilities required to implement telecommunications interception for law enforcement purposes. The Telecommunications Interception Ordinance of January 22, 2002, which lays out specific technical requirements, remains in force until its successor will be issued under the TKG 2004 by the German government.[2413] A few proposals for this law have already been circulated. However, there is still much discussion about how to include Voice over IP. Also, telephone monitoring has been on the increase since 1995, when there were 4,674 instances of monitoring, up to 29,017 in 2004.[2414] That equals a 500 percent increase within one decade. Four out of five wiretappings monitor cell phones. This renewed rise of interventions in secret communications gives the federal commissioners great concern for data security. For years, the

---

[2411] German Parliament (Bundestag) decision of February 17, 2005, available at <http://dip.bundestag.de/btd/15/045/1504597.pdf>; 64 Konferenz der Datenschutzbeauftragten des Bundes und der Länder, Trier October 24-25, 2002, available at <http://www.bfd.bund.de/information/DS-Konferenzen/64dsk_ent1.html>.

[2412] Response of the German government (Bundesregierung) of January 26, 2005, to parliamentary question, reference number (Drucksache) 15/4725, available at <http://dip.bundestag.de/btd/15/047/1504725.pdf>.

[2413] Ordinance concerning the Technical and Organizational Implementation of Measures for the Interception of Telecommunications (Telekommunikations-Überwachungsverordnung - TÜKV) of January 22, 2002, available at http://www.bmwa.bund.de/Redaktion/Inhalte/Pdf/TKUEV-deutsch-englisch,property=pdf.pdf; Steve Gold, "German Carriers Told to Install Cyber-Snooping Tech," Newsbytes, October 25, 2001.

[2414] Heise online, "Telefonüberwachungen 2004 wieder stark gestiegen," March 31, 2005, available at <http://www.heise.de/newsticker/meldung/58104> (in German).

commissioners have appealed to prosecution authorities to use this means sparingly.[2415]

The so called "*Grosser Lauschangriff*" ("Big Eavesdropping Attack") formed part of the Law for the Enhancement of the Fight against Organized Crime, which became effective in 1999, and was intended to provide the legal basis for police to survey potential criminals. In April 1998, Article 13 of the Constitution (*Grundgesetz*) that provides for the inviolability of private homes was amended in order to allow police authorities to place bugging devices in private homes (provided there is a court order).

In March 2004, the German Federal Constitutional Court ruled[2416] that significant portions of the avesdropping Law infringed the Constitution, or Basic Law, especially Article 1 on human dignity and Article 13 on the inviolability of private homes.[2417] The court held that certain communications are protected by an absolute area of intimacy wherein citizens can communicate privately without fear of government surveillance.[2418] This includes conversations with close family members, priests, doctors and defense attorneys, but excludes conversations about crimes that have already been committed or the planning of future crimes. However, to justify surveillance between the target and such persons of trust, the government must show that "there is strong reason to believe that the content of conversation does not fall in the area of intimacy,"[2419] and that the crime is "particularly serious."[2420] Once a specially protected conversation begins, the eavesdropping must stop immediately and any recordings of that portion of the conversation must be erased.

The German legislature was granted a transitional period until June 2005 to comply with the court's decision, and the German Government

---

[2415] Press information 12/05 of the Federal Data Protection Commissioner (*Bundesdatenschutzbeauftragter*) of March 31, 2005, "Telefonüberwachungen auch 2004 wieder stark gestiegen," available at <http://www.bfd.bund.de/Presse/pm20050331.html> (in German).

[2416] Federal Constitutional Court (*Bundesverfassungsgericht*) decision of March 3, 2004, reference number: 1 BvR 2378/98, available at <http://www.bverfg.de/entscheidungen/rs20040303_1bvr237898.html> (in German).

[2417] Basic Law for the Federal Republic of Germany, I. Basic Rights, Articles 1, 13, available at <http://www.bundesregierung.de/en/Federal-Government/Function-and-constitutional-ba-,10222/I.-Basic-rights.htm>.

[2418] C. Schröder, "Wiretap in Germany," German American Law Journal: American Edition (March 11, 2004), available at <http://www.recht.us/amlaw/2004/03/11>.

[2419] *Id.*

[2420] University College of London, Faculty of Laws, Institute of Global Law, "German Legal News - Constitutional Law," available at <http://www.ucl.ac.uk/laws/global_law/legal-news/german/index.shtml?constitution>.

(*Bundesregierung*) submitted draft legislation.[2421] The draft tries to incorporate the findings of German legal researchers who found severe flaws in the legal basis and application of technical surveillance.[2422] Under scrutiny by the Conference of German Data Protection Officers, they ask for improvements in the legal definitions of the absolute protected sphere of an individual's intimacy and about what constitutes a conversation with people of special trust.[2423]

In 2001, the *Bundestag* (the German Parliament) passed a law that added to the Criminal Procedural Code (StPO) further means of investigation into electronic communications. It serves as the legal basis for police and law enforcement to access "telecommunications connection data" for the investigation of serious crimes. The law took effect in January 2002 and requires telecommunications service providers to disclose data, such as time and duration of use, place of use and identifying numbers.[2424] In October 2004, the Parliament extended its application until January 1, 2008, together with a request to the Federal Government (*Bundesregierung*) for a detailed report until June 30, 2007, containing causes, results and the exact number of measures taken under this law.[2425] According to a survey, 75 percent of conducted telephone wiretapping actions violated the law. In most instances of wiretapping, law enforcement agencies did not inform the subjects after the eavesdropping took place, contrary to what is stipulated by the law.[2426]

Location Privacy

Germany also implemented in the StPO the possibility of using a so-called IMSI-Catcher system to track individuals trough the location of their cell phones. The law, which entered into force on August 14, 2002, provides law enforcement with the ability to obtain, upon court request and from the time it is granted, the

---

[2421] Draft law of the German Government (*Bundesregierung*) of September 22, 2004, for acoustic surveillance of private homes, available at <http://www.bmj.de/media/archive/753.pdf> (in German).

[2422] Expert referee of the Max Planck Institute for Foreign and International Criminal Law on technical surveillance in private homes available at <http://www.bmj.de/media/archive/787.pdf> (in German) and - second - expert referee of the Max Planck Institute for Foreign and International Criminal Law on wiretapping, available at <http://www.bmj.de/media/archive/134.pdf> (in German).

[2423] 68. Konferenz der Datenschutzbeauftragten des Bundes und der Lände, Saabruecken October 28-29, 2004, available at <http://www.bfd.bund.de/information/DS-Konferenzen/68dsk_ent1.pdf> (in German).
2424 Federal Bulletin, BGBL I 2001, 3879, available at <http://217.160.60.235/BGBL/bgbl1f/b101073f.pdf> (in German).
2425 Decision of the Parliament (Bundestag) of October 21, 2004, reference number 15/3349, 3971, available at <http://www3.bundesrat.de/coremedia/generator/Inhalt/Drucksachen/2004/0845_2D04_28zu_29,property=Dokument.pdf> (in German).

[2426] "*Dreiviertel aller Lauschangriffe rechtswidrig,*" *Der Spiegel* Online, January 9, 2003, available at <http://www.spiegel.de/politik/deutschland/0,1518,229958,00.html> (in German).

data of individuals' movements and their cell phone device number (IMEI number - International Mobile Equipment Identity) for a period of up to six months.[2427] The location of a mobile phone can further be conducted with silent SMS that is covered by general investigation powers in criminal cases.[2428] Silent SMS means that an empty message is sent to a mobile phone, which allows for some approximation of its whereabouts, but it does not report itself to the respective user.

The Federal Constitutional Court (*Bundesverfassungsgericht*) has ruled that the police may use GPS technology to track suspects driving motor vehicles in cases of serious crimes even without a judicial warrant.[2429] The Court approved §100c StPO to be consistent with the Constitutional principle of clarity and definiteness and when allowing police to use "all technical observational means" to investigate suspicious behaviour that might be considered a crime of substantial significance. However, the Court stressed that Parliament had to monitor the fast technological developments in this field and may have to correct laws if the risks for fundamental rights caused by technical surveillance increase. Parliament also has to ensure by procedural rules that law enforcement agencies (*e.g.* from different Länder or the Federal level) do not subject citizens to uncoordinated surveillance measures. The "additive effect" on fundamental rights has to be kept in mind.

In 2004, a new regulation of the German Criminal Code (§201a StGB) took effect. This regulation protects private life against the invasion of privacy by the taking of pictures of persons in their apartments or other protected areas, *e.g.*, changing cabins. Furthermore, publishing and distribution of such photographs on the Internet is punishable as a criminal offense.

Citizens have challenged several times the tactics used by German law enforcement to uncover terrorist suspects. By February 2002, courts in Berlin and Frankfurt had upheld objections to the use of "computerized searches of government records" (or *Rasterfahndung*) to profile terrorist suspects based partly on religious identification.[2430] Other courts thought the search was legal. However, the Federal DPA stated that all data of persons not related to terrorist

---

[2427] 19. *Tätigkeitsbericht* – 2001/2002 at 54-55, available at <http://www.bfd.bund.de/information/19tb0102.pdf> (in German).

[2428] Response of the Federal Government from January 26, 2005 to the questionnaire of the Parliament, available at <http://dip.bundestag.de/btd/15/047/1504725.pdf> (in German).

[2429] Federal Constitutional Court (BVerfG), decision of April 12, 2005, reference number 2 BvR 581/01, available at <http://www.bverfg.de/entscheidungen/rs20050412_2bvr058101.html> (in German).

[2430] John Hooper, "German Courts Put Terror Hunt In Doubt," The Guardian, February 2, 2002, available at <http://www.guardian.co.uk/international/story/0,3604,643720,00.html>.

activities have to be deleted immediately and new evaluations have to be carried out to test its efficiency.[2431] Despite concerns raised by the public and the obvious inefficiency of the *Rasterfahndung* initiated after September 11, 2001, Germany submitted in April 2002 to the EU a proposal to make it possible to conduct investigations using this surveillance tool (*Rasterfahndung*) throughout the Union to help combat terrorism.[2432]

In April 1998, a law was passed that allows the *Bundeskriminalamt* (Federal Police) to run a nationwide database of genetic profiles related to criminal investigations and convicted offenders. One month later, the *Bundesgrenzschutz* (Border Protection Forces), originally a paramilitary border police force but now responsible for guarding railways and stations, received permission to check persons' identities and baggage without any concrete suspicion.[2433]

The Information and Communications Services Act of June 13, 1997, actually comprises a few legal statutes or amendments designed for electronic communications and information services in computer networks.[2434] Specifically its Article 2 contains the Act on the Protection of Personal Data Used in Tele-Services, which is under federal regulatory oversight. Quite to the contrary, media services fall as content in the responsibility of the *Länder.* Therefore, data protection in media services is governed by the Media Services State Agreement of the *Länder* and their data protection officers monitor compliance with these rules. However, a coherent legislation of data protection in telecommunications and media services is about to be enacted, which will bring the regulatory oversight under the auspices of the Federal Data Protection Officer (BfD).[2435]

Moreover, Article 3 of the Information and Communications Services Act sets forth the legal requirements for digital signatures, which were made legally binding to be in line with the EU Directive on a Community framework for

---

[2431] *"Pressemitteilung des Bundesbeauftragten für den Datenschutz zum Tätigkeitsbericht* 2001/2002," May 7, 2003, available at <www.bfd.bund.de/Presse/pm20030507.html> (in German).

[2432] Jelle van Buuren, *"Rasterfahndung* at European Level?," Telepolis, April 4, 2002, available at <http://www.heise.de/tp/english/inhalt/te/12274/1.html>.

[2433] "New Powers for the Border Police: Checks Anywhere at Any Time," Fortress Europe, FECL 56 (December 1998).

[2434] Information and Communication Services Act (*Informations- und Kommunikationsdienste-Gesetz - IuKDG*) of June 13, 1997, <http://www.iid.de/iukdg/gesetz/iukdge.html>; *See also* Resolution of the Conference of Data Protection Commissioners of the Federation and the Länder of April 29, 1996 on key points for the regulation in matters of data protection of online services, available at <http://datenschutz-berlin.de/sonstige/konferen/sonstige/old-res2.htm>.

[2435] Response of the Federal Government from January 26, 2005 to the questionnaire of the Parliament, available at <http://dip.bundestag.de/btd/15/047/1504725.pdf> (in German).

electronic signatures (1999/93/EC).[2436] In January 2002, the German government announced plans to provide, within three years, more than 200,000 federal employees with the ability to sign electronic documents with chip cards containing encrypted keys. Such signatures would hold the same legal weight as handwritten signatures on paper documents.[2437]

Direct marketing issues are newly addressed by Section 7 of the German Unfair Competition Act. According to its general clause, it is unfair to annoy market players, *e.g.*, consumers, inappropriately.[2438] By default this applies to clearly unwanted advertisements, unsolicited commercial phone calls, marketing methods making use of automated calling machines, fax machines or e-mail (spam) without prior consent, and any direct marketing that cannot be linked back to the senders' identity. Direct marketing via e-mail is not prohibited as spam under the conditions that (1) an organization has received the e-mail address in the context of selling goods or services to the customer; (2) the organization uses the e-mail contact for marketing of very similar products and services; (3) the customer has not opposed the use of his e-mail for further direct marketing; and (4) at the time of the collection and each usage of the e-mail address clearly sets out the right to opt-out from direct marketing via e-mail. Cold calling of consumers is a violation of Unfair Competition Law.[2439]

By 2006 the electronic healthcare card will be introduced. This card has administrative and medical functions and can contain a patient's identification and emergency healthcare information, prescriptions, therapies and diagnoses. Patients will be able to use the card to fill prescriptions and disclose healthcare information to physicians on a voluntary basis.[2440] The patient has it in his hands if personal information will be at all disclosed or to which of the physicians information on the card will be disclosed. Access to the electronic healthcare

---

[2436] Directive 1999/93/EC of the European Parliament and of the Council of 13 December 1999 on a Community framework for electronic signatures, available at
<http://europa.eu.int/smartapi/cgi/sga_doc?smartapi!celexapi!prod!CELEXnumdoc&lg=EN&numdoc=31999L 0093&model=guichett>; *see also* "Fifth Annual Report on the Situation Regarding the Protection of Individuals With Regard to the Processing of Personal Data and Privacy in the European Union and in Third Countries," Data Protection Working Party, March 6, 2002, Part II, 37, available at
<http://europa.eu.int/comm/internal_market/privacy/docs/wpdocs/2002/wp54en_2.pdf>.

[2437] Rick Perera, "German Federal Employees Get Digital Signatures," CNN.com, January 21, 2002, available at <http://www.cnn.com/2002/TECH/ptech/01/21/german.government.idg/index.html>.

[2438] German Unfair Competition Act, available at <http://217.160.60.235/BGBL/bgbl1f/bgbl104s1414.pdf> (in German).

[2439] *Id.*

[2440] "Healthcare Groups Agree Parameters for Health Card," World Data Protection Report, vol. 2, issue 6 (June 2002). *See generally* about the specific privacy issues related to the Health Card, 65. *Konferenz der Datenschutzbeauftragten des Bundes und der Länder*, Dresden, 27, March 28, 2003, available at <http://www.bfd.bund.de/information/DS-Konferenzen/65dsk_ent1.html> (in German).

card by physicians requires proof of professional credentials and is recorded every time. By 2008 the Ministry of Health has to submit an evaluation of the card on data protection.

In June 2001, the German Ministry of the Economy and Labor presented a software prototype that would let consumers make anonymous Internet purchases and payments. The software was scheduled for general availability for testing in 2002. This is part of a project called Data Protection in Teleservices, the goal of which is to develop software that can accommodate data privacy law requirements. The Ministry of the Economy and Labor announced that 79 percent of online shops fail to adequately inform customers about their data privacy rights, and that 84 percent of Germans have privacy concerns about surfing the web. The program meets the quality criteria for Internet data privacy protection and the Teleservices Data Privacy Law.[2441]

Open Government

Four of the *Länder* already have their own Freedom of Information Laws (FOI) in effect.[2442] The *Land* of Brandenburg has the right of access to governmental records in its constitution and adopted a FOI law in 1998.[2443] Later, Berlin, Schleswig-Holstein, and Nordrhein-Westfalen also adopted FOI laws. On the federal level, FOI legislation was proposed for five years but the administration has been reluctant to agree on a draft statute. Eventually, Members of Parliament from the ruling coalition parties grew impatient for a draft and presented their own.[2444] On December 17, 2004, the German Parliament (*Bundestag*) had its first reading on a FOI Law.[2445] *Länder* FOI Commissioners published a statement about the draft law that criticizes the scope of the restrictions to the right of access.[2446] It seems likely that the Bill will be passed and enter into force in January 2006, thereby closing the gap in transparency between Germany and all

---

[2441] "German Government Searches Net Music Lovers' Homes," BNA World Data Protection Report, May 2001.

[2442] *See* for an overview <http://www.informationsfreiheit.de/info_deutschland/index.htm>.

[2443] FOI Brandenburg (*Akteneinsichts- und Informationszugangsgesetz* ("AIG"), 1998), available at <http://www.lda.brandenburg.de/sixcms/detail.php?id=68313&template=allgemein_lda> (in German).

[2444] Draft of a federal Freedom of Information Law, available at <http://dip.bundestag.de/btd/15/044/1504493.pdf> (in German) and <http://www.freedominfo.org/news/germany/FOI_Ger_1204.pdf> (in English).

[2445] EGovernment News of January 14, 2005, "German freedom of information law in the works", available at <http://europa.eu.int/idabc/en/document/3771/194>.

[2446] EDRI-gram of December 29, 2004, "Freedom of Information Law in German Parliament," available at <http://www.edri.org/edrigram/number2.25/foia>.

other Member States of the European Union (except Cyprus, Luxembourg, and Malta).

Since 1990, a law[2447] has allowed access to the files of the *Stasi (Ministerium für Staatssicherheit)*, the security service of former East Germany, for individuals and researchers. The law created a Federal Commissioner for the Records of the State Security Services of the former German Democratic Republic, which has a staff of 2,400 piecing together shredded documents and making files available.[2448] Many of the files were destroyed in 1989, but in 1990, the US Central Intelligence Agency was able to obtain the names, aliases and payment histories of 4,000 spies who worked in various countries for the *Stasi* or informers from the Soviet Union. At the beginning, the US Government refused to give the files to the German government until December 1999, claiming that it would harm the people in the files.[2449] Between 2000 and 2003, copies of the so-called Rosenholz files were returned on 381 CDs. They contain the microfiches of 290,000 individuals' files, 57,400 of which are about other *Stasi* affairs.[2450] There are more than 200.000 requests per year, half of which are individual requests to personal *Stasi* files.[2451]

In May 2000, files about former Chancellor Helmut Kohl's telephone calls were found to be missing from the archives when they were going to be used to investigate corruption. The *Stasi* had conducted extensive wiretapping of Kohl for years.[2452] In late 2000, Kohl's lawyers launched legal action to prevent the publication of transcripts of his telephone conversations recorded by the *Stasi*. The government wanted to release those because it believed they were of historical interest. Kohl's lawyers argued that the information had been gathered illegally.[2453] In July 2001, the Federal Administrative Court ruled that information collected by the *Stasi* about Kohl could not be disclosed to researchers or the media without Kohl's express consent. Subsequently, the German Parliament amended the *Stasi* Files Act to allow Kohl's files to become accessible by the media, at least to some extent.[2454] The amendment, which came

---

[2447] *See* the Stasi Records Act, available at <http://www.bstu.de/englisch/index.htm> (English translation).

[2448] Web site at <http://www.bstu.de/home.htm>.

[2449] "U.S.-Held Files Seen Uncovering E. German Spies," Reuters, February 4, 1999.

[2450] *See* on Rosenholz <http://www.bstu.de/mfs/rosenholz> (in German).

[2451] Press release of December 10, 2004 of the Federal Commissioner Birthler, available at <http://www.bstu.de/aktuelles/presse2004/1210_aufloesung.htm>.

[2452] "Stasi Files on Kohl's Tapped Calls Vanish," The Times, May 17, 2000.

[2453] "Kohl Sues to Gag Stasi Files," BBC News, December 8, 2000.

[2454] E-mail from Alexander Dix, Commissioner for Data Protection and Access to Information, Brandenburg, to EPIC, December 23, 2003 (on file with EPIC).

into force in September 2002, allows *Stasi* files to be disclosed to journalists and researchers, even where the subject is a victim of surveillance, if the information requested is linked with the political function or office of the person in question.[2455] Kohl again brought suit, this time claiming that this amendment was unconstitutional. His claim was dismissed. The case was appealed to the Federal Administrative Court. On June 23, 2004, this court upheld most of its original 2001 judgment, interpreting the amendment to the *Stasi* Files Act restrictively, with the effect that large parts of the files concerning the former chancellor will not be disclosed to the media. The court took the view that the *Stasi* violated the principles of the rule of law when spying on people, and that victims of such practices should therefore have control over whether this information is given to the media. However, researchers will still be allowed to access *Stasi* files with personal data if further disclosures to the public would be effectively prohibited. In March 2005, parts of the archive on former Chancellor Kohl were released to journalists and researchers under orders not to publish them, while parts of the documents referring to Kohl's personal life were blacked out.[2456]

Germany enacted several provisions intended to deter terrorist activity after the September 2001 attacks in the US. The Counter-Terrorism Act, which took effect in January 2002, comprehensively changed several existing laws. Among the most prominent revisions are those that create legal bases for biometric identification in passports and identity cards; make it easier for authorities to share information; allow the BND to request user information from ISPs, airlines, and travel agencies; and create a speech framework database to make possible speech recognition of asylum seekers.[2457] The issuance of travel documents with biometric identifiers, *i.e.*, facial data and fingerprints – all required for entering into the United States – will start in Fall 2005. Biometric ID cards are planned for 2007.[2458] The German implementation is largely based on a regulation of the Council of Europe of December 13, 2004 on standards for security features and biometrics in passports and travel documents, that itself relies on the recommendation of the International Civil Aviation Organization.[2459] In

---

[2455] Act Regarding the Records of the State Security Service of the Former German Democratic Republic (Stasi Records Act), v. 20.12.1991 (Federal Law Gazette I S. 2272), available at <http://www.bstu.de/rechtl_grundl/stug/stugenglisch.rtf>.

[2456] Deutsche Welle, current affairs of March 24, 2005, available at <http://www.deutsche-welle.de/dw/article/0,1564,1528457,00.html>.

[2457] *See Terrorismusbekämfungsgesetz* BGBl 2002, I, 361, available at <http://www.bmi.bund.de/Annex/de_15999/Terrorismusbekaempfungsegsetz_PDF-Datei.pdf>.

[2458] Response of the German Government (*Bundesregierung*), available at<http://dip.bundestag.de/btd/15/046/1504616.pdf> (in German).

[2459] Council regulation of December 13, 2004, on standards for security features and biometrics in passports and travel documents issued by Member States, available at <http://register.consilium.eu.int/pdf/en/04/st15/st15152.en04.pdf>.

Germany, there will be no centralized database containing biometrical identifiers. To access the biometric information, the holder of the passport will have to perform an active motion – a precaution against unrecognized read-out of the machine-readable information.[2460]

In 2005, a new system to electronically collect tolls for trucks using the national highways was launched. The system tracks vehicles through GPS (Global Positioning System) and cellular phone networks. According to a common standpoint of the DPAs in 2001,[2461] the Federal government implemented special data protection measures in the laws governing toll systems: data collection and processing is limited only for the purpose of billing; all data must be deleted after the payment; and all data collected from vehicles that are not subject to a toll must be immediately deleted.[2462] German authorities have also recently proposed implementation of a video surveillance system at toll collection points, to ensure that trucks from other countries are paying the proper tolls on the autobahn.[2463] Video footage would be compared against a central database. Privacy and data security groups have protested this proposal, citing the possibility for using the data for purposes other than toll-collection. Indeed, although this surveillance data is only supposed to be used for toll-collection and enforcement purposes, the German police recently gained access to the data when trying to locate a stolen garbage truck.[2464] The Federal Government (*Bundesregierung*) recently stated that it is not aware of any access by law enforcement to information of the toll system.[2465] Independently from the toll system, in the State of Hessen the new Police Law of December 2004 permits the electronic scanning of vehicles' number plates that are then automatically matched with a database of searched vehicles.[2466]

[2460] Press release of the Federal Data Protection Officer (*Bundesdatenschutzbeauftragter*) of December 2, 2004, available at <http://www.bfd.bund.de/Presse/pm20041202.html> (in German); Response of the German Government (*Bundesregierung*),available at <http://dip.bundestag.de/btd/15/046/1504616.pdf> (in German).

[2461] 62. *Konferenz der Datenschutzbeauftragten des Bundes und der Länder*, October 24-26, 2001, available at <http://www.bfd.bund.de/information/DS-Konferenzen/62dsk_ent3.html> (in German).

[2462] *Gesetz zur Änderung des Fernstrassenbauprivatisierungsgesetzes*, BGBl. I 2002 Nr. 63, 3442, available at <http://217.160.60.235/BGBL/bgbl1f/bgbl102s3442.pdf>; Response of the Federal Government from January 26, 2005 to the questionnaire of the Parliament, available at <http://dip.bundestag.de/btd/15/047/1504725.pdf> (in German).

[2463] E-mail from Bettina Winsemann, Staff Member, STOP1984, to the Electronic Privacy Information Center, July 9, 2004 (on file with EPIC).

[2464] Christiane Schulzki-Haddouti, "Fahnder wollen Daten aus LKW-Mautsystem" (Investigators Want Data from Truck Mautsystem"), Heise online, October 31, 2003, available at <http://www.heise.de/newsticker/meldung/41560> (in German).

[2465] Response of the Federal Government from January 26, 2005 to the questionnaire of the Parliament, available at <http://dip.bundestag.de/btd/15/047/1504725.pdf> (in German), at 30 (in German).

[2466] Heise News of December 15, 2004, "Hessen dehnt Polizeibefugnisse deutlich aus," available at <http://www.heise.de/newsticker/meldung/54298> (in German).

There are several other video surveillance projects in Germany which have generated a response from privacy and data protection advocacy groups. For example, a private group called *Der Grosse Bruder* (Big Brother)[2467] has created a map of Munich, highlighting all the video surveillance cameras installed there.[2468] In 2003, the *Humanistische Union* (Humanistic Union)[2469] sued a Berlin shopping center employing a video surveillance system with a range of vision that included a public street.[2470] In Weimar, Germany, a local newspaper protested the installation of video surveillance cameras that watched the entrance of a newspaper building (along with medical and political offices), and the local government eventually uninstalled the cameras.[2471]

The revision of the credit sector of the economy imposes rules for banks to disclose client data to the Federal Institution for the Supervision of the Credit Economy (FISCE).[2472] The FISCE will store data about all owners of bank accounts or depots and is required to transfer them to other public agencies upon request. Banks also have to run special surveillance programs to detect suspicious money transfers. In a recent statement, the data protection commissioners urged banks to inform their clients in writing and obtain a written consent.[2473] Starting on April 1, 2005 and in order to tackle tax evasion (*Gesetz zur Förderung der Steuerehrlichkeit*), banks have to transfer their customers' account information (name, account number but no information on account movements or the amount of money stored on the account) to the Federal Agency of Finance if so requested.[2474] This Law has been challenged before the Constitutional Court for an alleged violation of Article 2 (1) Basic Law. The court refused to grant preliminary injunction, since an ministerial ordinance, issued shortly before the

---

[2467] Homepage at <http://dergrossebruder.org>.

[2468] Munich Atlas at <http://dergrossebruder.org/main.php?id=74000>.

[2469] Homepage at <http://www.humanistiche-union.de>.

[2470] Stefan Krempl, "Urteil schränkt Videoüberwachung ein" ("Judgement Limits Video Monitoring"), Heise online, December 12, 2003, available at <http://www.heise.de/newsticker/meldung/43130> (in German).

[2471] Peter Nowak, "Weimarer Provinzposse mit Kamera," Telepolis, October 27, 2003, available at <http://www.heise.de/tp/deutsch/inhalt/te/15950/1.html> (in German).

[2472] Christian Schröder, Germany Prepares Extension of Anti-Money Laundering Law, 18 Int'l Enforcement L. Rep. 315 (2002); "Maßnahmen zur Bekämpfung der Terrorismusfinanzierung und der Geldwäsche in Deutschland," (Ministry of Finance Publishing New Measures to Fight Terrorism Financing and Money Laundering), June 19, 2002, available at <http://www.bundesfinanzministerium.de/Finanz-und-Wirtschaftspolitik/Terrorismusbekaempfung-.833.12650/Massnahmen-zur-Bekaempfung-der-Terrorismusfinanz.htm> (in German); G*esetz zur Verbesserung der Bekämpfung der Geldwäsche und der Finanzierung des Terrorismus* (*Geldwäschebekämpfungsgesetz*), BGBl. I 2002, at 3105 ff.

[2473] 63. *Konferenz der Datenschutzbeauftragten des Bundes und der Länder*, March 7-8, 2002, available at <http://www.bfd.bund.de/information/DS-Konferenzen/63dsk_ent4.html> (in German).

[2474] Response of the Federal Government of January 26, 2005 to the questionnaire of the Parliament, available at <http://dip.bundestag.de/btd/15/047/1504725.pdf>, at 6 (in German).

decision, assured that data can be gathered only if there is specific suspicion and if there is no other way to gain the same evidence by less infringing means.[2475] This, however, does not allow any prediction on the outcome of a final decision which is not expected until the end 2005.

In 2004, a German healthcare insurance company conducted a mass DNA screening with 6,000 volunteers in order to find the genetic disposition for a rare disease.[2476] With regards to genetic diagnostics, the DPAs stress that new opportunities to test human genetic code (DNA) for different purposes must be regulated in order to prevent misuse of the genetic data. The commissioners point out that no one should be forced to take any genetic tests. They also require that the use of data gained through genetic tests not legally approved and without explicit consent of the concerned person should be criminalized.[2477] With secret genetic paternity testing, another aspect of genetic privacy came in the spotlight.[2478] The Federal Court of Justice decided in January 2005 that evidence stemming from an anonymous paternity test is inadmissible in court because it violates the right of child and mother to control the use of their personal information.[2479] Fathers cannot normally rely on such tests when challenging their paternity in such proceedings. This decision, which was welcomed by the German Conference of Data Protection Commissioners, has led to a public debate as to whether clandestine paternity tests should be made a criminal offence. The Minister of Justice has proposed this but has met with strong political and public opposition. Any such regulation would be difficult to enforce against providers offering such services online from abroad.[2480] Presently, a draft for a genetic diagnostic law is being discussed that is, besides other aspects of genetic privacy, supposed to rule out anonymous paternity testings.[2481]

[2475] Federal Constitutional Court (BVerfG), decision of March 22, 2005, reference number 1 BvR 2357/04 und 1 BvQ 2/05, press release available at <http://www.bverfg.de/cgi-bin/link.pl?presse> (in German).

[2476] Response of the Federal Government (*Bundesregierung*) of November 16, 2004, reference number: 15/4221, available at <http://dip.bundestag.de/btd/15/042/1504221> (in German).

[2477] Press release of the Federal Data Protection Officer (*Bundesdatenschutzbeauftragter*) of January 13, 2005, available at <http://www.bfd.bund.de/Presse/pm20050113.html> (in German); 65. *Konferenz der Datenschutzbeauftragten des Bundes und der Länder*, Dresden, March 27-28, 2003, available at <http://www.bfd.bund.de/information/DS-Konferenzen/65dsk_ent1.html> (in German);.

[2478] Antonia Loick, "Anonymous Paternity Tests – A Violation of the Right to Control the Use of One's Personal Information", Goethe-Institut, January 2005, available at <http://www.goethe.de/kug/ges/soz/thm/en310103.htm>.

[2479] Federal Court of Justice (BGH), decisions of January 12, 2005, reference numbers: XII ZR 60/03, XII ZR 227/03.

[2480] *E.g.* <http://www.papacheck.de> is offering tests worldwide from Germany.

[2481] Response of the Federal Government (*Bundesregierung*) of November 16, 2004, reference number: 15/4221, available at <http://dip.bundestag.de/btd/15/042/1504221> (in German); Press release of the Federal Data Protection Officer (*Bundesdatenschutzbeauftragter*) of January 13, 2005, available at <http://www.bfd.bund.de/Presse/pm20050113.html> (in German).

RFID

In May 2003, the German retail giant Metro started a trial project to introduce a new cashing and customer convenience program with small chips, called Radio Frequency Identification (RFID) chips, at their Metro Future Store. The chips will be attached to all products. When queried by a radio device, RFID chips respond by transmitting a unique ID code. It therefore allows customers to pay and checkout automatically by pushing a loaded trolley past a sensor. Combined with an automatically readable customer client card, the system would allow the tracking of all purchases and the linking to the customer's identity.[2482] Metro claimed that the RFID chips could easily be deactivated, thus erasing any privacy invasions, but their process for deactivation leaves intact the unique identifying number on the RFID chip, so even "deactivated" cards can be traced back to their origin.[2483] In March, 2004, Metro halted the trial program in response to protests from digital rights groups regarding possible privacy violations.[2484] Outcry was particularly forceful upon discovery that Metro had placed RFID devices in their "Extra Future Card" (personal customer shopping card) without notifying consumers.[2485] This use of RFID was uncovered by a German NGO called FoeBuD by taking X-ray photos of the card.[2486] FoeBuD also staged two protests, one in front of the Metro Future Store and one at a "pro-RFID" conference, and has recently been granted money by the *Bewegungsstiftung*[2487] (a German group which supports and promotes social movements and reform projects) to develop the "privatizer," a small device which consumers could use to find hidden and embedded RFID chips in consumer products.[2488] In a recent speech, the Federal Data Protection Commissioner pointed out the privacy

---

[2482] "Retail Future: Painless Checkout, Knowing Scanners," Reuters, May 14, 2003 <http://www.forbes.com/home_europe/newswire/2003/05/14/rtr970418.html>.

[2483] E-mail from Bettina Winsemann, Staff Member, STOP1984, to EPIC, July 12, 2004.

[2484] "German Revolt Against RFID", The Register, March 1, 2004, available at <http://www.theregister.co.uk/2004/03/01/german_revolt_against_rfid/>.

[2485] *See* FoeBuD, RFID web page at http://www.foebud.org/rfid/; Under § 6(c) of the BDSG, notice must be provided to data subjects of communications with "intelligent" RFID (devices with integrated processors), thus prohibiting secret reading or writing of personal information. However, Germany does not yet have any regulations specifically addressing "non-intelligent" RFID, which still create a privacy risk, as they can be linked to personal information held elsewhere without violating § 6(c). (E-mail from Christian Schröder, former Law Clerk with EPIC, June 18, 2004 (on file with EPIC).)

[2486] FoeBuD, RFID web page available at <http://www.foebud.org/rfid/>.

[2487] Bewegungsstiftung <http://www.bewegungsstiftung.de/>.

[2488] E-mail from Bettina Winsemann, Staff Member, STOP1984, to EPIC, July 12, 2004 (on file with EPIC); *See also "Funkchip-Kontrolle für Konsumenten"* (Radio Chip Control for Consumers) <http://www.google.com/search?q=foebud+privatizer&ie=UTF-8&oe=UTF-8>.

implications of RFID, and called on the legislature to make provisions on RFID tags.[2489]

Tickets for the 2006 Football World Cup in Germany will be RFID-chipped and enable authorities to track the movements of the individualized spectator during the event.[2490] The application forms for tickets requires a large number of personal information, *i.e.* passport number, nationality, and day of birth.

Germany has no workplace privacy law because the Federal Government has not come up yet with a draft legislation on the subject, although the German Parliament has requested it several times.[2491] The Federal Data Protection Officer, Peter Schaar, also cites a need for a data protection statute regarding the use of employees' personal data in the context of the monitoring of web surfing and the protection of the employers' computer systems against viruses and spam.[2492]

There is a recent proposal to introduce an obligatory "smart jobcard" for all employees in Germany.[2493] The proposal is motivated by the reduction of employers' costs of certification in social security matters. Data such as current employer, salary and working hours would be stored in a centralized database, which all social security entities could access on request, with consent of the owner of the job card. However, the *Länder* data protection commissioners claim that this project constitutes a systematic data collection without a specific purpose, and therefore violates the right of self-determination as enumerated by the Constitutional Court. The commissioners also feared that the use of the social security number (*Rentenversicherungsnummer*) as a personal identification number would create serious privacy implications. At a conference on April 25, 2004, the data protection commissioner for Schleswig Holstein proposed some standards for the jobcard, such as a right of access to stored information by the

---

[2489] Peter Schaar (Federal Data Protection Commissioner), "Datenschutz als Verbraucherschutz: Neue Herausforderungen am Beispiel von Smart Chips und Kundenkarten," April 5, 2004, available at <http://www.bfd.bund.de/aktuelles/akt20040513.pdf>.

[2490] Monika Ermert, "World Cup 2006 'Abused for Mega-surveillance Project', The Register of February 8, 2005, available at <http://www.theregister.co.uk/2005/02/08/world_cup_2006_big_brother_charges/>.

[2491] Response of the Federal Government from January 26, 2005 to the questionnaire of the Parliament, available at <http://dip.bundestag.de/btd/15/047/1504725.pdf> (in German).

[2492] Peter Schaar also questions proposals to reform the Electronic Signature Statute, which the Parliament wants to change to require all certification centers to disclose the identity of all signature key owners to law enforcement, intelligence, or tax agencies upon request. The law as it stands merely stipulates the disclosure in cases where the signature owner is using a pseudonym. Peter Schaar, *supra.*

[2493] E-mail from Christian Schröeder, *supra.*

employee, encryption of the data using a public key, and restricted access to the database.[2494]

International Obligations

Germany is a member of the Council of Europe and has signed and ratified the Convention for the Protection of Individuals with Regard to Automatic Processing of Personal Data (Convention No. 108)[2495] and later signed an Additional Protocol to this convention.[2496] It has also signed and ratified the European Convention for the Protection of Human Rights and Fundamental Freedoms (Convention No. 005).[2497] In November 2002, Germany signed the Convention on Cybercrime but has not yet ratified it.[2498] It is a member of the Organization for Economic Cooperation and Development (OECD) and has adopted the OECD Guidelines on the Protection of Privacy and Transborder Flows of Personal Data.

Republic of Georgia

Constitutional Privacy Framework

Constitution of Georgia guarantees the right to privacy in Article 20 of the Constitution.[2499] This article sets out guarantees against arbitrary search and seizures. Article 20 states: (1) Everyone's private life, place of personal activity, personal records, correspondence, communication by telephone or other technical means, as well as messages received through technical means shall be inviolable. Restriction of the aforementioned rights shall be permissible by a court decision or also without such decision in the case of the urgent necessity provided for by law; (2) No one shall have the right to enter the house and other possessions

---

[2494] *See Stellungnahme des Unabhängigen Landeszentrums für Datenschutz* (Statement of the Independent National Center for Data Security), available at <http://www.datenschutzzentrum.de/material/themen/jobcard/>.

[2495] Council of Europe, Legal Affairs, Treaty Office at <http://conventions.coe.int/Treaty/en/Treaties/Html/108.htm>.

[2496] Council of Europe, Additional Protocol to the Convention for the Protection of Individuals with regard to the Automatic Processing of Personal Data, Regarding Supervisory Authorities and Transborder Data Flows, available at <http://conventions.coe.int/Treaty/EN/searchsig.asp?NT=181&CM=8&DF=>.

[2497] Council of Europe, Legal Affairs, Treaty Office at <http://conventions.coe.int/Treaty/en/Treaties/Html/005.htm>.

[2498] Council of Europe, Convention on Cybercrime, available at <http://conventions.coe.int/treaty/EN/searchsig.asp?NT=185&CM=7&DF=09/01/02>.

[2499] Constitution of Georgia, adopted in 1995, available at: <http://www.parliament.ge/LEGAL_ACTS/CONSTITUTION/consten.html>

against the will of possessors, or conduct search unless there is a court decision or the urgent necessity provided for by law.

Data Protection Framework

Despite constitutional guarantees, there is no precise legislation for the protection of privacy or personal information. The Civil Code of Georgia, which entered into force in 1997, recognizes right to privacy, as a civil law tort.[2500] The code includes a very general article stating that person may demand retraction of information invading into his/her private life: "A person is entitled to demand in court the retraction of information that defames his honor, dignity, privacy, personal inviolability or business reputation unless the person who has disseminated such information can prove that it corresponds to the true state of affairs. The same rule applies to the incomplete dissemination of facts, if such dissemination defames the honor, dignity or business reputation of a person."

Under the Civil Code[2501] of Georgia, persons may seek damages if they can prove the culpability of the person who disseminated the information.[2502] These provisions of the Civil Code have not been applied in courts' practice very often. In 2000, the General Administrative Code of Georgia was adopted. The code includes a Freedom of Information chapter, which, among other freedom of information rights, introduces the term "personal secret."[2503] The notion of "personal secret" is also found in Article 10 of the Code: "Everyone may gain access to official documents kept by an administrative agency, and obtain a copy thereof, unless such documents contain state, professional, commercial, or private secrets."

The validity of certain restrictions on disclosure of private secret, along with other possibilities of closing or classifying documents is considered in the Administrative Code. Aiming to avoid complications and misunderstandings, the Code identified what is personal data and how should information be classified as secret. Article 27, clause (e) defines "personal data" as "public information that allows identification of a person." The definition of personal data as public information allowing identification of a person is insufficient for considering data

---

[2500] The Civil Code of Georgia, Article 18, adopted on June 26, 1997, available at <http://www.iris.ge/docs/translations/code_civil.doc>.

[2501] *Id.*

[2502] *Id.*

[2503] The General Administrative Code of Georgia, Article 27, adopted on June 29, 1999, available at <http://www.iris.ge/docs/translations/code_admin_general.doc>.

stored in any public agency inaccessible to any third party; therefore, the issue of banning access to information is specifically addressed by Article 27.

Pursuant to the Article 27 of the General Administrative Code, a data subject shall decide whether information should be deemed as personal secret: "The matter whether particular information constitutes a personal secret shall be decided by the information subject, except as otherwise prescribed by the law."[2504]

After the adoption of the General Administrative Code, there has been much debate about whether a separate law on personal data should be adopted. In 2003, NGOs started to work towards a separate law, among them were IRIS Georgia and Liberty Institute. Draft laws have been prepared, but there have been no other steps taken in order to initiate the legislation.

Nevertheless, in 2004, an important piece of legislation came into force after democratic breakthrough in Georgia: "Draft law on Freedom of Speech and Expression,"[2505] which has been prepared and lobbied by a non-profit organization Liberty Institute since 1998. In 1999, "Draft Law on Freedom of Speech and Expression" was adopted by the Georgian Parliament in the first hearing; however, the Parliament didn't vote on the draft law again that year. In 2004, the draft law gained the approval of the Council of Europe Experts[2506] and was finally adopted by the Georgian Parliament.

The law sets out free speech guarantees, decriminalizes criminal defamation, envisages high protection for political speech, and includes clear distinction between private and public persons and facts and value judgments.[2507] This law also includes several provisions that are relevant to the right to privacy in Georgia. In particular, the law introduces the test of "reasonable expectation of privacy."[2508] Under the law "personal secret" is defined as follows: "information having personal value that should be protected according to the law as well as the information or facts with respect to which a person has a reasonable expectation of inviolability of private life. Information on an administrative agency shall not

---

[2504] If any other law contains obligations to consider personal information secret, the information is classified. e.g. such obligation is established by the law of Georgia on Patients' Rights.

[2505] Draft Law on Freedom of Speech and Expression, adopted on June 24, 2004, available at <http://www.liberty.ge/geo/categories.php?genre_id=67&section_id=2&from=categories>.

[2506] The Council of Europe approved the law on March 25, 2002. For more information on this issue *see*, <http://www.coe.int/T/E/Human_Rights/Media/3_Assistance_Programmes/Legislatives_exp/Georgia/ATCM(2002)002_en.asp>.

[2507] The Law on Freedom of Speech and Expression, adopted on June 24, 2004, Article 1.

[2508] *Id.* at Article 1, clause (n).

be considered a private secret."[2509] In addition, the law includes another provision stating: "The freedom of expression shall not be restricted by the reason of inviolability of private life and protection of a personal secret with respect to an event that should be known to a person for the exercise of the public self-government in a democratic society."[2510] "Law on Freedom of Speech and Expression" has not been used in Georgian courts as of April 2005, thus relevant practice is not known.

Supervisory Authority

On the bases of Resolution No. 731 of June 16, 1992 of the government of Georgia, a State Inspection for the Protection of Secret Information was created. The Inspection was created by the "Law on Press and Other Means of Mass Media" adopted on August 10, 1991. On June 24, 2004, the "Law on Freedom of Speech and Expression" was adopted, which repealed the previous "Law on Press and other Mass media." The new law contains no mention of the State Inspection for the Protection of Secret Information.

Still, in 1997 the Inspection was listed under the independent state entities of the executive branch by the "Law on Structure and Rules of Procedure of the Executive Power." However, this was abolished by the "Law on Structure, Power and Activities of the Government of Georgia of 2004." In February 2004, the temporary provisions of the law ordered the functions of the State Inspection for the Protection of Secret Information to be transferred and implemented by the National Security Council of Georgia. However, in December 2004 the law was amended[2511] and the appropriate function has been transferred to the Ministry of Internal Affairs of Georgia. Unfortunately, it is not clear in what form this function is conducted by the Ministry, as there is no regulation adopted regulating the issue.

As for other agencies in respect of protecting secret information, the General Administrative Code of Georgia obliges all public entities to protect secret information kept therein from disclosure. Moreover, ministries and legal entities of public law are governed by normative acts, which establish principles for considering information secret and their protection.

[2509] *Id.*

[2510] *Id.* at Article 13, clause (3).

[2511] Amendments to the Law on Structure, Power and Activities of the Government of Georgia were passed on December 23, 2004.

Law enforcement wiretapping, search, seizure and electronic surveillance authority is regulated by Law of Georgia on Operative and Investigative Activities adopted in 1999.[2512] Aims of the operative and investigative activities are listed in Article 2[2513]: prevention and detection of crime; detection of person who fled prosecution; detection of property gained by illegal action, detection of lost persons and gathering of evidence for criminal prosecution. Activities covered by the law and relevant for privacy issues are: gathering of information and visual surveillance, seizure of correspondence, wiretapping and covert eavesdropping, seizure and control of electronic correspondence and electronic surveillance.

A warrant from a judge is only required for wiretapping, seizure and control of electronic correspondence and electronic surveillance. In cases of urgency, a warrant is not required; however, a judge should be notified within 48 hours. The judge may approve or disprove of the measure and order the destruction of information acquired.[2514] The decision of the judge is final and there are no mechanisms to challenge the legality of the measure. The aforementioned measures for the purposes of criminal prosecution are allowed for crimes that have the punishment exceeding two years' imprisonment. Under the Criminal Code of Georgia almost 90% of crimes fall under the category for which those measures could be used. The law does not provide high standards of proof for use of these measures; Article 7 of the law merely states that the motion to the judge should be motivated. The law does not include principle of minimization[2515] in surveillance and wiretapping measures. The law provides that operative and investigative measures are "strictly confidential" and their disclosure entails criminal prosecution under the Law on State Secrets,[2516] unless 25 years have passed since the application of the measure.[2517] Activities can be prolonged up to six months with motivated decision of the head of the agency and in

---

[2512] Law of Georgia on Operative and Investigative Activities, adopted on April 30, 1999, available at <http://www.parliament.ge/LEGAL_ACTS/1933.htm>.

[2513] *Id.*

[2514] *Id.* at Article 7.

[2515] Principle of minimization is currently not recognized under the Georgian legal system. See discussion *infra*.

[2516] Law on State Secrets of Georgia, adopted on October 29, 1996, available at <http://www.parliament.ge/LEGAL_ACTS/>.

[2517] *Id.* at Article 5.

extraordinary circumstances up to 12 months with consent of the General Prosecutor of Georgia.[2518]

Liberty Institute[2519] has been calling for the reform of Criminal Justice System. A concept paper with NGO recommendations[2520] has been prepared by the Liberty Institute, Association for Legal and Public Education, and Georgian Young Lawyers Association in this regard. Based on the concept paper the new government, which came to power after the Rose Revolution,[2521] created a working group to prepare the new Criminal Procedure Code Draft, which included NGO representatives. The working group has prepared the draft,[2522] which envisages new provisions for wiretapping and electronic surveillance activities concerning criminal prosecution. Those measures, according to the draft, can be used only for investigation of grave crimes,[2523] with warrant from court (no exception allowed in cases of urgency), for 30 days and upon strict supervision of the Liberty Judges.[2524]

Prosecution has to report to the Liberty Judge every 10 days during which the measures are being carried out, and Liberty Judge may order the discontinuance of the measure if principle of minimization[2525] is not observed and no relevant information is being obtained. Under principle of minimization, law enforcement officials are obliged not to monitor the conversation that is not relevant to the crime. The surveillance measures may be continued for another 30 days upon a firm motion of the prosecutor. The draft Criminal Procedure Code provides that wiretapping and covert eavesdropping can be used only as a last resort, and the prosecution has to demonstrate that other restrictive measures have been applied but were not effective.[2526] The person against whom the measures have been

---

[2518] *Id.* at Article 8.

[2519] Liberty Institute is a non-profit, non-political organization. More information about Liberty Institute can be found at <www.liberty.ge>.

[2520] The concept paper is available at <http://www.liberty.ge/geo/categories.php?genre_id=76&section_id=2&from=categories> (in Georgian).

[2521] Rose Revolution in Georgia refers to a peaceful 2003 revolution that displaced president Eduard Shevardnadze. For more information *see* <http://news.bbc.co.uk/2/hi/europe/4036145.stm>.

[2522] Draft on the Georgian Criminal Procedure Code. Draft cCode is being finalized and will be presented to the Georgian Parliament in the fall session in September 2005. English version is not available.

[2523] Grave crimes according to the Georgian Criminal Code are crimes punishable with more than 10 years of imprisonment.

[2524] A new category of judges who will approve pre-trial orders.

[2525] Principle of minimization is defined in the Draft Code as follows: "Investigative authorities who are conducting control and communications measures against a person should take appropriate measures not to monitor conversations which do not reveal information relevant to the investigation."

[2526] Draft Code, *supra* at Article 98.

used has to be notified after termination of the measure, and can challenge the legality of the action in court.[2527]

Draft code is being prepared by active participation of the Council of Europe and the United States Department of Justice experts. As of April 2005, the code is being finalized and will be presented to the parliament for the Autumn Session in September 2005.

Another draft law prepared by the Parliamentary Committee on Defense and Security is Draft Law on Counter-Surveillance.[2528] The draft law was prepared based on the United State Foreign Intelligence Surveillance Act (FISA). Under the draft law, which is not finalized, the President of Georgia upon the motion of the Prosecutor General may order surveillance measures without approval from courts. Measures may last up to one year.[2529] Prosecutor General has to elaborate minimization rules and attach the elaboration to the motion for the application of the measure presented to the court. Minimization rules are defined by the Draft Law as follows:

> "Minimization procedures." with respect to electronic surveillance, mean (1) specific procedures, which shall be adopted by the Prosecutor General of Georgia, that are reasonably designed in light of the purpose and technique of the particular surveillance, to minimize the acquisition and retention, and prohibit the dissemination, of nonpublicly available information concerning unconsenting Georgian persons consistent with the need of the Georgia to obtain, produce, and disseminate foreign intelligence information; (2) procedures that require that nonpublicly available information, which is not foreign intelligence information, shall not be disseminated in a manner that identifies any Georgian person, without such person's consent, unless such person's identity is necessary to understand foreign intelligence information or assess its importance; (3) procedures that allow for the retention and dissemination of information that is evidence of a crime which has been, is being, or is about to be committed and that is to be retained or disseminated for law enforcement purposes; and (4) procedures that require that no contents of any communication to which a Georgian person is a party shall be disclosed, disseminated, or used for any purpose or retained for longer than 72 hours unless a court order is obtained or unless the Prosecutor General of Georgia determines

---

[2527] *Id.* at Article 101.

[2528] Draft Law on Counter-Surveillance, 2005, prepared by Member of Parliament, Deputy Chairman of the Parliamentary Committee on Defense and Security Mr. Nick Rurua. Draft law is not final as of April 27, 2005 and may be subject to changes until it is presented to the Parliament.

[2529] *Id.* at Article 7.

that the information indicates a threat of death or serious bodily harm to any person.[2530]

Draft law also provides for creation of a special *collegium* of judges to consider motions under it. *Collegium* will be established by the Chairman of the Supreme Court from the judges of Tbilisi District Court. Decision of District Court *collegium* may be appealed to Special *collegium,* whose members will be taken from Supreme Court judges. Decisions of the *collegium* are confidential, unless legality of the measure has been challenged in court and has to be determined.

Major Privacy Case Law

Privacy claims are very rare in Georgian courts. They started to appear in 2001. Most of those claims are dealt with under the Civil Code, which includes provisions for the protection of privacy.[2531]

During 2004, only one lawsuit was presented to court by the victim of rape, whose name, address and other personal characteristics were published in Georgian Weekly Newspaper "Kviris Palitra."[2532] Victim of the crime has motioned the court to hold closed hearings. Court heard the case in closed hearings; however, it released the final judgment to the press by the court. Court has relied on the provision of the Criminal Proceedings Code, under which all the judgments are public, even though the hearing was held *in camera*.[2533] District court ruled in favor of the applicant and obliged the newspaper and journalist to pay GEL 5,000 for moral damages. The Supreme Court has affirmed the judgment. However neither district court nor Supreme Court explored the obligation of court, which heard the case, to protect the privacy of the victim.

NGO Advocacy Work

Liberty Institute, with financing from IREX,[2534] is preparing the textbook for lawyers, judges and students of law and journalism education programs on the protection of privacy. This textbook will compile decisions of the European Court of Human Rights under Article 8, decisions of the UK House of Lords, the

---

[2530] *Id.* at Article 2.

[2531] The Civil Code of Georgia, *supra* at Article 18.

[2532] S.S. v. Weekly "Kviris Palitra" and Megi Tsanava, Supreme Court of Georgia, 2004.

[2533] The Criminal Code of Georgia, Article 13, available at <http://www.parliament.ge/LEGAL_ACTS/.>.

[2534] International Research and Exchanges Board homepage <www.irex.org>.

United States Supreme Court and the Canadian Supreme Court. In addition, it will include the explanatory notes on Article 8 of the ECHR and documents of the European Union on Data Protection. Liberty Institute is promoting discussion in this field and lobbying for adoption of relevant legislation in order to guarantee effective mechanisms for protection of privacy in Georgia.

International Obligations

On April 27, 1999, Georgia signed the European Convention on Human Rights and ratified it on May 20, 1999.[2535] On November 21, 2001, Georgia has signed but has not ratified the Convention for the Protection of Individuals with regard to Automatic Processing of Personal Data.[2536]

Hellenic Republic (Greece)

Constitutional Privacy Framework

The Constitution of Greece recognizes the rights of privacy and secrecy of communications. Article 9 states: "(1) Every person's home is a sanctuary. The private and family life of the individual is inviolable. No home search shall be made, except when and as specified by law, and always in the presence of representatives of the judicial power. (2) Violators of the preceding provision shall be punished for violating the home's asylum and for abuse of power, and shall be liable for full damages to the sufferer, as specified by law."[2537] A constitutional amendment in 2001 added a new provision to this article granting individuals a direct right to protection of their personal information. The new provision, Article 9A, states: "All persons have the right to be protected from the collection, processing and use, especially by electronic means, of their personal data, as specified by law. The protection of personal data is ensured by an independent authority, which is established and operates as specified by law."[2538] Article 19 of the Constitution protects the privacy of communications. It states: "Secrecy of letters and all other forms of free correspondence or communication

---

[2535] Convention for the Protection of Human Rights and Fundamental Freedoms. (ETS no.: 005), available at <http://conventions.coe.int/Treaty/EN/CadreListeTraites.htm>.

[2536] Convention for the Protection of Individuals with regard to Automatic Processing of Personal Data (ETS no.: 108), available at <http://conventions.coe.int/Treaty/EN/CadreListeTraites.htm>.

[2537] Constitution of Greece (1975) as amended in 2001, available at <http://www.oefre.unibe.ch/law/icl/gr00c___.pdf > (translation of Constitution was made by Klitos Paraskevopoulos and Prokopis Sofras).

[2538] Id.

shall be absolutely inviolable. The guarantees under which the judicial authority shall not be bound by this secrecy for reasons of national security or for the purpose of investigating especially serious crimes shall be specified under law." The 2001 amendment, in addition to adding two new provisions to this article, establishes an independent authority, to supervise matters relating to telecommunications.[2539] Article 19(2) now states: "The matters relating to the establishment, operation and powers of the independent authority ensuring the secrecy of paragraph 1 shall be specified by law." Article 19(3) states: "The use of evidence acquired in violation of the present article and of articles 9 and 9A is prohibited."[2540]

Data Protection Framework

The Law on the Protection of Individuals with regard to the Processing of Personal Data (Data Protection Act) was approved by the Parliament in April 1997.[2541] Greece was the last member of the European Union (EU) to adopt a data protection law and its law was written to directly adopt the EU Data Protection Directive (1995/46/EC). The Act was also necessary for Greece to join the Schengen Agreement. There were major protests during the ratification of the Schengen Agreement for border controls and information sharing. According to news reports, police used tear gas to disperse a group of about 1,000 protesters, including Orthodox priests, when they tried to push their way into Parliament as the pact was being debated.[2542]

Data Protection Authority

Implemented to ensure basic privacy protection, the Data Protection Act not only established the Hellenic Data Protection Authority (DPA), but also a set of guidelines, principles and rules relating to the use, processing, storage and export of personal data in both electronic and manual files.[2543] The DPA was established in November 1997 as an independent authority set to monitor privacy violations in Greece. It was created to supervise the implementation of the Data

---

[2539] Id.

[2540] Id.

[2541] Law No. 2472 on the Protection of Individuals with regard to the Processing of Personal Data, available at <http://www.dpa.gr/Documents/Eng/2472engl_all.doc>.

[2542] The Reuters European Community Report, June 10, 1997.

[2543] 6.1. Greece - Data Protection Act <http://europa.eu.int/ISPO/legal/en/news/9709/chapter6.html>.

Protection Act and all regulations referring to the protection of personal data.[2544] It also exercises other powers delegated to it from time to time.

The DPA consists of 24 members. The Authority is composed of a judge of a rank corresponding at least to that of a Conseiller d'État as President.[2545] The Authority is assisted by a Secretariat that operates at the directorate level. It consists of three departments: a) Auditors' Department (11 employees), b) Communications Department (2 employees), c) Department of Administration and Budgetary Affairs (7 employees). Each of the departments has a supervisor. All departments are supervised by the Director.[2546]

The DPA enforces the Act. The Authority may impose on the controllers or on their representatives both administrative and penal sanctions. The administrative sanctions range from warning with an order for the violation to cease within a specified time limit, to the destruction of the file or a ban of the processing and the destruction of the relevant data.[2547] The penal sanctions include: punishment by imprisonment for up to three years and a fine amounting between GRD 1,000,000 and GRD 5,000,000.[2548]

The DPA is responsible for archival audits, issuing regulatory acts arising from legislation on data protection, and providing information and recommendations to interested parties to ensure compliance with data protection regulations. Its mandate includes issuing directives to enhance uniformity in implementation and to protect personal data vis-à-vis technological developments; assisting controllers in drafting codes of conduct; examining complaints; reporting violations; and issuing decisions related to the right to access information. The DPA grants permits for the collection and processing of sensitive personal data and is accountable for the interconnection of files, including sensitive data and the trans-boundary flow of personal data. The DPA's communications office is in charge of all public relations and communication with private and public services and institutions, the media, foreign data protection authorities, European Union authorities, and international organizations and institutions.[2549]

[2544] Homepage <http://www.dpa.gr/home_eng.htm>.

[2545] Law 2472/97, chapter D, article 16 (Composition of the Authority).

[2546] E-mail from Amalia Logiaki, Hellenic Data Protection Authority, to Ula Galster, International Policy Fellow, Electronic Privacy Information Center, May 31, 2005 (on file with EPIC).

[2547] Law 2472/97 chapter E, artciles 21-22. Other administrative sanctions include: a fine amounting between GRD 300,000 and GRD 50,000,000, a temporary revocation of the permit, a definitive revocation of the permit.

[2548] For further information *see*, sections 21-22 (Sanctions).

[2549] Homepage <http://www.dpa.gr/home_eng.htm>.

In 2004,[2550] the Greek Data Protection Authority received 626 complaints, 682 questions regarding data protection matters and 663 registrations to Robinson's List (list of persons who do not wish data relating to them to be submitted to processing for the promotion of sales and long distance services), conducted 36 controls to files, issued 66 decisions and three opinions.[2551] The majority of the complaints are examined by the Auditors Department. Some complaints are also examined by the Board.[2552] A decision or an answer is issued and the interested parties are notified.[2553]

On December 16, 2002, the head of the DPA, and its first President, Mr. Dafermos, resigned from his post when it had been made clear that the Parliament would not support him for a new term. Mr. Dafermos had just completed his first term and was replaced by Mr. Gourgourakis, a former high court judge. Although Mr. Dafermos had generally kept a low profile, he had aroused criticism from the Greek Church and the right-wing party (New Democracy) after repeatedly getting involved with religious issues that had generally remained undiscussed. Mr. Dafermos was subsequently appointed General Controller for the Public Administration.[2554]

To date the DPA has issued several dozen decisions, ranging from issues surrounding the Olympic games to the ISDN Caller-ID issue. Some of the more important issues worked on by the Greek DPA have included: (1) the credit-reporting system's (TEIRESIAS) white-list. The official bank-run credit-reporting system that purports to make a list not only for bad-debtors, but also for good-payers; (2) the processing of personal information during the Olympics; (3) data-matching among the Ministries of Public Transport, of Finance and of Public Security (the actual collection of fines is a Greek first); (4) ISDN Caller-ID; (5) The decision on the inclusion of the religion in the elementary and high school curricula (the "final straw" that outraged the Church and ended Mr. Dafermos's chances for a new term).[2555]

[2550] Compared to 2001 and 2002, the total number of complaints submitted to the DPA for the year 2003 decreased to reach 228. 23 were against banks, 129 for access to files, 16 against creditworthiness ascertainment companies, 22 against telecommunications companies, 15 against hospitals, 10 against CCTV, 11 against marketing companies and two against System Information Schengen. Since the entry into force of Greek law on the protection of personal data, the DPA has performed 51 audits on privacy policies and standards.

[2551] E-mail from Amalia Logiaki, *supra*,

[2552] *See* <http://www.dpa.gr/authority_eng.htm#pre>http://www.dpa.gr/authority_eng.htm#pre>.

[2553] E-mail from Amalia Logiaki, *supra*.

[2554] E-mail from Vagelis Papakonstantinou, Hellenic Data Protection Authority, Greece, to Erik J. Blum, Law Clerk, Electronic Privacy Information Center, June 1, 2003 (on file with EPIC).

[2555] *Id.*

Recently, the DPA struck down the use of biometric identity verification at the International Athens Airport.[2556] The biometric system sought to ensure that the passenger who checked in was the same at the person who actually boarded the airplane. While observing that such cases should be decided on a case-by-case basis, the DPA ruled that the collection and processing of iris and fingerprint data for verification of passenger identity was not permissible. Pursuant to the Greek Data Protection Act, the biometric data process was unlawful because the gathering of personal data exceeded its purpose. The DPA noted that passenger identity could be ascertained in a "milder way" by requiring passengers to show an identity card along with the airplane ticket.[2557]

In another recent decision the DPA invalidated the dissemination of a screening test results to an insurance company.[2558] The DPA again protected private health information when it outlawed references in official Greek law reports to the specific health conditions that were the reason for employment terminations.[2559] Private contact information was at issue in another recent decision. The DPA ruled that the Ministry of Internal Affairs, Public Administration and Decentralization could grant to the Greek Branch of the International Social Authority contact information for biological parents to their biological children. This information was intended to assist biological children to contact their biological parents, provided the Ministry had already received the biological parents' consent.[2560]

Prior to the national elections in March 2004, the DPA struck down the construction of a database of the "friends," but not already members, of the Panhellenic Socialist Movement (PASOK) party for the purposes of electing the new President of PASOK.[2561] The DPA ruled that the creation of such a database would violate the constitutional provision for secret ballot, as provided by Article 51 § 3 of the Greek Constitution.[2562]

[2556] Hellenic Data Protection Authority, Decision 52/05.11.2003, available at <http://www.dpa.gr/decision_eng.htm>.

[2557] Id.

[2558] E-mail from Fereniki Panagopoulou to Cédric Laurant, Policy Counsel, Electronic Privacy Information Center, June 25, 2004 (on file with EPIC). See also Hellenic Data Protection Authority, Decision 2/08.01.2004, available at <http://www.dpa.gr/decs.htm> (in Greek).

[2559] E-mail from Fereniki Panagopoulou, supra. See also Hellenic Data Protection Authority, Decision 54/20.11.2003, available at <http://www.dpa.gr/decs.htm> (in Greek).

[2560] E-mail from Fereniki Panagopoulou, supra. See also Hellenic Data Protection Authority, Decision 10/27.02.2004, available at <http://www.dpa.gr/decs.htm> (in Greek).

[2561] E-mail from Fereniki Panagopoulou, supra. See also Hellenic Data Protection Authority, Decision 6/06.02.2004, available at http://www.dpa.gr/decs.htm (in Greek).

[2562] Participation in the elections of the party President is strongly correlated to voters' selections in the general election. The DPA noted that participation in the nomination of the PASOK President may lead to the

In 2002, the DPA ruled on videophone practices that were used between a bank and another company, and involved clients talking to the bank's employees from the other company's premises.[2563] After filling in the relevant documents and before signing them, the client was asked to contact the competent bank employee by videophone in order to receive some clarifications about the documents and, then, to sign them. The complainant refused and the transaction was cancelled. The bank argued that the videophone was necessary to verify the customer's signature on the documents. The system involved a bi-directional communication with picture transmission, using a dial up ISDN line. The DPA held that the transmission of the picture did not entail the storage of sound and image data. Further, the system did not constitute a CCTV system since the nature of the communication line did not allow for continuous surveillance of the place. The DPA concluded that the data protection law was not violated for the reasons that (1) the personal data would not be processed to assemble a file and (2) that the data subject had given his prior consent.[2564]

Other action by the DPA included nine "controls" directed at five banks, the Ministry of Defense, one nursery clinic, one NGO, and one Internet provider (a private enterprise). It found that banks generally protected privacy well, but they needed to inform their customers better in the future. Discussion also surrounded "instant loans" for a relatively small amount (maximum EUR 3,000), which were practically given automatically by machines, although the machines have to record the customer's picture and electronically save his or her signature. Other areas also did well. One Internet company case related to an installed web-camera. The camera was intended to show the weather and not persons, therefore the company was allowed to keep it, but it was forced to register as a "data controller."[2565]

An example of judicial action includes a case setting terms and limits on the lawful processing of personal data for the purposes of direct

---

impression, especially in smaller cities, that the people who did not participate in the nomination process do not intend to vote in the forthcoming elections for the specific party. The DPA concluded that registering the "friends" of PASOK consisted, in view of the constitutional provision for secret ballot, of an inappropriate means to achieve the intended goal. The intended goal was only to identify those people who were involved in the process of electing the party President. This identification could have been achieved, according to the DPA, through other means that would not require registering those voters who voted in the nomination of the President of a specific party. E-mail from Fereniki Panagopoulou, *supra*.

[2563] Hellenic Data Protection Authority, Decision 55/16.9.2001, available at <http://www.dpa.gr/decision_eng.htm>.

[2564] British Institute of International & Comparative Law Report, May 16, 2003, available at <http://www.biicl.org>.

[2565] E-mail from Vagelis Papakonstantinou *supra*.

marketing/advertising and the ascertainment of creditworthiness.[2566] Another case established that the announcement of the name of someone involved in criminal activities by police authorities in a press release may happen only if (1) the announcement of the name or photograph or other data, specific or not, is of someone who is allegedly involved in criminal activity and is lawfully wanted in order to be arrested or (2) the announcement is of the arrest.[2567]

In the past few years, the DPA has issued directives relating to state identity cards, direct marketing, CCTV, DNA testing, and workplace surveillance. The DPA has also issued guidelines covering data protection in the workplace in particular surveillance of phone calls and e-mails.[2568] On May 4, 2000, in a controversial ruling, the DPA ruled that religious affiliations must be removed from state identity cards. The decision was opposed by the Greek Orthodox Church and led to massive protests and challenges to the ruling.[2569] The strong connection between the Greek Orthodox Church and the State is notable as there is no separation between Church and State.[2570] In March 2001, Greece's highest administrative court upheld the ruling finding that stating citizens' religious affiliation on the compulsory identity cards was unconstitutional.[2571] Prior to the ruling, Greece was the only member of the European Union that required citizens to list their religious beliefs on citizen identity cards. The new Greek identity cards do not include religion, even on a voluntary basis. In addition to the removal of religious affiliation, new identity cards also no longer include fingerprints, names and surnames of the cardholder's spouse, maiden names, professions, home addresses, or citizenship.

The DPA considers the trading of personal data for direct marketing or sales to be lawful under specific conditions and only with the consent of the individual or when the data is collected from public sources. It has specific guidelines for the ascertainment of credibility of information and only for specific purposes.[2572] In

---

[2566] Hellenic Data Protection Authority, Decision 050/20.01.2000, available at <http://www.dpa.gr/decision_eng.htm>.

[2567] Hellenic Data Protection Authority, Decision 67/12.6.2002, available at <http://www.dpa.gr/decision_eng.htm>.

[2568] Article 29 Data Protection Working Group Party, Fifth Annual Report on the Situation regarding the Processing of Individuals with Regard to the Processing of Personal Data and Privacy in the European Union and in Third Countries, Part II, March 6, 2002, available at <http://europa.eu.int/comm/internal_market/en/dataprot/wpdocs/wp54en_2.pdf>.

[2569] "Greek Church at War Over Plans to Change ID Cards," The Guardian, May 24, 2000.

[2570] E-mail from Fereniki Panagopoulou, *supra*.

[2571] "Greek Church Causes Fresh Identity Crisis," The Guardian, August 29, 2001. *See also* Decision 134/31.10.2001, available at <http://www.dpa.gr/decision_eng.htm>.

[2572] Hellenic Data Protection Authority, Decision 050/20.01.2000, available at <http://www.dpa.gr/decision_eng.htm>.

May 2000, the DPA issued a directive regarding direct marketing companies that were collecting personal data directly from mothers in maternity hospitals. The directive required that hospitals act as controllers by drafting a consent form for mothers who wanted to receive advertising literature to fill out. The hospital would then forward the consent form to marketing firms.[2573]

In September 2000, the DPA set out guidelines prohibiting the recording, use, monitoring, and retention of personal information through the use of CCTV on a regular, continuous, or permanent basis.[2574] Recording is only lawful when it is done for the protection of individuals or goods or for traffic violations and only under the principles of necessity and proportionality. In these exceptional cases, the DPA must grant permission, and the rules on accuracy and notification must be followed. With respect to crime prevention or repression, the DPA must grant special permission to judicial and legal authorities to use cameras, with strict guidelines for use and retention. In the year 2000, the DPA received five complaints concerning CCTV systems in the private sector, two of which were infractions. The DPA, upon examining these infractions, ordered the relocation of the cameras and the prior notification of individuals entering the area monitored by CCTV.[2575]

In November 2004, the DPA issued a warning to a company to refrain from making a record of web pages visited by employees for statistical purposes, while allowing the web pages which employees may visit to be restricted. Furthermore, a company should refrain from collecting and processing data regarding calls and in general communications (including electronic mail) at the workplace, unless it is absolutely necessary for organizing and monitoring the handling of such operation or of a set of business operations and in particular for monitoring expenses. The communication data recorded must be limited to those absolutely necessary and appropriate for fulfilling such purposes. In no event is such recording and processing of the entire number of or of the totality of communication data or of data of their contents permitted.[2576]

With respect to DNA analysis for the purpose of criminal investigation and prosecution, the DPA issued an opinion in 2001 expressing concern with the

---

[2573] Hellenic Data Protection Authority, Decision 523/18 -25.5.2000, available at <http://www.dpa.gr/decision_eng.htm>.

[2574] Hellenic Data Protection Authority, Directive on Closed Circuit Television Systems, 1122-26.09.2000, available at <http://www.dpa.gr/decision_eng.htm>.

[2575] Id.

[2576] Hellenic Data Protection Authority. Decision 61/2004, available at <http://www.dpa.gr/decision_eng.htm>.

methods and effects of collection of citizens' sensitive data. According to the opinion, the genetic analysis of DNA must be limited to the "non-codified section of DNA" and identity verification.[2577] The DPA advised that any methods that allow any conclusions about the personality traits of individuals from their DNA should be forbidden, including personality profiling.[2578] This method of investigation should only be used for verification of offenders' and victims' identity and for criminal investigations and should be destroyed once the fulfillment of the intended aim is achieved. Finally, the DPA does not support any effort to collect and analyze genetic material for preventative purposes.[2579]

According to the Human Rights Watch 2002 World Report, in August 2001, the DPA asked the government to discard a provision of the law compelling hospital staff and hotel employees to notify the police if undocumented migrants sought their services because it violated Greece's privacy protection laws.[2580]

In May 2001, there was a public outcry when it was revealed that "Megalos Adelfos," the local version of the television show "Big Brother," was soon to be aired in Greece. The National Council for Radio and Television requested details of the show to determine whether it would breach the country's privacy regulations.[2581] In July 2001, the DPA issued an order for the termination of the processing of personal data for the show.[2582] The show aired nonetheless. Citing privacy concerns, journalists and media students staged a protest outside the private Antenna network's headquarters.

According to the Hellenic Bank Association, a nonprofit legal entity that represents banks and other financial institutions operating in Greece and sets codes of banking ethics for its members, there are voluntary standards of confidentiality and banking secrecy that protect customers' financial records. These records can only be disclosed with the consent of the customers. However, the code also states that the exchange of consolidated information between banks relating to "groups of customers, as part of the electronic transfer of quantitative

---

[2577] Hellenic Data Protection Authority. Opinion.15/2001, available at <http://www.dpa.gr/decision_eng.htm>.

[2578] *Id.*

[2579] *Id.*

[2580] Human Rights Watch, World Report 2002 (New York 2001).

[2581] "Greek Protests Over Big Brother," The Herald (Glasgow), May 28, 2001.

[2582] Hellenic Data Protection Authority. Decision 1346-03.07.01, available at <http://www.dpa.gr/decision_eng.htm>.

data on transactions and/or for statistical purposes, does not constitute a breach of confidentiality."[2583]

Wiretapping and Surveillance Rules

While Law No. 2225/94 requires police who wish to conduct telephone taps to obtain court permission,[2584] in the past there were continuing reports of government surveillance, including illegal wiretapping and interception of mail of human rights groups, Orthodox religious groups, and activist members of minority groups.[2585] Although monitored in the past, in 2001 the Greek Helsinki Monitor reported that it was not monitored by security services.[2586]

In April 2001, the European Court of Human Rights, in the case of *Donald Peers v. Greece*, found that Mr. Peers was entitled to compensation for breach of privacy, under Article 8 of the European Convention, when prison administrators opened his mail while he was incarcerated for drug offences in Greece in 1994.[2587]

While the current Greek Penal Law does address some cybercrimes, the penalties for violators are generally not severe, and when Greece tries to reduce cybercrime, the laws it passes generally do not correct the problem.[2588] One example of this can be seen in the attempt of the Greek government, during the summer of 2002, to restrict electronic games. This was primarily done to stem the flow of illegal online gambling, but led to economic hardship for many arcade owners, Internet cafes and computer game stores. Many of them closed or were forced to pay big fines for violations of the law. A side effect of these closures was the even bigger support for illegal distribution of pirated copies of games. This ultimately led to its repeal.[2589]

[2583] Hellenic Banking Association, Code of Banking Ethics, available at <http://www.Hba.gr/English/iabout/profile.htm#h1>.

[2584] Law No. 2225/94.

[2585] United States Department of State, Greece Country Report on Human Rights Practices 2000, February 2001, available at <http://www.state.gov/g/drl/rls/hrrpt/2000/>; Human Rights Watch World Report, 2002, available at <http://www.hrw.org/wr2k2/>.

[2586] United States Department of State, Greece Country Report on Human Rights Practices for 2001, March 2002, available at <http://www.state.gov/g/drl/rls/hrrpt/2001/eur/8261.htm>.

[2587] *Id.*

[2588] Christos Panageas, Computer Crime and Misuse: The Case of Greece and the EU (2003) (unpublished B.S. thesis, City College of the University of Sheffield) (on file with EPIC).

[2589] *Id. See also* Amanda Castleman, "More Fallout Over Greek Game Ban," Wired.com, February 13, 2003, at <http://www.wired.com/news/games/0,2101,57305,00.html>.

In an interview in June 2002, the Minister of Public Order, Michales Chrysocoidis, stated that although cybercrime has not reached a top level in Greece, the Ministry of Public Order had received warning signs that forced it to consider creating a National Center to protect public and private electronic infrastructures from crimes performed through the Internet.[2590] Public organizations such as the Greek Telecommunications Organization and the Greek Electricity Organization, carrier organizations like Service of State Airways, and government organizations such as the National Intelligence Agency and the Greek police will all be involved in the National Center project. The Minister also added that private organizations should participate in the project as well and admitted that other European countries are ahead of Greece in similar activities.[2591]

Tough security measures, including military patrols, special commando units and more than 1,000 surveillance cameras were put in place for the 2004 Olympic Games in Athens.[2592] Greek law enforcement authorities were provided training and intelligence assistance from seven countries: Australia, Britain, France, Germany, Israel and Spain, and the United States.[2593] There was little concern over the violation of citizens' privacy through the use of these cameras.

In May 2004, the DPA approved a police request to operate closed-circuit television (CCTV) cameras on the streets during the "operational phase" of the Olympics, as long as the cameras are not used after the Games.[2594] According to the DPA's decision, the cameras could legally operate from July 1 until October 4, 2004. Other conditions were that the cameras not be set up in such a way that they film the entrances or interiors of homes or that they record the conversations of passers-by, and that there be adequate signposting informing citizens they are entering surveillance areas. The legal preconditions to using the video cameras include: (a) there is no receipt or record of images of the entrance or the interior of private homes; (b) the receipt and hearing of conversations of inhabitants or passing people is not possible; (c) the person is informed in a convenient and an adequate way before he enters the range of the video camera (adequate number of distinguishable signboards in visible places) in a place that is video recorded as well as the purpose of the video recording; (d) the rules of security system as

---

[2590] *Id.*

[2591] *Id.*

[2592] "Athens to Be on Full Alert for Games," The Ottawa Citizen, November 24, 2000.

[2593] "Olympics: More to It Than Games," The New York Times, July 24, 2001.

[2594] "Privacy Watchdog Approves Use of Street Cameras, But Only During Games," Kathimerini, May 5, 2004.

well as data storage are strictly followed; and (e) the maintenance of the data is permitted for a period of seven days.[2595]

In November 2004, the DPA allowed the continuation of the closed-circuit television on the streets for a period of six months, as long as it was used only for the car circulation and not for any other reason including the ascertainment of illegal acts other than those related to the car circulation. The use of cameras was allowed only in the roads of high circulation and not in the roads of low circulation or at places, squares, parks, pedestrian-precincts, and public assembly areas (e.g. entrance of theaters). The cameras were to be set in such a way that they did not film the entrances or interiors of homes, and the receipt of sound should not be possible.[2596] In a recent decision,[2597] the DPA considered the processing of sensitive data in the TV (love communication between a Bishop and an unknown person) as unnecessary for the purposes of public information.

In 1999, Greece created Article 5 of the Greek Code of Administrative Procedure (Law No. 2690/1999),[2598] which is a new Freedom of Information Act that provides citizens the right to access administrative documents created by government agencies. It replaces Law 1599/1986, which regulated the use of the Single Register Code Number (EKAM).[2599]

Recent Developments

The Greek Ministry of the Interior is actively engaged in the delivery of e-government projects, including the creation of a data and voice network connecting approximately 2,000 public bodies via the National Public Administration Network. "Additionally, we are promoting the further development of the Citizen Service Centers (KEP), developing information technology infrastructure and introducing contemporary tools in various government organizations," said Mr. Pavlopoulos, the Minister of Interior. The Minister spoke at the E-Government Forum organized by "The Economist" in Athens on October 19, 2004.[2600]

[2595] E-mail from Fereniki Panagopoulou, *supra. See also* Hellenic Data Protection Authority, Decision 28/03.05.2004, available at <http://www.dpa.gr/decs.htm> (in Greek).

[2596] Hellenic Data Protection Authority. Decision 63/2004.

[2597] Hellenic Data Protection Authority. Decision 25/2005.

[2598] <http://www.rz.uni-frankfurt.de/~sobotta/greecenew.htm>.

[2599] Law No 1599/1986 on the Relationship of a New Type of Identification Card and Other Provisions.

[2600] "E-government a Priority for Greece, Says Minister of the Interior," eGoverment news, October 22, 2004, available at <http://europa.eu.int/idabc/en/document/3409/337>.

The first Greek Digital City is being developed under the responsibility of the Municipality of Trikala[2601] with funding from the Greek Information Society Strategy.[2602] The e-Trikala initiative aims to improve everyday life by simplifying public transactions, reducing telecommunication costs, delivering new electronic services, and offering new methods to enable citizens to participate in policymaking.

International Obligations

Greece is a member of the Council of Europe (CoE) and has signed and ratified the Convention for the Protection of Individuals with Regard to Automatic Processing of Personal Data (ETS No. 108)[2603] and the European Convention for the Protection of Human Rights and Fundamental Freedoms (ECHR).[2604] In November 2001, Greece signed the CoE Convention on Cybercrime.[2605] Greece is also a member of the Organization for Economic Cooperation and Development (OECD) and has adopted the OECD's Guidelines on the Protection of Privacy and Transborder Flows of Personal Data.

Guatemala

Constitutional Privacy Framework

The Political Constitution of the Republic of Guatemala has established rules that cover individual human rights, but does not expressly defines "privacy" as a human right. The Constitution nevertheless protects some aspects of the right to privacy as follows:

- Correspondence and other forms of private communication are inviolable. They may only be intercepted or recorded pursuant to a court order and to formalities established by law. The secret of correspondence is guaranteed as well as phone communications, radio transmissions, telegrams and other products of modern technology. For tax or legal purposes and for cases of inspection, supervision, and state intervention, the disclosure of accounting

---

[2601] *See* <http://www.trikalacity.gr/> (in Greek).

[2602] *See* <http://en.infosoc.gr/>.

[2603] Signed February 17, 1983; enacted August 11, 1995; entered into force December 1995.

[2604] Signed November 28, 1950; enacted November 28, 1974; entered into force November 28, 1974.

[2605] Signed November 23, 2001.

records and other private documents may be required within the limits provided by law. The documents and information obtained against this article cannot be used and cannot produce evidence in a court.[2606]

- Every administrative act of the government is public. Any citizen has the right to obtain, at any time, reports, copies, photocopies, reproductions and certifications that he has requested. Every person has the right to access public documents, except for military and diplomatic documents or information.[2607]

- The administration of public files is a duty of the State and it is a right of the citizens to get access to them. Every person has the right to know and obtain any information about himself that contains any public record or database, as well as has the right to know the purpose of these records, and to correct and update them. The processing of records about political affiliations is prohibited, except if it is done by electoral authorities and political parties.[2608]

The Guatemalan Constitution also amplifies the scope of the Constitution and acknowledges that privacy can be protected as an individual human right in Article 44:

> Rights inherent to the human (individual human rights): the rights and guarantees that have been established in the Constitution do not exclude others, that although not expressly mentioned in the Constitution, are inherent to the human person.[2609]

Data Protection Framework

There is no comprehensive data protection legal framework applicable to the private sector. The Penal Code[2610] establishes penalties for the following

---

[2606] Article 24 of the Political Constitution of the Republic of Guatemala of 1985, available at <http://www.georgetown.edu/pdba/Constitutions/Guate/guate85.html> (in Spanish).

[2607] *Id.* at Article 30.

[2608] *Id.* at Article 31.

[2609] Constitutional Court Journal No. 39, case No. 334-95, page No. 52, sentence of March 26, 1996.

[2610] Penal Code, (*Código Penal*), Decree No. 17-73 of the Congress of the Republic of Guatemala with its modifications, available at <http://www.oas.org/juridico/mla/sp/gtm/sp_gtm-int-text-cp.pdf> (in Spanish).

offenses: prohibited records,[2611] the manipulation of information,[2612] and the abusive use of information.[2613]

There is no data protection law. *Habeas data*[2614] has not expressly been included in the Constitution or other applicable law in Guatemala, but some principles of *habeas data* can be inferred from the Constitution and the Guatemalan legal framework, even though there are no specific laws or rules that regulate *habeas data*. There is no data controller or other administrative entity that controls the data collection and use of private information.

On May 7, 2000, the Presidential Secretary of Strategic Analysis (SAE) announced the existence of a computer database containing names, personal information, and military secret codes of more than 650,000 people. This database appeared to have been compiled by military intelligence many years ago with a permanent copy remaining in the computer system of the Secretary of Strategic Analysis. The SAE gave a copy of this database to the Human Rights Ombudsman, who, in turn, offered public access to the database for those who wished to know if their names appeared on the list.[2615]

In June 2003, the Spanish Data Protection Agency (AEPD) organized the second Ibero-American Conference on the Protection of Personal Data in La Antigua (Guatemala). The result of this meeting is reflected in the Antigua Declaration (*Declaración de La Antigua*).[2616] It holds that the protection of personal data is a genuine fundamental right and recognizes that the processing of personal data can encourage the development of the Information Society in each Ibero-

---

[2611] Article 274 D of the Penal Code establishes the following: "Prohibited Records: will be penalized with prison of six months to four years or a criminal penalty of two hundred to one thousand Quetzales, the person who creates a data base or electronic records that can affect the intimacy of any person."

[2612] Article 274 E of the Penal Code provides: "Manipulation of information. It will be sanctioned with prison from one to five years and a criminal penalty of five hundred to three thousand Quetzales, the person who uses electronic records or software in order to hide, forge or alter the accounting information or the economic situation of an individual or an entity (Corporation)."

[2613] Article 274 F provides: "Use of information. The penalty of imprisonment for six months to two years and the criminal penalty of two hundred to one thousand Quetzals will be imposed to the person who, without authorization, uses without proper authorization from its owner, a database or electronic information, or who gets access by any means to this database or electronic data without authorization."

[2614] *Habeas data* is the right to know, update, and rectify information gathered about individuals in data banks and the records of public and private entities.

[2615] Report on Practices of Human Rights in 2000, available at <http://usembassy.state.gov/guatemala/wwwhhrs2.html>.

[2616] La Antigua Declaration, made on the occasion of the second Seminar on Personal Data Protection in Ibero-America, (*Declaración de La Antigua (Guatemala) con motivo del II Encuentro Iberoamericano de Protección de Datos Personales*), June 6, 2003, available at <https://www.agpd.es/upload/Declaracion_La%20Antigua.ing.PDF>, *see* also <https://www.agpd.es/index.php?idSeccion=348> (in Spanish).

American country. At the same time, the Declaration notes the necessity to encourage the implementation of measures that guarantee a high level of protection of personal data, the ideal being to have national regulatory frameworks in place. It also highlights the importance of establishing a permanent channel of dialogue and collaboration in data protection matters in the Ibero-American region. The Declaration also created the Ibero-American Data Protection Network (IADPN).2617

Despite the adoption of legal rules and case law on data protection, violations of privacy remain a big concern. Legislation has not kept up with the technology, leaving gaps in protection. Unlike most other countries, Guatemala does not have laws or regulations that directly address Internet privacy.

Open Government

In February 2005, a bill (No. 3165) to the Guatemalan Parliament was presented, titled "Public Information Access and Classification and Declassification of Classified State Information."2618 The bill regulates the right to access public information and personal data contained in public and private records. The bill also gives the state the power to classify and declassify sensitive state information.

Article 40 of Bill No. 3165 establishes, that every person whose personal data appears in archives, files, records, data files, databases or any form of information storage held in private or in public records, has the right to know everything that appears in his file; know the identity of the data controller; know the purpose for which his information is collected; to correct wrong personal information, or have false or inaccurate data erased or amended; and to delete sensitive data. The information requested must be provided within 72 hours of the request.

Guatemala has undertaken a freedom of information bill.2619 The bill establishes that any person may generally gain access to public administrative activities. This bill is still in discussion in the Parliament. During the discussion, members of the

---

2617 Ibero-American Data Protection Network homepage <https://www.agpd.es/index.php?idSeccion=350> (in Spanish).

2618 Republic of Guatemala Congress. Legislative Administration, register No. 3165, bill presented by Congressman Eduardo Zachrisson Castillo and Congresswoman Nineth Montenegro Cottom, available at <http://www.congreso.gob.gt> (in Spanish).

2619 Freedom of Information Bill, (*Proyecto de la ley de Libre Acceso a la Información*), available at <http://probidad.org/regional/index.php?seccion=legislacion/2001/039.html0> (in Spanish).

Guatemalan Republican Front (a political party in the opposition) introduced a series of amendments that promote secrecy instead of improving access to information.

International Obligations

Guatemala signed the American Convention on Human Rights (the Pact of San Jose, Costa Rica), the United Nations International Covenant on Civil and Political Rights[2620] and the Universal Declaration of Human Rights.

Special Administrative Region of Hong Kong

Constitutional Privacy Framework

On July 1, 1997, the People's Republic of China (PRC) resumed exercise of its sovereignty over Hong Kong and established it as a "Special Administrative Region" (SAR). Under the principle of "one country, two systems," the laws of the Hong Kong SAR were incorporated into the Chinese legal system by the enactment of the Basic Law, often described as Hong Kong's mini-constitution.[2621] Under this arrangement, the Hong Kong SAR enjoys a high degree of autonomy in creating privacy-related legislations.

The Basic Law of the Hong Kong SAR contains several privacy protections. Article 29 provides that the "homes and other premises of Hong Kong residents shall be inviolable. Arbitrary or unlawful search of, or intrusion into, a resident's home or other premises shall be prohibited." Article 30 provides that the "freedom and privacy of communications of Hong Kong residents shall be protected by law. No department or individual may, on any grounds, infringe

---

[2620] "States Parties to Covenant on Civil and Political Rights. Elect Nine Members to Human Rights Committee," 27 Meeting of the International Covenant on Civil and Political Rights, September 9, 2002, available at <http://www.un.org/News/Press/docs/2002/hr4623.doc.htm>.

[2621] Adopted on April 4, 1990 by the Seventh National People's Congress of the People's Republic of China at its Third Session. The authority of the Congress to establish a special administrative region and decide on the systems to be implemented there is given by Articles 31 and 62 (13) of the Constitution of the PRC. *See* Y. Ghai, Hong Kong's New Constitutional Order: The Resumption of Chinese Sovereignty and the Basic Law 56 (Hong Kong University Press 1997). Legally, the Basic Law should not be considered as the constitution of Hong Kong, although it may have certain constitutional functions. The relationship between the Chinese central government and the Hong Kong SAR government is not the one between the federal government and a state. Although the Hong Kong SAR is a highly autonomous administrative region of China, it has no independent sovereignty. The power over Hong Kong absolutely belongs to China and the central government delegates certain powers to the Hong Kong SAR through the Basic Law. The powers not delegated to the Hong Kong SAR remain vested with the central government.

upon the freedom and privacy of communications of residents except that the relevant authorities may inspect communications in accordance with legal procedures to meet the needs of public security or of investigation into criminal offenses."

Court Cases

In 2004 and 2005, there were three significant court rulings relating to intrusion into privacy. Two rulings were about the powers of the Independent Commission Against Corruption (ICAC), to search for and seize journalistic material.[2622] A subcommittee has been set up by the Legislative Council to follow up on the issues arising from the two judgments.[2623] Another court ruled that evidence gathered through covert surveillance is inadmissible in court because it breaches the constitutional right to privacy.[2624] The court decided that standing orders from the Independent Commission Against Corruption's guidelines did not qualify as "legal procedures" in Article 30 of the Basic Law because the commission's order could not be legitimate without any public discussion.[2625]

Statutes

In 1996, after six years of study by the Law Reform Commission,[2626] Hong Kong enacted a Personal Data (Privacy) Ordinance (PDPO).[2627] The ordinance came into effect in 1996, with the exception of the provisions concerning the transfer of data outside Hong Kong[2628] and data-matching.[2629] No substantial amendments to the ordinance have been made, other than the provision that provided that the ordinance prevails over any other ordinance in case of inconsistencies.[2630] However, the Standing Committee of the National People's

---

[2622] Wing Keung v. Sing Tao Limited and Hsu Hiu Yee (HCMP 1833/2004), Court of First Instance, August 10, 2004; So Wing Keung v. Sing Tao Limited and Hsu Hiu Yee (CACV 245/2004), Court of Appeals, October 11, 2004.

[2623] More information is available at <http://www.legco.gov.hk/english/index.htm>.

[2624] Ravina Shamdasani, "Secret taping breaks basic law, says judge." April 23, 2005, South China Morning Post.

[2625] *Id.*

[2626] Hong Kong Law Reform Commission, 1994 Report on the Law Relating to the Protection Of Personal Data (1994).

[2627] Personal Data (Privacy) Ordinance, Chapter 486, June 30, 1997; see generally M. Berthold & R. Wacks, Hong Kong Data Privacy Law: Territorial Regulation in a Borderless World (Sweet & Maxwell Asia 2002). 2628 Personal Data (Privacy) Ordinance, Chapter 486, § 33 (June 30, 1997), available at <http://www.pco.org.hk/english/ordinance/ordglance.html>.

[2629] *Id.* at §§ 30-32. The provisions relating to data matching subsequently came into force on August 1, 1997.

[2630] *Id.* at § 3.2.

Congress of the PRC found this amendment contravened the Basic Law and declared invalid.[2631]

Following the standard set by the Organization for Economic Cooperation and Development (OECD) 1980 Guidelines for Protection of Privacy and Transborder Flows of Personal Data, the PDPO adopts six "fair information principles" to regulate notice, collection, accuracy, use, security and access to "personal data," broadly defined as "any representation of information (including an expression of opinion) in any document, and includes a personal identifier."[2632] It also imposes additional restrictions on certain processing, namely data matching and direct marketing. The former requires the prior approval of the Privacy Commissioner, while the latter requires that a "data user" inform the "data subject" of the opportunity to opt-out from further approaches.[2633]

The ordinance applies to public and private "data users" and to manual and electronic records. Violations of the PDPO can be either criminal or civil offenses.[2634] However, under the Interpretation and General Clauses Ordinance,[2635] it is not applicable to PRC government agencies in the Hong Kong SAR.[2636] In June 1999, the High Court dismissed a legislator's civil suit over the failure of the then New China News Agency (NCNA) to respond within the PDPO-specified time frame to the legislator's request for information about herself in the agency's files, because the NCNA Director named in the suit was not in Hong Kong at the time the incident occurred. In October 2000, the Director of the NCNA, now known as the Liaison Office, served the legislator a writ requiring the legislator to pay his court costs, as is allowed under Hong Kong law. The pro-democracy legislator eventually paid her opponent's court costs with a combination of public donations and personal funds.[2637]

[2631] R. Denny and P. Yung, "Hong Kong" 3, *in* C. Millard & M. Ford, Data Protection Laws of the World, looseleaf (London: Sweet & Maxwell, 2002), no statutory amendment has been made to this effect.

[2632] Personal Data (Privacy) Ordinance, (Hong Kong), 1996, Chapter 486, § 2, "data."

[2633] *Id.* at § 35.

[2634] United States Department of State, 2004 Report on Human Rights Practices in Hong Kong, February 28, 2005, available at <http://www.state.gov/g/drl/rls/hrrpt/2004/41640.htm#hongkong>.

[2635] Interpretation and General Clauses Ordinance, Chapter 1.

[2636] *See* J. Holvast *et al.,* The Global Encyclopedia of Data Protection Regulation Hong Kong 4.B (Kluwer 2000).

[2637] United States Department of State, 2001 Report on Human Rights Practices in Hong Kong SAR, 2002, available at <http://www.state.gov/g/drl/rls/hrrpt/2002/18239.htm>.

Anti-Terrorism Measures

On June 30, 2004, the United Nations (Anti-Terrorism Measures) (Amendment) Ordinance 2004 was enacted. The Ordinance seeks to implement the United Nations Security Council Resolution 1373 and relevant international conventions against terrorism, and empower the head of security of the HKSAR government to freeze terrorist property. The measures introduced by the Ordinance against terrorist acts, associates, and terrorist property, and the new powers it creates to investigate, seize and detain property suspected to be terrorist property, may have implications on the rights guaranteed under various human rights provisions of the Basic Law on privacy. The Hong Kong Journalists Association is particularly worried about specific sections of the Ordinance that empower law enforcement agencies to require individuals to provide information or produce materials, to search premises for relevant materials, and to seize and retain such materials for the investigation of offenses under the Ordinance.[2638]

Regulatory bodies such as the Hong Kong Monetary Authority, the Office of the Commissioner for Insurance and the Securities and Futures Commission also have issued guidelines on money laundering to the financial industries under their respective supervision. These guidelines require the industry to observe stipulated standards and procedures in recordkeeping, customer identification and reporting of suspicious transactions. On June 8, 2004, the Hong Kong Monetary Authority issued a revised version of the Supplement to the Guideline on Prevention of Money Laundering. Paragraph 15 of the Guideline sets out specific obligations on the part of authorized institutions to identify and report transactions with terrorist suspects.[2639]

Data Protection Authority

The PDPO establishes an oversight body, the Office of the Privacy Commissioner (PCO), to promote and enforce compliance with statutory requirements.[2640] The PCO currently has a staff of 39 including the Commissioner and Deputy Commissioner.[2641] It is comprised of five divisions:

[2638] See, e.g., LC Paper No. CB(2)2915/03-04 available at <http://www.legco.gov.hk/yr02-03/english/bc/bc61/reports/bc61_rpt.htm>.

[2639] <http://www.info.gov.hk/hkma/eng/press/2004/attached/20040608e4a3.pdf>.

[2640] Personal Data (Privacy) Ordinance, (Hong Kong), 1996, c. 486, § 5.

[2641] Updated reports of PCO Staff and Organizational structure can be found in PCO Reports, published annually and also available online at <http://www.pco.org.hk/english/publications/annualreport.html>.

Administration, Corporate Communications, Operations, Legal and Policy.[2642] The PCO is required by law to publish an annual report and has done so since 1997.[2643] The Commissioner is given strong enforcement powers modeled on those contained in the United Kingdom Data Protection Act.[2644] In addition to investigating complaints, the commissioner may initiate independent investigations and conduct audits of selected data users. Some violations of the PDPO constitute criminal offenses. In other cases, an injured party may seek compensation through civil proceedings. If the Commissioner believes that violations may continue or be repeated, it may issue enforcement notices to direct remedial measures.[2645]

The Privacy Commissioner's Office (PCO) receives enquiries either through its telephone hotline, in person, or in writing.[2646] Not all the received complaints were formally investigated by the PCO for reasons ranging from the nature of the complaint being outside the provisions of the Ordinance to lack of *prima facie* evidence. Also many complaints were not formally investigated because the involved parties mediated a settlement. Between June 2003 and June 2004, the PCO investigated 1,109 complaints, completing 1,047 cases.[2647] Of these cases 26 were found to violate of the PDPO, but none resulted in prosecution.[2648] In fact, the PCO reported that the majority of the cases handled by its office are resolved through mediation. The PCO also indicated that the most frequent types of complaints received relate to Data Protection Principles 1, 3 and 4, which cover the collection, use, and security of personal data, respectively.[2649] The PCO reported that 953 complaints were received during the period from April 1, 2004 until March 31, 2005. Of these, 660 (69%) complaints were filed against private sector organizations, 168 (18%) complaints were against individuals and

---

[2642] <http://www.pco.org.hk/english/about/orgchart.html>.

[2643] *See* Personal Data (Privacy) Ordinance, (Hong Kong), 1996.

[2644] Data Protection Act 1998 (United Kingdom), 1998, c. 29.

[2645] As an example, a notice was issued in 2002 against a former telemarketer who had improperly collected and subsequently used personal information of hotel guests. *See* Privacy Commissioner for Personal Data, Annual Report 2001-2002, 26-27 (Hong Kong, PCO, 2002).

[2646] The PCO has indicated that in the period from June 2004 until June 2005, 14,609 enquiries were made via the PCO's telephone hotline and an additional 1,115 enquiries were received in writing. In the same period, a total of 889 complaints were filed with the Office of the Privacy Commissioner for Personal Data and a total of 35 investigations were commenced.

[2647] United States Department of State, 2004 Report on Human Rights Practices in Hong Kong, *supra*.

[2648] *Id.*

2649 Illustrative examples of anonymized cases highlighting 2002-2003 acts or practices found in contravention of the PDPO may be found in the PCO Annual Report. See Privacy Commissioner for Personal Data, Annual Report 2002-2003, 25-30 (Hong Kong, PCO, 2003).

For a more extensive review of Enquiry and Complaint Case Notes, see

<http://www.pco.org.hk/english/casenotes/case_enquiry.php> and

<http://www.pco.org.hk/english/casenotes/case_complaint.php>.

125 (13%) complaints were filed against public sector organizations (i.e. government departments and other public bodies).[2650] Fax spam complaints have increased 50 percent between 2003 and 2004, with a total of 36,000 complaints.[2651]

A compliance check is undertaken when the PCO identifies a practice in an organization that appears to be inconsistent with the requirements of the PDPO. In such circumstances, the PCO raises the matter in writing with the organization concerned, pointing out the apparent inconsistency and, where appropriate, inviting it to take remedial action. In many cases, the organization concerned undertakes immediate action to remedy the suspected breach. In other cases, organizations seek the advice of the PCO on the improvement measures that should be taken to avoid repetition of suspected breaches.

The Commissioner may issue codes of conduct to provide guidance on compliance with the ordinance's provisions. Codes are legally subordinate, but have evidentiary relevance in determining whether a contravention of the ordinance has occurred. To date the Commissioner has issued five codes: the Code of Practice on the Identity Card Number and other Personal Identifiers;[2652] the Code of Practice on Consumer Credit Data;[2653] the Code of Practice on Human Resource Management;[2654] the Code of Practice on Protection of Customer Information for Fixed and Mobile Service Operators[2655] and, most recently, a draft Code of Practice on Monitoring and Personal Data Privacy at Work.[2656] In 2000, the Privacy Commissioner jointly issued a voluntary code of practice and a consumer guide on how to deal with "spam" with the

---

[2650] Id.

[2651] Tony Lam (Acting Privacy Commissioner for Personal Data of Hong Kong SAR), "The Way Forward for Hong Kong in
Combating Spam, March 31, 2005," Jurisdiction Report presented at the 37th Meeting of the International Working Group on
Data Protection in Telecommunications (March 31 – April 1, 2005).

[2652] Privacy Commissioner for Personal Data, Code of Practice on the Identity Card Number and other Personal Identifiers (Hong Kong, PCO, 1997).

[2653] Privacy Commissioner for Personal Data, Code of Practice on Consumer Credit Data (Hong Kong, PCO, 2002). Issued on 27 February 1998, effective as of November 27, 1998; see also Privacy Commissioner for Personal Data, Consultation Paper on Amendments.

[2654] Privacy Commissioner for Personal Data, Code of Practice on Human Resource Management, (Hong Kong, PCO, 2000).

[2655] Privacy Commissioner for Personal Data, Press Release, "New Code Launched for Fixed and Mobile Service Operators to Protection Customer Information," June 17, 2002, available at
<http://www.pco.org.hk/english/infocentre>; see also Privacy Commissioner for Personal Data, Code of Practice on Protection of Customer Information for Fixed and Mobile Service Operators, (Hong Kong, PCO, 2002).

[2656] Privacy Commissioner for Personal Data, Code of Practice on Monitoring and Personal Data Privacy at Work, (Hong Kong, PCO, 2002).

Telecommunications Authority and the Hong Kong Internet Service Providers Association. In May 2001, the Privacy Commissioner held a public consultation on the Code of Practice for Consumer Credit Data.[2657] In February 2002,[2658] the Privacy Commissioner approved amendments that would make it easier for banks and other credit grantors to gain access to consumer credit reference files[2659] and retain credit data for a much longer period of time than previously allowed.[2660] To date, the PCO has not introduced a data users registration scheme for companies or individuals, although Part IV of the PDPO makes provisions for data user returns and their registration. However, it has been reported that the PCO is evaluating the feasibility of creating a registration system for certain data collectors such as online merchants and service providers.[2661] The registration proposal is aimed at curbing the menace of fraudulent websites that solicit personal information from visitors ostensibly for legitimate reasons only to then use the collected information to facilitate identity theft. Under the proposal, the PCO would publish a list of registered sites for use as a cross-reference for legitimacy before web users divulged their confidential information. The PCO has asserted that it is empowered to enact such a law, and also to levy fines as large as USD 10,000 and prison terms up to six months against violators.[2662] The recent economic downturn[2663] has led to some companies outsourcing data processing functions to jurisdictions that have weaker privacy protections for personal data, particularly mainland China and India.[2664] To date this development has largely gone unchecked by the Privacy Commissioner[2665]

[2657] Privacy Commissioner for Personal Data, Consultation Paper on Amendments to the Consumer Credit Data Code, May 25, 2001.

[2658] Privacy Commissioner for Personal Data, Press Release, "Privacy Commissioner Approves Amendments to the Consumer Credit Data Code," February 8, 2002, available at <http://www.pco.org.hk/english/infocentre/press.html>.

[2659] Privacy Commissioner for Personal Data, Code of Practice on Consumer Credit Data, (Hong Kong, PCO, 1998), § 3.1.

[2660] Id. at §§ 2.2, 2.4-2.5.

[2661] E. Yiu, "Register for Online Operators to Help Guard Personal Data," South China Morning Post, June 30, 2004.

[2662] Id.

[2663] See, e.g. E. Yiu, "Bankruptcies Triple in First Five Months," South China Morning Post, June 12, 2002, at 1; E. Yiu, "WebTrust Seal of Approval still Awaits First Client," South China Morning Post, January 30, 2002, at 2.

[2664] See, e.g. L. Leung, "HKMA Pushes Banks to Share Loan Histories," South China Morning Post, September 21, 2001, at 4; "Hong Kong's Monetary Authority Urged Banks to Share Data on Consumer Credit to Reduce Default Loans;" L. Beckerling, "Sharing Credit Data Offers Benefits all Round, Says HSBC," South China Morning Post, May 21, 2002 at 3; "Hong Kong's Biggest Lender Supports Sacrificing Privacy for the Good of Hong Kong;" "MAS Bars Visa's New Outsourced Service for Banks," The Straits Times, June 17, 2002, naming Hong Kong as an adoptee of a new "Verified by VISA," which Singapore's Monetary Authority rejected for privacy reasons.

[2665] Privacy Commissioner for Personal Data, Privacy, Security and Transborder Data Flows – Observations from Hong Kong, May 20, 2002, at 5.

because Section 33 of the PDPO, governing transborder data flows, has yet to be enacted.[2666]

During the period between April 2004 and March 2005, the PCO undertook 95 compliance checks in relation to alleged practices of data users that might be inconsistent with the requirements of the PDPO. Of the 95 compliance checks, 48 were directed against those placing blind recruitment advertisements. The majority of compliance checks (87) involved practices in private sector organizations. The remaining eight checks related to government departments and statutory bodies.[2667]

Wiretapping & Surveillance

The Telecommunications Ordinance[2668] and the Post Office Ordinance[2669] regulate the interception of communications. Wiretaps require authorization for interception operations at the highest levels of government, but a court-issued warrant is not required. The Hong Kong government has refused to reveal how often the Chief Executive uses his powers to authorize telephone wiretaps and interception of private mail.[2670] In 1999, an unofficial report estimated that the HKSAR government intercepted more than 100 conversations of private individuals a day.[2671] The vagueness of the intercept powers and the lack of procedural safeguards are inconsistent with Article 17 of the International Covenant on Civil and Political Rights, which is incorporated into Hong Kong's domestic law by Article 14 of the Bill of Rights Ordinance.[2672]

After the Tiananmen Square demonstrations in 1989, and in anticipation of the 1997 handover, Beijing insisted on an internal security provision in the Basic

---

[2666] Section 33 would prescribe several conditions for transborder transfer of personal data: "1) reasonable grounds for believing the country has in place a law which is 'substantially similar' to Hong Kong's; 2) where 1 is not true, the data subject must give explicit consent to the transfer; 3) alternatively, the data user must have reasonable grounds to believe that the transfer is 'for the avoidance or mitigation of adverse action against the data subject,' it is not practicable to obtain consent and if it were, the data subject would give it; 4) the data transferred is exempt under the PD(P)O; or 5) the data user has taken *all* reasonable precautions to ensure the data will not be used in contravention to Hong Kong law."

[2667] Further details regarding compliance check cases are available at <www.pco.org.hk/english/enquiries/topical_issues.html>.

[2668] Telecommunications Ordinance, Chapter 106, § 33.

[2669] Post Office Ordinance, Chapter 98, § 13.

[2670] United States Department of State, Country Report on Human Rights Practices 2001, March 2002, available at <http://www.state.gov/g/drl/rls/hrrpt/2001/eap/8289.htm>

[2671] "Phone Tap Figures to Remain Secret," South China Morning Post, October 1, 1998.

[2672] Bill of Rights Ordinance Chapter 383, § 8, Article 14, June 30, 1997, <www.women.gov.hk/eng/document/ govern/cedaw/cedaw_annexb_e.pdf>.

Law[2673] requiring Hong Kong to draft internal security laws to replace the archaic colonial regulations left behind by the British. In September 2002, the Hong Kong government released an "Article 23" consultation document[2674] proposing a long list of substantive amendments – including prohibiting acts of treason by foreign nationals, secession, sedition, subversion, or theft of state secrets, as well contacts with foreign political organizations – and procedural amendments, including new police investigatory powers.[2675]

The amendments were vague and overbroad. Human rights groups noted that Chinese laws with similar language have been regularly used to convict and imprison journalists, labor activists, Internet entrepreneurs and academics.[2676] Following wide public criticism, the government scrapped the sedition and treason offenses in January 2003 and promised to narrow the allowed uses of new warrantless searches to only senior police officials.[2677] However, the government stood firm on proscribing local groups affiliated with mainland organizations that have been banned on national security grounds.[2678] In July 2003, massive public protests and the defection of a key pro-business member of the government forced the Chief Executive Tung to delay the passage of the Article 23 amendments indefinitely.

The Hong Kong Bar Association said the national security bill was widely perceived to be "a real threat to the rights and freedoms of the residents of Hong Kong, in particular, to their freedom of political expression and of seeking information through the media."[2679] The United States and Europe have stated that they are pleased the Hong Kong government had decided to delay Article 23 legislation.[2680]

[2673] *Id.* at § 23.

[2674] Security Bureau, Proposals to Implement Article 23 of the Basic Law, September 2002, available at <http://www.info.gov.hk/sb/eng/23/content.html>.

[2675] Ian Buruma, "Real Lives: Watch Out - Extra Government Powers Granted as Security Measures Have a Nasty Habit of Sticking around," The Guardian (UK), November 19, 2002, at 7.

[2676] Human Rights Watch, "Open Letter to Hong Kong Chief Executive C.H. Tung," December 23, 2002, available at <http://www.hrw.org/press/2002/12/hongkong1223.htm>.

[2677] Keith Bradsher, "Hong Kong Security Laws Are Softened after Criticism," New York Times, January 29, 2003, at A7.

[2678] Cannix Yau, "Victory for Pressure Groups on Article 23," The Standard, January 29, 2003.

[2679] "The People's Right to Know," South China Morning Post, July 9, 2003, at 13.

[2680] Matthew Saltmarsh & Kelvin Chan, "US, Europe Support Delaying Legislation," South China Morning Post, July 9, 2003, at 2.

Hong Kong's anti-terrorism efforts since September 11, 2001, have largely focused on improved financial tracking.[2681] The original bill allowed the government unilaterally to declare a person a terrorist, while the courts would only serve as an appeal channel. However, legislators have said the government should go through the courts first as a way to minimize the risk of people being wrongly labeled terrorists. The deputy secretary for security, Timothy Tong, has said the government would consider amending the bill.[2682]

In September 2002, the Hong Kong government signed a customs declaration with the United States Customs Service to facilitate exchanges of airline passenger information and increase surveillance of shipping traffic.[2683] The government has also signed similar agreements with other Southeast Asian nations.

Workplace Surveillance

In 1999, the Hong Kong Law Reform Commission issued a consultation paper calling for "a code of practice on all forms of surveillance in the workplace for the practical guidance of employers, employees and the general public."[2684] In March 2002, the Commissioner responded with a more modest Draft Code of Practice on Monitoring and Personal Data Privacy at Work,[2685] which covers the monitoring of telephone calls, e-mail and computer usage and video surveillance.[2686] He specifically recognized, but excluded from treatment, other privacy-invasive practices such as drug testing, psychological profiling and productivity monitoring by automated equipment. These may yet be covered by future codes of practice.

Opinion surveys conducted in 2000 and 2001 indicated that approximately 64 percent of Hong Kong businesses use at least one of the following five surveillance methods: closed-circuit television, computer use (auditing), web-

[2681] News release, "Hong Kong Security Chief Details Anti-terrorism Efforts," Hong Kong Economic and Trade Office, May 14, 2002, available at <http://www.hongkong.org/press/sf_051402.htm>.

[2682] "Hong Kong Official Says Government to Consider Amending Anti-terrorism Bill," RTHK Radio 3 by BBC Worldwide Monitoring, June 15, 2002.

[2683] "Chinese Spokeswoman Says Beijing Backs Hong Kong's Anti-terrorism Efforts," Xinhua News Agency, September 26, 2002.

[2684] Law Reform Commission, Consultation Paper on Civil Liability for Invasion of Privacy (August 1999), available at <http://www.info.gov.hk/hkreform/reports/index.htm>.

[2685] Privacy Commissioner for Personal Data, Draft Code of Practice on Monitoring and Personal Data Privacy at Work, (Hong Kong, PCO, 2002).

[2686] E-mail from Stephen Lau, Privacy Commissioner for Personal Data, Hong Kong to Sarah Andrews, Research Director, Electronic Privacy Information Center (EPIC), June 11, 2001 (on file with EPIC).

browsing, e-mail, phone.[2687] Only about 22 percent of businesses engaged in surveillance had relevant written policies.[2688] A survey by the Hong Kong Institute of Human Resources Management found that in 2004, 84 percent of firms collected personal data from their employees. Nearly 60 percent of the corporations surveyed were also found to monitor the e-mails and digital files of their employees.[2689] Employers, trade association and trade unions have criticized the draft – particularly the definition of "e-mail" – as problematically vague and have suggested that the nature of the workplace will be affected by companies reacting with more restrictive policies on the use of e-mail and the Internet at work.[2690]

In response to growing concerns, the Office of the Privacy Commissioner released a set of guidelines for dealing with data collected at the workplace.[2691] The PCO's initial plan was a statutory code of practice. However, strong opposition to the draft by employers made the PCO proceed with non-binding guidelines.[2692] The guidelines are designed to standardize best practices at the workplace. Nonetheless, human rights group criticized the guidelines as "useless," because they are legally non-binding. Law Yuk-kai, director of the Hong Kong Human Rights Monitor, said that the current guidelines will not motivate employers to abide by the PDPO.[2693]

Smart ID Card Development

Since 1949, Hong Kong residents have carried laminated photo identity cards imprinted with biographical data and the cardholder's residency status. In 2002, the government introduced a smart identity card with a chip that contains a digital replica of the cardholder's thumbprint, immigration data, a digital

---

[2687] University of Hong Kong, Social Sciences Research Centre, 2001 Opinion Survey: Personal Data (Privacy) Ordinance: Attitudes and Implementation – Key Findings, 16 (April 2002), the percentage reporting use of the enumerated surveillance types did not appreciate in 2001.

[2688] *Id.* at 17 (compared to approximately 18 percent in 2000).

[2689] E. Tang, "Big Brother Is Watching You at Work." Global News Wire: Asia Africa Intelligence Wire December 11, 2004.

[2690] C. Buddle, "Keeping Orwell out of the Office," South China Morning Post, March 15, 2002, at 18; A. Li and P. Moy, "Unclear Code for Workplace Rejected," South China Morning Post, April 13, 2002, at 6; see also Privacy Commissioner for Personal Data, Draft Code of Practice on Monitoring and Personal Data Privacy at Work, 22-23 (Hong Kong, PCO, 2002): e.g. the draft code differentiates between inbound and outbound e-mail, stating that "monitoring of inbound e-mails can rarely be justified."

[2691] PCO Press Release, available at: http://www.pco.org.hk/english/infocentre/press_20041217.html

[2692] R. Rodwell, "Guidelines push privacy issues to the forefront; Incorrect monitoring in the workplace can quickly sour employer-staff relationships." South China Morning Post Jan 8 2005

[2693] Cally Cheng, "Workplace Privacy Guide Useless Human Rights Group," Global News Wire: Aisa Africa Intelligence Wire, December 18, 2004.

certificate and have room for other information, including medical and financial data and driving records.[2694] The government plans to replace all 6.8 million of the old cards by 2007.[2695]

In response to widespread sensitivity about privacy, Hong Kong's Secretary of Information Technology and Broadcasting stated in January of 2002 that there "will be no more data on the surface of the card, than the data that already appears" and that ". . . only minimal data will be stored in the card's chip. Except for essential immigration-related data and digital certificates, personal data in respect of non-immigration related applications will be kept at back-end computer systems of the concerned government departments. None of the proposed non-immigration applications (that is, using the card as a driving license and library card, storage of a digital certificate and change of address) will be mandatory. Cardholders will have a choice on whether to include the applications on the card."[2696] Further, any data stored in the chip will be encrypted, data for separate applications will be segregated and only authorized persons will have access to the data on the card.[2697]

In commenting on the initial proposal, the Privacy Commissioner expressed concerns about the danger of identity theft and the secondary use of the personal information that will be stored on the card.[2698] Sin Chung-kai, a Democratic Party legislator, who led the debate on the ID card issue, stated: "We're not opposed to people having to carry ID cards. The crux of the controversy is how much other information about a person should be stored on the card."[2699]

Early 2005, the HKSAR government disclosed the last of the four consultancy reports assessing the privacy impact of the Smart ID Card Project, an identity card replacement exercise that was implemented in August 2003.[2700] The Hong Kong Smart ID Card Replacement Exercise mandated that holders of existing identity cards also had to apply for smart ID cards from January 24 to March 12,

---

[2694] M. Landler, "Fine-tuning for Privacy, Hong Kong Plans Digital ID," New York Times, February 18, 2002, at C1.

[2695] M. Benitez, "ID Card Contract Awarded," South China Morning Post, February 27, 2002.

[2696] C. Yau, Letter to the Editor, South China Morning Post, January 25, 2002, at 13.

[2697] Id.; In a classic example of "function creep," in April 2002, a senior Immigration Department official said that more services and functions are being considered, including storing a person's blood type on the card for emergencies. A. Lo, "New ID Cards May Get Extra Functions," South China Morning Post, April 24, 2002, at 2, quoting Raymond Wong Wai-main, assistant immigration director.

[2698] PCO, Press Release, "Privacy Commissioner for Personal Data Expresses Views on ID Card Scheme," October 20, 2000.

[2699] Landler, supra.

2700 A summary of the Consultant׳s findings and the Privacy Commissioner for Personal Data׳s comments are available at <http://www.legco.gov.hk/yr04-05/english/panels/se/papers/secb2-858-1e.pdf>.

2005. The Replacement Exercise covered all Hong Kong residents, permanent and temporary.[2701] Failure to apply for a new card constituted an offense that could be prosecuted and subject to a penalty of HKD 5,000 (~USD 643).[2702] The multifunction smart ID card contains basic identity details such as the photograph, fingerprint biometric of each holder and can also contain an electronic certificate (e-Cert) for electronic transactions.[2703]

Recently, the smart ID card was criticized for being too complicated to use. For instance, e-Cert, embedded in smart ID cards was designed to promote electronic commerce transaction.[2704] More than HKD 240 million (~USD 31 million) were invested to develop and implement the e-Cert system. But a survey found that only 10 percent of those who newly obtained ID cards had used e-Cert. [2705] An additional HKD 10 million (~USD 1.3 million) will be invested in 2005-2006 to promote the use of e-Cert.[2706]

A private consultant of the Immigration Department has recently completed the fourth privacy impact assessment of smart identity cards. This is an overall post-implementation review of privacy protection measures relating to system controls, functionalities and manual procedures, in order to ascertain that all such measures have been suitably implemented and are operating effectively.[2707] The Immigration Department is now preparing a Code of Practice, which will provide guidance on the collection, use of, and access to, smart ID card data. It is meant to provide the basis of the privacy compliance audit of the Smart Identity Card System. The audit will be carried out after the Code of Practice has been approved.

In December 2000, an interdepartmental working group on computer crime issued a report for public consultation.[2708] The report proposed a series of measures, both legislative and administrative, to address computer-related crimes. Recommendations included strengthening the penalties for hacking and

---

2701 "Hong Kong Residents Born in 1952-53 Start Applying for Smart ID Cards," Xinhua News Agency, Beijing, January 24, 2005,

2702 *Id.*

2703 "Hong Kong Government Rolling Out ID Cards Based on Keycorp Technology," Australian Associated Press (AAP), July, 28 2004,

2704 Sylvia Hui, "Few Using too Complex Smart ID Cards," Financial Times: Asia Africa Intelligence Wire, May 26, 2005.

2705 *Id.*

2706 *Id.*

2707 More information is available at <http://www.legco.gov.hk/yr04-05/english/panels/se/papers/secb2-858-1e.pdf>.

2708 S. Chung Kai, Cyber Office Legislative Councillor (Information Technology), Cyber 2005 (Issue No. 7), December 14, 2000.

unauthorized access offenses,[2709] compelling the disclosure of encryption keys or decrypted text,[2710] and requiring Internet Service Providers to retain subscriber logs.[2711] The government is still considering how to implement these proposals.[2712]

Financial Sector

Hong Kong banks already share a "blacklist" of loan defaulters and borrowers who have court judgments issued against them,[2713] but faced with an unprecedented five-fold increase in bankruptcies in recent years, banks proposed an amendment to the PDPO allowing them to share even more personal data through a newly created third-party agency. The so-called "positive data-sharing agency" would be run by a private company and modeled after British and North American institutions.[2714] The agency would allow banks to share information between each other on the amount of a credit seeker's outstanding credit card debt, cards held, credit limit, past due accounts, residential mortgages and other types of consumer credit.[2715] The Hong Kong Monetary Authority and the Privacy Commissioner supported the proposal, but HKSAR legislators, consumer advocates and the public did not, citing privacy concerns.[2716] A representative of one of Hong Kong's largest banks responded to these concerns by saying that "privacy [was] no longer relevant."[2717]

As required by the PDPO, the Privacy Commissioner opened a public consultation on the credit issue in 2003 and proposed relaxing restrictions on data

---

[2709] Security Bureau, Inter-departmental Working Group on Computer Related Crime Report, (Hong Kong, 2000).

[2710] *Id.* at paragraph 5.14.

[2711] *Id.* at paragraph 8.22.

[2712] A. Creed, "Hong Kong Mulls Measures to Fight Computer Crime," Newsbytes, July 18, 2001.

[2713] L. Beckerling, "Public Gets Say on Credit Bureau," South China Morning Post, May 4, 2002.

[2714] J. Moir & L. Beckerling, "Privacy Goes Plastic," South China Morning Post, June 13, 2002.

[2715] L. Beckerling, "First Look at Sample Credit Risks Report," South China Morning Post, March 29, 2002.

[2716] *See* L. Leung, "HKMA Pushes Banks to Share Loan Histories," South China Morning Post, September 21, 2001, at 4; L. Beckerling, "Public Gets Say on Credit Bureau," South China Morning Post, May 4, 2002, at 1; E. Yiu, "Democrats to Consider Proposal for Credit Information Sharing," South China Morning Post, June 24, 2002, at 3, quoting Democratic Party financial affairs spokesman, Sin Chung-kai arguing that banks would only use credit sharing to boost profitability.

[2717] L. Beckerling, "Public Gets Say on Credit Bureau," South China Morning Post, May 4, 2002, at 1, quoting Anna Borzi of HSBC Securities stating "Privacy is over. There are already more things being recorded, coded and monitored than we can poke a stick at. If anybody seriously believes privacy can still be protected they are seriously deluded. That battle has been fought and lost."

sharing between banks.[2718] Specifically, amendments to the Consumer Credit Data Code would extend the period of retention of credit application data by a credit reference agency from 90 days to five years and extend the period for retention of file activity data from 12 months to five years. Further proposals would allow the release of file activity data by a credit reference agency to credit providers, and to prevent credit providers from accessing an individual's data held by a credit reference agency except where there was a relevant need to do so. Credit reference agencies began building positive information databases on applicants in June 2003, but it will be another two years before they are in full use.[2719]

In June 2003, some of the proposed revisions to the Code of Practice on Consumer Credit Data took effect.[2720] The revisions allowed positive credit data to be shared among credit providers. The Privacy Commissioner's Office characterized the revisions as a response to the rapid deterioration in credit card and personal loan defaults associated with the protracted economic downturn in the Hong Kong economy. The PCO sought to put in place safeguards to prevent the changes being exploited to infringe on privacy. For instance, a 24-month transitional period (expiring June 2005) was mandated before there could be full access to, and use of, contributed data. Also, a provision was included in the amendment to require credit reference agencies to submit their operational procedures and systems to an independent annual privacy compliance audit. Copies of audit reports are to be provided to the Privacy Commissioner for scrutiny and, where appropriate, comment. The first audit was undertaken and the Privacy Commissioner deemed the audit report satisfactory.[2721] The PCO has also pursued safeguards related to the process of sharing positive credit data and related statistical computations undertaken by the credit reference agency in determining whether individual credit scores were put in place, and has expressed its commitment to continuing to closely monitor the effect of the amendment.[2722]

[2718] *See* Privacy Commissioner for Personal Data, Code of Practice on Consumer Credit Data (Hong Kong, PCO, 2002); *see also* Privacy Commissioner for Personal Data, *Consultation Paper on Amendments to the Consumer Credit Data Code*, May 25, 2001.

[2719] Sebastian Tong, "Revised Privacy Code Comes into Effect," The Standard, June 3, 2003.

[2720] "Amendments to Code of Practice on Consumer Credit Data Gazettes Tomorrow," Press Release of the Hong Kong Privacy Commissioner's Office, May 22, 2003, available at <http://www.pco.org.hk/english/infocentre/press_20030522.html>.

[2721] "Privacy Commissioner Approves First Privacy Compliance Audit Report," Press Release of the Hong Kong Privacy Commissioner's Office, June 29, 2004, available at <http://www.pco.org.hk/english/infocentre/press_20040629.html>.

[2722] *Id.*

Video Surveillance

In early 2002, Hong Kong police proposed a pilot program to install a number of cameras in Lan Kwai Fong, a district of Hong Kong, aimed at preventing crime and controlling crowds.[2723] The cameras would be linked to a police station and footage would be held for three months. The plan was supported by the local business association, but not by many local businesses who felt the surveillance might affect people's willingness to come to the area. Lawmakers and human rights groups also opposed the plan, saying it was an invasion of privacy.[2724]

In May 2002, Hong Kong police bowed to public and legislative opposition and suspended the proposal. In a paper submitted to legislators, Deputy Secretary for Security Timothy Tong Hin-ming said police would study the privacy concerns of the scheme before consulting the public and the Privacy Commissioner again.[2725]

In 2004, however, the Home Affairs Department revealed that authorities had installed closed-circuit TV (CCTV) surveillance cameras in five different locations of Hong Kong, leading to the prosecution of 29 people for hygiene offenses.[2726] The violations included washing dishes, dumping trash, and relieving themselves in the streets. Although officials scaled down the original plan of installing 100 cameras in 18 districts of Hong Kong, Cindy Yu, spokeswoman of Home Affairs Department, noted that the program had "proven quite useful" and will be expanded.[2727]

Also in May 2002, the SAR Correctional Services Department (CSD) announced that it was installing thousands of surveillance cameras in all of Hong Kong's prisons – including dormitories, but not toilets – in an effort to prevent inmate gambling.[2728] Following the death of an inmate last year, legislators renewed questions regarding the use of surveillance cameras in prisons. In the past, the CSD has refused to detail what percentage of prisons were monitored by cameras

---

[2723] When asked for a specific example of the need for video surveillance in Lan Kwai Fong, Deputy Police Commissioner Dick Lee Ming-kwai cited a stampede in 1993 when 20 people were crushed to death on New Year's Eve.

[2724] S. Lau, "Business Backs Push for Video Surveillance," South China Morning Post, February 19, 2002, at 5.

[2725] C. Yeung and R. Ma, "Police Drop Spy Camera Scheme," South China Morning Post, May 14, 2002, at 2.

[2726] "Hygiene Violators Beware: Hong Kong Watching Alleys with Closed-Circuit Cameras," Associated Press, September 26, 2004.

[2727] *Id.*

[2728] S. Lee, "Closed-circuit Television Cameras to Monitor Inmates' Evening Activities," South China Morning Post, May 17, 2002, at 6.

or what the criteria is for their use to be deemed necessary. "In some cases, the images are used to assist prison staff's observation only and no recording function is provided. In other cases, automatic recording of the sequential images appearing on the monitor is provided," a CSD spokesman said. At least one legislator has said he plans to ask the department to disclose details of the number, function and purpose of surveillance cameras in all penal institutions.[2729]

Another scandal concerns mobile phone cameras. Following outcries over "up skirt" scandals overseas and in the absence of laws making cyber-voyeurism illegal in Hong Kong, some businesses – such as fitness clubs – have begun to ban the use of mobile phones with built-in cameras.[2730]

Privacy Commissioner Raymond Tang left the office in 2004 with a new appointment as a head of the Equal Opportunities Commission. Human Rights groups criticized Tang's new appointment because it will reduce two years off his term as a privacy commissioner.[2731] The Civil Human Rights Front and Hong Kong Human Rights Monitor, for instance, issued a joint statement that criticized Tang's departure for being premature, pointing out that his departure will have negative impact on the reliable watchdog operation of the office.[2732] Law Yuk-kai, director of the Hong Kong Human Rights Monitor, said that human rights protection body should maintain the stability of tenure, adding that government appointees should not leave the position prematurely.[2733] Roderick Woo, former lawyer, took over the office on August 1, 2005.[2734]

Hong Kong's Independent Commission Against Corruption (ICAC) prosecuted two people, in 1998 and 1999, for unauthorized disclosure of telecom subscriber data to debt collectors.[2735] In response to these incidents, ICAC issued a study that called for closer cooperation among the government agencies responsible for

---

[2729] Niall Fraser & Stella Lee, "Come Clean on Video Surveillance, Prison Chiefs Told," South China Morning Post, November 24, 2002, at 4.

[2730] Carolyn Ong, "Businesses Ban Camera Phones; Fitness Clubs Lead Way in Curbing Use of Mobiles amid Fears over Locker-room Privacy," South China Morning Post, July 8, 2003, at 1.

[2731] Ravina Shamdasani, "Privacy Commission Chief Chosen to Lead EOC; Human Rights Groups Question 5-year Appointment of Raymond Tang," South China Morning Post. December 16, 2004,

[2732] Paris Lord, "Rights Group Blasts Tang Switching Watchdog Posts," Financial Times: Asia Africa Intelligence Wire, December 16, 2004,

[2733] Id.

[2734] Matthew Lee, "Privacy Law Unclear, Says New Chief," Financial Times: Asia Africa Intelligence Wire. April 26, 2005.

[2735] S. Schwartz, "Phone Firms Urged to Adopt Pioneering Data Privacy Code," South China Morning Post, June 18, 2002, at 4. The type of data contemplated by the Code includes a customer's name, identity document number, residential address, etc., as well as service plan details, usage details, billing details, payment details.

telecommunications in Hong Kong.[2736] In June 2002, the Privacy Commissioner jointly launched a voluntary Code of Practice on Protection of Customer Information for Fixed and Mobile Service Operators with Hong Kong's Consumer Council, ICAC, and the Office of the Telecommunications Authority.[2737] The guidelines are the result of a year-long effort to gather the privacy rules for telecommunication companies into one document.

The Code covers the following five areas: policy on protection of customer personal data; technical measures for protection of customer personal data; location security; staff security; and transfer of customer personal data.[2738] Specifically, the Code calls on companies to establish a data classification policy based on degrees of sensitivity for personal data and risk of exposure. It also recommends controlling access on a "need-to-know" basis, the introduction of an ethics policy and the prevention of bribery. While the compliance with the guidelines in the Code is voluntary, the requirements listed in the code are not. For example, the Telecommunication Authority requires service providers to protect customers' data,[2739] the PDPO sets out strict rules for the use and distribution of personal data; and the ICAC has responsibility for all cases involving bribery in Hong Kong.

In 2003, Hong Kong SAR was hit hard by SARS (or "severe acute respiratory syndrome"). The government implemented quarantine measures that required any person who had come into close contact with a known SARS carrier to report daily for ten days to one of four designated medical centers throughout the city. However, legislator Lo Wing-lok expressed concern that cases might be underreported as people stayed away from clinics for fear of being identified in the press. "There should be provisions for privacy – otherwise people might be discouraged from going because they won't want their pictures appearing in the press," he said. In response, health officials proposed to transport quarantined individuals to the centers by private shuttles.[2740]

[2736] "Four Hong Kong Government Agencies Issue New Privacy Guidelines for Telecom Industry," BNA Privacy Law Watch, June 21, 2002.

[2737] Privacy Commissioner for Personal Data, Press Release, "New Code Launched for Fixed and Mobile Service Operators to Protection Customer Information," June 17, 2002.

[2738] Privacy Commissioner for Personal Data, Code of Practice on Protection of Customer Information for Fixed and Mobile Service Operators, 3-4 (Hong Kong, PCO, 2002).

[2739] Telecommunications licensees have a condition that the licensee shall not disclose information of a customer except with the consent of the customer and that the licensee shall not use information provided by its customers or obtained in the course of provision of service to its customers for purposes other than those related to the provision of service by the licensees.

[2740] Verna Yu, "Concerns over Privacy as the Quarantine Measures Kick In; A Legislator Fears that People May Be Discouraged from Attending the Clinics," South China Morning Post, March 31, 2003, at 3.

Spam

Hong Kong SAR plans to enact an anti-spam law by 2006. The law, planned in consultation with industry groups, will make spam illegal.[2741] Its purpose is to combat unsolicited e-mails, junk faxes, or automated telemarketing calls.[2742] Fixed-line and mobile operators are actively involved in creating a code of practice for telemarketing. However, Au Man-ho, director-general of the Telecommunications Authority, noted that the enactment will require further public discussion before taking effect.[2743] No specified timetable for enactment was set.

The Hong Kong government's latest anti-spam effort was the further development of anti-spam initiative (STEPS) that was announced on February 24, 2004. The STEPS initiative was to strengthen existing regulation by promoting technical solutions, educating people, and introducing statutory measures.[2744] In addition to the proposed law, the government announced that it would undertake public education campaign while continuously cooperating with businesses on blacklisting repeat spam offenders.[2745]

In 2005, Hong Kong joined the international community against spam. The Commerce, Industry, and Technology Bureau of Hong Kong signed a multilateral memorandum with Australia, South Korea, Malaysia, Philippines, New Zealand, and mainland China. The purpose of the international memorandum is to promote cooperation among nations in order to reduce spam passing through nations in the region.[2746] Hong Kong's involvement was prompted by a finding that 95 percent of spam originated from overseas countries such as the United States and South Korea.[2747]

[2741] Danyll Wills, "Eliminating Spam Requires Co-operation between Governments," South China Morning Post, April 12, 2005.

[2742] "Hong Kong Plans to Enact Anti-Spam Law," China Daily, June 13, 2005, available at <http://www.chinadaily.com.cn/english/doc/2005-06/12/content_450708.htm>.

[2743] *Id.*

[2744] Danyll Wills. "Eliminating Spam Requires Co-operation between Governments," South China Morning Post. April 12, 2005,

2745 Kathleen McLaughlin. "Hong Kong Drafting Anti-Spam Bill as Work Starts on Other Measures," The Bureau of National Affairs Report, March 7, 2005, available at
<http://subscript.bna.com/SAMPLES/pvl.nsf/4866a14be3b6f56685256ba3004dcb8b/16301751af2a1fd985256f bb0004572d?OpenDocument>.

[2746] "HK Joins International Community against Spam," Xinhua News Agency. April 27, 2005,

[2747] *Id.*

International Cooperation

The Hong Kong SAR is the European Union's tenth largest trading partner, while the EU is Hong Kong's third largest supplier after China and Japan. Total bilateral trade in 2002 amounted to approximately EUR 39 billion.[2748] The Commissioner has had informal discussions with the EU over the question of the adequacy of data protection under the EU Data Protection Directive, but has not received a formal reply.[2749] Hong Kong will likely not be deemed adequate before the enactment of Section 33 of the Ordinance.[2750]

Hong Kong is an active member of APEC negotiations as one of the drafters of the APEC Privacy Framework (the Framework). In June 2005, the country hosted the first APEC Electronic Commerce Steering Group (ECSG) technical assistance seminar. The PCO has taken an active role in developing Framework as the process moves into the implementation phase. In Hong Kong, privacy protections are derived from the provisions of the PCO and therefore have statutory backing. Indeed, every effort is being made to enhance those provisions, and the powers of the Privacy Commissioner, by seeking a number of amendments to the PCO.

However, the HKSAR government has not so far developed any substantive measure, or had any plan to implement the Framework. Nor has the PCO unveiled any specific plan to promote it.[2751] As of now, it is hard to know the exact ramificatiosn of the APEC Privacy Framework and the direction of its future implementation in Hong Kong. Given wide latitude for "local exceptions" under the APEC framework, it is doubtful that the APEC implementation will have any direct impact on Hong Kong privacy laws.

[2748] Fourth Annual Report by the European Commission on the Hong Kong SAR: Report from the Commission to the Council and the European Parliament, COM (2002) 450 final at 9.

[2749] Data Protection Working Party – Article 29, Fourth Annual Report on the Situation Regarding the Protection of Individuals with regard to the Processing of Personal Data and Privacy in the Community and in Third Countries Covering the Year 1999: Part II, May 17, 2001, 5019/EN/WP 46, 20. The Working Party entered into preliminary discussions on the level of protection in Hong Kong, but has not yet reported back.

[2750] Data Protection Working Party Opinion 7/2001 on the Draft Commission Decision (version August 31, 2001) on Standard Contractual Clauses for the Transfer of Personal Data to Data Processors Established in Third Countries under Article 26(4) of Directive, September 13, 2001, 95/465061/01/EN/Final WP 47, 3, describing the general principle that the data importer is bound by the data exporter's legislation. *See also* C. Raab *et al.* Application of a Methodology Designed to Assess the Adequacy of the Level of Protection of Individuals with regard to Processing Personal Data: Test of the Method on Several Categories of Transfer: Final Report, European Commission Tender No. XV/97/18/D, 17-22, 57-65, 103-107,142-148,178-181. 2751 For more information on the Initiative's implementation, *see* <http://www.pco.org.hk/english/infocentre/apec_ecsg1_2.html>.

In 2005, the HK government will decide whether the Interception of Communications Ordinance (IOCO) should come into operation. IOCO was enacted on June 28, 1997, but has not been signed into law pending a review. IOCO proposes that interception warrants be issued by High Court Judges. The review of this ordinance has taken longer than expected because of the highly technical and complex issues it covers.

Republic of Hungary

Constitutional Privacy Framework

Article 59 of the Constitution of the Republic of Hungary provides that "everyone has the right to the good standing of his reputation, the privacy of his home and the protection of secrecy in private affairs and personal data."[2752] "Everyone in the Republic of Hungary shall have the right to good reputation, the inviolability of the privacy of his home and correspondence, and the protection of his personal data."[2753] In 1991, the Supreme Court ruled that a law creating a multi-use personal identification number violated the constitutional right of privacy.[2754]

Data Protection Framework

The Hungarian law on data protection follows the model of general and sector-specific regulation. The most important principles of data protection, along with the conditions and guarantees of limiting the right to the protection of personal data, are laid down in a single, so-called general act. This act does not contain explicit authorizations for processing information, the mandatory rules associated with various types of data and different data controllers are collected in sector-specific acts. Without these sector-specific acts the content of the general act could not be put into effect and the principles defined in the general act would be translated into practice only to a minimal extent.

[2752] Constitution of the Republic of Hungary, Chapter XII, Article 59, unofficial translation available at <http://www.mkab.hu/content/en/encont5b.htm>.

[2753] *Id.*

[2754] Constitutional Court Decision No. 15/1991 (IV. 13.)-AB.

The Hungarian general act, the Data Protection Act of 1992[2755] (the Act), covers the collection and use of personal information in both the public and private sectors. It is a combined data protection and freedom of information act. Its basic principle is informational self-determination. As regards data protection, the Act sets out general provisions on the request, collection, handling and transfer of personal information and provides legal remedies to individuals whose rights are violated. The Hungarian data protection system follows the opt-in regime. Under the Act personal data may only be collected and processed with the freely given, specific and informed consent of the individual or if it is required by law. The individual must be fully informed of the purpose of the data processing. Only the data necessary to accomplish this purpose may be collected, and it may only be stored until that purpose is fulfilled. The data must be accurate, complete, and up to date. Individuals are granted the right to access their personal information and, where necessary, to request its correction or even deletion. Special protections are set out for "sensitive data," which is defined as data relating to "racial origin, nationality, and ethnic status, political opinion or party affiliation, religious or other conviction" or "medical condition, abnormal addiction, sexual life, trade-union membership and criminal record." This kind of data may only be processed where the subject has consented in writing or if it is based on an international agreement or required by law for the purpose of enforcing a constitutional right, national security purposes, crime prevention, or a criminal investigation.[2756] The Act also expressly prohibits the use of all-purpose identification numbers or codes.

January 1, 2004 marked the start of a new era in Hungarian data protection. The entry into force of the amendment of Act LXIII of 1992 on the Protection of Personal Data and Disclosure of Data of Public Interest, which harmonized the law with applicable European Union regulations, also instated changes regarding the classic role of the ombudsman in protecting privacy, and opened a new chapter in the history of the institution.[2757]

The Article 29 Data Protection Working Party of the European Commission recommended in September 1999 that the Commission and the Article 31 Committee note that Hungary ensures an adequate level of protection within the

---

[2755] Act No. LXIII of 1992 on the Protection of Personal Data and the Publicity of Data of Public Interest, available at <http://abiweb.obh.hu/dpc/legislation/1992_LXIIIa.htm>.

[2756] *See* Zita Orb, "Amended Rules on Data Protection," World Data Protection Report, Volume 1, Issue 1, January 2001 at 22.

[2757] E-mail from Attila Péterfalvi, Parliamentary Commissioner for Data Protection and Freedom of Information, to Ula Galster, International Policy Fellow, Electronic Privacy Information Center (EPIC), May 26, 2005 (on file with EPIC).

meaning of Article 25(6) of the EU Data Protection Directive.[2758] In July 2000, the European Commission formally adopted this position, thereby approving all future transfers of personal data to Hungary.

On May 1, 2004, Hungarian Republic joined the European Union. In order to fulfill the requirements of the EU Data Protection Directive (1995/46/EC) the Parliament amended the Act three times. In June 1999, it created a distinction between "data handling" (*i.e.*, data controlling) and "technical data processing."[2759] Another amendment came into force in 2004 that adopted some legal institutions from the Directive, such as automated individual decisions, data protection officials, and liberated the data flows to the Member States. The regulation on transborder data flows was specified in 2005. As a consequence of the implementation of the Directive, decisions relating to the regulation on data protection are partly out of the competence of Hungarian authorities.

On May 1, 2004, Hungary became a full member of the Working Party established under Article 29 of Directive 95/46/EC of the European Parliament and of the Council on the Protection of individuals with regard to the processing of personal data and on the free movement of such data – an independent consulting body operating on the side of the Commission, made up by the member states' privacy commissioners and/or other authority.[2760]

Many sector-specific acts contain rules for handling personal data including addresses,[2761] sector-specific identification codes,[2762] medical information,[2763] police information,[2764] public records,[2765] employment,[2766] telecommunications,[2767] and national security services.[2768] The Direct Marketing Act authorizes companies to process individuals' names and addresses for

---

[2758] European Union Article 29 Data Protection Working Group, Opinion 6/99 concerning the Level of Personal Data in Hungary, September 7, 1999, available at
<http://europa.eu.int/comm/internal_market/privacy/docs/wpdocs/1999/wp24en.pdf>.

[2759] Act No. LXXII. of 1999.

[2760] E-mail from Attila Péterfalvi, *supra*.

[2761] Act No. LXVI of 1992 on the Register of Personal Data and Addresses of Citizens.

[2762] Act No. XX of 1996 on the Identification Methods Replacing the Universal Personal Identification Number, and on the Use of Identification Codes.

[2763] Act No. XLVII of 1997 on the Use and Protection of Medical and Related Data.

[2764] Act No. XXXIV of 1994 on the Police (Chapter VIII: "Data Handling by the Police").

[2765] Act No. LXVI of 1995 on Public Records, Public Archives, and the Protection of Private Archives (Restricting Rules on the Publicity of Documents Containing Personal Data).

[2766] Act No. IV of 1991 on Furthering Employment and Provisions for the Unemployed.

[2767] Act No. C of 2003 on Electronic Communications, available at
<http://www.nhh.hu/english/menu4/m4_8.htm>.

[2768] Act No. CXXV of 1995 on the National Security Services, etc.

marketing purposes but requires consent for the processing of other information such as telephone numbers or e-mail addresses.[2769] There is no sector-specific legislation covering the Internet; however, the Data Protection Commissioner issued a recommendation[2770] in February 2001 calling for amendments or supplements to existing law to address this issue. The Criminal Code also has provisions on privacy.[2771]

Data Protection Authority

The Parliamentary Commissioner for Data Protection and Freedom of Information oversees the 1992 Act.[2772] Besides supervising the implementation of the Act and acting as an ombudsman for both data protection and freedom of information, the Commissioner's tasks include investigating complaints, maintaining the Data Protection Register, and providing opinions on draft legislation. Until 2004, the Commissioner's only effective power was provided by the Secrecy Act of 1995. Under this Act, the Commissioner is entitled to review and propose changes to the classification of state and official secrets. Since 2004, the Commissioner has also been entitled to order the blocking, deletion, or destruction of unlawfully processed data; prohibit the unlawful processing or technical processing of data, and suspend the transfer of data to foreign countries. The data controller concerned may institute court proceedings against these measures of the Commissioner. The first Commissioner (along with the three other Parliamentary Commissioners – one for human rights in general, his deputy, and one for the ethnic minorities) was elected on June 30, 1995, for a six-year term. The current Parliamentary Commissioner for Data Protection and Freedom of Information is Dr. Attila Péterfalvi. Dr. Péterfalvi has a staff of approximately 40 persons, including senior experts and a secretarial staff.[2773]

The Commissioner has been very active reviewing cases involving personal information. The Commissioner conducts about 900 examinations each year.[2774] In 2002, the number of complaints and investigations reached 538 while the

---

[2769] Act No. CXIX of 1995 on the Use of Name and Address Information Serving the Purposes of Research and Direct Marketing.

[2770] Recommendation of the Data Protection Commissioner on certain issues of handling data in connection with the Internet, Annual Report of the Parliamentary Commissioner for Data Protection and Freedom of Information 2001, at 101–107, *see also* <http://abiweb.obh.hu/adatved/indexek/2001/intro2.htm#sector4>

[2771] Criminal Code, Sections 177-178, available at <http://www.privacy.org/pi/countries/hungary/hungary_criminal_code.html>.

[2772] Homepage <http://www.obh.hu/>.

[2773] Data Protection Commissioner of Hungary homepage <http://abiweb.obh.hu/dpc/index.htm>.

[2774] Letters from László Majtényi, Parliamentary Commissioner for Data Protection and Freedom of Information, August 4, 1999 and July 11, 2000.

number of consultations was approximately 500 and the number of reports on draft law was 180. In 2003, the Commission received 70 percent more submissions than the previous year. In 2004, the number of the investigations reached 1,300, including 60 *ex officio* inspections and 80 international cases.[2775] There was a significant rise in the number of requests from both the government and citizens for Commission opinions on draft legislation, from 180 in 2002 to 354 in 2003. In 2004, this number increased to 450. According to the Commissioner, this increase was in part due to the country's accession to the European Union. Data protection cases increased by 72 percent, while those concerning freedom of information issues rose by 140 percent from the previous year.[2776] In 2000, the Commissioner was particularly astounded by the unprecedented rise in the number of complaints against private organizations.[2777] In 2003, the Commissioner noted the unprecedented workload with which both the government and citizens flooded the Commissioner's office. Commissioner Péterfalvi specifically noted the government's renewed attempts at creating additional records involving massive quantities of data. He also noted the high number of submissions from citizens as a "massive overall rise," which he felt "indicates increasing awareness of citizens of the right to the protection of personal data, and that they also know the avenues of redress."[2778]

In December 2001, the Hungarian Socialist Party (*Magyar Szocialista Párt*, or MSZP) sent three million campaign letters to their constituents on behalf of Péter Medgyessy, their candidate for the position of Prime Minister. Although the Party stated that it had used a telephone directory to collect the recipients' addresses, they actually sent their message to persons who only had a private telephone number. Attila Péterfalvi, the Data Protection Commissioner, opposing the opt-out model, ordered the MSZP to erase the databases that contained voters' addresses and the information about whether they wanted to get a second letter from the MSZP. The Socialist Party followed his opinion by destroying their databases.[2779]

[2775] E-mail from Attila Péterfalvi, *supra*.

[2776] Annual Report of the Parliamentary Commissioner for Data Protection and Freedom of Information 2003, available at <http://abiweb.obh.hu/dpc/index.htm>.

[2777] Annual Report of the Parliamentary Commissioner for Data Protection and Freedom of Information 2000, available at <http://www.obh.hu/adatved/indexek/besz/index.htm>.

[2778] Annual Report of the Parliamentary Commissioner for Data Protection and Freedom of Information 2003 and Annual Report of the Parliamentary Commissioner for Data Protection and Freedom of Information 2004, available at <http://abiweb.obh.hu/dpc/index.htm>.

[2779] Az adatvédelmi biztos beszámolója 2002 (The Report of the Data Protection Commissioner, 2002) <http://www.obh.hu/adatved/magyar/2002/2_1resz.htm#2_A1>; Hírösszefoglalónk, "Törvénysért_levelek. Adatvédelmi kifogás az MSZP névre szóló küldeményei miatt" ("Letters Violate the Law. Data Protection Objection because of MSZP's Mailing"), Népszabadság Online, March 13, 2002 <http://www.nol.hu/Default.asp?DocCollID=42277&DocID=42798#42798>.

In 2002, László Majtényi, ex-Data Protection Commissioner emphasized after the end of the elections, that the "political class" had not taken at all notice of the rights for informational autonomy. It all started in 2001 when the Department of Country Image (*Országimázs Központ*) sent its Country Traveler (*Országjáró*), a periodical to popularize the Hungarian Government headed by Viktor Orbán (1998-2002), to every household without obtaining the legal authorization to use the recipients' names and addresses.

In the spring of 2002, the resigning Minister of Finance, Mihály Varga, directed the National Pension Institute (*Országos Nyugdíjbiztosítási Igazgatóság*) to transfer the list of addresses of 1.5 million pensioners to the Hungarian Post Corporation. The Post was thus able to send the letter of Viktor Orbán (the resigning Prime Minister) to pensioners about the increase of the amount of their pension. The Hungarian Data Protection Commissioner held that it was not necessary to announce a new law affecting pensioners by personalized mailing, and while Orbán's letters did not harm anybody's constitutional rights for privacy, the letters did not comply with Hungarian data protection regulations.[2780]

In 2003, the deployment of closed circuit television (CCTV) systems by public authorities, primarily in Budapest, was in the headlines. Although it is mandatory to inform citizens about the installation and use of video surveillance cameras by notices on the walls of the buildings of the monitored areas, the authorities did not comply with that rule in 82 percent of the cases. Surveillance cameras now monitor almost every street and square of the downtown area. It has been reported that some of them have nighttime vision and face recognition capabilities. Authorities have claimed that video cameras are efficient tools against crime. When authorities planned to use their camera systems for purposes different from the ones that justified their original installation,[2781] Attila Péterfalvi, the Data Protection Commissioner, pointed out that the law prohibited this. The Commissioner investigated the case of the Budapest neighborhood of Terézváros where the mayor wanted to give rights to a private company to run the CCTV network, even though only the police have the right to process

---

[2780] "Az ombudsman szerint Orbán Viktor levele a nyugdíjasokhoz nem sértett törvényt" (The Ombudsman Says Viktor Orbáns' Letter to Pensioners Did not Violate the Law), Jogi Fórum, June 24, 2002 <http://www.jogiforum.hu/hir/102494000810697.php>.

[2781] As an example, a camera system monitoring payment on a highway was used later to identify those who had not fastened their safety belts.

personal data collected by cameras on public areas. The mayor later complied with the Commissioner's opinion.[2782]

Major Privacy Case Law

In June 2004, the Constitutional Court ruled[2783] that the provisions on controlling of personal data in the Act regulating the work of security guards[2784] are unconstitutional and furthermore annulled the right of security guards to search anyone's package or vehicle in a private area open to the public. The Constitutional Court has called upon the Parliament to amend the Act by December 31, 2004. The Parliament exceeded the deadline and enacted a new Act[2785] only in early May. In the meantime, security guards continued working on the basis of the annulled provisions, with the explicit support of the Ministry of Interior.[2786] Although the new Act complies with at least some aspects of the Constitutional Court decision, it also gives several anti-privacy powers to private security enterprises. It allows private companies to store CCTV records for about 30 days, and in post offices, banks, and similar institutions, for 60 days, without any legal purpose.[2787]

In December 2003, the Data Protection Commissioner began an investigation of the use of mobile phone cameras and voice recordings of people without their permission. Commissioner Péterfalvi said that multimedia messaging (MMS) transmission of such information qualifies as data handling, which is subject to the 1992 data protection law. Péterfalvi said at the time,

> Mobile providers and users of all MMS services should note that if a photo or voice recording allows to identify a natural person, taking and

---

[2782] Kiss Gábor, "Megfigyelt megfigyelök" ("Watching the Watchers"), Tech-tudomány, January 18, 2003 <http://www.index.hu/tech/jog/urbaneye/>; "Szabadtéri Big Brother Budapesten - nem önkéntes alapon" ("Open-air Big Brother in Budapest - Not on a Voluntary Basis"), Korridor, July 29, 2002 <http://www.korridor.hu/Archivum_index.php?cikk=100000037427&next=0&archiv=1>; Sándor Tünde, "Minden sarkon térfigyelö. Erzsébetváros teljes területét kamerák pásztázzák" ("There Is a Surveillance Camera at Every Corner. The Whole Area of Erzsébetváros Is Full of Cameras"), Népszabadság Online, July 24, 2002 <http://www.nol.hu/Default.asp?DocCollID=63989&DocID=61783#61783>.

[2783] Decision 22/2004 (VI.19.) AB.

[2784] Act No. IV of 1998 on Security Guards.

[2785] At the time of writing the new act has not as yet been promulgated. Its text is available at <http://www.parlament.hu/irom37/13634/13634.pdf>.

[2786] Letter from the Legal Department of the Ministry of Interior to Balázs Dénes, Executive Director of HCLU, January 17, 2005 <http://www.tasz.hu//download/BM%20v%E1lasz%20a%20ny%EDlt%20lev%E9lre1.pdf?id=13515&time=11 07187108&op=cont>.

[2787] Bill No. T/13634, Section 31 (2).

transmitting it without legal authorization or personal consent amounts to unlawful data handling and can lead to civil or, in some cases, penal responsibility.[2788]

In January 2004, the Data Protection Commissioner's Office informed Hungarian Airlines Malev that, in the transfer of passengers' personal data to the United States, the airline must provide sufficient notice and ability to consent. Malev was only informing the passengers at the airport. As a result, Malev began to inform and get written consent from passengers at the time they purchased their tickets. The Commissioner said, "It is not enough to inform passengers about the fact that their data are sent to the USA, their consent has to be asked for, and what is more, at a time when they can properly consider whether they want to travel with such conditions or not."[2789]

When Jerusalem-based Simon Wiesenthal Center started a campaign to hunt down surviving Nazi war criminals in Hungary, the Data Protection Commissioner investigated whether a foreign institute had the legal right to collect Hungarian data. Attila Péterfalvi found it to be illegal under European Union standards to transfer the personal data of suspected Nazi war criminals to Israel. The center suspended its actions in Hungary, although the director of the program called it an attempt to protect Nazi war criminals.[2790]

The Commissioner maintains close relationships with the data protection authorities in other central and eastern European countries. In December 2001, the Data Protection Commissioners from the Czech Republic, Hungary, Lithuania, Slovakia, Estonia, Latvia, and Poland signed a joint declaration agreeing to closer cooperation and assistance. The Commissioners formed the "Central and Eastern Europe Data Protection Authorities" and agreed to meet twice a year in the future, to provide each other with regular updates and overviews of developments in their countries, and to establish a common Web site for more effective communication.[2791] The Web site includes reports and a newsgroup for persons professionally dealing with personal data protection issues to exchange views and to discuss ethical, legal and technical-organizational proposals of solutions regarding the scope of freedom and

---

[2788] "Ombudsman Starts Inquiry into Cellphone Snapshots," Hungarian News Agency, December 13, 2003.

[2789] "Hungarian Airline to Request Advance Passenger Consent to US Use of Data," BBC Monitoring, January 21, 2004.

[2790] "Nazi Hunt Suspended in Hungary due to Data Protection Concerns," Hungarian News Agency, July 26, 2004.

[2791] E-mail from Karel Neuwirt, President, Office for Personal Data Protection, Czech Republic, to Sarah Andrews, Research Director, EPIC, May 15, 2002 (on file with EPIC).

limitations of personal data processing. Their next meeting will be held in Slovakia in 2005.[2792]

Wiretapping and Surveillance Rules

Surveillance by police requires a court order and is limited to investigations of crimes punishable by more than five years' imprisonment.[2793] Surveillance by national security services requires the permission of a specially appointed judge or the Minister of Justice, who can authorize surveillance for up to 90 days.[2794] In April 1998, the government issued a decree ordering phone companies that offer cellular service to modify their systems to ensure that they could be intercepted. The cost was estimated to be HUF 10 billion (~USD 50 million).[2795] It has been reported that the National Security Service (NSS) regularly install black boxes on Internet Service Providers (ISPs)' networks and intercept communications without warrants. Furthermore, signing a contract to allow full access to data by the NSS is a precondition for obtaining an ISP operating license.[2796]There have been several scandals involving spying on politicians, environmental activists and ethnic minorities. In March 2001, the Chairman of the Hungarian Coalition Party (SMK) reported that its members were being monitored and their communications bugged.[2797] In 1998 Prime Minister Viktor Orbán stated that members of the then-opposition political party FIDESZ were the targets of illegal secret surveillance by the secret services.[2798] A parliamentary committee was established to investigate the matter but its final report released in the spring of 2000 did not find evidence to support the allegations.[2799] In November 2001, the Justice Minister denied reports that there had been an increase in secret surveillance, saying that the number of authorizations for surveillance under this government was 25 percent less than under previous governments.[2800]

[2792] Central and Eastern Europe Data Protection Authoritites Web site, available at <http://www.ceecprivacy.org>.

[2793] Act No. XXXIV of 1994 on Police.

[2794] Act No. LXXV of 1995 on the National Security Services.

[2795] "Technical Costs of Phone Tapping Estimated at HUF 10bn," MTI Econews, April 17, 1998.

[2796] Act No. C of 2003 on Electronic Communications, available at <http://www.nhh.hu/english/menu4/m4_8.htm>.

[2797] "Hungarian Party's Phones Bugged," BBC Summary of World Broadcasts, March 8, 2001.

[2798] "Fidesz 'Bugging' Probe Underway," The Budapest Sun, September 3, 1998.

[2799] United States Department of State, Country Reports on Human Rights Practices 2000, February 2001, available at <http://www.state.gov/g/drl/rls/hrrpt/2000/eur/index.cfm?docid=774>.

2800 "Justice Minister Denies Increase in Secret Surveillance," BBC Worldwide Monitoring, November 20, 2001.

Open Government

The Hungarian Parliament created an investigative committee (*AKA Mécs-bizottság*, named after its head, Member of Parliament Imre Mécs) to investigate the political past of the members of the government because it was revealed that the new Prime Minister, Péter Medgyessy, had worked in counter-intelligence for a state security agency during the communist era. The political opposition tried to use this information against the governing party, arguing that the Prime Minister was a "spy"), which sparked a political battle between the political factions. The main privacy issue was whether the fact that someone who had worked as a "secret police agent" before the 90s could be considered "personal information," or whether the interest for open government and freedom of information trumped an individual's privacy rights and informational autonomy. The Data Protection Commissioner's position was that the investigative committee was established constitutionally, but it had no right to manage the personal data of government members. Nevertheless, a Hungarian daily magazine, *Magyar Hírlap*, published the names of 11 politicians who were "affected," *i.e.*, the names of the people who either worked for a secret agency, or whose name was only mentioned in a document of a spy agency. The investigative committee's head, László Mécs, published almost the same list of affected persons a week later.[2801]

The so-called Lustration Law (publicly known as the "Agent-Law"),[2802] enacted in 1994, stipulates a compromise solution between the accessibility of data relating to persons who cooperated with the secret police of the past regime in an unconstitutional way, and data relating to subjects of secret police reports, on the one hand, and the right to information privacy of all persons concerned, on the other. Originally the Hungarian solution was much less radical than the German model: the victims of surveillance could not learn the identity of the agents reporting on them, only the data reported on themselves; and the former agents fulfilling public functions in the new regime were allowed to resign hidden from public scrutiny. Consequently, the maximum sanction, namely, the publishing of the agents' names in the official gazette, could be applied only if they insisted on staying in function.

[2801] Péterfalvi Attila, August 6, 2002 <http://www.obh.hu/adatved/magyar/2002/mell12.htm#M_23>; "A Mécs-bizottság nem tehet közzé adatokat. Az ombudsman a bizottsági meghallgatás után is fenntartja véleményét," Népszabadság, August 27, 2002 <http://www.mszp007.hu/html/2002/08/nsz0827.htm>; Kovács Zoltán, "Frusztrációs eljárások" ("Frustrating Procedures"), Élet És Irodalom, October 11, 2002 <http://es.fullnet.hu/0241/monokli.htm>; "Ügynökmúlt - Mécs Imre nyilvánosságra hozta a listát" ("Past Agent. Imre Mécs Published the List"), Népszabadság Online, August 30, 2002 <http://www.nol.hu/Default.asp?DocCollID=69268&DocID=66460#66460>.

[2802] Act No. XXIII of 1994 on Supervision of Personnel in Certain Important Positions.

In 2003 a new law[2803] was enacted (while the 1994 law remained in force) with provisions on the rights of victims of surveillance to learn the names of the agents reporting on them and the right to make these names public (but only in the cases where the former agents are presently public figures), and the establishment of the Historical Archives of State Security Services, replacing the Office of History, where documents relating to the activities of the former secret police are to be kept. Despite these legislative developments, there has been a great deal of uncertainty concerning the contents, authenticity, and completeness of the former secret police documents, which gives rise to political blackmail and keeps the issue on the public agenda.

In early 2005 certain organizations posted allegedly reliable lists of former agents and collaborators of the secret police on the Internet[2804] that again stirred heated debates in political life and the press.[2805] Since late 2004 several Bills[2806] have been submitted to the Parliament from both the governing parties and those in opposition, including an amendment to the Constitution,[2807] on full accessibility of all former secret police documents, even on the mandatory posting of certain documents on the Internet. The Parliament is expected to decide on these Bills during its spring 2005 session.

In terms of access to information, the 1992 Act on the Protection of Personal Data and Disclosure of Data of Public Interest (the Act) guarantees access to information of public interest, which is defined as any information being processed by government authorities except for personal information. Exemptions can be made for state secrets or official secrets and information related to national defense, national security, criminal investigations, monetary and currency policy, international relations and judicial procedure. In June 2002, the Government announced that it would ask the Parliament to pass legislation authorizing the further opening of the secret police files from the Communist

---

[2803] Act No. III of 2003 on the disclosure of the secret service activities of the past regime and on the establishing of the Historical Archives of State Security Services.

[2804] The Political Capital Policy Research & Consulting Institute <http://www.politicalcapital.hu>, an anonymous person or organization on a free U.S. Web site <http://www.angelfire/zine2/szakerto90/>, and the weekly magazine *HVG* <http://hvg.hu/print/20050304hivatasoslista.aspx>.

[2805] Among others, the weekly magazine *Magyar Narancs* <http://www.mancs.hu/index.php?gcPage=/public/hirek/szam&id=437&mode2=1&mode3=1> and the daily *Népszabadság* <http://www.nol.hu/cikk/353852/)>or the weekly *Élet és Irodalom* <http://www.es.hu/pd/display.asp?channel=PUBLICISZTIKA0512&article=2005-0329-0854-54PMST>.

[2806] Bill No. T/14230 (February 4, 2005) to amend Act III of 2003, submitted by MPs of the governing Hungarian Socialist Party, available at <http://www.parlament.hu/irom37/14230/14230.pdf>; Bill No. T/14379 (February 11, 2005) on the handling and publicity of the secret documents of the party-state, submitted by MPs of the opposition party Fidesz, available at <http://www.parlament.hu/irom37/14379/14379.pdf>.

[2807] Bill No. T/15822 (21 April 2005), available at <http://www.parlament.hu/irom37/15822/15822.pdf>.

era.[2808] The announcement came following an admission by the Prime Minister that he had been a counter-intelligence officer in the secret police during that time.[2809] Hungary has enacted a law opening up secret service files and has been coordinating with the German Stasi archive to prosecute members of the communist regime. The law regulates the access to files for both victims of spying and former spies. Victims can find out who spied on them, but to prevent recriminations and revenge-taking, they are not given access to the spy's files.[2810]

Miscellaneous Developments

In July 2002, the National Radio and Television Council (ORTT), created by the Parliament in 1996 to defend free speech and warrant the independence of the media, published its Internet regulation plan.[2811] The plan provides for the application of the same rights and liabilities to online and offline newspapers, and to extend the traditional press regulations to online content providers. It also backed the use of a filtering system to prevent minors from being exposed to harmful content, and endorsed the idea of a "notice and takedown" procedure applicable to ISPs when they have to deal with infringement claims. The ORTT declared, however, that an ISP hosting Web space for free could not be responsible for its content, unless the ISP had known about the infringement and did not act upon it.[2812]

NGOs Advocacy Work

The annual Big Brother Award[2813] has been organized in Hungary since 2001 by a civil society organization, Technology for the People Foundation *(Technika az Emberért Alapítvány)*.[2814] Through an anonymous online voting system, anyone

---

[2808] Radio Free Europe, June 28, 2002.

[2809] Radio Free Europe, June 20, 2002.

[2810] "Former Dictatorships Hoping to Learn from German Stasi Archive," Deutsche Welle, May 12, 2004, available at <http://www.dw-world.de/english/0,3367,1432_A_1197738_1_A,00.html>.

[2811] Report contributors include employees of the Commissioner for Civil Rights and of the Commissioner for Data Protection and Freedom of Information, as well as some non-governmental organizations, *e.g.*, the Hungarian Content Providers' Association (MTE).

[2812] Navarro, "Internetszabályozási koncepcióval állt elö az ORTT. Az önszabályozás elönyt élvez" ("ORTT Came Forward with an Internet Regulation Plan. Self-regulation Will be Preferred") Tech-tudomány, June 19, 2002 <http://www.index.hu/tech/jog/ortt0619/>; "Az elektronikus úton végzett nyilvános kommunikáció tartalomszabályozásának alaptételei" (The Principles of Content Regulation of Electronically Publicized Communication) <www.ortt.hu/tanulmanyok/koncepcio_20020619.doc>.

[2813] The negative award, launched by Privacy International (http://www.privacyinternational.org) in the United Kingdom in 1998, followed by a growing number of other countries (*see* http://www.bigbrotherawards.org), to be given to those who did the most in violating people's privacy.

[2814] <http://www.bigbrotherawards.hu>.

---

can nominate a person or organization for the award, and vote for those shortlisted. In 2002, the present Data Protection Commissioner was on the shortlist of nominees because of the much-debated and widely publicized installation of CCTV cameras in his office building. In 2004, his name appeared again on the shortlist because of his controversial position on the use of CCTV cameras in department stores' changing rooms. This time he was awarded the Big Brother Award 2004 in the public vote category. His win has given rise to much controversy, even within the civil sector; nevertheless, it reflects the civil sector's discontent with certain positions and communiqués of the Commissioner.[2815]

In December 2004, Hungary signed the Council Regulation (EC) No. 2252/2004 of December 13, 2004, on standards for security features and biometrics in passports and travel documents issued by Member States.[2816] This regulation *inter alia* prescribes that all citizens of the EU provide their biometric facial image and fingerprints for inclusion in their new passports or travel documents. There were several attempts from privacy groups to prevent this regulation from being signed. The Parliamentary Data Protection Commissioner, Dr. Attila Péterfalvi' the former Commissioner, Dr. László Majtényi; and three Hungarian NGOs[2817] signed the "Open Letter to the European Parliament on Biometric Registration of All EU Citizens and Residents," written by Privacy International, Statewatch and European Digital Rights (EDRI).[2818] In line with this international protest, the Hungarian Civil Liberties Union (HCLU) has addressed the Hungarian members of the European Parliament and started a media campaign trying to change the government's position on this issue. Hungary eventually signed the biometric regulation, contrary to the Constitution, without consulting the Data Protection Commissioner and informing the public of its effects.

International Obligations

During the first half of 2005 Hungary presided over the Salzburg Forum (Salzburg Group), a regular and informal meeting of the Ministers of the Interior

---

[2815] The Commissioner, who personally took the award, published his position in his 2004 Annual Report, available at <http://abiweb.obh.hu/abi/beszamolok/2004/fuggelek1n.htm> (in Hungarian); the abbreviated English edition of the 2004 Report is in preparation.

[2816] Official Journal of the European Union L 385 Volume 47 (December 29, 2004), available at <http://europa.eu.int/eur-lex/lex/LexUriServ/site/en/oj/2004/l_385/l_38520041229en00010006.pdf>.

[2817] The Hungarian Civil Liberties Union, the Hungarian Helsinki Committee, and the Technology for People Foundation (TEA).

[2818] Privacy International, "PI Forges Coalition Calling on European Parliament to Stop Mass Fingerprinting Proposal," November 30, 2004 <http://www.privacyinternational.org/article.shtml?cmd[347]=x-347-85336&als[theme]=BTS%20Biometric%20Passports>.

of Austria, Czech Republic, Hungary, Poland, Slovakia, and Slovenia. The program[2819] of the April 22, 2005, meeting of the Forum included, *inter alia,* enlarging the Forum to Romania and Bulgaria (countries expected to join the EU in 2007), cooperating to protect witnesses, sharing reliable information on the country of origin in asylum procedures, and preparing to implement the Schengen Convention standards, the Visa Information System, and biometrics. The Hungarian Minister of Interior has put forward the idea of connecting EURODAC (the EU database on asylum seekers and illegal aliens) to criminal records, an idea that was fully supported by the five other ministers and has been proposed to the EU.[2820]

Hungary is a member of the Council of Europe (CoE) and has signed and ratified the Convention for the Protection of Individuals with Regard to Automatic Processing of Personal Data (Convention No. 108).[2821] It has signed and ratified the European Convention for the Protection of Human Rights and Fundamental Freedoms.[2822] Hungary ratified the CoE Convention on Cybercrime in late 2003, and it entered into force in July 2004.[2823] It is a member of the Organization for Economic Cooperation and Development (OECD) and has adopted the OECD Guidelines on the Protection of Privacy and Transborder Flows of Personal Data.

Republic of Iceland

Constitutional Privacy Framework

Article 66 of the 1944 Constitution (as amended in 1991) provided: "The home shall be inviolate. Houses may not be searched, nor may any letters or other documents be detained and examined, except by judicial ruling or by a special provision of law."[2824] In 1995 further amendments were made to the Constitution and the personal privacy provision is now contained in Article 72.

[2819] "A Salzburg Csoport belügyminiszterei Budapesten" (The Ministers of the Interior of the Salzburg Group in Budapest"), press release of the Ministry of Interior
<http://www.bm.hu/web/portal.nsf/archiv_hirek/A172785C44D51313C1256FE7003C2B6A>.

[2820] Parliament of the Republic of Hungary, minutes of the hearing taken before the Committee of European Affairs (February 22, 2005); *see also* " Ministry of Interior and Administration of the Republic of Poland Fruitful meeting of the Salzburg Group," July 19, 2004, available at
<http://www.mswia.gov.pl/eng_aktual_190704_salzburg.html>.

[2821] Signed May 13, 1993; enacted October 8, 1997; entered into force February 1, 1998.

[2822] Signed November 6, 1990; enacted November 5, 1992; entered into force November 5, 1992.

[2823] Signed November 23, 2001; ratified December 4, 2003; entered into force July 1, 2004.

[2824] Constitution of the Republic of Iceland, No. 33, June 17, 1944, as amended May 30, 1984, May 31, 1991, June 28, 1995 and June 24, 1999, available at <http://government.is/constitution/> (official English translation from Icelandic).

Data Protection Framework

As a member of the European Free Trade Association (EFTA), Iceland is obliged to ensure that its laws, in certain fields, are compatible with those of the European Union (EU). On January 1, 2000, the Act on the Protection of Individuals with regard to the Processing of Personal Data came into force. The Act replaced the Registration and Processing of Personal Data of 1989 (as amended) and was adopted to bring Iceland's data protection regime into compliance with the EU Data Protection Directive (1995/46/EC).[2825] It covers both automated and manual processing of personal information. It distinguishes between sensitive and non-sensitive data and includes specific restrictions on the use of video surveillance and national identification numbers. It instructs the Statistical Bureau of Iceland to maintain a registry of individuals not willing to allow the use of their names in product marketing.

Data Protection Authority

The Act established a new independent Data Protection Authority (*Persónuvernd* or DPA) to replace the former Data Protection Commission.[2826] *Persónuvernd* supervises implementation and compliance with the Act and any pursuant regulations or orders. It maintains the registry of activities and can investigate and issue rulings. It can impose fines for non-compliance and can seek criminal sanctions. The DPA is also responsible for supervising the handling of personal information in the Schengen Information System.[2827] *Persónuvernd* also has the authority to issue public guidelines and regulations. Over the last few years it has issued rules on consent, notification, security assessments, and systematic safety measures.[2828]

Persónuvernd handled 676 new cases in 2004.[2829] Altogether *Persónuvernd* handled 775 cases of which 691 were solved. Out of these 775 cases, 337 were complaints and questions from individuals, data controllers and institutions that

---

[2825] Act on the Protection of Individuals with regard to the Processing of Personal Data No. 77/2000, available at
<http://www.personuvernd.is/tolvunefnd.nsf/pages/A6B42A045297151D00256DB40053600B>.

[2826] Homepage <http://www.personuvernd.is/tolvunefnd.nsf/pages/english>.

[2827] Act on the Participation of Iceland in the Schengen Co-operation, No. 15/2000, and Act on the Schengen Information System, No. 16/2000.

[2828] *See* <http://www.personuvernd.is/tolvunefnd.nsf/pages/english>.

[2829] *Persónuvernd* handled 627 cases in 2003. During this period, it received 246 complaints and questions and engaged in 8 investigations of data processing by certain data controllers. While the number of such investigations was lower in 2003 compared with 2002, their range was wider. Since its establishment, *Persónuvernd* has received 1,691 notifications of personal data processing, 678 of them in 2003 alone.

were either solved with an opinion or a decision, some of them concerning bills or administrative regulations. From July 1, 2004, to April 30, 2005, *Persónuvernd* was involved in 42 investigations of data processing by certain data controllers, of which seven were solved formally with a decision or an opinion. In four of these cases, the data controllers were ordered or advised to undertake necessary privacy measures. The scope of most of these investigations was large, and many of them were due to be finished in 2005. As of July 2005, there are seven full-time staff. *Persónuvernd* does not expect its work to change significantly in the next year, though an emphasis on investigations may continue to increase.[2830]

National ID System

Every individual's identity (ID) number is publicly available and widely used, along with names, addresses and other personal information. For instance, day-to-day activities such as video rental are based on the personal ID numbers. This has implications for the privacy of sensitive data, which registration is based on the same personal ID numbers, facilitating the task of intruders and abusers of the data. The open access to personal ID numbers requires stronger privacy protections. Instead, several recent laws have been enacted that allow the creation of databases including sensitive personal information. Privacy advocates have criticized this trend, and said that the government has prioritized corporate interests over those of individuals concerned about the use of their personal data.

In December 1998, the Parliament approved the Health Sector Database Act to create a nationwide centralized database of medical records to be used for genetic research.[2831] In January 2000, the Minister of Health granted an exclusive 12-year license to operate that database to *Íslensk Erfðagreining ehf*, the Icelandic subsidiary of American bio-tech company deCODE Genetics, Inc.[2832] The database would incorporate non-personally identifiable data derived from the medical records held by Iceland's health services. Patients are to be granted a right to opt-out of the database by notifying the Director General of Public

---

[2830] *See* e-mail from Thordur Sveinsson, Legal Counsel, Icelandic Data Protection Authority (*Persónuvernd*) to Ula Galster, International Policy Fellow, Electronic Privacy Information Center, August 2, 2005 (on file with EPIC).

[2831] Act on a Health Sector Database No. 139/1998, December 17, 1998, available at <http://brunnur.stjr.is/interpro/htr/htr.nsf/pages/gagngr-log-ensk>.

2832 Operating License issued to Íslensk erf agreining ehf, State Reg. No. 691295-3549, for the Creation and Operation of a Health Sector Database, Ministry of Health and Social Security, January 2000, available at <http://brunnur.stjr.is/interpro/htr/htr.nsf/Files/oplic/$file/oplic.pdf>.

Health, and over 20,000 had chosen to opt-out of the database by June 2003.[2833] The database is to be used to "develop new or improved methods of achieving better health, prediction, diagnosis and treatment of disease, to seek the most economic ways of operating health services, and for making reports in the health sector." Measures to ensure security and privacy in the operation of the database must meet standards and conditions set out by the DPA. In 2000, the DPA issued regulations on the general security terms.[2834] The government's National Bioethics Committee reviews deCODE's research protocols while the DPA strips data of all personal identifiers, encrypts all identification numbers using an algorithm, and oversees maintenance of all personalized data.[2835]

The operating company is specifically authorized to use the data in the database for financial profit and, as long as confidentiality is ensured, to link it with other databases containing genealogical or genetic data. The company is reportedly spending USD 200 million over a period of five years to research the country's genetic pool in order to find the genes related to common illnesses such as cancer, asthma, schizophrenia, Alzheimer's and Parkinson's diseases. According to one estimate presented at an international conference on human genetics in May 2001, the database will be worth approximately USD 14 billion.[2836]

This proposal has been very controversial and is hotly debated both in Iceland and with medical and privacy experts around the world. In Iceland, the Association of Icelanders for Ethics in Science and Medicine (*Mannvernd*) is leading the opposition to the project. *Mannvernd* reports that as of June 30, 2003, 20,426 people had opted out of the database.[2837] The Icelandic Medical Association is also opposing the effort and many doctors are refusing to hand over their patients' records without consent.[2838] In April 1999, the World Medical Association supported the Icelandic Medical Association's opposition to the database,[2839] and adopted in 2002 a Declaration on Health Databases[2840] that

---

[2833] Opt-Out Graph, Association of Icelanders for Ethics in Science and Medicine (Mannvernd), available at <http://www.mannvernd.is/english/optout.html>.

[2834] General Security Terms of the Icelandic Data Protection Commission, Document No. 1, January 19, 2000,available at
<http://www.personuvernd.is/tolvunefnd.nsf/pages/C9519A42E967537E002569180036F54C>.

[2835] Richard Merli, "Privacy Concerns Loom Large for Genetic Databases," Pharmaceuticals Insider, July 9, 2003 <http://www.kpmginsiders.com/>.

[2836] J. C. Bear, "What Is A Person's DNA Worth? Fair Compensation For DNA Access, Faculty of Medicine Memorial University of Newfoundland," report presented at the 10th International Congress of Human Genetics, Vienna, May 2001, available at <http://www.mannvernd.is/english/articles/jb_fair_compensation.html>.

[2837] *See* Opt Out Graph *supra.*

[2838] *See* <http://www.icemed.is/english/default.htm>.

[2839] "World Medical Association Opposes Icelandic Gene Database," EBMJ, April 24, 1999.

protects patients' interests with regard to the creation of central health databases.[2841] At their annual meeting in Santiago de Compostela, Spain, in September 1998, the European Data Protection Commissioners recommended that the Icelandic authorities reconsider the project in light of the fundamental principles laid down in the European Convention for the Protection of Human Rights and Fundamental Freedoms (ECHR), the Council of Europe Convention for the Protection of Individuals with Regard to Automatic Processing of Personal Data (Council of Europe's Convention No. 108) and its Recommendation (97) 5 on Medical Data, and the EU Data Protection Directive. In 1998, at the request of the Icelandic Medical Association, security expert Dr. Ross Anderson evaluated the proposed system. He concluded that the privacy and ethical implications of the proposed database were "outside the boundaries of what would be acceptable elsewhere in Europe" and advised the association to oppose its establishment.[2842]

Since 2002, development on the database has been postponed, as the company has been unable to come to an agreement with the Icelandic DPA or Iceland's National Bioethics Committee about proposed uses of the data, and the company has been unable to establish who would fund the project.[2843]

Major Privacy Case Law

In November 2003, the Icelandic Supreme Court issued a key ruling[2844] that transfer of a dead patient's health data to the proposed database would infringe the privacy rights of the deceased's descendants, casting further doubt over the feasibility of the Health Sector Database. The court ruled in favor of an 18-year old who sought to prevent the transfer of her dead father's health records, ending her 4-year fight for this right. Even though the data would be anonymous and encrypted, information about the child could be inferred from data related to the father's hereditary characteristics. The court also noted that linkage with other

---

[2840] Declaration on Ethical Considerations Regarding Health Databases October 6, 2002, available at <http://www.wma.net/e/policy/d1.htm>.

[2841] The Guidelines lay down a policy on confidentiality, against which the creation of national health databases should be judged: they establish controls over the use and disclosure of personal health information; require patients' consent if the inclusion of their health information on a database involves disclosure to a third party; and allow patients to withdraw their health information from databases. Press release of the World Medical Association, General Assembly, Washington, USA, October 2-6, 2002 <http://www.wma.net/e/press/2002_5.htm>.

[2842] Ross Anderson, "The deCODE Proposal for an Icelandic Health Database," March 1998, available at <http://www.cl.cam.ac.uk/~rja14/iceland/iceland.html>.

[2843] Alison Abbott, "Icelandic Database Shelved as Court Judges Privacy in Peril," Nature, May 13, 2004, at 118.

[2844] Icelandic Supreme Court, November 27, 2003, judgment No. 151/2003.

---

genetic and genealogical databases increased the possibility of improper identification.[2845] In its judgment, the court noted that it was unclear what information in the HSD would be encrypted, and that persons could be identified from medical record data other than names and adresses. Futhermore, the law did not adequately ensure that health information in the database would not be personally identifiable, in spite of the law repeatedly claiming so. The court concluded that: "even though individual provisions of Act No. 139/1998 repeatedly stipulate that health information in the Health Sector Database should be non-personally identifiable, it is far from adequately ensured under statutory law that this stated objective will be achieved." In light of these circumstances, and taking into account the principles of Icelandic law concerning the confidentiality and protection of privacy, the Court concluded that the right of the 18-year-old in this matter must be recognized, and her court claims, therefore, upheld.[2846]

The court's ruling suggests that the 1998 Health Sector Database Act may be unconstitutional, being contrary to the Constitution's privacy clause. The government, however, anticipates that the Act and database may still be salvaged,[2847] and deCODE has played down the decision's significance on its current operations.[2848] DeCODE has already begun work with 110,000 living individuals who have provided informed consent. Consent forms vary, however, and research subjects are sometimes asked to sign open consent forms, permitting any research use of their samples.[2849] So far, deCODE is not permitted to use the collected samples in the study on the unrelated diseases.[2850] This court ruling killed whatever was left of deCODE's original project to create a country-wide computerized database of medical records.[2851] It also sets a precedent for the privacy rights of the deceased. The law is still in effect, however, and so is the license. The Health Ministry officials have said that amendments to the law in accordance with the court ruling are being prepared.[2852]

[2845] Abbott, *supra* note 20.

[2846] A professional (legal) English translation from Icelandic of the court ruling can be found at <http://www.mannvernd.is/english/>

[2847] "deCODE's Court Opposition," Nature Biotechnology, May 2004 at 500.

[2848] *Id.*

[2849] Karen J Maschke, Navigating an Ethical Patchwork—Human Gene Banks, Nature Biotechnology 23, 539 - 545 (2005).

[2850] Abbott, *supra* note 20.

[2851] Annas GJ, Family Privacy and Death - Antigone, War, and Medical Research, New England Journal of Medicine 352: 501-5 (2005).

[2852] Interview, in Icelandic, with Guðríður Þorsteinsdóttir, head of unit at the Ministry of Health, in the Icelandic Medical Journal 91, 362 (2005), available at <http://www.laeknablad*ld*.is/2005/04/nr/1949>.

Ultimately the Health Sector Database (HSD) has not been created, *i.e.* data has not been entered into the database, The licensee, deCODE Genetics, does not expect to operate the database and has therefore reversed the license fee in its accounts in the annual report. DeCODE puts the blame on the Data Protection Authority (DPA) for lack of security clearance, and on the main Icelandic hospital, the Landspítali National University Hospital for the lack of agreement about access to medical records therein. The DPA, on the other hand, claims that deCODE repeatedly changed the design of the database, requiring revision of the security requirements. The hospital doctors actively opposed the transfer of medical record data without patient consent. In its annual report to the U.S. Security and Exchange Commission,[2853] deCODE explained that it had not obtained a data transfer agreements with the National University Hospital (NUH). DeCODE stated, "No such agreement with the NUH has been consummated, and the IHD has not been commercialized primarily because the Icelandic Data Protection Authority has not issued the required security certification."

In August 2004, an announcement appeared on the website of the U.S. National Institute of Health, offering grants and cooperation between American and Icelandic scientists on HSD research.[2854] According to the announcement, "NIH representatives have identified several opportunities for expanding collaboration between U.S. and Icelandic scientists. Even though the Health Sector Database is not yet complete, other opportunities for collaboration exist." The NIH said that there are opportunities to "(1) use tissues and information in biobanks and other repositories for research, (2) use, for research, information in the genealogy databases and other databases, (3) conduct research with Icelandic volunteers, and (4) collaborate with research groups and private companies in Iceland."[2855]

The HSD is described in the announcement as if it already existed, and in positive terms only. Normal research subject protection was not considered necessary. The U.S. Health and Human Services Office for Human Research Protections determined that: "research with the Health Sector Database does not constitute human subjects research under the HHS human subject protections regulations codified at 45 CFR part 46, because researchers would receive only aggregated data from this database and are prohibited by Icelandic law from having access to the raw or coded data that would enable linkage to an

---

[2853] 10-K form, page 73, 16 March 2005, available at
<http://sec.gov/Archives/edgar/data/1022974/000104746905006706/a2153601z10-k.htm>.
[2854] *See* <http://grants2.nih.gov/grants/icelandic_research.pdf>.
[2855] *Id.*

individual." Furthermore, a U.S. query to the HSD would not require review by the Icelandic National Bioethics Committee, nor by the US Institutional Review Board, according to the announcement.

In May 2000, the Government enacted the Act on Biobanks.[2856] This Act sets rules for the "collection, keeping, handling and utilization of biological samples from human beings" to ensure confidentiality and prohibit discrimination. The Act requires informed consent from the person for the collection of samples. However, this requirement does not apply to samples in biobanks that already exist, such as the Health Sector Database and the deCODE biobank, which is expected to be connected to the former. In certain cases, the specimens can even be used for research in spite of the donor's opposition.[2857] The Act came into force in January 2001.

In October 2000, the Commission ruled that four researchers in pharmacology and geriatrics, who had been granted a permit for a research project into Alzheimer's disease, had breached the terms of the permit by collecting the medical records of people who were not participants in the Alzheimer project. The research project was financed by, and conducted in association with, *Islensk Erföagreining ehf.*[2858]

Under the Law on Criminal Procedure, wiretapping, tape recording or photographing without consent requires a court order and must be limited to a short period of time. After the recording is complete, the target must be informed and the recordings must be destroyed after they are no longer needed.[2859] Complaints against the orders can be submitted to the Supreme Court. A recent Supreme Court judgment allows news reporters to record telephone interviews without first informing the interviewee. Chapter XXV of the Penal Code also penalizes violations of privacy such as violating the secrecy of letters and revealing secrets to the public.

In June 2001, Keflavik International Airport began incorporating facial recognition software, FaceIT, into its video surveillance system. A police spokesperson said that the surveillance was being used to "identify known

---

[2856] Act on Biobanks No. 110/2000, May 2000, available at
<http://brunnur.stjr.is/interpro/htr/htr.nsf/pages/Act-biobanks>.

[2857] Winickoff, D. Biosamples, Genomics, and Human Rights: Context and Content of Iceland's Biobanks Act, Journal of BioLaw and Business, Volume 4, Number 2, 11-17 (2000).

[2858] "Illegal Research on Alzheimer," Icelandic State Radio News Service, October 28, 2000, translation by Mannvernd at <http://www.mannvernd.is/english/news/alzheimer.illegal.html>.

[2859] Articles 86-87, Law on Criminal Procedure.

criminals and false asylum seekers" without disturbing European citizens' rights to travel freely under the Schengen Agreement.[2860]

In 2003, the Minister of Justice passed a Regulation on Foreigners, No. 53/2003, requiring lodging businesses such as hotels, hostels, or camps to maintain registers of their guests. These registers are to be retained for two years and may be accessed by the police at any time. This provision is based on Article 54 of the Act on Foreigners, No. 96/2002, authorizing the Minister of Justice to pass rules governing the duties of lodgers. The rule might also be construed to apply to private homes, lodging foreign guests, requiring notification to the Directorate of Immigration. *Persónuvernd* offered criticism of this provision prior to its enactment.

Like many countries in Europe in 2003 and 2004, Iceland has had to respond to requests by the United States Department of Homeland Security's Bureau of Customs and Border Protection (CBP) for airline passenger data, including Advanced Passenger Information System (APIS) and Passenger Name Record (PNR) data. As a party to the European Economic Area Agreement, Iceland was bound by the May 2004 agreement between CBP and the European Commission governing the scope of data to be transferred and the protections afforded to the data. *Persónuvernd* sought to ensure that data from Iceland and Icelandair would not be processed or retained differently than data from other European airlines.

Two major security-related bills were presented to the Parliament by the Minister of Justice in 2004. One bill, which became law (No. 20/2004), amended the Act on Foreigners, No. 96/2000, allowing significant governmental intrusions based on suspicion of sham or forced marriages. The act allows body and house searches where there is suspicion that the sole aim of a marriage is to give one spouse the right to stay in Iceland, or where there is suspicion that the marriage is forced. The act also allows genetic testing of foreigners claiming kinship to Icelandic citizens as the basis for their right to reside in Iceland, and it creates a presumption of a sham or forced marriage where there is reasonable suspicion of such a condition. Although the DPA offered significant criticism of the act, it was only able to effect a change to the standard for allowing body and house searches for suspect marriages, requiring that it be absolutely beyond doubt that the search would be allowed by a judge.

The DPA participated with greater effect on a second bill, amending the Act on the Procedure of Criminal Cases, No. 19/1991. One provision allowed for

---

[2860] "Icelandic Airport Installs New Surveillance Software," Airline Industry Information, June 20, 2001.

wiretaps without prior judicial approval, provided that approval was obtained within 24 hours of the wiretap. The DPA and other groups, including the Icelandic Federation of Lawyers, strongly criticized this provision, and it was removed prior to enactment.

Throughout 2003 and 2004, there was also significant debate regarding the retention of network traffic data, including the retention of IP numbers in computer logs, to facilitate investigation of crimes such as child pornography. The State Police Chief proposed requiring retention of network traffic data for at least six months, claiming concordance with European legislation providing exceptions to the general rule requiring disposal of such data after billing and transmission purposes have been fulfilled. The DPA responded that such data retention would need to be narrower in scope and limited in time.

Wiretapping and Surveillance Rules

An amendment to the Telecommunications Law was introduced in April 2005. The bill provided the police with the access to IP numbers, phone numbers, as needed for investigation purposes, up to one year after their use, without obtaining a court order.[2861] This was opposed by many, and led to the amendment of the bill. In the version enacted in May 2005, telecommunication firms shall only store data such as IP numbers for 6 months, but the police still have access to such data without a court order.[2862] The new law shortens the originally proposed period for which the service providers are obliged to store information, from one year to 6 months. The original bill also proposed that the provider should store the time and length of a call and the amount of data transferred to and from the user should be registered. The new law however, stipulates that the providers shall only store the date of the call and the amount of data sent to the user. In addition, the final version of the bill, enacted in May, did not require users to present their personal identification document when purchasing phone cards, as proposed by the original bill, but instead the law now permits officials to collect information on users of such cards.[2863]

[2861] Draft amendment 1102 April 2005 to the Telecommunication Act. Article 7 provides: "Minimum registration shall ensure that the telecommunication firm can provide information regarding which of its customers had a specific phone number, IP number or user name, and provide information on all of the user's connections, the time, length, who the link was to, amount of data transferred, both to and from the user." *See* <http://www.althingi.is/altext/131/s/1102.html>.

[2862] Law 78/2005, (amendment to the 1993 Telecommunication act) Article 7, available at <http://www.althingi.is/altext/131/s/1473.html>.

[2863] Law 81/2003 with amendments, the Telecommunication Act, available at <http://www.althingi.is/altext/stjt/2003.081.html>.

In Iceland, court orders can be obtained almost immediately, usually the same day, which raises questions about the importance of granting police access without a court order. The parliamentary majority noted that public interest in this instance was weighted against the privacy rights of individuals.[2864] Purported public interest prevailed and the police access to data without a court order was legalized.

Paradoxically, police, in their evaluation of the bill submitted to the Parliament, argued that court practice was such that police only succeeded in obtaining court orders for access to this information if the sentence for the alleged crime would be more than eight years or if there is high public or private interest at stake. The police would not have been able to investigate Internet crimes, except for the most serious cases, if the bill had not been passed.[2865]

Open Government

The Freedom of Information Act of 1996 (*Upplysingalög*) governs the release of documents.[2866] Under the Act, individuals (including non-residents) and legal entities have a legal right to official documents without having to show a reason for the request. There are exceptions for national security, commercial and personal information. Copyrighted material can be provided to requestors but it is then their responsibility if they republish the materials in a manner inconsistent with the copyright. Denials can be appealed to the Information Committee. There are often delays in the release of documents. Recently, the government refused to release a memorandum on a court case on the grounds that it was an internal government document. The Supreme Court ordered its release, because it had previously been shown to non-official parties.

Health Privacy

In 2003, the Parliament passed a bill on prescription databases, permitting the State Health Insurance Institution (the Institution) to register data from all doctors' prescriptions of medicines. The purpose of creating such a database is to prevent abuse of prescription drugs and to give an overview of the nation's drug consumption. The Director of Public Health will control access to personal data.

[2864]*See* Parliament majority proposal for amending the bill, available at
<http://www.althingi.is/altext/131/s/1369.html> (in Icelandic).

[2865] *See* Morgunblaðið (daily newspaper), available at
<http://mbl.is/mm/frettir/frett.html?nid=3411828;restrict=1> (in Icelandic).

[2866] Act No. 50/1996, available at <http://www.rz.uni-frankfurt.de/~sobotta/Enskthyd.doc>.

As a result of the DPA's opposition to the draft bill, the bill was modified to implement encryption means to protect the personal data. *Mannvernd* pointed out that the Director of Public Health had no need to have access to information about most of the medicines and prescriptions covered by the Act, since there was no potential of abuse or threat to the health of the population, and that the collection of sensitive information by the State Health Insurance Organization would compromise the integrity of that establishment, thereby endangering the trust of their clients. *Mannvernd* additionally argued that there was a danger that the database could be used later for different purposes than the original ones, as this had already been the case in the past. It recommended that sensitive information only be collected in case of absolute necessity.

In April 2005, the Institution announced it was going to increase surveillance, both of disability payment recipients and of their doctors.[2867] The medical director of the Institution claimed in the media that recipients lie and pretend to live alone or not to work, in order to receive higher disability payments. The same director also demanded access to doctors' medical records, in order to verify patient contact as a basis for doctors' claims for reimbursement.[2868] Patients complain that they find it difficult to rely on the institution for disability payments when it also has a triple surveillance role (monitoring the disabled, the doctors and prescriptions) in addition to the health insurance role. In addition to *Mannvernd*, the Icelandic Federation of Lawyers has worked as an advocate for privacy interests in Iceland in certain instances.

International Obligations

Iceland is a member of the Council of Europe (CoE) and has signed and ratified the CoE Convention No. 108.[2869] It has signed and ratified the ECHR.[2870] In

---

[2867] "The State Health Insurance Institution is substantially increasing its surveillance of whether people on insurance payments break the rules they have to comply with in order to receive those payments," according to Sigurður Thorlacius, medical director of the Institution. "It is not only the illicit work which is said to occur among individuals on disability payments," Thorlacius said. "Many are lying to us. Individuals with children claim they are not in cohabitation. That means they receive much higher payments from us. That leads to suffering for those in dire need, relying solely on our payments, because of those who lie to us about their situation." The newspaper Fréttablaðið, April 28, 2005, p. 1. Similar accusations were made by the director of the Institution in other media.

[2868] Law 154/2001, paragraph 8, amending Law 117/1993, paragraph 47 provides: "The Institution's doctors, or dentists if relevant, are permitted to examine the part of the medical record that forms the basis of the invoice to the Institution," available at <http://www.althingi.is/lagas/131a/1993117.html>.

[2869] Signed September 27, 1982; enacted March 3, 1991; entered into force July 1, 1991 <http://conventions.coe.int/>.

[2870] Signed November 4, 1950; enacted June 29, 1953; entered into force September 3, 1953 <http://conventions.coe.int/>.

November 2001, it signed, but has not ratified, the CoE Convention on Cybercrime (ETS No.185).[2871] It is a member of the Organization for Economic Cooperation and Development (OECD) and has adopted the OECD Guidelines on the Protection of Privacy and Transborder Flows of Personal Data.

Republic of India

Constitutional Privacy Framework

The Constitution of 1950 does not expressly recognize the right to privacy.[2872] However, the Supreme Court first recognized in 1964 that there is a right of privacy implicit in the Constitution under Article 21, which states, "No person shall be deprived of his life or personal liberty except according to procedure established by law."[2873]

Data Protection Framework

There is a general right of personal privacy recognized in Indian law. Police must obtain warrants to conduct searches and seizures, except in cases where exigent circumstances exist. Police must justify warrantless searches in writing to the nearest magistrate with jurisdiction over the offense. However, the authorities in Jammu and Kashmir, Punjab, and Assam have special powers to search and arrest without a warrant.[2874] Invasion of privacy by private persons is not governed by the Constitution, though unlawful attacks on the honor and reputation of a person can invite an action in tort and/or criminal law.[2875]

There is no general data protection law in India, though some provisions exist in other regulations. The Public Financial Institutions Act of 1993 codifies India's

---

[2871] Signed November 30, 2001.

[2872] India Constitution, available at <http://indiacode.nic.in/coiweb/welcome.html>.

[2873] Kharak Singh v. State of UP, (1964) 1 SCR 332; *see* R.C. Jain, National Human Rights Commission, India, Indian Supreme Court on Right to Privacy, July 1997.

[2874] Business Line - Internet Edition, "Nasscom Urges Laws for Data Protection," <http://www.indiaserver.com/businessline/2000/06/29/stories/152939t5.htm>. Bureau of Democracy, Human Rights, and Labor, *supra* Section 1f.

[2875] As the civil law pertaining to defamation is not codified, the courts have to apply the corresponding rules of the English Common Law. In 1994 the Supreme Court decided in the *Auto Shankar* case that every citizen has the right to safeguard his or her privacy and that nothing could be published on areas such as the family, marriage and education, "whether truthful or otherwise," without the citizen's consent, but carved an exception to this rule for material based on public records and information about public officials' conduct that is "relevant to the discharge of their duties"; *see* "Failure to Define Law on Privacy Could Cost Society Dear," Times of India, August 26, 2001.

---

tradition of maintaining confidentiality in bank transactions. Privacy in telecommunications has also been regulated by the Telecom Regulatory Authority of India (TRAI), which regulates all telecommunication services in the country. The Common Charter of Telecom Services for adoption by all Telecom Service providers provides, "All Service Providers assure that the privacy of their subscribers (not affecting the national security) shall be scrupulously guarded."[2876]

The rise of business process outsourcing (BPO) operations and call centers in India has placed the government under increasing pressure to implement a data protection law that conforms to US and European data protection standards.[2877] The National Task Force on IT and Software Development had submitted an "IT Action Plan" to Prime Minister Vajpayee in July 1998 calling for the creation of a "National Policy on Information Security, Privacy and Data Protection Act for handling of computerized data." It examined the United Kingdom Data Protection Act as a model and recommended several cyber laws including ones on privacy and encryption. However, no action has been taken following these suggestions.[2878]

The National Association of Software and Service Companies (NASSCOM) has continued to urge the government to pass a data protection law to ensure the privacy of information supplied over computer networks and to meet US and European data protection standards.[2879] Press coverage of the growing privacy concerns in the US over data sent to India as well as continued pressure from EU companies have lead NASSCOM and other industry leaders to move for increased privacy protection in India. This protection may take the form of a Safe-Harbor agreement similar to the US and EU privacy framework.[2880] NASSCOM has also identified State-specific data privacy laws with which Indian regulations must apply, including the Health Insurance Portability and Accountability Act (HIPAA), the Gramm-Leach-Bliley Act, and California's

---

[2876] Telecom Regulatory Authority of India, "TRAI for Introduction of Common Charter of Telecom Services By All the Service Providers" 2005, Section Three (3), available at
<http://www.trai.gov.in/commonchart24feb05.htm>.

[2877] John Ribeiro, "Indian Law May Satisfy Data Protection Concerns," Computerworld, April 21, 2004, available at
<http://www.computerworld.com/securitytopics/security/privacy/story/0,10801,92557,00.html?f=x10>.

[2878] National Task Force on IT & SD, Basic Background Report, June 9, 1998
<http://it-taskforce.nic.in/bgr14.htm>; "Asia/Pacific," Privacy Knowledge Database, April 11, 2005
<http://www.privacyknowledgebase.com/document.jsp?docid=REFDPASP#Republic%20of%20India>.

[2879] "Inadequate Cyber Laws Hurting Indian Firms," Hindustan Times, May 25, 2005, available at
<http://www.hindustantimes.com/news/181_1375119,001300460000.htm>.

[2880] Margaret P. Eisenhauer, "Privacy and Security Law Issues in Off-shore Outsourcing Transactions," Hunton & Wiliams, February 15, 2005.

identity protection law, SB 1386.[2881] NASSCOM has suggested changes to the Information Technology Act 2000 that would conform to US and EU privacy laws and allow India to negotiate with the EU for recognition as a country that offers an adequate level of protection for personal data[2882] and has issued a statement that it hopes the provisions will be in place by the end of 2005.[2883] Foreign companies are currently relying on contractual obligations to impose privacy protection standards for customers.[2884]

The push for data protection laws comes in the wake of fraud and identity theft in the BPO industry. In February 2003, India convicted its first cyber-criminal when a Delhi High Court sentenced Arif Azim on the charges of online cheating. In this case, Arif Azim, while working for a call centre near Delhi stole credit card information that belonged to an American citizen and used it to order a color television and a cordless phone.[2885] In April 2005, a fraud scheme was discovered involving employees of an Indian call center.[2886] Employees convinced Citibank account holders in the United States to reveal their personal identification numbers, which were used to obtain more than USD 400,000.[2887]

To combat concerns about potential employee fraud, NASSCOM has announced that it is working on a central employee database that would keep updated information on employees working in the IT and BPO sector. The proposal is still in an initial stage, and no specifics of the database have been released.[2888]

[2881] NASSCOM, "Indian Privacy Law," 2002 <http://www.nasscom.org/artdisplay.asp?cat_id=652>.

[2882] "Inadequate Cyber Laws Hurting Indian Firms," Hindustan Times, May 25, 2005, available at <http://www.hindustantimes.com/news/181_1375119,001300460000.htm>.

[2883] NASSCOM, "NASSCOM Outlines Plan to Protect Privacy," May 31, 2005 <http://www.nasscom.org/artdisplay.asp?Art_id=4371>.

[2884] John Ribeiro, "Indian Law May Satisfy Data Protection Concerns," Computerworld, April 21, 2004, available at <http://www.computerworld.com/securitytopics/security/privacy/story/0,10801,92557,00.html?f=x10>.

[2885] "India Poised to Tighten Data Protection Law," ComputerWeekly.com, April 22, 2004, available at <http://www.computerweekly.com/Articles/2004/04/22/201936/Indiapoisedtotightendataprotectionlaw.htm>.

[2886] Narayanan Madhavan, "India Plans IT Staff Registry to Help Stop Fraud," USA Today, May 17, 2005, available at <http://www.usatoday.com/tech/news/computersecurity/infotheft/2005-05-17-india-it-registry_x.htm>.

[2887] Erica Lee Nelson, "India Fortifies its Data Security," The Washington Times, May 28, 2005, available at <http://washingtontimes.com/business/20050527-103942-3132r.htm>.

[2888] "India Faces Outsourcing Labor Shortage," The New York Times, June 7, 2005, available at <http://www.nytimes.com/aponline/business/AP-India-Labor-Shortage.html?>; NASSCOM, "NASSCOM to Set Up Employee Database," April 20, 2005 <http://www.nasscom.org/artDisplay.asp?art_id=4247>.

On June 14, 2004, the Reserve Bank of India submitted for public comments a report of the Working Group on Financial Conglomerates.[2889] The group suggested criteria for identifying financial conglomerates, establishing a monitoring system for capturing intra-group transactions and exposures amongst conglomerates, as well as mechanisms for inter-regulatory exchange of information with respect to conglomerates. The group also proposed that a "designated entity" be established within each group or conglomerate and be first identified within each of them. The entity is to be assigned the responsibility of providing data, with respect to all financial subsidiaries or associates constituting the conglomerate, to its regulator, which would be the Principal Regulator for the entire conglomerate. Therefore a Principal Regulator is to be established for each conglomerate. The group suggested that the designated entity would have to submit periodic reports to the principal regulator and that a complete database of all information received from all conglomerates would be maintained at the nodal cell further RBI to address issues arising out of data disaggregation. Each designated entity may also submit the information to RBI. Modalities of electronic data submission and database issues are to be developed later on. The responsibility of collating data from all other group entities and submitting the same to their principal regulator therefore lies with the designated entity. The Principal Regulator would notify the name of the designated entity.

Wiretapping and Surveillance Rules

Wiretapping is generally regulated under the Telegraph Act of 1885, which gives the police authority to tap phones and intercept mail to aid an investigation.[2890] There have been numerous wiretap scandals in India, resulting in a 1996 decision by the Supreme Court that wiretaps are a "serious invasion of an individual's privacy."[2891] The Court also set out guidelines for wiretapping by the government that define who can tap phones and under what circumstances. Only the Union Home Secretary, or his counterpart in the states, can issue an order for a wiretap. The government is also required to show that the information sought cannot be obtained through any other means. The Court mandated the development of a high-level committee to review the legality of each wiretap.[2892]

[2889] Reserve Bank of India, "Report on Monitoring of Financial Conglomerates," June 14, 2004 <http://www.rbi.org.in/index.dll/53601?OpenStory?fromdate=06/14/2004&todate=06/14/2004&s1secid=0&s2secid=0&secid=21/0/0&archivemode=0>.

[2890] Bureau of Democracy, Human Rights, and Labor, *supra* at Section 1f.

[2891] Peoples Union for Civil Liberties (PUCL) v. The Union of India & Another, 18 December 1996, on Writ Petition (C) No. 256 of 1991.

[2892] South Asia Human Rights Documentation Centre, Alternate Report and Commentary to the United Nations Human Rights Committee on India's Third Periodic Report under Article 40 of the International

---

Recordings or transcripts of tapped phone calls are not generally accepted as primary evidence in Indian courts, however such evidence was admissible in terrorist cases under the Prevention of Terrorism Act (POTA) and the Unlawful Activities (Prevention) Act (UAPA).[2893] According to prominent NGOs, the mail of many NGOs in Delhi and in strife-torn areas continues to be subjected to interception and censorship, despite the Supreme Court prohibition of unauthorized taps.[2894] In recent years, the Government Enforcement Directorate, which investigates foreign exchange and currency violations, searched, interrogated, and arrested thousands of business and management professionals, often without search warrants.[2895]

In May of 2000, the government passed the Information Technology Act, a set of laws intended to provide a comprehensive regulatory environment for electronic commerce.[2896] The Act also addresses computer crime, hacking, damage to computer source code, breach of confidentiality and viewing of pornography. A variety of tools are provided to authorities to investigate cyber-crime. Section 69 allows for interception of any information transmitted through a computer resource and requires that users disclose encryption keys or face a jail sentence of up to seven years. The section also gives tremendous powers to the Controller of Certifying Authorities (CCA) to direct interception of any information transmitted through any computer resource. This direction is only to be given if the CCA is satisfied that it is necessary or expedient so to do in the interests of the following: the sovereignty or integrity of India, the security of the state, friendly relations with foreign states, public order, or for preventing incitement to the commission of any cognizable offence.[2897] Section 44 imposes stiff penalties on anyone who fails to provide requested information to authorities. Section 80 allows deputy superintendents of police to conduct searches and seize suspects in public spaces without a warrant. This section in particular appears to be targeted at users of cybercafés, where an estimated 75 percent of Indian Internet users access the Web.[2898]

Covenant on Civil and Political Rights, July 1997, available at
<http://www.hri.ca/partners/sahrdc/alternate/fulltext.shtml>.

[2893] Bureau of Democracy, Human Rights, and Labor, *supra* at Section 1f.

[2894] South Asia Human Rights Documentation Centre, *supra.*

[2895] Bureau of Democracy, Human Rights, and Labor, *supra* at Section 1f.

[2896] Information Technology Act 2000, No. 21 of 2000. available at
<http://www.mit.gov.in/itbillonline/it_framef.asp>.

[2897] *Id.*

[2898] Siddharth Varadarjan Sarai Reader 2001: The Public Domain, "Policing the Net - The Dangers of India's New IT Act" <http://www.sarai.net/journal/pdf/133-135%20(bill).pdf>.

After widespread public outcry, sections requiring cybercafés to create detailed records about their customers' browsing habits were dropped; however, many sections of the Act place strict regulations on the use of computers and the Internet. The Act provides for censoring information on the Internet on public morality grounds and imposes strict penalties for involvement in the electronic publishing of materials deemed obscene by the government.[2899] The Act considers "unauthorized access to certain types of electronic information" a crime.[2900]

Chapter III of the IT Act gives electronic records and digital signatures legal recognition. Chapter VI authorizes the Government to appoint a CCA, who will license certifying authorities before they can operate in India and will act as the repository of all digital signature certificates issued under the Act.

Following the enactment of the IT Act, the Ministry of Information Technology adopted the Information Technology (Certifying Authorities) Rules in October 2000 to regulate the application of digital signatures and to provide guidelines for Certifying Authorities.[2901] The digital signature regime in India became operational in February 2002. The CCA has also appointed numerous licensed Certifying Authorities including Safe Script, National Informatics Centre, the Institute of Development and Research in Banking Technology, and Tata Consultancy Services.

In March 2000, the Central Bureau of Investigation set up the Cyber Crime Investigation Cell (CCIC) to investigate offences under the IT Act and other high-tech crimes.[2902] The CCIC has jurisdiction over all of India and is a member of the Interpol Working Party on Information Technology Crime for South East Asia and Australia. Similar cells have been set up at the state and city level, for example in the state of Karnataka and the city of Mumbai. The National Police Academy in Hyderabad has prepared a handbook on procedures to handle digital evidence in the case of computer and Internet-related crimes.[2903] The government is also considering establishing an Electronic Research and Development Centre of India to develop new cyber-forensic tools. India's Intelligence Bureau is

---

[2899] *Id.*

[2900] Bureau of Democracy, Human Rights, and Labor, "India," Country Reports on Human Rights Practices, Section 2a (2004) available at <http://www.state.gov/g/drl/rls/hrrpt/2004/41740.htm>.

[2901] Information Technology (Certifying Authorities) Rules 2000. <http://www.mit.gov.in/rules/rulesfinal.htm>.

[2902] *See* Cyber Crime Investigation Cell homepage, <http://cbi.nic.in/cyber1.htm>.

[2903] Sardar Vallabhbhai Patel National Police Academy, "Inauguration of Police Training Network," <http://www.svpnpa.gov.in/milestone.asp>.

reported to have developed an e-mail interception tool similar to the Federal Bureau of Investigation's Carnivore system, which it claims to use in anti-terrorist investigations.[2904] In April 2002, India and the United States launched a cyber-security forum to collaborate on responding to cyber-security threats.[2905]

There is currently no law governing the use of hidden cameras in India. Digital cameras and other mobile devices are categorized as "computers" in the IT Act of 2000, but there are no specific provisions impacting the use of digital cameras and no provisions governing privacy in the Act.[2906] In 2001, a prominent exposé of government corruption by the web portal Tehelka sparked a growing debate on the appropriate balance between the press and personal privacy. Telehka's investigative journalists covertly filmed high-level officials accepting bribes and army officers groping call girls as part of their exposé on how official corruption operates in India.[2907] While some critics admit that the journalists did shed much-needed light on a murky subject, they argue that there should be some restrictions on the behavior of the press.[2908] India authorizes the use of illegally obtained evidence that would therefore allow journalists to present such evidence in court. Similar questions arose in relation to the transcripts of tapped phone calls released to the press in a match-fixing scandal surrounding the national sport of cricket in April 2000.[2909]

The Government of India initiated steps for enacting a law on convergence in late 2001. The proposed Communications Convergence Bill of 2001 was considered by Parliament's Standing Committee on Information Technology, which gave detailed recommendations at the end of 2002 and forwarded them to the government. No action has been taken in recent years to enact the bill, although government and industry critics have pushed for passage of the bill.[2910] The bill aims to create a "super regulator," the Communications Commission for India, to

---

[2904] Siddaharth Srivastava, "E-mail Users Beware, Big Brother is Watching," Times of India, December 24, 2001, available at <http://www.blythe.org/nytransfer-subs/Covert_Actions/India:_E-mail_users_beware,_Big_Brother_is_watching>; *see also* "India: Interception of E-Mails, Electronic Data," BNA World Data Protection Report, March 2002.

[2905] Media Note. "United States and India Launch New Phase of Cyber Security Cooperation," US Department of State, November 10, 2004, available at <http://www.state.gov/r/pa/prs/ps/2004/38080.htm>.

[2906] Pavan Duggal, "License to Shoot," Yahoo News, India, December 25, 2004, available at <http://in.news.yahoo.com/041224/48/2in9n.html>.

[2907] Mukund Padmanabhan, "Sex, Bribes, and Videotape," The Hindu, September 8, 2001, available at <http://www.hinduonnet.com/thehindu/2001/09/08/stories/05082523.htm>.

[2908] Rajeev Dhavan, "Tehelka: What Next?" The Hindu, September 7, 2001, available at <http://www.hinduonnet.com/thehindu/2001/09/07/stories/05072523.htm>.

[2909] Manoj Joshi, "Phone-Tap Laws May Trip Cronje Case," April 15, 2000.

[2910] Draft bill, available at http://www.tiaonline.org/policy/regional/asia/conbill.pdf;"Get On With Convergence," Economic Times, September 13, 2004; "Plethora of Business Opportunities," Business Line (Hindu), February 7, 2005.

oversee voice and data (including telecom, broadcasting, and Internet) communications.[2911] Chapter XIV of the Bill covers the interception of communications and penalties for unlawful interception. Section 63 has been criticized by business groups for placing a significant burden on service providers to provide the government information about their customers, and allow law enforcement to intercept any communication under a very low standard.[2912]

Anti-Terrorism Measures

In March 2002, the Indian Parliament, in a rare joint session, passed the Prevention Of Terrorism Act (POTA) over the objections of several Opposition parties and in the face of considerable public criticism. The National Human Rights Commission, an independent government entity, criticized the measure, finding that the existing laws were sufficient to combat terrorism.[2913] The law codified the Prevention of Terrorism Ordinance that in turn built on the repealed Terrorists And Disruptive Activities (Prevention) Act (TADA). In September 2004, POTA was repealed following heavy criticism that its provisions were frequently misused against Muslims.[2914] However, many aspects of POTA, including the legal definition of terrorism and specific ordinances dealing with the financing of terrorism, were added onto the Unlawful Activities (Prevention) Act (UAPA).[2915]

POTA gave law enforcement sweeping powers to arrest suspected terrorists, intercept communications, and curtail free expression.[2916] Critics argued that the experience of TADA and POTA showed that the power had often been misused for political ends by authorities and that POTA had done little to curb those excesses. Chapter V of POTA dealt with the interception of electronic communications, which also created an audit mechanism that included some provision for judicial review and parliamentary oversight.

[2911] Communications Convergence Bill of 2001, available at <http://www.tiaonline.org/policy/regional/asia/conbill.pdf>.

[2912] *See* US India Business Council, Comment to GOI on Draft Communications Convergence Bill, available at <http://www.tiaonline.org/policy/submissions/USIBCConvergenceSubmission.pdf>.

[2913] National Human Rights Commission, "Prevention of Terrorism Bill, 2000: NHRC's Opinion," available at <http://nhrc.nic.in/disparchive.asp?fno=456>.

[2914] "India Withdraws Anti-Terror Law," BBC News, September 17, 2004, available at <http://news.bbc.co.uk/2/hi/south_asia/3665098.stm>.

[2915] Bureau of Democracy, Human Rights, and Labor, *supra.*

[2916] Prevention of Terrorism Act of 2002, Act No. 15 of 2002. available at <http://www.satp.org/satporgtp/countries/india/document/actandordinances/POTA.htm>.

In certain high-risk states such as Jammu and Kashmir, search warrants are not required and the government from time to time bans the use of cellular telephones, long distance phones, and cybercafes. India's Enforcement Directorate, which investigates foreign exchange and currency violations, searches, interrogates, and arrests business professionals, often without a warrant.

On December 13, 2001, five heavily armed intruders and gunmen attacked the Indian Parliament. A case was duly registered, investigated and prosecuted under the provisions of POTA, enacted partly in response to this event. The trial court judge convicted the accused persons. On appeal, the New Delhi High Court held that intercepted telephone conversations of the three persons charged under POTA for plotting the attack on the Parliament were not admissible evidence, although the High Court had previously held that telephone conversations could qualify as admissible evidence under the Indian Evidence Act, the Indian Telegraph Act and the Indian Penal Code, and that trial court is allowed to consider the intercepts under these laws while deciding the case. The Central Bureau of Investigation appealed the High Court order and on September 5, 2003, the Supreme Court set the Delhi High Court judgment aside, allowed the appeal and decided that intercepted communications between the accused in the House of Parliament are admissible.

The Maharashtra Control of Organised Crime Act (MCOCA) was promulgated in 1999, reportedly to combat organized crime and terrorism. The Gujarat Control of Organised Crime Bill (GUJCOC), which is similar to MCOCA, was passed in 2004 after sections which gave blanket powers to district collectors and district superintendents of police to intercept and record telephonic and other means of communications were deleted following suggestions that they violated the privacy of citizens.[2917]

MCOCA's repeal has been the main demand of human rights activists. However, police officials feel that its provisions were justified. The Public Prosecutor for Greater Mumbai insists that MCOCA has been "sparingly used" and that there is "little allegation of misuse."[2918] According to another public prosecutor, however, "no judge in his right mind" would grant bail to a person indicted under MCOCA, since the provisions allowing bail practically mandate an indirect acquittal before trial.[2919] Other sources of contention among the legal and human

---

[2917] Ujjwal Kumar Singh, "Repeal of POTA," Economic and Political Weekly, August 14, 2004, available at <http://www.epw.org.in/showArticles.php?root=2004&leaf=08&filename=7548&filetype=html>.

[2918] "Police Officials against Repeal of MCOCA, " The Hindu, June 3, 2004, available at <http://www.hindu.com/2004/06/04/stories/2004060401501200.htm>.

[2919] Neil Pate, "Scraping MCOCA Is not the Solution," Times News Network, June 01, 2004, available at

rights communities are Sections 14 through 17 of MCOCA. These provisions deal with authorizing the interception of wire, electronic and telephonic communications. Nowhere is it specified that permission from a competent authority is required before an individual's privacy is invaded.[2920]

Recent Privacy Case Law

In 2004, the Court re-examined the development of the right of privacy in India when it declared the Indian Stamp Act, as amended in 1986, violated the right of privacy.[2921] The 1986 Andhra Pradesh amendment of the Act allowed investigators to invade the home of suspects who possessed documents "tending" to prove or leading to the discovery of any tax fraud. The Court noted that it had previously followed seminal cases in the US in creating a right to privacy "of the person," and that this Act directly violated that established right of "personal liberty."[2922] Exceptions to the right of privacy were noted, however. As the Supreme Court articulated, "the right is not absolute," and the State can intrude on a person's privacy "if it has reasonable basis or reasonable materials to support [the intrusion]."[2923]

In February 2005, the Supreme Court found that unsolicited calls to mobile phones violated the right to privacy. The Court asked the legislature to take steps to protect cell phone users from unsolicited calls.[2924] The Court also sent notices explaining its decision to telecom operators and several multinational banks believed to be active in telemarketing of loans and credit cards through cell phone messaging.[2925]

Known as the world's largest democracy, voting in India[2926] is open to those 18 years or older, but is not mandatory. In May 2004, more than 670 million registered voters, voting at nearly 800,000 polling locations during several phases spanning weeks, completed their first all-direct recording electronic (DRE) -

---

<http://timesofindia.indiatimes.com/articleshow/713365.cms>.

[2920] Neil Pate, *supra*.

[2921] Dist. Registrar & Collector, Hyderabad & Anr. Vs Canara Bank, Appeal (civil) 6350-6374 of 1997 (2004).

[2922] *Id.* citing Govind v. State of MP, (1975) 2 SCC 148; Griswold v. Connecticut 381 US 479 (1965).

[2923] *Id.*

[2924] Vir Sign, "India Moves to Silence Cell Spam," USA Today, April 13, 2005, available at <http://www.usatoday.com/tech/world/2005-04-13-csm-india-spam_x.htm?csp=34>.

[2925] "India Seeks Curbs on Mobile Spam," BBC News, February 8, 2005, available at <http://news.bbc.co.uk/1/hi/business/4245397.stm>.

[2928] Constitution of Ireland, available at <http://www.taoiseach.gov.ie/upload/publications/297.htm>.

voting-technology election. There are 11 completely different scripts, alphabet systems, used throughout the Nation of India and the government recognizes 18 official languages. The Indian Census has identified more than 200 different dialects, which had to be accommodated by the voting system. The technology afforded more privacy for language minorities throughout the country. This achievement did not come without complications; more than 40 deaths occurred as a result of election violence. There were also reports of hired partisans taking control of some polling locations and employing the skills of computer science and engineering graduates to manipulate the technology at those sites. The problems identified with this election period were greatly minimized by the efforts of civil society groups who, with the assistance of government officials, were successful in getting public candidates to file disclosure affidavits, correcting voter registration lists, educating voters, and better enforcing election ethics laws.[2927]

Republic of Ireland

Constitutional Privacy Framework

Although there is no express reference to a right to privacy in the Irish Constitution, the Supreme Court has ruled an individual may invoke the personal rights provision in Article 40.3.1 to establish an implied right to privacy.[2928] This article provides, "The State guarantees in its laws to respect, and, as far as practicable, by its laws to defend and vindicate the personal rights of the citizens." It was first used to establish an implied constitutional right in the case of *McGee v. Attorney General*,[2929] which recognized the right to marital privacy. This case has been followed by others such as *Norris v. Attorney General*[2930] and *Kennedy and Arnold v. Ireland.*[2931] In the latter case, the Supreme Court ruled that the illegal wiretapping of two journalists was a violation of the constitution, stating:

> The right to privacy is one of the fundamental personal rights of the citizen which flow from the Christian and democratic nature of the State . . . . The nature of the right to privacy is such that it must ensure the dignity and freedom of the individual in a democratic society. This can

---

[2929] 1974 I.R. 284.
[2930] 1984 I.R. 36.
[2931] 1987 I.R. 587.

not be insured if his private communications, whether written or telephonic, are deliberately and unjustifiably interfered with.[2932]

Data Protection Framework

In 1988, the Data Protection Act was passed to implement the 1981 Council of Europe (CoE) Convention for the Protection of Individuals with Regard to Automatic Processing of Personal Data. The Act regulates the collection, processing, keeping, use and disclosure of personal information processed by both the private and public sectors. However, before its amendment, the Act applied only to information automatically processed. Individuals have a right to access and correct inaccurate information. Information can only be used for specified and lawful purposes and cannot be improperly used or disclosed. Additional protections can be ordered for sensitive data. Criminal penalties can be imposed for violations. There are broad exemptions for national security, tax, and criminal purposes. Misuse of data is also criminalized by the Criminal Damage Act 1991.

As a member of the European Union, Ireland should have amended this Act and extended its scope to implement the European Data Protection Directive by October 1, 1998. In January 2000, the European Commission initiated a case before the European Court of Justice against Ireland and four other countries for failure to implement the Directive on time.[2933] In December 2001, certain provisions of the Directive were implemented by the European Communities (Data Protection) Regulations, 2001. The regulations took effect in April 2002 and governed the transfer of personal information to third countries (*i.e.* non-European Economic Area countries). The Data Protection (Amendment) Act (the Act) was finally enacted in July 2003, repealing the regulations and purporting to give effect to the EU Data Protection Directive.

The Act amends the existing law in several ways. The definition of "data" is extended to manual as well as automated files, although this extension will not be fully effective until October 2007. The Act also broadens the definition of "processing" to performing "any" operation on the data.[2934] The rights of individuals in the areas of notice, access and consent are also improved. Section

---

[2932] Constitution of Ireland, *supra.*

[2933] European Commission, Press Release, "Data Protection: Commission Takes Five Member States to Court," January 11, 2000, available at <http://europa.eu.int/comm/internal_market/en/media/dataprot/news/2k-10.htm>.

[2934] Section 2(a)(v).

6B, as inserted by the 2003 Act, introduces a right in relation to automated decision making. It provides that decisions that significantly affect a data subject (such as work performance, creditworthiness, reliability or conduct) may not, in the absence of consent, be taken automatically without human input.

The Act also clarifies, and in many cases increases, the responsibilities of data controllers. It provides additional protection for "sensitive" data, defined as information relating to racial or ethnic origin, political opinions, religious or philosophical belief, trade union membership, physical or mental health, sexual life, the commission or alleged commission of an offence and any proceedings arising therefrom.[2935] Except in extreme circumstances, data controllers must get explicit consent before processing sensitive data, and must provide additional safeguards.[2936]

The Data Protection (Amendment) Act also provides for a number of measures concerning those involved in direct marketing. Under previous data protection legislation, information garnered from sources required by law to be publicly available (such as the electoral register) was exempt. Under the 2003 Act, an individual now has the right to object to use of this data for direct marketing purposes, and the controller must inform the individual of this right. In addition, the Electoral Amendment Act 2001 makes provision for the establishment of an edited electoral register similar to a system already deployed in the United Kingdom. Local authorities must now prepare two versions of the electoral register, a full one that can only be used for electoral and statutory purposes, and an edited version that will contain the names and addresses of those who have indicated their willingness to be contracted by commercial entities.[2937] It is an offence to ignore the edited register.[2938]

Data Protection Authority

Unless specifically exempted under regulations issued by the Data Protection Commissioner (DPC), all data controllers are required to be registered. The Act increases the powers of the DPC and a provision is made for "prior checking" of applications for registration that may potentially cause substantial harm to data subjects. The DPC may also carry out investigations he or she considers

---

[2935] Section 2(a)(i).
[2936] Section 2B as inserted by the 2003 Act.
[2937] Section 4.
[2938] Section 10.

appropriate to ensure compliance and to issue Codes of Practice. Finally, the new Act creates specific exemptions for "journalistic, artistic, or literary" processing.

The office of the DPC oversees the enforcement of data protection laws. The Office of the DPC consists of 21 staff members.[2939] The Commissioner has powers to investigate complaints, prosecute offenders, sponsor or publish codes of practice, and supervise the registration process.[2940] Under Section 10 of the Data Protection Acts, 1988 and 2003, the Commissioner must investigate any complaints that he receives from individuals who feel that personal information about them is not being treated in accordance with the Act, unless he is of the opinion that such complaints are "frivolous or vexatious." The Commissioner notifies the complainant in writing of his decision regarding the complaint. The Commissioner's decision can be appealed to the Circuit Court.[2941]

In 2004, the Commissioner received 385 complaints, of which 131 were in relation to alleged contravention of the Privacy in Electronic Communications Regulations (S.I. No.535 of 2003) by unsolicited direct marketing chiefly on mobile phones.[2942]\This is an increase over 2003 with 258 complaints; 2002, with 189 complaints and 2001 with 233 complaints.[2943] The majority of complaints in 2003 concerned access rights (28 percent), direct marketing (29 percent) and disclosure (19 percent).

Each year the Data Protection Commissioner publishes a number of case studies from issues that had to be dealt with during the year. Some of the 2004 case studies concerned:

> *Legal privilege and access to medical data.(1/04)*
> An employee on sick leave was requested to attend a doctor nominated by the employer. His employment was terminated subsequently, and he brought proceedings against the company. On making a request for the medical report, he was denied on the basis that the report was privileged by virtue of Section 5(1)g. The issues was resolved by reference to the

---

[2939] E-mail from Aileen Harrington, Data Protection Commissioner's office, to Ula Galster, International Policy Fellow, Electronic Privacy Information Center, June 10, 2005 (on file with EPIC).

[2940] *See generally* Data Protection Commissioner <http://www.dataprivacy.ie>.

[2941] E-mail from Aileen Harrington, *supra*; for more information on the DPC investigation procedures and tools of empowerment, *see*
<http://193.178.2.158/ViewDoc.asp?fn=/documents/legal/4c.htm&CatID=22&m=e>; *see also*,
<http://193.178.2.158/viewdoc.asp?m=m&fn=/documents/guidance/3gm11.htm>.

[2942] Office of the Data Protection Commissioner, Annual Report 2004, p. 11, available at
<http://www.dataprivacy.ie/documents/annualreports/annual_report_2004.pdf>.

[2943] *Id* at 13.

purpose for which the employee was requested to attend the doctor: there was no reference to his attendance being required in relation to any potential legal proceedings. The DPC was conscious of privilege being used unjustifiably as a veil to restrict access.

Credit checks and affordable housing.(6/04)
A local authority required applicants for affordable housing to request details of their financial standing from the Irish Credit Bureau (Credit referencing agency). Guidelines had already been published to the effect that data stored on a credit referencing database should be used only for bona fide credit referencing purposes, and not for local authorities to assess the financial standing of applicants. By requiring the applicants request the information, the local authority was circumventing the requirement that only members of the Irish Credit Bureau could use the service. The DPC also approved of the principle of practical obscurity whereby some personal information that must be made available to the public should not be put online.

Procedures for ensuring barring orders are respected.(7/04)
A wife changed telephone account details from the name of her husband, who was subject to a barring order, to her own name. However he succeeded in having voicemail codes changed so he could access her voicemail, and on closing the account the final statement was sent to his address. Eircom, the communications company did not know how the matter arose, but said the husband had perhaps "spun a plausible story." The company reviewed its procedures in light of the complaint.

Other case studies concerned: an employer contacting the referees even though consent to do so was expressly withheld until a later stage, the use of a political party database by a charity to solicit donations, and inadvertent disclosure of data by a Health Board.

The number of data controllers registered rose to 4,618 during 2003, and by a further 19% in 2004. In January 2001, the DPC issued regulations[2944] requiring all telecommunications companies and Internet service providers (ISPs) to register with his office.[2945] This was the first time the Commissioner had

---

[2944] The Data Protection (Registration) Regulations 2001.

[2945] Office of the Data Protection Commissioner, "Data Protection Commissioner Requires Telecommunications Industry and Internet Service Providers to Register," News Release, (January 9, 2001), available at <http://www.dataprivacy.ie/7nr0101.htm>.

exercised his power to create additional categories of operators required to register.

In addition to investigations and regulations, the Commissioner has issued public criticism of poor data practices. Most notably, in November 2001 the Commissioner began an investigation into Irish mobile phone operators Eircell and Digifone when it was revealed that they were holding customer "locator records" for more than six years, stating that they believed they were required to do so under the law.[2946] Also in 2001, the Commissioner criticized members of the legal profession for their low level of compliance with the registration requirement,[2947] and ultimately two legal firms were prosecuted in February 2004 for their failure to register.

Whereas under the 1988 Act the Commissioner only had the power to approve codes drawn up by trade associations, the 2003 Act gives the Commissioner the power to propose and prepare codes, which, if approved by the *Oireachtas* (Parliament), will have binding legal effect. The preparation of codes of practice for the employment area, An Garda Síochána (Police), and the Funds, banking, insurance and financial services sectors is ongoing.

In May 2002, the European Communities (Data Protection and Privacy in Telecommunications) Regulations were signed into law.[2948] These regulations give effect to EU Directive 1997/66, which concerns data protection in the telecommunications sector. This directive was, however, replaced within five years by Directive 2002/58, which applies the principles of the general data protection Directive, 1995/46, to the communications sector.[2949] The new directive was transposed into Irish law by the European Communities (Electronic Communications Networks and Services) (Data Protection and Privacy) Regulations 2003.[2950]

The regulations strengthen the rules concerning direct marketing. In particular, unsolicited communications to individuals by means of fax, SMS, or automated

---

[2946] Karlin Lillington, "Irish Know Where You've Been," Wired News (November 9, 2001), at <http://www.wired.com/news/privacy/0,1848,48251,00.html>.

[2947] Office of the Data Protection Commissioner, Annual Report 2001, available at <http://www.dataprivacy.ie/images/annual_report_2001.pdf>.

[2948] Statutory Instrument No. 192 of 2002.

[2949] Directive 2002/58/EC, "Directive on Privacy and Electronic Communications," (July 12, 2002), available at <http://europa.eu.int/eur-lex/pri/en/oj/dat/2002/l_201/l_20120020731en00370047.pdf>.

[2950] Statutory Instrument No. 535 of 2003, available at <http://www.dataprivacy.ie/documents/legal/SI5352003.doc>.

calling are prohibited unless the individual "opts in" to receiving such.[2951] Where the recipient of the call is a company, they must state they do not wish to receive the communications.[2952]

In the case of unsolicited telephone calls made by human operators, persons may not be contacted if they have opted out, or if they have registered that they do not wish to receive such calls on the National Directory Database (NDD).[2953] The regulations provide for an amended version of the NDD,[2954] which lists those unwilling to receive unsolicited telephone calls.

On July 21, 2005, more than 12 months later than originally planned, the NDD became fully operational. The three mobile telephone operators in Ireland chose to opt-out all their customers. The Privacy in Electronic Communications Regulations accounted for 131 complaints received by the DPC in 2004. Billy Hawkes replaced Joe Meade as Data Protection Commissioner in July 2005.

Wiretapping and Surveillance Rules

Wiretapping and electronic surveillance are regulated under the Interception of Postal Packets and Telecommunications Messages (Regulation) Act.[2955] The Act followed a 1987 decision of the Supreme Court ruling that wiretaps of journalists violated the constitution (see above). In October 2001, the *Taoiseach* (Prime Minister) publicly apologized on behalf of the State to three journalists whose phones were tapped during the 1980s as part of an effort to control leaks from the government. The *Taoiseach* apologized for "the inappropriate invasion of their privacy and interference by the State with their role as journalists."[2956] In its June 1998 Report on "Privacy, Surveillance and the Interception of Communications,"[2957] the Law Reform Commission recommended legislation to make illegal the invasion of a person's privacy through secret filming, taping and eavesdropping, and the publication of information received from such surveillance.

[2951] Regulation 13 (1).

[2952] Regulation 13 (2).

[2953] Regulation 14.

[2954] The central phone directory that lists subscribers from all the telecommunications companies in Ireland.

[2955] Interception of Postal Packets and Telecommunications Messages (Regulation) Act, June 6, 1993, available at <http://www.irishstatutebook.ie/1993_10.html>.

[2956] "Apology for Phone Tapping," The Irish Times, October 26, 2001.

[2957] 1998 Report on "Privacy, Surveillance and the Interception of Communications (LRC 57 -1998), available at <http://www.lawreform.ie/publications/data/lrc99/lrc_99.html> .

The issue of traffic or communications data retention has been a controversial data protection issue in Ireland since 2002. In November 2001, an investigation by the DPC showed Irish mobile phone operators were holding customer "locator records" for more than six years. In 2002, the government introduced a requirement for telecommuications service providers to retain customers' communications data, using secondary legislation that received minimal parliamentary consideration. In January 2003, the DPC, which itself operates under the auspices of the Department of Justice, Equality and Law Reform, initiated proceedings for judicial review on the basis that the government was "using an 'invalid' Ministerial Direction to unconstitutionally store citizens' phone, fax and mobile phone data."[2958]

Due to the lack of progress in regularizing the legislative framework, the DPC issued enforcement notices in January 2005 requiring that, by May 2005, the telecoms companies hold data for a maximum of 12 months. Due to a last-minute amendment, the Criminal Justice (Terrorist Offences) Act 2005 introduced a three-year period of data retention. It is unfortunate that in the course of debate the Minister for Justice, Michael McDowell stated: "The Bill is largely to do with the introduction of provisions into Irish law to extend our law in an adequate way to deal with international terrorism, as is required by various international instruments to which we are party." No international instruments as yet require data retention for a period of 36 months, and proposals put forward for such during the Irish Presidency of the EU were rejected. It is also unfortunate that given the length of time the government had to publish legislation on the issue, and despite repeated promises of dedicated legislation, they chose to insert the provisions as a last-minute amendment into a largely unrelated bill.[2959]

Anti-terrorism Measures

The Criminal Justice (Terrorist Offences) Act 2005 largely has its origins in the European Union Framework Decision on Combating Terrorism. As a result they share an overly broad and vague definition of "terrorist activity."[2960] The most controversial aspect of the new Act was the data retention measures.

[2958] Karlin Lillington, "Court Threat for State over Privacy," Irish Times, May 26, 2003, available at <http://www.statewatch.org/news/2003/may/17ireland.htm>.

[2959] Karlin Lillington, "McDowell's Sneaky Data Law Heralds Surveillance State," Irish Times, March 25, 2005.

[2960] Section 4.

The Offences Against the State Act 1939 is the primary piece of anti-terrorist legislation in Ireland. Part 2 of the Act defines certain offences that are considered to be offences against the state. Part 3 introduced the concept of an illegal organization, a provision which has seen much use though the years in securing the conviction of members of the provisional IRA and other organizations involved in the conflict in Northern Ireland.

Section 52 of the Offences Against the State Act 1939 has also been subjected to addition judicial scrutiny in recent years. Section 52 provides that a person suspected of an offence under the Offences Against the State Act must account for his movements or actions during any specified period and divulge all information relating to the commission or intended commission of an offence. Although the section was found to be constitutional in *Heaney v. Ireland*,[2961] the European Court of Human Rights found the men, who received six-month sentences for failing to account for their movements, had been denied the right to a fair trial (Section 6.1 of the Convention) and the presumption of innocence (Section 6.2 of the Convention). In *Quinn v. O'Leary & Ors*,[2962] a case with similar facts, it was held by a judge that the plaintiff was entitled to have his conviction set aside on the basis of the European Convention of Human Rights, although the government was not obliged to repeal the offending legislation. The issue has not been yet been considered in light of the implementation of the European Convention on Human Rights Act 2003.

Recent Development Related to Privacy

On June 1st, 2004, the Department of Communications, Marine and Natural Resources announced it was to create a mandatory register for 3G mobile phones, the aim of which would be to protect children. The register was originally to be in place before the service was rolled out, however following lobbying by the mobile phone industry this proposal has been shelved. It is reported that the government is instead considering the mobile phone industry's alternative proposals which are likely to involve some form of content filtering.[2963]

In 1998, the *Oireachtas* passed the Social Welfare Act, which creates a unique personal identification number for use in dealing with public agencies. The Personal Public Service Number (PPSN) replaced the "Revenue and Social Insurance" (RSI) number that, for years, was used only for social welfare and tax

---

[2961] [1996] 1 IR 580.

[2962] High Court, April 23, 2004, available at <http://www.bailii.org/ie/cases/IEHC/2004/103.html>.

[2963] Jamie Smyth, "Government U-turn on National 3G Register," Irish Times, October 20, 2004.

purposes. Its operation has been strengthened and expanded in a piecemeal manner by Acts in 1999, 2000, 2002, 2003, and 2004. The PPSN is used as a unique personal identifier in communications between the individual and specified state agencies, such as government departments, hospitals, local authorities, and educational institutions. Employers may also use the PPSN for interaction with state bodies (most notably the Revenue Commissioners), while some state agencies have used the PPSN as a unique identification number for their own employees.[2964] Most recently, tenants have been obliged to divulge their PPSN to landlords for the purposes of registering with the Private Residential Tenancies Board.[2965]

The Act allows for the exchange of personal data between prescribed bodies in certain circumstances, and its provisions in this respect are expressly exempt from the Data Protection Act. The Register of users of the PPSN maintained by the Department of Social and Family Affairs (DSFA) bears testament to the zeal with which various state agencies have engaged in data matching and exchange exercises.[2966] It is an offence for anyone other than a state agency (or person or body acting on their behalf) to attempt to obtain an individual's PPSN. However, the wide-scale use of the PPSN suggests that identity theft may become an issue. The DPC criticized this scheme while it was debated, stating that "the proposed sharing of personal data, obtained and kept by legally separate entities, for such diverse purposes is fundamentally incompatible with . . . the basic tenets of data protection law."[2967] In February 2004, the DSFA issued a code of Practice on the use of the PPSN,[2968] which recognizes its potency and its status as personal data under the Data Protection Acts, but does not attempt to unduly constrain its use. The *Gardaí* and armed forces, at present, are prohibited from collecting and using the PPSN for matters other than those related to their own members. The Immigration Act of 2003, however, gives power to the *Gardaí* to use the PPSN in relation to non-EU nationals.[2969]

The development of the PPSN is part of a much larger project to modernize public services and develop a fully functioning e-Government. In 1999, an

---

[2964] The Department of Education uses the PPSN as the main identifier on primary and post-primary teacher payrolls, while Cork County Council intends to use it for similar purposes.

[2965] <http://www.oasis.gov.ie/housing/renting_a_flat_or_house/private_residential_tenancies_board.html>.

[2966] Register of users of the PPS Number, available at <http://welfare.ie/topics/ppsn/rou.html>.

[2967] Irish Data Protection Commissioner, Annual Report, at 35 (1996); *see also* "Remarks by the Data Protection Commissioner on the Bill to the Dail Select Committee on Social, Community and Family Affairs" (March 4, 1998).

[2968] Personal Public Service Number Code of Practice, available at <http://welfare.ie/topics/ppsn/cop.html>.

[2969] Immigration Act 2003, available at <http://www.ucc.ie/law/irlii/statutes/2003-26.php>.

independent government agency, known as Reach, was established by government order to oversee this project, and progress since that date has been steady. Reach is charged with implementing a central Public Service Broker, which will be developed by BearingPoint Inc. The PSB will comprise three main elements: a) a user interface that will serve as a single point of access to public services, b) an XML-based framework that will allow data be shared asynchronously between public services, and c) a service fulfillment layer that will provide government agencies with a standard set of tools to deliver services electronically. Personal data about citizens will be held in secure vaults and be released to the public agencies in the course of particular transactions.[2970] Concern has been raised, however, about whether there are sufficient safeguards with the large number of agencies that will be able to access the "Inter Agency Messaging System" (IAMS). The currently IAMS is used to transfer life event information between the General Registrar's Office and the DSFA, and a more advanced version is used by the Department of Agriculture and Revenue Commissioners.[2971]

Every individual with a PPS Number is listed in the Central Records System (CRS). The CRS comprises of 5.5 million entries, and a further 500,000 dormant entries relating to people who no longer have reason to use their PPSN, either due to a failed asylum application or emigration.

Full access to the CRS is available to all employees of the Client Identity Services in the Department of Social and Family Affairs, while other departments may get limited access on the basis of making a "business case" to the Client Identity Services Section. The database is populated electronically by the General Registers Office.

Although at present the system does not incorporate an ID card per se, a Public Services Card (PSC) is being developed as an individual's key to access his or her personal data and the connected public services, using the PPSN as a unique identifier. In June 2004, the Minister for Social and Family Affairs, Mary Coughlan, announced the establishment of an expert group to report on a standardized framework to replace five separate state-issued cards with a single PSC. The terms of reference for this group include the investigation of whether such a card may "be used by the cardholder as a proof of age card and wider use

---

[2970] European Commission's IDA (Interchange of Data between Administrations) on Reach, "Building an E-government Services Broker in Ireland," available at <http://europa.eu.int/ISPO/ida/jsps/index.jsp?fuseAction=showDocument&parent=whatsnew&documentID=2668>.

[2971] For more information, see the Reach Services website at <www.reach,ie>.

by the cardholder as a secure token of identity generally."[2972] The working party has not yet reported, but they are expected to suggest the introduction of the Public Services Card.

Michael McDowell, the Minister for Justice has also stated that UK ID card developments may necessitate an Irish ID card, due to the common travel area between the two countries.[2973] However, he is not personally in favor of such a scheme and "the onus is on people who argue for it rather than against it."[2974]

The Irish government has chosen to comply with the US requirement of a biometric passport for visa waiver countries by providing a "secure printed digital photograph" without encoding any information electronically on the card. It is the only European government to take this minimalist approach.[2975]

In 2003, the DPC expressed concern that while "[a] Public Awareness Survey . . . revealed that people regarded protection of personal privacy as being very important," many people "[were] not fully aware of [their privacy rights]."[2976] The study, which surveyed 1,200 Irish people, found that "people's anxieties about intrusions into their privacy have increased [since a similar study in 1997]."[2977] However, public debate on privacy or e-government matters is virtually non-existent.

Ireland is recognized as having modern copyright and electronic signature laws, and while it was once regarded as being superior in this respect to much of the EU, this is a gap which has considerably narrowed in recent years.[2978] In July

---

[2972] Mary Couglan Minister for Social and Family Affairs, press release, "Simple Access to Public Services from the State on the Cards," June 29, 2004, available at
<http://www.reach.ie/publications/downloads/NewPublicServicesCard.doc>.

[2973] Although a London School of Economics report disputes the necessity of such, "An Assessment of the UK Identity Cards Bill and its Implications," London School of Economics, March 2005, page 29, available at
<http://www.lse.ac.uk/collections/pressAndInformationOffice/newsAndEvents/archives/2005/IDReport.htm>.
[2974] Carl O'Brien, "McDowell says ID cards may be introduced," Irish Times, January 17, 2005.

[2975] "US Lawmakers Question the Need for Microchips in European Passports," IDABC e-Government News, 26 April 2005, available at <http://europa.eu.int/idabc/en/document/4220/194>; however, it should be noted that the new type passport announced on December 10, 2004, will have a polycarbonate page capable of holding a chip of some description if one is introduced, *see*
<http://foreignaffairs.gov.ie/information/display.asp?ID=1660>.

[2976] Office of the Data Protection Commissioner, "People Are not Fully Aware of Their Privacy Rights says Data Protection Commissioner," Media Release, April 30, 2003.

[2977] Office of the Data Protection Commissioner, "Privacy Fears on the Increase, Warns Data Protection Commissioner," Media Release, January 13, 2003, available at
<http://www.dataprivacy.ie/docs/Press_Release_-_Privacy_Fears_on_the_Increase,_warns_Data_Pr/225.htm>.
[2978] A recent Accenture Report ranked Ireland in 11th place for the second year a row, available at
<http://www.accenture.com/xdoc/ir/locations/ireland/insights/egovernment.pdf>.

2000, the E-Commerce Act was implemented, granting legal recognition to e-signatures, e-writings and e-contracts. However, adoption of such in the public sector has been disappointing.[2979] It is hoped that the Public Services Broker going live in May 2005 will help in the provision of services electronically.[2980]

The Copyright and Related Rights Act, which permits surprise searches and enacts stiff penalties against software theft, came into force in November 2000. Ireland's implementation of the European Union E-Commerce Directive (2000/31/EC) makes it one of the only European countries to place the burden of opting out of "spam" on the consumer.[2981] However, this must be considered something of an anomaly in light of the recent implementation of the Directive on Privacy and Electronic Communications.

The issue of employee monitoring is also causing growing concern in Ireland. In 2000, the Manufacturing, Science and Finance Union (MSF) called for national and European Union legislation to limit the use of electronic surveillance in the workplace.[2982] In March 2002, Amarach Consulting released a survey finding that one in four employees say that their use of the Internet in the workplace is monitored or restricted.[2983]

Voting is available to those 18 years or older, but is not obligatory.[2984] In February 2002, the government allowed the use of electronic voting to be tested in public elections. An Interim Report of the Commission on Electronic Voting, dated April 29, 2004, rejected the use of direct recording electronic (DRE) voting machines in the upcoming elections.[2985] The report states that "publication of ballot results in full . . . can in theory . . . allow voters to identify themselves in a context of corruption or intimidation,"[2986] which could undermine the integrity of an election. This e-voting technology report led to the decision to abandon electronic voting in Ireland for the June 2004 EU elections.[2987]

[2979] *See also*, M. McDonagh and F. White, Electronic Signatures; the Legal Framework and the Market Reality in Ireland, Commercial Law Practitioner, (2003) 10 C.L.P.228-236 September 2003.

[2980] Ciaran Buckely, "E-government for everyone," Electric News Network, April 22, 2005, available at <http://www.enn.ie/frontpage/news-9602543.html>.

[2981] "Republic Puts 'Spam' Burden on the Consumer," The Irish Times (June 29, 2001).

[2982] "Law to Limit Monitoring of Workers Urged," The Irish Times (March 7, 2000).

[2983] Amarach Consulting, "Big Brother Watching Irish Internet Users," Press Release, March 14, 2002, available at <http://www.amarach.com/news/amarachpressrelease_14_03_02.doc>.

[2984] CIA Country Fact Book, January 1, 2004, available at <http://www.cia.gov/cia/publications/factbook/>.

[2985] Interim Report of the [Ireland] Commission on Electronic Voting on the Secrecy, Accuracy and Testing of the Chosen Electronic Voting System. April 29, 2004, available at <http://www.cev.ie/htm/report/V02.pdf>.

[2986] *Id.*

[2987] Mark Hennessy & Mark Brennock, "E-voting Abandoned for Elections in June," Irish Times, May 1, 2004, available at <http://www.ireland.com/newspaper/front/2004/0501/213310571HM1EVOTE.html>.

The Freedom of Information Act (the FOI Act) was approved in 1997 and went into effect in April 1997.[2988] The FOI Act creates a presumption that the public can access documents created by government agencies and requires that government agencies make internal information on their rules and activities available. The Office of the Information Commissioner enforces the Act. On April 11, 2003, the government passed a series of restrictive amendments to the Freedom of Information Act.[2989] The amending legislation was widely criticized by the opposition, press and, indirectly, by the Ombudsman. The amendments resulted in more central control over information and the restriction of all information, instead of just a subset. Specifically, the amendment: doubled the time-restriction on government records, regardless of content; introduced processing fees on information requests under the Act; broadened the definition of "government" under the Act; increased government exemptions to information requests; and granted ministers the ability to suppress information release, without appeal, by another ministry or public body. However, in the same year, the government endorsed Emily O'Reilly as the next Ombudsman and Information Commissioner; she is an outspoken critic of the recent amendments to the FOI Act.[2990] Ms. O'Reilly, a well-respected journalist, is the first replacement commissioner since the office was created.

In a review of the operation of the amending legislation, Ms. O'Reilly found that overall use of the Act had fallen by 50 percent while requests for non-personal information fell by 75 percent. In relation to journalists using FOI Act, there had been an 83 percent drop in requests. The fees structure introduced by the amendment can largely be blamed for this sharp decline. The Information Commissioner has called for a reappraisal of fees, which can amount to EUR 240 when retrieval, internal appeal, and appeal to the Information Commissioner are considered.[2991]

[2988] "Freedom of Information, 1997—Short Guide," Department of Finance, available at
<http://www.finance.gov.ie/viewdoc.asp?DocID=821>.

[2989] Freedom of Information (Amendment) Act (April 11, 2003), available at
<http://www.oic.gov.ie/2546_3c2.htm>.

[2990] Mark Brennock, "Emily O'Reilly to be Appointed as State's Next Ombudsman," Irish Times, March 26, 2003, available at
<http://www.ireland.com/newspaper/front/2003/0326/1270181268HM1OMBUDSMAN.html>.

[2991] Review of the Operation of the Freedom of Information (Amendment) Act 2003, available at
<http://www.oic.gov.ie/261e/Review.pdf>.

International Obligations

Ireland is a member of the Council of Europe (CoE) and has signed and ratified the Convention for the Protection of Individuals with Regard to Automatic Processing of Personal Data (ETS No. 108).[2992] It has also signed and ratified the European Convention for the Protection of Human Rights and Fundamental Freedoms.[2993] However, unlike every other European signatory country, Ireland has not incorporated this Convention into national law. In February 2002, Ireland signed the CoE Convention on Cybercrime.[2994] Ireland is also a member of the Organization for Economic Cooperation and Development (OECD) and has adopted the OECD Guidelines on the Protection of Privacy and Transborder Flows of Personal Data.

State of Israel

Constitutional Privacy Framework

Israel's Constitution operates as a body of "basic laws" that are interpreted by the courts.[2995] In terms of a constitutional right to privacy, Section 7 of the Basic Law on Human Dignity and Freedom (1992) states that: ""(a) All persons have the right to privacy and to intimacy. (b) There shall be no entry into the private premises of a person who has not consented thereto. (c) No search shall be conducted on the private premises or body of a person, nor in the body or belongings of a person. (d) There shall be no violation of the confidentiality of the spoken utterances, writings or records of a person"[2996] According to Supreme Court Justice Mishael Cheshin, this law elevated the right of privacy to the level of a basic right.[2997]

[2992] Signed December 18, 1986; enacted May 25, 1990; entered into force August 1, 1990.

[2993] Signed November 11, 1950; enacted February 25, 1953; entered into force September 3, 1953.

[2994] Signed February 28, 2002.

[2995] The State: The Law of The Land, Israel Ministry of Foreign Affairs, February 1, 2004 <http://www.mfa.gov.il/MFA/Facts%20About%20Israel/State/THE%20STATE-%20The%20Law%20of%20the%20Land>.

[2996] The Basic Law: Human Dignity and Freedom (5752 - 1992), passed by the Knesset on the 21st Adar, 5754, March 9, 1994, available at <http://www.mfa.gov.il/mfa/go.asp?MFAH00hi0>.

[2997] Alon Kaplan & Paul Ogden eds., Israeli Business Law: An Essential Guide (Boston: Kluwer Law International) 1997, at 30.01.

Data Protection Framework

The Protection of Privacy Law regulates the processing of personal information in computer data banks in an effort to protect privacy.[2998] The law sets out 11 categories of prohibited activities and provides for civil and criminal penalties for violating individual privacy.[2999] Evidence acquired through infringement of privacy is inadmissible under the Privacy Law, although courts have the discretion to make exceptions.

The Privacy Law contains broad exemptions for police and security services as well as a wide range of defenses.[3000] For example, actions in good faith or in furtherance of the public interest are statutory defenses. The law also sets up basic privacy regulations relating to surveillance, publication of confidential information, criminal records, and the legal obligations of the government with respect to confidential information. The Privacy Law was last amended in 1996 to broaden the databases covered and increase penalties for violations.[3001]

The Credit Data Service Law of 2002 created a shared center for storing consumers' credit information among different competing creditors and break up the dominance of the two banks that controlled most credit information.[3002] The law gives consumers access to their information, the opportunity to correct information collected (including "positive" records, such as evidence of good credit), and features a procedure for opting out of collection. Some politicians have argued, however, that it unduly invades privacy by automatically sharing credit information and penalizing those who opt out of the database.[3003]

Unauthorized access to computers is punished by the Computer Law of 1995.[3004] Many routine activities prohibited by this law, such as accessing a computer or erasing information, are illegal only when performed without proper

---

[2998] The Protection of Privacy Law 5741-1981 (hereinafter Privacy Law), 1011 Laws of the State of Israel 128, amended by the Protection of Privacy Law (Amendment) 5745-1985.

[2999] Privacy Law, *supra* at Chapter 1, Section 5. It should be noted that, although, until recently, Section 2 of the Privacy Law was usually interpreted by Israeli courts (in view of Section 3 of the Privacy Law) as applying only to individuals (and not to corporations). However, in February 2002, Tel Aviv District Court Judge Yehuda Zaft ruled that Section 2(5) of the Privacy Law may be used to protect the privacy of corporations as well. This issue has not been reviewed yet by the Supreme Court. *See* Civil Case (Tel Aviv) 2324/01 Multilock Ltd. v. Rav Bariach Hashkaot Ltd. and Others.

[3000] Privacy Law, *supra* at Chapter 3, Section 18-19.

[3001] Law of April 11, 1996.

[3002] Credit Data Service Law, 5762-2002.

[3003] "MKs to Duke it out in Credit Data Service Law Battle," Israel Business Arena, July 5, 2001.

[3004] The Computer Law (5755-1995), 1534 Laws of the State of Israel 366, *see* Miguel Deutch, Computer Legislation: Israel's New Codified Approach, 14 J. Marshall J. Computer & Info. L. 461 (Spring 1996).

authorization.[3005] In June 2002, an Israeli teenager was sentenced under this law to 18 months in jail for masterminding a series of high-profile hacks into the computer systems at the Massachusetts Institute of Technology, the National Aeronautics and Space Administration, the Federal Bureau of Investigations, the United States Air Force and the United States Department of Defense.[3006] An appeals court overruled the teenager's original sentence of six months community service after the Israeli government, under pressure from the United States, pushed for a stricter sentence.[3007]

The Postal and Telegraph Censor, which operates as a civil department within the Ministry of Defense, has the power to open any postal letter or package to prevent harm to state security or public order.[3008] The 1996 Patient Rights Law imposes a duty of confidentiality on all medical personnel.[3009] The Genetic Information Law of 2000 protects the rights of individuals with respect to their DNA samples and their genetic information. The Genetic Information Law and existing ethical guidelines cover most issues of informed consent, confidentiality, and rules of access for both identified and non-identified DNA samples or genetic information in the individual or family-based, small-scale collections.[3010] Criminal records are governed by the Criminal Register and Rehabilitation Law, which allows more than 30 government agencies to access the records.[3011]

The obligation to maintain bank secrecy stems from Israel's adoption of English bank laws in 1922, by Section 46 of the British Order-in-Council.[3012] The obligation of bank secrecy is limited to consumers and not to companies.[3013] The obligation includes information regarding clients' accounts, transactions effected through the account and the collateral toward the account.[3014]

[3005] Id.

[3006] Boaz Guttman, "The Analyzer: Following the State's Appeal," May 6, 2002, available at <http://www.4law.co.il/206.pdf>.

[3007] Bob Sullivan, "Analyzer Gets 18-Month Jail Term," MSNBC, June 6, 2002.

[3008] Regulation 89 of the Mandatory Defence (Emergency) Regulations, 1945.

[3009] Patient Rights Law, 5756-1996.

[3010] "Population Based Large-Scale Collections of DNA Samples and Databases of Genetic Information," in Report of the Bioethics Advisory Committee of the Israel Academy of Sciences and Humanities, December 2002, at 2.

[3011] Criminal Register and Rehabilitation Law, 5741-1981.

[3012] Nahum Bitterman, "The Extent of the Obligation of Secrecy," Israeli Business Law: An Essential Guide (Kluwer Law International 1996).

[3013] Id.

[3014] Id.

On September 28, 1995, the Israeli-Palestinian Interim Agreement on the West Bank and the Gaza Strip was signed by the Israeli Government and the Palestine Liberation Organization (PLO). Annex III of the Agreement, the Protocol Concerning Civil Affairs contains Article 33, which provides that Israeli and Palestinian social welfare systems will cooperate to protect the confidentiality and individual privacy in the exchange of personal information.[3015]

Wiretapping and Surveillance Rules

The Secret Monitoring Law of 1979 governs the interception of communications.[3016] The law prohibits individuals from "listening in" on others' conversation by using a device without a permit or the consent of a party to the conversation.

The law was amended in 1995 following a finding by the State Comptroller that police were abusing wiretap procedures. Although the amendments sought to tighten procedures, they also expanded the Secret Monitoring Law to cover new technologies, such as mobile phones and computer communications, including e-mail. In addition, the amendments increased penalties for illegal taps while allowing interception of privileged communications, such as those with a lawyer or doctor.[3017]

The President of the District Court must authorize police to intercept any form of wire or electronic communication, or plant a microphone for a period up to three months, which can be renewed. The Chief Military Censor may also intercept international conversations to or from Israel for purposes of censorship.[3018] Intelligence agencies may wiretap people suspected of endangering national security after receiving written permission from the Prime Minister or Defense Minister. Police and other law enforcement agencies must present an annual report to the *Knesset's* (the Israeli Parliament's) Constitution, Law and Justice Committee detailing such activities. According to the Israeli government, the number of wiretap orders "has averaged roughly 1,000 to 1,100 annually over the last several years. Roughly half of these wiretap permits are given in connection

---

[3015] Israeli-Palestinian Interim Agreement on the West Bank and the Gaza Strip, Annex III: Protocol Concerning Civil Affairs, Article 33, Sept. 28, 1995, available at <http://www.mfa.gov.il/MFA/Peace+Process/Guide+to+the+Peace+Process/THE+ISRAELI-PALESTINIAN+INTERIM+AGREEMENT+-+Annex+III.htm#app-33>.

[3016] The Secret Monitoring Law, 5739-1979, Laws of the State of Israel, vol. 33, at 141-146.

[3017] *Id.*

[3018] Herb Keinon, "Shas Disputes Linking Wiretap to Yishai-Deri Rivalry," The Jerusalem Post, November 27, 1998.

with drug-related offences."[3019] Although courts are supposed to weigh privacy concerns against law enforcement needs before authorizing wiretaps, authorization is, in practice, almost automatic upon request. The 2005 police report said that district courts approved 1,089 police requests for wiretaps and rejected six, an approval rate of 99.5 percent.[3020]

Data Protection Authority

Under the Privacy Law, personal information contained in databases is protected. All holders of data banks containing more than 10,000 names or various confidential information must register with the Registrar of Databases and report their purpose, use, means of data collection, and data security measures implemented.[3021] The law limits the use of information in these databases to the purposes for which they were intended, and database holders must provide access to database subjects. Under the Privacy Law, individuals have a right to access their personal information held in both government and private sector databanks.

The Registrar of Databases within the Ministry of Justice enforces the Privacy Law with regard to databases. The Registrar maintains the register of databases and can deny registration if it is believed that a database is being used for illegal activities. The Registrar also investigates Privacy Law violations.[3022] Pursuant to the Privacy Law, every individual may inspect information about herself in a database and the owner of the database must provide for such inspection in Hebrew, Arabic, or English.[3023] The most recent figures available show that in 1998, 5,200 databases were registered.[3024] A Public Council for the Protection of Privacy has also been set up to advise the Justice Minister on legislative matters related to the Protection of Privacy Law and its subsidiary regulations and orders.

[3019] United Nations Human Rights Committee, Israel CCPR/C/81/Add.13 (Initial State Party Report) April 9, 1998, available at
<http://www.unhchr.ch/tbs/doc.nsf/184758d9fcd7a2b1c12565a9004dc312/ff05b8854986b0398025662f005675 74?opendocument>.

[3020] Ha'aretz Ze'ev Segal, "A Sweeping License to Invade Privacy," Haartez, June 15, 2005, available at
<http://www.Ha'aretzdaily.com/hasen/pages/ShArt.jhtml?itemNo=312763&contrassID=2&subContrassID=4& sbSubContrassID=0&listSrc=Y>.

[3021] Debbie L. Rabina, "Access to Government Information in Israel: Stages in the Continuing Development of a National Information Policy," International Federation of Library Associations and Institutions, August 13, 2000, available at <http://www.ifla.org/IV/ifla66/papers/018-160e.htm>.

[3022] *See* Ministry of Justice, Registrar of Databases at <http://www.mfa.gov.il/mfa/go.asp?MFAH00hx0>.

[3023] Privacy Law, *supra* at Chapter 2, Section 13.

[3024] United Nations Human Rights Committee, Israel CCPR/C/81/Add.13 (Initial State Party Report) April 9, 1998, available at
<http://www.unhchr.ch/tbs/doc.nsf/184758d9fcd7a2b1c12565a9004dc312/ff05b8854986b0398025662f005675 74?opendocument>.

The Council sets guidelines for the protection of computerized databases and guides the work of the Registrar of Databases. The European Commission considers that Israel's data protection laws are likely to offer an adequate level of protection for personal data transferred to Israel from countries in the European Union.[3025] In the last decade, the Registrar's Office has advanced measures to increase database registration.[3026] The Registrar of Databases may appoint inspectors to examine databases and enforce compliance with registration laws. In 2003, it was reported that the Registrar's Office was encountering budgetary difficulties and, as a result, difficulties in efficiently exercising its authority

Anti-terrorism Measures

In March 1998 the Finance Minister granted the Director of the Bureau for Counterterrorism full access to all Israeli taxation authorities' databases. The authorization gave the Bureau access to the financial records of any citizen in Israel, including the status of their bank account "for urgent cases of preventing terrorist acts."[3027]

Israel contracted Electronic Data Systems in 1999 to install a biometrics-based border control system, using hand geometry and facial recognition technology, to monitor the entrance and exit through the Gaza Strip of about 50,000 Palestinians workers.[3028] Israel also installed a biometrics identification system in Tel Aviv's Ben Gurion Airport. Frequent travelers who submit biographic information and biometric hand-geometry data may use automatic inspection kiosks to go through airport security. Travelers use a credit card for initial identification and then scan their palms into the kiosk to verify identity. The machine prints a receipt that allows the traveler to proceed through security. As of 2001, nearly 80,000 Israeli citizens have enrolled in the biometric identification system.[3029]

As part of the disengagement process, the Israeli Defense Ministry announced the creation of a new high-tech border crossing north of the Gaza Strip in January

---

[3025] "Global Data Protection and Security Issues in the Cards Arena," Cards International, September 26, 2001.

[3026] Rabina, *supra*.

[3027] *Id.*

[3028] "Consortium Led by EDS Wins Award to Develop Leading-edge Biometric Border Crossing System for the Israeli Borders," EDS News Releases, Sept. 6, 1999, available at <http://www.oti.co.il/objects/PR_19990906_Bazel-EDS%20et%20al.pdf#search='Consortium%20Led%20by%20EDS%20Wins%20Award%20to%20Develop%20Leadingedge%20Biometric%20Border%20Crossing%20System'>.

[3029] John Mesenbrink, "Biometrics Plays Big Role in Airport Safety," Security, December 1, 2001.

2005. Security guards will monitor individuals video surveillance cameras as they pass through "identification stations" where their identities are verified using existing ID cards and biometrics.[3030]

Major Privacy Case Law

Alonial, et. al v. Ariel McDonald is a case involving copyright between McDonald's and well known basketball player Ariel McDonald. The Supreme Court of Israel affirmed that Israel's Privacy Law protects personal rights and interests, and not economic rights.[3031]

In October 2004, the Jerusalem District Court rejected Yigal Amir's petition to stop the broadcast of a TV movie shown on the ninth anniversary of the assassination of Prime Minister Rabin, for which Amir was convicted.[3032] Amir had argued that film footage showing him in his jail cell dressed in his underwear violated his privacy rights.

In 2002, several public-sector workers from the police and various government departments were convicted of acceptance of bribes, violation of privacy, illegal use of classified databases, and conspiracy for selling information from a classified database on the country's inhabitants.[3033]

In June 2000, the Tel Aviv District Court held that the State could not order an Internet service provider (ISP) to collect subscriber e-mails to provide to the police, finding that the practice was the equivalent of an illegal wiretap. However, the Court determined[3034] that, when balanced against individual privacy rights, police could request e-mails already collected by the ISP from subscribers against whom an indictment is pending, and could use those e-mails upon indictment if a court found the collection to be justifiable – even if it was illegal at the time of seizure.[3035]

[3030] "Hi-Tech Security Crossing to be Built on Gaza Border," January 19, 2005, available at <http://israelnn.com/news.php3?id=75505>.

[3031] Civil Appeal No. 8483/02 March 30, 2004, available at <http://www.israelbar.org.il/english_inner.asp?pgId=20382&catId=246>.

[3032] "District Court Rejects Amir Privacy Appeal," IsraeINN, October 26, 2004 <http://israelnn.com/news.php3?id=71046>.

[3033] "46 Indicted for Selling Confidential Data," The Jerusalem Post, December 5, 2001.

[3034] MC 90868/00 Netvision Ltd. v. Israel Defense Forces & others (unpublished).

[3035] Alon in Ha'aretz, *supra*.

Several people, including Ma'ariv publisher Opher Nimrodi, were convicted in 1998 of ordering wiretaps on business people and media personalities, including a government minister.[3036] In November 1998, wiretaps were discovered on the phone of then-Labor and Social Affairs Minister Eli Yishai. A rival internal political faction was suspected. In 1996, an Israeli Defense Forces employee was prosecuted for misusing the phone records of a journalist.[3037]

Recent Developments

A bill was introduced in February 2004 concerning mobile telecommunications companies. Such companies would be prohibited from providing an employer location details of a cellular phone carried by an employee.[3038]

As of June 2005, three other bills are pending in the *Knesset*. In early 2005, a bill was introduced that would bring universities and public colleges within the ambit of the Freedom of Information (FOI) Law. The bill has not yet passed, although it has been met with some oppositon.[3039] In January 2005, the *Knesset* passed a first reading of a bill that would require Supreme Court approval for placing a wiretap on the telephone of a member of Parliament in order to allow members to perform their duties free from concerns about monitoring or privacy invasions.[3040] It is unclear whether this bill will become law. Also pending is a bill to protect the privacy of the poor.[3041] The bill would prohibit media from taking pictures of people waiting in line to receive food because such attention may deter individuals in need from coming forward to receive assistance.

At the beginning of June 2005 the Knesset approved an amendment to the Criminal Procedure Law. The amendement authorizes Israel Police to collect DNA samples from suspects taken in for questioning and convicts in custody. The justification for the genetic data bank is to allow police to cross-reference DNA profiles from crime scenes with the data banks of criminals and suspects in order to identify serial offenders in crimes against persons, property or

---

[3036] "Media Wiretapper Found Guilty," The Jerusalem Post, September 4, 1998.

[3037] Evelyn Gordon, "IDF Officer Involved in Phone Record Scandal Accuses Others of Involvement," The Jerusalem Post, July 11, 1996.

[3038] *Knesset* Bill No. p/1842.

[3039] Yuval Yoaz, "We are All Still in the Dark," Ha'aretz, June 8, 2005, available at <http://www.Ha'aretz.com/hasen/pages/ShArtVty.jhtml?sw=privacy+law&itemNo=585620>.

[3040] "Eavesdropping Law Passes First Reading," IsraelNN.com, January 18, 2005, available at <http://israelnn.com/news.php3?id=75542>.

[3041] "Bill Introduced to Protect the Privacy of the Poor," IsraelNN.com, April 20 2005, available at <http://israelnn.com/news.php3?id=80564>.

security.[3042] An individual acquitted of charges will have his or her DNA retained in the data bank for seven years. A convicted offender's DNA will be kept for 20 years. The police have set a target of genetically mapping 20,000 samples annually.[3043]

NGO Advocacy WorkIn May 2004, the Supreme Court accepted a petition submitted by the Association for Civil Rights in Israel (ACRI) in 1998. In its petition, ACRI challenged the right of hundreds of clerks in various government authorities and commercial banks to have access to the Israeli Population Registry.[3044] Also, in May 2004, an internationally funded NGO, Peace Now, was under investigation for possible breaches of the espionage provisions of the Israeli Penal code for allegedly photographing and conducting surveillance of Israeli settlement areas and security breaches where Israeli civilians were later killed in attacks.[3045]

In late May 2005, the year-old Israeli branch of the Movement for Freedom of Information, petitioned an administrative court in Tel Aviv to order the Israeli Defence Forces (IDF) to reveal the "formula" by which the IDF's psychotechnical diagnosticians rank new recruits, thus determining their military service path, *i.e.*, whether she or he will become an officer, serve in the Ordinance Corps, become a pilot or be assigned non-combative roles.[3046] Israeli NGOs, particularly environmental groups, have been turning to courts to obtain information when access requests have been denied by government offices.[3047]

[3042] Ze'ev Segal, "A Sweeping License to Invade Privacy," Ha'aretz June 15, 2005, available at http://www.Ha'aretzdaily.com/hasen/pages/ShArtVty.jhtml?sw=privacy+law&itemNo=587768>; "Police Permitted to Take Blood from Suspects," IsraelINN.com, June 2, 2005, available at <http://israelnn.com/news.php3?id=83152>.

[3043] Jonathan Lis, "Police to start DNA Bank of Suspects, Convicts," Ha'aretz, June 15, 2005, available at <http://www.Ha'aretzdaily.com/hasen/pages/ShArtVty.jhtml?sw=privacy+law&itemNo=587768>.

[3044] Naama Yashuvi (Kim Weiss, trans.), The State of Human Rights in Israel 2003-2004, available at <http://www.acri.org.il/english-acri/engine/story.asp?id=182#sub_6>.

[3045] " 'Peace Now' Under Investigation for Espionage Activities," May 21, 2004, available at

<http://www.israelnn.com/news.php3?id=62808>.

[3046] Yuval Yoaz, "We are all still in the dark," Ha'aretz, June 8, 2005, available at <http://www.Ha'aretz.com/hasen/pages/ShArtVty.jhtml?sw=privacy+law&itemNo=585620>.

[3047] David Banisar, "Israel," Freedom of Information and Access to Government Records Around the World, May 2004 at 44, available at <http://www.freedominfo.org/survey/global_survey2004.pdf>.

Open Government

The Israeli Supreme Court ruled in *Shalit v. Peres* that there was a fundamental right for citizens to obtain information from government.[3048] The Freedom of Information Law was approved unanimously by the *Knesset* in May 1998. The law allows any citizen or resident to access records held by government offices, local councils and government-owned corporations.[3049] Requests for information must be processed within 30 days. Courts can review government decisions refusing to disclose information.

In Israel, the Freedom of Information Law[3050] applies to some government institutions such as government ministries, the President's Office, the *Knesset*, the state comptroller and the public organizations that Office oversees, the courts, the local authorities, statutory corporations, government corporations and companies under the control of the local authorities. However, several public bodies are not currently required by law to be open and transparent regarding access to information.

International Obligations

Israel is a signatory to the International Covenant on Civil and Political Rights,[3051] which provides at Article 17 that: 1) No one shall be subjected to arbitrary or unlawful interference with his privacy, family, home or correspondence, nor to unlawful attacks on his honour and reputation, and 2) Everyone has the right to the protection of the law against such interference or attacks.

[3048] H.C. 1601-4/90 Shalit et al. v. Peres et al., 44(3) P.D. 353; *see, also* Rabina, *supra.*

[3049] Banisar, *supra*, at 44.

[3050] Freedom of Information Law 5758-1998.

[3051] International Covenant on Civil and Political Rights, G.A. res. 2200A (XXI), 21 U.N. GAOR Supp. (No. 16) at 52, U.N. Doc. A/6316 (1966), 999 U.N.T.S. 171, entered into force March 23, 1976, available at <http://www.unhchr.ch/html/menu3/b/a_ccpr.htm>.

Italian Republic

Constitutional Framework

The Italian Constitution, adopted in 1948, has several limited provisions relating to privacy.[3052] Article 14 states, "(1) Personal domicile is inviolable. (2) Inspection and search may not be carried out save in cases and in the manner laid down by law in conformity with guarantees prescribed for safeguarding personal freedom. (3) Special laws regulate verifications and inspections for reasons of public health and safety, or for economic and fiscal purposes." Article 15 states, "(1) The liberty and secrecy of correspondence and of every form of communication are inviolable. (2) Limitations upon them may only be enforced by decision, for which motives must be given, of the judicial authorities with the guarantees laid down by law."[3053]

Data Protection Framework

A new Privacy Code[3054] relating to the protection of personal data was enacted by a Legislative Decree of June 30, 2003 No. 196.[3055] The Code replaced the Data Protection Act (which was enacted on December 31, 1996, after 20 years of debate,[3056] to fully implement the European Union (EU) Data Protection Directive) and the various decrees enacted after 1996 to regulate data protection in specific sectors, such as security requirements,[3057] the processing of medical information,[3058] the processing of information for journalistic,[3059] scientific or

---

[3052] Constitution of the Italian Republic (*Costituzione della Repubblica Italiana*), available at <http://www.notarlex.it/codici.jsp>.

[3053] *Id.* at Article 15.

[3054] Available at <http://www.garanteprivacy.it/garante/document?ID=727068> (in Italian and English).

[3055] "Italy Enacts a New Privacy Code," BNA World Data Protection Report Vol. 3, Issue 9, September 2003, at 19.

[3056] *Legge* No. 675 (December 31, 1996), amended by *Decreto Legislativo* No. 123 (May 9, 1997) and *Decreto Legislativo* No. 255 (July 28, 1997), available at <http://www.privacy.it/dl1997123.html>; *Legge* No. 676 (December 31, 1996), *Delega al Governo in materia di tutela delle persone e di altri soggetti rispetto al trattamento dei dati personali*, available at <http://www.privacy.it/legge96676.html>.

[3057] Decree of the President of the Republic (*Decreto del Presidente della Repubblica*) No. 318 (July 28, 1999), available at <http://www.garanteprivacy.it/garante/navig/jsp/index.jsp?folderpath=Normativa%2FItaliana%2FLeggi+e+decreti+legislativi>.

[3058] Legislative Decree (*Decreto Legislativo*) No. 282 (July 28, 1999), available at <http://www.garanteprivacy.it/garante/navig/jsp/index.jsp?folderpath=Normativa%2FItaliana%2FLeggi+e+decreti+legislativi>.

---

research purposes,[3060] and personal data held by public bodies.[3061] The new Privacy Code (the Code) therefore covers all the requirements from previous data protection decrees, as well as from the EU Directive on Privacy and Electronic Communications (2002/58/EC) and some codes of conduct already approved by the Italian Data Protection Authority. The Code creates more protections for data subjects while simplifying the applicable rules. The Code is arranged in three sections with the first containing provisions dealing with the rules applicable to the processing of personal information in the public and private sector; the second dealing with "special requirements," which would apply in those specific sectors, such as debtors or the health sector; and the third concerning administrative and judicial issues.[3062] Violators of the Code may also face harsh administrative or criminal penalties. Although the Code has been in effect since January 1, 2004, individuals or organizations processing data had until June 30, 2004, to implement the required measures in order to comply with the new standards.

Supervisory Authority

The Italian Data Protection Code is enforced by the Supervisory Authority for Personal Data Protection (*Garante per la Protezione dei Dati Personali*, or *Garante*).[3063] The *Garante* maintains a register of databases, conducts audits and enforces the laws. The *Garante* can also audit databanks not under its jurisdiction, such as those relating to intelligence activities. The Decree on the Internal Organization of the *Garante*[3064] establishes the procedures for keeping the Register of Data Processes and regulates access to the register by citizens, or for investigations, registrations and inspections. As of June 2004, the *Garante* had 93 people on staff. In March 2005, the new members of the collegiate panel

---

[3059] Legislative Decree (*Decreto Legislativo*) No. 171.(May 13, 1998), available at
<http://www.garanteprivacy.it/garante/navig/jsp/index.jsp?folderpath=Normativa%2FItaliana%2FLeggi+e+decr
eti+legislativi>.

[3060] Legislative Decree (*Decreto Legislativo*) No. 281 (July 30, 1999), available at
<http://www.garanteprivacy.it/garante/navig/jsp/index.jsp?folderpath=Normativa%2FItaliana%2FLeggi+e+decr
eti+legislativi>.

[3061] Legislative Decree (*Decreto Legislativo*) No. 135 (May 11, 1999), available at
<http://www.garanteprivacy.it/garante/navig/jsp/index.jsp?folderpath=Normativa%2FItaliana%2FLeggi+e+decr
eti+legislativi>.

[3062] *Id.*

[3063] "*Garante Per La Protezione Dei Dati Personali*," available at <http://www.dataprotection.org/>.

[3064] *Decreto del Presidente della Repubblica* No. 501 (March 31, 1998), reprinted in *Gazzetta Ufficiale* No. 25 (February 1, 1999), available at <http://193.207.119.193/MV/gazzette_ufficiali/25/2.htm>; the decree was subsequently partly repealed by the Data Protection Code.

---

of the *Garante* were appointed by Parliament; they are Giuseppe Chiaravalloti, Giuseppe Fortunato, Mauro Paissan, and Franco Pizzetti.[3065]

The *Garante* is responsible for carrying out many activities. Enforcement actions the *Garante* carries out are mainly based on the reaction to complaints lodged by data subjects for failure to exercise their rights (access, rectification, deletion) and on inspection or audit activities that are carried out either *ex officio* (based on an annual action plan identifying specific sectors and/or processing operations) or following complaints and reports.

Significant enforcement activities were carried out in the biometrics sector. The *Garante* stopped two initiatives by public bodies considering the use of fingerprint-based systems. In one case, the data controller required low-income university students and/or scholarship recipients to submit their fingerprints if they wanted to receive discounted access to restaurants and shops. In another, a local municipality required their employees to be fingerprinted to check their attendance at the workplace. The Italian DPA argued that use of biometrics-based mechanisms was disproportionate compared with the purposes to be achieved, and that specific privacy safeguards (such as enhanced security measures) were necessary given the highly sensitive nature of biometric information.[3066]

Moreover, the *Garante* carries out enforcement action by, for example, issuing penalties to entities that omit to notify data subjects that they process their data. Sixteen entities, both public and private, were fined in June 2004 because they had not submitted, or delayed submitting, the notification of processing operations concerning highly sensitive data (genetic, biometric and health data, as well as data concerning sex life, etc.). The inspections carried out by the Italian DPA jointly with an *ad hoc* squad of the Finance Police (*Guardia di Finanza*) found that several health care units, medical laboratories and a bank did not abide by the newly enacted Data Protection Code. This Code considerably simplifies notification requirements by making it mandatory only in specific cases, *i.e.* cases that involve the processing of highly sensitive data or entail specific risks for data subjects' fundamental rights and freedoms. In addition to being fined EUR 10,000 to 60,000, depending on the circumstances, the entities

---

[3065] Italian Data Protection Authority, Country Report on Italy Presented at the Meeting of the International Working Group on Data Protection in Telecommunications (Italian DPA's Report), March 31 - April 1, 2005 (on file with EPIC).

[3066] "Recent Examples of Enforcement Actions Carried Out by Data Protection Authorities," Article 29-Data Protection Working Party, (Article 29 WP Report) January 2005, available at <http://europa.eu.int/comm/justice_home/fsj/privacy/docs/wpdocs/2004/wp101a_en.pdf>.

in question were banned in some cases from using the personal data in their possession, as provided by the Data Protection Code.[3067]

In particular, this institution deals with many complaints from the public and requests for information. During the period between January 1, 2003 and March 31, 2004,[3068] queries were broken down in the following manner:

- 38,180 requests for information and clarification could be dealt with via the telephone help desk;
- 4,080 claims and reports were dealt with in writing;
- 834 answers were provided to specific questions/requests for clarification;
- 775 complaints were dealt with in connection with the failure by data subjects to exercise their rights (this is a strictly regulated type of proceeding, which is to be finalised within 50 days from its start);
- 464 requests for access to and/or verification of the information contained in the Schengen Information System were complied with;
- 9,791 notifications of data processing operations were entered into the relevant register;
- 69 on-the-spot audits were carried out;
- 5,754 answers were provided to citizens by the *Garante*'s front office via e-mails, faxes and/or letters.[3069]

When looking at some of the figures in greater detail, from the calls that were dealt with via the help desk, about 40 percent had to do with clarification on the provisions set out in the new Data Protection Code, 10 percent related to the activities of credit reporting agencies, five percent dealt with spamming and unsolicited communications, and about 30 percent concerned miscellaneous issues.

The *Garante* dictates the direction for the implementation of data protection in Italy. In October 1998, the *Garante* decided that phone companies need not conceal phone numbers on bills and they should allow for anonymous phone cards to protect privacy. Between December 2000 and February 2001, the *Garante* made several declarations on privacy issues: decided whether employees are entitled to access information about them included in evaluation reports

---

[3067] *Id.*

[3068] This time period was used because the information was gathered from the Annual Report recently submitted to the Italian Parliament.

[3069] E-mail from Antonio Caselli to Dina Mashayekhi, IPIOP Clerk, Electronic Privacy Information Center, June 22, 2004, (on file with EPIC).

drafted by their employers;[3070] provided that political associations can not collect e-mail addresses from the Internet to send unsolicited political messages;[3071] regulated the processing operations of the Italian armed forces corps; found that the *Carabinieri* failed to comply with the Data Protection Law;[3072] ruled that the personal information on identification badges worn by employees who are in regular contact with the public should be relevant and not excessive to the purpose;[3073] ruled that banks cannot take fingerprint scans of those entering the premises since doing so would be disproportionate to their security needs;[3074] and found that in insurance liability cases, the personal data in medical expert opinions must be accessible to the data subject, but may be temporarily deferred in order not to affect the outcome of the investigation.[3075]

The *Garante* carries out several different functions with regards to data protection. For example, in 2001, the *Garante* issued a Code of Conduct and Ethics Regarding the Processing of Personal Data for Historical Purposes, including guidelines on the protection of personal data in election activities such as campaign literature and elections.[3076] In 2002, the *Garante* released a report on the treatment of personal data obtained through general video surveillance.[3077] The report sets forth concerns related to such surveillance, and addresses the obligations of a data collector to protect information and the rights of those whose person are observed.[3078] In 2003, the *Garante* launched a public information television campaign to inform the public of their rights with regards to the collection of personal data.[3079] In the same year, the *Garante* began work

---

[3070] Italian Data Protection Commission, "Employee Evaluation Data Are Personal Data," February 6, 2001, available at <http://www2.garanteprivacy.it/garante/frontdoor/1,1003,00.html?LANG=2>.

[3071] Italian Data Protection Commission, "The Garante Says No to Political Spamming," January 11, 2001, available at <http://www2.garanteprivacy.it/garante/frontdoor/1,1003,,00.html?LANG=2>.

[3072] Italian Data Protection Commission, "Italy: Flawed Data Protection Approach by a Police Corps," January 11, 2001, available at <http://www2.garanteprivacy.it/garante/frontdoor/1,1003,,00.html?LANG=2>.

[3073] Italian Data Protection Commission, "Employee's Badges: Less Personal Data for More Privacy," December 11, 2000, available at <http://www2.garanteprivacy.it/garante/frontdoor/1,1003,,00.html?LANG=2>.

[3074] Italian Data Protection Commission, "No Taking of Fingerprints to Enter a Bank," December 11, 2000, available at <http://www2.garanteprivacy.it/garante/frontdoor/1,1003,,00.html?LANG=2>.

[3075] Italian Data Protection Commission, "Right of Access—Personal Data Included in Medical Expert Opinions for Insurance Purposes: Access May be Deferred," December 28, 2000, available at <http://www2.garanteprivacy.it/garante/frontdoor/1,1003,,00.html?LANG=2>.

[3076] Italian Data Protection Commission, "Personal Data and Elections-Instructions for Use," March 7, 2001, available at <http://www2.garanteprivacy.it/garante/frontdoor/1,1003,,00.html?LANG=2>.

[3077] Italian Data Protection Commission, "Relazione 2002—Nuovi diritti, riservatezza, dignita della persona: sei anni dalla legge 675," 11750/02/IT, WP 67, available under "Attivita dell'Authorita" at <http://www.<http://www.garanteprivacy.it/garante/navig/jsp/index.jsp?folderpath=Attivit%E0+dell%27Autori t%E0%2FRelazioni+annuali+al+Parlamento%2F2002>.

[3078] *Id.*

[3079] "Non e' una firmetta!," Newsletter of the *Garante per la Protezione dei Dati Personali*, No. 163 (March 17-23, 2003), available at <http://www.garanteprivacy.it/garante/doc.jsp?ID=66974>.

on a do-not-call scheme to deter unwanted marketing calls.[3080] In addition, nearly every year the *Garante* hosts a conference in Rome. Topics have ranged from human genetics to the future of privacy.[3081]

Wiretapping and Surveillance Rules

Wiretapping is regulated by Articles 266-271 of the Penal Procedure Code and may only be authorized in the case of legal proceedings.[3082] Government interceptions of telephone and all other forms of communications must be approved by a court order. The law on computer crime includes penalties on interception of electronic communications.[3083] Interception orders are granted for 15 days at a time and can be extended for the same length of time by a judge. The judge also monitors procedures for storing recordings and transcripts. Any recordings or transcripts that are not used must be destroyed. The conversations of religious ministers, lawyers, doctors or others subject to professional confidentiality rules can not be intercepted. There are more lenient procedures for anti-Mafia cases. Some 44,000 orders were approved in 1996, up from 15,000 in 1992.[3084] A June 2002 report indicated that Rome, by itself, had nearly 13,000 wiretaps during the period of a year.[3085]

In February 2005, the Italian mobile operator TIM, one of the largest in Italy, issued a unique warning that the number of wiretaps had reached a limit. In a fax sent to all Italian public prosecutors, TIM said that it had already over-stretched its capability of simultaneously intercepting between 5,000 and 7,000 mobile phones. New requests would have to be processed on a "first come, first served" basis.[3086] Even more rare in the current secretive environment of law enforcement, the Italian Minister of Justice Roberto Castelli has provided the newspaper *Repubblica* with statistics about the number of wiretaps and costs.

[3080] "Nuovi elenchi telefonici: chiarezza nelle informazioni agli abbonati," Newsletter of the *Garante per la Protezione dei Dati Personali*, No. 163 (February 24-March 2, 2003), available at <http://www.garanteprivacy.it/garante/doc.jsp?ID=34804>.

[3081] *See generally, Garante per la Protezione dei Dati Personali,* available at <http://www.garanteprivacy.it>.

[3082] *Decreto del Presidente della Repubblica* No. 447, *Approvazione del Codice Procedura Penale* (September 22, 1988).

[3083] *Legge* No. 547 (December 23, 1993).

[3084] French Commission Nationale de Contrôle des Interceptions de Sécurité, Annual Report (1996).

[3085] British Broadcasting Corporation Worldwide Monitoring, "Italian News Agency ANSA review of the Italian press for 7 Jun 02," (June 7, 2002).

[3086] "Italian GSM Provider Warns: too Many Wiretaps," EDRi-gram newsletter Number 3.4, February 24, 2005. Available at <http://www.edri.org/edrigram/number3.4/wiretap/>; *see also*, "Too Many Wiretaps in Italy," MobileMonday.Net, February 27, 2005, available at <http://www.mobilemonday.net/mm/story.php?story_id=4141>.

The number of wiretaps has doubled every two years, he said, from 32,000 intercepts in 2001, to 45,000 in 2002, to 77,000 in 2003. He estimated the number of wiretaps in 2004 to be 100,000, costing the Department of Justice approximately EUR 300 million in reimbursements. In 2003, the Department of Justice spent EUR 225 million on intercepts, EUR 230 million in 2002 and EUR 165 million in 2001. With 58 million inhabitants and 100,000 intercepts in 2004, the number of judicial intercepts per 100,000 inhabitant reaches 172.[3087]

In October 2001, the Italian Parliament passed a decree[3088] in which the offense of criminal association for purposes of terrorism was re-defined; however, the blanket surveillance of communications by law enforcement bodies was expressly ruled out. Telephone tapping and electronic surveillance were facilitated but only with authorization and under the supervision of judicial authorities, and, only with regard to very serious offences. Additional safeguards apply to the use of investigational findings and the prohibition to disclose such findings.[3089]

On June 21, 2005, the Italian collective and Internet service provider (ISP) Austistici/Inventati discovered a major police backdoor in their server, which hosts a large number of web sites, mailboxes, mailing lists and Internet services for NGOs, grassroots activists and public interest associations. The Italian *Polizia Postale* (Postal Police) installed the backdoor the year before after the *Procura di Bologna* (Office of the Public Prosecutor of Bologna) ordered a seizure during an investigation of the anarchist collective Crocenera. The police gained access to the private SSL certificate stored on the server and installed several tools to monitor, intercept and decrypt all the traffic going through the server – that is, traffic that was not directly relevant to the investigations. This included the communications of more than 30,000 subscribers of the ISP, whose basic rights to privacy and presumption of innocence, as granted under the Italian constitution, have been violated.

Italy also has several laws relating to workplace surveillance,[3090] statistical information, electronic files, and digital signatures.[3091] For example, the Workers

---

[3087] *Id.*

[3088] Decree No. 374/2001, converted into Act No. 438/2001.

[3089] On January 7, 2003, Giuseppe Pisanu, the Italian Interior Minister, went before parliament to address terrorism concerns. His testimony was supplemented by a "report in which he warned of a growing climate of 'widespread political illegality' which must be monitored and combated," "Italy: Interior Minister Link Terrorism and Activists," Statewatch News Online, February 2003, available at <http://www.statewatch.org/news/2003/feb/02italy.htm>.

[3090] *Legge* No. 93 (March 29, 1983).

Charter prohibits employers from investigating the political, religious or trade union opinions of their workers, and in general, on any matter that is irrelevant for the purposes of assessing their professional skills and aptitudes.[3092] The 1993 computer crime law prohibits unlawfully using a computer system and intercepting computer communications.[3093]

The Italian authorities quieted impassioned speech on various occasions in 2002. Prompted by the Catholic Church, Italian officials seized local web sites that portrayed religious figures alongside sexual imagery and harsh language.[3094] Officials asserted justification based on the illegality of blasphemy in Italy and because such depictions "offended the 'dignity of the people.' "[3095] Later in the year, a group of activists were arrested for forming a "subversive association."[3096] According to a report, the protestors were "accused of political conspiracy by association aimed at disrupting the exercise of government . . . by '[organizing] and provoking clashes between numerous demonstrators and the police to make public order unmanageable,' and of continuous distribution of subversive propaganda, sometimes using Internet, to 'violently subvert the economic order of the State.' "[3097] The activists were ultimately released, but remained under investigation.[3098]

Radio Frequency Identification

The *Garante* has paid considerable attention to the development of radio frequency identification (RFID) technology. An initial in-depth analysis of this issue was carried out by addressing the way in which the new technology might impact the conditions for the exercise of individuals' freedoms, as well as the

---

[3091] *Decreto del Presidente della Repubblica* No. 513 (November 10, 1997), available at <http://www.privacy.it/dpcm19990208.html>.

[3092] *Legge* No. 300, § 8 (May 20, 1970).

[3093] *Legge* No. 547 (December 23, 1993).

[3094] "Italian Police Censor US-Hosted Sites," Global Internet Liberty Campaign Newsletter, 6:5, July 23, 2002; *see also* "Italy Gags 'Porno' Virgin Mary sites," BBC News Online, July 10, 2002, available at <http://news.bbc.co.uk/hi/english/world/europe/newsid_2119000/2119780.stm> and Associated Press, "Italian police shut down U.S.-based porn sites," USATODAY.com, July 10, 2002, available at <http://www.usatoday.com/tech/news/2002/07/10/italy-porn.htm>.

[3095] "Italian Police Censor US-Hosted Sites" *supra.*

[3096] "Italy: Activists Arrested for 'Subversive Association,' " Statewatch News Online, November 2002, available at <http://www.statewatch.org/news/2002/nov/06italy.htm>.

[3097] *Id.*

[3098] "Update: Italy: Activists Freed, but Still Under Investigation," Statewatch News Online, February 2003, available at <http://www.statewatch.org/news/2003/feb/02italy.htm>.

---

issues that are bound to arise in a data protection perspective following implementation of the technology.[3099]

In December 2004, the *Garante* opened a consultation on privacy issues related to RFID tags, loyalty cards, digital TV (*e.g.*, pay-per-view) and video-telephoning.[3100] The Winston Smith Project,[3101] an Italian NGO, has responded with a legal proposal to control the use of RFID tags. First, the organization wants legal rules that oblige manufacturers to make RFID tags easily identifiable and removable. Second, the organization says the presence, type and position of RFID tags must be clearly advertised on the packaging of an article or the article itself. Third, the group requires permanent deactivation of RFID tags when buying the product or when usage of the tag has ended. Fourth, the group urges that all data collected by RFID readers be treated as personal data, to which all privacy principles apply. Fifth, the group says collection, storage and further processing should only happen within the boundaries of a strict and publicly known goal. In case of additional processing or conservation for a longer time, companies should notify the Data Protection Authority. Furthermore, the groups says these rules should not only apply to RFID-related data, but to all kinds of new electronic databases, such as GSM location data, web log files and data generated by wireless networks.[3102]

Recently, some Italian fashion retailers have begun, or expressed intentions to begin, attaching RFID tags to clothing in order to track store inventory.[3103] Another benefit, according to the proponents of RFID, is that "[t]he technology creates a seamless shopping experience designed to enhance customer relationships."[3104] According to opponents, "the transmitter would let the retailer identify and track customers," and "sensors hidden in the retailer's clothing could be used to create a global surveillance network."[3105] Against a backlash of negative publicity to the United Colors of Benetton's announcement that it would begin to use RFID, the clothing retailer quickly issued a reassurance to customers

---

[3099] Italian DPA's Report, *supra*.

[3100] Italian Data Protection Authority, Consultation on RFID, available at
<http://www.garanteprivacy.it/garante/doc.jsp?ID=1078227>.

[3101] Homepage <http://www.winstonsmith.info/pws/index-e.html>.

[3102] "Answer to RFID consultation Italian Privacy Authority," EDRi-gram newsletter Number 3.1, January 12, 2005, available at http://www.edri.org/edrigram/number3.1/; *see also,* Legal proposal from the Winston Smith Project (03.01.2005), available at <http://www.winstonsmith.info/proposta_di_legge_rdp_v5.rtf>.

[3103] "Prada Personalizing Customer Experience at New York Epicenter Store Using Texas Instruments RFID Smart Labels," Business Wire, April 23, 2002.

[3104] *Id.*

[3105] Ann Bednarz, "Privacy Concerns Dog Initial RFID Plans," Network World, April 28, 2003.

that no RFID technology was currently incorporated into their clothing line, though they reserved the right to implement it at any time.[3106]

One of the most recent deployments of RFID technology concerns human subdermal RFID implants. Such implants have already been tested in Italy, for instance in order to store and make available, where necessary, information on a patient's health, or to check access to high-security areas, or even to ensure quick payments in various commercial transactions.[3107]

Also in 2004, Italy's market for counterfeit products[3108] was shaken when the state enacted stronger regulations on anti-piracy.[3109] The new Anti-Piracy Act applies to music and film, offering wider protection for copyrighted works and subjecting offenders to greater punishments for statutory violations. While the Act was still in its proposal stage, the Italian *Associazione Software Libero* started an online petition against the legislation.[3110] The Italian police, authorized by the legislation, have begun "combing through the e-mail accounts of thousands of Italians they suspect of having downloaded music and films to swap on the Internet."[3111]

On March 3, 2005, the Italian government closed an agreement with 50 organizations from the music, video, publishing and information technology industries to fight copyright infringements by organizing public "sensibilization" campaigns. The agreement was launched during the well-known Sanremo pop music festival. Prepared by three ministers (of Technological Innovation, Culture and Communications) the agreement was signed by, among others, RAI (the state-owned TV and radio-broadcasting corporation), Microsoft, BSA, Philips, Mediaset (the largest private TV broadcasting corporation in Italy), Sony, Tiscali, Telecom Italia, AIIP (the Italian association of Internet Providers) and two consumer organizations (Adiconsum and UNC).[3112] The agreement is supposed

---

[3106] *Id.*; *see also* "Benetton: No Microchips Present in Garments on Sale," United Colors of Benetton Press Release, April 4, 2003, available at <http://www.benetton.com/press>.

[3107] Italian DPAs Report *supra*.

[3108] Italy is the third largest global producer of counterfeit products "and Europe's greatest consumer of counterfeit products." Laurence Morel-Chavillet,"Anti-counterfeiting in Europe - a Difficult Struggle," IPR No. 4, October 2002, available at <http://www.statewatch.org/news/2002/nov/06italy.htm>.

[3109] *Decreto Legislativo* No. 68 (April 29, 2003), available at <http://www.altalex.it>.

[3110] "Petition against Copyright Law in Italy," EDRi-gram, Number 4, March 12, 2003, available at <http://www.edri.org/cgi-bin/index?id=000100000055 .>; *see generall,y Associazione Software Libero online* at <http://www.softwarelibero.it>.

[3111] "Italian Police Cracking down on Illegal Music Downloads," GigaLaw.com Daily News, June 4, 2003. Available at <http://www.gigalaw.com/newsarchives/2003_06_03_index2.html>.

[3112] "Italian Agreement to Fight Copyright Infringements," EDRi-gram Number 3.5, May 10, 2005, available at <http://www.edri.org/edrigram/number3.5/sanremo>; dee also, text of the Sanremo Agreement, available at

to produce codes of conduct to which all Internet service providers and other distribution platforms, rightsholders and the audio-visual production industry would voluntarily adhere. Notwithstanding the enthusiasm of the promoters of the initiative, however, the Sanremo agreement is problematic in several ways. For example, the third recital of the agreement guidelines binds the signatories to "favour the development and the adoption of Digital Rights Management (DRM) systems respecting principles of interoperability, technological neutrality and ease of content use by end users." Nowhere in the Sanremo agreement does it address any of the well-known problems DRM systems can present, such as privacy issues, contractual and/or factual overturn of "fair use" provisions and user exceptions in copyright law, the stifling of research activities and the over-favoring of rightsholders through legal protection of TPMs (Technical Protection Measures).

A decree-law issued in March 2004 increased the responsibilities of Internet service providers (ISPs) and now makes them report who among their users engages in peer-to-peer file-sharing.[3113] If the ISPs fail to monitor and control their users, they will be automatically liable for their subscribers' activities. At the end of May 2004, Italy passed one of the world's toughest laws against piracy and file-sharing.[3114] Penalties include a prison term of up to three years and fines that can exceed USD 300,000. The Culture Ministry said that the law was necessary to protect the intellectual property rights of artists in light of the growing popularity of peer-to-peer networks.

The compulsory limit for the data retention of telephone traffic was increased from 30 months to four years in February 2004 as a result of an Act (No. 45/2004)[3115] issued further to a decree proposed by the Italian government.[3116] The latter decree (No. 354/2003) had been approved by the government cabinet as a result of "the extraordinary need and urgency for the regulation of the modes of storage of traffic data relating to telephone and Internet communications, so as to prevent its loss in case its acquisition should prove necessary for the scope of

---

<http://www.innovazione.gov.it/ita/news/2005/cartellastampa/sanremo/Linee_Guida.pdf> (in Italian).

[3113] *Decreto Legislativo* No. 72 (March 22, 2004), enforcing urgent actions to fight the illicit diffusion of audio-visual works, and to sustain movie and entertainment activities.

[3114] Aidan Lewis, "Italy Passes Tough Internet Piracy Law," USA Today, May 28, 2004, available at <http://www.usatoday.com/tech/news/techpolicy/2004-05-28-italy-piracy-law_x.htm?POE=TECISVA>.

[3115] *Legge* No. 45 (February 26, 2004), available at <http://www.garanteprivacy.it/garante/navig/jsp/index.jsp?folderpath=Normativa%2FItaliana%2FLeggi+e+decreti+legislativi> (in Italian).

[3116] EFF Italy, "Civil Rights and Ambiguity of Crime 'Prevention'," January 24, 2004., available at <http://www.alcei.it/english/actions/crimprev.htm>.

the repression of particularly serious crimes."[3117] Also following the advice provided by the Italian Data Protection Authority, the Act passed in February 2004 applied the expanded retention period to telephone traffic data only. The relevant requirements will unfold in the following manner: during the first 24 months service providers must retain telephone traffic data in case it is required for the investigation of criminal offences, and, during the final 24 months, stricter access guidelines will be attached whereby it can be requested for more serious crimes only, including terrorism.[3118]

Unsolicited E-mails ("Spam")

The newly approved Privacy Code of Italy considers the sending of unsolicited e-mails to be a very serious offence.[3119] If an individual is found guilty of sending spam and trying to profit from such e-mails, he could face up to three years in prison. Since many companies are losing a large amount of bandwidth as a result of dealing with spam, the Italian government has now made spam an act of theft. Italy is one of the first countries to implement legislation that actively deals with combating spam. Critics remain skeptical of Italy's law, because many of the sources of spam are from outside the country and therefore outside the Italian court's jurisdiction. Italy is currently one of the few European countries to be fully compliant with EU Directive 2002/58/EC, which prohibits the sending of unsolicited e-mail.[3120]

The sending of "spam," however, is an ever-recurring topic, not only as regards commercial messages, but also in connection with "political marketing." In 2004, the *Garante* issued two provisions. The *Garante* took part in meetings in which fixed and mobile telephony operators, consumer associations, and ISP associations participated. These meetings were focused on the drafting of a self-regulatory code.[3121]

[3117] "Italy to Retain Communications Data for Five Years," Statewatch, available at
<http://www.statewatch.org/news/2004/jan/03italy-dataretention.htm>.

[3118] *See* Section 132 of the Data Protection Code.

[3119] Will Sturgeon, "Italy Plans to Jail Spammers," Silicon.com, September 5, 2003, available at
<http://www.silicon.com/research/specialreports/thespamreport/0,39025001,10005895,00.htm>.

[3120] "EU Directive on Privacy and Electronic Communications enters into force," Interchange of Data between Administrations, November 3, 2003, available at
<http://europa.eu.int/ISPO/ida/jsps/index.jsp?fuseAction=showDocument&parent=whatsnew&documentID=1722>.

[3121] Italian DPA's Report *supra*.

Throughout 2003, Italy enacted several laws that contain provisions which effectively compromise the privacy rights of its citizens. For example, Act No. 140 from June 20, 2003,[3122] contains provisions on interceptions and acquisitions of reports concerning conversations and/or communications of MPs as intercepted within the framework of judicial proceedings concerning third parties. This Act provides, in particular, for the need to destroy reports and recordings concerning irrelevant interception activities.[3123] The latter provision is related to general data protection principles, in that its violation may also entail the impossibility of using the personal data being processed – as per Section 11 of the Data Protection Code.

Legislative Decree No. 269 of September 30, 2003,[3124] converted with amendments into Act No. 326 of November 24, 2003,[3125] sets out the requirements to monitor health care expenditure. During the process leading to the conversion of the legislative decree, the *Garante* drew Parliament's attention to the sensitive issues raised by Section 50 in the decree, providing, *inter alia*, for the establishment of a database containing the fiscal identification codes of all health care beneficiaries in order to monitor health care expenditure. The *Garante* pointed out that the purpose the decree sought was undoubtedly in line with streamlining supervision over the state's expenditure; however, the tools envisaged to that end might jeopardize citizens' rights to the protection of their personal data – in particular the data concerning health, which are covered by special safeguards.[3126]

On January 1, 2005, the Italian Electronic Health card was launched. Together with e-prescriptions, the e-Health card is a key element of the Italian national e-Health Program, which aims at controlling public health expenses while improving communication between health professionals and delivering better services to patients. The card, which contains a magnetic stripe but no chip, also features the European e-health insurance card information on the back. They are used in conjunction with the National Healthcare Expenditure Monitoring

---

[3122] *Legge* No. 140 (June 20, 2003).

[3123] *Id.* at § 6.

[3124] *Decreto Legislativo* No. 269 (September 30, 2003).

[3125] *Legge* No. 326 (November 24, 2003).

[3126] Indeed, it would arguably always be possible to trace each data subject's medical history based on the information concerning prescriptions and specialists' advice. The *Garante* pointed out that the legislation in force already sets forth procedures to monitor health care expenditure without setting up centralised databases, and stressed that the need to increase the effectiveness of such procedures should not result in limiting the right to personal data protection. According to the *Garante*, in order to comply with personal data protection legislation, the monitoring system would have to prohibit the processing of identification data, and the setting up of a centralized database, if any, should be based exclusively on the use of anonymized data. E-Mail from Antonio Caselli, *supra*.

System, commonly referred to as the "TS System." Designed to monitor and manage each phase of the public health expenditure cycle, from drug prescription to service delivery, the system will allow Italian authorities to enhance controls on the healthcare benefits of each citizen. The TS System is coordinated by the Italian Revenue Agency and implemented by Sogei[3127] in those regions where e-health cards are being issued. Distribution of the cards has already started in the Regions of Abruzzi, Umbria, Emilia Romagna, Veneto and Lazio. The government will progressively introduce the e-health card in other regions, with the objective of issuing 15 million cards by April 2005.[3128]

Major Privacy Case Law

In addition to legislative action, there have been a number of decisions on the judicial front that have dealt with the right to privacy. A decision by the Council of State (*Consiglio di Stato*) addressed the relationship between the right of access and the right to privacy, ruling that the laws in force do not provide general guidance on how to balance these two rights. The decision allows an administrative body holding sensitive data to assess each specific situation in order to determine whether access is necessary or not to establish or defend a claim that is at least equal to the data subject's claim to privacy.[3129] In another decision concerning this issue, the Council of State ruled that the right of access, albeit in its "softened" version, *i.e.*, as the right to inspect records, should override the right to privacy if knowledge of the information is required to exercise the right of defence with regard to circumstances amounting to a criminal offence.[3130] Furthermore, in two decisions issued in 2003, the Court of Cassation (*Corte di cassazione*), which is the highest court in Italy, ruled that non-pecuniary damage should be construed as a wide-ranging category including all cases in which there is violation of a value pertaining to human beings. Among the cases the Court considered to entitle to protection against the damage caused by the violation of individual-related interests devoid of pecuniary value, the use of unlawful means in collecting personal data was expressly mentioned.[3131]

[3127] Homepage <http://www.sogei.it/>.

[3128] *See* "Italy eServices for Citizens," eGovernment News, January 12, 2005, available at <http://europa.eu.int/idabc/en/document/3768/353>.

[3129] *Cons. Stato*. 4002/2003 Foro It. V. Stato.

[3130] *Cons. Stato*. 9276/2003 Foro It. V. Stato.

[3131] Cass. 8827/2003, 8828/2003.

The public prosecutor's office of Rome has requested the relevant judicial authorities to allow the seizure of Indymedia Italy's web site, on the ground of violation of the Italian penal law on insult to the catholic religion (*vilipendio della religione cattolica*) and insult to the Pope's figure (*vilipendio della figura del Papa*). Someone, using Indymedia's content management system (which allows everyone to freely upload all kinds of material), published a fake photo of Pope Benedictus XVI dressed as a Nazi official. This was a clear reference to the Pope being a member – albeit, as he put it in various interviews, "not a real enthusiast" – of the *Hitlerjugend* (the Hitler Youth). Even though the constitutionality of the law on insult to the Catholic religion, that is being invoked as a weapon against Indymedia Italy, is itself quite doubtful (on the basis that it is discriminatory towards other religions and in general not really compatible with the supposedly lay nature of the Italian State) the public prosecutor has nevertheless decided to issue an international judicial action. He is now is waiting for the authorization of the Italian Ministry of Justice in order to prosecute for insult to the Pope's figure. Since the Pope is a foreign head of state, a formal authorization by the minister is necessary.[3132]

In two important employment cases, the *Garante* found that the organizational arrangements made by the data controllers (*i.e.*, the employers) were not in line with the security measures required under the Data Protection Code. In particular, a company was fined because it had allowed dissemination of sensitive data concerning an employee and her family members, when the information should have remained within the employee's personal file. In another case, a public body was ordered to adopt all the necessary security measures to prevent unauthorized staff from accessing personal files. In this case, information on an employee's family circumstances had been used by other colleagues to support a complaint against that employee's allegedly unjustified leave of absence. Even though one of the colleagues was authorized to access employees' personal files, she had used the data for personal purposes unrelated to her official duties.[3133]

The *Garante* has also made several decisions concerning important issues over the past year regarding video surveillance, biometrics and access to personal data contained in clinical records. A decision adopted by the *Garante* on April 29, 2004 referred to the basic principles on video surveillance and described the general requirements to be fulfilled by any video surveillance system. Guidance

---

[3132] "Italian Prosecutor Demands Take down of Indymedia Italy," EDRi-gram Number 3.9, May 4, 2005, available at <http://www.edri.org/edrigram/number3.9/indymedia>.
[3133] Article 29 WP Report *supra*.

was also provided in respect of specific data processing operations concerning the use of video surveillance in schools, hospitals, on board transportation means, and at the workplace. The *Garante* reserved the right to take *ad hoc* measures in particular situations on a case-by-case basis. It was determined that the basic criteria should be the respect for citizens' fundamental rights and freedoms and personal dignity, with particular regard to privacy, identity and personal data protection.[3134] Accordingly, the *Garante* stated that individuals may not be deprived of the right to move without interferences that are incompatible with a free democratic society,[3135] such as those resulting from invasive and oppressive data acquisitions in respect of an individual's whereabouts and movements. The *Garante* also drew inspiration from the guidelines issued by several international and Community fora such as, in particular, the Council of Europe's guidelines on video surveillance of May 20 - May 23, 2003[3136] and the documents drafted by the European data protection authorities within the framework of the Article 29 Working Party.[3137]

The *Garante* considered the use and appropriateness of biometrics in relation to a project called S-Travel, which considered initial tests at the Athens and Milan Malpensa airports. Biometric authentication technologies, using fingerprints and/or iris scans, with particular regard to check-in and boarding operations, were the main issue. The *Garante* stated that it was necessary to comply with data minimization and proportionality principles, as well as with data relevance and non-excessiveness requirements. In the case at issue, the technologies to be implemented were only partly suitable for achieving enhanced security of airport controls. Furthermore, the collection of biometric data related to both fingerprints and iris scans of both eyes was found to be excessive and disproportionate compared with the purposes of the processing.

Finally, in a decision from July 2003, the *Garante* specified the conditions in which the right to privacy and the right of access to clinical records held by

---

[3134] *See* § 2(1) of the Data Protection Code.

[3135] *See* Article 8 of the European Human Rights Convention as ratified in Italy by *Legge* No. 848/1955.

[3136] Council of Europe, European Committee on Legal Co-operation (CDCJ), Report Containing Guiding Principles for the Protection of Individuals with regard to the Collection and Processing of Data by Means of Video Surveillance, May 20-23, 2003, available at <http://www.coe.int/T/E/Legal_affairs/Legal_co-operation/Data_protection/Documents/Reports/Q-Report%20guiding%20principles%20video.asp#TopOfPage>.

[3137] Article 29 Data Protection Working Party, Opinion 4/2004 (WP 89) on the Processing of Personal Data by means of Video Surveillance, February 11, 2004, available at <http://europa.eu.int/comm/internal_market/privacy/docs/wpdocs/2004/wp89_en.pdf>; Article 29 Data Protection Working Party, Working Document on the Processing of Personal Data by means of Video Surveillance (WP 67), November 25, 2002, available at <http://europa.eu.int/comm/internal_market/privacy/docs/wpdocs/2002/wp67_en.pdf>.

health care institutions could be balanced. This is an issue arising mostly in connection with the requests made by defense counsel carrying their own investigations in order to access records containing data relating to health and/or sex life. In particular, the so-called "equal importance" principle holds that the processing of personal data in order to enable access is only allowed if the right to be defended through the request for accessing administrative records is at least as important as the data subject's rights, or else consists in a personal right or another fundamental, inviolable right or freedom. In other words, the defendant's rights must be equal to, or outweigh, the other individual's fundamental right to privacy.

The Italian government has also been in the process of developing a National Services Card, an identification card that may include biometric data in the future and will give the user access to e-government services.[3138] According to current plans, the ID card contains personal data including the holder's blood type and fiscal code coupled with a digital signature. The personal data and digital signature are stored on the card's microchip and can only be released if the holder gives permission by inserting a PIN code. The information is not yest stored on any central database. The cards were first launched in 2001 but have not been widely distributed. The goal is to replace older identification cards with these new cards over the next five years.[3139] In December 2004, the Italian ogvernment issued the final technical and security regulations for the National Services Card (*Carta Nazionale dei Servizi* or CNS). Combined with a reader, the CNS chip card will allow users to access and pay for e-government services. Public administrations will have the possibility to issue CNS cards and will be able to combine both the e-Health and the CNS cards in a single document.[3140]

On March 31, 2005, the Law No. 43/2005 was adopted. The Law provides for the demise of paper ID documents and their replacement by electronic ID cards by the end of 2005. As of January 1, 2006, all new ID documents issued in Italy will be electronic.[3141]

[3138] "Italian Government Ready to Roll out Electronic ID cards," Interchange of Data Between Administrations, April 19, 2004, available at <http://europa.eu.int/idabc/>.

[3139] *Id.*

[3140] "Italian Prosecutor Demands Take down of Indymedia Italy," EDRi-gram Number 3.9, May 4, 2005 a,vailable at <http://www.edri.org/edrigram/number3.9/indymedia>.

[3141] EGovernment News, *supra.*

NGO Advocacy Work

In May 2005, Italy's Big Brother Awards (organized by Privacy International and the Winston Smith Project, in association with 14 other organizations) announced this year's winners. Telecom Italia (Italy's leading, formerly public, telephone service provider) won the "People's Lament" Award, which is automatically granted to the person or body that receives the largest number of nominations from the public. Italian Prime Minister Silvio Berlusconi won an award as a result of his office sending every Italian mobile phone a text message inviting them to vote in Italy's European elections. Giuseppe Fortunato, a lawyer, won the "Life-Time Menace" Award. He is "one of the few persons" who has had a firm sentence passed against him for "serious crimes against privacy" in 2002, for accessing telephone company records, and using them for his personal gain.[3142] Fortunato was recently voted in as a member of the *Garante* by a commission; a majority of its members are from the Italian government coalition.

International Obligations

Italy is a member of several organizations that influence the country's treatment of privacy and personal data. Most notably, Italy is part of the Council of Europe (CoE). Italy signed and ratified the CoE's Convention for the Protection of Individuals with Regard to Automatic Processing of Personal Data.[3143] In addition, Italy ratified the European Convention for the Protection of Human Rights and Fundamental Freedoms[3144] and signed the CoE's Convention for Cyber-crime, but has not ratified it yet.[3145] Italy is a member of the Organization for Economic Cooperation and Development (OECD) and has adopted the OECD Guidelines on the Protection of Privacy and Transborder Flows of Personal Data.

[3142] "Italy/Spain: Big Brother Awards," Statewatch News Online, June 15, 2005 (23/25), available at <http://www.statewatch.org/news/2005/jun/03italy-spain-big-brother.htm>; for more information, *see* "Big Brother Award for new member Italian DPA," EDRI-gram Number 3.11, June 2, 2005, available at <www.edri.org/edrigram/number3.11/>.

[3143] European Treaties Series ("ETS") Nos. 108, 181 (enacted July 1, 1997).

[3144] ETS No. 5 (ratified on October 26, 1955).

[3145] ETS No. 185 (signed on November 23, 2001).

Japan

Constitutional Privacy Framework

Article 13 of the Constitution provides that "the right to life, liberty, and the pursuit of happiness shall . . . be the supreme consideration in legislation and in other governmental affairs." In 1963, the Supreme Court first recognized the substantial right to privacy under Article 13 of the Constitution. Since then, the right of privacy has been established under Article 13 by the courts' precedents and has been applied to specific cases through the general provisions of tort law in the Civil Code. However, until recently, Japan had no statute with respect to the processing of personal data in the private sector, for which the Japanese government followed a policy of self-regulation, especially regarding electronic commerce.

The Basic Law on Personal Information Protection

On May 30, 2003, the Act Concerning the Protection of Personal Information (also called the Personal Information Protection Act, or referred to here as "the Act") was eventually enacted after a long controversy in the *Diet* (the Japanese Parliament).[3146] The Act is divided into two parts: 1) "Basic ideals and

---

[3146] Since the summer of 1999, lawmakers had been working on the Personal Information Protection Bill, which would provide a framework for both governmental and commercial usage of personal information. The proposed legislation required that such private and public entities abide by "five basic principles." (Japan Proposed Law Concerning Protection of Personal Information (Unofficial Transcript, available at <http://www.kantei.go.jp/jp/it/privacy/houseika/hourituan/030307houan.html> (in Japanese); "Cabinet Approves Bill to Protect Personal Info," Yomiuri Shinbun, March 28, 2001.) These five principles were: 1) to explicitly specify the purpose for data collection and hold to the scope of that purpose; 2) to gather personal information "by lawful and appropriate means;" 3) to maintain the data accurate and up to date; 4) to protect the security of personal information; and 5) to infuse transparency into the collection and use of data. Further, the bill specifically required private businesses to disclose to individuals any personal information collected from them and the purposes of such collection; it also prohibited companies from sharing personal information with third parties. ("Bill Must Serve Freedom of the Press," Yomuiri Shinbun, March 28, 2001.) Journalists feared that, because government officials would be the ultimate arbiters as to what constitutes exempted "reporting," they would exclude articles that pry too deeply into their own misdeeds. ("New Tokyo Law May Out End to 'Exposes,'" Straits Times (Singapore), June 1, 2001.) In March 2000 ("Current Diet Unlikely to OK Info Bill," Yomiuri Shinbun, June 3, 2001), and again in 2001, the Prime Minister's Cabinet approved the bill and submitted it to the *Diet*. ("Bill on Data Protection Approved by Cabinet," Japan Times, March 28, 2001.) However, deliberations on the bill were once again delayed due to continued criticism by media groups and opposition parties. (Advisory Panel to Japanese Government Drafts Law to Protect Personal Information, BNA Daily Report for Executives, June 8, 2000.) After a long controversy in the *Diet*, the bill was repealed in December 2002. Soon after, the ruling parties revised it, responding to public criticism that it would, among other concerns, violate freedom of the press. In response to criticism from opposition parties and the media, the ruling coalition dropped the contentious "five basic principles" from the bill and provided exemption clauses for the press. Broadcasters, newspapers, news agencies and other reporting organs, including individuals and writers were exempted from the application of the clauses. ("Diet Begins Debate on Watered-down Privacy Bills," The Japan Times, April 9, 2003.) The revised bill was approved in the Cabinet meeting in March 2003.

principles" that will serve for future legislation on the protection of privacy, both in the public and private sectors (Chapter 1 to 3), and 2) "General Provisions" on personal information protection in the private sector (Chapter 4 to 6).[3147] The Act defines that "personal information" as the information that relates to "living individuals," which can be used to identify specific individuals by name, date of birth, or other description (Article 2, Section 1). The "General Provisions" part details how businesses have to handle personal information,[3148] duties that are derived from the data protection principles of the OECD Privacy Guidelines.[3149] To promote the self-regulatory system and complaint handling of personal information in the private sector, the Act allows a Minister in charge to approve a "Certified Personal Information Protection Organization," which handles complaint settlement concerning personal information (Articles 37 to 49). Each Minister implements the Act for the area he is in charge of and is authorized to issue recommendations or orders to businesses dealing with personal information. Those who refuse to follow ministers' orders could face up to six months in prison or a fine of not more than JPY 300,000 (~USD 2,683). The Act also provides that ministers in charge must not exercise their authority to issue orders to those who provide information to the media. The Act was fully enforced from April 1, 2005.[3150]

[3147] The privacy legislation preceding the new 2003 Act was the 1988 Act for the Protection of Computer Processed Personal Data Held by Administrative Organs (the "1988 Act"). It was the first act on privacy protection and governed the use of personal information in computerized files held by government agencies. (The Act for the Protection of Computer Processed Personal Data Held by Administrative Organs, Act No. 95, December 16, 1988 (Kampoo, December 16, 1988)). Additionally, some local governments had enacted similar laws: the Prefecture of Kanagawa had legislation that protects privacy in both the public and private sectors. (Kanagawa Prefecture Ordinance on the Protection of Personal Data, Ordinance No. 6, March 30, 1990.) The 1988 Act was based on the OECD Privacy Guidelines and imposed duties of security, access, and correction. Agencies had to limit their collection to relevant information and publish a public notice listing their file systems. Information collected for one purpose could not be used for a purpose "other than the file holding purpose."

[3148] "Businesses Handling Personal Information" refers to a business that uses personal information databases, etc., for business operations, but excludes "organs of the national government." "Local public entities," "independent administrative corporations, etc." and Persons designated by government ordinance (Article 2).

[3149] The Cabinet Office, Commentary on Personal Information Protection Act, available at <http://www5.cao.go.jp/seikatsu/kojin/kaisetsu/index.html>; general provisions include "Specification of Purpose of Use," "Limitations on the Purpose of Use," "Appropriate Acquisition," "Notification of Purpose of Use in Acquisition," "Securing Accuracy of Data Content," "Security Control Measures," "Supervision of Employees," "Supervision of Delegates," and "Restrictions on Providing Information to Third Parties."

[3150] Provisions for the basic principles of personal information protection and national and local governments' obligations and some provisions such as the "Basic Ideals" and the "Duties of the Government and Local Public Entities" came into force on May 30, 2003, whereas other provisions such as the "Duties of an Enterprise that Handles Private Personal Information," the "Competent Minister," the "Promotion of the Protection of Personal Information by a Private Body," "Exemptions," and "Penal Provisions" came into force on April 1, 2005.

Four Laws Related to the Protection of Personal Information

On May 23, 2003, the *Diet* passed, in addition to the Act itself, another package of four personal information protection bills that include two laws that cover private businesses, government organizations and independent administrative agencies.[3151] Four laws related to the protection of personal information were promulgated on May 30, 2003 as well: 1) The Act concerning the Protection of Personal Information Held by Administrative Organs, which originally governed the use of personal information in computerized files, was completely amended to govern paper-based data as well as computerized data. The 2003 Act sets new criminal provisions for government officials who leak personal information without proper justification;[3152] 2) the Information Disclosure and Personal Information Protection Council Establishment Act; 3) the Act concerning the Protection of Personal Information Held by an Independent Administrative Agency; and 4) The Act concerning the Preparation of Related Laws for the Enforcement of the Act concerning the Protection of Personal Information Held by Administrative Organs.

Guidelines for Industry

The Cabinet Office announced that each Ministry is drawing up guidelines for protecting personal information, corresponding to industrial classifications by the fall of 2004. By March 31, 2005, each Ministry had published 30 individual guidelines in 20 industry areas in order to prompt personal information protection in the private sector.[3153]

The Ministry of Finance, Wealth and Labor, and the Ministry of Internal Affairs and Communications (MIC) planned to introduce legislation to protect personal information, including individual credit data, medical data, and data in the field of broadcast by the end of 2004.[3154] On January 27, 2005, the Cabinet Office announced that the government had enacted new legislation in the medical, financial and telecommunications sectors.[3155]

[3151] "Japan Passes Personal Information Protection Bills," Mainichi Daily News, May 23, 2003.

[3152] The Act for Protection of Personal Data Held by Administrative Organs of 2003, Articles 53-55.

[3153] The Cabinet Office, Guidelines for the Personal of Information Protection, March 31, 2005, available at <http://www5.cao.go.jp/seikatsu/kojin/gaidorainkentou.html>; *see also,* Japan Privacy Resource, List of Ministry Guidelines under the Personal Information Protection Act, available at <http://www.privacyexchange.org/japan/JapanGuidelines.html> (English).

[3154] "Industry Guidelines on Personal Information Is Being Established," Nihon Keizai Shimbun, June 11, 2003.

[3155] "Individual Personal Information Laws Were Passed on," Nihon Keizai Shimbun, January 28, 2005.

Privacy Mark System

In February 1998, the Ministry of International Trade and Industry (MITI) established a Supervisory Authority for the Protection of Personal Data to monitor a new system for the granting of "privacy marks" to businesses committing to the handling of the personal data in accordance with the MITI guidelines, and to promote awareness of privacy protection for consumers. The "privacy mark" system is administered by the Japan Information Processing Development Center (JIPDEC) – a joint public/private agency promoting e-commerce and designing regulatory guidelines on the information technology industry.[3156] Companies that do not comply with the industry guidelines will be excluded from relevant industry bodies and not granted the privacy protection mark. It is assumed that market forces will then penalize them. However, in addition, the new Supervisory Authority will investigate violations and make suggestions as necessary to the relevant administrative authorities.[3157] An analysis of the marks done for the European Union by four academic privacy experts found that there were serious shortcomings in the system.[3158] In the first two years of the JIDPEC program, companies seeking certification were dominated by businesses that handle personal information, such as marriage bureaus; in total, the JIPDEC awarded about 140 licenses.[3159] In May 2000, the JIPDEC agreed with BBBOnline, a division of the US-based Better Business Bureau, to mutually recognize each other's privacy protection marks. Because of growing concerns for privacy among the public, the number of companies holding "privacy marks" has increased. By June 13, 2005, 1,562 companies had been awarded privacy marks by JIPDEC.[3160]

Constitutional Scheme for Free Speech

Article 21 of the 1946 Constitution states, "1) Freedom of assembly and association as well as speech, press and all other forms of expression are guaranteed. 2) No censorship shall be maintained, nor shall the secrecy of any means of communication be violated." Article 35 states, "1) The right of all

---

[3156] Homepage <http://www.jipdec.or.jp/security/privacy/index-e.html>.

[3157] Nigel Waters, "Reviewing the Adequacy of Privacy Protection in the Asia Pacific Region," IIR Conference Information Privacy - Data Protection, June 15, 1998, Sydney; *see also,* Ministry of International Trade and Industry, "Japan's Views on the Protection of Personal Data" (April 1998).

[3158] Raab, Bennett, Gellman & Waters, European Commission Tender No. XV/97/18/D, Application of a Methodology Designed to Assess the Adequacy of the Level of Protection of Individuals with Regard to Processing Personal Data: Test of the Method on Several Categories of Transfer, September 1998.

[3159] "Japan, US Bodies Ink Deal on Data-privacy Certification," The Yomiuri Shimbun, May 19, 2000.

[3160] Japan Information Processing Development Corporation <http://privacymark.jp/>.

persons to be secure in their homes, papers and effects against entries, searches and seizures shall not be impaired except upon warrant issued for adequate cause and particularly describing the place to be searched and things to be seized. . . . 2) Each search or seizure shall be made upon separate warrant issued by a competent judicial officer."[3161]

Regulation on the Internet

In response to the Internet Provider Responsibility Law of 2001 (IPRL), which restricts the liability of Specified Electronic Telecommunications Service Providers when they disclose customers' information,[3162] Japanese Internet Service Providers (ISPs) issued in 2002 the Guidelines for protecting privacy and honor under the IPRL (The Guidelines).[3163] The guidelines limit dissemination of private information without specific consent, allow ISPs to delete user information, and require them to maintain information posted by users about public figures.[3164] The first test case involved Yahoo Japan. On March 31, 2003, the district court of Tokyo ordered Yahoo to identify and disclose information on one of its users, who had posted a defamatory comment about the plaintiff on Yahoo's bulletin board.[3165] This case is the first one that tested how the IPRL has to be interpreted.

The year 2002 also saw the implementation of two new anti-spam laws. The laws allow Internet users and text-enabled mobile phones to opt out of spammers' contact lists, and require that all unsolicited commercial e-mail be clearly identified. MIC enforces the law, imposing fines of up to JPY 500,000 (~USD 4,170) for failure to comply. Another law enforced by MITI is intended to protect consumers. Repeat or egregious offenders can be fined up to JPY 3 million (~USD 25,000) or two years in prison.[3166] Corporate offenders can face up to JPY 300 million (~USD 2.5 million) in fines.

In response to increasing privacy invasion on Internet bulletin boards, MIC, along with the Human Rights Bureau of the Ministry of Justice and Internet industry stakeholders, announced that they would review the Guidelines in order

---

[3161] Constitution of Japan, November 3, 1946, available at
<http://www.solon.org/Constitutions/Japan/English/english-Constitution.html#CHAPTER_III>.

[3162] Law No. 137, 2001 was promulgated on November 30, 2001.

[3163] <http://www.telesa.or.jp/guideline/pdf/provider_041006_2.pdf>.

[3164] "Japanese ISPs, Carriers, Users Release Guideline for ISP Privacy Protection Duties," Bureau of National Affairs Privacy Law Watch, April 17, 2002.

[3165] "The Court First Ruled that ISP Disclose Name of its User," Mainichi Shimbun, March 31, 2003.

[3166] Toru Takahashi, "2 New Laws Aimed at Cutting Spam," Daily Yomiuri, July 2, 2002.

to require ISPs to delete private information from web sites.[3167] The new Guidelines were published in October 2004. They allow the regional Civil Liberties Bureaus under the Ministry of Justice to send ISPs official requests demanding that the names or photographs of teenage criminal suspects be deleted from the web sites they manage. Since such demands are not legally binding, ISPs can refuse to comply. In such cases, however, ISPs are required to explain their refusal to comply.[3168]

Wiretapping

Wiretapping traditionally has been considered a violation of the Constitution's right of privacy and has been authorized only a few times. However, in August 1999, the *Diet* passed the controversial Communications Interception Law authorizing wiretapping of phone or faxes, and monitoring e-mail, when investigating cases involving narcotics, gun offenses, gang-related murders and large-scale smuggling of foreigners.[3169] Under the new law, which went into effect in August 2000, the use of wiretaps is restricted to prosecutors and police officers at the rank of superintendent and above, and requires police officers to obtain warrants from district court judges in order to use wiretaps. The warrants are good for 10 days and can only be extended for a total of 30 days. Further, the presence of a third, independent party, such as an employee of Nippon Telegraph and Telephone Company, is required during monitoring. Finally, police and prosecutors must in principle notify individuals who have been monitored within 30 days after the investigation. Strict penalties are possible for those who abuse the wiretap policy.[3170] The National Police Agency (NPA) and Ministry of Justice (MOJ) recently requested about JPY 170 million (~ USD 1.6 million) in 2001 for the development of a "temporary mailbox" technology for intercepting e-mail.[3171]

The Federation of Bar Associations, journalists and trade unions opposed the wiretap law.[3172] Opponents argue that *Diet* proponents of wiretapping forced a vote on the bill before the legislatures could host a full airing of the potential

---

[3167] "Govt to Tighten Rules on Web Privacy," Daily Yomiuri, July 30, 2004.

[3168] "Internet Providers Face Crackdown over Hosting Info on Teen Criminals," Mainichi Daily News, July 29, 2004.

[3169] Reuters, June 1, 1999; *see also*,
<http://web.archive.org/web/20010406074226/http://www.jca.ax.apc.org/~toshi/cen/wiretap.intr.html>.

[3170] "Diet Passes Wiretap, ID Bills," Asia Intelligence Wire, August 13, 1999.

[3171] Toshimaru Ogura, "Toward Global Communication Rights: Movements against Wiretapping and Monitoring in Japan," October 30, 2000.

[3172] "Diet Eyes Allowing Police to Bug Phones," Mainichi Daily News, June 16, 1998.

privacy problems it would create.[3173] Professor Toshimaru Ogura, of the Japanese Net Workers against Surveillance Taskforce (NaST) and Toyama University, asserts the law does not restrict the storage and use of information gathered, possibly providing the government with a mandate to maintain databases on citizens that can be shared by other domestic—and possibly foreign—agencies.[3174] Further, Professor Ogura argues that the MOJ officials have a free hand to broadly intercept communications from innocent people in the process of targeting criminals; for example, the MOJ proposed in a *Diet* session that it could tap all of the in/outcoming phone calls of a shipping company in an effort to capture drug smugglers.[3175]

The new law was applied for the first time in May 2002 to break up a Tokyo drug ring. Police monitored cell phones and e-mail based on a warrant, and arrested nine suspects.[3176]

Many have protested the wiretapping law as too large a grant of power, including one lawmaker who sued alleging the police had illegally tapped his phone.[3177] Over 180,000 people have signed a petition for the repeal of the wiretapping law. The signature-collecting Committee for the Repeal of the Wiretapping Law submitted the petition to the *Diet* on May 24, 2000.[3178] In August, NTT asked that its employees not be required to be present when taps are installed, saying it would likely have a detrimental effect on company performance.[3179] Wiretapping is also prohibited under Article 104 of the Telecommunications Business Law and Article 14 of the Wire Telecommunications Law.[3180]

In June 1997, the Tokyo High Court upheld a lower court's finding that the Kanagawa Prefectural Police had illegally wiretapped the home telephone of a senior member of the Japanese Communist Party. The court awarded damages of JPY 4 million (~USD 36,600).[3181] Several NTT employees have also been caught selling information about customers.[3182] Several companies that provide

---

[3173] Ogura, *supra*; "Police Gain Right to Tap Phone Email," The Standard, August 15, 2000.

[3174] Ogura, *supra*.

[3175] *Id.*

[3176] World Data Protection Report 2, 6, June 2002.

[3177] "Prosecutors Drop Bug Case by Lawmaker, TV Asahi," Yomiuri Shinbun, December 29, 2000.

[3178] *See* NaST <http://www.jca.apc.org/privacy/>.

[3179] "DoCoMo Rrges NPA not to Seek Tapping Aid," Yomiuri Shimbun, August 16, 2000.

[3180] Telecommunications Business Law, LAW No. 86 of 25 December 1984), as amended last by Law No. 97 of 20 June 1997.

[3181] "Police Wiretapping," Mainichi Daily News, June 29, 1997.

[3182] "NTT Staffers Leaking Customer Information," Newsbytes, July 2, 1999.

for pre-paid cellular phone service announced in May 2000 that, in order to prevent crime, they would start requiring users to provide identification before using the service.[3183]

In a controversial international development during the summer of 2001, a New Zealand researcher testified before the European Union that New Zealand was intercepting electronic transmission from Japanese embassies as part of the Echelon spy network.[3184] He claimed that the United States was primarily interested in information on Japan's economic influence in the South Pacific.[3185] A group of Japanese civic groups requested that their government lodge a complaint against the US and the four other suspected member nations of Echelon: New Zealand, Australia, the United Kingdom, and Canada.[3186]

Surveillance Technology

The Ministry of Transportation announced in June 1999 a plan to issue "Smart Plates" license plates with embedded IC chips. These new licenses could be issued as early as 2004,[3187] and will contain driver and vehicle information and be used for road tolls and traffic control.[3188] Since 1986, the National Police Agency has also operated a comprehensive video surveillance system called the "N-system" in at least 540 locations on expressways and major highways throughout the country; it automatically records the license plate number of every passing car.[3189] Whenever a "wanted" car is detected, the system immediately issues a notice to police.[3190] Eleven motorists filed a lawsuit challenging the system in 1997. The latest model of N-system can also photograph the faces of drivers.[3191]

In response to rising crime rates, Tokyo police have been operating surveillance cameras on utility poles and buildings to monitor pedestrians in the several densely populated districts of the city.[3192] Lawyers opposing the move assert that

---

[3183] "Prepaid Cell Phone Companies to Require," Kyodo News Service, May 12, 2000.

[3184] "Japanese Diplomatic Dispatches Infiltrated by English-speaking Spies," Mainichi Shinbun, June 27, 2001.

[3185] *Id.*

[3186] "Japanese Call To Shut out Satellite Spy Group," The Age, June 28, 2001.

[3187] "NPA Reports on IC Chip Data to Be Implanted in Licenses," Kyodo News Services, June 21, 2001.

[3188] "License Plates to Bear IC Chips with Driver, Auto Info," Comline, June 09, 1999.

[3189] "Cameras to Give Police in Kabukicho 'Peep' Show," Japan Times, June 5, 2001.

[3190] Christian Science Monitor, April 8, 1997.

[3191] Ogura, *supra.*

[3192] "Big Brother's Cameras Silently Go on the Beat in Tokyo," The Nikkei Weekly, April 26, 2004.

this surveillance is unconstitutional, pointing to a 1969 Supreme Court decision against a police officer who secretly photographed a student activist in Kyoto.[3193] Other areas of the country are following Tokyo's lead, but many privacy groups, such as NaST[3194] and the Consumers Union of Japan[3195] are reporting on video surveillance and publicizing all new camera installations. Suginami ward, one of Tokyo's largest wards, enacted an ordinance to limit the rapid increase in the number of security cameras being set up in public areas following heightened concerns about privacy in the community.[3196]

In August 2002, it was revealed that the Bureau of Customs (agency affiliated with the Ministry of Finance) had installed surveillance cameras at Japan's two international airports. The bureau has refused to make public their locations and number "for security concerns."[3197]

Radio Frequency Identification (RFID) Technology

Major RFID manufacturers in Japan include NEC, which recently became the first Japanese firm to join the EPC Global standards body[3198] and Hitachi, which manufactures the 0.3 millimeter square Mu chip.[3199] RFID applications are fairly widespread in Japan. On March 22, 2004, after several months of testing, the East Japan Railway Co., Ltd., began formally offering an RFID-enabled "e-money" system to customers using its "Suica" card, allowing customers to shop at 196 convenience stores and restaurants located in 64 stations.[3200] During the last two years, RFID tags have quickly become widespread. The Ministry of Economy, Trade and Industry (METI) formed an industry consortium aimed at reducing the cost of RFID tags to JPY 5 (~USD 0.05) each within two years, in order to encourage use.[3201] While IC tags have some value for retailers, giving detailed information on goods, including not only prices but production places and distribution channels, there are fears that personal information, such as

---

[3193] Japan Times, June 5, 2001.

[3194] <http://www.jca.ax.apc.org/privacy/>.

[3195] <http://www1.jca.apc.org/nishoren/>.

[3196] Yomiuri Shimbun, March 18, 2004.

[3197] "Surveilance Camera at Narita International Airport," ASCII24 Inside Story, August 26, 2002, available at <http://ascii24.com/news/inside/2002/08/08/637794-000.html>.

[3198] "NEC to Join EPCglobal," JCN Network, May 21, 2004, available at <http://www.japancorp.net/Article.Asp?Art_ID=7368>.

[3199] "Hitachi Unveils Smallest RFID Chip," RFIDJournal.com, May 14, 2003, available at <http://www.rfidjournal.com/article/articleview/337/1/1/>.

[3200] "JR East to Extend E-Money Service with 'Suica' Smartcard," NE Asia News, February 19, 2004.

[3201] "METI to Form Consortium to Cut IC Tag Price to 5 Yen," Japan Today, March 25, 2004.

purchase history and location data, may be disclosed to third parties.[3202] Joint guidelines released by MIC and METI on June 8, 2004 call for consumers to be given options on how they might interfere with the reading of tags but appear to say nothing about rights to have the tag removed or destroyed.[3203] The guidelines provide that: 1) consumers must be notified of the presence of RFID tags; 2) consumers have the right to choose whether they want to use the tags; 3) RFID tag users must provide information about the public benefits of RFID tags; 4) the Personal Information Protection Act applies when there is matching between RFID tag-related data and databases; 5) tag users must restrict their use of personal information gathered through RFID tags; 6) tag users must ensure the accuracy of the personal information recorded through RFID tags; 7) appointment of information administrators; and 8) accountability and provision of information to consumers.[3204]

In February 2005, NTT Data Corp. announced that it had developed a security system using integrated circuit tags designed to signal the whereabouts of children as a means of protecting them against a growing trend of kidnapping among schoolchildren.[3205] Some municipal and private schools have started testing this IC-tag tracking system.[3206]

Privacy in the Workplace

Private surveillance is also on the rise. The Japan Institute of Labor reported that 35 percent of Japanese companies are monitoring their employees' e-mail and web use.[3207] Companies cited fear of viruses, sexual harassment, and other concerns as the reasons for workplace surveillance.

[3202] "Japan Moves to Protect Privacy to Promote Radio Tags," Jiji Press Ticker Service, February 23, 2004.

[3203] "Japanese RFID Privacy Guideline Released," June 8, 2004, RFIDBuzz.com, available at <http://www.rfidbuzz.com/news/2004/japanese_rfid_privacy_guideline_released.html>; *see also* Nikkei BP, June 8, available at <http://nikkeibp.jp/wcs/leaf/CID/onair/jp/flash/312386> (in Japanese).

[3204] The RFID Guidelines contain the following headings: "1. Purpose; 2. Scope; 3. Notification of the presence of RFID tags; 4. Ultimate right of consumer to choose to deactivate RFID tags; 5. Obligation to provide information on benefits of RFID tags; 6. Presumption for application of the Personal Information Protection Act to information stored on RFID tags; 7. Restriction on usage of personal data gathered from RFID tags; 8. Ensuring accuracy of personal information stored on RFID tags; 9. Assignment of Information Administrators for RFID-related issues; 10. Accountability to consumers; *see also,* Nihon Keizai Shimbun, June 8, 2004.

[3205] "NTT Data to Electronically Tag Kids," The Daily Yomiuri (Tokyo), February 22, 2005.

[3206] *Id.*

[3207] "35% of Companies Monitor Online Browsing, Email by Employees," Japan Today, May 14, 2002, available at <http://www.japantoday.com/e/?content=news&cat=4&id=215446>.

Cybercrime Treaty

Japan is a member of the Organization for Economic Cooperation and Development (OECD) and a signatory to the OECD Guidelines on Privacy and Transborder Data Flows. Japan participated as a non-member observer country in the negotiations on the Council of Europe Convention on Cybercrime and signed the Convention in November 2001.[3208] In April 2004, the Congress ratified the Convention on Cybercrime. In order to implement the Convention, the government started to amend related acts, including the Criminal Code and the Code of Criminal Procedure. The Japanese Federation of Bar Associations opposes the proposed amendments.[3209]

Medical Privacy

In March 2000, it was discovered that a research company had secretly conducted genetic tests on 1,000 blood samples obtained from people who had donated blood to the Japanese Red Cross Society. The Health and Welfare Ministry launched an investigation in November 1999 into reports that a dealer was selling private information on people receiving medical treatment, including their clinical histories. Several months later, Tohoku University in Sendai and the National Cardiovascular Center in the Osaka Prefecture city of Suita also disclosed that they had studied the genes of blood donors without obtaining their consent. A poll conducted by the Mainichi newspaper suggests that this is standard practice, finding that 70 percent of medicine faculties in 64 universities around Japan are conducting gene tests.[3210] Health and Welfare Minister Yuya Niwa said that the ministry is investigating the case and will consider setting up laws regulating such leakage of patients' medical data.

On December 17, 2004, METI released Guidelines for the Protection of Personal Information in Businesses That Use Human Genetic Information. The Guidelines require businesses using genetic information to give prior notification of the

---

[3208] Convention on Cybercrime, Chart of signatures and ratifications, available at
<http://conventions.coe.int/>.

[3209] Mainichi Shimbun, June 28, 2004. The Japanese Federation of Bar Associations especially opposes the following suggested amendments: 1) the enhancement of the penal clause for data security in the Criminal Code; 2) the expansion of punishable conducts in the Child Pornography Act; 3) the procedural provision which allows investigating authorities to preventive seizures without writ from the court; and 4) the expedited preservation of stored computer data. *See* Japan Federation of Bar Associations, Opinion concerning Ratification of Cyber Crime Treaty, available at
<http://www.nichibenren.or.jp/jp/katsudo/sytyou/iken/data/2004_23.pdf>.

[3210] Manabu Yoshikawa and Yasuyoshi Tanaka Mainichi Shimbun, "Ethicists OK Gene-sample Research," Mainichi Daily News, May 8, 2000.

purpose of use of the genetic data, as well as get written consent from data subjects.[3211]

The National Police Agency (NPA) revealed that the police are creating a system to collect DNA samples from criminal suspects upon obtaining court permission to do so, and to enter them into a database. The NPA had already started running a database on DNA collected from crime scenes. But the agency had been carefully discussing whether to create a database of DNA taken from crime suspects as such information is considered private information.[3212]

Freedom of Information in Local Governments

The Law Concerning Access to Information Held by Administrative Organs (also called Freedom of Information Law) was approved by the Diet in May 1999 and went into effect in April 2001.[3213] The law allows any individual or company to request government information in electronic or printed form. A nine-person committee in the Office of the Prime Minster receives complaints about information that the government refuses to make public and examines whether the decisions made by the ministries and agencies were appropriate. Government officials still have broad discretion to refuse requests but requestors are able to appeal decisions to withhold documents to one of eight different district courts. According to the MIC, 2,950 of 3,170 cities and prefectural governments enacted a Freedom of Information Ordinance by April 1, 2004.[3214]

The Resident Registry Network System

In the same anti-crime package of bills under which the wiretapping law was passed, the *Diet* also provisionally approved the Basic Resident Registers Law, granting Tokyo the authority to issue an 11-digit number to every Japanese citizen and resident alien, and requiring all citizens and resident aliens to provide basic information – name, date of birth, sex, and address. The registered data is computerized and connected to the nationwide Resident Registry Network System (RRNS, also called "Juki-Net") created by the law. The government

---

[3211] Guidelines for the Protection of Personal Information in Businesses That Use Human Genetic Information, available at <http://www.meti.go.jp/feedback/downloadfiles/i41227dj.pdf>.

[3212] "Japan's Police Have Decided to Keep a DNA Database on Crime Suspects, Officials Said," Mainichi Shimbun, April 28, 2005.

[3213] The Law Concerning Access to Information Held by Administrative Organs, available at <http://www.somucho.go.jp/gyoukan/kanri/translation.htm>.

[3214] <http://www.soumu.go.jp/s-news/2004/040730_8.html>.

planned to expand the use of the registry code to offer administrative services "more efficiently" via this network.[3215] The RRNS was partly launched on August 5, 2002. However, some local governments, such as the city of Yokohama, the nation's largest municipality, have decided not to participate in the network, and some local assemblies decided to postpone the launch of the system.[3216] The six local governments refused to log on to RRNS because of concerns for personal information security.[3217] On July 26, 2002, a group of academics, journalists and Tokyo citizens filed a suit against the state over the network, alleging that the network system invades the right of privacy and is unconstitutional.[3218] The METI said it would introduce an electronic information security audit system by year-end to address public concerns. On August 22, 2002, METI officials set complete audit guidelines that conform to international rules and entrust independent auditing companies to inspect whether computer network systems of municipalities and businesses are sufficiently secure in protecting private information.[3219] On August 25, 2003, all of the prefecture's 34 municipal offices launched full RRNS operations.

The Nagano Prefecture carried out hacking, using a computer from outside the local body offices with a LAN connection and through the Internet, to verify the vulnerability of the RRNS system between September and November 2003.[3220] Their results found that access to private information on residents was accessible with local area network (LAN) connections, both from within and outside local body offices. Part of the tests also reportedly showed that it was possible to falsify personal data in the network and send it to servers nationwide.[3221] The Saga Prefectural Police arrested a 46-year-old man on suspicion of illegally obtaining a resident registry card of another man in September 2003. It is alleged that he used the card to borrow several hundred thousand yen from many consumer finance firms. This is the first arrest made over illegal use of RRNS.[3222]

[3215] "Diet Passes Wiretap, ID Bills," Asia Intelligence Wire, August 13, 1999.

[3216] "Yokohama to Give Choice, Kokubunji to Boycott Registry," Japan Economic Newswire, August 2 2002.

[3217] "Government Starts the Resident Registry Network System," The Daily Yomiuri, August 6, 2002.

[3218] "Seek Injunction against the Residents Registration Network," Nihon Keizai Simbun, July 27, 2003.

[3219] "Public Records: Japanese Officials Plan Security Audit On New Resident Registration Program," Privacy Law Watch, August 23, 2003.

[3220] "Nagano Gov't Hackers Easily Infiltrate 'Big Brother' Network," Mainichi Daily News, December 16, 2003.

[3221] Id.

[3222] "1st Arrest Made over Illegal Juki Net Use," The Daily Yomiuri, February 8, 2004.

In May 2002, the Defense Agency revealed that more than 550 municipalities across the nation had provided the Agency with registered personal data on teenagers that should not have been divulged.[3223] The Defense Agency received information from those municipalities, such as the occupation and health condition of teenagers' parents, which does not appear in the registration cards that anyone can access pursuant to the Basic Resident Registers Law. Such cards only contain residents' names, addresses, dates of birth and gender. The agency has used information to assist the Self-Defense Forces' (SDF) recruitment activities.[3224] The Defense Agency also revealed that collection activity for SDF had been conducted since 1966.[3225]

On May 31, 2005, The Kanazawa District Court ordered the government to delete personal information from the RRNS about 28 plaintiff-residents of the Ishikawa Prefecture.[3226] The court explicitly stated that the government violated the right to privacy considered in the Constitution as the right to control one's own information, and held that all residents' information was subject to privacy rights, and, therefore, that individuals' consent was required when it forcibly placed the plaintiffs' personal information on the RRNS.[3227] The Court, however, dismissed the plaintiffs' demand for compensation from the government.[3228] A day after this decision, the Nagoya District Court ruled that the RRNS does not violate privacy rights under the Constitution.[3229] The Nagoya District Court held that residents' names, addresses, birth dates and genders, plus 11-digit resident codes stored in the network that people can access over the network, "do not need to be highly protected." It held that the plaintiff's rights and legal interests had not been infringed upon.[3230] In both Nagoya and Kanazawa, the plaintiffs who comprised members of the Tokai and Ishikawa branches of a nationwide association against RRNS, insisted that their rights to privacy, guaranteed under Article 13 of the Constitution, were in jeopardy as the network shared basic personal information with the central and local governments.[3231] Similar

---

[3223] "Municipalities Gave Data to SDF Inappropriately," Japan Economic Newswire, May 19, 2002. This case is unclear as to whether or not it violates the law.

[3224] Id.

[3225] "Defense Agency Collated Secret Data on Recruits for its Ranks," The Japan Times, April 23, 2003.

[3226] "Court Orders Government to Delete Residents' Personal Information from Registry Network," Mainichi Daily News, May 30, 2005.

[3227] "Juki Net Clouds Privacy Rights," The Daily Yomiuri, June 2, 2005,

[3228] Id; "The Defendant Ishikawa Prefecture Appealed to the Higher Court afterward," Mainichi Shimbun, June 7, 2005.

[3229] "Court Rules Juki Net not a Violation of Privacy," The Daily Yomiuri, June 1, 2005.

[3230] Id.

[3231] Id.

lawsuits, filed at 13 district courts, have focused on whether RRNS infringes on people's privacy rights.[3232]

Personal Data Leaks

In June 2002, the Defense Agency revealed that it had been collecting names of people requesting information via the new law and cross-referencing the list with private information, such as the political affiliations of the requestor.[3233] While it is as yet unclear whether the list constitutes a clear violation of the law, it has sparked a huge outcry by the public, including calls for the resignation of defense officials.[3234] On February 12, 2004, the Tokyo District Court ruled that a list compiled by the Defense Agency on people who sought information from it violated their privacy, and ordered the government to pay JPY 100,000 (~USD 915,600) in compensation to a writer who was on the list.[3235]

According to the Cabinet Office's survey on the protection of personal information, 69 percent of people in Japan are worried that their personal information may be leaked from public entities and private firms, up drastically from 39.8 percent in a previous survey in 1989.[3236] The year 2004 saw many massive data leaks cases. It came to light that personal data of about 4.6 million subscribers to Yahoo BB (Broad Band Phone Service) Internet access service was leaked by its employees. The case is unprecedented in Japan in terms of volume.[3237] The Metropolitan Police Department arrested four persons for allegedly blackmailing Softbank Corp. – the company that operates Yahoo BB – as well as an affiliate, including the company employees, by threatening to leak confidential customer data they had illegally obtained from those companies. Softbank Corp. allowed several people to share the same ID and password to access its database. Stolen information included each subscriber's name, address, phone number, subscription starting date and e-mail address, but did not include credit card details.[3238] Three of Yahoo BB's customers launched a damages suit

---

[3232] *Id.*

[3233] "MSDF Officer Compiled Personal Data on People Seeking Defense Agency Info," Japan Times, May 29, 2002.

[3234] "Private Data Kept by All SDF Arms," Japan Times, June 4, 2002.

[3235] "Court Rules Defense Agency's Info List Illegal, Violates Privacy," Japan Economic Newswire, February 12, 2004.

[3236] "69% Worried about Personal Information Leaking: Survey," Japan Economic Newswire, December 6, 2003.

[3237] "Yahoo! BB subscriber info leaked," The Daily Yomiuri, February 25, 2004, at 1.

[3238] *Id.* As an apology to its customers, Softbank sent them JPY 500 gift certificates, a measure that could have cost the company about JPY four billion. Taiga Uranaka, "Softbank Offers 500 to Yahoo! BB Users, Confirms Data Leak on Millions," The Japan Times, February 28, 2004.

against the service operator Softbank Corp. before the Osaka District Court over the massive leak of customer information. The three plaintiffs, Yahoo BB's customers, are demanding JPY 100,000 each in compensation.[3239]

There were other similar cases that resulted from failures in proper management of personal data involving such companies as Sanyo Shinpan Finance Co., one of the major consumer finance firms (up to two million customers' personal data),[3240] consumer credit company Nihon Shinpan (up to 100,000 customers),[3241] Suntry (75,000),[3242] major travel agent Hankyu Express (620,000),[3243] DSL service provider ACCA Networks (about one million),[3244] teleshop service JAPANET TAKATA (660,000),[3245] and Cosomo Oil (920,000).[3246] According to the Ministry of Public Management, 52 cases involving major leaks of personal information were reported during the past three years.[3247] In June 2002, the NPA and the Metropolitan Police Department reported that, in May 2002, the names, addresses and other personal information of some 50,000 visitors of the web site of Kommy Corp. (a beauty-treatment service firm), had been leaked. There were other similar cases involving such entities as YKK Architectural Products Inc., All Nippon Airways World Tours Co. and Nihon University. Police authorities also warned that the massive leaks of personal information resulted from simple errors in web site design.[3248]

On May 12, 2004, METI's Information Security Subcommittee resolved to call on the Government to amend the Criminal Code to include a criminal offense of "information theft." The Subcommittee called for the theft of information to attract the same penalties as the theft of any tangible object. Japanese law does not currently penalize the unauthorized electronic transfer of information, and the Personal Information Protection Act does not penalize individuals. METI will work with the Ministry of Justice and the Cabinet Office on the proposal to amend the law.[3249]

[3239] "Internet Customers Sue Yahoo! BB Operator over Info Leak," Mainichi Daily News, May 17, 2004.

[3240] Nihon Keizai Shimbun, May 11, 2004.

[3241] *Id.* April 26, 2004.

[3242] *Id.* March 30, 2004.

[3243] *Id.* June 2, 2004.

[3244] *Id.* May 25, 2004.

[3245] *Id.* May 9, 2004.

[3246] *Id.* June 8, 2004.

[3247] "Bills on Personal Data Seek Balance," The Daily Yomiuri, May 8, 2003.

[3248] "Police Call for Security Steps to Prevent Online," Japan Economic Newswire, June 5, 2002.

[3249] "METI To Seek Law against Information Theft," Nihon Keizai Shimbun, May 15, 2004.

On June 17, 2005, the United States company MasterCard International revealed that the security system in CardSystems, a company handling MasterCard's data processing, had been breached and an unauthorized individual had been able to infiltrate its network and access the data of more than 40 million cardholders in the world.[3250] Effects from the data breach are being felt around the world. Because 26 Japanese card issuers are linked to MasterCard, their customers had to be notified that they were at risk of having fraudulent charges placed on their accounts as a result of the breach.[3251] More than 120 Japanese customers have thus far reported fraudulent activity.[3252]

Voting Privacy

Voting in Japan is voluntary for those 20 years of age or older.[3253] In 2001, the law governing elections in cities, towns, and villages was changed to allow electronic voting. Electronic voting was conducted at the municipal level for the first time in 2002, when the city of Niimi in the Prefecture of Okayama allowed their use in a mayoral and local assembly election.[3254] More than 15,000 voters at 43 polling locations in Niimi cast votes on touch-screen voting machines. The Public Management Ministry plans to revise the Public Office Election Law to allow the use of electronic voting for national elections.[3255] Before the use of electronic voting, all ballot selections were handwritten by voters and counted by hand.[3256]

The Hashemite Kingdom of Jordan

Constitutional Privacy Framework

As with many languages, Arabic has no equivalent to the English word "privacy," although there exist more specific – and less ambiguous – words that pertain to any discussion of privacy rights.[3257] While the concept of privacy

---

[3250] "Banks Unsure Which Cards Were Exposed in Breach," The New York Times, June 21, 2005,

[3251] "6TH LD: Security Breach in US Affects More than 300 Cards in Japan," Japan Economic Newswire, June 21, 2005,

[3252] *Id.*

[3253] CIA, The Country Fact Book, Japan, available at <http://www.cia.gov/cia/publications/factbook/geos/ja.html#Govt>.

[3254] "Electronic Voting Opens New Doors," Mainichi Daily News, June 24, 2002.

[3255] "Electronic Vote Eyed for '04 Poll," The Daily Yomiuri, January 4, 2002.

[3256] *Id.*

[3257] For example, the term "*khususi*" meaning "personal."

exists in the Arab world, its content and meaning differ from Western notions.[3258] Traditional Arab privacy does not connote "the 'personal,' the 'secret' or the 'individuated space,' rather it concerns two core spheres – women and the family."[3259] Thus, while privacy as a cultural value is entrenched in the Jordanian state, privacy as a legal right is as yet an evolving concept.

The Jordanian Constitution specifically recognizes a limited right to privacy, but these rights are regularly circumscribed by law or practice. Article 10 of the Constitution stipulates, "[d]welling houses shall be inviolable and shall not be entered except in the circumstances and in the manner prescribed by law."[3260] Jordanian law is founded on Islamic law or *shari'ah* and elements of the Napoleonic Code.[3261] Article 10 can be directly traced to both the *Qur'an* and the *Sunnah* – the body of precedent sayings, acts and tacit approvals of the Prophet Mohammed – which together form the basis of the *shari'ah*.[3262]

Article 18 of the Constitution stipulates, "[a]ll postal, telegraphic and telephonic communications shall be treated as secret and as such shall not be subject to censorship or suspension except in circumstances prescribed by law." In practice, however, authorities often do not respect these constitutional restrictions. According to human rights reports, security officers monitor telephone conversations and Internet communications, read private correspondence, and engage in surveillance of persons who are considered to pose a threat to the government or national security.[3263] Unlawful telephone surveillance, in

---

[3258] *See* Ahmad Moussalli, The Islamic Quest for Democracy, Pluralism, and Human Rights, 129 (University Press of Florida 2001). "Thus the state, which is responsible for securing people's rights, must work within a just context. For instance, the right to privacy – the prohibition of espionage or intruding in the private life of people – cannot be secured without such a context. Islamic jurists' views on this point can be summarized by saying that the privacy of the people could not legitimately be invaded if there was no apparent misconduct or violation of the law. The sanctity of privacy was earlier postulated by the Prophet [Mohammed] himself and can also be found in the *Qur'an*; the Prophet prohibited entering any residence without the owner's permission. Hanbali, Hanafi, Shafi'i, and some Maliki [jurists have agreed that a person can defend his privacy and even hurt the offender without incurring punishment [footnotes omitted]." Hanbali, Hanafi, Shafi'i, and Maliki are four of the five religious authorities of the *Sunni* school, which is one of the most important sects of Islam.

[3259] Fadwa El Guindi, Veil, Modesty, Privacy and Resistance, 81-82 (Berg 1999).

[3260] Constitution of the Hashemite Kingdom of Jordan, adopted January 1, 1952, available at <http://www.kinghussein.gov.jo/constitution_jo.html>.

[3261] CIA World Factbook 2002, available at <http://www.cia.gov/cia/publications/factbook/geos/jo.html>.

[3262] Umar Moghul, Approximating Certainty in Ratiocination: How to Ascertain the *'Illah* (Effective Cause) in the Islamic Legal System 4 J. Islamic Law 125, 135 (1999). Unlike English common law, which is secular, Islamic law is based on divine sources: the *Qur'an* and the *Sunnah*. *'Illah* is the reason for which a particular law is believed to have been established by God. The *'illah* of asking permission before entering a private home is given in the text itself when the Prophet says that "permission is required because of viewing." Regardless of the potential awkwardness of adapting ancient text to the modern concept, it could be said that the *'illah* therefore protects the privacy of the home.

[3263] United States State Department, Country Report on Human Rights Practices in Jordan, 2003, available at <http://www.state.gov/g/drl/rls/hrrpt/2003/27930.htm>.

particular, has become such a frequent issue in the courts that it has been the object of complaint by some judges.[3264]

Other regular privacy or related rights abuses include arbitrary arrest and detention; lack of transparent investigations and accountability within the security services; prolonged detention without charge; denial of due process of law stemming from the expanded authority of the State Security Court and interference in the judicial process; harassment of members of opposition political parties; and significant restrictions on freedom of speech, press, assembly, and association.

Data Protection Framework

Jordan has no data protection or privacy law, and it remains difficult for Jordanians to exercise their information privacy rights.[3265] However, a few laws already provide some level of privacy protections. While still relatively low, Internet penetration and e-commerce are expanding. Coupled with this growth, concerns about privacy and data collection are also developing. Less than three years ago, the majority of potential e-commerce users felt that their rights of privacy were not protected under then-current laws. There are domestic and international pressures for the government to address these issues.[3266]

Recently, the Royal Scientific Society conducted a study on e-commerce and its effect on labor and found that Jordan was one of the leading countries in adjusting its laws to conform to technological evolution, which encouraged local companies to start electronic businesses.[3267] This could be attributed to the aforementioned pressure put on the government. According to another study, would-be e-commerce users feel that their privacy is not protected by the way the law is written.[3268]

In July 1999, Jordan drafted a plan to establish the requisites for a knowledge-based economy, including: modern cyber laws, new information technology (IT) infrastructure, an IT-oriented educational system, and the latest generation in

---

[3264] *Id.*

[3265] Akhal Al Ahmad, The Virtual Law Firm: Privacy Issue World Wide Activities Middle East – Jordan, available at <http://vlf.juridicum.su.se/master99/staff/akhal/privacy.html>.

[3266] Obeidat Mohammad, "Consumer Protection and Electronic Commerce in Jordan – An Exploratory Study," The Public Voice in Emerging Market Economies Conference, 2001.

[3267] "Jordan: RSS Study Examines Effect of E-Commerce on Labor Practices," Financial Times Information, December 15, 2004.

[3268] Obeidat Mohammad, *supra.*

telecommunications.[3269] A key goal of the public/private REACH Initiative[3270] has been to establish a supportive regulatory and legal environment for e-commerce; a dozen important legislative changes have been promulgated, with more on the way.[3271] The achievements of the IT sector through REACH have included 15 new laws dealing with labor, telecommunications, private shareholding and IP, education sector reform and private-public partnerships.[3272] Unlike Malaysia's Multimedia Super Corridor program, after which it is modeled, privacy or data protection legislation is noticeably absent from the REACH agenda. However, several amendments and regulations have significant implications for privacy rights, including the Electronic Transactions Act, regulations for Internet cafés, and amendments to the Telecommunications Act.[3273]

The Electronic Transactions Act (ETA) prohibits authentication institutions from disclosing the secrets of any client[3274] and provides additional sanctions for any person who commits a crime by electronic means.[3275] Furthermore, the act gives the Telecommunication Regulatory Commission the "right to monitor the source of any radio waves to ascertain the licensing of that source, without this being considered as breach of the confidentiality of communications or violation of the provisions of the Laws in force."[3276]

In December 2000, regulations were promulgated under the ETA to govern the operation and licensing of Internet cafés. The regulations required that the government license all Internet cafés and that all owners[3277] and managers[3278] be

---

[3269] Owen Clegg, "Malaysia Is Example to Follow," Jordan Times, April 23, 2001.

[3270] REACH is an acronym standing for: Regulatory Framework; Enabling Environment and Infrastructure; Advancement of National IT Programs; Capital and Finance; Human Resource Development.

[3271] Ghassan Joha, "Reach 2.0: Initiative to Develop IT Sector," Arabia.com, July 16, 2000, available at <http://web.archive.org/web/20031016212731/http://www.arabia.com/jordan/business/article/english/0,5127,37 69,00.html>.

[3272] Sarah Ryan, "Information Technology Sector Highlighted as an Example of Organizing Private Sector Clusters." Jordan Times. December 20, 2004, available at <http://www.jordanembassyus.org/12202004005.htm>.

[3273] Wassel Al Mashagbeh & Brendan Gannon, "Expanding the Usage of the Internet and Bridging the Digital Divide," Jordan Times, June 1, 2001, available at <http://www.jordanembassyus.org/0612001004.htm>.

[3274] Electronic Transactions Law No. (85) of 2001, § 37 (December 31, 2001), available at <http://www.bakernet.com/ecommerce/e-transactions%20law.doc>.

[3275] Id. at § 38.

[3276] Telecommunications Law No. 13 and its Amendments of 1995, Article 62, available at <http://www.trc.gov.jo/Static_English/chap%209.shtm>.

[3277] Instructions for Regulating the Work of the Internet Centers and Cafés and the Bases for their Licensing for the Year 2001, § 4 (December 2001), available at <http://www.reach.jo/Downloads/Legislative/Internet_Cafes_Regulations.pdf> [Internet Café Regulations].

[3278] Id. at § 17.

Jordanian nationals, of "good conduct and manners," and without any felony or misdemeanor convictions affecting honor or public morals. More controversially, the regulations stipulated that Internet cafés must collect user names and any available unique personal identifiers (*i.e.* national ID number), the time of use, the fixed IP address of the Internet access point and monthly log files showing which sites had been visited and by whom.[3279] Internet cafés were also required to block and filter any site containing "any visual, audible or printed materials that provoke sexual instincts, slandered religious beliefs or promoted the use of drugs, tobacco and medical drugs, gambling sites or sites that showed the method of manufacturing of materials for military uses in an illegitimate manner."[3280] Further, all Internet point-of-access were required to be in public halls open to the public and not in a closed or private room.[3281] A public security team would periodically perform inspection tours of all cafés.[3282] While café personnel were required to maintain the confidentiality of all personal data pertaining to the user and any information relevant to their use of the network,[3283] they were also required to submit such information to authorities when requested in accordance with the law.[3284]

In response to negative reactions from the REACH private-sector participants, the government quickly retracted the regulations in January 2001.[3285]

Amendments to the Telecommunications Act provide that "telephone calls and private telecommunications shall be considered confidential matters that shall not be violated"[3286] and that any person who "withholds a message . . . copies or reveals a message or tampers with the data related to any subscriber, including unpublished telephone numbers and sent or received messages,"[3287] or who discloses the content of any private communication "which came to his knowledge by virtue of his post or who records the same without any legal basis, shall be punished" by imprisonment, a fine or both.[3288] Similarly, "any person who intercepts, obstructs, alters or strikes off the contents of a message carried

---

[3279] *Id.* at § 6(1)-(2).

[3280] *Id.* at § 6(4).

[3281] Internet Café Regulations, *supra* at § 13.

[3282] *Id.* at § 12.

[3283] *Id.* at § 6(3).

[3284] *Id.* at § 11(2).

[3285] "Gov't Nixes New Net Cafe Regulations," Jordan Times, January 29, 2001; Maia Malas, "Jordan Joins Debate over Internet Access Controls," Jordan Times, December 1, 2001.

[3286] Telecommunications Law of 1995, § 56 (amended February 17, 2002), available at <http://www.trc.gov.jo/Static_English/chap%208.shtm>.

[3287] *Id.* at § 77.

[3288] *Id.* at § 71.

through the telecommunications networks or encourages others to do so, shall be punished" by imprisonment, a fine or both.[3289]

In 2004, Jordan along with Egypt, Tunisia, and Morocco signed the Agadir Process, a European Union-led effort to integrate the Mediterranean region into global trade and to create stable business environments.[3290] These events indicate a shift in Jordan's stance on data protection as industry speculation in the country points to further legal consultation concerning procedures and regulation of conducting trade and commerce with the countries of the European Union.[3291] This has led to the belief that the European Union's data protection regime is potentially compatible with some Middle Eastern countries Islamic beliefs (which many of their laws resonate from) and values when compared to the United States system of self-regulation.[3292]

National ID

The government imposes some limits on freedom of religion and notes individuals' religious affiliation (except for *Druze* and *Baha'is*, and other unrecognized religions) on the national identity card and in the "family book" (a national registration record that is issued to the head of every family and that serves as proof of citizenship) of all citizens. Atheists must associate themselves with a recognized religion for official identification purposes.

In September 2001, the government rolled out a new national identification smart card. The new cards feature stronger security measures and will replace the current national identification card. According to the government, however, they also carry more personal information, notably voter registration information.[3293] Jordan has also implemented a smart health card system in the capital. Doctors, pharmacies, hospitals, laboratories and radiology centers in Amman have electronic access to patient insurance and medical information through a card-based system of electronic record storage. Personal information contained on these cards includes everything from blood type to benefits status.[3294]

[3289] *Id.* at § 76.

[3290] "Commissioner Patten Attends Signature of Agadir Agreement," Europa World, February 27, 2004, available at <http://www.europaworld.org/week166/commissionerpatten27204.htm>.

[3291] Ryan Moshell, Comment:…and then There Was One: The Outlook for A Self-Regulatory United States amidst A Global Trend toward Comprehensive Data Protection, 37 Texas Tech Law Review 357 (2005).

[3292] *Id.*

[3293] Rana Husseini, "New National ID to Include Voter Information," Jordan Times, August 29, 2001.

[3294] News Release, "Cardlogix, NatHealth, IdealSoft, and Innovonics Provide Smart Card Medical Records to Country of Jordan," Cardlogix, April 9, 2000.

International Obligations

In 2000, Jordan signed several international agreements that will likely assist in propagating international standards for privacy protection into domestic law, including its acceptance to the World Trade Organization, a trade partnership agreement with the European Union and a joint statement on electronic commerce with the United States. The first two agreements call for the liberalization of trade and stipulate the incorporation of measures to facilitate the development of, among other things, information privacy rights with respect to the processing of personal data, and assurances of minimal restrictions on the free flow of personal data between jurisdictions. The third agreement explicitly recognizes that both the public and the private sectors need to be involved in the protection of privacy for e-commerce to flourish, and sets the Organization for Economic Cooperation and Development Guidelines on the Protection of Privacy and Transborder Flows of Personal Data as an appropriate basis for policy development.[3295] None of these agreements have legal force, but they are potential indicators of future policy. On June 10, 2003, the EU's Association Agreement with Jordan went into effect during the Euro-Mediterranean "Barcelona Process."[3296] Jordan is a signatory to the United Nations Declaration of Human Rights.

Republic of Latvia

Statutory Rules of Privacy

Article 96 of the Latvian Constitution established a fundamental human right to privacy: "Everyone has the right to inviolability of their private life, home and correspondence."[3297] All laws protecting privacy apply to citizens and noncitizens equally.[3298]

The Law on Personal Data Protection was adopted by the Parliament on March 23, 2000, and came into force in January 2001. The law is based on standard fair

---

[3295] US-Jordanian Joint Statement on Electronic Commerce, available at
<http://www.jordanusfta.com/documents/joint_statement_on_e-commerce.pdf>.

[3296] Human Rights Watch World Report 2003: Middle East and North Africa Overview, 2003, available at <http://www.hrw.org/wr2k3/mideast.html>.

[3297] Constitution of the Republic of Latvia, available at
<http://www.saeima.lv/LapasEnglish/Constitution_Saturs.htm>.

[3298] The United States State Department report on Human Rights Practices 2002, Bureau of Democracy, Human Rights, and Labor for the year, Latvia Country Report on Human Rights Practices.

information practices and is fully compliant with the EU Data Protection Directive.

Data processing systems in the areas of "public safety, combating of crime or national security and defense" or those maintained "by institutions specially authorized by law" are exempt from this registration procedure. Nevertheless, personal data protection does apply to the police sector.[3299] A further exemption from the Act is provided for "official secret matters" regulated by the Law on Official Secrets. The Law distinguishes personal data related to criminal offences, criminal records, judicial procedures in criminal cases and closed civil cases can only be processed by persons prescribed by law in the occasions provided by law.

Supervisory Authority

Supervision over personal data protection shall be carried out by the *Datu valsts inspekcija* (Data State Inspectorate), an institution established in 2001 and currently under the jurisdiction of the Ministry of Justice"[3300] Data State Inspectorate has staff of about 17 employees as of June 2005. It is charged with making decisions and reviewing complaints, making formal recommendations, issuing permission for the transfer of information abroad, and maintaining and inspecting the national register of data processing systems. Data State Inspectorate is also authorized to impose administrative penalties for violations of personal data processing.[3301]

In 2004, the Inspection considered 137 applications and imposed 18 administrative punishments (in 14 cases the penalty has been financial). Approximately 10% of all the complaints are related to the health sector.[3302] Throughout the year, there were 407 consultations provided to data controllers and citizens (by written answers as well as direct communication). In the beginning of the year, the Inspectorate launched a three-month public awareness campaign on the right to data protection.

[3299] Latvia's Contribution to the Regular Report from the Commission on Latvia's Progress Towards Accession (National Progress Report), June 2002, available at
<http://www.am.gov.lv/files/e/national_progress_report_2002.pdf>.

[3300] The Law on Personal Data Protection, Article 29, effective since January 1, 2004

[3301] *Id.;* as of July 2003, 35 complaints had been received.

[3302] E-mail from Aiga Balode, to Ula Galster, International Policy Fellow, Electronic Privacy Information Center, May 1, 2005 (on file with EPIC).

During 2004, the Inspectorate has accredited 45 internal and eight external data protection auditors.[3303] Also in 2004, the Inspectorate received 818 applications for system registration, in total 705 systems were registered. The register is available online.[3304]

Wiretapping and Surveillance Rules

Violation of the confidentiality of correspondence, information in the form of transmissions over a telecommunications networks and other information is liable to criminal punishment.[3305] On October 28, 2004, the Law on Electronic Communications was adopted.[3306] The Law on Electronic Communications replaced the Law on Telecommunications; it contains the provisions of the EU Directive on privacy and electronic communications (2002/58/EC) and has a chapter regulating data protection in the electronic communications sector. Article 68 of the Law on Electronic Communications states that the service provider is prohibited from disclosing information on users or subscribers as well as information on received electronic communications services or value added services. The Law gives the right to the interception or surveillance of communications only to the officials of bodies performing investigatory operations and only in the cases specified by law. In addition, the processing of traffic data and location data is regulated by the Law on Electronic Communications.[3307]

The new Criminal Procedure Law,[3308] which is intended to replace the Soviet time regulation of 1961, will be adopted in May 2005. Amongst other issues, the Law elaborates on the role and process of acquiring electronic evidence. According to this regulation, investigation officers have powers to obligate an information system manager to ensure immediately that certain data necessary for the purposes of investigation is preserved unchanged and may not be revealed to any third persons whatsoever. But it is only after receiving permission of a judge that the officer can require a manager to reveal data stored in the system.[3309] There are also new rules on applying means of investigation

---

[3303] According to information providing by Egins Āletrs, Head of Information Division of the Data State Inspectorate, July 13, 2005.

[3304] E-mail from Aiga Balode, *supra*; *see also*, <http://www.dvi.gov.lv>.

[3305] Criminal Code, Article 144 as of July 2005.

[3306] Entered into force on December 1, 2004.

[3307] Law on Electronic Communications, available only in Latvian at <http://www.likumi.lv/doc.php?id=96611>.

[3308] Criminal Procedure Law, Latvijas Vestnesis, May 11, 2005, effective from October 2005.

[3309] *Id.* at Articles 191 and 192.

conducted without individual's consent or knowledge, such as wiretapping, control of data stored in an electronical storage system, control of transferred data, video and audio control of a certain place or person, and tracking of a person can be executed only with a permission of a judge. The new law has outlined more detailed guidelines for implementation of discretionary powers of responsible officers and the court.

Article 143 of the Criminal Law prescribes liability for illegal entry into a residence unit against the will of the person residing there. Article 144 of the Criminal Law provides that the intentional violation of the secrecy of personal correspondence or information transmitted over telecommunications networks, as well as the intentional violation of the secrecy of such information and software provided for use in connection with electronic data processing, is punishable by coercive community service or a fine of up to five minimum monthly salaries.[3310]

The Criminal Procedure Code provides an exhaustive list of situations when public agencies have a right to interfere with the right of a person to the inviolability of privacy in family life, residence and correspondence, in compliance with the procedure prescribed by the abovementioned Code. The Law lists the following procedural activities – search of the residence, search of the person, inspection, observation, seizing the property, seizing the post and telegraph correspondence, tapping telephone conversations and acquiring information from technical means, investigation experiment and the verification of testimonies on site.[3311]

One is allowed to tap conversations over the telephone and other means of communication of the suspect or the accused person, on the basis of a decision of court or a judge, in the specific criminal case, if there are sufficient grounds to believe that tapping conversations or the acquisition of information through technical means can provide information relevant to the case. One is also allowed to gain information from the technical means that are used by the suspect or the accused person. The decision on tapping conversations or the acquisition of information through technical means is sent to the police for execution. If the threat of violence, extortion or other illegal acts has been directed against the victim, the witness or other persons participating in the case, conversations of these persons over the telephone or other means of communication can be tapped

---

[3310] The Criminal Law, available at <http://www.ttc.lv/New/lv/tulkojumi/E0032.doc>.
[3311] Id.

without a decision by court or a judge, following the application submitted by these persons and with their consent.[3312]

The Law "On Operative Activity" and the Criminal Procedure Code include norms that do not permit an arbitrary and unjustified interference in the right of a person to the inviolability of residence and correspondence. Under Article 8 of the above Law, the operative control of correspondence, the operative acquisition of information from technical means, the operative tapping of non-public conversations (also over the telephone, electronic and other means of communication) and the operative entry is to be performed with the approval of judges. The permission to perform these operative activities may be issued for a period of up to three months and, in the event of justified necessity, it may prolonged, but only for the period of time that the operative proceedings concerning the person are undertaken. In exceptional cases, i.e., when there is a need of acting without delay to prevent a threat to vital public interests, an act of terrorism or subversive activity, a murder or some other serious crime, or if there is actual threat for the life, health or property of a person or the person's close relatives, the above operative activities can be performed without the judge's approval. The prosecutor must be notified about them within 24 hours, while the judge's approval must be received within 72 hours. If the officers fail to do so, the performance of operative activities must be terminated. In addition, Article 5 of the above Law stipulates that if the person under observation holds the opinion that the operative activity has violated his or her lawful interests and freedoms, the person has the right to submit a complaint to the prosecutor, who after a review issues a statement on the compliance of officials of operative activities to law, or the person may submit a claim in court.[3313]

There is no separate binding regulation on use of surveillance technologies; issues arising out of such cases are dealt in accordance with principles and norms of data protection law. However, in 2004 the Inspection prepared a non-binding recommendation comprising basic principles that should be followed by those willing to use such technologies in accordance with the rule of law.

A case, which has received a considerable public attention, arose in the end of April 2005 when a widely known lawyer publicly announced concerns that his office phones were being tapped. The Council of Sworn Advocates referred the

---

[3312] *Id.*

[3313] "Periodic Report Of The Republic Of Latvia On The Implementation Of The 1966 International Covenant On Civil And Political Rights In The Republic Of Latvia During The Period From 1995 Till 2002," available at <http://www.mkparstavis.am.gov.lv/en/?id=58>.

case to Prosecutor General's Office, which subsequently denied the claims and refused to start criminal proceedings on the issue.[3314]

Anti-terrorism Measures

In 2004, there have been several amendments to the existing legislation, which on the account of fight against terrorism, have loosened the rules guaranteeing protection of personal data in credit institutions. Coordinated amendments were made to laws on credit institutions on the Prevention of the Laundering of the Proceeds from Crime and Law on Financial Instruments.

Though the basic principle in the law on credit institutions renders that information about a client and his dealings is protected information, the lawmakers have widened the scope of exceptions. It now ensures that information on clients (existent and potential) and their dealings have to be revealed to institutions mentioned in the law in the amount required by the law. The law now mentions 13 occasions when full information on the client must be given to institutions mentioned in law, with or without the consent of a judge in some cases.[3315]

In November 2004, the Cabinet of Ministers accepted a Concept on Establishment of Anti Terrorism Centre, a document that entails establishment of a new specialized department within the institutional structure of the Security Police. The department would mainly conduct analytical and planning activities.

Major Privacy Case Law

In 2003, the Riga City Council refused to release to journalists information on bonus salaries received by its officials on the occasion of national celebration. After some public discussion and interference of the responsible minister, the Council agreed to provide information to the major daily newspaper "Diena," which published an article including the facts obtained from the Council.[3316] An employee whose data was included in the publication claimed satisfaction of moral damages from the Inspectorate, holding that information was released following "irresponsible action" and "order" of the Inspectorate. The claim was

---

[3314] Neatkariga Rita Avize, April 15, 2005 and BNS, June 15, 2005.

[3315] Law On Credit Institutions, Article 63.

[3316] Ivars Āboliņš "Arī domes ierindas darbiniekiem lielas prēmijas [Employees of the City Council Have Received Substantial Premium Sallaries]," Diena, December 6, 2003.

dismissed. The Court held that "Personal Data Protection law does not limit the freedom of press and [its] right to receive information."[3317] Law on Budgets of Local Governments[3318] provides that process of elaboration and spending of the budget must be open/ transparent.

Law on Official Secrets[3319] establishes that information on the economic situation of the country, execution of budget, and rates of salaries, benefits, preferences and guarantees granted to officials and employees of the state and local government institutions cannot be declared information of restricted access.[3320]

Since 2001, there have also been several cases concerning protection of privacy brought before Constitutional Court of Latvia and ECHR both by Latvian citizens and non-citizens. The Latvian Constitutional Court ruled in January 2005 that the norm of the Criminal Law, which envisages criminal liability for the "use of narcotic or psychotropic substances without a physician's designation," doesn't violate the right to private life. The Court stated that the norm shall be regarded as a restriction of the right to inviolability of private life, but the restriction is constitutional because it is aimed at the protection of public safety and it is needed in a democratic society as the health of an individual is inherent not only of personal but also of social value; the Court also took into consideration the spread of narcomania in the State and its special dangerousness.[3321]

The *Mentzen* case concerned the law requiring personal names of foreign origin to be "Latvianized" in official documents. The Latvian Constitutional Court ruled that the law does implicate the constitutional right to privacy, but the restriction was declared constitutional because it protected "the rights of other inhabitants of Latvia to use the Latvian language on all of Latvia's territory and to protect the democratic order."[3322] The European Court on Human Rights (ECtHR) dismissed

---

[3317] Judgment of the Center District of Riga, May 13, 2004, No. C-27085004;C-850/04/7 (not published) page 3, paragraph 9; *see also*, Article 5 of the Law on Personal Data Protection.

[3318] Law on Budgets of Local Governments., April 4, 1995, at Article 6.

[3319] Law on Official Secrets, October 29, 1996 at Article 5 available at <http://www.ttc.lv/New/lv/tulkojumi/E0612.doc>.

[3321] Judgment of the Latvian Constitutional Court in case No. 2004-17-01 "On the Compliance of the Norm 'Use of Narcotic and Psychotropic Substances without a Physician's Designation,' Included in the First Part of Section 253² of the Republic of Latvia Criminal Law with Article 96 of the Republic of Latvia Satversme," January 26, 2005, available at <http://www.satv.tiesa.gov.lv/ENG/Spriedumi/17-01(04).htm>.

[3322] Judgment of the Latvian Constitutional Court of December 2, 2001, No. 2001-04-0103.

the application, stating the alleged violation is such that would be necessary in a democratic society.[3323]

Another case, *Tatjana Slivenko and Others v. Latvia*, was filed by the wife and daughter of a former member of the Russian military. The family was denied residency and expelled from the country on the basis of the 1994 agreement with Russia on troop withdrawal. The ECtHR held in October 2003 that the applicants' removal from Latvia constituted an interference with their "private life" and their "home" within the meaning of Article 8 (1) of the European Convention for the Protection of Human Rights and Fundamental Freedoms (ECHR) and that Latvia had therefore violated Article 8 of the Convention.[3324]

The case of *Sisojeva and Others v. Latvia* was also brought by the family of a former Russian military official. The ECtHR held, by five votes to two, that there had been a violation of Article 8 (right to respect for private and family life) of ECHR, and held by six votes to one that the Latvian government had complied with their obligations under Article 34 of the Convention (rights to communicate with the Court without interference). The case concerned applicants' right of residency in Latvia. The first two applicants had come to Latvia at the end of the 1960s; the third applicant was born in Latvia in 1978. The ECtHR acknowledged that during these many years the applicants have developed personal, social and economic ties with Latvia that are to be considered within the context of the private life. The ECtHR considered that the Latvian authorities' prolonged refusal to recognize the applicants' right to permanent residence in Latvia constituted interference with their right to respect for their private life, noting, however, that Latvia had acted in compliance with the law and had therefore pursued the legitimate aim of the "prevention of disorder." The ECtHR awarded each of the applicants EUR 5,000 for non-pecuniary damage (total EUR 15,000), which is EUR 40,800 less than requested by the applicants. The ECtHR rejected the applicants' claims to receive compensation for pecuniary damage and court expenses (approximately LVL 4,850).[3325]

[3323] More information available at the Web page of the Representative of the Government of the Republic of Latvia before International Human Rights Organizations, <http://www.mkparstavis.am.gov.lv/en/>.

[3324] European Court of Human Rights, Slivenko v. Latvia, Application No. 48321/99, October 9, 2003, available at <http://hudoc.echr.coe.int/Hudoc1doc2/HEJUD/200310/slivenko%20-%2048321jf.gc%2009102003e.doc>; for an outline of the case, *see*, "International Law in Brief, Developments in International Law," The American Society of International Law, November 4, 2003, available at <http://www.asil.org/ilib/ilib0619.htm>.

[3325] Sisojeva et autres c. Lettonie, No. 60654/00. "European Court of Human Rights Delivers its Judgment on the Case 'Sisojeva and Others v. Latvia,' " Ministry of Foreign Affairs of the Republic of Latvia, press release, available at <http://www.am.gov.lv/en/news/press-releases/2005/June/16-1/>.

Recent Developments

The legal status of Data State Inspectorate has caused repeated concerns during the last few years and has been alleged to undermine independence and effectiveness of the institution. Independence is one of the main requirements by international standards, such as the EU Data Protection Directive. This problem has been patrly solved by the Concept of the Status of Independent Institution soon[3326] to be adopted by the Cabinet of Ministers, which includes Inspectorate as one of the institutions whose effective functioning can be seriously undermined if working within the institutional structure of subordination and therefore political power. The last necessary step will be amendments in the Constitution requiring the assent of 2/3 of 100 parliamentarians. Several laws were adopted from June 1, 2004 through April 30, 2005 that concern the right to privacy.

According to the Law on Establishment and Use of National Data Base of DNA adopted on June 17, 2004,[3327] the national database of DNA has to be established. This database will be used in the investigation of crimes. The law provides that the following information will be stored in the national database: profiles and data about the suspect, accused person, defendant or convict, and information on the DNA profiles and data of unrecognized dead bodies, missing persons and traces of biological origin. This information is classified as restricted access information. The Law on Establishment and Use of National Data Base of DNA regulates also the exchange of results of genetic research of DNA with other countries and international organizations.[3328]

In 2002, the Latvian Parliament passed a law introducing compulsory identity cards for all residents. It requires all citizens and non-citizens of Latvia over the age of 15 to be issued machine-readable ID cards that would also be a means for creating personal e-signatures. Introduction of ID cards was set for 2005, but has recently been postponed to year 2007.[3329]

The Electronic Document Law, transposing the EU Directive on a Community Framework for Electronic Signatures (1999/93/EC),[3330] was passed by the

---

[3326] The document has not been adopted as of July 2005.

[3327] Entered into force on January 1, 2005.

[3328] Law on Establishment and Use of National Data Base of DNA, available at <http://www.likumi.lv/doc.php?id=90819> (in Latvian).

[3329] Amendments to Personal Identification Documents Law of April 20, 2004.

[3330] Directive 1999/93/EC of the European Parliament and of the Council of 13 December 1999 on a Community Framework for Electronic Signatures, Official Journal L 013, January 19, 2000, at 0012 – 0020,

Parliament on October 31, 2002. The law defines the legal status of an electronic document and a digital signature. The introduction of electronic documents and electronic signatures has been in the limelight during 2004 and 2005. The parliament has amended the initial law in order to clarify issues concerning legal status of e-documents and digital signature. The law presently states that, with certain exceptions as to private contracts, e-format has a juridical force identical to traditional documents and signatures.

The main problems identified here are the lack of unified center for certification service and absence of uniform carriers of electronic signatures (due to postponing introduction of ID cards).[3331] According to the law, the Data State Inspectorate is established as a supervisory institution of reliable certification service providers, and shall perform their accreditation.[3332]

The new Law on Civil Registration Records was adopted on March 17, 2005.[3333] This law will replace the Law on Civil Registration and regulate the registration of marriage, birth and death in registry office. The Law on Civil Registration Records states that cause of death will no longer be indicated on death certificates.[3334]

NGO Advocacy Work

There are no visible NGO activities aimed at raising citizens' awareness of their rights and duties under data protection legislation. To some degree, advocacy work has been done by organizations working with specific issues, such as patient rights, within the framework of their conventional activities.

Open Government

The Law on Freedom of Information (FOIL) was adopted by the Latvian Parliament on October 29, 1998 and signed into law by the President in November 1998. It guarantees public access to all information held by state

---

available at
<http://europa.eu.int/smartapi/cgi/sga_doc?smartapi!celexapi!prod!CELEXnumdoc&lg=EN&numdoc=31999L0093&model=guichett>.

[3331] Interview with J. Reirs, Special Assignments Minister for Electronical Governance, available at <http://www.eparvalde.lv>.

[3332] Data State Inspectorate, Annual Report 2003, available at <http://www.dvi.gov.lv/eng/about/reports/2002/>.

[3333] Entered into force on April 15, 2005.

[3334] Law on Civil Registration Records, available at <http://www.likumi.lv/doc.php?id=104832>.

---

administrative institutions and local government institutions in "any technically feasible form" not specifically restricted by law. Public bodies must respond to requests for information within 15 days. According to FOI,L there are several exemptions from the basic principle: the information is for internal use of an institution; it is a trade secret not relating to public procurements or information about the private life of an individual; or if it concerns certification, examination, project, tender and similar evaluation procedures, and (a recent addition) information for the use of the service, mainly concerning information received from NATO and other international institutions relating to state security. Finally, the FOIL introduces a wide exception allowing other legitimate grounds for restricting public access to be defined by other laws (e.g. criminal procedure, law on police, other laws governing particular institutions).

Appeals can be made internally to a higher body or directly to a court. The law was amended in 2003 to give the Data State Inspectorate_oversight authority starting in January 2004.[3335] In practice, however, Inspectorate experiences considerable problems with implementing this task due to the lack of resources, administrative capacity, and, in contrast to oversight of data protection issues, Inspectorate has no competence to punish any violations of FOIL.

Some recent examples on FOI issues relate to openness of public finance. Since 2003, there have been repeated discussions on whether the Capital's City Council should reveal the names and exact amount of bonus payments received by its officials (the case has been described above). After one of its employees, who claimed disclosure of data constituted breach of his privacy, had lost the case against a major daily newspaper, "Diena," the Council changed the practice and now publishes the information.

An emerging issue is the necessity of publishing almost complete information on incomes and expenditures of government officials contained in the now-public part of their annual financial declaration (in accordance with the law on prevention of conflicts of interests of public officials, and approximately 46,000 – 50,000 people must make the declaration). The dispute involves the necessity of publishing information on relatives who have to be indicated in the declaration, according to the law.

[3335] EGovernment Factsheet, Latvia-Legal Framework, available at <http://europa.eu.int/idabc/en/document/1167/402>.

International Obligations

Latvia joined the Council of Europe (CoE) in 1995 and held the six-month rotating presidency from November 2000 to May 2001. It has signed and ratified both the ECHR[3336] and the CoE Convention for the Protection of Individuals with Regard to Automatic Processing of Personal Data (Convention No. 108).[3337]

In the framework of the Article 29 Working Group (established by Article 20 of Directive 95/46/EK), Latvia along with other EU countries have been working to coordinate their data protection policies. The European Convention on the Suppression of Terrorism was ratified on April 20, 1999. On December 22, 2004, Latvia ratified the Protocol Amending the European Convention on the Suppression of Terrorism.

Republic of Lithuania

Constitutional Privacy Framework

Article 22 of the Constitution states, "The private life of an individual shall be inviolable. Personal correspondence, telephone conversations, telegraphs messages, and other intercommunications shall be inviolable. Information concerning the private life of an individual may be collected only upon a justified court order and in accordance with the law. The law and the court shall protect individuals from arbitrary or unlawful interference in their private or family life, and from encroachment upon their honor and dignity."[3338]

Data Protection Framework

Lithuania's predominant data protection regulation, the Law on Legal Protection of Personal Data (LLPPD),[3339] was passed in 1996 and has since been amended multiple times to account for both domestic and European concerns. In 1998, the LLPPD was extended to regulate computerized information held privately, in

---

[3336] Signed February 10, 1995; ratified July 26, 1996; entered into force July 26, 1996.

[3337] Signed October 31, 2000; ratified May 30, 2001; entered into force September 1, 2001.

[3338] Constitution of the Republic of Lithuania (Approved by The Citizens of the Republic of Lithuania in the Referendum on October 25,1992 as amended on March 20, 2003, No. IX-1379), available at <http://www.litlex.lt/Litlex/Eng/Frames/Laws/Documents/CONSTITU.HTM>.

[3339] The Law on Legal Protection of Personal Data (No. I-1374, 1996) (State News, 1996, No. 63-1479).

addition to data publicly held.[3340] It was further amended in 2000[3341] to insure compliance with the EU Directives on Data Protection and Telecommunications, and in 2002[3342] to further bring Lithuania in line with European data protection standards.

The appearance of data protection law in Lithuania was mainly fostered by Lithuania's political aim to become a member of the EU and, consequently, the wish to intercept the *Acquis Communautaire*. These aims, together with many references to the EU directives, are stated in the *travaux préparatoires* of all six amendments to the LLPPD. The negative side of this process is that there were no discussions about data protection in the media, no publications and no academic texts in the field before the enactment of the law. All academic texts discussing problems of legal protection of personal data were published long after the enactment of the law. Academic research, professional consultations, as well as public awareness campaigns in the field are currently widely encouraged by the Data Protection Authority and academics.[3343]

Lithuania became a full member of the EU on May 1, 2004.[3344] Lithuania was accepted as one of 10 new members for membership into the EU in October 2002.[3345]

Three stages in the wording of the data protection law can be distinguished. Between 1996 and 1998, the scope of its application was limited to personal data processed in the public sector, and the law did not apply to "relations regulated by other laws"[3346] and thus was just a secondary law. Between 1998 and 2002, the LLPPD was extended to regulate privately held, in addition to publicly held, computerized information.[3347] The LLPPD was significantly altered in 2000[3348] to ensure compliance with the EU Data Protection and the Privacy and Electronic Communications Directives. Special provisions were added to cover the processing of personal data in various sectors and for various purposes, including social security, social care, health care, scientific research, direct marketing,

---

[3340] Law No.VII-662, March 12, 1998.

[3341] Law No. VIII-1852, July 17, 2000 (State News, 2000, No.64-1924).

[3342] Law No. IX-719, February 6, 2002.

[3343] *E.g.*, Department of Legal Informatics of the Law University of Lithuania.

[3344] Lithuania Country Brief March 2004, Australian Government Department of Foreign Affairs <http://www.dfat.gov.au/geo/lithuania/country_brief_lithuania.html>.

[3345] Lithuania voters supported the agreement to become a member of the EU by 91 percent during an election held in May 2003. *Id.*

[3346] Law on Legal Protection of Personal Data, No. I-1374, 1996 (State News, 1996, No.63-1479).

[3347] Law on Legal Protection of Personal Data, No.VII-662, March 12, 1998. (State News, 1998, No.31-819).

[3348] Law on Legal Protection of Personal Data, No. VIII-1852, July 17, 2000 (State News, 2000, No.64-1924).

statistics and telecommunications. The 2002 amendments[3349] to the LLPPD further strengthened data subjects' rights and covered the processing of personal data for purposes of elections, referenda and citizens' legislative initiative.

After 2003, the aim of the LLPPD radically changed. The current law seeks "protection of an inviolability of an individual's right to private life with regard to the processing of personal data"[3350] in comparison with previous wording of the LLPPD which aimed at balancing individual's interests with processor's. Special provisions devoted to the processing of personal data in public registers, credit and solvency data were also included in the wording of the LLPPD.

The stated purpose of the Law on Legal Protection of Personal Data is to protect the private lives of people by establishing the rights of individuals and regulations for data processors. Individuals are entitled to know about the processing of their personal data; have access to that data; familiarize themselves with the processing method; demand rectification or destruction of their personal data; and object to the processing of their personal data. These rights are, however, contingent upon several enumerated exceptions, such as national security, law enforcement and important economic or financial interests of the state. In addition to these rights, the data subject, who has sustained damage as a result of unlawful processing of personal data, or any other acts or omissions by the data controller, the data processor or any other persons, in violation of the provisions of the LLPPD shall be entitled to claim compensation for pecuniary and non-pecuniary damage caused to him. The extent of pecuniary and non-pecuniary damage shall be determined by court. Most of these rights are further detailed in the LLPPD and most of them are contingent upon enumerated exceptions. The increase of personal complaints regarding the processing of personal data corroborates that individuals care about their informational privacy and examine their rights effectively.[3351]

Once consent from the data subject is obtained, data processors are subject to both regulations on both their means and ends. Personal data can only lawfully be processed if used for predefined purposes such as compliance with a legal obligation or as a necessary adjunct to a commercial transaction. The use must be accurate, fair, lawful, and not excessive in relation to the predefined purpose. Finally, personal data can only be further disclosed under a personal data

---

[3349] Law on Legal Protection of Personal Data, No. IX-719, February 6, 2002 (State News, 2002, No.64-1924); Law on Legal Protection of Personal Data, No.IX-970, June 20, 2002 (State News, 2002, No.68-2769).

[3350] Law on Legal Protection of Personal Data, No.IX-1296, January 21, 2003 (State News, 2003, No.15-597).

[3351] Activity Reports of State Data Protection Inspectorate of the year: 1997-2000, 2001, 2002, first quarter of the year 2003.

disclosure contract, specifying the purposes for which the data will be used and the conditions and procedures of its use.

As a complement to the protections described above, in 1998 the Code of Administrative Offenses[3352] was supplemented with monetary penalties for unlawful personal data processing,[3353] unlawful state information systems processing.[3354] Furthermore, the amendments to the articles 23 and 26 of the LLPPD were prepared and entered into force on April 24 2004.[3355] Article 23 speaks about the fees, specified by the government, that the State Data Protection Inspectorate (SDPI) may demand for assisting the data subject in exercising his/her right of access to his/her personal data. The amendment eliminated a provision that such fees shall not exceed the expenses of the data collection and rendering of the service. The fee now starts at LTL 3 and goes up till LTL 500 (data collected from each additional data controller adds LTL 1).[3356]

Amendment to Article 26 of the LLPPD sought to specify the cases when prior checking is necessary. The amendment provides that prior checking will not be carried out when personal data are intended to be processed by non-automated means, and when sensitive data are intended to be processed for internal administration purposes.[3357] In addition, in 2005 the SDPI intends to submit amendments to the LLPPD relating to the use of personal identification number and processing of personal data for statistical purposes.[3358]

The implementation of Article 24 of the LLPPD, regarding the control of data security in private sector, is being left without further attention by the SDPI, to whom the implementation of the LLPPD is in general assigned. In addition, the Law on State Registers3359 provides further controls on the use and legitimacy

---

[3352] State News, 1998, No.40-1065. *See* Data Protection Development Programme for the Year 2002-2004, II, Current Statement, available at <http://www.ada.lt/en/legal.html>.

[3353] "Notification on data processing," available at <http://www.ada.lt/dok-rekom/dv_forma_nauja_20030701.doc> (in Lithuanian).

[3354] *See* Ona Jakstaite, "Regulating Data Security in Lithuania," Baltic IT Review.

[3355] Law on the Amendment of Articles 23 and 26 of the Law on Legal Protection of Personal Data, April 13, 2004, State News No. 60 – 2120 <http://www3.lrs.lt/cgi-bin/preps2?Condition1=231531&Condition2=>.

[3356] Government Bylaw Regarding the List of the State Fees, Approval of the Rules on Payment and Return, and the Fee Amounts, No. 1458, December 15, 2000 (State News, 2000, Nr. 108-3463), available at <http://www3.lrs.lt/cgi-bin/preps2?Condition1=256178&Condition2=>.

[3357] Activity Report of the State Data Protection Inspectorate for the year 2004, available at <http://www.ada.lt/dok-veikla/ataskaita2004.doc>.

[3358] *Id.*

[3359] The Law on the Public Registers (August 13, 1996, No. I-1490), (State News, 1996, No.86-2043), available at <http://www.ada.lt/en/docs/Ist_reg.htm>.

of state data registers that contain personal information, and mandates that data registers may only be erased or destroyed in cooperation with the SDPI.

Data Protection Authority

In order to enforce the provisions of the Law on Legal Protection of Personal Data and the Law on State Registers, the State Data Protection Inspectorate was established in 1996 in order to supervise and monitor the implementation of the Law on Legal Protection of Personal Data and the Law on State Registers.[3360] The SDPI started to function practically in 1997 and since then has attained much power to supervise and monitor the processing of personal data *ex ante* as well as *ex post*. Before data processing takes place, the data processor shall inform the SDPI, which registers the processor and has the power to carry out prior checking.[3361] After processing is carried out, the SDPI checks its lawfulness, handles appeals for denial of access to records, and grants authorizations to data controllers to disclose personal data to data recipients in third countries. Other functions of the SDPI include examination of personal requests and complaints, assistance to data controllers and data subjects, and composition of methodological recommendations on the protection of personal data.

The office previously operated within the Ministry of Public Administration Reforms and Local Authorities but was granted full independence under the Law on Legal Protection of Personal Data of 2000. From 2000 on, it is a government institution financed from the state budget. The SDPI is accountable to, and its regulations approved by, the government. The status of the SDPI is a specific one because, while under the executive power, it is competent to inspect and control the processing of personal data by legislative bodies. So far, nobody in Lithuania has disputed the competence of the SDPI although such discussions are likely to take place due to indistinctness of legislative and executive powers.

The structure of the Inspectorate is the following: Director of the Inspectorate, two Deputy Directors, chief assistant, chief financier, chief specialist, administrator, and four divisions. The number of full-time positions available is 30. In 2004, the number of full-time positions divided into specified organizational units or departments is 25. The Inspectorate also consists of five

---

[3360] Government of Republic of Lithuania Resolution No.1185 Concerning the Setting up of the State Data Protection Inspectorate, October 10, 1996 (State news, 1996, No.100-2293).

[3361] Recommended form approved by Order No. 1T-28 of 29 January 2004 of the Director of the State Data Protection Inspectorate, "Notification of automated processing," January 29, 2004, available at <http://www.ada.lt/en/docs/apras_pranesimas.doc>.

members in the Legal Division, six in the Prevention Division, six in the Information and Technologies Division, six in the Complaints Investigation, and, finally, six in the International Cooperation division.[3362]

During 2004 the SDPI reviewed 87 complaints, made 365 controls (128 of them at the SDPI's own initiative),[3363] answered 18 requests from Convention ETS No. 108 member states, prepared 136 conclusions regarding the prior checking. In total, the SDPI provided 1,885 consultations.[3364] Information was provided to the mass media 49 times[3365] and the SDPI participated in the TV and radio programs 20 times.[3366] Furthermore, the SDPI was approached by the Social Welfare Division of the Russian Embassy to grant a permit for providing personal data to Russian Federation for payment of pensions for those who live in Lithuania. The SDPI reasoned that such permission was redundant since such data providing itself complies with Article 28(4)(4) of the LLPPD,[3367] which includes an exception for where it is necessary to provide personal data due to important public interest.[3368]

In 2004, an increase in the activity of data controllers in comparison with 2003 was noted. A rather great amount of consultations was provided to the marshals regarding the filling of the form on Notification of Personal Data Processing by Automated Means. Furthermore, when the schools started to process students' sensitive data (on health and nationality), the SDPI experienced an increase of the consultations for the prior checking at the end of the year 2004.[3369]

In 2004, the SDPI received 91 complaints regarding the possible violations of personal data processing[3370] and prepared 27 administrative law infringement protocols. In 18 of these cases, the court recognized that there was an Administrative Law infringement, in 12 the court gave warnings, in six cases the court imposed fines, two cases were terminated, and seven are still undergoing the court proceedings.[3371]

[3362] E-mail from Neringa Kaktavi i t , State Data Protection Inspectorate, to Ula Galster, International Policy Fellow, Electronic Privacy Information Center, May 2, 2005 (on file with EPIC).

3363 Activity Report of the State Data Protection Inspectorate for the year 2004, *supra*.

[3364] *Id.*

[3365] *Id.*

[3366] *Id.*

[3367] LLPPD Article 28. Transfer of Personal Data to Data Recipients in foreign Countries.

[3368] Activity Report of the State Data Protection Inspectorate for the year 2004, *supra*.

3369 *Id.*

3370 *Id.*

3371 *Id.*

In 2004, the SDPI gained full membership status in the Working Party on the Protection of Individuals with regard to the Processing of Personal Data set up under Article 29 of the Directive 95/46/EC of the European Parliament and of the Council. After the ratification of the Europol Convention3372 on April 22, 2004 and its entering into force on September 1, 2004, as well as the ratification of the Convention on the Use of Information Technology for Customs Purposes3373 on May 1, 2004 and its entering into force on August 1, 2004, the SDPI became a full member of the Joint Supervisory Authorities of Europol, Schengen and Customs.3374 The SDPI together with the Joint Supervisory Body of Europol, seeking better implementation of the Europol Convention requirements and in order to guarantee the lawful processing of personal data organized the seminar on October 29, 2004 on the supervision of personal data processing according to the Europol Convention.3375

In March 2004, with the funding and support from the EU the Phare Programme Twinning Project, "Strengthening Administrative and Technical Capacity of Personal Data Protection," was launched between two partners: Lithuania and Austria. The respective beneficiaries were the SDPI and its Austrian counterpart, the Ludwig Boltzmann Institute of Human Rights in Vienna. The project finishes in June 2005. More than 30 data-protection specialists from Austria, Germany, France, Spain and the Netherlands participated in different activities of the Project. Among the most important objectives are: the improvement of the capacity of the SDPI; trainings for data controllers, judges and officials of authorities besides the SDPI; and preparation of the Commentary on the LLPPD, which should be available on the SDPI website when the project is completed.

The SDPI prepared a strategic plan for the development of data protection and measures of implementation for the years 2002-2004.3376 The plan had three main objectives: to create a reliable and efficient data protection system in harmonization with European Union regulations; to foster an environment that respects constitutional rights to privacy; and to encourage the development of privacy enhancing technologies. However, the SDPI employs an interesting

---

3372 Europol Convention, State News, 2004, No. 113-4202, available at
<http://www3.lrs.lt/cgi-bin/preps2?Condition1=238239&Condition2=>.

3373 Convention on the Use of Information Technology for Customs Purposes, State News, 2004, No. 36-1188, available at
<http://www3.lrs.lt/cgi-bin/preps2?Condition1=228195&Condition2=>.

3374 Activity Report of the State Data Protection Inspectorate for the year 2004, *supra*.

3375 Activity Report of the State Data Protection Inspectorate for the year 2004, *supra*.

3376 The State Data Protection Inspectorate, Data Protection Development Programme for the Years 2002-2004, available at <http://www.ada.lt/en/legal.html>.

practice attempting to foresee the number of the complains in upcoming year. For instance in the SDPI's Activities Plan for the year 2004, the SDPI planned to receive and review 50 individual complaints, to answer 10 requests from the member states of Convention No. 108, and to provide 1,200 consultations.[3377] Thus, the organization of the work of the SDPI is still reminiscent of the model of the planned economy, which has been widely used in the Soviet times. Even though Lithuania has been an independent state for more than 15 years, there is still a lot of room for a change, especially in the organization of the work and elimination of bureaucracy within the institution itself in order to achieve the greater efficiency. This also stems from the decision *O.Jakstaite v. Prime Minister*,[3378] where the petitioner, the SDPI Director Ms. Jakstaite, appealed the judgment of the Vilnius Circuit Administrative Court to the Supreme Administrative Court of Lithuania for annulment of the Prime Minister's decree. The decree imposed on the SDPI Director an official sanction, namely, a severe reprimand for breach of principles and rules of ethics of state servants' activities, as well as, infringement of principles of objectivity and proportionality. Vilnius Circuit Administrative Court indicated that the SDPI selected an authoritarian management style, where by (oral or written) orders it was precisely directed what, when, and how to do something, when employees were expected to do all that on time, while being under the continuous assessment. The SDPI Director often used to adopt all decisions *ex-parte* and employees had no actual influence on decision-making.[3379] They were, in fact, forced to recognize adopted decisions and to execute them without reservations. Incapability by the petitioner to formulate clear and concrete tasks to employees resulted in a waste of time and did not produce any useful results, since documents prepared by employees and their other work was repeatedly corrected.[3380] The representative of the Prime Minister in the case stated that the internal rules of the SDPI are too strict.[3381] Furthermore, it was determined that Ms. Jakstaite was often behaving in an unprofessional manner, and thus, raised the mistrust of the society and commercial entities, whose activities in the data protection field are controlled by the SDPI.[3382] It was also established that the SDPI had often been expressing different opinions on the same issues. The investigation established many cases of instructions by the SDPI Director to employees to correct the letters

---

[3377] Activity Report of the State Data Protection Inspectorate for the Year 2004, *supra*.

[3378] O. Jakstaite v. Prime Minister, April 22, 2005, No. A10 – 459 – 05, Supreme Administrative Court, available at <http://www.lvat.lt/Default.aspx?item=nutart>.

[3379] *Id.*

[3380] *Id.*

[3381] *Id.*

[3382] O. Jakstaite v. Prime Minister, *supra*.

comparable to the ones already signed by the Director.[3383] There were also cases when the same permission was issued to one business entity and not issued to another. The SDPI Director objected to a statement by traders that the SDPI had no unanimous opinion.[3384] The Supreme Administrative Court concluded that the Director of the SDPI, Ms. Jakstaite, breached principles and rules of ethics of state servants' activities and violated the objectivity and proportionality principles embedded in Article 4 of the Law on Public Administration.[3385]

There is no encouragement of self-regulation of data controllers and codes of conduct of data protection in the law. Supervision of data protection is exclusively concentrated in the hands of the SDPI. Thus, the effectiveness of data protection rests on the powers of this sole institution. Such a situation creates additional burdens for the free movement of personal data and, at the same time, induces more power to be attributed to the SDPI. The last tendency could be illustrated by the newest legislative initiative to amend the Administrative Code to empower the SDPI to issue an administrative protocol. Under the actual wording of the Administrative Code, the SDPI is empowered to sue the infringer of the LLPPD before an administrative court.

The SDPI maintains close relations with the data protection authorities in other central and eastern European countries. In December 2001, the Data Protection Commissioners from the Czech Republic, Hungary, Lithuania, Slovakia, Estonia, Latvia and Poland signed a joint declaration agreeing to closer cooperation and assistance. The Commissioners agreed to meet twice a year in the future, to provide each other with regular updates and overviews of developments in their countries, and to establish a common website for more effective communication.[3386]

Telecommunications Privacy

Although it appears that Lithuania has implemented a comprehensive legal and governmental regime for the protection of personal data, the concepts, duties and rights conferred are still unfamiliar. Compliance with the laws, while growing, still has much room to improve. In April 2004, Lithuania's largest Internet Service Provider (ISP), Lietuvos Telekomas (Lithuanian Telecom), wireless

---

[3383] *Id.*

[3384] *Id,*

[3385] *Id.*

[3386] E-mail from Karel Neuwirt, President, Office for Personal Data Protection, Czech Republic, to Sarah Andrews, Research Director, Electronic Privacy Information Center, May 15, 2002 (on file with EPIC).

operators Omnitel and Bite, and copyright protection associations LATGA-A, AGATA, BSA Lietuva and FGPA decided to join together to combat Internet piracy.[3387]

The Constitution and the law limit government observation of, and intrusion into, individuals' privacy. Under a criminal procedure law, as well as a Law on Operative Activities,[3388] wiretapping requires a warrant issued by the Prosecutor General or a judge. Police and security services may, with this warrant, engage in surveillance and monitoring activities on the grounds of national security, law enforcement, and important financial or economic interests of the state.[3389] In 2003, there were reports that the government did not respect the legal prohibition against arbitrary interference with privacy, family, home, and correspondence. "It was assumed widely that law enforcement agencies had increased the use of a range of surveillance methods to cope with the expansion of organized crime."[3390] In practice, the boundaries of lawful surveillance are still being determined, with the emergence of new national and international case law.[3391] The United States Department of State Human Rights Report reports that in December 2003, "a parliamentary commission concluded that the Government's anti-corruption service and the Presidency had violated the law by seeking and providing information about persons who were not seeking public office" and that "[t]he media . . . reported that doctors occasionally divulged confidential data about patients to employers and others."[3392]

[3387] "Lithuania's Telecommunications Leaders Join Hands in Fight against Internet Piracy." Baltic News Service, April 26, 2004.

[3388] Law on Operative Activities, 1991. available at <http://www3.lrs.lt/cgi-bin/preps2?Condition1=212375&Condition2=>.

[3389] United States Department of State, Country Reports on Human Rights Practices, Lithuania, 2003, available at <http://www.state.gov/g/drl/rls/hrrpt/2003/27850.htm>.

[3390] Id.

[3391] According to the United States Department of State Human Rights Report for the year 2001: "In July 2001, in the case of Juozas Valasinas v. Lithuania . . . the European Court of Human Rights found that officials in his correctional institution were reading his correspondence without the approval of the court. During the first half of the year, the Parliament controller confirmed a violation of prisoner's correspondence rights. Pursuant to a change in the law, since April prisoners' complaints to courts, the Parliament controller, and human rights groups have not been censored, and censorship of their private correspondence has been subject to stricter control by prison authorities. Local media reported that the security services monitored the activities of the nongovernmental organization Collegiate Association for the Research of the Principle, Jehovah's Witnesses, and a visiting member of the Russian Vissarion Church. In May, a member of the Parliament complained that a government agency had monitored his cell phone calls in 2000, when he was not yet a member of the Parliament; a printout of his calls were published in a national daily newspaper during a political dispute. "United States Department of State, Country Reports on Human Rights Practices, Lithuania, 2001, available at <http://www.state.gov/g/drl/rls/hrrpt/2001/eur/8287.htm>.

[3392] United States Department of State, Country Reports on Human Rights Practices, Lithuania, 2003, *supra*.

The Law on Telecommunications also contains provisions requiring ISPs to implement retention measures for data (identifications and content) transmissions through common access telecommunications networks, and to provide them free of charge to criminal investigators and other law enforcement authorities according to the government-established procedures. Those data retention measures never came into force as they were repealed after a constitutional challenge before the Constitutional Court in 2002.[3393] The Court found that such provisions are unconstitutional to the extent that they require unlimited and non-government subsidized data retention. The Court held that only data retention measures that are necessary for ISPs' ordinary business activities might be justified and considered reasonable. Thus ISPs are effectively entitled to decide on the scope and length of data retention, with due regard to data protection laws.

On April 15, 2004, the Parliament adopted Law No. IX-2135 on Electronic Communications,[3394] which practically substituted the former Law on Telecommunications. The new law implements all of the EU directives of 2002 on electronic communications, including the EU Directive on Privacy and Electronic Communications (2002/58/EC), and is aimed at regulating the operation of electronic communications in Lithuania.[3395]

Wiretapping and Surveillance Rules

Recently, the government adopted a resolution that affects Internet privacy.[3396] The Resolution introduces data retention requirements for hosting service providers. They are required to log operations with data and content hosted on their servers and to provide them free of charge, along with the personal data of the individual and entities using the hosting services, to criminal investigators and other law enforcement authorities. However, the obligation to provide such data is limited to data necessary for normal business operations, following the September 2002 Constitutional Court decision.[3397]

[3393] Constitutional Court of the Republic of Lithuania, Ruling on the compliance of Paragraph 2 of Article 27 of the Republic of Lithuania Law on Telecommunications (…), September 19, 2002, available at <http://www.lrkt.lt/dokumentai/2002/r020919.htm>.

[3394] <http://www3.lrs.lt/cgi-bin/preps2?Condition1=232036&Condition2=> (in Lithuanian).

[3395] See Petrauskas Lideika, Update June 2004, Infolex.lt, June 2004, available at <http://www.infolex.lt/portal/ml/start.asp?act=legupd&lang=eng&biulid=87>.

[3396] The Resolution No. 290 of March 5, 2003 on Procedures for Control of Harmful Information and Distribution of Restricted Information in Publicly Accessible Computer Networks.

[3397] Constitutional Court of the Republic of Lithuania, Ruling of September 19, 2002, *supra*.

In 2004, the press announced that the State Security Department has the ability to tap unrestrictedly the cell phones of the people.[3398] The representatives of the major telecommunication companies admitted that, taking into account current technical possibilities for the operational activity services to intercept the phone calls, the companies couldn't control whether the officers are tapping only those subscribers, which are indicated in the court order.[3399] There is a lack of the detailed procedure guaranteeing that the officers would control only those subscribers, which are indicated in the court order and only during the foreseen period of time.[3400] The institution nominated for the control of electronic communications, i.e. the State Security Department, is the same institution that conducts operational activities and pretrial investigations.[3401] The Report of the Human Rights Monitoring Institute (HRMI) states that this is a malpractice and suggests the control of electronic communications should be allocated to another institution than the State Security Department.

One of the most severe human rights violations that occurred in 2004 was the publicizing of private phone conversations while conducting an operational activity.[3402] Some private phone calls were publicized after the presidential scandal emerged.[3403] Furthermore, the phone conversations of the Parliament members suspected of being corrupted and private persons were publicized.[3404] These conversations were broadcast on TV, radio and publicly discussed.[3405] The heads of the law enforcement institutions, the Deputy General Prosecutor and the Head of Vilnius Board of the Special Investigation Service, called for publicizing the private conversations between the Parliament members and private persons.[3406]

The Special Investigation Service tapped the phone of the mayor of Vilnius city; later on nspecial agent of this service handed the telephone records over to journalists.[3407] The agent received only the strict warning from the Head of the

---

[3398] Human Rights in Lithuania 2004: Overview, 2nd Periodic Report of Human Rights Monitoring Institute (2005), available at
<http://www.hrmi.lt/downloads/structure//zmogaus_teisiu_ig2005_liet.pdf>.
[3399] Id.
[3400] Id.
[3401] Id.
[3402] Human Rights in Lithuania 2004, *supra*.
[3403] Id.
[3404] Id.
[3405] Id.
[3406] Human Rights in Lithuania 2004, *supra*.
[3407] Liuminata Mockute, "The Man of the Week, Invisible and Inaudible Agent of the Special Investigation Service, Takes Over the Mission of the Judge," Republika, February 19, 2005, at 4.

Special Investigation Service, who admitted that the agent caused a lot of trouble to the Special Investigation Service. However, the agent's actions were evaluated in a liberal manner. The Head of the Special Investigation Service also denied that the agent acted with the knowledge of the superior officers.[3408]

In 2004, the Criminal Police Bureau and the General Prosecutor's Office found out that Telekom had equipment that was collecting excessive data, i.e., the identification codes and login passwords of the bank account owners, which were transmitted by DTMF[3409] signals while on the phone.[3410] Telekom alleged that equipment was used to prevent telephone fraud. The pre-trial investigation was based on the articles of the Criminal Code foreseeing the liability for unlawful violation of the correspondence privacy, privacy of other messages, parcels or telephone conversations (Article 166), for unlawful collection of information about private life of the person (Article 167), and for unlawful possession of the equipment, software, passwords, login codes and other data used for committing a crime (Article 198(2)). However, the General Prosecutor's Office terminated the pre-trial investigation, because it found that equipment was acquired lawfully, although it admitted that part of the data was collected and stored unlawfully. However, the collection was said to have occurred accidentally, without "guilt." The General Prosecutor's Office referred to the SDPI and the Communication Regulation Service asking to destroy unlawfully collected data. Telekom took measures to improve their equipment in order to comply with the requirements of the law. However, the public opinion survey showed that 71 percent of the population of Lithuania thought that the mentioned equipment was used for wiretapping.[3411]

The Chairman of the Human Rights Monitoring Institute (later HRMI) Steering Committee said that there was no serious liability foreseen for interception of the phone calls and for distribution of such records. Furthermore, there is no clear procedure for when such calls may be intercepted and when the calls cannot be tapped.[3412] There is no need to have a very serious proof that a crime was committed.[3413] The mere assumption that such a crime could be committed is

---

[3408] Id.

[3409] DTMF stands for Dual-Tone Multi-Frequency.

[3410] Ainis Gurevicius, Vytene Stasaityte, "Scandal of the Telekom – the Crime without the Penalty," Respublika, October 19, 2004, at 3.

[3411] Human Rights in Lithuania 2004, supra.

[3412] Dalia Gudaviciute, "The Words Hunters Bluster without Limitations," (interview with the Chairman of the Human Rights Monitoring Institute Steering Committee), Respublika, March 1, 2005, at 4.

[3413] Id.

sufficient for starting the wiretapping.3414 After this happens, it is not necessary to submit the case to the court. In addition, nobody explains what happens with the records.3415 The records may be stored in the archives, copied and later on distributed for various purposes. Moreover, there is a huge potential to intercept all phone calls of important people.3416

The Law on Electronic Communications and the LLPPD govern the protection of data, collected and stored by the electronic communication providers, from accidental or unlawful destruction, alteration or disclosure. The supervision for implementation of this duty is allocated to the SDPI, which at present pays little attention to this issue.3417

In 2005, the HRMI suggested enacting a stricter liability for the violations of data protection. The Code of Administrative Law Infringements foresees the fines up to LTL 1000 (about EUR 290) for violations of personal data processing; the fine for the repeated offense is up to LTL 2000. This clearly is not proportional to the hazards of invading the private life while collecting and processing personal data in electronic communications.3418

On June 26, 2003, the Parliament (*Seimas*) of the Republic of Lithuania passed a resolution to ensure the protection of personal information managed by government agencies.3419 There are specific privacy protections in laws relating to telecommunications,3420 radio communications,3421 statistics,3422 the population register,3423 and health information.3424 The Criminal Code provides for criminal responsibility for violations of the inviolability of a residence, infringement on secrecy of correspondence and telegram contents, on privacy of telephone conversations, persecution for criticism, secrecy of adoption, slander,

---

3414 *Id.*

3415 *Id.*

3416 Dalia Gudaviciute, *supra.*

3417 Human Rights in Lithuania 2004, *supra.*

3418 *Id.*

3419 Resolution of the *Seimas* of the Republic of Lithuania on the Guaranteeing of Personal Data Protection in State Institutions (in Lithuanian) June 26, 2003, available at<http://www3.lrs.lt/cgi-bin/preps2?Condition1=214375&Condition2=>.

3420 Law No. IX-2135 on Electronic Communications of April 15, 2004, available at <http://www3.lrs.lt/cgi-bin/preps2?Condition1=232036&Condition2=> (in Lithuanian), replacing the Law No. I-1109 on Telecommunications of November 30, 1995.

3421 Law on Radio Communication, November 7, 1995, No.I-1086, available at <http://www.litlex.lt/Litlex/Eng/Frames/Laws/Documents/366.HTM>.

3422 Law on Statistics, October 12, 1993, No.I-270.

3423 Law on the Population Register, January 23, 1992, No. I-2237.

3424 Law on the Health System, July 19, 1994, No.I-552.

desecration of graves and impact on computer information. The new Criminal Process Code requires a judge's authorization for the search of premises of an individual. The seizure, monitoring, and recording of information transmitted through telecommunications networks or surveillance must also be court-ordered.[3425] Civil laws provide for compensation for moral damage because of dissemination of unlawful or false information demeaning the honor and dignity of a person in the mass media.[3426] In February 2001, the European Court of Human Rights (ECtHR) accepted two cases against Lithuania filed by a former prosecutor and a former tax inspector who allege that their privacy was violated when they were fired from their positions and prohibited from taking certain posts in the private sector because of their previous collaboration with the KGB.[3427] On July 27, ECtHR concluded that the ban on the applicants seeking employment in various private-sector spheres, in application of Article 2 of the KGB Act, constituted a disproportionate measure, even having regard to the legitimacy of the aims pursued by that ban and, thus, found a violation of Article 14 of the Convention taken in conjunction with Article 8.[3428] In another case, the applicants, also former KGB agents, complained that the loss of their jobs, respectively, as a private-company lawyer and barrister, and the ban on their employment in various private-sector spheres until 2009, breached their privacy. The Court recalled the case of *Sidabras and Džiautas* explaining that the applicants' complaints were very similar, albeit wider: they related not only to their hypothetical inability to apply for various private-sector jobs until 2009 (as in *Sidabras and Džiautas*), but they also concerned their actual dismissal from existing employment in that sector. Consequently, the ECtHR found a violation of Article 14 of the Convention, taken in conjunction with Article 8.[3429]

The journalist's right not to disclose the source of information provided in this law was approved in an October 21, 2002 decision of the Constitutional Court. The Court emphasized that this right shall not be exercised only in a case where there is a valid court order to disclose such information, and where such

---

[3425] United States Department of State, Country Reports on Human Rights Practices, Lithuania, 2003, *supra*.

[3426] United Nations Human Rights Committee, Consideration of Reports Submitted by States Parties Under Article 40 of the Covenant, Initial reports of States parties due in 1993, Addendum, Lithuania, 1996, available at <http://www.hri.ca/fortherecord1997/documentation/tbodies/ccpr-c-81-add10.htm>.

[3427] "Strasbourg Probing 2 Cases Of Ex-KGB Agents Vs. Lithuania," Baltic News Service, February 8, 2001.

[3428] Sidabras and Dziautas v. Lithuania, ECtHR, Applications Nos. 55480/00 and 59330/00, July 27, 2004, available at <http://cmiskp.echr.coe.int/tkp197/view.asp?item=5&portal=hbkm&action=html&highlight=Lithuania&session id=2323085&skin=hudoc-en>.

[3429] Rainys and Gasparavicius v. Lithuania, Applications Nos. 70665/01 and 74345/01, April 7, 2005, available at <http://cmiskp.echr.coe.int/tkp197/view.asp?item=4&portal=hbkm&action=html&highlight=Lithuania&session id=2323085&skin=hudoc-en>.

disclosure is needed for the public interest. On the other hand, in the same decision the Court approved the right to publicize private information on public figures when such disclosure raises reasonable public interest, or does not cause any harm to the affected individual. The Inspector of Journalistic Ethics in his Report for 2003 – 2004 urges to amend Article 8 of the Law on the Provision of Information to the Public as contradicting to Articles 25(3) and (4) of the Constitution.

Article 8 of the Law foresees that the processing of personal data carried out for the purposes of providing information to the public or for the purposes of artistic or literary expression, as well as, other purposes is supervised by the Inspector for Journalistic Ethics. The Inspector indicated that mass media often violated the privacy, especially when the information was provided about antisocial, less educated persons.[3430] These people more often refer to the TV Channel LNK "Court"[3431] than to the courts of the Republic of Lithuania.[3432] The Inspector for Journalistic Ethics also indicated that mass media often benefit from the lack of legal knowledge of these people and their "desire" to become popular.[3433]

While reviewing the complaints, the Inspector of Journalistic Ethics noted that the data protected by the LLPPD, such as personal identification number, family status, incapacities for work, health, are too often publicized without the public interest. In particular, he drew attention to publicized information about debtors (those indebted to the mobile communication companies, municipality companies).[3434] The Inspector of Journalistic Ethics said in his report that a public announcement of debtors in the newspapers and other mass media initiated by the creditors is not lawful and violates the rights of these persons. Creditors do not have a right to disseminate information about debtors' solvency.[3435] Some of the companies consider this an effective measure in the fight against the debtors' insolvency.[3436] However, publicizing such information should not become a precedent in the democratic society.[3437]

[3430] *See,* Analytical Overview of the Inspector of Journalistic Ethics for the year 2003-2004, April 25, 2005, available at

<http://www3.lrs.lt/docs2/WXY5QEC1XB.DOC>.

[3431] LNK (Laivas ir Nepriklausomas Kanalas/ Free and Independent Channel) is a TV channel in Lithuania, "Court" is one of their programs imitating a real court.

[3432] *See* Analytical Overview of the Inspector of Journalistic Ethics, *supra.*

[3433] *Id.*

[3434] Activity Report of the Inspector of Journalistic Ethics for the Year 2003 – 2004, April 13, 2004, available at <http://www3.lrs.lt/pls/inter/w3_viewer.ViewTheme?p_int_tv_id=2564&p_kalb_id=1&p_org=0>.

[3435] *Id.*

[3436] Activity Report of the Inspector of Journalistic Ethics, *supra.*

[3437] *Id.*

Article 14(2)(3) of the Law on Provision of Information to the Public (LPIP) states that information about the private life of the person can be publicized without the consent of the person, when publicizing of the information does not cause harm to the person, when information helps to disclose crimes or infringements of the laws, and when the information is provided while discussing the case in the open court hearing. The Inspector of Journalistic Ethics expressed doubts, whether this article does not contradict Article 22 of the Constitution, which does not provide any reservations on the protection of right to private life.3438 Furthermore, it is not clear who has to decide whether the information is not causing harm to the person.[3439] Moreover, the definition of the public person provided by the law is also vague.[3440] The Inspector notes that it is rather difficult to unambiguously apply such a definition in practice. Such indetermination can lead to unreasonable violations of the right to the private life of these persons, who even though participate in the public life but have no real influence on public life and, thus, their private life should not be narrowed unreasonably.3441 At present, it is only clear that the public person, i.e. the one whose publicity does not raise any doubts, cannot expect privacy.3442

The Inspector of Journalistic Ethics suggested that the LPIP should contain provisions imposing special requirements for the information disseminated via the Internet, defining the liability for publicizing of information in the Internet, and creating a new self-control institution to supervise the observance of these requirements3443 Article 14 of the LPIP[3444] should be amended by adding the provision which would guarantee the protection of the private life when the information about the person is collected and not only when information is prepared and disseminated.3445

Mr. Alvaro Gil-Robles, Commissioner for Human Rights of the Council of Europe noted that the right to private life is either not known or hardly identified

---

3438 *Id.*

3439 *Id.*

3440 Activity Report of the Inspector of Journalistic Ethics, *supra.*

3441 *Id.*

3442 *Id.*

3443 *Id.*

3444 Law on Provision of Information to the Public, July 2, 1996, No. I-1418 (as amended by State News, 2004, No. IX – 2176), available at <C:\Documents and Settings\Asmeninis\My Documents\Phare\Laws on the registers\Law on Provision of Information.htm>; *see also,* Article 14 of the law, under Protection of Privacy section, stating: "When producing and disseminating public information, a person's right to have his personal and family life respected must be ensured."

3445 Activity Report of the Inspector of Journalistic Ethics, *supra.*

by the majority of Lithuanians. They very rarely appeal to courts or other institutions, such as the Ombudsman, regarding the infringement of the right to privacy.3446 Also, NGOs have expressed concerns about increasing violations of privacy laws by the media and business groups and by increased violations on monitoring of the Internet.3447 The Commissioner recommended responding appropriately, in particular by implementing existing legislation, to ensure the protection of personal and private data, as well as, regulating the use of information in the case of public persons. Furthermore, it is of the utmost importance to develop legal education and explain to people the content of the right to privacy and ways of protecting it.3448

The HRMI reported that in 2004 there was an active trade in computer software, which allowed controlling of the work process of an employee's computer. Such control creates unlimited possibilities to observe the work of the employee. The HRMI said that the employee has a right to the protection of his/her private life. The ECHR does not exclude the person's right to private life at the workplace, for example, the use of the phone in the work place falls within the scope of the employee's private life.[3449] The HRMI also said that the education of the users about the hazards to their privacy augmented by the Internet is very important. However the SDPI, with the exception of a very few complaints, does not control unlawful processing of personal data in the Internet environment.[3450] As this occurrence is a global one, international cooperation in this area is needed.[3451]

Furthermore, the HRMI said that the number of video surveillance of the person's private life has increased. More and more companies and organizations established such systems in public places. In practice, there is a need for strict observance of the requirement to inform people properly about the existence of the video surveillance.[3452] The SDPI have not yet made a systemic legal analysis on the use of video surveillance measures and limited itself to the review of single complaints.[3453]

3446 Council of Europe, Office of the Commissioner for Human Rights, Report on the Visit to Lithuania, Doc. No. CommDH(2004)6 (Fe), February 12, 2004, available at
<http://www.coe.int/T/E/Commissioner_H.R/Communication_Unit/CommDH%282004%296_E.doc>.
3447 Id.
3448 Id.
3449 Human Rights in Lithuania 2004, supra.
3450 Id.
3451 Id.
3452 Id.
3453 Human Rights in Lithuania 2004, supra.

The survey on "How the Society Evaluates the Human Rights Situation in Lithuania" was assessing the level of tolerance for interfering with the private life of the respondent and of the public person.3454 Respondents totaling 1,005,3455 from 19 cities and 59 villages, participated in the survey. Almost 80 percent of the respondents evaluated negatively the possibility to publicize their telephone conversations, but only about one-fifth of the respondents thought that publicizing the conversations of a well-known politician would violate his or her right to private life.3456 For most of the people, the decisive criterion on admissibility to limit private life is the person's status in the society.3457 The threshold for the privacy protection of the well-known politicians, i.e. public person, is rather low.3458 Only 22 percent of the respondents envisaged the problem regarding the disclosure of personal data, in this case the disclosure of personal identification number.3459 HRMI in its survey determined that every third legal act requires disclosure of the personal identification number, and, thus, it concludes that the principle of proportionality is not observed.3460 It is no wonder that in such an environment the public circulation of PIN became the daily routine.3461 The survey indicates that the right to the immunity of the private life is less important for the rural population and those receiving small income. However, this result must be viewed through the prism of their poor social status in general, when the concern for elementary survival prevails over concern for other human rights.3462

Mass media were very often highlighting the issues of processing of the personal data and violating the personal data protection.3463 Together with the wiretapping scandal, the issue of publicizing the KGB reserve list was widely discussed. The Chairman of the Seimas, Mr. Paulauskas, supported the idea of publicizing the KGB reserve list. However, the Law on Documents and Archives foresees that

---

3454 Survey "How the Society Evaluates the Human Rights Situation in Lithuania," results presented by the Human Rights Monitoring Institute in the BNS press conference, Vilnius, January 17, 2005, *available at* <http://www.hrmi.lt/news.php?strid=1010&id=2208>.

3455 *See* <http://www.hrmi.lt/downloads/structure//tyrimo_pristatymas_20050117.pdf>.

3456 *Id.*

3457 Survey "How the Society Evaluates the Human Rights Situation in Lithuania," *supra*.

3458 *Id.*

3459 *Id.*

3460 Human Rights in Lithuania 2004, *supra* .

3461 Survey "How the Society Evaluates the Human Rights Situation in Lithuania," *supra*.

3462 *Id.*

3463 Activity Report of the State Data Protection Inspectorate for the year 2004, *supra*.

access to the documents and files of the Special USSR services is limited for up to 70 years after their preparation.[3464]

Recent Developments

Recently, Lithuania started to issue passports with biometric data to the Lithuanian diplomats. It is expected that the citizens should receive such passports in 2006.[3465] The passports have 20 security measures.[3466]

In the past year, the data protection issues in the courts' practice started to emerge. The HRMI reports that the use of technical measures during the court hearings is not properly regulated.[3467] The Law foresees wide possibilities for the use of video recording and other technical measures during the court hearings; however, there are no comprehensive rules for storage and destruction of the collected data.[3468]

Article 123(3) of the Civil Procedure Code foresees that if the person delivering the procedural document does not find the addressee at home or at his/her workplace, one of the options to deliver the document is to hand it over to the administration of the addressee's workplace. However, it should be noted that such document contains not only the plaintiff's, but also the defendant's personal data, which should not be accessible to the employer, unless the employer is the party to the case.[3469]

One of the examples of a decreasing importance of personal data protection in the courts' practice is a wide spread of using full names and last names in the publicized court's decisions. However, this violation of privacy is not yet addressed thoroughly in Lithuania. The courts in their decisions still frequently include excessive personal data of the parties to the case. The examples include personal identification numbers, addresses, sometimes even indicating the personal identification numbers which should not necessarily be contained in the publicly accessible decisions and thus, jeopardize the interests of the parties.

[3464] Vytene Stasaityte, "The Publicizing of the KGB Reserve is Blocked by the Laws," Respublika, January 14, 2005, at 2.

[3465] "Modern Passports to the Lithuanian Diplomats," Lietuvos Rytas, May 3, 2005 (in Lithuanian).

[3466] *Id.*

[3467] Human Rights in Lithuania 2004, *supra.*

[3468] *Id.*

[3469] Seminar "Data Processing in the Courts," by Dr. Krause, Vilnius, April 21, 2005.

One of the emerging trends in the Lithuanian administrative courts' practice is to punish violators of the LLPPD with merely a warning. Such practice has negative consequences, since it sets up a low threshold to value the privacy of the individuals and it sends the negative message to the society as a whole. Furthermore, it leads to the conclusion that the courts still do not understand the importance of personal data protection.

Major Privacy Case Law

The case law in the data protection field is not very extensive. One of the reasons for this status quo is such that the right to privacy is still a novelty in the laws of Lithuania and in the courts' practice. Furthermore, many people still do not grasp the concept of this right to privacy and consequently, do not value it.[3470] Lithuanians rarely refer to the courts or other institutions due to the violations of their private life.[3471] In the more rural settlements away for the city-centers people, perceive the boundaries of private life in a very liberal way.[3472] However, the case law regarding the right to privacy is gradually developing.

In 2005, ECtHR once more found that Lithuania violated right to respect for private and family life[3473] embedded in Article 8 of the Convention for the Protection of Human Rights and Fundamental Freedoms.[3474] The applicant's admissible complaints concerned the opening up and reading by the prison administration of all his letters to and from the State authorities, NGOs and private persons such as his family, relatives, friends and legal counsel. The Court noted that interference with the applicant's right to respect for his correspondence could only be justified if such interference would be "in accordance with the law," pursued a legitimate aim and was necessary in a democratic society in order to achieve that aim.[3475] The interference had a legal basis, namely the provisions of the Detention on Remand Act and Remand Prisons Internal Rules, and the Court was satisfied that it pursued the legitimate aim of "the prevention of disorder or crime." However, as regards the necessity of the interference, the

---

[3470] Dalia Gudaviciute, "The Words Hunters Bluster without Limitations," (interview with the Chairman of the Human Rights Monitoring Institute Steering Committee), Respublika, March 1, 2005, at 4.

[3471] Activity Report of the Inspector of Journalistic Ethics, *supra*.

[3472] *Id.*

[3473] Jankauskas v. Lithuania, ECHR, Application no. 59304/00, February 24, 2005, available at <http://cmiskp.echr.coe.int/tkp197/view.asp?item=1&portal=hbkm&action=html&highlight=Lithuania&session id=2213420&skin=hudoc-en>.

[3474] Convention for the Protection of Human Rights and Fundamental Freedoms, available at <http://www.echr.coe.int/Convention/webConvenENG.pdf>.

[3475] Jankauskas v. Lithuania, *supra*.

government had not explained why the control of all the applicant's letters addressed to him and coming from the outside world was indispensable. The Court explained that the government's reason, namely the fear of the applicant's absconding or influencing his trial, may have been a basis for a certain form of interference with part of his correspondence, such as, for example, checking of some correspondence of non-legal nature or his correspondence with certain persons of dangerous provenance. However, the Court said that this fear alone could not be sufficient to grant the remand prison administration an open license for indiscriminate, routine checking of all of the applicant's correspondence, in particularly the applicant's letters from his legal counsel.3476 The Court also did not find any reason to justify the censorship by the prison administration of the applicant's letters to State authorities. Overall, the government has not presented sufficient reasons to show that such a total control of the applicant's correspondence with the outside world was "necessary in a democratic society." Consequently, the Court found a violation of Article 8 of the Convention.

The Supreme Court indicated that the right to the private life and privacy is not violated, if the elements of the publication content do not create a possibility to identify a person, about whom the information in the publication is provided.3477 In this decision, the Supreme Court concluded that the first instance court reasonably rejected the claim and the court of appeals left the decision without the changes after the courts were not able to determine that the publicized information in the article was in particular about the plaintiff's private life. In another case, the Supreme Court also explained that a public person is not under the same defense of honor and dignity as the private one because the higher behavior requirements are set for the public person then for the private one. Therefore, the public person has to tolerate the publicized information (even though it is not precise in full) or opinion about him.3478

According to Article 2.24(6) of the Civil Code, the person's liability is waived, when distributed data failed short of reality, if publicized data were about the public person, about his state or social activity but the person, who publicized the data proves that he was acting honestly in order to acquaint society with that person.3479 The Supreme Court interpreted Article 2.24(6) of the Civil Code

---

3476 *Id.*

3477 J. Varapnickiene-Mazyliene v. Vilnius City Children Rights Defense Service, November 29, 2004, No 3K-3-600/2004, Supreme Court of the Republic of Lithuania, Overview of the Supreme Court Cassation Practice for the year 2004, at 13 - 14.

3478 V. Vizbaras v. I. Dzedulioniene, February 17, 2004, No. 3K-3-56/2004, Supreme Court of the Republic of Lithuania, Overview of the Supreme Court Cassation Practice for the year 2004, at 14.

3479 J. Kaliacius v. I. Starosaite-Zvaguliene, October 27, 2004, No. 3K-3-579/2004, Supreme Court of the Republic of Lithuania, Overview of the Supreme Court Cassation Practice for the year 2004, at 14.

noting that the person who distributed the data interfering with the reality about the public person is released under the respective conditions of the Civil Code, but the person is not released from rectifying the information, which interfere with reality and degrade the honor and dignity of the public person.[3480]

The Supreme Court expressing opinion on Article 8 of the Convention for the Protection of Human Rights and Fundamental Freedoms and person's right to private life, entrenched in the national laws, indicated that the violation of the right to private life can be understood as filming of a private person in his/her private tenure without his consent, distribution or publicizing of the video record in which the private person is recorded without his/her consent and similar[3481]. The substantiation measures can be the photos, audio and video records, made without infringing the law.[3482] Admissibility of the substantiation measure is understood as receiving of information, constituting the content of the proof, without violating procedures set by the laws.[3483] Upon assessing the admissibility of the video record as the substantiation measure, it should be decided, whether this proof was received without violation of the rights and interests of the data subjects who are recorded in the video record, in particular their right to privacy.[3484] The Supreme Court indicated that in the present case the filming was conducted in the shop premises belonging to the defendant, the salesroom, i.e. the public place, the filmed persons were in labor relations with the defendant and materially liable for carried work. Such filming cannot be regarded as violation of the private person's rights, therefore, information in the video record has to be recognized as a proper proof, when considering the labor duties violation.[3485] This proof shall be assessed and analyzed together with other evidence in the case. On the basis of these arguments the Supreme Court repealed the decision of the appellate instance court, where it was decided that the discussed video records violated person's right to his private life and, thus, could not be regarded as admissible measure of substantiation.[3486]

[3480] Id.

[3481] P. Lasas v. JSC "VP Market," November 2, 2004, No 3K-3-643/2004, Supreme Court of the Republic of Lithuania, Overview of the Supreme Court Cassation Practice for the Year 2004, at 67.

[3482] Id.

[3483] Id.

[3484] Id.

[3485] P. Lasas v. JSC "VP Market," supra, at 67.

[3486] Id.

In another case, the Supreme Court indicated that person's right to privacy is not absolute.3487 Immunity of private life can be restricted due to personal non-material values and their compatibility with the rights and lawful interests of other persons; if the person abuses his/her right to privacy (when acting dishonestly one defends himself or herself with privacy), so in single cases it might be reasonably denied to defend the person's right to privacy.3488 The plaintiff worked as a sales clerk. From the point of view of the territory the sphere of the private life consists of a person's living accommodations, as well premises, which the person uses for his housekeeping or professional activities or similar.3489 The public workplace is not a person's private sphere. The salesmen cannot require that their privacy be guaranteed at their workplace, i.e. in the salesroom; therefore, surveillance of the salesroom and the salesmen's work is not secret surveillance of person's private life.3490 The defendant, owner of the store, installed video cameras in public locations, i.e. in the salesroom above the working place of the saleswomen (cash register) in order to prevent the law infringements and crimes.3491 The work of the saleswoman was public character activity, therefore she could not require to guarantee her privacy at her work place.3492 The plaintiffs made an Administrative Law infringement; her behavior was dishonest in the workplace, even unlawful, therefore the plaintiff cannot use violation of her right to privacy in her defense.3493

The SDPI received complaints from a couple of people with regard to the processing of personal data by the General Prosecutor's Office, the Secretariat of the Chairmen of the Seimas, and Seimas Anticorruption Commission. The complainants asked the SDPI to determine whether these institutions lawfully and reasonably processed complainants' personal data. During the control it was found that the Commission, when releasing the copy of the notification about the suspicion to the mass media representatives, provided excessive amount of personal data, i.e. personal identification number, residence address, and did not implement proper organizational and technical measures for accidental and unlawful disclosure of personal data.3494 For these violations, the SDPI prepared

---

3487 J. Bartasiuniene v. Public Institution "Humana people to people Baltic," May 3, 2004, No. 3K-3-289/2004, Supreme Court of the Republic of Lithuania, Overview of the Supreme Court Cassation Practice for the Year 2004, at 67 – 68.
3488 *Id.*
3489 *Id.*
3490 *Id.*
3491 J. Bartasiuniene v. Public Institution "Humana people to people Baltic," *supra.*
3492 *Id.*
3493 *Id.*
3494 Activity Report of the State Data Protection Inspectorate for the year 2004, *supra.*

an Administrative Law infringement protocol for the chairmen of the Commission, which later was submitted to the court. The court, however, did not find Administrative Law Infringement.3495

The SDPI received another complaint, where the complainant was asking what was the source of the information received by the "Political Party and Organization Homeland Union" and for what purposes it was processing his personal data. During the control the SDPI found out that the party received electors' lists from the Central Electoral Committee. The chairperson of the party authorized the representative of the party to process data of the general electors list and to be responsible for maintaining the confidentiality of personal data. The Central Electoral Committee following the signed act ttransmitted the data to the representative of the political party. The representative copied the data received in the CD and distributed it to the members of the party in order to use this data for the election agitation. The representative was unable to specify to whom he handed over the mentioned lists. He only explained that the data were handed over to many members of the party. The SDPI prepared an Administrative Law infringement protocol on the grounds of the failure of the representative to implement proper organizational and technical measures for protecting the data from accidental or unlawful destruction, altering, disclosure, as well as any other unlawful processing. The protocol was submitted to the court, which gave a warning to the violator.3496

Open Government

The 1996 Law on the Provision of Information to the Public provides for a limited right of access to official documents and to documents held by political parties, political and public organizations, trade union and other entities.[3497] A more comprehensive "Law on the Right to Receive Information from the State and Municipal Institutions" was enacted on January 11, 2000.[3498] However, there are few examples of the practical application of this law.

There were some new developments with regard to various registers. At the beginning of 2004, the Information Systems on the Administration of the

---

[3495] *Id.*

[3496] *Id.*

[3497] Law on the Provision of Information to the Public, July 2 1996 No.I-1418 (as amended on January 23, 1997), available at <http://www.lrtv.lt/en_lrtvm.htm>.

[3498] Memorandum on the Submission of Article 19 Critique - Lithuanian Draft Law on "The Right to Receive Information," available at <http://www.article19.org/docimages/404.doc>.

Debtors, which included both natural and legal persons, started to operate.3499 On average, there are more than 340,000 records and 100,000 requests made each month. In December 2004, the requests increased to 200,000 per month.3500 In 2005, the Electronic Internal Waters Vessels Register was created.3501 The register will interact with other state registers and information systems and will guarantee the effective distribution of information to the data subjects, such as marshals judicial institutions and Tax Inspectorate.3502

For the first time, in the history of Lithuania, the Social Insurance Fund will provide data by electronic means to the private companies.3503 The Board of the Social Insurance Fund signed contracts for providing data with a couple of banks and soon the Board will contract with the leasing companies.3504 The banks will only have partial access to the data stored in the Social Insurance Fund's database. They will be allowed to access the data concerning their client's solvency. The banks will be able to access the database only after receiving a written consent of the client. In addition, they will be able to access the data about client's employment or work history, salary as well as any received pensions or one-time payments.3505 Access to the database will be provided for a certain fee at the bank's request.

In 2005, an investigation was started concerning a copy of the Social Insurance Fund's database allegedly sold for LTL 10,000 (about EUR 2,900) to special investigation officers, who pretended to be potential purchasers.3506 The copy contained 20 GB of data on the income of 1.5 million workers and 100,000 companies, names, surnames, workplaces and home addresses.[3507]

International Obligations

Lithuania is a member of the Council of Europe (CoE) and in June 2001 ratified the Convention for the Protection of Individuals with Regard to Automatic

---

3499 "News flow. Debts,", Lietuvos Rytas, March 4, 2005, at 11.
3500 *Id.*
3501 "The Electronic Internal Waters Vessels Register Created," Respublika, February 23, 2005, at 28.
3502 *Id.*
3503 Mantas Dubauskas, "The Country Banks will not Require Any More Piles of Notes," Lietuvos Rytas, February 10, 2005, at 10.
3504 Martynas Zilionis, "Data about Salary – Directly from the Social Insurance Fund," Respublika, March 12, 2005, at 17.
3505 *Id.*
3506 Justinas Vanagas, "Trade in Social Insurance Fund's data," Lietuvos Zinios, April 30, 2005.
3507 *Id.*

Processing of Personal Data (Convention No. 108).[3508] It has signed and ratified the European Convention for the Protection of Human Rights and Fundamental Freedoms[3509] and the CoE Convention on Cybercrime.[3510] On May 1, 2004, Lithuania jointed the European Union.

Grand Duchy of Luxembourg

Constitutional Privacy Framework

Article 28 of the Constitution states, "(1) The secrecy of correspondence is inviolable. The law determines the agents responsible for the violation of the secrecy of correspondence entrusted to the postal services. (2) The law determines the guarantee to be afforded to the secrecy of telegrams."[3511]

Data Protection Framework

Luxembourg's Act concerning the Use of Nominal Data in Computer Processing was adopted in 1979.[3512] The law regulates individually identifiable automated personal records in both public and private computer files. All databanks including personal data have to be authorized, and data subjects have the right to access their personal data and correct it if inaccurate. The law also requires licensing of systems used for the processing of personal data.[3513]

The Data Protection Act of 2002[3514] governs the processing and use of personal data. It implements the European Union (EU) Data Protection Directive

---

[3508] Convention for the Protection of Individuals with regard to Automatic Processing of Personal Data (ETS no.: 108). Signed February 11, 2000; ratified June 1, 2001; entered into force October 1, 2001, available at <http://conventions.coe.int/Treaty/EN/CadreListeTraites.htm>.

[3509] Convention for the Protection of Human Rights and Fundamental Freedoms. (ETS no.: 005). Signed May 14, 1993; ratified June 20, 1995; entered into force June 20, 1995, available at <http://conventions.coe.int/Treaty/EN/CadreListeTraites.htm>.

[3510] Signed June 23, 2004; ratified March 18, 2004; entered into force July 1, 2004, available at <http://conventions.coe.int/Treaty/Commun/ChercheSig.asp?NT=185&CM=8&DF=&CL=ENG>.

[3511] Constitution of the Grand Duchy of Luxembourg.

[3512] Act on the Use of Nominal Data in Computer Processing, March 31, 1979; *see* Charles E.H. Franklin, Business Guide to Privacy and Data Protection Legislation 306 (1996).

[3513] A good outline of the law is available at <http://www.privacyexchange.org/legal/nat/omni/luxemsum.html>.

[3514] Loi du 2 août 2002 relative à la protection des personnes à l'égard du traitement des données à caractère personnel (Data Protectiona Act of 2002), *Mémorial*, A-91, August 13, 2002, at 1836-1854, available at <http://www.etat.lu/legilux/DOCUMENTS_PDF/MEMORIAL/memorial/a/2002/a0911308.pdf> (in French); <http://www.cnpd.lu/loi_langue_anglaise.pdf> (English translation).

(1995/46/EC).[3515] The law[3516] goes beyond the framework of the EU directive by covering not only natural, but also moral, persons. It contains specific provisions on the processing of medical data by health services,[3517] the processing of personal data for surveillance purposes[3518] and in the workplace.[3519] iHowever, n April 2004, the European Commission threatened legal action against Luxembourg and seven other countries for failing to incorporate the EU Directive on Privacy and Electronic Communications (2002/58/EC).[3520]

In May 2005, a new law[3521] implemented the provisions of the EU Directive on Privacy and Electronic Communications. The law states that any service provider must retain traffic and location data for a period of 12 months for the purposes of prevention, investigation, detection and prosecution of criminal offences. It also adopts an "opt-in" system for unsolicited electronic communications; the use of automated calling systems, fax machines or e-mail for the purposes of direct marketing is prohibited without obtaining the subscriber's prior consent, unless the service provider can make use of the specific exceptions mentioned in the EU directive. The law provides for criminal sanctions (imprisonment and fines) for breach of the provisions related to spam and unsolicited communications. A court may ban any illegal processing, together with a penalty payment. The *Commission nationale pour la protection des données* (CNPD) (see below) was consulted during the drafting of the bill.

[3515] Luxembourg should have amended this law by October 1, 1998. In January 2000, the European Commission initiated a case before the European Court of Justice against Luxembourg and other countries for failure to implement the directive on time; *see* European Commission, Data Protection: Commission Takes Five Member States to Court, January 11, 2000, available at <http://europa.eu.int/comm/internal_market/en/media/dataprot/news/2k-10.htm>. A new bill was eventually drafted and submitted to Parliament in October 2000, and enacted in August 2002.

[3516] For more information on the law, *see* the exhaustive analysis made by Steve Jacoby & Catherine Dauger de Caulaincourt, AGEFI Luxembourg, December 2002 and February 2003; *see also* Dossier de presse quant à la presentation de la Commission nationale pour la protection des données <http://www.gouvernement.lu/salle_presse/actualite/2002/12/12biltgen/dossierpresse.pdf> (in French).

[3517] Data Protection Act of 2002, *supra* at Article 7

[3518] *Id.* at Article 10.

[3519] *Id.* at Article 11; on the particular issue of the processing of personal data by employers in the workplace, *see* Guy Castagnero, L'actualité du droit du travail: la protection des données personnelles des travailleurs, AGEFI Luxembourg, April 2003, available at <http://www.agefi.lu/mensuel/Article.asp?NumArticle=5364>.

[3520] Associated Press, "EU Issues Order on Internet Privacy," Toronto Star, April 2, 2004, at E05.

[3521] Law "Privacy in Electronic Communications" of May 30, 2005 (Loi du 30 mai 2005 (1) relative aux dispositions spécifiques de protection de la personne à l'égard du traitement des données à caractère personnel dans le secteur des communications électroniques et (2) portant modification des articles 88-2 et 88-4 du Code d'instruction criminelle), *Mémorial*, A-073, June 7, 2005, at 1168-1173, available at <http://www.legilux.public.lu/leg/a/archives/2005/0730706/0730706.pdf#page=26>.

In December 2004, a Grand Duchy Ruling[3522] established the conditions in which some data controllers may designate a person in charge of data processing and compliance with the data protection law. In doing this, they could avoid having to comply with the notification requirements to the Commission.

Data Protection Authority

The Data Protection Act of 2002 created a new data protection authority, the *Commission nationale pour la protection des données*[3523] (CNPD). Created on December 12, 2002,[3524] the CNPD is an independent agency whose task will be to control the processing of personal data in Luxembourg and ensure compliance with data protection regulations.[3525]

On May 3, 2004, the CNPD rendered opinions on two bills, one on the freedom of speech in the media[3526] and the other on a law amending the Law of August 2, 2002 to transpose the EU Directive on Privacy and Electronic Communications (2002/58/EC).[3527] On August 7, 2003, the CNPD established directives simplifying the notification for certain types of personal data processing that is not likely to infringe on data subjects' freedoms and fundamental rights.

A Grand-Ducal decree of August 1979 created the *Commission à la protection des données nominatives* (the Commission). The Commission is charged with overseeing the law and assisting the Minister of Justice with the management of the National Register of Databanks. If an application for personal data processing is granted, and there is an objection raised, or if the application is refused, or the original authorization is withdrawn for some reason, an appeal can be made to the Disputes Committee of the Council of State. The Minister for Justice maintains a national register of all systems containing personal information. Public sector personal data systems can only be established upon the issuance of

---

[3522] Règlement grand-ducal relatif à la désignation des chargés de la protection des données. *Mémorial* A-200, December 20, 2004.

[3523] Commission Nationale pour la Protection des Données homepage <http://www.cnpd.lu/>.

[3524] *See* Le Gouvernement du Grand-Duché de Luxembourg, Actualité gouvernementale: Présentation de la Commission Nationale pour la Protection des Données, available at <http://www.gouvernement.lu/salle_presse/actualite/2002/12/12biltgen/>.

[3525] *See* Article 32, Data Protection Act, for the details of its competences.

[3526] Délibération No. 6 bis 1/2003 relative à l'avis sur le projet de loi No. 4910 sur la liberté d'expression dans les médias, October 17, 2003, available at <http://www.cnpd.lu/projet4910.pdf>.

[3527] Délibération No. 2/2004, Avis sur le projet de loi No. 5181 relatif aux dispositions spécifiques de protection des personnes des personnes à l'égard du traitement des données à caractère personnel dans le secteur des communications électroniques et portant modification de la loi du 2 août 2002, February 20, 2004, available at <http://www.cnpd.lu/projet5181.pdf>.

a special law or regulation. The Advisory Board reviews such proposed laws or regulations. In 1992, the law was amended to include special protection requirements for police and medical data. In 1993, the law was modified to establish an independent control authority pursuant to the Schengen Agreement.

In October 2004, after having communicated with various actors covered by the 2002 data protection legislation (including business organizations and associations, public administrations, non-profit associations and health services), the CNPD launched a national information and advertising campaign (with press advertising, posters, information booklet) to target the public. The campaign was aimed at raising awareness of individuals' rights in relation to personal data and of legal rights of control under the data protection legislation.[3528]

Also in October 2004, the CNPD released an opinion about a new bill regulating identification procedures using genetic information in a criminal context.[3529] The CNPD criticized certain provisions of the bill that deal with the scope of the definition of "DNA profile" as "personal data," the number of persons who would have to be subject to DNA testing in the context of a criminal investigation, and the retention of DNA data.

Wiretapping and Other Government Surveillance

Articles 88-1 and 88-2 of the Criminal Code regulate telephone tapping.[3530] Judicial wiretaps are authorized if it can be shown: that a serious crime or infringement, punishable by two or more years imprisonment, is involved; that there is sufficient evidence to suspect that the subject of the interception order committed or participated in the crime; or received or transmitted information to, from, or concerning the accused; and that ordinary investigative techniques would be inadequate under the circumstances. Orders are granted for one-month periods and may be extended repeatedly as long as the cumulative period does not exceed one year. Administrative wiretaps may also be authorized for national security reasons by a special tribunal appointed by the head of government. These interceptions are granted for three months at a time and must stop once the

---

[3528] *See* Commission Nationale pour la Protection des Données, Data Protection and Privacy, October 27, 2004, available at <http://www.cnpd.lu/BrochureUK.pdf>.

[3529] Commission Nationale pour la Protection des Données, Avis concernant le projet de loi No. 5356 relatif aux procédures d'identification par empreintes génétiques en matière pénale et portant modification du Code d'instruction criminelle, Délibération No. 78/2004 du 8 octobre 2004, available at <http://www.cnpd.lu/782004.pdf>.

[3530] Articles 88-1 - 88-4 of the Criminal Code, Law of 26 November 1982, modified by the law of July 7, 1989.

requested information is received. The communications of persons bound by professional secrecy rules cannot be intercepted and any recordings of such must be destroyed immediately. Information gathered during judicial and administrative interceptions, but not subsequently used, must be destroyed. In the case of judicial warrants, persons who were the subject of the warrant will sometimes be informed of the action taken. This law was highly criticized by human rights activists and the Socialist Workers Party when it was first introduced. In fact the law was challenged on numerous occasions before the European Court of Human Rights. That court, however, ruled that the law violated neither Article 8 (concerning the right to private and family life) nor Article 13 (concerning the right to due process) of the European Convention on Human Rights.[3531]

Statutory Rules Related to Privacy

A law on electronic commerce that implements three European Union directives (Directive 1999/93 on Electronic Signatures, Directive 2000/31/EC on Electronic Commerce, and Directive 1997/7 on Distance-Selling) was adopted in August 2000.[3532] This law contains provisions on the privacy rules certification authorities have to comply with, spamming, and the liability of online service providers. A Grand-Ducal regulation on electronic signatures, electronic payments and the creation of the Electronic Commerce Committee was adopted on June 1, 2001. On July 5, 2004, the legislator amended the Law on Electronic Commerce to establish the "opt-in" regime for unsolicited commercial communications and add various provisions on consumer protection.[3533] A law enacted in May 30, 2005[3534] transposes part of the EU "telecommunications regulatory package" by establishing new rights for consumers and

---

[3531] Commission nationale de contrôle des interceptions de sécurité, (France) 8e Rapport d'activité 1999, at 66-67.

[3532] Loi du 14 août 2000 relative au commerce électronique modifiant le code civil, le nouveau code de procédure civile, le code de commerce, le code pénal et transposant la Directive 99/93 relative à un cadre communautaire pour les signatures électroniques, la Directive relative à certains aspects juridiques des services de la société de l'information, certaines dispositions de la Directive 97/7 concernant la vente à distance des biens et des services autres que les services financiers, *Mémorial*, September 8, 2000, at 2176, available at <http://www.chd.lu> under "Portail Documentaire," "recherche d'archives," "recherche avancée," "Dossier parlementaire No. 4641."

[3533] Law of July 5, 2004 modifying the Law of August 14, 2000 on Electronic Commerce (Loi du 5 juillet 2004, modifiant la loi du 14 août 2000 relative au commerce électronique), *Mémorial*, A-125, July 16, 2004, at 1848, available at <http://www.legilux.public.lu/leg/a/archives/2004/1251607/2004A18481.html> (in French); *see*, for more details, Sandrine Munoz, "Le Luxembourg modifie sa loi relative au commerce électronique – Analyse," available at <http://www.droit-technologie.org/1_2.asp?actu_id=1047>.

[3534] Law on Networks and Electronic Communications Services (Loi du 30 mai 2005 sur les réseaux et les services de communications électroniques), Mémorial, A-073, June 7, 2005, at 1144,-1159, available at <http://www.legilux.public.lu/leg/a/archives/2005/0730706/0730706.pdf#page=2>.

---

telecommunications users, and corresponding obligations for network and publicly available electronic communications service providers.

The Numerical Identification of Natural and Legal Persons Act of 1979[3535] provides for the introduction of an identity number, consisting of 11 digits (including digits to represent date of birth and sex, nationality, marital status and spouse's name) for every resident in the country, and a numbering system for companies. The law contains specifications for use of this number: the identification number and other related information can only be used by the public services that are authorized to have access to the index, and is restricted to an internal use. These specifications are loosely drafted, however, and allow the number to be widely circulated. The data protection authority is said to be monitoring the adoption of this number closely.[3536]

There are also sectoral laws on privacy relating to telecommunications[3537] and banking secrecy. Luxembourg's status as a financial haven ensures that unwarranted surveillance of individuals is forbidden. This may change as Luxembourg comes under increasing pressure to amend its financial confidentiality laws to permit greater access to personal financial records by European and American investigators.

In December 2001, the Commission of Surveillance of the Financial Sector (*Commission de Surveillance du Secteur Financier*) released practical and technical guidelines to financial services companies that intend to promote the protection of customers' privacy and the confidentiality of their financial information when launching new online financial services.[3538]

[3535] Loi du 30 mars 1979 organisant l'identification numérique des personnes physiques et morales, available at <http://www.etat.lu/ECP/30-3-79.doc>; Règlement grand-ducal du 7 juin 1979 déterminant les actes, documents et fichiers autorisés à utiliser le numéro d'identité des personnes physiques et morales, available at <http://www.etat.lu/ECP/7-6-79.doc>. Règlement grand-ducal modifié du 21 décembre 1987 fixant les modalités d'application de la loi du 30 mars 1979, available at <http://www.etat.lu/ECP/21-12-87.doc>.

[3536] The Council of Europe, The introduction and use of personal identification numbers: the data protection issues, 1991, available at <http://www.coe.fr/DataProtection/Etudes_Rapports/epins.htm>.

[3537] Law of March 21, 1997 on Telecommunications (Loi du 21 mars 1997 sur les télécommunications), available at <http://www.etat.lu/ILT/co/legal/loi-t.htm>; Grand Duchy Ruling of December 22, 1997 (Règlement grand-ducal du 22 décembre 1997 fixant les conditions du cahier des charges pour l'établissement et l'exploitation de réseaux fixes de telecommunications), available at <http://www.etat.lu/ILT/co/legal/lic-b.htm>.

[3538] Commission de Surveillance du Secteur Financier, Services financiers par Internet (Résultats du recensement Internet au 31 décembre 2000 et recommendations portant sur les aspects prudentiels), December 2001, available at <http://www.droit-technologie.org/redirect.asp?type=legislation&legis_id=95&url=legislations/CSSF_services_financiers_sur_int ernet_decembre2001.pdf>.

Open Government

There is no general freedom of information law in Luxembourg. Under the 1960 Decree on State Archives, the archives are open to the public, but citizens must make a written request explaining why they want access and ministers have broad discretion to deny requests.[3539] The government announced in August 1999 that it was planning to develop a new press bill including a right to access records.[3540]

International Obligations

Luxembourg is a member of the Council of Europe (CoE) and has signed and ratified the Convention for the Protection of Individuals with Regard to Automatic Processing of Personal Data (ETS No. 108).[3541] It has signed and ratified the European Convention for the Protection of Human Rights and Fundamental Freedoms.[3542] In January 2003, Luxembourg signed the CoE Convention on Cybercrime, but has not ratified it.[3543] It is a member of the Organization for Economic Cooperation and Development (OECD) and has adopted the OECD Guidelines on the Protection of Privacy and Transborder Flows of Personal Data.

Republic of Macedonia

Constitutional Privacy Framework

The Constitution of the Republic of Macedonia[3544] recognizes the rights of privacy, data protection and secrecy of communications. Article 25 states: "Each citizen is guaranteed the respect and protection of the privacy of his or her personal and family life and of his or her dignity and repute." Article 26 states:

[3539] Arrêté grand-ducal fixant l'organisation et les conditions de fonctionnement des Archives de l'Etat.

[3540] Le programme gouvernemental: Accord de coalition PCS/PDL, August 1999, available at <http://www.gouvernement.lu/gouv/fr/gouv/progg/coalfr.html#1>.

[3541] Signed January 28, 1981; ratified February 10, 1988; entered into force June 1, 1988.

[3542] Signed November 11, 1950; ratified September 3, 1953; entered into force September 3, 1953.

[3543] Signed January 28, 2003.

3544 Published in the Official Gazette of the Republic of Macedonia, Nos. 52/91, 01/92, 31/98, 91/01, 84/03. The Constitution is available at the website of the Constitutional Court <http://www.usud.gov.mk>, and the website of the President <http://www.president.gov.mk>.

"(1) The inviolability of the home is guaranteed. (2) The right to the inviolability of the home may be restricted only by a court decision in cases of the detection or prevention of criminal offences or the protection of people's health. Article 18 states: "(1)The security and confidentiality of personal information are guaranteed. (2) Citizens are guaranteed protection from any violation of their personal integrity deriving from the registration of personal information through data processing." Equally guaranteed is the freedom and confidentiality of correspondence. Article 17 states: "(1) The freedom and confidentiality of correspondence and other forms of communication is guaranteed. (2) Only a court decision may authorise non-application of the principle of the inviolability of the confidentiality of correspondence and other forms of communication, in cases where it is indispensable to a criminal investigation or required in the interests of the defence of the Republic."

Data Protection Framework

Several laws regulate the right of privacy in the Republic of Macedonia. The new Law on Personal Data Protection (LPDP) was adopted on January 25, 2005.[3545] The LPDP explicitly identifies the exceptions from its application, focused on processing of personal data performed by natural persons purely for personal or household activities, processing of personal data in criminal procedure, as well as protection of the interests of security and defence of the Republic of Macedonia.[3546] According to the law, the personal data shall be processed fairly and lawfully, in conformity with the law and shall be collected for specified, explicit and legitimate purposes and shall be processed in a manner according to these purposes; they shall be adequate, relevant and not excessive in respect to the purposes they are collected or processed for.[3547] The data shall be accurate, complete and updated as needed. Inaccurate or incomplete data, having in mind the aims for which they were collected or processed, will be erased or rectified. The personal data shall be kept in a form that enables identification of the subject of personal data for not longer than it is necessary to fulfill the purposes for which the data were collected or for which they are further processed. The data controllers are responsible for complying with the abovementioned principles concerning the quality of personal data.[3548]

[3545] No. 07/05.

[3546] LPDP at Article 4.

[3547] *Id.* at Article 5.

[3548] *Id.* at Article 5, paragraph 2.

The LPDP, in accordance with the Council of Europe (CoE) Convention No. 108, provides that consent of the data subject is mandatory for processing of personal data. Exceptions from the aforementioned rule are also specified. Personal data can be processed without the consent of the subject if it is necessary for performance of a contract where the subject of personal data is a contracting party, or upon a request of the subject of personal data, prior to entering into a contract; for compliance with a legal obligation of the data controller; for protection of the vital interests of the subject of personal data; for performance of activities of public interest or of official authority vested in the data controller or a third party to whom the data were disclosed.[3549]

Furthermore, the law prohibits processing of special categories of personal data. All exceptions are defined by the law. The LPDP stipulates that processing must be specially designated and protected, while transfer through a telecommunications network may be carried out if the data are specially protected with encryption methods to render them unreadable during transmission.[3550]

The rights of the data subject include the right to examine the data collection; the right to submit a request to rectify, erase or block the processing of personal data, if the data are incomplete, inaccurate or out of date, or if their processing is not in conformity with the provisions of this law; and the right to request that their personal data are not used for advertising purposes.[3551] Furthermore, the LPDPguarantees that no court decision that produces legal effects concerning the performance of certain person can be based solely on automated data processing, the purpose of which is evaluation of certain personal aspects relating to that person.

The LPDP also established an obligation for data controllers to notify the Directorate for Protection of Personal Data before performing wholly or partly automatic processing operation and an obligation of the data controller to submit data on any newly opened collection of personal data, as well as change of data from the existing personal data collections.[3552] The records from the Central Register kept by the Directorate are publicly accessible, and they are published in

---

[3549] LPDP at Article 6.

[3550] *Id.* at Article 8.

[3551] *Id.* at Article 10.

[3552] *Id.* at Article 29, paragraph 1: "Data Controller is obligate to submit a report to the Directorate, containing data which is in accordance to the article 27 of the law, before performing wholly or partly automatic processing of personal data. Data Controller is obligate to report the Directorate for each change of the data from the existing personal data collections."

the Official Gazette of the Republic of Macedonia.[3553] Additionally, transfer of personal data to other countries can be performed only if the third country provides an adequate level of protection of personal data.

Data controllers can make personal data available on the basis of a written request submitted by the user, if the data are needed to perform activities within the legally established scope of competences of the user. The LPDP stipulates a prohibition on providing personal data processing that cannot be carried out in accordance with the provisions of this law, and the purpose for requesting such personal data must be in accordance with specific, clear and lawful purposes for which personal data is collected.[3554]

The constitutional guarantee of protection of personal data is also regulated by the Criminal Code.[3555] The "abuse of personal data" Is considered a crime under the Criminal Code. The punishment for this criminal offence consists of a prescribed fine or prison sentence of up to one year for the perpetrator who, contrary to conditions established by law and without the consent of the citizen, collects, processes or uses his personal data. The same fine is provided for the person who will break into computerized information systems of personal data with the intention to use the data for himself or herself or another person in order to gain benefit or to cause harm to another person. The criminal offence "abuse of personal data" has an aggravated form if it is committed by officials carrying out their duty, and that punishment is a prison sentence of three months to three years. The attempt to commit such a crime is also punishable. With the new amendments of the Criminal Code in 2004, legal persons can also be perpetrators of the primary form of this crime and be punished with a fine.[3556]

[3553] LPDP at Article 30.

[3554] *Id.* at Article 34, paragraph 1 and 3: "(1) Data Controller can make personal data available on the basis of a written request submitted by the user, if the data are needed to perform activities within the legally established scope of competencies of the user. (3) Providing personal data whose processing, i.e. use cannot be carried out in accordance with the provisions of this Law is prohibited."

[3555] Criminal Code, No. 37/96, 80/99, 4/02, 43/03 and 19/04, available online at <http://www.mlrc.org.mk/law/CriminalCode.htm>.

[3556] Criminal Code, Article 149: "(1)A person who collects, processes or uses personal data from a citizen without his permission, contrary to the conditions determined by law, shall be punished with a fine, or with imprisonment of up to one year. (2)The punishment from item 1 shall apply to a person who penetrates a computerized information system of personal data, with the intention of using them in order to attain some benefit for himself or for another, or to inflict some harm upon another. (3)If the crime from items 1 and 2 is committed by an official person while performing his duty, he shall be punished with imprisonment of three months to three years. (4)The attempt is punishable. (5) If the crime from item 1 is committed by a legal entity shall be punished with a fine."

The Law on Organisation and Operation of State Administrative Bodies[3557] provides that state administrative bodies do not disclose data related to national security, official and business secrets, and personal data of citizens in accordance to the law that governs protection of personal data of citizens.

The Law on Voter's List[3558] protects the personal data collected in accordance with the LPDP and they must not be used for any purpose other than for exercising citizens' voting right in accordance with the Law on Voter's List. Any citizen may, within the period determined with this law, file a request for registering, amending or deleting data in the copies of the voter's list provided for public inspection in case they or any other citizen are not correctly registered on the list. Copies of the voter's list, with data related to the ordinal number, surname, name, gender, date of birth and address, are provided to registered political parties and to independent candidates.[3559]

Basic personal data on citizens is recorded in the Registry of Births, Marriages and of Deaths. Registry books are kept, protected and used in in accordance with the Law on Personal Identification Records.[3560] The original copy, the certificate from a registry, as well as a transcript or a copy for entry in a registry, are issued upon request of the person to whom the data in those documents refer. The documents are also issued to a concerned party, such as a legal entity or body when there is legal interest established by law. The person to whom the data relates or an interested person who has a direct legal interest established by law, has the right to inspection of registries or the documents and decisions upon which entries are made in the registries.

The Law on Reporting Dwellings and Residence of Citizens[3561] stipulates that the Ministry of the Interior provides protection from unauthorised access and use of the data contained in the records on the dwelling, change of home address and residence of the citizens.

The personal data on asylum seekers, recognized refugees and persons under humanitarian protection, as well as the data on their residence and the rights they enjoy in the Republic of Macedonia are contained in the Central Collection of Data, established, processed and used by the Ministry of the Interior (Asylum

---

[3557] Nos. 58/00 and 44/02.

[3558] Nos.42/02 and 35/04, available at<http://faq.macedonia.org/politics/elections/law.on.voters.lists.html>.

[3559] Law on Voter's List, Part III: "Protection of the personal data of the Voter's list," Article 28.

[3560] Nos. 08/95 and 38/02.

[3561] Nos. 36/92, 12/93 and 43/00.

Section). The above collection of data is established, processed and used by the person handling the collection in accordance with the provisions of the LPDP. In accordance with the Law on Asylum and Temporary Protection,[3562] the data from the Central Collection of Data cannot be exchanged with the country of origin of the person to whom such data relates or with the country of origin of the members of his family.

The personal identification number of the citizen is a unique designation on the identification documents of the citizen. In accordance with the Law on Personal Identification Number,[3563] the Ministry of the Interior designates a personal identification number to the citizen according to the place of registration of the newborn child in the Registry of Births kept on the territory of the Republic of Macedonia. The Ministry of the Interior provides for the retention, use and protection of the data from unauthorised access in accordance with law.

Law enforcement officers, in accordance with the Code of Police Ethics,[3564] are obliged to adhere to the citizens' right to privacy in accordance with the Constitution and the laws of the Republic of Macedonia. The collection, retention and use of personal data by the police is performed in accordance with law and the ratified international agreements for protecting personal data, restrictively and to the extent necessary for carrying out legal duties.

The Law on Classified Information[3565] establishes the measures and activities for protecting classified information. The measures and activities for security of individuals, such as issuing a security certificate, are significant. The satisfaction of the conditions for issuing a security certificate is established through a security audit carried out upon previous written consent of the person to whom a security certificate is to be issued. The data from the completed security questionnaire are used for the purposes of the audit. The law comprises the NATO and EU standards on classified information.[3566]

The Law on State Statistics[3567] regulates the protection of individual data (of natural or legal persons) collected and processed for statistical purposes. The individual data related to a legal or natural person, collected and processed for

---

[3562] No. 49/03.

[3563] No. 36/92.

[3564] No. 03/04.

[3565] No. 9/04.

[3566] "Macedonian Parliament resumes 53rd session," February 10, 2005, MT. net News, available at <http://vesti.mt.net.mk/English/vest.asp?id=149389>.

[3567] No. 54/97.

statistical purposes, are confidential data and as such can be used as separate data for statistical purposes only. By exception, access to such data is allowed for scientific purposes (without the identification data about the data subject). Publication or preparation of statistical data must be conducted in a form preventing the identification of the data subject, unless the data subject has agreed to such publishing. Data providers are notified of the data protection. The measures and techniques for protecting individual data collected and processed for statistical purposes are established in a Rulebook on the Measures and Techniques on the Protection of Individual Data Collected for Statistical Purposes (SSO internal document), adopted by the Director of the State Statistical Office. A Commission for Protection of Data has been established within the above state administrative body to supervise the protection of data.[3568]

Illegal invasion of the privacy of communications are prohibited and punishable. In accordance with the new Law on Electronic Communications[3569] the holders, operators of telecommunication networks and means, as well as the providers of public telecommunication services are obliged to provide inviolability of message confidentiality within their technical abilities. Furthermore, the law contains provisions regulating protective measures for providing networks and services, communication confidentiality, caller or connecting line identification, and location information that is not traffic information, automatic call diverting, etc.

The Law on the National Bank of the Republic of Macedonia[3570] obligates the members of the Council of the National Bank and the employees of the National Bank to keep official and business secrets. This obligation binds these persons for five years following the end of their membership in the Council of the National Bank. The data that are official or business secrets may be provided only upon written request of the court. Furthermore, the Banking Law[3571] establishes the persons who may not reveal data and information established as a business secret of the bank by law, statute and other bank acts. The obligation to keep a business secret that persists after the termination of employment with the bank also relates to persons with special rights and responsibilities, bank employees and other persons with access to bank operations. The data on savings and bank deposits of natural and legal entities, as well as data on the account

---

[3568] The website of State Statistical Office is available at <http://www.stat.gov.mk/>. According to the LPDP, Commission for Protection of Data is to be elected six months after the law goes into force, August 1, 2005. That is why the commission still does not have a homepage.

[3569] No. 13/05 adopted on February 22, 2005.

3570 Nos. 03/02, 51/03, 85/03 and 40/04.

[3571] Nos. 63/00, 103/00, 70/01, 37/02, 51/03, 85/03, 83/04.

operations of natural and legal persons, are business secrets of the bank. The above data may be provided only in the following cases: (1) If the client provides written consent to reveal the data; (2) Upon written request or order of the competent court; (3) Upon written request of the national bank for the purpose of supervision, or another body authorised by law; or (4) If the data are provided to the Directorate for Money Laundering Prevention, in accordance with law. Additionally, in accordance with the Law on Securities,[3572] the management and the employees of the Central Securities Depositary, as well as certified auditors, are obliged to keep the confidentiality of the data learned through their employment, unless they are obliged to provide such information in accordance with specified law.

Other regulations partially or indirectly regulate the privacy right. The Law on Single Registry of the Population in the Republic of Macedonia[3573] provides for the introduction, retention and contents of the single automated registry of the population in the Republic of Macedonia, the competent authority for keeping the registry, the protection of the data from the registry and the processing, publishing and use of the data from the registry.

The Law on Personal Identification Records of the Insured and Beneficiaries of Pension and Disability Insurance Rights[3574] provides for protection of the in such records. This protection encompasses undertaking measures and activities for protecting the data from: unauthorised access, unauthorised processing, prevention of destruction, loss, modification, abuse and unauthorised use of the data.

The Law on Keeping Labour Records[3575] stipulates that the data contained in such records can be used for statistical purposes and for other official needs. Legally established data can also be used by individuals to whom the mentioned data refer to in order to exercise their rights.

The Law on Social Care[3576] provides an obligation for the social security institution and the employees to keep professional and official secrets. The Law protects the data and the facts discovered during procedures and decisionmaking

---

[3572] Nos. 63/00, 103/00, 34/01, 04/02, 37/02, 31/03, 85/03 and 96/04.

[3573] Published in the Official Gazette of the SRM, No. 46/90.

3574 Published in the Official Gazette of the Republic of Macedonia, No. 16/04.

[3575] No. 16/04.

[3576] No.50/97, 16/00, 17/03 and 65/04.

concerning the rights of beneficiaries of social security, of legal family protection, and on the competencies established by criminal regulations.

Furthermore, the Law on Family[3577] establishes that the data on adoptions are an official secret. The Law on Health Care[3578] specifies that health sector workers are obliged to take care of patients, to respect their dignity, to adhere to medical ethics and to keep professional secrets. The obligation to keep professional secrets refers, to any worker who use medical records or in any way (in performing their tasks) comes across data contained therein. In accordance with the Law on the Protection of the Population from Contagious Diseases,[3579] the reporting of AIDS and the HIV infection, as well as microbiological findings for Treponema pallidum, Neisseria gonorhoeae, congenital infections with the Rubella virus, Tohoplasma gondii and Chlamydia gondii is anonymous.

Data Protection Authority

The LPDP foresees establishment of a Directorate for Protection of Personal Data, as an independent supervisory authority over the legality of processing of personal data, no later that August 9, 2005. The LPDP provisions regulate the establishment of the Directorate as an independent and autonomous state body with a capacity of a legal entity. The Directorate is managed by a director who is appointed and dismissed by the Parliament of the Republic of Macedonia, upon a nomination by the Government of the Republic of Macedonia. The Director is appointed for a five-year term, with the right to be re-elected twice. The director and the deputy director of the Directorate are accountable to the Parliament of the Republic of Macedonia. The director and the employees of the Directorate must keep as official secrets the data that they have encountered in their work, both during the terms of office or employment within the Directorate and afterward.

The Directorate will: assess the legality of the processing of personal data; publish the principles of processing of personal data and ensure that the Data Controllers respect them; investigate and has access to the collections of personal data established by data controllers, according to type of subjects and aims; control the operations for processing of personal data that data controllers use; collect data necessary for proper performance of its tasks; maintain a central register of collections of personal data; maintain records on transfer of personal data to other countries; receive reports or complaints related to processing of

---

[3577] No. 80/92, 09/96, 38/04 and 83/04 – consolidated text.
[3578] No. 38/91, 46/93, 55/95, 17/97 – consolidated text and 10/04.
[3579] No. 66/04.

personal data by data controllers; issue prohibitions of further processing of personal data to data controller; provide opinion on the secondary legislation of the Data Controllers; and perform other tasks established by law.

If violations of the provisions of the LPDP in the course of processing of personal data are found, the data controller must, within 30 days from the date when the violations were detected: bring its work in line with the provisions of this law and remove the reasons that led to the violations; complete, update, correct, disclose or maintain the confidentiality of the personal data; adopt additional measures for protection of the collection of personal data; interrupt the transfer of personal data to other states; secure the data or their transfer to other entities; and erase the personal data. Against a decision of the director, an administrative dispute can be initiated.[3580]

Wiretapping and Surveillance Rules

The Constitution of the Republic of Macedonia in Article 17 guarantees the freedom and confidentiality of correspondence and other forms of communication. In 2003, an amendment of this article was made in order to regulate wiretapping and other surveillance authorities. The new Article 17 provides for violation of the confidentiality of correspondence and other forms of communication, only in cases where it is indispensable to prevent or to discover a crime, to a criminal investigation or required in the interests of the defence of the Republic. These violations can be imposed only with a court decision based on a procedure according to a law that is adopted with 2/3 majority in the Parliament.[3581]

Although the constitutional changes were made to allow such law to be brought, the Law on Surveillance of the Communication is still in the government procedure and has not been adopted. Therefore, wiretapping and electronic surveillance remain illegal. However, a case involving alleged illegal wiretapping by the former director of the Bureau for Security and Intelligence,. Dosta Dimovska, was made public in 2001. At that time, the President of Republic of Macedonia Boris Trajkovski pardoned[3582] Ms. Dimovska and another person involved in the case therefore making impossible for criminal charges to be filed.

[3580] LPDP at Article 47, paragraphs 1 and 2.

[3581] Constitution of the Republic of Macedonia, *supra*.

[3582] President Boris Trajkovski proclaimed absolution of Ms. Dosta Dimovska and Mr. Aleksandar Cvetkov for their involvement in the wiretapping scandal, several days after the charges against her were filed (Dnevnik, April 9, 2003, available at <http://217.16.70.236/?pBroj=2122&stID=16821)l> (in Cyrillic)), claiming that the

Search of homes and personal search and seizure are regulated in the Law on Criminal Procedure.[3583] In general, a judge's warrant must be issued prior to such searches.

NGOs' Advocacy Work

Foundation Metamorphosis,[3584] in coordination with other actors,[3585] participated in the creation of the National Strategy for Information Society of the Republic of Macedonia.[3586] As a result, the e-citizens pillar of the Strategy clearly identified the "lack of clear privacy rules for storing the personal and secret data in electronic form, especially in the private sector, which leads to possibilities of abuse," and the need "to define the entire environment and good practice for respect of data privacy," including development of joint system to combat cybercrime, development and implementation clear security standards. The action plan for e-lawmaking includes a mid-range goal of reform of the court system to provide "efficient and effective protection of privacy and data from abuse," and a designated e-security activity Action Plan of creating or improving the appropriate laws.

In March 2004, Foundation Metamorphosis initiated activities on creating a program for protection of privacy through research, raising public awareness through sharing of information and networking activities with local and international partners, based on examination of ICT-related privacy issues and their implications to society at large. Another example of privacy-related activities of the NGOs include the initiative of the First Children's Embassy in

---

case was used as a "personal attack" for political purposes and could "harm the functioning of the security system." This effectively prevented the completion of the investigation, and incited condemnations both from the media (Branko Geroski, "Ako ima pravda, kje ima i impichment" (If there's justice, an impeachment must take place) Dnevnik, April 11, 2003, available at <http://217.16.70.236/?pBroj=2124&stID=16907>) and legal experts ("Dosta Dimovska pomiluvana za prislushkuvanjeto" (Dosta Dimovska pardoned for the wiretapping) Radio Free Europe, Macedonian edition, April 8, 2003, available at <http://www.makdenes.org/programs/aktuelnosti/ma/2003/04/8C6CE77B-EB22-4C0F-897F-2EDA35E09DEC.ASP>) who called for the President's impeachment. Then Prime Minister Branko Crvenkovski also reacted to this act, qualifying it as "extremely irresponsible use of the constitutional powers with grave political implications," but had no comment on the impeachment issue ("Crvenkovski iznenaden od odlukata na Trajkovski" (Crvenkovski Surprised by Trajkovski's decision), MIA, April 8, 2003, available at <http://www.idividi.com.mk/vesti/svet/192097/index.html>.

[3583] Nos. 15/97, 74/04.

[3584] The website of Foundation Metamorphosis is available at <http://www.metamorphosis.org.mk>.

[3585] Members of the National Task Force and NGOs included in the e-citizens discussion group, such as Free Software Macedonia, whose website is available at <http://www.slobodensoftver.org.mk>.

[3586] National Strategy for Information Society of Republic of Macedonia is available on the site of the Committee for Information Technology <http://www.kit.gov.mk>.

the World Megjashi,[3587] Association for the Rights of the Child, and the Helsinki Committee for Human Rights in Republic of Macedonia[3588] advocating for government action in the case of amateur porn movie distributed via cybercafés,[3589] focusing on the child abuse aspect of the case, while mentioning the breach of privacy and the assault on dignity. In addition, the Centre for Civil and Human Rights[3590] and Macedonian Association for Free Sexual Orientation[3591] raised the issue of privacy in context of their objections to treatment of homosexual members of the armed forces[3592] and in general,[3593] respectively.

Freedom of Information Laws

Free access to information, the freedom of reception and transmission of information are guaranteed by the Macedonian Constitution.[3594] In July 2003, the non-governmental sector in Macedonia initiated a process for drafting FOI law. Unfortunately, the law has not yet been adopted. FOI draft law is in the second phase of the parliamentary procedure, and it is scheduled to be adopted in summer 2005. The law is expected to take effect on January 1, 2006.

Draft law determines which public bodies are responsible for providing information and establishes a State commission[3595] for prevention of right to access to information, whose main function is to be an appeal administrative body. The draft law guarantees a free insight into public sector information and

---

[3587] The website of the First Children's Embassy in the World Megjashi is available at <http://www.megjashi.org.mk>.

[3588] Helsinki Committee for Human Rights in Republic of Macedonia <http://www.mhc.org.mk>.

[3589] "NVO iniciraat krivichna postapka za avtorot na amaterskiot porno film" (NGOs Initiate Court Action Against Author of Amateur Porn Movie), A1 TV, December 29, 2005, available at <http://www.a1.com.mk/vesti/vest.asp?VestID=41223>. Note: The movie included sexual intercourse of an adult male (24) with an underage girl (16).

[3590] The website of the Centre for Civil and Human Rights is available at <http://www.cgcp.org.mk>.

[3591] The website of the Macedonian Association for Free Sexual Orientation is available at <http://www.masso.org.mk>, respectively.

[3592] "Homoseksualcite vo ARM izednacheni so predavnicite" (ARM Treats Homosexuals and Traitors the Same), Dnevnik, February 11, 2005, available at <http://217.16.70.236/?pBroj=2681&stID=48868>.

[3593] "Vo Makedonija homoseksualcite ne se priznaeni nitu zashtiteni" (Homosexuals in Macedonia Remain Unrecognized and Unprotected), Utrinski vesnik, September 18, 2004, available at <http://217.16.70.245/?pBroj=1579&stID=22652&pR=22>.

[3594] Article 16 of the Constitution·

[3595] FOI Draft Law is in the second phase of the parliamentary procedure and it is scheduled to be adopted in September 2005. The law will go into force in January 2006. Article 45: "Commission members and their deputies shall be appointed within two months following the date of entry into force of the present Law at latest." That is why they currently do not have a homepage.

costs of transcripts are limited only to material costs.[3596] Some types of information, such as personal data, or information important for national security are excluded from public sector information.[3597]

Also the Law on Local Self-Government of the Republic of Macedonia recognizes the right for informing the public. Article 8 states: "(1) The organs of the municipality, the council committees, and public agencies established by the municipality shall be obliged to inform the citizens about their work, as well as about the plans and programs which are of importance for the development of the municipality without any compensation, in a way determined by the statute. (2) The municipality shall be obliged to enable access to the basic information about the services that it provides to its citizens, in a way and under conditions determined by the statute of the municipality."[3598]

In July 1999, Republic of Macedonia signed and ratified the Convention on Access to information, Public participation in decision-making and Access to justice in environmental matters (Arhus Convention).[3599]

Computer and Cybercrime Related Provisions

Computer crimes are regulated by Article 251 of the Criminal Code.[3600] This act was added to the Criminal Law in 1996. It is included in chapter 23, Criminal Acts against Property of the Republic of Macedonia.

Law enforcement professionals base their actions on the provisions of the LPDP and must obtain a court order (a warrant) in order to obtain information from private companies, such as internet providers (ISPs) or cybercafés. None of the major five ISPs displays a public copy of their privacy policy, and the Internet access or web hosting contracts do not include information about it or the rights

---

[3596] FOI Draft Law, Article 29, "(1)Inspection of the information requested shall be free of charge. (2)The information requester shall pay appropriate material costs for the obtained written summary, photocopy or an electronic record of the information requested. (3)The Government of the Republic of Macedonia will determine the amount of the material costs payable mentioned in paragraph 2 herein."

[3597] FOI Draft Law, Article 6: "(1) Information holders shall deny access to information requested in case the information concerned: 1.1. information based on a Law which regulates information representing classified information with an appropriate degree of secrecy given according the law; 1.2. personal data whose revelation means violation of the protection of the personal data in accordance to the LPDP; 1.3. information concerning individual data for legal and natural persons, gathered, processed and given for statistical aims."

[3598] Published in the Official Gazette of the Republic of Macedonia, No.5/2002.

[3599] No.40/1999.

[3600] Criminal Code, *supra.*

of users according to the LPDP, or internal procedures and responsibilities for dealing with sensitive information.

Cybercafés operate under the Law for Entertainment Games and Games of Chance,[3601] and are not required to implement additional standards in regard to protection of the privacy of the users. The only provision in that law related to privacy is the obligation of confidentiality in regard to winning or losing.[3602] As a result, customers use the cybercafés at their own risk, and a number of cases of publishing excerpts of private conversations (IMs, IRC) suggests that many cafés retain activity logs and monitor the traffic in their establishments, without making that clear to their customers. Users are also threatened by other users, who use low security in the cafés to install spyware and harvest data.

Very few Macedonian websites in general display privacy protection clauses explaining what type of data they gather from each visit and what they use it for. Such examples include the sites of ISPs (with one exception),[3603] portals, media companies (all newspapers and TV stations), and state bodies (Government, President, Assembly, Ministries).

Media Laws and Practice

According to representatives of both the regulatory Broadcasting Council of the Republic of Macedonia[3604] and the Association of Journalists in Macedonia,[3605] media laws in Macedonia do not specifically address the protection of privacy. Article 62 of the Law on Broadcasting[3606] includes provision of the right to response and correction if a medium publishes incorrect data, but includes no sanctions for revealing personal data.

[3601] *See* <http://www.finance.gov.mk/gb/laws/law_on_games_of_chance.pdf> (unofficial English translation); *see also*, Draft Law for Modification and Amendment to the Law on Games of Chance and Entertainment Games, Official Gazette of the Republic of Macedonia No 10/97 and 54/97, available at <http://www.finance.gov.mk/gb/laws/amandments_law_on_games_of_chance.pdf> (unofficial English translation).

[3602] Law for Entertainment Games and Games of Chance at Article 82.

[3603] MT.net provides privacy provisions in their Legal remark, available at <http://www.mt.net.mk/Content/PravnaNapomena.asp> (in Macedonian. MT.net uses the same privacy policy of its mother company, the Macedonian Telecom, which was developed for the purposes of landline telephony. (Personal inquiry with the staff of the legal department.)

[3604] Broadcasting Council of the Republic of Macedonia websitet <http://www.srd.org.mk>.

[3605] Association of Journalists in Macedonia website <http://www.znm.org.mk>.

[3606] Published in the Official Gazette of the Republic of Macedonia, No.20/97 and 70/03.

Article 7 of Code of Journalists of Macedonia,[3607] adopted by the Association and enforced by the Council of Honour states: "The journalist shall respect the privacy of every person, except in cases when that is on the contrary with the public interest." Members of the association are "obliged to respect the personal pain and grief," and must obtain consent of parent or guardian to interview or photograph children or persons "with special needs, who are not able to decide rationally." [3608] Both above sources indicated that, to their knowledge, nobody complained about any journalistic breach of privacy during the examined period, while they had numerous suits against journalists for slander and libel.

A search commenced with "Najdi," the Macedonian search engine[3609] that indexes online news sources, provides an illustration of low media interest in the area of privacy. The search[3610] revealed 120 articles from June 1, 2004 to April 30, 2005 containing forms of the word "privacy" (keyword: privatnost, in Cyrillic), constituting 0.12%) of the total of 96,808 pages from that period.

The following breakdown provides a rough illustration of the trends in the media. Namely, only 43% of the listed privacy-related articles referred to various forms of the actual notion of privacy in the country, while the rest were either referring to developments abroad (54%) or were irrelevant (horoscopes).

Of the articles dealing with privacy in Macedonia: 31% dealt with mutual accusations of politicians during election and referendum campaigns, and the issue of their right to stay away from the public eye; 27% dealt with the life of local celebrities, with the term "privacy" ("privatnost") often incorrectly used instead of "private life" ("privaten zhivot"); 21% referred to other privacy-related issues, such as search and seizure, sanctity of the home, privacy in health care and in public sector enterprises; 11% dealt with NGO activism; 8% discussed reactions to the new wiretapping law, and 2% included a review of anti-spyware software.

[3607] Code of Journalists of Macedonia <http://www.znm.org.mk/EN/code.asp>.

[3608] Id. at Article 9.

[3609] Najdi! – the Macedonian search engine is available at <http://najdi.org.mk>.

[3610] The URL for this particular search is <http://najdi.org.mk/najdi?query=%EF%F0%E8%E2%E0%F2%ED%EE%F1%F2%2A&metaname=swishdefault&sort=timestamp&lat2cyr=on&dr_e_year=2005&dr_s_mon=6&dr_s_year=2004&dr_s_day=1&dr_e_day=30&dr_o=13&dr_e_mon=4&start=0>. Please note that the above results referr to search commenced June 1, 2005. Najdi! constantly updates its list of sources and results may vary as archives of new sites are indexed.

The Republic of Macedonia is a member of the Council of Europe and has signed and ratified the Convention for the Protection of Individuals with Regard to Automatic Processing of Personal Data No. 108.[3611] Furthermore, the Republic of Macedonia has signed and ratified the European Convention for the Protection of Human Rights and Fundamental Freedoms,[3612] and in June 2004 ratified the CoE Convention on Cybercrime.[3613] The LPDP is compatible and aligned with the standards and the criteria set forth by the European Parliament and the European Council Directive on the Protection of Individuals with Regard to the Processing of Personal Data and on the Free Movement of Such Data 95/46/EC of 1995.

Malaysia

The Constitution of Malaysia does not specifically recognize a right to privacy,[3614] but does provide a conclusive list of fundamental rights, including freedom of assembly, speech and movement.[3615] This restrictive list of rights is due to the fact that, at the time of the drafting of the Constitution in 1956, the objective was to create a balance in maintaining a homogeneous nation embodying multi-racial, multi-religious, and multi-cultural people under a common flag, and to destroy the imminent threat of Communist influence that was prevalent at the time.[3616] Proceeding from such a foundation, which emphasizes state security vis-à-vis combating communism, the government has circumscribed these rights by law or practice, increasingly so in the name of anti-terrorism.[3617]

[3611] Published in the Official Gazette of the Republic of Macedonia, No. 07/05. Convention for the Protection of Individuals with regard to Automatic Processing of Personal Data (ETS no.: 108), available at<http://conventions.coe.int/Treaty/EN/CadreListeTraites.htm>.

[3612] Convention for the Protection of Human Rights and Fundamental Freedoms (ETS no.: 005), available at <http://conventions.coe.int/Treaty/EN/CadreListeTraites.htm>.

[3613] Published in the Official Gazette of the Republic of Macedonia, No. 41/04. Convention on Cybercrime (ETS no.: 185), available at <http://conventions.coe.int/Treaty/en/Treaties/Html/185.htm>

[3614] Ultra Demision v. Kook Wei Kuan, 5 CLJ 285 (2004).

[3615] Constitution of Malaysia, available at <http://www.helplinelaw.com/law/constitution/malaysia/malaysia01.php>; *see also* Caslon Analytics Privacy Guide Asia <http://www.caslon.com.au/privacyguide6.htm#Malaysia>.

[3616] Federation of Malaya Constitutional Commission, 1956-1957 Report at paragraph 161.

[3617] The Malaysian government also bans membership in unregistered political parties and unregistered organizations. US State Department, Country Reports on Human Rights Practices 2004, Malaysia, available at <http://www.state.gov/g/drl/rls/hrrpt/2004/41649.htm>.

Statutory Laws

The most controversial of Malaysia's laws remains the Internal Security Act (ISA), which was enacted in the 1960s in response to Communist insurgency. The ISA has been used to suppress both political opposition and peaceful dissent.[3618] The ISA allows police to enter and search the homes of persons suspected of threatening national security without a warrant; police may also seize evidence. The lack of independent judicial oversight is the most fervent criticism of the ISA. Judicial review of arrests under the ISA is limited to questions of procedure; at no point are authorities required to produce either evidence or detailed charges. Police regularly use the ISA to search homes and offices, seize books and papers, monitor conversations, and take persons into custody without a warrant.[3619] Persons arrested under the ISA as potential threats to national security or public order can be held for up to two years, renewable indefinitely, without being charged.[3620] The government does not disclose the number of people so held, but civil rights groups estimate it is in the hundreds. Most of these individuals are allegedly connected to Islamic terrorist groups, but the use of the phrases "terrorist threat" and "terrorist" have increased markedly since September 11, 2001, and is now used to describe a litany of individuals or actions that previously would not have been so classified. The ISA does not provide precise definitions or criteria for determining whether an individual poses a threat.[3621] The Malaysian government has yet to offer public evidence against any of the detainees held under allegations of terrorism or bring them to trial.[3622] Many alleged terrorists are connected to political opposition parties.[3623] The ISA has been used in the past to intimidate and restrict political dissent.[3624]

Prior to September 11, 2001, there had been much public pressure – both from inside and outside the country – to repeal the ISA in favor of a more constrained

---

[3618] Human Rights Watch, World Report 2005, Malaysia, available at <http://hrw.org/english/docs/2005/01/13/malays9822.htm>.

[3619] US State Department, Country Reports on Human Rights Practices 2003, Malaysia, available at <http://www.state.gov/g/drl/rls/hrrpt/2003/27778.htm>.

[3620] Amnesty International, Report 2005, Malaysia, available at <http://web.amnesty.org/report2005/mys-summary-eng>.

[3621] *Id.*

[3622] Human Rights Watch, World Report 2005, Malaysia, *supra.*

[3623] Fergus Shiel, "Rights Abuses Spread after 9/11," The Age (Melbourne), April 16, 2003, at 6. Minister Dr. Rais Yatim, of the Prime Minister's Department *Datuk Seri*, has argued that a broad legal definition of "terrorism" is necessary in order to effectively combat terrorist threats and has noted that the United States has adopted a similar stance with the passage of the USA PATRIOT Act. For a discussion of Malaysian Prime Minister Mohamed's definition of "terrorism," see Abdul Haseeb Ansari, Terrorism, National Integrity and Human Rights: A Critical Appraisal 3 Malayan L.J. 205 (2002).

[3624] *See id.*

security law, but the government has taken no action and is now unlikely to do so.[3625] Minister Yatim has stated that laws like the ISA[3626] are even more relevant post-September 11, and that "submission to idealistic rights was not realistic . . . in safeguarding domestic integrity and security." The Prime Minister responded to criticism of the ISA by stating that "if someone commits an act that violates the human rights of the majority, then he . . . will lose his basic rights."[3627] In 2003, opposition leaders and human rights organizations called on the government to repeal the ISA and the other laws that deprive persons of the right to defend themselves in court.[3628] The National Human Rights Commission (*Suhakam*) publicly recommended that the government rewrite the ISA to ensure it is not used against political opponents.[3629]

Prime Minister Abdullah Badawi, who took office in October 2003, has begun to remedy some of the abuses under the ISA. In 2004, Abdullah provided journalists with access to the notorious Kamunting Detention Center where ISA detainees are held. Further, the government announced that *Suhakam* would investigate allegations of abuse at short-term detention centers where detainees are held before they are sent to Kamunting. However, the government continues to bar the independent monitoring or investigation of Kamunting.[3630]

Other laws with implications for privacy include the Anti-Corruption Act, the Companies Act, and the Penal Code.[3631] The Anti-Corruption Act empowers the Attorney General to authorize the interception of mail and wiretapping of telephones in corruption investigations.[3632] Information obtained in this manner is admissible evidence in a corruption trial.[3633]

The Companies Act grants the Registrar of Companies broad powers to block or disband organizations deemed prejudicial to national security or the national interest. This authority has been used to prevent international human rights

---

[3625] Shiel, *supra*.

[3626] "Penal Code to Be Amended to Include Anti-Terrorism Provisions," New Straits Times, June 15, 2003, at 4. Minister Yatim announcing that the Penal Code would be amended to include new anti-terrorism provisions that the government had previously considered tacking on to the ISA.

[3627] "Malaysian PM Says No Need to Respect Human Rights of Those Who Violate Them," translated by BBC Monitoring Asia Pacific from Bernama News Agency, December 21, 2002.

[3628] US State Department Report 2003, *supra*.

[3629] *Id.*

[3630] Human Rights Watch, World Report 2005, *supra*.

[3631] MECM Cyberlaws <http://www.ktkm.gov.my/comm/cyberlaws.html>. For a discussion and critique of some of the more important provisions of the CCA, *see* Sulaiman Azmil, Crimes on the Electronic Frontier - Some Thoughts on the Computer Crimes Act 3 Malayan L.J. 59 (1997).

[3632] US State Department Report 2004, *supra*.

[3633] *Id.*

organizations from establishing domestic operations. Section 509 of the Penal Code provides criminal penalties for insulting "the modesty of any person" or "intruding upon the privacy of [any] person" by uttering any word, sound or gesture, or exhibiting any object, intending that such word or sound shall be heard, or that such gesture or object shall be seen by such person.

Cyberlaws

Malaysia is generally regarded as having comprehensive cyberlaws.[3634] These laws include the Digital Signature Act 1997, the Communications and Multimedia Act 1998, the Computer Crimes Act 1997, the Telemedicine Act 1997, and the Optical Discs Act 2000.[3635]

The Communications and Multimedia Act (CMA) prohibits unlawful interception of communications, establishes rules for searches of computers, mandates access to encryption keys, and authorizes police to intercept communications without a warrant if a public prosecutor believes that a communication is likely to contain information relevant to an investigation.[3636] In addition, provisions of the CMA allow the government to close web sites if they are deemed to be indecent, obscene, or offensive.[3637] In practice, the provisions of the CMA that restrict telecommunications interception appear to be regularly ignored or overridden by other statutes, including the ISA and the CCA.[3638] There are regular reports of illegal wiretapping, including of former Deputy Premier Anwar Ibrahim in 1998. Later that same year, police detained four people under the ISA on suspicion of spreading rumors of disturbances in Kuala Lumpur. Inspector General of Police Tan Sri Abdul Rahim Noorsaid told the media that the suspects were detained after police tracked their activities on the Internet with the assistance of Internet service provider (ISP) Mimos Berhad.[3639] The provider later claimed that it did not monitor the activities of its subscribers.[3640] In addition, the government may invoke the both the CMA and

---

[3634] "M'sia Drafting Another Three Cyberlaws," Bernama – The Malaysian National News Agency, March 2, 2004.

[3635] Ferina Manecksha, "Gaining Better Understanding of Cyberlaws," New Straits Times – Computimes, February 23, 2004.

[3636] Communications and Multimedia Act of 1998, available at <http://www.cmc.gov.my/legisframe.htm>.

[3637] "Difficult Task of Internet Policing," New Straits Times, May 30, 2004.

[3638] Abu Bakar Munir & Mohammad Yasin, Privacy and Data Protection: A Comparative Analysis with Special Reference to the Malaysian Proposed Law (Sweet & Maxwell 2002).

[3639] Tony Emmanuel, "Rumours over Internet: Four to Be Charged Soon," New Straits Times, September 24, 1998.

[3640] "E-mail not Screened, Says Service Provider," New Straits Times, August 17, 1998.

the CCA when it believes the Internet is being used to spread lies or malicious rumors. The government has attempted to track down the sources of malicious e-mails and prosecute them. To do so, the government enlists Mimos, the government-owned technology firm, to trace the source of malicious e-mails.[3641] A recent development involves the sale of pornographic materials for download to mobile phone users. Though no arrests have yet been made for this practice, under the CMA those caught can be fined MYR 50,000 (approximately USD 13,160) or one year in jail or both.[3642]

The Computer Crime Act (CCA) was modeled after the United Kingdom's Computer Misuse Act of 1990. It allows police to inspect and seize a suspect's computer equipment without a warrant. Suspects are also required to turn over all encryption keys for any encrypted data on their equipment.[3643]

Three additional bills have also been proposed recently: the Personal Data Protection Act (PDPA), the Electronic Transaction Act (ETA) and the Electronic Government Activities Act (EGAA). The ETA is a law of general application that provides a legal framework for electronic transactions, while the EGAA aims at removing all procedural and administrative impediments for e-government activities. The latter bill should enable the government to conduct electronic transactions or issue approvals that have the same legal standing as a manual transaction or approval by letter.[3644]

National Identity Card

Malaysians generally have the right to travel, live, and work where they please; however, the government restricts these rights in some circumstances. The eastern states of Sabah and Sarawak have the right to control immigration and to require citizens from peninsular Malaysia and foreigners to present passports or national identity cards for entry. The adoption of a national identity smart card makes tracking citizens easier.

[3641] Chow Kum Hor, "Uphill Task to Police E-mails," New Straits Times, September 17, 2004.

[3642] Izwan Ismail, "Combating Indecency in Mobile Content," New Straits Times, March 31, 2005.

[3643] Computer Crimes Act of 1997, available at
<http://www.ktkm.gov.my/template01.asp?Content_ID=440&Cat_ID=4&CatType_ID=78&SubCat_ID=126>.

[3644] *See* Manecksha, *supra*; Kasim, *supra; see also* "Attorney-General Calls for Review of Existing Laws," Bernama -- The Malaysian National News Agency, April 7, 2004.

Malaysia was one of the first countries in the world to use a chip-based identification card that is also a multipurpose smart card.[3645] Since 1999, the Malaysian government has been gradually phasing in a multipurpose national identity smart card, which it intends all Malaysians to adopt by the end of 2005.[3646] The card, known as "MyKad," incorporates both photo identification and fingerprint biometric technology.[3647] MyKad currently has seven functions other than identification: driver's license, passport information, health information, e-cash function (referred to as electronic purse, or e-purse), toll payment (or Touch 'n Go), automated teller machine, and public key infrastructure. As of January 2005, as part of the National Roll Out project, all 96 National Registration Department (NRD) offices were equipped to load smart card applications to MyKad cards.[3648] The card's ATM function is the least attractive feature, and banks have discouraged customers from using the card for such purpose.[3649] So far, the value-added MyKad applications have seen little usage. The Director-General of the NRD, Datuk Wan Ibrahim Wan Ahmad, said that the low usage might be due to perception, apprehension, or lack of awareness. However, users have expressed frustration that service providers do not yet support the applications.[3650]

MyKad is currently optional, but it automatically replaces other forms of expired identification and is quickly becoming a *de facto* requirement to access certain government and private-sector services. In December 1998, the government began requiring cybercafés to obtain name, address, and identity card information from patrons. However it lifted this requirement in March 1999.[3651] In some cases there may be penalties for not carrying the card. In 1998, the government announced that persons not carrying identification cards risk being detained by immigration authorities.[3652] It is the government's intention that all Malaysians over the age of 12, or 18 million citizens, will be registered in the MyKad system by the end of 2005.[3653] While registration is currently free, those who register

---

[3645] Anna Maria Samsudin, "All Offices Equipped to Issue Smart Cards," New Straits Times, January 28, 2005.

[3646] "Privacy of MyKad Holders to Be Protected by Law," New Straits Times, May 19, 2004, at 6.

[3647] "Wise Up to Role of Smart Card," The Star, December 15, 2002.

[3648] Anna Maria Samsudin, "Eight MyKad Applications Launched Nationwide," Bernama – The Malaysian National News Agency, January 27, 2005.

[3649] "Privacy of MyKad Holders to Be Protected by Law," *supra*; *see also* "Free Upgrade of MyKad to 64K," New Straits Times, June 16, 2004, at 5.

[3650] Fauziah Muhtar, "Hope for More MyKad Usage Opportunity," New Straits Times – Computimes, December 23, 2004.

[3651] "Cabinet: Cybercafes not Subjected to Restrictions," New Straits Times, March 18, 1999.

[3652] Annie Freeda Cruez, "Malaysians Told: Carry ICs or Risk Detention," New Straits Times, May 14, 1998.

[3653] Muhtar, *supra*.

after the end of 2005 will be charged. As of April 2005, three million Malaysians were still unregistered. Many express discomfort with the all-in-one feature of MyKad. Others do not feel compelled to use MyKad while there are still other means to perform the transactions. The government has announced, however, that MyKad will be the sole identification document permitted for dealing with government agencies effective January 1, 2006.[3654] Those under the age of 12 are encouraged to apply for a junior version of the MyKad, which differs only in its lack of a photograph and thumbprint biometric. In addition, every baby born in 2003 or later is provided with MyKad as a "lifelong identification document and a personal database."[3655]

The Malaysian government originally proposed placing the religious affiliation of all citizens on the MyKad, but complaints from the country's non-Muslim ethnic groups prompted the government to limit such identification to Muslims only. In January 1999, it was announced that Islamic religious authorities in the capital, Kuala Lumpur, would be equipped with portable card readers in order to instantly verify the vows of Muslim couples found in "close proximity." In 2002, the Prime Minister proposed adding marital status and voting constituency information to the cards for the benefit of religious authorities and to minimize electoral fraud, respectively. Both proposals were sharply criticized by opposition Member of Parliament Teresa Kok as being an unnecessary invasion of privacy.[3656] The anonymity of balloting is already a matter of concern for privacy advocates, even without MyKad. Traditional ballots are marked with a serial number that can be matched against a voter's name. While there is no evidence that the government has ever tracked individual votes, some opposition leaders allege that the potential to do so has had a chilling effect on some voters, particularly civil servants.

With so much personal information stored on the MyKad, even proponents of the card have acknowledged inherent privacy risks: "[h]aving the smart card will probably increase theft . . . because the attraction is there. There is a lot of personal information stored [on the card], including buying patterns which would attract (card cloning) syndicates," according to industry analyst Jafizwaty Ishahak. Recently, the NRD admitted that the practice of surrendering identity cards to security guards before entering certain premises may need to be changed because of privacy concerns.[3657] The Consumers Association of Penang has

---

[3654] *Id.*; Ahmad Kushairi, "Sparking Interest in MyKad," New Straits Times – Computimes, April 14, 2005.

[3655] Muhtar, *supra.*

[3656] News Release, "Government Proposal to Add Marital, Constituency Information to MyKad Should Be Debated," MP for Seputeh Teresa Kok, September 27, 2002.

[3657] Rosnazura Idrus, "Leaving MyKad at Guardhouse under Review," New Straits Times, July 9, 2003.

argued that the cards make individuals' personal and confidential information too vulnerable and has recommended that the proposed Personal Data Protection Act address these risks specifically.[3658] The Federation of Malaysian Consumers Associations criticized the government for not implementing clear guidelines or consulting with the public on how MyKad is to be used, by whom and for what purpose. The Federation also challenged the security of the system, contending that the storage of personal information in a centralized database makes it vulnerable to tampering and sabotage. Later, in 2004, the Bar Council chief severely criticized the security and privacy risks related to the use of MyKad, and sought strong privacy laws to protect cardholders against potential misuse, pointing out that personal data contained on the card could easily be accessed.[3659] It is widely known that anyone with a card reader can access all information contained in the MyKad.[3660] In response to such critiques, the government is now reportedly drafting a bill to ensure the privacy of MyKad users and protect the information associated with it against unauthorized use.[3661]

Users can access the personal information stored on their MyKad at government kiosks and offices after biometric authentication of their fingerprint. Access to personal information by others is hierarchical or compartmentalized. For example, only certain medical officers have access to sensitive health information. However, access to some personal information held in the MyKad system seems to be available, remotely via a network, to a wide range of third parties, including hotels, restaurants and ticket agents. Determining who has access to what information and for what purpose remains difficult for Malaysians.

The health information contained in MyKad includes allergies, blood type, and chronic diseases. In June 2004, the health application was still in a pilot phase, being tested at the Putrajaya Hospital. Full implementation of MyKad's health information was expected to be completed by the end of 2004.[3662]

Another privacy concern regarding MyKad is loss. In 2004, more than 200,000 MyKads were reported lost.[3663] Some individuals have lost their MyKad repeatedly. The government intends to adopt a policy that would involve

---

[3658] "Smart IC Open to Abuse," The Star, April 18, 2001.

[3659] "Bar Council Chief Seeks Laws to Protect MyKad Data," New Straits Times, April 3, 2004, at 8.

[3660] "Privacy of MyKad Holders to Be Protected by Law," supra.

[3661] Id.; see also A. Shukor Rahman, "Evaluating Risks in MyKad," New Straits Times, October 20, 2003, at 21.

[3662] Rozana Sani, "Protecting Personal Info," New Straits Times – Computimes, October 18, 2004.

[3663] Samsudin, supra.

recording the statements of those who lose their card more than five times. There are proposals being considered that would allow the ministry and police to carry out investigations before allowing those who had lost their card more than five times to apply for a replacement.[3664]

Freedom of Information

Rights pertaining to freedom of information do not exist in Malaysia.[3665] Due to the absence of this right, the government has sometimes directly restricted the release of information deemed embarrassing or prejudicial to national interests. For example, the government has had a policy of prohibiting public disclosure of air pollution readings and deaths due to dengue fever.[3666]

Activist groups are advocating adoption of Freedom of Information (FOI) laws in Malaysia. A National Seminar on Freedom of Information Legislation was held in Kuala Lumpur in September 2004. Legal experts, NGOs, journalists, and FOI specialists plan to build a coalition to promote FOI legislation in Malaysia. The groups also recommend that all secrecy provisions in other laws should be reviewed, and amended or repealed if necessary, within three years. In addition, the groups will push for an independent administrative oversight body and review of FOI laws by Parliament at least every five years.[3667]

Data Protection

Former Prime Minister Dr. Mahathir Mohamad characterized data protection principles as a burden on business and an impediment to effective policing. However, e-commerce concerns and the desire to comply with the adequacy provisions of the European Union Data Protection Directive, have led the Malaysian Ministry of Energy, Communications and Multimedia (MECM) to begin drafting a new personal data protection bill.[3668] The initial draft of the bill,

---

[3664] "Coming Down Hard on Losers of MyKad," New Straits Times, December 31, 2004.

[3665] In Malaysia today there is an absence of freedom of information laws. However, there is a growing debate over the need for such a statute. In the words of HRH Sultan Azlan (Former King and Lord President of Malaysia): "I believe that we need a Freedom of Information Act, under which members of the public have a right of access to specifically requested public records, and that these should be made available, as of right, within a reasonable time. A Freedom of Information Act will greatly improve the quality of trust in this country." [1986] JMCL at 22.

[3666] US State Department Report 2004, *supra*.

[3667] Santha Oorjitham, "Activists: Freedom of Information the Key to Clean Government," Malaysia General News, September 30, 2004.

[3668] Ministry of Energy, Communications and Multimedia
<http://www.ktkm.gov.my/template01.asp?Content_ID=368&Cat_ID=4&CatType_ID=84>.

the Personal Data Protection Bill 1998, was seen to have reflected the European Union Directive. However, after September 11, 2001, the government has taken a more restricted approach in the introduction of the Personal Data Protection Bill 2003. This bill seeks to adopt rights similar to the American "Safe Harbor" approach.

The Personal Data Protection Bill 2003 was supposed to be enacted by 2004,[3669] but has been repeatedly delayed. The bill has been submitted to the Attorney-General Chambers.[3670] Proponents believe that the Act will provide increased confidence for online transactions by protecting individuals' data privacy.[3671] The legislation establishes common guidelines to regulate the handling and use of personal data by any person or organization.[3672] The legislation regulates the transfer of consumer data by institutions to third parties whether during the collection, use or further processing of the data. Under the Act, the type of data that may be disclosed to third parties and that which requires the owner's permission before release, would be clearly specified.[3673] The proposed law sets out seven data protection principles to govern the processing of personal data – notice, choice, disclosure, security, data integrity, access, and enforcement. If enacted, the Act will establish a government-appointed data protection commissioner with the power to monitor and enforce compliance, promote public awareness of the law, encourage trade bodies to prepare industry codes of practice, and cooperate with counterparts in foreign countries.[3674] Proposed penalties for violating the law will include punitive fines of up to MYR 250,000 (approximately USD 65,790) and imprisonment for up to 12 years for a serious offense.[3675] The Act also provides for the establishment of a tribunal to assist in the exercise of the Commissioner's powers and functions in the public interest. While the detailed operation of the tribunal will be left to regulation, it is presumed it would function as an appellate body. Although its ramifications and effects are far-reaching, legal observers have emphasized that the proposed Act does not attempt to prohibit the collection, holding, processing or use of personal

---

[3669] "Proposals for a Personal Data Law," World Data Protection Report, November 2003.

[3670] Sharifah Kasim, "Key Issues to Push ICT," New Straits Times, February 2, 2004, at 1.

[3671] Rozana Sani, "Longer Wait for Legal Online Protection," New Straits Times – Computimes, February 21, 2005.

[3672] Cynthia Peterson, "Law for Online Data Protection Soon," New Straits Times – Computimes, April 14, 2005.

[3673] Rozana Sani, "Tackling Grey Areas when Tabling Bills," New Straits Times, January 1, 2004, at 2; see also "Attorney-General Calls for Review of Existing Laws," Bernama – The Malaysian National News Agency, April 7, 2004.

[3674] Loh Chyi Jen, "Framing the Country's Privacy Laws," New Straits Times, July 18, 2001.

[3675] World Data Protection Report, November 2003, supra; Sani, "Tackling Grey Areas when Tabling Bills," supra.

data, nor does it deal with access to any information collected. In other words, they argue, the proposed law is not a law relating to privacy or freedom of information.[3676]

Malaysia announced plans in November 2001 to provide data protection and Internet law training for its judges, public prosecutors and police officers in anticipation of the enactment of the PDPA.[3677] The Prime Minister's Department said training for the judiciary and law enforcement would "better equip them to deal with computer-related crimes."[3678]

Freedom of Assembly, Speech and Press

Under the Constitution, freedom of assembly may be limited in the interest of security and public order. The government regularly monitors public assemblies (defined as gatherings of more than three people)[3679] through the issuance of permits under the Police Act. While the decision to grant permits theoretically rests with district police chiefs, in practice, senior police officials and political leaders influence grants and denials. In July 2001, the government ceased issuing permits for all political meetings throughout the country.[3680] This significantly impeded the ability of opposition parties, particularly the Islamic party, to communicate with their supporters and to fundraise. In May 2005, a Malaysian royal commission called for reform of security laws, including the Police Act. The commission argued that the need to get police permission to hold a public gathering "is against the basic freedom needed by a democratic society to function, where this right is enshrined in the Federal Constitution." The commission found that issuance of permits was often selective and biased against meetings to be held by opposition groups.[3681]

The Constitution provides that freedom of speech and of the press may be restricted by legislation "in the interest of security [or] public order."[3682] In

---

[3676] Khaw Lake Tee, The Proposed Malaysian Personal Data Protection Law – Some Salient Features 3 IPPP UM Research Bulletin No. 3.

[3677] "Training for Judges, Prosecutors to Keep in Touch with Cyber World," New Straits Times-Management Times, November 30, 2001.

[3678] "Judiciary to Have Data Protection Training," World Data Protection Report, February 2002.

[3679] "Malaysian Royal Commission Urges Security Law Review, Police Reform," Kyodo News International, May 16, 2005.

[3680] United States State Department Country Report, on Human Rights Practices in Malaysia, 2002, available at <http://www.state.gov/www/global/human_rights/hrp_reports_mainhp.html>.

[3681] "Malaysian royal commission urges security law review, police reform," *supra*.

[3682] Constitution of Malaysia, *supra*.

practice, the law is frequently used to restrict or intimidate dissenting political speech. The media continues to face significant government resistance and is limited in its criticism of government policy.[3683] The media is subject to a variety of laws limiting free expression and daily monitoring and control.[3684] All newspapers and magazines must be licensed by the government, and the Sedition Act prohibits public comment on issues defined as sensitive, such as racial and religious matters. In practice, the Sedition Act, the Official Secrets Act (OSA), criminal defamation laws, and other laws have been used to restrict and discourage dissenting political speech.[3685]

The Malaysian government has gone after political dissenters who express their views online.[3686] In January 2003, an independent news web site, Malaysiakini.com,[3687] published an anonymous letter critical of the government, and its office was subsequently raided by police. The police seized about 20 computers containing potentially sensitive information, including the addresses of letter writers who had requested confidentiality.[3688] It appears that the government's 1999 pledge not to regulate content on the Internet, in part to attract international investment to its high-tech sector, was a hollow one. Before that, in 1996, Malaysia introduced the Multimedia Super Corridor Bill of Guarantee, which stated that the government would "ensure no Internet censorship."[3689] However, the Bill of Guarantee permits government efforts to combat elements that have the potential to jeopardize the country's sovereignty or the way of life of its people.[3690] In October 2003, the government announced that it had forwarded its nine-month-long investigation to the attorney general for a decision on whether to prosecute.[3691] The government continued to deny Malaysiakini journalists formal press accreditation, although its reporters were reportedly

---

[3683] Human Rights Watch, World Report 2005, *supra*.

[3684] *Id.*

[3685] US State Department Report 2004, *supra.*

[3686] "Internet Crackdown: Asian Governments Combat Net Content Through its Users: Flashbacks, Updates, and Nostalgia," Telecom Asia, February 1, 2005.

[3687] Malaysiakini, which started operating in November 1999, is known for being one of the few independent media voices, and the leading independent Internet news outlets, in Malaysia. "It is one of a handful of print and online publications that offer an alternative view to Malaysia's largely pro-government mainstream media, much of which is owned by large corporations affiliated with UMNO [or United Malay National Organization, the ruling party in Malaysia]." "Malaysia: End Intimidation of News Website," Human Rights Watch, October 8, 2003 <http://www.hrw.org/press/2003/10/malaysia100803.htm>.

[3688] News Release, "Malaysia - Police Raid Offices of Malaysiakini.com News Web Site," Reporters Sans Frontières, January 20, 2003; "Independent Internet Daily's Offices Raided," Canadian Journalists for Free Expression, January 20, 2003.

[3689] Human Rights Watch, October 8, 2003, *supra.*

[3690] Sharifah Kasim, "Effort to Monitor Internet Content," New Straits Times – Computimes, May 27, 2004.

[3691] *Id.*

---

allowed to cover government functions and ministers' press conferences.[3692] The government has continued to promise that it will not censor the Internet, while making notable exceptions to this policy.[3693]

The government places some restrictions on academic freedom, particularly regarding the expression of unapproved political views, and has enforced restrictions on teachers and students who expressed dissenting views. In March 2002, the government began to require that all civil servants sign a pledge of loyalty to the government, and in May 2002 it required that university faculty and students sign the same pledge. Opposition leaders and human rights activists claimed that this was intended to restrain political activity among civil servants, academics, and students.[3694] Earlier, in August 2001, the Malaysian Bar Council ruled that body searches by school authorities to look for tattoos on students were a gross violation of privacy and should only be conducted if a student is suspected of having committed an offense. The searches had been primarily carried out on students in religious and residential schools who were believed to have been targeted by occult groups.[3695]

Recent Developments

The government decided in 2004 to install closed circuit television (CCTV) cameras in major cities with the purpose of curbing snatch thefts. Local councils installed the cameras in public spaces such as bridges, light rail transportation or bus stations, night markets and dark lanes. CCTV systems are connected to district police stations where images are monitored. Also, 237 additional CCTVs are scheduled to be installed at KL International Airport (KLIA) by the end of 2005, adding to the 1,266 CCTVs already there.[3696] The Internal Security Ministry reported in 2004 that the installation of CCTVs has proven effective – Kuala Lumpur had a 50 percent drop in snatch thefts, while the country as a whole saw a 26.2 percent drop in such thefts.[3697] Bar Council chairman Khutubul Zaman Bukhari has expressed his view that there is no need to incorporate privacy safeguards for the use of CCTV in Malaysia" proposed Personal Data

---

[3692] US State Department Report 2003, *supra.*

[3693] "Internet Crackdown: Asian Governments Combat Net Content Through its Users: Flashbacks, Updates, and Nostalgia," *supra.*

[3694] US State Department Report 2003, *supra.*

[3695] "Body Searches 'Violate Students' Privacy'," New Straits Times, August 4, 2001.

[3696] "CCTV Installation at KLIA to Complete Before Year-End," Bernama – The Malaysian National News Agency, April 14. 2005.

[3697] "Computerised System to Enable Speedier Police Response to Crime Scene," Bernama – The Malaysian National News Agency, December 1, 2004.

Protection Act, as long as the images recorded "are used for the sole purpose of preventing criminal acts."[3698]

Some critics assert that CCTV could be used not only against snatch thieves but also to spot and nab courting couples caught on camera displaying affection in public, which is not allowed in Malaysian society.[3699] For a period of time, the state of Malacca recruited peepers, vulgarly referred to as *mat skodeng*, to spy on young people to stop the moral deterioration of youth.[3700] This effort has since been called off.[3701] In April 2005, the Malaysian Parliament Human Rights Caucus expressed its opposition to moral policing pursuant to religious and municipal laws aimed at regulating private behavior.[3702] In addition, the Caucus recommended that the government tighten rules and regulations with respect to human rights and privacy.[3703] In March 2005, the Caucus was presented with a joint statement of the Citizens Against Moral Policing representatives entitled "The State Has No Role In Policing Morality."[3704] The statement was endorsed by 52 NGOs, three political parties, and 242 individuals, including three Cabinet ministers, 20 Members of Parliament, and one state executive councilor.[3705] The statement expressed concern about the infringement of human rights and individual privacy caused by moral policing by religious enforcement officials.[3706] Citizens Against Moral Policing was formed after a number of recent cases where enforcement officers allegedly violated individual privacy and personal dignity.[3707] More and more Malaysians are speaking out against moral policing.[3708] The government has told state Islamic departments that they must seek police permission before conducting raids on Muslims alleged to be committing immoral acts.[3709]

[3698] Abdul Razak Ahmad, "Smile, You Aren't on Camera Yet," New Straits Times, July 11, 2004.

[3699] *See id.*

[3700] Syed Nadzri, "Danger of the Overzealous, Voyeuristic Moral Guardians," New Straits Times, January 13, 2005.

[3701] Syed Nadzri, "Civil Liberties Trampled on with Impunity"; "Malaysia Restricts 'Moral Policing,'" United Press International, March 26, 2005.

[3702] "Caucus Against Moral Policing," New Straits Times, April 5, 2005; "Parliament Human Rights Caucus Calls for Guidelines on Moral Laws," Bernama – The Malaysian National News Agency, April 4, 2005.

[3703] "Caucus Against Moral Policing," *supra*; "Parliament Human Rights Caucus Calls for Guidelines on Moral Laws," *supra*.

[3704] "Parliament Human Rights Caucus Calls for Guidelines on Moral Laws," *supra*.

[3705] *Id.*

[3706] *Id.*

[3707] "Caucus Against Moral Policing," *supra*.

[3708] Syed Nadzri, "Civil Liberties Trampled on With Impunity," New Straits Times, April 7, 2005.

[3709] "Malaysia Restricts 'Moral Policing,'" *supra*.

A three-month trial period for the use of MyKad to enter the state of Sarawak began in May 2005. The Immigration Department was to install 12 card readers linked to the NRD at eight points of entry in the state. The machines would read the MyKad and, if the card were found to be genuine, would issue a receipt valid for a three-month stay in the state.[3710] If the trial period is successful, the procedure will be implemented for the whole of Sabah and Sarawak, with 27 machines installed at all entry points.[3711] Use of MyKad would eliminate the need to complete an immigration form or to show a passport.[3712] However, those without a MyKad can still use this prior procedure. Though the procedure for entry to Sabah and Sarawak may change, the conditions for entry remain the same.[3713]

Due to concerns about procedural safeguards for issuing MyKads, the NRD made plans in February 2005 to do away with the MyKad for permanent residents and the MyKid children's identity card and replacing them with different cards. The card to be issued to those with permanent resident status will be called MyPR.[3714]

In May 2005, the police introduced a plan to fingerprint all newborn babies in an effort to combat crime. The proposal involves taking palm and foot prints of newborns, which would be stored in a computer database to be used in criminal investigations in later years. While prints grow as an individual matures, officials assert that computer software exists to match the changes and keep the database up to date. Police argue that the thumbprint required for the MyKad is inadequate because premeditated crimes such as rape and murder are increasingly sophisticated.[3715] Police believe that this system would help improve the national crime-solving rate of 45 percent.[3716] However, this plan has met opposition from lawyers, human rights activists, and others who argue that the proposal is unconstitutional and treats innocent children as potential criminals.[3717]

Most government agencies plan to implement Oracle Corporations' citizen data hub. This database would include information on individuals including

---

[3710] "MyKad Entry Procedure Trial Begins May 1 in Sarawak," Bernama – The Malaysian National News Agency," April 12, 2005.

[3711] *Id.*; "MyKad for Entry Into Sabah, Sarawak Only Procedural, Says Ongkili," Bernama – The Malaysian National News Agency, April 8, 2005.

[3712] "MyKad Entry Procedure Trial Begins May 1 in Sarawak," *supra.*

[3713] "MyKad for Entry Into Sabah, Sarawak Only Procedural, Says Ongkili," *supra.*

[3714] "NRD to Adopt Stricter Procedures," New Straits Times, February 15, 2005.

[3715] Baradan Kuppusamy, "Rights Groups Condemn Plan to Fingerprint Babies; Police Proposal 'Unconstitutional and Illogical,'" South China Morning Post, May 6, 2005.

[3716] Dennis Wong, "Marked at Birth," New Straits Times, May 3, 2005.

[3717] Kuppusamy, *supra.*

background, educational achievements, and health records. Proponents argue that that the database will allow government agencies to create and maintain a comprehensive, accurate citizen data repository for better decisionmaking, improved response times, and better citizen services.[3718]

In 2005, the government began implementing a biometric system to keep a record of foreigners in the country.[3719] The program is intended to detect illegal immigrants and foreign workers entering and leaving Malaysia.[3720] Those with a criminal record will not be admitted into the country.[3721] The Home Affairs Minister has also reported that a biometric system will record the fingerprints, photographs, and background of foreigners being held at temporary detention camps throughout the country.[3722] As of October 2004, 6,000 immigrants had been recorded in the system.[3723]

International Commitments

Since September 11, 2001, Malaysia's relationship with the United States has changed dramatically. Prior to the attacks, the US had been publicly critical of Malaysia's human rights record and its misuse of the ISA. Since the attacks, "Malaysia has cooperated extensively with the US in counterterrorism efforts, regularly sharing intelligence information and offering access to ISA prisoners for interrogations." Together, the countries established the Southeast Asia Regional Center for Counter Terrorism in Malaysia in 2003. The US has provided assistance and training for the center.[3724]

Since September 11, 2001, the Malaysian government has made money-laundering detection and enforcement a priority and has enlisted regional and international cooperation. The government recently concluded an agreement to exchange financial intelligence information with several countries, including Australia and the United States,[3725] and to facilitate data and intelligence

---

[3718] "Government Agencies to Implement Oracle Citizen Data Hub," Bernama – The Malaysian National News Agency, March 12, 2005.

[3719] "13.1Mln MyKads Issued, 10,000 Unclaimed – Abdul Rahman," Bernama – The Malaysian National News Agency, December 9, 2004; "Work Permits Using Biometric System to be Introduced Next Year," Bernama – The Malaysian National News Agency, August 21, 2004.

[3720] "Work Permits Using Biometric System to be Introduced Next Year," *supra*.

[3721] "13.1Mln MyKads Issued, 10,000 Unclaimed – Abdul Rahman," *supra*.

[3722] Bernama, October 18, 2004, *supra*.

[3723] *Id.*

[3724] *Id.*

[3725] Allesandra Fabro, "Intelligence Deal with Malaysia," Australian Financial Review, February 5, 2003, at 11.

exchange under the Anti-Money Laundering Act 2001.[3726] In addition, Bank Negara Malaysia is supporting the International Monetary Funds (IMF's) Special Data Dissemination Standards initiative as part of Malaysia's efforts to encourage greater transparency in the global financial system.[3727]

Malaysia made plans in October 2004 to implement use of the MyKad as a border pass for those traveling between Malaysia and Thailand, Singapore, and Brunei. The Home Affairs Minister reported that the system would be used to monitor the movement of Malaysians and other nationals in and out of their home countries. Card readers would be placed at all entry points in the country.[3728]

Malaysia is a member of the Association of Southeast Asian Nations (ASEAN), which is comprised of 10 nations. In 2004, this body assumed a more prominent role in regional affairs, "providing a forum for member states to discuss increased cooperation and information sharing on security issues."[3729] However, ASEAN has not made human rights a priority and has failed to speak out on issues including Malaysia's denial of due process to ISA detainees.[3730] In 2001, ASEAN made plans to harmonize immigration regulations and develop a regional smart card to allow full freedom of movement within the member nations.[3731] ASEAN hopes to implement the plan by 2009.[3732]

The Asia Pacific Coalition Against Unsolicited Commercial E-mail (APCAUCE), which includes member groups from Australia, Hong Kong, China, India, Korea, Malaysia and New Zealand, held a Net Abuse Workshop in Kuala Lumpur in February 2004, a July 2004 workshop in Kathmandu, Nepal, and a 2005 workshop in Kyoto, Japan.[3733] The Malaysian government does not support national legislation on unsolicited commercial e-mail, or spam, but instead favors consumer education and action by Internet service providers (ISPs).[3734]

[3726] "ISA Has 'Saved Nation from Many Disasters,' " New Straits Times, November 20, 2002, at 6.

[3727] "Economic Surveillance to Remain Integral in Regional Discussions," Bernama – The Malaysian National News Agency, March 23, 2005.

[3728] "M'sia to Use Smart Card in Place of Border Pass," Bernama – The Malaysian National News Agency, October 18, 2004.

[3729] Human Rights Watch, World Report 2005, *supra*.

[3730] *Id.*

[3731] Kevin Woodward, "Going Global With National ID," Card Technology, June 1, 2005.

[3732] *Id.*

[3733] See <http://www.apcauce.org/>.

[3734] "Asian Countries Join US-Led Coalition Against Spam," Channel NewsAsia, March 16, 2004.

Malaysia is a signatory to the Universal Declaration of Human Rights, but the legislation that created the National Human Rights Commission (*Suhakam*) restricts the application of the Declaration to those "fundamental liberties provided for" in the Constitution and to those provisions consistent with the Constitution. In 1999, prior to *Suhakam's* creation, opposition leaders and NGOs, including the Bar Council, criticized the definition of human rights as too narrow.

However, following former *Suhakam* Chairman Musa Hitam's October 2001 statement that human rights would need to take a backseat to the fight against terrorism, the Commission has assumed a lower profile in carrying out its mission and has not often publicly challenged the government on sensitive subjects. The new Chairman of the Commission, former Attorney General Abu Talib, appears to favor a low-key, behind-the-scenes approach to promoting human rights.[3735]

Malta

Constitutional Privacy Framework

Article 38 of the Constitution of Malta provides individuals protection against arbitrary searches and seizures. To conduct a search, police officers must obtain warrants under reasonable grounds of suspicion. The Minister of Home Affairs or the Prime Minister may issue wiretap warrants, but only in circumstances that relate to national security.[3736]

Data Protection Framework

In May 2004, Malta joined the European Union. In order to comply with the EU Data Protection Directive 2002/58/EC, the Republic of Malta enacted the Data Protection Act[3737] in 2001, which entered into force on July 15, 2003. The Ministry for Information Technology and Investment is charged with enforcing data protection in Malta. Pursuant to the Act, the Republic named a Data Protection Commissioner and a Data Protection Appeals Tribunal in March 2002. The Act outlines nine principles to ensure the protection of personal

---

[3735] "Body Searches 'Violate Students' Privacy,'" New Straits Times, August 4, 2001.

[3736] *See* 2002 United States State Department Country Report on Human Rights Practices, available at <http://www.state.gov/g/drl/rls/hrrpt/2002/18380.htm>.

[3737] Data Protection Act, Chap. 440, Act XXVI of 2001, available at <http://www.privacyinternational.org/countries/malta/ Data%20Protection%20Act%20CHAPT440.pdf>.

information.[3738] Data collectors must state to individuals the specific purpose for the collection of information,[3739] and the data may not be used for other purposes.[3740] The Act also contains accuracy requirements, mandating that "reasonable measures" be taken to "complete, correct, block or erase data to the extent that such data is incomplete or incorrect."[3741] Regarding consent, an individual's "unambiguous" consent is required in order to process personal information[3742] (absent several exceptions) and "explicit" consent it necessary in order to process "sensitive personal data."[3743]

Data Protection Authority

Malta has a Data Protection Commissioner (the Commissioner), the Ombudsman, who independently investigates complaints. The Ombudsman may investigate complaints against government agencies as well as complaints against private individuals. In addition, the Data Protection Act, establishes the following obligations of the Commissioner:

> to carry out inspection or investigation and considering any complaint and for such purpose require the production of any documents and have access to the premises where data is kept;

> to create and maintain a public register of all processing operations being notified by Data Controllers;

> to encourage the drawing up of suitable codes of conduct by the various sectors;

> to order the blocking, erasure or destruction of data, to impose a temporary or definitive ban on processing, or to warn or admonish the controller;

> the Commissioner is also required to collaborate with supervisory authorities of other countries to the extent necessary for the performance of his duties and participate in the EU for a of data protection authorities;

3738 Data Protection Act, Part III § 7; see also Frank C. Dimech, "Protecting Yourself. . .from Data Protection," October 2002, available at <http://www.cdf.com.mt/pages/docs/DATA%20PROTECTION.PDF>.

3739 Data Protection Act, Part III § 7(c).

3740 Id. at § 7(d).

3741 Id. at § 7(h).

3742 Id. at § 9. Unambiguous consent may not be passive (e.g., opt-out) (See PART III of the Data Protection Act). However, the consent need not be explicit, and consent may be implied through certain actions an individual takes.

3743 Id. at § 12(2).

to enforce the provisions of the Act and in cases of violation, the Commissioner may impose administrative fines or institute court proceedings.[3744]

Since the Data Protection Act was brought into force until the end of 2003, the Commissioner has received 77 substantive complaints,[3745] which covered issues ranging from incorrect processing of personal data, right of access to personal data, excess collection of personal data, breach of a consumer's confidentiality, collection of personal data without prior consent, abusive processing of personal data, etc. The provisions of the Data Protection Act impose an obligation on data controllers to notify the processing operations in relation to the personal data being processed. As per L.N.154 of 2003 as amended by L.N.162 of 2004, the notification deadline was extended to July 14, 2004 and the notification fee reduced to a flat rate of Lm10 payable annually. Data Controllers who have no employees are exempted from the notification fee, also exempted are NGOs who are exempted from the payment of Income Tax. Companies whose only personal data is that contained in the Articles registered with the Registrar of companies are not required to notify. To date, 9,000 notifications reached the DPA Office.[3746] The Commissioner's staff consists of a technical unit with a legal professional, an IT professional and an executive compliance and seven support staff.[3747]

The Malta Communications Authority regulates the telecommunications industry as mandated by the Telecommunications Regulation Act.[3748] The Authority was established in 2001 under the authority of the Malta Communications Authority Act.[3749] In 2003, the Authority enacted Telecommunications (Personal Data and Protection of Privacy) Regulations.[3750] The Regulations contain provisions to help telecommunications subscribers maintain their privacy. The Regulations require telecommunications providers to inform their subscribers of the existence of situations where their information may be unintentionally made available to

---

[3744] E-mail from Ian Deguara, Head Information Unit, Office of the Commissioner for Data Protection of the Republic of Malta, to Ula Galster, International Policy Fellow, Electronic Privacy Information Center, August 1, 2005 (on file with EPIC).

[3745] In 2003, the Commissioner received 14 substantive complaints.

[3746] E-mail from Ian Deguara, *supra*.

[3747] *Id.*

[3748] Chapter 399, Act XXXIII of 1997, available at <http://www.privacyinternational.org/countries/malta/telecomm%20regs%20act.pdf>.

[3749] Chapter 418, Act XVIII of 2000, available at <http://www.privacyinternational.org/countries/malta/comm%20authority%20act%20chapt418.pdf>.

[3750] Telecommunications (Personal Data and Protection of Privacy) Regulations, available at <http://www.mca.org.mt/library/show.asp?id=210&lc=1>.

third parties.[3751] The Regulations also require telecommunications carriers to provide the option of disabling caller ID functions.

Directive 2002/58/EC in the field of electronic communications has been transposed in subsidiary legislation under both the Data Protection Act and the Electronic Communications (Regulation) Act.[3752] The secondary legislation provides an obligation for both authorities, the Office of the Data Protection Commissioner and the Malta Communications Authority, to mutually collaborate with the objective of ensuring effective data protection implementation in the sector.[3753]

The Press Act sets forth the boundaries of acceptable content for the press.[3754] The Act makes it unlawful to "impute ulterior motives to the acts of the President of Malta" or to "insult, revile or bring into hatred . . . the person of the President." The Act also establishes libel and slander laws. The Seditious Propaganda (Prohibition Ordinance)[3755] makes it illegal to print material that is likely to encourage seditious activity. The Act allows the government to obtain a warrant to intercept and open mail suspected of containing seditious material.[3756]

The Constitution prohibits such arbitrary interference with privacy, family, home and correspondence. In 2003, the government generally respected these prohibitions in practice and violations were subject to effective legal sanctions. Only police officers with the rank of inspector or above are allowed to issue search warrants based on reasonable grounds for suspicion of wrongdoing. Security services may intercept communications, such as tap telephones, but only under specific written authorization of the Minister for Home Affairs or the Prime Minister. [3757] In 2003, such actions were permitted only in cases related to national security, including combating organized crime.[3758] These authorizations were reviewed by a special commission and a security committee, under the

---

[3751] *Id.* at § 8.

[3752] Chapter 399, Act VII of 2004, available at
<http://docs.justice.gov.mt/lom/legislation/english/leg/vol_12/chapt399.pdf>.

[3753] E-mail from Ian Deguara, *supra.*

[3754] Press Act, Chapter 248, Act XL of 1974, available at
<http://www.privacyinternational.org/countries/malta/press%20act%20chapt248.pdf>.

[3755] Chapter 71, Ordinance XIX or 1932, available at
<http://www.privacyinternational.org/countries/malta/seditious%20propaganda%20act.pdf>.

[3756] *Id.* at § 3.

[3757] United States Department of State Country, Bureau of Democracy, Human Rights, and Labor, Report on Human Rights Practices (2003), Malta country report, February 25, 2004, available at
<http://www.state.gov/g/drl/rls/hrrpt/2003/27853.htm>.

[3758] *Id.*

oversight of the Prime Minister, the Leader of the Opposition, and the Ministers for Home and Foreign Affairs.[3759]

Recent Developments

Since its launch in April 2003, the Malta Public Service Intranet has been steadily increasing its features and attracting a growing number of users. The main development brought by the second phase of the Public Service Intranet (PSI), which started in September 2004, was the creation of secure, reserved areas that allow user groups to share restricted documents such as presentations, minutes and news items.[3760]

The government of Malta has initiated the research phase of a program aimed at switching all voice communications between central departments to Voice over Internet Protocol (VoIP). The Office of the Prime Minister's Central Information Management Unit (CIMU)[3761] and Malta Information Technology and Training Services Ltd (MITTS)[3762]– a government-owned company supplying IT systems and services to government departments – are currently working on a project to implement VoIP communications between ministries. CIMU will lead the project from the business aspect, while MITTS will be coordinating the technical side. A Project Review Board has defined a short to medium term strategy – involving the migration to VoIP of each individual department – and a long-term strategy that will connect all departments together so as to achieve cost savings in intra-governmental calls. Switching to VoIP is not a complete novelty for the Maltese public sector. In 2003 the Ministry for the Family and Social Security[3763] implemented a VoIP system connecting it to all its agencies.[3764]

International Obligations

Malta is a member of the Council of Europe (CoE) and has signed and ratified the European Convention for the Protection of Human Rights and Fundamental

---

[3759] Id.

[3760] "Maltese public sector Intranet supports communities of practice," eGoverment news, March 1, 2005 available at <http://europa.eu.int/idabc/en/document/3951/5791>.

[3761] See <http://www.cimu.gov.mt/htdocs/index.asp>.

[3762] See <http://mitts.gov.mt/default.aspx>.

[3763] See <http://www.msp.gov.mt/>.

[3764] "Maltese public sector to migrate to Voice over IP," eGovernment news, March 29, 2005, available at <http://europa.eu.int/idabc/en/document/4061/5791>.

Freedoms,[3765] as well as the Convention for the Protection of Individuals with Regard to Automatic Processing of Personal Data (Convention No. 108).[3766] In January 2002, the Maltese government signed the CoE Convention on Cybercrime, but the Parliament has not ratified yet.[3767]

United Mexican States

The Constitutional Framework

The Constitution protects the right to privacy, which traditionally includes the inviolability of the domicile and correspondence. The Constitution protects the person, his/her family, documents or possessions, and the confidentiality of correspondence; the immunity can only be broken by written order of the competent authority (Article 16).

Article 16 of the Constitution of 1917 provides, in part:

> One's person, family, home, papers or possessions may not be molested, except by virtue of a written order by a proper authority, based on and motivated by legal proceedings.[3768]

> "In all search warrants, that only the judicial authority will be able to produce, it must be expressed in writing the place that is to be inspected, the person or people whom are to be arrested and the objects that are searched for, so as to limit to the stated issues the proceedings, and in concluding them, a detailed record must be written in the presence of two witnesses proposed by the occupant of the place that was inspected or in their absence or refusal, by the authority that practiced the proceedings.

> "Private communications are inviolable. The Law will provide a criminal sanction to any act that attempts against the freedom and privacy of private communications. Exclusively the federal judicial authority, at the request of the federal authority that is empowered by the law or by the holder of the Ministerio Público (prosecutor authority) of the

---

[3765] Signed December 12, 1966; ratified January 23, 1967; entered into force January 23, 1967.

[3766] Signed January 15, 2003; ratified February 28, 2003; entered into force June 1, 2003.

[3767] Signed January 17, 2002.

[3768] *Constitución Política de los Estados Unidos Mexicanos* (Mexican Constitution), available at <http://info4.juridicas.unam.mx/ijure/fed/9/> (in Spanish), <http://www.cddhcu.gob.mx/leyinfo/doc/1.doc>, <http://www.cddhcu.gob.mx/leyinfo/pdf/1.pdf> or <http://www.cddhcu.gob.mx/leyinfo/zip/1.zip>.

corresponding federal entity, will be able to authorize the intervention of any private communication. The competent authority, in writing, will have to find and motivate the legal causes of the request, and also the kind, the subjects, and the duration of the intervention. The federal judicial authority will not be able to grant these authorizations in issues of electoral, fiscal, mercantile, civil, labour, or administrative character, or in the case of the communications of the person under arrest with his/her defender.

"The authorized interceptions will adjust to the requirements and limits anticipated in the law. The results of the interventions that do not fulfil these requirements will lack all value as evidence.

"The administrative authority may make home visits only to certify compliance with sanitary and police rules; the presentation of books and papers indispensable to verify compliance with the fiscal laws may be required in compliance with the respective laws and the formalities prescribed for their inspection. Correspondence will be free from all inspection, and its violation will be punishable by law.

Statutes and Federal Legislation

There are 27 statutes that deal with privacy issues and personal data protection in Mexico. They are very different laws, covering various issues.[3769] The most recent laws are related to finance and banking, consumers' rights and credit information. The legal landscape has been enriched in 2003 with decrees issued on the Federal Law of Transparency and Access to the Government Public Information (LFTAIPG).[3770] The main contribution of the LFTAIPG has been to standardize the principles under which the diverse organs of the State must process citizens' personal data, including especially the safeguard of the consent and purpose specification principles, and the guarantee of the rights of access and correction. However, the law lacks sufficient protections to provide greater levels of security for the processing of private data; better and suitable law enforcement mechanisms and authorities are needed.

[3769] The Federal legislation is available on the website of the Mexican House of Representatives, Honorable Congress of the Union at <http://www.cddhcu.gob.mx/leyinfo/> (in Spanish); some statutes that already deal with the right to privacy and make reference to personal data, can be looked up at <http://profesor.uia.mx/aveleyra/comunica/privacidad/leyes2.htm> (in Spanish).

[3770] <http://www.cddhcu.gob.mx/leyinfo/zip/244.zip> or <http://www.cddhcu.gob.mx/leyinfo/doc/244.doc>. Last reforms are available at <http://www.cddhcu.gob.mx/leyinfo/decre/ltaipg_110504.doc>.

There is not yet a comprehensive data protection law in Mexico. Provisions in the Federal Consumer Protection Law, however, place restrictions on direct marketing and credit reporting agencies. The Mexican E-Commerce Act took effect on May 29, 2000. This law amends the Civil Code, the Commercial Code, the Rules of Civil Procedure and the Consumer Protection Act. It covers consumer protection, privacy, digital signatures and electronic documents. It includes a new article in the Federal Consumer Protection Act giving authority to the government "to provide for the effective protection of the consumer in electronic transactions or concluded by any other means, and the adequate use of the data he provides " (Article 1.VIII); and to coordinate the use of the Code of Ethics by providers, including the principles of this law. The law also creates a new chapter in the Consumer Law entitled: "Rights of Consumers in electronic transactions and transactions by any other means."[3771]

The 1939 General Means of Communication Law (*Ley de Vías Generales de Comunicación*), provides penalties for interrupting communications and divulging secrets.[3772] Article 383 of this law provides that employees and civil servants devoted to the service of electric communications are obliged to keep absolutely secret the content of the messages whose transmission or reception has been under their supervision, or of those messages that they know by virtue of their job; as well as not to disclose any information pertaining to such messages other than the signatories, recipients or a competent authority.

The information transmitted through networks and telecommunication services shall be kept confidential except for the information that by its own nature is considered public or where there is an order from a competent authority (Article 49 of the Federal Telecommunications Law (*Ley Federal de Telecomunicaciones*)).[3773] It is strictly prohibited to intercept, disclose or make use of messages, news or information that are not for the public domain and are received through radio communication devices (Article 66 of the Federal Law of Radio and Television (*Ley Federal de Radio y Televisión*)).[3774]

[3771] The new Article 76 now provides: "This article will be applied to the relation between providers and consumers in transactions effectuated by electronics means. The following principles must be observed: (I) Providers shall use information provided by consumers in a confidential manner, and shall not be able to transfer it to third parties, unless there is express consent from the consumer or a requirement from a public authority. (II) Providers must use technical measures to provide security and confidentiality to the information submitted by the consumer, and notify the consumer, before the transaction, of the characteristics of the system. . . . (VI) Providers must respect consumer decisions not to receive commercial solicitations."

[3772] Ley de Vías Generales de Comunicación, December 30, 1939, at Articles 571, 576, 578, available at <http://profesor.uia.mx/aveleyra/comunica/privacidad/leyes2.htm> and go to "lvgc571-578.html".

[3773] <http://www.cddhcu.gob.mx/leyinfo/txt/118.txt>.

[3774] <http://www.cddhcu.gob.mx/leyinfo/txt/114.txt>.

Every professional is strictly obliged to keep the secrets of matters entrusted by his/her clients, except for the compulsory information set forth in other laws (Article 36 of the Regulation of Article 5 of the Federal Constitution pertaining to the Exercise of Professions in the Federal District (*Ley Reglamentaria del Artículo 5 Constitucional*)).[3775]

The Federal Consumer Protection Law (*Ley Federal de Protección al Consumidor* or FLCP) aims at protecting consumers who carry out transactions through the use of conventional, electronic, optic means, or any other technology (Section VIII, Article 1).[3776] The customer should always know the kind of personal data that the commercial providers have collected from him. This right includes free access to that data and the right to correct it, including the right to know who are the third party companies that know the customer's personal data (Article 16).[3777] Commercial messages or advertising sent to consumers should indicate the business's contact information and the name of the *Procuraduría Federal del Consumidor* (Consumers Agency, or PROFECO) (Article 17).[3778] The consumer is entitled to directly opt-out from any business's direct marketing scheme. PROFECO may develop, where applicable, a consumers' public registry listing all persons who opted out (Article 18).[3779] Businesses are prohibited from using consumers' personal information for marketing or advertising purposes if their names are on the PROFECO's opt-out list or if consumers have directly requested opt-out from them (Article 18*bis*).[3780] Businesses have to protect the confidentiality of information that consumers provided to them. They shall not disclose it or transmit it to third parties except with the consumer's express written authorization (opt-in) or by petition of a judicial authority (Section I, Article 76*bis*). Authorities and tribunals are prohibited from obtaining information on merchants' private accounting systems (Article 42 of the Code of Commerce (*Código de Comercio*)).[3781]

The Law of Protection and Defense of the User of Financial Services (*Ley de Protección y Defensa al Usuario de Servicios Financieros* or LPDUSF)[3782] provides the legal framework for the protection and defense of the rights and

---

[3775] <http://www.cddhcu.gob.mx/leyinfo/zip/208.zip>.
[3776] <http://www.cddhcu.gob.mx/leyinfo/zip/113.zip>.
[3777] *Id.*
[3778] *Id.*
[3779] *Id.*
[3780] *Id.*
[3781] <http://www.cddhcu.gob.mx/leyinfo/zip/3.zip>.
[3782] <http://www.cddhcu.gob.mx/leyinfo/txt/64.txt>.

interests of users of financial services rendered by private and public institutions duly authorized, as well as those rendered by the social sector. This law also regulates the organization, procedures and functioning of the National Commission for the Protection and Defense of Users of Financial Services (*Comisión Nacional para la Protección y Defensa de los Usuarios de Servicios Financieros* or CONDUSEF), which is in charge of promoting, advising, protecting, and defending the rights and interests of users before financial institutions; judging their conflicts on an impartial basis, and promoting legal equity in the relations between them.

The LPDUSF protects the disclosure of the banking, fiduciary and securities secrets by mandating the CONDUSEF maintain strict reserve on the information and documents that the CONDUSEF may know as part of its duties and that is related to deposits, services or any other kind of transactions carried out by financial institutions. CONDUSEF shall be legally entitled to provide information only in case such information or documents is requested by a judicial authority, and by virtue of a sentence duly resolved in trial (Article 13).[3783]

Public functionaries of the National Commission are personally liable for breaching the duty of confidentiality or secret provided in Article 13 of the LPDUFS, obliging them to repair any damage and loss caused as a result of disclosing banking, fiduciary or securities secrets (Articles 14-15).[3784] There are other laws protecting the disclosure of the banking, fiduciary and securities secret.[3785] A public official involved in matters related to the application and interpretation of tax must keep all declarations and data provided by tax contributors or third parties confidential (Article 69, Fiscal Code of the Federation (*Código Fiscal de la Federación*)).[3786]

People are entitled to have their data rectified when incomplete, inaccurate or obsolete, and have the right to complain before administrative and judicial authorities when the principle of confidentiality has been breached (Article 37 of the Geographic and Statistics Information Law (*Ley de Información Estadística y Geográfica*)).[3787] The information and data disclosed by individuals for statistical

---

[3783] *Id.*

[3784] *Id.*

[3785] The Credit Institutions Law (*Ley de Instituciones de Crédito*) Articles 117, 117 bis and 118; Securities Market Law (*Ley del Mercado de Valores*) Article 25; Saving and Popular Credit Law (*Ley de Ahorro y Crédito Popular*) Article 34; Investment Partnerships Law (*Ley de Sociedades de Inversión*) Article 55; and the Law to Regulate Credit Information Partnerships (*Ley para Regular las Sociedades de Información Crediticia*) (Section I Articles 18, 28, 37, 38, 39 and 52).

[3786] <http://www.cddhcu.gob.mx/leyinfo/zip/8.zip>.

[3787] <http://www.cddhcu.gob.mx/leyinfo/txt/41.txt>.

purposes, or coming from civil or administrative registries, shall not be communicated in any nominative form. It shall not be used as evidence before any administrative or fiscal authority (Article 38).[3788]

The General Population Act (*Ley General de Población*) regulates the National Registry of Population and Personal Identification.[3789] The purpose of the Registry is to register all persons making up the country's population using data enabling their identity to be certified reliably. The aim is ultimately to issue the citizen's identity card, which will be the official document of identification, fully endorsing the data contained in it concerning the holder.[3790] When a person is incorporated in the National Registry of Population, an identification keyword[3791] is assigned to the citizen (Article 91 of the General Population Act (*Ley General de Población*)). This keyword is used to register and identify Mexicans on an individual basis. That identification has the particularity of conferring a unique code for each citizen with which one can have direct access to multiple personal data. A unique code increases the risk of file interconnection.[3792]

All documents and information provided by citizens to the Federal Electoral Registry shall be held strictly confidential and shall not be communicated or disclosed, except when the Federal Electoral Institute is a party in legal trials, remedies or proceedings and acts to comply with its legal obligations or upon the petition of a competent judge. (Article 135, Section III, of the Federal Code of Institutions and Electoral Proceedings (*Código Federal de Instituciones y Procedimientos Electorales* or COFIPE)).[3793]

In 1981, the Penal Code was amended to include the interception of telephone calls by third parties. There are penalties for disclosing by any means, including personal mail, any secret or confidential communication known or received by virtue of employment, occupation or position, and the sanction may vary depending on whether the person renders professional or technical services,

---

[3788] *Id.*

[3789] <http://www.cddhcu.gob.mx/leyinfo/txt/140.txt>.

[3790] *See* United Nations Commission on Human Rights, "Question of the follow-up to the guidelines for the regulation of computerized personal data files: report of the Secretary-General prepared pursuant to Commission decision 1995/114," available at
<http://www.hri.ca/fortherecord1997/documentation/commission/e-cn4-1997-67.htm>.

[3791] The keyword is called "Unique Key-Word of the Population Registry" (*Clave Única del Registro de Población*, or CURP).

[3792] Portugal and Argentina, which suffered military dictatorial regimes, prohibited such personal identification numbers unless the number was to be associated by itself with particular individuals. France also prohibits the interconnection of files.

[3793] <http://www.cddhcu.gob.mx/leyinfo/zip/5.zip>.

whether the person is a functionary or public official, or whether the secret disclosed or published may be of industrial character. There are sanctions that range from six to 12 years of imprisonment and a fine for those who reveal, disclose, or unduly use to the detriment of others, information or images obtained during the interception of a private communication (Articles 210, 211 and 211*bis* of the Federal Criminal Code (*Código Penal Federal*)).[3794]

The Federal Law Against Organized Crime (*Ley Federal contra la Delincuencia Organizada*) passed on November 7, 1996, allows for electronic surveillance with a judicial order and details the conditions in which a judicial authority might authorize the interception of private communications (Articles 16-28).[3795] Authorities, officials and persons involved in the interception of private communications shall strictly keep the confidentiality of their content. Also, the law provides fines and imprisonment sanctions to public officials and employees that reveal, disclose or improperly use against the prejudice of another person information or images obtained in the course of an interception of private communications whether authorized or not. The law prohibits electronic surveillance in cases of electoral, civil, commercial, labor, or administrative matters and expands protection against unauthorized surveillance to cover all private means of communications, not merely telephone calls. The Federal Law against Organized Crime has been widely criticized by Mexican human rights organizations as violating Article 16 of the Constitution.[3796]

[3794] <http://www.cddhcu.gob.mx/leyinfo/zip/9.zip>.

[3795] <http://www.cddhcu.gob.mx/leyinfo/zip/101.zip>.

[3796] ("Exigen siete ONG la renuncia del titular de Seguridad Publica," La Jornada, October 7, 1997.). They noted that the ruling party *Partido Revolucionario Institucional* (PRI) "to keep the opposition in check" had historically used telephone espionage ("Con la reforma anticrimen, el espionaje entraría a la Constitución," La Jornada, April 28, 1996). There are numerous reports of illegal wiretapping. In September 2001, 13 people were arrested on suspicion of involvement in the illegal wiretapping of state government employees and former employees. The wiretapping was allegedly run out of the state governor's office, which has denied any involvement (United States Department of State, Country Report on Human Rights Practices 2001, March 2002, available at <http://www.state.gov/g/drl/rls/hrrpt/2001/>). In December 2000, President Vicente Fox formed a committee to review the practices of CISEN, the Government civilian intelligence agency, following allegations of illegal phone tapping. In March 1998, a large cache of government electronic eavesdropping equipment that had been used since 1991 to spy on members of opposition political parties, human rights groups and journalists was discovered in Campeche ("Spy Network Stuns Mexicans, Raid Opens Door to Exposure of Government Snooping," The Washington Post, April 13, 1998). Thousands of pages of transcripts of telephone conversations were uncovered along with receipts for USD 1.2 million in Israeli surveillance equipment. More than a dozen other cases of government espionage in four other states were exposed, ranging from hidden microphones and cameras found in government offices in Mexico City to tapes of a state governor's telephone calls. Every government agency identified with the electronic surveillance operations – the federal attorney general and interior ministry, the military, the national security agency and a plethora of state institutions – denied knowing anything about them ("Anger as Big Brother Spy Tactics Exposed," The Guardian (London), April 14, 1998). Since he was elected, President Fox promised to eliminate the security police division that is responsible for much of the illegal government wiretapping in Mexico.

The United States-Mexican border has been an area of increased surveillance. Mexican authorities now routinely perform "security sweeps" of homes in areas bordering the United States.[3797] On the United States side, biometric facial recognition systems have been implemented by the Immigration and Naturalization Service[3798] at the *Mesa de Otay* border crossing (San Diego-Tijuana) for frequent United States commuters to Mexican *maquiladora* factories. The biometric data is stored with driver's license numbers, vehicle registration numbers and passport status information in an INS database. When a commuter in the program approaches the United States border, a transponder under his vehicle sends a signal to the checkpoint booth, activating the database and displaying the driver's image. Other commuters use a voice-activated device in addition to the facial scan.[3799]

Federal Law Initiatives on Privacy and Protection of Personal Data

Three different bills on personal data protection were reviewed in the last five years. One by Representative Luis Miguel Barbosa Huerta (PRD); another by Senator Antonio García Torres (PRI), and the new amended version of Senator García Torres's bill, as approved by the Senate. The first two more or less follow the old or more recent Spanish data protection legislation. The third one, the Draft Initiative of Decree Issuing the Federal Law of Protection of Personal Data, is the first initiative enacted by the Mexican Congress dealing with privacy and the protection of personal data.[3800] The draft bill was largely based on the European Union Data Protection Directive and the Spanish Law on Protection of Personal Data of 1999.

The Draft Initiative Issuing the Federal Law of Protection of Personal Data was approved in the Senate on April 30, 2002. This bill adopts, for the most part, the language of the EU Data Protection Directive and contains a provision restricting the transfer of personal data to third countries that do not provide an adequate level of protection and that may likely create non-tariff barriers and distortion to international trade for Mexico. This bill still needs to be reviewed in the House of Representatives. The House of Representatives, through the Commission of Economy, will organize a workshop on data protection to discuss and analyze the bill with public, private and academic sectors, and experts.

[3797] "En marcha, amplia operación anticrimen en la frontera con Estados Unidos," La Jornada, November 5, 1996.

[3798] Now called the Department of Homeland Security's Bureau of Customs and Border Protection.

[3799] "Human Bar Codes," The San Diego Union-Tribune, May 13, 1998.

[3800] This draft bill was published in the Mexico's Parliamentary Gazette of September 7, 2001.

National Authority of Personal Data

There is a National Authority of Personal Data only for the Federal Public Administration (President, Attorney General, Ministries and State-owned enterprises): the Federal Institute of Access to Public Information (IFAI, or *Instituto Federal de Acceso a la Información Pública*).

Senator Garcia Torres's newest initiative seems to contemplate building up a new national authority of personal data, the *Instituto Federal de Protección de Datos Personales*. Besides IFAI, there are multiple organs for the protection of data, belonging to different branches of the State, related to the right of access to public information. As it is now conceived, IFAI has no authority when the personal data is in the hands of private people or entities, even those destined to provide information.

Mexico lacks a law to regulate the processing of personal information by private entities. Nowadays there are several separate governmental agencies dealing with personal financial data: the Ministry of Finance (SHCP), the Central Bank (BANXICO), the National Banking and Stock Exchange Commission (*Comisión Nacional Bancaria y de Valores,* or CNBV), the Financial Service Users Agency (CONDUSEF), the Consumers Agency (PROFECO), and the vast amount of public information offices (*Unidades de Enlace*) established after the enactment of the Transparency and Public Information Law (LFTAIPG). There are many other offices as well.[3801] IFAI, as the data protection authority, is undertaking the efforts to give Mexico a modern framework for personal data protection and security, departing from the federal public administration. In 2005, there is an ongoing political conflict about the competence to regulate personal data between IFAI and Secretary of the Public Function (*Secretaría de Función Pública*, or SFP).

Related Non-Governmental Organizations

There are currently no public interest organizations specializing exclusively in advocacy and legal protection of privacy rights. There are, on the other hand,

---

[3801] Pursuant to *Ley Orgánica de la Administración Pública Federal*, Article 26, there are 18 *Secretarias* (Ministries) and one *Consejeria Juridica* in the Central Public Administration. There are also the *Administracion Publica Paraestatal* (decentralized organs, corporations with public investment, national banks, national credit organizations, national insurance and guarantees organizations, trusts). For an analysis of the extent of the personal data managed by the Federal Public Administration in Mexico, *see* <http://profesor.uia.mx/aveleyra/comunica/privacidad/dp-apf.htm> and <http://www.ifai.org.mx/lisdap//listado.pdf>.

various associations and centers dedicated to the study, publication and promotion of transparency, right to know and access to public information.[3802]

In February 2003, the former Commission of Trade and Industrial Promotion of the House of Representatives (the former Commission of Trade) organized a workshop on data protection legislation to find out and hear the points of view on the impact that the two draft bills would have if approved, and to get the perspective from the private sector on privacy-related issues such as opt-in and opt-out approaches, the collection and processing of personal data of individuals, and online and offline transborder data flows. During a six-month period of weekly meetings, the participants did not reach a consensus on either bill or a viable approach that the legislation should follow.[3803]

Access to Public Government Information

The Federal Law of Transparency and Access to Public Government Information (*Ley Federal de Transparencia y Acceso a la Información Pública Gubernamental,* or FLTAIPG),[3804] in force since June 12, 2003, guarantees access to all interested individuals to the information in possession of the three branches (legislative, executive and judicial) of the Federal Union of Mexico; the constitutional autonomous entities (such as the *Comisión Nacional de Derechos Humanos* (National Commission for Human Rights), the *Banco de México*, and the *Instituto Federal Electoral*); or the entities with legal autonomy (such as IFAI or the *Auditoría Superior de la Federación*); as well as any other federal entity. This law is compulsory for all federal public officials.

The FLTAIPG established a new government entity: the Federal Institute of Access to Public Information (IFAI, or *Instituto Federal de Acceso a la Información*) to supervise the implementation of the law and promote the right to access information. It also adjudicates on the petitions regarding access to information and the protection of personal data in the possession of government

---

[3802] Freedom of Information Mexico (LIMAC) (*Libertad de Información México*); Foundation Information and Democracy - FIDAC (*Fundación Información y Democracia*); *Proyecto Atlatl*; the *Universidad Nacional Autónoma de México* (UNAM) in the Law Research Institute, (*Instituto de Investigaciones Jurídicas*) and Law School (*Facultad de Derecho*) of the *Universidad Nacional Autónoma de México* (UNAM), the Center for Research and Economic Teaching - CIDE (*Centro de Investigación y Docencia Económica*), and the *Programa Iberoamericano de Derecho de la Información, Universidad Iberoamericana* (UIA). For a survey of the NGO's process, *see* Talli Nauman, Mexico's Right-to- Know movement Citizen's Action in the Americas No. 4, February 2003 <http://www.americaspolicy.org/citizen-action/series/04-rtk.html>. For a listing of some of the NGOs *see* <http://www.americaspolicy.org/citizen- action/series/04-rtk_body.html#Mexican>.

[3803] The documents, feedback and testimonies of the Data Protection Legislation Workshop are available at <http://148.243.10.8/comcome/principal/mesaselectronico.asp> (in Spanish).

[3804] <http://www.cddhcu.gob.mx/leyinfo/zip/244.zip>.

entities and agencies. IFAI is also responsible for ensuring compliance with the privacy and data protection provisions of the FLTAIPG.[3805]

The main contribution of the LFTAIPG has been to standardize the principles under which the diverse organs of the State shall manage citizen's personal data. The law also safeguards the principles of notice, consent, and purpose specification, and guarantees the rights of access and correction. However, the law lacks sufficient guarantees to protect the security of data processing activities, and lacks adequate enforcement mechanisms. After the LFTAIPG was enacted, new related laws were enacted as well, for all the branches of Government.[3806]

There are administrative and judicial instances to enforce the law regarding access to government public information and personal data. In order to guarantee the minimum rights written down in the law, there are procedures to access and correct personal data, as well as to appeal for review, in both cases before an administrative instance. The data subject can use the *Juicio de Amparo* a safe, fast and effective procedure for persons to safeguard their constitutional individual, or an ordinary civil procedure before a court. If the Federal Personal Data Protection Law is enacted, it will introduce a procedural action, known in other countries as *habeas data*, from which shall derive administrative actions, and new procedures within the judicial system (Juzgados de Distrito), as well as new associated criminal provisions.

[3805] This law also provides a definition of personal data, information, reserved information and personal data system (Article 3); a full chapter on reserved and confidential information (Article 13 -20); a full chapter on protection of personal data (Articles 20-26); a chapter on IFAI (Articles 33-39); access to information requests and the internal procedure of the linking administrative units (unidades de enlace) (Articles 40-48); the legal procedure and remedies before IFAI (Articles 49-60); access to information to other compelled bodies and organizations (Articles 61-62), and a full chapter on liability and sanctions (Articles 63-64).

[3806] Those regulations were, at the level of the executive branch, the regulation for the application of the LFTAIPG; IFAI's internal bylaws (IFAI's internal regulatory statute); IFAI's Guidelines for information request; IFAI's Recommendations for the identification of reserved and confidential information in the public administration; the Form to request personal information and for demanding personal data correction and modification; the Guidelines for information classification. At the level of the judicial branch, the Agreement for accountability and public information; the Guidelines for the conservation and classification of information of the Supreme Court of Justice; the Guidelines for the conservation and classification of information of the Federal Judicial Counsel; the Guidelines for the conservation and classification of information of the Electoral Court and Administrative Tribunals: the Agreement for accountability (transparency) and public information of the Federal Court of Tax and Administrative Justice; the Regulation for the Transparency and Information Access of the Federal Court of Labour Arbitration; the Regulation for the Transparency and Information Access of the Agrarian Courts. At the level of the legislative branch, the Regulaton for the Accountability (Transparency) and Public Information Access of the Representatives Chamber; the Parliamentary Agreement for the Accountability (Transparency) and Access to Governmental Public Information in the Chamber of the Senate. At the level of the Constitutional Autonomous Organs:, the Regulation for the Accountability (Transparency) and Public Information Access of the Federal Electoral Institute; the criteria of the Banco de Mexico to classify reserved and confidential information; the Regulation for the Accountability (Transparency) and Public Information Access of the Human Rights National Commission. *See* <http://profesor.uia.mx/aveleyra/comunica/privacidad/correlacion-leyes.htm>.

Mexico has subscribed to, and ratified, the main international conventions related to the fundamental right to privacy.[3807] Mexico is a member of the Organization for Economic Cooperation and Development (OECD), but still has to implement the OECD Guidelines on the Protection of Privacy and Transborder Flows of Personal Data. Mexico has signed the American Convention on Human Rights, and the United Nations (UN) Guidelines for the Regulation of Computerized Personal Data Files adopted by General Assembly Resolution 45/95 of December 14, 1990.[3808] Both sets of Guidelines will have great impact on public policy and on the new legislative and administrative provisions that Mexico is about to implement.

Due to case law of the Supreme Court[3809] international treaties have an immediately inferior hierarchy to that of the Constitution, but superior to federal laws.

Recent developments

On June 14, 2003, the Constitutional Congress of the State of Colima enacted Decree No. 356,[3810] which contains the Personal Data Protection Law. The purpose of Colima's Data Protection Law is to protect and guarantee the protection of personal data as a fundamental human (Article 1). Colima is the first state that has enacted a privacy and data protection legislation in the Mexican Republic and even before the Federal Legislative Power. Colima's Data Protection Law has been in full effect since June 15, 2003 and its provisions have not yet been interpreted by Colima's local courts or by the Supreme Court. It is

---

[3807] Universal Declaration of Human Rights (1948) Article 12; Articles 5, 9 and 18 of the American Declaration of Rights and Duties of Mankind (1948); the International Pact of Civil and Political Rights (1966) Article 17; The American Convention of Human Rights or Pact of San José, Costa Rica (1969) Article 11; The Convention regarding Children's Rights (1989) Article 16. Also the International Agreement on Fed Telecommunications (Nairobi, 1982) Articles 18, 22 and 27, published in the Official Federal Diary ("DOF") on June 29, 1984, and nowadays substituted by the Constitution and Agreement of the International Union of Telecommunications, Nice, France, June 30, 1989, and ratified by Mexico on April 26, 1991, and published in the DOF March 3, 1992. A synoptic view of the texts specifically dealing with privacy in those Treaties subscribed by Mexico is available <http://profesor.uia.mx/aveleyra/comunica/privacidad/ti.htm>.

[3808] <http://www.unhchr.ch/html/menu3/b/71.htm>. Assembly General Resolution 44/132, UN Document A/44/49 (1989). The General Assembly of the Organization of the United Nations adopted on December 14, 1990 the Resolution 45/95, that deals with the limits for the regulation of the computer files of personal data (Document E/CN.4/1990/72). United Nations Guidelines and Principles can be consulted in in English at <http://193.194.138.190/html/menu3/b/71.htm>.

[3809] *Amparo en revisión* 1475/98 and Tesis P.LXXVII/99. *Semanario Judicial de la Federación y su Gaceta, novena época*, v. X, November 1999, at 46. *See* Manuel Becerra Ramírez, Jorge Carpizo, Edgar Corzo Sosa, Sergio López Ayllón, *Cuestiones Constitucionales 3* (July-December 2000), available at <http://www.juridicas.unam.mx/publica/rev/cconst/cont/3/cj/cj7.htm>.

[3810] <http://www.congresocol.gob.mx/leyes/ley-proteccion-datos-pers.htm>.

---

also not known how Colima's Data Protection Law is working in practice since it has been in effect for only a very short time.

Though there are several,[3811] three matters have mainly caught the attention of the media with regard to privacy. The first one is the prosecution of companies that disclosed Mexicans' personal information to US companies in violation of the principle of consent. Those companies made use of various databases such as the federal electoral census database, the vehicle register database, and the driver license database, in order to sell the data they contained to the US company Choicepoint which supplied data to various US government agencies, including the former Immigration and Naturalization Service, the Department of Justice and Federal Bureau of Investigation. The facts were already known more than a year before,[3812] but the case was not known in Mexico until after the newspaper *Reforma*, of Mexico City, broke the news on April 13, 2003. From that point forward, the case became important in the public agenda.[3813]

Diverse control measures were implemented at the US-Mexico, and Mexico-Guatemala borders. The fight against terrorism has pushed the US to adopt biometrics as a tool to identify Mexican nationals.[3814] Private companies began to sell chips for medical purposes, but also to be able to locate persons.[3815]

Secret government files detail several human rights violations of the past (including the "dirty war" and slaughters of 1968,[3816] 1971,[3817] as well as the

---

[3811] Among them, *see* "CNDH finds violations to privacy in INBA and makes a recommendation" <http://www.cndh.org.mx/Principal/document/Comunicacion_Social/boletines/jun2003/bol_084.htm>; the US Department of State Human Rights Report 2002 includes other cases. *See* <http://www.state.gov/g/drl/rls/hrrpt/2002/> and <http://www.state.gov/documents/organization/19593.doc> at 1. f). Other cases are referred in *Reporte Situación de los Derechos Humanos en México de la Oficina del Alto Comisionado de las Naciones Unidas para los Derechos Humanos en México*, available at <http://www.gobernacion.gob.mx/archnov/diagdhm.pdf> and at <http://www.cinu.org.mx/prensa/especiales/2003/dh_2003/index.htm>. *See* particularly *Recomendación 14*, at VIII, and chapter 2.3.1 *Otros Derechos Civiles, Derecho a la Libertad de Expresión y Derecho a la Información*, at 64 and related notes (196-221).

[3812] *See generally* <http://www.epic.org/privacy/choicepoint/default.html>, and especially <http://www.epic.org/privacy/publicrecords/inschoicepoint.pdf>.

[3813] *See* news articles on the ChoicePoint case at <http://profesor.uia.mx/aveleyra/comunica/privacidad/noticias/>, *see also* <http://www.cpsr-peru.org/privacidad/datos_personales/choicepoint/noticias/> (in Spanish).

[3814] *See* <http://www.eluniversal.com.mx/pls/impreso/noticia.html?id_nota=157874&tabla=notas>.

[3815] Jorge Medellín, "Este año, microchip para localizar personas," El Universal online, July 17, 2003, available at <http://www.eluniversal.com.mx/pls/impreso/noticia.html?id_nota=158107&tabla=notas>.

[3816] Kate Doyle, "Tlatelolco Massacre: Declassified US Documents on Mexico and the Events of 1968," The National Security Archives <http://www.gwu.edu/%7Ensarchiv/NSAEBB/NSAEBB10/intro.htm>. The declassified documents are available at <http://www.gwu.edu/%7Ensarchiv/NSAEBB/NSAEBB10/nsaebb10.htm>.

abuses of the Secret Police Corps from the late 60s until the early '80s,[3818] and the social and *guerilla* fighters movements in the '70s.[3819] The opening of those files occurred before the LFTAIPG entered into force. It will not be considered confidential any information related to the investigation of serious violations of fundamental rights or crimes against mankind (*delitos de lesa humanidad*) that appear in the public files.

Negotiations between the United States and the European Union in regard to the protection of personal data led to some agreements being made.[3820] On July 19, 2004, a new Regulation of the Code of Commerce regarding Lenders of Services of Certification[3821] (*Reglamento del Código de Comercio en Materia de Prestadores de Servicios de Certificación*) was added to the Electronic Commerce Act, to which the General Rules regarding Lenders of Services of Certification (*Reglas generales a las que deberán sujetarse los prestadores de servicios de certificación*) were added on August 10, 2004.[3822] Both regulations include the rules and procedures for the implementation of a public key infrastructure and the emission of public certificates.

Mongolia

Constitutional Privacy Framework

The Constitution of Mongolia recognizes the right to personal liberty and safety under Aection 13 of Article 16. That article states: "No one may be searched, arrested, detained, persecuted, or restricted of liberty save in accordance with procedures and on grounds determined by law. No one may be subjected to torture, inhuman, cruel, or degrading treatment. Where a person is arrested his or her family and counsel shall be notified within a period of time established by law of the reasons for the arrest. The privacy of citizens, their families, correspondence, and homes shall be protected by law."[3823]

[3817] Kate Doyle, "The Corpus Christi Massacre," The National Security Archives, June 10, 2003, available at <http://www.gwu.edu/~nsarchiv/NSAEBB/NSAEBB91/>.

[3818] A review of the news is available at <http://profesor.uia.mx/aveleyra/comunica/privacidad/noticias/>.

[3819] Kate Doyle, "Human Rights and the Dirty War in Mexico," The National Security Archive, May 11, 2003, available at <http://www.gwu.edu/~nsarchiv/NSAEBB/NSAEBB89/>.

[3820] *See* the relevant parts at <https://www.agpd.es/upload/Acuerdo_de_asociacion_economica_con_Mexico.pdf>.

[3821] <http://www.firmadigital.gob.mx/reglamentopsc.doc>.

[3822] <http://www.firmadigital.gob.mx/reglasPSCfinal.doc>.

[3823] Constitution of Mongolia of 1992, available at <http://www.parl.gov.mn/top/law_english/el_54.htm>.

Data Protection Framework

In the past, a special law regulating relations connected with personal secrecy did not exist. The adoption of the Law on Personal Secrecy by the State Great Hural (the Parliament) in 1995 therefore was a novelty in the legal practice of Mongolia, attesting to the legalization of the protection of human rights, honor and reputation. With this law a significant step forward has been made in the direction of guaranteeing human rights and freedoms and realization of the concept that in settling civil suits and disputes the courts shall not apply legislation that contradicts the Constitution, the general foundations of the Civil Code of Mongolia, and any decisions that set the norms pertaining to State administration.[3824]

The Law on Personal Secrecy (Privacy Law) of Mongolia defined the right in more detail, and categorized it as the following five types: secrecy of correspondence; secrecy of health information; secrecy of property; secrecy of family; and other secrecy, which is defined by laws.[3825] Aimed at protecting human rights, honor and dignity, this law includes within personal secrecy any information, documentation and material object defined by the pertinent laws of Mongolia as secret. The significance of determining the types of personal secrecy and the grounds and procedure for making it public in the law is twofold. First, it establishes that information pertaining to human health, property, correspondence and family is secret. Second, it creates a legal basis for revealing such data in cases when this is unavoidable for reasons of national security, national defense, public health and legal interests. This law also establishes the right of citizens to sue anyone who divulges their personal secrets.[3826]

According to the Privacy Law, the government should also protect citizens' secrets in accordance with procedures and on grounds determined by law.[3827] Only officials of authorized state organizations have access to personal data of citizens that is kept in accordance with procedures and on grounds determined by law. In addition, the law prohibits revealing a person's private information that was gained in accordance with procedures and on grounds determined by law.

[3824] UN Fourth Periodic Report of States Parties due in 1995: Mongolia, 14/06/99. CCPR/C/103/Add.7. (State Party Report), available at <http://www.hri.ca/fortherecord2000/documentation/tbodies/ccpr-c-103-add7.htm>

[3825] The Law on Personal Secrecy of Mongolia 1995 at Article 4.

[3826] UN Fourth Periodic Report of States Parties: Mongolia, *supra* at Note 2.

[3827] *Id.* at Article 5.

According the Privacy Law, the court will fine a person who breaks the law and reveals a person's private data in an unauthorized manner.[3828]

The National Program for Improving Human Rights was approved on October 24, 2003. The goals of the program were: make the Privacy Law more distinct; develop an information list that contains citizens' secrecy, family secrecy, correspondence secrecy, health secrecy, property secrecy, etc.; conduct training for officials dealing with citizens' secrecy who are employed at all types of organizations including public, private, and civil society organizations; and raise responsibility of the officials by obliging them to take an oath, etc.[3829]

About 20 laws, such as Health Law, Donors Law, Insurance Law, and Tax Law, were brought to conformity with the Privacy Law. Further, the Criminal Code and the Code of Criminal Procedure incorporate detailed provisions guaranteeing the security of privacy. The criminal legal protection against the violation of individuals' privacy was established in Article 18[3830] of the Criminal Code entitled "Crimes against the citizens' political and other rights and freedoms." Violations of privacy imply the legal liability (e.g. criminal, administrative, material, etc.) of those who unlawfully cause any of the following: violation of the legislation by the intelligence activities;[3831] violation of the privacy of correspondence;[3832] disclosure of private secrets;[3833] and violation of home.[3834]

If a person violates the Criminal Code, courts can impose upon him a penalty such as fine, enforcing to work, arresting three to six months, and imprisoning up to three years. According to the Criminal Code, a person who illegally obtains computer data will face criminal penalty.[3835]

Wiretapping and Surveillance Rules

The law of Intelligence Operation determines the lawful disclosure of private secrets. According to the law, only a few organizations have a right to conduct "executive work." These organizations include Intelligence, military intelligence

---

[3828] *Id.* at Article 8.

[3829] The National Programme for Improving Human Rights, Article 2.1.3.

[3830] Criminal Code of Mongolia, available at <http://www.parl.gov.mn/top/law_enlish/el_o4.htm>.

[3831] *Id.* at Article 133.

[3832] *Id.* at Article 135.

[3833] *Id.* at Article 136.

[3834] Criminal Code of Mongolia, *supra* at Article 137.

[3835] *Id.* at Article 227.

organization, police, enforcement agency (established by a court decision), and the Border Intelligence Agency.[3836] Those organizations are allowed to conduct surveillance (telephone and mail correspondence), to make secret inspection (including home, organization, vehicles, luggage, and things), and to use special equipment enabling them to that intercept communications. However, they must first obtain prosecutor's written permission.[3837] Moreover, the prosecutor must supervise all of their activities.[3838]

In Mongolia, the Intelligence is responsible for registration of the surveillance equipment and for control of its usage. The prosecutor's office exercises control on registration of surveillance equipment. However, the law of Intelligence Operation does not include any regulation on the production or import of surveillance equipment. Moreover, the law does not ban the import, sale, possession, or use of surveillance equipment by citizens and organizations, and does not establish any legal ground for system of amenability on wrongdoers.

According to the Law on Approval of the List for State Secrets, the reports, news, studies of executive works, documents of special funds, documents of crimes under control or investigation, and other related issues[3839] are considered state secrets. Therefore, one cannot know how many people were investigated secretly, and who uses the surveillance equipment and for what purposes.

Telecommunications Privacy

Currently, there are no standards set up for telecommunications and postal offices, or mobile phone and Internet service providers (ISP) regarding the protection of communication privacy. No monitoring system has been established concerning whether a person secretly surveys transmissions, etc. There is no nationwide rule for registering all cases that investigate secretly a person's privacy with the permission of an authorized organization.

In 2000, the National Human Rights Commission of Mongolia, which includes the Human Rights Ombudsman, was established by Parliament. The commission is charged with the promotion and protection of human rights, and with monitoring the implementation of the provisions of human rights and

---

[3836] Law of Intelligence Operation, Article 9.

[3837] *Id.* at Article 11.

[3838] *Id.* at Article 23.

[3839] Law on Approval of the List for State Secrets, Articles 1.50, 1.53.

freedoms[3840] enshrined in the constitution of Mongolia, laws and international treaties to which Mongolia is party. The commission published human rights status reports[3841] in 2002, 2003 correspondingly, and distributed it government and broad public.

The Information Security Law is under development. Last year, the working group on information security draft law was established by presidential decree. However, the draft is not yet finalized or publicized.

Open Government

Recently, Ministry of Justice of Mongolia drafted the Freedom of Information Law. However, it is not clear when the law will be submitted to the Parliament. In September 2004, the international anti-corruption non-governmental organization Transparency International (TI) included Mongolia (for the first time since 1999) in its annual "Perceptions of Corruption" survey. Mongolia ranked 85 out of 145 countries and its score (3 out of 10, where 10 is the "best") is "poor."[3842] In addition, United Nations Development Programme (UNDP) surveys of Mongolia, conducted in 1999 and again in 2002 and 2003, also indicate a growing and serious entrenchment of bureaucratic and political corruption in Mongolia.[3843] The current Mongolian government has agreed to consider signing and ratifying this convention in 2005 and to amend its laws to bring them into compliance with the provisions of the convention. Draft anti-corruption legislation is under consideration by Parliament.[3844]

With regard to the Information and Communication Technologies (ICT) sector, the joint committee of Ministry of Justice, and ICT Authority drafted the law on ICT. The draft law is under discussion, and plans are to submit it for Parliament discussion in the spring session of 2005.

International Obligations

In the past 15 years, Mongolia has made key progress in terms of respect human rights, including protecting privacy, but much remains to be done to ensure to

---

[3840] The National Human Rights Commission homepage <http://www.nhrc-mn.org>.

[3841] *See* <http://www.nhrc-mn.org/doclinks.asp?group=reports>.

[3842] For more information see <http://www.transparency.org.>.

[3843] *See* <http://www.undp.org.in/>.

[3844] "2005 Investement Climate Statement-Monolia," U.S. Department of State Report, available at <http://www.state.gov/e/eb/ifd/2005/42091.htm>.

full consistency with international law. Currently, Mongolia has ratified more than 20 international human rights conventions, and around 25 conventions of the international labor organizations. However, Mongolia has not yet joined the following international conventions concerning automatic personal data processing: Convention for the Protection of Individuals with Regard to Automatic Processing of Personal Data (Convention No. 108);[3845] European Convention for the Protection of Human Rights and Fundamental Freedoms;[3846] and European Council Directive on the Protection of Individuals with Regard to the Processing of Personal Data and on the Free Movement of such Data 95/46/EC of 1995.

Kingdom of the Netherlands

Constitutional Privacy Framework

The Constitution grants citizens an explicit right to privacy.[3847] Article 10 states: "(1) Everyone shall have the right to respect for his privacy, without prejudice to restrictions laid down by, or pursuant to, Act of Parliament. (2) Rules to protect privacy shall be laid down by Act of Parliament in connection with the recording and dissemination of personal data. (3) Rules concerning the rights of persons to be informed of data recorded concerning them, of the use that is made thereof, and to have such data corrected shall be laid down by Act of Parliament." Article 12 states: "(1) Entry into a home against the will of the occupant shall be permitted only in the cases laid down by, or pursuant to, Act of Parliament, by those designated for this purpose by, or pursuant to, Act of Parliament. (2) Prior identification and notice of purpose shall be required in order to enter a home under the preceding paragraph, subject to the exceptions prescribed by Act of Parliament. A written report of the entry shall be issued to the occupant." Article 13 states, "(1) The privacy of correspondence shall not be violated, except in the cases laid down by Act of Parliament or by order of the courts. (2) The privacy of the telephone and telegraph shall not be violated, except in the cases laid down by Act of Parliament, by or with the authorization of those designated for this purpose by Act of Parliament." The *Hoge Raad* (the highest court) is not allowed

---

[3845] Convention for the Protection of Individuals with regard to Automatic Processing of Personal Data (ETS no.: 108), available at<http://conventions.coe.int/Treaty/EN/CadreListeTraites.htm>.

[3846] Convention for the Protection of Human Rights and Fundamental Freedoms.
(ETS no.: 005), available at <http://conventions.coe.int/Treaty/EN/CadreListeTraites.htm>.

[3847] Constitution of the Kingdom of the Netherlands 2002, available at
<http://www.minbzk.nl/uk/constitution_and/publications/the_constitution_of>.

to review acts of parliament, although proposals to make this possible are being discussed.

In May 2000, the government-appointed Commission for Constitutional Rights in the Digital Age presented proposals to make existing constitutional rights more technology-independent. According to this proposal, Article 10 will be expanded to the right of persons to be informed about the origin of data recorded about them and the right to correct that data. Article 13 would be made technology-neutral and would give the right to confidential communications. In November 2004, the Dutch government announced that proposals to amend the Constitution would be delayed in order to incorporate upcoming international developments regarding human rights and the information society such as the Council of Europe's recommendation "Human Rights and the Rule of Law in the Information Society." The recommendation was adopted by the Council of Europe on May 13, 2005.[3848]

The Personal Data Protection Act of 2000[3849] (PDPA) is a revised and expanded version of the Data Registration Act of 1998 that brings Dutch law in line with the European Union Data Protection Directive (95/46/EC) and regulates the disclosure of personal data to countries outside of the European Union. The law went into effect in September 2001 and is scheduled for an evaluation in 2006.

Data Protection Authority

The Dutch data protection authority (*College Bescherming Persoonsgegevens*, or CBP) exercises supervision of the operation of personal data files in accordance with the PDPA.[3850] Previously known as the *Registratiekamer*, the CBP's functions have remained largely the same with the implementation of the PDPA, although it has been given new powers of enforcement. It can now apply administrative measures and impose fines for non-compliance with a decision. It can also levy fines, of up to EUR 4,540, for breach of the notification requirements. Otherwise, the CBP advises the government, deals with complaints submitted by data subjects, institutes investigations and makes recommendations to controllers of personal data files.

[3848] Declaration of the Committee of Ministers on human rights and the rule of law in the Information Society, available at <http://www.minbzk.nl/contents/pages/42826/declaration.pdf>

[3849] Personal Data Protection Act 2000, unofficial translation available at <http://www.dutchdpa.nl/documenten/en_pdpa.htm>.

[3850] <http://www.dutchdpa.nl/>.

In 2004, the CBP investigated 409 complaints. The CBP also dealt with 56 *ex-officio* investigations, nine complaints concerning codes of conduct, 34 advisories to government on new legislation. The CBP also conducted 2,778 information and advisory services (letters and e-mails): 2,778 and 4,866 telephone helpdesk.[3851] The Dutch DPA has 64.5 full-time positions. The following are the main departments/positions: three commissioners (full-time); legal department; intervention, complaints and appeals department; investigations department; communication and front office; and, support staff.[3852] The CBP generally relies on a network of privacy officers within companies and (government) institutions to produce annual privacy reports and discuss procedures with the CBP. Currently, there are 170 privacy officers in the Netherlands. The CBP issues reports on a regular basis about the implementation of and compliance with privacy regulations. In April 2002, it issued updated guidelines on e-mail and Internet privacy in the workplace. The guidelines favor of a balanced and common-sense approach to e-mail and Internet monitoring at the workplace. It concludes that, although employees retain a reasonable expectation of privacy in the workplace, employers should be entitled to monitor e-mail and Internet use under certain conditions.[3853]

In its 2004 annual report,3854 the CBP expresses its concern about the current public debate in which there has, for some years, "been a strong erosion and politicisation of the term 'privacy.' " Privacy seems to be looked upon as "a vaguely defined interest that supposedly prevents administrators and professionals from realising politically and socially desirable objectives."3855 The report also mentions the popular "privacy-bashing" among politicians, administrators and chiefs of police. Government officials criticize privacy "as an obstacle to action and as a hiding place for defaulters, fraudsters and other malicious persons"3856 but, according to the CBP, this criticism is mostly "a recurring cover for the lack of decisiveness or successful action on the part of organisation in question."3857 "In the eyes of some parties the Dutch DPA is an 'administrative burden' rather than the 'privacy watchdog.' "3858

[3851] E-mail from S. Artz, Legal adviser, Dutch Data Protection Authority, to Ula Galster, International Policy Fellow, Electronic Privacy Information Center, May 3, 2005 (on file with EPIC).

[3852] *Id.*

[3853] Dutch Data Protection Authority, Working well in Networks, April 2002, English summary available at <http://www.cbpweb.nl/en/documenten/EN_av_21_Working_well_in_networks.htm>.

[3854] *College Bescherming Persoonsgegevens*, Annual Report for the Year 2004, May 2005, with English summary available at <http://www.cbpweb.nl/downloads_jaarverslagen/jv_2004.pdf>.

[3855] *Id.*

[3856] *Id.*

[3857] *Id.*

[3858] *College Bescherming Persoonsgegevens*, Annual Report for the Year 2004, May 2005, *supra.*

The CBP's 2004 annual report also mentions various new acts and government plans to new methods and powers for combating terrorism. The CBP is especially critical of the so-called Counter-terrorism Info Box, a information-sharing infrastructure in which the security services, the police, the Public Prosecution Service and the IND (Immigration and Nationalization Service) participate. The system facilitates the comprehensive collection, linking and analysis of information about groups and persons as the key to preventing terrorism. For this purpose, the government finds it necessary to extend its investigative powers. It announced it would reduce the legal criterion for the authorization of such actions as tapping telephones, monitoring Internet use and surveillance from "suspicion or reasonable suspicion of involvement" to "indications of involvement." According to the plan, the mere fact that a citizen acts suspiciously is sufficient reason to put him under surveillance to assess whether the suspicion is justified or not. The CBP concluded that the necessity for an expansion of the powers to collect information had not been demonstrated and that the proposed far-reaching coordination of the gathering of information fails to recognize the separate legal responsibilities and powers of intelligence services and the police. The report also discusses European data retention proposals, passenger data sharing with the United States, the new biometric passport, the duty of identification, camera surveillance, the Citizens Service Number and data-sharing between doctors and insurance companies under the new Health Insurance Act.[3859]

Pursuant to the Personal Data Protection Act (PDPA), the Decree on Regulated Exemption[3860] has been enacted to exempt certain organizations from the registration requirements of the PDPA. There are also sectoral privacy laws regulating the Dutch police,[3861] medical exams,[3862] medical treatment,[3863] social security,[3864] the search of private homes,[3865] and the employment of minorities.[3866]

[3859] *Id.*

[3860] Decree on Regulated Exemption, May 7, 2001.

[3861] Dutch Police Registers Act 1990.

[3862] Dutch Medical Examinations Act 1997.

[3863] Dutch Medical Treatment Act 1997.

[3864] Dutch Social Security System Act 1997, Compulsory Identification Act.

[3865] Dutch Act on the Entering of Buildings and Houses 1994.

[3866] Dutch Act on the Stimulation of Labor by Minorities 1994.

Interception of communications is regulated by the Criminal Code and requires a court order.[3867] The intelligence services do not need a court order for interception, but obtain their authorization from the Minister of Interior. The Special Investigation Powers Act, which came into effect in February 2000, streamlines criminal investigatory methods.[3868] A Telecommunications Act was approved in December 1998, requiring all telecommunication providers to have the capability to intercept all traffic (phone and Internet) with a court order.[3869] The bill was enacted after Internet service provider (ISP) XS4ALL, refused to conduct a broad wiretap of the electronic communications of one of its subscribers.[3870] The costs of installing the required wiretap technology will have to be financed by the telecommunications providers themselves. The Netherlands Radiocommunications Agency is responsible for enforcing the wiretap capabilities of the telecommunication sector.[3871] Internet provider XS4ALL launched a court case in March 2005 against the Dutch State, seeking compensation for the cost of making its network ready for wiretaps. XS4ALL claims to have invested about EUR 500,0000 since the end of 2001 to comply with the requirements for lawful interception, a significant percentage of its net profit. XS4ALL considers it unreasonable that these costs are not reimbursed, because these investments are made purely in the general interest of law enforcement and do not benefit the provider in any way. According to XS4ALL, the law requiring providers to pay for the costs of wiretapping is a violation of property rights and an obstruction to freedom of speech. Moreover, the cost division also violates the principle of equal discharge of public burdens and European rules on free movement of services.[3872] By a decree,[3873] the government ordered a dramatic reduction in cost reimbursement to telecommunication companies for the handover of personal data or wiretaps. Since April 1, 2005, the companies only receive EUR 13 for a wiretap and EUR 6.75 for an extensive investigation into historical traffic data.

A survey by the Dutch Ministry of Justice in 1996 found that law enforcement in the Netherlands intercept more telephone calls than their counterparts in the

---

[3867] Article 125m of the Code of Criminal Procedure.

[3868] *See* Ministry of Justice, Fact Sheet on the Special Investigation Powers Act, available at <http://www.justitie.nl/english//Publications/factsheets/bob.asp?ComponentID=35268>.

[3869] Telecommunications Act 1998.

[3870] <http://www.xs4all.nl/uk/overxs4all/aftappen/aftappen.html>.

[3871] Home Agentschap Telecom homepage <http://www.agentschap-telecom.nl/>

[3872] XS4ALLl subpoena, English translation available at: <http://www.xs4all.nl/nieuws/pdf/XS4ALLdagvaarding-en.pdf>.

[3873] Decree on cost reimbursement for legal access to telecommunications, Ministry of Economic Affairs, 1 April 2005, <http://www.bof.nl/docs/OPT_Concept_regeling_aftapkosten_23_maart_2005.pdf>.

United States, Germany or Britain.[3874] According to a 2003 report by the German Max Planck Institute for Foreign and International Criminal Law, Italy and the Netherlands are the wiretap champions of the Western world.[3875] The Parliamentary Commission of Investigations into Police Methods released a 4,700-page report in 1996. The report was critical of the legal framework of police surveillance[3876] and found that there was a failure among judges, prosecutors and other officials to limit police abuses. Some researchers say that the reason for the high number of wiretaps is that the Netherlands limits other forms of investigations, such as police infiltration.[3877] A 2003 Freedom of Information Act request by the privacy and civil liberties organization Bits of Freedom[3878] resulted in the release of 1998 statistics that reveal that law enforcement wiretapped 10,000 telephone numbers.[3879] The Minister of Justice refused to deliver statistics from previous years stating that those were not available to him. After publication of the statistics by Bits of Freedom, Members of Parliament asked the government to record such statistics in the future but the Minister of Justice answered that it did not see the benefit of doing so.[3880] The official position of the Dutch government is that it does not know how often it wiretaps its citizens. However, in the Public Prosecution Service annual report of 2004 it is mentioned that the number of telephone and the Internet wiretaps is still on the rise. Costs for arranging wiretaps have risen by 30% compared to 2003.[3881] In recent years several high profile cases drew public attention to flaws in the organization and overview of interception. In a criminal case *State v. Baybasin*,[3882] expert witnesses, both former law enforcement and military intelligence interception employees, testified, after reviewing the evidence, that the intercepted telephone recordings had been tampered with. A July 2003 report by the CBP criticized the unlawful police practice of recording calls between

---

[3874] Tappen in Nederland, WODC, 1996.

[3875] *Rechtswirklichkeit und Effizienz der Überwachung der Telekommunikation* [.], Max Planck Institute for Foreign and International Criminal Law, June 2003, available at <http://www.iuscrim.mpg.de/verlag/online/Band_115.pdf>.

[3876] Parliamentary Investigations Commission Van Traa, 1996.

[3877] De telefoontap in grote opsporingsonderzoeken, WODC, June 2004, also available at <http://www.ministerievanjustitie.nl/b_organ/wodc/publicaties/overige/pdf/jv0404bok.pdf>.

[3878] Bits of Freedom <http://www.bof.nl>.

[3879] <http://www.bof.nl/docs/aftapbrief.html>.

[3880] Answers to Parliament questions, Tweede Kamer, 2002-2003, Aanhangsel Handelingen, nr. 1035 and nr. 1553, and 2003-2004, Aanhangsel Handelingen, nr. 219.

[3881] Public Prosecution Service Annual Report 2004, May 2005, available at <http://www.om.nl/pg/documents/om2005/Jaarbericht-2004.pdf>.

[3882] Higher Court Den Bosch, July 30, 2002, LJN-number AE5920.

suspects and their lawyers.[3883] In March 2005, the Dutch association of criminal defense lawyers (NVSA) lost a court case (preliminary proceedings) demanding an immediate stop to the practice of wiretapping their confidential telephone conversations with clients. The Court ruled that these conversations do not per definition fall under the professional secrecy. Dutch lawyers fear a "back room" atmosphere, where lawyers have to secretly make appointments with their clients, possibly even at secret locations.[3884] An August 2003 analysis order by the Ministry of Justice into the security and vulnerability of police wiretap facilities was conducted by PricewaterhouseCoopers.[3885] One of the report's alarming conclusions was that, within the police organization, little access control to intercepted communication was enforced. The report also found that suppliers of interception equipment conducted maintenance and installed upgrades through remote access without supervision by Dutch authorities.

In September 2004, a new Act came into force that amends the powers to request telecommunications data. The law (*Vorderen gegevens telecommunicatie*) enables the public prosecutor to request traffic data from providers of public telecommunications networks and services. This power may be applied in cases where there is suspicion of a serious offense on which a term of imprisonment of four years or more may be imposed. A subscriber's information can be requested by any investigating officer in the event of a suspicion of a criminal offense. A proposal to notify suspects after the subscriber's data was requested was not accepted by Parliament. Members of the Senate questioned the scope of the powers requested and required mandatory registration of all data retrievals in order to review their proportionality and effectiveness.

Anti-terrorism Measures

In August 2004, the Crimes of Terrorism Act came into force. Recruitment of fighters for the Islamic armed struggle or *jihad* and conspiracy to commit a serious act of terrorism will each be a separate punishable criminal offense under the Act. The maximum prison sentences for crimes such as homicide, gross maltreatment, hijacking or kidnapping will be higher if they have been

---

[3883] CBP, *Onderzoek naar de waarborging van de vertrouwelijke communicatie van advocaten bij de interceptie van telecommunicatie*, July 17, 2003, available at
<http://www.cbpweb.nl/documenten/rap_2003_beroepsgeheim_advocaten.htm>.

[3884] "No ban on wiretapping of Dutch lawyers", EDRI-gram newsletter, number 3.6 March 24, 2005, available at <http://www.edri.org/edrigram/number3.6/wiretap>.

[3885] A & K-analyse op een vijftal interceptie organisaties en -systemen, PricewaterhouseCoopers, August 2003, available at <http://www.bof.nl/docs/kwetsbaarheid_tapkamers.pdf>.

committed with a "terrorist purpose." In addition, the conspiracy to commit serious acts of terrorism will be made a separate punishable criminal offense.

The Netherlands do not have a mandatory data retention requirement for telecommunications. There is, however, an obligation to store location data from pre-paid GSMs for a three-month period. The proposal from the European Ministers of Justice to introduce mandatory data retention has resulted in a fierce public and political debate in the Netherlands. The Dutch government is in support of the proposal but has failed to explain to the Dutch parliament basic issues regarding proportionality, effectiveness and costs. After a public access request, Bits of Freedom obtained a 2003 police report that states that traffic data is seldom essential in criminal investigations. Most cases can be solved without access to traffic data, with the exception of large fraud investigations. The Minister of Justice did not send the report to parliament claiming it was "not representative."[3886] In April 2005, the Minister of Justice announced that new research would be conducted into the necessity and effectiveness of mandatory data retention. According to a December 2004 study[3887] by KPMG into the costs of mandatory data retention, Internet providers will face investments of millions of euro. The Dutch study is the only government study in Europe, so far, that made the costs of data retention public. In November 2004, 246 Dutch ISPs and 23 other organizations send a petition to parliament asking for attention to the negative effect on innovation, privacy and costs. In April 2005, Bits of Freedom and the Dutch Consumer Association asked parliament to consider the effect on the freedom of communication, costs and the lack of proven necessity.[3888]

There have been several proposals over past years to grant law enforcement increased authority. In 2001 the Mevis Committee issued a report proposing a wide range of increased powers for police to allow them to carry out "pro-active investigations" (*verkennend onderzoek*). The proposals would grant police access, without the need to obtain judicial warrants, to the personal information of whole groups of citizens stored by a wide variety of private entities, such as banks, telephone companies, credit card companies, hospitals and travel agents, in order to determine crime patterns.[3889] The Mevis Committee specifically recommended that telecommunications data be excluded from the constitutional

---

[3886] The use of (historic) traffic data in law enforcement, Rotterdam police, April 2003, available at <http://www.bof.nl/docs/rapport_verkeersgegevens.pdf>

[3887] Onderzoek naar de opslag van historische verkeersgegevens van telecommunicatieaanbieders, KPMG, December 2004, with English summary available at <http://www.bof.nl/docs/bewaarplicht_KPMG.pdf>.

[3888] Bits of Freedom and the Dutch Consumer Association, letter to Parliament, April 2005, available at <http://www.bof.nl/briefverkeersgegevens.html>.

[3889] Jelle van Buuren, "Dutch Law Enforcement Should Get Easier Access to Personal Data Stored by Companies," Telepolis, May 21, 2001.

right to confidential communications, stating that it should not be necessary for police to always obtain a warrant to intercept communications.[3890] A draft law with the Mevis proposals *(Wet vorderen gegevens)* was passed by the House of Representatives and is now being considered by the Senate. The Federation of Organisations of Libraries (FOBID) has asked the Senate in the April 2005 letter not to pass the law fearing a chilling effect on the use of libraries when law enforcement is able to seize library records.

In October 2001, the Government released an Action Plan containing 43 specific measures to be taken to combat terrorism and promote security.[3891] Among these were proposals to expand information and security agencies; promote better cooperation among information and security services and the police; develop biometric identifiers; expand investigative and prosecuting capacity; regulate the use of strong encryption and force Trusted Third Parties to use key escrow or key recovery techniques to enable access to encrypted communications; ensure the quick implementation of the 1998 interception requirements for ISPs (above); expand satellite interception capacity to combat terrorism and "investigate further" the issue of data retention by telecommunications operators.

Proposals for mandatory key escrow for Trusted Third Parties were left behind after the release of a 2002 joint government and industry report examining costs and possible benefits. The report concluded that costs were high and law enforcement rarely ran into difficulties posed by encryption.[3892] Law enforcement can, however, order anyone, but for a suspect, who can reasonably be considered to know the means of encryption, to decrypt information encountered during an investigation. Failure to cooperate can be punished with a maximum of three months' imprisonment.[3893] Intelligences services can order anyone to cooperate. Failure to comply with the request from an intelligence service is punishable with up to six months' imprisonment if it was not intentional, and with up to two years' imprisonment if it was intentional.[3894] In November 2003, the introduction of a commercial, software-based, encrypted GSM, the Cryptophone,[3895] led to questions in Parliament. The Minister of Justice was asked if it was possible to outlaw the Cryptophone. He answered, however, that no legal constraints on encryption are in place and that the

---

[3890] Report of the Mevis Commission, May 2001.

[3891] Ministry of Justice, Plan of Action for Combating Terrorism and Promoting Security, October 5, 2001.

[3892] Parliament, Tweede kamer, 2002-2003, 26581, No. 2.

[3893] Article 125k of the Code of Criminal Procedure.

[3894] Intelligence and Security Services Act 2001.

[3895] Cryptophone homepage <http://www.cryptophone.nl/>.

Cryptophone provided the protection of a legitimate right of privacy in communications.[3896]

The Intelligence and Security Services Act also authorizes the interception, search and keyword scanning of satellite communications. It allows intelligence services to store intercepted communications for up to one year. Previously, irrelevant communications had to be deleted immediately. Encrypted data can be stored for an unlimited time to facilitate possible decryption in the future. In 2003, the National SIGINT Organization (NSO) was established. The NSO will operate all satellite communications interception by the Dutch intelligence services. The interception capabilities will expand from two satellite dishes at Zoutkamp to 20 dishes at Burum. The NSO has bought part of the satellite ground station of the commercial satellite company Xantic at Burum and will intercept communications alongside the commercial activities at the location.

Recent Developments Related to Privacy

In January 2005, compulsory identification[3897] for all persons from the age of 14 came into force . The Extended Compulsory Identification Act is intended to increase general public safety. Many critics have stated that the government failed to clarify the need to broaden the identification requirements. The proposal is widely seen as a symbolic gesture to satisfy public concerns about security and crime and will have huge civil liberties consequences. The new law will not require citizens to carry identification but to show one if asked by police. No new identification card will be introduced; the existing passport and driver license will be used. About 5,300 persons a month are fined for not being able to show their ID, mostly because of minor offenses such as bicycling without a light.[3898]

Like all EU countries the Netherlands are working on the inclusion of biometrics in their passport. Both fingerprints and facial images will be used in contactless chip in the Dutch passport.[3899] In January 2005, the Minister of the Interior announced plans to also store the biometric data in a central database, enabling

---

[3896] Answers to parliament questions, Tweede Kamer, 2003-2004, nr. 891.

[3897] Compulsory Identification, Ministry of Justice, October 2004, available at
<http://www.justitie.nl/english/Themes/more_themes/compulsary_identification/index.asp>.

[3898] Identificatieplicht: 5300 boetes per maand, Bits of Freedom, May 2005, available at
<http://www.bof.nl/nieuwsbrief/nieuwsbrief_2005_9.html>

[3899] Biometry in passports, page maintained by Professor of Software Security and Correctness Bart Jacobs, available at <http://www.sos.cs.ru.nl/research/society/passport/>.

the identification of persons that do not carry a passport[3900] through fingerprints or face recognition.

In February 2005, the DNA Testing of Convicted Persons Act came into force. The law makes it possible to take DNA samples of all persons that are convicted of crimes carrying a maximum penalty of four years or more. The mouth swab sample will be investigated by the Netherlands Forensic Institute (NFI) in order to determine the DNA profile.[3901]

In March 2005, the Netherlands National Commission for Unesco published recommendations on human rights and Internet, following a conference held on February 4 and 5. The recommendations focus on privacy, the right of freedom of expression and the right to communicate, including access to the vast cultural, educational and scientific heritage of mankind. On privacy, the recommendations call on States to "[a]cknowledge that privacy is an indispensable prerequisite to the right of freedom of expression and the right to communicate. Online as well as off-line, readers, listeners and viewers have a right to the same high level of privacy and anonymity. If online access to information is tracked and tied to detailed personal profiles, self-censorship is imminent and - more important still - the public debate and the rule of law are eroded."[3902]

Starting in 2004, the use of covert video surveillance in public places requires notice. The Hidden Camera Surveillance Act 2003 (*Heimelijk Cameratoezicht*) makes it unlawful to use hidden cameras in public places without notification. The use of hidden cameras in the workplace remains lawful if there is a suspicion of criminal behavior and if workers are notified of the likelihood of video surveillance. Journalists can still use hidden cameras for their work. A November 2003 report by the Dutch Data Protection Authority concludes that about half of the local governments that use camera surveillance for public order purposes had not evaluated its effectiveness. Only one in five monitors the camera is live, which puts its usefulness into serious questioning according to the DPA.[3903] In April 2005, the House of Representatives passed the Camera Surveillance Act, which enables the retention of images up to four weeks and also facilitates the

---

[3900] Databank vingerafdrukken alle Nederlanders, Bits of Freedom, February 2005, available at <http://www.bof.nl/nieuwsbrief/nieuwsbrief_2005_3.html>.

[3901] "DNA Samples to be Taken from Convicted Persons," Ministry of Justice, February 2005, available at <http://www.justitie.nl/english/press/press_releases/archive/archive_2005/020205dna_samples_to_be_taken_from_convicted_persons.asp>.

[3902] Internet, Human Rights and Culture, Unesco Netherlands, March 2005, available at <http://www.unesco.nl/main_6-2.php>.

[3903] Cameratoezicht in de openbare ruimte, CBP, November 2003, available at <http://www.cbpweb.nl/documenten/rap_2003_vct_in_openbare_ruimte.stm>.

use of cameras for law enforcement purposes, where before the main purpose of camera surveillance was keeping public order.

In March 2002, ISP XS4ALL won a court case preventing well-known spam company Abfab from sending unsolicited commercial e-mail to its subscribers. Abfab appealed the decision but went bankrupt as a result of the negative publicity.[3904] The Supreme Court ruled in March 2004 that the provider "has exclusive rights to its computer capacity, transmission capacity and customer base (its computer system)" and may therefore forbid Abfab to send spam to its subscribers. Although the ruling confirms the possibility of ISPs to block spam, it goes much further and allows proprietary rights to prevail over freedom of speech, even in cases that have nothing to do with spam.

In 2003 and 2004 the transfer of passenger name records (PNR) to the United States was heavily debated in the Dutch media. After it was uncovered that US airline company Northwest Airlines transferred PNR to the National Aeronautics and Space Administration (NASA),[3905] Bits of Freedom requested that the Dutch Data Protection Authority investigate the transfer. Northwest is a partner of the Dutch airline KLM, the two companies operate code-sharing and integrated reservations. Bits of Freedom argued that large quantities of data from Dutch KLM passengers are likely to have been transferred to NASA. The DPA declined an investigation, saying it was likely a one-time event.[3906]

In May 2004, the Parliament passed the law on e-commerce (*Wet elektronische handel*) that implements the EU E-Commerce Directive (2000/31/EC). Under the law, hosting providers risk liability for apparently illegal content from their customers. Once they are notified, and the unlawfulness is "apparent," providers should take immediate action to block or remove the content. There is no unified notice and takedown procedure in the Netherlands that implements these legal obligations. In September 2004 Bits of Freedom conducted research into the notice and takedown procedure at Dutch ISPs by sending a bogus complaint through a Hotmail account about a webpage containing a public domain text. Seven out of 10 of the Internet providers in the Netherlands removed the text by the famous Dutch author Multatuli (who died in 1887), without even looking at the webpage, or verifying the identity of the plaintiff.[3907]

[3904] *See* XS4ALL News web page at <http://www.xs4all.nl/uk/news/overview/abfab.html>.

[3905] <http://www.epic.org/privacy/airtravel/nasa/>.

[3906] College Bescherming Persoonsgegevens homepage at <http://www.cbpweb.nl/documenten/med_uit_z2004-0310.htm>.

[3907] The Multatuli Project, Bits of Freedom, October 2004, <http://www.bof.nl/docs/researchpaperSANE.pdf>.

Since 2003 Dutch courts has ordered several foreign gamble web sites to make their sites inaccessible t Dutch Internet users. Dutch casinos and lotteries, which operate with a mandatory permit, argued that foreign web sites have an unfair competitive advantage. Gambling is widespread in the Netherlands but the Dutch government claims that it is maintaining a tight control that is being surpassed by Internet gambling.

In May 2004 the EU Directive on Privacy and Electronic Communications (2002/58/EC) was partly implemented by outlawing spam. Senders of commercial electronic messages will need prior consent of the e-mail address holder. During a hearing in Dutch Parliament in August 2003, Bits of Freedom asked for an obligation for senders to prove prior consent. An amendment including this proof of consent was added into the law. The ban on spam does not cover work e-mail addresses, a concession made after a fierce industry lobby to prevent such a proposal. Several persons and companies have since been fined for spamming. Also, proposals have been announced to include work e-mail addresses in the law, after the direct-marketing industry failed to agree on self-regulation regarding business-to-business e-mail marketing.

Major Privacy Case Law

Brein, the joint anti-piracy program of the entertainment industry, announced in April 2005 it would start 32 court cases against individual alleged peer-to-peer users. In order to obtain the identifying data of the users behind IP addresses from which music was unlawfully uploaded, Brein has sued five Dutch Internet providers. The providers had agreed to forward complaints from the copyright holders to their customers but refused to reveal the customers' identities. In total, Brein sent 50 cease and desist letters, demanding the recipient identify him- or herself, agree to pay an average fine of EUR 2,100, and sign a unlimited binding agreement to never "directly or indirectly be involved in any way or have an interest in unlawfully distributing materials on the Internet." If ever again caught in such a very broadly defined act, the signed agrees to pay a fine of EUR 5,000 per day.[3908] In June 2004, the Appeals Court of Amsterdam ruled in the case *Lycos v. Pessers* against webportal Lycos where the identity of one of its customers was demanded for alleged defamation.[3909] Although the Appeals Court

---

[3908] "New Wave of Lawsuits against European P2P Users," EDRI-gram, Number 3.8, April 20 2005, available at <http://www.edri.org/edrigram/number3.8/P2P>.

[3909] "Court attacks Dutch internet anonymity," EDRI-gram, July 2004, <http://www.edri.org/edrigram/number2.14/anonym>

acknowledged that the content on the website was not "apparently unlawful," the court nevertheless felt that Lycos was required to hand over the user's identity. A final ruling at the highest court is expected in the summer of 2005.[3910]

The Netherlands have seen little public debate about the use of RFID technology in retail and supermarkets until now. The main reason is that very few pilot projects in stores exist that make use of RFID tags with unique serial numbers (such as the Electronic Product Code, the EPC). ECP.NL, an e-commerce industry platform, has begun to write a first report on the privacy implication of RFID (the report is expected in June 2005). Bits of Freedom has published a position paper on RFID,[3911] as has the small ChristenUnie fraction in Parliament.[3912]

NGO Advocacy Work

In October 2004, Bits of Freedom organized the third Dutch Big Brother Awards.[3913] The awards were granted to EU Commissioner Bolkestein for his deal on passenger data with the US, Digidoor (a database for schools with personal data about students and no apparent design measures that provide privacy or security of the data) and the National Job Centres for spying on the Internet usage of their visitors. The EU mandatory data retention proposal got an award as "Most Appalling Proposal."[3914]

The Freedom of Information Act of 1991 is based on the constitutional right of access to information. It creates a presumption that documents created by a public agency should be available to everyone. Information can be withheld if it relates to international relations of the state, the "economic or financial interest of the state," investigation of criminal offenses, inspections by public authorities, or personal privacy. However, these exemptions must be balanced against the importance of the disclosure. Requesters can appeal denials to an administrative court that renders the final decision.

[3910] Court proceedings in Dutch, page maintained by Lycos, available at <http://www.lycos.nl/rechtzaak/>.

[3911] RFID position paper, Bits of Freedom, December 2004, available at <http://www.bof.nl/rfid/RFIDpositionpaper.html>.

[3912] Report on RFID, ChristenUnie, May 2005, available at <http://www.tweedekamer.christenunie.nl/index.php?Hoofd=/nieuws.php&tekstId=1000>.

[3913] The Big Brother Awards grant individuals, governmental entities or organizations awards for the most egregious privacy violations for which they have been responsible. The event is organized every year by Privacy International and affiliated non-governmental organizations around the world.

[3914] Dutch Big Brother Awards 2004 <http://www.bigbrotherawards.nl/index_uk.html>.

International Obligations

The Netherlands is a member of the Council of Europe (CoE) and has signed and ratified the CoE's Convention for the Protection of Individuals with Regard to Automatic Processing of Personal Data (ETS No. 108).[3915] It has signed and ratified the European Convention for the Protection of Human Rights and Fundamental Freedoms. In November 2001, the Netherlands signed, but has not ratified, the CoE's Convention on Cybercrime.[3916] It is a member of the Organization for Economic Cooperation and Development (OECD) and has adopted the OECD Guidelines on the Protection of Privacy and Transborder Flows of Personal Data.

New Zealand

Constitutional Privacy Framework

Article 21 of the New Zealand Bill of Rights Act 1990 states "Everyone has the right to be secure against unreasonable search or seizure, whether of the person, property, or correspondence or otherwise."[3917] The New Zealand Court of Appeal has interpreted this provision in several cases as protecting the important values and interests that comprise the right to privacy.[3918]

Data Protection Framework

New Zealand's Privacy Act of 1993 came into force on July 1, 1993, and has been amended several times.[3919] It regulates the collection, use and dissemination of personal information in both the public and private sectors. It also grants to

---

[3915] Signed May 7, 1982; ratified May 28, 1993; entered into force September 1, 1993.

[3916] Signed November 23, 2001.

[3917] Bill of Rights Act, 1990, Chapter 4, Section 21, available at
<http://www.oefre.unibe.ch/law/icl/nz01000_.html>.

[3918] Tim McBride, "Recent New Zealand Case Law on Privacy: Part I: Privacy Act and the Bill of Rights Act," Privacy Law & Reporter, January 2000, at 107.

[3919] Privacy Act 1993, available at <http://www.knowledge-basket.co.nz/privacy/legislation/1993028/toc.html>; Privacy Amendment Act 1993, available at <http://www.privacy.org.nz/slegisf.html>; Privacy Amendment Act 1994, available at <http://www.privacy.org.nz/slegisf.html>; Privacy Amendment Act 1996, available at <http://rangi.knowledge-basket.co.nz/gpacts/public/text/1996/an/142.html>; Privacy Amendment Act 1997, available at <http://rangi.knowledge-basket.co.nz/gpacts/public/text/1997/an/142.html>; Privacy Amendment Act 1998, available at <http://rangi.knowledge-basket.co.nz/gpacts/public/text/1998/an/057.html>; Privacy Amendment Act 2000, available at <http://rangi.knowledge-basket.co.nz/gpacts/public/text/2000/an/076.html>; and Privacy Amendment Act 2002, available at <http://rangi.knowledge-basket.co.nz/gpacts/public/text/2002/an/073.html>.

individuals the right to have access to personal information about them held by any agency. The Privacy Act applies to "personal information," which is any information about an identifiable individual, whether automatically or manually processed.[3920] Recent case law has held that the definition also applies to mentally processed information.[3921] The news media are exempt from the Privacy Act in relation to their news activities.

The Act creates 12 Information Privacy Principles generally based on the 1980 Organization for Economic and Cooperation Development (OECD) Guidelines and the information privacy principles in Australia's Privacy Act 1988. In addition, the legislation includes a new principle that deals with the assignment and use of unique identifiers. The Information Privacy Principles can be individually or collectively replaced by enforceable codes of practice for particular sectors or classes of information. At present, there are three complete sector-specific codes of practice in force: the Health Information Privacy Code 1994, the Telecommunications Information Privacy Code 2003, and the Credit Reporting Privacy Code 2004.[3922] There are several codes of practice that alter the application of single information privacy principles: the Superannuation Schemes Unique Identifier Code 1995, the Justice Sector Unique Identifier Code 1998, and the Post-Compulsory Education Unique Identifier Code 2001.[3923] In addition to the information privacy principles, the legislation contains principles relating to information held on public registers; it sets out guidelines and procedures in respect to information matching programs run by government agencies, and it makes special provisions for the sharing of law enforcement information among specialized agencies.

The Broadcasting Act of 1989 requires broadcasters to maintain standards that are consistent with "the observance of good taste and decency . . . the maintenance of law and order and the privacy of the individual."[3924] It establishes a Broadcasting Standards Authority (BSA) to oversee enforcement and to rule on complaints. The BSA has ruled on several privacy cases.[3925] Recently, particular

---

[3920] *See* Paul Roth, "What is 'Personal Information'?," 20(1) New Zealand Universities Law Review 40 (2002).

[3921] *See* Re Application by L – Information stored in person's memory (1997) 3 HRNZ 716 (Complaints Review Tribunal).

[3922] Available at <http://www.privacy.org.nz/comply/codes.html>. The Privacy Commissioner may issue codes of practice that modify the Information Privacy Principles set out in the Privacy Act to take into account the special characteristics of specific industries, agencies or types of personal information. These provisions may be more stringent or less stringent than the principles.

[3923] "How to Comply with the Privacy Act," available at <http://www.privacy.org.nz/comply/comptop.html>.

[3924] Available at <http://www.spectrum.net.nz/archive/acts.shtml>.

[3925] *See, e.g.*, Tim McBride, "Recent New Zealand Case Law on Privacy: Part II: the Broadcasting Standards Authority, the Media and Employment," Privacy Law & Reporter, February 2000, at 133.

controversy surrounded several television broadcasts that unreasonably intruded on the privacy of children. In March 1999, one program, widely publicized in advance, revealed the results of a DNA paternity test live on TV with mother, father and young child present.[3926] The Broadcasting Amendment Act of 2000, which came into effect on July 1, 2000, empowers the BSA to encourage the development and observance by broadcasters of codes of broadcasting practice in relation to the privacy of the individual.

In April 2005, the government introduced the Crimes (Intimate Covert Filming) Amendment Bill, which will amend the Crimes Act 1961 by creating three new offense provisions relating to the making of intimate visual recordings, the possession of intimate visual recordings, and the publishing, import, export, or sale of intimate visual recordings. The legislation is aimed at the surreptitious visual recording of another person in intimate circumstances without the person's consent or knowledge and in circumstances that the person would reasonably expect to be private (such as secret recording with a mobile phone camera of people undressing in a locker room). This legislation follows on from recommendations made by the Law Commission in 2004.[3927]

Data Protection Authority

The Office of the Privacy Commissioner is an independent oversight authority that was created prior to the Privacy Act by the 1991 Privacy Commissioner Act, which focused on the supervision of information matching among government departments.[3928] The Privacy Commissioner oversees compliance with the Privacy Act 1993, but does not function as a central data registration or notification authority. The Privacy Commissioner's principal powers and functions include promoting the objects of the Act, monitoring proposed legislation and government policies, dealing with complaints at first instance, approving and issuing codes of practice, and authorizing special exemptions from the information privacy principles, and reviewing public sector information matching programs. In June 2002, the Commissioner had 18 full-time and six part-time staff members.

Complaints by individuals are initially filed with the Privacy Commissioner, who then attempts to conciliate the matter. In the 2003-2004 fiscal year, there were 934 new complaints received. By contrast, in the year ending June 2002, the

---

[3926] "DNA Test Matches Father and Son on TV," The Dominion (Wellington), March 30, 1999.

[3927] Study Paper 15, Intimate Covert Filming, Wellington, June 2004.

[3928] Homepage <http://www.privacy.org.nz/>.

office received 1,044 new complaints and 6,772 inquiries, 1,049 complaints (new and from the year before) were closed during the year, and 85 percent were resolved without issuing a final opinion.[3929] The Commissioner regards the power to investigate and to require answers during investigations as "a vital element" in securing such a high conciliation rate. When conciliation fails, the Director of Human Rights Proceedings[3930] or the complainant (if the Director of Human Rights Proceedings is unwilling) can bring the matter before the Human Rights Review Tribunal, which can issue decisions and award declaratory relief, issue restraining or remedial orders, and award special and general damages up to NZD 200,000 (~USD 115,000).[3931]

Privacy Commissioner Marie Shroff has argued that privacy laws and press freedom are similar in that they both involve offering some protections and empowerment to citizens.[3932]

Current issues of concern include the growing aggregation of New Zealanders' DNA in public data banks.[3933] The permanent collection of these genetic profiles is arousing the interest of privacy and civil liberties groups, which are concerned that a population-wide database of DNA is being created, without public awareness, debate, or proper controls.

Commentators also note that in New Zealand it is widely accepted that employers are able to monitor all e-mails sent on work computers.[3934] A new health law, the Health (National Cervical Screening Programme) Amendment Act 2004, is raising privacy complaints because the once-private relationship between more than a million New Zealand women and their gynecologists has been undermined by new legislation on the National Cervical Screening Programme (NCSP), according to women's health advocate Barbara Robson.[3935] The legislation allows evaluators to investigate the case histories of any woman enrolled in the

---

[3929] New Zealand Privacy Commission, Annual Report for the Year Ended 30 June 2003, available at <http://www.privacy.org.nz/>.

[3930] The Director of Human Rights Proceedings is an official appointed under the Human Rights Act of 1993.

[3931] This limit can be raised by application to the High Court.

[3932] Commissioner Shroff is also quoted as saying, "Privacy is not about keeping secrets, but about retaining a level of control over your own information. . . . Although privacy concerns are sometimes positioned as being in opposition to press freedom, I don't see that as being the case." Gamble Warren, "Freedom to Publish," The Press (Christchurch), May 1, 2004, at 8D.

[3933] Courtney Dave, "Who's in Charge of DNA Bank?," The Press (Christchurch), April 28, 2004, at 15A.

[3934] Andrew Kelly, "NZ Bosses Free to Read Staff E-mails," The Dominion Post (Wellington), April 10, 2004 at 5.

[3935] Rankin Janine, "Privacy 'Undermined' by New Law," The Evening Standard (Palmerston North), March 4, 2004, at 3.

program without seeking her consent.[3936] The legislation is aimed at reducing death from cervical cancer through early detection screening. The Ministerial Inquiry into the Under-Reporting of Cervical Smear Abnormalities in the Gisbourne Region in April 2001 reported that privacy measures in the Health Act 1956 presented barriers to the effective functioning of this program, as women with detected abnormalities were unable to be contacted, and the efficacy of the screening program was unable to be evaluated. The new legislation aims to inform women about the screening program, and gives them the right to opt out of it if they do not wish their data be seen by evaluators.

Major Privacy Case Law

A landmark Employment Court ruling in April 2004 gave Air New Zealand the right to conduct random drug tests on its workers in "safety-sensitive areas."[3937] This was the first comprehensive decision on the issue in New Zealand. While the court ruled that the national airline may not impose random tests for drugs or alcohol across its workforce, it may undertake random testing of workers in certain circumstances: in safety sensitive areas; to carry out pre-employment testing of workers before they join the company; testing of workers whose behavior suggests they have taken drugs; and workers involved in an accident or near-miss.

In March 2004, the New Zealand Court of Appeal rejected broadcaster Mike Hosking's complaint of breach of privacy over the intended publication of photographs taken of his twin baby daughters on a public street.[3938] This was one of the very few privacy tort cases that went before the Court of Appeal in 2004.

The High Court ruled in July 2000 that the implementation of a nationwide driver's license system with a digitized photograph that was required by the 1998 Land Transport Act was legal. The law creates a national database of digitized photographs. The individual challenging the law appealed the ruling. The Court of Appeals rejected her appeal in April 2001, saying much of the case was based on misconceptions of the law.[3939]

[3936] *Id.*

[3937] NZ Amalgamated Engineering Printing and Manufacturing Union Inc v. Air New Zealand Ltd. (AC 22/04, 13 April 2004, Goddard CJ; Travis Colgan JJ),

[3938] Hosking v. Runting, [2003] 3 NZLR 385, available at <http://www.brookers.co.nz/legal/judgments/Default.asp?doc=2003\ca101.htm#Number1>.

[3939] "Photo Licence Appeal Rejected," The Dominion (Wellington), April 12, 2001.

In the summer of 2001, the Mental Health Commission began a study of privacy procedures in mental health services. The Privacy Commissioner participated in the work of the review board. In February 2002, the board issued its report, "A Review of the Implementation of the Privacy Act and Health Information Privacy Code by Mental Health Units of District Health Boards."[3940] The Law Commission reviewed the legal protection of privacy rights and the 1993 Privacy Act, and produced a discussion paper in February 2002, titled "Protecting Personal Information from Disclosure," for public comment.[3941] However, this exercise has apparently been abandoned.

The Criminal Investigations (Blood Samples) Act of 1995 authorized the establishment of a national DNA databank. Police are required to obtain an order from a High Court judge before a compulsory test can be conducted, and they can take samples only from suspects of violent crimes and convicted burglars. Voluntary samples from anyone can be included in the databank. In October 2000, police were ordered to reduce the number of voluntary DNA samples due to budgetary concerns. By 2002, however, it was reported that police were being advised to increase this number again and to try to obtain voluntary samples from anyone arrested with a prior criminal record.[3942] In February 2001, the Justice Minister announced that he planned to introduce legislation to allow DNA samples to be taken from burglary suspects.[3943] As of June 2004, the total number of DNA profiles stored in a DNA databank in New Zealand was 42,844. Of these, 36,439 were obtained by consent and 6,239 were obtained by compulsion orders.[3944] By contrast, in June 2003, the total number of DNA profiles stored in the national database was 33,892 (up from 24,001 in 2002). Of these, 28,614 were obtained by consent and 5,116 were obtained by compulsory order.[3945] In May 2002, a new NZD 3,000,000 (~USD 2,000,000) laboratory was opened in Auckland for the purpose of forensic DNA testing.[3946] Testing was carried out by the Institute of Environmental Science and Research (ESR).

[3940] Available at <http://www.mhc.govt.nz/publications/Publications/Privacy%20Review.pdf>.

[3941] Available at <http://www.lawcom.govt.nz/>. The New Zealand Law Commission is a statutory body that is charged with examining issues of law reform. It does so either on its own initiative or on reference by the government.

[3942] "Police DNA Drive," The Evening Post (Wellington), March 21, 2002.

[3943] "Police Say They Can Afford Bigger DNA Database," The Dominion (Wellington), February 13, 2001.

[3944] New Zealand Police Annual Report 2004, available at <http://www.police.govt.nz/resources/2004/annual-report/annual-report.pdf>.

[3945] New Zealand Police Annual Report 2003, available at <http://www.police.govt.nz/resources/2003/annualreport/>.

[3946] "DNA Laboratory to Be Ready in May," The Dominion (Wellington), February 23, 2002.

Wiretapping and Surveillance Rules

The New Zealand Crimes Act and Misuse of Drugs Act govern the use of police interception powers.[3947] Interception warrants authorize not just the interception of communications but also the placing of listening devices. A judge authorizes warrants where there are reasonable grounds to believe that certain offenses have been committed or are being contemplated. Emergency permits may be granted for the bugging of premises and, following the 1997 repeal of a prohibition, for telephonic interceptions. Those who disclose the contents of illegally intercepted private communications face two years in prison. However, those who disclose the contents of lawfully intercepted private communications are merely liable for a NZD 500 (~USD 290) fine.

In 2003-2004 the New Zealand police sought, and were granted, 18 interception warrants under the Misuse of Drugs Act. Nine renewed interception warrants were sought and granted under the Act.[3948] Under the Crimes Act, 15 interception warrants were granted and no renewals were sought. By contrast, in 2002-2003 the police sought and obtained 37 (new and renewed) interception warrants under the Misuse of Drugs Act and nine (new and renewed) interception warrants under the Crimes Act. No emergency permits were granted under the Crimes Act.[3949] In 2003-2004 a total of 93 warrants (new and renewed) were obtained under the Telecommunications Amendment Act 1997, whereas 85 warrants were obtained in 2002-2003 for obtaining call data analyzers (pen registers and trap-and-trace devices that obtain call information but not the contents of communications).

The New Zealand Security Intelligence Service (NZSIS), established under the New Zealand Security Intelligence Service Act of 1969,[3950] is also permitted to carry out electronic interceptions. The NZSIS has a staff of 145 full-time equivalents (up from 132 and 115 respectively from the previous years) and an annual budget of NZD 17 million (~USD 11,475,000). The majority of its work is devoted to threats to national security.[3951] The qct was amended in 1999 to allow for the NZSIS to enter premises to install wiretaps following a Court of

---

[3947] Part XIA, Crimes Act 196; Misuse of Drugs Act 1978.

[3948] New Zealand Police Annual Report 2004, *supra.*

[3949] New Zealand Police Annual Report 2003, *supra.*

[3950] New Zealand Security Intelligence Service Act of 1969, available at
<http://www.legislation.govt.nz/browse_vw.asp?content-set=pal_statutes>.

[3951] John Armstrong, "SIS Gives MPs New Details of NZ Terrorist Links," New Zealand Herald, December 9, 2000, available at
<http://www.nzherald.co.nz/storydisplay.cfm?thesection=news&thesubsection=&storyID=163879>.

Appeal case that prohibited the entering of premises without a warrant. The amendment also created a "foreign interception warrant."[3952] Another amendment created a Commissioner of Security Warrants to jointly issue warrants with the Prime Minister.[3953] The Minister in Charge of the NZSIS is required to submit an annual report to the House of Representatives. During the year ending June 2004, the Minister reported that 16 domestic interception warrants were in force. Of these, 13 were new interception warrants and three were carried over from the previous year. The average length of time that these warrants were in force was 165 days.[3954] According to the Minister's report, "the methods for interception and seizure used were listening devices and the copying of documents." The report also stated that foreign interception warrants were in force during the year but does not give any statistics for these warrants. Issues investigated during the 2003-2004 fiscal year included the following: information from a foreign national relating to the security of a foreign country; apparent links between individuals in or from New Zealand and international terrorist activities; individuals in New Zealand seeking to raise funds for terrorist organizations; links in New Zealand to weapons of mass destruction development programs overseas; people operating in New Zealand and overseas to procure dual-use equipment or technology for foreign governments; and foreign intelligence organizations conducting covert activity in New Zealand.

One agency not governed by the restrictions imposed on law enforcement and the NZSIS is the Government Communications Security Bureau (GCSB), the Signals Intelligence (SIGINT) agency for New Zealand. The GSCB was established by Executive Authority in 1977 and focuses on foreign intelligence. Operating as a virtual branch of the US National Security Agency, this agency maintains two intercept stations at Waihopai and Tangimoana. The Waihopai station routinely intercepts trans-Pacific and intra-Pacific communications and passes the collected intelligence to NSA headquarters. David Lange, a former Prime Minister of New Zealand, said that he and other ministers were told very little about the operations of GCSB while they were in power. Of particular interest to GCSB and NSA are the communications of the governments of neighboring Pacific island states.[3955] GCSB was specifically exempted from the provisions of the Crimes Act in 1997.[3956]

[3952] New Zealand Security Intelligence Service Amendment Act 1999.

[3953] New Zealand Security Intelligence Service Amendment (No. 2) Act 1999.

[3954] Report of the New Zealand Security Intelligence Service to the House of Representatives for the year ended 30 June 2002, available at <http://www.nzsis.govt.nz/ar02/part2.html>.

[3955] Nicky Hager, Secret Power: New Zealand's Role in the International Spy Network (Nelson, NZ: Craig Potton 1996).

[3956] Crimes (Exemption of Listening Device) Order 1997 (SR 1997/145).

The Government Communications Security Bureau Act was enacted in 2003. This enactment places the GCSB on a statutory footing. In August 2001, the government announced that it set up a new unit within the Government Communications Security Bureau dedicated to the protection of the nation's critical infrastructure from cyber threats by Internet hackers or computer viruses. The Centre for Critical Infrastructure Protection (CCIP) was scheduled to begin operations in April 2002.[3957]

The Government has created major new surveillance powers for these state agencies. New Zealand's Parliament passed the Crimes Amendment Bill,[3958] effective October 1, 2003, which grants broader powers to police and security agencies to intercept electronic communications.[3959] The Crimes Amendment Act, overwhelmingly passed by Parliament in July 2003, gives intelligence agencies additional powers to intercept communications, with High Court approval, while also criminalizing similar unauthorized activities as well as the distribution or possession of computer hacking programs.[3960] The controversial anti-hacking legislation gives police explicit authority to intercept electronic communications. The new law makes it illegal to intercept, access, use or damage data stored on computers without proper authorization. It also makes the sale, distribution or possession of hacking programs illegal.[3961] The Act prohibits the unauthorized interception of electronic communications and makes hacking and denial of service attacks illegal, but would grant exemptions to the police, the NZSIS and the GCSB, allowing them to secretly hack into individuals' computers and intercept e-mail, text messages, and faxes. Police are required to specify a person, place, and specific electronic address, phone number, or similar facility when applying for an interception warrant.

Even more controversial was the Telecommunications (Interception Capabilities) Act 2004. Similar to the United States Communications Assistance for Law Enforcement Act (CALEA) of 1994, this legislation would require all Internet Service Providers (ISPs) and telephone companies to upgrade their systems so that they would be able to assist the police and intelligence agencies, including the Government Communications Security Bureau (GCSB) and Security Intelligence Service (SIS), intercept communications. The Bill would oblige

---

[3957] Adam Creed, "New Zealand Center to Combat Cyber Threats," Newsbytes, August 8, 2001.

[3958] Crimes Act of 1961, as amended, available at <http://www.netlaw.co.nz/crime.cfm?PageID=28>.

[3959] Francis Till, "Police Win Intercept Rights," The National Business Review, July 11, 2003, at 31.

[3960] Associated Press, "NZ Police Get Tech Crime Powers," AustralianIT, July 4, 2003.

[3961] Crimes Act of 1961 (as amended), available at <http://www.legislation.govt.nz/browse_vw.asp?content-set=pal_statutes>.

telecommunications companies and ISPs to intercept phone calls and e-mails at the behest of the police and security services.[3962] The legislation would also require a telecommunications operator to decrypt the communications of a customer if that operator had provided the encryption facility.[3963] It would not require individuals to hand over encryption keys.

Prior to introducing these proposals, the government sought the advice of the New Zealand Law Commission on whether such a requirement would violate Section 21 of the New Zealand Bill of Rights on unreasonable searches and seizures. In its report, issued in February 2002, the Law Commission concluded, "[T]he existence of comparable obligations in other democracies establishes reasonably conclusively either that the search is not thereby rendered unreasonable or that if there is a limitation of the rights described in Section 21 it can be demonstrably justified in a free and democratic society." The Commission recommended that the law be amended to impose an obligation on third parties to provide all reasonable and necessary information and assistance (including passwords and decryption keys) to enable law enforcement officers to access, copy or convert the data into intelligible form.[3964]

Anti-terrorism Measures

Since the terrorist attacks on September 11, 2001, the New Zealand government has been working to strengthen counter-terrorism laws.[3965] Before September 11, 2001, New Zealand was a party to only eight of the 12 conventions that the international community had negotiated over the last 30 years. However, according to Foreign Minister Phil Goff, as of December 2003. New Zealand is a party to all 12 United Nations terrorism conventions.[3966]

The Terrorism Suppression Act 2002 was enacted on October 17, 2002 to put in place certain measures to combat terrorism, as well as implement New Zealand's obligations under the Bombings Convention, the Financing Convention, the Anti-

---

[3962] Tom Pullar-Strecker, "Bugging Bill Fears Unfounded," New Zealand Infotech Weekly, November 17, 2003, at 2.

[3963] "Interception Capability – Government Decisions," New Zealand Government Executive Press Release, March 21, 2002, available at <http://www.executive.govt.nz/speech.cfm?speechralph=37658&SR=0>.

[3964] New Zealand Law Reform Commission, Study Paper 12, "Electronic Technology and Police Investigations: Some Issues," February 2002, available at <http://www.lawcom.govt.nz/Documents/Publications/SP%2012%2028-2-02.pdf>.

[3965] Phil Goff, "NZ Now Party to All 12 UN Terrorism Conventions," December 23, 2003, available at <http://www.beehive.govt.nz/ViewDocument.cfm?DocumentID=18735>.

[3966] Id.

Terrorism Resolution, and (as added by the Terrorism Suppression Amendment Act 2003) the Nuclear Material Convention and the Plastic Explosives Convention. The act creates the offense of "terrorist bombing," and contains measures that aim at combating the financing or other support of terrorist acts. The act also provides for the designation of terrorist entities.

In June 2005, the Terrorism Suppression Amendment Act (No. 2) was enacted to update the original 2002 Act in two important respects: to ensure that the designation of terrorist entities under the original legislation does not expire (which would have placed New Zealand in violation of UN Security Council resolutions), and to bring New Zealand law into more complete compliance with Security Council and OECD-based Financial Action Task Force requirements to criminalize the act of providing financial support to terrorist organizations. The legislation also tightens the requirements relating to international and domestic wire transfer of funds and the cross-border transfer of cash by couriers. Further anti-terrorist and anti-money-laundering measures are being considered. The parliamentary Foreign Affairs, Defence and Trade Committee is currently engaged in reviewing the Terrorism Suppression Act and is scheduled to report back to the House of Representatives before December 1, 2005.[3967]

The government introduced the Counter-Terrorism Bill on December 17, 2002, which has not yet been enacted. This measure, intended to implement obligations arising from international conventions relating to the suppression of terrorism, proposes to introduce new and sweeping criminal offenses.[3968] The bill introduces powers to search and seize computer databases, and to seize and detain goods at border checks if there is cause to suspect that the recipient is "eligible" for designation as a terrorist. It also establishes a regime for the use of tracking devices (defined as devices which, "when installed in or on any thing, may be used to help ascertain, by electronic or other means, the location of any thing or person"). The bill could force individuals to disclose their passwords, even in non-terrorism related investigations, or else face three months in jail or a fine of NZD 2,000 (~USD 1,350).

[3967] New Zealand Government, Press Release, "Goff on Terrorism Suppression Amendment Bill," June 17, 2005.

[3968] Phil Goff, "Counter Terrorism Act Boosts Government Fight against Terrorism," October 22, 2003, available at <http://www.beehive.govt.nz/ViewDocument.cfm?DocumentID=18168>. According to Prime Minister Helen Clark, New Zealand has not taken any special measures after the March 2004 bombings in Madrid, Spain, because it already had extra counter-terrorism capabilities in place following the September 11, 2001 attacks. Kevin Taylor, "NZ Anti-terrorism Measures in Place, Says Helen Clark," The New Zealand Herald, March 16, 2004.

Other recent parliamentary measures implicate privacy and data protection interests. These include the Border Security Bill 2003 and the Maritime Security Act 2004. The aim of the Border Security Bill is to strengthen border control measures against terrorism and trans-national crime, including drug smuggling, across both travel and trade sectors.[3969] It also seeks to establish the framework to enable New Zealand to respond to the United States' Container Security Initiative. The Maritime Security Act adds to the framework of laws seeking to reduce the risk of terrorism to international shipping.[3970] New Zealand is a party to the 1974 International Convention for the Safety of Life at Sea (SOLAS). The Maritime Security Bill was intended to give effect to these requirements under the SOLAS Convention.[3971]

Unsolicited E-mails

New Zealand does not yet have anti-spam legislation. InternetNZ,[3972] a non-profit Internet interest group, created the Anti-Spam Task Force, which counts the New Zealand Direct Marketing Association among its members. The group has met with the New Zealand government, held a conference in November 2003, funded a member to attend the OECD Conference on Spam, and worked with the press. The group encourages all ISPs to refer their customers to their Web site, which includes advice to individuals and businesses, and a discussion of legislative activity in the country. In February 2004, the Telecommunications Carriers Forum adopted the SMS Anti-Spam Code.[3973] It has been ratified by Telecom, Vodafone, TelstraClear, TUANZ, WorldxChange, CallPlus, BCL, Vector Communications, and the Direct Marketing Association. The Internet Society of New Zealand, the Direct Marketing Association, and the Telecommunications Carriers Forum are currently developing a voluntary industry code of practice, which is intended to work in conjunction with the government's proposed legislation in this area. The code will provide for a greater level of detail in order to assist direct marketers in complying with the new law.[3974] The government is expected to enact legislation in this area in the near future, modeled on the Australian law. A proposed Unsolicited Electronic

---

[3969] Rick Barker, "Putting New Zealand Security on the Front Foot," May 20, 2004, available at <http://www.beehive.govt.nz/ViewDocument.cfm?DocumentID=19768>.

[3970] Ministry of Transportation, Maritime Security, available at <http://www.transport.govt.nz/business/maritime/maritime-security.php>.

[3971] Id.

[3972] Stop Spam homepage <http://stopspam.net.nz>.

[3973] Available on the Telecommunications Carriers Forum website: <http://www.tcf.org.nz/outputs/>.

[3974] See Action on Anti-spam Code: Working Party Convened," available at <http://www.internetnz.net.nz/news/040205aspam.htm>.

Messages Bill will apply to e-mails, text messages, and instant messaging services. Opt-in provisions will apply to commercial messages, and opt-out provisions to non-commercial marketing messages that promote an organization's aims or ideals.[3975]

Transborder Dataflows

New Zealand is one of several countries involved in negotiations with the European Commission concerning the "adequacy" of its privacy regime in relation to the European Union Data Protection Directive (1995/46/EC). Since 1998 the Commission has been urging the Government to introduce two minor amendments to the Privacy Act in order to secure a finding of adequacy. The first amendment would remove the existing requirement that in order to make an access or correction request, an individual must be a New Zealand citizen or permanent resident, or present in New Zealand at the time the request is made. The second would introduce a limited data export control to regulate the transfer of personal information outside New Zealand. On December 12, 2000, these changes were finally included in the Statutes Amendment Bill[3976] and submitted to Parliament. Accordingly, it was expected that these amendments would be approved and enacted without delay.[3977] In the fall of 2001, however, one party withdrew its support of one of the amendments. In his annual report for the year ending June 30, 2001, the Privacy Commissioner encouraged "those responsible for the business of the House of Representatives [to] ensure that whatever vehicle these amendments proceed in is given priority." There has been no apparent progress on this issue. The Statutes Amendment Bill has not yet been re-introduced.

Open Government

The Official Information Act of 1982[3978] and the Local Government Official Information and Meetings Act of 1987[3979] are freedom of information laws

---

[3975] *See* the Cabinet paper "Legislating Against Unsolicited Electronic Messages Sent for Marketing or Promotional Purposes (Spam)," available on the website of the Ministry of Economic Development <http://www.med.govt.nz/pbt/infotech/spam/cabinet/paper-one/index.html>, and the government's press release: "Minister Unveils Anti-Spam Law Proposal," available at <http://www.beehive.govt.nz/nz/ViewDocument.aspx?DocumentID=22285>.

[3976] A statutes amendment bill is a procedure designed for the introduction of non-controversial legislation.

[3977] Office of the Privacy Commissioner, Press Release, "Proposed Amendments to the Privacy Act Addressing the Questions of Adequacy under the EU Data Protection Directive, December 15, 2000, available at <http://www.privacy.org.nz/media/prppaam.html>.

[3978] Official Information Act 1982, available at <http://www.ombudsmen.govt.nz/official.htm>.

governing the public sector. The Official Information Act is seen as an important weapon to oversee the actions of the executive and ministers.[3980] There are significant interconnections between this freedom of information legislation and the Privacy Act in subject matter, administration, and jurisprudence, so much so that the three enactments may be viewed, in relation to access to information, as complementary components of one overall statutory scheme. The Office of the Ombudsman supervises enforcement.[3981] The Ombudsman hears around 1,100 complaints each year under the Official Information Act and 170 each year under the Local Government Official Information and Meetings Act. The Privacy Commissioner and the Ombudsmen work closely together where Official Information Act requests involve privacy issues.

International Obligations

New Zealand is a member of the Organization for Economic Cooperation and Development (OECD) and has adopted the OECD Guidelines on the Protection of Privacy and Transborder Flows of Personal Data.

Self-governing Territories

The Privacy Act does not apply to self-governing territories associated with New Zealand, the Cook Islands and Niue, nor does it apply to the soon-to-be self-governing territory of Tokelau.

Federal Republic of Nigeria

Chapter IV, § 37 of the 1999 Constitution of the Federal Republic of Nigeria declares that "the privacy of citizens, their homes, correspondence, telephone conversations, and telegraphic communications is hereby guaranteed and protected."[3982] The Constitution also allows courts to exclude certain parties from judicial proceedings for "the protection of the private lives of parties."[3983]

[3979] Local Government Official Information and Meetings Act 1987, available at
<http://www.ombudsmen.govt.nz/local.htm>.

[3980] Richard Worth, "Bill Boosts Secrecy Powers," The National Business Review (New Zealand), May 21, 2004, at 32.

[3981] Homepage <http://www.ombudsmen.govt.nz/>.

[3982] 1999 Constitution of the Federal Republic of Nigeria, Chapter IV, § 37, available at <http://www.nigeria-law.org/ConstitutionOfTheFederalRepublicOfNigeria.htm>.

[3983] *Id.* at Chapter IV, §36 (4)(a).

However, the Constitution's ban on secret societies[3984] raises concerns regarding the privacy of association.

National Information Technology Development Association

The principal body for Nigerian information technology policy is the National Information Technology Development Agency (NITDA), a sub-agency of the Nigerian Communications Commission. NITDA developed a Nigerian Information Technology (IT) Policy, which was approved by the Nigerian Federal Executive Council in 2001.[3985] The IT Policy identifies some of its objectives as, "promot[ing] legislation (Bills & Acts) for the protection of on-line, business transactions, privacy and security,"[3986] and "enhanc[ing] freedom and access to digital information at all levels while protecting personal privacy."[3987] The IT Policy names as one of its strategies, "[e]nsur[ing] the protection of individual and collective privacy, security, and confidentiality of information."[3988]

The menace of fraudsters soliciting victims via e-mail prompted the Nigerian government in 2002 to create a National Committee to address the problem.[3989] NITDA was involved in this process, and one of the committee's recommendations was a draft Cybercrime Act that included a Data Retention Provision that declared, "[a]ll service providers under this Act shall have the responsibility of keeping all transactional records of operations generated in their systems and networks for a minimum period of five years."[3990] This provision raised privacy concerns as the draft Act defined "service providers" as "Internet service providers, cybercafés, communications service providers, application service providers, any individual or body corporate that deploys information and communication technology resources in Nigeria."[3991] This broad definition of service providers could have extended the five-year data retention requirement to virtually all Internet communications in Nigeria. In the final draft of the Act,

---

3984 *Id.* at Chapter IV, §38 (4).

3985 "The Nigerian National Information Technology Policy," Jidaw Systems website <http://www.jidaw.com/policy.html>.

3986 "Nigerian National Policy for Information Technology: USE IT" iv, available at <http://www.nitda.gov.ng/docs/policy/ngitpolicy.pdf>.

3987 *Id.* at 32.

3988 *Id.* at 33.

3989 Sam Olukoya, "Nigeria Grapples with E-Mail Scams," BBC News Online, April 23, 2002, available at <http://news.bbc.co.uk/1/hi/world/africa/1944801.stm>.

3990 Femi Oyesanya, "The Nigerian Patriot A[ct] Is Coming: Compliments of NITDA," Gamji.com News, July 6, 2004, available at <http://www.gamji.com/article3000/NEWS3569.htm>.

3991 *Id.*

however, the five year requirement has been eliminated.[3992] New requirements have been added to ensure that information service providers retain records of traffic and transactions on their networks, which must be made available to security agencies upon request.[3993] Another concern is that the data retention provision provides no definition for "transactional records."[3994] This term has the potential to cover a wide range of data and intrude on individuals' privacy.[3995]

Nigerian Evidence Act

The Nigerian Evidence Act protects the confidentiality of communication during marriage. It provides that no husband or wife shall be compelled to disclose any communication made to him or her during marriage by his or her spouse; nor shall he or she be permitted to disclose any such communication unless the person who made it, or that person's representative, consents, except in suits between married persons or proceedings in which one married person is prosecuted for certain specified offenses.[3996]

Sharia – Islamic Law

The operation of *Sharia* Law[3997] in 12 northern Nigerian states[3998] also raises issues of privacy. Of particular concern is a provision in several states for the punishment of adultery by stoning to death.[3999] While no one has been stoned for adultery under the *Sharia* laws, several accused Nigerian women have had to undergo judicial proceedings in which, by necessity, the consideration of the details of their sexual lives have been the basis for both their prosecution and defense.[4000] Criminalization of *zina*, or sexually related offenses, is used to deprive both men and women of their rights to privacy and to freedom of

---

[3992] Femi Oyesanya, "Nigeria: Data Retention: A Cautionary Exploration (I)," Business Day, March 23, 2005, available at <http://www.businessdayonline.com/index.php?fArticleId=6712>.

[3993] *Id.*

[3994] Balancing Act News Update, Issue No. 210, available at <http://www.balancingact-africa.com/news/back/balancing-act_210.html>; Oyesanya, "The Nigerian Patriot Act is Coming."

[3995] Balancing Act News Update, Issue No. 210, *supra.*

[3996] Evidence Act, Laws of the Federation of Nigeria, 1990, Cap 112.

[3997] The *Sharia* is a body of Islamic law that governs not only aspects of religious faith, but also offers dictates for the conduct of everyday secular activities.

[3998] Dan Isaacs, "Nigerian in Crisis over Sharia Law," BBC News Online, March 26, 2002, available at <http://news.bbc.co.uk/1/hi/world/africa/1893589.stm>.

[3999] *Id.*

[4000] *Id.*

expression and association.[4001] Since 2000, at least 10 individuals have been sentenced to death and dozens have been sentenced to amputation or flogging.[4002] While *Sharia* courts continue to issue death sentences, no sentence has been implemented since 2002.[4003] The number of sentences issued by *Sharia* courts has decreased, and authorities seem to be reluctant to carry out sentences.[4004] In 2004, appellate courts overturned three death sentences.[4005]

National Identity Card System

A national identity card system was first conceived in 1979 by then-Military Head of State, General Obasanjo.[4006] The Department of National Civic Registration was established at that time, with the responsibility of issuing national identity cards.[4007] Since then, however, there have been many bumps in the implementation process.[4008] In February 2003, the Nigerian government, headed by President Obasanjo, launched an extensive National Identification Card Drive in which everybody over 18 years of age was eligible to participate.[4009] While registration for the identity card is not compulsory, those who choose to participate are required to provide information that includes name, age, sex, address, occupation, state of origin, local government area, height measurement, thumbprint, and passport photograph.[4010] While possession of an identity card is not required, it may be necessary to have a card to obtain government services.[4011] Of Nigeria's estimated 120 million inhabitants, about 60 million citizens are eligible to register for the national identity card.[4012] During

---

[4001] Amnesty International, Report 2005, Nigeria, available at <http://web.amnesty.org/report2005/nga-summary-eng>.

[4002] "Nigeria: Under Islamic Law, Rights still Unprotected," Human Rights Watch, September 21, 2004, available at <http://hrw.org/english/docs/2004/09/21/nigeri9364.htm>.

[4003] Human Rights Watch, World Report 2005, Nigeria, available at <http://hrw.org/english/docs/2005/01/13/nigeri9883.htm>.

[4004] *Id.*

[4005] Amnesty International, Report 2005, Nigeria, *supra.*

[4006] "SAGEM Resumes ID Cards Production," Africa News, June 3, 2004.; "Nigeria: Collect Your ID Cards, FG Urges," Africa News, March 6, 2005.

[4007] "Nigeria: Collect Your ID Cards, FG Urges," *supra.*

[4008] "SAGEM Resumes ID Cards Production," *supra.*

[4009] Nigerian Information Service Center, "National Identity Card for Nigerians," February 20, 2003, available at <http://www.nigeriaembassyusa.org/022103_2.shtml>.

[4010] "Nigerians Register for National Identity Card from Today," NigeriaBusinessInfo.com, February 18, 2003, available at <http://www.nigeriabusinessinfo.com/id-card180203.htm>.

[4011] "Bad Start for Nigerian ID Scheme," BBC News, February 19, 2003, available at <http://news.bbc.co.uk/2/hi/Africa/2780235.stm>.

[4012] *Id.*

the registration period from February to March of 2004, 52 million Nigerians registered for the cards.[4013]

Despite allegations that the identity card contract was corruptly awarded, in 2004 the government reaffirmed its commitment to the project and announced that the first batch of cards were ready for collection.[4014] In June 2004, Sagem, the contractor producing the identity cards, returned to Nigeria to begin producing the cards, after having left the country following corruption allegations.[4015] Production of all cards for registered Nigerians is expected to be completed by mid-2005.[4016] The cards are being produced and distributed state by state.[4017] As of March 2005, the cards have been distributed in the Federal Capital Territory (Abuja) and five states – Bayelsa, Yobe, Ogun, Benue, and Adamawa.[4018] The latest identity card scandal involves allegations that millions of aliens have registered for national identity cards, thus defeating one of the objectives of the system.[4019] To respond to this, the Minister of Internal Affairs has requested that the Nigeria Immigration Service strictly monitor identity card distribution.[4020]

The identification card system was intended to provide data for government planning, to assist in identification of illegal immigrants, and to enhance national security and cohesion.[4021] The identity card may also assist the Nigerian Police in investigation and control of crime.[4022] In addition, the Ministry of Internal Affairs anticipates that the identity card project will resolve the conflict between the north and south over which region is more populous.[4023] The system is opposed by some northern politicians who fear that the identification card may be used to verify other population records, including voter rolls.[4024]

Many Nigerians, especially those in the northern part of the country, objected to use of the national identity card to obtain voter cards for the elections of April

---

[4013] "SAGEM Resumes ID Cards Production," *supra*.

[4014] Iyefu Adoba, "FG Restates Commitment to ID Card Project," This Day, June 9, 2004, available at <http://allafrica.com/stories/200406090330.html>.

[4015] "SAGEM Resumes ID Cards Production," *supra*.

[4016] Adoba, "FG Restates Commitment to ID Card Project," *supra*.

[4017] *Id.*

[4018] "Nigeria: Collect Your ID Cards, FG Urges," *supra*.

[4019] "Nigeria: Shocker over National Identity Card Scheme," Africa News, March 6, 2005.

[4020] *Id.*

[4021] "Bad Start for Nigerian ID Scheme," *supra*; "Obstacles to National I.D. Card Project Identified," This Day (Nigeria) – AAGM, November 9, 2004.

[4022] "Obstacles to National I.D. Card Project Identified," *supra*.

[4023] "National ID Card Will Reconcile Nigerians," Africa News, August 9, 2004.

[4024] "Bad Start for Nigerian ID Scheme," *supra*.

and May 2003.[4025] However, because the methods of the Independent National Electoral Commission (INEC) produced a tally of validly registered voters that was almost identical to the number of persons registered under the national identity card program (about 61 million), it turned out there was no need to use the national identity card to obtain a voter card.[4026]

Freedom of Information

Under current practices, most government information in Nigeria, even basic facts and information, is classified as top secret.[4027] In addition, a number of laws prevent civil servants from divulging official facts and figures.[4028] The most significant of these laws is the Official Secrets Act, which makes it an offense for civil servants to give out government information and for anyone to receive or produce such information. In addition, government departments often withhold information from one another.[4029]

A Freedom of Access to Information Bill is pending in the Nigerian National Assembly. In 1999, a Freedom of Information Bill was introduced in the House of Representatives. It was first introduced by a private initiative of human rights advocates.[4030] However, the legislature's four-year term passed without a vote on the bill.[4031] The draft bill would have allowed citizens and non-citizens to make information requests, mandated the annual publication of certain operational records by every government institution, and provided several exemptions to the disclosure requirement (*e.g.*, certain international affairs and defense matters, certain law enforcement and investigation information, and information of a personal nature).[4032] The bill was resubmitted to the current National Assembly in 2003.[4033] The Freedom of Access to Information Bill 2004 seeks to provide access to public records while protecting those records that should not be public

---

[4025] T.A. Akinyele, "The 2003 Nigerian Elections that Broke the Jinx," West Africa Review, available at <http://www.westafricareview.com/issue5/akinyele.htm>.

[4026] *Id.*

[4027] Sam Olukoya, "Rights-Nigeria: Passage of Freedom of Information Bill Stalled," IPS-Inter Press Service, June 21, 2004, available at <http://www.ipsnews.net/Africa/interna.asp?idnews=24297>; "Nigeria; Mother of All Democratic Dividends: Benefits of FOI Bill," Africa News, November 17, 2004.

[4028] Olukoya, "Rights-Nigeria: Passage of Freedom of Information Bill Stalled," *supra*.

[4029] *Id.*

[4030] Wahab Abdulah, Tunde Sesan & Margaret Odeyemi, "Atiku, Attah Back Freedom of Information Law," Vanguard (Nigeria) – AAGM, May 4, 2005.

[4031] Olukoya, "Rights-Nigeria: Passage of Freedom of Information Bill Stalled," *supra*.

[4032] Freedom of Information Bill 1999, available at <http://www.internews.org/mra/freeinfo/freeinfo.htm>.

[4033] Olukoya, "Rights-Nigeria: Passage of Freedom of Information Bill Stalled," *supra*.

knowledge.[4034] The bill facilitates greater access to federal, state, and local government information.[4035] The bill defines "public record" as "a document in any form having been prepared or having been or being used, received, or possessed or under the control of any public or private bodies relating to matters of public interest."[4036] However, the bill protects an officer who refuses to release the information or record requested if it is deemed to contain information "the disclosure of which may be injurious to the conduct of international affairs and the defence of the Federal Republic of Nigeria."[4037] The category of "injurious" information includes "trade secret, financial, commercial or technical information that belongs to the Government of the Federal Republic of Nigeria or any State or Local Government thereof."[4038] Based on fears of public officials about unrestricted access to information by those who are not Nigerian citizens, the bill would provide access to Nigerians only.[4039] The bill has been vigorously promoted by the Freedom of Information Coalition, a group of more than 100 media groups, business interests, and human rights organizations.[4040] The bill was passed by the House in August 2004,[4041] but it must still be passed by the Nigerian Senate and signed into law by the Executive.[4042]

The Lagos State Government is also drafting a Freedom of Information Bill.[4043] The state Commissioner of Information and Strategy has indicated plans to set up an information center where researchers could obtain information about state governance.[4044] Lagos State has also indicated plans to translate the 1999 Constitution into Yoruba language.[4045] According to the state Commissioner of Information and Strategy, this will enable people at the grassroots level to know their rights.[4046]

[4034] "Nigeria; House Commences Debate on Freedom of Information Bill," Africa News, August 6, 2004.

[4035] "Nigeria; House Passes Freedom of Information Bill," Africa News, August 26, 2004.

[4036] Id.

[4037] Id.

[4038] Id.

[4039] "Nigeria; House Commences Debate on Freedom of Information Bill," supra.

[4040] Olukoya; "Campaign on Freedom of Information Bill Begins," This Day (Nigeria), August 2, 2004.

[4041] "Nigeria; House Passes Freedom of Information Bill," supra.

[4042] "Nigeria; Freedom of Information Bill," Africa News, October 25, 2004.

[4043] "Nigeria: Lagos to Send Freedom of Information Bill to National Assembly," Africa News, May 29, 2004.

[4044] Id.

[4045] Id.

[4046] Id.

Recent Developments

The Internal Affairs Ministry has begun introduction of a new Harmonised ECOWAS Passport, which will replace the country's previous passport.[4047] The new passport is electronic and contains an individual's biometric features – fingerprints, eyes, and face.[4048] The government intends to issue the new passport, and withdraw the old one, in 2005.[4049] Nigeria anticipates being one of the first countries to have a biometric passport.[4050]

To help control the current crime wave in Nigeria, in May 2005 the Federal Executive Council, a body composed of the President and his Ministers, approved NGN 297 million (approximately USD 2.21 million) for the purchase and installation of automated fingerprinting machines for the Nigeria Police.[4051] The machines will be installed at the Police Force Headquarters in Abuja, state commands, and other police posts throughout the nation.[4052] The Nigerian government has also begun to create a database for the prison service that will contain photographs of inmates throughout the country.[4053]

To enhance security at the University of Lagos, in March 2005 the University administration announced that its students would be required to carry fingerprint cards.[4054] This development is partly in response to a violent student protest at the University in January 2005.[4055] The school was closed for two months, and reopened in March following a re-registration process that included issuance of fingerprint cards.[4056] To be issued a card, students were required to supply photographs of themselves and their guarantors, provide personal data, and sign an undertaking to be of good conduct.[4057]

[4047] "ID Card Production Resumes," Africa News, June 16, 2004.

[4048] "Nigeria: Issuance of Identity Cards to Resume on 8 November," BBC Monitoring International Reports, November 4, 2004.

[4049] *Id.*

[4050] *Id.*

[4051] "Fingerprinting Equipment to Aid Police," Nigeriafirst.org <http://www.nigeriafirst.org/article_3932.shtml>.

[4052] *Id.*

[4053] "Nigeria: Issuance of Identity Cards to Resume on 8 November," BBC Monitoring International Reports, November 4, 2004.

[4054] "Nigeria: Unilag Students Get Finger-Print Identity Cards," Africa News, March 31, 2005.

[4055] *Id.*

[4056] *Id.*

[4057] *Id.*

International Commitments

Representatives from the Nigerian legislature participated in the Study Group on Access to Information in July 2004, along with representatives from Fiji Islands, India, South Africa, Trinidad and Tobago, British Columbia, Scotland, and Ghana.[4058] To help prevent terrorism at sea and in ports, the United Nations has sponsored a biometric identity verification system that could affect 1.2 million maritime workers.[4059] Nigeria is one of only three countries to have ratified the International Labor Organization (ILO) Seafarers Identity Documents Convention 2003, which implements this international biometric identity verification system.[4060] The Convention requires ratification by two countries, and came into force in February 2005.[4061] Ratifying states will be required to issue new documents that conform to the standards for converting two fingerprints into a biometric template that will be stored in an internationally standardized barcode printed on the Seafarers' Identity Document.[4062]

Kingdom of Norway

Constitutional Privacy Framework

The Norwegian Constitution of 1814 does not have a specific provision dealing with the protection of privacy.[4063] The closest provision is Article 102, which prohibits searches of private homes except in "criminal cases." More generally, Article 110(c) of the Constitution places state authorities under an express duty to "respect and secure human rights."[4064] In 1952, the Norwegian Supreme Court held that there exists in Norwegian law a general legal protection of "personality," which embraces a right to privacy. This protection of personality exists independently of statutory authority but helps form the basis of the latter

---

[4058] "PanAfrica: Parlimentarians Call for Greater Access to Information," Africa News, July 14, 2004.

[4059] "Biometric Identity Verification System Comes into Force," The Press Trust of India, February 11, 2005.

[4060] *Id.*

[4061] *Id.*

[4062] *Id.*

[4063] The Constitution of the Kingdom of Norway, English version available at <http://odin.dep.no/odin/engelsk/norway/system/032005-990424/> (this URL (as of May 20, 2005) links to the text of the Constitution as it existed in 1995; more recent amendments to the Constitution, particularly to Article 100 (freedom of speech – *see infra*), are not reflected therein); the current Norwegian version (*Kongeriget Norges Grundlov*), with latest amendments as of September 30, 2004, is available at <http://www.lovdata.no/all/nl-18140517-000.html>.

[4064] Lee A. Bygrave & Ann Helen Aaro, Norway, International Privacy, Publicity and Personality Laws 333 (M. Henry ed., 2001).

(including data protection legislation), and can be applied by the courts on a case-by-case basis.[4065] A statutory protection for privacy is granted by Section 390 of the Criminal Code 1902. Section 390 provides a penalty for violations of privacy caused by "public disclosure of information relating to personal or domestic affairs."[4066]

The Norwegian Constitution also protects freedom of speech (Article 100). Persons may not be legally liable for disseminating or receiving information, ideas, or messages if the information can be justified under the rubric of freedom of expression (*i.e.*, the seeking of truth, the promotion of democracy, or the expression of an individual opinion) (Article 100(2)). Postal communications may be censored only within certain State institutions and by leave of a court of law (Article 100(4)).

Data Protection Framework

The Electronic Communications Act of 2003 and its accompanying regulations implement the requirements of the European Union (EU) Directive on Privacy and Electronic Communications (2002/58/EC). Under Section 2-9 of the Act, telecommunications providers must safeguard the secrecy of the content of telecommunications.[4067] The duty of confidentiality, however, does not prevent such information from being given to the prosecuting authority or the police, or to another authority pursuant to the law.[4068] The Act has reduced some safeguards on electronic communications provided for in the Telecommunications Act of 1995, which the Electronic Communications Act replaced. Previously, customers could provide a minimum of personal information when purchasing a mobile phone. By using unregistered cell phones and anonymous cash cards, individuals could communicate almost undetected. Article 6-2 of the accompanying regulation states that all electronic communication providers must keep records of all their end users. The consequence of this provision is that mobile phone cash cards can no longer be sold anonymously.[4069]

[4065] *Id.* at 340.

[4066] *Id.* at 334.

[4067] The Electronic Communications Act (*ekomloven*), July 4, 2003, No. 83, available at <http://www.npt.no/iKnowBase/FileServer/ekom_eng.pdf?documentID=7922> (unofficial English translation).

[4068] *Id.*

[4069] E-mail from Morten Foss, Legal Adviser, The Norwegian Post and Telecommunications Authority, to Kenneth Farrall, IPIOP Law Clerk, Electronic Privacy Information Center (EPIC), June 14, 2004 (on file with the EPIC).

Data Protection Authority

The regulation of personal data and information in Norway was formerly governed by the Personal Data Registers Act of 1978, but this law has been replaced by the Personal Data Act of 2000 (PDA).[4070] The PDA protects the right to privacy by setting out safeguards to ensure that personal data are processed in accordance with fundamental respect for the right to privacy, including the need to protect personal integrity and private life and to ensure adequate quality of personal data (Section 1). Enforcement of the PDA is overseen by The Data Inspectorate (*Datatilsynet*), a body originally set up in 1980.[4071] The Inspectorate is placed under the administrative wings of the Ministry of Labor and Government Administration, but is otherwise expected to function completely independently of government or private sector bodies. The Inspectorate employed 30 staff members as of May 2005, 12 of whom are lawyers, five are engineers, three are information personnel, and the rest hold administrative positions.[4072]

The responsibilities of the Inspectorate include verifying compliance with statutes and regulations that apply to the processing of personal data and that errors or deficiencies are rectified; identifying risks to protection of privacy; and providing guidance on measures to avoid or limit such risks.[4073] Complaints are normally handled by written procedures, but also by guidance meetings, by phone calls and e-mail. In terms of complaints enforcement, the Data Inspectorate has the tools mentioned in Sections 47 – 49 in the Act of April 14, 2000 No. 31 relating to the processing of personal data (Personal Data Act).[4074]

The Data Inspectorate handled approximately 3,800 complaints and investigations, as well as, a 100 inspections from June 1, 2004 to April 30, 2005.[4075] In the same period, the Data Inspectorate answered roughly 13,000

[4070] The Data Inspectorate's homepage <http://www.datatilsynet.no/>.

[4071] *Id.*

[4072] E-mail from Gunnel Helmers, Data Inspectorate, Norway, to Kenneth Farrall, IPIOP Law Clerk, EPIC, June 30, 2004 (on file with EPIC).

[4073] *Id.*

[4074] E-mail from Gunnel Helmers, Data Inspectorate, Norway, to Ula Galster, International Policy Fellow, EPIC, April 29, 2005 (on file with EPIC). For more information on the Data Inspectorate's investigation procedures and tools of empowerment, *see* <http://www.datatilsynet.no.htest.osl.basefarm.net/upload/Dokumenter/regelverk/lov_forskrift/lov-20000414-031-eng.pdf>.

[4075] From June 1, 2003 to June 1, 2004, the Data Inspectorate answered approximately 3,500 incoming letters. This figure includes the whole range from small to extensive complaints and 141 written submissions. In the period from November 2003 to June 2004, the Inspectorate's answering service responded to 6,000 telephone calls.

telephone calls and e-mails, the most frequent topics of which were workplace privacy (13 percent of the calls), video surveillance (10 percent of the calls), unwanted telephone sales and direct marketing.[4076] About one half of the calls came from private individuals with rights according to the PDA, and the other half from different organisations and enterprises with duties according to the PDA.[4077] Decisions of the Inspectorate may be appealed to a quasi-judicial body, the Data Protection Tribunal (*Personvernnemnda*). Decisions of the Tribunal may be appealed to civil courts on questions of law.[4078]

Although Norway is not a member of the European Union, the PDA was designed to bring Norwegian law into compliance with the EU Data Protection Directive.[4079] The PDA covers all data that may be linked directly or indirectly to individuals.[4080] The PDA applies to both the public and private sectors, and it covers both manual and computerized registers (Section 3). As a point of departure, the PDA requires that the Data Inspectorate be notified in advance of data-processing operations (Sections 31-32). In some instances, a license must be acquired from the Data Inspectorate in order to process data. This is generally the case, for example, with the planned processing of sensitive information, such as information on racial origin, religion, or criminal record (Section 33), and with the processing of personal data by the insurance, banking and telecommunications sectors (Chapter 7 of the regulations to the Act). The Inspectorate also has the power to make onsite visits to data register licensees to determine compliance with the Act (Section 44). The PDA provides strong protections for data subjects about whom data has been collected. The Act provides that all persons have a right to demand access to information which concerns them (Section 18). Also, according to the Act, all incorrect data must be corrected (Section 27), and all persons shall have the right to block their name from use in direct marketing (Section 26). The Act also restricts the flow of personal data to other countries in accordance with the rules laid down in Articles 25 and 26 of the EU Data Protection Directive (Sections 29-30). Again, similar to the EU Directive, data subjects must be informed that their personal data is being collected and of the name of the controller collecting the personal data (Sections 19-20). New in relation to the EU Directive, however, is that the Act imposes a duty of informing the subject when, on the basis of a personal profile, either the data subject is approached or contacted, or a decision directed at the data subject is made.

[4076] *Id.*

[4077] E-mail from Gunnel Helmers, *supra*.

[4078] Bygrave & Aarø, at 337.

[4079] *Id.* at 336.

[4080] Lee A. Bygrave, Data Protection Law: Approaching Its Rationale, Logic and Limits 48 (The Hague: Kluwer Law International, 2002).

In such a case, the data subject must be automatically informed of the data controller's identity, the data constituting the profile, and the source of these data (Section 21). Violations of the Act are punishable by fines or imprisonment (Sections 46 *et seq.*).[4081]

A decision of principle by the Data Protection Tribunal in late 2002 defines the scope of the Act, specifically as it applies to human biological material such as blood samples. The tribunal's decision overturned a Norwegian Data Inspectorate ruling on a case involving a medical researcher who wished to take human blood samples from his work at a university hospital with him to his new job.[4082] The Data Inspectorate ruled that blood samples constituted "personal information" for the purposes of the Act. On appeal, the decision was reversed by a majority of the Data Protection Tribunal, applying a view of "data" and "information" typical in the fields of informatics and information science. Further, the decision reflected a concern that the Act should not be radically extended in scope without such an extension being considered in Parliament.[4083]

A more recent decision of principle by the Data Protection Tribunal defines the ambit of the PDA as it applies to audiotape recordings.[4084] The tribunal found that audiotape recordings of a person's telephone conversation – recorded without the consent of that person by the other party to the conversation – do not fall within the scope of the PDA, thus reversing the earlier decision by the Data Inspectorate on the issue. According to the Tribunal, such recordings *per se* could not constitute a "register" or "file" for the purposes of Section 3(1)(b), as they are not organized in a way that facilitates ready identification of specific individuals. The tribunal also found that the recordings could not qualify as a processing of personal data by automatic means (Section 3 (1)(a)), because manual intervention was needed to initiate and conclude the recording operation.

[4081] *See also* Bygrave & Aarø, *supra*, at 339-340.

[4082] *See* appeal decision in case 8/2002, available at <http://www.personvernnemnda.no/vedtak/2002_8.html>.

[4083] Lee A. Bygrave, "The Body as Data? Reflections on the Relationship of Data Privacy Law with the Human Body," edited text of speech given at an international conference organized by the Office of the Victorian Privacy Commissioner on the theme "The Body as Data," Federation Square, Melbourne, September 8, 2003, available at <http://www.privacy.vic.gov.au/dir100/priweb.nsf/download/CF51D885BA101AACCA256E050012CBA5/$FILE/Bygrave%20paper.pdf>.

[4084] *See* appeal decision in case 1/2005, available at <http://www.personvernnemnda.no/vedtak/2005_1.html>.

Wiretapping and Surveillance Rules

The PDA provides specific rules for video surveillance. Video surveillance that does not create actual files falls under weaker protection than regular personal data registers. However, if the surveillance results in the actual recording of pictures, then the surveillance falls under the Act and the Data Inspectorate must be informed (Section 37). The Inspectorate has the power to intervene and prohibit the surveillance if it does not conform with the Act. If the video surveillance is performed in a public place, there must be clear notice given, such as through use of a warning sign (Section 40). However, the Criminal Procedure Act of 1981 allows police to perform covert video surveillance of public areas if the surveillance is permitted by court order and is of "essential significance" for investigating suspected criminal conduct that can result in more than six months imprisonment (Section 202(a)).

General exemptions to the Personal Data Act are made for processing of data for purely private or purely artistic, literary or journalistic purposes (Sections 3 and 7). Processing of data for historical, statistical, or scientific purposes is also treated leniently (*see, e.g.*, Section 11(2)). Some data registers kept for purposes of policing and/or national security are also taken outside the control competence of the Data Inspectorate (Chapter 1 of the regulations to the Act).

The Personal Data Act is expected to undergo a comprehensive review followed by changes to some of its provisions.[4085] For example, the decision by the Court of Justice of the European Communities in the criminal proceedings against Bodil Lindqvist[4086] has led to a change in policy of the Norwegian Data Inspectorate.[4087] The Inspectorate had exempted from the Act the posting of personal data on homepages for ostensibly private or domestic purposes. The *Lindqvist* decision, however, states that the exemption for "private" processing does not apply when the data can be accessed by an indefinite number of persons. Unless personal data posted on a web site is restricted so that only a small number of persons can legally access the material, the disclosure of this data now

---

[4085] Email from Lee A. Bygrave, Associate Professor, Faculty of Law, University of Oslo, to Kenneth Farrall, IPIOP Law Clerk, EPIC, June 11, 2004 (on file EPIC).

[4086] *See* decision of November 6, 2003 in Case C-101/01.

[4087] *See* EU Data Protection Directive (1995/46/EC), OJEC of November 23, 1995 No L. 281 p. 31, Article 3(2), second indent, available at
<http://europa.eu.int/smartapi/cgi/sga_doc?smartapi!celexapi!prod!CELEXnumdoc&lg=EN&numdoc=31995L0046&model=guichett>.

falls within the scope of the European Data Protection Directive and the PDA.[4088]

Wiretapping normally requires the permission of a court and is initially limited to four weeks.[4089] The total number of telephones monitored was 360 in 1990, 467 in 1991, 426 in 1992, 402 in 1993, 541 in 1994 and 534 in 1995.[4090] A Supervisory Board reviews the warrants to ensure the adequacy of the protections. A Parliamentary Commission of Inquiry was created in 1994 to investigate the post-World War II surveillance practices of Norwegian police and security services. The Lund Commission delivered a 600-page report in 1996, causing a great deal of public and political debate on account of its finding that much of the undercover surveillance practices, including wiretapping of left-wing political groups until 1989, had been instituted and/or conducted illegally and that the courts had not generally been strong enough in their oversight.[4091] This included keeping files on children as young as 11 years old.

Anti-terrorism Measures

A recent report from an official Norwegian commission has tackled the controversial issue of balance between crime prevention and privacy in the light of global terrorism and organized crime.[4092] One proposal in the report involves reducing current restrictions on police bugging of non-telephonic conversations between criminals, a practice known as "*romavlytting*" in Norwegian. Although similar proposals have been made in the past, there are indications that some conservative politicians who have previously opposed such a measure now support it.[4093]

A recent law proposal now suggests that ISPs are mandated to retain registered traffic data for one year for law enforcement purposes.[4094] The proposal has not passed the Parliament yet, but is due to be discussed after April 2005.[4095]

[4088] *Id.*

[4089] *See generally* Criminal Procedure Act, Chapter 16 a.

[4090] Government of Norway report to the UN Human Rights Commission, CCPR/C/115/Add.2, May 26, 1997.

[4091] "Judicial Inquiry into Norwegian Secret Surveillance," Fortress Europe Circular Letter (FECL) 43 (April/May 1996), available at <http://www.fecl.org/circular/4305.htm>.

[4092] *See "Mellom Effektivitet og Personvern,"* NOU 2004:6.

[4093] E-mail from Lee Bygrave, *supra.*

[4094] *See* "Between Efficiency and Data Protection – Police Methods to Prevent Crime," NOU 2004:6.

[4095] E-mail from Gunnel Helmers, *supra.*

Another official commission has recently issued a major report concerning the regulation of personal data registers established by the police, of which there are many types.[4096] The report, which has not raised much controversy, recommends the enactment of a new statute to regulate specifically the establishment and use of such registers.[4097] A proposition based on an ILO convention proposes that the national governments shall issue biometric ID cards to seafarers. The ID cards are proposed as a safeguard against terrorism. An amendment was also proposed to the regulations regarding object security based on the need to secure objects against terrorism and crime. The proposed amendment prepares for a somewhat increased use of security clearances, access controls and camera surveillance.[4098]

Provisions of the Criminal Procedure Act allow for wiretapping without court permission in two circumstances. First, Section 216(a) allows wiretapping for narcotics investigations and in connection with cases involving national security, albeit with the permission of a magistrate court. Second, Section 216(b) allows wiretapping in connection with some less serious offenses but requires the permission of a magistrate court.

New legislation to monitor the secret services was approved in 1995 following the Lund Commission's recommendations.[4099] The legislation created a new Control Committee to monitor the activities of the Police Security Services, the Defense Security Services, and the Defense Intelligence Services. The former Minister of Justice and the head of the Norwegian security police (POT) were forced to resign from the government in 1996 after it was revealed that the POT had placed a member of the Lund Commission under surveillance and requested a copy of her *Stasi* file from the German authorities four times.[4100] Later it was discovered that the POT had also investigated several key members of the Parliament who have oversight over the agency.[4101] In 1997, the Parliament agreed to allow people who were under surveillance by the POT to review their records and to obtain compensation if the surveillance was unlawful. The POT has records on more than 50,000 people.[4102] The period for allowing access to these records has now terminated.

[4096] See "*Kriminalitetsbekjempelse og Personvern*," NOU 2003:21.

[4097] *Id.*

[4098] E-mail from Gunnel Helmers, *supra.*

[4099] Act No. 7 of February 3, 1995 on the Control of the Secret Services.

[4100] "Minister Resigns," Statewatch Bulletin, November-December 1996, Vol. 6, No 1.

[4101] "Minister Steps back after New Snooping Scandal," FECL 49 (December 1996/January 1997), available at <http://www.fecl.org/circular/4906.htm>.

[4102] "Parliament Says People Can See Files," Statewatch Bulletin, May-June 1997, Vol. 7, No. 3.

Many other laws contain provisions relevant to privacy and data protection. These include the Administrative Procedures Act of 1967 and the Criminal Code of 1902.[4103] The Criminal Code first prohibited the publication of information relating to "personal or domestic affairs" in 1889.[4104] The Criminal Code also prohibits the unauthorized opening of sealed correspondence, including cracking security mechanisms.[4105] The Criminal Code also prohibits covert monitoring or recording of telephone conversations or other conversations in closed settings.[4106] In December 2000, a Norwegian news service reported that Norwegian military and police intelligence units entered into an agreement with the country's 15 largest companies to perform Internet surveillance.[4107] The system was reported to be similar to the US FBI's Carnivore system, which intercepts and monitors any information sent across the Internet. The Norwegian Justice Department confirmed the existence of the system, but sources claimed that it has not been implemented on a large scale. The Norwegian Parliament has demanded a review of the project, which was created to defend the national information technology infrastructure.

Open Government

The 1970 Act on Public Access to Documents in the (Public) Administration provides for public access to government records. Under the Act, there is a broad right of access to records. The Act has been in effect since 1971. The Act does not apply to records held by the Parliament, the Office of the Auditor General, the Ombudsman for Public Administration, or other parliamentary institutions. There are exemptions for internal documents; information that "could be detrimental to the security of the realm, national defense or relations with foreign states or international organizations"; subject to a duty of secrecy; "in the interests of proper execution of the financial, pay or personnel management"; the minutes of the Council of State, photographs of persons entered in a personal data register; complaints, reports and other documents concerning breaches of the law; answers to examinations or similar tests; and documents prepared by a ministry in connection with annual fiscal budgets. The King can make a determination that historical documents in the archive that are otherwise

---

[4103] *See generally* Bygrave & Aarø, *supra*, at 334-335.

[4104] *See* Prof. Dr. Juris Jon Bing, Data Protection in Norway, 1996, available at
<http://www.jus.uio.no/iri/rettsinfo/lib/papers/dp_norway/dp_norway.html>.

[4105] Bygrave & Aaro, *supra*, at 334.

[4106] *Id.*

[4107] Digi.no, available at <http://www.digi.no/d2.nsf/frames/b9569727*1913023575>.

exempted can be publicly released. If access is denied, individuals can appeal to a higher authority under the act and then to a court.

In June 2003, a new money laundering law was passed. It requires employees in financial, gaming, and other institutions involved in the transfer of funds to notify the Norwegian Economic Crime Unit if they suspect that a client may be laundering funds.[4108]

In addition to data protection regulations that contain privacy provisions, Norway has addressed privacy issues stemming from threats of terrorism and human rights violations. The European Convention on Human Rights and Fundamental Freedoms of 1950 (ECHR) and the International Covenant on Civil and Political Rights of 1966, both of which contain a catalogue of basic human rights, including express rights to privacy, have recently been incorporated into Norwegian law.[4109] In April 2002, the Norwegian Parliament adopted amendments to the Norwegian Penal Code, which include prohibitions against "terrorist acts."[4110] Many privacy advocates and non-governmental organizations have expressed concern that the prohibition against "terrorist acts" is too broad and imprecise, and may result in persons becoming victims of arbitrary, inaccurate, or politically motivated charges.[4111]

Norway has also agreed to support United Nations (UN) Security Council Resolution 1368, which reconfirms the right to individual or collective self-defense, and Resolution 1373, which outlines the measures member states of the UN must implement in order to prevent and suppress terrorist activities.[4112] Other steps Norway has taken to counteract terrorism are: to call for the establishment of the International Criminal Court in The Hague, to ratify all UN Conventions against international terrorism in force, and to sign the UN Convention for the Suppression of the Financing of Terrorism.[4113] To safeguard human rights and fundamental freedoms in light of the threat of terrorism, the Norwegian government granted the Norwegian Institute for Human Rights the status of a

---

[4108] "New Money Laundering Law Passed," Aftenposten, May 29, 2003, available at
<http://www.aftenposten.no/english/business/article.jhtml?articleID=554420>.

[4109] Bygrave & Aaro, *supra.*

[4110] International Helsinki Foundation (IHF) Report, "Human Rights in the OSCE Region: Europe, Central Asia and North America 2003 (Events 2002)"<http://www.ihf-hr.org/viewbinary/viewdocument.php?doc_id=2261>.

[4111] *Id.*

[4112] UN GAOR 56th Sess. Plen. Item 166: Measures to Eliminate International Terrorism (Statement by H.E. Mr. Ole Peter Kolby Ambassador Permanent Representative) (2001), available at
<http://www.un.org/terrorism/statements/norwayE.html>.

[4113] *Id.*

signatures.[4139] While some people expressed concerns about the privacy and security safeguards of the database that will hold signers' information, the bill expressly states which information shall be available and which shall remain confidential.[4140]

Voting Privacy

Voting in Paraguay is compulsory for those between the ages of 18 and 75.[4141] The penalty for not voting is a fine.[4142] In 2001, Paraguay entered into an agreement, which was partly funded by the United States, to hold a rehearsal election using electronic voting (e-voting) technology. The test of e-voting was made possible through two agreements signed between the Superior Court of Electoral Justice of Paraguay and the Organization of American States, as well as with the Electoral Superior Court of Brazil, which provided technical support and the ballot boxes used in the voting process. The rehearsal project was conducted in seven municipalities, each involving the participation of 1.56 percent of the voter population. Citizen participation in the voting process increased from an average of 54 percent to 78 percent in some locations. Voters were universally supportive of e-voting.

Open Government

In July 2001, Congress passed Law No. 1728[4143] to regulate Article 28 of the Constitution about the access to information available in public records. Although the law states that access should be freely granted, several complaints from civil society[4144] persuaded the Executive Branch to veto the law, arguing that the procedure for obtaining information was extremely complicated and the exceptions to the information that might be provided were too broad. In August 2001, following the Presidential Veto, a bill proposing new text for a Law of Access to Public Information was presented to Congress by an alliance of several

---

[4139] Alvaro Lafuente, "Nace una Herramienta de Negocios: Firma Digital," Portal Paraguayo de Noticias, October 25, 2004, available at <http://www.ppn.com.py/html/noticias/entrevistas/firma_digital.asp>.

[4140] Id.

[4141] The World Fact Book, available at <http://www.cia.gov/cia/publications/factbook/geos/pa.html#Govt>.

[4142] Nobody, however, has ever been compelled to pay the fine.

[4143] Law No. 1728, available at <http://www.bibliojuridica.org/libros/3/1156/31.pdf> (in Spanish).

[4144] Cristian Nielsen, "La Prensa de Paraguay ante el Barranco de la Censura," Medios y Libertad de Expresión en las Americas, August 27, 2001, available at <http://www.libertad-prensa.org/nielsen.html>.

non-governmental organizations,[4145] which have been very active at promoting the right to freedom of information.[4146] Congress has not approved yet approved the bill.[4147]

International Obligations

Paraguay ratified the 1948 Universal Declaration of Human Rights,[4148] the 1966 International Covenant on Civil and Political Rights,[4149] and the American Convention on Human Rights (ACHR).[4150] The ACHR provides that every person has "the right to have his honor respected and his dignity recognized." Additionally, "no one may be the object of arbitrary or abusive interference with his private life, his family, his home, or his correspondence, or of unlawful attacks on his honor or reputation. And everyone has the right to the protection of the law against such interference or attacks."

Republic of Peru

Constitutional Privacy Framework

Different articles of the 1993 Constitution protect the privacy and secrecy of communications and private documents, the inviolability of the home, the freedom of the press, freedom of expression, and access to public information. Article 2 states, "Every person has the right:

> To be assured that information services, whether or not they are computerized, public or private, will not release information affecting one's personal and family intimacy.

[4145] Consumers and Users Association of Paraguay (ASUCOP) is a non-governmental organization that has performed remarkable work to defend and increase awareness of consumers' rights.

[4146] Propuesta de Ley de Acceso a la Información Pública, August 22, 2001, available at <http://www.probidad.org/regional/legislacion/2001/006a.html>.

[4147] Interview with Juan Vera, President, ASUCOP, January 5, 2005, available at <http://www.asucop.org>.

[4148] Signed and ratified on December 10, 1948. *Declaración Universal de los Derechos Humanos*, available at <http://www.un.org/spanish/aboutun/hrights.htm>.

[4149] Signed on December 16, 1966; ratified on June 10, 1992. *Pacto Internacional de Derechos Civiles y Políticos*, available at <http://www.aidh.org/uni/Formation/02Pacte2_e.htm>.

[4150] Signed on November 22, 1969; ratified on August 18, 1989. Convención Americana sobre Derechos Humanos. Pacto de San José de Costa Rica, available at <http://www.oas.org/juridico/spanish/firmas/b-32.html>.

To his honor and good reputation, personal and family intimacy, and his own voice and image. Every person affected by inaccurate or injurious statements contained in any medium of social communication has the right to free, immediate and proportional[4151] rectification, notwithstanding other legal responsibilities.

To the inviolability and secrecy of private documents and communications. Communications, telecommunications, or documents stemming therefrom, may only be opened, seized, intercepted, or tapped with a bench warrant and pursuant to all the guarantees provided by law. Confidentiality must be maintained regarding all matters not related to the reason of the search. Private documents obtained in violation of this principle are not admissible before a court. Books, receipts, as well as accounting and administrative documents are subject to inspection or auditing by the proper authorities, in accordance with the law. They may not be removed or seized without a court order.

To the inviolability of his home. No one may enter the home or conduct any investigation or search without authorization from the inhabitant or a court warrant, except in the case of *flagrante delicto* or of a very serious danger. Exceptions for reasons of health or serious risk are governed by law.

To freedom of conscience and religion, individually or as a member of a group. No one may be persecuted for his ideas or beliefs. There is no such thing as a crime of opinion. . . .

To freedom of information, opinion, expression, and the dissemination of thoughts through the spoken or written word or in images, by any means of social communication, and without previous authorization, censorship, or impediment whatsoever, and in accordance with the law. Crimes committed by means of books, the press, or other media of social communication are outlined in the Penal Code and will be tried in a court of law. Any action that suspends or closes any organ of expression or prevents its free circulation also constitutes a crime. The right to inform and express opinions includes the right to find means of communication.

To request information that one needs without disclosing the reason, and to receive that information from any public entity, within the period

---

[4151] Proportionate to the degree of fault.

specified by law, at a reasonable cost. Information that affects personal intimacy and that is expressly excluded by law or for reasons of national security is not subject to disclosure. Banking secrecy and confidentiality concerning taxes may only be lifted at the request of a judge, the National Prosecutor, or a congressional investigative commission in accordance with the law and provided that such information relates to the case."[4152]

All these constitutional rights are included, in one way or another, in Article 1, which provides that "the protection of the person and the respect for his dignity are the supreme goal of society and the State."

The right of informational self-determination is partially protected by the action of *habeas data*. In Peru, *habeas data* is used to refer to the constitutional procedure which protects not only the right of a person to access information about himself (right to informational self-determination (Constitution, Article 2.6), but also the right to access whatever information an individual may require from any public body (freedom of information and access to government records (Constitution, Article 2.5).[4153] However, *habeas data* is a redress mechanism used only after the damage has been done.[4154] In several sentences, the Constitutional Tribunal has mentioned the right of informational self-determination, which is not specifically mentioned in the Peruvian Constitution, as "one that gives an individual the ability to request the rectification of inexact information about himself, contained in databases or registries."[4155]

On May 28, 2004, the Code of Constitutional Procedures was enacted. It regulates the procedures of *habeas corpus*, *amparo*, and *habeas data*, established by Articles 200 and 202.3 of the Constitution.

[4152] Constitution of Peru, Articles 2.6, 2.7, 2.10, 2.9, 2.3, 2.4, and 2.5, available at <http://www.asesor.com.pe/teleley/biblioteca/constitucional/5000f.htm>, <www.idlo.int/texts/leg6577.pdf>.

[4153] Habeas data provision, Article 200, Subsection 3 of the 1993 Constitution of Peru, is a constitutional guarantee that protects against any act or omission by whatever authority, whether a state employee or a private person, that would reduce or jeopardize the rights of the individual as contained in Article 2, Subsections 5-6, available at <http://www.asesor.com.pe/teleley/biblioteca/constitucional/5000f.htm>, <www.idlo.int/texts/leg6577.pdf>.

[4154] Tribunal Constitucional, Expediente 0666-96-HD/TC. Published on July 8, 1998, available at <http://www.tc.gob.pe/jurisprudencia/1998/0666-1996-HD.html>.

[4155] Tribunal Constitucional <http://www.tc.gob.pe/jurisprudencia/2003/0700-2003-HC Resolucion.html>.

Peru does not have comprehensive data protection legislation. However, numerous specific legal regulations protect privacy, and the Ombudsman, in some cases, does the work of a data protection agency.[4156] In August 2004, the Ministry of Justice published a report about a bill on data protection. It contains provisions related to general data protection principles pursuant to the Peruvian Constitution, and is based on the European Union Data Protection Directive and the Spanish Data Protection Acts of 1992 and 1999. It contains provisions on data subjects' rights, data controllers' obligations, the supervisory authority as well as sanctions. If the bill is passed, existing data protection regulations (including bank, disabilities and credit card regulations) would have to be adapted to it.[4157]

In August 2001, Peru enacted a data protection law covering private credit reporting agencies called *Centrales Privadas de Información de Riesgos* (CEPIRS).[4158] These private companies are in charge of collecting and processing the credit risk information of individuals and companies whose information is recorded in databases. The law regulates the incorporation of credit bureaus, qualifications for shareholders, and the sources of information they can use. Similar to Article 11 of the EU Data Protection Directive, it sets out the information that must be provided to the data subject when the data has not been obtained from him or her. In addition, the law prohibits credit bureaus from collecting sensitive information, data violating the confidentiality of bank or tax records, inaccurate or outdated information, bankruptcy records older than five years, and other debtors' records five years after the debt has been paid. It provides that credit agencies must adopt security measures, and that individuals have the following rights: 1) the right to access their personal data; 2) the right to modify or delete their personal data; 3) the right to rectify personal data that is illegal, inexact, erroneous or has expired; and 4) jurisdictional trusteeship or jurisdictional protection (*tutela jurisdiccional*). The law also creates a strict liability regime. The Agency for Consumer Protection of the National Institute for the Defense of Competition and the Protection of Intellectual Property

---

[4156] Constitution of Peru, Article 162: "It is the duty of the Ombudsman to defend constitutional rights and fundamental personal rights and those of the community; and to supervise the fulfillment of the duties of state administration and public services to the citizenry. . . . He has the right to initiate law proposals, and may propose measures to facilitate the fulfillment of the functions of the office."

[4157] Bill on data protection, available at <http://www.minjus.gob.pe/minjus/PROYECTODELEY.PDF>.

[4158] *Ley que regula las centrales privadas de información de riesgos y de protección al titular de la información*, Law 27489, available at <http://www.leyes.congreso.gob.pe/Imagenes/Leyes/27489.pdf>.

(INDECOPI)[4159] is in charge of applying fines for violation of the law, and issuing injunctions to correct errors.

Any person has the right to request, for a fee and without having to disclose the reason for doing so, copy of the documentation that exists in the Public Registries. However, Article 128 of the General Regulation of Public Registries, relating to the publicity of the registries, provides: "[w]hen the information requested affects the right to privacy (*intimidad*), this information can only be granted to those who demonstrate legitimate interest, according to the regulations established by the National Superintendent of the Public Registries."[4160]

Public Registries handle information that may be sensitive. This might include, for example, information from the Personal Registry such as judicial rulings regarding someone's mental status, separation agreements between spouses, or child custody rulings. The office of Lima (and several of the main registry offices in Peru) has an online service for subscribers. Soon, the interconnection between all offices of Public Registries in Peru will be completed, making it possible to access them from any computer connected to the Internet.

Statutory Rules Related to Privacy

The Civil Code of 1984 considers the intimacy of private life, in all its aspects, as worthy of legal protection, subject only to limitations where there is consent by the person concerned, a social interest, or a reason of public order. Article 14 of the Civil Code states that "personal and family intimacy may not be made public without the consent of the person." This article aims at regulating snooping, and other behavior that interferes with someone's private life, or that constitutes an illegal search of a person's goods or properties.[4161]

Article 69 of the Penal Code[4162] establishes that "anyone who has completed a penalty or security measure[4163] imposed on them by the court must be rehabilitated in society without further proceedings. The rehabilitation produces the following effects: . . . 2. The cancellation of their criminal, judicial and police

---

[4159] Comisión de Protección al Consumidor del Instituto Nacional de Defensa de la Competencia y de la Protección de la Propiedad Intelectual.

[4160] Superintendencia Nacional de los Registros Públicos <http://www.orlc.gob.pe>.

[4161] *See* Carlos Fernández Sessarego, Derecho de las Personas 59 (Studium 1987).

[4162] *Código Penal* (Penal Code), available at <http://www.leyes.congreso.gob.pe/CodigoP.htm>.

[4163] *Id.* Security measures are those that aim at preventing a dangerous person from committing new crimes. Examples of such security measures provided for in the Peruvian Penal Code are internment and ambulatory treatment.

official records. These certificates do not have to express the penalty nor the rehabilitation." In crimes against the honor (insult, calumny, defamation), Article 135 states that "the evidence is never admitted by the court in any case if: . . . 2. [t]he imputation pertains to personal and family intimacy, or a crime against sexual freedom."

Article 154 of the Penal Code states that "a person who violates personal or family privacy, whether by watching, listening to, or recording an act, a word, a piece of writing or an image, using technical instruments or processes and other means, shall be punished with imprisonment for no longer than two years." Article 157 criminalizes the disclosure of sensitive data including "political and religious convictions" and other aspects of private life.

Article 161 of the Penal Code establishes "that a person who unlawfully opens a letter, document, telegram, radio telegram, telephone message, or other document of a similar nature that is not addressed to him, or unlawfully takes possession of any such document even if it is open, shall be liable to imprisonment of not more than two years and to a fine of between 60 and 90 days." A sentence of not less than one year, and not more than three years, is to be given to any "person who unlawfully interferes with, or listens to, a telephone or similar conversation." Public servants guilty of the same crime must serve not less than three and not more than five years, and must be dismissed from their post. A person who unlawfully tampers with, deletes, or misdirects, "the address on a letter or telegram," but does not open it, "is liable to 20 to 52 days of community service."

The Organic Law of the National Identification Registry and Civil Status (1995) created an autonomous agency which may "collaborate with the exercise of the functions of pertinent political and judicial authorities in order to identify persons" but is "vigilant regarding restrictions with respect to the privacy and identity of the person" and "guarantees the privacy of its registered individuals' personal data." The Law also requires all persons to carry a national identity document featuring a corresponding number, photograph, and fingerprint.[4164]

In January 2002, a law creating a National Registry of Persons with Disabilities was adopted.[4165] The registry is administered by the National Council of Integration of Persons with Disabilities (CONADIS).

[4164] *Ley Orgánica del Registro Nacional de Identificación y Estado Civil*, Law 26497, July 11, 1995, available at <http://www.leyes.congreso.gob.pe/Imagenes/Leyes/26497.pdf>.

[4165] *Ley General de la Persona con Discapacidad*, Law 27050, available at <http://www.leyes.congreso.gob.pe/Imagenes/Leyes/27050.pdf>.

Article 140 of the General Banking and Insurance Law prohibits financial institutions, as well as their directors and workers, from providing any information regarding their clients' transactions, except upon written authorization from the clients, or unless the transactions fall within one of the banking secrecy provisions (Articles 142 and 143).[4166]

In May 2004, El Comercio, the most important newspaper in Lima, provided an extensive report that revealed the sale of databases on CDs, costing USD 20 each, by data dealers based in popular hardware and software stores. The CDs contain data on approximately 60,000 Peruvian citizens, including their names, addresses, fixed and mobile telephone numbers, e-mails, employment, consumer habits, economic activities, etc. Information is also "segmented" into various categories: lawyers, architects, doctors, notaries, executive women, university professors, "top companies," and NGOs. The information is upgraded every six months, according to the data dealers.[4167]

On April 12, 2005, a new law (Law No. 28493[4168]) was enacted to regulate the use of unsolicited commercial e-mails ("spam"). The law does not determine whether the user has to grant his express authorization to receive spam (opt-in), or reject it once he has received it (opt-out). It indicates that all spam that originates from Peru must contain specific items of information such as the word "publicity" in the subject of the message, the name of the natural or legal person who sent the spam, and a valid and active e-mail address that can be used to opt-out. Spam is considered illegal when it does not fulfill Article 5, when the e-mail contains false or misleading information, or when the sender of spam does not comply with opt-out requests. The law also provides damages for individuals being spammed.[4169]

Article 4 of the Law of Telecommunications[4170] states that "all persons have the right to the inviolability and secrecy of their telecommunications. The Ministry of Transports, Communications, Housing and Construction is in charge of protecting this right." Every concession contract of public services of

---

[4166] <http://www.sbs.gob.pe/normas/leyes/LeyGeneral-Febrero2004.doc>.

[4167] El Comercio, May 10, 2004, at A2.

[4168] *Ley que regula el uso del correo electrónico comercial no solicitado* (SPAM), April 12, 2005, available at <http://www.cpsr-peru.org/spam/anti-spam/>.

[4169] Juan Carlos Lujan, "En julio quedará reglamentada ley contra el 'spam mail' en el Perú," available at <http://www.elcomercioperu.com.pe/EdicionImpresa/Html/2005-05-13/impVidayFuturo0305641.html>; *see also* Katitza Rodríguez y Palmira Puglianini, "Spam nuestro de cada día," April 24, 2005, available at <http://www.cpsr-peru.org/spam/ndp>.

[4170] *Texto Unico Ordenado de la Ley de Telecomunicaciones*, D.S. 013-93-TCC, available at <http://www.mtc.gob.pe/secom/mlegal/leyes/ley.htm>.

telecommunications has to indicate the guarantees that service providers must offer to ensure the secrecy of communications. What constitute very serious infractions to the concession contract are: "the interception or unauthorized interference of services of telecommunications that are not available for free use by the general public" and the "spreading of the existence or content, or the publication, or any other use, of all type of data obtained by means of the interception or interference of the services of telecommunications not meant for general public use."[4171]

The General Regulation of the Law of Telecommunications provides that "it is a violation of the secrecy of telecommunications for a person, who is not the one who originates nor is the addressee of a communication, to deliberately remove, intercept, interfere, change or alter its text, turn aside the course, publish, disclose, use, try to know; or facilitate for another person to know about the existence or content of any communication. . . . The concessionaires of public services of telecommunications are forced to safeguard the secrecy of telecommunications and protect personal data. They also have to adopt the reasonable measures and procedures to guarantee the inviolability and secrecy of the communications; as well as to maintain the confidentiality of their users' personal information obtained in the course of business, except if users have provided their prior, written and express consent, or if there is a judicial warrant. The holders of private services of telecommunications will have to adopt their own security measures to provide for the inviolability and secrecy of telecommunications."[4172]

Wiretapping and Other Government Surveillance

According to Article 16 of the Civil Code, "the mail, communications of any sort or voice recordings, when they are confidential or refer to personal and family private life, cannot be wiretapped or disclosed without their author and addressee's assent. The publication of the personal or family memories, requires in any case the author's authorization. When the author or recipient has died . . . his heirs get the right to consent for him. If there is no agreement between heirs, the judge decides. The prohibition of the posthumous publication made by the author or the recipient cannot extend beyond 50 years from his death."

[4171] Law of Telecommunications, Article 52-f, Article 87, numerals 4 and 5.

[4172] *Texto Unico Ordenado del Reglamento General de la Ley de Telecomunicaciones*, D.S. 027-2004-MTC, published on July 15, 2004, Article 13.

In April 2002, Peru passed a new law to govern the interception of communications and private documents.[4173] Under this law, a judicial warrant is needed to seize documents or intercept communications. The law requires telecommunications operators to provide all necessary technical assistance and facilities to carry out interceptions. The powers may be used in the investigation of crimes, including kidnapping, child traffic, drug traffic, customs violations, terrorism, crimes against humanity, and treason.

In the recent past there have been numerous reports of abuse of surveillance of the National Intelligence Service (*Servicio de Inteligencia Nacional*, or SIN). The SIN conducted widespread surveillance and illegal phone tapping of government ministers and judges assigned to constitutional cases, beginning in the early 90s. Army agents used sophisticated Israeli phone-tapping equipment to monitor telephone conversations, and copies of the conversations were delivered to Vladimiro Montesinos, the head of Peru's intelligence service.[4174] The SIN maintained close ties with the U.S. Central Intelligence Agency, including a covert assistance program to combat drug trafficking.[4175] The SIN has allegedly conducted a nationwide surveillance campaign with the sole purpose of intimidating political opposition figures, including the former UN General Secretary Javier Pérez de Cuéllar while he ran for President against Alberto Fujimori.[4176] In 2003, a parliamentary commission investigated the telephone wiretapping carried out during the government of Alberto Fujimori. It discovered that Vladimiro Montesinos had used the Office of Electronic Information (DIE) of the SIN to carry out telephone monitoring. For that purpose, the DIE activated 29 interception points in Lima and Callao, of which only 20 have been deactivated.[4177] In February 2005, 95 people were charged with phone tapping and illicit association, among other crimes.[4178]

According to the parliamentary commission, some of this surveillance equipment is still in operation. This presumption is based upon reports of telephone wiretapping made after the deactivation of the SIN operation. In September 2003,

---

[4173] Law 27697, *Ley que otorga facultad al fiscal para la intervención y control de comunicaciones y documentos privados en caso excepcional*, Diario Oficial El Peruano, April 12, 2002, available at <http://www.leyes.congreso.gob.pe/Imagenes/Leyes/27697.pdf>.

[4174] "Former Agent Accuses Peru Spy Chief," Associated Press, March 17, 1998. *See also* <http://en.wikipedia.org/wiki/Vladimiro_Montesinos>.

[4175] 1998 Human Rights Watch Report, available at <http://www.hrw.org/hrw/worldreport/Americas.htm>.

[4176] "Former UN Chief Charges Peru Tapped His Phone," Reuters, August 4, 1997.

[4177] The equipment used by the DIE for the interception of fixed and cellular telephones was manufactured in Israel, Germany, and the United States. More than 100 units were involved. In downtown Lima, six interception points were implemented where practically all public, private, newspaper and even ecclesiastical, organizations, were controlled. Diario El Comercio, Lima.

[4178] La República, February 27, 2005, at 12-13.

journalists denounced the pursuit of this operation by the current intelligence service agency. The head of intelligence was dismissed after he admitted spying on journalists. He alleged that the investigation only studied how "confidential information"[4179] (*información reservada*) was filtered from the government to the press.

Telephone monitoring is being carried out by former staff of the intelligence service (technicians in telecommunications) working freely in the job market. Between 2001 and 2003, the National Intelligence Council has conducted several operations attempting to break up the clandestine wiretapping network that uses wiretap equipment that belonged to the prior SIN established by the Fujimori's government. This network is believed to have 80 wiretapping units and electronic espionage operating in seven cities, including Lima, and its members may have international contacts in Panama, Colombia, Venezuela, Brazil, and Chile.[4180]

On July 29, 2004, the new Code of Criminal Procedures, Legislative Decree 957, was published in the Official Gazette. The controversial Article 205 allows police, without an order from the prosecutor's office or a judge, to require identification and investigate the identity of any person, where considered necessary to prevent a crime, or to obtain useful information relating to a punishable offense. Under Article 206, for felony offenses, when it is necessary to discover and locate the participants to a socially disturbing crime and safeguard evidence of such a crime, the police, by notifying the prosecutor, may place guards on public thoroughfares, places, and establishments. These guards may identify the persons who are traveling to, or are present in, those places, search vehicles, and stop and search individuals' personal effects, in order to check whether these persons are carrying illegal or dangerous substances or instruments. In this case, the police will establish a Register of Public Police Checks.[4181]

Video surveillance is regulated in Article 207. It gives the prosecutor's office the authority to photograph, do detective work, and/or use special technical measures to observe the residence of a suspect at the prosecutor's or police's request in the case of investigations for serious or violent crimes, or for involvement in criminal organizations.[4182] In the Miraflores district of Lima, 25 video surveillance cameras have been installed in the main streets and parks. The

---

[4179] Information that is exempt under the freedom of information law.

[4180] La República, March 14, 2004, at 15.

[4181] <http://www.cpsr-peru.org/bdatos/peru/privacidad/cpp/>.

[4182] <http://www.cpsr-peru.org/bdatos/peru/privacidad/videovigilancia/>.

cameras have visualization fields of 360 degrees, massive zooming power, and are connected to two surveillance control rooms, including the National Police emergencies station.[4183]

In July 2000, a Computer Crimes Act was adopted and codified in Article 207(A)(B)(C) of the Penal Code.[4184] The Act prohibits unlawful access, use, interference, or damage to a system, database, or network of computers. Sanctions include up to five years' imprisonment. In 2000, a Law on Electronic Signature and Electronic Signature Certification was enacted. The law establishes that electronic signatures in contracts and agreements shall be equally valid and effective as those on paper.[4185]

In November 2003, the Parliament passed a law that compels administrators of Internet cafés to install a browsing filter or mechanism that makes it impossible to display pornographic content.[4186] In addition, local authorities of several districts of Lima passed similar regulations that also include penalties such as fines and the permanent closure of the business.

Miscellaneous Developments

In 2005, local authorities of Santiago de Surco, another district in Lima, announced the mandatory use of radio frequency identification (RFID) devices for the identification of dogs of dangerous races.[4187] In 1992, during Alberto Fujimori's government, several anti-terrorism laws were enacted that allowed criminal prosecutions of civilians in military courts, anonymous tribunals, secret hearings, life sentences, and the criminalization of behaviors that could not legitimately be considered acts of terrorism. The Constitutional Tribunal concluded on January 3, 2003, that those laws constituted an excessive punishment, violated the Constitution (Article 139), as well as the Universal Declaration of Human Rights (Articles 8, 9, 10, and 11), the International Pact of Civil and Political Rights (Articles 9 and 14), and the Inter-American Convention of Human Rights (Article 8).[4188]

[4183] Miraflores Boletín Informativo, Year 2, July 2004, at 5.

[4184] Law 27309, Diario Oficial El Peruano, July 17, 2000, incorporating Article 207 A, B y C of the Penal Code.

[4185] *Ley de Firmas y Certificados Digitales*, Law 27269, May 26, 2000, modified by Law 27310, July 15, 2000 <http://www.cpsr-peru.org/bdatos/peru/firma/digital/>.

[4186] *Ley que Prohíbe el Acceso de Menores de Edad a Páginas Web de Contenido Pornográfico*, Law 28119.

[4187] Dominical de La República, May 9, 2004, at 19.

[4188] Sentencia del Tribunal Constitucional, Expediente N° 010-2002-AI/TC, published on January 4, 2003, available at <http://www.tc.gob.pe/jurisprudencia/2003/0010-2002-AI.html>.

On February 12, 2003, President Alejandro Toledo promulgated Legislative Decree 922. Article 12 of the Decree states that "oral hearings for the crime of terrorism will be public. The public and media outlets will have access to the courtroom. However, the use of video cameras, tape recorders, cameras and similar technology is prohibited."[4189]

NGO Advocacy

CPSR-Perú and Privaterra organized trainings in privacy and secure communications for human rights and NGOs doing research and journalism in Peru and Colombia.[4190]

Open Government

A Law of Transparency and Access to Public Information was adopted in August 2002 and amended in January 2003.[4191] Under the law, every person has the right to request information, without having to explain why, in any form from any government body or private entity that offers public services or executes administrative functions. Documentation funded by the public budget is considered public information. Public bodies must respond within seven working days. There are three exceptions: for national security information, the disclosure of which would cause a threat to the territorial integrity and/or survival of the democratic systems and intelligence or counterintelligence activities; reserved information about crimes and external relations; and confidential information relating to pre-decisional advice, commercial secrets, ongoing investigations, and personal privacy. Information relating to human rights violations and the Geneva Convention of 1949 cannot be classified. The courts, Congress, the General Comptroller, and the Ombudsman can in some cases obtain exempted information. Once administrative procedures are completed and access to documents is rejected, the requestor can claim access to courts under Law 27584[4192] or under Law 26301 for the constitutional *habeas data*.[4193] In practice, *habeas data* is faster and more effective.

[4189] *See* <http://www.ifex.org/es/content/view/full/33608/>.

[4190] CPSR-Perú <http://www.cpsr-peru.org>, Privaterra <http://www.privaterra.org>.

[4191] *Ley de transparencia y acceso a la información pública*, Law 27808, modified by Law 27927, both consolidated in a unified text approved by Supreme Decree 043-2003-PCM. A history of the development of the bill is available at <http://www.freedominfo.org/news/peru2/>.

[4192]*Ley que regula el Proceso Contencioso Administrativo*, Law 27584, December 7, 2001.

The law also requires government departments to create Web sites and publish data on their organization, activities, regulations, budget, salaries, costs of acquisition of goods and services, and official activities of high-ranking officials. Detailed data on public finances has to be published every four months on the Ministry of Economy and Finance's Web site.[4194] The Constitutional Tribunal has clearly set down that the right of access to public information imposes upon public administration entities the duty to inform, and ruled that the information that is provided must not be false, incomplete, fragmentary, or confusing.[4195]

International Obligations

Peru is a signatory of the 1948 Universal Declaration of Human Rights, the 1966 International Covenant on Civil and Political Rights, and the American Convention on Human Rights. The American Convention provides that every person has "the right to have his honor respected and his dignity recognized." Additionally, "no one may be the object of arbitrary or abusive interference with his private life, his family, his home, or his correspondence, or of unlawful attacks on his honor or reputation. And everyone has the right to the protection of the law against such interference or attacks."

Perú accepted the jurisdiction of the Inter-American Court of Human Rights on January 21, 1981. It withdrew from the jurisdiction of that court in July 1999, but returned on January 12, 2001. According to Article 205 of the Constitution, "after exhausting internal remedies, those who consider themselves denied the rights recognized in the Constitution may resort to international tribunals or organs constituted by treaty or agreement to which Peru is a party."

[4193] Law 26301, aprueban Ley referida a la aplicación de la acción Constitucional de Habeas Data, May 2, 1994, available at <http://www.asesor.com.pe/teleley/bull505.htm>.

[4194] Campaign for this law was led by the *Consejo de la Prensa Peruana* (The Peruvian Press Council is a NGO of media owners that works on freedom of press and freedom of information) and other organizations such as the *Instituto Prensa y Sociedad* (the Press and Society Institute is a NGO of national and Latin American journalists, affiliated with Reporters Without Borders and the International Freedom of Expression Exchange (IFEX) of Canada that protects freedom of the press and freedom of information and fights against corruption). The amendment to the law incorporated a revised exemption for national security that was negotiated by the Peruvian Press Council and the armed forces. *See* <http://www.freedominfo.org/news/peru1/>. The law also included almost all of the proposals concerning national security restrictions that the Peruvian Press Council and the Ombudsman had put forward. *See* <http://www.freemedia.at/wpfr/Americas/peru.htm>.

4195 Tribunal Constitucional <http://www.tc.gob.pe/jurisprudencia/2003/1797-2002-HD.html>.

Republic of the Philippines

Article III of the Philippine Constitution contains the Bill of Rights. Section 1 of the Bill of Rights states that the "Congress shall give highest priority to the enactment of measures that protect and enhance the right of all the people to human dignity."[4196] Section 2 protects "the right of the people to be secure in their persons, houses, papers, and effects against unreasonable searches and seizures of whatever nature and for any purpose ... shall be inviolable, and no search warrant or warrant of arrest shall issue except upon probable cause to be determined personally by the judge after examination under oath or affirmation of the complainant and the witnesses he may produce, and particularly describing the place to be searched and the persons or things to be seized."[4197] Privacy is addressed in Section 3(1), which states that "privacy of communication and correspondence shall be inviolable except upon lawful order of the court, or when public safety or order requires otherwise, as prescribed by law."[4198] It further states that "any evidence obtained in violation of this or the preceding section shall be inadmissible for any purpose in any proceeding." Section 7 grants Filipinos the right to gain access to "information on matters of public concern ... and to documents and papers pertaining to official acts, transactions, or decisions, as well as to government research data used as basis for policy development."[4199]

Although there is currently no general data protection law, the Philippine government attempted in 2003 to address issues of secure data transfer and consumers' right to privacy. In 2003, the Information Technology and E-Commerce Council (ITECC) proposed a data privacy and cyber security law.[4200] This law was expected to adhere to the strict EU standards of data privacy, despite the difficulty of negotiating the differences between the policies of the EU and the US, one of With the Cybercrime Prevention Act of 2003, the ITECC struggled to craft a law that would satisfy the contrasting privacy needs of the EU and the United States.[4201] The proposed Act was not able to gain enough support and was replaced by the Commission on Information and Communication in

---

[4196] Constitution of the Philippines, Art. III, § 1.

[4197] *Id.* at § 2.

[4198] *Id.* at § 3(1).

[4199] *Id.* at § 7.

[4200] Eleanore C. Sanchez, "Technology Body Drafts Data Privacy Measure," Business World, April 16, 2003, at 3.

[4201] *Id.; see also* Eleanore C. Sanchez, "ITECC Mulls Data Privacy Law Proposal," BusinessWorld Online, March 14-15, 2003, available at <http://itmatters.com.ph/news/news_03142003a.html>.

CITC in 2004.[7] The CITC has a specific mandate "to preserve the rights of individuals to privacy and confidentiality of their personal information"[4202] The CITC has yet to propose a new cybercrime law. However, much like the ITECC proposal, any future data privacy law is expected to address hacking as well as "the issues of violation of privacy, and censorship of content such as pornography."[4203]

Despite the lack of a current data protection law, there is a recognized right of privacy in civil law.[4204] The Civil Code of the Philippines states that "[e]very person shall respect the dignity, personality, privacy, and peace of mind of his neighbors and other persons," and punishes acts that violate privacy by private citizens, public officers, or employees of private companies.[4205]

Article 26 of the Civil Code states that "every person shall respect the dignity, personality, privacy and peace of mind of his neighbors and other persons. The following and similar acts, though they may not constitute a criminal offense, shall produce a cause of action for damages, prevention and other relief: (1) Prying into the privacy of another's residence; (2) Meddling with or disturbing the private life or family relations of another; (3) Intriguing to cause another to be alienated from his friends; (4) Vexing or humiliating another on account of his religious beliefs, lowly station in life, place of birth, physical defect, or other personal condition."[4206] Article 32(11) of the Civil Code states that "any public officer or employee, or any private individual, who directly or indirectly obstructs, defeats, violates or in any manner impedes or impairs the privacy of communication and correspondence shall be liable to the latter for damages."[4207]

The Philippines has only one law on data transfer, Presidential Decree (P.D.) No. 1718 entitled "Providing for Incentives in The Pursuit of Economic Development Programs by Restricting The Use of Documents and Information Vital to The National Interest in Certain Proceedings and Processes." While the law was passed in 1980, it lacks force because rules and regulations have not been issued to allow enforcement. Broadly, P.D. 1718 prohibits the export of all documents

---

[7] Executive Order No. 3334, "Abolishing ITECC …," <http://www.ops.gov.ph/records/eo_no334.htm>.

[4202] Commission on Information and Communications Technology Charter available at, <http://www.cict.gov.ph/index.php?option=com_content&task=view&id=45&Itemid=82>.

[4203] Maricel E. Estavillo, "Ecommerce Law Stands Amid Tech Ambiguities," BusinessWorld Online, June 14, 2004, available at <http://itmatters.com.ph/features/features_06142004-2.html>.

[4204] Ople v. Torres, 293 S.C.R.A. 150 (S.C., July 23, 1998) (Phil.).

[4205] Civil Code, Art. 26.

[4206] Id.

[4207] Id. at Art. 32(11).

and information from the Philippines to other countries that may adversely affect the interests of Philippine corporations, individuals, or government agencies. P.D. 1718 contains exceptions for exportation of information that are a matter of form, in connection with business transactions or negotiations that require them, in compliance with international agreements, or made pursuant to authority granted by the designated representative of the President.[4208]

Bank records are protected by the Bank Secrecy Act[4209] and the Secrecy of Bank Deposits Act.[4210] The acts provide that deposits with banks or banking institutions are confidential and may not be examined, inquired, or looked into absent "exceptional circumstances." Those circumstances include: the written permission of the depositor, cases of impeachment, court orders in cases of bribery or dereliction of duty of public officials, cases where the money deposited or invested is the subject matter of litigation, and cases covered by the Anti-Graft and Corrupt Practices Act.[4211] The Anti-Money Laundering Act of 2001 allows exceptions to the Bank Secrecy Act and the Secrecy of Bank Deposits Act.[4212] Section 9(c) of the Act requires banks, insurance companies, financial institutions, and "other entities administering or otherwise dealing in currency, commodities, or financial derivatives"[4213] to report to the Anti-Money Laundering Council of the *Bangko Sentral ng Pilipinas* all transactions (including series or combinations of transactions) in excess of PHP four million (~USD 75,000).[4214] The institution does not have to report the transaction if it involves a "properly identified client and the amount is commensurate with the business or financial capacity of the client; or those with an underlying legal or trade obligation, purpose, origin, or economic justification."[4215] The Act does provide neither explicit definitions of a "properly identified client," nor a method for determining values commensurate with a particular financial capacity. Those who are compelled to report covered transactions to the AMLC are also prohibited from communicating that they have made such a report to anyone.[4216] Those who do communicate or publish the existence of a report or any

---

[4208] Christopher Lim, E-com Legal Guide, The Philippines, Baker & McKenzie, Manila, January 2001, available at <http://www.bakerinfo.com/apec/philapec_main.htm> (June 2, 2003).

[4209] Bank Secrecy Act, Republic Act No. 7653.

[4210] Secrecy of Bank Deposits Act, Republic Act No. 1405.

[4211] Natividad Kwan and Cornelio B. Abuda, Internet Banking – Key Legal Considerations, Baker & McKenzie, Manila, November 2000.

[4212] Republic Act No. 9160, § 7(c).

[4213] *Id.* at §3(a).

[4214] *Id.* at § 3(b).

[4215] *Id.*

[4216] Republic Act No. 9160, *supra* at.§9(c).

information connected with one are criminally liable.[4217] In 2003, the Act was amended to allow the AMLC unfettered access to deposits accounts without a court order.[4218]

The Supreme Court ruled in July 1998 that Administrative Order No. 308, the Adoption of a National Computerized Identification Reference System, introduced by former President Ramos in 1996, was unconstitutional. The Court found the order would "put our people's right to privacy in clear and present danger .... No one will refuse to get this identity card for no one can avoid dealing with government. It is thus clear as daylight that without the ID, a citizen will have difficulty exercising his rights and enjoying his privileges." While stating that all laws invasive of privacy would be subject to "strict scrutiny," the Court also was careful to note that, "the right to privacy does not bar all incursions to privacy."[4219] Then-president Joseph Estrada reiterated his support for the use of a national identification system in August 1998, stating that only criminals are against a national ID.[4220] Justice Secretary Serafin Cuevas authorized the National Statistics Office (NSO) to proceed to use the population reference number (PRN) for the Civil Registry System-Information Technology Project (CRS-ITP) on August 14, claiming that it is not covered by the decision.[4221]

However, President Gloria Arroyo, who was newly re-elected in May 2004, has stepped up efforts to revive the national ID scheme. Presidential spokesma Ignacio Bunye was quoted by the Manila Times of December 1, 2003 as asserting the necessity of the ID system for "peace and order," to facilitate transactions, and to reduce the number of IDs currently required.[4222] Bunye has sought to allay privacy concerns by explaining that, "the data that we would give once we apply for this ID are the information that we usually provide when applying for an ATM card or an SSS (Social Security System) ID."[4223] Proponents of the ID scheme argue that it will reduce crime and be constitutional because it would be backed not by an Executive Order like the former ID scheme

---

[4217] *Id.*

[4218] Bangko Sentral ng Pilipinas, "AMLA Admendments to Intensify Fight vs. Dirty Money" http://www.bsp.gov.ph/archive/News_2003/2003-02/news-02042003a.htm.

[4219] "Philippine Supreme Court Decision of the National ID System," *supra.*

[4220] Leotes Marie T. Lugo, "Erap Wants National ID System (Only Criminals Disagree with It, Says the President)," Business World, August 12, 1998, at 12.

[4221] Opinion Number 91; *see* "Foundation Laid for Proposed Nat'l ID," Business World, August 14, 1998, at 11.

[4222] Ma. Theresa Torres, "Congress Told: Pass Law for National ID," Manila Times, December 1, 2003., available at <http://www.manilatimes.net/national/2003/dec/01/yehey/top_stories/20031201top7.html>.

[4223] *Id.*

the Supreme Court had ruled invalid, but rather by a congressionally passed law.[4224] There, however, continues to be opposition to the bill.[4225]

In May 2000, the ILOVEYOU e-mail virus was traced to a hacker in the Philippines, focusing international attention on the country's cyberlaw regime.[4226] Lacking specific laws on hacking and cybercrime, prosecutors were only able to gain a warrant under the Access Devices Regulation Act of 1998,[4227] a law intended to punish credit card fraud that outlaws the use of unauthorized access devices to obtain goods or services broadly.[4228]

On the heels of the virus attack, in May, the Electronic Commerce Act of 2000 was signed into law.[4229] Section 33 of the Act mandates a minimum fine of PHP 100,000 (~USD 1,900) and a prison term of six months to three years for unlawful and unauthorized access to computer systems. Section 31 provides that only individuals with legal right of possession shall be granted access to electronic files or electronic keys. Section 32 imposes an obligation of confidentiality on persons receiving electronic data, keys, messages, or other information not to convey it to any other person.[4230]

In June 2001, the Philippine National Bureau of Investigation brought the first formal hacking and piracy charges under the Electronic Commerce Act. The charges involved two former employees of a business school who allegedly broke into the school's computer system and stole an undisclosed amount of proprietary digital material.[4231]

While restrictions on search and seizure within private homes are generally respected, searches without warrants do occur.[4232] More recently, Communist organizations have complained of a "pattern of surveillance" of their activities.[4233] Members of the *Bayan Muna* political party reported that offices

---

[4224] "Gov't to Push for National I.D. System-Palace," press release December 12, 2003, available at <http://www.freewebs.com/no2id/newid.html>.

[4225] Manila Times Editorial, "Scary ID System," Manila Times, December 3, 2003, available at <http://www.manilatimes.net/national/2003/dec/03/yehey/opinion/20031203opi1.html>.

[4226] Lim, *supra.*

[4227] Access Devices Regulation Act of 1998, Republic Act No. 8484.

[4228] *Id.*

[4229] Electronic Commerce Act of 2000, Republic Act No. 8792.

[4230] Kwan and Abuda, *supra.*

[4231] "Philippines' NBI Clamps Down on 'Cyberthieves'," Metropolitan Computer Times, (June 13, 2001), available at http://www.findarticles.com/p/articles/mi_m0NEW/is_2001_June_13/ai_75495014.

[4233] US Department of State Country Report on Human Rights Practices 2002, Philippines, March 2003.

and a clinic catering to their members were ransacked.[4234] The United Church of Christ of the Philippines also reported the ransacking of their human rights, peace, and interfaith offices, in what many consider to be acts of political intimidation.[4235]

The Act to Prohibit and Penalize Wire Tapping and Other Related Violations of the Privacy of Communication and for Other Purposes[4236] contains a notwithstanding clause that supersedes all inconsistent statutes.[4237] Section 1 states that all parties to a communication must give permission for a recorded wiretap or intercept and makes it illegal to knowingly possess any recording made in prohibition of this law, unless it is evidence for a trial, civil or criminal.[4238] Section 2 assesses liability for any person who contributes to the actions described in Section 1.[4239] Section 3 provides certain exceptions to the conditions found in Sections 1 and 2 but adopts stringent criteria for wiretap warrants, including the identity of the wiretap target; who may execute the warrant; reasonable grounds that a crime has been, is or will be committed; and, a reasonable belief that the evidence obtained via the wiretap will aid in a conviction or prevention of a crime.[4240] Further, predicate offenses – or offenses for which a court may authorize a wiretap – are limited to several particularly onerous severity.[4241] Section 4 states that any communication obtained in violation of this Act shall not be admissible as evidence in any court.

Despite the legal prohibitions on wiretapping, illegal wiretaps appear to be a continuing problem. In June 2005, charges were filed against a high ranking government official for illegally taping a conversation of President Arroyo.[4242]

U.S. Department of State, Bureau of Democracy, Human Rights, and Labor, Philippines: Country Report on Human Rights Practices for 2003, available at <http://www.state.gov/g/drl/rls/hrrpt/2002/18261.htm>.

[4234] Id.

[4235] Id.; see also Jowel F. Canuday, "UCCP's Human Rights, Peace, Interfaith Offices Ransacked," MindaNews, January 6, 2003, available at <http://www.mindanews.com/2003/01/2nd/arn07uccp.html>.

[4236] Act to Prohibit and Penalize Wire Tapping and Other Related Violations of the Privacy of Communication and for Other Purposes, Republic Act No. 4200, June 19, 1965.

[4237] Id. at § 5.

[4238] Id. at § 1.

[4239] Penalties include imprisonment, disqualification from public office or deportation, in the case of a foreigners.

[4240] Republic Act No. 4200, § 3.

[4241] Offences falling into this category include: crimes of treason, espionage, provoking war and disloyalty in case of war, piracy, mutiny in the high seas, rebellion, conspiracy and proposal to commit rebellion, inciting to rebellion, sedition, conspiracy to commit sedition, inciting to sedition, kidnapping as defined by the Revised Penal Code, and violations of Commonwealth Act No. 616, punishing espionage and other offenses against national security.

[4242] Sun-Star Network Online, "Wiretapping, sedition raps readied against Ong," June 13, 2005, available at <http://www.sunstar.com.ph/static/net/2005/06/13/wiretapping.sedition.raps.readied.against.ong.html>.

The incident has heightened awareness surveillance and wiretapping threats within the Philippine government.[4243]

Section 5 of the Rape Victim Assistance and Protection Act of 1998, stipulates that "any stage of the investigation, prosecution and trial of a complaint for rape, the police officer, the prosecutor, the court and its officers, as well as the parties to the complaint shall recognize the right to privacy of the offended party and the accused." It further states that a police officer, prosecutor or court may order a closed-door investigation, prosecution or trial and that the name and personal circumstances of the offended party and/or the accused, or any other information tending to establish their identities, and such circumstances or information on the complaint shall not be disclosed to the public.[4244] Section 3 provides for the establishment of a rape crisis center in every province and city "for the purpose of: ensuring the privacy and safety of rape victims."[4245]

Section 8 of the Proposed Rule on Juveniles in Conflict (the Rule) with the Law stipulates that "the right of the juvenile to privacy shall be protected at all times. All measures necessary to promote this right shall be taken, including the exclusion of the media."[4246] Section 9 of the Rule, dealing with the fingerprinting and photographing of a juvenile, states "while under investigation, no juvenile in conflict with law shall be fingerprinted or photographed in a humiliating and degrading manner," and stipulates procedural guidelines such as separate storage of fingerprint files from adult files; restricted access by prior authority of the Family Court; and automatic destruction if no charges are laid or when the juvenile reaches the age of majority (21).[4247] Section 26(k) of the Rule confers a duty on the Family Court to respect the privacy of minors during all stages of the proceedings.[4248]

[4243] Fel V. Maragay, "How hi-tech is wiretapping in RP?," Manila Standard Today, June 8, 2005, available at <http://www.manilastandardonline.com:8080/mnlastd/?page=politics02_june08_2005>; China View.com, "Philippine govt admits security threat with wiretapping of Arroyo," June 7, 2005, available at

<http://news.xinhuanet.com/english/2005-06/07/content_3055971.htm>.

[4244] Rape Victim Assistance and Protection Act of 1998, No. 8505, § 5.

[4245] Id. § 3(d).

[4246] Proposed Rule on Juveniles in Conflict With the Law A. M. NO. 02-1-18-SC (April 15, 2002), available at <http://www.chanrobles.com/amno02118sc.htm>, § 8.

[4247] Id. at § 9.

[4248] Id. at § 26.

The Local Government Code of the Philippines[4249] provides that all *barangay*[4250] "proceedings for settlement shall be public and informal provided that the . . . chairman . . . may upon request of a party, exclude the public from the proceedings in the interest of privacy, decency, or public morals."[4251] Section 14 of Alien Social Integration Act of 1995[4252] provides that "information submitted by an alien applicant pursuant to this Act, shall be used only for the purpose of determining the veracity of the factual statements by the applicant or for enforcing the penalties prescribed by this Act."[4253]

The use of biometric technologies has been rising in the Philippines. Since March of 1996, dozens of companies and government agencies have adopted fingerscan technologies in applications ranging from time management and payroll systems to security access control. Many companies use the technology primarily to reduce fraudulent time card punching.[4254] Banks use the technology to reduce fraudulent transactions and to promote security. Additionally, GTE and IriScan, Inc. introduced iris-scan technology in 1998 to ensure the security of online transactions. Other uses of biometric technology in the Philippines include the dispensation of health care and social services; privacy systems for database and records protection; travel security systems with passport, ticket, and baggage verification; business, residence, and vehicle security with access and operator authentication; processing and circulation control in the corrections or prison environment; and portable systems for on-scene recognition of individuals for use in law enforcement.[4255] National ID proposals also typically include fingerprints as part of the information available on the ID card.[4256]

The Code of Conduct and Ethical Standards for Public Officials and Employees[4257] mandates the disclosure of public transactions and guarantees access to official information, records or documents. Agencies must act on a

---

[4249] Local Government Code of the Philippines.

[4250] As the basic political unit, the *barangay* serves as the primary planning and implementing unit of government policies, plans, programs, projects, and activities in the community, and as a forum wherein the collective views of the people may be expressed, crystallized and considered, and where disputes may be amicably settled.

[4251] Local Government Code of the Philippines, § 414.

[4252] Alien Social Integration Act of 1995, No. 7919.

[4253] *Id.* at § 14.

[4254] The Government Service Insurance System, National Computer Center, Philippine Tourism Authority, Department of Social Welfare and Development, and the Light Railway Transit Authority use the fingerscan as a means to ensure that employees are actually at the worksite.

[4255] "Biometrics System Usage Rises," Business World, February 17, 1998, at 14.

[4256] *See, e.g.,* Lira Dalangin-Fernandez, "Arroyo backs national ID system," inq7.net, February 18, 2005, available at <http://beta.inq7.net/common/print.php?index=1&story_id=27929&site_id=39>.

[4257] Republic Act No. 6713.

request within 15 working days from receipt of the request. Complaints against public officials and employees who fail to act on request can be filed with the Civil Service Commission or the Office of the Ombudsman.

Terrorism has continued. In 2003, the government, in an effort to be a menace in the Philippines in 2003 and 2004. There were bomb attacks by Islamist terrorists in March and April 2003.[4258] Part of the government's anti-combat terrorism measures has been the 2003 installation of, installed an Airport Identification Computer System at the Ninoy Aquino International Airport.[4259] The system called PISCES (Personal Identification SecuritySecure Comparison and Evaluation System) was designed to screen for potential terrorists attempting to travel to the United States while they are still in their country of origin's airport. PISCES collates and processes facial images, fingerprints, and biographical information and is purportedly linked to US government databases, allowing for exchange of passenger information.[4260] The Philippine Bureau of Immigration is currently planning to integrate an Advanced Passenger Information system with PISCES to improve border security.[4261]

In February 2005, there were three terrorist bombings in three Philippine cities. The "Valentine's Day bombings" took place in Makati, Davao, and General Santos.[4262] The bombings led to the creation of an anti-terrorism bill.[4263] Through the proposed bill, President Arroyo "wants to institute a national identification system and … give the authorities broad powers that include wiretapping, arresting subjects without warrants and detaining them for longer periods of time."[4264] There is opposition to the bill from human rights organizations and from within the government.[4265]

[4258] April 2, 2003 <http://news.bbc.co.uk/1/hi/world/asia-pacific/2910073.stm>.

[4259] Jonathan M. Hicap, "NAIA Survillance System Linked to FBI Computers." Manila Times. September 25, 2003 <http://www.manilatimes.net/national/2003/sept/25/top_stories/20030925top11.html>.

[4260] Wayne Madsen, "The Business of the Watchers: Privacy Protections Recede as the Purveyors of Digital Security Technologies Capitalize on September 11," Multinational Monitor, Vol 23, No. 3, March 2002, available at <http://multinationalmonitor.org/mm2002/02march/march02corp3.html>.

[4261] "New Border Control Scheme Eyed to Boost Fight vs. Terror," What's On & Expat, April 24, 2005, <http://www.whatson-expat.com.ph/articles/2005/apr24/localnews.htm>.

[4262] Paul Alexander, "Militant Bombings Hit Philippines," Associated Press, February 14, 2005, <http://www.cbsnews.com/stories/2005/02/14/world/main673870.shtml>.

[4263] Privacy International "Philippines Anti-Terrorism Bill," May 25, 2005 <http://www.privacyinternational.org/article.shtml?cmd%5B347%5D=x-347-224693>.

[4264] Carlos H. Conde, "Manila Pushes Anti-Terror Bill," International Herald Tribune, February 23, 2005, available at <http://www.iht.com/articles/2005/02/22/news/manila.html>.

[4265] Edre U. Olalia, "Anti-Terrorism Bill: More Monstrous than the Monster Itself," Bulatlat, May 1- 7, 2005, available at <www.bulatlat.net/news/5-12/5-12-atb.htm>; National Union of Journalists of the Philippines, "A Media Petition against the Anti-Terrorism Bill," Cyberdiario], March 23, 2005, available at <http://www.cyberdyaryo.com/statements/st2005_0323_03.htm>.

Subsection (9) of Section 4 of the anti-terrorism bill classifies cyberspace attacks as acts of terrorism. Such attacks include "committing any unlawful act against networks, servers, computers or other information and communication systems."[4266] Section 18 incorporates the Anti-Money Laundering Act into the bill and authorizes ban.[4267] Section 19 allows for wiretapping through the Anti-Wire Tapping Act.

Republic of Poland

Constitutional Privacy Framework

The Polish Constitution recognizes the rights of privacy and data protection. Article 47 states, "Everyone shall have the right to legal protection of his private and family life, of his honor and good reputation and to make decisions about his personal life." Article 49 states, "The freedom and privacy of communication shall be ensured. Any limitations thereon may be imposed only in cases and in a manner specified by statute." Article 51 states, "(1) No one may be obliged, except on the basis of statute, to disclose information concerning his person. (2) Public authorities shall not acquire, collect nor make accessible information on citizens other than that which is necessary in a democratic state ruled by law. (3) Everyone shall have a right of access to official documents and data collections concerning himself. Limitations upon such rights may be established by statute. (4) Everyone shall have the right to demand the correction or deletion of untrue or incomplete information, or information acquired by means contrary to statute. (5) Principles and procedures for collection of and access to information shall be specified by statute."[4268]

Data Protection Framework

The Law on the Protection of Personal Data (LPPD) was approved in October 1997 and took effect in April 1998.[4269] The law is based on the European Union

---

[4266] Phillippines Anti-Terrorism Bill, § (4)(9).

[4267] *Id.* at § 18.

[4268] The Constitutional Act of 1997, English version available at
<http://www.sejm.gov.pl/english/konstytucja/kon1.htm>.

[4269] Law on the Protection of Personal Data, Dz.U. nr 133, poz. 833, October 29, 1997. Unified text available in the Journal of Laws of 2002 No. 101, item 926 with later amendments. Full English text of the Act can be downloaded from the official Web site of the Inspector General for Personal Data Protection, at
<http://www.giodo.gov.pl/144/j/en/>.

(EU) Data Protection Directive (1995/46/EC). Under the Law, personal information relating to identity may only be processed upon the fulfillment of at least one of the conditions the LPPD requires to be met for lawful personal data processing. Special rules are provided for the processing of sensitive data, which is defined as data relating to race, ethnic origin, religion or philosophical beliefs, political opinions, party or trade-union membership, as well as the processing of data concerning health, genetic code, addictions or sexual preferences, convictions, and other decisions issued in court or administrative proceedings. Everyone has the right to control the processing of his or her personal data contained in the filing systems, and has the right to be informed whether such databases exist and who administers them; queries should be answered within thirty days. Upon finding out that data is incorrect, inaccurate, outdated or collected in a way that constitutes a violation of the Act, citizens have the right to request that the data be corrected, filled in or withheld from processing.[4270] Personal information cannot generally be transferred outside of the European Economic Area unless the third country has "comparable" protections. The law sets out administrative and criminal sanctions for violations. A 1998 regulation from the Minister of Internal Affairs and Administration set out standards for the security of information systems that contain personal information,[4271] but was replaced by the regulation of 2004.[4272]

In August 2001, the Act was amended in order to bring it into full compliance with the EU Data Protection Directive.[4273] Among other changes, the amendment redefined the term "personal data;" introduced a new provision relating to final decisions issued solely on the basis of automated processing of personal data; introduced a new provision on data processing in relation to performance of a contract; adjusted the lawful processing provision; and inserted a scientific research clause. On May 1, 2004, the day of Poland's accession to the European Union, the Amendments to the Act on the Protection of Personal Data entered into force. [4274] These amendments brought into effect the regulation regarding the

---

[4270] "The Info Boom's Murky Side," Warsaw Voice, November 9, 1997.

[4271] The Regulation of June 3, 1998, by the Minister of Internal Affairs and Administration as regards Establishing Basic, Technical and Organizational Conditions Which Should Be Fulfilled by Devices and Information Systems Used for the Personal Data Processing, Journal of Laws, June 30, 1998, No. 80, item 521.

[4272] Regulation of April 29, 2004, by the Minister of Internal Affairs and Administration as regards personal data processing documentation and technical and organisational conditions which should be fulfilled by devices and computer systems used for the personal data processing, Journal of Laws 2004, No. 100, item 1024.

[4273] Act of August 25, 2001, amending the Act on Personal Data Protection, Journal of Laws, No. 100, item 1087.

[4274] *See* <http://www.giodo.gov.pl/259/id_art/195/j/en/>. The text of the Amendment to the Act is available on the Web site <http://www.giodo.gov.pl/272/j/en/>.

prior checking of sensitive data, the transfer of personal data to a third country, and specified some of the controller's duties.

Data Protection Authority

The Inspector General enforces the LPPD.[4275] Ewa Kulesza was appointed as the first Inspector General for the Protection of Personal Data by the Polish Parliament in April 1998 and continues to hold the post. Her second 4-year term ends in May 2006.

The Inspector General has six central duties: to supervise compliance of data processing with the provisions on the protection of personal data; to consider complaints and issue administrative decisions; to comment on proposed new laws and regulations that impact upon data protection; to maintain a central registry of databases; to initiate and undertake activities to improve the protection of personal data; and to participate in the work of international organizations and institutions involved in personal data protection. The Inspector General for Personal Data Protection is an independent authority and performs her duties assisted by the Bureau of the Inspector General (Bureau). The functioning of the Bureau is determined by regulation of the President of the Republic of Poland.[4276] The Bureau secures performing the tasks due to the Inspector General's power conferred upon by the Act and other provisions in force.

Registration details must include the name and address of the data controller, the scope and purpose of the data processing, methods of collection and disclosure, and the security measures. The specimen of a notification of the data filing system to registration by the Inspector General is constituted in the Appendix to the Regulation of April 29, 2004. An Inspector has the right to access data, check data transfer and security systems, and determine whether the information gathered is appropriate for the purpose that it is supposed to serve.[4277] The office monitors the activities of all central government, local government and private institutions, individuals and corporations. As of June 2004, the Bureau had 117 staff members.[4278] The Bureau is structured into several departments.[4279]

[4275] Homepage <http://www.giodo.gov.pl>.

[4276] The Regulation of May 29, 1998 by the President of the Republic of Poland. As regards granting the statutes to the Bureau of the Inspector General for the Protection of Personal Data, Journal of Laws 1998, No. 73, item 464 with later amendments, available at <http://www.giodo.gov.pl/272/j/en/>.

[4277] "A One-Woman Orchestra," Warsaw Voice, June 21, 1998.

[4278] In June 2003, the Bureau had 112 staff members, up from 102 in June 2002.

[4279] The Legal Department prepares answers to the legal questions being lodged; analyzes legal acts with regard to their compliance with the LPPD; prepares legal opinions for the Inspector General, the Director of the

The organizational structure of the Office of the General Inspector for Personal Data Protection has not been modified. The Complaints Department consists of 15 employees and a secretary who administers the flow of documents within the department and between the Complaints Department and other organizational units of the Bureau.[4280] The Complaints Department institutes proceedings on the basis of complaints launched by individuals. The Bureau also carries its activities out *ex officio* when it receives information of possible violations of the LPPD.[4281]

During the period of July 1, 2005 to April 30, 2005,[4282] the Bureau of the Inspector General received 811 complaints that were investigated by the employees of the Bureau.[4283] In general, the issues that are most often raised in the complaints include: the collection of excessive personal data (in particular by banks, insurance companies, employers, telecommunications operators, social assistance centers, administrations of justice, and law enforcement bodies); disclosure of data from medical documents, records of criminal proceedings, or various records collected by public bodies (*e.g.*, motor vehicle or census records); public disclosure of debtors' data and their transfer to professional debt collectors; the legal basis of data processing for the purpose of direct marketing or political campaigns; appropriate means of ensuring the security of personal data (*e.g.*, data contained in employees' files in case of bankruptcy); and the legal basis and scope of processing on the Internet.[4284] The Bureau has, from its inception, conducted an education campaign in an attempt to educate citizens,

---

Bureau and the other departments. The Inspection Department performs inspection activities in order to assess the compliance of processors with the appropriate provisions of the LPPD; works on projects to the decisions issued as a result of inspections; demands institution of disciplinary proceedings against persons found to be guilty of the negligence during inspections, and prepares notifications of committed offences addressed to law enforcement. The Registration Department keeps the register of personal data filing systems, accepts applications for data filing system registration, drafts decisions on refusal of data filing system registration and other letters connected with registry procedure, and issues certificates on personal data filing systems. The Computer Department carries out inspection activities together with the Inspection Department, assesses the requests for registration of data filing systems with regards to compliance with technical and organizational requirements for processing systems, and secures the access to the Bureau's computer system. The Complaints Department considers complaints and motions concerning the compliance with the provisions on personal data protection, drafts decisions issued in cases it examines, drafts notifications on committed offences addressed to law enforcement bodies, and requests inspections on the basis of complaints received. Letter from Mr. Jaroslaw Trelka, *supra.*

[4280] E-mail from Ewa Kulesza, the Inspector General for Personal Data Protection, Poland, to Ula Galster, International Policy Fellow, Electronic Privacy Information Center, May 4, 2005 (on file with EPIC).

[4281] LPPD, *supra.*

[4282] In 2003, the Bureau answered 1,482 enquiries concerning the binding provisions on data protection and the interpretation of the Act, considered 753 complaints, gave 374 legal opinions on bills, conducted 184 inspections at data controllers' facilities in order to assess the compliance of the data processing with the provisions on personal data protection, registered 3,461 data filing systems, issued 522 decisions, and addressed 74 notifications of committed offences provided for by the provisions on personal data protection. Letter from Ms. Alina Szymczak, Director of the Bureau of the Inspector General for Personal Data Protection, Poland, to Samantha Liskow, Law Clerk, Electronic Privacy Information Center, June 11, 2004 (on file with EPIC).

[4283] E-mail from Ewa Kulesza, *supra.*

[4284] Letter from Mr. Jaroslaw Trelka, *supra.*

government officials and the private sector on the provisions of the Act. Some of the more significant decisions issued by the Inspector General in 2001 were to prohibit: telecommunications and insurance companies from making photocopies of identity cards at the time of entering into a contract to provide their services; banks from using their former clients' personal data for marketing purposes; and employers from processing data on employees' sexual life during recruitment. The Inspector has also opened an investigation into a brokerage house that accidentally disclosed clients' personal data on the Internet.[4285] In 2003, the Inspector General ordered Polish telecommunications operators to limit the scope of data collected by them to the extent allowed by the telecommunications law.[4286]

Administrative proceedings initiated by the individual complaint are subject to the duty of fulfilling the requirements stipulated by the Code of Administrative Procedure or by the Act of September 9, 2004 on Stamp Duty. The Code of Administrative Procedure, which by the power of Article 22 of the LPPD is applicable to all proceedings conducted by the Inspector General unless the LPPD states otherwise, provides that any case should be investigated within a one month period. However, in complicated cases this period can be prolonged up to two months.[4287]

The entire proceeding is conducted solely in writing. The authority addresses the entities, which according to the complainant have breached provisions of the LPPD, with a request for explanations and for any documents confirming the right to process personal data of the complainant. Once the documentation has been collected, the evidence is analyzed. If there is a recognized breach of provisions on personal data protection, the Inspector General orders, by means of administrative decision, restoration of the proper legal state.[4288]

The Inspector General for Personal Data Protection, pursuant to the provisions of the LPPD, may also react on the breach of the Act by initiating disciplinary proceedings or notification of crime commitment. In the surveyed period, the Inspector General issued 238 administrative decisions and 51 notifications of crime commitment. Furthermore, the Inspector General addressed the data controllers with documents containing the interpretation of legally binding

---

[4285] E-mail from Igor Kowalewski, International Relations Officer, Bureau of the Inspector General for Personal Data Protection, to Sarah Andrews, Research Director, Electronic Privacy Information Center, June 20, 2002 (on file with EPIC).

[4286] Letter from Ms. Alina Szymczak, *supra*.

[4287] E-mail from Ewa Kulesza, *supra*.

[4288] *Id.*

provisions applicable in the individual case and principles governing the due personal data processing.[4289]

In addition, the Complaints Department may, in case of individual complaints and in cases conducted *ex officio,* request that the Inspection Department inspect the premises of the data controller against whom the proceedings are being conducted. As of April 2005, the inspectors of the Bureau carried out 102 inspections (including 75 instituted at the request of the Complaints Department and 19 instituted at the request of the Personal Data Files Registration Department).[4290]

In the Polish personal data protection legal system it is the Inspector General that registers personal data files (also referred to as personal data filling systems) and not the controllers themselves. In the surveyed period the Inspector General registered in the preliminary registry 2,695 personal data filling systems.

The separate category of administrative decisions pertains to the registration of personal data filling systems. In this regard the Inspector General issued 257 decisions: 109 decisions on denial of registration of the data filing system, 52 decisions on discontinuing the proceedings, and 96 decisions on striking of the filing system from the registry. From July 1, 2004 to April 30, 2005, the Inspector General also issued 405 addresses to the data controllers indicating the practices that either do or may violate provisions on personal data protection.[4291]

In November 2001, the Inspector General, in conjunction with the Council of Europe, hosted a major conference on data protection.[4292] In September 2004, the Inspector General hosted the 26th International Conference on Privacy and Personal Data Protection in Wroclaw, Poland, under the theme "The Right to Privacy – the Right to Dignity." The annual meetings involve national authorities of personal data protection, the Council of Europe, the European Commission, scientists, economic entities, public institutions and human rights organizations.[4293]

[4289] *Id.*

[4290] *Id.*

[4291] E-mail from Ewa Kulesza, *supra.*

[4292] European Conference on Data Protection, "Council of Europe Convention 108 for the Protection of Individuals with regard to Automatic Processing of Personal Data: Present and Future," November 19-20, 2001, Warsaw (Poland).

[4293] <http://www.giodo.gov.pl/259/id_art/175/j/en/>.

The Inspector General also participated in the Public Voice conference, organized by the Electronic Privacy Information Center, in Wroclaw on the theme "Privacy in a new Era; Challenges Opportunities, Partnerships."[4294] Dr. Kulesza, who gave the opening address, expressed support for NGO participation in the work of the data protection commissioners and proposed future collaborations. The conference featured panel discussions on "Privacy Laws and Developments," "Best Practices for Data Protection Agencies: The Citizen's Perspective" and "Civil Society Collaborations and Regional Focus." Several privacy commissioners participated, including Peter Hustinx (European Data Protection Supervisor), Karel Neuwirt (Data Protection Commissioner for the Czech Republic), Jennifer Stoddart (Privacy Commissioner for Canada), David Loukidelis (Privacy Commissioner for British Columbia Canada), Raymond Tang (Privacy Commissioner for Hong Kong), Frank Work (Information and Privacy Commissioner for Alberta), and Peter Schaar (Chair of the Article 29 Working Group).

The Bureau also maintains close relationships with the data protection authorities in other central and eastern European countries. In December 2001, the Data Protection Commissioners from the Czech Republic, Hungary, Lithuania, Slovakia, Estonia, Latvia, and Poland signed a joint declaration agreeing to closer cooperation and assistance.[4295] The Commissioners have been meeting twice a year. The fourth meeting took place at the end of April 2003 in Budapest.[4296] The sixth Meeting of the Central and Eastern European Data Protection Commissioners was held in Riga, Latvia, in May 2004.

With regard to the harmonization efforts with *Acquis Communitaire*, the Bureau of the Inspector General has been preparing for the Polish accession to the European Union structures for some time. The Inspector General and her representatives have attended meetings (as observers) of such institutions as Article 29 Working Party, Europol Joint Supervisory Body, Schengen Joint Supervisory Authority, and Customs Joint Supervisory Authority. On May 1, 2004, the Inspector General became a member of the Article 29 Working Party. Since November 1, 2004, Poland has also been a party to the Europol Convention and the Europol Joint Supervisory Body. Currently Poland is in the course of becoming a party to the Convention on the Use of Information Technology for Customs Purposes.[4297]

[4294] *See* <http://www.thepublicvoice.org/events/wroclaw04/>.

[4295] <http://www.giodo.gov.pl/234/j/en/>.

[4296] Agenda and meeting notes available at Central and Eastern Europe Data Protection Authorities Web site <http://www.ceecprivacy.org/main.php?s=1>.

[4297] E-mail from Ewa Kulesza, *supra*.

Statutory Rules Related to Privacy

There are sectoral laws in place to deal with the processing of medical and financial data. The 1996 Act on the Profession of a Doctor imposes a duty of confidentiality in relation to patient information on medical professionals, subject to certain exceptions. The Constitutional Tribunal ruled in March 1998 that requiring doctors to identify, on sick leave certificates, the disease of the patient violated patients' right to privacy. The Banking Act of 1997 imposes a requirement of secrecy on banks in relation to an individual's banking activities and identity, and limits the exchange and disclosure of personal data among banks and third parties except for the purpose of assessing credit risks or investigating fraud. However, broad exemptions are granted to state entities. In April 2000, the Constitutional Tribunal dismissed a challenge to the rights of Polish tax authorities to request confidential information about any individual's bank accounts, bonds and securities. The court held that these powers were important in the fight against bribery and money laundering.[4298]

Chapter 33 of the 1997 Penal Code, "Offences against the Protection of Information," deals, among other things, with computer related offences. Unauthorized access to computer systems, computer eavesdropping, interference with data, and computer sabotage are crimes punishable by up to eight years' imprisonment. The code also prohibits telecommunications fraud, the handling of stolen software, computer espionage, and causing harm from interference with automatic data processing.[4299]

Major Privacy Case Law

On October 12, 2004, the Supreme Administrative Court delivered a significant judgment concerning the transfer of personal data.[4300] This judgment followed the cassation claim against the decision of the Regional Administrative Court examining the legality of the decision of the Inspector General for Personal Data Protection. The Court in its decision has affirmed the illegality of the transfer of debtor's personal data (as a result of the transfer of receivables) to a debt

---

[4298] "Constitutional Tribunal Allows Treasury to Screen Bank Accounts," Polish News Bulletin, April 12, 2000.

[4299] Andrzej Adamski, "Computer Crime in Poland: Three Years' Experience in Enforcing the Law," presented to the Council of Europe Conference on Cybercrime, Budapest, November 2001, available at <http://www.coe.int/T/E/Legal%5FAffairs/Legal%5Fco%2Doperation/Combating%5Feconomic%5Fcrime/Cybercrime/International_conference/3National_reports.asp#TopOfPage>.

[4300] Number of the judgment: OSK 769/04.

collection company without a prior approval of the debtor. Inspector General has decided that any transfer of personal data must be preceded by an individual consent of the debtor. The fact that Polish law allows for the transfer of receivables does not constitute a sufficient justification for making personal data available to third parties without the approval of the debtor. It is also insufficient to reserve such a right in the model contract. Both the Regional and Supreme Administrative Courts have shared this view.

However, in the judgment of December 16, 2004, the Supreme Administrative Court adopted a different standpoint. The Court decided that transfer of receivables can be considered as a legitimate interest of the data controller and the transfer of data of the data subject is allowed without his or her consent. After a long deliberation, the Supreme Administrative Court (composed of seven judges) in the judgment of June 6, 2005, revoked the view expressed in the judgment of December 16, 2004. Therefore, it has been established that the processing or the transfer of personal data within the transfer of receivables does require the consent of the data subject. The lack of consent cannot be justified by a legitimate interest of the data controller.[4301]

Wiretapping and Other Government Surveillance

The Government of Poland carries out a large number of wiretaps with limited oversight. Under the Criminal Code, the use of wiretaps shall be authorized by the court, after an appropriate motion by the Prosecutor. The Minister of Justice, in consultation with the Minister appropriate for the communication issues, the Minister of Defense and the Minister appropriate for the internal affairs, specified, in the way of the regulation the manner of the control and technical requirements of wiretaps and how to carry out the wiretap.[4302] The law specifies for which cases the interception of communications may be authorized. In exceptional cases, the police may initiate a wiretap at the same time as they apply for authorization. Furthermore, under the Police Code, electronic surveillance may be used for the prevention of crime as well as for investigative purposes. The government does not usually release statistics on the number of wiretaps applied for and authorized, tending to view this as a state secret. In 1997, the reports of numbers of wiretaps varied from 2,000 to 4,000.[4303] There are

---

[4301] Number of the judgment: sygn. I OPS 2/05.

[4302] The Regulation of June 24, 2003 by the Ministry of Justice.

[4303] Some Remarks on Human Rights Protection in Poland (in connection with the fourth periodic report of Republic of Poland on implementation of the International Covenant on Civil and Political Rights), Helsinki Foundation for Human Rights, available at <http://www.hfhrpol.waw.pl/en/index.html>.

unsubstantiated reports that these numbers increased further in 1999 and 2000.[4304] The United States Department of State, in its annual Country Reports on Human Rights Practices, has been consistently critical of high number of wiretaps authorized in Poland. In its most recent report, despite the fact that no credible estimate existed of the number of police wiretaps, the U.S. government agency wrote, "[t]here was no independent judicial review of surveillance activities, nor was there any control over how the information derived from investigations is used. A number of agencies have access to wiretap information, and the Police Code allows electronic surveillance to be used for the prevention of crime as well as for investigations."[4305]

In its 1999 report, the United Nations Human Rights Committee said it was "concerned that the Prosecutor (without judicial consent) may permit telephone tapping and that there is no independent monitoring of the use of the entire system of tapping telephones." The Committee recommended that Poland "review these matters so as to ensure compatibility with article 17 [of the International Covenant on Civil and Political Rights], introduce a system of independent monitoring, and include in its next report a full description of the system by then in operation."[4306]

Various proposals to expand law enforcement surveillance capabilities over the last few years have been put forward. In July 2001, amendments to the Police Act gave the police increased powers to monitor individuals in public places including through the use of video surveillance. The International Helsinki Committee noted in its 2002 report that the amendments "were dubious in terms of the right to privacy."[4307] The Ministry of Internal Affairs and Administration announced in January 2000 that it was setting up a new unit of 1,500 officers to combat organized crime, based on the United States Federal Bureau of Investigation. The new unit will have the power to conduct electronic surveillance and create extensive databases.[4308] Efforts to require all service operators (including mobile phone and Internet Service Providers) to install equipment, to facilitate this increased monitoring, are also going forward. There are serious concerns within the Bureau about the Polish Executive Regulation of

---

[4304] United States Department of State, Country Reports on Human Rights Practices 2001, March 4, 2002, available at <http://www.state.gov/g/drl/rls/hrrpt/2001/eur/8321.htm>.

[4305] United States Department of State, Country Reports on Human Rights Practices 2003, February 25, 2004, available at <http://www.state.gov/g/drl/rls/hrrpt/2003/27858.htm>.

[4306] United Nations, Report of the Human Rights Committee, A/54/40, October 21, 1999.

[4307] International Helsinki Federation for Human Rights, "Human Rights in the OSCE Region: The Balkans, the Caucasus, Europe, Central Asia and North America," Report 2002 (events 2001) available at <http://www.ihf-hr.org/reports/AR2002/country%20links/Poland.htm>.

[4308] "New Police Unit to Combat Organised Crime," Polish News Bulletin, January 4, 2000.

February 22, 2003, adopted pursuant to the Telecommunications Law. The provisions of this regulation impose upon telecommunications network operators the obligation to ensure the public security bodies have access to information sent through telecommunications networks for the purpose of national defense, state security and public order.[4309]

Amendments to the Police Act[4310] have been made by the Telecommunication Act.[4311] They focus on disclosing and processing a caller ID by the Police. The amendments also concern network terminals and/or telecom devices used in the connection, data generated during the connection or attempts to connect to particular telecom devices or network terminals, and the circumstances and a type of connection. Currently they may be disclosed to and processed by the Police only in order to prevent or detect a crime. The above-mentioned data may be disclosed at a written request by the Police Commander in Chief and/or a Regional Commander, or at an oral request of a policeman having a written authorization of the above-mentioned authorities. Telecom operators shall disclose to the policemen the data mentioned in the request of an appropriate Police unit. Materials obtained by the Police, which contain information relevant to the criminal proceedings, are transferred to the office of the prosecutor of relevant competence. Materials obtained by the Police, which do not contain information significant to criminal proceedings, shall be immediately destroyed by a specially formed committee, which shall also provide officially recorded evidence of the destruction. Data shall be disclosed to the Police at the cost of a telecommunications operator. Despite the opinions of the Police and state security services, operators are not obliged to register (identify) the pre-paid users. However, after bomb attacks in Madrid and London, a new legislation in this regard is at the preparatory stage.

In February 2003, legislation was enacted exempting officials from the law of "lustration" if they cooperated with intelligence and counterintelligence agencies. The law of lustration is designed to expose collaborators with the Communist-era secret police by requiring sworn affidavits that may be reviewed by a court. The Constitutional Tribunal in June 2003 found the legislation to be procedurally unconstitutional, but a new, similar law was enacted in October.[4312]

[4309] The Regulation of January 24, 2003 by the Minister of Infrastructure – Journal of Laws of 2003, No. 19, item 166. (The concern is mentioned in the Mr. Trelka's letter, *supra*.)

[4310] The Police Act of 6 April 1990, Journal of Laws of 2002, No 7, item 166, with changes.

[4311] The Telecommunication Act of 16 July 2004, Journal of Laws of 2004, No 171, item 1800.

[4312] United States Department of State, Country Reports on Human Rights Practices 2003, *supra*.

The information about cooperation with above mentioned intelligence and counterintelligence agencies are gathered by the Institute of National Remembrance (*Instytut Pamieci Narodowej* -IPN).[4313] IPN is authorized to reveal such information in the cases specified by the Act of 18th December 1998 on IPN.[4314] The Inspector General for Personal Data Protection has pointed out that the legal conditions of disclosure of the data are unclear.

The Constitutional Tribunal (*Trybunal Konstytucyjny* - TK) also found unconstitutional, in April 2004, an act regarding the Internal Security and Intelligence Agencies that allowed officers to observe and record events in public places. Public groups had opposed the act on numerous grounds, including that it violated the right to privacy.[4315] According to a recent decision of the TK,[4316] the powers of Polish fiscal inspectors are too extensive. They were broadened by the 2003 Act on Provincial Fiscal Courts and will expire in 2006. At present, fiscal inspectors have nearly unlimited rights to collect, store and use personal information, register events in public places, install tapping devices, and register call attempts. The information obtained in this way can be archived and stored even after it becomes useless for the inspectors. The Act has been appealed against by MPs from Law and Justice (*Prawo i Sprawiedliwosc* - PiS) and the League of Polish Families (*Liga Polskich Rodzin* - LPR). In their opinion, fiscal inspectors are currently capable of collecting personal information in a secret and uncontrolled manner, which infringes the constitutional right of privacy. The TK agreed that such powers should only be available to the inspectors in special circumstances.[4317]

Controversy still surrounds the expanded national identification (ID) system. The Electronic Census System (PESEL) number, which has been issued since the mid-1970s, is the biggest collection of personal data in Poland. Every identity card contains a PESEL number, which is a confirmation of the owner's date of birth and sex. The system is fully computerized. The Government began issuing the new ID cards in January 2001.

[4313] Homepage <http://www.ipn.gov.pl/index_eng.html>.

[4314] *Ustawa o Instytucie Pamieci Narodowej -Komisji cigania Zbrodni przeciwko Narodowi Polskiemu*, Journal of Laws December 19, 1998, available at http://www.ipn.gov.pl/index.html (in Polish).

[4315] "Court Says Parts of Secret Services Law Unconstitutional," BBC Worldwide Monitoring, April 20, 2004 (source Polish Radio 1, Warsaw, in Polish, April 20, 2004).

[4316] *See* <http://www.trybunal.gov.pl/eng/>.

[4317] "TK States Fiscal Inspectors' Powers Are Too Extensive," Polish New Bulletin, June 21, 2005, issue of Puls Biznesu p. 5 (on file with EPIC).

Anti-terrorism Measures

Poland has given priority to the fight against organized crime. The Police Act was amended in August 2001 to give the police more operational powers (authorization to check bank and insurance accounts of suspects). Considerable efforts were made to equip the police with the latest technological tools (the central automated system for identifying fingerprints was extended to regional and local levels).[4318]

As regards the surveyed period (July 1, 2004, to April 30, 2005) there have been no new security laws introduced or proposed of which the Inspector General would be aware because of the advisory function of the authority. However, taking into account that terrorism seems to be closely related with organized crime, it needs to be stressed that during the said period the Bureau of the Inspector General for Personal Data Protection had received a number international agreements on cooperation in combating organized crime. These agreements may affect personal data protection, as the law enforcement agencies would be allowed to exchange personal data necessary to fight this form of criminal activity.[4319]

As regards the fight against terrorism, Poland has ratified the main conventions, such as the UN Convention for the Suppression of Terrorist Financing[4320] and is preparing to accede to the Convention on Mutual Assistance in Criminal Matters between the Member States[4321] when it has joined the European Union.[4322]

Open Government

The Parliament approved the Act on Access to Public Information in September 2001. It went into effect in January 2002. The Act creates a presumption of access to information held by all public bodies, private bodies that exercise public tasks, trade unions, and political parties. The bodies are also required to

---

[4318] "Poland Adoption of the Community *Acquis*," Summary of the Legislation available at
<http://europa.eu.int/scadplus/leg/en/lvb/e22106.htm> (last updated April 13, 2004).

[4319] E-mail from Ewa Kulesza, *supra*.

[4320] United Nations Convention for the Suppression of Terrorist Financing adopted by the General Assembly of the United Nations on December 9, 1999, available at
<http://untreaty.un.org/English/Terrorism/Conv12.pdf>.

[4321] Council of Europe Convention on Mutual Assistance in Criminal Matters between the Member States, May 29, 2000 [Official Journal C 197, 12.07.2000] available at
<http://europa.eu.int/scadplus/leg/en/lvb/l33108.htm>.

[4322] Summary of the Legislation, *supra*.

publish material online. There are exemptions for official or state secrets, confidential information, personal privacy, and business secrets. Appeals are made to a court. In July 2003, the Polish Access to Public Data Bill came into force, requiring thousands of public institutions, such as local government, political parties and schools, to put public information on Web sites.[4323] The Public Data Bulletin, a system of Internet sites, serves to collect these informational sites in one place.[4324]

Poland enacted the Classified Information Protection Act in January 1999 as a condition to entering North Atlantic Treaty Organization (NATO).[4325] The act covers classified information or information collected by government agencies whose disclosure "might damage interests of the state, public interests, or lawfully protected interests of citizens or of an organization." There have also been efforts to deal with the files of former employees of the communist era secret police. A law creating a National Remembrance Institute (IPN) to allow victims of this secret police agency access to records was approved by the Parliament in October 1998. The files were opened to the public in February 2001.[4326] The Screening Act of 1997 created a special commission to examine the records of government officials who might have collaborated with the secret police. The Commission began work in November 1998. Under the Data Protection Act, individuals have the right to access and correct records that contain personal information about them from both public and private bodies. However, in November 2003 the government asked Parliament to amend the law on the protection of secret information; that amendment introduces 64 forms of information to be declared top secret and classified. The amendment also allows officers to mark any information as classified that might be "inconvenient" for them.[4327]

Recent Developments

The National Council of Radio and Television, (*Krajowa Rada Radiofonii i Telewizji*),[4328] which is a regulatory body for Polish broadcasters of TV and radio (both public and commercial) similar to the US FCC, has produced a document

---

[4323] Journal of Laws No 112, item 1198, available at <http://home.online.no/~wkeim/files/poland-foia.htm>.

[4324] *See* <http://www.bip.gov.pl/> (in Polish).

[4325] The Classified Information Protection Act of 22 January 1999.

[4326] *See* "Freedom of Information and Access to Government Records Around the World," *supra.*

[4327] International Helsinki Federation for Human Rights, Human Rights in the OSCE Region: The Balkans, the Caucasus, Europe, Central Asia and North America, Report 2004 (events 2003), available at <http://www.ihf-hr.org/documents/doc_summary.php?sec_id=3&d_id=3860>.

[4328] Homepage <http://www.krrit.gov.pl>.

called Polish State's Strategy on Electronic Media for the years 2005-2020 (*Strategia panstwa polskiego w dziedzinie mediow elektronicznych na lata 2005-2020*).[4329] In the document, they have included various plans, ideas and legislative proposals, including regulation and rating of the Internet content, and even the licensing of the radio and television broadcasted in the Internet, similar to the licensing that now exists for the traditional radio and television.[4330]

On February 18, 2005 the lower chamber (*Sejm*) of the Parliament voted almost unanimously on passing the Computerization Act,[4331] which is supposed to foster the development of e-government in Poland. The Computerization Act is an instrument for the modernization of the Polish public administration and the coordination of the country's computerization. Among other things, the new legislation: gives citizens and businesses the right to contact public authorities electronically; establishes the Plan for Information Society Development in Poland and a number of projects of public interest; provides for the technological neutrality of IT systems used by the public sector; sets the minimum requirements for IT systems used for the fulfillment of public administration tasks, for public registers, and for the electronic exchange of data between public entities; and introduces an interoperability framework for public sector IT systems, in order to facilitate seamless communication both among public bodies and between government and citizens and businesses.4332

NGOs Advocacy Work

The Polish Constitution sets out the necessary foundations for the NGOs existence in the articles 12 and 58. The two basic types of non-governmental organizations in Poland are associations and foundations, regulated respectively by the Law on Associations[4333] and the Law on Foundations.[4334]

[4329] Available at: <http://www.krrit.gov.pl/stronykrrit/opracowania/strategiapp.pdf> (in Polish).

[4330] *See* <http://www.fkn.pl/news/id__16717, *See also*, http://www.vagla.pl, Freedom and Capitalism, the libertarian portal, formerly of the "UPR" party at: http://e-upr.org, http://liberator.org.pl.

[4331] Computerization Act (*Ustawa o Informatyzacji*), February 17, 2005, available at <http://www.mnii.gov.pl/_gAllery/79/57/7957.pdf> (in Polish).

[4332] "Polish Computerization Act passes Parliament's vote," eGovernment news, available at <http://europa.eu.int/idabc/en/document/3926/585>. *See also*, the Ministry of Science and Information Society Technologies, press release, available at <http://www.mnii.gov.pl/mnii/index.jsp?place=Lead07&news_cat_id=13&news_id=1927&layout=6&page=text> (in Polish).

[4333] Act of April 4th 1989 The Law of Associations (Journal of Laws No 79, item 855, 2001, with changes).

[4334] Act of April 6th 1984 The Law of Foundations (Journal of Laws No 46, item 203, 1991, with changes).

The Polish history of relations between the government and the civil society groups is quite brief. It was only after 1989 when a development of civil society began. Thus, even though Poland is now the EU Member State, there have not been any significant developments in this area. Civil society is still weak and its influence on policy making is relatively small.[4335]

Legal grounds for the cooperation between the public authorities and the NGOs are established in the Act on Public Benefit and Volunteer Work.[4336] This act provides a framework for such cooperation. It also imposes an obligation on public administration to cooperate with the NGOs in the field of public tasks. This obligation concerns cooperation not only with "public benefit organizations" but also all with other NGOs involved in the area of public tasks.

The cooperation may take forms of: entrusting NGOs with the performance of public tasks; reciprocal feedback concerning all activities planned; consulting NGOs on draft normative acts in areas relating to their statutory acts; and setting up joint advisory teams of relevant public administration authorities with the participation of the NGOs representatives.

Unfortunately, in practice the civic sector is quite underdeveloped in the sense of NGOs capacity. Therefore, in many instances public institutions might be under the impression that the majority of the NGOs they had invited to consultation processes have been unable to participate. This is true, especially in the case when a very short consultation period has been offered.[4337]

Furthermore, there are informal criteria such as organization size, good personal contacts of the NGOs leaders with civil servants or networking structure, and limited possibilities for civic sector development because small or newly set up NGOs have no access to information or to funding.[4338]

The most frequent problems reported by the representatives of auditors offices, which co-operated with the NGOs, involved the lack of internal organization,

---

[4335] UN Country Program document for Poland (2004-2005), DP/DCP/POL/1, 5 August 2003.

[4336] Act of April 24th 2003 on Public Benefit and Volunteer Work.

[4337] Grażyna Rokicka and Paweł Rokicki, "National Report on Assessing and Reviewing the Criteria of Representativeness of Civic NGOs -Poland" available at <www.activecitizenship.net/documenti/Poland.doc>. *See also*, the project "Assessing and Reviewing the Criteria of Representativeness of Civic NGOs," promoted by Active Citizenship Network, (ACN), available at <http://www.activecitizenship.net/home.html>.

[4338] *Id.*

poor management, lack of specified procedures, and clearly specified responsibilities.[4339]

International Obligations

Poland is a member of the Council of Europe (CoE) and has signed and ratified the European Convention for the Protection of Human Rights and Fundamental Freedoms. In May 2002, it ratified the CoE Convention for the Protection of Individuals with Regard to Automatic Processing of Personal Data (ETS No. 108).[4340] In November 2001, it signed, but has not ratified, the CoE Cybercrime Convention (ETS No. 185).[4341] Poland is a member of the Organization for Economic Cooperation and Development (OECD) and has adopted the OECD Guidelines on the Protection of Privacy and Transborder Flows of Personal Data. In November 2001, Poland ratified the United Nations Convention of 2000 against Transnational Organised Crime (the Palermo convention[4342]). Poland has also yet to sign the Council of Europe Convention on Computer-related Crime. On May 1, 2004, Poland joined the European Union.

Republic of Portugal

Constitutional Privacy Framework

The Portuguese Constitution has extensive provisions on protecting privacy, secrecy of communications and data protection.[4343] Article 26 states, "(1) Everyone's right to his or her personal identity, civil capacity, citizenship, good name and reputation, image, the right to speak out, and the right to the protection of the intimacy of his or her private and family life is recognized. (2) The law establishes effective safeguards against the abusive use, or any use that is contrary to human dignity, of information concerning persons and families. (3) A person may be deprived of citizenship or subjected to restrictions on his or her civil capacity only in cases and under conditions laid down by law, and never on political grounds."[4344] Article 34 states, "(1) The individual's home and the

---

[4339] *Id.*

[4340] Signed April 21, 1999; ratified May 23, 2002; entered into force September 1, 2002.

[4341] Signed November 23, 2001.

[4342] *See* <http://europa.eu.int/scadplus/leg/en/lvb/l33088.htm>.

[4343] Constitution of the Portuguese Republic, available at <http://www.parlamento.pt/ingles/cons_leg/crp_ing/index.html>.

[4344] *Id.* at Article 26.

privacy of his correspondence and other means of private communication are inviolable. (2) A citizen's home may not be entered against his will, except by order of the competent judicial authority and in the cases and according to the forms laid down by law. (3) No one may enter the home of any person at night without his or her consent. (4) Any interference by public authority with correspondence or telecommunications, apart from the cases laid down by law in connection with criminal procedure, are prohibited."[4345]

In 1997, Article 35 of the Constitution was amended to give citizens a right to data protection. The new Article 35 states, "1. All citizens have the right of access to any computerized data relating to them and the right to be informed of the use for which the data is intended, under the law; they are entitled to require that the contents of the files and records be corrected and brought up to date. 2. The law shall determine what is personal data as well as the conditions applicable to automatic processing, connection, transmission and use thereof, and shall guarantee its protection by means of an independent administrative body. 3. Computerized storage shall not be used for information concerning a person's ideological or political convictions, party or trade union affiliations, religious beliefs, private life or ethnic origin. Such storage is only allowed when there is express consent from the data subject, authorization is provided for under the law with guarantees of non-discrimination, or as long as it is not possible to identify individuals in the case of data processing done for statistical purposes. 4. Access to personal data of third parties is prohibited, aside from exceptional cases as prescribed by law. 5. Citizens shall not be given an all-purpose national identity number. 6. Everyone shall be guaranteed free access to public information networks and the law shall define the regulations applicable to the transnational data flows and the adequate norms of protection for personal data and for data that should be safeguarded in the national interest. 7. Personal data kept on manual files shall benefit from protection identical to that provided for in the above articles, in accordance with the law."[4346]

Data Protection Framework

The 1998 Act on the Protection of Personal Data adopts the European Union (EU) Data Protection Directive requirements into Portuguese law.[4347] It limits

---

[4345] *Id.* at Article 34.

[4346] *Id.* at Article 35.

[4347] Act No. 67/98 of October 26, 1998.,Act on the Protection of Personal Data (transposing into the Portuguese legal system Directive 95/46/EC of the European Parliament and of the Council of 24 October 1995

the collection, use and dissemination of personal information in manual or electronic form. It also applies to video surveillance or "other forms of capture, processing and dissemination of sound and images." It replaces the 1991 Act on the Protection of Personal Data with Regard to Automatic Processing.[4348]

In August 18, 2004, the parliament enacted Law No. 41/04,[4349] which implemented the EC Directive on Privacy and Electronic Communications (2002/58/EC) without incorporating the Directive's Article 13 on unsolicited communications. That article had already been implemented in Law No. 7/04,[4350] which also implemented the EC's Directive on Electronic Commerce (2000/31/EC). Law No. 41/04 also repealed Law No. 69/98,[4351] which implemented the EC Telecommunications Privacy Directive (1997/66/EC).

In January 2005, the Health Ministry published a regulation[4352] adding HIV and AIDS to the list of diseases with compulsory notification by any doctor to the Epidemic Surveillance Center of the National Health Institute. The stated objective is to identify the epidemic pattern of the disease. The form in question included all the data needed to identify a specific individual, including the person's full name. That was corrected in a later regulation[4353] that defined a form approved by the National Data Protection Commission where the personal information was reduced.

Data Protection Authority

The National Data Protection Commission (*Comissão Nacional de Protecção de Dados*, or CNPD) is charged with controlling and enforcing the laws on protection of personal data.[4354] The Commission functioned as part of the National Parliament until 2004. In 2004, it became an independent agency that is directly responsible to the Parliament.[4355] Its functions are to register existing

on the protection of individuals with regard to the processing of personal data and on the free movement of such data), available at <http://www.cnpd.pt/bin/legis/nacional/lei_6798.htm>.

[4348] Law No. 10/91 - *Lei da Protecção de Dados Pessoais face à Informática*, amended by Law No. 28/94 of August 29, 1994, *Aprova medidas de reforço da protecção de dados pessoais*.

[4349] Law No. 41/04, *available at* <http://www.anacom.pt/template20.jsp?categoryId=127240&contentId=22754>.

[4350] Available at <http://www.anacom.pt/template20.jsp?categoryId=98047&contentId=164733>.

[4351] Law No. 69/98, available at <http://www.cnpd.pt/bin/legis/nacional/lei_6998.htm>.

[4352] Regulation No. 103/2005, available at <http://www.dre.pt/pdfgratis/2005/01/017B00.PDF#page=39>.

[4353] Regulation No. 258/2005, available at <http://www.dre.pt/pdfgratis/2005/03/053B00.PDF#page=71>.

[4354] Homepage <http://www.cnpd.pt/>.

[4355] Law No. 43/2004, available at <http://www.dre.pt/pdfgratis/2004/08/194A00.PDF#page=21>.

databases with private data, authorize and control such databases, issue directives, and oversee the Schengen Information System (SIS). The number of investigations conducted has risen steadily from five in 1994 to 42 in 1997, 78 in 1998, 151 in 2000, 223 in 2001 and 211 in 2002. The number of referrals for criminal prosecution to the Public Prosecution Service is very low due to the existence of a fine system for the transgressions. There was one referral in 2001 and two in 2002. The Commission applied 22 fines in 2001, totaling EUR 52,000 and 119 in 2002, totaling EUR 435,000. The Commission authorized 483 databases in 2000, 486 in 2001, and 638 in 2002, for a total of 4,285 approvals between 1993 and 2002.[4356] The Commission handled 223 inspections in 2001, and 211 in 2002, mostly in the private sector.[4357] It issued opinions on obtaining subscriber information from telecommunications providers, access to marketing databases by the Criminal Investigation Police, denied access by the Information and Security Service to the information system of the Aliens and Frontiers Department, and approved transborder data flows to the United States when the transferee company promised to protect the personal data collected pursuant to European data protection legal standards.[4358] In June 1997, the Supreme Administrative Tribunal upheld the Commission's decision in a case against a shoe company that used smart cards to control employees' bathroom visits.[4359]

In 2003, the CNPD published "Guidelines on Privacy in the Workplace."[4360] These guidelines establish that information and contents of phone calls, e-mails and Internet access for private use of a worker is protected as private data and must be respected as such by the employer. In 2004, the CNPD published guidelines on the usage of Radio Frequency Identification (RFID) technology,[4361] biometrics[4362] and surveillance systems.[4363] These guidelines establish the need for the registration of the databases connected to these systems, and determine the criteria for the use of such systems to comply with data protection principles.

[4356] Estatisticas 2001 & 2002, Tratamentos Legalizados por Ano, available at <http://www.cnpd.pt/bin/relatorios/estat/200102/estat0102.htm>.

[4357] *Comissão Nacional para a Protecção de Dados*, 2001-02 Report, available at <http://www.cnpd.pt/bin/relatorios/anos/relat01-02.htm>.

[4358] <http://www.cnpd.pt/bin/decisoes/decisoes.asp>.

[4359] Annual Report, 1997, § 5.2, available at <http://www.cnpd.pt/bin/relatorios/anos/relat97.htm>.

[4360] *Comissão Nacional para a Protecção de Dados*, "*Princípios sobre a Privacidade no Local de Trabalho,*" October 29, 2002, available at <http://www.cnpd.pt/bin/orientacoes/principiostrabalho.htm>.

[4361] *Comissão Nacional para a Protecção de Dados*, "*Identificação por radiofrequência,*" January 13, 2004, available at <http://www.cnpd.pt/bin/decisoes/2004/htm/del/del009-04.htm>.

[4362] *Comissão Nacional para a Protecção de Dados*, Principles for the use of biometric data in controlling access and monitoring hours worked, February 26, 2004, available at <http://www.cnpd.pt/bin/orientacoes/principiosbiometricos.htm>.

[4363] *Comissão Nacional para a Protecção de Dados*, "*Princípios sobre o tratamento de videovigilância,*" April 19, 2004, available at <http://www.cnpd.pt/bin/orientacoes/principiosvideo.htm>.

Also in 2004, the CNPD performed an audit on the usage of personal health data in hospitals.[4364] The conclusions included: around half of the personal data databases in hospitals are illegal; with an exception of the video surveillance systems, there are no mechanisms to ensure patient's access to his or her personal data; and personal data is normally supplied for medical research without even informing the authorities (the CNPD) who have the responsibility of approving such transactions. The report also recommends the usage of online requests for analysis as the paper version "is always a target for the general curiosity – both in the archives and the services it flows through – there not being any effective mechanisms to assure the impossibility of inquiry."[4365]

Wiretapping and Surveillance Rules

The Penal Code has provisions against unlawful surveillance and interference with privacy.[4366] Evidence obtained by any violation of privacy, including that of the home, correspondence or telecommunications, without the consent of the interested party is null and void.[4367] An inquiry was opened in October 1994 on illegal surveillance of politicians after microphones were discovered in the offices of a state prosecutor and several ministers.[4368] The Portuguese government ordered cellular telephone companies to assist with surveillance in October 1996.[4369] There are also specific laws on the SIS,[4370] computer crime,[4371] and counseling centers.[4372]

[4364] *Comissão Nacional para a Protecção de Dados, "Relatório de Auditoria ao Tratamento de Informação de Saúde nos Hospitais"* November 9, 2004, available at
<http://www.cnpd.pt/bin/relatorios/outros/Relatorio_final.pdf>.

[4365] *Id.* at 72.

[4366] Penal Code, Chapter VII, §§ 190-98, available at
<http://www.verbojuridico.net/download/cpenal95_2001.zip>.

[4367] Code of Penal Procedure, Article 126, paragraph 3, available at
<http://www.verbojuridico.net/download/cpp_2004.zip>.

[4368] "Bug Found in Portuguese State Prosecutor's Office," Reuters European Business Report, April 27, 1994.

[4369] "Portugal to Tap Mobile Phones in Drugs War," Reuters World Service, October 9, 1996.

[4370] Law No. 2/94 (*Estabelece os mecanismos de controlo e fiscalização do Sistema de Informação Schengen*), available at <http://www.cnpd.pt/bin/legis/nacional/lei_294.htm>.

[4371] Law No. 109/91 (*Sobre a criminalidade informática*) (Law on Computer Crime), available at
<http://www.cnpd.pt/bin/legis/nacional/lei_10991.htm>.

[4372] This law creates a duty of confidentiality for counseling centers, Article15, Law No. 3/84 (*Educação sexual e planeamento familiar*), available at <http://www.apf.pt/leis/lei01.htm>.

Recent Developments Related to Privacy

In 2001 the previous Portuguese government first launched the Portuguese citizen card project. Now the project has been brought to full speed and implementation is expected by 2006. The card, officially called "citizen common card" ("*cartão comum do cidadão*"), will combine ID, tax, social security, health insurance and electoral information. The card was originally expected to be phased in during 2003 but was blocked at the feasibility study stage. The new Portuguese government has now brought the project back to the limelight with a view to start distributing the card in 2006.[4373]

The card will not include a single identification number, because such a number is explicitly forbidden by Article 35 of the Portuguese Constitution. In addition, there will not be a single, common database consolidating all the information contained in the card. The government has said this will ensure that citizens' rights and freedoms will be protected, but organizations such as the Portuguese Association for Consumer Rights[4374] remain unconvinced and have warned against the potential dangers of an electronic citizen card, including the access to personal and health data by a growing number of public and private bodies.[4375]

Open Government

Law No. 65/93 of August 26, 1993 (*Regula o Acesso aos Documentos da Administrção* or Law on the Regulation of, and Access to, Administrative Documents) provides for access to government records in any form by any person.[4376] Documents can be withheld for "internal or external security," secrecy of justice, and personal privacy.[4377] Documents with personally identifiable information can only be accessed by the subject of that information or third parties with "direct, personal and legitimate" interest.[4378] The access to government documents is overseen by the Commission for Access to Administrative Documents (CADA), an independent parliamentary agency. The CADA can examine complaints, provide opinions on access, and decide on

---

[4373] "Portugal – Identification & Authentication/eServices for Citizens," eGovernment News, May 17, 2005, available at <http://europa.eu.int/idabc/en/document/4298/353>.

[4374] Homepage <http://www.apdconsumo.pt/>.

[4375] Portugal – Identification & Authentication/eServices for Citizens, *supra*.

[4376] Law No. 65/93, including alterations made by Laws No. 8/95 and 94/99, available at <http://www.cada.pt/paginas/lada.html>.

[4377] Perguntas Frequentes, <http://www.cada.pt/paginas/faq.html>.

[4378] *Id.*

classification of systems. CADA's decisions are not binding, so if an agency continues to deny access, further appeal can be made to an administrative court. CADA issued 177 opinions in 1998, 231 in 1999, 333 in 2000, 260 in 2001, 259 in 2002, and 310 in 2003.[4379]

International Obligations

Portugal is a member of the Council of Europe (CoE) and has signed and ratified the CoE Convention for the Protection of Individuals with Regard to Automatic Processing of Personal Data (ETS No. 108) (Convention No. 108).[4380] In November 2001, it signed the CoE Convention on Cybercrime (ETS No. 185) but has not ratified it.[4381] It has signed and ratified the European Convention for the Protection of Human Rights and Fundamental Freedoms.[4382] It is a member of the Organization for Economic Cooperation and Development (OECD) and has adopted the OECD Guidelines on the Protection of Privacy and Transborder Flows of Personal Data.

Romania

Constitutional Privacy Framework

The Romanian Constitution[4383] adopted in 1991 recognizes under Title II (Fundamental Rights, Freedoms and Duties) the rights of privacy, inviolability of domicile, freedom of conscience and expression. Article 26 of the Constitution states, "(1) Public authorities shall respect and protect intimacy, family and private life. (2) Any natural person has the right to freely dispose of himself unless by this he causes an infringement upon the rights and freedoms of others, on public order or morals." Article 27 states, "(1) The domicile and the residence are inviolable. No one may enter or remain in the domicile or residence of a person without consent. (2) Derogation from provisions under paragraph (1) is permissible by law, in the following circumstances: for carrying into execution a warrant for arrest or a court sentence; to remove any danger against the life, physical integrity or assets of a person; to defend national security or public

---

[4379] Estatísticas, <http://cada.pt/paginas/estatistica.html>.

[4380] Signed May 14, 1981; ratified September 2, 1993; entered into force January 1, 1994.

[4381] Signed November 23, 2001.

[4382] Signed September 22, 1976; ratified November 9, 1978; entered into force November 9, 1978.

[4383] <http://www.cdep.ro/pls/dic/act_show?ida=1&idl=2&tit=2#t2c2s0a26>.

order; to prevent the spread of an epidemic. (3) Searches may be ordered only by a magistrate and carried out exclusively under observance of the legal procedure. (4) Searches at night time shall be prohibited, except in cases of *flagrante delicto*." Article 28 states, "Secrecy of the letters, telegrams and other postal communications, of telephone conversations and of any other legal means of communication is inviolable." According to Article 30, "(6) Freedom of expression shall not be prejudicial to the dignity, honour, privacy of person, and the right to one's own image."

Data Protection Framework

In November 2001, the Parliament enacted Law No. 676/2001 on the Processing of Personal Data and the Protection of Privacy in the Telecommunications Sector[4384] and Law No. 677/2001 for the Protection of Persons concerning the Processing of Personal Data and the Free Circulation of Such Data.[4385] These laws follow very closely the European Union Telecommunications Privacy (1997/66/EC) and Data Protection (1995/46/EC) Directives respectively.

Law No. 676/2001 provides for specific conditions under which privacy is protected with respect to the processing of personal data in the telecommunications sector. The law applies to the operators of public telecommunications networks and the providers of publicly available telecommunications services who, in the context of their activities, process personal data. The regulatory authority established by Law No. 676/2001 was originally the Ministry of Communication and Information Technology, but it was changed by the Government Emergency Ordinance No. 79/2002 for the National Regulatory Authority for Communication (NRAC).[4386] No specific department was created to take care of the application of Law No. 676/2001.

In 2004, Law No. 676/2001[4387] was practically replaced by Law No. 506/2004 closely following Directive 2002/58/EC of the European Parliament and the Council on personal data processing and privacy protection in the electronic communications sector.[4388]

[4384] <http://www.riti-internews.ro/lg676.htm>.

[4385] <http://www.avp.ro/leg677en.html>.

[4386] <http://www.anrc.ro/en/index.htm>.

[4387] Official Monitor no. 1101, November 25, 2005.

[4388] Directive 2002/58/EC, Official Journal of the European Community no.L.201/31.07.2002.

The new law entered into force on November 17, 2004, and it divides the task of enforcing the personal data protection law, between two institutions: the National Regulatory Authority for Communication (NRAC) for issues related to electronic communications and the People's Advocate Office with regard to issues related to privacy. In this sense, the National Regulatory Authority for Communication (NRAC) has competence in relation to: security measures for electronic communication; non-compliance with invoice issuing conditions; infringement of the obligations regarding the presentation and restriction of calling and connected line identification.

Law No. 677/2001 applies to the processing of personal data, made, totally or partially, through automatic means, as well as to the processing through means other than automatic, which are part of, or destined to, an evidence system.

Supervisory Authority

The supervisory authority for Law No. 677/2001 is the Ombudsman (also called "The People's Advocate").[4389] The Organizational and Functional Regulations of the Ombudsman were changed in order to provide the creation of a special Private Information Protection Office (PIPO), concerned with the protection of individuals in relation to private data processing. This specialized structure established for the implementation of the data protection legislation should have 19 posts.

The Law 506/2004 empowers the People's Advocate Office with the competence related to: listening, recording, storing and any other form of interception and surveillance of communications and related traffic data; use of an electronic communication network with the purpose of storing the stored information in the terminal equipment of a subscriber or user or obtaining access to it; traffic data processing; location data processing; subscriber directories; and sending spam.

A report of the European Union criticized the implementation of the legislation in the domain of personal data protection: "However, progress in implementing personal data protection rules has only been limited. There are grounds for concern regarding the enforcement of these rules: enforcement activities are far below levels in current Member States and additional posts have not been filled during the reporting period,"[4390] and "As regards enforcement and administrative

---

[4389] *See* <http://www.avp.ro>.

[4390] *See* "2004- Regular Report On Romania's progress towards accession," available at <http://europa.eu.int/comm/enlargement/report_2004/pdf/rr_ro_2004_en.pdf>.

capacity, contrary to the announcement of June 2003 that the number of positions in the Directorate for the Protection of Individuals' Rights as regards Personal Data Processing (part of the office of the Romanian People's Advocate) would be increased to 20, the actual staffing level remained at 14 employees." According to the People's Advocate website in April 2005, presently there are 15 people working in this division.

The situation significantly improved in 2004, when the number of people employed within the personal data protection division of the People's Advocate institution increased. In addition, data protection and the obligations related to this domain, were discussed at several seminars addressed to the specific sectors (hotels, tourism, Internet services, health, financial-bank etc). The number of registered personal data processing operators has also increased significantly (five times higher than in 2003).[4391]

In 2002, the Ombudsman adopted several orders in order to implement the Law No. 677/2001.[4392] Furthermore, in 2003 the Ombudsman proposed a normative act establishing a notification fee; to that effect, Law No. 476/2003 was adopted.[4393]

The procedure for solving the complaints submitted to the supervisory authority is stipulated by Article 25 of Law No. 677/2001. Pursuant to these provisions, the complaint cannot be submitted to the supervisory authority earlier than 15 days from the time a complaint is submitted that deals with the same problem to the data controller. In order to solve the complaint, the supervisory authority may listen to both the respective person and the data controller or, if applicable, the person who represents the interests of the respective persons. If the complaint is justified, the supervisory authority is empowered to order the temporary interruption or ceasing of the data processing, the partial or total erasure of the processed data, and may also notify the criminal bodies or bring a lawsuit.[4394]

[4391] Bogdan Manolea, *Institutional Framework for Personal Data Protection in Romania*, presented at Conference "Personal Data Protection – Policy and Practice in the EU Accession and New Member States," Sofia, April, 8 2005, available at <http://www.apti.ro/DataProtection_ro.pdf>.

[4392] Ombudsman Order No. 52 (April 18, 2002) for the approval of the minimum security measures for data processing constituting the basis of the operators to adopt technical and organizational measures in order to guarantee a proper level of legal security of data processing, Official Monitor, June 5, 2002; Ombudsman Order No. 53 (April 18, 2002) for the approval of standardized notification forms, Official Monitor, June 5, 2002; Ombudsman Order No. 54 (April 18, 2002) for the determination of situations requiring the notification of data processing that falls under Law No. 677/2001, Official Monitor, June 5, 2002; Ombudsman Order No. 75 (June 4, 2002) to establish specific measures and procedures to provide a satisfactory level of protection for data subjects, Official Monitor, June 26, 2002.

[4393] Official Monitor, No. 814, November 18, 2003.

[4394] E-mail from Ioan Muraru, People's Advocate, to Cédric Laurant, Policy Counsel, Electronic Privacy Information Center, July 4, 2004 (on file with EPIC).

As a rule, a complaint cannot be addressed by the supervisory authority, unless a judicial procedure involving the same parties and the same subject matter has been already initiated and the applicant does not provide a proof of previously approaching the data controller. In case of non-compliance with the provisions of Law No. 677/2001, the supervisory authority may partially or completely delete, suspend or terminate the data being processed. The authority may also notify the criminal prosecution bodies or may file complaints to a court of law. In addition, some cases of infringement of the law may involve the contravention sanctions imposing a fine on the infringer.[4395]

In 2003, the Ombudsman issued Order No. 6 of January 29, 2003, which establishes standard contractual clauses for the transfer of personal data to third countries that do not provide an adequate level of protection.[4396]

For the period of July 1, 2004 to April 22, 2005, there were 1,303 registered notifications filled by 1,204 data controllers. For the notifications regarding the international transfers of personal data, 49 authorisations were issued. For the same period, four investigations were performed in both public and private sectors.[4397] Seventeen complaints filed according to Law No. 677/2001 concerned infringements of the rights guaranteed by this law, in the field of finance – banking or direct marketing.[4398] The total number of data controllers registered with the supervisory authority to date is 2,381.[4399]

In the Activity Report of the People's Advocate Institution for 2004, Chapter 4 is dedicated to the *Activity of the People's Advocate as a supervisory authority for personal data processing*.[4400] The report was submitted for debates to the both Chambers of the Parliament on January 31, 2005.

[4395] E-mail from Virgil Cristian Cristea, Director of the People's Advocate Office, to Ula Galster, International Policy Fellow, Electronic Privacy Information Center, April 27, 2005 (on file with EPIC).

[4396] Official Monitor No. 151, March 10, 2003.

[4397] In 2003 the Ombudsman only ordered four prior controls and eight investigations, performed both at public and private operators. In a public statement the President of the Ombudsman, Ioan Muraru, declared that the designation of this institution as the surveillance authority for personal data processing is against the purpose on this institutions and asked the Parliament to transfer these tasks to other public institutions. He believed that such an institution requires very specialized personnel and the Ombudsman does not and cannot have such structures. He asked for a specialized Control Authority on Personal Data Processing. "*Avocatul Poporului îsi declină competentele privind protectia datelor cu caracter personal*" (The Ombudsman Declines Responsibilities on Personal Data Protection) Azi, February 13, 2004, available at <http://www.azi.ro/arhive/2004/02/13/social.htm#stirea2>.

[4398] E-mail from Virgil Cristian Cristea, *supra.*

[4399] *Id.*

[4400] Romanian Ombudsman Annual Report 2004 available at <http://www.avp.ro/statnoie.html>.

The report for 2004 of the People's Advocate Office states: "As compared to 2003 there is a visible progress; the number of personal data processors increased 5 times and the number of notifications increased by 300%. Until now, a total of 97 notifications have been registered concerning personal data transfer abroad. Out of these 97 notifications, in 2004, 57 transfer notifications were registered. The progress is quite remarkable in this sector also in comparison to the previous years the notifications for transfer of personal data abroad have increased by 196.5%, as compared to 2003. For the transfer abroad of personal data, in 2004, 53 authorizations were issued out of the total number of 66."[4401]

According to the 2004 Report, the People's Advocate Office provided 943 consultations involving enforcement of the obligations foreseen by the law 677/2004. The consultations were conducted by phone or in a written form. Moreover, the People's Advocate has approved two codes of conduct that included specific norms for the protection of personal data. The two codes of conduct were adopted by the Association of Leasing Companies from Romania[4402] and by Direct Marketing Romanian Association.[4403]

The Romanian Government was not much concerned with the frequent lack of enforcement of the law on data protection. However, the indication of this unsatisfactory status quo in the European Union country report for 2004 made the authorities in Bucharest anxious. Thus, in a short time a meeting to discuss data protection issues was organized. The meeting included the key governmental institutions: the Consultative Council of August 30, 2004, in charge of the integration with the EU, the Ministry of Internal Affairs, the Ministry of the EU Integration and the People's Advocate. Despite the fact that no representative of the NGO sector was invited to participate in this debate, one of the conclusions of the meeting stated: "The civil society can play a bigger role in educating the people on personal data protection and in supporting the public administration in this field."[4404]

A draft act on the creation, organization and operation of the National Authority for the Surveillance of Personal Data Processing was quickly prepared and available for public commentary on the website of the Ministry of the EU

[4401] Id.

[4402] Notice n. 2 / 15 June 2004 published in the Official Monitor no. 627 from July 9, 2004.

[4403] Notice n. 3 / 15 September 2004 published in the Official Monitor no. 874 from September 24, 2004.

[4404] See the press release at <http://groups.yahoo.com/group/romania_eu_list/message/16950>.

Integration on October 9, 2004.[4405] The same unmodified draft was submitted to the Parliament on December 7, 2004.

The act aims at establishing the "National Authority for the Control and Supervision of Personal Character Data Processing" (ANSPDCP). The New Authority shall have at its disposal all necessary resources (logistical, human capital-dedicated specialists, administrative structures, as well as financial means) in order to ensure efficient and correct promotion and implementation of the Law. The Authority shall have a President with the rank of Ministry and a Vice-President with the rank of Secretary of State, both appointed by the Romanian Senate (the Romanian upper Parliamentary Chamber). The Permanent Bureau of the Senate shall appoint the candidates for the two positions, after consulting the proposals addressed by the parliamentary groups from the two Parliamentary Chambers. In order to ensure continuity in the activity of data protection, the draft law stipulates that the New Authority shall become operational within 90 days after the Law comes into force and stipulates clear responsibilities for the new institution. It also regulates the transfer of the database from the People's Advocate Office to the New Authority.[4406]

The proposed draft is, undoubtedly, a step ahead to a better protection of personal data. The president and the vice-president of the ANSPDCP are appointed by the Senate, for a 5-year period. The possibility of employing a maximum number of 50 people within this authority is also foreseen.

The draft law aiming at establishing the "National Authority for the Control and Supervision of Personal Character Data Processing" (ANSPDCP) was criticized on several occasions.[4407] Nevertheless, the Chamber of Deputies approved the proposed draft on March 8, 2005, in its initial form. Although amendments or re-discussions have been proposed by the opposition members, they were rejected due to procedural matters or non-compliance with EU requirements.

In addition, the declaration of the People's Advocate at the plenum of the Deputy Chamber[4408] meant to support this normative act. However, it created confusion

---

[4405] Ministry of the European Integration homepage <www.mie.ro>.

[4406] Precu Corneliu, "Romanian Data Protection Legislation in a European Context," 2005, Master Thesis, The Master Programme in Law and IT, Stockholm University.

[4407] For further discussion on this issue *see* Bogdan Manolea - Institutional Framework for Personal Data Protection in Romania, presented at Conference "Personal Data Protection – Policy and Practice in the EU Accession and New Member States," 8 April - Sofia. Document available at <http://www.apti.ro/DataProtection_ro.pdf>.

[4408] Available at <http://www.cdep.ro/pls/steno/steno.stenograma?ids=5812&idm=6> (in Romanian).

as to treating this matter seriously by the government and the Ombudsman himself.

> "I want to inform you that the experts in Brussels have agreed with the draft, to the letter, there are reports from Brussels, therefore, these drafts were accepted only after the conviction was created in Brussels that this authority will be entirely autonomous, totally independent. And this autonomy and independence, eventually, was approved, to say so, only if the president and vice-president will be appointed by a parliament assembly so that it may be no subordination to the Government or the ministries ... *No doubt you can bring, I know, improvements, amendments. I repeat*, within the report that has been sent from Brussels, which exists with the documents submitted by the Government to the Parliament, it is very clear, sometimes, I repeat, to the letter, how such a project should look like. It is a question that is related to our acceptance in the European Union if I may say so although this matter is beyond me somehow."[4409]

The Draft act was adopted by the Senate with no changes on April 11, 2005. Finally the law was signed by the Romanian President on May 3, 2005, and became Law No. 102/2005.[4410]

In 2002, Law No. 365/2002 on Electronic Commerce[4411] adopted the opt-in principle for unsolicited commercial e-mails ("spam").[4412] Law No. 506/2004 also regulates spam. The new law states that the use of electronic mail for the purposes of direct marketing without the prior explicit consent of the user will be sanctioned with a fine between ROL 50 million (approx. EUR 1,250) and ROL 1 billion (approx. EUR 25,000). For companies with a turnover that exceeds ROL 50 billion, the fine could amount to as much as 2% of revenues. Other provisions regulate the subscribers' right to choose not to be included in printed or electronic directories and to consent to use of personal data in the directory. Companies that infringe this right are subject to a fine between ROL 300 million (approx. EUR 7,500) and ROL 1billion (approx. EUR 25,000). The new law further stipulates that the provider of a publicly available electronic communications service must

---

[4409] *Id.*

[4410] Official Monitor, No. 391 of May 9, 2005, available at <http://www.legi-internet.ro/autoritate_date_pers.htm> (in Romanian).

[4411] Available at <http://www.legi-internet.ro\en\e-commerce.htm>.

[4412] Art. 6 (1) provide that "commercial communications through electronic mail are forbidden, except where the recipient has expressly consented to receive such communications."

take appropriate measures to safeguard the security of its services, and to inform subscribers and users in relation to any risk of a security breach.[4413]

In 2002, the National Audiovisual Council[4414] issued regulations regarding privacy and television and radio programs in Decision No. 80 of August 13, 2002 Regarding the Protection of Human Dignity and the Right to Protect One's Own Image established a few privacy principles: Article 6 states, "(1) Any person has a right to privacy, privacy of his family, his residence and correspondence. (2) The broadcasting of news, debates, inquiries or audio-visual reports on a person's private and family life is prohibited without that person's approval." According to Article 7, "It is forbidden to broadcast images of a person in his or her own home or any other private places without that person's approval; (2) It is forbidden to broadcast images of a private property, filmed from the inside, without its owner's approval."

Law No. 451/2004 concerning temporal marks has been added to the Romanian portfolio of laws regulating electronic and Internet activity. A temporal mark shows when an electronic document is created or signed. The registration of temporal marks must be maintained for at least 10 years.

It is usually used to verify an electronic signature, the validity of the electronic signature certificate in the Internet auctions and when there is a requirement for a certain date for the copyrighted materials. The law also regulates the liability of temporal mark services providers, who are responsible for losses suffered by customers as a result of the provider's failure to comply with the provisions of the law. Providers are required to contract a liability insurance policy or obtain a warranty certificate from a financial institution. The Law entered into force on December 5, 2004.[4415]

Wiretapping and Surveillance Rules

The interception of telephone calls, the opening of correspondence and other similar actions are regulated by Law No. 51/1991 on National Security in Romania and Law No. 26/1994 on Police Organization.[4416] Article 13 of Law

---

[4413] Romania Legal Market Newsletter, December 2004, available at<http://www.salans.com/publications/pdf/pub1450lang1.pdf>.

[4414] Homepage <http://www.cna.ro>.

[4415] Romania Legal Market Newsletter, December 2004, available at <http://www.salans.com/publications/pdf/pub1450lang1.pdf>.

[4416] Nicolae Volonciu, Penal Procedure Treatise, 509-514 (Ed. Padeia 1999).

No. 51/1991 allows the interception of calls in case of crimes against the state, only as a result of a mandate issued by the General Prosecutor of the Office related to the Supreme Court. The mandate has a maximum duration of six months with the possibility of extension by up to three months by the General Prosecutor. According to Article 16 of the same law, the means to obtain information may not infringe citizens' fundamental rights and freedoms, *i.e.,* their private life, honor or reputation, or to subject those rights and freedoms to legal restrictions. The citizens who believe that their rights have been infringed, can appeal to the Commissions of Human Rights of the two Chambers of the Parliament. According to Article 17 of Law No. 26/1994, which aims at preventing organized crime and serious infringements in the interest of a criminal investigation, the police can require the Prosecutor's Office to intercept calls and open correspondence pursuant to Law No. 51/1991.

In 1996, the Criminal Code was modified by Law No. 41/1996, which introduced a new section on the use of audio and video recordings for interception purposes. The section establishes the conditions under which video and audio recordings may be carried out, including the interception of telephone calls. Therefore, according to Article 91 of the Criminal Code, the recordings on magnetic tape can be used as evidence if the following conditions are complied with: there are reasons to believe that a crime has been, or is about to be, committed; the criminal deed related to which the recording is made is a crime investigated ex-officio; the use and efficiency in finding out the truth; and the authority that carries out the wiretap has been properly authorized to do so. The authority competent to issue such an authorization is the prosecutor designated by the General Prosecutor of the Office related to the Court of Appeals. The authorization to wiretap is given for a period of up to 30 days. The authorization can only be extended for very substantiated reasons.

The law also compels law enforcement authorities to report specific information about their wiretapping: the authorization given by the prosecutor, the number of the telephones among which the calls take place, the names of the people carrying out the conversations, and, if known, the date and time at which each communication took place, and the item number of the roll or tape on which the recording is made.

Similar provisions related to the recording of traffic data were introduced by the Law on Anti-Corruption No. 161/2003[4417] in order to prevent and combat cybercrime. Romanian law does not provide for the retention of traffic data by

---

[4417] Official Monitor No. 279, April 21, 2003, available at <http://www.legi-internet.ro/en/cybercrime.htm>.

Internet service providers (ISPs). The law provides that, only in emergency and properly motivated cases, law enforcement can expeditiously obtain the preservation of computer or traffic data if they could be destroyed or altered, and if there are good reasons to believe that a criminal offense by means of computer systems is being, or is about to be, committed, and for the purpose of gathering evidence or identifying the wrongdoers. During the criminal investigation, the preservation is undertaken by the prosecutor, pursuant to an appropriate ordinance and at the request of the investigative body or ex-officio, and during trial, by a court settlement. This ordinance is valid only for no longer than 90 days, and can be exceeded only once by a period not longer than 30 days.

Most of the cases involving invasion of privacy concerned the illegal interception of telephone calls. Several complaints were filed, especially by Opposition members.[4418] The president of the Senate Human Rights Commission recently declared[4419] that a hearing of those people who complained on these issues should take place in the Commission. The Foundation Horia Rusu organized a public debate on those issues on April 14, 2003.[4420] Two Opposition deputies presented a draft law[4421] that would establish the conditions pursuant to which telephone calls could be intercepted so as to limit the intrusion into people's privacy. The draft provides that the warrant authorizing interception could be issued only by a judge and that, later on, the person wiretapped would have to be informed about the reasons of wiretapping. Other cases involved the invasion of privacy of several Romanian TV stars.[4422]

At the beginning of 2005, several cases appeared in the press with regard to that the Romanian secret service intercepting phone call of journalists and other public figures. On January 27, 2005, the Chief of the Romanian Secret Service (SRI) Ioan Timofte explained[4423] that several phones of some Romanian and foreign journalists in Romania were intercepted for several months. The reason was that they were suspected for sabotage and crimes against Romanian National security. The Romanian Press Club and the Board of the Foreign Press in

---

[4418] Such as Dan Carlan, vice-president of the Liberal Party; Iasi Count, Dorin Marian, ex-counsellor of the former President Emil Constantinescu.

[4419] Roxana Ristache, "Interception of Telephone Calls from Iasi in Attention of the Senate," Cotidianul, April 16, 2003.

[4420] Ovidiu Banches, "The Citizen Threatened by National Safety," Ziua, April 15, 2003.

[4421] Draft law No. 207/2002 amending Law No. 51/1991 on the National Security of Romania.

[4422] "Extensions of Free Speech against Privacy?" Cotidianul, April 19, 2002, available at <http://www.cotidianul.ro/anterioare/2002/reportaj/rep1521apr.htm>.

[4423] Dan Bucura, Gabriela Stefan, "There are paid and recruited journalists by foreign information services," Adevarul, January 27, 2005.

Romania Association have protested[4424] and demanded SRI to publicly announce the name of the journalists that were supervised. SRI refused the demand, claiming that they cannot reveal information that may affect national security. The Defense Commissions in the Romanian Parliament, after a hearing of the people involved have considered that the interceptions were legal.[4425] Another case involved the Anticorruption Prosecutor (PNA) from the Mures County (Andreea Ciuca, ex-president for the Mures Tribunal) who has monitored the phones of more than 70 local journalists, local and national press headquarters and lawyers for more than 13 months from April 24, 2003 to May 25, 2004.[4426] No relevant information was offered by PNA to explain this case.

Even the UK liberal MEP Emma Nicholson has accused the Romanian secret service of spying on her. Emma Nicholson said that the surveillance was "predictable and obvious," according to an article in Austria's Der Standard on February 8, 2005. Her comments follow similar ones made by former Dutch MEP Orie Oostlander. Mr. Oostlander, a Christian Democrat and also involved in drawing up reports on Romania, claimed that he has been under surveillance by the Romanian Secret Service.[4427]

Anti-terrorism Measures

Following the international events with regard to terrorism, Romania has adopted specific legislation that directly attempts to combat terrorism. Law No. 508/2004[4428] establishes the conditions in which the Investigating Division on Terrorism and Organized Crime, a new unit created within the Prosecutor's Office from the Supreme Court of Justice, will operate. The unit has the authority to investigate the crimes related to terrorism. Moreover, the unit may require the surveillance or interception of electronic communications as well as investigation of computer systems. However, the final decision in this respect will be taken solely by a judge, according to the Romanian Penal Procedural Code.

[4424] Hotnews.ro, "SRI Does Not Publicize the Bames of the Surveilled Journalists," February 1 2005, available at <http://www.hotnews.ro/articol_14162-SRI-nu-face-publice-numele-ziaristilor-urmariti.htm>.

[4425] Ion M. Ionita, "Virgil Ardelean Pretends That the Intention to Intercept Journalists Calls Started from a Provocation," Adevarul, January 27, 2005.

[4426] Adina Anghelescu, Razvan Savaliuc, "PNA has illegally intercepted the journalists phones," Ziua, February 3, 2005.

[4427] Honor Mahony, "Romanian Secret Service Accused of Spying on MEP," Euobserver.com, February 8, 2005.

[4428] Official Monitor No. 1089, November 23, 2004.

A new law on combating and preventing terrorism was passed in November 2004 (Law No. 535/2004[4429]), changing the previous normative acts[4430] that were in force since 2001. The law offers the possibility for the surveillance or interception of electronic communications, as well as for investigation of computer systems, if there are activities that might be considered threats to national security. These activities need to be approved by the Prosecutor General Prosecutor within the Supreme Court of Justice and authorized by the Supreme Court's judges. The warrant for interception or investigation cannot exceed six months.

Recently draft law was initiated[4431] by four parliamentarians from the Social Democrat Party (PSD) that offers different procedures for authorizing the interception of communications in the cases involving the national security. According to the draft law, the interception of communications would in some cases be possible without a warrant from a judge. A warrant would not be requested in case of new interception equipments being tested or when the improvements of the interception equipments are being made.

In special cases that involve national security the interception could be started without the warrant provided the authorization for the interception for communications is requested from a judge in maximum 48 hours since the interception started. The draft law explicitly refuses the right to appeal the authorization of any communications interception. The draft law also foresees the creation of the Technical Center for National Security – a special body that would collect and manage all the information gathered in the course of these interceptions.

The draft law was heavily criticized by the press,[4432] civil society[4433] (especially Transparency International and Pro Democracy Association) as well as former dissidents like Mircea Dinescu,[4434] who have all accused the former communist

---

[4429] Official Monitor No. 1161, December 8, 2004.

[4430] Emergency Ordinance No .141/2001 on Punishing Terrorist Acts, Official Monitor No. 691, October 31, 2001.

[4431] *See* the draft law submitted to the Parliament on August 25, 2005, available at <http://www.cdep.ro/pls/proiecte/upl_pck.proiect?idp=6486&cam=2> (in Romanian).

[4432] Emilia Sercan, Silviu Sergiu, "Big Brother Project, pattered by PSD," available at <http://www.evz.ro/dezvaluiri/?news_id=192544> (in Romanian), Evenimentul Zilei, July 25 2005,

[4433] Razvan Ghoerghe, "Intercepting Without Warrant," Ziua, July 22, 2005, available at <http://www.ziua.net/display.php?id=181243&data=2005-07-23> (in Romanian).

[4434] Mircea Dinescu, "The Loneliness of the Microphone," Gandul, July 26, 2005, available at <http://www.gandul.info/2005-07-26/actual/singuratatea_microfonului_de_cursa_lunga>; see also, Adina Anghelescu, Razvan Savaliuc, "PNA Has Illegally Intercepted the Journalists' Phones," Ziua, February 3, 2005.

Security Forces of following old habits. The law was also criticized by the Liberal Party, by one of its ministers.

Open Government

The Law regarding Free Access to Information of Public Interest was approved in October 2001.[4435] The law allows any person to ask for information from public authorities and state companies. The authorities must respond in a maximum of 30 days. There are exemptions for national security, public safety and order, deliberations of authorities, and personal data. Those whose requests have been denied can appeal to the agency concerned or to a court.

The 1999 Law on the Access to the Personal File and the Disclosure of the *Securitate* as a Political Police[4436] allows Romanian citizens to access their *Securitate* (secret police) files. It also allows public access to the files of those aspiring for public office. The law sets up the National Council for the Search of Security Archives (CNSAS)[4437] to administer the *Securitate* archives.

The Law on Protecting Classified Information was enacted in April 2002 at the behest of North Atlantic Treaty Organization.[4438] Its drafters used an expansive view of classification that will limit access to records under the access to information law. The law was strongly criticized by the Opposition and civil society.[4439]

Law No. 64/2004 was adopted to ratify the Cybercrime Convention on November 23, 2001.[4440] Many provisions of this Convention, especially the definitions of the crimes, were incorporated into Title III (on Preventing and Fighting Cybercrime) of the Anti-Corruption Law No. 161/2003.[4441] Additional

---

[4435] <http://www.publicinfo.ro/INITIAT/Legea%20accesului%20engl.pdf>.

[4436] Law No. 187/1999 available at <http://www.cnsas.ro/legeeng.html>.

[4437] Homepage <http://www.cnsas.ro/indexeng.html>.

[4438] Law No. 182/2002, Official Monitor, April 12, 2002, available at <http://www.crji.go.ro/legeainfclas.htm> (in Romanian).

[4439] *See* The Association for the Defense of Human Rights in Romania – The Helsinki Committee (APADOR-CH). The Limits to Information in Romanian, available at <http://www.apador.org/limits.htm>.

[4440] Official Monitor No. 343, April 20, 2004, available at <http://www.legi-internet.ro/ratifcybercrime.htm> (in Romanian).

[4441] Official Monitor No. 279, April 21, 2003, available at <http://www.legi-internet.ro/en/cybercrime.htm>.

---

laws deal with privacy issues, such as the Patient's Rights Law[4442] or the Law on Combating and Preventing the Traffic of Human Beings.[4443]

In the draft of the new Penal Code,[4444] an article provides that the infringement of a person's right to privacy by using remote means of interception to get data, information, images or sounds from home or other similar private property without its owner's consent or by breaking the law, is punished with an imprisonment of two to five years. It is also prohibited to disseminate data, information, images or sounds obtained in one of the ways set out in Paragraph 1 of Article 204. Some Romanian NGOs[4445] have requested the elimination of this article, because, in its current wording, it limits the freedom of expression and the debate of matters of public interest. The new version of the Penal Code[4446] will enter into force on June 29, 2005. The former Article 204 is now replaced by Article 209, which provides that it is not a crime to make a photo or to film a building from public places."[4447]

Government Decision No. 952 of August 14, 2003[4448] calls for the establishment of an Integrated Informational System (SII). The SII is a database that will centralize the information held by all public institutions on natural and legal persons. It may become the electronic arm of the Romanian Intelligence Service (SRI). Both the Association for the Defense of Human Rights in Romania – Helsinki Committee (APADOR-CH) and the media criticized this decision by arguing that the Government Decision was not legal, and because of the threats the decision raises for certain fundamental rights, especially the right to privacy.[4449]

[4442] Law No. 46/2003, Chapter IV.

[4443] Law No. 678/2001, Article 26, Paragraph 2.

[4444] Available at <http://www.just.ro/bin/proiecte/cod_penal.htm> (in Romanian).

[4445] Such as APADOR-CH and the Association for Promoting and Protecting the Freedom of Expression (APPLE).

[4446] Official Monitor No. 575, June 29, 2004.

[4447] "Practically, it may be considered a crime even if a journalist takes pictures of an official's villa without permission because the villa is inside the yard and taking pictures of whatever is inside the yard violates the official's right to privacy. Of course, not listing these deeds as crimes does not mean that privacy remains unprotected, only that it has to be protected by civil, not criminal laws. If there is no political will to eliminate this incrimination, the draft should at least be modified by introducing a provision to stipulate that the deed is not a crime if it refers to aspects of private life impeaching over a person's capacity to exercise a public function." APADOR–CH Report on 2003 – available at <http://www.apador.org/rapoarte/anuale/report2003.htm>.

[4448] Official Monitor No. 631, September 3, 2003.

[4449] APADOR-CH considers that the government resolution refers to a decision of the Supreme Defence Council (CSAT), which could not be substituted to the Parliament's. APADOR-CH's representative Manuela Stefanescu said: "We do not know to whom this integrated information system is subordinated; we do not know to whom it is of use, and it is extremely dangerous to create a superpower, especially without the slightest guarantee that the personal data will be protected. . . . Furthermore, natural and legal persons lack any means of

APADOR-CH filed an administrative complaint with the Government, based on Article 5 of Law 29/1990 on administrative courts, pointing out that the decision was illegal and violated the right to privacy, and requesting that the decision be annulled or withdrawn.[4450] The government rejected all objections. As a consequence, the APADOR-CH as a legal entity, and two of its members as individuals, filed a court complaint considering that the decision has seriously infringed upon the subjective right to privacy of APADOR-CH's members (as well as of all other people), a right guaranteed by Article 26 of the Constitution and Article 8 of the European Convention of Human Rights. The court has not yet made a decision .

International Obligations

Romania signed the European Union Association Agreement in 1993, became founding member of the WTO in 1995 and joined the CEFTA in 1997. Romania also signed the Council of Europe Cybercrime Convention on November 23, 2001, and ratified it by adopting Law No. 64/2004.[4451]

In 2001, Law No. 682/2001 was enacted to ratify the Council of Europe (CoE) Convention for the Protection of Individuals with Regard to Automatic Processing of Personal Data (Convention No. 108). The Additional Protocol to the Convention for the Protection of Individuals with Regard to Automatic Processing of Personal Data, Regarding Supervisory Authorities and Transborder Data Flows, was adopted in Strasbourg on November 18, 2001 and was ratified by Law No. 55/2005.[4452]

Russian Federation

Constitutional Privacy Framework

The Constitution of the Russian Federation recognizes rights of privacy, data protection and secrecy of communications. Article 23 states, "1. Everyone shall

---

controlling the way in which the data centralized in this mammoth system will be used. . . .".Evenimentul zilei, September 29, 2003, available at <http://www.evz.ro/english/?news_id=132980>.

[4450] *See* the complaint in the APADOR-CH 2003 report available at
<http://www.apador.org/rapoarte/anuale/report2003.htm>.

[4451] Official Monitor No. 343, April 20, 2004, available at <http://www.legi-internet.ro/ratifcybercrime.htm> (in Romanian).

[4452] E-mail from Virgil Cristian Cristea, *supra.*

have the right to privacy, to personal and family secrets, and to protection of one's honor and good name. 2. Everyone shall have the right to privacy of correspondence, telephone communications, mail, cables and other communications. Any restriction of this right shall be allowed only under an order of a court of law." Article 24 states, "1. It shall be forbidden to gather, store, use and disseminate information on the private life of any person without his/her consent. 2. The bodies of state authority and the bodies of local self-government and the officials thereof shall provide to each citizen access to any documents and materials directly affecting his/her rights and liberties unless otherwise stipulated under the law." Article 25 states, "The home shall be inviolable. No one shall have the right to enter the home against the will of persons residing in it except in cases stipulated by the federal law or under an order of a court of law."[4453]

Data Protection Framework

According to the federal Law on Information, Informatization and the Protection of Information (LIIPI),[4454] government data resources are open for general use except for documented information of limited access (data relevant to state secrets and confidential information). Personal data is considered confidential information. The law states, in particular, that collection, storage, use and distribution (processing) of information pertaining to the private life of a natural person without his or her permission, shall be prohibited, except for processing implemented on the basis of judicial warrant.[4455] The term "personal data" and some guarantees for personal data protection appear in new laws, in particular, the Tax Code,[4456] the Labor Code[4457] and the federal Law on Statements of Civil Status. Also, confidentiality of information has been mentioned in various laws relevant to professional secrets.[4458]

[4453] Constitution of the Russian Federation, available at
<http://www.russianembassy.org/RUSSIA/CONSTIT>.The Constitution of the Russian Federation was adopted by national voting on December 12, 1993. The previous Constitution (which was adopted in 1977 by the Supreme Soviet of the USSR) included weaker privacy guarantees.

[4454] Russian Federation Federal Law No. 24-FZ, Law of the Russian Federation on Information, Informatization and Information Protection, January 25, 1995, available at <http://www.datenschutz-berlin.de/gesetze/internat/fen.htm> (extracts).

[4455] *Id.* at Article 11.

[4456] Tax Code, Article 84, Part 1.

[4457] Labor Code, Articles 85-90; *see also,* "Improved Russian Labor Code Entered Into Force," Vol. 8, No. 2, International Law Update, February 2002.

[4458] Law "On Banks and Banking Activity," Principles of legislation of the Russian Federation with regard to citizens' health protection, Family Code, Tax Code, etc.

According to Articles 11 and 21 of the LIIPI, the list of personal data and the ways it is protected are to be stipulated by special federal law. The Russian Parliament has not yet approved this law. Two bills about personal data were proposed in 1998 and in 2000 but have not been passed by the Parliament.

In Russia (especially in Moscow and St. Petersburg) illegal collection and distribution of data on private persons and organizations is commonplace. Quite popular are databases on purchase/sale of cars, car owners, passport data and foreign passport data of Russian citizens, data on real estate (purchase and sale of apartments, their parameters, location and proprietors), databases of taxpayers, and information about people wanted for crimes and those who have been previously convicted. Cheap CDs with such databases are easily available on the streets and the Internet. At the beginning of 2003, Mobile Telesystems (MTS), a mobile phone company, suffered a massive security breach that led to the sale of CDs with MTS's entire database of several million customers. By law, MTS was required to share information about its customers with the police and government agencies. MTS said that the database had been stolen, and the company had started its own internal investigation without seeking help from law enforcement agencies. The company refused to provide details as to the results of this investigation, so they are unknown. Widespread speculation and comments from an MTS spokesperson indicate that the data was leaked by a low-paid employee from a government agency.[4459] In May 2003, Russian media wrote about a similar database theft case in St. Petersburg. In autumn 2004, CDs appeared with detailed information about income of taxpayers.

In the last couple of years, the number of websites that offer databases have grown rapidly. Some online shops appeared where one can use a virtual basket, quantity discounts and online assistance. Some websites offered Webmoney payment system to their customers. There are shops that allow prepaid online access to databases.[4460]

Data Protection Authority

Russian legislation does not establish a central regulatory body for data protection. Some efforts are being carried out by regional ombudsmen, *e.g.*, the

---

[4459] Sabrina Tavernise, "Personal Data Is Pirated from Russian Phone Files," New York Times, January 23, 2003, available at
<http://www.nytimes.com/2003/01/23/business/worldbusiness/23DATA.html?ex=1054440000&en=fee2785ba6eafbb5&ei=5070>.

[4460] Human Rights Network, Privacy in the Russian Internet (Human Rights Publishers, 2005), available at <http://privacy.hro.org/docs/report2005> (in Russian).

Ombudsman of the region of Perm that initiated an investigation on the practices of a local communications company that used clients' phone numbers for commercial purposes. In his report of 2000, the federal Ombudsman suggested introducing a law on privacy protection, but this idea has not been put into practice. In his report of 2003, the federal Ombudsman for the first time considered privacy as a fundamental freedom.[4461]

In April 2005, President Putin signed the Federal Law, which created the new institution, and in a sense, collective ombudsman: The Public Chamber. President suggested the idea of the creation of this institute as an anti-terrorism measure after the Beslan tragedy.[4462] Its role will be to analyze draft legislation and public expertise of the government's decisions involving the public interest. However, some Russian leaders of the civil society organizations do not think the Chamber will promote civil society to participate in the decision-making process of the state.[4463] The law will come into effect on July 1, 2005. The Public Chamber will have 126 members and during the first month after the Law has been passed the President will appoint 42 members of the Chamber. The other 2/3 will be nominated by civil society federal organizations.[4464]

Information Technologies

A special "Department K" within the Ministry of Internal Affairs and its branches in cities of Russia are responsible for investigation of crimes in a sphere of information technologies. The number of cybercrimes grows in Russia every year. In 2001, the number of illegal accesses to computer information was 1,576. In 2004, the number of cybercrimes rose approximately 8,000.[4465] Most cases relate to unauthorized access to computer systems and networks and the distribution of pirated software, though sometimes Department K deals with cases of breaches of privacy. Among 1,673 cases that were initiated by Department K in the first half of 2004, only 2.4% related to illegal disclosure of

[4461] See generally, <http://www.ombudsman.gov.ru> (in Russian). See also, Federal Constitutional Law on the Commissioner for Human Rights in the Russian Federation, available at <http://www.anticorruption.bg/ombudsman/eng/readnews.php?id=6085&lang=en&t_style=tex&l_style=defaut>.

[4462] " Putin Signed the Law on the Public Chamber," April 4, 2005, available at <http://news.izvestia.ru/politic/news94422> (in Russian).

[4463] Jeremy Bransten, "Russia: New Public Chamber Criticized As 'Smokescreen,'" CDI Russia Weekly, March 18, 2005, available at <http://www.cdi.org/russia/346-5.cfm>.

[4464] The Federal Law No. 32-FZ of April 4, 2005 on "Public Chamber," available at <http://www.rg.ru/2005/04/07/obshestv-palata-dok.html>.

[4465] Human Rights Network, Privacy in the Russian Internet (Human Rights Publishers, 2005), available at <http://privacy.hro.org/docs/report2005> (in Russian).

personal data.[4466] One of the recent examples is the case against the owners of the website sherlok.ru. They offered to post on the Internet public information about phone conversations of "Beeline" (one of three biggest cellular phone systems in Russia) customers: phone numbers of outgoing/incoming calls and length of conversations of specific "Beeline" subscriber. The infringers used sherlok.ru website to serve their clients The police brought charges against two active and one former staff members of the mobile company. The company actively helped to seize the criminals.[4467]

In April 2005, the prosecutor's office accused a computer engineer from Nizhny Novgorod of the disclosure of sensitive personal data of the managers of the industrial complex where he worked, including phone numbers and income details. The young man published this information on his webpage. The court ordered a small fine of RUB 400 (less than USD 15). The spokeswoman for the prosecutor's office admitted this case to have no precedents in the past.[4468]

Wiretapping and Surveillance Rules

The 1995 Communications Law protects secrecy of communications. A new version of this law came into force on January 1, 2004. The tapping of telephone conversations, scrutiny of electronic communications, delay, inspection and seizure of postal mailings and documentary correspondence, receipt of information therein, and other restriction of communications secrets are allowed only with a court order.[4469] The Law on Operational Investigation Activity that regulates surveillance methods used by secret services requires a court-issued warrant.[4470] The law was amended in December 1998 by the State *Duma*. Guarantees for the protection of privacy were emphasized and additional controls imposed on prosecutors. Article 5 of the Law provides that an investigative structure must secure people's privacy. The Law also provides: "If one believes that some actions of bodies conducting operational investigation have infringed on an individual's rights or freedoms, the individual has the right to appeal to a

[4466] "Department K of the Ministry of Internal Affairs: the Number of IT Crimes in Russian Federation Doubles each Year," CNews.ru, October 11, 2004, available at
<http://www.cnews.ru/newsline/index.shtml?2004/10/11/166497> (in Russian).

[4467] N. Khaytina, "Vympelcom staff stole databases," ComNews.ru, November 29, 2004, available at <http://www.comnews.ru/index.cfm?id=12754> (in Russian).

[4468] "A Milky Hacker," Computer Crime Research Center, April 15, 2005, available at <http://www.crime-research.org/news/15.04.2005/1157>,

[4469] Russian Federation Federal Law "On communication" No. 15-FZ, Article 32; adopted by the State *Duma* on January 20, 1995.

[4470] The Federal Law No. 144-FZ of August 12, 1995.

court, a prosecutor, or to a higher body that carries out investigative activities." Article 6 of the federal Law on Federal Security Services of the Russian Federation has a similar provision:[4471] "If a person has not been convicted during a legally established procedure, then all materials obtained during this operational investigation must be archived for a period of one year (in compliance with the Law on Operational Investigations) and subsequently deleted." However this provision is virtually revoked by the following addition: ". . . unless official interests or justice require otherwise."[4472] In December 1999, the law was amended to allow surveillance by the tax police, the Ministry of Internal Affairs, Border Guards, the Kremlin Security Service, the Presidential Security Service, the parliamentary security services and the Foreign Intelligence Service.[4473] In 2001, the following provision was added to the Law:[4474] "Audio recordings and other materials resulting from interception and wiretapping of the conversation of persons being out of criminal proceedings must be deleted within six months after the wiretapping is over with an appropriate protocol.[4475] The judge must be notified three months before materials reflecting the results of operational investigations, implemented on the basis of a court warrant, are deleted." Disclosure of data that affects someone's privacy without his or her consent is legally prohibited unless otherwise stipulated by federal laws. The Law on Federal Security Service of the Russian Federation contains no requirement for the deletion of data but stipulates that the information shall not be transferred to anyone else.

The Federal Security Service (FSB) has conducted phone tapping using the "SORM" system (or "System of Operative Investigative Activities"). In 1998, information about a new SORM-2 system that applies to the Internet was revealed. SORM-2 requires Internet Service Providers (ISPs) to install surveillance devices and high-speed links to local FSB departments, which would allow the FSB to directly access Internet users' communications, although with a warrant requirement.[4476] These rather expensive devices and links are to be paid for by the ISPs themselves. While most ISPs have not publicly resisted FSB's demands to install SORM-2, one ISP in Volgograd, Bayard-Slaviya

---

[4471] The Federal Law No. 40-FZ of April 3, 1995.

[4472] Article 5 of the Federal Law "On operational investigations" of August 12, 1995 (the Federal Law No. 144-FZ of 1995).

[4473] "Police Get Window of Access to E-mail," The Moscow Times, January 13, 2000.

[4474] This amendment has been introduced by the Federal Law No. 26-FZ of March 20, 2001.

[4475] The "protocol" is an official paper, a form that must be completed and signed to certify that the data was deleted.

[4476] "Russia Prepares to Police Internet," The Moscow Times, July 29, 1998. More information in English and Russian is available from the Moscow Libertarium Forum <http://www.libertarium.ru/libertarium/sorm/>.

Communications, challenged the FSB's demands. The local FSB and the Ministry of Communications attempted to have the ISP's license revoked[4477] but backed off after the ISP challenged their decision in court.

The existence of SORM-2 was confirmed by the State Committee of the Russian Federation on Communication and Informization (*Goskomsvyaz*, now the Ministry of Communications) as Order No. 47 in March 27, 1999, and Order No. 130, in July 25, 2000, which was registered with the Ministry of Justice on August 9, 2000. Order No. 130 was immediately challenged in the Russian Supreme Court by Pavel Netupsky, a St. Petersburg journalist. Although the Court upheld SORM-2, it ruled part 2.6 illegal, and therefore made sure that ISPs would know whom the FSB is monitoring.[4478] Netupsky lost on all other counts. SORM-2 has now been implemented, although FSB representatives have not provided any evaluation of how effective SORM-2 has been for the prevention and investigation of criminal activities, and there have been no announced arrests as of yet. Although the FSB insists that there have been no violations of privacy, its assertions cannot be verified as Russia lacks the appropriate supervisory and independent body to control FSB's activities. ISPs are used to avoid comments on any issues connected with SORM-2.

Governmental proposals concerning digital rights tend to be intrusive. In the beginning of April 2000, the Committee of the State *Duma* for Information Policy introduced a bill on Regulation of the Russian Segment of the Internet that raised many critiques. The Russian Internet community did its best to prevent this bill from becoming a law and suggested an alternative bill on the State Policy of the Russian Federation Pertaining to the Development and Use of the Internet.[4479] On May 18, 2000, parliamentary hearings took place to discuss the bill and the legislation relevant to the Internet. Most of its participants agreed that there was "no need for a special law applicable to the Internet."[4480] However, in June 2004, the Moscow major Yuri Luzkov published a contradictory article with the main idea of establishing control over the Internet. Soon afterwards Lyudmila Narusova, member of the higher chamber of the Russian Parliament, confirmed

---

[4477] In Russia a license is necessary for providing Internet services. ISPs have to meet license terms and conditions including cooperation with secret services.

[4478] "Supreme Court Rules Phone-Tapping Clause in Decree to be Illegal," BBC World Monitoring, September 28, 2000.

[4479] Alexander Kostinsky and Sergei Smirnov, "Hello! The Parliament Is listening!," Internet.ru, May 19, 2000, available at <http://www.internet.ru/articles/n_r9z1.esp>.

[4480] Human Rights Network, Privacy in the Russian Internet (Human Rights Publishers, 2003), available at <http://www.hro.org/docs/reps/privacy/2002/eng/>.

that a law on the Internet is being prepared in the Parliament.[4481] In April 2005, Dmitry Frolov, the spokesman of the Federal Security Service (a successor to KGB, the governmental institution taht deals with national security issues), declared that the Service should get more authority to control the Internet, including some forms of freedom of expression and access to information.[4482]

The Federal Law on Commercial Secret was enacted on July 29, 2004.[4483] The law regulates the disclosure of "commercial secrets" and how its confidentiality can be protected. It also defines information that may not be considered commercial secret, and establishes a list of information that may constitute commercial secret, including but not limited to, the number of employees, the system of remuneration, labor conditions including safety arrangements, work-related injuries, occupational morbidity figures, and vacancies; as well as past infringements to the Russian Federation legislation and ensuing prosecutions. The law expressly stipulates that the owner of commercial secrets is the employer.

In May 2004, President Putin signed the Presidential Decree on "Measures of Providing Information Safety to the Russian Federation in the International Information Exchange Area," which forbids the connection of information networks, communication networks and autonomous computers to the Internet and other networks of the international information exchange, if they contain state and official secrets and other information that can be withheld.[4484]

Despite these clear restrictions, President Putin declared that he does not approve of administrative restrictions of the Internet networks: "The Internet is the most democratic way of the dissemination of information, and reasonable restrictions of the criminal use of the Internet should not have influence on freedom of information."[4485] However, some Russian officials have another standpoint. They claim that the Internet should be under control of the state. Minister of Foreign Affairs Sergey Lavrov said that some Internet sites are propagandizing

---

[4481] "Russian Parliament Plans to Regulate Internet," MosNews, June 3, 2004, available at <http://www.mosnews.com/news/2004/06/03/internet.shtml>.

[4482] "Russia's FSB Demands Control Over Internet," MosNews, April 28, 2005, available at <http://www.mosnews.com/news/2005/04/28/fsbinternet.shtml>

[4483] Federal Act No. 98-FZ.

[4484] Decree of President of the Russian Federation on "Measures of Providing the Information Safety of the Russian Federation in International Information Exchange Area" No. 611 of May 12, 2004.

[4485] "President Putin doesn't approve administrative restrictions of Internet," December 23, 2004, available at <http://www.nta-nn.ru/?id=70291>.

intolerance and violence.[4486] The draft on new mass media law is being prepared. The new law is supposed cover the Internet as well, however, it lacks a realistic regulation mechanism. In October 2004, there was a holding meeting for the Commission of the Council of the Federation (Upper Chamber of the Parliament) regarding the information policy on which the concept of the new mass media law has been considered. The draft was prepared by the Industrial Committee,[4487] with cooperation from the Ministry on Affairs of the Press, Broadcasting and Mass Communications.[4488] During the meeting Alexander Kotenkov, who represents the President in the Council of Federation, declared that all Internet sites should have permanent IP addresses in order to define the information resource. However, officials could not resolve the issue of whether the Internet sites are traditional mass media or not. In some cases, Internet sites could be considered mass media. For example, according to the Decision of the Supreme Court, when detractive and false information are put on the Internet site, which has been legally registered as mass media, it should be regulated by the Russian mass media legislation.[4489] If it is impossible to find out the person who disseminated detractive and false information, judicial protection is certainly possible. The registration of Internet sites as electronic editions of mass media is carried out in the Federal Service regarding Supervision of Observance of the Legislation, in the field of Mass Communications and Protection of a Cultural Heritage. The registration is carried out voluntarily and assumes the fulfillment of Civil Code and also Mass Media Legislation.[4490]

Anti-terrorism Measures

Anti-terrorist campaigns that the United States government promoted worldwide after the terrorist acts of September 11, 2001 have influenced Russian legislation. On December 20, 2000, the State *Duma* approved amendments to federal laws on Terrorism and on Mass Media in first reading. Although these amendments did not specifically concern online privacy, they seriously limited distribution of

---

[4486] Ministry of International Affairs: Internet must be under control of the State, of November 2004, available at <http://lenta.ru/internet/2004/11/17/lavrov/>.

[4487] Industrial Committee, created in September 2002, is a non-profit organization. Members include heads of the state and commercial mass media and information agencies -- basically leaders of the mass media business.

[4488] On March 9, 2004, this Ministry was abolished and transformed into the Ministry of Culture and Mass Communications of the Russian Federation. Decree of the President of the Russian Federation on "System and Structure of the Federal Bodies of Executive Power" No. 314 of March 9, 2004.

[4489] Decree of the Plenary Session of the Supreme Court of the Russian Federation on "Court Practice for Cases on Protecting of Honor and Dignity and also Business Reputation of persons and Legal Persons" No. 3 of February 24, 2005 .

[4490] A. Richter, "Legal Basis of the Journalism," Institute of the Information Law Issues, Moscow, 2004.

"extremist materials" via the Internet (even though "extremism" and "extremist materials" were not defined in Russian law at the time). On April 30, 2002, the President announced a bill on Counteraction to Extremist Activities. The bill contained broad definitions of "extremist activities" and, some critics argued, enabled a wide range of public protest actions to be viewed as extremism. The first draft contained an article relevant to the Internet: ISPs were forced to censor materials on their servers and remove or block "extremist sites." This article was later replaced with the indistinct reference to other legislation, and the controversial procedure of Internet monitoring and censorship was dropped.[4491] After the terrorist attack in Moscow of October 2002,[4492] the State *Duma* quickly adopted several amendments to the laws on Mass Media and Terrorism, banning any distribution of information that could impede anti-terrorist actions.[4493] In December 2004, the State *Duma* approved (in the first reading) a counter-terrorism bill that introduced a new concept, "state of a terrorist emergency," and a detailed elaboration of a "counter-terrorist operation." Most MPs (385) voted for the bill, 47 parliamentarians voted against it and one abstained from voting. The new regime of a "state of a terrorist emergency" may be announced in case Russian law enforcement bodies receive information about a terrorist act prepared but failed to check this information. The regime may last up to 60 days. It may cover the territory of several settlements or the whole country. During the "state of terrorist emergency," all popular actions are banned, freedom of movement and some other rights are constrained. As of the beginning of June 2005, the bill has not passed all three reading in the Russian parliament.[4494]

According to Article 53 of the Federal Law on Communications, the data about telecommunications users are confidential and are protected by Russian laws.

Russian legislation provides criminal liability for the invasion of privacy. The Criminal Code provides a penalty for violation of the immunity of private life,[4495] violation of secrecy of communications,[4496] and infringement of home

---

[4491] The Law "On Counteraction Extremist Activity" No. 114-FZ of July 25, 2002. *See also* Declan McCullagh, "Russia Poised to Restrict Net Activities," CNET, June 24, 2002, available at <http://news.com.com/2100-1023-938810.html>.

[4492] On October 23, 2002, a group of Chechen terrorists captured about 800 hostages in one of Moscow theaters. They demanded taht the Russian government withdraw its troops from the territory of Chechnya. The terrorist attack ended with the death of all terrorists and 129 of the hostages. Since 1999, Russia has been at war in Chechnya.

[4493] The Russian government considers the war in Chechnya to be a "counter-terrorist" operation.

[4494] Nabi Abdullaev, "Duma Seeks to Grant FSB Sweeping Powers," The St. Petersburg Times, December 21, 2004, available at <http://www.sptimes.ru/archive/times/1031/news/n_14479.htm>.

[4495] Criminal Code at Article 137.

[4496] *Id.* at Article 138.

inviolability.[4497] The Criminal Code also provides liability for unauthorized access to legally protected computer information.[4498] The Criminal Code includes sentences such as fines, forced labor, arrest, a ban on the right to hold certain positions or to be engaged in a certain activity and, in some cases, imprisonment for a period of up to five years.[4499] The maximum fine is RUB 300,000.[4500] According to the Civil Code,[4501] privacy is a legally protected non-property right. Attached to this right are personal dignity, personal immunity, honor and good name, business name, personal secret and family secret. If an individual suffers physical or moral damages by violation of his or her personal non-property rights or some other non-material welfare rights, as well as in other cases provided by the law, a court can force the person invading privacy to provide financial compensation.[4502] The Administrative Code (effective since July 1, 2002) states that "infringement of a legally established procedure of collection, storage, use or distribution of information about citizens (personal data)" shall lead to a warning or penalty.[4503] The Administrative Code also establishes liability for disclosure of information if access to it is restricted by federal law.[4504] The illegitimate refusal by a public official to submit information to a person is also an administrative breach of the law.[4505]

The United Nations Human Rights Committee expressed concerns about the state of privacy in Russia in 1995 and recommended the enactment of additional privacy laws. It noted: "The Committee is concerned that actions may continue which violate the right to protection from unlawful or arbitrary interference with privacy, family, home or correspondence. It is concerned that the mechanisms to intrude into private telephone communication continue to exist, without a clear legislation setting out the conditions of legitimate interference with privacy and providing for safeguards against unlawful interference. The Committee urges that legislation be passed on the protection of privacy, as well as strict and positive action be taken, to prevent violations of the right to protection from unlawful or arbitrary interference with privacy, family, home or correspondence."[4506]

[4497] *Id.* at Article 139.

[4498] *Id.* at Article 272.

[4499] Criminal Code, *supra* at Article 272, Part 2.

[4500] For the period of spring 2005, RUB 300,000 is about USD 10,800.

[4501] Civil Code, Article 150, Part 2.

[4502] *Id.* at Article 151.

[4503] Administrative Code, Article 13.11.

[4504] *Id.* at Article 13.14.

[4505] *Id.* at Article 5.39.

[4506] United Nations Human Rights Committee, Comments on Russian Federation, U.N. Doc. CCPR/C/79/Add.54 (1995), available at <http://sim.law.uu.nl/SIM/CaseLaw/uncom.nsf/0/9172bc5146972b6dc125663c00343b49?OpenDocument>.

The Fifth Periodical Report of the Russian Federation on the Implementation of the International Covenant on Civil and Political Rights of 2002 provides that in the period of four years 42 persons were convicted for violations of privacy, 61 for the violation of the secrecy of communications. According to the report, the number of persons convicted for breaching the inviolability of the home for the same period is much higher (5,476 persons). This apparently shows the lack of the enforcement required for the investigation of crimes related to the breach of privacy, as well as the lack of governmental oversight and independent institutions that could monitor how privacy laws are implemented. Law enforcement structures used to refer to the lack of legal grounds and, in particular, to the lack of clear legal procedures about how to collect, process, store, transfer and disclose personal data. The constitutional right of personal privacy is usually considered insufficient to provide a legal basis for criminal proceedings. People usually choose not to turn to courts when their privacy is violated for several reasons: lack of laws and procedures that could be effectively used by plaintiffs; monetary damages in all cases are usually small; people do not consider privacy as a fundamental right and do not believe it can be effectively protected from interference.[4507]

Recent Developments

In January 2002, the government adopted the federal program "Electronic Russia" for the period 2002-2010. The program has provisions about freedom of search, access, transfer, production and distribution of information, and privacy safeguards for any legally protected information available on information systems. For these purposes, the authors of the program have proposed to elaborate an effective ground for regulations. This basis should extend to the regulation of issues of information security and realization of citizens' constitutional rights. However, the confidentiality was not mentioned as a major governmental policy issue. One of the tasks in this program is described as a "legal solution of the problems concerning performance of operational investigations through computer networks." Other program items include the electronic circulation of documents, business information security, etc. The Russian Ministry for Communication and Information and the Ministry for Economic Development and Trade of the Russian Federation are the leading coordinator for this program.

[4507] Human Rights Network, Privacy in the Russian Internet (Human Rights Publishers, 2005), available at <http://privacy.hro.org/docs/report2005> (in Russian).

The notion of "privacy policy" has not yet become commonplace in Russia. Few web sites ensure the privacy of their customers. ISPs take appropriate measures to control spam after receiving consumer complaints. Freeware and shareware programs for the protection of personal privacy of Internet users are available on Russian servers.[4508]

Russian Federation does not have an explicit law that would restrict the spam (unsolicited commercial e-mail). However, on July 14, 2004, the Moscow Municipal *Duma* proposed the legislative initiative to make amendments on the resistance of sending spam for some legal acts. This draft was considered by the Committee of the State *Duma* on the Information Policy, which did not support it. In late December 2004, deputies of Moscow's Municipal *Duma* recalled the draft because the Ministry of Information Technologies and Communications and Committee on Information of State *Duma* (the lower chamber of the Russian Parliament) created a working group for a new draft.[4509]The Minister of Information Technologies and Communication of the Russian Federation, Leonid Rejman, did not approve of the strict measures against spam and regulating the Internet as a whole.[4510]

National ID System

Russia has a national ID system. Each person older than 14 years of age must have a personal document (internal passport) that can be obtained at a local department of the Ministry of Internal Affairs. This passport is used as the main ID document and is necessary for many activities, including the purchase of train and plane tickets. Each passport bears a residency permit stamp (the so-called *propiska*). Russian courts (including the Supreme Court in 1998) have asserted that this permission regime is unconstitutional. Moscow authorities insist that the *propiska* is only a notification procedure. However, for those attempting to move to Moscow, bureaucrats can make this registration a painful and complicated process. Without *propiska* it is difficult get a well-paid job, get full public medical aid, children cannot attend public schools, etc. Moscow police used to stop people at streets and fine them if they did not carry their *propiska*.[4511]

[4508] *Id.*

[4509] "Legislative Initiative of Moscow Municipal *Duma* on the Struggle with Spam will be Recalled from State *Duma*", January 27, 2005 available at <http://www.securitylab.ru/52167.html>.

[4510] *See* <http://antispam.rin.ru/news.htm>, March 24, 2005.

[4511] *See, e.g.,* Chris Riley, "Moscow's Heart of Darkness," NBC News, August 7, 1998, available at <http://msnbc.msn.com/id/3072234/#BODY>.

In recent years, officials, both at federal and Moscow levels, announced several times that a new system of electronic IDs would be introduced in the near future. According to these statements, the new system would supplement, and later replace, internal passports.[4512] In January 2004, the Russian Ministry of Economical Development announced plans to build a national system that would connect existing major public databases through a new ID system. According to the Ministry, each newborn Russian will be assigned a unique ID. Other people will get IDs, too. No central database will be created but a new governmental body responsible for data processing may be created later on. Access to these databases is promised to be "easy" for common people.

The Russian national ID system will change according to the Presidential Decree concerning Creation of the Interdepartmental Work Group on Preparation for Passport and Visa Documents of the New Generation, which was signed on September 18, 2005. ThegGroup will control the creation of all the necessary legal, technical and financial conditions for using of the new biometric passports, according to the international standards in Russia before January 1, 2006.[4513]

A biological passport will contain digitalized image information of its owner: it will be possible to trace and scan the images at airports. There will be a special section for digital fingerprints in the ID system as well. The final decision pertaining to the type of information to be uploaded in the passport chip has not yet been made. It will probably be a blood group or a taxpayer's identification code.[4514]

International Obligations

Russia is a member of the Council of Europe (CoE) and has signed and ratified the European Convention for the Protection of Human Rights and Fundamental Freedoms.[4515] The Russian Federation has signed the CoE Convention for the

---

[4512] Mayakinfo.ru, available at <http://www.mayakinfo.ru/news.asp?msg=676>; "Gref: electronic Ids may replace passports in 6-8 years," Russia Journal Daily, June 10, 2003, available at http://www.russiajournal.com/print/russia_news_38527.html.

[4513] The Presidential Decree on "Creation of the Interdepartmental Work Group on Preparation for Passport and Visa Documents of the New Generation" No430-RP, September 18, 2004, available at <http://document.kremlin.ru/doc.asp?ID=024260>.

[4514] "EU requires new biometrical passports for Russia as a condition to join the world community," PRAVDA.ru, March 24, 2005, available at <http://english.pravda.ru/main/18/90/362/15164_passport.html>.

[4515] Signed February 28, 1996; ratified May 5, 1998; entered into force May 5, 1998, available at <http://conventions.coe.int/>.

Protection of Individuals with Regard to Automatic Processing of Personal Data (ETS No. 108) but has not ratified it.[4516]

Russia participated in the negotiations on the CoE Convention on Cybercrime which was opened for signature in November 23, 2001.[4517] The Convention requires Member States to establish criminal offences under their domestic laws regarding various computer or computer-related crimes, including unauthorized access to a computer system and unauthorized interception of a data transmission. As of May 2005, Russia has not yet signed the treaty.

Autonomous Russian Republics

The Constitutions of 16 republics of Russian Federation reproduce Articles 23, 24 and 25 of the Federal Constitution. Constitutions of Bashkortostan and Ingushetya stipulate the same guarantees with different wording. The Constitution of Bashkortostan incorporates the addendum, allowing a search only on the basis of a judicial warrant. In other cases, there are fewer privacy safeguards than in the federal Constitution, or even no safeguards at all (Karelia, Kalmykia). There are no essential differences between the constitutions of the republics and federal privacy guarantees.[4518]

Republic of San Marino

The Act on Collection, Elaboration and Use of Computerized Personal Data was enacted in 1983 and amended in 1995.[4519] The Act applies to any computerized filing system or data bank, both private and public. It prohibits the collection of personal and confidential data through fraudulent, illegal or unfair means. It requires that information is accurate, relevant and complete. Any individual is entitled both to inquire whether his or her personal data have been collected or processed, to obtain a copy, and to require that inaccurate, outdated, incomplete, or ambiguous data, or data whose collection, processing, transmission, or preservation is forbidden, be rectified, integrated, clarified, updated, or canceled. The creation of a data bank requires the prior authorization of both the State Congress (the Government) and the Guarantor for the Safeguard of Confidential

---

[4516] Signed November 8, 2001, available at <http://conventions.coe.int/>.

[4517] <http://conventions.coe.int/>.

[4518] Human Rights Network, Privacy in the Russian Internet (Human Rights Publishers, 2005), available at <http://privacy.hro.org/docs/report2005> (in Russian).

[4519] Regulating the Computerized Collection of Personal Data, Law No. 70 of May 23, 1995; revising Law No. 27 of March 1, 1983, amended by Law No. 70/95.

and Personal Data. There are additional rules for sensitive information. Infringements can be punished by means of administrative sanctions or penalties. There were a number of Regency's Decrees issued under the 1983 Act that remained in force after the 1995 revisions.[4520] The Regulation on Statistical Data Collection and Public Competence in Data Processing[4521] regulates data processing within the Public Administration.

The Guarantor enforces the Act for the Safeguard of Confidential and Personal Data, and is a judge of the Administrative Court. The Guarantor can examine any claim or petition relating to the application of the above-mentioned law and pass judgment whenever the confidentiality of personal data is violated. His judgment can be appealed to a higher court. The release of information to other countries is conditioned on the prior authorization of the Guarantor, who must verify that the country to which confidential information is being transmitted ensures the same level of protection of personal data as that established in Sammarinese legislation.

Under pressure from the Organization for Economic Cooperation and Development (OECD), San Marino has agreed to amend its tax laws and, if necessary, weaken financial privacy standards, in order to facilitate better "exchange of information in tax matters."[4522]

San Marino is a member of the Council of Europe but has not signed nor ratified the Convention for the Protection of Individuals with Regard to Automatic Processing of Personal Data (Convention No. 108). It has signed and ratified the European Convention for the Protection of Human Rights and Fundamental Freedoms.[4523]

[4520] Decree No. 7 of March 13, 1984, Establishment of a State Data Bank as Provided for by Article 5 of Law No. 27 of March 1, 1983; Decree No. 7 of June 3, 1986, Integration to Decree No. 7 of March 13, 1984, Establishing a State Data Bank; Decree No. 140 of November 26, 1987, Procedures for the Establishment of Private Data Banks.

[4521] Regulation on Statistical Data Collection and Public Competence in Data Processing, Law No. 71 of May 23, 1995.

[4522] "The War on Tax Havens," The National Post, September 4, 2001.

[4523] Signed November 16, 1988; ratified March 22, 1989; entered into force March 22, 1989.

Republic of Singapore

Constitutional Privacy Framework

The Singapore Constitution is based on the British system and does not contain any explicit right to privacy.[4524] The High Court has ruled that personal information may be protected from disclosure under a duty of confidences.[4525]

Statutory Rules Related to Privacy

There is no general data protection or privacy law in Singapore.[4526] The government has been aggressive in using surveillance to promote social control and limit domestic opposition.[4527] Singapore has no governmental authority affiliated with privacy or data protection, except for a small privacy division within the Ministry of Finance.[4528] The idea of data protection legislation has been officially "under review" by the government for 13 years. A Straits Times survey revealed that 80 percent of readers feel that personal information contained in databases is too freely accessible.[4529] For purposes of e-commerce, the National Internet Advisory Committee proposed the Model Data Protection Code (MDPC) for the Private Sector in February 2002[4530] and the National Trust Council implemented it in 2003,[4531] though businesses will not be required to adopt its provisions.[4532] The MDPC spells out certain standards for the collection and use of customer data by merchants that the National Trust Council certifies.[4533]

In September 1998, the National Internet Advisory Board released an industry-based self-regulatory "E-Commerce Code for the Protection of Personal Information and Communications of Consumers of Internet Commerce"

[4524] Constitution of the Republic of Singapore, September 1963, available at <http://www.oefre.unibe.ch/law/icl/sn00000_.html>.

[4525] X v. CDE1992 2 SLR 996.

[4526] *See* <http://bakerinfo.com/apec/singapec_main.htm#Privacy>.

[4527] *See* Christophen Tremewan, The Political Economy of Social Control in Singapore (St. Martin's Press, 1994).

[4528] Report of the National Internet Advisory Board 1997/1998, September 1998; *see also* Susan Long, "Guess Who's Reading Your Personal Data Today?" Singapore Press Holdings, May 18, 2002.

[4529] Long, *supra.*

[4530] "Consultation on Protection Regime," BNA World Data Protection Report, Volume 2, Issue 4, April 2002.

[4531] Chua Hian Hou, "By 2009, No One Will Have Any Secrets...," Straits Times, June 11, 2005.

[4532] "Voluntary Singapore Web Codes to Protect Privacy," Reuters, February 5, 2002.

[4533] Chua Hian Hou, *supra.*

("Code")[4534] The Code encourages providers to ensure the confidentiality of business records and personal information of users, including details of usage or transactions. It prohibits the disclosure of personal information, and requires providers not to intercept communications unless required by law. The Code also limits information collection, prohibits the disclosure of personal information without informing consumers and giving them an option to stop the transfer, ensures accuracy of records, and provides a right to correct or delete data.[4535] In 1999, the Code was adopted by CaseTrust – a joint project operated by the Consumers Association of Singapore, CommerceNet Singapore Limited and the Retail Promotion Centre in Singapore – and incorporated into its code of practice as part of an accreditation scheme promoting good business practices among store-based and web-based retailers (CaseTrust is).[4536] The Info-Communications Development Authority (IDA), the lead agency in charge of e-commerce regulation, announced in March 2000 that it would endorse the TRUSTe system as "an industry 'trustmark' seal."[4537]

Development of anti-spam legislation was initiated in May 2004. IDA announced a multifaceted approach including legislation, public education and self-regulation of the marketing industry.[4538] IDA and the Attorney General's Chambers of Singapore (AGC) issued a joint report proposing the legislative strategy for anti-spam legislation and recommended an opt-out approach.[4539] The report also recommends requiring advertisers to label marketing e-mail as such and prohibiting fake return e-mail addresses.[4540] The laws are expected to be finalized in 2005.[4541]

The Singapore AntiSpam Resource Centre web site was launched in May 2004 "to provide a central anti-spam repository for the public and industry." The site includes information for consumers, including reviews of anti-spam software and

---

[4534] Kien Keong Wong and Ken Chia (Baker & McKenzie Singapore), "E-com Legal Guide, Singapore," January 2001, available at <http://www.bakerinfo.com/apec/singapec_main.htm#Privacy>.
[4535] Id.
[4536] Id.
[4537] "Infocomm Development Authority Helping Singaporeans Go Online," March 2000, available at <http://www.ida.gov.sg>.
[4538] See Infocomm Development Authority of Singapore, "Multi-Pronged Measures Developed to Curb E-Mail Spam in Singapore," Press Release, May 25, 2004, available at <http://www.ida.gov.sg/idaweb/marketing/infopage.jsp?infopagecategory=&infopageid=I2884>.
Id.
[4540] Joint Infocomm Development of Authority of Singapore and Attorney-General Chambers of Singapore Report, Proposed Legislative Framework for the Control of Email Spam, (2004) available at <http://www.ida.gov.sg/idaweb/pnr/infopage.jsp?infopagecategory=infoecon:pnr&versionid=1&infopageid=I2883>.
[4541] "Singapore Drawing Up New Anti-Spam Laws," Channel NewsAsia, May 25, 2004.

free software downloads, and information about Singapore's proposed anti-spam legislation and how consumers can comment on the proposal.[4542] The Singapore Information Technology Federation, a group of technology security companies such as Brightmail and Symantec, held an anti-spam forum on June 22, 2004, bringing together government, industry and trade associations, IT companies and academics to discuss legal, policy and technical anti-spam solutions.[4543]

Early 2005, the Internet Industry Association of Singapore (IIAS) was launched and kicked off two nationwide initiatives regarding privacy and offensive content on the Internet. IIAS, a non-profit organization representing the views of the Internet industry, will set up a privacy portal for consumers about spam, phishing and other security issues.[4544]

Employer monitoring of employee phone calls, e-mails, and Internet usage is also permissible under Singapore law. Under Singapore property law, workplace e-mail, telephone and computer contents are the property of the employer. Thus, if an employee loses his job because of the contents of his communications technology, he has no grounds for defense based on an invasion of privacy.[4545]

The Banking Act prohibits disclosure of financial information without the permission of the customer.[4546] Numbered accounts can also be opened with the permission of the authority. The High Court can require the disclosure of records to investigate drug trafficking and other serious crimes. The Monetary Authority of Singapore (MAS) issued new "Know Your Customer" guidelines to banks in May 1998 on money laundering. Banks are required to clarify the economic background and purpose of any transactions of which the form or amount appear unusual in relation to the customer, finance company or branch office concerned, or whenever the economic purpose and the legality of the transaction are not immediately evident.[4547] Banks must report suspicious transactions to MAS. In 2002, the Credit Bureau asked CaseTrust to accredit its procedures and systems to allay consumer financial privacy concerns.[4548]

4542 See <http://www.antispam.org.sg/>.

4543 <http://ssc.sitf.org.sg/default.aspx>.

4544 Dalena Lee, "IIAS to Set up a Privacy Portal for Consumers," Straits Times, March 7, 2005.

4545 "Boss is Spying on You – And He Has the Right," Straits Times, October 10, 2000.

4546 Banking Act, Chapter 19, available at <http://www.mas.gov.sg>.

4547 "Guidelines on Prevention of Money Laundering," Monetary Authority of Singapore, May 26, 1999, available at <http://www.mas.gov.sg>.

4548 Leong Chan Teik, "New Bank Credit Bureau Will Get Accredited," Straits Times, June 4, 2002.

Homosexual acts are crimes under the Penal Code.[4549] Singapore also has laws against sodomy. However, authorities rarely enforce them.[4550] Gay activists in the country have long called for their repeal. Although attitudes towards gays have become more tolerant over the years, including in the workplace, the discussion of such issues in public fora and mass media remains highly sensitive.[4551]

Limitations to Freedom of Speech and Censorship Rules

The Singaporean Constitution protects the freedom of speech but permits restrictions. The government significantly restricted freedom of speech and the press in practice through intimidations and pressures, leading to the practice of self-censorship among journalists. The U.S. State Department Report on Human Rights Practices on Singapore states, "there continued to be some limited progress towards greater openness in 2004, including a moderate level of ongoing debate in newspapers and on the Internet on various public issues."[4552]

In 2002, the Singapore government created the Media Development Authority (MDA) to regulate media content – including Internet, radio, television, and radio.[4553] MDA formed through a merger of the existing Singapore Broadcasting Authority (SBA), the Films and Publications Department (FPD), and the Singapore Film Commission (SFC) with the goal of uniting various forms of media under a single authority.[4554] Like its predecessor SBA, MDA has assumed the strict approach towards regulating the Internet. All Internet Service Providers (ISPs) and Internet Content Providers (ICPs) are required to comply with the Internet Code of Practice[4555] and the Class License Provisions.[4556] ISPs are required to register with the, along with ICPs who promote the discussion of political or religious topics relating to Singapore.[4557] ISPs are required to deny

---

[4549] Sections 377 and 377A of the Penal Code classify them as sexual acts "against the order of nature" and "outrages on decency" respectively.

[4550] In recent memory, no homosexual has been prosecuted for what he does in the privacy of his home. Lydia Lim, "Time to Reach out and Talk?" Straits Times, March 19, 2005.

[4551] Id.

[4552] US Department of State, Report on Singapore, Country Reports on Human Rights Practices 2004, February 28, 2005, available at <http://www.state.gov/g/drl/rls/hrrpt/2004/41659.htm>.

[4553] Media Development Authority of Singapore Act (Act 34 of 2002), available at <http://statutes.agc.gov.sg>. This statutory board operates under the authority of the Ministry of Information and the Arts.

[4554] <http://www.mda.gov.sg/aboutus/index.html>.

[4555] Internet Code of Practice, available at <http://www.mda.gov.sg/medium/internet/i_codenpractice.html>.

[4556] Class License Provisions, available at<http://www.mda.gov.sg/medium/internet/i_classlicence.html>.

[4557] Id. at § 2-3.

access to sites identified by MDA as containing prohibited material.[4558] Likewise, ICPs may not broadcast prohibited material or entertain discussion on prohibited themes.[4559] Prohibited material includes pornography, material that "advocates homosexuality or lesbianism," and material that "glorifies, incites or endorses ethnic, racial or religious hatred, strife or intolerance," among other prohibitions.[4560] Political content, especially during elections, is regulated.[4561] "Over the boundary markers" – religion, race and government criticism – is strictly enforced while other issues, though still subject to regulation, have not traditionally been enforced as strictly.[4562]

The Minister of Information, Communication, and the Arts appointed a Censorship Review Committee in 2002 to examine censorship policies related to broadcast media and to make recommendations.[4563] The committee released their report in July 2003. The findings recognized that young and artistic communities are restricted by current censorship rules, but reported that the majority of Singaporeans are satisfied with the censorship regime.[4564] The report recommended increased access to films under a more granular rating system and additional television programming allowing relaxed content restrictions after prime time.[4565] Although the report recognized that the Internet has wrought significant changes to access to media, it recommended that ISPs "should develop and subscribe to a code of conduct and put greater effort in protecting the young by developing an effective filtering system within a period of two years."[4566] Prominent members of the arts community call the recommendations "cosmetic," demanding a shift away from censorship – through editing or banning – and towards regulation of the audience permitted to view the work.[4567]

In March 2000, the Minister for Home Affairs created a "Speaker's Corner" based on a similar concept in London. The Speaker's Corner is a designated area

---

[4558] Internet Code of Practice, *supra*, at § 3.

[4559] *Id.* at § 3(3).

[4560] *Id.* at § 4.

[4561] John O'Callaghan, "Singapore Calls November 3 Election," Reuters, October 24, 2001, available at <http://www.thinkcentre.org/article.cfm?ArticleID=1183>.

[4562] E-mail from Milagros Rivera to Patrick Mueller, IPIOP clerk, Electronic Privacy Information Center, July 2, 2004 (on file with EPIC).

[4563] *See* the Censorship Review Committee's web page <http://www.mda.gov.sg/content/CRC_executive.html>.

[4564] "Report of the Censorship Review Committee 2003," July 2003, available at <http://www.mda.gov.sg/MDA/documents/Censorship_Review_2003.pdf>.

[4565] *Id.*

[4566] *Id.*

[4567] "Arts Community Says Proposed Changes to Censorship Are Largely Cosmetic," Channel NewsAsia, September 5, 2003.

where individuals can publicly speak without an official permit.[4568] However, pursuant to Singapore's Public Entertainments and Meeting Act, speakers are required to register with the local police station and show their national ID cards or passports.[4569] As a result, speech in the Speaker's Corner is subject to censorship. Speakers are not allowed to discuss banned topics such as race or religion. In July 2002, Chee Soon Juan, a candidate running for office, was effectively barred from running for office for discussing religion.[4570] There are report that Chee was banned for actions resulting from his failure to procure the official permit for the Speaker's Corner.[4571] During his speech at the Speaker's Corner, he criticized the government for banning Muslim girls from wearing headscarves in schools.[4572]

Also in connection with the Speaker's Corner, law enforcement officials hold a speaker's personal information for five years.[4573] Home Affairs Minister Wong Kan Seng said that the records are kept for investigative purposes to ensure that the speaker has registered.[4574] The police reportedly investigated several human rights activists, who staged a peaceful rally in Speakers Corner in December 2000, for the offense of "assembly without a permit."[4575] In 2004, the government partially relaxed its restrictions on indoor public events and the level of ongoing debate in newspapers and on the Internet on various public issues was moderate.[4576]

Wiretapping and Other Government Surveillance

Law enforcement authorities have extensive networks to gather information and conduct surveillance, as well as sophisticated capabilities to monitor telephone and other private conversations. Court warrants are not required for such surveillance. The law allows the government to monitor Internet use. Authorities are believed to routinely monitor telephone conversations and Internet use, as

---

[4568] Jake Lloyd-Smith, "Singapore's Curbs on Free Speech Look Set to Stay," November 27, 2002.

[4569] *Id.*

[4570] Agence France-Presse "Singapore Opposition Leader Barred from Polls over Religious Speech," July 30, 2002.

[4571] E-mail from Sinapan Samydorai, President, Think Centre, to Patrick Mueller, IPIOP Clerk, Electronic Privacy Information Center, July 5, 2004 (on file with EPIC).

[4572] *Id.*

[4573] "Singapore To Get Speakers' Corner," Asian Wall Street Journal, April 25, 2000.

[4574] "Keeping Records of Speakers," Straits Times, May 9, 2000.

[4575] "Police Begins Human Rights Violations," ThinkCentre, January 30, 2001 <http://www.thinkcentre.org/article.cfm?ArticleID=410>.

[4576] US Department of State, Report on Singapore 2004, *supra.*

well as monitor opposition politicians and government critics. According to the US State Department Report on Human Rights Practices of Singapore, there are no confirmed reports of such practices in 2004.[4577]

In July 1998, the Singapore government enacted three major bills concerning computer networks. They are the Computer Misuse (Amendment) Act (CMA), the Electronic Transactions Act and the National Computer Board (Amendment) Act. CMA prohibits the unauthorized interception of computer communications.[4578] It also provides the police with additional powers of investigation, and makes it an offense to refuse to assist the police in an investigation. CMA also grants law enforcement broad power to access data and encrypted material when conducting an investigation. In November 2003, CMA was revised, allowing the government to arrest an individual on suspicion of computer hacking, with penalties up to SGD 10,000 (~USD 5,950) or up to three years' imprisonment.[4579] This power of access requires the consent of the Public Prosecutor. The Electronic Transactions Act (ETA) was enacted in July 1998 to create a legislative framework for electronic transactions. It imposes a duty of confidentiality on records obtained under the act and imposes a maximum SGD 10,000 fine and 12-month jail sentence for disclosing those records without authorization. IDA and AGC began work in February 2004 to update ETA[4580] in order to cover new services and technologies, including biometrics, radio frequency identification (RFID), Wi-Fi, WiMax and others, by the end of 2005.[4581] Police have broad powers to search any computer and to require disclosure of documents for an offense related to the act without a warrant.[4582] More broadly, the government has wide discretionary powers under the Internal Security Act, the Criminal Law Act, the Misuse of Drugs Act, and the Undesirable Publications Act to conduct searches without warrants, as is normally required, if it determines that national security, public safety or order,

---

[4577] Id.

[4578] Computer Misuse Act (Chapter 50A), available at
<http://www.ida.gov.sg/idaweb/pnr/infopage.jsp?infopagecategory=infoecon:pnr&versionid=1&infopageid=1234>.

[4579] E-mail from Sinapan Samydorai, President, Thin Centre, to Patrick Mueller, IPIOP Clerk, Electronic Privacy Information Center, July 2, 2004 (on file with EPIC); see "Computer Misuse [Amendment] Act," ThinkCentre, November 13, 2004 <http://www.thinkcentre.org/article.cfm?ArticleID=2229>.

[4580] Press Release, Infocomm Development Authority of Singapore, "IDA and AGC Seek Views on Proposed Amendments to the Electronic Transactions Act," February 19, 2004, available at
<http://www.ida.gov.sg/idaweb/media/infopage.jsp?infopagecategory=infocommindustry.mr:media&versionid=1&infopageid=I2695>.

[4581] Raju Chellam, "Electronic Trading Law Ready to Be Upgraded; Law not Updated since Coming into Effect during Dotcom Boom," Straits Times, June 23, 2005.

[4582] Electronic Transactions Act (Act 25 of 1998), available at
<http://www.ida.gov.sg/idaweb/pnr/infopage.jsp?infopagecategory=regulation:pnr&infopageid=I1934&versionid=1>.

or the public interest are at issue.[4583] Defendants have the right to request judicial review of such searches.

The Telecommunications Authority of Singapore (TAS) governed electronic surveillance of communications until it was merged with the National Computer Board in the late 1990s and eventually became part of IDA.[4584] The government has extensive powers under the Internal Security Act and other acts to monitor anything that is considered a threat to "national security."

Government-owned or government-controlled companies operate all ISPs.[4585] Each person in Singapore wishing to obtain an Internet account must show his national ID card to the provider to obtain an account.[4586] ISPs reportedly provide, on a regular basis, information on users to government officials without complying with legal requirements. In 1994, Technet – then the only Internet provider in the country serving the academic and technical community – scanned through e-mail of its members looking for pornographic files. According to Technet, they scanned the files without opening the mails, looking for clues like large file sizes. In September 1996, a man was fined USD 43,000 for downloading sex films from the Internet. It was the first enforcement of Singapore's Internet regulation. The raid followed a tip-off from Interpol, which was investigating people exchanging pornography online. Afterwards, SBA told citizens that it does not monitor e-mail messages, chat groups, sites people access, or what they download.[4587]

In 1999, the Home Affairs Ministry scanned 200,000 users of SingNet ISP at the request of the company looking for the "Back Orifice" program without telling the subscribers. TAS determined that the ISP had violated no law, but nevertheless SingNet apologized for the scans and the National Information Technology Committee announced that it would create new guidelines.[4588] IDA released guidelines in January 2000.[4589] Under the guidelines, a subscriber's

---

[4583] US Department of State, Country Reports on Human Rights Practices 2000, February 2001, available at <http://www.state.gov/g/drl/rls/hrrpt/2000/>.

[4584] E-mail from Milagros Rivera to Patrick Mueller, IPIOP Clerk, Electronic Privacy Information Center (EPIC), July 2, 2004 (on file with EPIC).

[4585] Garry Roday, "The Internet and Social Control in Singapore," Pol. Sci. Q. Volume 113, No. 1, Spring 1998.

[4586] Id.

[4587] Straits Times, September 27, 1996.

[4588] "ISPs To Get Guidelines On Scanning," Straits Times, May 12, 1999.

[4589] "Guidelines for IASPs on Scanning of Subscribers' Computers," Infocomm Development Authority of Singapore, for IASPs on Scanning of Subscribers' January 6, 2000, available at <http://www.ida.gov.sg/Website/IDAContent.nsf/dd1521f1e79ecf3bc825682f0045a340/7c22304fecdd8affc825685e0035f9eb?OpenDocument>.

explicit consent must be obtained before scanning can occur. The scanning must be minimally intrusive and must not intercept web browsing or electronic communications. A November 1999 study by the Singapore Polytechnic's business administration found that 60 percent of consumers said they were not ready for virtual shopping cited privacy concerns.[4590]

Although the Constitution gives citizens the right to move freely throughout the country, the government has limited this right in a few instances. For example, it requires all citizens and permanent residents over the age of 15 to register and carry identification cards.[4591] The government is also active in some areas normally considered private, in pursuit of what it considers the public interest. For example, the government continues to enforce ethnic ratios for publicly subsidized housing, where the majority of citizens live and own their own units, designed to achieve an ethnic mix more or less in proportion to that in the society at large.[4592]

Video surveillance cameras are commonly used for monitoring roads and preventing littering in many areas.[4593] In 1995, the government proposed that cameras be placed in all public spaces in Tampines, a neighborhood in Singapore, including corridors, lifts, and open areas such as public parks, car parks and neighborhood centers, and that the cameras broadcast on the public cable television channel.[4594] Authorities increasingly have installed closed-circuit television (CCTV) cameras in areas chosen because of residents' complaints about illegal prostitution and fights.[4595] They plan on installing more over time based on consultation with residents and tenants about where they are most needed.[4596] Recently, authorities called for the use of cameras in the streets to beef up security against terrorism, especially in places with a higher incidence of crime and those popular with the public.[4597] After the July 2005 terrorist bombings in London, authorities began to look into deploying CCTV on buses,

---

[4590] "Not Many Ready To Cyber-Shop, Says Poll," Straits Times, November 18, 1999.

[4591] US Department of State, Report on Singapore 2004, *supra.*

[4592] US Department of State, Country Reports on Human Rights Practices 2000, February 2001, available at <http://www.state.gov/g/drl/rls/hrrpt/2001/eap/8375.htm>.

[4593] "Video Cameras To Monitor Traffic at 15 Junctions," Straits Times, March 12, 1995; "Surveillance System Set Up in Jurong East," Straits Times, July 16, 1996.

[4594] "Do We Really Want an All-Seeing Camera?" Straits Times, July 13, 1995.

[4595] Tanya Fong, "Anti-Crime Cameras to Go up in more Areas; Success in Boat Quay, Little India and Newton. Next on the List is Geylang," Straits Times, February 23, 2005.

[4596] *Id.*

[4597] Li Xueying, "More 'Eyes' to Help Fight Terror; Public Areas and Streets to Have more CCTV Cameras – They Will Help Defuse Potential Terrorist Activities as well as Deter Crimes," Strait Times, November 7, 2004.

trains, lifts, carparks, housing estates, schools and other public areas.[4598] Despite the extensive and arguably invasive monitoring, most Singaporeans support placing surveillance cameras in public places, according to a 2000 survey conducted by the Straits Times.

Efforts against Terrorism

The Internal Security Act (ISA) is legislation aimed at countering the perceived threats to national security, including international terrorism. ISA has provisions for arrest and detention without warrant or judicial review if police authorities determine that national security, public safety and order, or the public interest is at risk. It has been used to deal with security threats, and, recently, the government employed it against suspected terrorists. The opposition called for its abolition many times, which the government rejected every time. The minister of Home Affairs, at the direction of the president, has broad discretion under ISA to order detention without filing charges, if the president determines that a person poses a threat to national security. At the end of 2004, 36 detainees were being held as suspected terrorists.[4599] In 2004, the government continued to rely on preventive detention to investigate terrorism cases, sometimes infringing on citizens' privacy rights.[4600]

In response to the terrorist attacks in the United States on September 11, 2001, Singapore strengthened its anti-terrorist efforts by passing laws that codified United Nations resolutions to punish criminally the funding of terrorist activities and the making of false terrorist threats.[4601] In this respect, Parliament passed the Terrorism (Suppression of Financing) Act in July 2002, which punishes those found sheltering or dealing with the property of terrorists, and withholding financial information of terrorist acts.[4602]

In June 2002, Singapore proposed that Asian and European law enforcement agencies organize a system to share intelligence information to combat terrorism and organized crime.[4603] In November 2003, the Computer Misuse Act was

---

[4598] Goh Chin Lian, "More CCTV Cameras for Housing Estates; Police Explore Idea to Boost Security; Cameras on Buses, Trains Considered," Straits Times, July 25, 2005.

[4599] US Department of State, Report on Singapore 2004, *supra*.

[4600] *Id.*

[4601] "Singapore Tightens Anti-Terrorist Laws," BBC News, November 13, 2001, available at <http://news.bbc.co.uk/hi/english/world/asia-pacific/newsid_1653000/1653797.stm>.

[4602] Terrorism (Suppression of Financing) Act (No. 16 of 2002), available at <http://statutes.agc.gov.sg>.

[4603] "European Union/ASEM – Calls For Restraint in Middle East and Kashmir," European Report, June 12, 2002.

amended to allow authorities to launch pre-emptive actions against suspected hackers based on "credible information" linking the suspect to planned attacks on sensitive information networks.[4604] Reporters Without Borders warned against potential abuses, because the amendment allows continuous surveillance of suspects through real-time monitoring software.[4605]

In late 2003, Singapore's Home Affairs Minister urged countries to develop biometric-enabled passports in order to "prevent terrorist from moving freely."[4606] During his five-nation tour of Asia in 2004, US Secretary for Homeland Security Tom Ridge met with Singapore defense officials to "explore opportunities for closer cooperation as part of the international exchange and sharing of information and knowledge."[4607]

Miscellaneous Developments

In March 2003, the Ministry of Finance and the Central Provident Fund Board created "SingPass," the "online equivalent of the Identity Card."[4608] SingPass is a single, user-created password Singaporeans must use to access electronic government services.[4609] Individuals over the age of 15 may apply for SingPass, and it will be automatically issued to individuals who register for a national identity card.[4610] Singaporeans can access electronic government services through the "eCitizen portal."[4611]

In early 2001, the Ministry of Health launched MeetDoc.com, an Internet-accessible medical database.[4612] MeetDoc.com holds all patients' records from all hospitals and clinics in Singapore and is available to government and private doctors in Singapore and abroad. Because records are accessible only with a

---

[4604] Amit Chanda, "New Singaporean Law to Enable 'Pre-Emptive' Action against Cyber-Terrorists," World Markets Analysis, November 11, 2003.

[4605] Reporters Without Borders, "The Internet Under Surveillance" (October 13, 2003).

[4606] Johnson Choo, "Singapore Urges Use of Biometric Passports to Restrict Terrorists' Movements," Channel News Asia, November 21, 2003, available at
<http://www.channelnewsasia.com/stories/singaporelocalnews/view/58376/1/.html>.

[4607] "Singapore, US Officials Hold Talks on Terrorism," Xinhua General News Service, March 8, 2004.

[4608] "Singpass: One Password for E-Services," February 24, 2003, available at
<http://www.ida.gov.sg/Website/IDAContent.nsf/dd1521f1e79ecf3bc825682f0045a340/e7641f18ddbcf758482
56ced003710d3?OpenDocument>.

[4609] "SingPass Opens the Door to E-Services," Business Times (Singapore), February 25, 2003.

[4610] Id.

[4611] <http://www.ecitizen.gov.sg>.

[4612] Edmund Tee, "Get All Your Medical Data Online," Straits Times, February 17, 2001.

patient's username and password, physicians must obtain a patient's permission before obtaining medical information.

An extensive Electronic Road Pricing (ERP) system for monitoring road usage went into effect in 1998. The system collects information on an automobile's travel from smart cards ("CashCards") plugged into transmitters in every car (in-vehicle units, or IUs) and in video surveillance cameras.[4613] ERP collects tolls. Video surveillance cameras monitor drivers attempting to circumvent the system. About 1,500 summonses were issued in a six-month period in 2003-2004 for such violations.[4614] The service claims that the data will only be kept for 24 hours and does not maintain a central accounting system. In 2005, a new generation of smarter ERP IUs is being evaluated that could function automatically without the need to insert cash cards, for example any time a vehicle passes under a gantry or enters into an ERP-equipped carpark.[4615] Whether it is implemented may depend on political and social acceptance because of current privacy concerns.[4616]

In April 2003, Singapore added SARS to the Quarantine Act, a law that had previously been dormant for 27 years.[4617] Measures taken to combat SARS included contact tracing and the thermal-imaging detection of body temperatures in public places.[4618] To prevent violation of quarantine orders, the government ordered a 10-day quarantine of individuals suspected of having SARS.[4619] Security officials installed cameras into the home of individuals who had received quarantine orders and required them to appear before the camera at specific intervals.[4620] Also, officials would call the suspected individual's home as an additional check to enforce the quarantine, and his telephone company would be ordered to block any attempt to forward home phone calls to mobile

---

[4613] "You're on Candid Camera," Straits Times, September 2, 1998.

[4614] "Surveillance Cameras Pick Up More Motorists Trying to Avoid ERP Charges," Channel NewsAsia, April 27, 2004.

[4615] Christopher Tan, "Plans for Smarter and Sleeker ERP Device; It Works even if CashCard Is not Inserted in in-Vehicle Unit," Straits Times, August 1, 2005. A government official hinted that the ERP system may one day be satellite-tracked, which would enable authorities to charge ERP fees based on the distance a driver travels and may replace the fixed road tax in place today.

[4616] Id.

[4617] Julie Robotham, "Tougher Laws to Keep SARS Under Control," Sydney Morning Herald. April 7, 2003, available at <http://www.smh.com.au/articles/2003/04/06/1049567566823.html>.

[4618] Richard Paddock and Sonni Effron, "SARS Under Control in Singapore, WHO Says." Los Angeles Times, June 1, 2003 at A4.

[4619] Chua Mui Hoong, "Govt's Sars Action Swift, But Shows Up Lack of Checks," Straits Times, May 10, 2003.

[4620] Id.

phones to make sure that the individual does not leave the home.[4621] The government also planned to use electronic wristbands if suspected individuals did not answer phone calls.[4622] One man in Singapore was sentenced to six months in prison for "repeatedly flouting home quarantine orders."[4623]

Radio frequency identification (RFID) tags first appeared in Singapore in 1988, when the Electronic Library Management System deployed a book management and checkout system featuring 120,000 RFID tags.[4624] Later, in 2000, the National University of Singapore Library unveiled a multi-library system utilizing more than two million RFID tags, making it the largest library RFID project in the world.[4625] In 2004, IDA announced a three-year USD 10 million plan to spur greater RFID use,[4626] which was later matched by the industry to invest in RFID trial projects and infrastructure development.[4627] IDA committed itself to developing international RFID standards, aligning the frequency spectrum, and initiated talks with United States RFID development leaders, including Auto-ID Labs at the Massachusetts Institute of Technology.[4628] In 2005, RFID increasingly attracted the attention of the major technology players of the region that consider RFID as a huge revenue generator in years to come in several areas, such as airports, seaports and retail logistics applications. However, major concerns remain such as cost, lack of common standards and privacy.[4629]

IDA launched a trial program in February 2004 to stimulate the development of ultra-wideband technology. This will be used in products that "can see through walls and track vehicles or objects."[4630]

Late in 2004, the government launched a giant e-government project, a portal (www.gov.sg) that draws together around 1,600 different services through various ministry Web sites and will allegedly offer everything from sports ground bookings to collecting payments for traffic fines, credit card bills and TV

[4621] *Id.*

[4622] *Id.*

[4623] "Singapore Man Sentenced to Six Months in Jail for Violating Home Quarantine Orders," Associated Press Newswires, May 9, 2003.

[4624] Tony Santiago, "Singapore Plunges into RFID Tags," Electrical Engineering Times, May 17, 2004, at 38.

[4625] *Id.*

[4626] Infocomm Development Authority of Singapore, "RFID Identified as Next Growth Area for Singapore ICT Industry," press release, May 5, 2004, available at
<http://www.ida.gov.sg/idaweb/marketing/infopage.jsp?infopagecategory=&infopageid=12845>.

[4627] Pek Tiong Gee, "Tech@Work: RFID Action for Tech Majors," Straits Times, January 17, 2005.

[4628] Infocomm Development Authority of Singapore, *supra.*

[4629] Pek Tiong Gee, *supra.*

[4630] "Singapore to Test Technology that Sees Through Walls," Wall Street Journal, February 25, 2004.

licenses. Another project is the national electronic payment hub, which high cost has been factored in under the e-Government action plan II, that started last year with a USD 1.3 billion budget. It would enable people to pay their government bills, town council fees, or even mobile phone subscriptions by going to a single Web site.[4631] The government has said that its data privacy protection code – which controls how the government processes, uses and shares information – would apply to any public-private sector project. The code restricts the sharing of information among government agencies to the specific purpose for which the information was collected. It also prohibits agencies from disclosing data to commercial companies without explicit approval from the individual concerned. Private companies that would connect with the government to provide services on the www.gov.sg Web site would have to comply with the same rules.[4632] However, the government has not determined yet what penalties would apply for breach of these rules. Most importantly, there are still critical concerns about the potential information security risks these projects raise. They involve data access, sharing and management, the integrity and accuracy of the data, and the potential for hacking and fraud.[4633]

The Bioethics Advisory Committee of Singapore (BAC) drew up guidelines to ensure that individuals undertake genetic testing voluntarily and to protect their privacy and the confidentiality of their information. Among the 24 recommendations BAC issued, one is that the results of genetic tests should not be disclosed to third parties, unless the person concerned consents.[4634]

Singapore ranked 13th in a global Information Society Index survey carried out late 2004 by American research company International Data Corp. The survey reveals that the country's censorship laws and a lack of data protection legislation meant it was not as ready as its Asian neighbors South Korea and Hong Kong to successfully compete in the information economy.[4635]

[4631] Grace Chng, "Locking up Security Risks for e-Govt Site," Straits Times, November 8, 2004.

[4632] Natalie Soh, "Steps in Place to Ensure Privacy, Security; Issue of Confidentiality Taken very Seriously, Says IDA," Straits Times, October 29, 2004.

[4633] Grace Chng, *supra*.

[4634] "Genes that Tell on You," Editorial, Straits Times, April 11, 2005; "Chance to Have Say on Genetic Research," Straits Times, May 6, 2005.

[4635] Chua Hian Hou, "S'pore Lags in Tech Ranking," Straits Times, November 10, 2004.

Singapore became a member of the United Nations (UN) Organization on September 21, 1965[4636] and enshrined the Universal Declaration of Human Rights in its Constitution.[4637] In spite of this, it has not yet ratified the two primary UN human rights instruments: the International Covenant on Civil and Political Rights and the International Covenant on Economic, Social and Cultural Rights.[4638]

Slovak Republic

Constitutional Privacy Framework

The 1992 Constitution provides for protections for privacy, data protection, and secrecy of communications. Article 16 states, "(1) The inviolability of the person and its privacy is guaranteed. It can be limited only in cases defined by law." Article 19 states, "(1) Everyone has the right to the preservation of his human dignity, personal honor and good reputation, and the protection of his name. (2) Everyone has the right to protection against unwarranted interference in his private and family life. (3) Everyone has the right to protection against the unwarranted collection, publication, or other illicit use of his personal data." Article 22 states, "(1) The privacy of correspondence and secrecy of mailed messages and other written documents and the protection of personal data are guaranteed. (2) No one must violate the privacy of correspondence and the secrecy of other written documents and records, whether they are kept in private or sent by mail or in another way, with the exception of cases to be set out in a law. Equally guaranteed is the secrecy of messages conveyed by telephone, telegraph, or other similar means."[4639]

[4636] United Nations, List of Member States <http://www.un.org/Overview/unmember.html>.

[4637] Thinkcentre.org, "Singapore: Constitutional Rights," November 8, 2004 <http://www.thinkcentre.org/article.cfm?ArticleID=2486>.

[4638] University of Minnesota, Human Rights Library, Ratification of International Human Rights Treaties – Singapore <http://www1.umn.edu/humanrts/research/ratification-singapore.html>.

[4639] Act No. 460 of September 1, 1992 Constitution of the Slovak Republic (September 1, 1992), available at <http://www.slovakia.org/sk-constitution.htm>.

Data Protection Framework

The Act on Protection of Personal Data in Information Systems was approved in February 1998 and went into effect on March 1, 1998.[4640] The Act replaces the previous 1992 Czechoslovakian legislation.[4641] It limits the collection, disclosure and use of personal information by government agencies and private enterprises either in electronic or manual form. It creates duties of access, accuracy and correction, security, and confidentiality on the data processor. Processing of information on racial, ethnic, political opinions, religion, philosophical beliefs, trade union membership, health, and sexuality is forbidden. Special protections are provided for sensitive data, defined as data revealing "racial or ethnic origin, political opinions, religious or philosophical beliefs, trade-union membership and data concerning health or sex life and conviction." Transfers to other countries are limited unless the country has "adequate" protection. All systems are required to be registered with the Statistical Office of the Slovak Republic.[4642]

Data Protection Authority

The Act created a new office, the Inspection Unit for the Protection of Personal Data (*Úrad na ochranu osobných údajov*), headed by the Commissioner for Personal Data Protection (the Commissioner), to supervise and enforce the Act.[4643] The Commissioner is appointed by the Government on the basis of a recommendation by the President of the Statistical Office. Mr. Pavol Husar took office as the first Commissioner in February 1999. The Commissioner monitors the implementation of the law, reviews registered systems, inspects the processing of personal data in information systems, receives and handles complaints concerning the violation of personal data protection in information systems, initiates corrective actions whenever a breach of legal obligations is ascertained, and participates in the preparation of generally binding regulations in the field of personal data. The Commissioner is required to file an annual report on the status of data protection with the Government and the National Council (parliament).

[4640] Act No. 52 of February 3, 1998 on Protection of Personal Data in Information Systems, available at <http://www.statistics.sk/webdata/english/acts/act5298/act5298.htm>.

[4641] Act of April 29, 1992 on Protection of Personal Data in Information Systems (No. 256/92).

[4642] Registration is governed by the Decree of the Statistical Office of the Slovak Republic of 11 May 1998, available at <http://www.statistics.sk/webdata/english/acts/155decre/155decre.htm>.

[4643] Homepage <http://www.dataprotection.gov.sk/>.

As of April 2005, the office had 28 employees, including 10 legal professionals, five information technology professionals and six support staff.[4644] In January 2001, the Commissioner said publicly that the act was going to be much more vigorously enforced and large fines imposed for violations, including non-registration. He noted that there were only 400 information systems registered when the number should really be around 20,000.[4645]

One of the top priorities for the Inspection Unit over the last few years has been to secure amendments to the Act on Protection of Personal Data in Information Systems in order to bring it into full compliance with the EU Directive.[4646] In September 2001, a draft amendment to the Act was submitted to the Legislative Council of the government for approval. In November 2001, the Legislative Council reviewed the draft and made several recommendations, including the establishment of a new independent supervisory authority, to be called the Office for Personal Data Protection. At the Council's request, the Commissioner drafted a completely new Act to incorporate these changes and resubmitted it in December 2001. The new bill was approved by the Government and submitted to Parliament in February 2002. Many of the bill's provisions dealt with restructuring the supervisory authority. It also created new protections for the processing of sensitive information, defined as information relating to race or ethnic origin, political views, religion or philosophical beliefs, membership in political parties, participation in political movements or trade unions, health, and sex life. It also places restrictions on the processing of the national identity number. The bill failed to become law when, in late June 2002, the President refused to sign it on the grounds that it did not clearly define the establishment of the new office. He also objected to the proposed implementation date of July 1, 2002, stating that it would interfere with the general election planned for September 2002. Under the election laws at the time, political parties were required to submit petition sheets containing over 10,000 signatures and including signatory's identity numbers (so called "birth numbers"), a requirement that would contradict the new law. On July 3, 2002, the Parliament passed an amended bill taking into account these objections.[4647]

[4644] E-mail from Daniel Valentovic, Inspection Unit for the Protection of Personal Data, Slovakia, to Ula Galster, International Policy Fellow, Electronic Privacy Information Center (EPIC), May 27, 2005 (on file with EPIC).

[4645] "Large Fines to be Imposed for Abuse of Personal Data in Slovakia," BBC Worldwide Monitoring, January 25, 2001.

[4646] Id.

[4647] "Slovak MPs Approve Personal Data Protection Law," BBC Worldwide Monitoring, July 3, 2002.

On September 1, 2002, a bill known as Act. No. 428 of July 3, 2002 on Protection of Personal Data, went into effect. The law establishes the Office for Personal Data Protection (OPDP) and purports to provide a higher degree of protection to the subjects of data collectors.[4648] In particular, subjects of data collection are given the right to obtain a copy of their data from the controller.[4649] Moreover, the law imposes new duties on controllers, who are to secure better protection of personal data and to take safeguards to mitigate the risk of infringement of personal data. The law also allows the Office to publish or issue in specific situations binding statements (measures). The law enables the imposition of stricter sanctions[4650] for violation of the act's provisions.[4651]

The Addendum to the Report on Slovakia's Progress in its Integration into the European Union states:

> The National Council of the Slovak Republic adopted Personal Data Protection Act No. 428/2002 Coll. with effect from 1 September 2002. The Act ensures full compatibility with European Parliament and Council Directive 95/46/EC on the protection of individuals with regard to the processing of personal data and on the free movement of such data. The Act also accounts for written recommendations of Commission experts who examined the protection of personal data in the Slovak Republic.[4652]

The Act No. 428/2002 Coll. was amended at the beginning of 2005 by Act 90/2005 Coll.[4653] The old Act of 2002 creates a basement for the newest version of the Act.

The Office for Personal Data Protection (OPDP) is involved in the wide spectrum of activities. In 2004, the OPDP issued 105 administrative decisions, as well as 694 opinions to data controllers. The OPDP also performs advisory services regarding legislative proposals (the total number of advices in 2004 was 151) and

---

[4648] Introduction of the Chairman of the Office, available at
<http://www.dataprotection.gov.sk/buxus/generate_page.php3?page_id=423>.
[4649] Id.
[4650] Id.; for example, fines of up to USD 287,000.
[4651] Id.
[4652] "Addendum to the Report on Slovakia's Progress in its Integration into the EU" 38 (2002) available at <http://www.vlada.gov.sk/eu_en/>.
[4653] Act 90 Coll of 2005 on Personal Data Protection (Zákon č. 428/2002 Z. z. o ochrane osobných údajov v znení zákona č. 602/2003 Z. z., zákona č. 576/2004 Z. z. a zákona č. /2005 Z. z.) received in e-mail from Daniel Valentovic, (in Slovakian only) (on file with EPIC).

conducts explanatory proceedings (the total number in 2004 was 37).[4654] The OPDP also orders public opinion surveys at the Institute for Public Opinion Surveys Research of the Statistical Office of the Slovak Republic (*Ústav výskumu verejnej mienky, Štatistického úradu SR*) on the subject of the awareness of rules concerning the personal data protection. The OPDP also participates in the process of publishing specialized booklets for target groups. Booklets contain information about data protection duties addressed to personnel professionals, health care employees, schools and municipalities. As of February 2005, there were 4,300 data controllers registered with the OPDP.[4655]

The Office of Personal Data Protection maintains close relations with the data protection authorities in other central and eastern European countries. In December 2001, the Data Protection Commissioners from the Czech Republic, Hungary, Lithuania, Slovakia, Estonia, Latvia, and Poland signed a joint declaration agreeing to closer cooperation and assistance. The Commissioners agreed to meet twice a year in the future, to provide each other with regular updates and overviews of developments in their countries, and to establish a common website for more effective communication.[4656]

Wiretapping and Surveillance Rules

Under the 1993 Police Law, the police are required to obtain permission from a court or prosecutor before undertaking any telephone tapping or mail surveillance.[4657] This type of activity is supposed to be used only in cases of extraordinarily serious premeditated crimes or crimes involving international-treaty obligations. However, the communist-era secret police still remain in positions of power and over the years there have been many public revelations of illegal wiretapping of opposition politicians, reporters and dissidents.[4658] In 2001, there were allegations that members of the SMK and SMER parties were being

---

[4654] The number of written proceedings: (on a percentage basis) 16 percent; the number of conducted inspections/audits (on a percentage basis): 43 percent; the number of conducted proceedings related to prior checking: 16; Since inception of the Office of Personal Data Protection in September of 2002 through April 30, 2003, the office received 36 complaints of data subjects. The office undertook nine inspections, issued five measures, referred two cases to criminal justice agencies, and registered 1,752 information systems.

[4655] E-mail from Daniel Valentovic, *supra.*

[4656] E-mail from Karel Neuwirt, President, Office for Personal Data Protection, Czech Republic, to Sarah Andrews, Research Director, EPIC, May 15, 2002 (on file with EPIC).

[4657] Code of Criminal Procedure, Articles 86 to 88.

[4658] "Hungarian Politicians in Slovakia Are Being Bugged," CTK National News Wire, February 21, 1995; "Deputy Brings Charges Against Slovak Secret Services Spokesman," CTK National News Wire, August 21, 1997.

monitored and their telephones tapped.[4659] Active monitoring of the Church of Scientology by the Ministry of the Interior was also reported.[4660] Under the Criminal Code, police require a judicial search warrant to enter a private home and the court may only issue this warrant with good cause. Police are required to present the warrant before conducting the search or within 24 hours. There are continuing reports of Roma homes being entered without warrants.[4661]

There are legal protections for privacy in the Civil Code. Article 11 states, "everyone has the right to the preservation of his personality, mainly of life and health, personal honor and human dignity as well as privacy, name and exhibitions of personal nature." There are also computer-related offenses linked with the protection of a person (unjustified treatment of personal data).[4662] The Slovak Constitutional Court ruled in March 1998 that the law allowing public prosecutors to demand to see the files or private correspondence of political parties, private citizens, trade union organizations and churches, even when not necessary for prosecution, was unconstitutional. Court chairman Milan Cic said this was "not only not usual, but opens the door to widespread violation of peoples' basic rights and their right to privacy."[4663] Moreover, there are sector-specific privacy provisions to protect an individual's medical, financial and tax records.[4664] A draft new media law, containing provisions on the protection of privacy and rights of correction, is also moving forward.[4665]

In April 2005, the Slovak government announced plans to start issuing biometric passports by September 1, 2006. New passports introduced by the Slovakian government in April 2005 have better security features than the previous travel document and, although they do not currently include any biometric identifier, are "biometric-ready." According to Interior Minister Vladimir Palko, a digital facial image of the holder will be included in passports starting in September 2006, while a fingerprint scan will be added starting March 1, 2008. The

---

[4659] US Department of State Country Reports on Human Rights Practices – 2001, March 2002, available at <http://www.state.gov/g/drl/rls/hrrpt/2001/eur/8338.htm>.

[4660] Id.

[4661] Id.

[4662] European Commission, Agenda 2000 - Commission Opinion on Slovakia's Application for Membership of the European Union, Doc 97/20, July 15, 1997.

[4663] "Court Rules Law on Public Prosecutors Unconstitutional," CTK National News Wire, March 4, 1998.

[4664] Act No. 277/1994 on Health Care; Act No. 21/1992 on Banks (later cancelled and replaced by Act. No. 483/2001 on Banks); Act No. 511/1992 on Tax Fee Administration; *see* "Data Protection Laws of the World," Christopher Millard and Mark Ford, Clifford Chance, Sweet & Maxwell 2000.

[4665] "Culture Ministry to Draft Own Media Law," BBC Worldwide Monitoring, February 9, 2001.

biometric passports will provide Slovakia with further arguments to negotiate visa-free travel to the United States for its citizens.[4666]

Anti-terrorism Measures

The head of Slovakia's Parliamentary Defense Committee, Robert Kaliňák is calling for a new law on terrorism. Kaliňák said: "The law would define priority tasks for security forces. These priority tasks would include monitoring the movements of dangerous materials and people deemed potentially dangerous in Slovakia." Kaliňák believes that new legislation would be more effective in the fight against terror than what is currently in place (*i.e.* the monitoring of telephone calls). The law would also help coordinate intelligence services, the head of the Committee claims. Kaliňák plans to draft the legislation this autumn, together with defense committee members.[4667]

Open Government

The Act on Free Access to Information was approved by the Parliament in May 2000. It sets broad rules on disclosure of information held by all "Obligees," which means state agencies (including parliament, government, courts, etc.) municipalities, legal entities established by law and by state agencies, as well as legal entities and natural persons that have been given the power by law to make decisions in the area of public administration.[4668] There are limitations on information that (a) is classified; (b) constitutes a trade, bank, or tax secret; (c) is a tax secret; (d) is a bank secret; (e) is intellectual property; (f) would violate privacy; (g) was obtained "from a person not required by law to provide information, who upon notification of the Obligee instructed the Obligee in writing not to disclose information"; (h) is information published regularly by the Obligee under a special act; (i) "concerns the decision-making power of the courts and law enforcement bodies"; or (j) identifies localities of protected animals and plants, minerals and fossils. The information requests to obligees must be disposed without undue delay, but not later than in 10 days. Appeals are made to higher agencies and can be reviewed by an administrative court.[4669]

[4666] "Slovakia to Issue Biometric Passports in 2006," eGoverment news, April 12, 2005, available at <http://europa.eu.int/idabc/en/document/4095/587>.

[4667] "MP calls for new anti-terrorism law," The Slovak Spectator, July 27, 2005, available at <http://www.slovakspectator.sk/clanok.asp?cl=20427>.

[4668] Act on Free Access to Information, available at <http://www.civil.gov.sk/SNARCHIV/uk_the_act_on_free_access_to_information.htm>.

[4669] E-mail from Vlado Pirosik, Public Interest Lawyer, Environmental Lobbying Facility, Slovak Republic, to

During the implementation of this Act in practice, some difficulties have been found in cases regarding appeals against decisions made by obligees that do not have their own superiors, e.g. municipalities, the National Property Fund of SR, etc. In these cases, it is not clear what is the appropriate appellate body. For example, in the case of municipalities, two different provisions of two different acts collide. On one hand, the Act on Free Access to Information states in Article 19 that, "if it is a decision of the municipal office, the decision on the appeal shall be made by the mayor." In practice, this is not possible because the municipal office is alo an executive body of the mayor. On the other hand, Act No. 369/1990 on Municipalities states in Article 13 that, "in administrative proceedings the mayor is the administrative body." This means that the mayor is the only body that is allowed to make first-degree administrative decisions. The municipal office is not allowed to do this. Under Article 27 of the Act on Municipalities, the court is the appellate body to the mayor's decision on the rights and responsibilities of natural persons or legal entities in matters of self-governance, including the disclosure of information. During more than the three years of implementing the Act on Free Access to Information, there has been no adjudication that would unify these two contradicting provisions of two different acts. Moreover, since January 1, 2003, several provisions in Act No. 99/1963 on Civil Court Procedure have changed. Among them are provisions that are important for proceedings of the court as an appellate body to the mayor's decision in matters of self-governance. The most important change is that the requester can file an appeal against the court adjudication to a higher court, a step that was not possible before. Courts have no obligatory time limit within which they must decide. The consequence of this change in the Act on Civil Court Procedure is that the process for obtaining information can be extended indefinitely, while the value of the information originally requested declines in value.

There are also separate requirements for disclosure of environmental information that covers private organizations. New requirements became effective January 1, 2001[4670] and revoked Act 171/1998 of the National Council on Free Access to Environmental Information. In February 2001, the government approved a draft

---

John Baggaley, Law Clerk, EPIC, July 11, 2003 (on file with EPIC). The Act on Free Access to Information stipulates the duty for obligees to provide information "without undue delay, but not later than in ten days." If a requester does not get the information from either the obligee or from the appellate body (in the previous administrative proceedings), the requester has the right (Article 19, paragraph 4) to access the administrative court and let the court review both the administrative decisions. If the requester decides to use this right, from the moment she files a civil action, the proceeding is governed not by the Act on Free Access to Information, but by Act 99/1963 on Civil Court Procedure. Under this act, there is no obligatory time limit imposed upon the courts. Typically, in Slovakia, this procedure takes five to six months.

[4670] Act on Free Access to Information, available at <http://www.elaw.org/resources/text.asp?ID=331>.

law on Protection of Confidential Information to harmonize the handling of classified documents with NATO standards, despite the Data Protection Commissioner's objections that it violated human rights.[4671]

In July 2005, it was reported that the Interior Ministry sought to change the existing free access to information law, which gives citizens the right to get information from public and municipal authorities. If the changes are introduced, a public official who withholds information will no longer be committing an offense. At present, a bureaucrat who fails to provide information requested by a citizen can be fined up to SKK 50,000 (~ USD 1,570) and be suspended from the job for up to two years. In the Interior Ministry's proposal, however, the offence clause would be left out of the freedom of information law. Jana Pôbišová, of the Interior Ministry, said that this is because the state or municipal employees do not act as private entities, but rather in the name of legal entities, the state or municipal authorities, and should therefore not be punished as individuals. Activists claim, however, that if the clause is eliminated, it will be virtually impossible to identify who is responsible for withholding information.[4672]

Major Privacy Case Law

In situations that are not regulated by detailed provisions of the acts,[4673] the public administration has the discretion to interpret and apply general legal terms, such as "privacy" or "honor," in conformity with the Constitution, and thus may consider that the right to privacy is in certain cases[4674] restrained in favor of the right to information. The obligation of the public administration to consider constitutional principles[4675] was recognized by the Slovak Constitutional Court in the ruling II. ÚS 44/00, where held that making a film record of policemen performing their official duties is not an invasion of their right to privacy and should be allowed.

[4671] "Government Approves New Version of Law on Confidential Information," BBC Summary of World Broadcasts, March 2, 2001.

[4672] "Ministry Proposes Changes to Law on Access to Information," The Slovak Spectator July 22, 2005, available at <http://www.slovakspectator.sk/clanok.asp?cl=20370>.

[4673] In instances, where the general legal terms as "privacy" or "honor" are applied – for example under Section 11 of the Slovak Civil Code "A natural person has a right to the protection of his personality, honor, dignity, privacy, name and personal expressions."

[4674] *See* judgment II. ÚS 44/00 of the Slovak Constitutional Court.

[4675] Principle, that all laws shall be interpreted and applied in conformity with the Constitution. For instance Article 152 Paragraph 4 of the Constitution stipulates this principle.

Another serious problem arises when the information about official duties (performing within public administrative bodies or institutions public functions) is considered personal data. This information is often withheld. For instance, the Ministry of Foreign Affairs refused to provide information about the names and functions of its employees to protect their personal data. Currently, two legal actions have been brought against the Ministry to the Regional court in Bratislava.[4676] At the end of the 2004, the Cabinet approved rewards for high state officials. However, when journalists asked the Cabinet to disclose the amount of the rewards or concrete sums and persons' names, the Cabinet responded that this information could not be disclosed on data protection grounds.[4677]

On May 30, 2001, the National Council of the Slovak Republic adopted Act. No. 241 on the Protection of Confidential Information. Most of the law became effective in July, 1, 2001, the rest on November, 1, 2001. This Act was in effect until April 30, 2004, when it was replaced by Act No. 215/2004 on the Protection of Confidential Information adopted by the National Council of the Slovak Republic. One of the most important changes brought by this new Act is in the method of creation of the Confidential Information List. According to the old wording, this list was created by the National Security Authority in the form of a regulation. The wording of the new Act states that the Confidential Information List is created by the head of each authority that deals with confidential information. That means that one of the duties of the head of the authority is to determine the fundamental scope of classified information, and unless he or she determines otherwise, to decide on the period of, change to, and extinction of, the security classification level. The information can be classified as a confidential information only in fields stipulated by the Government of the Slovak Republic in regulation No. 216/2004.

On August 19, 2002, the National Council of the Slovak Republic adopted the Act on Access to Documents Concerning the Activities of the State Security Services between 1939 and 1989 and on Establishment of the Institute of National Memory Act No. 553/2002 Coll (National Memory Act). The National Memory Act allows Slovak citizens and foreigners to request access to documents containing information about the applicants that was collected and maintained by the state security services between 1939 and 1989. The Act

---

[4676] These are pending cases and have not been decided yet. Numbers of court proceedings are: 1S 64/05 and 2S 94/05.

[4677] PRAVDA, December, 10 2004, available at
<http://spravy.pravda.sk/sk_domace.asp?r=sk_domace&c=A041209_183102_sk_domace_p02>.

purports to provide historians, victims, and their relatives with access to documents collected by the former state security services.[4678]

The National Memory Act sets forth the principles for evidence, collection, registration, disclosure, and management of certain documents created and maintained by the security services of the German Third Reich and the former Soviet Union as well as the Czechoslovak and Slovak security agencies in the so-called "totality era," the period from April 18, 1939, to December 31, 1989. Specifically, the National Memory Act deals with documents concerning crimes committed on Slovak nationals as well as Slovak citizens of other nationalities. The crimes in question include (i) Nazi crimes, (ii) communist crimes, (iii) other crimes against peace, humanity, or war crimes, and (iv) other retaliations for political reasons.[4679]

International Obligations

Slovakia is a member of the Council of Europe and has signed and ratified the Convention for the Protection of Individuals with Regard to Automatic Processing of Personal Data (ETS No. 108).[4680] In August 2001, it signed, and later ratified, the Additional Protocol to Convention 108 regarding supervisory authorities and transborder data flows.[4681] It has signed and ratified the European Convention for the Protection of Human Rights and Fundamental Freedoms.[4682] Slovakia joined the Organization for Economic Cooperation and Development (OECD) in September 2000. On May 1, 2004 Slovakia joined the European Union.

[4678] E-mail from Zuzana Babicová, Office for Personal Data Protection, Slovak Republic, to John Baggaley, EPIC, June 16, 2003 (on file with EPIC).

[4679] Id.

[4680] Signed April 14, 2000; ratified September 13, 2000; entered into force January 1, 2001, available at <http://conventions.coe.int/Treaty/Commun/QueVoulezVous.asp?NT=108&CM=1&DF=10/09/04&CL=ENG>

[4681] Ratified on January 1, 2004, available at <http://www.coe.int/T/E/Legal_affairs/Legal_co-operation/Data_protection/Documents/International_legal_instruments/Amendements%20to%20the%20Convention%20108.asp>.

[4682] Signed February 21, 1991; ratified March 18, 1992; entered into force January 1, 1993, available at <http://conventions.coe.int/>.

Republic of Slovenia

Constitutional Privacy Framework

The right to privacy appears in two forms in the 1991 Slovenian Constitution,[4683] as an individual right of a private character, and as a human right, meaning that it also has a public nature.[4684] Privacy rights are covered in the second section of the Constitution, which protects various aspects of privacy. Article 35 on the Protection of the Right to Privacy and of Personal Rights states, "The physical and mental integrity of each person shall be guaranteed, as shall be his right to privacy and his other personal rights." Article 37 on the Protection of Privacy of Post and Other Means of Communication states, "The privacy of the post and of other means of communication shall be guaranteed. In accordance with the statute, a court may authorize action infringing on the privacy of the post or of other means of communication, or on the inviolability of individual privacy, where such actions are deemed necessary for the institution or continuance of criminal proceedings or for reasons of national security."[4685]

Data Protection Framework

Since May 1, 2004, Slovenia is a new member of European Union, which means that all EU directives are effective in the country. Slovenia enacted in 1999 the Personal Data Protection Act (PDPA) based on the EU Data Protection Directive and the Council of Europe (CoE) Convention for the Protection of Individuals with Regard to Automatic Processing of Personal Data (Convention No. 108). In this law, private entities may process personal data only if they have obtained individuals' written consent, or if law regulates the data processing. Article 38 of the Constitution states, "The protection of personal data relating to an individual shall be guaranteed. Any use of personal data shall be forbidden where that use conflicts with the original purpose for which it was collected. The collection, processing and the end-use of such data, as well as the supervision and protection of the confidentiality of such data, shall be regulated by statute. Each person has

---

[4683] Constitution of the Republic of Slovenia 1991, available at <http://www.sigov.si/us/eus-usta.html>.

[4684] *Komentar Ustave Republike Slovenije* (Comments about the Constitution of the Republic of Slovenia) 369 (Sturm & Lovro eds., Ljubljana, *Fakulteta za podiplomske drzavne in evropske studije* 2002).

[4685] The means of communication are interpreted in the widest sense of the word: it may include telephone communications, e-mails, SMS messages and the like, since the form or content of communication is irrelevant in this context. Privacy protection also applies to private telecommunication systems, as well as traffic data, which are also an integral part of communications (*i.e.*, telephone numbers, data about the duration of a communication or the quantity of data transmitted, etc.) *Id.* at 395-396.

the right to be informed of the personal data relating to him which has been collected and has the right to legal remedy in the event of any misuse of that data."[4686]

On January 1, 2005, a new version of the PDPA came into force. The new act, which modernizes the previous version from 2001, follows some changes in the area of personal data processing that occurred in the recent years. PDPA now covers automatic decisionmaking, use of video surveillance cameras, biometrics, collecting of data about entrances and leavings from premises. PDPA meets all requirements of the 1995 EU Data Protection Directive.[4687]

Data Protection Authority

Supervision of the Act is performed by the Inspectorate for Personal Data Protection (the Inspectorate) within the Ministry of Justice and the Human Rights Ombudsman. The Inspectorate began work in September 2001 and, as of July 2002, employed three persons. The Human Rights Ombudsman employs two persons responsible for data protection. The Ministry of Justice remains responsible for maintaining the database registry. The Home Policy Committee within the National Assembly also performs oversight of the Act.[4688]

The PDPA is subject to supervision by inspection agencies. The report for 2004 is not available yet, but in the Inspectorate's 2003 report,[4689] inspectors again have noted an increase in complaints (60 in 2003), which is probably the consequence of greater awareness of individuals about their rights. The majority of complaints concerned the sending of unsolicited commercial messages (via e-mail and ordinary mail)[4690] and the publication of personal data on the Internet. Furthermore, the Inspectorate conducted 18 other inspections and supervisions of the implementation of the provisions of the DPDA. These inspections and supervisions were performed mostly in the field of health service, the educational

---

[4686] Constitution of the Republic of Slovenia 1991, *supra.*

[4687] Directive 95/46/EC of the European Parliament and of the Council of October 24, 1995, on the protection of individuals with regard to the processing of personal data and on the free movement of such data, Official Journal L. 281, 23/11/1995 p. 0031 - 0050.

[4688] E-mail from Joze Bogataj, Data Protection Inspector, to Sarah Andrews, Research Director, Electronic Privacy Information Center (EPIC), July 12, 2002 (on file with EPIC).

[4689] Slovenian Data Protection Inspectorate, Annual Report 2003, available at <http://www.sigov.si/mp/index.php?vie=content&gr1=orgVSst&gr2=insVrsOsb#03>.

[4690] General Consumers Inspector received 58 complaints about spam, but he was only able to take measures against spammers from Slovenia and not from abroad. Letter from the General Consumers Inspector Roman Kladošek to Matej Kovacic, Junior Researcher at the Faculty of Social Sciences, University of Ljubljana, Slovenia, June 24, 2004 (on file with EPIC).

system, public authority, employment, closed circuit television video surveillance, the management of multi-occupied buildings, and employment.[4691] About 1,025 database administrators have registered in the Joint Personal Data Catalogue, the register of all databases containing personal data, which is within the competence of Ministry of Justice.[4692]

The PDPA applies the principles contained in Convention No. 108. The Convention and the PDPA provide that everything that is not explicitly allowed in connection with personal data collection and processing is prohibited. The first version of the PDPA was enacted in 1990, with amendments dating from 1999 and 2001. Public entities may only process personal data for which they have been granted legal authorization, while private entities must receive written consent from individuals. Persons whose personal data are gathered must be informed in advance of the purpose of the collection of data (by giving their written consent or where the purpose of collection is authorized by law). In principle, personal data can be gathered and stored for only as long as needed to meet that objective, and deleted or blocked once the objective is met. All exemptions must be defined in the law. Use of video surveillance in the workplace is allowed only under special circumstances (if it is necessary for security of the people or wealth, protecting secret data or business secrets and this purpose cannot be achieved by less intrusive means). Employees must be presented with a written notice about this measure, the same applies to the use of biometrics in the private sector.

The PDPA also defines in detail the duties of the data controller. It is prohibited to use the same identifier in databases maintained in the areas of public safety, state security, defense, judiciary and health. The connection between these databases is allowed only if there is a legal basis or the individual has given his or her written consent. The data controller of such databases must enable access to the individual free of charge within fifteen days of receiving his or her request, as well as provide a copy of an individual's personal data within thirty days of receiving the request. If a data controller fails to fulfill this obligation, he or she must provide a motivation for doing so in writing. In case an individual's personal data are transferred to recipients, the data controller must supply, at that individual's request, the list of recipients within a thirty-day deadline.

[4691] E-mail from Joze Bogataj, Data Protection Inspector. Slovenian Data Protection Inspectorate, to Cedric Laurant, Policy Counsel, EPIC, July 2, 2004 (on file with EPIC).
[4692] Id.

If an individual provides evidence that his or her personal data were gathered in breach of the law, the data controller must delete the data, or update and correct them if the data were inaccurate or incomplete. The data controller must bear those costs, and must also keep a separate catalogue for each database, which contains, among other things, a detailed description of the kind of data gathered and the manner in which they are gathered, the purpose of their use and the duration of storage, the list of their users and a description of how they are secured. Furthermore, the Ministry of Justice, which is responsible for the protection of personal data, must keep a register of all databases containing personal data. Information in this register is provided by data controllers and is publicly available on the Internet.

Special protections are set out for "sensitive data," defined as data on racial or other origins, political, religious or other beliefs, trade union membership, sexual behavior, criminal convictions and medical data. This data must be specially labeled and may only be transferred across telecommunications networks if it is protected by "encryption methods" and an "electronic signature" that can guarantee illegibility. The law also imposes cross-border restrictions providing that data may only be transferred to countries that have a data protection legal framework as adequate as the Slovenian one. Article 62 explicitly states that there are no cross-border restrictions for the EU member states.

Video Surveillance

Video surveillance is covered in PDPA and Private Protection Act that was enacted in November 2003. PDPA requires that administrators of video surveillances system publish a notice about video surveillance. The notice must contain information about who is and where they are performing video surveillance, and where an individual can get information about data retention periods. The video surveillance system must be protected from unauthorized access. Article 43 of Private Protection Act allows video surveillance systems to be operated only by private guards with a license. The law contains provisions about maximum retention periods of video and audio data. It also mandates video surveillance users to notify people about the monitoring. Failure to notify can carry penalties of up to EUR 12,500.

Privacy of Communications

The right to privacy of communication is guaranteed by the Constitution and is also covered by Article 150 of the Penal Code that prescribes sanctions for the violation of the secrecy of means of communication. This article prohibits unauthorized opening of letters and other postal messages and interception of messages transmitted via telecommunications networks, or reading of their contents without opening a letter or other postal messages. Similarly, it prohibits unauthorized acquaintance with the content of a message transmitted by telephone or other telecommunications equipment, as well as the unauthorized forwarding of someone's letter to a third party. Article 151 further prohibits the publication of private communications without consent by the authorized person.

Privacy of communication may only be invaded by a court order, and if such an invasion is deemed necessary for the purpose of criminal proceedings, or in order to protect the security of the state. In Slovenia, this area is regulated by the Criminal Proceedings Act and the Slovenian Intelligence and Security Agency Act (SISAA) and carried out by the police and Slovenian Intelligence and Security Agency (SOVA).

The Criminal Proceedings Act includes a detailed list of criminal offences and cases in which the privacy of communications may be invaded (with a court order), but the SISAA is not as specific. For example, it stipulates that state security is threatened by "activities aimed against . . . the strategic interests of the Republic of Slovenia," but experts draw attention to the problems potentially arising from such a wording that enables broad interpretations of "strategic interests" in contrast to other more well-defined criminal offences. However the SOVA does not prosecute criminal offenders. If it deals with a suspected criminal offence, it must provide information about it to the director general of the police force and the public prosecutor. SOVA is compelled to inform the Prime Minister about its activities and findings, as well as the President of the Republic, the President of the National Assembly and other ministers if these activities are related to their fields of competence.

In general, a judge's warrant must be issued prior to a house search or telephone tapping. A new Law on the Police, adopted in 1998, allows secret observation and following, and secret police collaboration, to be authorized under very special circumstances by a General Police Director.[4693] However, the wording of the SISAA allows for potential abuse on the part of the SOVA, because it could result in SOVA acquiring too easily a court warrant for communications interception.

[4693]5 Article 49, Law on the Police, July 18, 1998.

Electronic Communications

On May 1, 2004, the Electronic Communications Act came in effect. This Act regulates Internet communications; is compatible with the EU Privacy and Electronic Communications Directive, and replaces the former Telecommunications Act. Article 104 is about traffic data. It requires that subscribers and users' traffic data processed and stored by an operator, be erased or made anonymous as soon as it is no longer needed for the transmission of a message. Operators may store and process traffic data required for billing and interconnection payments only until payment for services or if they have the user's prior consent. Location data other than traffic data relating to users may be processed only in anonymous form or on the basis of the user's prior consent, according to Article 106. Article 107 states that operators shall be obliged at their own expense to ensure adequate equipment and appropriate interfaces enabling lawful interception of communications in their networks, and minister for information society shall prescribe the equipment and determine appropriate interfaces in ordinance, with agreement with the minister for internal affairs, the minister for defense, and the director of SOVA.

On June 1, 2004, an important discussion took place at a meeting among representatives of the Ministry of Information Society, the Ministry of the Interior, police authorities and some Internet service providers (ISPs) (including a representative of SISPA, the Slovenian ISP association) to discuss the implementation of the requirement of the Electronic Communications Act that compels operators to pay the expenses for equipment enabling lawful interception of communications in their networks.[4694] Since these expenses are estimated to be between EUR 100,000 and EUR 700,000 per operator, small ISPs have a good reason to fear for their survival. In response to those concerns, representatives of the Ministry of the Interior and the police proposed to create one central interception center to decrease the costs per operator.[4695] Concerns were also shared that small ISPs may not have enough people and expertise to operate interception devices. The police offered to help manage them. Ordinance for implementation of Internet surveillance has not been adopted yet.

[4694] Not all Slovenian ISPs are members of SISPA.

[4695] Proceedings from the meeting: Ministry of Information Society, Realisation of lawful interception of telecommunications traffic which flows over the Internet, June 1, 2004 (on file with EPIC).

The Penal Code

The Penal Code specifies sanctions for an invasion of territorial privacy in Articles 149 and 152. Article 149 prohibits unauthorized recording or image taking of individuals or their premises if such an act entails a serious invasion of privacy. Article 152 specifies sanctions for the violation of dwellings through an unauthorized entry into, or search of, private facilities, or an attempt to do so. Intrusion into a computer system is the subject of Article 242, but such an intrusion is punishable only if it is connected with business dealings, and made with the aim of acquiring illegal property-related benefits, or causing material harm to others.[4696] Article 154 provides for sanctions and prohibits any use of personal data that is in breach of the law, or any intrusion into an electronic database for the purpose of obtaining some item of information for personal use or for a third party's use. Article 225 also prohibits unauthorized access to an unprotected database, the modification and copying of its content or the insertion of viruses. The conditions under which personal data may be gathered, processed and used are regulated by the PDPA.

Miscellaneous Developments

Police have a right to take a picture, fingerprints and saliva samples from suspects, as provided by Article 149 of the Criminal Proceeding Act. Police also can use DNA samples for criminal investigations.

Slovenia has ID cards. The ID Card Act requires all adults to have and carry a valid ID card with a photograph (Article 2) and to show it to authorities when required. Non-compliance with this requirement carries fines of up to EUR 420.

Slovenia is included in the US visa waiver program and is required to produce biometric passports. However, due to technical and institutional ambiguities, authorities declared that biometric passports could not be produced until 2006.

Other regulations partially or indirectly relate to privacy. Unlawful invasions of the privacy of communications are prohibited and sanctioned. The Electronic Communications Act deals with surveillance and confidentiality of telecommunications. A court order is always required, but the legislation follows

---

[4696] Unfortunately, this wording could lead to a situation in which an intrusion into a computer system not resulting in material harm, or not yielding other kinds of benefit for the intruder, would not be sanctioned. In such a case Article 309, which sanctions the production or acquisition of tools for intrusion into a computer system, has to be applied.

EU trends by requiring that telecommunications service providers gather extensive information. An ordinance about interfaces and software for lawful interception of telecommunications, adopted under the former Telecommunications Act, is still effective and requires mobile operators to supply on request information about the location of a mobile telephone user. Article 72 of the Electronic Communications Act requires operators to provide the location of a device that has been used to make a call to emergency numbers.

The Law on National Statistics regulates the privacy of information collected for statistical purposes.[4697] In July 2000, the Health Insurance Data Collections Act came into force. The Act sets out restrictions on the collection, use and exchange of health data.[4698]

On May 3, 2005, the Electronic Central Register started to operate in Slovenia. This is a reference electronic population register enabling authorized administrators to access the population registry electronically. Public Administration Minister Gregor Virant said that it would make public administration more efficient. The register will combine the three separate registries that were kept on paper. It will include all information associated with births, deaths and marriages, as well as name changes, adoptions, recognitions of fatherhood and divorces. At the same time, an electronic register of households was set up. This means that all registers associated with administrative bodies have now been computerized. The project was launched in 2004 and cost SIT 216 million (EUR 900,000), which includes the upgrade of the population register as well as the registers of foreigners and citizenships.[4699]

Article 50 of the Postal Services Act states that providers of postal services should enable an authorized body to access, on the basis of a court order, the content of post. Both telephone operators and providers of postal services must ensure an indelible record of such moves.

The revised Consumer Protection Act (CPA) that was enacted in January 2003 incorporates the EU E-Commerce Directive (2000/31/EC). Article 45a states that companies (*e.g.*, direct marketing companies) may use the automatic telephone dialing system only with consumer's previous consent. The same is true for fax messages and e-mail messages (*i.e.* spam). The company must also exclude the

---

[4697] Law on National Statistics, July 25, 1995.

[4698] *Id.*

[4699] "E-Register of Births, Deaths and Marriages Launched," Public Relation and Media Office, available at <http://www.uvi.si/eng/slovenia/publications/slovenia-news/2014/2018/>.

consumer from the contact list if he or she makes such a request. The fines average EUR 4,200 for physical persons and EUR 12,600 for companies. The CPA only protects individuals, but Article 109 of the Electronic Communications Act of 2004 protects companies from receiving spam.

The Labor Relations Act prohibits employers from asking employees or employment candidates questions about family matters, marital status, pregnancy, or other information that is not work-related.[4700]

There is no regulation of cryptography in Slovenia. The Electronic Commerce and Electronic Signature Act and the PDPA are even encouraging the use of cryptography and digital signatures. Slovenia also has a right against self-incrimination, which means that a suspect is not compelled to reveal his cryptographic keys.[4701]

An international study (SIBIS 2003) showed that the concern for privacy/confidentiality, as well as, for data security among the Internet users is relatively low in Slovenia, especially in comparison to 25 EU member states and to the US.[4702]

Past Cases of Importance

In late 1998, Slovenian journalist Tomaz Ranc published some articles that were based on confidential information. Police obtained a list of phone numbers he had called and a list of the telephone numbers of the people who called him so they could identify his confidential information sources. The police obtained that list without a court order. Ranc then complained and the court ruled that authorities had violated his human rights when they had attempted to establish his sources by acquiring the list of the telephone numbers he had called.[4703]

In October 2001, it was reported that, in response to the September 11 attacks in the United States, the SOVA began monitoring the e-mails and telephone

---

[4700] Article 26 of the Labor Relations Act.

[4701] Article 5 of the Criminal Proceedings Act.

[4702] Vasja Vehovar, Bojana Lobe, Matej Kovacic, *Confidentiality concern and on-line shopping.* Paper prepared for the "Consumer WebWatch and Consumers International First International Workshop and Roundtable on Web Credibility: Building Trust on the Web," Ljubljana, June 8-9, 2003, available at <http://www.ris.org/uploadi/editor/vehovar_paper_consumersinternational.doc>.

[4703] UNPAN report about Slovenia, available at <http://unpan1.un.org/intradoc/groups/public/documents/nispacee/unpan007961.pdf>.

communications of prominent academics and NGO activists.[4704] In June 2002, the Parliamentary Commission for the Supervision of Work of Security and Intelligence Services started investigating the allegations that the Slovene police and SOVA were secretly wiretapping Peter Ceferin, the lawyer of a man accused of human trafficking.[4705] The same lawyer was the target of secret observation at the beginning of 2004. After a complaint and the publication of the case, the police said that they had received an anonymous denunciation. It turned out that the person performing the observation was a policeman who was not on duty at the time and was presumably acting as a private citizen. There were also questions as to whether SOVA had been secretly wiretapping some political activists for political purposes.[4706]

Probably one of the biggest recent privacy abuses took place in April 2003. Someone set up a website (www.udba.net) and published the personal data of about 1.5 million individuals from Slovenia (almost the whole population of the country). The information published was part of archives of the previous communist regime's secret service (the UDBA), later renamed National Security Service (SDV). In that archive (called the Central Active File) were persons' names, surnames, dates of birth, nationalities, secret service dossier number, and all criminal offenses of which a person had only been suspected. The persons listed were not only SDV agents, but also individuals who came in contact with the repressive organs of the previous communist regime: political opponents, traffic offenders, criminals, and even people who were just put under surveillance at their employer's request. Among them were prominent politicians and public persons. On April 17, 2003, the Inspector for Personal Data Protection ordered Slovenian ISPs to block access to the udba.net website. In a few days almost all the media had published how to avoid the blocking and started a wide public debate about Internet censorship. Some legal experts also claimed that the

---

[4704] International Helsinki Federation for Human Rights, "Human Rights in the OSCE Region: The Balkans, the Caucasus, Europe, Central Asia and North America" Report 2002 (events 2001), available at <http://www.ihf-hr.org/reports/AR2002/country%20links/Slovenia.htm>.

[4705] "Slovene Inquiry Commission Investigates Wiretapping Allegations," BBC Worldwide Monitoring, June 28, 2002.

[4706] Professor Mocnik from the Faculty of Arts, University of Ljubljana, Slovenia, recently wrote a public protest based on information published on June 7, 2003 in one of the main newspapers in Slovenia (DELO). The article asserts that the Parliamentary Commission for Supervision of Security and Intelligence Services has been secretly informed about the activities of various Slovenian extremist and militant anti-globalization groups. Professor Mocnik remarks that Slovenian anti-globalization groups are not militant and violent, since all their protests have been peaceful and without a single riot, although anti-globalization groups are strongly opposing current Slovenian foreign policy, and have a remarkable influence on the public opinion and the media. Professor Mocnik concludes that the SOVA surveillance is probably politically motivated, available at <http://www.mladina.si/tednik/200324/clanek/kolumna/>.

Inspector's action was unlawful,[4707] because it ordered ISPs to block the access to, rather than close, the controversial website. The Inspectorate's decision was motivated by the fact that the website is not located on a server based in Slovenia but in a country (Thailand) over which the Inspectorate does not have any jurisdiction. After a few days the Inspectorate repealed its order, explaining that it could not be enforced, and was void as a result. Regardless, the Inspectorate's action has probably been problematic in a legal sense, because inspectors ordered ISPs to block the access and not shut down the website itself,[4708] and despite the censorship debate it is obvious that there has been a great abuse of individuals' personal data.

In 2003 a Slovenian business journal sold CD-ROMs containing e-mail addresses of Slovenian Internet users. Despite criticism of such practices, the addresses had been collected from public sources. The Slovenian search engine Najdi.si is also collecting e-mail addresses. To allay critiques, the website enables individuals to remove their e-mail addresses from the database and took technical measures to prevent automatic harvesting of addresses by spider bots.

In October 2004, the National Bank of Slovenia published information about the Bank's account holders on the Internet. It resulted in the ability to access searchable database of names of account holders and their addresses (though not complete addresses), tax numbers and account numbers. The data were published in accordance with the Monetary Transactions Act that required that data should be made public. However, the Inspector for Personal Data Protection found that requirement problematic and temporary blocked access to the website.[4709] The case is not closed yet and the problem still raises public debates.

On October 2, 2004, one day before election silence (on the day before elections and on election day political parties are not allowed to advertise themselves), one of the cellular phone operators, Simobil sent about 117,000 SMS messages with advertisements for one of political parties. Due to the technical problems, some SMS messages were delivered after election silence started. About 70,000 SMS messages have been delivered in the time of election silence to the users of competitive operator Mobitel. Mobitel informed their users that received the

---

[4707] Makarovic Bostjan, *Ali in kako lahko drzava pravno ureja dogajanje na internetu?* (May the state regulate the Internet and how?) *Informatika in pravo* (Information Technology and Legal Issues) 4 (2003).

[4708] *Id.* The author claims that ISPs are not processing personal data, because they just provide access to the data, although they are not aware of the content of the data. However, since the problematic website is located outside Slovenian jurisdiction, it seems that the Inspectorate has no legal instrument to sanction that kind of a violation.

[4709] Decision of the Inspector for Personal Data Protection, from October, 5, 2004 (on file with EPIC).

message in question on October 3 that the message was sent by their competitor and that the message is illegal. There has been a vigorous public debate about sending SMS spam (later it was found that political advertising is not a spam) and possible violation of election silence (it was found that the violation was not intentional). Some questions were also raised with regard to the privacy issues. The fact that Mobitel was able to identify those users who received political SMS message from another cellular phone operator after election silence began implies that Mobitel was recording traffic data about incoming SMS messages. This activity is prohibited by the Electronic Communications Act.[4710] Unfortunately, neither the police nor the Inspector for Personal Data Protection addressed these privacy questions, but some privacy activists and journalists are still investigating.[4711]

Access to Public Information

Every person has the right to acquire information held by a public body, according to Article 39 of the Slovenian Constitution. In 2003, the Access to the Public Sector Information Act (APSIA)[4712] was enacted. It determines which public bodies are responsible for providing information and establishes an independent body, the Deputy for Access to Public Sector Information, whose main function is to be an appeal administrative body. The APSIA guarantees a free insight into public sector information and costs of transcripts are limited only to material costs. All public sector information must also be provided on the Internet, according to Article 10. Some types of information, such as personal data, or information important for national security are excluded from public sector information. The Ministry of Information Society is also required to issue a catalogue of public institutions that are bounded to APSIA. Slovenian Freedom of Information legislation is based on the guidelines of Article XIX[4713] and is harmonized with all the European laws dealing with access to public information. The new version of the APSIA Act is being prepared. If it is adopted, it will extend the right to access public information with the introduction of the so-called "public interest test." The test allows Deputy to decide that some information must be made public, even when the legal exceptions to the contrary exists, if the greater public interest in that information prevails. Another proposed

---

[4710] Zakon o elektronskih komunikacijah (ZeKOM) (Electronic Communication Act), Official Journal RS, No. 43/04 (on file with EPIC).

[4711] Kovacic Matej. *Zakoniti nadzor v Sloveniji*, 2. del (Legal Surveillance In Slovenia, part two), Slo-Tech, October 28, 2004, available at <http://www.slo-tech.com/clanki/04020/04020.shtml>.

[4712] APSIA is available at <http://www.dostopdoinformacij.si/index.php?id=253#236>.

[4713] *See* <http://www.article19.org/>

change is that commercial use of public information will not be free of charge as it is now.

The APSIA catalogue includes almost all governmental institutions; however, the first version of the catalogue did not include SOVA. A representative from the Ministry of Information Society said it had been explicitly requested that SOVA be excluded from the catalogue (which had been adopted by the government), but in his opinion this request was illegal.[4714] In July and August 2004, a request for access to public information was sent to SOVA and to the court's department in charge of issuing warrants for secret service and to the police. The request concerned information about annual statistical overview of their investigative activities (especially the secret ones - wiretapping, secret observing, etc.). The court turned down the request. The Secret Service answered partially - they sent information about the number of public orders that they issued and number of purchases of special equipment, but they refused to answer the other questions.[4715] However, a SOVA representative publicly said they have "about 10 wiretaps annually" and a Defense Department's Secret Service representative said they have "less than 5 wiretaps annually."[4716] The fact that they officially responded to the said request refuted their claims that they were not bounded by the APSIA. The Court's and SOVA's decisions were appealed to the Deputy for Access to Public Sector Information. The Deputy decided that revelation of requested information is not reasonable and rejected the appeal.[4717]

The police answered all the questions and the statistics of some of their surveillance activities are shown in the chart below:

Year	1998	1999	2000	2001	2002	2003
Number of wiretaps	318	287	318	453	505	472
Secret observations	328	306	232	476	476	195
Number of persons wiretapped	176	163	151	199	222	168
Number of persons observed	N/A	132	N/A	389	469	386

[4714] E-mail from representative of the Ministry of Information Society to Matej Kovacic, Junior Researcher at the Faculty of Social Sciences, University of Ljubljana, Slovenia, July 8, 2004 (on file with EPIC).

[4715] Kovacic Matej. *Zakoniti nadzor v Sloveniji*, 1. del (Legal Surveillance in Slovenia, part one), Slo-Tech, September, 3, 2004, available at <http://www.slo-tech.com/clanki/04014/04014.shtml>.

[4716] Statements of representatives on a POP TV on August, 26, 2004, available at <http://24ur.com/bin/article_print.php?id=2045241>.

[4717] Decision of the Deputy for Access to Public Sector Information about appeal against SOVA's decision, available athttp://www.dostopdoinformacij.si/index.php?id=290; Decision of the Deputy for Access to Public Sector Information about appeal against Supreme court's decision, available at <http://www.dostopdoinformacij.si/index.php?id=348>.

Since Slovenia has a Deputy for Access to Public Sector Information, there have been intense discussions about the right to be informed versus the right to privacy. A lot of public discussions revolved around the decision to block access to the udba.net website. At the end of 2003, the Inspector for Personal Data Protection suggested police representatives stop providing information that will make identification of suspects possible to the public, since there is no legal basis for the release of that information.[4718] In practice, it means that the police may only provide information about the event, its location and the age of the persons involved, but no more initials of their names. That decision provoked several protests from journalists and reporters, who used that information for criminal stories.

There were some cases where private pornographic pictures were stolen from home computers and published on the Internet, and one case where journalists identified member of a parliament participating in an anonymous Internet sex forum and published the whole story together with presumably naked pictures of him.[4719]

International Obligations

Slovenia is a member of the Council of Europe (CoE) and has signed and ratified Convention No. 108.[4720] It has also signed and ratified the European Convention for the Protection of Human Rights and Fundamental Freedoms.[4721] In May 2004, Slovenia ratified the CoE Convention on Cybercrime[4722] and the Additional Protocol with provisions against racism and xenophobia in virtual networks.[4723]

[4718] Mail from Jože Bogataj, Data Protection Inspector to Matej Kovacic, Junior Researcher at the Faculty of Social Sciences, University of Ljubljana, Slovenia, February 12, 2004 with press release of inspektro from January 15, 2004 in an attachment (on file with EPIC).

[4719] Modic, Max. 2005. Krivi, ker seksajo. Mladina, February, 7, 2005, available at <http://www.mladina.si/tednik/200506/clanek/slo-tema--max_modic/index.print.html-l2>.

[4720] Signed November 23; 1993; ratified May 27, 1994; entered into force September 1, 1994.

[4721] Signed May 14, 1993; ratified June 28, 1994; entered into force June 28, 1994.

[4722] Convention on Cybercrime (CETS No.: 185), available at <http://conventions.coe.int/Treaty/Commun/QueVoulezVous.asp?NT=185&CM=8&CL=ENG>.

[4723] Additional Protocol to the Convention on Cybercrime, Concerning the Criminalisation of Acts of a Racist and Xenophobic Nature Committed through Computer Systems (CETS No.: 189), available at <http://conventions.coe.int/Treaty/Commun/QueVoulezVous.asp?NT=189&CM=8&CL=ENG>.

Republic of South Africa

Constitutional Privacy Framework

Section 14 of the South African Constitution of 1996 states, "Everyone has the right to privacy, which includes the right not to have – (a) their person or home searched; (b) their property searched; (c) their possessions seized; or (d) the privacy of their communications infringed." Section 32 states, "(1) Everyone has the right of access to – (a) any information held by the state, and; (b) any information that is held by another person and that is required for the exercise or protection of any rights; (2) National legislation must be enacted to give effect to this right, and may provide for reasonable measures to alleviate the administrative and financial burden on the state."[4724] The interim Constitution contained equivalent provisions to Section 14 and Section 32.[4725]

The South African Constitutional Court has delivered several judgments on the constitutional right to privacy. These deal with legislation prohibiting the possession of indecent or obscene photographs[4726] and child pornography,[4727] searches and seizures[4728] and the criminalization of prostitution.[4729] The court's interpretation of the right is a mixture of US and European jurisprudence. On the one hand, the court has emphasized that the roots of the right lie in the value of human dignity.[4730] On the other hand, the court has defined the right, along US lines, as protecting an actual (or subjective) expectation of privacy that society is prepared to recognize as reasonable.[4731]

[4724] The Constitution of the Republic of South Africa, Act 108 of 1996, available at <http://www.info.gov.za/constitution/1996/96cons.htm>.

[4725] Section 13 and 23 of the *interim* Constitution (Act 200 of 1993). The Constitutional Court's jurisprudence interpreting the privacy right in the *interim* Constitution remains authoritative for the right in the 1996 Constitution. The *interim* Constitution's access to information right was however confined to information held by organs of state. The *interim* Constitution was in force between April 1994 and February 1997.

[4726] Case v. Minister of Safety and Security 1996 (3) SA 617 (CC) (wide and vague apartheid-era prohibition on possession of pornography a violation of right to privacy). All judgments of the South African Constitutional Court are available online at <http://www.concourt.gov.za>.

[4727] De Reuck v. Director of Public Prosecutions (Witwatersrand Local Division) 2004 (1) SA 406 (CC) (justifiable to limit the right to privacy to protect children from the exploitation and degradation inherent in child pornography).

[4728] Bernstein v. Bester NO 1996 (2) SA 751 (CC); Mistry v. Interim National Medical and Dental Council of South Africa 1998 (4) SA 1127 (CC).

[4729] S v. Jordan 2002 (6) SA 642 (CC) (no significant privacy interests in the act of prostitution).

[4730] *Id.* at paragraph 81.

[4731] Bernstein v. Bester *NO* 1996 (2) SA 751 (CC) paragraph 67. Judgments of the South African Constitutional Court are available at <http://www.constitutionalcourt.org.za>.

The constitutional right to privacy also has application in private litigation.[4732] Recent decisions have considered the effect of the right in litigation seeking to prevent the publication of intimate photographs of a quasi-celebrity,[4733] an action for damages to compensate for publication of an inaccurate report that a person had been arrested for terrorism[4734] and the filming of the activities of members of a helicopter club by a competitor seeking evidence of contraventions of aviation safety regulations.[4735] There is currently no general statutory protection of privacy or general data protection legislation in South Africa.

Data Protection Framework

In early 2000, the South African Law Reform Commission was requested by Parliament to investigate the introduction of privacy and data protection legislation. The request was made at the time that Parliament was considering the Promotion of Access to Information Act (the Act). Drafts of the Act contained a chapter proposing the regulation of access to, and dissemination of, personal information held in private and public "data banks." Parliament took the view that these matters would be better regulated by a comprehensive purpose-specific data protection statute and the chapter was removed from the Access to Information Act as finally enacted. The Law Reform Commission (the Commission), having researched the matter, then published an Issue Paper on Privacy and Data Protection in August 2003.[4736] The Issue Paper makes a number of preliminary recommendations that closely track the provisions of the European Union (EU) Data Protection Directive. This is to be expected since the Directive, by requiring a basic level of data protection in countries doing business with the EU, is an important impetus for the law-reform initiative. The Commission recommends that legislation be enacted to govern the collection, use and dissemination of personal information in both the public and private sectors,

---

[4732] The South African Bill of Rights has both direct and indirect application in so-called "horizontal" disputes (disputes not involving state actors or legislation).

[4733] Prinsloo v. RCP Media Ltd t/a Rapport 2003 (4) SA 456 (T) (injunction available to prevent publication of purloined photographs of notorious surgically-improved Pretoria lawyer).

[4734] Independent Newspapers Holdings Ltd v. Suliman 2005 (7) BCLR 641 (SCA) (no privacy interests in information and photographs of person publicly arrested at airport), available at <http://wwwserver.law.wits.ac.za/sca/summary.php?case_id=12818>.

[4735] Huey Extreme Club v. McDonald t/a Sport Helicopters 2005 (1) SA 485 (C), (extensive, continuous filming an invasion of privacy that is not justified by the need to promote aviation safety).

[4736] Available at <http://wwwserver.law.wits.ac.za/salc/issue/issue.html>. An Issue Paper is the first stage in the Law Reform Commission's research process. It consists of a document identifying the broad issues for consideration in the development of new legislation and requesting public comment on these issues. The second stage is reached when a Discussion Paper is published, containing draft legislation. This is only published to seek comment and the process is completed by the publication of a Report which contains the Commission's recommendations to the Cabinet on draft legislation.

and calls for the creation of a specialized Commission. The Commission is likely to publish draft legislation for comment in the second half of 2005. It will then issue a final report and recommendations to the Minister of Justice in the first half of 2006. The legislative process is likely to take at least a year after that.

The Interception Act

The Regulation of Interception of Communications and Provision of Communication-related Information Act 70 of 2002 (the Interception Act) is the product of several proposals of the South African Law Reform Commission. In November 1998, the Commission recommended amendments to facilitate the monitoring of cellular phones and Internet service providers (ISPs).[4737] On July 18, 2001, a Bill was introduced into Parliament, proposing the repeal and replacement of the Interception and Monitoring Prohibition Act 127 of 1992. According to Johnny de Lange, Chairperson of the Parliament's Portfolio Committee on Justice and Constitutional Development, the Bill "aims to regulate the interception and monitoring of certain communications . . . to regulate authorized telecommunications monitoring," and "to prohibit the provision of certain telecommunication services which do not have the capacity to be monitored."[4738] Following 18 months of limited consultation with stakeholders, the Interception Act was enacted in December 2002. It will enter into force on a date to be proclaimed by the President in the Government Gazette.

The passage of the Interception Act had initially been delayed, pending finalization of the Council of Europe Convention on Cybercrime, which, if ratified, would require member states and non-member signatories to enact measures consistent with the Convention.[4739] South Africa is one of four non-member signatories to the Convention, along with the United States, Canada and Japan.[4740] The Interception Act conforms to the requirements of the Convention.

The Interception Act was considered and passed as several unauthorized surveillance incidents had come to light in the last few years. In 1996, it was revealed that the South African Police Service had been monitoring thousands of

---

[4737] Discussion Paper 78 (Project 105), Review of Security Legislation, The Interception and Monitoring Prohibition Act 127 of 1992 (November 1998), available at
<http://www.law.wits.ac.za/salc/discussn/monitoring.pdf>.

[4738] Adv. Johnny de Lange, Press statement, available at
<http://www.polity.org.za/govdocs/pr/2001/pr0718c.html>.

[4739] Specifically, Chapter II, Article 3, Council of Europe, Convention on Cybercrime. ETS No. 185.

[4740] Signed November 23, 2001.

international and domestic phone calls without a warrant.[4741] The opposition Democratic Party announced in November 1999 that it had found surveillance devices at its parliamentary offices and national headquarters.[4742] In February 2000, the government apologized to the German government after the media reported that an intelligence operative had placed spy cameras outside the German Embassy.[4743]

The purpose and essence of the Interception Act remains similar to all previous versions. The Act prohibits wiretaps and surveillance, except for law enforcement purposes. It requires that all telecommunications services, including Internet Service Providers (ISPs), make their services capable of being intercepted before they could offer them to the public. There is a provision for the Minister to exempt ISPs from these provisions. However, while exemptions can be made from the requirement to enable a network for surveillance purposes, ISPs that are exempt will be required to contribute to a fund that will be used to purchase centrally held surveillance equipment. This equipment will be used on a rotational basis as needed by smaller ISPs that are required to comply with a surveillance request by law enforcement.

Generally, providers will be required to pay for the costs of making their systems wiretap-enabled. No model of cost sharing is proposed at this stage, and the state will be responsible for the costs of connecting central interception centers to telecommunications providers. Criminal penalties are also included should a service provider refuse to comply with the provisions of the Act or assist law enforcement. Repeat offenders might, in addition, face the revocation of their service license granted under the Telecommunications Act.[4744]

Several amendments made by Parliament during the consideration of the Interception Act widened the scope of the legislation. The definition of "communication" has been augmented to include all "direct" and "indirect" communications, which together cover all traffic, signaling and other call-related information, as well as the content of such communications. Amendments include: an expanded list of grounds for obtaining a wiretap order, including a wiretap to ascertain the location of a person in the case of an emergency;[4745] an

---

[4741] "Newspaper Uncovers 'Unlawful' Tapping by Intelligence Units," The Star, February 21, 1996.

[4742] "Democratic Party Outraged by Bugging of Its Offices," Africa News, November 23, 1999.

[4743] "South Africa Admits to Spying on German Embassy," Reuters, February 6, 2000.

[4744] Act No. 103 of 1996, as amended.

[4745] Section 8.

expanded range of interception directions that can be granted,[4746] such as decryption orders;[4747] and an augmented list of offences under the Act,[4748] which includes being in possession of a stolen cellular phone and failure to report a stolen, lost or damaged SIM (Subscriber Identity Module) card.

Provisions on data retention require all telecommunication service providers (TSPs) to gather detailed personal data on individuals and companies (including photocopies of identity documents) before signing contracts or selling SIM cards for pre-paid mobile services. Provisions require that such data is made available to law enforcement agencies when requested. There is no limit specified for the length of time TSPs are required to retain personal data, but a requirement to store communication-related information is currently limited to 12 months.

The Minister has several broad powers in the Interception Act, including the discretion to stipulate in a directive all technical and security requirements for networks to be capable of surveillance, including capacity, the systems to be used, the facilities and devices to be acquired, the type of communication-related information to be stored, and the period for which such specified information must be stored. The first draft of the directive was released in August 2004 and addresses all of these issues.[4749] A consultation process has been initiated calling for opinions from interested persons in the telecommunications sector. The directive will become operational within six months of promulgation of the Interception Act.

The National Intelligence Agency (NIA) announced in February 2000 that it was creating a signals intelligence service based on the model of the United Kingdom's GCHQ.[4750] The NIA will have the authority to intercept all postal, telephone and Internet communications under the auspices of crime control and national security, actual or potential threats to public health and safety, and to

---

[4746] These include: broad interception direction; an archived communications direction (any communication related information in the possession of a telecommunications service provider (TSP) and which is being stored by that TSP for up to one year, regarding the transmission of the indirect communication) and real time (real time information on an ongoing basis without interception) or supplementary direction, or a combination thereof. Also on application are entry warrants (to rig premises and intercept postal articles) and decryption directions. All can be obtained as oral directions when urgent circumstances prevail.

[4747] Section 21.

[4748] Chapter 9.

[4749] *See* Notice 1601, Government Gazette, Vol. 470, 4 August 2004, available at <http://www.info.gov.za/gazette/notices/2004/26644.pdf>. *See also* "Draft Directive for Telecommunication Service Providers who have not been issued with the Directive for mobile cellular operators, fixed line operators or Internet Service Providers" available at <http://www.doc.gov.za/images/Directive_PTNV.pdf> and "Draft Directive for value added Network (VAN) Licence holders providing Internet Services," available at <http://www.doc.gov.za/images/DraftDirISP_v4_1.pdf>.

[4750] "South Africa to Set up Signals Intelligence Centre," Reuters, February 7, 2000.

assist foreign law enforcement agencies with interception regarding organized crime or terrorism, under a mutual assistance agreement.[4751] In January 2004, the Department of Communications called for proposals by technology firms to create interception centers to intercept, monitor and store e-mail and cell phone messages.[4752]

At the time of writing, the Interception Act had yet to come into force. While the various stakeholders prepare for the Interception Act comes into operation, several problems are beginning to emerge. Various operational requirements appear impractical and hard to implement. An example is the requirement that before an Internet service contract can be concluded, ISPs are required to verify the identity of the subscriber. As many Internet users subscribe online, this creates many difficulties. Moreover, ISPs now have to verify identities and retain copies of identity documents. Another impediment to the Act's enforcement is the question of who will bear the great costs associated with the implementation and maintenance of the monitoring and storage equipment required for ISPs to fulfill their obligations under the new legislation.

It is projected that, once it is in force, the Interception Act will have an impact on the privacy of communications in the workplace through some of the exceptions to the general prohibition of interception and monitoring, particularly Section 5 (interception with the prior consent of a party to the communication) and Section 6 (interception for business purposes, or as referred to in comparable foreign legislation – "the business exemption"). Before the enactment of Section 5 of the Interception Act, the interception of electronic communications in the workplace in South Africa was primarily regulated through electronic communications policies or employee consent agreements embedded in the employment contract.[4753] The business exemption (Section 6) appears to allow employers to intercept and store the e-mail messages of their employees, for transactional, record-keeping and network security purposes, that are sent in the course of company business over the company's telecommunications network and upon reasonable efforts to notify the parties of the communication of the possibility of interception.

[4751] Section 13(5).

[4752] "Plans for Spy Centres Sought," Business Day, January 6, 2004.

[4753] This trend can be observed in the growing number of cases concerning interception of e-mail in the workplace, *e.g.*, Bamford & Others v. Energizer (SA) Ltd [2001] 12 BALR 1251 (P) (employees suspended for forwarding e-mails with pornographic, sexist and racist nature) and Cronje v. Toyota Manufacturing [2001] 3 BALR 213 (CCMA) (an employee was suspended for circulating a racist e-mail).

The Electronic Communications and Transactions Act (ECTA) has been in operation since August 2002.[4754] The main purpose of the Act is to facilitate e-commerce by creating legal certainty and promoting trust and confidence in electronic transactions. It provides for functional equivalence of electronic documents, recognition of contracts, digital signatures, electronic filing and evidence etc.[4755] The Act also contains statutory provisions on cybercrime and creates several computer crime offences. These include: unauthorized access to data; interception of, or interference with data; computer -elated extortion; fraud, and forgery[4756] aimed at interfering with commercial activities and hacking. Other provisions restrict ISP liability;[4757] promote consumer rights; criminalize spam, and require all websites engaged in "offering goods or services for sale, for hire or for exchanges by way of an electronic transaction" to provide information about the security and privacy policy of the website.[4758] Websites that collect personal information may voluntarily subscribe to certain principles in the Act intended to protect a person's privacy, but are not required to do so.

Chapter II of the ECTA directs the Minister of Communications to develop a national "e-strategy" within two years of the commencement of the Act. Amongst the matters to be addressed by the e-strategy are the closing of the "digital divide" through programs aimed at providing Internet connectivity to disadvantaged communities and encouraging the private sector to initiate schemes to provide universal access.

The ECTA provides for the registration of all cryptography providers and services and government accreditation of authentication providers. A new "cyber inspectorate" will monitor websites and public information systems and investigate compliance by cryptography and authentication providers.[4759]

Included in the ECTA is a provision authorizing the Minister to declare both public and private databases critical in the "national interest" or the "economic

---

[4754] Act 25 of 2002. Available at <http://www.info.gov.za/gazette/acts/2002/a25-02.pdf>.

[4755] Chapter III.

[4756] Chapter XIII.

[4757] By incorporating notice and take down procedures; mere conduit recognition and safe harbor provisions. Liability will only attach where an ISP has direct knowledge of illegal or objectionable material and fails to take effective action as required by law.

[4758] The Act does not require websites to have a security or privacy policy, nor does it prescribe what such a policy should contain. If a website does happen to have a policy, it is usually based on the codes of conduct of various associations in the data collection sector.

[4759] Inspectors are given investigative, search and seizure powers, subject to obtaining a warrant (which may be issued by any court). They may also exercise these powers without a warrant if they have reason to believe that a warrant would be issued to them on application, and if delaying the search to obtain a warrant would defeat its purpose.

and social well-being of South Africa." Once declared, the Minister can require the database to be registered, including all information about its location and the types of data stored. The law also authorizes the Minister of Communications to determine technical standards and set procedures for the general management of critical databases, their security and disaster recovery procedures.[4760]

South Africa does not have a data protection authority but has a Human Rights Commission (HRC), which was established under Chapter 9 of the Constitution. The HRC's mandate is to protect and investigate infringements of the fundamental rights guaranteed in the Bill of Rights, and to take steps to secure appropriate redress where human rights have been violated. The Commission has limited powers to enforce the Promotion of Access to Information Act.[4761]

Finacial Privacy

South Africa has a well-developed financial system and banking infrastructure. Despite the sophistication of the financial sector, the privacy of financial information is weakly regulated by a code of conduct for banks issued by the Banking Council. The current Code (in place since 2000) has recently been revised and will be replaced with effect from October 1, 2004.[4762] Adherence to the Code is voluntary and it is expressly declared to be not legally binding. Financial institutions subscribing to the Code undertake not to share personal information of their clients without consent except in the public or "where [banks'] interests require disclosure.' Information may be disclosed to third-party credit risk management services with prior consent, or after notice to the client.

Important new legislation, the Financial Intelligence Centre Act 38 of 2001 (FICA), aimed at preventing money laundering was passed by Parliament in 2001 and the bulk of its provisions came into effect in 2003. Along the lines of similar legislation in other jurisdictions, the Act creates the Financial Intelligence Centre, a supervisory and investigative body that receives and analyzes information regarding suspected money-laundering activities supplied to it by financial institutions, and disseminates reports to the criminal investigative authorities, the intelligence services and the revenue service. Banks and other financial institutions are required to verify the identity of their customers, to maintain a considerable body of information about customers and their transactions, and must report suspicious transactions to the Centre. The bulk of customers would

---

[4760] Chapter XI.

[4761] Act No. 2 of 2000.

[4762] *See* <http://www.banking.org.za>.

have to provide FICA-related information until September 2005. Non-compliance will bring restrictions on clients' ability to transact on their accounts.

The weakness of banks' data security measures were exposed in a well-publicized case of identity theft in 2003. A hacker was able to gain access to the account and password details of the Internet banking accounts of a number of bank customers by using commercially available keystroke-logging spyware. The publicity given to the case – unusual because banks usually keep bank fraud cases confidential – resulted in upgrades to security by most commercial banks offering Internet banking services.[4763]

Credit bureaus are currently self-regulated by a Code of Conduct administered by the Credit Bureau Association (CBA). After an investigation by the government's Consumer Affairs Committee into the ability of the CBA to enforce its code, the government proposed legal regulation of the industry. The draft regulations were published for comment in April 2003. They propose strict limitations on the types of information that may be held by credit bureaus and the period of time for which information can be held. The draft regulations also require access to credit information by consumers to ascertain the accuracy of the information credit bureaus hold on them and require procedures to allow consumers to dispute inaccurate data in the files.[4764]

Smart Card

The Cabinet approved a plan in March 1998 to issue a multipurpose smart card that combines access to all government departments and services with banking facilities. In the long term, the smart card was intended to function as passport, driver's license, identity document and bankcard, and was to be linked to fingerprint information.[4765] In 2003, a commission recommended major changes to the project. In February 2004, the report of the transaction advisors on the feasibility of procuring the new identity document through a public/private partnership recommended against the partnership. In 2005, the Department of Home Affairs awarded a contract for the cleaning of its database as the next step towards the rollout of the Hanis identity card system. It is expected that the first smart ID cards will be issued by the end of 2006. The first recipients of the cards

---

[4763] "Hacker Cleans out Bank Accounts," Sunday Times, July 20, 2003.

[4764] The draft regulations are available at <http://www.info.gov.za/gazette/notices/2003/24738b.pdf>.

[4765] "Smart Cards to Replace ID Books in SA in 2001," Africa News, February 1, 2000.

will be beneficiaries of the state social development grants.[4766] A similar project has already been started by the South African Post Office (wholly government-owned) in the North West Province where social pensioners are provided with a Postbank account for receiving their social services grant. The account is linked to a smart card containing the thumbprint and ID photo of the pensioner in encoded form.[4767]

In 2004, the Department of Home Affairs began a pilot program to issue 30,000 smart cards to refugees (persons granted political asylum). In the Department's view, this program is an initial step towards a planned rollout of six million smart cards per year over a five-year period. The full program entails the conversion of 30 million paper-based sets of records into the Department's electronic document management system. The government agency aims to eventually produce "an integrated biometric database of all people the Department deals with – citizens, residents, refugees, illegal foreigners."[4768]

Open Government

The Promotion of Access to Information Act (PAIA) came into operation on March 9, 2001.[4769] The Act is a general freedom of information law, modeled on the FOI laws of the United States and Commonwealth jurisdictions. It is, however, unusual and groundbreaking in at least two respects. First, it is based on, and backed up by, a specific constitutional right of access to information, entrenched in the Bill of Rights.[4770] Second, this right and, as a consequence, the Act are applicable not only to information in government hands but also to information held in the private sector.[4771] There is no freedom of information commission to monitor the implementation of the Act or to provide dispute-resolution services. Instead, the South African Human Rights Commission is charged with monitoring the use of the Act, publicizing the rights that it creates, assisting members of the public to make requests, conducting research and publishing explanatory material about the Act. Disputes about alleged

---

[4766] "Nqakula: Parliamentary Media Briefing," May 5, 2005 available at <http://www.polity.org.za/pol/speech/2005/?show=66960>.

[4767] "No More Pension Queues in the North West Province," SAPO Press Release, available at <http://www.sapo.co.za/cms/viewHTMLarticle.asp?parentid=456&parentlevel=4&Stamp=False>.

[4768] Deputy Minister of Home Affairs, Malusi Gigaba: Home Affairs Department Budget Vote 2004/2005.

[4769] Act 2 of 2000.

[4770] Section 32 of the 1996 Constitution. The section grants a right of access to "any information held by the state" and to "any information . . . held by another person and that is required for the exercise or protection of any rights."

[4771] "Concerns Raised over Access to Information Act," Mail & Guardian, May 10, 2001.

maladministration of the Act (*e.g.*, requests for information not answered, indexes of records not submitted as required by the Act) can be heard by the Public Protector (the South Africa's Ombudsman). Disputes about the substance of a refusal of a request for information can be resolved by applying to the ordinary courts.[4772]

Concern has been expressed from various quarters (including the Human Rights Commission) about the ineffectiveness of the Act's dispute-resolution processes. Litigation is widely recognized as being too inaccessible and cumbersome to be an effective tool of to enforce the freedom of information rights in the Act and in the Constitution.[4773]

On paper, the Act grants extensive freedom of information rights. However, it is more difficult to assess the effectiveness of these rights in practice. First, because the Act is not yet completely operational, it will not be possible to draw accurate conclusions about the success or failure of the Act until "manuals" (indexes of records)[4774] are published.[4775] Second, a vital resource for researchers - the statistics on the use of the Act, to be compiled by the Human Rights Commission - have not yet been published. There are no comprehensive empirical studies available on the implementation of the Act. In their absence, much of the evidence available to researchers is anecdotal. Requesters have reported that PAIA requests are often dealt with extremely slowly or, more troublingly, are simply ignored.[4776] There appears to be widespread ignorance of the requirements of the Act, even of its existence, in the public sector.[4777]

However, there have been a number of high profile cases involving the use of PAIA. For example, the leader of the Opposition made a successful request to the Presidency and the Ministry of Justice for records relating to a number of controversial presidential pardons of prisoners who had been refused amnesty by the Truth and Reconciliation Commission.[4778] One of the most active users of the

---

[4772] Application can be made either to the High Court or to a magistrates' court. The courts have wide powers to inspect the disputed records and to order disclosure of records.

[4773] "Information Law not Accessible to Public – HRC," Business Day, February 3, 2004.

[4774] The "manuals," or indexes of records, are intended to provide essential guidance for requesters about how to make a request and what can be requested from a particular body.

[4775] The deadline for public and private bodies to submit manuals has been extended on three occasions and is currently August 31, 2005.

[4776] "Few Groups Aware of Act on Access to Information," Business Day, October 14, 2002.

[4777] A survey conducted by the Open Democracy Advice Centre revealed that 54 percent of the public bodies contacted by the Centre were unaware of the Act, 16 percent were aware of the Act but did not implement it and only 30 percent were aware of it and implementing it. "Few Groups Aware of Act on Access to Information," Business Day, October 14, 2002.

[4778] "Leon Set to Get Data on Pardons," Business Day, October 15, 2002.

Act – the South African History Archive (SAHA), a NGO that collects and archives apartheid-era documentation – has retrieved large quantities of classified material from military archives and documents collected by the Truth and Reconciliation Commission. While SAHA has had some important victories, the organization suggests that use of the Act has been limited because the culture of freedom of information has not taken root yet and because PAIA has been poorly publicized.[4779] The Institute for Democracy in South Africa has launched a campaign to use the access rights granted by the PAIA to require political parties to disclose the sources of their funding.[4780] Predictably enough, the requests for this information were not met with transparency by political parties, and the organization has begun a court process to test the principles at stake.[4781]

There appears to have been little use by requesters of the private-sector provisions of the Act, but the extent to which the Act has had an impact on the private sector is almost impossible to measure.[4782] Certainly, the Act's requirements that private bodies publish indexes of their records have largely been ignored.[4783]

Anti-terrorism Measures

Even before the terrorist acts of September 11, 2001, South Africa had been revising its anti-terrorism laws. A draft anti-terrorism Bill was tabled for debate in Parliament and was the subject of public hearings at the Portfolio Committee on Safety and Security. The Bill was widely criticized as unconstitutional for its far-ranging provisions with regard to personal freedoms, detention, bail, and wide police search and seizure powers. The proposed Bill initially defined an act of terrorism as "an unlawful act committed in or outside the Republic" while a "terrorist organization" was defined as "an organization declared as such by the Minister of Safety and Security and which is likely to intimidate the public or a

---

[4779] *See* <http://www.wits.ac.za/saha/programme.htm>.

[4780] Political party funding is currently unregulated in South Africa. There are no limits on the amounts of funding a party can receive, nor are there any disclosure requirements.

[4781] *See* <http://www.idasa.org.za/pdf/1043.pdf>.

[4782] The Human Rights Commission's duty to compile statistics on the use of the Act applies only with respect to requests made to public bodies.

[4783] Widespread failure by both public and private bodies to comply with the Act's publication requirements resulted in the Minister of Justice granting a six-month extension on the Act's deadline for compliance until February 2003, a second extension until August 2003 and a third (ostensibly "final") extension until August 2005. Missing from the Act is a sanction for non-compliance with this requirement. Legislation introduced in the Parliament during 2003, but not yet enacted, proposes to correct this by granting a power to the Minister of Justice to prescribe a penaly of up to two years' imprisonment for failure to produce a manual as required by the Act. *See* the Judicial Matters Second Amendment Bill 41 of 2003.

segment of the public, or is likely to carry out a convention offence."[4784] This broad definition of a "terrorist" and "terrorist organization" could extend to legitimate protest activity. Interest groups have argued for a more precise definition that will reduce the chances of arbitrary state action against individuals or organizations.

Other concerns pertain to the wide powers given to the Minister of Safety and Security, the National Directorate of Public Prosecutions, and general law enforcement agencies, and the right given to the state to declare organizations as terrorist organizations. NGOs that made submissions on the Bill raised concerns that its far-ranging provisions pose a threat to personal freedom, freedom of expression and freedom of the media. In particular, the powers given to the police and prosecuting authorities to act *ex parte*[4785] against individuals and organizations simply on the basis of unspecified "reasonable grounds" have been cause for concern.[4786] Many submissions also noted that the new proposed Bill may also be unnecessarily duplicative of legislative resources as there are approximately 22 existing laws that can already adequately deal with "terrorism" crimes without placing constitutional freedoms at risk. Perhaps, and most significantly, the leading trade union organization the Congress of South African Trade Unions (COSATU) opposed the bill on the ground that its definition of terrorism could lead to the outlawing of legitimate strike activities.

The draft legislation was passed by the National Assembly[4787] in November 2003. However, after introducing the law in a redrafted form (now titled the Protection of Constitutional Democracy against Terrorist and Related Activities Bill) in the second chamber of Parliament in February 2004, the government announced, under the threat of a nationwide strike by COSATU, that it was delaying a vote on the legislation until after the April 2004 elections. The government re-introduced the draft legislation in July 2004.

[4784] A "convention offence" is defined in the Bill schedule as including "interfering with or seizure or exercising control of an aircraft or damaging an aircraft, or murdering or kidnapping an internationally protected person."

[4785] Note of the Editor: on behalf of one party only.

[4786] The Legal Resources Centre (LRC), in a submission to Parliament, criticized a section of the Bill giving the Safety and Security Minister powers to make regulations concerning any matter that may or must be prescribed in terms of this legislation and any other matter "which is necessary or expedient" to prescribe for the proper implementation of this legislation. The LRC urged that any regulations prepared should be tabled in Parliament prior to them being published for comment in the Government Gazette.

[4787] One of the chambers of Parliament.

Recent Developments

In June 2004, *The Star* newspaper reported that the South African Post Office was planning a joint venture with the private company Intimate Data to launch a National Address Database (NAD),[4788] which would contain personal information on millions of South Africans.[4789] Documents issued to the press by Intimate Data suggest that personally identifiable information, including sensitive data such as income segmentation derived from enumerator area, date of birth, gender, ethnic group, alternate addresses for an individual, and alternate contact details such as phone numbers, will be available to subscribers of the product. The reported sources of the personal data to be featured in NAD are the national voters roll, the Department of Home Affairs, parastatals such as the State broadcaster and telecommunications monopoly, the State Pension fund and census data. So far only the Electoral Commission has denied supplying data to the project.[4790] The Post Office later clarified their intention as not aimed at selling personal data, but only to provide address-verification services to client companies.[4791] The government continues to express support for NAD.[4792] The Post Office, together with the Department of Communications, has in 2005 piloted an addressing system at Ga-Rasai, Brits, in the North West province.[4793]

Republic of (South) Korea

Constitutional Privacy Framework

The Constitution of the Republic of Korea provides for the protection of secrecy and liberty of private life.[4794] Article 16 states, "All citizens are free from

---

[4788] The website of the product is available at <http://www.nad.postoffice.co.za/>.

[4789] "State to Sell Your Privacy," The Star, June 15 2005, available at <http://www.thestar.co.za/index.php?fSectionId=129&fArticleId=2113150>.

[4790] National Common Voters' Roll, Electoral Commission Release, June 15, 2004, available at <http://www.info.gov.za/speeches/2004/04072309451003.htm>.

[4791] "Post Office Dives for Cover, June 16, 2004, available at <http://www.thestar.co.za/index.php?fSectionId=129&fArticleId=2114859>

[4792] "Presentation by Minister of Minerals and Energy, Phumzile Mlambo-Ngcuka, on behalf of the Economic Cluster II Sector," February 18, 2005, where Minister Mlambo-Ngcuka stated that "[i]n the next few months, together with the South African Post Office and Statistics South Africa, the Department of Communications will be launching the National Address Database and Registry, whose aim is to ensure that all South Africans have addresses."

[4793] South Africa Year Book 2004/2005, at 135.

[4794] Constitution of The Republic of Korea, Chapter II (Rights and Duties of Citizens), § 16; Section 9 further stating that "it shall be the duty of the State to confirm and guarantee the fundamental and inviolable human rights of individuals."

intrusion into their place of residence. In case of search or seizure in a residence, a warrant issued by a judge upon request of a prosecutor has to be presented."[4795] Article 17 states, "the privacy of no citizen shall be infringed."[4796] Article 18 states, "The privacy of correspondence of no citizen shall be infringed."[4797] In general, the government respects the integrity of the home and family.[4798]

The protection of human rights in South Korea, including the right to a fair trial before an independent and impartial tribunal, is still in its infancy. It was only in November 2001 that a commission was created to police the actions of the state in this context. This commission has been beset with problems in fulfilling its role due to a lack of autonomy and political independence, as well as other structural problems.[4799]

In April 2005, during its 61st session in Geneva, the United Nations Human Rights Commission (UNHRC) severely criticized the judiciary for its lack of impartiality and independence, and particularly for applying a presumption of guilt rather than a presumption of innocence, in violation of the United Nation's International Covenant on Civil and Political Rights that South Korea ratified.[4800] In the specific context of the judicial system, South Korea has massive institutional problems, which allow injustices, particularly in politically charged cases.[4801] The "practice of initiating unfair prosecutions against political enemies of the ruling party is also not uncommon."[4802]

[4795] However, Korean courts are willing to "rubber stamp" practically all prosecutors' requests. "Courts are issuing warrants for search and seizure almost automatically upon request from Public Prosecutors and . . . the issue of search and seizure warrants is being abused." "Courts' Issue of Warrants for Search and Seizure at the Rate of 99.3%," Edaily, October 14, 2004 <http://news.naver.com/news/read.php?mode=LSD&office_id=018&article_id=0000212219&section_id=102&menu_id=102>.'

[4796] Korean Constitution, *supra* at § 17.

[4797] *Id.* at § 18.

[4798] US Department of State, Bureau of Democracy, Human Rights, and Labor, South Korea (Republic of) Country Report on Human Rights Practices for 2003 at <http://www.state.gov/g/drl/rls/hrrpt/2003/27776.htm>.

[4799] Asia Pacific Human Rights Network, "National Human Rights Commission of Korea: Miles To Go," September 2004.

[4800] "Skewed Judiciary Undermines Human Rights: The Prosecution in South Korea Exercises near Complete Control over the Pre-trial and Trial Process," Human Rights Features, April 11-17, 2005 ("A recent high profile case in point is that of Un-Yong Kim, the Vice President of the International Olympic Committee and founder of World Taekwondo Federation. Observers have described him as a "prisoner of conscience" who is being scapegoated by South Korean politicians since Pyeongchang's failure to win the 2010 Winter Olympic Games bid in 2003. The Supreme Court concluded in its verdict on 14 January 2005: "Since Mr. Kim failed to give convincing and rational explanations on why he drew the money and how he spent it, it can be inferred that he used the public money for personal purposes"), available at <http://hrdc.net/sahrdc/hrfchr61/pdf/issue5-v8.pdf>.

[4801] *Id.*

[4802] *Id. See also*, "Justicial Murder: The Judiciary Must Speak Out Now," Break News, September 14, 2004, available at <http://news.naver.com/news/read.php?mode=LSD&office_id=106&article_id=0000000464&section_id=100&menu_id=100>.

Within the past few years, South Korea has undergone a political purge of sorts, culminating in impeachment proceedings against President Moo-Hyun Roh in the National Assembly in March 2004. During that period and hence, scores of the National Assemblymen and business leaders have been prosecuted or imprisoned. President Roh gave the prosecutors "free rein" to investigate politicians and political parties for alleged corruption and even "encouraged" investigations targeting certain members of the ruling Uri Party.[4803] Following an investigation into illegal campaign funds during the December 2002 presidential elections, which resulted in the inauguration of Moo-Hyun Roh as the President on February 25, 2003, "the prosecution indicted 40 politicians, including 23 incumbent lawmakers, most of whom resigned or were not re-elected. In October 2004, the Supreme Public Prosecutor's Office announced that it had indicted another 46 lawmakers for alleged election law violations during the April 2004 parliamentary elections."[4804]

According to Amnesty International, the "[l]aws regarding arrest and detention are vague, and prosecutors have had wide latitude."[4805] For example, the National Security Law (NSL) defines espionage in broad terms and permits the authorities to monitor, detain and arrest persons who are suspected of engaging in "anti-state" activities. Between January 2003 and July 2003, 43 persons were arrested for violating the NSL, and nine persons remained in custody as of the end of 2004. The case of Professor Du-Yul Song, a German citizen of Korean origin, who was convicted of supporting the North Korean regime through his academic activities as a professor at Münster University, attracted protests from the German government as well as international human rights organizations.[4806] The UNHRC has termed the NSL "a major obstacle to the full realization of the rights enshrined in the International Covenant on Civil and Political Rights."[4807]

[4803] US Department of State, Country Report on Human Rights Practices - South Korea 2004, Section 3: Respect for Political Rights, February 2005, available at
<http://www.state.gov/g/drl/rls/hrrpt/2004/41647.htm>.
[4804] Id.
[4805] Id. at Section 1.d: Arbitrary Arrest or Detention.
[4806] Amnesty International Report 2004 - South Korea, "He Was a Prisoner of Conscience," available at
<http://web.amnesty.org/report2005/kor-summary-eng>; see also "German Government Welcomes the Release of Professor Du-Yul Song," Kookmin Ilbo, July 22, 2004 ("Regarding the repeated arguments by the Korean Public Prosecutor's Office and the Court that Professor Song described North Korean Communists sympathetically in his academic writings, the [ARD German TV] channel pointed out that 'In Germany this kind of misbehaviour would be clear violations of academic freedom and freedom of speech.' ")
<http://news.naver.com/news/read.php?mode=LOD&office_id=005&article_id=0000170762>.
[4807] Id.

South Korea has adopted a data protection regime similar to the United States and Japan, with one act covering the public sector and sectoral legislation for the private sector.[4808] The statute in the former category is the 1994 Act on the Protection of Personal Information Maintained by Public Agencies,[4809] which is generally applicable to the automated processing of personal data in the public sector, but not to manual records.[4810] This statute has a provision recommending that private entities respect the data protection principles in the statute, but it has no appropriate administrative or enforcement mechanism to that effect.[4811]

The Act on the Protection of Personal Information Maintained by Public Agencies imposes an obligation on public agencies to maintain records of personal information databases and to report these databases to the Ministry of Government Administration and Home Affairs (MOGAHA), the ministry responsible for the Act.[4812] The MOGAHA publishes lists of these databases in an official journal, which is publicly available.[4813] In addition, the MOGAHA can request relevant information from the data holding entities and issue opinions on their data processing practices.[4814] A data subject has a right of access to, and correction of, personal information held by public agencies.[4815] The Act establishes a Data Protection Review Commission, under the Premier's Office, headed by the Vice-Minister of the MOGAHA, to recommend and review proposals on improving data protection policy.[4816]

The Act has been criticized for its ineffectiveness.[4817] The MOGAHA has placed little emphasis on rigorous application of the legislation and reportedly has little will to uphold privacy versus administrative efficiency. In January 1999, the Act was amended to give even more power to the MOGAHA, streamline the procedure for access to personal information by data subjects, and limit exemptions to disclosure. However, there remains no independent oversight of government application of the Act.

[4808] C. Chung and I. Shin, "On-Line Data Protection and Cyberlaws in Korea" 27 Korean J. of Int'l and Comp. L. 21, 24 (1999).

[4809] Act No. 4734, last amended by Act No. 5715, January 29, 1999.

[4810] *Id.* at §§ 1, 2(3).

[4811] Chung and I. Shin, *supra* at 31.

[4812] Act No. 4734 § 6.

[4813] *Id.* at §§ 7-8.

[4814] *Id.* at §§ 18-19.

[4815] *Id.* at §§ 12, 16.

[4816] Act No. 4734 § 20.

[4817] Chung and I. Shin, *supra* at. 21, 33.

Acts governing the collection, use and disclosure of personal information in the private sector include the Protection of Communications Secrets Act (1993) (*a.k.a.,* "Anti-Wiretap Law");[4818] the Telecommunications Business Act (1991);[4819] the Medical Service Act (1973);[4820] the Real Name Financial Transactions and Secrecy Act (1997);[4821] the Use and Protection of Credit Information Act (1995);[4822] the Framework Act on Electronic Commerce (1999);[4823] and the Digital Signatures Act (1999).[4824]

As early as 1997, legislators and academics proposed a general privacy law for the private sector.[4825] However, the government proposed, and later adopted, a narrower alternative that targeted only the information and telecommunications industries. The Act on Promotion of Information and Communications Network Utilization and Data Protection (the Act),[4826] modeled after the German Online Service Data Protection Act of 1997,[4827] came into effect in 2000. The Act adopts common "fair information principles"[4828] and rules for the collection, use, and disclosure of personal data by "providers of information and communications services," such as common carriers, Internet service providers and other intermediaries, particularly content providers. The Act also covers specific off-line service providers such as travel agencies, airlines, hotels, and educational institutes.

The Act requires that "data users" seek consent from "data subjects" for the collection, use, and disclosure of data to a third party "beyond the notification as prescribed in the Act or the limit specified in a standardized contract for the

---

[4818] Act No. 4650, last amended by Act No. 7138, January 29, 2004. Article 3 (Protection of Secrets of Communication and Conversation), paragraph 1 of this Act provides that "No person shall censor any mail, wiretap any telecommunications, provide the communication confirmation data, record or listen to conversations between others that are not made public, without recourse to this Act, the Criminal Procedure Act or the Military Court Act."

[4819] Act No. 4394, last amended by Act No. 7165, February 9, 2004.

[4820] Act No. 2533, last amended by Act No. 7148, January 29, 2004.

[4821] Act No. 5493, last amended by Act No. 7189, March 12, 2004.

[4822] Act No. 4866, last amended by Act No.7110, January 29, 2004.

[4823] Act No. 5834, last amended by Act No. 6614, January 19, 2002.

[4824] Act No. 5792, last amended by Act No. 6585, December 31, 2001.

[4825] *See* C. Chung, "International Developments in the Data Protection and Some Proposals for Korean Legislation," Korean J. of Info. Soc. (1997).

[4826] Act No. 5835, last amended by Act No. 7142, January 29, 2004.

[4827] *Gesetz zur Regelung der Rahmenbedingungen für Informations und Kommunikationsdienste*: IuKDG, Ch. 2.

[4828] The fair information principles of the Act are derived from the eight principles found in the OECD Guidelines on the Protection of Privacy and Transborder Flows of Personal Data, September 23, 1980, OECD, available at <http://www.oecd.org/document/20/0,2340,en_2649_34255_15589524_1_1_1_1,00.html>.

---

utilization of the information and communication services."[4829] Data users should collect as little personal data as is necessary[4830] and are prohibited from collecting sensitive personal information, including ideology, faith and medical data without explicit consent of the data subject.[4831] However, consent is not required when it is necessary to give effect to a contract, adjust fees, or when the personal information is provided after having been rendered unidentifiable to the individual, such as for the compilation of statistics, academic research or market surveys.[4832] The Act allows the data subject to withdraw consent for the collection, use and disclosure of data at any time and requires the data user to comply, unless the preservation of such personal information is required by another Act. Further, every data subject has a right to access and correct his or her personal information.[4833]

A data user must obtain consent from an appropriate legal guardian when collecting, using or disclosing personal information from children under 14, and may request appropriate minimum information of the guardian in order to effect that consent. A legal guardian has a right to access and correct the child's personal information. Upon receiving a guardian's request for correction, the data user must cease to use or disclose erroneous information until they have made the correction.[4834]

The Act prohibits one from sending unsolicited commercial e-mail contrary to an addressee's explicit refusal of such e-mail.[4835] All unsolicited commercial e-mail must contain the word "Advertisement" in the subject line of every message and must contain opt-out instructions and contact information for the sender.[4836] Additionally, several direct marketers established the Association for the Improvement of the E-Mail Environment in early 2002 to help cope with the increasing number of unsolicited commercial e-mails problem in Korea.[4837] In March 2004, the Ministry of Information and Communication (MIC) fined 68

[4829] Act No. 5835, § 16 (2).

[4830] Id. at § 16(1).

[4831] Id. at § 4.

[4832] Id. at 3. But see L. Sweeney, The Identifiability of Data, (forthcoming), discussing the ease of re-identifying ostensibly de-identified data.

[4833] Act No. 5835, § 18(2).

[4834] Id. at § 18(4).

[4835] Id. at § 19(3).

[4836] Id. at 5. Due to the volume of unsolicited commercial e-mails, the government is contemplating an amendment that would curtail distribution and punish senders. Further, the amendment proposes the addition of "Adult" or "Consent" in the subject line of each and every unsolicited commercial e-mail and punitive measures for their senders who use false contact information or hinder technologically their tracing or deletion.

[4837] Personal Information Dispute Mediation Committee of the Korea Information Security Agency, "Personal Data Protection in Korea," August 2002, at 12 (available at <http://www.cyberprivacy.or.kr/inter.htm>).

online marketers – more than half of the 120 fined in all of 2003 – in an effort to achieve the government's goal of reducing the number of spam e-mails by half.[4838] According to Internet service operators in Korea, more than four out of every five e-mails sent in Korea in 2003 were spam.

The government imposes criminal and administrative penalties for breaches of data protection principles. The processing of personal information without consent or beyond the scope of the purpose for which the collection was made, attracts either penalties of up to one year in prison or a fine of KRW 10 million (USD 9,856).[4839] Data subjects may file damage claims for breaches of the Act with the Personal Information Mediation Committee or with a court. The onus is on the data user to prove either good faith intentions to comply, or non-negligence.[4840]

There is significant overlap between the aforementioned act, the Framework Act on Electronic Commerce (FAEC) and the Digital Signatures Act (DSA). For this reason and others, some legal commentators have called for comprehensive reform.[4841] The FAEC requires data users to give data subjects sufficient information regarding the purpose of collection.[4842] Under the FAEC, the data user must obtain explicit consent from the data subject before collecting personal information, and is prohibited from using the personal information collected for inconsistent purposes.[4843] Additional requirements of the FAEC include appropriate security,[4844] and a right of access, correction or deletion.[4845] The DSA prohibits an individual from fraudulently using another person's private key or issuing a key.[4846] It also has data protection provisions[4847] similar to the

---

[4838] "Korea to Half Spams this Year," Korea Times, March 19, 2004, available at <http://search.hankooki.com/times/times_view.php?terms=spam+code%3A+kt&path=hankooki3%2Ftimes%2Flpage%2Ftech%2F200403%2Fkt2004031917570311800.htm>.

[4839] Act No. 5835 at § 30. Additionally, § 32 imposes lesser administrative penalties of KRW 5 million for violations of other data protection principles.

[4840] Personal Information Dispute Mediation Committee of the Korea Information Security Agency, "Personal Data Protection in Korea," August 2002 at 4.

[4841] See C. Chung and I. Shin, supra at 42-43, citing the lack of an appropriate oversight authority as the major weakness of the Korean data protection regime; I. Kim, "A Study on the Data Protection Act" 26 Public Law 2 (June 1998) (in Korean); I. Lee, "Trends in the Korean Data Protection Legislation" Road to the Information Society (November 1999) (in Korean).

[4842] Act No. 5834, §§ 30-31.

[4843] Id. at § 13(2).

[4844] Id. at § 13(3).

[4845] Id. at § 13(4).

[4846] Act No. 5792, §§ 19-23.

[4847] Id. at § 24.

Electronic Commerce Act and penalties equal to the Act on Promotion of Information and Communications Network Utilization and Data Protection.

With more than 70 percent of the population with frequent online access and more than 85 percent with e-mail accounts,[4848] the protection of personal information has become a critical issue in the country. In February 2005, the MIC proposed to develop a new online identification system to replace the use of resident registration numbers.[4849]

In October 2000, the MIC proposed a cybercrime prevention system to combat an increase in fraud, gambling, and privacy intrusion on the Internet. The system would establish a monitoring network, a cyber conflict coordination committee, and damage control centers.[4850] In March 2001, the MIC announced that it would invest KRW 277.7 billion (USD 237 million) over the next five years to develop the country's information security industry, including public-key infrastructure, biometrics, and high-density/high speed ciphers.[4851]

In December 2001, the MIC established the Personal Information Dispute Mediation Committee, as an alternative to civil litigation, to facilitate a prompt, convenient and appropriate settlement of data protection disputes.[4852] Members of the Committee, which includes lawyers, IT engineers, professors, consumer advocates and industry representatives, are appointed for three-year terms.

Both data subjects or data users can initiate mediation, free of charge. The Committee first engages in informal fact-finding and makes non-binding recommendations for settlement. If parties cannot reach a settlement, they can begin formal mediation. If parties fail to reach a mediated settlement, they can pursue matters in a competent civil court. They can also bypass the Committee process altogether and go directly to court.[4853]

The Korea Association of Information and Telecommunication (KAIT) has instituted a privacy trust mark for websites and other online businesses that satisfy appropriate data processing standards. Regarding personal information,

---

[4848] "Portals Criticized over Privacy Standards," Korea Herald, May 31, 2005, available at <http://www.koreaherald.co.kr/archives/result_contents.asp?id=200505310041&query=internet>.
[4849] Id.

[4850] "Ministry of Information to Set up Cyber Crime Prevention System," Korea Herald, October 16, 2000.
[4851] "Gov't Unveils 5-Year Plan for Security Technology," Korea Herald, March 14, 2001.
[4852] Personal Information Dispute Mediation Committee of the Korea Information Security Agency, "Personal Data Protection in Korea," August 2002, at 8-9.
[4853] Id.

qualified trust mark applicants provide notice and purpose of collection, use and disclosure. In addition, the applicants provide special treatment for children under 14, and offer remedies for data subjects.

In June 2004, the Korea Information Security Agency (KISA) found that many Korean Internet websites pose a threat to personal information privacy. The agency reported that thousands of websites that collect personal information about subscribers, including resident registration numbers, remain vulnerable to security breaches.[4854] To address this problem, KISA planned to conduct more investigations, levy administrative penalties on offending websites, and solicit feedback on privacy problems from users.

In May 2005, the People's Solidarity for Participatory Democracy reported, based on a survey of 15 Internet portals, that most Korean Internet portals still require customers to provide a large amount of personal information, even their resident registration numbers (a 13-digit system whereby an individual's age, gender, place of birth and other private data, are stored and tracked by the government), without clarifying how the personal data will be used and without obtaining their individual consent.[4855]

Furthermore, the MOGAHA proposed a bill, which requires approval by the National Assembly to become law, that bars Korea's 35,000 public institutions from exchanging private information about citizens without permission. The bill, however, includes an exemption for public authorities dealing with national security affairs, criminal investigations, and tax audits.

Extending the doctrine of privacy law, Korean courts have tacitly recognized a "right of publicity," an individual's right to control the commercial use of his or her identity.[4856] Plaintiffs in invasion of privacy and defamation tort cases have the burden of proving that both the facts and the standard for the action are met.[4857] If successful, plaintiffs are entitled to compensatory relief for damages resulting from as little as "hurt feelings."[4858] Putative damages, however, are

---

[4854] "Agency Says the Web is Quite a Leaky Place," JoongAng Daily, June 15, 2004
<http://joongangdaily.joins.com/200312/04/200312040128212409900090609061.html>.

[4855] "Portals Criticized over Privacy Standards," Korea Herald, May 31, 2005, available at
<http://www.koreaherald.co.kr/archives/result_contents.asp?id=200505310041&query=internet>.

[4856] H. Nam, "The Applicability of the Right of Publicity in Korea," 27 Korean J. of Int'l and Comp. L. 45, 49 (1999); see also W. Han, "Infringement of the Right of Publicity and Civil Liability," 12 Human Rights and Justice 109, 116 (1996) (in Korean).

[4857] H. Nam, supra, at 88.

[4858] Id.

unavailable.[4859] Actions related to the right of privacy or defamation are rarely brought before Korean courts due to the cultural dislike against bringing private matters into such a public forum.[4860]

In an attempt to resolve the tension between the right of privacy and the constitutionally protected "freedom of speech and press"[4861] or "freedom of the arts,"[4862] Korean courts have held that "a decedent's right of privacy should be recognized only if his personal honor would be severely injured."[4863] In another case, a Seoul court found that five female university students were entitled to damages when a *Newsweek* photographer published a photo of them at school without their permission in conjunction with an unfavorable accompanying article.[4864]

The ruling Uri Party introduced and passed a controversial media bill, effective July 28, 2005, that limits the market share of any one daily newspaper to 30 percent.[4865] The new legislation also makes it illegal for the combined market share of any three newspapers to be more than 60 percent.[4866] The country's largest circulation newspapers are adversely affected by this legislation.[4867] In addition, Uri Party plans to restrict the total amount of advertising that a newspaper can carry.[4868] The NGO community[4869] and media associations[4870]

[4859] *Id.*

[4860] *Id.* at n. 122; *but see* "Grassroots Pro-privacy Movements on the Rise," BNA World Data Protection Report, November 2001, at 8, as evidence that Koreans are generally concerned about privacy issues.

[4861] Constitution of Korea, Article 21.

[4862] *Id.* at Article 22, Clause 1.

[4863] *Marianne Sim Lim v. Jin-Myung Kim*, Seoul Dist. Ct., 94 Kahab 9230 (June 23, 1995), involving a "model novel" which depicted the life of the deceased subject in a fictional manner.

[4864] *Sun-Jeong Kwon, Hyun-Ju Kim and Yun-Hwa Kim v. Newsweek Inc.*, Seoul Civil Dist. Ct., 92 Gadan 57989 (July 8, 1993).

[4865] "Roh's Media Reform Policy under Review," Korea Times, March 2, 2005, available at <http://news.naver.com/news/read.php?mode=LSD&office_id=040&article_id=0000019963&section_id=108&menu_id=108>

[4866] *Id.*

[4867] US Department of State, Country Report on Human Rights Practices – South Korea 2004, Section 2.a: Freedom of Speech and Press, available at <http://www.state.gov/g/drl/rls/hrrpt/2004/41647.htm>.

[4868] *Id.*

[4869] "Foreign Watchdog Hits out at Seoul over Media Bills: The International Press Institute Disagrees with Two Recently Passed Bills Restricting South Korean Press Freedoms," Strait Times, January 15, 2005, available at <http://www.asiamedia.ucla.edu/article.asp?parentid=19822>.

[4870] "Roh's Attacks on Press Freedoms Dangerous, Says WAN President," Korea Herald, June 1, 2005, available at <http://www.koreaherald.co.kr/archives/result_contents.asp?id=200506010034&query=world%20newspaper%20congress>.

have expressed concerns that the law would be used to control the printed press sector.[4871]

In November 2003, the government introduced a revised version of the Terrorism Prevention Bill that expands the power of the National Intelligence Service[4872] (NIS) to enact anti-terrorism measures. The bill was originally introduced in November 2001 but failed to secure the requisite number of votes in the National Assembly in April 2002. Human rights organizations, including Amnesty International, have criticized the bill's Article 4 provision creating a Counter-Terrorism Center, under the command of the secretive NIS, and its Article 8 provision denying the rights of non-citizens who are suspected of being "terrorists" to apply for asylum.[4873] In its current form, the bill's Article 13, which concerns spreading false information regarding terrorists, and the expansion of the NIS' power to recommend the deportation of foreign nationals, is under intense scrutiny from the human rights community in South Korea.[4874]

State security services have a history of conducting surveillance of political dissidents. The Korean Government designed the Protection of Communications Secrets Act of 1993 and the reform of the NIS to curb government surveillance of civilians.

The Protection of Communications Secrets Act lays out broad conditions under which the monitoring of telephone calls, mail, and other forms of communication is legal.[4875] This Act requires government officials to secure a judge's permission before placing wiretaps, or, in the event of an emergency, soon after placing them. The Act also provides jail terms for persons who violate this law. Some human rights groups argue that a considerable amount of illegal wiretapping, shadowing, and surveillance photography still occurs, and they assert that the

---

[4871] In May 2005, in its Press Freedom Report, the Korea Journalist's Club (an organization founded in 1977 that comprises some 400 senior journalists) marked the nation's freedom of the press at 54.6 points on a scale of 0 (meaning *no* press freedom) to 100 (meaning *complete* press freedom), a 5.4 point decrease from last year, and claimed that "Korea's situation of press freedom, which has steadily deteriorated under President Roh Moo-Hyun's rule . . . is now closer to the fringe of press control." "Freedom of Press Worsens in Korea," Korea Times, May 31, 2005, available at
<http://news.naver.com/news/read.php?mode=LSD&office_id=040&article_id=0000022694&section_id=108&menu_id=108>.

[4872] The National Intelligence Service is formerly known as the National Security Planning Agency, or colloquially referred to as the Korean Central Intelligence Agency, *a.k.a.,* the KCIA.

[4873] "The Revised Terrorism Prevention Bill: Fear of Increased Human Rights Abuses," Amnesty International, October 10, 2003; *see also* Amnesty International, Republic of Korea (South Korea), "Terrorism Prevention Bill: Granting Greater Scope for Increased Human Rights Violations," April 11, 2002, available at <http://web.amnesty.org/library/index/engasa250032002>.

[4874] *Id.*

[4875] Act No. 4650.

lack of an independent body to investigate whether police have employed illegal wiretaps hinders the effectiveness of the Anti-Wiretap Law.[4876]

The Anti-Wiretap Law sets out "broad conditions under which the government may monitor telephone calls, mail, and other forms of communication, for up to two months in criminal investigations and four months in national security cases."[4877]

On October19, 2004, during the annual national audit, the National Assembly's Legislative and Judiciary Committee accused the Supreme Public Prosecutor's Office (SPPO) of conducting "'surveillance'" activities outside the boundaries of collection of criminal information, and even resorting to such deceptive means as falsification of identity and impersonation.[4878]

The NIS has been under attack due to alleged illegal wiretapping. Politicians of the opposition Grand National Party (GNP) charged that the NIS illegally wiretapped conversations during their election campaigns.[4879]

South Koreans have long had to live with widespread surveillance and wiretapping abuses by intelligence and police officials under successive regimes. In October 1998, President Kim Dae-Jung ordered a full-scale probe into illegal wiretapping. Rep. Hyong-Oh Kim of the opposition GNP stated that he believed that over 10,000 taps were actually placed in 1998.[4880] The government proposed amendments to the Protection of Communications Secrets Act in November 1999 that would allow victims of illegal wiretapping to sue in court, limit the number of crimes for which wiretapping is allowed, and provide for notice to targets of wiretapping. The government set up a wiretapping complaint center under the

---

[4876] US Department of State, Country Report on Human Rights Practices – South Korea 2004, Section 1.f: Arbitrary Interference with Privacy, Family, Home, or Correspondence, available at <http://www.state.gov/g/drl/rls/hrrpt/2004/41647.htm>.

[4877] *Id.*

[4878] Scene of National Audit, "Criticism against Surveillance on Pretext of Collection of Criminal Data," Yonhap News, October 19, 2004
<http://news.naver.com/news/read.php?mode=LSD&office_id=001&article_id=0000794552&section_id=102& menu_id=102>.

[4879] Kyung-Ho Kim, "Three Nabbed in Wiretapping Inquiry – Roh Spurs on Prosecution as Lawmakers Refuse to be Questioned," Korea Herald, March 19, 2003. These charges were based on leaked documents GNP politicians obtained from the NIS alleged to reveal the wiretapping. *Id.*

[4880] "Kim Hyong-o Says more than 10,000 May Be Exposed to Gov't Taps," Korea Times, February 13, 1999.

MIC in October 1999.[4881] The UNHRC heard testimony on Korean wiretapping at its meeting in October 1999.[4882]

In 1998, several opposition legislators broke into the NIS liaison office in the National Assembly and removed documents that they claim substantiated allegations that the NIS was conducting surveillance of Assembly members.[4883] The members further alleged that their homes, offices, and cellular telephones were tapped. These members called for either tightening or abolishing a provision in the existing law that allows government officials to obtain retroactive judicial permission to monitor a conversation (especially a cellular telephone call) in the event of an emergency.[4884]

According to the opposition GNP, public prosecutors, police and many governmental bodies, such as the SPPO, the National Police Agency (NPA), the National Tax Administration (NTA), the Financial Supervisory Service (FSS), the Financial Intelligence Unit (FIU), the Fair Trade Commission (FTC) and the Central Election Management Committee (CEMC), are not only indiscriminately monitoring bank accounts, but there has also been a sharp rise of wiretapping incidents by investigating authorities, with a high risks to infringement of human rights.[4885] Furthermore "a considerable number of these surveillances have been carried out without proper legal procedures such as obtaining a warrant or the consent of the individual concerned, but simply at the convenience of the investigating authorities."[4886]

The MIC disclosed that there were 917 cases of government wiretappings in the first half of 2004, an increase of 14.8 percent from the second half of 2003.[4887] As to the means of communications, there were 148 cases of mobile phone tapping (a 42 percent increase from 2003), 239 cases of Internet/PC communications tapping (a 24.5 percent increase),[4888] and 530 cases of landline

---

[4881] "Government to Operate Eavesdropping Complaint Center," Korea Herald, October 30, 1999.

[4882] United Nations Human Rights Committee, Summary record of the 1,792nd meeting: Republic of Korea. 22/11/99. CCPR/C/SR.1792, (November 22, 1999).

[4883] US Department of State, Country Report on Human Rights Practices – South Korea 2000 at s. (f), available at <http://www.state.gov/g/drl/hrrpt/2000/>.

[4884] Id.

[4885] "Government's Intrusion into Privacy Is Excessive" Maeil Gyungjae [The Economic Daily], October 19, 2004, available at <http://news.naver.com/news/read.php?mode=LSD&office_id=009&article_id=0000400141&section_id=101&menu_id=101>.

[4886] Id.

[4887] Id.

[4888] Id.

telephone tapping (a 5.4 percent increase).[4889] As to the types of tapping, there were 149 cases of voicemail or text message taps (a 43.4 percent increase), and 768 cases of eavesdropping on conversations (a 10.5 percent increase).[4890]

According to an MIC report, the number of location-tracking services furnished by mobile phone service providers to state investigation agencies in 2004 has significantly increased over those in 2003.[4891] Government authorities such as the NPA and the NIS tracked mobile phone users in 16,497 instances just during the first half of 2004.[4892] The total number of cases was 20,773 in 2003, a 62.3 percent increase over the 12,184 cases in 2002.[4893]

On November 9, 2004, 16 national legislators of the opposition GNP, including Rep. Young-Se Kwon, submitted a proposal to the National Assembly to revise the current law regulating the privacy of communications.[4894] The proposed bill would require investigators to obtain the approval from a district court judge before tracking the location of a mobile phone user. The bill also requires mobile phone operators to inform customers when state agencies track their location without their knowledge within three months of providing the information to the authorities.[4895] The current law permits government agencies to track a mobile phone user's location for their investigation so long as a district prosecutor's office agrees.[4896]

Through material submitted by the Ministry of Finance and Economy (MOFE) and other agencies to the National Assembly, it was also discovered that even in non-emergency cases, which only require the senior prosecutor's consent – rather than a court approval – public prosecutors obtained telecommunications records by breaking the rule in 40 percent of the cases.[4897] There were 124,893 cases of

[4889] Id.

[4890] Id.

[4891] "Location-Tracing Sparks Privacy Concerns", Korea Times, November 16, 2004, available at <http://news.naver.com/news/read.php?mode=LSD&office_id=040&article_id=0000016873&section_id=108&menu_id=108>.

[4892] Id.

[4893] Id.

[4894] Id.

[4895] Id.

[4896] Id.

[4897] "Sharp Rise in Tappings of Mobile Phone Text Messages and Voice Mailboxes by Government Investigative Agencies," JoongAng Daily, November 24, 2004, available at <http://news.naver.com/news/read.php?mode=LSD&office_id=025&article_id=0000532790&section_id=102&menu_id=102>.

disclosures of telecommunications data, an increase of 24.3 percent compared to the same period in 2003.[4898]

These 2004 statistics represent significant and continuing increases well above the numbers of previous years. According to statistics released by the MIC in 2003, the number of wiretapping cases increased to 1,665 in 2003, up 11.8 percent from 2002. Requests to check criminal suspects' communication records and their identities also jumped by 36.3 percent and 48.1 percent to 44,500 and 61,405 cases, respectively.[4899] Emergency wiretapping, which is conducted without approval from the court, fell to 31 cases in 2003 from 39 in 2002 and 69 in 2001.[4900] The NIS conducted 853, approximately half of the total wiretapping cases in 2003, followed by the prosecution's 514 and the police's 180.[4901] However, the MIC tends to disclose only the numbers of wiretapping cases under the "Restricting Measures for Crime Investigations" of the Protection of Communications Secrets Act.[4902] In 2003, bugging of mobile phone instant messages and emails increased by 27.8 percent to 216 cases, while wiretapping for fixed-line phones and the Internet grew by 8.3 percent and 10.7 percent, respectively.[4903]

In July 2004, employees of Samsung SDI, a subsidiary of the Samsung Group, accused the company of secretly tracking former and current employees through their mobile phones, in order to prevent them from establishing a labor union.[4904] Jea-Min Kang, 41, the last among four employees of Samsung SDI's Suwon factory who filed lawsuits against the company, had been threatened by Samsung officials to quit the company.[4905]

[4898] "Government's Intrusion into Privacy Is Excessive," Maeil Gyungjae [The Economic Daily], October 19, 2004, available at
<http://news.naver.com/news/read.php?mode=LSD&office_id=009&article_id=0000400141&section_id=101&menu_id=101>.

[4899] "Wiretapping Cases up 12 Percent," Korea Times, February 11, 2004, available at
<http://news.naver.com/news/read.php?mode=LSD&office_id=040&article_id=0000009009&section_id=001&menu_id=001>.

[4900] Id.

[4901] Id.

[4902] "Sharp Rise in Tappings of Mobile Phone Text Messages and Voice Mailboxes by Government Investigative Agencies," JoongAng Daily, November 24, 2004, available at
<http://news.naver.com/news/read.php?mode=LSD&office_id=025&article_id=0000532790&section_id=102&menu_id=102>.

[4903] "Wiretapping Cases up 12 Percent," Korea Times, February 11, 2004, available at
<http://news.naver.com/news/read.php?mode=LSD&office_id=040&article_id=0000009009&section_id=001&menu_id=001>.

[4904] "Location-Tracing Sparks Privacy Concerns," Korea Times, November 16, 2004, available at
<http://news.naver.com/news/read.php?mode=LSD&office_id=040&article_id=0000016873&section_id=108&menu_id=108>.

[4905] Id.

In May 2005, Richard Wacker, the President and Chief Executive Officer of Korea Exchange Bank (KEB) discovered that a Korean director at KEB had secretly installed a CCTV camera inside his office during interior remodelling.[4906] Although KEB suspended the unnamed director, allegations still remain among foreign businessmen of being subjected to illicit surveillance by their Korean counterparts and to other acts of industrial espionage.

Earlier, in March 2005, Yun-Joo Jung, the President and CEO of Korea Broadcasting Service (KBS), the state broadcasting service, had been urged by the labor union to step down in an eavesdropping scandal involving the management's alleged secret recording of a union meeting.[4907]

South Korean courts routinely accept recordings, or transcripts of recordings, as admissible evidence in both civil and criminal proceedings. The Supreme Court ruled in October 2002 that it is not illegal for a party to a phone call to record the phone conversation secretly without the other party's knowledge, although the recording of a phone conversation by a third party without the consent of both parties to the phone call is illegal.[4908] In August 2004, the Seoul Central District Court ruled that it was not illegal for a journalist to publish a recording that he made of a phone conversation without the other person's consent.[4909]

Fresh on the heels of similar developments in Hong Kong, the MIC stated in December 2001 that mobile service providers have been neglecting rules regarding user privacy and that companies need to clarify their legal obligations with respect to subscriber privacy. The MIC has proposed a measure to require mobile phone companies to require location-detecting technology in their

---

[4906] "KEB Director Installs CCTV at CEO's Office," Korea Times, May 3, 2005, available at
<http://news.naver.com/news/read.php?mode=LSD&office_id=040&article_id=0000021814&section_id=108&menu_id=108>.

[4907] "KBS CEO Urged to Step Down for Eavesdropping Scandal," Korea Times, March 25, 2005, available at
<http://news.naver.com/news/read.php?mode=LSD&office_id=040&article_id=0000020804&section_id=108&menu_id=108>.

[4908] "Third party's Recording of Phone Conversation without Consent of Both Parties to the Phone Call Is Illegal," Kookmin Ilbo, October 14, 2002, available at
<http://news.naver.com/news/read.php?mode=LSD&office_id=005&article_id=0000122348&section_id=102&menu_id=102>.

[4909] "Not Illegal to Write Article Based on Secret Tape Recording," Edaily, August 3, 2004, available at
<http://news.naver.com/news/read.php?mode=LSD&office_id=018&article_id=0000188418&section_id=102&menu_id=102>; see also "Publishing Article Based on Secret Tape Recording of Conversation Is not Unlawful," OhMyNews, August 3, 2004, available at
<http://news.naver.com/news/read.php?mode=LSD&office_id=047&article_id=0000048896&section_id=102&menu_id=102>.

phones.[4910] The measure would allow mobile service providers to offer location information to third parties under specific conditions.[4911] Privacy advocates are concerned about the proposed measure, particularly because Korean mobile service providers have a bad track record of protecting consumer information. Most recently, provider Korea Telecom Freetel (KTF) admitted that a data leak occurred when an Internet site revealed the exact location of KTF subscribers with GPS-enhanced mobile phones.[4912]

Unauthorized phone taps – through the illegal use of interception equipment and radio frequency devices – have also been increasing at an alarming rate.[4913] According to the MIC, 1,026 illegal phone taps were reported to government authorities and private security companies in 2004.[4914] As of May 2005, another 418 incidents were reported, increasing the number of cases to 6,009 since 2000.[4915] Law enforcement authorities have been able to prosecute the offenders in just 177 of the cases.[4916]

Despite rising public awareness over violations of privacy, in 2005, the Ministry of Justice (MOJ) has been pushing a controversial new law that grants government authorities greater freedom to gather evidence through phone taps by requiring landline and wireless telephone companies to implement new surveillance technologies.[4917] The MOJ is in discussions with the MIC and expects to complete the law by August 2005.[4918]

South Korea has one of the world's highest concentrations of mobile-phone users. As the quality of photos taken by phone cameras improves, there is rising concern about possible privacy abuses. In November 2003, the MIC introduced regulations to protect against the surreptitious taking of photos in public areas such as locker rooms and swimming pools. Starting in 2004, mobile phone manufacturers are required to design camera-enabled mobile phones to make

---

[4910] Sung-Jin Yang, "Push for Location-Based Service Law Confronts Obstacles," Korea Herald, March 25, 2003.

[4911] Id.

[4912] Id.

[4913] "Illegal phone taps increasing sharply," Korea Herald, June 15, 2005, available at <http://www.koreaherald.co.kr/archives/result_contents.asp?id=200506150043&query=illegal%20phone%20taps>

[4914] Id.

[4915] Id.

[4916] Id.

[4917] "Illegal Phone Taps Increasing Sharply," Korea Herald, June 15, 2005, available at <http://www.koreaherald.co.kr/archives/result_contents.asp?id=200506150043&query=illegal%20phone%20taps>.

[4918] Id.

"camera shutter" sounds, of at least 64 decibels, when a picture is taken.[4919] The *Korea Times* reported that the MIC was drafting a new bill to prohibit individuals from taking photographs of others using camera phones without prior consent.[4920]

According to the US State Department, it was "difficult to estimate the number of political prisoners because it was not clear whether particular persons were arrested for exercising the right of free speech or association, or were detained for committing acts of violence or espionage."[4921] Amnesty International reports that the Korean government continued to require released political prisoners to report regularly to the police under the Social Surveillance Law.[4922]

Under the National Security Law, it is forbidden for South Koreans to listen to North Korean radio in their homes or read books published in North Korea if the government determines that they are doing so to help North Korea. However, in 1999 the government made it legal for South Koreans to view North Korean satellite telecasts in their private homes. The government also allows the personal perusal of North Korean books, music, television programs, and movies as a means to promote understanding and reconciliation with North Korea. Student groups make credible claims that government informants are posted on university campuses.[4923]

The Use and Protection of Credit Information Act of 1995 protects credit reports.[4924] In July 2001, three large credit card companies were fined under this law. The companies were found to have disclosed personal information on their customers (including bank account numbers, pay levels and credit card transaction records, and customer identifiers such as names, addresses, phone numbers and resident-registration numbers) to insurance companies without giving notice to their customers or obtaining their consent in advance.[4925] The Postal Services Act protects postal privacy.[4926]

4919 "Phone Camera Makers Are Told to Use 'Click' to Protect Privacy," JoongAng Daily, November 12, 2003.
4920 "Camera Phone to Require Shutter Sound from Next Year," Korea Times, November 11, 2003, available at <http://times.hankooki.com/lpage/tech/200311/kt2003111120385111810.htm>.
4921 US Department of State, Country Report on Human Rights Practices – South Korea 2004, Section 1.e: Denial of Fair Public Trial, available at <http://www.state.gov/g/drl/rls/hrrpt/2004/41647.htm>.
4922 *See* Amnesty International, Republic of Korea (South Korea): On trial for defending his rights: the case of human rights activist Suh Jun-sik; under the law, some released prisoners are required to report to the police when moving or traveling, available at <http://www.web.amnesty.org/ai.nsf/index/ASA250181998>,.
4923 US Department of State, Country Report on Human Rights Practices – South Korea 2003, available at <http://www.state.gov/g/drl/hrrpt/2003/>.
4924 No. 4866, Enforcement Decree for the Act Relating to Use and Protection of Credit Information.
4925 "Stricter Privacy Protection," Korea Herald, July 19, 2001.
4926 Act No. 542, last amended by Act No. 6196, January 21, 2000.

Since January 2002, Korea has maintained a DNA database of missing children.[4927] Registry in the database is voluntary, and it is available to parents and children in orphanages.[4928] The Supreme Public Prosecutor's Office (SPPO) analyzes the samples, and the information is stored in a database maintained by Biogrand, a private company.[4929] Privacy advocates are concerned that the SPPO, an office engaged in criminal prosecutions, collects the DNA samples.[4930] The SPPO maintains that they do not have access to personally identifiable information aside from age and sex when they receive a DNA sample, and that the database's use is strictly for family relationships.[4931] Privacy advocates are nevertheless wary because there are no specific laws that address DNA information.[4932] As such, there is the potential for abuse and extending the database's function.

Open Government

The Official Information Disclosure Act is a "freedom of information act" that allows Koreans to demand access to government records. It was enacted in 1996 and went into effect in 1998.[4933] The Supreme Court ruled in 1989 that there is a constitutional right to information "as an aspect of the right of freedom of expression, and specific implementing legislation to define the contours of the right was not a prerequisite to its enforcement."[4934]

On November 25, 2001, South Korea created the National Human Rights Commission (NHRCK) to independently investigate human rights violations, including privacy violations, and offer remedies when applicable.[4935] The NHRCK is comprised of 11 Commissioners and 167 staff. According to the US State Department Human Rights Report, women enjoy equal access to education, but face job discrimination in the private sector and are at a disadvantage because

---

[4927] E-mail from Kim Nak ho, Department of Communications, Soul National University to Waseem Karim, Law Clerk, Electronic Privacy Information Center (EPIC), July 5, 2002 (on file with EPIC).

[4928] *Id.*

[4929] *Id.*

[4930] *Id.*

[4931] *Id.*

[4932] *Id.*

[4933] Wholly amended by Act No. 7127, January 29, 2004.

[4934] Right to Information (1 KCCR 176, 88 HunMa 22, Sep. 4, 1989), available at <http://www.ccourt.go.kr/english/case4.html>.

[4935] *See* MD Presswire, November 12, 2002.

of some government agencies' preferential hiring of men.[4936] Violence and sexual harassment against women continue to be serious problems despite recent legislation and other initiatives to protect women. High incidences of domestic violence are reported.[4937] Women's groups say that rape and sexual harassment generally are not prosecuted and that convicted offenders often receive light sentences.[4938] Prostitution is "illegal, but widespread," and South Korea remains "a country of origin, transit and destination" whereby women are trafficked for sexual exploitation.[4939]

In March 2003, the Korean Ministry of Education and Human Resources launched the National Education Information System (NEIS), a nationwide database that links the information of over 10,000 school and education agencies.[4940] The purpose of the NEIS is to enable schools to share education information with each other.[4941] Various organizations opposed the implementation of the NEIS due to the threat that the system poses on the privacy of students and teachers, including the National Teacher's Union, which organized a strike.[4942] Furthermore, the NHRCK recommended that the Ministry of Education abandon maintaining three categories of information (school management information, student academic records, and health and enrollment records) within the NEIS, determining that the Ministry lacked the legal foundation to implement NEIS in this manner, and the threat that the system posed to privacy was significant.[4943] As a result of the opposition, the

---

[4936] US Department of State, Korea (Republic of) Country Report on Human Rights Practices for 2004, section 5: Discrimination, Societal Abuses and Trafficking in Person, available at <http://www.state.gov/g/drl/rls/hrrpt/2004/41647.htm>.

[4937] Amnesty International Report 2003 - South Korea, available at <http://web.amnesty.org/report2004/kofr-summary-eng>.

[4938] Freedom in the World 2003: The Annual Survey of Political Rights and Civil Liberties (Freedom House 2003).

[4939] US Department of State, Country Report on Human Rights Practices – South Korea 2004, Section 5: Discrimination, Societal Abuses and Trafficking in Person, available at <http://www.state.gov/g/drl/rls/hrrpt/2004/41647.htm>.

[4940] "Privacy or Convenience," Korea Herald, May 22, 2003.

[4941] Among the stated goals "are setting up the national standardization of educational content, evenly distributing educational information among different regions, and establishing more rational educational policies," Launching the National Education Information System (NEIS), available at <http://www.moe.go.kr/English/Policy/pds_v.php?number=28&db=bbs13_1_5&tb=engmoebbs2002&gubun=o pi&mod=&keyset=&searchword=>.

[4942] Participants in the strike were also opposed to pressure from the World Trade Organization to open Korea's educational sector to foreign competitors. "Teachers Union to Launch Strike Against NEIS," Yonhap English News, March 26, 2003.

[4943] Among the risks cited by the NHRCK was the potential for hackers to steal information from the system. Id. The Commission stated that the kind of information that the system contained about a student was so intimate that it demanded constitutional protection. "Privacy or Convenience," Korea Herald, May 22, 2003.

government decided that they would rethink the NEIS after gathering more information.[4944]

On April 19, 2005, it was asserted during a National Assembly session that the MIC "had purchased private information of fingerprints and facial skeletal features without a clear-cut legal basis."[4945] Rep. Hae-Suk Suh of the Uri Party argued: "Over two years since 2002, the MIC has spent [KRW] 2.8 billion to establish a database on vital information of 5,620 people including minors. . . . The government continues to amass personal identification data on the grounds that it is useful for the commercialization of biometrics."[4946] The MIC admitted that its affiliate, the Korea Information Security Agency (KISA), has "carried out the collection of 3,600 fingerprints and 2,020 facial skeletal features," but denied any wrongdoing, pointing out that the Act on Promotion of Information and Communications Network Utilization and Data Protection (DPA) stipulates that "the MIC can ferret out measures for protection of individual information together with the KISA."[4947]

International Obligations

South Korea is a member of the Organization for Economic Cooperation and Development (OECD) and has adopted the OECD Guidelines on the Protection of Privacy and Transborder Flows of Personal Data.[4948]

Kingdom of Spain

Constitutional and Data Protection Framework

The Spanish Constitution recognizes the right to personal privacy, secrecy of communications, and the protection of personal data. Article 18 of the Constitution states, "(1) The right of honor, personal, and family privacy and identity is guaranteed. (2) The home is inviolable. No entry or search may be made without legal authority except with the express consent of the owners or in

---

[4944] Hyung-Jin Kim, "Controversial Education Database under Review," Korea Herald, May 20, 2003.

[4945] "Ministry Buys Individual Information for Research", Korea Times, April 20, 2005, available at <http://news.naver.com/news/read.php?mode=LSD&office_id=040&article_id=0000021481&section_id=108&menu_id=108>.

[4946] *Id.*

[4947] *Id.*

[4948] OECD Guidelines on the Protection of Privacy and Transborder Flows of Personal Data, available at <http://www.oecd.org/document/18/0,2340,en_2649_34255_1815186_1_1_1_1,00.html>.

the case of a *flagrante delicto*. (3) Secrecy of communications, particularly regarding postal, telegraphic, and telephone communication, is guaranteed, except for infractions by judicial order. (4) The law shall limit the use of data processing to guarantee personal and family honor, the privacy of citizens, and the full exercise of their rights."[4949]

The first Spanish Data Protection Act (LORTAD) was enacted in 1992, and was succeeded in 1999 by an amended Data Protection Act (LOPD) that brought Spanish law in line with the European Union Data Protection Directive.[4950] The LOPD applies to information held by the public and private sectors. The law establishes the right of citizens to know what personal data is contained in electronic records and grants citizens the right to correct or delete incorrect or false data in those records. Additionally, the LOPD also restricts the disclosure of personal information to a third party by requiring the consent of the individual to the specific purpose for which the data was collected. Additional protections are also provided for sensitive personal data. Consumer groups, however, are concerned about the law's provisions allowing use of information without consent unless the consumer has opted out of such use. In 1999, regulations on the secondary measures required to be taken to protect electronic data systems were issued in accordance with the LOPD.[4951]

Data Protection Authority

The Spanish Data Protection Agency (*Agencia Española de Protección de Datos*, or AEPD) is charged with enforcing the LOPD.[4952] In 2000, the country's data protection laws and the AEPD's authority to enforce those laws was challenged and the Constitutional Tribunal of Spain issued three judgments clarifying the

---

[4949] Constitution of Spain, as amended August 1992, available at
<http://www.congreso.es/ingles/funciones/constitucion/cons_t_preliminar.htm>.

[4950] *See* Organic Law 5/1992 of October 29, 1992 Regulating the Automated Processing of Personal Data), Ley Orgánica 5/1992 de 29 de Octubre 1992, de Regulación del Tratamiento Automatizado de los Datos de Caracter Personal (LORTAD), enacted on January 14, 2000, available at
<http://noticias.juridicas.com/base_datos/Derogadas/r0-lo5-1992.html>; *see also* Organic Law 15/1999 of December 13, 1999 on the Protection of Personal Data (LOPD), (Ley Orgánica 15/99 de 13 de Diciembre 1999 de Protección de Datos de Carácter Personal (LOPD), available at
<http://www.igsap.map.es/cia/dispo/17643.htm>.

[4951] *See* Royal Decree No. 994/1999 of June 11, which approves the regulation on mandatory security measures for the computer files which contain personal data (Real Decreto 994/1999, del 11 de junio, por el que se aprueba el Reglamento de medidas de seguridad de los ficheros automatizados que contengan datos de carácter personal), available at <https://www.agpd.es/upload/reglamento_ingles_pdf.pdf>.

[4952] *See* Spanish Data Protection Authority (AEPD) homepage
<https://www.agpd.es/index.php?idSeccion=8>; *see also* <https://www.agpd.es> (in Spanish).

issues that arose.[4953] The first was a constitutional challenge against the 1992, law for breach of the provisions of the country's constitution relating to distribution of power between the State and other agencies (in this case the AEPD). The court rejected this challenge. The second concerned another constitutional challenge which was originally brought against the 1992 law but which carried over to the 1999 law. This judgment upheld the constitutionality of the law generally, although the court struck down certain provisions allowing government agencies to transfer personal information on Spanish citizens without a citizen's permission. The court ruled that these provisions infringed on the privacy rights guaranteed to citizens by Title 18 of the Spanish Constitution.[4954] The third case concerned an employer's processing of an employee's health data. The court ruled that the applicant's constitutional privacy rights were breached when the employer noted the employee's medical diagnosis on the sick leave records.

As part of their enforcement of the country's data protection laws, the AEPD maintains a registry of information databases in Spain and can investigate violations of the LOPD. In December 2001, the number of registered information databases was 271,875. In 2002, it reached 328,649, and in 2003, there were 470,000 registered information databases.[4955] As of April 30, 2005, there were 556,104 registered information databases, of which 506,796 were held by private entities, and 49,308 were held by public bodies or entities.[4956] Additionally, in 2003, 574 complaints were investigated by the agency, and there were 568 defense of citizens' rights procedures (*procedimientos de tutela de derechos*), 163 infringement procedures against the private sector, and 28 against the public sector. In comparison, in 2004 there were 978 complaints investigated, 654 defense of citizens rights procedures, 366 infringement procedures against the private sector and 28 against the public sector. The AEPD also investigated a number of "spam" cases in 2004, initiating 86 investigations and 10 sanction procedures involving small- and medium-size businesses.[4957]

[4953] Judgements Nos. 290/2000, 292/2000, and 202/1999 respectively. Summaries available in European Union Article 29 Data Protection Working Party, Fifth Annual Report.

[4954] Judgement No. 292/2000.

[4955] General Subdirectorate for Inspection, 2003 Reports by the AEPD, (La Agencia en cifras. Subdirección General de Inspección, Memorias 2003 de la AEPD), available at
<https://www.agpd.es/upload/Canal_Documentacion/Memoria/Memoria_2003/La%20Agencia%20en%20cifras.%20Subdirecci%F3n%20General%20de%20Inspecci%F3n.pdf> (in Spanish).

[4956] Estadísticas Mensuales Registro General de Protección de Datos, April 2005
<https://www.agpd.es/upload/Informa%20AEPD/est200504.pdf>.

[4957] Report from Dra. Mercedez Ortuño, Data Inspector Agencia Española de Protección de Datos, to Cédric Laurant, Director, International Privacy Project, EPIC, February 24, 2005 (on file with EPIC).

Another fundamental enforcement activity of the Spanish Data Protection Agency is the Sectorial Inspection Programmes, which annually audit various public and private sector businesses in order to ensure compliance with data protection legislation.[4958] Since its inception, the Sectorial Inspections have carried out investigative actions and have imposed penalties on various businesses including some in the healthcare and telecommunications sector.[4959] In the telecommunications industry, the most common problem the AEPD has had to deal with is the fraudulent pre-assignment of telephone lines without the knowledge or consent of the person concerned. In September 2000, the AEPD also fined Telefónica, the Spanish telephone company, EUR 60,000 (~USD 73,000) for a glitch in its computer systems that allowed improper access to customer files.[4960] Another problem addressed by the AEPD is unsolicited marketing. A decision concerning unsolicited direct sales calls, using automatic call services, declared that an offense had been committed by the marketing company because it could not be shown that the person affected had given consent to the marketing. The AEPD also carried out actions to safeguard citizens' rights (access to, rectification of, and deletion of personal information records) that did not involve issuing penalties, and which were limited to accepting or rejecting claims made by the public to the AEPD.

In January of 2001, a ESP 180 million (EUR one million) fine was issued to Zeppelin, the television company producing the Spanish version of the show "Big Brother," for releasing personal information on those who tried out for the show.[4961] A ESP 100,000 fine was also issued to *Caja Insular de Ahorros de Canarias* in February 2001, and *Microsoft Ibérica* was fined ESP 10 million in April of 2001, for improper use of client information.[4962] The agency has also investigated the University of Zaragoza on allegations that the university sold alumni information without permission.[4963] In 2002, the AEPD also considered the case of the company Inlander, which was accused of storing personal data of

---

[4958] Report from Dra. Mercedez Ortuño, Data Inspector, Agencia Española de Protección de Datos, to Cédric Laurant, Director, International Privacy Project, EPIC, December 22, 2004 (on file with EPIC).
[4959] *Id.*
[4960] "Protección de Datos Multa con 10 millones a Telefónica por el acceso en internet a la facturación de sus clientes," El País, September 29, 2000.
[4961] " Por la fuga de datos en 'Gran Hermano' la AEPD multa con un millón de euros a la productora Zeppelín" (Zeppelin production fined one million euros by the AEPD for the disappearance of personal details relating to Big Brother), Expansión, January 6, 2001.
[4962] Article relating to the fining of a savings bank for unjustly blacklisting certain individuals, appearing in El País, (Multada una caja de ahorros por mantener en la lista de morosos a quien ya no lo era protección de datos recuerda que no se pueden consignar antiguas deudas como Saldo O), El País, February 17, 2001; "Microsoft Ibérica, sancionada por utilizar datos de sus clientes" (Microsoft Iberica is fined for using personal data of its customers), Cinco Días, April 18, 2001.
[4963] "Public Prosecutions Office Summons University of Zaragoza over Passing on of Personal Data," (El defensor del pueblo requiere a la Universidad de Zaragoza sobre la venta de datos), El País, June 4, 2001.

Spanish citizens on a US-based database and failing to take security measures to protect private personal data.[4964] Appeals against any decisions of the AEPD may be brought before an administrative court. In 2000, however, 54 such appeals were brought, and the court upheld the decisions of the AEPD in the majority of these cases.[4965]

An important debate took place in 2003 regarding employers' access to employees' e-mails. The first case involved a Deutsche Bank employee who was dismissed for spending too much time sending private e-mails during working hours. The employer had obtained the list of private e-mails the employee had sent. That list had been obtained without any adequate authorization from a judge. This case was fought on the basis that the firing was unlawful. The Superior Court of Catalunya ruled in favor of the bank. On appeal, the employee made the claim that his employer had intruded upon his right to privacy. After losing again, the employee brought his claim before the Supreme Court. An out-of-court settlement was reached before the final ruling was issued. The Superior Court of Catalunya, however, held that electronic mail is the employer's tool and is lent to the employee, therefore, the employee cannot expect any privacy. In other cases, however, the court has found in favor of the employee. In January 2003, the trade union (*Comisiones Obreras*) requested from the *La Caixa* bank that it remove from its internal rules a regulation that allowed the bank to monitor its employees' e-mails to check whether they were working. On January 23, 2004, a court (the *Audiencia Provincial de Madrid*) held that the installation of spyware software to monitor an employee's e-mail, even though the purpose may have been to prove the employee's absenteeism, is illegal, pursuant to Article 197.1 of the Penal Code.[4966]

The 1998 General Telecommunications Act (LGT) guaranteed the right of individuals to use strong cryptography but also contained a provision allowing for a mandatory key recovery system. This provision was strongly opposed by civil liberties advocates.[4967] Subsequent changes to the LGT, however, incorporated Article 52. Although the revision allowed for the use of

---

[4964] Laia Raventós, "*Multado un ISP Español por Alojar Datos en Estados Unidos*," *Ciberpaís*, August 29, 2002.

[4965] European Union Article 29 Data Protection Working Party, Fifth Annual Report on the Situation Regarding the Protection of Individuals with Regard to the Processing of Personal Data and Privacy in the European Union and in Third Countries Covering the Year 2000, Part II, March 6, 2002, available at <http://europa.eu.int/comm/internal_market/en/dataprot/wpdocs/wp54en_2.pdf>.

[4966] "Caso COAPI. Espiar a un trabajador puede ser constitutivo de delito," <http://www.bufetalmeida.com/sentencias/coapi.html>.

[4967] *See* Global Internet Liberty Campaign, "New Spanish Telecommunications Law Opens a Door to Mandatory Key Recovery Systems," July 1998, available at <http://www.gilc.org/crypto/spain/gilc-crypto-spain-798.html>.

cryptography to protect information that is circulating on networks, it also imposed a few restrictions for encryption product manufacturers, network operators and end users. Among these restrictions was the compelling of these individuals to notify the General Administration of the State regarding the means of encryption used. A more recent amendment, Article 36, also makes it more likely that a key escrow will soon be created by the government,[4968] even though the government had promised in April 2003, that such a modification in the law would not occur. In its final version, the law is sufficiently ambiguous for it not to be directly applicable, although it still could become the basis for a law creating a key escrow system. The new Article 36 does not change much from the former Article 52 which compelled the notification of the algorithms used, but still remains ambiguous with regard to any reference to the creation of a key escrow system.[4969]

In June 2002, the Parliament approved the controversial Law of Information Society Services and Electronic Commerce (LSSI),[4970] which entered into force on October 12, 2002. The law prohibits the distribution of spam, requires web hosting companies to police content and shut down websites involved in illegal activities, and mandates retention for one year of Internet users' traffic data.[4971] This latter requirement was a late addition to the proposal, which had been under consideration for nearly two years. It was introduced following the approval, in May 2002, by the European Parliament of the EU Directive on Privacy and Electronic Communications, which contained a provision allowing for data retention. Prior to passage, the AEPD, in a formal submission to the Government, expressed its opposition to the routine storage of traffic data.[4972] Opponents have vowed to challenge the law before the Constitutional Court arguing that it breaches constitutional rights to privacy, freedom of expression and presumption of innocence.[4973]

[4968] The amendment provides that end users may be compelled to notify the government information on "the keys, algorithms, or any other encryption procedure used, including the technical information regarding the systems used for [encryption]."

[4969] See "No al articulo 36 Restricciones a la Criptografía: La Nueva Ley General de Telecomunicaciones Impone la Obligación de Revelar las Claves de Cifrado," March 2003, available at <http://www.spain.cpsr.org/02042003.php>; Mercé Molist, "El Congreso no Aclara el Depósito del Cifrado en la Ley de Telecomunicaciones," El País, June 12, 2003.

[4970] <http://www.setsi.mcyt.es/legisla/internet/ley34_02/sumario.htm>.

[4971] See generally EPIC's LSSI webpage, available at <http://www.epic.org/privacy/intl/lssi.html>.

[4972] Letter from Emilio Aced Felez, June 27, 2002, supra.

[4973] "Foes Vow to Challenge Spanish Internet Law," Associated Press, July 1, 2002.

Under the criminal code, interception of electronic communications requires a court order.[4974] There have been several scandals in Spain over illegal wiretapping by the intelligence services. In 1995, Deputy Prime Minister Narcis Serra, Defense Minister Julian Garcia Vargas, and military intelligence chief Gen. Emilio Alonso Manglano were forced to quit following revelations that they had monitored the conversations of hundreds of people, including King Juan Carlos.[4975] More recently, Juan Alberto Perote, the former head of operations of the *Centro Superior de Información de la Defensa* (CESID, the Spanish secret service, which was part of the armed forces until it was replaced by the CNI in 2002), was found guilty on April 12, 2005, and sentenced to four months in prison. In the first trial in 1999, Manglano and Perote both received sixth-month sentences and five CESID officers were sentenced to six months, although the Constitutional Tribunal annulled this ruling on March 29, 2004 after it deemed that the judge who heard the case was not impartial. Charges brought against Emilio Alonso Manglano and the five CESID officers by private individuals and groups placed under surveillance were dropped. Perote criticised the decision against him, claiming that his director, Manglano, and members of the Socialist Party government of the time knew about "this activity," which was carried out between 1983 and 1991.[4976]

An exclusionary rule applies to evidence collected by means of illegal wiretaps or bugs, and in November of 2000, the Barcelona High Court (*Audiencia de Barcelona*) threw out a case because the evidence was so tainted.[4977] In May of 2001, prosecutors asked for 12-year sentences for each of two detectives accused of placing illegal wiretaps.[4978] In December 2004, the Supreme Court claimed that "the approval of an adequate regulation for telephone interceptions" cannot be postponed, after acquitting two suspected drug traffickers because telephone interceptions used to sentence them in the *Audiencia Nacional* were deemed to be irregular. The Court added that Spain has already been condemned by the

---

[4974] Ley Orgánica 11/1980 de 1 de Diciembre 1980 (December 1, 1980). Penal Code, Sections 196-199.

[4975] "Spain Socialists Seek Opposition Apology on Bugging," Reuters, February 6, 1996.

[4976] "Perote, condenado a cuatro meses de arresto por las escuchas del Cesid," El País, April 13, 2005; and "Cuatro meses de prisión para Perote por las escuchas del Cesid," El País, April 4, 2005.

[4977] "Secreto Communicaciones Audienceia Invalida Pruebas Obtenidas por "Pinchazo" Telefono," Spanish Newswire Services, November 23, 2000.

[4978] "Pinchazos Telefonicos: Fiscalia Pide 24 Años Paragraph Detectives por Pinchar Telefonos," Spanish Newswire Service, May 7, 2001.

European Court of Human Rights for failing to specify the nature of offenses that can give rise to these interceptions and to fix a time limit for them.[4979]

In early 2004, the National Police Corps (*Cuerpo Nacional de Policía*) and the Civil Guard (*Guardia Civil*) reportedly started using a new software program, SINTEL, that enables them to directly tap into telephonic communications without the need to get prior court authorization. SINTEL, which was designed by an October 2001 secret agreement, works in real time. In addition to recording the content of the communication, the software also provides the identity of both callers and the place from which they are calling.[4980]

Anti-terrorism Measures

The terrorist attack on a Madrid commuter line on March 11, 2004 was followed by announcements of a raft of measures to be introduced with regards to the problem of Islamist terrorism, most notably those of placing "radical" imams and former *mujahedins* (Muslims who fought in Afghanistan or the Balkans) under surveillance, and of establishing databases in order to establish their numbers.[4981]

The draft National Defence Law,[4982] published on March 31, 2005, seeks to expand the scope of activities by the National Intelligence Centre (*Centro Nacional de Inteligencia*, or CNI),[4983] by directing it to "contribute . . . in obtaining, evaluating and interpreting the necessary information to prevent and avoid any risk or threat that affects the independence and integrity of Spain, national interests and the stability of the State of law and its institutions" (Article 28). The words "risk or threat" alter the wording of the decree that established the CNI, which envisaged its scope as preventing and avoiding "danger, threat or aggression against," which cannot be interpreted as widely. Experts cited in *El País* newspaper suggested that "risk that affects the integrity of Spain" is so ambiguous as to be liable to be interpreted as giving the intelligence service a role in countering political proposals such as the so-called *Plan Ibarretxe*,

---

[4979] "El Supremo cree inapalazable regular el control de telefonos." El País, December 13, 2004.

[4980] "Policía y Guardia Civil Pueden Pinchar Los Teléfonos Informáticamente," February 19, 2004, available at <http://www.nodo50.org/tortuga/article.php3?id_article=204>.

[4981] "Censo de ex muyahidines e imanes radicales," El País, May 30, 2004.

[4982] Proyecto de Ley Orgánica de la defensa nacional 121/000031, Boletín Oficial de las Cortes Generales, March 31, 2005.

[4983] Spain's secret service agency.

---

proposed by the *lehendakari* (head of the Basque government) to change the status of the Basque autonomous region.[4984]

Additionally, there are two new laws related to the fight against terrorism. These two laws are written to complement each other and directly impact the field of data protection by creating new databases in public ownership. The first law aims at preventing and freezing terrorism funding.[4985] It sets up the Commission for Monitoring the Funding of Terrorist Activities. This institution has the authority to freeze funds, bank accounts, and other financial assets belonging to entities or persons linked to terrorist activities. It develops its findings within the administrative sphere and collaborates with the judiciary to transmit its conclusions to the judge in criminal trials. The law establishes the obligations of financial entities (*e.g.*, banks, credit entities, exchange bureaus) and all subjects referred to in the law against money laundering (Law 19/2003, described below) to collaborate in providing all the information required (including personal data) in relation to frozen funds. This law also provides that, with regard to the provisions of the LOPD, the files created by the Monitoring Commission will be considered files in public ownership, and therefore exempt with regard to the rights of access, rectification, and cancellation.

The second regulation is Law 19/2003 regulating the movement of money and international transactions and enacted in July 2003.[4986] This law works to prevent money laundering and is closely linked with the law regarding the funding of terrorist activities. It was approved as a modification to the law of 1993 preventing money laundering. The new rule also incorporates into national legislation, Directive 2001/97 on the prevention of money laundering.[4987]

This law will apply not only to terrorist crimes, illegal drug trafficking, and organized crime (current situation) but also to all other serious crimes (punishable with more than three years in prison) and related money-laundering

---

[4984] *"El borrador permite al servicio secreto investigar cualquier riesgo que afecte a la integridad de España,"* *El País*, March 18, 2005.

[4985] Ley 12/2003, de 21 de mayo, de prevención y bloqueo de la financiación del terrorismo, (Law 12/2003 of May 21 on preventing and freezing terrorism funding), available at
<http://noticias.juridicas.com/base_datos/Admin/l12-2003.html> (in Spanish); *see also*
<http://www.igsap.map.es/cia/dispo/26927.htm>.

[4986] Ley 19/2003, de 4 julio, sobre régimen jurídico de los movimientos de capitales y de las transacciones económicas con el exterior y sobre determinadas medidas de prevención del blanqueo de capitales, available at
<http://www.igsap.map.es/cia/dispo/26927.htm> (in Spanish).

[4987] Directiva 2001/97/CE del Parlamento Europeo y del Consejo, de 4 de diciembre de 2001 sobre Blanqueo de capitales: prevención de la utilización del sistema financiero (European Parliament and Council Directive 2001/97/EC of December 4, 2001 related to Money laundering: Preventing use of the financial system), available at <http://europa.eu.int/scadplus/leg/es/lvb/l24016.htm>.

activities. The law also imposes new obligations on subjects, such as auditors, external accountants (not only internal company accountants), and tax advisors. Notaries, lawyers and attorneys must also collaborate with full respect to professional secrecy and without prejudice to the constitutional right to defense.

Recent Developments

In the 2004 opinion on "The Qualification of the IP Address as Personal Data,"[4988] the AEPD ruled that IP addresses can be considered "personal data" and therefore, that every data controller that processes such information has to comply with the LOPD requirements. Failure to comply may subject the violator to fines of up to EUR 300,000 (~USD 366,000).[4989]

In December 2004, the director of the AEPD, José Luis Piñar, complained about the lack of funding and personnel in the agency, noting that its budget for 2005, EUR 7 million (~USD 8,5 million), is the lowest budget for any independent Spanish body. Mr. Piñar also noted that the agency's 16 inspectors, who work in pairs, are organized into only eight inspection teams that are responsible for enforcement across the entire country.[4990]

Also in December 2004, 12 persons from different social movements in the region of Catalunya filed a complaint in the AEPD as a result of the alleged inclusion of their personal data and photographs in an illegal database of a "political" nature held by the National Police force's *Brigada Provincial de Información* (Provincial Information Brigade). The plaintiffs have no criminal records, but are part of a group of 30 people whose photographs were shown to three persons accused of throwing molotov cocktails against the police station in Sants (a neighbourhood in Barcelona) on October 3, 2004, during their interrogation. This procedure would have been legal if the people whose photographs were shown had criminal records, and a further concern is that the photographs that were shown were not from their national ID cards (DNI), but had been taken during their participation in public activities. The plaintiffs claimed that Article 7.4 of the 1999 LOPD was contravened, as it forbids "databases created with the exclusive scope of storing personal data that reveals

---

[4988] Agencia Española de Protección de Datos, "Carácter de dato personal de la dirección IP," (Informe 327/03), available at <https://www.agpd.es/index.php?idSeccion=390> (in Spanish).

[4989] Marta Escudero & Javier Maestre, "Como Consecuencia, Muchos Webmasters Deberán Registrar Sus Ficheros en la Agencia," July 5, 2004, available at <http://www.kriptopolis.com/more.php?id=201_0_1_0_M>.

[4990] "Solo tenemos dieciseis inspectores para todo el territorio nacional," interview, Expansión, December 7, 2004.

the ideology, trade union membership, religion, beliefs, racial or ethnic origin, or sexual habits." The police denied holding a database to identify people related to social movements, and that it only uses a database of citizens with judicial precedents, although it also admitted using a database for investigations, which operates under the control of the data protection authority.[4991]

On January 5, 2005, AEPD Instruction number 1/2004 (dated December 22, 2004) was published in the Spanish Official Journal (*Boletín Oficial del Estado*, or BOE), decreeing that, in the interest of transparency and to promote public knowledge of its decisions, the AEPD would publish all of its resolutions on its website within a month from the day after the persons concerned had been informed of a decision.[4992] The only exception would be with regard to the registration of databases in its record of authorised information databases.

Two issues on which the AEPD has been particularly active in 2004 and 2005 is the combating of "spam" and encouraging small- and medium-size businesses (*pequeñas y medianas empresas* – PYMES) to register their databases in the RGPD. Although registry of information databases is compulsory, only 10 percent of PYMES that are active on the Spanish territory are complying with the law.[4993] With regard to "spam," the AEPD announced the signing of a Memorandum of Understanding on February 23, 2005 with the US Federal Trade Commission. This memorandum is aimed at establishing an administrative cooperation between Spain and the United States in order to combat the problem of "spam." The AEPD also announced that almost a hundred investigations have been launched in relation to this phenomenon, and these investigations have given rise to 14 legal actions for breaches of data protection rules, of which six have been resolved. Of these six resolved cases, two were classified as "serious breaches," two as "minor breaches," and in the remaining two, proceedings were discontinued.[4994] In general, however, fines of up to EUR 30,000 (~USD 36,600) are applicable for breaches of anti-spam regulations.

On December 11, 2003, the Parliament enacted the Law on Digital Signatures. The legislation established an electronic identification card (*DNI electrónico*) that includes a certificate used to generate a digital signature. The card, to be

---

[4991] "12 activistas de Barcelona denuncian que la policía les incluye en un fichero ilegal," El País, December 30, 2004.

[4992] Instrucción 1/2004, de 22 de diciembre, de la Agencia Española de Protección de Datos sobre la publicación de sus resoluciones <https://www.agpd.es/upload/Canal_Documentacion/legislacion/Estatal/Instruccion1-2004.pdf>.

[4993] "Solo el 10% de las PYMES españolas cumple la Ley de Protección de Datos", Atlántico, April 13, 2005.

[4994] AEPD, press statement, February 23, 2005, available at <https://www.agpd.es/upload/Prensa/Nota%20eeuu.pdf>.

fully rolled out by 2007, would allow individuals and businesses to digitally sign documents – and provide the same value as a regular handwritten signature. The government seeks to encourage the development of electronic commerce and promote consumer confidence in Internet-based transactions.[4995] The electronic ID card will include two elements: a chip with information relating to the citizen's identity and electronic signature, as well as biometric data (fingerprint and photograph). Privacy groups criticize the law because, as they assert, it would make the card compulsory for all and would create a huge database of citizens' personal data that would be subject to serious security risks. They have urged that the project be revised to ensure the full protection of Spanish citizens' privacy.[4996]

The Commission on Liberties and Information Technology (*Comisión Libertades e Informática*, or CLI)) complained about the lack of debate with regards to the introduction of the planned electronic ID card,[4997] warning that measures that are to be introduced may contravene fundamental rights, such as the rights to privacy and to the protection of personal data.[4998] It also stressed that it will be important for adequate security measures to be adopted in relation to the introduction of this identification document, as it may contain elements that will make it possible to access sensitive personal information about cardholders, such as race and religious affiliation in the case of photographs. In a plenary session of the Senate, the Ministry of Interior announced that it would delay the introduction of the electronic ID card, and planned to launch a pilot scheme in 2006 with a view to its nationwide implementation in late 2007 or early 2008. The CLI hopes that the delay will allow time for a public debate on the guarantees that are needed to safeguard the rights and freedoms of citizens, particularly in relation to the inclusion of biometric data in the document. The CLI has also warned about the possibility that DNA details be included, and that it would be illegal for it to include medical information (or to turn the ID card into a multipurpose document required to have access to health services), as was suggested in February 2004, by the former Minister of Public Administration, Julia García Valdecasas.[4999]

[4995] "La Ley de la Firma Electrónica entra en vigor," Redes and Telecoms, December 12, 2003, available at <http://www.redestelecom.com/Actualidad/Noticias/Comunicaciones/Legislaci%C3%B3n/20031212036>.

[4996] "El DNI Electrónico se Tramitará en España el Próximo Año," El País, May 5, 2003.

[4997] "El DNI Electrónico no puede incluir datos personales ajenos a la identificación," IBLNEWS, October 4, 2004.

[4998] "La CLI advierte que el contenido del DNI Electrónico no puede incluir datos de carácter personal," Asociación de Internautas, May 20, 2005, available at <http://www.internautas.org/html/1/2934.html>.

[4999] *Comisión de Libertades e Informática* press statement, 19.2.2004.

In October 2004, the Employment and Social Affairs Ministry presented the draft Regulation implementing the Aliens Law (Spain's immigration legislation), after it was modified by the Organic Law 14/2003. Implementing Article 15 of the law, the Regulation instructs land, air, and sea carriers to pass on passenger data to Spanish border authorities before take-off as an early stage of border controls. Carriers will also be required to help immigration authorities track down people who have overstayed their visas by compiling dossiers of passengers who fail to make use of their return ticket.[5000] The establishment of a Central Register of Foreigners under Article 109, to be managed by the *Dirección General de Policía* (General Direction of Police), is also under consideration. It is expected to hold details about a foreign visitor, including the information contained in travel documents and the foreigner identification number card.[5001] The database will also hold information regarding any legal decisions or permissions to exit or enter the country that have been taken with respect to a foreign national. This information will be made available to the State Secretariat on Immigration and Emigration and is subject to data protection under the LOPD. Foreigners will also be obliged to provide details of any change in their condition or personal situation (*i.e.* civil status) within one month.[5002]

On September 10, 2002, the Computer Professionals for Social Responsibility Spain (CPSR-ES) organized the first Big Brother Awards event in Spain.[5003] They have been held every year since then. On October 30, 2004, in their third edition, Telefónica (Spain's leading telecommunications service provider), Zara (a manufacturer and retailer in the fashion sector) and the *Sociedad General de Autores Española* (the Spanish Authors' Association, or SGAE) received awards for the negative consequences of their actions on privacy. Among other concerns, Telefónica received a EUR 420,000 (~USD 512,000) fine for illegally making customer data available, and because of the lack of protection of customer data on its telefonicaonline.com website in June 2004 after a glitch in its computer system. The award given to Zara was a result of its use of identification chips using RFID technology in some of its products.[5004]

[5000] The entry requirements for nationals of third countries requiring visas to enter Spain are: possession of a visa (tourist visas are valid for three months), a return ticket, and a fixed amount of money.

[5001] The foreigner identification number card is the equivalent of a national ID card for foreigners, which carries a fingerprint, compulsory for anyone with a visa or permit to reside in Spain for over six months.
5002 Proyecto de Reglamento de la Ley Orgánica 4/2000, de 11 de enero, sobre derechos y libertades de los extranjeros en España y su integración social, October 2004.

[5003] See Spanish Big Brother Awards website <http://www.es.bigbrotherawards.org:81/en/>.
5004 "La Gran Familia BBA 2004 – Crónica oficiosa," Boletín Enigma, n.28, December 3, 2004, available at <http://www.ugr.es/~aquiran/cripto/enigma/boletin_enigma_28.htm#4>.

In July 2003, in one of Europe's largest crackdown on P2P users, a Spanish law firm announced that they would file a complaint on behalf of 32 software producers and four Spanish industry groups against 4,000 individuals for infringement of the copyright laws by allegedly having swapped files over peer-to-peer networks. Experts disagree as to whether there is an "intent to profit" on users' part since Spanish law only prohibits individuals to share files when profit is sought.[5005] Civil liberties and Internet user groups asserted that they doubted whether the case was valid under Spanish law, calling it "a scare tactic to dampen the use of P2P systems."[5006] By the end of August 2003, the Technological Research Brigade of the National Police denied having received any lawsuit request from the law firm. In January 2005, following a meeting with the SGAE, the Education and Science Minister, María Jesús San Segundo, announced that the LSSI should be reformed to make ISPs responsible for the contents hosted by their customers, as a means of combating P2P file exchange networks and the illegal copying of products such as books, CDs and films.[5007]

International Obligations

Spain is a member of the Council of Europe (CoE) and has signed and ratified the Convention for the Protection of Individuals with Regard to Automatic Processing of Personal Data (Convention No. 108).[5008] It has signed and ratified the European Convention for the Protection of Human Rights and Fundamental Freedoms.[5009] In November 2001, Spain signed the CoE Convention on Cybercrime.[5010] It is a member of the Organization for Economic Cooperation and Development (OECD) and has adopted the OECD Guidelines on the Protection of Privacy and Transborder Flows of Personal Data.

[5005] Julia Scheeres, "Spanish Firms Target File Traders," Wired News, July 23, 2003, available at <http://www.wired.com/news/digiwood/0,1412,59720,00.html>.

[5006] Matthew Broersma & Munir Kotadia, "European Firms Threaten Mass P2P Lawsuit," CNET News.com, August 1, 2003, available at <http://news.com.com/2100-1027-5058666.html>.

[5007] Arturo Quirantes Sierra, "¡A vueltas con la LSSI... Otra vez!," January 29, 2005, available at. <http://www.ugr.es/~aquiran/cripto/tribuna/2005-01-29_lssi2005.htm>.

[5008] Signed January 28, 1982; ratified April 31, 1984; entered into force October 1, 1985.

[5009] Signed November 24, 1977; ratified October 4, 1979; entered into force October 4, 1979.

[5010] Signed November 23, 2001.

Republic of Sri Lanka

Constitutional Privacy Framework

The 1978 Constitution[5011] of the Democratic Socialist Republic of Sri Lanka does not explicitly recognize the right to personal privacy as a basic fundamental right. In 1997 and 2000, the proposed versions of the draft Constitution considered the right to privacy and family life as a fundamental right. The proposed October 1997 Constitution's Article 14 (1) specifically stated, "Every person has the right to have his or her private and family life, home, correspondence and communications respected, and shall not be subjected to unlawful attacks on his or her honour and reputation."[5012]

In Sri Lanka there are two recent cases related to individual privacy, one related to the interception of communications (*Hewamanna v Attorney General*)[5013]; the other related to privacy and freedom of the press (Sunday Times defamation case in 2000). In both cases the Supreme Court of Sri Lanka highlighted the importance of the individual's right to privacy.

The government has not introduced any specific legislation that protects individual privacy or collection of personal information. The only legislation that refers to this area is the Telecommunication Act No. 27 of 1996,[5014] which regulates the interception of communications. According to Section 53 and 54 (1) of this act, the interception of telecommunication transmissions and the disclosure of their contents is an offense subject to penalties, including imprisonment.

The common law in Sri Lanka does not recognize any right to the protection of personal information. It only permits "peripheral protection"[5015] or remedial action for invasions of privacy stemming from the inappropriate use of personal data.

[5011] <http://www.loc.gov/law/guide/srilanka.html>.

[5012] Draft Bill (No. 372) to repeal and replace the Constitution of the Democratic Socialist Republic of Sri Lanka, available at <http://www.priu.gov.lk/cons/2000constitutional Bill/Index2000constitutionalBill.html>.
[5013] 1999 ICHRL 31:8 March 1999.

[5014] <http://www.trc.gov.lk/act2.htm>.

[5015] This means that there is no direct common law protection and the law only covers the cases where there is a breach of confidential information or a liability for invasion of privacy. *See* P. Mahanamahewa, "Internet, e-Business and Privacy Concerns," July 20, 2003 <http://www.sundaytimes.lk/July 20, 2003>.

The rapid developments in information and communications technologies in Sri Lanka have significantly affected the current legal system. Many privacy experts in Sri Lanka state that there is a need for new laws that adequately regulate new technologies.

The absence of a data protection law and a data protection authority in Sri Lanka is a real threat to the recently introduced e-Sri Lanka program.[5016] The e-Sri Lanka program aims to computerize all government departments in the country and facilitate electronic documentary service, as opposed to the traditional government service that still processes everything manually.

The government is currently in the preliminary stages of introducing a new data protection law. Under the e-Government project, the Population Registry and the e-Citizen ID Program are currently being considered to improve the services delivered to citizens.[5017]

In 2003, the Parliament passed the Information and Communication Technology Act No. 27[5018] to provide for the establishment of a national policy on information and communication technology and for the preparation of an action plan. Under this act, the Information and Communication Technology Agency (ICTA) is in charge of the implementation of the national policy in both the public and the private sectors. The agency functions as the single highest body involved in information and communications technology policy to the nation. It also assumes the role of implementing the e-Sri Lanka initiative.[5019]

In October 2004, pursuant to a decision of the Cabinet of Ministers, the ICTA has been specifically mandated and authorized to implement the e-Sri Lanka Project and to recommend to the Cabinet the appropriate regulatory and policy framework required for the development of Information and Communication Technologies (ICTs) in Sri Lanka. The Cabinet's decision is consistent with the ICT Act of 2003, which requires the ICTA to provide consultation and formulate policies for ICTs before the government adopts them.[5020] In November 2004, the ICTA set up a working committee to write the first draft of the ICT policy for the government.[5021] The document was circulated amongst members of the ICTA

[5016] *See* <http://www.esrilanka.lk>.

[5017] *See* <http://www.icta.lk/Insidepages/programmes/Re-engineering_Government1.asp>.

[5018] *See* <http://209.1053.13/Default.asp>.

[5019] *See* <http://209.10.53.13/Inside pages?e-Laws/e-Laws.asp>.

[5020] *See* Draft ICT Policy for the Government, at 3.

[5021] *See* <http://www.icta.lk/Insidepages/programmes/IctPolicyForGovernment.asp>.

working and focus groups, and to academic members, to obtain their views. ICTA has now made the document public and available for comments.[5022] The emphasis is now on adopting legislation to facilitate electronic transactions and to prepare a Code of Practice for Data Protection, in consultation with the private sector. A committee has been set up for this task with the association of the Ceylon Chamber of Commerce. Likewise, an e-Security Working Group has been established, with the participation of state agencies and other stakeholders, to review legal and technical aspects of e-commerce.[5023]

The Draft ICT Policy would require each government agency to appoint a Chief Innovation Officer (CIO). This CIO would be responsible for the promotion and development of ICTs within the agency, and would be the interface between a government agency and other organizations. The implementation of the ICT policy is likely to promote Sri Lanka's objective of being an information society for all. The policy will not be a static document, as the ICTA will frequently update it as required, taking into account changing trends in the environment, the technology and business processes.[5024]

The Draft Policy requires data protection issues to be addressed in accordance with the government's Information Security Policy. Citizens' e-mail addresses gathered from government web sites[5025] will not be divulged, made available or sold to third parties. Also, personally identifiable information obtained through government web sites shall not be kept for longer than is necessary and only for the purpose for which it was obtained.[5026]

In September 2002, the Ministry of Mass Communications proposed a National Communication Policy on the availability of affordable and effective choices of communications for citizens.[5027] Section 6.3 specifically addresses privacy violations by telecommunications operators and service providers. The Telecommunication Regulatory Commission, part of the Ministry of Mass Communications, has set up basic guidelines that should be complied with by

---

[5022] *See* <http://www.icta.lk/Insidepages/downloadDocs/Draft%20ICT%20Policy%20for%20Government.pdf>.
[5023] <http://www.icta.lk/Insidepages/downloadDocs/ICT%20Legal%20Reforms%20-%20Country%20Report.pdf>
[5024] *Id.*, at 12.
[5025] *See, e.g.*, <http://www.pubad.gov.lk>, <http://www.immigration.gov.lk/html/visa/info.html> and <http://www.boi.lk/>.
[5026] *See, id*, 12, Section 0104 and 010401.
[5027] National Communication Policy on Availability of Affordable and Effective Choices of Communications for the Citizens, September 2002, available at <http://www.trc.gov.lk/pdf/ncpn.pdf>.

individuals who want to set up call centers in Sri Lanka.[5028] According to a recent workplace privacy survey, the majority of employees and executive managers are seriously worried about the privacy of their communications in the workplace.[5029]

The Prevention of Computer Crime Bill of 2003[5030] was approved by the Cabinet of Ministers and presented to the Sri Lanka Parliament recently. This act aims at combating computer crime in Sri Lanka.[5031] This act shall apply where: (a) a person commits an offence under this act while being present in Sri Lanka; (b) the computer program, data or information affected or which was to be affected, by the act which constituted an offence under this act, was at the material time within Sri Lanka; (c) the facility or service, including any computer storage or processing or communication facility, used in the commission of an offence under this act was based in Sri Lanka; or (d) loss or damage is caused by the commission of an offence under this act in Sri Lanka to a person resident in Sri Lanka.[5032] The act also addresses computer misuse;[5033] unlawful obtention of data;[5034] child pornography;[5035] cyber-stalking;[5036] strict liability for offences against national security;[5037] national economy and public safety;[5038] and unauthorized disclosure of confidential information and illegal interception of data.[5039] Part 11 of the act creates a panel of experts from police departments and other persons who possess expertise in the field of information technology for the purposes of investigations under the act.

Another bill pending for cabinet approval is the Electronic Transaction bill. This would provide for the legal recognition of electronic transactions and other transactions carried out by means of electronic communications commonly

---

[5028] *See* <http//www.trc.gov.lk/notice_cc.htm>.

[5029] *See* P. Mahanamahewa, "Guidelines for Establishing an E-mail and Internet Monitoring Policy in the Workplace," <http://www.cssl.lk/nitc2005.htm>.

[5030] *See* <http://www.justiceministry.gov.lk>.

[5031] Its most important features are: Section 13, which makes the illegal interception of data an offence; Section 15, which makes the unauthorized disclosure of information enabling access to a service an offence; and Section 23, which provides for the appointment of a panel of experts in the field of information technology for investigation purposes.

[5032] The Prevention of Computer Crime Bill of 2003, Section 2(1).

[5033] *Id.* at Section 7.

[5034] *Id.* at Section 11.

[5035] *Id.* at Section 12.

[5036] Prevention of Computer Crime Bill of 2003, *supra* at Section 14.

[5037] *Id.* at Section 8(a).

[5038] *Id.* at Section 8(b), (c).

[5039] *Id.* at Section 13.

referred to as "electronic commerce."[5040] The act is based on the UNCITRAL Model Law on E-Commerce 1996[5041] and the 2001 UNCITRAL Model Law on Electronic signatures.[5042] On September 22, 2004, the Cabinet of Ministers decided that legislation on electronic transactions should be prepared by the Legal Draftsman's Department in conjunction with the ICTA. As regards the protection of intellectual property rights, the Intellectual Property (IP) Act No. 36 of 2003 replaced the Code of Intellectual Property Act No. 52 of 1979. The new IP Act[5043] contains several new provisions that pertain to the protection of software, trade secrets and integrated circuits.

Open Government

A Freedom of Access to Official Information Bill 2003 is awaiting cabinet approval.[5044]

International Obligations

Sri Lanka became a member of the United Nations Organization on December 14, 1955,[5045] and ratified the International Covenant on Civil and Political Rights (ICCPR) and the International Covenant on Economic, Social and Cultural Rights (ICESCR) in 1980.[5046] Sri Lanka ratified the UN Convention on the Rights of the Child (1991), and the Parliament subsequently enacted the National Child Protection Act No. 50 of 1998.[5047] Sri Lanka also ratified the UN

[5040] *See* S. Marsoof, Legislation for Commerce and Data Protection in Sri Lanka, Information Technology Conference, Bar Association, Colombo, Sri Lanka (2004).

[5041] <http://www.jus.uio.no/lm/un.electroni.commerce.model.law.1996/doc>.

[5042] <http://www.jus.uio.no/lm/un.conventions.membership.status/un.electroni.signature.model.law.2001>.

[5043] <http://www.dailynews.lk/2005/04/19/fea13.htm>.

[5044] <http://www.humanrightsinitiative.org/programs/ai/rti/international/laws_papers/srilanka/foibill-critique-v2-feb04.pdf>.

[5045] <http://www.un.org/overview/unmember.html>.

[5046] <http://www.law.emory.edu/Ifl/legal/srilanka.htm#text>.

[5047] *See* <http://www.childprotection.gov.lk/L1NCPAACT.htm>. Under this Act, the National Child Protection Authority (NCPA) has been established to protect and promote children's rights. The National Child Protection Authority is the Central Agency for coordinating and monitoring action on the protection of children. The NCPA can take appropriate steps where necessary for securing the safety and privacy protection of children involved in criminal investigation and criminal proceedings. On September 8, 2000 Sri Lanka signed and ratified the optional protocol to the Convention on the Rights of the Child on the involvement of children in armed conflicts (<http://sim.law.uu.nl>), and on May 8, 2002 the government of Sri Lanka signed the Optional Protocol to the Convention on the Rights of the Child on the Sale of Children, Child Prostitute and Child Pornography (<http://www.unhchr.ch/html/mennz/6/crctreaties/status.opsc.htm>). The NCPA recently established the "Cyber Watch" Unit, which monitors websites patronized by paedophiles. Its goals are to prevent the use of Sri Lankan children for the purposes of child pornography and other forms of commercial sexual exploitation. (*See* <http://www.childprotection.gov.lk/pdfs/200203/Annual/Rep.pdf>).

Convention on the Elimination of All Forms of Discrimination Against Women (1981).[5048] Sri Lanka became a member of the International Labour Organization (ILO) in 1948 and has since ratified 39 ILO Conventions.[5049]

Kingdom of Sweden

Constitutional Privacy Framework

Sweden's Constitution[5050] consists of four fundamental laws: the Instrument of Government, the Act of Succession, the Freedom of the Press Act, and the Fundamental Law on Freedom of Expression. These laws serve as a basis for the Swedish political decision-making and contain several provisions relevant to data protection and citizens' freedoms and rights. For example, Section 2 of the Instrument of Government Act of 1974[5051] provides for the protection of individual privacy. Section 13 of Chapter 2 of the same instrument also states that freedom of expression and information – which are constitutionally protected pursuant to the Freedom of the Press Act of 1949[5052] – can be limited with respect to the "sanctity of private life." Moreover, Section 3 of the same chapter provides for a right to protection of personal integrity (privacy) in relation to automatic data processing. The same article also prohibits non-consensual registration of persons purely on the basis of their political opinion. The European Convention on Human Rights (ECHR) has been incorporated into Swedish law in 1994. The ECHR is not formally part of the Swedish Constitution but has, in effect, similar status.

Data Protection Framework

The Swedish Personal Data Act (PDA) or *personuppgiftslagen* (PUL) was enacted in 1998 to bring Swedish law into conformity with the requirements of the European Union (EU) Data Protection Directive (95/46/EC).[5053] The PDA essentially incorporates the EU Data Protection Directive into Swedish law. It

---

[5048] *See* <http://www.womens-affair.gov.lk>WWW.womens-affair.gov.lk>.

[5049] *See* <http;//www.labour.gov.lk/documents/f_rectify.htm>.

[5050] Swedish Constitution, English version available at <http://www.riksdagen.se/english/work/constitution.asp>.

[5051] *Regeringsformen*, SFS 1974:152.

[5052] *Tryckfrihetsförordningen*, SFS 1949:105.

[5053] *Personuppgiftslagen*, SFS 1998:204, English version available at <http://www.sweden.gov.se/sb/d/3288/a/19577>.

regulates the establishment and use, in both public and private sectors, of automated data files on physical/natural persons. The Act replaced the Data Act of 1973, which was the first comprehensive national act on privacy in the world.[5054] The 1973 Act continued to apply until October 2001 with respect to processing of personal data initiated prior to October 24, 1998. An extended transition period, up to 2007, is allowed for pre-existing manual files. An amendment of Section 33 of the Act entered into force in January 2000 in order to align even closer to the EU Data Protection Directive standards on the transfer of personal data to third countries.

Besides the PDA, there is also specific legislation regarding processing of personal data in different specified sectors. Some examples include the Health Care Register Act of 1998,[5055] the Police Data Act of 1998,[5056] the Land Register Act of 2000,[5057] the Schengen Information System Act of 2000,[5058] and the Act on processing of personal data within Social Services of 2001.[5059] Other statutes with provisions relating to data protection include the Secrecy Act of 1980,[5060] the Credit Information Act of 1973,[5061] the Debt Recovery Act of 1974,[5062] and the Administrative Procedure Act of 1986.[5063] In sectors that fall within the scope of the EU Data Protection Directive, the specific legislation takes into account the Directive's rules.[5064]

The PDA provides liberal exemptions for freedom of expression. It specifically states that in the case of a conflict, the existing protections for freedom of the press (Freedom of the Press Act)[5065] and freedom of speech (Freedom of Expression Act)[5066] will prevail. The majority of the provisions in the PDA are also exempted in regard to processing that is carried out exclusively for journalistic purposes, or artistic or literary expression. In 2001, the Swedish Supreme Court ruled that the operator of a Web site dedicated to the criticism of

---

[5054] *Datalagen,* SFS 1973:289.

[5055] SFS 1998:544.

[5056] SFS 1998:622.

[5057] SFS 2000:224.

[5058] SFS 2000:344.

[5059] SFS 2001:454

[5060] SFS 1980:100.

[5061] SFS 1973:1173.

[5062] SFS 1974:182.

[5063] SFS 1986:223.

[5064] *See* for example the Health Care Register Act of 1998 and the Credit Information Act of 1973.

[5065] SFS1949:105, available at <http://www.riksdagen.se/english/work/constitution.asp>.

[5066] SFS 1991:1469 and 2002:209, available at <http://www.riksdagen.se/english/work/constitution.asp>.

several Swedish banks and bank officials did not violate the PDA, as he was protected by the exemptions for journalistic purposes.[5067] In another case, where a church volunteer had published information about church employees on the Internet without their consent, the Göta Court of Appeal decided in 2004 that this was not a matter of processing for journalistic purposes, or artistic or literary expression.[5068] The Court found that, in this case, the right to privacy outweighed the freedom of expression and the processing conflicted with several provisions in the PDA. However, due to the circumstances in this case, it was not to be seen as a serious offense, and the church volunteer was not convicted. The Court of Appeal's decision did not include the question of whether publication on the Internet means that data has been transferred to a third country. The charges in this respect had been withdrawn following a decision by the EC Court of Justice.[5069]

In 2002, the Parliament adopted new rules on voluntary publishing licenses.[5070] The rules on freedom of the press and freedom of expression apply to printed publications, radio and television, films, etc., and do not – in principle – apply to the Internet. With the new rules, anyone may apply for and obtain such a license, and thereby extend the rules on freedom of the press and expression to their Web site. This means that the keeper of a Web site who has obtained a publishing license will be able to process personal data without having to comply with the provisions in the PDA.[5071] Specific privacy problems have occurred in this context regarding publication of credit information and phone directories on the Internet. Following remarks from the data protection authority, a specific inquiry has been set up within the Ministry of Justice to analyze whether the new legislation conflicts with provisions that aim at protecting privacy.[5072] The problem regarding phone directories has been commented in a report by the National Post and Telecom Agency, who said that the new legislation might be in conflict with the EU Directive on Privacy and Electronic Communications.[5073]

[5067] Supreme Court, June 12 2001, *see* Nytt Juridiskt Arkiv (NJA) 2001 at 409, available at <http://www.rattsinfosok.dom.se/lagrummet/index.jsp> (in Swedish).

[5068] Göta Court of Appeal, April 7 2004, case B 747-00.

[5069] EC Court of Justice, November 6, 2003, case C-101/01, available at <http://curia.eu.int/en/transitpage.htm>.

[5070] Chapter 1, section 9 of The Fundamental Law on Freedom of Expression, SFS 1991:1469 and 2002:209, available at <http://www.riksdagen.se/english/work/constitution.asp>.

[5071] The Swedish Radio and TV Authority <http://www.rtvv.se/uk/Swedish_Radio_and_TV_Authority>.

[5072] Ministry of Justice (JU) nr 2003:04, *see* terms of reference 2003:58, available in Swedish at <http://www.riksdagen.se/debatt/dir/index.asp>.

[5073] EC Directive 2002/58 of July 12, 2002, concerning the processing of personal data and the protection of privacy in the electronic communications sector, OJ L 201, 31.7.2002, p. 37.

The agency recommended that this conflict also be examined in the Ministry of Justice inquiry.[5074]

The PDA, and the EU Data Protection Directive on which it is based, has been criticized for being too restrictive. For instance, the PDA currently includes within its definition of "data processing," applications such as word processing, Web publishing, and e-mail. Sweden thus submitted a proposal to the EU on amending the Directive to adopt a "misuse model."[5075] This model separates data processing into two categories: one including applications not structured to facilitate retrieval of personal data (such as word processing and e-mail); and the other including databases and other data structures created for easy retrieval of data. Processing of information within the first category would only be punished if it resulted in harm to the data subject, while processing of information in the second category would be subject to the current protections.[5076] The Swedish "misuse model" aims to concentrate more on the prevention of misuse or abuse of personal data than on the everyday processing of such personal data. The proposal did not lead to an amendment of the EU Data Protection Directive.

The Ministry of Justice also began an inquiry to determine how the misuse model could be applied to the PDA within the requirements of the EU Data Protection Directive.[5077] The report in February 2004 proposed that the processing of personal data in unstructured material, such as continuous text, sound and images, be exempt from the great majority of handling regulations in the PDA. The proposal means that the handling regulations in the PDA would not be applicable, *i.a.,* to everyday processing like production of continuous text in word processing software, publication of such text on the Internet, and e-mail correspondence – on condition that the material is not intended to be included in a database with a personal data-related structure. Instead, the exempt processing operations would be regulated by one simple rule designed to provide protection from the misuse of personal data, *i.e.,* processing would not be permitted if it involves an improper intrusion on privacy. Also, the right of access for the registered person would be maintained with some exceptions. The report is under consideration of the Ministry of Justice.

[5074] See the Report on a Swedish strategy to secure Internet infrastructure, by the National Post and Telecom Agency, page 51 (PTS-ER-2005:7), available in English at
<http://www.pts.se/Dokument/dokumentlista.asp?SectionId=2253>.

[5075] Ministry of Justice, "Misuse Model", available at <http://www.sweden.gov.se/sb/d/2771/a/15554>.
27 *Datalagen*, SFS 1973:289.

[5077] Review of the PDA, Översyn av personuppgiftslagen, Swedish governmental investigation SOU 2004:6', an English summary is available at <http://www.regeringen.se/sb/d/108/a/2673>.

The EU Directive on privacy and electronic communications (2002/58/EC) was essentially implemented in July 2003 by the entry into force of the Electronic Communications Act (ECA).[5078] The provision on unsolicited e-mail in this Directive was implemented in April 2004 when the Swedish Marketing Act was amended to reflect the Directive in this respect.[5079] As a result of this amendment, direct marketing by e-mail now requires prior consent. The National Post and Telecom Agency is in charge of supervising compliance with the Electronic Communications Act.[5080] Monitoring of the Marketing Act, including the provisions on unsolicited e-mail, falls under the scope of the Swedish Consumer Agency.[5081]

The provisions on privacy in publicly available electronic communications services are found in Chapter 6 of the ECA. This includes provisions on security in public communications networks, processing of traffic and location data, cookies, public directories, etc. The Personal Data Act of 1998 applies to processing of personal data in electronic communications networks and services to the extent that the ECA does not stipulate otherwise. The National Post and Telecom Agency recently published a report describing spyware functions that Internet users – usually unknowingly – download or in other ways are affected by and which may violate the privacy of the user.[5082] The report provides security tips on how Internet users can protect themselves. Further to an assignment by the Government, the Agency has in another report proposed a strategy to improve the security of the Internet in Sweden and to enhance the protection within critical Internet functions against manipulated information.[5083] The Agency has *i.a.* emphasized the importance of enhancing the level of user knowledge and awareness about security on the Internet.

Data Protection Authority

Compliance with the PDA is monitored by the Data Inspection Board (DIB), *Datainspektionen.* The DIB is a central government agency and carries out its functions independently. As of April 2005 the DIB has 39 employees.[5084] The

---

[5078] SFS 2003:389.

[5079] SFS 1995:450, § 13b.

[5080] Homepage <http://www.pts.se>.

[5081] Homepage <http://www.konsumentverket.se>.

[5082] *See* the report on Spyware and closely related phenomena, by the National Post and Telecom Agency, (PTS-ER-2005:15), available in English at <http://www.pts.se/Dokument/dokumentlista.asp?SectionId=2253>.

[5083] Report PTS-ER-2005:7, *supra.*

[5084] Homepage <http://www.datainspektionen.se>.

agency handles complaints from individuals concerning processing of personal data. From June 1, 2004 to April 30, 2005, the DIB handled 380 complaints about personal data processing. The DIB has discretion to decide which complaints to pursue, but complainants always receive a response as to whether an investigation is initiated, and the outcome of any investigation.[5085] The DIB also carries out investigations on its own initiative. From June 1, 2004 to April 30, 2005, the DIB conducted 52 field inspections, 127 inspections via questionnaires, and 95 more limited inquiries via telephone and mail. The agency also focuses on pro-active work such as information and regulatory activities.[5086]

The PDA requires that automated processing of personal data be notified to the DIB.[5087] As of April 30, 2005, 2,624 processing operations were notified and included in the agency's register. Several exemptions from the notification duty apply, for example, if an entity appoints a personal data representative. As of April 2005, there are 3,342 personal data representatives registered with the DIB. Some processing operations that are likely to involve particular risks for improper intrusion of privacy must be notified for prior checking.[5088] From June 1, 2004 to April 30, 2005, 117 such processing operations were notified to the DIB. These notifications primarily concerned processing of personal data in research activity.

Initiatives have also been taken to use biometric data outside the government authority sector. In 2004 and 2005, the DIB handled several requests from schools regarding the use of fingerprint-recognition devices for allowing access to school canteens. The DIB said that processing of biometric data for this purpose was not compatible with the necessity and proportionality principles prescribed by the PDA and the EU Data Protection Directive. The fact that consent would be obtained from the students or their parents did not change this view. The County Administrative Court in Stockholm has confirmed some of the DIB's decisions in this respect – other appeals are still pending.[5089]

[5085] *Id.*

[5086] E-mail from Elisabeth Wallin, Data Inspection Board, to Ula Galster, International Policy Fellow, Electronic Privacy Information Center, May 1, 2005 (on file with EPIC).

[5087] SFS 1998:204, § 36.

[5088] SFS 1998:204, § 41.

[5089] *See* the DIB's file on biometrics, available at <http://www.datainspektionen.se/temasidor/biometri.shtml>.

With regard to privacy in the health and medical sector, the use of information technology has increased. While information technology can facilitate documentation of health and medical care, and contribute to using resources more efficiently, it also involves new challenges in terms of privacy and data protection. The National Board of Health and Welfare has proposed in a report that the Act on Patients' records should explicitly allow that one comprehensive record is kept for each patient.[5090] The Board has said that using one record covering all occasions when a patient has sought medical care at different care providers would even further reduce the time spent on documentation of medical treatment. Moreover, the Board has said that this requires that obstacles in terms of secrecy do not exist and that possibilities are given to jointly process personal data. The DIB has pointed to several problems that this proposal poses from both a secrecy perspective and a privacy point of view.[5091]

Personal data processing in the health and medical sector is currently regulated by the Health Care Register Act of 1998 and the Patients' Records Act of 1985. In 2004, an inquiry with the task to review personal data processing in health and medical care for quality evaluation purposes was also given the task to review personal data processing in health and medical care in general.[5092] The inquiry shall, in particular, examine issues relating to electronic patients' records, the exchange of information between different medical care providers and how the individual patient can be given access to information about him or her via the Internet. In this analysis, the inquiry is instructed to find the balance between privacy on one hand and the advantages for society and patients' security on the other hand. The Government Offices are also analyzing the handling of patients' records and other information about individuals' health within insurance companies.[5093]

A related question was answered by the DIB in February 2005. A county council in Sweden had decided to create a joint patients' records system where all medical staff (doctors and nurses) within the county could access all information. However, certain sensitive data could be blocked. Considering the Health Care Register Act, which states that access to information in health care registers

---

[5090] Referred to in terms of reference nr 2004:95, by the Ministry of Health and Social Affairs, available in Swedish at <http://www.riksdagen.se/debatt/dir/index.asp>.

[5091] The Data Inspection Board's opinion of September 5, 2002, case 991-2002, available at <http://www.datainspektionen.se/infobestall/infomaterial/remissvar.jsp>.

[5092] *See* terms of reference nr 2004:95, *supra*.

[5093] *Id.*

should be reserved for those who need the information in their work, the DIB took the view that the county council's rules on access were much broader than the legislation intended. The Board required the county council to provide rules for access to patients' records that clearly take into account what is required for the staff members to be able to carry out their work.[5094]

In 1999, the Swedish government established a Committee to study workplace privacy issues. In March 2002, the Committee issued a proposal recommending specific legislation to protect the personal information of current and former employees, and employment applicants in both the private and public sectors.[5095] The proposal has not led to legislation.

Recently, the question of collecting and storing DNA information about all Swedish citizens has been subject to public debate. In June 2004, proposals were made to widen the scope of DNA use in law enforcement.[5096] According to current legislation, DNA samples fall under the rules in Chapter 28 of the Code of Judicial Procedure and rules in the Police Data Act of 1998. The inquiry tasked with reviewing the current legislation suggested introducing specific rules regarding DNA samples in law enforcement and allowing such samples to be taken from persons who are arrested, taken into custody, or suspected of crimes that can lead to imprisonment, but also from other persons if it is required in the investigation of such crimes. According to the inquiry's report, results from DNA analyses should be put into the DNA register kept by the National Police Board regarding persons who are suspected of, or sentenced for, crimes where the penalty includes imprisonment. The current rules on the DNA register only allows registration of those who have been convicted of a crime that involves a penalty of more than two years' imprisonment. According to Section 24 of the Police Data Act, registration must be limited to such data that provides information about identity – other DNA information must not be registered. The inquiry suggested that information in the register should be deleted when the preliminary investigation is withdrawn or when charges against the individual in question have been withdrawn or rejected. Information regarding persons who have been convicted should continue to be retained until the person is deleted

---

[5094] Decision of the Data Inspection Board of February 22, 2005, case 1459-2004, available in Swedish at <http://www.datainspektionen.se/nyhetsarkiv/nyheter/2005/februari/2005-02-23.shtml>.

[5095] "Sweden Concerns over Employer Monitoring," BNA World Data Protection Report, Volume 2, Issue 4, April 2002. The proposal is available at <http://naring.regeringen.se/propositioner_mm/sou/pdf/sou2002_18a.pdf> (in Swedish with summary in English).

[5096] Ministry publications series 2004:35, *Genetiska fingeravtryck*, July 7 2004, Ministry of Justice, available in Swedish at <http://www.regeringen.se/sb/d/108/a/27189>.

from the register of convicted persons in accordance with the specific rules in the Act of 1998.

The right to privacy has been subject to discussion in Sweden since the 1960s. In recent years, new attention has been drawn to this question. This discussion has concerned in particular the balance between privacy and efficient law enforcement, and also privacy in relation to information technology in general. In April 2004, the Ministry of Justice set up an inquiry with the task to analyze legislation related to privacy to see if this legislation adequately protects privacy. The inquiry shall analyze the relationship between existing coercive measures and surveillance methods, and the protection of privacy. It shall also examine whether the constitutional provision on the right to privacy in relation to automated personal data processing, in Chapter 2, Section 3, of the Instrument of Government, needs to be amended so as to have the same legal implication as the provisions on other constitutional rights and freedoms. The inquiry consists of members of Parliament and privacy experts and shall present their results by the end of March 2007.[5097]

ID Cards and Travel Documents

Sweden is implementing Council Regulation No. 2252/2004 on Standards for Security Features and Biometrics in Passports and Travel Documents Issued by Member States. The new biometric passports, based on the International Civil Aviation Organizations (ICAO)[5098] specifications, will be introduced in Sweden on October 1, 2005. The passport will contain a digital facial image that will be stored in a chip included in the passport.[5099] The biometric data that can be retrieved from the facial image are to be destroyed immediately after the delivery of the passport to the applicant or after a passport check. No other kinds of data than those already registered will be entered into the centralized register of passports.[5100]

Identification of individuals within public administration is based on the system of national identification numbers. Such numbers have been used in Sweden since the 1940s. Since 1994, the data protection legislation includes restrictions

---

[5097] Terms of reference 2004:51, the Ministry of Justice, available at <http://www.riksdagen.se/debatt/dir/index.asp>.

[5098] See <http://www.icao.org>.

[5099] See <http://www.polisen.se/inter/nodeid=33591&pageversion=1.html>.

[5100] See fact sheet from the Ministry of Justice, (Ju 05.04) March 2005, available in Swedish at <http://www.regeringen.se/content/1/c6/04/02/02/aa286ad5.pdf>.

on the use of identification numbers. Under Section 22 of the PDA, national identification numbers may only be processed without consent if the processing is clearly justified with regard to the purpose of the processing, the importance of secure identification, or some other substantial reason.

Plans are made to introduce national ID cards. This card will include information about nationality and will also contain a chip for storage of electronic certificates, which enables the cardholder to fill in tax-return forms or sign payments via the Internet. Swedish citizens traveling in the Schengen area will also be able to use an ID card instead of a passport to prove their nationality. The national ID card will not be mandatory.[5101]

Wiretapping and Surveillance Rules

The 1998 Act on General Video Surveillance restricts the use of such surveillance.[5102] In principle, video surveillance in places to which the public has access requires a permit from the County Administrative Board. In certain situations, it is sufficient to notify the County Administrative Board about the surveillance. The notification duty applies to post offices, banks, and stores where the surveillance only covers entrances, exits, and cash points. In a few other situations neither a permit nor notification is required. In all cases, the Act requires that clearly visible notices about the video surveillance are posted. Penalties for breach of the law include fines or a maximum imprisonment of one year. The Act has been subject to review by an inquiry that presented its report in November 2002.[5103]

Secret camera surveillance, wire surveillance and wiretapping require a court order according to the specific Act on secret camera surveillance[5104] and to Chapter 27 of the Code of Judicial Procedure. A specific Act of 1952 widens the scope for using these measures if specific risks for national security are involved.[5105] In 2003, the scope of the 1952 Act was extended to terrorist crimes referred to in the legislation that implements the EU Framework decision of June 13, 2002, on combating terrorism (2002/475/JHA).[5106] The limited period of

---

[5101] *See* <http://www.polisen.se/inter/nodeid=33595&pageversion=1.html>.

[5102] SFS 1998:150.

[5103] Swedish Government Official reports (SOU) 2002:110, *Allmän kameraövervakning*, Ministry of Justice, available at <http://www.regeringen.se/sb/d/108/a/437>.

[5104] SFS 1995:1506.

[5105] SFS 1952:98.

[5106] Section 1 amended by SFS 2003:151.

validity of the 1952 Act and of the 1995 Act on secret camera surveillance has been prolonged numerous times and both Acts now apply until the end of 2007.[5107] The Government has submitted a report to Parliament every year with details of all of electronic surveillance conducted. According to the 2003 government report[5108] to the Parliament, the use of secret surveillance increased "considerably" in 2002.[5109] Only two wiretapping requests were turned down by courts, and 533 were permitted, many for drug-related investigations. In addition, hundreds of demands for wire surveillance were permitted, along with 33 demands for camera surveillance. The Swedish Helsinki Committee (SHC), a non-governmental organization that monitors human rights compliance with the Helsinki agreement of 1975, has concluded that the state authorities' right to interfere in the private life of citizens, as allowed in certain instances by Swedish law, continued to lack both the necessary legality and transparency.[5110] The SHC has called for an independent assessment of the necessity and effectiveness of secret surveillance methods used in Sweden. However, in connection to the prolongation of the legislation,[5111] the Government stated that combating crimes related to national security have been given increased priority and that secret camera surveillance, wire surveillance, and wiretapping are all efficient tools for investigating terrorist and other serious crimes. The Government said there were good reasons for making the 1952 Act and the Act on secret camera surveillance permanently applicable, but for now settled for yet another prolongation.

In March 2005, the Ministry of Justice presented a bill to Parliament concerning surplus information, derived from the use of secret surveillance.[5112] Secret surveillance may result in information that does not relate to the crime on which the decision to initiate surveillance is based. This information may nevertheless be relevant in the investigation of other crimes, according to the Ministry. The right to use surplus information in other crimes is currently not regulated in Swedish law. According to the Ministry's proposal, such information ought to be made available for use also in the investigation of crimes other than those causing the secret surveillance. Restrictions are proposed for less serious offenses. The Ministry also suggested that surplus information about planned

---

[5107] SFS 2004:617.

[5108] Government report to the Parliament in November 2003 (*Regeringens skrivelse* 2003/2004:36) (reporting on 2002 figures); available upon request at <ordermottagningen@riksdagen.se>.

[5109] International Helsinki Federation for Human Rights, Human Rights in the OSCE Region: The Balkans, the Caucasus, Europe, Central Asia and North America, Report 2004 (events 2003), available at <http://www.ihf-hr.org/documents/doc_summary.php?sec_id=3&d_id=3860>.

[5110] International Helsinki Federation for Human Rights (IHF) Annual report 2004, available at <http://www.ihf-hr.org/documents/doc_summary.php?sec_id=3&d_id=3860>.

[5111] Government bill 2003/04:74, at 8-9.

[5112] Government bill 2004/05:143.

criminal activity should be made available in order to prevent crime. The Government bill is expected to be discussed in Parliament in June 2005.[5113]

Internal security is the responsibility of the Security Police, also known as National Security (Intelligence) Service or SÄPO, an independent agency under the overall control of the National Police Board. Oversight is conducted by the Register Board, which was established in 1996.[5114]

On the EU level, Sweden and a few other countries came forward with a proposal for new EU Framework rules on mandatory retention of traffic data in 2004. The proposal aims at harmonizing the rules on retention of traffic data throughout the EU in order to facilitate judicial cooperation in criminal matters. All traffic data generated in publicly available electronic communications, such as telephony or the Internet, would have to be retained by service providers for law enforcement purposes. The data would have to be kept for a minimum period of one year and a maximum period of three years.[5115] The proposal has been criticized from a privacy and fundamental rights point of view, and also from service providers because of its cost and lack of efficiency.[5116]

Sweden has also in 2004 laid a proposal for new EU Framework rules on exchange of information between law enforcement authorities.[5117] The proposal would require law enforcement authorities in EU Member States to supply certain information and intelligence to such authorities in other EU Member States, upon request, for the purpose of investigating crimes, particularly serious offenses and terrorist acts. This proposal has been criticized by privacy groups as being too broad and going far beyond the relatively narrow range of offenses covered by other EU instruments, such as the Europol Convention.[5118]

[5113] *See* the Parliaments website:
http://www4.riksdagen.se/debatt/dokstatus.aspx?doktyp=betankande&bet=2004/05:JuU28

[5114] Iain Cameron & Dennis Töllborg, Internal Security in Sweden, in J.P. Brodeur, P. Gill & D. Töllborg (eds), Democracy, Law and Security: Internal Security Services in Contemporary Europe (Ashgate 2002).

[5115] Draft Framework decision on the retention of data processed and stored in connection with the provision of publicly available electronic communications services etc. (8958/04), the Council of the European union, available at <http://register.consilium.eu.int/pdf/en/04/st08/st08958.en04.pdf>.

[5116] Fact sheet from the Government Offices, 2004/05:FPM23, available in Swedish at <http://www.riksdagen.se/debatt/faktapm/fpm.asp?dok_id=GS0623>'; Article 29 Working Party Opinion 9/2004, WP 99 available at <http://europa.eu.int/comm/internal_market/privacy/workinggroup/wp2004/wpdocs04_en.htm>.

[5117] Draft Framework decision on simplifying the exchange of information and intelligence between law enforcement authorities of the Member States of the European Union, in particular as regards serious offences including terrorist acts (10215/04), the Council of the European Union, available at <http://register.consilium.eu.int/pdf/en/04/st10/st10215.en04.pdf>.

[5118] Council Act of July 26, 1995, drawing up the Convention based on Article K.3 of the Treaty on European Union, on the establishment of a European Police Office (Europol Convention), OJ C 316, 27.11.1995, p. 1.

Miscellaneous Developments Related to Privacy

In June 2003, the Ministry of Finance appointed a delegation, the 24/7 Agency Delegation, to stimulate the development and use of electronic services in the public sector.[5119] The Ministry declared that the public sector should be exemplary as an active user of information and communication technology (ICT) in its own activities and in collaboration with businesses and the public. This development has, according to the Ministry, gained momentum and, in several ways, brought about simplifications and improvements for Swedish citizens in their dealings with public agencies. Registering and deregistering vehicles, applying for jobs, submitting income-tax declarations, and requesting temporary parental benefit were mentioned as examples of public services available through ICT.

To realize the full potential of government e-services in terms of efficiency and quality, co-ordination was considered necessary. The Government thus appointed the Government Interoperability Board (GIB), *e-nämnden*.[5120] According to the board, the use of ICT in e-government requires that adequate trust be established in the relationships among public administration and citizens and companies. Authorities that cooperate must rely on each other in terms of access to and exchange of information. Citizens and companies must trust the way in which public administration provides electronic services and protects privacy. The GIB has proposed directions and guidelines on how information security work shall be conducted within public administration with regard to electronic information exchange with other agencies or with citizens and companies.[5121]

In order to facilitate the identification of victims of the tsunami in Asia in December 2004, the Parliament decided in January 2005 to allow information from the Swedish PKU-register[5122] to be used for identification purposes in the case of accidents or other occurrences involving multiple deaths.[5123] The PKU-register contains information about blood samples that have been routinely collected from newborn babies in Sweden since 1975. The information is referable to each individual. The PKU-register is regulated by the Biobanks in

---

[5119] Terms of reference nr 2003:81, available in English at <http://www.24sju.se/index.php?dir=25>.

[5120] Web site in English available at <http://www.e-namnden.se/enamnden/templates/Page____492.aspx>.

[5121] *Id.*

[5122] A register kept by Huddinge hospital used mainly for screening for certain metabolic diseases such as phenylketonuria (PKU).

5123 See press release from the Swedish Parliament on January 7, 2005, available at <http://www.riksdagen.se/english/work/press/200405/pku.asp>.

Medical Care Act of 2002[5124] and the information may only be used for research purposes. The decision to extend the purpose to identification is limited in time and applies until the end of June 2006.

Anti-terrorism Measures

In 2002, the Swedish Parliament approved two anti-terrorism laws in order to implement the UN Convention on the Suppression of the Financing of Terrorism[5125] and the Framework Decision of the European Union Council on Combating Terrorism.[5126] The Act on Criminal Responsibility for Terrorist Crimes entered into force in July 2003 and classifies certain crimes – such as murder or kidnapping – as terrorist acts when committed against countries, their institutions or their citizens with the aim of intimidating, altering or destroying political, economic or social structures.[5127] Strict punishments apply. The SHC noted, in addressing an appeal to the Swedish Government, that the definition of terrorist crimes in the Act is unclear, and that neither the Act nor the EU Decision addresses the issue of how to draw the line between politically motivated violence and terrorism.[5128] In July 2003, the Parliament also adopted an Act on surrender from Sweden[5129] in accordance with the European Union Council Framework Decision of June 13, 2002, on the European arrest warrant (2002/584/JHA).[5130] The Act came into force in January 2004. At the same time, a new Act on Joint Investigation Teams for Criminal Investigations came into force.[5131] The Act applies to joint investigation teams for criminal investigations set up between authorities in Sweden and those in one or more EU Member States. The Act implements the European Union Council Framework decision of June 13, 2002, on joint investigation teams 82002/465/JHA).[5132] The Act contains rules on, for example, conditions for the use of information received through a joint investigation team.[5133]

[5124] SFS 2002:297.

[5125] *See* <http://untreaty.un.org/English/Terrorism.asp>.

[5126] Council Framework Decision of June 13, 2002, on combating terrorism, EU Official Journal L 164, June 22, 2002, at 3-7 <http://europa.eu.int/eur-lex/en/search/search_lif.html>.

[5127] SFS 2003:148.

[5128] International Helsinki Federation for Human Rights (IHF) Annual report 2004, *supra*.

[5129] SFS 2003:1156, available in English at <http://www.sweden.gov.se/sb/d/3288/a/19568>.

[5130] EU Official Journal L 190, July 18, 2002, page 1-20, <http://europa.eu.int/eur-lex/en/search/search_lif.html>.

[5131] SFS 2003:1174, available in English at <http://www.sweden.gov.se/sb/d/3288/a/19568>.

[5132] EU Official Journal L 162, June 20, 2002, page 1-3, <http://europa.eu.int/eur-lex/en/search/search_lif.html>.

[5133] See sections 5 – 7 of the Act 2003:1174.

Voting Privacy

Voting is open to those age 18 and older but is not mandatory.[5134] National elections are managed by the Swedish Election Authority or *Valmyndigheten,* which was established in July 2001.[5135] The Election Authority is responsible for all voting material from voter registration cards to paper ballots, including development of and support for the information technology systems used during the election process. The Election Authority keeps a register with voter registration information for the purpose of producing voter registration cards.[5136] Voter registration information is also kept in secured files at the Central Bureau of Statistics.[5137] Voting can take place by mail or by going to a local post office. Post offices when used as polling locations are available from 18 days before the election and on Election Day. Voting at post offices has grown in popularity among voters. At this time other public locations such as libraries are being explored as possible alternative poll locations. Voting secrecy is highly valued. Ballots are cast on paper ballots that are placed in envelopes, which are then given to a poll official to place in the appropriate ballot box. Citizens are free to observe all polling and vote counting.

The Swedish government established the Election Authority to achieve best practices in the administration of elections. This system has a high level of trust in the process and the organization of elections. The Election Authority project that the first Internet Voting may occur around the year 2010.

Open Government

Sweden is a country that has traditionally adhered to the Nordic tradition of open access to government files. The world's first freedom of information act was the *Riksdag's* (Swedish Parliament's) Freedom of the Press Act of 1766. The Act required that official documents should "upon request immediately be made available to anyone making a request" at no charge. The Freedom of the Press Act is now part of the Constitution and provides that "every Swedish citizen shall have free access to official documents." Restrictions in several situations are stipulated in the Secrecy Act.[5138] Decisions by public authorities to deny access

---

[5134] CIA Country Fact Book, January 1, 2004, available at <http://www.cia.gov/cia/publications/factbook/>.

[5135] Homepage <http://www.val.se>.

[5136] SFS 2001:183.

[5137] European Commission CyberVote Report (IST-1999-20338), available at <http://www.eucybervote.org/MSI-WP6-D21-v1.0.pdf>.

[5138] SFS 1980:100.

to official documents may be appealed to general administrative courts and, ultimately, to the Supreme Administrative Court. The Parliamentary Ombudsman has some oversight functions for freedom of information.

International Obligations

Sweden is a member of the Council of Europe and has signed and ratified the Convention for the Protection of Individuals with Regard to Automatic Processing of Personal Data (ETS No. 108).[5139] It has also signed and ratified the European Convention for the Protection of Human Rights and Fundamental Freedoms.[5140] In November 2001, Sweden signed, but has not ratified, the Council of Europe Convention on Cybercrime (ETS No. 185).[5141] An additional protocol to the Convention concerning the criminalization of acts of a racist and xenophobic nature committed through computer systems was signed on January 28, 2003. The Swedish Parliament also decided in October 2004 to approve an EU Framework decision on attacks against information systems.[5142] Sweden is a member of the Organization for Economic Cooperation and Development (OECD) and has adopted the OECD Guidelines on the Protection of Privacy and Transborder Flows of Personal Data.

Swiss Confederation (Switzerland)

Constitutional Privacy Framework

Article 36(4) of the 1874 Constitution guaranteed, "[t]he inviolability of the secrecy of letters and telegrams." This constitution was repealed and replaced by public referendum in April 1999. The new constitution, which entered into force on January 1, 2000, greatly expanded the older privacy protection provision. Article 13 of the new constitution states: "All persons have the right to the respect of their private and family life, home, mail and telecommunications. All persons have the right to be protected against abuse of their personal data."[5143]

[5139] Signed January 28, 1981; ratified September 29, 1982; entered into force October 1, 1985.

[5140] Signed November 28, 1950; ratified February 4, 1952; entered into force September 3, 1953.

[5141] Signed November 23, 2001.

[5142] *See* Government bill 2003/04:164 and the Swedish Parliament's Web site <http://www4.riksdagen.se/debatt/dokstatus.aspx?doktyp=betankande&bet=2004/05:JuU4>.

[5143] *Constitution of Switzerland*, 1999, "Bundesverfassung der Schweizerischen Eidgenossenschaft vom 18. April 1999" (BV, SR 101), <http://www.admin.ch/ch/d/sr/c101.html>. In addition to the Constitution, every federal law and regulation is available in an online directory. In this report, we generally link to the German versions ("*Systematische Rechtssammlung*" SR: <http://www.admin.ch/ch/d/sr/sr.html>). However, there are

Data Protection Framework

The Federal Data Protection Act of 1992 (*Loi fédérale sur la protection des données* or LPD) regulates personal information held by federal government and private bodies.[5144] The act requires that information be legally and fairly collected and places limits on its use and disclosure to third parties. Federal agencies must register their databases. Private companies must register if they regularly process sensitive data or transfer the data to third parties. Transfers to other nations must be registered and the recipient nation must have adequate data protection laws. Individuals have a right of access to correct inaccurate information. There are criminal penalties for violations.

Almost each of the 26 Swiss Cantons (states) has a separate data protection law and its own data protection commissioner. However, as some cantons are small, some data protection commissioners are employed only by 10 percent of their working time for this purpose. In order to exchange opinions and collaborate, the cantonal data protection officers founded the association "DSB+CPD.CH" in March 2000. In 2003-2004, the association published a critical opinion on the EPID project (see below), and in June 2004, a detailed list of web resources on computer security and "safer surfing."[5145]

To date, the Federal Parliament is discussing a revision of the Data Protection Act, which in some parts provides better regulations, while at the same time proposing a major change in a new Article 17a. This article would federal authorities to create new databanks and to process personal data without previous regulation by the law, "if major public interest does not allow a postponement of data processing or if a testing phase is required." In these cases, the government only has to produce a regulation (decree).[5146]

---

version avialable in French ("Recueil systématique du droit fédéral" (RS) <http://www.admin.ch/ch/f/rs/rs.html>) and in Italian ("*Raccolta sistematica del diritto federale*" <http://www.admin.ch/ch/i/rs/rs.html>).

[5144] *Bundesgesetz über den Datenschutz, DSG vom 19. Juni 1992 (Stand 2000)* (Swiss Data Protection Statute from June 19, 1992 (in the updated version of 2000) DSG, SR 235.1), available at <http://www.admin.ch/ch/d/sr/c235_1.html> (in German). For an English translation *see* <http://www.edsb.ch/e/gesetz/schweiz/index.htm> or <http://www.ics.uci.edu/~kobsa/privacy/switzerland.htm>.

[5145] Association of Data Protection Commissioners <http://www.dsb-cpd.ch>; Brochure on "Safer Surfing" <http://www.dsb-cpd.ch/d/publikationen/broschuere_sicherheit_d.pdf>; Link list on "Safer Surfing" <http://www.datenschutz.ch/index/sichersurfen.htm?id=9254>.

[5146] *Eidgenössisches Justiz- und Polizeidepartement: Entwurf zur Teilrevision dess Bundesdatenschutzgesetzes*, (Federal Department of Justice and Police: Pre-draft for a Partial Revision of the Federal Data Protection Act), August 2001, available at <http://www.ofj.admin.ch/themen/datenschutz/vn-ber-d.pdf>. A report by the controlling delegation of the National Council of the Federal Parliament (*Geschäftsprüfungskommission des Nationalrates* [GPK-N]) has been published in April 2004, together with a statement of the Government. See *Bericht der Geschäftsprüfungskommission des Nationalrates [GPK-N] vom 21. November 2003, sowie*

In June 1999, the European Union Data Protection Working Party determined that Swiss law was adequate under the European Union Directive.[5147] In July 2000, the European Commission formally adopted this position, thereby approving all future personal data transfers to Switzerland. On October 20, 2004, the Commission of the European Union confirmed this approval.[5148] However, as long as the revision of the Data Protection Law is pending, Switzerland cannot formally ratify the Data Protection Protocol of the European Council.[5149]

Data Protection Authority

The LPD created the office of a Federal Data Protection Commissioner (the Commissioner, or EDSB).[5150] The Commissioner maintains and publishes the Register for Data Files,[5151] supervises federal government and private bodies, provides advice, issues recommendations and reports, and conducts investigations. The Commissioner also consults with the private sector. The

---

Stellungnahme des Bundesrates vom 24. März 2004, in: Bundesblatt vom 06. April 2004 / Nr. 13 S. 1413 bzw. S. 1431: <http://www.admin.ch/ch/d/ff/2004/index0_13.html>. While the National Council (*Nationalrat*) refused to discuss the project on March 3, 2004, (*i.e.*, to send it back to the commission for revision), the smaller chamber decided to discuss it. The consultation process is going on, without any decision being taken so far. The National Council (*Nationalrat*) is the larger chamber of the Swiss Federal Parliament, representing the population, while the State Council (*Ständerat*) is the smaller chamber, representing the 26 *cantons*. Switzerland is governed by the collective Federal Council (*Bundesrat*), with seven members (ministers). Information about the political system in Switzerland can be found at <http://www.parlament.ch/e/homepage.htm>.

[5147] Data Protection Working Party, Article 19, Opinion 5/99 on the Level of Protection of Personal Data in Switzerland, June 7, 1999, available at <http://europa.eu.int/comm/dg15/en/media/dataprot/wpdocs/wp22fr.pdf>.

[5148] The Commission of the European Communities: "The application of Commission Decision 2000/518/EC of 26 July 2000 pursuant to Directive 95/46/EC of the European Parliament and of the Council on the adequate protection of personal data provided in Switzerland," SEC (2004) 1322, Brussels, 20.10.2004, available at <http://europa.eu.int/comm/justice_home/fsj/privacy/docs/adequacy/sec-2004-1322_en.pdf&e=10313>; the decision is based on the "Commission Decision of 26 July 2000 pursuant to Directive 95/46/EC of the European Parliament and of the Council on the adequate protection of personal data provided in Switzerland (notified under document number C(2000) 2304), 2000/518/EC," Official Journal L 215, 25/08/2000 P. 0001-0003, available at <http://europa.eu.int/eur-lex/lex/LexUriServ/LexUriServ.do?uri=CELEX:32000D0518:EN:HTML>. *See also* European Union Press Release, "Commission Adopts Decisions Recognising Adequacy of Regimes in United States, Switzerland and Hungary," July 27, 2000, available at <http://europa.eu.int/comm/internal_market/en/media/dataprot/news/safeharbor.htm>. The English report of the EU Commission from January 11, 2005 is also available at <http://dsbzg.instanthost.ch/dsbzg/content.nsf/A89C8AC5E2CBE4CBC1256FA70029B10B/$File/CH_EU_DS _Schutzniveau.pdf>.

[5149] *Zusatzprotokoll zum Übereinkommen des Europarats zum Schutz des Menschen bei der automatisierten Verarbeitung personenbezogener Daten* (Série des traités européens STE Nr.108).

[5150] Homepage <http://www.edsb.ch/>.

[5151] According to official information by the EDSB office, there are approximately 1,200 individuals or companies registered, according to Article 11 of the Swiss Federal Act on Data Protection of June 19, 1992. E-mail from Eliane Schmid, EDSB office; to Cédric Laurant, Policy Counsel, Electronic Privacy Information Center, July 8, 2004. (on file with EPIC.)

---

office publishes a detailed annual report,[5152] as well as leaflets, summaries of press articles and critical statements, *e.g.*, on the medical tariffing system Tarmed (see below), on the telecom provider Orange SA collecting sensitive data of their employees, or on the governmental project to introduce a unique ID number for all Swiss residents (EPID).[5153] Further, the office is advising governmental agencies on issues of data protection. In 2004, there were 23 employees in this office. However, the Federal Data Protection Commissioner has only limited possibilities for interventions: he can only submit "suggestions" (*Empfehlungen*) or ask the Data Protection Commission to review a case. Decisions of this commission can then be submitted to the Federal Court (*Bundesgericht*). The last decision of the Data Protection Commission published on its website dates back to October 31, 2003. On August 29, 2003, the Commission decided that the pharmaceutical company Roche was not allowed to systematically take samples of the urine of its apprentices (*Lehrlinge*) in order to test them for the use of illegal drugs.[5154] In 2000, Roche received a Swiss "Big Brother Award" for its testing of apprentices.[5155]

Annually, the EDSB deals with 1,500 to 2,000 complaints, investigations and requests. Among these, there are questions of individuals, media inquiries, long-term supervision of operational proceedings in private enterprises, as much as, in the federal administration, and comments on legislation at the hearing stage. According to the ESDBD, between April 1, 2004 and March 31, 2005 the subject matters were divided approximately as follows: 24% general information; 18% IT, telecommunication; 8% insurance matters; 13% various questions concerning data protection; 6% matters relating to employment and workplace; 8% justice, police and internal security; and 2% to 6% each for health, finance, trade/economy, basic rights, defense and statistics/research.[5156]

[5152] *Annual report*, nr. 11, published on July 5, 2004, available at <http://www.edsb.ch/d/doku/jahresberichte/tb11/index.htm>, also available in French at <http://www.edsb.ch/f/doku/jahresberichte/tb11/index.htm>.

[5153] EPID means "*Einheitlicher Personenidentifikator*," *see* <http://www.edsb.ch/d/themen/weitere/epid/edsb-papier-epid_d.pdf> and "Register Would Give Everyone ID Number," New York Times, January 7, 2004. After protests, the EPID project was revised in 2003-2004: instead of one unique ID number, there is now a plan to introduce about six different ID numbers for different areas. In spring 2004, the law went into a second political consultation process. Traditionally, in Switzerland, new law projects are presented to the "interested public" for consultation (*Vernehmlassungsverfahren*, consultation process). This is mainly to prevent opposition that would require a formal referendum on the bill.

[5154] "*Urteil der Eidgenössischen Datenschutzkommission vom 29. August 2003, Widerrechtliche Bearbeitung von Personendaten. Drogentests während der Lehre 68.68*," <http://www.vpb.admin.ch/deutsch/cont/aut/aut_1.2.3.5.html>. Members of the commission, <http://www.admin.ch/ch/d/cf/ko/index_111.html>

[5155] Big Brother Awards Switzerland, "Hall of Shame," <http://www.bigbrotherawards.ch/diverses/hallofshame>.

[5156] E-mail from Eliane Schmid, EDSB office, to Ula Galster, International Policy Fellow, Electronic Privacy Information Center, April 26, 2005 (on file with EPIC).

Besides the Data Protection Act,[5157] there are also legal protections for privacy in the Civil Code[5158] and the Penal Code.[5159] There are also special rules relating to workers' privacy from surveillance,[5160] telecommunications information,[5161] health care statistics,[5162] professional confidentiality including medical and legal data,[5163] medical research,[5164] and identity cards.[5165]

The identity card is machine-readable as is the new passport, which became effective on January 1, 2003. On September 15, 2004, the Swiss government decided that the next edition of Swiss passports should include a chip with biometric data. The decision is based on a feasibility study by the Federal Police "Fedpol," commissioned in September 2003. This should allow Swiss citizens to fulfill the requests introduced by the US government after September 11 2001, requiring that every visitor without a visa be able to present a passport with a biometric identity tag.[5166] In April 2005, the Swiss government declared that such a passport would be available only by September 2006 or later, due to the coordination of similar efforts of the European Union (EU).[5167] In Spring 2005 it

---

[5157] For an overview of legal regulations concerning Data Protection, *see* <http://www.admin.ch/ch/d/sr/23.html#235>.

[5158] Section 28 of the *Zivilgesetzbuch* (ZGB, SR 210), Civil Code, December 10, 1907, <http://www.admin.ch/ch/d/sr/c210.html>.

[5159] *Code pénal, Titre troisième: Infractions contre l'honneur et contre le domaine secret ou le domaine privé,* Art. 173-179. *Schweizerisches Strafgesetzbuch* (StGB) *vom 21. Dezember 1937* (SR 311.0) <http://www.admin.ch/ch/d/sr/c311_0.html>.

[5160] Section 328 of the *Obligationenrecht* (OR, SR 22) <http://www.admin.ch/ch/d/sr/22.html>, *Code of Obligations. See* International Labour Organization, Conditions of Work Digest, Volume 12, 1/1993.

[5161] *Fernmeldegesetz* (FMG, SR 784.10), available at <http://www.admin.ch/ch/d/sr/c784_10.html>, *Telecommunications Law* (LTC) of 30 April 1997.

[5162] *Office fédéral de la statistique, La protection des données dans la statistique médicale,* 1997 <http://www.admin.ch/bfs/stat_ch/ber14/statsant/ff1403c.htm>.

[5163] *Code pénal,* Art. 320-322, *Schweizerisches Strafgesetzbuch* vom 21. Dezember 1937 (StGB, SR 311.0) <http://www.admin.ch/ch/d/sr/c311_0.html>.

[5164] *Verordnung vom 14. Juni 1993 über die Offenbarung des Berufsgeheimnisses im Bereich der medizinischen Forschung* (VOBG, SR 235.154) <http://www.admin.ch/ch/d/sr/c235_154.html>, *Ordonnance du 14 juin 1993 concernant les autorisations de lever le secret professionnel en matière de recherche médicale (OALSP).*

[5165] *Bundesgesetz vom 22. Juni 2001 über die Ausweise für Schweizer Staatsangehörige* (Ausweisgesetz, AwG, SR 143.1) <http://www.admin.ch/ch/d/sr/c143_1.html>, and the corresponding regulation *Verordnung vom 20. September 2002 über die Ausweise für Schweizer Staatsangehörige* (Ausweisverordnung, VAwG, SR 143.11) <http://www.admin.ch/ch/d/sr/c143_11.html>, replacing the older *Ordonnance du 18 mai 1994 relative à la carte d'identité suisse.*

[5166] "Pilotprojekt für Biometrie-Pässe," Media release of the Justice and Police Department EJPD of September 15, 2004, available at (http://www.ejpd.admin.ch/doks/mm/content/mm_view-d.php?mmID=2192&mmTopic=Ausweise). An official 10-point FAQ on biometrical data in the Swiss passport is available at <http://www.fedpol.admin.ch/FAQ_Pass/d/faq_pass.htm>.

[5167] "Biometrischer Schweizer Pass: Einführung frühestens im September 2006," Media release of the Swiss Justice and Police Departement EJPD of 13 April 2005, available at<http://www.ejpd.admin.ch/doks/mm/content/mm_view-d.php?mmID=2386&mmTopic=Ausweise>.

---

was not clear what biometrical data should be included in which format in the Swiss and EU passports.

Banking records are protected by the Swiss Federal Banking Act of 1934. This act was passed to guarantee strong protections for the privacy and confidentiality of bank customers. However, Switzerland has come under increasing pressure from the European Union and the Organization for Economic Cooperation and Development (OECD) to weaken these laws and provide greater access to bank records for the purposes of tax collection. The adoption of the "Schengen agreement" would provide a solution to the conflicts (see below). In reality, banking data have been transmitted illegally to the US in at least one case described at the end of this chapter.

Anti-terrorism Measures

Under the headlines of "fighting against terrorism" (especially after the September 11, 2001 attack in the United States), Switzerland expanded domestic surveillance, and established and strengthened collaboration agreements, especially with the US and the EU. On September 4, 2002, a secret "Operative Working Arrangement" was signed, establishing a close "joint operative exchange of officers"[5168] (see *PHR 2004*). On June 24, 2004, the Swiss Attorney General (*Bundesanwalt)* concluded that the Swiss banks "did not play a major role" in financing the September 11, 2001 attacks. Still, some accounts of financing companies have been blocked, and some cases handed over to a federal investigative judge. At the end of the first step of the investigations, the Swiss Attorney General declared the end of the "Operative Working Arrangement."

On March 3, 2005, the Swiss government signed an agreement on the issue of the disclosure of air travelers' data from the airline company "Swiss" to US authorities. The immigration branch of the US Department of Homeland of Security will receive information on 34 categories of data from every passenger.[5169] The US authorities will be allowed to store this data for 3.5 years,. The request by US authorities has been criticized because the disclosure of data

---

[5168] The "Arrangement" was signed by the Swiss Attorney General (*Bundesanwalt*, General Federal Prosecutor), Mr. Valentin Roschacher for Switzerland, and by US Attorney General John Ashcroft and US Deputy Secretary at the Department of Treasury, Kenneth Dam for the US. In June 2004, the Swiss newspaper "Facts" published a facsimile of the agreement <http://www.facts.ch/dyn/magazin/schweiz/382176.html>.

[5169] Media release of the Swiss Department of Traffic, Energy and Communication (UVEK) of March 4, 2005, available at
<http://www.uvek.admin.ch/dokumentation/medienmitteilungen/artikel/20050304/02207/index.html?lang=de>.
The department also published a list of the 34 data categories in PDF format, available at
<http://www.uvek.admin.ch/imperia/md/content/gs_uvek2/d/verkehr/luftfahrt/1.pdf>.

violates the Swiss Data Protection Law, which allows the transfer of data to another state only if the other nation has a similar data protection legislation, which is not the case of the US. The Swiss agreement has been coordinated with a similar agreement between the EU and the US on this issue.[5170]

Cooperation with the European Union

Switzerland is not a member of the EU, but has some special agreements with the EU. Some of these bilateral agreements were signed in 2000 and 2001. In May 2004, the government decided to sign another set of agreements ("Bilaterale II").[5171] However, these contracts will have to be approved by the citizens by a referendum that has been demanded, mainly by some national conservative parties.[5172] The referendum will take place on June 6, 2005. It is very likely that Switzerland will ratify the Schengen and Dublin Conventions. The Schengen agreement[5173] aims at creating a pan-European Security Zone, thus shifting the borders between European nations to the external borders of Europe. Inside Europe, people would be able travel without the traditional border police control, while travelers from and to Europe would face strengthened border controls. However, the national police forces will be allowed to execute "mobile controls" in the 30 km range along the borders, as well as in train stations, inside of trains and at airports. This means that all persons will *de facto* have to carry an ID document, which was not compulsory until now in Switzerland.[5174]

Further, the Schengen Convention would establish a close cooperation among police forces, in order to combat international "criminal tourism" (*Kriminaltourismus*). The core subject of this agreement is the Schengen Information System (SIS), a pan-European database that records personal

---

[5170] On May 28, 2004, the EU signed an agreement with the US on the disclosure of PNR data. However, the European Parliament decided to present the case to the Court of Justice of the European Communities.

[5171] "Botschaft zur Genehmigung der bilateralen Abkommen zwischen der Schweiz und der Europäischen Union, einschliesslich der Erlasse zur Umsetzung der Abkommen (Bilaterale II) vom 1. Oktober 2004," published in the Bundesblatt nr. 44/09 on November 9, 2004, pp. 5965-6564, available at <http://www.admin.ch/ch/d/ff/2004/index0_44.html>.

[5172] A new law adopted by Parliament does not enter into force if a referendum is sought within 100 days. To be valid, the signature of 50,000 electors must be obtained in favor of a popular ballot. On the Swiss legislative procedure in general *see* <http://www.admin.ch/ch/e/gg/index.html>.

[5173] *See* <http://www.ejpd.admin.ch/d/dossiers/schengen/>; for a critical overview *see e.g.* the documentation of the group "Solidarité sans frontières" (SOSF), available at <http://www.sosf.ch/publikationen/intro/intro.html>

[5174] This rule is most likely against a 1983 decision by the Swiss federal court, which held that identity controls are only allowed in case of a disruptive situation ("*situation troublée*"). *Bundesgerichtesentscheid* BGE 109 Ia 146, available at <http://www.polyreg.ch/bgeleitentscheide/Band_109_1983/BGE_109_IA_146.html>.

information on people who have been arrested, migrants, and missing objects[5175] (*Fahndungsdatenbank*) by the national police forces. In the spring of 2004, SIS consisted of 10 million entries. In 2003, 1.2 million data sets concerned persons, but only 1.6 percent of these persons had been the subject of an international warrant. The majority of files concerned persons from non-EU member states. The SIS database is not only a tool against crime, but also a tool for repression against immigration. SIS is operated by the EUROPOL, and by joining the Schengen agreement, Swiss police officers will have full online access to the SIS database. The Swiss Department of Justice and Police (EJPD) calls the SIS "a revolutionary step for police work." Collaboration in the EUROPOL will be "faster and more efficient than with Interpol." Other parts of the Schengen Convention cover the cross-border observation by national police forces and the exchange of police officers.

The Dublin Convention, created in 1990, establishes a European cooperation agreement to process applications from asylum seekers. It will allow Switzerland to access "Eurodac," the pan-European database of fingerprints of asylum seekers and migrants.[5176] According to the Dublin Convention, asylum requests are checked only by one EU member state whose decision becomes binding for all other member states.

There are several bilateral agreements on police cooperation between Switzerland and many other nations in Europe, which expand the types of collaboration among law enforcement authorities. The Swiss Federal Police is, in this regard, exchanging information and data with other countries.[5177] Concrete

---

[5175] <http://www.fact-index.com/s/sc/schengen_information_system.html>. For a critical review of the SIS *see e.g.* the documentation of the group "Solidarité sans frontières" (SOSF) at
<http://www.sosf.ch/publikationen/intro/intro.html>, as well as Heiner Busch "Lieber Pest oder Cholera?" in WOZ Die Wochenzeitung Nr. 14/2004, April 1 2004. For information on SIS in English *see .e.g.*
statewatch.org, "From the Schengen Information System to SIS II and the Visa Information (VIS): the Proposals Explained" (48 pages / February 2005), available at
<http://www.statewatch.org/news/2005/may/analysis-sisII.pdf>, as well as the 12 page update of May 2005 by statewatch.org, "SIS II fait accompli? Construction of the EU' Big Brother Database Underway - New Analysis", available at <http://www.statewatch.org/news/2005/may/sisII-analysis-may05.pdf>. By checking the Governmental Report (*Botschaft*) on the Schengen Agreement, the data protection officer of the Canton Zug found 233 hits in his quick survey. However, this does not mean that personal data is protected. The *Botschaft* has been published in the Bundesblatt Nr. 44/2004 (November 9, 2004), pp. 5965-6564, available at
<http://www.admin.ch/ch/d/ff/2004/5965.pdf>. For other agreements in the same context, see
<http://www.admin.ch/ch/d/ff/2004/index0_44.html>

[5176] After a revision of the regulation "Verordnung über die Bearbeitung erkennungsdienstlicher Daten" by the Swiss Government on May 12, 2004, the Swiss border police is allowed to collect fingerprints of all persons they expect to be illegally trying to immigrate to Switzerland, and to store these data in the national database called AFIS, from June 1, 2004 on. The revision has to be regarded as a preparation for the joining of the Eurodac database. See "Verordnung über die Bearbeitung erkennungsdienstlicher Daten vom 21. November 2001" (SR 361.3), available at <http://www.admin.ch/ch/d/sr/c361_3.html>.

[5177] *E.g.*, in April 2002, the Swiss government signed an agreement with Europol on exchanging information as well as police agents. The government promised to submit the agreement to Parliament in a later stage.

collaboration has been tested in the case of international political and economic meetings, like the G8 meeting in Geneva in June 2003 and the World Economic Forum meeting in Davos in January 2004. In January 2005, the Swiss government published an agreement on the collaboration with Europol, signed in September 2004. The agreement allows both parties to establish "exchange officers."[5178]

Switzerland is a member of the unofficial "Club de Berne," renamed in April 2004 to "Counter Terrorist Group/CTG" (see *PHR 2004*). According to different sources, the club was founded in Berne in 1971 as a loose federation (*Zusammenschluss*) of national European intelligence service leaders. Today, club seems to consist of members of 27 nations. In 2002, the mysterious club has been honored with a Swiss "Big Brother Award" in the "lifetime award" Category.[5179]

Police and Intelligence Agencies' Activities

The Swiss police system is traditionally strongly organized by the 26 *cantons*. Every canton has its own police force. However, in the last few years there have been substantial efforts to build up a central "Federal Police" corps (Fedpol), based in Berne.[5180] Fedpol has mainly investigative duties. For this purpose, a Federal Criminal Police has been built up since 1994.[5181] Other duties include the "prevention" of crimes. Fedpol publishes an annual report on "national security."[5182] Most of the expansion of Fedpol has been done in order to "fight against organized crime and terrorism." In order to "fight cybercrime" a specific task force was established in 2003, the "Coordination Unit for Cybercrime Control" (CYCOS).[5183] In December 2004, the Swiss government opened the

---

[5178] *See* Botschaft, Bundesbeschluss and Abkommen (Aggreement, SR 0.360.268.2) in Bundesblatt Nr. 6/2005 of February 15, 2005, pp.983ff., available at <http://www.admin.ch/ch/d/ff/2005/index0_6.html>.

[5179] *See* <http://www.bigbrotherawards.ch/diverses/hallofshame>.

[5180] *See* <http://www.fedpol.ch>, with an impressive organization chart: <http://www.fedpol.ch/e/portrait/Visio-Fedpol-2004-e-internet.pdf>.

[5181] *"Bundesgesetz über kriminalpolizeiliche Zentralstellen des Bundes vom 7. Oktober 1994"* (ZentG, SR 360) <http://www.admin.ch/ch/d/sr/c360.html>.

[5182] *"Bericht Innere Sicherheit der Schweiz 2004,"* published on May 26, 2005, available at <http://www.fedpol.ch/d/aktuell/berichte/biss_2004_d.pdf> (in German). The report is edited by the Fedpol section "Service for Analysis and Prevention," DAP (*Dienst für Analyse und Prävention),* which is the political Swiss "preventive State Security Police," part of the Swiss Federal Police, ex-BUPO, *Bundespolizei.*

[5183] "Coordination Unit against Cybercrime" (CYCOS, KOBIK in German) <http://www.cybercrime.admin.ch/e/index.htm>. The CYCOS is a cooperating project between the Confederation and most of the Swiss Cantons. In 2005, the Canton Zurich decided to participate as well. According to a newspaper report, CYCOS received about 6,500 hints from the public, most of them regarding child pornography and child abuse. During 2004, CYCOS forwarded 450 cases to the competent cantonal

---

consultation process on a revision of the Penal Code (*Strafgesetzbuch, StGB*[5184]), which consists mainly of regulating the criminal liability of Internet providers, stating: content providers should be fully liable for documents which are prohibited by law; hosting providers should not be liable at all; while access providers should be liable only if they participate actively in offering such documents. A second consultation process has been opened on a bill aiming at centralizing the investigations of cybercrime cases at the Federal Police.[5185]

Although the cooperation has been extended in various fields, there are still some tensions between Fedpol and cantonal police forces, and also inside governmental agencies. Therefore, the Controlling Commission of the Swiss Parliament (*Geschäftsprüfungsdelegation, GPDel*) is demanding a more efficient coordination of the different intelligence agencies of the Swiss Army and the Federal Police.[5186]

Legally, the activities of the Fedpol are mainly based on the *Bundesgesetz über Massnahmen zur Wahrung der inneren Sicherheit* (BWIS).[5187] This law was enacted in July 1, 1998 following a scandal in the autumn of 1989, when members of a parliamentary investigative commission (the *Parlamentarische Untersuchungskommission*, or PUK) discovered huge databases of citizens in the premises of the Federal Police (the political police) and the Federal Prosecutor (*Bundesanwaltschaft*).[5188]

The former Federal Police, now called the Service for Analysis and Prevention, is part of the Federal Office for Police Matters, which also includes the Federal Criminal Police. It hosts two databanks, including ISIS (the Information System

---

attorneys (2003: 100 cases). Source: Niels Anner, "Erfolge der Internet-Polizei", NZZ am Sonntag, February 6, 2005).

[5184] Swiss Penal Code, *Strafgesetzbuch*, SR 311.0, available at <http://www.admin.ch/ch/d/sr/311_0/index.html> (in German, French and Italian).

[5185] *See* media release by the Federal Justice Departement (EJPD): "Die Netzwerkkriminalität verstärkt bekämpfen. EJPD schickt zwei Gesetzesentwürfe in die Vernehmlassung," December 10, 2004, available at <http://www.ofj.admin.ch/themen/netzwerkkrim/> (in German and French).

[5186] *See e.g.* wab. "Für Parlamentarier gar nicht 'hervorragend', " in NZZ, November 22, 2004, p.13.

[5187] *Bundesgesetz über Massnahmen zur Wahrung der inneren Sicherheit vom 21. März 1997* (BWIS, SR 120) <http://www.admin.ch/ch/d/sr/c120.html>.

[5188] The commission found about 900,000 folders, called "*Fichen*" (hence "*Fichenskandal*"), on persons, most of whom were not suspected of having committed any offenses. Most of the folders had to be destroyed. At this time, there was no legal basis for the collection of these folders. In 1991, a citizens' committee launched a popular initiative to abolish the political police. Surveillance should only be possible on the grounds of a criminal investigation. The vote on the initiative was postponed by the government for years. In June 1998, nine years after the scandal 75 percent of the voters said no to the initiative. The federal government had saved its political police, which since the beginning of the nineties had been completely modernized and, by July 1, 1998, received for the first time a legal basis with the Law on Measures for Maintaining Internal Security (BWIS).

for Internal Security), which replaced the old paper files of the federal police.[5189] In April 2004, ISIS contained files on 60,477 persons who are considered terrorists, violent extremists or possible spies.[5190] Files are opened on "preventive" grounds, which means that no criminal investigation is required. However, data resulting from criminal investigations, and thus also from telephone surveillance, can be maintained for preventive purposes, even if the person is acquitted before a court. The other databank is JANUS,[5191] which contained files of 62,500 persons in July 2001 and 83,700 in March 2004, most of them being registered for alleged drug trafficking, since registration of consumers is not allowed. Files in JANUS can be created on the grounds of simple suspicion. In July 2001, the records on the 62,500 suspected target persons (*Stammpersonen*) also contained 116,500 references to third persons who are not suspected.[5192]

The database GEWA of the Fedpol section on money laundering (*Meldestelle Geldwäscherei)* contained 10,884 persons and 4,170 companies in February 2004.[5193] The database for "searched people and objects" (*Fahndungsdatenbank*) RIPOL contained 142,625 entries for persons in January 2004, most of them are searched for because of minor offenses.[5194] In February 2004, the main Fedpol register IPAS (*Personen- und Aktennachweissystem*) contained entries on 641,446 persons.[5195] IPAS is organized as an index to other databases, including the database of fingerprints AFIS and of genetic profiles EDNA (see below).[5196]

[5189] ISIS: *Verordnung über das Staatsschutz-Informations-System (ISIS-Verordnung) vom 30. November 2001* (SR 120.3), <http://www.admin.ch/ch/d/sr/c120_3.html>.

[5190] Heiner Busch, "Das neue Schweizer Wettfichen," in WOZ Die Wochenzeitung nr. 9, March 3, 2005, p.6.

[5191] *Verordnung über das Informationssystem der Bundeskriminalpolizei (JANUS-Verordnung) vom 30. November 2001 (Stand am 22. Januar 2002)* (SR 360.2) <http://www.admin.ch/ch/d/sr/c360_2.html>. JANUS is the fusion of three information systems that have been built up during the nineties, and had been maintained separately until 1998: DOSIS, which held data on investigations in drug trafficking; ISOK, the information system on "organized crime;" and FAMP, which includes information about forged money, trafficking human beings (prostitution) and illicit pornography.

[5192] Among them, 13,500 are so-called "contact persons"; 13,000 are telephone subscribers (with their names and addresses); and about 90,000 are telephone numbers with only fragmentary information to the respective persons (Conseil national *01-1068 – Question ordinaire de Dardel – Personnes enregistrées dans les systèmes de données JANUS et ISIS – Réponse du Conseil fédéral du 5 septembre 2001* <http://www.parlament.ch/afs/data/f/gesch/2001/f_gesch_20011068.htm>).

[5193] Heiner Busch, "Das neue Schweizer Wettfichen,",*supra* at p.6.

[5194] The acronym RIPOL stands for "le système de recherches informatisées de police." *see Verordnung über das automatisierte Fahndungssystem* (RIPOL-Verordnung, SR 172.213.61) vom 19. Juni 1995, *see* <http://www.admin.ch/ch/d/sr/c172_213_61.html>-

[5195] IPAS is an acronym for "informatisiertes Personennachweis-, Aktennachweis- und Verwaltungssystem im Bundesamt für Polizei", based on the *IPAS-Verordnung vom 21. November 2001* (SR 361.2), see <http://www.admin.ch/ch/d/sr/c361_2.html>.

[5196] Heiner Busch, "Das neue Schweizer Wettfichen," *supra* at p.6.

Currently the Swiss government is preparing a bill that should include the legal basis for JANUS, IPAS and RIPOL in one single law on police databases.[5197] In the same context, the government plans a new information system called "Police Index," to facilitate the collaboration with the cantonal and with foreign police authorities.

A revision of the BWIS is currently planned. The directors of the Federal Police and the Intelligence forces are demanding an extension of their capabilities, *e.g.*, to be allowed to spy inside private apartments or to tap telecommunications, even without the concrete suspicion of a crime. Further, the revision should include the possibility to operate secret "undercover agents" (*verdeckte Ermittler*), even for the means of "prevention," that is, in cases where no concrete crime is under investigation.[5198] Since January 1, 2005, the police are allowed to operate as undercover special agents.[5199] The majority of the Parliament accepted the governmental proposal, arguing that this would be "a necessary tool against organized crime," like terrorism and money laundering. Finally, the police forces are also demanding access to ONYX, the Swiss military satellite telecom interception system similar to ECHELON (see below).

On the legal basis of the BWIS, the government decreed a regulation which compels all institutions "executing an official duty" to report any suspicion of a "terrorist activity" to the federal police.[5200] These institutions include universities, hospitals, and train carriers. The regulation was first released in November 1, 2001, in the aftermath of the attacks of September 11, 2001, to sunset after one year. It was extended for another year, and in November 2003 was extended for two more years.[5201]

The Department of Justice and Police (EJPD) is preparing a new law including measures against racism, against so-called hooliganism, and against propaganda

---

[5197] "*Bundesgesetz über die polizeilichen Informationssysteme des Bundes (BPI)*," documents are available at <http://www.fedpol.admin.ch/d/brennpunkt/index.htm>. direct link at <http://www.fedpol.ch/d/aktuell/medien/050304_BPI_Vorentwurf_d.pdf>. The consultation process is going on until June 15, 2005. (in general on the Swiss consultation procedure: <http://www.admin.ch/ch/e/gg/pc/index.html>).

[5198] *See e.g.* Markus Steudler: "Der Staat will wieder lauschen," NZZ am Sonntag, 1. Mai 2005, p.11, <http://nzz.ch/2005/05/01/il/articleCRX8R.html>.

[5199] *Bundesgesetz über verdeckte Ermittlung* (BVE) vom 20. June 2003 (SR 312.8) <http://www.admin.ch/ch/d/sr/c312_8.html>, and the regulation (decree) *Verordnung vom 10. November 2004 über die verdeckte Ermittlung* (VVE, SR 312.81), <http://www.admin.ch/ch/d/sr/c312_81.html>.

[5200] *Verordnung betreffend die Ausdehnung der Auskunftspflichten und des Melderechts von Behörden, Amtsstellen und Organisationen zur Gewährleistung der inneren und äusseren Sicherheit* (SR 120.1)

[5201] In Switzerland, the citizens can demand a referendum on every law regarding domestic politics by collecting 50,000 signatures in the delay of 100 days – but they can not ask for a referendum in the case of a regulation (*Verordnung*, decree).

of violence.[5202] The law is paving the way for the establishment of a centralized national database on so-called "hooligans" in the legal framework of the BWIS (see above), providing the basis for the exchange of data with other nations. Currently, there is a consultation process on the subject of another bill "against hooliganism."[5203] The new law would allow the police forces (a) to ban a person to enter a certain area in a city for a certain time (access restriction, *Rayonverbote*), (b) to ban a person to travel to another country (traveling restriction, *Ausreiseverbote*), (c) to oblige a person to present himself personally at a police station during a manifestation (*Meldeauflage*), and (d) police custody (*Polizeigewahrsam*). On a first look and according to official statements, these measurements are aimed at combating "hooliganism" in the context of sport events. The government underscore that both the database and the four additional measures would be essential in view of the next European Football Championship (TM), scheduled for 2008 in Switzerland and Austria. However, critics fear that the term "hooliganism" would not be restricted to football fans, since the law covers all kinds of "large public events," including political demonstrations.

A kind of a practical test for some of the new measures was executed in Zurich on December, 5 2004 when the Zurich police stopped more than 400 football fans from the rival FC Basel on a suburban train station, banned them from participation at the football match, collected the personal data of the fans and transmitted them to the Federal Police, where the data was added to the POLIS database.[5204] Similar procedures were tested in winter 2004-05 at political manifestations against the World Economic Forum (WEF) in the cities of Winterthur and Berne.[5205] These two cities changed their local laws, including the possibility for police forces to ban certain people from entering certain areas of the city (*Rayonverbote*), even the people haven't committed any crime. The new laws are aimed mainly against alcoholics, "punks" and loitering people, in order to force actions of "city cleaning." The cities of Zurich and St. Gall are

---

[5202] *Bundesgesetz über Massnahmen gegen Rassismus, Hooliganismus und Gewaltpropaganda(Entwurf)* and press release <http://www.ejpd.admin.ch/doks/mm/2003/030212c-d.htm>.

[5203] "Hooliganismus soll stärker bekämpft werden," Media release of the FedPol issued on 23.03.2005, available at <http://www.fedpol.ch/d/aktuell/medien/03231.htm>, with a link to the new bill "Bundesgesetz über Massnahmen gegen Gewaltpropaganda und Gewalt anlässlich von Sportveranstaltungen (Entwurf vom 01.03.05)," available at <http://www.fedpol.ch/d/aktuell/medien/GesetzesE_Massn_d.pdf>. The deadline for the consultation procedure on this bill is June 24, 2005.

[5204] *See e.g.* WOZ Die Wochenzeitung, 9.12.2004, as well as a lot of other press articles. The Basel fans organized a collective suit against the Zurich police.

[5205] The World Economic Forum is a private event organized since 2000 in the alpine village Davos, supported by large multinational companies, as well as by the Swiss Government. In the context of the WEF in Davos in January 2004, police forces blocked access to the mountain village, collected data on more than 1,000 peaceful demonstrators and transmitted the data to the Federal Police, in order to cross-check it with the ISIS database (*see PHR 2004*).

discussing the introduction of similar laws. Daniele Jenni, a lawyer in Berne, is opposing these regulations because he says they contradict the Swiss constitution. Particularly, these laws are violating the right of association and the right of meeting in public places, he says.[5206] Mr. Jenni is defending people who are accused of contradicting the law. In some cases, he is preparing to continue his opposition by calling the Federal Court (*Bundesgericht*).[5207] In October 2004, Jenni's opposition was honoured by the audience of the fifth Swiss "Big Brother Award" ceremony with a "Winkelried Award," which is the only positive prize, given for opposition against privacy intrusions.[5208]

Interception of Telecommunications

Until the beginning of 2002, telephone tapping was governed by Article 179 *octies* of the Penal Code and corresponding regulations in the federal, the military and the cantonal Penal Procedure Codes.[5209] Due to liberalization of the telecommunications sector by the 1997 Telecommunication Act, the government issued a regulation that established a specialized agency, *Le Service des Tâches Spéciales* (Special Services, or STS), within the Department of the Environment, Transport, Energy and Communications (UVEK), to administer wiretaps.[5210] The STS now is a link between the special services of the different private and state-owned telecommunications companies and the public prosecutors, who issue interception orders. under the previous regulation, every interception order had to be confirmed by a prosecution chamber of the federal court or by the cantonal high court.

[5206] Swiss Constitution, *Bundesverfassung*, SR 101, available at <http://www.admin.ch/ch/d/sr/c101.html>, Art. 22 on Versammlungsfreiheit, Art. 23 on Vereinigungsfreiheit. See also the *Dossier Wegweisungen* (in German only)available at <http://www.stadt-wohnen.ch/aktuell/stadt_wegweisung.php>. *See also* the juridical expertise elaborated by the lawyer Viktor Györffy for the Green Party of the city of Zurich, available at <http://www.gruenezuerich.ch/download/gutachten.pdf>.

[5207] *See* <http://www.danielejenni.ch>.

[5208] *See* <http://www.bigbrotherawards.ch/halloffame>.

[5209] Articles 66-73, *Bundesgesetz vom 15. Juni 1934 über die Bundesstrafrechtspflege* (SR 312.0, Federal Criminal Procedure Code, *Procédure pénale fédérale*), <http://www.admin.ch/ch/d/sr/c312_0.html>, and: *Loi du 23 Mars 1979 sur la protection de la vie privée* (Law on the Protection of Privacy, March 23, 1979).

[5210] *Telecommunications Law* (LTC) of April 30, 1997. *Ordonnance du 1er décembre 1997 sur le service de surveillance de la correspondance postale et des télécommunications* (December 1, 1997), available at *Ordonnance du 31 octobre 2001 sur la surveillance de la correspondance par poste et télécommunication* (OSCPT), RS 780.11 from October 31, 2001, <www.admin.ch/ch/f/rs/c780_11.html>, in German Decree on the Monitoring of Mail Correspondence and Telecommunications. Until 2002, the technical procedures for wiretapping were carried out by a special service within former Telecom PTT (now Swisscom), the state monopoly company. The STS has been established in 2003 in order to technically establish a link between the requests of the judges and the data of the telecom providers. However, with the new system "Metamorphose" being introduced now, the DBA is also registering the requests in its own database, keeping copies of the data for up to one year.

From April 1, 2003 on, the Swiss telecom providers have to keep a log for six months of all communication traffic data,[5211] to comply with the new Federal Law on the Surveillance of Mail and Telecommunications.[5212] Implementation of this law will require that the respective telephone companies constantly track phones and store the data collected. Whereas until 2003 interception was possible in all investigations relating to crimes and offenses (crimes for which a prison sentence can be issued), the new law prohibits any preventive interception and provides, for the first time, for a catalogue of offenses. In the case of investigations on crimes and offenses described in the catalogue, an instruction judge (*Untersuchungsrichter*), with the allowance of the prosecution chamber, can order providers to hand over the archived data. The same catalogue is relevant for real-time interception cases. In this case, a judge can compel a provider to install a direct connection of all telecommunications to the STS.[5213] In March 2003, the catalogue of criminal offenses allowing interception has been extended, introducing provisions against the "financing of terrorism."[5214]

On October 21, 2003, the Federal Court decided in a unanimous vote that, in the case of wiretapping, the Federal Prosecutor has the duty to inform the persons

---

[5211] "Traffic data" means the technical data of the connections (*Kommunikationsranddaten*) sent by their customers by telephone, fax or the Internet. These data include the time, the sender and receiver's dial number, as well as – in the case of mobile phones – the geographical location.

[5212] *Bundesgesetz zur Überwachung des Post- und Fernmeldeverkehrs* (BÜPF, SR 780.1) (*Loi fédérale sur la surveillance de la correspondance postale et des telecommunications*) <www.admin.ch/ch/f/rs/c780_1.html>, available at <www.admin.ch/ch/f/rs/c780_1.html> and its implementing decree, *Ordonnance du 31 octobre 2001 sur la surveillance de la correspondance par poste et télécommunication* (OSCPT), RS 780.11 from October 31, 2001, available at <www.admin.ch/ch/f/rs/c780_11.html> (*Verordnung zur Überwachung des Post- und Fernmeldeverkehrs* (VÜPF, SR 780.11)), available at <http://www.admin.ch/ch/d/sr/c780_11.html>.

[5213] However, this does not include communication by way of ADSL, WLAN, voice-over-IP, MMS and SMS-over-GPRS, *see* the article "Taube Lauscher", facts October 7, 2007, p.26. While at the beginning of the 1990s about 500 interception orders were issued annually, the number has continuously increased to about 2,000 orders since 1996 (2,138 cases). (Conseil National, Heures de Questions: Session d'hiver 1999, *Réponse du Conseil fédéral concernant les écoutes téléphoniques* (Answer by the Federal Council, Decembre 20, 1999,) available at <http://www.parlament.ch/afs/data/f/gesch/1999/f_gesch_19993427.htm>.) To these orders, another 2,000 cases of disclosure of traffic data have to be added. Furthermore, Swiss authorities ordered 2,430 telephone taps in 2000 compared with 2,046 the previous year. More than a third of them were ordered in connection with a suspected breach in drugs law, an 18 percent increase ("Phonetapping on the Increase," July 23, 2003, available at <http://www.swissinfo.org/sen/Swissinfo.html?siteSect=111&sid=1000096>). In 2002, lawful interception concerned 6,646 telephones, 2/3 of the mobile phones, that is 1,551 more than in 2001. Almost 3,000 real-time observations were established in 2002. The tariff for lawful interceptions according to BÜPF has been changed for April 1, 2004. For Internet Service Providers, there are only two tariffs since then. One is for requests of past data from log files and it is CHF 538 flat (IP address, login number, email log). The other one is CHF 1,326 flat for real-time transmission of e-mail messages. Since it is always a flat rate no matter how long the interception (or logs, up to six months) is, some suspect that law enforcement will always opt for maximum period just in case. Statistics for the years 1998-2003 are available at <http://www.uvek.admin.ch/kommunikation/dba/unterseite2/index.html?lang=de>. In regards to the Internet traffic, the newspaper "Sonntagszeitung" calculated a projection of about 3,000 ex-post requests per year (Michael Soukup: "Sorgen mit dem Datenhunger", Sonntagszeitung 30.01.2005, p.102.)

[5214] *See* <http://www.admin.ch/ch/d/as/2003/3043.pdf>.

observed after surveillance has been carried out, including information about the reasons of the monitoring.[5215]

In a March 2004 revision of the Penal Code (*Strafgesetzbuch*), commercial companies are allowed to keep logs of phone conversations with their clients, even without their consent, for the purpose of securing evidence. However, they are not allowed to analyze this data for marketing purposes, or to give this data to third parties.[5216]

Prepaid Mobile Phone Cards

In March 2003, the National Council (*Nationalrat*) passed a law that made it illegal to purchase cell phone SIM cards without providing personal information. The National Council was following the decisions of the smaller chamber (*Ständerat*, or Council of States), which had decided to pass such a law in December 2002 in the context of the UN Convention for the Suppression of the Financing of Terrorism.[5217] From July 2004 on, every prepaid SIM card issued after November 1, 2002 has to be registered by presenting an officially accepted identity document. Asylum seekers often do not have such a document and are

---

[5215] Federal Court, BGE 8G.109/2003 of 21.10.2003, no publication. There have been numerous public revelations of illegal wiretapping. A 1993 inquiry found that phones used by journalists and ministers in the Swiss Parliament were tapped (Statewatch bulletin, Volume 3, Number 1, January-February 1993). The data protection commissioner also accused the Swisscom (Telecom PTT at that time), the state telephone company, of illegally wiretapping telephones. In February 1998, an agent for Israel's Mossad Secret Service was arrested by the Swiss authorities for attempting to tap the phone of a Lebanese immigrant whom he believed had links to the Hezbollah. On July 7, 2000 the Swiss court handed down a one-year sentence to be suspended for two years ("Swiss Court Hands Mossad Spy a Suspended One-year Sentence," Associated Press, July 10, 2000).

[5216] Presumably with the exception of giving away such data to investigating police forces, in the case that a judge ordered it. see: *Änderung des Art. 179 quinqies StGB, Abs. 1, Bst. b) vom 1. März 2004* (AS 2004 823). *Schweizerisches Strafgesetzbuch* (Code Penal) vom 21. Dezember 1937 (SR 311.0) <http://www.admin.ch/ch/d/sr/c311_0.html>, with the new article 179 quinqies: <http://www.admin.ch/ch/d/as/2004/823.pdf>.

[5217] Topic *02.052 – Uno-Übereinkommen gegen Terrorismusfinanzierung und Bombenterrorismus* <http://www.parlament.ch/afs/data/d/gesch/2002/d_gesch_20020052.htm>. According to a New York Times report: "following testimony from a Swiss federal prosecutor, Claude Nicati, that the Swisscom cards had become popular with [Al] Qaeda operatives." ("How Tiny Swiss Cellphone Chips Helped Track Global Terror Web," New York Times, March 4, 2004, available at <http://www.nytimes.com/2004/03/04/international/europe/04PHON.html?ex=1079384398&ei=1&en=efa2261 f4a39d7e9>). According to the telecom providers, more than two million prepaid SIM cards have been sold in Switzerland. Approximately one-third of all mobile phone customers in Switzerland are using a card of this type. In order to comply with the new regulation, the Swiss government released a revision of the regulation VÜPF on June 23, 2004, forcing all Swiss telecom providers to sell their mobile SIM cards only if the customer provides a proof of identity. This rule came into force on August 1, 2004. According to telecom providers, approximately 300,000 prepaid SIM cards have been sold anonymously since July 2002. For all these cards, the providers have to organize the registration ex post by sending the customers a text message (SMS) asking them to register personally. If these customers fail to prove their identity, the providers were compelled to block their SIM cards after October 31, 2004 (*See* Revision of the VÜPF, *Verordnung zur Überwachung des Post- und Fernmeldeverkehrs* (VÜPF, SR 780.11) <http://www.admin.ch/ch/d/sr/c780_11.html>, *Änderung vom 23. Juni 2004* <http://www.uvek.admin.ch/imperia/md/content/gs_uvek2/d/kommunikation/20.pdf>).

thus excluded from using mobile phones. In order to allow asylum seekers to use mobile phones, human rights groups organized a network of Swiss people "sponsoring" their name for the purchase of SIM cards.[5218] Opposition against the new law also comes from attorneys (saying it is "not useful") and from telecommunications companies (saying it is "too expensive"). In March 2004, the Swiss Attorney General (*Bundesanwalt)* announced that tracking prepaid mobile phone cards (SIM cards) released by the Swiss telecom provider Swisscom helped the US intelligence find terrorists in Afghanistan.[5219]

Electronic Warfare and Satellite Telecom Interception

In October 2003, the Swiss government introduced a new regulation on electronic warfare.[5220] The regulation allows the military forces to disrupt civilians' mobile phone communications and regulates radio interception, including the interception of satellite communications. Since the end of the 1990s, Switzerland has been building up a system for satellite interception of the COMINT type (Communications Intelligence), similar to the UK/USA "Echelon" system. The Swiss system, first called "Satos-3" then ONYX, started its operations in April 2000. All three operational sites are planned to be working by the end of 2005. Like the "Echelon" system, ONYX interception operates with software filtering the content of satellite communications for specific keywords.[5221]

The preventive Police Section DAP[5222] is demanding access to the ONYX data and would like to be allowed to give orders for preventive interceptions. In February 2005, the parliamentary Security Commission of the *Ständerat* presented a list of additional measures "to combat terrorism and organized

---

[5218] *See* <http://www.augenauf.ch>.

[5219] The New York Times wrote: "The investigation helped narrow the search for one of the most wanted men in the world, Khalid Shaikh Mohammed, who is accused of being the mastermind of the September 11 attacks." and explained, citing "a senior intelligence official based in Europe," "They thought these phones protected their anonymity, but they didn't [. . .] Even without personal information, the authorities were able to conduct routine monitoring of phone conversations." *See* Don Van Natta Jr. and Desmond Butler, "How Tiny Swiss Cellphone Chips Helped Track Global Terror Web," New York Times, March 4, 2004, available at <http://www.nytimes.com/2004/03/04/international/europe/04PHON.html?ex=1079384398&ei=1&en=efa2261f4a39d7e9>).

[5220] *Verordnung vom 15. Oktober 2003 über die elektronische Kriegführung* (VEKF, SR 510.292), Inkrafttreten am 1. November 2003, <http://www.admin.ch/ch/d/sr/c510_292.html>. Art. 10 on "disturbing telecommunication". The regulation is based on the "Military Law" (*Militärgesetz* MG, SR 510.10), available at <http://www.admin.ch/ch/d/sr/c510_10.html>.

[5221] For more detailed information on the Swiss ONYX system, *see* Switzerland chapter of *PHR 2004*.

[5222] DAP is the *Dienst für Analyse und Prävention* at the Swiss Federal Police, *see* <http://www.fedpol.ch>. Until now, the DAP did not have direct access to the ONYX data collected by the military intelligence services (SND, Strategischer Nachrichtendienst).

crime," e.g. asking the government to allow the Swiss Attorney General to access the military "electronic warfare systems" and to give orders to intercept communications "by terrorists."[5223]

According to media reports, the ONYX system is being technically updated. For 2005, the government asked for a credit of 186.1 Mio. CHF for new military projects. A 10 Mio. part of this credit seems to be "top secret," not even the parliamentary "finance commission" knows any details. On November 27, 2003, the usually well-informed journalist Bruno Vanoni theorized that this credit could be used for a technical update of the ONYX project, now called "Malachit."[5224] In the first reading, the *Nationalrat* (larger chamber of the parliament) rejected the proposal, but in the second reading, it was accepted by 101 to 68 votes.[5225]

In December 2004, a hidden audio surveillance installation has been found in the "Salon Français" of the United Nations "Palais des Nations" in Geneva. It is not clear who owned the installation. It is not clear if Swiss Authorities will be allowed to investigate the case, because of the United Nations "extraterritoriality".

DNA Samples, Biometry, and Genetic Screening

In July 2000, a regulation on the collection and storage of genetic profiles was introduced, allowing the Swiss administration – by way of a new Agency called AFIS Services – to establish and operate a centralized database with DNA profiles of persons and stains.[5226] The Federal Office has collected data for the police since August 1, 2000. All samples taken by the police are given a unique identifier, so that the name of the suspect is never disclosed to laboratory employees. The regulation states that police forces are allowed to collect DNA samples only in case the offense committed is listed in a catalogue.[5227] However,

---

[5223] "05.3006 Po. Sicherheitspolitische Kommission SR (21.2.2005) Effizientere Bekämpfung von Terrorismus und organisiertem Verbrechen," available at
<http://www.parlament.ch/afs/data/d/gesch/2005/d_gesch_20053006.htm>.

[5224] Bruno Vanoni, "Rütteln am geheimen neuen Abhörprojekt", in Tages-Anzeiger, 27.11.2004, p.3; and Bruno Vanoni, "Keine Kürzung beim neuen geheimen Abhörprojekt," in Tages-Anzeiger, 02.12.2004, p.2.

[5225] Amtliches Bulletin, Nationalrat, Winter session 2004, 1.12.2004, Geschäft "04.047 Voranschlag der Eidgenossenschaft 2005", Budgetposten "3210.001 Projektierung, Erprobung und Beschaffungsvorbereitung (PEB)", *AB 2004 N 1844 / BO 2004 N 1844,* available at
<http://www.parlament.ch/ab/data/d/n/4706/114076/d_n_4706_114076_114090.htm#114154>

[5226] *Verordnung über das DNA-Profil-Informationssystem* (EDNA, SR 361.1)
<http://www.admin.ch/ch/d/sr/c361_1.html>.

[5227] EDNA, Article 5, for details on the procedure *see also* W.Bär, Adelgunde Kratzer & M. Strehler, "Swiss Federal DNA Profile Information System – EDNA," available at
<http://www.promega.com/geneticidproc/ussymp12proc/abstracts/bar.pdf>.

this catalogue not only includes crimes like murder, sexual offenses, life endangerment and rape, but also theft (*Diebstahl*). Further, there are reports (and lawsuits) of cases where the police have taken DNA samples of persons who did not commit any of these offenses.[5228] By the end of 2003, EDNA contained 45,313 DNA profiles. One year later, it had almost 60,000.[5229] On January 1, 2005, the EDNA regulation was replaced by a formal law,[5230] which does not have a catalogue of offenses at all.

In March 2004, the majority of the National Council decided to allow life insurance companies to review previous DNA analyses of persons in case they want to sign a contract with a life or a voluntary insurance company against invalidity. The bill was approved by the smaller chamber (*Ständerat*) in June 2004 and again in October 2004. The deadline for a referendum passed on January 27, 2005 without a request for a public ballot; the new law will enter into force soon.[5231]

Revision of the Law on Asylum

In May 2004, the National Council discussed a revision of the Law on Asylum.[5232] The revision would allow the collection of biometric data of immigrants and would allow the police to transmit data of asylum seekers to their home nation, even before the request of the asylum seeker is decided upon. A minority in the National Council criticized the fact that this rule would place asylum seekers and their relatives in danger. Despite the opposition, the National Council accepted the revision by 2/3 of the votes on May 5, 2004. The law still

---

[5228] *See e.g.* Heiner Busch, "Die Wattestäbchenattacke", in WOZ Die Wochenzeitung, Nr. 26/2004, available at <http://www.woz.ch/artikel/archiv/10141.html>, as well as reports at <http://switzerland.indymedia.org/demix/2004/11/28078.shtml>. For a critical comment on DNA samples see also Markus Hofmann "DNA-Profile - die Lieblinge der Polizei," in: Neue Zürcher Zeitung NZZ, March 4, 2005, p.13. According to this article, every sample costs about 295 CHF.

[5229] Heiner Busch, "Das neue Schweizer Wettfichen" in WOZ Die Wochenzeitung nr. 9, March 3, 2005, p.6.

[5230] *Bundesgesetz über die Verwendung von DNA-Profilen im Strafverfahren und zur Identifizierung von unbekannten oder vermissten Personen (DNA-Profil-Gesetz, SR 363* <http://www.admin.ch/ch/d/sr/c363.html>, as well as the corresponding regulation (decreee) *(DNA-Profil-Verordnung,* SR 363.1 <http://www.admin.ch/ch/d/sr/c363_1.html>). For the discussion in the parliament *see* (Nationalrat, Amtliches Bulletin, 20.06.03-08h00) <http://www.parlament.ch/ab/data/d/n/4619/86799/d_n_4619_86799_86951.htm>. In September 2002, the majority of the National Council decided, against the recommendation of the preparing commission, not to include any catalogue in the new law on DNA profiles. After the tsunami disaster in December 2004 in Southeast Asia, a lot of DNA samples of Swiss relatives of missing tourists have been taken.

[5231] *Bundesgesetz über genetische Untersuchungen beim Menschen* (Parliamentary number 02.065, SR 814.02, Bundesblatt Nr. 41, 19 October 2004, pp.5483ff, available at <http: http://www.admin.ch/ch/d/ff/2004/5483.pdf)>. For a summary of the parliamentary discussion *see* <http://www.parlament.ch/afs/data/d/rb/d_rb_20020065.htm> (in German).

[5232] *Asylgesetzrevision, see* "Dossier Asylgesetz" of the Swiss Parliament and *"Sondersession 3.-5. Mai 2004: Überblick über die Entscheide des Nationalrats,"* available at <http://www.parlament.ch/do-asylgesetz>.

---

has to be discussed by the second chamber (*Ständerat*). Humanitarian organizations, including Amnesty International, are criticizing Switzerland for restricting the rights of asylum seekers. The Social Democratic Party sought to organize a referendum, asking for a public ballot, if the bill will not meet minimal humanitarian standards.[5233]

Revision of the Law on Foreigners

In May 2004, the National Council began to debate the revision of the Law on Foreigners.[5234] The larger chamber of the Federal Parliament decided to include biometric data in foreigners' identity documents. The law would also provide a definite legal basis for the Central Register of Foreigners, which now holds data on about 4.5 million persons. In order to avoid so-called "faked marriages" (*Scheinehen*), the law provides that marriage officers (*Zivilstandsbeamte*) would be allowed to investigate the "honesty" of bi-national marriages. In June 2004, the National Council passed the law, despite strong opposition in the parliamentary commission concerned. The second chamber (*Ständerat*) discussed the bill in March 2005 and introduced even more severe restrictions for foreigners.[5235] The bill now goes back to the National Council.

Surveillance Cameras

More and more public transport companies are introducing CCTV in their vehicles. After a pilot test in 2002 and 2003, the Swiss Federal Railway company SBB (now a private company, but still owned by the state) announced a large project to install surveillance cameras in trains.[5236] Until 2003, such surveillance was not allowed by law, neither was the operation of CCTV systems in train stations. In December 2003, a regulation was subsequently introduced, allowing the SBB to operate CCTV systems in train stations and inside trains.[5237]

[5233] Media release of the Socialdemocratic Party of May 17, 2005, available at <http://www.sp-ps.ch/aktuell/communiques_detail.htm?view_Communiques_OID=344>.

[5234] *Ausländergesetzrevision*, Dossier <http://www.parlament.ch/do-auslaendergesetz> and the *Bundesgesetz über die Ausländerinnen und Ausländer (AuG, Entwurf)* <http://www.admin.ch/ch/d/ff/2002/3851.pdf> (Parliamentary nr. 02.024).

[5235] Discussion in the Parliament (*Ständerat*) available at <http://www.parlament.ch/ab/data/d/s/4707/122615/d_s_4707_122615_122623.htm>.

[5236] *See* media release <http://www.sbb.ch/gs/press/press_0303_d.htm#210303Kamera,berwachung>.

[5237] *Verordnung über die Videoüberwachung durch die Schweizerischen Bundesbahnen SBB (Videoüberwachungsverordnung SBB, VüV-SBB)* SR 742.147.2, <http://www.uvek.admin.ch/imperia/md/content/gs_uvek2/d/verkehr/schienenverkehr/vuev/1.pdf>, as well as the media release of the Department UVEK, December 5, 2003, available at <http://www.uvek.admin.ch/dokumentation/medienmitteilungen/artikel/20031205/01748/index.html>.

The city police of Zurich bought a new mobile camera system with capabilities for automatic car plate recognition (AFNES) to be operated in Zurich. It will be able to identify car plates and compare the results with the national database RIPOL. With closer connections to EU justice and police agencies, Switzerland will likely also gain direct access to European car plate databases. According to some sources, the use of an automatic plate recognition system is planned on at least one Swiss highway tunnel in order to control speed limits.[5238]

The growth of video surveillance in Switzerland is helped by the cameras getting smaller, cheaper and more sophisticated. This is especially true for the systems operated by private entities, such as shopkeepers or house owners. Also, more sport stadiums are installing CCTV cameras. However, opposition against camera surveillance is growing as well. The committee of the Swiss "Big Brother Awards" has been organizing several "excursions" on the subject of surveillance cameras in Zurich and released a map with camera locations in a city district of Zurich, as well as in the Zurich Main Train Station.[5239] The Federal Data Protection Commissioner published a leaflet explaining the legal conditions for private individuals to operate video surveillance cameras.[5240]

Unmanned Aerial Vehicles

The Swiss Air Force started operating Unmanned Aerial Vehicles (*Drohnen*) of the type "ADS 95 Ranger." They are produced in Switzerland by the company RUAG in Emmen LU, in collaboration with Israeli companies. On January 6, 2004, on a test flight, a military UAV observed a civil car driving into a forest near Lucerne. The operators informed the local police patrol, who amended the car passengers for smoking marijuana.[5241] According to a media report, the Swiss Air Force is operating one to four UAV test flights every day. The images of the cameras are registered and stored for up to six months.

In honor of this privacy invasion, the Air Force received one of four Swiss "Big Brother Awards 2004."[5242] On Easter Holiday 2005, the Army offered their

---

[5238] "Abschnittsgeschwindigkeitskontrolle," planned for the Belchentunnel from 2005 on, *see* <http://www.radar.ch/Infoblitz/0304.pdf> (especially p. 2).

[5239] *See* <http://www.bigbrotherawards.ch/kameras/>.

[5240] *See* <http://www.edsb.ch/e/doku/merkblaetter/video.htm>.

[5241] *See* "Von der Luftwaffe beim Kiffen erwischt", NZZ am Sonntag on May 23, 2004, <http://www.nzz.ch/2004/05/23/il/page-article9M50A.html> (in German). During the Olympic Games in Athens, Greece in Summer 2004, Swiss surveillance "Zeppelins" were used to observe the city.

[5242] *See* <http://www.bigbrotherawards.ch/hallofshame>.

UAVs to cantonal police forces in order to observe north-south traffic on the Gotthard route. For the celebration of the International Worker's Day on May 1, 2004, the Zurich police asked the Air Force about using UAVs to observe the rally in Zurich from the air. These examples show a strengthened collaboration between military and police forces.

Face Recognition

At the Zurich "Unique" airport, the cantonal Police of Zurich tested a pilot system for automatic face recognition between February and June 2003. Officially, the *Farec* (Face Recognition system, mainly aims at recognizing people trying to immigrate without identity documents. This is the first test worldwide of face recognition in the context of boarder controls. During the test phase, 1,003 passengers of 277 flights were registered by *Farec*. In 81 cases, a search in the database followed, with 10 hits and 17 fails. In December 2004, the Zurich Cantonal Government (*Regierungsrat*) provided a legal regulation (decree, *Verordnung*), extending the test phase until the end of 2006.[5243] Although quite skeptical about the usefulness of the system, the data protection officer of the canton Zurich accepted the decree.[5244]

Private Surveillance

Customer loyalty programs (*Kundenbindungsprogramme*) are still expanding. According to the largest retail chain in Switzerland, Migros, more than one out of two households in Switzerland has a grocery shopping card. Data from the largest competitor, COOP, is similar. Smaller companies are also issuing their own cards. There is a growing risk that customers' databases are being merged, thus providing increasingly detailed data profiles. As an example, in 2004, the second-largest Swiss retailer, COOP, established a collaboration with the largest Swiss telecom provider, Swisscom, to share their respective "bonus points." Both companies stress that the exchange program consists only of aggregated data (*i.e.*

[5243] *Verordnung über den Einsatz eines biometrischen Gesichtserkennungssystems am Flughafen Zürich vom 8. Dezember 2004*, (Nr. 551.113, available at
<http://www.sk.zh.ch/internet/sk/de/mm/mm_2004_quartal_4/285_gesichtserkennung.ContentList.0002.Docum ent.tmp/Verordnung%20%FCber%20den%20Einsatz%20eines%20biometrischen%20Gesichtserkennungssyste ms%20a>). *See also* the media release issued by the *Regierungsrates* on December 16, .2004
(http://www.sk.zh.ch/internet/sk/de/mm/mm_2004_quartal_4/285_gesichtserkennung.html). *See also* Marcel Gyr, "Weiterer Test des Gesichtserkennungssystems," in: Neue Zürcher Zeitung NZZ, December 17, 2004, p.53.

[5244] *See, e.g.*, Neue Zürcher Zeitung, 23. August 2002, No. 194, p.37, and *id.*, and Stefan Hohler, "Phase 2 für 'Frühwarnsystem'" in Tages-Anzeiger December 17,.2004.

bonus points), and that they do not exchange nor merge detailed information about specific customers.

Police forces are increasingly trying to get access to data collected by private companies. The political police DAP at Fedpol is demanding systematic access to data of financial intermediaries, like banks.[5245]

The largest retailer, Migros, is involved in a research program on RFIDs (radio frequency identification tags) at the University of St. Gall, together with SAP and other software companies.[5246] Until now, the has not been large-scale commercial use of RFID in Switzerland, with the exception of some ski lifts in mountain resort areas. Also, RFIDs are increasingly used as access control devices by companies, libraries, schools, etc. In August 2002, the Swiss Federal Railway Company SBB decided to postpone their project of RFID-based contactless train tickets called "EasyRide." On the other hand, "Kindercity," an entertainment center for children in Volketswil near Zurich, introduced RFID tags to control their young guests.[5247]

Insurance companies are interested in data about their customers. In summer 2003, the company Winterthur admitted that it used to keep secret data files on "risky customers," without informing either the Federal Data Protection Commissioner or the customers, and thus not allowing their costumers to correct inaccurate data.[5248] Further, according to media reports in May 2004, some insurance companies are systematically using lie detectors (*Lügendetektoren*) in their call centers in order to detect if customers are lying when reporting their losses or damages (*Schäden*) without notifying them of this fact.

In the context of a large reorganization of the billing system of medical services provided by doctors and hospitals, the association of private health insurance companies (*Krankenkassen*), Santésuisse, is forcing the new tariff system

---

[5245] .Markus Steudler: "Der Staat will wieder lauschen." NZZ am Sonntag, May 1, 2005, p.11.

[5246] Auto-ID Center at the University of St. Gall at <http://www.m-lab.ch/>.

[5247] Laurent Burkhalter, "Kindercity, enfants à puces," a TV report by the station Télévision Suisse Romande, *Nouvo*, émission du 28 octobre 2004, available at <http://www.nouvo.ch/55-1>.

[5248] According to the Federal Law on Data Protection, every systematically organized database on personal data has to be registered by the Federal Data Protection Commissioner. (This rule may be abrogated in the current revision proposal). Further, the law states the right of everyone to get information about their personal data in the database, as well as the right to correct wrong data – with the exception of "secret data bases." In this case, the Federal Data Protection Commissioner has the duty to act as an intermediary. *See Bundesgesetz über den Datenschutz* (DSG, SR 235.1) vom 19. Juni 1992 (Stand am 3. Oktober 2000), available at <http://www.admin.ch/ch/d/sr/c235_1.html>. For an English translation *see* <http://www.ics.uci.edu/~kobsa/privacy/switzerland.htm> or <http://www.edsb.ch/e/gesetz/schweiz/index.htm>.

Tarmed. According to this system, medical service providers have to include detailed ICD-10-Codes[5249] in their bills, which are being handed over the insurance companies. By this system, the insurance companies get access to sensitive data about their customers. Although there have been critiques and protests by customers and doctors, as well as by Data Protection Commissioners, the Tarmed system is officially in operation since January 1, 2004. In October 2004, the TARMED system of santésuisse has been honored by the fifth Swiss "Big Brother Award" in the category Business.[5250]

In the case reported by the Swiss advocacy group "bigbrotherawards.ch", the Swiss Banking Company "Postfinance" has transmitted banking data illegally to the US: A customer ordered a payment to another Swiss Bank (UBS) in favor of the Child Aid Agency "Camaquito" in Cuba. As the payment has been blocked by the "US Department of the Treasury" (sic!) it became clear that US authorities have insight in banking data. The Federal Data Protection Officer urged "Postfinance" to change their procedure on transmitting data to the US, or at least to inform their clients clearly about the possibility of such transmissions.[5251]

Freedom of Information

In some cantons, the data protection law is at the same time a "Freedom of Information Law" (*Öffentlichkeitsgesetz*), and the data protection officer has the duties of a Freedom of Information Protection Officer as well. According to such laws, all official documents should be publicly available and citizens have a legal right to receive information - except if a document is declared as confidential. Other cantons and the Confederation are preparing a similar law.[5252] However, the first consultations among interested parties are revealing considerable opposition, *e.g.* in the canton of Zurich.

[5249] IDC stands for International Code of Diseases. The International Statistical Classification of Diseases and Related Health Problems (commonly known by the abbreviation ICD) is published by the World Health Organization. It is currently in its tenth edition, known as the ICD-10. *See* <http://www.yourencyclopedia.net/International_Code_of_Diseases>.

[5250] *See* the Swiss Big Brother Awards "Hall of Shame" at <http://www.bigbrotherawards.ch/diverses/hallofshame#shame>, Category "Business."

[5251] The story is documented at <http://www.enterag.ch/hartwig/cuba/postfinance.html> (in German).

[5252] For the Confederation, *see* the proposal for a *Bundesgesetz über das Öffentlichkeitsprinzip der Verwaltung* (*Öffentlichkeitsgesetz*, BGÖ; SR 152.), published in the Bundesblatt 2004, pp. 7269ff. (<http://www.admin.ch/ch/d/ff/2004/7269.pdf>) and the corresponding governmental report (*Botschaft*) at <http://www.ofec.admin.ch/themen/oeffprinzip/bot-d.pdf>. The delay for a referendum was passed on April 7, 2005 without any request for a referendum. For an overview of this law, *see* <http://www.ofj.admin.ch/themen/oeffprinzip/intro-d.htm> (in German). Critics of the new law argue that it contains too many exceptions.

By April 2005, a revision of the regulation (decree) on Land Registers (*Grundbuchverordnung*), dating back to 1910, has been put into force by the Government.[5253] The cantons are now allowed to publish parts of the register on the Internet.

International Obligations

Switzerland is a member of the Council of Europe (CoE) and has signed and ratified the Convention for the Protection of Individuals with Regard to Automatic Processing of Personal Data (Convention No. 108) in 1997.[5254] Switzerland has also signed and ratified the European Convention for the Protection of Human Rights and Fundamental Freedoms (ECHR).[5255] On 13 May 2005, Switzerland signed Protocol 14 to the ECHR, amending the Convention's control system, at the 114th session of the Committee of Ministers of the Council of Europe held in Strasbourg.[5256] In November 2001, Switzerland signed, but has not ratified, the CoE Convention on Cybercrime.[5257] It is a member of the Organization for Economic Cooperation and Development (OECD) and has adopted the OECD Guidelines on the Protection of Privacy and Transborder Flows of Personal Data.

Republic of China (Taiwan)

Constitutional Privacy Framework

Article 12 of the 1946 Republic of China Constitution states, "The people shall have freedom of privacy of correspondence."[5258] Additionally, the Constitution

---

[5253] *Grundbuchverordnung*, (GBV; SR 211.432.1, <http://www.admin.ch/ch/d/sr/c211_432_1.html>. The changes have been published in the official publication of laws (AS) at <http://www.admin.ch/ch/d/as/2005/1343.pdf>. For an overview in English, *see* <http://www.ofj.admin.ch/themen/gba/intro-e.htm>.

[5254] "*Übereinkommen zum Schutz des Menschen bei der automatischen Verarbeitung personenbezogener Daten. Abgeschlossen in Strassburg am 28. Januar 1981. Von der Bundesversammlung genehmigt am 5. Juni 1997. Schweizerische Ratifikationsurkunde hinterlegt am 2. Oktober 1997. Für die Schweiz in Kraft getreten am 1. Februar 1998*" (Übersetzung des französischen Originaltextes, Translation of the original in French, RO 2002 2847). SR 0.235.1) <http://www.admin.ch/ch/d/as/2002/2847.pdf>. Signed October 2, 1997; ratified October 2, 1997; entered into force February 1, 1998.

[5255] EMRK, signed in Rome on November 4, 1950, accepted by the parliament on October 3, 1974, ratified on November 28, 1974 <http://www.admin.ch/ch/d/sr/0_101/index.html>.

[5256] *See* <http://www.ofj.admin.ch/themen/menschenrechte/prot14emrk-com-e.htm>.

[5257] Signed November 23, 2001.

[5258] Constitution of the Republic of China, Adopted by the National Assembly on December 25, 1946, promulgated by the National Government on January 1, 1947, and effective from December 25, 1947, available at <http://www.president.gov.tw/1_roc_intro/index_e.html>.

protects many rights that have an impact on privacy, such as free exercise of religion (Article 13) and freedom of association (Article 14).[5259]

Data Protection Framework

The most important statutory privacy provision in Taiwan is the Computer-Processed Personal Data Protection Law, enacted in August 1995.[5260] The Act governs the collection and use of personally identifiable information by government agencies and many areas of the private sector. It requires that "[t]he collection or utilization of personal data shall respect the rights and interests of the principal and such personal data shall be handled in accordance with the principles of honesty and credibility so as not to exceed the scope of the specific purpose."[5261] Individuals have a right of access to and correction of their data, the ability to request cessation of computerized processing and use, and the ability to request deletion of their data. Data flows to countries without privacy laws can be prohibited, and damages can be assessed for violations. The Act also establishes separate principles for eight categories of private institutions: credit information organizations, hospitals, schools, telecommunications businesses, financial businesses, securities businesses, insurance businesses, and mass media, as well as "other enterprises, organizations, or individuals designated by the Ministry of Justice and the central government authorities in charge of concerned end enterprises."[5262] Numerous scandals involving leaks of personal information from government and private entities to crime syndicates have resulted in calls for lawmakers to strengthen the law.[5263] In 2004, the Cabinet approved a draft amendment that would significantly increase the maximum penalty for those who release personal data. If approved, violators would face a possibility of five years imprisonment or a fine of TWD one million (~USD 31,700).[5264]

[5259] *Id.*

[5260] Computer-Processed Personal Data Protection Law of August 11, 1995, available at <http://www.virtual-asia.com/taiwan/bizpack/legalcodes/cpdpl.htm>.

[5261] *Id.*

[5262] *See generally* for an overview on the current status of personal data protection in Taiwan, in particular on the inadequacy of the Computer-Processed Personal Data Protection Law, Tyng-Ruey Chuang, "Personal Data Protection in Taiwan: Whose Business?" 53-70 National Policy Quarterly, vol. 2, No. 1 (March 2003), available at <http://www.iis.sinica.edu.tw/~trc/npq2003.pdf> (in Chinese with English abstract).

[5263] *See, e.g.*, Jimmy Chuang, "Ministry Looks to Protect Privacy," Taipei Times, July 2, 2003; "DPP Seeks Tighter Rules on Personal Data," China Post, April 24, 2004; "Compensation Sought for Victims over Leaks of Personal Data," China Post, June 1, 2004.

[5264] Ko Shu-ling, "Change Data-Protection Law: Cabinet," Taipei Times, September 9, 2004, available at <http://www.taipeitimes.com/News/taiwan/archives/2004/09/09/2003202190>.

Supervisory Authorities

There is no single privacy oversight body to enforce the Act. The Ministry of Justice enforces the Act for government agencies. For the private sector, the relevant government agency for that sector enforces compliance. For example, the Criminal Investigation Bureau (CIB) arrested several people in November 1998 for selling lists of more than 15 million voters and personal data of up to 40 million individuals in violation of the Act.[5265]

Wiretapping and Surveillance

Several laws control spying or surveillance by private parties. Article 315 of Taiwan's Criminal Code states that a person who, without reason, opens or conceals a sealed letter, or other sealed document belonging to another, may be punished under the law. The 1996 Telecommunications Law states "Unauthorized third parties shall not receive, record or use other illegal means to infringe upon the secrets of telecommunications enterprises and telecommunications messages. A telecommunications enterprise should take proper and necessary measures to protect its telecommunications security."[5266] The Act was amended in October 1999 to increase penalties for illegal telephone taps to TWD 1.5 million (~USD 44,000) and up to five years in prison.

Illegal wiretapping by the government has been a widespread problem in Taiwan for years. Previously, under the martial law-era Telecommunications Surveillance Act and Code of Criminal Procedure, judicial and security authorities simply had to file a written request with a prosecutor's office to wiretap a suspect's telephone calls. In June 1999, the Parliament approved the Telecommunication Protection and Control Act to impose stricter guidelines on when and how wiretaps can be used, although they can still be approved for broad reasons such as "national security" and "social order." The act also requires telecommunications providers to assist law enforcement and sets technical requirements for interception, which is opposed by mobile phone providers.[5267] In 1998, the Supreme Court ruled that evidence obtained through illegal wiretaps was not admissible in a criminal trial.

[5265] "Police Arrest Data Thieves," China News, November 10, 1998.

[5266] Telecommunications Law 1996, February 5, 1996.

[5267] "Private Cellular Firms Feel Threatened by Wiretap Law," Taipei Times, November 13, 1999.

The Prosecutor General's Office revealed in 1999 that more than 15,000 people were subject to wiretapping, including for "political intelligence" in the first half of 1999.[5268] According to the United States State Department, the number of wiretaps was reduced to 3,377 in 2000 and 6,505 in 2001 following the enactment of the new law.[5269] However, according to the Ministry of Justice (MOJ), the number of approved wiretaps rose to approximately 10,000 in 2002 and 13,834 in 2003, apparently due to vote-buying investigations during local and national elections.[5270] The increase in total wiretap authorizations continued, reaching 19,485 in 2004. In an effort to stem this problem, the MOJ is pushing legislators to transfer wiretap authority from prosecutors to judges.[5271] In January 2000, a wiretap was found at the campaign office of presidential candidate (now President) Chen Shui-bian.[5272] Independent presidential candidate James Soong alleged in November 1999 that the government was tapping his campaign and home phones.[5273]

The new law also regulates wiretapping by the intelligence services, which previously operated without any supervision. In October 2000, Chin Huei-chu, a People First Party legislator, accused the Military Intelligence Bureau (MIB) of conducting political surveillance domestically. The MIB denied the allegations, saying that all intelligence work was directed solely at mainland China.[5274] Many legislators also claim that the National Security Bureau (NSB), which oversees national law enforcement, routinely monitors the phone conversations of politicians. This charge is also denied by the NSB.[5275]

Recent Developments

Under the HIV Prevention Law, the government can demand that foreigners who have been in Taiwan for more than three months take an HIV test and may deport

---

[5268] "Surveillance Must not Be Abused," China News, November 7, 1999.

[5269] United States Department of State, Country Reports on Human Rights Practices 2001, March 4, 2002, available at <http://www.state.gov/g/drl/rls/hrrpt/2001/eap/8294.htm>.

[5270] United States Department of State, Country Reports on Human Rights Practices 2003, February 25, 2004, available at <http://www.state.gov/g/drl/rls/hrrpt/2003/ 27767.htm>.

[5271] Sofia Wu, "MOJ Reaffirms Commitment to Tightening Wiretapping Authorization," Central News Agency-Taiwan, March 24, 2005.

[5272] "'Taiwan's Watergate,' Says Chen after Wiretap Found," Taipei Times, January 26, 2000.

[5273] "Soong Aides Make Wiretapping Claim," China News, November 4, 1999.

[5274] "Military Intelligence Bureau Denies Political Surveillance at Home," British Broadcasting Corporation, October 11, 2000.

[5275] Jimmy Chuang, "NSB Denies Bugging Lawmakers," Taipei Times, April 5, 2002, available at <http://www.taipeitimes.com/news/2002/04/05/print/0000130595>.

them if they test positive.[5276] This is a liberalization of the earlier rule, which called for mandatory deportation of HIV-positive foreigners.[5277] In 2004, Article 71 of the Medical Treatment Law was amended to guarantee patients the right to obtain copies of their medical records upon request. Though hospitals can be fined up to TWD 10,000 (~USD 294) for refusal to comply with the law, many continue to require physician approval before providing patients with copies of their records.[5278]

In 1997, the Taiwanese government proposed a new national ID card called the "National Integrated Circuit Card." The plan called for a smart card-based system with more than a hundred uses for the card including ID, health insurance, driver's license, taxation, and possibly small-value payments. Following public outcry based on the privacy implications of the plan, the government held hearings to evaluate it again. Eventually, the government abandoned the plan[5279] in favor of a traditional paper ID.[5280] However, the Household Registration Law will require citizens over age 14 to submit all 10 fingerprints upon receipt of their renewed national ID cards in July 2005, which the Cabinet plans to use to establish a national fingerprint bank. A proposal to abolish the fingerprinting requirement is pending in the legislature.[5281] Additionally, the ruling Democratic Progressive Party reversed its prior position and is now seeking to have the fingerprinting provision ruled unconstitutional.[5282]

Another heavily criticized scheme is a national health insurance integrated circuit (IC) card system using the national ID number, also compulsory, that stores sensitive personal information (such as ICD-9 code for illness classification) on the patient's health insurance IC card.[5283] Introduced in 2001,[5284] IC cards were issued to 99 percent of citizens by 2004.[5285] The card was initially intended to

---

[5276] "Legislature Revises HIV Prevention Law regarding Foreigners Found to Be Positive," Taipei Times, July 1, 2000.

[5277] An Enforcement Ordinance of the HIV Prevention Law.

[5278] Joy Su, "Hospitals Slow to Show Records," Taipei Times, June 17, 2004.

[5279] "When Smart Cards Get too Smart," The Industry Standard, September 7, 1998.

[5280] Tsai Ting-I, "Fingerprint Law likely to Be Axed," Taipei Times, January 1, 2002, available at <http://www.taipeitimes.com/news/2002/01/01/print/0000118132>.

[5281] Ko Shu-ling, "Yu Says Cabinet Will Obey Law over Fingerprint Bank," Taipei Times, May 30, 2004.

[5282] "Major Parties Oppose DPP's Backpedal on Fingerprinting Plan," China Post, May 30, 2005.

[5283] Tyng-Ruey Chuang, "The Health Insurance IC Card System and Personal Data Protection," Liberty Times, August 6, 2002, available at <http://www.libertytimes.com.tw/2002/new/aug/6/today-o1.htm#o4> (in Chinese).

[5284] Chuang Chi-ting, "Paperless Health-cards Unveiled," Taipei Times, November 12, 2001, available at <http://www.taipeitimes.com/news/2001/11/12/print/0000111165>.

[5285] Cecilia Fanchiang, "New IC Health Insurance Card Expected to Offer Many Benefits," Taiwan Journal, January 2, 2005.

store only enough information to make patient registration easier, but it now includes "a record of every major illness, injury, organ donation and prescription." Results of diagnostic tests are also stored on the IC card.[5286] As the National Health Insurance Act only requires a "health insurance certificate" for the purpose of identifying a person's insurance status, a compulsory IC card-based system that stores personal medical data is viewed as violating the Computer-Processed Personal Data Protection Law.[5287] Use of the national health insurance IC card at all hospitals and clinics became compulsory in 2004.[5288]

Voyeurism and scandalous revelations in the media have prompted new demands for enhanced privacy protection. A video of a Taipei City Council member allegedly engaged in sexual relations with her married lover – shot with a hidden pinhole camera – was released by a gossip magazine in 2002.[5289] Pornographic videos of female subjects taken without their knowledge have turned up on the Internet.[5290] In March 2002, President Chen's daughter was forced to publicly deny that a hidden "pinhole" video of an intimate couple was of her and her future husband.[5291] In response, lawmakers are looking to strengthen the 1999 criminal law (Article 315) punishing circulation of illegally recorded activities. Currently, the law mandates prison terms of five years or fines of TWD 50,000 (~USD 1,470).

Taiwan is one of only a few non-Muslim states to criminalize adultery.[5292] This law corresponds to a strong social condemnation of sexual adventurism, which encourages the media to look for indiscretions among the famous. In July 2001, Taiwan industries announced the production of special mobile "spy phones." The phones have a special chip that is supposedly able to pick up sounds and voices in the near vicinity of the phone. Dialing a special code can remotely activate the

---

[5286] Cecilia Fanchiang, "Private Information to Be Stored on Cards Issued by Health Bureau," Taiwan Journal, January 7, 2005.

[5287] *See generally* the Alliance for Personal Data Protection Web site <http://www.tahr.org.tw/PDPA/index.htm> (in Chinese).

[5288] Joy Su, "New Health Cards Become Compulsory Despite Fears," Taipei Times, January 2, 2004.

[5289] Tsai Ting-I, "Legislators Target Hidden Cameras," Taipei Times, March 12, 2002, available at <http://www.taipeitimes.com/news/2002/03/12/print/0000127325>.

[5290] Tsai Ting-I, "Legislators Demand Tougher Legislation for Candid Cameras," Taipei Times, March 6, 2002, available at <http://www.taipeitimes.com/news/2002/03/12/print/0000126529>.

[5291] Lawrence Chung, "Stop Fanning such Voyeurism, Taipei Government Tells Media," Straights Times (Singapore), March 2, 2002.

[5292] "Adultery: the Pursuit of Happiness – or a Crime against the State?" Asiaweek, November 16, 2001.

chip. They are being marketed toward housewives as a means to spy on their husbands to see if they are having extra-marital affairs.[5293]

An increasing number of Taiwanese access the Internet in cybercafés,[5294] and Taiwan has new regulations for browsing in such establishments. The city of Taipei implemented a law in 2002 banning cybercafés within 200 meters of a school and limiting the hours children can enter the cafés. In response to protests by owners of cybercafés, the national government superceded the Taipei law with new regulations. Now, the popular shops must be at least 50 meters from schools, but need not restrict hours for children ages 15 to 18.[5295] Also, the management of the cafés agreed to keep customers from accessing "questionable" material, but they are not required directly to monitor Internet use.[5296]

The Ministry of Economic Affairs (MOEA) established a radio frequency identification (RFID) development program in 2003, and hopes to capitalize on potential markets for the technology.[5297] The MOEA also funded a program that developed several RFID sensors to monitor vital statistics of patients and track employee movement in hospitals.[5298]

Under the updated Sexual Violation Prevention Law, "high risk" sex offenders are required to wear electronic tags after their release from jail. In an attempt to reduce sex crimes, serial rapists and attempted escapees are required to wear RFID bracelets so that police can monitor movements and verify curfew compliance.[5299]

NGO Advocacy Work

In addition to producing an annual human rights report, the Taiwan Association for Human Rights (TAHR) has campaigned against the many ID card proposals

---

[5293] "Taiwan Wives Can Spy on Spouses with Special Phone," Straits Times (Singapore), July 22, 2001.

[5294] "Taiwan Internet Usage at Cybercafes up 9.2% in Two Years," Chinese Information and Cultural Center, July 8, 2001, available at <http://www.taipei.org/teco/cicc/news/english/e-07-08-01/e-07-08-01-13.htm>.

[5295] "Government Unveils Net Café Provisions," Taiwan Headlines, December 5, 2001, available at <http://www.taiwanheadlines.gov.tw/20011205/20011205s1.html>.

[5296] Adam Creed, "Taiwan Drafts New Rules for Internet Cafes," Washington Post, December 6, 2001.

[5297] Owen Chu, "Radio Tags Point Way to Potential Market," Taipei Journal, August 6, 2004.

[5298] Owen Chu, "Hospitals Apply RFID to Disease Control," Taiwan Journal, December 10, 2004.

[5299] "Taiwan to Order Sex Criminals to Wear Electronic Tagging Devices," Agence France-Presse, March 17, 2005.

in Taiwan.[5300] In July 2002, TAHR created and coordinated the Personal Information Protection Alliance, which consisted of more than 50 civil societies and non-governmental organizations.[5301] The alliance was formed to protest several government schemes that require citizens to submit sensitive personal data.[5302] Although the alliance was unable to prevent the introduction of the health IC card, it has brought significant attention to the issue using creative protest methods.[5303]

Open Government

In 2002, the executive branch introduced open government legislation. It is doubtful that the proposal will become law as previous attempts in 1999, 2000, and 2001 failed to win approval from the legislative branch. The Law on Opening Government Information would make unclassified government documents easier to access.[5304] While a comprehensive freedom of information act has not been passed, the government has instituted reforms to try to limit the number of documents marked "classified."[5305]

Kingdom of Thailand

Constitutional Privacy Framework

In 1997 Thailand enacted a new constitution.[5306] Among the rights conferred upon citizens are rights of privacy and rights to government information, but both of those rights may be qualified in the interest of society. The relevant parts are:

[5300] Chiting Serena Chuang, "Human Rights Concerns in An Information Society," World Summit on The Information Society Asian Regional Conference, January 13, 2003, available at <http://www.tahr.org.tw/site/english/wsis-chuang.htm>.

[5301] *Id.*

[5302] *See* the Personal Information Protection Alliance Web site <http://www.tahr.org.tw/site/PDPA/2003.03.14.htm> (in Chinese).

[5303] *See, e.g.* Caroline Hung, "Pro-Privacy Protesters Break Eggs," Taipei Times, May 29, 2004, available at <http://www.taipeitimes.com/News/taiwan/archives/2004/05/29/2003157386>; Joy Su, "New Health Cards Become Compulsory Despite Fears," Taipei Times, January 2, 2004, available at <http://www.taipeitimes.com/News/taiwan/archives/2004/01/02/2003086023>.

[5304] Ko Shu-ling, "Executive Yuan Approves Bill to Boost Transparency," Taipei Times, September 5, 2002, available at <http://www.taipeitimes.com/News/taiwan/archives/2002/09/05/166852>.

[5305] Dennis Engbarth, "State Secrets Act Approved," Taiwan News, January 15, 2003, available at <http://www.etaiwannews.com/Taiwan/2003/01/15/1042591734.htm>.

[5306] Constitution of the Kingdom of Thailand, B.E. 2540 [hereinafter Constitution], available at <http://www.krisdika.go.th/pdfPage.jsp?page=eng&type=laws&lawType=law1&lawCode=%25c306&lawID=%25c306-10-2540-A0001>. Unless otherwise noted, all documents are the official translations promulgated by

Section 34. A person's family rights, dignity, reputation or the right of privacy shall be protected.

The assertion or circulation of a statement or picture in any manner whatsoever to the public, which violates or affects a person's family rights, dignity, reputation or the right of privacy, shall not be made except for the case which is beneficial to the public.

Section 37. A person shall enjoy the liberty of communication by lawful means.

The censorship, detention, or disclosure of communication between persons, including any other act disclosing a statement in the communication between persons, shall not be made except by virtue of the provisions of the law specifically enacted for security of the State or maintaining public order or good morals.

Section 58. A person shall have the right to get access to public information held by a State agency, State enterprise or local government organization, unless the disclosure of such information shall affect the security of the State, public safety or interests of other persons which shall be protected as provided by law.[5307]

Data Protection Framework and Freedom of Information

Thailand's Official Information Act (OIA),[5308] passed one month before approval of the 1997 Constitution, provides citizens with substantial rights to government information. The OIA creates two main types of rights: rights of access to government records and rights to control government-held personal information. It establishes an administrative board, the Official Information Council (OIC),[5309] and a judicial division known as Information Disclosure Tribunals (IDTs)[5310] to implement and enforce the OIA.

---

the Office of the Council of State, *see* Office of the Council of State, Law Library
<http://www.krisdika.go.th/about.jsp?head=3>.

[5307] Constitution, *supra*, at § 34, 37, 58.

[5308] Official Information Act, B.E. 2540 (1997), available at
<http://www.krisdika.go.th/lawHtmStaticContent01.jsp?frm=tmp&page=eng&lawType=law2&lawCode=%A2
03&lawID=%A203-20-2540-001>.

[5309] *Id.* at § 27.

[5310] *Id.* at § 35; the OIA divides power to decide cases between the OIC and IDT's, *see Id.* at §§ 28, 33, 37, 38.

Chapters 1 and 2 of the OIA create a duty upon the government to disclose information, limited by several exceptions.[5311] Those exceptions permitting nondisclosure include threats to national security or harm to individuals, hindrance of law enforcement, and confidentiality of medical records and other personal information.[5312]

Chapter 3 limits the government's use of personal data and confers a right upon citizens to retrieve and correct that data.[5313] A state agency may only retain personal information "insofar as it is . . . necessary" for the agency's purposes and must discard it immediately thereafter,[5314] and agencies generally may not exchange data with other agencies or third parties unless personally identifiable information is stripped from the data.[5315] Agencies must also publish the types of information they retain and the ways in which that information is used,[5316] and they must give individuals a right to see their own records and correct them.[5317]

While the OIA protects personal data *vis à vis* the government, the law makes no such restrictions on private parties. Currently in development within several government agencies is a data privacy act that would regulate private use of information.[5318] The proposed data privacy act is intended to be comprehensive and strongly protective of rights.[5319] The drafts were described as "the basis for the fundamental right to personal data protection," and they would potentially

---

[5311] *Id.* at §§ 7–20.

[5312] *Id.* at § 15; the Act also contains a provision giving immunity to officials who in good faith erroneously release documents that another official ordered to be withheld, *Id.* at § 20.

[5313] Official Information Act, *supra* at §§ 21–25.

[5314] *Id.* at § 23(1).

[5315] *See id.* at § 24; other exceptions include written consent from the people whose data are being transferred, disclosure to planning or census agencies who "have the duty to keep the personal information undisclosed," and law enforcement or safety purposes. *Id.* Agencies must keep, and individuals have a right to see, an audit trail of how data was exchanged. *Id.*

[5316] *See id.* at § 23(3); agencies dealing with intelligence or security are exempt from this clause, *see id. at §* 22.

[5317] *Id.* at § 25; the Act requires the agency to disclose to requesting individuals whether they have a right to opt out of giving information to the agency *id.* at § 23(5); t also requires that information be stored in "an appropriate security system . . . to prevent improper use" of the data, *id.*

[5318] Sasiwimon Boonruang, "Saving Private Data," Bangkok Post, September 15, 2004, ICT and OIC have both developed versions of data protection laws.

[5319] *See, e.g.,* Pateep Methakunavudhi, "A Guideline for Data Protection Legislation in Thailand," Computers and Society, September 1998. This law is part of a package of six laws that the National Information Technology Committee (NITC) was charged to devise. *See* Thaweesak Koanantakool, E-Commerce in Thailand <http://www.nectec.or.th/users/htk/e-commerce/intro.html>. The other five are laws on Computer Crime, Electronic Data Interchange (electronic contracting), Digital Signatures, Electronic Funds Transfer, and Universal Access to Information. *Id.* The Electronic Data Interchange law appears to have been enacted as the "Act on Electronic Transaction"; the others seem to be still in the drafting or debate stages. *See* Thai Law Reform Commission, Legislations (listing all enacted laws) <http://www.lawreform.go.th/lawDocumentMain.jsp?groupType=L>; Thailand ICT Laws <http://www.ictlaw.thaigov.net/> (in Thai).

even prohibit transfer of data overseas (a provision that worries some businesses).[5320]

Privacy Case Law

In the past few years, citizens have made frequent use of the OIA. Between November 1998 and June 2004, 326 cases were filed before the IDT, 262 of them in or after 2002.[5321] From January through October 2000, there were 144 complaints and 64 appeals submitted to the OIC.[5322] A number of controversial cases have made their way into the press.[5323] In one case,[5324] a girl who failed the entrance examination to a state-run school requested the test scores of herself and other students who were accepted.[5325] In a series of decisions by the OIC, the IDT, and even the civil and supreme courts, the right of access to test scores was upheld and enforced.[5326] This decision was made amidst the protests and countersuit of parents of other students, who claimed that their privacy rights were violated by the disclosure of their test scores; the courts held that the results of a "public competition were not personal information" and thus unprotected.[5327]

[5320] Boonruang, *supra*. One scholar working on an early draft of the bill, noting that it drew from a wide body of existing laws and other sources, including two papers by Electronic Privacy Information Center Executive Director Marc Rotenberg, declared that the draft "fully addresse[d] all the major issues" that had been raised. Methakunavudhi, *supra*, at 29–30.

[5321] OIC makes available descriptions and dates (but not decisions) of IDT cases. *See* Office of the Official Information Commission, Information Disclosure Tribunal Reports, at <http://www.oic.go.th/new2/ver4/oicnewweb2/content_eng/report.htm>. The numbers were collected by counting the decisions reported therein. *See id.*

[5322] Nakorn Seriak, "Challenges of Thailand's Freedom of Information," Conference on Freedom of Information and Civil Society in Asia, April 13, 2001 <http://www.foi-asia.org/Thailand/NSreport.html>.

[5323] *See id.*; Kittisak Prokati, "Information Access and Privacy Protection in Thailand," Conference on Freedom of Information and Civil Society in Asia, April 13, 2001 <http://www.foi-asia.org/Thailand/KPreport.html>.

[5324] One source cites the case as "Entrance examination result disclosure (Decision No. S1/1998)." Chungtong Opassiriwit, Thailand: A Case Study in the Interrelationship between Freedom of Information and Privacy (2002) 9 Privacy Law and Policy Reporter 42 (2002), available at <http://www.austlii.edu.au/au/journals/PLPR/2002/42.html>.

[5325] Prokati, *supra*.

[5326] *Id.*

[5327] *Id.* In a somewhat happy ending, the disclosed scores revealed the school's discriminatory admittance procedures and resulted in reforms of the school entrance examination system.

Wiretapping and Surveillance

Despite the constitutional and statutory protections of communications privacy,[5328] and perhaps because of the constitutional exception for law enforcement,[5329] wiretapping is prevalent throughout Thailand. In January 2004, partly in response to the terrorist situation, the Special Case Investigation Act was adopted to increase police powers for certain "special cases," such as terrorism or organized crime.[5330] Among those increased powers are permissions to search persons, houses, or vehicles when there is "reasonable ground" for suspecting a special case;[5331] to retrieve financial and other records;[5332] and to retrieve telephone and electronic communications (but only with a judicial warrant).[5333]

In December 2004, the deputy police commissioner asked the government to enact a law permitting warrantless, judicially unsupervised wiretaps and searches.[5334] Reaction was swift: within one day, opposition condemned the government's attempt to override civil liberties and human rights.[5335] Only two days after the proposal was reported, Deputy Prime Minister Visanu Krue-ngarm rejected the proposal, primarily on the grounds that the current laws gave the police sufficient power to investigate suspected terrorists.[5336]

Wiretapping has also been used in Thailand to thwart organized crime. The Money Laundering Control Act creates a police power to "have access to . . . communicated data or computer data" when there is "reasonable ground" to

---

[5328] Telegraph and Telephone Act, B.E. 2477 § 25 (1934) (prohibiting the "divulg[ing of] a telegraphic or telephonic message in whole or in part")
<http://www.krisdika.go.th/pdfPage.jsp?page=eng&type=laws&lawType=law2&lawCode=%25b704&lawID=%25b704-20-2477-001>.

[5329] Constitution, *supra* at § 37 (disallowing wiretapping "except by virtue of the provisions of law . . . for security of the State").

[5330] *See* Special Case Investigation Act, B.E. 2547 § 21 (2004) (translator unknown)
<http://www.dsi.go.th/dsi/news_index.jsp?id=105>.

[5331] *Id.* at §§ 24(1)–2. The power to search is limited procedurally; the officer must submit a justifying statement in writing.

[5332] *Id.* at §§ 24(3)–4. It is not clear whether the holder of the records is permitted to decline.

[5333] *See id.* at § 25.

[5334] "Security Decree for Deep South: Police Seek Sweeping Powers," The Nation, December 2, 2004.

[5335] *See, e.g.,* "The Week That Was: Police Approve Tougher Measures," The Nation, December 5, 2004; Yuwadee Tunyasiri, "Visanu: No Need for New Law," Bangkok Post, December 3, 2004 (quoting Senator Kraisak Choonhavan, who worried about the impact of the proposal on "the rights and freedom of innocent people"); "Editorial: Do Not Rush into Anti-Terror Decree," The Nation, December 3, 2004 (suggesting that the "extreme measures" proposed are part of the "administration's shameful record on human rights").

[5336] Yuwadee Tunyasiry & Manop Thip-Osot, "Govt Security Decree U-Turn," Bangkok Post, December 4, 2004.

suspect money laundering.[5337] The government has used this wiretapping power to thwart organized crime and promote the war on drugs.[5338] Telephone bugging is apparently so prevalent that phone operators have complained about excessive government demands for wiretaps.[5339]

The Thai police have exercised surveillance powers in other forms as well. One Internet Service Provider (ISP), who reportedly worked closely with the Thai police's new cybercrime division, suggested that anonymity of users on the Internet is the major stumbling block in the investigation of Internet crimes.[5340] Police now are working with ISPs to track Internet users and the websites they visit.[5341] Also, the police planned in 2004 to install video surveillance cameras in the southern provinces, presumably to watch for terrorist activities.[5342] The US Department of State's report on human rights in Thailand acknowledged these practices, noting that, "at times, security forces infringed on citizens' privacy rights."[5343]

Political wiretapping is no less common. The Thai Rak Thai party has been accused by politicians and human rights activists of wiretapping political opponents.[5344] In a well-publicized demonstration, the Democratic party installed a satellite communications system with "anti-phone bugging equipment to keep [the party's] poll secrets from being tapped into."[5345] And in a controversial incident in June 2004, several reporters discovered a microphone in the Ministry of Information and Communications Technology (ICT) press room.[5346] ICT first claimed that the microphones were used for testing the sound system[5347] and then

---

[5337] Money Laundering Control Act, B.E. 2542 § 46 (1999)
<http://www.krisdika.go.th/pdfPage.jsp?page=eng&type=laws&lawType=law2&lawCode=%25bb40&lawID=%25bb40-20-2542-A0001> (a judicial warrant is also required.)

[5338] *See* "Drug Syndicate Members Held," Bangkok Post, July 3, 2004; *see also* "Mob in Govt Crosshairs," The Nation, September 7, 2004 (calling for greater powers to deter international organized crime).

[5339] *See* Komsan Tortermvasana, "Phone Operators Ask for NTC Help on Taps," Bangkok Post, October 15, 2004.

[5340] *See* Wassayos Ngamkham, "Special Unit to Hunt Down Internet Felons," Bangkok Post, February 17, 2003.

[5341] "Thailand Moves to Crack Down on Web Content," Newsbytes, July 26, 2004.

[5342] *See* "Surveillance Cameras for the South," The Nation, April 17, 2004.

[5343] US Department of State, Bureau of Democracy, Human Rights, and Labor, *supra*.

[5344] *See* "TRT Campaign Launch: They're Evading Key Issues," The Nation, October 18, 2004; *see also* "Law Enforcement: Wiretapping Story 'Untrue'," The Nation, October 16, 2004 (Justice Minister denying allegations that the administration was wiretapping opponents).

[5345] Mongkol Bangprapa, "Democrats Unwrap New High-Tech Election HQ," Bangkok Post, June 21, 2004.

[5346] "Spy Charges after Mikes Uncovered," Bangkok Post, June 15, 2004.

[5347] *Id.*

claimed it was part of a crude communications system.[5348] Journalists were up in arms, outraged at the violation of their journalistic confidentiality.[5349]

The Mobile Phone Card Controversy

For many years, mobile phone service in Thailand was sold anonymously, through the use of pre-paid SIM cards that consumers could purchase in stores.[5350] However, the recent terrorism has led government officials to retract that anonymity, creating new avenues for potential abuse of mobile phone customer data and a loss of privacy in that marketplace.

Many of the terrorist acts in the South have involved homemade bombs set off by mobile phones modified to trigger the explosions.[5351] This led government officials to propose requiring SIM card purchasers to show identification. The first report that such an idea was being considered was on April 5, 2005.[5352] Only 13 days later, with almost no intervening debate in the media, the major telecommunications organizations and agencies such as ICT held a meeting, the result of which was a sudden announcement that SIM card purchasers would need to present identification.[5353] The plan was passed by agreement among the parties; no legislation was involved.[5354] Several individuals have expressed their support for this program as a step forward in preventing terrorist acts,[5355] and a

---

[5348] "Editorial I: Doubts Linger over ICT Explanation," The Nation, June 22, 2004.

[5349] See id.

[5350] A Subscriber Identity Module card, or SIM card, is a type of smart card that is inserted into a mobile phone and used to uniquely identify the caller (for the purpose of charging him/her for airtime). See Radiotelephone Installation for Prepayment Operation with Security Protection, U.S. Patent No. 5,301,234 (filed October 10, 1991). In Thailand, as in many other countries, mobile phone users purchase pre-paid cards, rather than subscribing to a service, so those purchases can be made anonymously. See Waedao Harai & Muhamad Ayub Pathan, "Bombs Injure Six Soldiers in Narathiwat," Bangkok Post, April 18, 2005.

[5351] See B Raman, "Thai Militants Turning Tech Savvy," Asia Times, April 6, 2005 <http://www.atimes.com/atimes/Southeast_Asia/GD06Ae03.html>. A review of the two major English-language Bangkok papers between June 2004 and April 2005 reveals at least 10 bombings set off by phones, four of them in the first 17 days of April 2005. See, e.g., "Carriers Back SIM Sign-Ups," The Nation, April 18, 2005.

[5352] "Misuse of Mobile Phones Worries Authorities," Bangkok Post, April 5, 2005.

[5353] Yuwadee Tunyasiri & Komsan Tortermvsana, "IDs to Be Mandatory for SIM Cards," Bangkok Post, April 19, 2005. The plan is scheduled to go into effect on May 10, 2005. "Prepaid Phone SIM Purchase to Require ID from May 10," Bangkok Post, April 22, 2005. It also requires foreigners in the country to declare their numbers, but it does not yet require the registration of existing mobile phone users, "Mobile Phones: Foreigners Must Give Numbers," The Nation, April 23, 2005.

[5354] Tunyasiri & Tortermvsana, supra.

[5355] See, e.g., Kamol Hengkietisak, "Keep Politics out of Numbers Game," Bangkok Post, April 24, 2005 (letter to the editor) ("It's time Sim card for use in mobile phone [sic] is put under control for national security interests").

poll taken contemporaneous to the agreement found that the people generally supported it.[5356]

However, substantial criticism of the proposed plan has come from all sides. ICT Minister Suvit Khunkitti worried that mere identification of SIM card buyers wouldn't stop terrorists who could use "several communications tools. . . to set off explosions."[5357] Others noted that fake ID cards could easily be used,[5358] or SIM cards could be illegally bought or brought from neighboring countries,[5359] so the plan would ultimately fail. Several decried the invasion of privacy inherent in the plan,[5360] some going so far as to suggest that ICT had "ulterior motives" to misuse the personal information.[5361]

National ID Cards

Thailand has assigned national ID cards for a number of years.[5362] Recently, the national government decided to replace the ID cards with new smart cards.[5363] They plan to distribute 64 million cards at a cost of THB 7.8 billion (~USD 191 million) between 2005 and 2009.[5364] Additionally, unlike the current cards that are issued to individuals 15 years or older, new cards would be mandatory from birth.[5365] The cards will be capable of storing substantial amounts of personal data, including the cardholder's name, address, age, religion, medical

---

[5356] "Public Backs SIM Plan: Poll," The Nation, April 20, 2005 (two polls were taken; one found a 79 percent support rate and the other 59 percent).

[5357] Tunyasiri & Tortermvsana, *supra*.

[5358] *Id.* (Bangkok Senator Seri Suwannapanont); "Prepaid Proposals Worry Operators," The Nation, April 19, 2005 (telecom director Thana Thienachariya).

[5359] "Bombers Can still Use Malaysian SIM Cards," Bangkok Post, April 21, 2005.

[5360] "IDs Required for SIM Cards in May," The Nation, April 22, 2005 (phone operators stating that personal customer information should be confidential and only disclosed upon court order); "Rights Secondary in Mobile ID Plan," Bangkok Post, April 20, 2005 ("Some customers feared an invasion of privacy and possible identity theft from revealing their ID card numbers"); *cf. id.* ("Prime Minister Thaksin Shinawatra said the registration. . . would not infringe on consumer rights")

[5361] "Anti-Terror Measures: Mobile ID Plan Flawed, Say Experts," The Nation, April 19, 2005 (quoting an unidentified "telecom industry observer"); "Letters to the Editor: Prepaid Mobile Phones Are Just One Technology That Terrorists Could Use," The Nation, April 22, 2005 ("Either someone shot from the hip or there is a deeper agenda behind the registration of prepaid SIM cards.").

[5362] *See* State Official Identification Card Act, B.E. 2542 (1999) <http://www.lawreform.go.th/lawDocumentDetailTXT.jsp?isMainChild=IS_MAIN&specific=&groupType=L&mainDocID=270&from=alphabetic&char=8&groupID=13&docID=270&x=#>.

[5363] *See, e.g.,* "Smart Card Launch 'By Mid-April'," Bangkok Post, March 3, 2005.

[5364] *See* "Microchip ID: The Act of Cards," The Nation, March 20, 2005; Bangkok Post, *supra* note 66. Technical problems with the cards are currently delaying their release. *See* "New ID Cards Not So Smart," Bangkok Post, April 28, 2005.

[5365] "ID to be Mandatory from Birth," The Nation, March 9, 2005.

---

information, biometric data, familial status, and even financial information.[5366] Thailand is also interested in designing a secure electronic passport.[5367]

Three factors seem to be driving this move to smart ID cards. First, a major goal of the Thai government is to put the nation at the forefront of technology. Radio Frequency Identification (RFID) and smart card technology are used frequently in Thailand, with applications ranging from tracking voting machines[5368] to storing cars in automated parking garages.[5369] Second, Thailand has engaged in a major electronic government undertaking; smart ID cards would provide the keys of access for citizens to use the state's online services.[5370] Third, in response to the terrorist activity in Southern Thailand,[5371] the government sees smart ID cards as a mechanism to create security.[5372]

Criticism against the smart card proposal has been substantial. At the Smart Cards and Society Conference, held at Chulalongkorn University in November 2004, several human rights and privacy advocates criticized the government for pushing an intrusive identification system while the country still lacked a data protection law, and called for public debate on the subject.[5373] These criticisms about potential misuse of data indeed have weight; one proposed use of the smart cards is to track students' post-graduate incomes in order to assess their student loan payments.[5374] One columnist, in addition to noting the privacy problems with the smart ID card project,[5375] also stated his fear that the cards would widen the digital divide between the technology-rich urban population and the rural

---

[5366] *See* "Microship ID: The Act of Cards," *supra.*

[5367] Suchalee Pongprasert, "Passport Changes: Greater Security Promised When Electronics Used," The Nation, April 11, 2005.

[5368] Jiranpan Bonnoon & Asina Pornwasin, "Electronic Democracy: Voting Machines Imminent," The Nation, September 20, 2004.

[5369] Chatrarat Kaewmorakot, "Traffic: Hi-Tech Projects to Tackle Congestion," The Nation, March 14, 2005.

[5370] *See, e.g.,* "A Year of Impressive Progress: National ID Card," The Nation, December 31, 2004; *see also* Sirikul Bunnang, "Education Spending to Increase B100BN," Bangkok Post, February 26, 2005 (Prime Minister suggesting that smart cards could be used to track students' educational progress and improve schools).

[5371] *See* the section on SIM cards for an overview of the terrorist activity.

[5372] *See* "Beware of Muslim Impersonators," The Nation, October 25, 2004 (noting also that smart cards will be rushed to the southern provinces because of law enforcement's need for them).

[5373] *See* Onnucha Huttasingh, "Smart Cards Called Threat to Privacy," Bangkok Post, November 12, 2004; Pongpen Sutharoj, "UK Expert Urges Debate on Smart ID Card," The Nation, November 15, 2004; *see also* Kriengsak Chareonwongsak, "Smart Cards, Smart Choices," Bangkok Post, July 18, 2004 (calling for the freedom to opt out of the ID card system or remove information from the card at will). The Interior Ministry has suggested that people will in fact be able to choose what information is stored. "Citizens to Get Say over Smart Card Data," The Nation, March 12, 2004.

[5374] *See* Phermsak Lilakul, "Student Loans: Plan to Ease Repayment Burden," The Nation, September 13, 2004.

[5375] Don Sambandaraksa, "In Defence of Smartcards," Bangkok Post, June 2, 2004.

people.[5376] And one scholar has suggested that the smart ID card system is contrary to Buddhist principles of governance.[5377]

Republic of Turkey

Constitutional Privacy Framework

Section Five of the 1982 Turkish Constitution is entitled, "Privacy and Protection of Private Life."[5378] Article 20 of the Turkish Constitution deals with individual privacy and states, "Everyone has the right to demand respect for his private and family life. Privacy of individual and family life cannot be violated."[5379] Article 20 prohibits the search or seizure of any individual, his private papers, or his belongings unless there exists a decision duly passed by a judge in cases explicitly defined by law, and unless there exists an order of an agency authorized by law in cases where delay is deemed prejudicial. Article 22 preserves the secrecy of communication and states that, "Communication shall not be impeded nor its secrecy be violated, unless there exists a decision duly passed by a judge in cases explicitly defined by law, and unless there exists an order of an agency authorized by law in cases where delay is deemed prejudicial."[5380] In October 2001, in a move aimed at improving its chances of joining the European Union, Turkey passed the Constitutional Amendment Bill, containing 34 proposals for amendments to the Constitution.[5381] Several of the proposals strengthen the basic rights and freedoms of individuals, including increased protection for privacy of the person and the home.[5382]

[5376] Don Sambandaraksa, "Grass Not Greener on Other Side of Digital Divide," Bangkok Post, December 8, 2004.

[5377] Krisana Kitiyadisai, "Smart ID Card in Thailand from a Buddhist Perspective," Second Asia-Pacific Computing and Philosophy Conference, January 9, 2005, <http://www.stc.arts.chula.ac.th/cyberethics/papers/Krisna-Smart%20ID-buddhist.doc>. Buddhism is the official religion of the king. Constitution, *supra* at § 9. Professor Krisana's paper also presents an excellent overview of the criticisms of the smart ID card program.

[5378] Constitution Republic of Turkey, available at <http://www.mfa.gov.tr/GRUPI/Anayasa/i142.htm>.

[5379] *Id.* at Article 20.

[5380] *Id.*

[5381] Nick Thorpe, "Mixed Reactions to Turkey's Reforms," BBC News, October 5, 2001, available at <http://news.bbc.co.uk/hi/english/world/europe/newsid_1580000/1580238.stm>.

[5382] US Department of State, Country Reports on Human Rights Practices - 2001, March 4, 2002, available at <http://www.state.gov/g/drl/rls/hrrpt/2001>.

Data Protection Framework

In light of the negotiations for entry to the European Union, Turkey made substantial progress in the last three years to establish a national data protection regime. At the core of these efforts is the Draft Data Protection Act (DDPA), which has been worked on for three years.[5383] The draft establishes the protection of privacy in the public and private sphere on a new legal basis. It protects the personal data handled either by persons or entities, with the aim of protecting natural persons. The law will be applicable to both automated and manual data processing. The DDPA has a special standing in view of EU entry efforts. It aims to protect the right of personality and the fundamental rights of persons who are the subjects of data processing.

The DDPA protects personal data of natural persons. It regulates data processing that applies in principle to both the government agencies and to private data processors. The protection of the person whose data is processed is strengthened. The draft is shaped by the effort to reconcile the interests of personal data protection and the legitimate need of administration offices and business enterprises for processing personal data in an adequate manner. However, the DDPA is not applicable to personal data that a natural person converts exclusively for personal use. According to the draft, those who live under the same "roof" are subject to this exception.[5384]

The draft contains the following rules: General conditions for the legal standard of data processing; rights of personal data subjects; rules for data processing under private and public law; structure and obligations of the supervisory authority; data registry; registration of the data collection; data transfer to other countries; obligation to register data transmission; and penal provisions: the legislature intends to legislate offences against privacy, which will be subject to civil, administrative and criminal sanctions.[5385]

For the time being the protection of personal rights within the Turkish national legislation is regulated in the Civil Code. Pursuant to Article 24 of the Civil Code, an individual whose personal rights are violated unjustly has a right of civil action. However, there is little criminal liability for such violations of personal rights.

[5383] *See* <http://www.adalet.gov.tr/kanun/newfolder/kisiselveri.htm>.
[5384] *Id.*
[5385] *Id.*

Due to the delay in adopting the DDPA, there exists a gap with regard to the substantial as well as, the criminal rules. The new Criminal Code[5386] that entered into force on June 1, 2005, plans to punish data protection violations. This will be the first time that criminal rules on data protection will be enforced. Unfortunately as long as the DDPA remains unadopted, the legal status of the criminal provisions will be lacking statutory basis, therefore are bound to be declared void by the Turkish Constitutional Court.

The new Criminal Code regulates felonies against the private life and the private sphere. These felonies may be pursued *ex officio*, where the offences concern the storage, illegal transfer or data retention. The following felonies on data protection are established in the section 9 of the Turkish Criminal Code: Violation of the communication secrecy; wire-tapping; storage of personal data; and, illegal transfer of personal data.[5387]

Under the current Turkish Criminal Code, computer-related offenses can be prosecuted pursuant to Amendment 3756, "Crimes on Informatics."[5388] Articles 195-200 of the Turkish Criminal Code govern freedom of communication through letters, parcels, telegram and telephone. Government officials are required, subject to various exceptions, to obtain a judicial warrant before monitoring private correspondence. In 1990, a parliamentary commission on human rights was established with the power to monitor the human rights situation in Turkey and abroad. Currently, the commission consists of 25 parliamentarians, three consultants and four secretaries. Since its inception, the commission has pursued some twenty cases on its own initiative. Most of these cases relate to alleged violations of physical integrity.[5389] Turkey is also a member of the Council of Europe and has recognized the right of its citizens to individually petition the European Court of Human Rights.[5390]

[5386] Official Gazette dated: 12/10/2004 – No.: 25611, Act No: 5237 Date of Acceptance: 26/9/2004.

[5387] *Id.*

[5388] Turkish Criminal Code, Amendment No. 3756 (June 14, 1991) *cited in* National Report: Turkey at the Council of Europe Conference on Cybercrime, Ministry of Justice (November 22, 2001), available at <http://www.legal.coe.int/economiccrime>.

[5389] *See* Commission On Human Rights, Question of the Human Rights of All Persons Subjected to any Form of Detention or Imprisonment: Promotion and protection of the right to freedom of opinion and expression, report of the Special Rapporteur, Mr. Abid Hussain, submitted pursuant to Commission on Human Rights resolution 1996/53 Addendum Mission to Turkey, Distr. General E/CN.4/1997/31/Add.1, February 11,1997 available at <http://www.unhchr.ch/html/menu4/chrrep/3197a1.htm>.

[5390] *See* "Turkey and the Council of Europe," available at <http://www.coe.int/T/e/com/about_coe/member_states/e_tu.asp#TopOfPage>.

A Turkish law extending the state press restrictions to the Internet was passed amid much opposition in May 2002.[5391] The law, called the Supreme Board of Radio and Television Bill No. 4676,[5392] places the Turkish Internet under the regulatory authority of the Supreme Radio and Television Board (RTUK).[5393] Turkish President Ahmet Necdet Sezer has expressed disapproval of the provisions,[5394] although the Supreme Court has already upheld some portions of the law.[5395]

A Law on the Right to Information[5396] was officially published in October 2003 and went into effect on April 24, 2004.[5397] The law allows the public to request information from government agencies. It provides for the withholding of confidential private information, and the review of disputed information requests by a Board, as well as a right to sue. However, there are questions on the adequacy of the law's implementation mechanism.[5398] For instance, many government ministries' Right to Information offices have not yet been established.[5399]

Due to recent expansions in the global trend towards electronic commerce, new means for supporting e-commerce are currently being introduced in Turkey.[5400] Recently, the Electronic Commerce Coordination Commission was formed within the Undersecretariat of Foreign Trade to prepare a Draft Law for Electronic Data, Electronic Contract and Electronic Signature Code.[5401] The Commission has completed the Draft Law, and the Electronic Signature Code came into force on July 23, 2004. The Act was prepared under the guidance of the EU Directive and taking into account the practice of member states such as

---

[5391] Jonathan Evans, "Turkey Passes Strict Net Law," Wired News, May 15, 2002, available at <http://www.wired.com/news/politics/0,1283,52558,00.html?tw=wn_story_related>.

[5392] Yaman Akdeniz, Internet Governance and Freedom in Turkey 3 (2003). available at <http://www.cyber-rights.org/documents/osce_turkey_paper.pdf>.

[5393] Dorian Jones, "Turkey Tightens Controls on the Net," BBC News Online, May 28, 2002, available at <http://news.bbc.co.uk/1/hi/sci/tech/2006759.stm>.

[5394] Id.

[5395] Asian School of Cyberlaws News, "Turkey Court Upholds Internet Law," available at <http://www.asianlaws.org/cyberlaw/archives/06_02_turkey.htm>.

[5396] Law on the Right to Information (No. 4982), available at <http://www.freedominfo.org/news/turkey/lawengl.pdf>.

[5397] "New FOI Law in Turkey Posted, Campaign Underway for Implementation," FreedomInfo.Org News, available at <http://www.freedominfo.org/news/turkey/>.

[5398] "The Elephant in the China Shop," Turkish Time, February 15 - March 15, 2004, available at <http://www.turkishtime.org/25/88_1_en.asp>.

[5399] BilgilenmeHakki.Org, "The Turkish Right to Information Act Comes into Force, April 26, 2004 Press Release, available at <http://www.bilgilenmehakki.org/foi_tr_26april.pdf>.

[5400] "Draft E-Signature Law to Be Issued," BNA World Data Protection Report vol. 3 (January 2003).

[5401] Id.

Germany, France, Austria, and Belgium. In addition the E-signature Regulation and Communique entered into force on January 6, 2005.[5402]

Under this law, certificate service providers are subject to the following obligations related to data protection: (a) The certification service provider may collect personal data only to the extent, necessary for the purposes of issuing a certificate. Sharing data with a third party is permissible only with the consent of the person whose personal data is being processed; (b) The certification service provider may not disclose the certificate to third parties without the consent of the certificate owner; and, (c) The certification service provider has to prevent third parties from collecting personal data without the written consent of the owner of such personal data. The certificate service provider may transfer/use personal data only with consent of the owner of such data.[5403]

The Turkish Ministry of Justice has been working on data protection legislation for several years without success.[5404] Promisingly, in mid-2003, the draft Law on the Protection of Personal Data (Kisisel Verilerin Korunmasi Kanunu Taslagi) was completed. It is based on the 1981 Council of Europe Convention and the European Data Protection Directive (1995/46/EC).[5405] The draft law provides, among other things, that subjects should be informed and consent to data collection, that data should be processed in line with the declared collection purpose, and that a supervisory authority termed the Institution of Protection of Personal Data (Kisisel Verileri Koruma Yksek Kurulu) be established.[5406] There was a possibility that the draft law might be enacted in 2004, as the government initiated E-Transformation Turkey Project had included this goal in its Short Term Action Plan.[5407]

In June 2004, the DPPA was revised and was passed by the Ministry of Justice to the Prime Ministry. So far, it has not been promulgated. A detailed criticism to

---

[5402] All legal documents are avalaible at: <http://www.tk.gov.tr>.

[5403] Id.

[5404] Turkish Republic Foreign Trade Office, E-Commerce Laws Working Party Report, May 8, 1998. A summary is available at <http://kurul.ubak.gov.tr/e-ticaret.html> (in Turkish).

[5405] Yaman Akdeniz, Internet Governance in Turkey 18 (Yaman Akdeniz 2004), available at <http://www.policy.hu/akdeniz/osi_ya_final_rp.pdf>.

[5406] Elif Altinsoy, "Turkish Draft Law on Personal Data Protection," University of Stockholm Virtual Law Firm, December 5, 2003, available at <http://vlf.juridicum.su.se/vlf/main.asp?Content=ShowContent&Show=News&ID=39>.

[5407] The E-Transformation Turkey Project was established via a Prime Minister's Circular (2003/12), dated February 27, 2003, while the Short Term Action Plan came into effect with a Prime Minister's Circular (2003/48) published in the Turkish Official Gazette, No. 25306 on December 4, 2003. Yaman Akdeniz, Internet Governance in Turkey 24-26 (Yaman Akdeniz 2004), available at <http://www.policy.hu/akdeniz/osi_ya_final_rp.pdf>.

the Turkish DDPA draft was published for the first time last year.[5408] However in the last two years, the group of lawyers of the annual "Turkey IT Congress"[5409] discussed international data protection issues. But, a detailed criticism on the DDPA draft by the said subgroup of lawyers was published in the annual report of 2004.

Wiretapping and Surveillance Rules

Despite the existing laws and regulations, the right to privacy of private communications is not well-respected in Turkey. There is widespread illegal wiretapping by the government. For instance, in 1997, a parliamentary committee discovered that the General Directorate of Security, a body under the Ministry of Internal Affairs charged with police powers, listened in on telephone communications.[5410] In December 1999, the deputy head of Ankara's police intelligence division, Zafer Aktas, was convicted for his role in a taping scandal that involved the bugging of the Prime Minister's telephones.[5411] In March 2000, the Turkish Interior Ministry was sued by the Chairman of the Supreme Court's Eighth Department, Naci Unver, upon his discovery that his official phone had been bugged. The Interior Ministry defended this wiretapping,[5412] although its Minister later stated that new guidelines would be issued soon and punishment for illegal wiretaps would be forthcoming.[5413] No such guidelines were issued.

In 2001, there were continued allegations of telephone wiretapping of the Istanbul Governor,[5414] the Foreign Ministry,[5415] and a Parliamentary deputy from the Motherland Party.[5416] The Interior Ministry denied the allegations,[5417] but on

---

[5408] Nilgün Başalp, Kişisel verilerin Korunması ve Saklanması (Data Protection), Ankara 2004.

[5409] The Turkish IT meeting takes place with participation of universities, press, public and private sector. The goal of the annual meetings is to define clear tasks to transform the Turkish society into an active information society. The congress is divided into six sub-groups, which the group of lawyers is also under, which worked recently on a report on the DPA draft.

[5410] "Acting Security Director Confirms All Telephones Bugged," BBC Worldwide Monitoring, April 14, 1997 and "No Privacy on the Phone Lines," Asia Times, April 16, 1997 at 8.

[5411] "Turk Policeman Convicted in Phone Tapping Scandal," Reuters, December 6, 1999.

[5412] "Comedy of Phone Bugging," Milliyet, March 16, 2000.

[5413] Hürriyet, March 13, 2000.

[5414] "Istanbul Police Chief Denies Ordering Governor's Phone Tapped," BBC Worldwide Monitoring, April 22, 2001.

[5415] "Turkish Foreign Ministry Investigates Wiretapping Allegations," BBC Worldwide Monitoring, May 3, 2001.

[5416] "Turkish Speaker Concerned over Tapping of Phones without Court Order," BBC Worldwide Monitoring, May 10, 2001.

[5417] "Interior Ministry Denies Illegal Wiretapping,' BBC Worldwide Monitoring," May 4, 2001.

June 15, 2001, released a decree establishing an Inspection Delegation.[5418] In May 2002, the Wiretapping and Investigation Committee, a sub-committee of the Human Rights Investigation Committee, issued its final report finding that cellular phones are easily monitored by operating companies and that the Mafia engages in illegal wiretapping.[5419] In June 2004, it was reported that the Turkish National Intelligence Organization, a security arm of the government, had admitted to bugging the telephone of the British Ambassador in Ankara.[5420] This admission came after newspaper journalist Fikret Bila included a transcript of a bugged phone conversation with the British Ambassador in a book he wrote. Bila was subsequently charged with revealing state secrets.[5421]

Regarding the privacy of digital communications, in April 2000, the government introduced a new bill proposing the establishment of a Council for the Security of National Information and its Duties within the Prime Minister's office. The Council was to address issues including data protection, encryption and security of information systems.[5422] The draft bill was heavily criticized and eventually dropped. In February 2002, a scandal broke following the publication in a weekly magazine of the private e-mails of the EU's ambassador to Turkey,[5423] and from March to April of 2003, an increase in digital attacks by hackers in Turkey was reported.[5424]

On February 6, 2004, the Telecommunications Authority enacted a new data security regulation.[5425] This regulation is in principle a summary of the European Union directive on data protection in the electronic communications.[5426] It regulates the following topics: security of communication; duty to disclose the risks with regard to network security; privacy of communication; processing of data; call number display; lists of participants; and spamming.

[5418] "Body Probing Phone Tapping to Be Set up," BBC Worldwide Monitoring, June 15, 2001.

[5419] "Parliamentary Report Reveals Illegal Wiretapping by Mafia, GSM Operators," Istanbul Hurriyet, May 24, 2002 (FBIS Translated Text).

[5420] "Legal, International Scandal over Suspected Phone Tapping," Turkish Probe, June 13, 2004 (Financial Times Information Translated Text).

[5421] Suna Erdem, "Turkey Taps British Diplomat's Phone," London Times, June 12, 2004.

[5422] Elif Unal, "Turkey Debates Cyberspace Controls," Reuters.

[5423] "Fogg Email Scandal Said Attempt to Discredit Pro-EU Circles at Home," Istanbul Milliyet, February 12, 2002 (FBIS Translated Text).

[5424] "Turkish Hackers Begin to Challenge Brazilians to Claim Top Spot," Mena Report Reporters, June 2, 2003.

[5425] See <http://www.tk.gov.tr>.

[5426] Directive 97/66/EC, available at <http://www.dataprotection.ie/viewdoc.asp?m=l&fn=/documents/legal/6aiii.htm>.

Currently, the Ministry of Finance is preparing the Draft Code on Electronic Invoice and Electronic Commercial Books. By the end of this year, it is expected to be in force in Turkey. Furthermore, the Undersecretary of the Prime Ministry for Foreign Trade, the Electronic Commerce Commission and the Ministry of Justice jointly established a Working Group on the problems of Electronic Commerce in the EU and in Turkey. Finally, there are also published studies[5427] and significant working groups about computer forensics.[5428]

Major Privacy Case Law

A large number of cases against Turkey for violations of human rights have been brought before the European Court of Human Rights. For instance, in 1996, the Court in *Akdivar and others v Turkey*, a case concerning attacks on a village in southeast Turkey, ruled that the deliberate burning of villagers' homes and their contents was an unjustified and serious interference with the right to respect for their family lives, in violation of Article 8 of the European Convention.[5429] In July 2001, the Interior Minister released a circular, "Violation of Decisions of European Court of Human Rights," advising officials to respect individuals' rights, so as to improve the country's record before the Court and other democratic nations.[5430] Among other issues, the Minister specified that, in order to comply with Article 8 of the European Convention on Human Rights, judicial authorization is necessary before houses can be searched. However, there were several more adverse rulings after the Interior Minister's directive. For instance, in June 2002, the European Court ruled that relatives of Kurdish villagers who disappeared following a raid by the Turkish army in 1994 were entitled to compensation for violations of their right to privacy.[5431] And in November 2003, the European Court of Human Rights ruled against Turkey in two cases, one of

---

[5427] Leyla Keser, Adli Bilişim (Computer Forensic), Ankara 2004; Istanbul Bilgi University IT Law Center and Istanbul Police Headquarters, Booklet on Computer Forensic (Adli Bilişim), Istanbul 2004.

[5428] Istanbul Bilgi University, IT Law Center, available at <http://bthukuku.bilgi.edu.tr/>; the Izmir Institute of Technology, College of Engineering, Department of Computer Engineering organized on May 19-20, 2005 a two-day workshop on these topics, available at
<http://adlibilisim.iyte.edu.tr/AdliBilisim2005Web/Select.do?id=anasayfa>

[5429] Akdivar and others v Turkey, 1 Eur. Ct. H.R. 137 (1996).

[5430] "Interior Minister Issues Circular Warning of Human Rights Violations," BBC Worldwide Monitoring, July 25, 2001.

[5431] Orhan v. Turkey, App. No. 25656/94, Eur. Ct. H.R. (June 18, 2002).

which involved a finding that Turkey had violated several rights of 16 detained barristers, including their right to the respect of their private and family life.[5432]

The practice of "virginity testing" in Turkey also raises concerns relating to the bodily integrity and privacy of women. Under the practice, women are subjected to gynecological examinations ostensibly to determine if they have ever had sexual intercourse.[5433] Encouragingly, in 2002, the Turkish government rescinded a law that allowed forced virginity testing of school girls.[5434]

International Obligations

Turkey signed the Convention for the Protection of Individuals with Regard to Automatic Processing of Personal Data (Convention No. 108) in 1981 but has not yet ratified it.[5435] It has signed and ratified the European Convention for the Protection of Human Rights and Fundamental Freedoms,[5436] and has been a member of the Organization for Economic Co-operation and Development since 1961.

Republic of Uganda

Constitutional Privacy Framework

The Constitution of the Republic of Uganda[5437] recognizes the right to privacy as a human right.[5438] Article 27 of the Constitution provides:

> No person shall be subjected to unlawful search of the person, home or other property of that person; or unlawful entry by others of the premises

---

[5432] "European Court Rules against Turkey," Turkish Daily News, November 15, 2004 (Financial Times Information Translated Text).

[5433] Chante Lasco, Virginity Testing in Turkey: A Violation of Women's Human Rights 9 Human Rights Brief 10 (2002), available at <http://www.wcl.american.edu/hrbrief/09/3turkey.cfm>.

[5434] "Turkey Scraps Virginity Tests," BBC News Online, February 28, 2002, available at <http://news.bbc.co.uk/1/hi/world/europe/1845784.stm>.

[5435] Convention for the Protection of Individuals with Regard to Automatic Processing of Personal Data (ETS No. 108), available at <http://conventions.coe.int/Treaty/en/Treaties/Html/108.htm>.

[5436] Signed November 11, 1950; ratified May 18, 1954, entered into force May 18, 1954, available at <http://conventions.coe.int/Treaty/en/Treaties/Html/005.htm>.

[5437] Constitution of the Republic of Uganda, available at <http://www.parliament.go.ug/Constitute.htm>.

[5438] See generally, E.M. Bakibinga, "Managing Electronic Privacy in the Telecommunications Sub-sector: The Ugandan Perspective," paper presented at the African Electronic Privacy and Public Voice Symposium held on December 6, 2004, Cape Town, Republic of South Africa, available at <http://www.thepublicvoice.org/events/capetown04/bakibinga.doc>.

of that person. No person shall be subjected to interference with the privacy of his home, correspondence, communications or other property.[5439]

The right to privacy, however, is not an absolute right, as it can be derogated from by lawful means. Article 43 provides that in the enjoyment of the prescribed rights and freedoms, no person shall prejudice the fundamental or other human rights and freedoms of others or the public interest.[5440]

The Constitutional Court addresses questions relating to the interpretation of the Constitution. Article 137(4) of the Constitution empowers the Constitutional Court to grant an order of redress, should it determine that a law or act or omission by any person or authority is inconsistent, or in contravention with, a constitutional provision.[5441] Where necessary, it refers the matter to the High Court, to investigate and determine the appropriate redress.

Privacy Supervisory Authority

The Constitution established the Uganda Human Rights Commission (UHRC) to oversee the enjoyment of all rights provided for in the Constitution.[5442] The Uganda Human Rights Commission Act provides in greater details the powers, functions, and structure of the UHRC, as well as the procedure and mechanisms for handling complaints before it.[5443] The UHRC has engaged in significant monitoring of activities in contentious areas of human rights, especially in the activities of security agencies. The commission has the powers and general mandate to address all complaints arising out of human rights abuses. It is entrusted with the duty to initiate investigations of human rights violations; have access to and monitor detention conditions; conduct educational and other activities to promote human rights awareness; and monitor and make recommendations for government compliance with its international obligations. The UHRC can subpoena any witness or document, order the release of any detained person, and recommend payment or compensation, or any other legal remedy after it learns of the existence of a human rights abuse.

[5439] Constitution of the Republic of Uganda, *supra* at Article 27.

[5440] *Id.* at Article 43.

[5441] *Id.* at Article 137(4).

[5442] *Id.* at Article 50.

[5443] Uganda Human Rights Commission Act, Cap 24, Vol. 2, Laws of Uganda, Revised Edition 2000.

Uganda does not have a Data Protection Authority. The UHRC is therefore the body handling the complaints that arise out of issues concerning the abuse of privacy.

Data Protection Framework

The Uganda Communications Act (UCA) establishes the Uganda Communications Commission (UCC) to carry on functions related to communications services and operations in Uganda and also to ensure compliance with international standards and obligations relating to communications by receiving and investigating complaints and taking necessary responsive action.[5444] Any operator[5445] has to ensure that there is no unlawful divulgence, interception or disclosure,[5446] with some exceptions in accordance with a court order or in public emergency. Telecommunication companies have cooperated with security agencies requiring information such as traffic data and calling line identification. A person who sustains loss or damage as a result of any act or omission contrary to UCA may sue and recover for the loss or damage suffered.[5447] However, Uganda's courts lack adequate capacity to address privacy issues – privacy being a relatively new area in the jurisprudence of Uganda – and in the absence of proper guidelines, the process can easily be abused.

The Uganda Posts and Telecommunications Act provides for secrecy of telephone communications and telegrams. It permits interception and disclosure only in the case public emergency or in the interest of public safety or tranquility under the direction of the Minister responsible for internal security.[5448] The Penal Code Act empowers a police officer not below the rank of inspector or any other officer authorized by the Attorney General to detain, open and examine any package or article that he suspects contains prohibited publications or information prejudicial to security and to detain such person for purposes of prosecution.[5449]

[5444] Uganda Communications Act (UCA), at Section 4.

[5445] Any licensee providing communications services under the UCA.

[5446] UCA, *supra* at Section 66.

[5447] *Id.* at Section 73; Under this section, the UCA does not prevent any person from being prosecuted, under any other law in force, for an act or omission that constitutes an offense. Therefore, courts may apply other laws concerning privacy such as the Penal Code Act (Cap 120, Laws of Uganda) and the Uganda Posts and Telecommunications Act (Cap 107, Laws of Uganda).

[5448] There have been a number of prosecutions concerning offenses pertaining to stealing postal material and secrecy of telegrams in the lower courts; *see* Uganda v. Grace Kitaka, Case No: HQS-CO-0061-2003 and Uganda v. Kiiza Joe Masajjage & Anor, Case No: BUG-CO-1042-2004, both of which are still undergoing inquiries.

[5449] Cap 120, Vol. 6, Laws of Uganda, Revised Edition 2000.

In the communications sector, emphasis has been on trade liberalization rather than consumer protection issues. Save for the provisions in the UCA and license terms and conditions requiring respect for privacy, there are no regulations or guidelines. Operators have a duty to observe consumer privacy through the mastermind operator/customer agreement. A number of complaints that have arisen have been addressed directly to the operator responsible for the unauthorized and unlawful release of the traffic data in contention.

The Evidence (Banker's Books) Act[5450] empowers courts to permit a party to a legal proceeding to inspect and take copies of any entries in a banker's record. In the absence of guidelines, courts have resorted to requiring the court order applicant to attach a copy of relevant documents so the courts can check on the likelihood of abuse of the process. There have, in fact, been instances in which individuals used law enforcement officers to unlawfully access bank records, in breach of a customer's privacy. This is due to a lack of guidelines or procedural rules that could enable better implementation of the law.

The Press and Journalists Act requires journalists to comply with laws prohibiting publication that improperly infringes on the privacy of an individual.[5451] However, the professional code of ethics in the Fourth Schedule to the Act does not contain a provision on the respect of privacy.

The Uganda Consumers Protection Association handles all matters concerning consumer interests. Since most people do not vigilantly pursue matters where a breach of privacy occurs, few complaints arise.

Wiretapping and Other Government Surveillance

The Suppression of Terrorism Act permits an authorized officer to intercept the communications of a person and otherwise conduct surveillance of that person.[5452] The Act allows interception of letters and postal packages, telephone calls, fax messages, e-mails, and bank records, and allows rigorous security checks and surveillance of persons or premises. According to the government-owned daily newspaper, the President of Uganda stated that communication between opposition politicians and members of the Lord's Resistance Army

---

[5450] Cap 7, Vol. 2, Laws of Uganda, Revised Edition 2000.

[5451] Cap 105, Vol. 5, Laws of Uganda Revised Edition 2000.

[5452] The Suppression of Terrorism Act No. 14 of 2002.

(LRA)[5453] have been monitored.[5454] This surveillance comes in the wake of the 1998 bombings of the United States embassies in Nairobi, Kenya, and Dar-es-Salaam in Tanzania, the September 11, 2001 terrorist attacks in the United States, and the continued instability in Northern Uganda.

Open Government

The right of access to information is also provided for in the Constitution. Article 41 provides that: "Every citizen has a right of access to information in the possession of the State or any other organ or agency of the State, except where the release of the information is likely to prejudice the security or sovereignty of the State or interfere with the right to the privacy of any other person."[5455]

The Access to Information Act was enacted by Parliament in 2005. It contains the only statutory definition of privacy available in Uganda: "the right of a person to keep his or her matters and relationships secret." This Act also provides that the right of access should not interfere with the right to privacy.[5456] It remains to be seen how the implementation of this law will affect the state of privacy in Uganda.

International Obligations

Uganda is a signatory to a number of international human rights legal instruments, namely the Universal Declaration of Human Rights and the International Covenant on Civil and Political Rights. Uganda therefore has obligations pertaining to the duty to ensure respect for personal privacy.

[5453] The Lord's Resistance Army and Movement are listed as terrorist groups under the Schedule to the Suppression of Terrorism Act. No. 14 of 2002.

[5454] New Vision Reporter, "Museveni Warns MPs – MPs who Communicate with LRA Will Be Hanged'," New Vision, Vol. 18, No. 217, September 10, 2003, at 1; "Museveni Raps Kony Backers," New Vision, Vol. 18, No. 271, November 14, 2003, at 2.

[5455] Constitution of the Republic of Uganda, *supra* at Article 41.

[5456] The Access to Information Act was enacted by the Parliament on March 13, 2005 and presented to the President for Assent.

Ukraine

Constitutional Privacy Framework

The Constitution of Ukraine guarantees the right of privacy and data protection.[5457] Article 31 states, "Everyone is guaranteed privacy of mail, telephone conversations, telegraph and other correspondence. Exceptions shall be established only by a court in cases envisaged by law, with the purpose of preventing crime or ascertaining the truth in the course of the investigation of a criminal case, if it is not possible to obtain information by other means." Article 32 states, "No one shall be subject to interference in his or her personal and family life, except in cases envisaged by the Constitution of Ukraine. The collection, storage, use and dissemination of confidential information about a person without his or her consent shall not be permitted, except in cases determined by law, and only in the interests of national security, economic welfare and human rights. Every citizen has the right to examine information about himself or herself, that is not a state secret or other secret protected by law, at the bodies of state power, bodies of local self-government, institutions and organizations. Everyone is guaranteed judicial protection of the right to rectify incorrect information about himself or herself and members of his or her family, of the right to demand that any type of information be expunged, and also the right to compensation for material and moral damages inflicted by the collection, storage, use and dissemination of such incorrect information." There is also a right of freedom of information. Article 34 states: "Everyone has the right to freely collect, store, use and disseminate information by oral, written or other means of his or her choice." Article 50 states, "Everyone is guaranteed the right of free access to information about the environmental situation, the quality of food and consumer goods, and also the right to disseminate such information. No one shall make such information secret."

Data Protection Framework

There have been efforts to enact a data protection act for several years. However, as of June 2004, no data protection act has been enacted. A draft Law on Personal Data Protection (No. 2618) passed first hearings on May 15, 2003, and has not yet been submitted for second hearings. This draft law was submitted by Members of Parliament Rodionov, Nikolaenko, Yukhnovsky, Tolochko, and Sytnyk,

---

[5457] Constitution of Ukraine, adopted at the Fifth Session of the *Verkhovna Rada* of Ukraine, June 28, 1996, available at <http://alpha.rada.kiev.ua/const/conengl.htm>.

and drafted by communications experts, employees of the State Committee on Communications and Information, and the Ministry of Internal Affairs. In June 2001, Mr. Zadorozhniy (then Chief of the Parliament Committee on Legal Policy, currently the Representative of the President in the Parliament) introduced an alternative draft bill on Personal Information to the Parliament. The bill was prepared with the assistance of Mr. A. Pazyuk, Director of Privacy Ukraine. The draft covers public and private sectors, provides natural persons with the right to informational self-determination. It includes special provisions concerning sensitive data (racial origin, nationality, trade union membership, political, philosophical and religious beliefs, medical and health data, and data on criminal offenses) and imposes limitation of data transfer to third countries with inadequate level of data protection. The draft proposes the establishment of independent authority for supervision. The National Agency on Personal Data Processing Supervision would be empowered to conduct investigations, impose sanctions, maintain a national register of databases, and to adopt or approve codes of fair information practices proposed by the private sector. The draft would require amendments to the Constitution to provide for the appointment of the National Agency chief nominated by the President of Ukraine and subject to the authority of the Parliament. The Agency would be required to submit annual reports to Parliament. MP Zadorozhniy's draft has received positive evaluation by the experts of the Council of Europe in 2001 as it is based on the Convention for the Protection of Individuals with Regard to Automatic Processing of Personal Data (ETS No. 108) (Convention No. 108) and the EU Data Protection Directive (1995/46/EC). At the same time, the direct marketing industry opposed strong data protection rules. The main obstacle for the adoption of a data protection legal framework in Ukraine is the misunderstanding of the role of a data protection commissioner and the unwillingness to establish an additional public body with effective powers of control.

The new Civil Code, which entered into force on January 1, 2004, introduced a number of sectoral privacy-related safeguards within Book II (Personality Rights). It ensures a tort cause of action for the violation of an individual's personal privacy interest in his or her health status, personal life, personal papers, correspondence, and inviolability of business reputation. The Code enables an individual to control the publicity of his or her image in photographs, artistic pieces, and movies, as well as safeguard the inviolability of one's name.

Before Bill No. 2618, a draft bill on Data Protection, prepared by the State Committee of Communications and Computerization, had been introduced to the Cabinet of Ministers for consideration in December 1999. The draft was loosely based on the Convention No. 108 and the State of Hesse's (Germany) 1970 Data Protection Act and focused on property rights for privacy control.

The biggest violations of the right to privacy are associated with the privacy of communication. The legislation does not provide clear reasons for information retrieval from communication channels (wiretapping of telephones, mobile phones or keeping track of e-mail messages and Internet browsing), a specific period of such information retrieval and the circumstances under which such information should be destroyed and how it may be used. The guarantees of legitimacy of information retrieval from communication channels are insufficient. As a result, no one can monitor the number of permits and necessity of eavesdropping, while persons, to whom such actions were applied, are not aware of them and, thus, cannot appeal against such actions in the court of law or otherwise protect their right to privacy.[5458]

The Law on Telecommunications No. 1280-IV was enacted on November 18, 2003.[5459] It provides certain guarantees for privacy protection. Operators and providers have to protect the secrecy of personal data (Article 34). Consumer's personal data and data on telecommunication services can be provided to third parties with the data subject's consent or on the conditions provided by law. Subscribers' personal data may only be included in directories with the data subject's permission. The Law does not restrict personal data collection by service providers but prohibits further dissemination.[5460] The National Regulatory Commission for Communication (NRCC) is empowered to protect consumer's rights (including data protection) (Article 21). As of today, the NRCC is not yet operational since the President has not yet appointed its members.

The Act on the Operational Investigative Activity (OIA) of February 18, 1992, empowers law enforcement agencies to conduct surveillance. The agencies are obliged to obtain a warrant under the court procedure as implemented by the Act of the Supreme Court Plenary Session of November 1, 1996.[5461] The Statute does not provide wiretapping procedure rules. Those are regulated by secret rules, adopted by the joint Ministry of Internal Affairs and State Committee as Communications Order No. 745/90 of September 30, 1999. The applications are

---

[5458] "Human rights in Ukraine 2004," Report of human right organizations, Kharkiv, Folio, 2005, page 92.

[5459] The laws of Ukraine, as well as other legislative documents, can be found on the website of the Parliament of Ukraine <http://zakon.rada.gov.ua>.

[5460] E-mail from Andriy Pazyuk, Privacy Ukraine, to Cédric Laurant, Policy Counsel, Electronic Privacy Information Center (EPIC), July 9, 2003 (on file with EPIC).

[5461] Directive of the Supreme Court of Ukraine, No. 9 of November 1, 1996, on referring to the Constitution in Administering Justice.

registered and include the names of officials, and the date and type of communications. Statistical data on wiretapping activity is not publicly available. Under Article 11 of the Act, priests, doctors, and lawyers cannot be asked about information concerning their clients, and any such information cannot be used as evidence in court. However, in practice, the courts regularly use such information. The special services investigated the Kazakhstan Energy Grid Operating Company in June 2000 for the illegal tapping of employee conversations and charged one employee with a violation of the criminal code.[5462]

On January 18, 2001, a new law was passed amending the OIA Act of 1992. The new Act clarifies the offenses for which surveillance may be used and significantly improves procedures for judicial supervision and oversight. Individuals are not granted full access to the personal data collected by police during the investigation and are allowed only to receive an explanation of the human rights implications of the surveillance. The Act prohibits the dissemination of information about undisclosed crimes, information that might damage an open investigation, a person's interest or the security of the State. The disclosure of State secrets is also prohibited. An Order of the Chief of the Security Service dated March 1, 2001 defines a State secret as data relating to "the preparation, performance and results of secret OIA measures used against persons who are preparing or have committed especially dangerous or heinous crimes against the State."

Wiretapping and Surveillance Rules

During 2004, political shadowing in Ukraine grew extraordinarily in scale and the problem became public. The shadowing spread to people's deputies, presidential candidates, heads of governmental authorities. On August 10, 2004, the people's deputies of Ukraine who accompanied presidential candidate Viktor Yuschenko noticed a car that spied on the presidential candidate in Crimea. Militia officers who arrived on the scene discovered that a person who was detained at the place of spying had a directed action microphone, wiretapping devices, photo and video equipment. An extraterritorial surveillance car was packed with materials about Yuschenko obtained through tracking. There were also different surveillance devices, 12 different number plates of the car, and an official task of the Interior Ministry of Ukraine to place Yuschenko under

---

[5462] "Power Company Denies Involvement in Telephone Tapping," BBC Summary of World Broadcasts, June 2, 2000.

surveillance. Other documents, which were found in the car, also provided information on another presidential candidate of Ukraine, Nataliya Vitrenko.[5463]

Head of the Information Research Department of the Field Service Division at the Agency of the Interior Ministry of Ukraine in Chernihiv oblast, Lieutenant Colonel Serhiy Kordyk, informed that the secret services received a verbal instruction to check those who have the same last names as opposition leaders to make sure whether "there is possible kinship between them." According to Kordyk, a person was found in Chernihiv oblast with the last name Yuschenko; they thoroughly checked the information and reported to respective authorities that Yuschenko from Chernihiv is not a son of the people's deputy of Ukraine, Head of Our Ukraine Block, Viktor Andriyovych Yuschenko. The children of the latter are."[5464]

Law enforcement authorities were also very actively involved in the presidential election campaign in Ukraine, acting on the side of the presidential candidate and Prime Minister of Ukraine, Viktor Yanukovych. Interior bodies collected personal data about public activists and organized mass detention thereof for no valid reason.[5465]

On February 17, 2005, Head of the Security Service of Ukraine Oleksandr Turchynov notified about the institution of criminal proceedings on charges of illegal wiretapping of telephone talks of the former opposition leaders, in particular, Viktor Yuschenko and Yulia Tymoshenko.The case was instituted pursuant to part 2 of Article 379 "Illegal Use of Surveillance Devices". According to the Head of the Security Service of Ukraine, the wiretapping of opposition politicians was illegal and of very high scale, with the decision about the wiretapping approved at the highest level. Documents were filed to court in order to obtain a permit for wiretapping and eavesdropping of a person who had broke the law, and the court authorized such actions. At the same time, the documents that were furnished to the court contained telephone numbers of other persons, which in turn allowed the wiretapping of other persons.[5466]

Oleksandr Turchynov notified that in Ukraine the required wiretapping equipment is currently owned by various governmental authorities, in particular, the Ministry of Interior, the State Frontier Service, Tax Militia of the State Tax

---

[5463] Internet edition Ukrainian Monitor, available at
<http://foreignpolicy.org.ua/ua/headlines/politics/elections/index.shtml?id=3535>.

[5464] Internet human rights edition RUPOR, available at <http://www.rupor.org/index.php?id=1092743112>.

[5465] Report on file with Roman Romanov.

[5466] Internet Media Ukrainska Pravda, available at <http://www2.pravda.com.ua/archive/?50217-6-77>.

Administration, the Department for Execution of Punishments, and intelligence agencies.[5467]

Specific data about the scope of wiretapping of telephone talks in Ukraine are not known since the official statistics are not provided by governmental authorities. However, it was reported that in 2002 the courts issued over 40,000 authorizations. It was officially confirmed that in 2003 the Appellate Court of Chernivtsi oblast, which is the smallest region of Ukraine, issued 823 permits for wiretapping in communication channels.[5468]

As of June 13, 2002, the Ukrainian Prosecutor-General's Office has suspended the investigation into the case against former security officer Mykola Melnychenko who was granted United States political asylum after he publicized wiretapped conversations of Ukrainian President Leonid Kuchma suggesting the president's involvement in illegal activities.[5469] The tapes made in the president's office are said to implicate President Leonid Kuchma in the journalist's murder and several other crimes.[5470] Ukraine wants Melnychenko extradited for divulging state secrets.

Another high-profile incident of illegal wiretapping occurred in 2002. Investigators launched a criminal investigation into the bugging of telephone conversations between the Kiev mayor Oleksandr Omelchenko and the leader of the popular centre-right political party block "Our Ukraine," Viktor Yushchenko, during a 2001 election campaign.[5471] In Ukraine, it is a criminal offense to publicize private conversations, as well as to secretly record them. The leaders of the all-Ukrainian public movement "For Honesty in Politics" first published the recordings at a news conference on January 9, 2002. The wiretapping is believed to have been carried out in Kiev and investigators do not rule out the possibility that it was done legally by law enforcement agencies as part of a criminal investigation directed at non-public or -state figures.[5472]

[5467] Internet Media Tribuna, available at<http://www.tribuna.com.ua/news/2005/02/17/23536.html>.

[5468] Yevhen Zakharov. "Criminal Investigation Activities and Privacy of Communications" in a book. *Freedom of Information and Right to Privacy in Ukraine*, second volume, Kharkiv, Folio, 2004, pages 45-60.

[5469] "Ukraine Suspends Tape Scandal Inquiry, Wants Whistle-Blower Extradited," BBC Worldwide Monitoring, June 13, 2002.

[5470] The tapes are available at <http://www.wcfia.harvard.edu/academy/melnychenko/records.htm>.

[5471] "Latest Tape Scandal Triggers Probe into Phone Tapping," BBC Worldwide Monitoring, January 11, 2002.

[5472] "Prosecutor Warns Organizers of Recent Tape Scandal of Imprisonment," BBC Worldwide Monitoring, February 6, 2002.

A wide publicity was given to the situation concerning recordings of conversations held at the office of the former President of Ukraine, Leonid Kuchma. The audio tapes kept in possession of the former presidential guard, Mykola Melnychenko, contained the information about possible involvement in grave crimes of heads of state, but it is likewise the information, which can constitute a state secret. The wiretapping of the Ukrainian President's office was illegal. At the same time however, the recorded data can shed light upon the crimes and help to solve them. Political discussions keep going in Ukraine as to whether the whole archive of Mykola Melnychenko's recordings should be made public.[5473]

The Ukrainian Supreme Council has supported a resolution to create a parliamentary ad hoc commission to investigate violations of the confidentiality of telephone conversations.[5474] Last year, the Supreme Council parliament renewed prosecutor supervision over people's and politicians' constitutional right to privacy of telephone conversations and correspondence.

The Department of Special Telecommunication Systems and Information Safeguard of the Security Service of Ukraine is authorized under an April 2000 Presidential *Ukase*[5475] to adopt regulations on the protection of information in data transmitting networks, as well as to establish the "application of the tools for the protection of state information resources."[5476] The Presidential Ukase, although in force, is not observed. To implement provisions of this *Ukase*, the Parliament of Ukraine should adopt new laws and amend others. The situation with this *Ukase* is typical in Ukraine when a law although enacted is not implemented and does, as a result, not influence the social and political life of the country. In July 2000, President Kuchma signed the *Ukase* on "development of national content of the global informational network (Internet) and wide access to this network in Ukraine." It sets rules on digital signatures, information security and protection of information "which can not be published according to the law."[5477]

In 2004, active discussion was held around the proposal to establish a Unified State Register of Individuals and other state registers to contain personal data, in particular, the register of electors. On November 16, 2004, the Parliament

---

[5473] *See* <http://www.glavred.info/eng/index.php?news=102811131>.

[5474] "Ukrainian Parliament Sets up ad hoc Body to Investigate Wiretap," BBC Worldwide Monitoring, March 7, 2002.

[5475] Act of the President of a regulatory nature.

[5476] Presidential *Ukase* No. 582/2000 of April 10, 2000.

[5477] Ukase of July 31, 2000, No. 928/2000.

(*Verkhovna Rada*) of Ukraine rejected a bill on registration of individuals in Ukraine. The Committee for European Integration of the Parliament (*Verkhovna Rada*) of Ukraine recommended that the Parliament should reject the bill on registration of individuals in Ukraine as the bill that does not meet the regulations of the European Union, obligations of Ukraine to the Council of Europe and contravenes the Constitution of Ukraine.

However, under Decree No. 500 "On Establishment of the Unified State Register of Individuals," dated April 30, 2004, the President of Ukraine approved, for no legal cause, the creation of the Unified Register. Under the Decree, such functions were vested into the Ministry of Interior on the basis of the Uniform State Automated Passport System ("USAPS").

However, under Decree No. 457/2005, dated March 10, 2005, President Yuschenko revoked previous decisions of then-President Kuchma regarding the creation of the Unified State Register of Individuals (Presidential Decree, dated April 30, 2004), thereby revoking the intention to introduce a new sample passport in the form of a plastic card.[5478]

Under the revoked Decree of President Kuchma, a passport of the Ukrainian citizen would have contained a page of machine-readable data (so called "data page") between the cover and the first page. It also intended to include a digital picture of the passport holder, data about a type of passport, code of the State, passport number, full name, nationality, date of birth, PIN, sex, place of birth, date of issuance and a passport along with the issuing body, passport validity period and signature of passport holder.

Currently, the main electronic classifier, which is the basis for collection and processing of the personal data of Ukrainian citizens, is an ID code provided by the State Tax Administration.[5479] The scope of its use constantly grows and extends far beyond the goal for which it was originally introduced – tax accounting. Failure to obtain an identification code would make it impossible to be legally employed, be provided with retirement benefit, exercise the right to education, be granted scholarships and unemployment benefit, register subsidies, open bank accounts, and register oneself as a business entity, etc.

[5478] Public Relations Department of the Interior Ministry of Ukraine, available at <http://mvsinfo.gov.ua/official/2005/03/031805_1.html>.

[5479] ID code is a 14-digit number, first four digits are date of birth starting from 1.01.1900, next four digits are a personal number among people born the same day, the ninth digit is related to sex, and the tenth is the "control digit." For more information, *see* <http://www.khpg.org/index.php?id=944254613>.

Anti-terrorism Measures

The Law of Ukraine "On Combating Terrorism"[5480] came into effect in March 2003. Its adoption resulted in amendments, which were introduced to other laws and which, in particular, considerably restricted guarantees of secrecy in banking, access to information, and extended powers of the Security Service of Ukraine in terms of telecommunication monitoring.

On August 6, 2003, the action plan was adopted by the Cabinet of Ministers of Ukraine, which is aimed at ensuring the enforcement of the Law of Ukraine "On Combating Terrorism." The plan also stipulates the development by the Security Service of Ukraine of a an amendment to the law "On Freedom of Conscience and Religious Organizations," which should provide for "a mechanism of registration of new religious organizations whose centers are located abroad, provided that preliminary legal, religious, medical and psychological examination of religions they practice is conducted."[5481] However, all such initiatives were rejected by the Parliament (*Verkhovna Rada*) of Ukraine.

Ukrainian law-enforcement bodies, to counteract political opposition during the 2004 election campaign, used a set of measures envisaged by the law for combating terrorism. An explosion was set off in autumn at one of Kyiv's markets. Kyiv militiamen implicated oppositional youth political associations in this crime. Searches were conducted in the premises of the public campaign "PORA"[5482] in different Ukrainian regions. The Security Service of Ukraine conducted a search of the apartment of PORA's campaign leader, Mykhailo Svystovych, in the town of Irpin. Explosive materials were earlier found in the PORA premises in Kyiv and Chernihiv and activists were detained.[5483] Representatives of the law-enforcement bodies publicly called the PORA campaign a terrorist organization.[5484] The institution of criminal proceedings on charges of creation and participation in the activities of the "terrorist organization," allowed for criminal investigations against activists of opposition organizations. Members of the campaign claimed that they had nothing to do with the explosive materials found and law enforcement officials failed to provide evidence that the explosive materials belonged to the activists.[5485]

[5480] The Law of Ukraine "On Combating Terrorism," available at <http://zakon.rada.gov.ua>.

[5481] http://zakon.rada.gov.ua.

[5482] PORA campaign official website <http://www.kuchmizm.info>.

[5483] Internet edition *Podrobnosti,* available at<http://www.podrobnosti.ua/accidents/2004/10/16/152088.html>.

[5484]Available at <http://www.proua.com/news/2004/10/19/114937.html>.

[5485] *Id.*

The Security Service of Ukraine takes the initiative of expanding its powers by making reference to the international principles of combating terrorism. Thus, measures of monitoring Internet users and Ukrainian Internet network segment regulation are launched in order to counteract the so-called "computer terrorism." Therefore, the Security Service of Ukraine referring to recommendations of the Parliamentary Assembly of the Council of Europe on combating terrorism put forward the initiative of developing bills "On Protection of Information in Data Communication Networks," "On Regulation of the Ukrainian Segment of the Internet Network" and "On Telecommunications Monitoring."[5486]

The last of the above bills was subject to a wide discussion in 2004. Non-governmental organizations of human right activists, Internet providers, and network users criticized the Security Service of Ukraine proposals and developed an alternative bill, "On Interception of Telecommunications."

The bill, developed jointly by the *Internet Association of Ukraine* (IAU), public organizations *Ukrainian Internet Community* (UIC) and *Kharkiv Human Rights Group,* provides for the creation of a system of automated remote interception of telecommunications – a protected special-purpose telecommunications network, to which the following facilities are connected: interception devices installed directly in the telecommunications operator's networks; arbitrary terminals installed within judicial authorities issuing permits for interception of telecommunications; on-line terminals installed within investigation divisions conducting criminal investigation, counter-intelligence, and intelligence and prejudicial inquiries; recording terminals installed at the office of the Human Rights Commissioner (Ombudsman) of the Parliament (Verkhovna Rada) of Ukraine. Persons to whom interception was applied should be informed of the interception period and the content of the information gathered through these means. In addition, the Ombudsman should annually publish statistical reporting about the interception of communications in Ukraine. The interception period may not exceed six months. The interception is solely applied to individuals suspected of committing grave offences and felonies (Article 10 of the draft law).[5487] This bill was carried through six Committees of the Verkovna Rada (the Parliament) of Ukraine as the bill stipulating efficient privacy protection procedures and the Cabinet of Ministers of Ukraine subsequently revoked the bill "On Telecommunications Monitoring."[5488]

[5486] Legal Bulletin of Ukraine, January 26, 2002.

[5487] Available at <http://www.rada.gov.ua:8080/pls/zweb/webproc4_1?id=&pf3511=17622>.

[5488] Human Rights in Ukraine in 2004. Report of human right organizations, Kharkiv, Folio, 2005, page 99.

In September 1999, President Leonid Kuchma proposed regulations requiring that Internet service providers install surveillance devices on their systems based on the Russian SORM system. The regulations had to be withdrawn because of a constitutional issue and he proposed a bill to implement them. The bill was attacked by the Parliament and withdrawn. In June 2000, several high government officials (including the deputy chair of the security service, the chair of the headquarters of the Ministry of Defense, and the chair of the Presidential Committee on informational security) held closed meetings with representatives of the major Ukrainian ISPs to discuss new SORM regulations. A working group released a document announcing that the group had agreed to implement surveillance capabilities based on the European ENFOPOL 98 initiative and create a working group on filtering and monitoring of unlawful information.[5489] The large ISPs are expected to support the regulations to eliminate competition from smaller ISPs who will not be able to afford the new systems.

An opportunity of use of SORM systems has never been discussed in Ukraine. In 2000, during a conference on information security issues, two Internet associations were created: the Internet Association of Ukraine[5490] and the Association of the Internet Market Players of Ukraine.[5491] When the State Committee on Communications and Information understood that it was difficult to enact a law establishing telephone tapping and making ISPs install tap equipment, they issued Instruction No. 122 in June 2002 that compels state bodies' ISPs to get a certification at the Department of Special Telecommunication Systems and Information Safeguard of the Security Service, that requires the use of special wiretap equipment. Currently, only one Ukrainian ISP has already been granted such certification. Other ISPs refuse to apply for certification and go on working with state bodies.

The chief of the National Security Service (SBU) Yuri Radchenko stated at a press conference on July 14, 2001, that the SBU "ha[d] no plans to control the Internet in Ukraine but that it would rather like to register all Ukrainian Internet users."[5492] In October 2001, the Council of National Security and Defense took a decision that was enacted by the *Ukase* of the President on The Measures for the

---

[5489] *See* Andriy Pazyuk, "Ukrainian ISPs Demonstrate Their Willingness to Be Subservient to Big Brother," Privacy Ukraine, July 7, 2000.

[5490] Homepage <http://www.inau.org.ua/>.

[5491] Homepage <http://www.auriu.org/>.

[5492] Yuri Radchenko, "Automatic Electronic Surveillance of the Citizens: Worldwide Reality and Ukrainian Prospects," Zerkalo Nedeli, Mirror-Weekly, No. 28 (352), July 28 – August 3, 2001, available at <http://www.zn.kiev.ua/nn/show/352/31695/>.

Improvement of National Information Policy and Safeguards of Information Security of December 6, 2001 (No. 1193/2001). The *Ukase* directed the Cabinet of Ministers to elaborate and introduce draft laws compelling ISPs and electronic media to obtain licenses, monitor Internet traffic, and store Internet traffic data for a period of six months. It was President Kuchma's second attempt to require Ukrainian providers of communication services to install at their own expenses wiretapping equipment as a requirement to obtain a state license. The first attempt was *Ukase* No. 737/99 of June 27, 1999, supplemented with the draft law introduced to the Parliament on June 29, 1999. The Parliament of Ukraine considered the presidential proposal but turned it down by an Enactment of September 7, 1999 (No. 1016-14), and since then, the Cabinet of Ministers has not introduced any similar bill to the Parliament.

There are several other laws that control personal information.[5493] The cabinet approved the creation of a Single State Automated Passport System in January 1997 as a component of the State Register of Population.[5494] The system will be used as an internal ID system and hold both textual and graphical data about every Ukrainian. The text data will include: first, patronymic and last name, date of birth, sex, identification number, date of registration and residence, data of another state citizenship, data of passport and its duplicates, data of employment and education, matrimonial status, data of husband/wife and children, military draft status, date of documents for traveling abroad, and memoranda (disability care, restriction for traveling abroad). The graphical information will include: identifier, biometrics data and signature. Religious conservatives demonstrated in opposition to the application of personal identification numbers approved by the Act on State Register of Natural Persons – Taxpayers.[5495] The Parliament approved an amendment to the statute in July 1999 allowing for an alternative system of registration to be used for persons with religious grounds for opposing identity numbers.[5496] There are also laws relating to tax information,[5497] social insurance,[5498] domicile registration,[5499] retirement insurance,[5500] unemployment insurance,[5501] criminal investigations,[5502] juvenile records,[5503] former

---

[5493] *See* Andriy Pazyuk, Privacy Ukraine Privacy of Data Subject in Ukraine, 1999, for more details on the laws, available at <http://www2.datatestlab.com/privacy/>.

[5494] The Statutory Order of the Cabinet of Ministers (CM) of January 20, 1997 (No 40).

[5495] "On State Register of Natural Persons – Taxpayers" of December 22, 1994 (No.320/94).

[5496] Statute of July 16, 1999 (No.1003-XIV) on the alterations to the Statute on State Register of Natural Persons – Taxpayers.

[5497] Law on State Register of Natural Persons – Taxpayers of December 22, 1994 (No. 320/94).

[5498] The Basic Legislation of Ukraine on Obligatory State Social Insurance, January 14, 1998 (No. 16/98).

[5499] The MIA Order, February 3, 1992 (No. 66).

[5500] Statutory Order of the CM, June 4, 1998 (No. 794).

[5501] The Statutory Order of CM, May 27, 1998 (No. 578).

prisoners,[5504] military service records,[5505] medical records,[5506] and HIV and AIDS records.[5507]

The Ordinance of the President of Ukraine on the Establishment of the Unified State Register of Physical Persons No. 500/2004 of April 30, 2004 authorized the Ministry of Internal Affairs (MIA) to register persons by place of residence and to keep records of the Unified State Register of Physical Persons. The Ordinance also authorizes the MIA to improve the domestic personal identification document (national passport) and to bring it into accordance with European requirements, particularly with the decisions of the 2001 Warsaw Conference on Combating Terrorism.

The Parliament of Ukraine adopted a new edition of the Criminal Code on April 5, 2001. The new code includes several articles relating to privacy violation and will go into effect in September 2001. Article 132 prohibits dissemination of information about AIDS or other incurable diseases data by medical personnel. Dissemination of other confidential medical data by a doctor is punishable under Article 145. Article 162 provides for criminal liability for unlawful entrance, search and seizure. Article 163 criminalizes the unlawful wiretapping or interception of electronic communications. Article 168 provides liability for disclosing confidential information regarding child adoption. Finally, Article 182 on "Breaching the Inviolability of Private Life" provides that the "[u]nlawful collection, storage, usage or dissemination of confidential information related to a person without consent or the dissemination of such information in a public speech, or production or in the mass-media, is punishable by a fine of up to 50 multiple tax free incomes or correctional labor of up to two years or imprisonment of up to six months or limitation of liberty of up to three years."

Considering that the Constitutional Court of Ukraine has interpreted "confidential information" to include all personal data related to individual, the broad scope of Article 182 poses a real threat to freedom of speech. In order to address this

---

[5502] The Order of Office of Public Prosecutor, December 21, 1995 (No. 22/835); The MIA Order, January 14, 1994 (No. 190).

[5503] The Law on Organs and Services on Juveniles and Dedicated Educational Institutions for Juveniles, January 1995 (No. 20/95); Ministry of Education Order, December 27, 1994 (No. 362).

[5504] The Law on Administrative Control the Former Prisoners, December 1, 1994 (No. 264/94).

[5505] Department of Defense Orders of June 27, 1995 No. 165, 166 approved the Regulation on Military Record Maintained at the Place of Employment or Study (Public or Private) and the Regulation on Military Domiciliary Registration.

[5506] Law of September 19, 1992.

[5507] Law on the Prevention of AIDS Contamination and Social Aid on Civilians (adopted on March 3, 1998) as well as Article 13 of the Discipline of Medical Inspection on HIV Results, Registration of HIV and AIDS Persons and Medical Care (approved by the Statutory Order of the Cabinet of Ministers, December 18, 1998).

issue, the draft bill on Personal Information (introduced in June 2001) proposes that this article be amended to criminalize only the use of personal data for unlawful actions that endanger the life or health of the person concerned.

Recent Developments

Recent amendments to the Law on Prevention of Money Laundering No. 249-IV of November 28, 2002 provides for the establishment of a new executive public body authorized to undertake financial monitoring. Starting on January 1, 2005, it will replace the Department for Financial Monitoring of the Ministry of Finance. This body will use the database records of the State Unified Information System for its activities in the area of the prevention of money laundering and terrorism financing. The database has been established by the Enactment No. 1896 of December 10, 2003 of the Cabinet of Ministers pursuant to the Financial Action Task Force on Money Laundering (FATF)'s Recommendations,[5508] as a separate part of the National System of Confidential Communications. It contains comprehensive data of different natures and resources from different state registers, and is accessible to the range of public executive and law enforcement bodies. It includes criminal records, data on lost passports, vehicle registration information, data on financial and other types of licenses, financial violations, import-export custom clearance records, tax register data, financial accounting records, investments, some commercial data, and border control records. The system will be fully operational by 2006.

In respect of the adoption procedure, the Ukrainian legislation disregards the interests of the adopted child. The secrecy of adoption is guaranteed by allowing adoptive parents to register themselves as the child's parents (Article 229 of the Family Code) and to change the reference to the child's place of birth within a six-month period and his/her date of birth (Article 230 of the Family Code). Disclosure of the adoption secret results in criminal punishment (Article 168 of the Criminal Code of Ukraine). However, the child's right to know his/her natural parents (Article 7 of the UN Convention on the Rights of the Child) and right to preserve his/her individuality (Article 8 of the UN Convention on the Rights of the Child) are absolutely disregarded. Furthermore, the law contains provisions about privacy of adoption in relation to the very child (part 2 of Article 226 of the Family Code).[5509]

[5508] The Forty Recommendations (2003), available at <http://www1.oecd.org/fatf/40Recs_en.htm>.

[5509] N. Petrova,"Right to respect for private and family life: civil and legal aspects in the legislation and judicial practice of Ukraine" in *The European Convention on Human Rights: general provisions, practice of application, Ukrainian context* Revised by O.L. Zhukovska. – K.: CJSC VIPOL, 2004, page 403.

Another problem is the issue of forced medical examination and interference of law-enforcement bodies into the family life of persons with untraditional sexual orientation. For example, law enforcement bodies still provide the State Statistics Committee with the information about discovered homosexuals and keep record thereof as constituting the AIDS-risk group[5510].

The All-Ukrainian Network of People Living with HIV reports the disclosure of the medical diagnosis of HIV-infected persons. HIV-infected persons are losing employment opportunities and access to social services. In Simferopol, a person was erroneously diagnosed with HIV and then suffered the disclosure of the HIV-infection diagnosis, brought a suit in court.[5511]

Major Privacy Case Law

The European Court of Human Rights has acknowledged the admissibility of six cases relating to Ukraine dealing with the infringement of the right of convicted persons to private life through correspondence, receipt of parcels, postal packets, limitation of the number of meetings with their relatives and conditions provided for such meetings. For the cases *Poltoratsky v. Ukraine, Kuznetsov v. Ukraine, Aliev v. Ukraine, Nazarenko v. Ukraine, Dankevych v. Ukraine, Khokhlych v. Ukraine*, the Court admitted the violation of Article 8 of the Convention for the above reasons.

The European Convention on Human Rights, ratified by Ukraine in July 1997, requires Ukraine to refrain from impeding the applications of any persons in the country to the European Court of Human Rights. However, applicable Ukrainian legislation does not provide for any confidentiality procedure with regard to the correspondence sent from places of confinement to the European Court in Strasbourg. Currently, only letters, applications, proposals and complaints directed to the Authorized Officer of the Parliament (*Verkhovna Rada*) of Ukraine for Human Rights and the Prosecutor, are not examined by administrative institutions for execution of punishments. The bill developed by the Ministry of Justice, proposes some changes to the Criminal Punishment Execution Code and the Law of Ukraine "On Pretrial Detention." The bill proposes to establish, at the legislative level, the prohibition of any examination

---

[5510] Report on the performance of interior bodies in their fighting against prostitution, detection of risk group, and the results of their AIDS-examination, approved by the Order No. 436 of the State Statistics Committee of Ukraine, as of December 10, 2002.

[5511] *Nasha Zhizn (Our Life)* bulletin, No. 1(5), 2004, page 27, available at <http://www.network.org.ua>.

of correspondence sent from places of confinement to the European Court of Human Rights.[5512]

In February 2005, the European Court of Human Rights delivered a judgment admitting the violation by Ukraine of Article 8 of the European Convention on Human Rights. The court ordered payment of damages in the amount of EUR 8,000 to the Ukrainian national Romuald Novoseletsky residing in Ussuriysk (Russian Federatinon). The funds are to be paid in compensation for material as well as non-material damages. The former category stems from the loss of goods from Mr. Novoseletsky's apartment, during the time that somebody else was living in his apartment, accordingly to the authorization issued by some governmental institution. The plaintiff also suffered from non-material damage that was caused by the impossibility to reside in his own apartment with his family for a long period of time. The European Court of Human Rights admitted that, as a result of the unlawful decision, Mr. Novoseletsky had to live with a family that was not his own, which constituted an infringement of his right to private and family life (right to privacy).[5513]

Open Government

The 1992 Act on Information[5514] defines only general principles of citizens' access to information personally related to them. The Act provides a right of access to government records. Individuals have the right to get access to information concerning them (Article 9). Exceptions are to be defined by law. There are methods for making official information public, including disclosing it to interested persons orally, in writing or in other ways (Article 21). Article 23 of the Act prohibits the collection of personal data without the data subject's consent.[5515] Any data subject has the right to know about data collection (Article 23). The right to obtain non-covert information is limited (Article 29), although there are many exceptions to this rule (Article 37). The author of a rejected or postponed request has a right to appeal the decision to a higher echelon or court (Article 34). There is limited access to the files of the former secret police under the Act "on rehabilitation of victims of political repressions," which gives the

---

[5512] Internet edition on human rights *RUPOR*, available at <http://www.rupor.org/index.php?id=1092437416>.

[5513] *Id.*

[5514] Statute on Information adopted by Parliament on October 2, 1992 (No. 2657-XII).

[5515] The Constitutional Court of Ukraine ruled in October 1997 that Article 23 prohibited not only the collection of information, but also the storage, use and dissemination of confidential personal information without the individual's consent. Verdict of the Constitutional Court of Ukraine concerning the case of the official treatment of Articles 3, 23, 31, 47, 48 of the Law of Ukraine on Information and Article 12 of the Law on the Prosecutor's Office (case of K. G. Ustimenko), October 30, 1997.

rehabilitated citizen or his heirs the right to read his personal file kept in the KGB archives. There are exceptions for national security and economic well-being reasons. Information that would affect another individual's rights and freedoms is also exempted. Confidential information includes, in particular, information about a person such as education, marital status, state of health, date and place of birth, property status and other personal details.

Access to public and private archives is regulated by the Law on National Archival Fund and Archival Bodies of December 24, 1993 (No. 3814-XII) in the version of the Law of December 13, 2001 (No. 2888-III). Article 16 provides that archival bodies have the right to limit access to documents owned by state or local communities containing state secrets, or other secrets protected by the laws until the documents are declassified by state secrecy experts. The Law on State Secret of November 21, 1999 regulates the duration of access limitation. It ranges from five to 30 years depending on the level of secrecy. Public access to confidential personal data, the disclosure of which could threaten life or the inviolability of the home, is barred for 75 years. It is possible to get access to such documents with the permission of the data subject or his heirs. Access is permitted to the staff of archival bodies, courts, law-enforcement and tax bodies if provided by laws.

On May 11, 2004, the Ukrainian Parliament (*Verkhovna Rada*) adopted the Law on Amendments (No. 1703-IV) to amend a number of laws in the field of protection of state secret, administrative liability for the illegal use of wiretapping, access to information, etc. The right of printed media journalists to freely receive, use, disseminate and store information will be limited to information that has "open access" status (amendments to Articles 2(1) and 26(2) of the Law on Printed Mass Media). After the law had been initially adopted in July 2003, it was strongly opposed by the EU representatives, the Organization for Security and Cooperation in Europe (OSCE), the International Federation of Journalists (IFJ), domestic NGOs, and the Parliamentary Committee on freedom of speech and information. In an open address, a number of NGO representatives and politicians appealed to the President not to promulgate the law as far as its provisions violate the Constitution of Ukraine and global freedom of information standards. Due to external and internal pressure, a number of amendments were introduced at the final stage, improving the final draft. The Law on Amendments introduces the term "state-owned confidential information." This includes all information owned by the state and used by state entities, bodies of local self-government, as well as organizations and companies with mixed ownership. Access to this data is restricted. The authority to establish rules for storing and using documents containing confidential information owned by the state is given to the government (amendments to Article 30 of the Law on Information). According to the Law, it is not allowed to classify as confidential environmental information, information on disasters, statistical data, information on violations of human rights and breaches of law, as well as information that should be publicly accessible according to domestic and international laws. The Cabinet of Ministers of Ukraine is empowered to adopt a list of what is considered "confidential information" taking into consideration the provisions of the Ukrainian Constitution and international law obligations (including the provisions of Article 10 of the European Convention on Human Rights).[5516]

International Obligations

Ukraine is a member of the Council of Europe (CoE) but has not signed or ratified the Convention No. 108. However, a task force of the Ministry of Justice of Ukraine started its work in 2005. It includes non-governmental organizations operating in the field of privacy rights protection. Within 2005, Ukraine plans to ratify Convention No. 108 and, at the same time, to introduce required amendments to the national legislation. Ukraine has signed and ratified the European Convention for the Protection of Human Rights and Fundamental Freedoms, which forms part of its national legislation.[5517] In November 2001, Ukraine signed, but has not ratified yet, the CoE Convention on cybercrime. The European Parliament supported the European Union Common Strategy towards Ukraine in a vote on March 15, 2001, but at the same time, it urged rapid changes to many current Ukraine policies.[5518]

United Kingdom of Great Britain and Northern Ireland

Constitutional Privacy Framework

The United Kingdom (UK) does not have a written constitution. The Human Rights Act provides for a limited incorporation of the European Convention on Human Rights (ECHR) into domestic law, including the right of privacy.[5519] The Act came into force on October 2, 2000. Thus far, the courts have cautiously implemented the rights. A right of privacy is slowly emerging in the cases from

---

[5516] EDRi-gram No. 2.10, May 19, 2004, available at <http://www.edri.org/cgi-bin/index?id=000100000150>.

[5517] Signed November 9, 1995; ratified September 11, 1997; entered into force September 11, 1997.

[5518] "European Union/Ukraine: Parliament Debates Strategy and Tactics," Europe Information Service, Euro-East, March 27, 2001.

[5519] Human Rights Act 1998 (c. 42), available at <http://www.hmso.gov.uk/acts/acts1998/19980042.htm>.

the law of confidence that has been used as far back as 1849 to protect the unauthorized disclosure of personal information.[5520] The House of Lords acting as the highest court ruled in October 2003 that there is no general common law tort for invasion of privacy and that the ECHR does not require the UK to adopt one.[5521] However, the Lords ruled in May 2004 that a tabloid newspaper violated model Naomi Campbell's privacy under Article 8 by publishing that she was undergoing drug treatment and printing pictures of her leaving the treatment center.[5522] More recently, the Court of Appeals ruled in May 2005 that following the European Court of Human Rights (ECtHR) case on Princess Caroline, there is an obligation of states to protect individuals from invasions of their personal lives and a duty on courts to follow that obligation.[5523]

There is a long history of recognizing privacy from government intrusion in the UK. The statesman William Pitt in the 18th century said, "The poorest man may in his cottage bid defiance to all the force of the Crown. It may be frail; its roof may shake; the wind may blow through it; the storms may enter, the rain may enter - but the King of England cannot enter; all his forces dare not cross the threshold of the ruined tenement!"[5524]

However, the current privacy picture in the UK is decidedly grim. The Labour government's political stance to appear tough on crime and its large Parliamentary majority have resulted in an unprecedented number of new laws limiting rights, including freedom of assembly, privacy, freedom of movement, the right of silence, and freedom of speech in the past seven years. There has been a vast expansion in the use of electronic surveillance, biometrics, surveillance cameras, computer databases, DNA testing and other intrusive technologies.[5525] The previous Home Secretary, David Blunkett, was described by one commentator as the "judicial equivalent of a football hooligan" for his personal attacks on judges, civil rights campaigners and political figures (including those from his own party) who opposed his proposals for limiting civil

---

[5520] Prince Albert v. Strange, 1 Mac & G 25 (1849).

[5521] Wainwright and another v. Home Office, (2003) UKHL 53, (2003) 4 All ER 969. October 16, 2003.

[5522] Campbell v. MGN Ltd (2004) UKHL 22, 2 WLR 1232. May 6, 2004; *see also* Information Commissioner – Annual report and accounts for the year ending March 31, 2003, July 2003, available at <http://www.informationcommissioner.gov.uk/>.

[5523] Douglas v. Hello (2005) EWCA Civ 595.

[5524] William Pitt, Earl of Chatham, Speech on the Excise Bill in Bartletts Familiar Quotations, 10th ed. (1919); *see also e.g.* Entick v. Carrington, 95 Eng. Rep., 807 K.B. (1765).

[5525] For a comprehensive overview of recent developments in the deployment of surveillance technologies in the UK, see FIPR, Technology development and its effect on privacy & law enforcement, February 2004, available at <http://www.informationcommissioner.gov.uk/cms/DocumentUploads/Report%20Parts%201%262.pdf>.

liberties and giving himself more powers.[5526] However, he was sacked as Home Secretary for abusing his powers in 2004. The May 2005 elections saw Labour reelected but with a substantial loss of its majority in Parliament and it is expected that controversial proposals to further limit civil liberties will be less likely to be approved.

Data Protection Framework

The Parliament approved the Data Protection Act in July 1998 to implement the European Union Data Protection Directive.[5527] The legislation, which came into force on March 1, 2000, applies to records held by government agencies and private entities. It creates eight data protection principles based on the Directive to be followed. These provide for limitations on the use of personal information, access to, and correction of, records and requires that entities that maintain records register with the Information Commissioner.

The Act is quite complex and is considered not very effective at promoting privacy and implementing the EU Directive.[5528] It has been described by the courts as a "cumbersome and inelegant piece of legislation."[5529] The Information Commissioner noted in his 2004 report that it "is not the most elegant or easily understood statute. It is not written for the casual reader." Its complexity results in it being often incorrectly cited as a justification for the mishandling of data by public and private authorities.[5530] The Commissioner has committed to providing clearer guidance of the law and improving the "fair processing notices" to give individuals better information about how their personal information is being collected and used.

The protections it does offer are being undermined. The Court of Appeals issued a controversial decision in December 2003 narrowing the definition of personal information protected under the Act and limiting individuals' right to access

---

[5526] Simon Jenkins, "The Judicial Equivalent of a Football Hooligan," The Times, June 23, 2004.

[5527] Data Protection Act 1998 (c. 29) <http://www.hmso.gov.uk/acts/acts1998/19980029.htm>. replacing Data Protection Act 1984 (c. 35), available at <http://www.hmso.gov.uk/acts/acts1984/1984035.htm>.

[5528] *See e.g.*, Bainbridge D. *et al.*, Tilting the Windmills – Has the New Data Protection Law Failed to Make a Significant Contribution to Rights of Privacy, 2 Jnl of Information, Law and Tech (2000), available at <http://elj.warwick.ac.uk/jilt/00-2/bainbridge.html>.

[5529] Campbell v. MGN Ltd, Court of Appeal (Civil Division), (2002) EWCA Civ 1373, (2003) QB 633. October 14, 2002 (Opinion of Lord Phillips).

[5530] *See* Final Report of the Bichard Inquiry regarding problems of police understanding the DPA rules (2004), available at <http://www.bichardinquiry.org.uk/>; "Couple with No Gas Found Dead," BBC News Online, December 22, 2003, (British Gas blaming deaths of elderly couple on DPA after BG cut off gas to apartment).

personal information held in manual files.[5531] The Lord Chancellor's Department also held a consultation in 2002 on restricting individuals' access to their own files under the Data Protection Act after several politicians and prominent people obtained their own records and found that government officials were secretly trying to undermine their efforts to obtain information from government bodies.[5532] The European Commission has sent a letter of formal notice to the UK government that it may not be in compliance with the EU Data Protection Directive, although both the EU and UK governments have refused to release the letter.[5533]

The government is pressing to allow public bodies to be able to share more information.[5534] There have been a series of proposals in the name of e-government, population registration and local government. A proposal for the creation of electronic life records was withdrawn in December 2004 after two parliamentary committees found the regulations the government proposed exceeded the authority of the law.[5535] The Children Act, approved in November 2004,[5536] created a national database of all children and parents in the United Kingdom. Access to this database would be widely available. Children's advocates and the Parliamentary Joint Committee on Human Rights expressed concern that it violates Article 8 of the ECHR and criticized the bill.[5537] The government admitted that it might violate the ECHR but claimed that it was proportional because it involved children. A slim 12-vote majority in the Parliament approved it.

The Crime and Disorder Act 1998 provides for information sharing and data matching among public bodies in order to reduce crime and disorder. There are

---

[5531] Durant v. Financial Services Authority, (2003) EWCA Civ 1746.

[5532] A Lord Chancellor's Department Consultation Paper Data Protection Act 1998: Subject Access, October 2002, available at <http://www.lcd.gov.uk/consult/foi/dpsacons.htm>; Response to the Consultation Paper Data Protection Act 1998: Subject Access, July 2003, available at <http://www.dca.gov.uk/consult/foi/dpsaresp.htm>; *see* "Ashcroft Memos May Spur Data Law Repeal," The Guardian, February 5, 2002 and "MP Challenges Secrecy Culture," The Guardian, June 27, 2001.

[5533] "European Commission suggests UK's Data Protection Act is deficient," Out-Law. July 15, 2004.

[5534] Lord Chancellor's Department Consultation Paper, For Your Information: How Can The Public Sector Provide People with Information on, and Build Confidence in, the Way It Handles Their Personal Details?, April 2003, available at <http://www.lcd.gov.uk/consult/datasharing/datashare.htm>; Performance and Innovation Unit (PIU), "Privacy and Data-sharing: The way Forward for Public Services," April 2002, available at <http://www.number-10.gov.uk/su/privacy/index.htm>; Office of National Statistics, The Population Register Proposal, available at <http://www.gro.gov.uk/Images/wpeng_tcm69-3581.pdf>.

[5535] Office of National Statistics, Modernizing Civil Registration, available at <http://www.statistics.gov.uk/registration/whitepaper/default.asp>; Ministerial Statement on the Modernisation of Civil Registration, 1 March 2005, available at <http://www.gro.gov.uk/Images/FST_Statement_010305_tcm69-15715.pdf>.

[5536] Children Act 2004, (C. 31). Available at http://www.hmso.gov.uk/acts/acts2004/20040031.htm.

[5537] Joint Committee On Human Rights - Nineteenth Report, September 8, 2004.

also several other laws that affect privacy, most notably those governing medical records[5538] and consumer credit information.[5539] Other laws with privacy components include: the Rehabilitation of Offenders Act 1974, the Police Act 1997, the Broadcasting Act 1996, Part VI, and the Protection from Harassment Act 1997. The House of Commons Culture Media and Sport Committee recommended the adoption of a privacy law relating to the media in June 2003, but the Government immediately rejected the proposal.[5540]

Under a voluntary moratorium agreed to between the government and insurance industry in 2001 and renewed in March 2005, insurance companies will not demand or use the results of genetic tests for policies under GBP 500,000 unless approved first by the Genetics and Insurance Committee until 2011. Only the test for Huntington's disease has been approved. Tests done for a research study do not have to be disclosed.[5541] However, family history information can still be used. The level of protection for employees is less clear.[5542] The Information Commissioner released the final section of the Employment Practices Data Protection Code in December 2004, which relates to workers' health data.[5543]

Data Protection Authority

The Office of the Information Commissioner is an independent agency that maintains the register and enforces the Data Protection and Freedom of Information Acts.[5544] The Commissioner, Richard Thomas, was appointed in 2002. As of March 2004, there were 251,702 databases registered with the Commission, up from 211,251 in the previous year.[5545] The agency received 11,664 requests for assessment and inquiries, and 68,000 phone enquiries in 2003-2004. There were eight convictions for unlawfully obtaining or selling of personal data. The Commissioner is also responsible for enforcing the

---

[5538] Access to Medical Reports Act 1988 and the Access to Health Records Act 1990.The Health and Social Care Act 2001. Mostly repealed by the Data Protection Act 1998.

[5539] Consumer Credit Act, 1974.

[5540] House of Commons Culture, Media and Sport Committee, Privacy and Media Intrusion, Fifth Report of Session 2002–03, June 2003.

[5541] Concordat and Moratorium on Genetics and Insurance, March 2005, available at <http://www.abi.org.uk/Display/File/Child/106/Concordat_and_Moratorium.pdf>.

[5542] See Genewatch, "Genetic Testing in the Workplace," June 2003, available at <http://www.genewatch.org/HumanGen/publications/Reports/GeneticTesting.pdf>.

[5543] Information Commissioner's Office, The Employment Practices Data Protection Code - Part 4: Information About Workers' Health, December 2004.

[5544] Homepage of the Information Commissioner: <http://www.dataprotection.gov.uk/>.

[5545] See Information Commissioner – Annual Report July 2004, July 2004, available at <http://www.informationcommissioner.gov.uk/>.

Telecommunications (Data Protection and Privacy) Regulations and received 1,670 complaints for breaches of the regulations.

There is also a poor culture of security for the protection of personal information. Personal information from government computers is regularly disclosed inadvertently or for profit.[5546] The Inland Revenue found in 2003 that there were 226 cases of employees illegally accessing the records and selling, or maliciously using, information.[5547] The Information Commissioner reported 14 pending cases in 2004 against employees of police forces for illegal access to the Police National Computer, and noted continuing problems of illegal access by employees of the Department of Works and Pensions, Inland Revenue and the Driver and Vehicle Licensing Agency (DVLA). The Foundation for Information Policy Research (FIPR) estimates that more than 200,000 illegal requests for information are made each year by private investigators under false pretenses. There are also plans for a central database of all health records under the National Health Service that has few limits on access.[5548]

Wiretapping and Surveillance Rules

Interception of communications is regulated by the Regulation of Investigatory Powers Act 2000 (RIPA).[5549] Part I authorizes the Home Secretary to issue warrants for the interception of communications and requires Communications Service Providers to provide a "reasonable interception capability" in their networks. The Home, Northern Ireland or Foreign Secretaries of State and the Scottish First Minister normally authorize telephone taps for national security purposes. It further allows any public authority designated by the Home Secretary to access "communications data" without a warrant. This data includes the source, destination and type of any communication, such as mobile phone location information and partial web browsing logs (but the full URL is considered content subject to a warrant). Part III allows senior members of the

---

[5546] *See* "Internal Breach Sparks Met Review," BBC News, June 15, 2004; "Lives Ruined as NHS Leaks Patients' Notes," The Observer, June 25, 2000; "Fraudster Squad," The Guardian, September 21, 2002.

[5547] "Tax Records 'for Sale' Scandal," BBC Online, January 16, 2003.

[5548] *See* Moritz Y. Becker, A formal Security Policy for an NHS Electronic Health Record Service, University of Cambridge, Computer Laboratory, March 2005, available at <http://www.cl.cam.ac.uk/TechReports/UCAM-CL-TR-628.html>.

[5549] Regulation of Investigatory Powers Act 2000. (c. 23), available at <http://www.legislation.hmso.gov.uk/acts/acts2000/20000023.htm>, replacing Interception of Communications Act 1985, 1985 (c. 56), available at <http://www.butterworths.co.uk/academic/lloyd/Statutes/communications.htm>; *see* Y. Akdeniz, N. Taylor, C. Walker, Regulation of Investigatory Powers Act 2000 (1): Bigbrother.gov.uk: State Surveillance in the Age of Information and Rights, Criminal Law Review 73-90 (February 2001) available at <http://www.cyber-rights.org/documents/crimlr.pdf>.

civilian and military police, customs, and members of the judiciary to demand that users hand over the plaintext of encrypted material, or in certain circumstances decryption keys themselves. This has not been implemented yet, but the Surveillance Commissioner wrote in his 2004 report that, "I am assured that the need to implement Part III of RIPA is being kept under review." Part II sets rules on other types of "human intelligence" powers that had not been previously regulated under UK law. Many legal experts, including the Information Commissioner, believe that many of the provisions violate the ECHR. The Home Office has issued several codes and regulations.[5550]

In 2003, there were 1,983 warrants for interceptions issued in England and Scotland under RIPA, up from 1,466 in 2002.[5551] There were also 2,844 modifications of warrants in 2003. The government refused to disclose the number of national security interceptions. The process is overseen by the Interception of Communications Commissioner, a former high court judge who appears to act more as a cheerleader for the technique.[5552] Every year the Commissioner has found errors but has also decreed that they were not deliberate and were remedied. He found 39 errors in 2003 that included tapping wrong numbers such as the mobile number of the officer, not the suspect. The Investigatory Powers Tribunal hears complaints from individuals that they have been subject to illegal surveillance. It received 130 complaints in 2002. It operates in secret and has never upheld a case of illegal wiretapping. In January 2003, it ruled that its procedures should be changed so that some of its hearings may be made public.[5553]

There is a long history of illegal wiretapping of political opponents, labor unions and others in the UK.[5554] In the late 1970s and '80s, MI5, Britain's security service, tapped the phones of many left-leaning activists including current MPs and members of the Government. The ECtHR has strongly criticized the practices of the law and this has resulted in several significant changes to the law. In 1985, the ECtHR ruled that police interception of individuals' communications

---

[5550] *See* Home Office RIPA pages, <http://www.homeoffice.gov.uk/crimpol/crimreduc/regulation/>.

[5551] Report of the Interception of Communications Commissioner for 2003, 22 July 2004. For a historical overview, *see* Statewatch, Telephone Tapping and Mail-opening Figures 1937-2001, available at <http://www.statewatch.org/news/2003/jan/teltap01.htm>.

[5552] He noted in his 2003 report that, "I have been impressed by the quality, dedication and enthusiasm of the personnel carrying out this work on behalf of the government and the people of the United Kingdom." *See* correspondence between Commissioner and PI, available at <http://www.privacyinternational.org/countries/uk/surveillance/interceptioncomm.html>.

[5553] In the Matter of Applications Nos. IPT/01/62 and IPT/01/77, January 23, 2003.

[5554] *See, e.g.,* Patrick Fitzgerald & Mark Leopold, Stranger on the Line, Bodley Head 1987.

was a violation of Article 8 of the ECHR,[5555] which resulted in the adoption of the Interception of Communications Act 1985. The ECtHR ruled in 1997 that police eavesdropping of a policewoman violated Article 8, which resulted in the adoption of RIPA.[5556]

In October 2004, two UK servers for Indymedia, an independent media organization, were seized at the request of US authorities on behalf of Swiss and Italian authorities. The seizure was based on a US court order served on the corporate parent of the server company based in Texas but without separate UK authorization. It was returned several days later but it is still unclear who seized it and what was done with the information on it.[5557]

Unsolicited Commercial E-mails

The Privacy and Electronic Communications (EC Directive) Regulations 2003 came into force in December 2003.[5558] The regulations implement the EU Directive on Privacy and Electronic Communications (2002/58/EC). They place new rules on cookies and require opt-in for most e-mail and SMS spam. The Information Commission said in April 2004 that the office needed additional powers to stop spammers from continuing to conduct their activities while under investigation, and that it was unlikely that there would be any prosecutions before 2005.[5559] Several UK bodies have signed a Memorandum of Understanding with the US Federal Trade Commission and related Australian government bodies in July 2004 to facilitate cooperation in anti-spam efforts under the regulations.

[5555] Malone v. United Kingdom (A/95): (1991) 13 EHRR 448.

[5556] Halford v. United Kingdom (Application No 20605/92), 24 EHRR 523, June 25, 1997.

5557 See <http://www.eff.org/Censorship/Indymedia/>.

5558 The Privacy and Electronic Communications (EC Directive) Regulations 2003, SI 2003 No. 2426, September 18, 2003, available at http://www.hmso.gov.uk/si/si2003/20032426.htm; The Privacy and Electronic Communications (EC Directive) (Amendment) Regulations 2004, available at <http://www.opsi.gov.uk/si/si2004/20041039.htm>; See also "Spam": Report of an Inquiry by the All Party Internet Group, October 2003, available at <http://www.apig.org.uk/spam_inquiry.htm>.

5559 "UK Spammers off the Legal Hook for Another Year," Silicon.com, April 16, 2004. British Information Commissioner Richard Thomas discussed the difficulties of enforcing European anti-spam directive rules at an April 2004 global privacy symposium sponsored by White & Case. He noted the absence of an international system to track down violators, and the UK's "very weak enforcement process," which gives the Information Commission no injunctive powers. He also complained about the Information Commission's lack of resources. See John Herzfeld, "U.K. Anti-Spam Enforcement Hindered by National Boundaries, Official Says," Privacy & Security Law Report, Vol. 3, No. 18, May 3, 2004, at 531.

In December 2001, the Parliament approved the Anti-terrorism, Crime and Security Act (ATCS).[5560] The law allows the Home Secretary to issue a code of practice for the voluntary "retention of communications data by communications providers" for the purpose of protecting national security or preventing or detecting crime that relates to national security. It only applies to data that is already being held by the communications service providers (CSPs) for business purposes. The Code of Practice was approved in December 2003.[5561] Under it, some communications data can be retained for up to one year. An opinion commissioned by the Office of the Information Commissioner found that the access to information retained under the act for non-national security purposes would violate human rights and would be unlawful.[5562] The government has proposed modifying the ATCS and RIPA to make data retention mandatory and expanding its use to include serious crimes, not just terrorism offenses.[5563] A leaked submission by the police and intelligence services to the Home Office in 2000 proposed a seven-year data retention scheme.[5564]

There has been considerable controversy about who has access to communications data held by CSPs. In June 2002, the Home Office announced that the list of government agencies allowed under RIPA to access communications data was being extended to more than 1,000 different government departments including local authorities, health, environmental, trade departments and many other public authorities. This resulted in a substantial public outcry, especially after the Surveillance Commissioner admitted in his annual report that "I clearly cannot carry out meaningful oversight of so many bodies without assistance" even before the proposed expansion.[5565] Home Secretary David Blunkett announced a few weeks later that he had "blundered"

[5560] Anti-terrorism, Crime and Security Act 2001, available at
<http://www.hmso.gov.uk/acts/acts2001/20010024.htm>.

[5561] The Retention of Communications Data (Code of Practice) Order 2003, SI 2003 No. 3175, December 4, 2003; Retention of Communications Data Under Part 11: Anti-Terrorism, Crime & Security Act 2001 - Voluntary Code of Practice, available at <http://www.legislation.hmso.gov.uk/si/si2003/draft/5b.pdf>.

[5562] Opinion of Ben Emmerson QC and Helen Mountfield, Matrix Chambers, July 2002, available at
<http://www.privacyinternational.org/countries/uk/surveillance/ic-terror-opinion.htm>.

[5563] Home Office, Counter-Terrorism Powers: Reconciling Security and Liberty in an Open Society: A Discussion Paper, February 2004; *See* C. Walker & Y. Akdeniz, "Anti-Terrorism laws and Data Retention: War Is Over?" 54(2) Northern Ireland Legal Quarterly 159-182 (2003), available at <http://www.cyber-rights.org/documents/data_retention_article.pdf>.

[5564] NCIS Submission on Communications Data Retention Law, August 2000, available at <http://www.statewatch.org/news/dec00/02ncis.htm>.

[5565] Report of the Chief Surveillance Commissioner for 2000-2001, Cm 5360, January 2002.

and withdrew the order.[5566] A more restricted order was adopted in December 2003.[5567]

Police Activities

The Police and Criminal Evidence Act 1984 (PACE) allows police to enter and search homes without a warrant following an arrest for any offense. Police have the right to stop and search any person on the street on grounds of suspicion. Following arrest, a body sample will be taken for inclusion in the national DNA database.[5568] The House of Lords ruled in 2004 that DNA and fingerprints could be kept even if the person was not convicted.[5569] The police stopped and searched 721,900 persons and 12,500 vehicles under the Act in England and Wales in 2003-04, down 18 percent from the previous year. Stops for anti-terrorism reasons under the Terrorism Act 2000 remained steady at around 33,000, which resulted in 491 arrests.[5570] However, the NGO Statewatch estimates that many of the terrorism stops are made under PACE or other legislation and the official figures are only half of the actual numbers, There were also a substantial number of road checks by the Home Office, which admits that one arrest was made for every 1,069 vehicles stopped in 2003-04, down from one in 6,393 in 2002-03.

A Surveillance Commissioner who reviews other investigatory techniques under RIPA Part II and PACE provides some further oversight.[5571] According to his last report, there were 2,483 authorizations including 447 for "intrusive" authorizations for break-ins into homes under the Police Act 1997 and Part II of RIPA between April 2003 and March 2004.[5572] The Commissioner ordered that five be quashed for lack of adequate justification. There were 26,986 authorizations by law enforcement and 6,398 from other bodies for directed surveillance in the same period. The Commissioner stated that he plans to

---

[5566] "Blunkett Shelves Access to Data Plans," The Guardian, June 19, 2002.

[5567] Regulation of Investigatory Powers (Communications Data) Order 2003, available at <http://www.opsi.gov.uk/si/si2003/20033172.htm.>; Amended by Statutory Instrument 2005 No. 1083, The Regulation of Investigatory Powers (Communications Data) (Amendment); Order 2005, available at <http://www.opsi.gov.uk/si/si2005/20051083.htm>.

[5568] Criminal Justice and Public Order Act 1994, available at <http://www.legislation.hmso.gov.uk/acts/acts1994/Ukpga_19940033_en_1.htm>.

[5569] Regina v. Chief Constable of South Yorkshire Police, (2004) UKHL 39.

[5570] Home Office, Arrests for Notifiable Offences and the Operation of Certain Police Powers under PACE 18/04 England and Wales, 2003/04, December 16, 2004; See also Anti-terrorist Stop and Searches Target Muslim Communities, but Few Arrests, Statewatch Bulletin, Vol. 13 No. 6, November-December 2004-05-09.

[5571] Homepage <http://www.surveillancecommissioners.gov.uk/>.

[5572] Annual Report of the Chief Surveillance Commissioner for 2003-04.

"monitor technological developments closely, such as body scanners, facial recognition and automatic number plate recognition to ensure that their use does not transgress legislation for the protection of privacy."

Video Surveillance

There has been a proliferation of CCTV cameras in hundreds of towns and cities in Britain. It is now estimated that there are over four million cameras in Britain, one for every 14 residents, a 300 percent increase in just three years.[5573] The camera networks can be operated by police, local authorities or private companies, and are partly funded by Home Office grants. Their original purpose was crime prevention and detection, though in recent years the cameras have become important tools for city center management and the control of "anti-social behavior." Many of the systems have been enhanced with technology for facial recognition but the jurisdictions that have installed the systems have admitted that the technology has yet to result in an arrest. In London, a system for "congestion charging" uses a sophisticated number plate recognition system to charge motorists who drive into central London during business hours. It was later revealed that the system was organized in cooperation with the intelligence services that use it with facial recognition systems to monitor the drivers of the cars.[5574] The government announced in January 2005 that it was expanding its pilot program of automatic number plate recognition nationwide.[5575] Traffic cameras have also spread across the country.

There has been growing criticism of the use of the cameras. The ECtHR ruled in January 2003 that a Council's release of CCTV footage of an attempted suicide for a campaign on CCTV that resulted in the person being identified publicly violated Article 8 of the ECHR.[5576] Motorists across the UK have engaged in vandalism of traffic cameras and they are widely criticized for being used for fundraising rather than traffic safety.[5577] There is also a growing body of literature that the cameras are not nearly as effective as the proponents claim. A Home Office study released in 2005 found many problems with the systems. In all but one area studied, crime did not show a statistically significant decrease

---

[5573] "Nowhere to Hide as Britain Tops CCTV League, "Sunday Times, April 18, 2004.

[5574] "Security Role for Traffic Cameras," The Observer, February 9, 2003.

[5575] *See* <http://www.pito.org.uk/what_we_do/identification/anpr.htm>.

[5576] Peck v. the United Kingdom (application No. 44647/98), January 2003, available at <http://www.echr.coe.int/Eng/Press/2003/jan/Peckjudeng.htm>.

[5577] "Speed Camera at Accident Black Spot Is Blown up," Daily Telegraph, February 8, 2003; See also <http://www.speedcam.co.uk/gatso2.htm>; <http://www.safespeed.org.uk/main.html>.

and even increased in a majority of areas for unknown reasons. CCTV also did not improve perceptions about safety significantly and did not change behaviors. In nearly half of the areas, support for CCTV and its perceived effectiveness declined once it was installed. On the design of the system, the study found that many systems were installed without clear objectives based on feelings that CCTV was "a good thing," a perceived need to "catch up" if other jurisdictions had already installed then, and a pressure to bid for it based on the existence of funding more than actual need. Technical consultants were often not challenged on the installation of the systems and police were not consulted adequately.[5578] The Scottish Centre for Criminology found that the cameras did not reduce crime, nor improve public perception of crime problems.[5579] A study in June 2002 found that in many areas with CCTV crime increased and street lighting is a more effective deterrent.[5580]

National ID

There has been no national ID card in the UK since 1952, when the House of Lords ruled that requiring the disclosure of the card was not lawful and the National Registration Act was repealed.[5581] Since that time, the issue has come up every few years and has been soundly rejected each time due to public opposition. Shortly after September 11, 2001, then-Home Secretary Blunkett again proposed the card but was forced to back away after it was severely criticized. The government has subsequently promoted the card as a means to prevent illegal immigration, reduce identity theft, improve public services, and finally again to prevent terrorism, depending on the topical public debate at any given time. The vast majority of responses to a Home Office consultation were against the proposal.

A consultation and draft bill was released in April 2004 over opposition from several cabinet ministers including the former Home Secretary, now Foreign Secretary Jack Straw.[5582] The bill was strongly opposed by a wide variety of

---

[5578] Home Office Research, Development and Statistics Directorate, "Home Office Research Study 292 Assessing the impact of CCTV," February 2005, available at
<http://www.homeoffice.gov.uk/rds/pdfs05/hors292.pdf>.

[5579] Homepage <http://www.scotcrim.u-net.com/researchc.htm.>.

[5580] NACRO, "To CCTV or not to CCTV," June 28 2002, available at
<http://www.nacro.org.uk/templates/publications/briefingItem.cfm/2002062800-csps.htm>.

[5581] Willcock v. Muckle, June 26, 1951; *See* Privacy International UK ID Card Page for more details., available at <http://www.privacyinternational.org/issues/idcard/uk/>.

[5582] Home Office, Legislation on Identity Cards, April 2004, available at
<http://www.homeoffice.gov.uk/docs3/identitycardsconsult.pdf>.

groups including the Conservative party (the official opposition which initially supported it), the Liberal Democrat party (the third largest political party), the Law Society, and the Information Commissioner. A public opinion poll commissioned by Privacy International found several million people would conduct civil disobedience and one million would go to jail before they submitted to the new card.[5583] The House of Commons approved the bill in February 2005. The government was forced to drop the bill in the House of Lords due to a lack of time before the election and the anticipation that it would have faced serious opposition and possible defeat in the House of Lords.

Following the election, the government announced in the Queen's Speech that the ID card was a top legislative priority and reintroduced the bill in May 2005. It is largely unchanged from the previous version. It requires the creation of a central National Identity Register and the issuing of "voluntary" ID cards. The cards would include biometric identifiers. There are heavy penalties for a large number of new offenses including failing to register to receive a biometric scan, and to update a home address. It gives the Home Secretary the power to issue regulations to vastly expand its scope, including making the card mandatory without needing changes to the law. It also creates a mostly powerless National Identity Scheme Commissioner, who can only review unauthorized disclosures. The card will be phased in over 10 years starting in 2007-08 by replacing existing drivers licenses and passport cards. It would cost at least GBP 15 billion to implement but the government is refusing to release its cost estimates, claiming "commercial confidentiality." Public opinion polls have shown a dropping off of support from 80 percent to little more than half supporting it before being told of the more controversial provisions.

On June 28, 2005, the UK government narrowly won a vote on its identity card proposals in the House of Commons. The previous day the UK Information Commissioner, Richard Thomas, expressed strong concerns over the government's plans for a biometric national identity card and database. He particularly criticized the scheme's "disproportionate and excessive" storage of personal information and the wide range of uses that would "permit function creep into unforeseen and perhaps unacceptable areas of private life."[5584]

[5583] "A Nation Divided: Views of the British Public on the Government's Proposed National Identity Card," UK public survey commissioned by Privacy International & conducted by YouGov, May 2004, available at <http://www.privacyinternational.org/isses/idcard/uk/idpollanalysis.pdf>.

[5584] Heated Debate on ID Cards in the UK," EDRI-gram newsletter, June 29, 2005, number 3.13, available at <http://www.edri.org/edrigram/number3.13/>.

E-Voting

In 2003, the United Kingdom conducted an electronic voting test during the Ipswich Borough elections held on May 1, 2003.[5585] Voters were allowed to cast votes by use of a telephone touch-tone voting system, by text messaging, over the Internet, or at a polling location. There are concerns that voter privacy may be compromised in the casting of electronic ballots.[5586] It is also pointed out by some that the secret ballot could be threatened if precautions are not taken to shield voter choices from illegitimate interest.[5587]

Open Government

The Freedom of Information Act (FOI) was enacted in November 2000.[5588] However, its full implementation was delayed until 2005, the slowest implementation of any FOI law in the world. The Act has received considerable criticism as being insufficient and weaker in some areas than the previous non-binding code of practice. In the short period that it has been in effect, it has received considerable interest and use and appears to be working for at least some types (mostly non-controversial) of information. However, the legal advice from the Attorney General was released following its partial leak to the press just before the election. In June 2002, the Scottish Parliament approved a Freedom of Information Act[5589] that is regarded as somewhat stronger than the UK Act. It also went into effect in January 2005.

International Obligations

The UK is a member of the Council of Europe (CoE) and has signed and ratified the CoE Convention for the Protection of Individuals with Regard to Automatic Processing of Personal Data (Convention No. 108)[5590] and the European

---

[5585] Voting result, Ipswich Borough Council Local Election, May 1, 2003, available at <http://www.psr.keele.ac.uk/area/uk/loc03/pages/Ipswich/wwwipswichgovuk/election2003/votingpatterns.htm> and Resolution authorizing the Ipswich Borough election, available at <http://www.odpm.gov.uk/stellent/groups/odpm_localgov/documents/page/odpm_locgov_023172.pdf>.

[5586] Dr. N. Ben Fairweather & Professor Simon Rogerson, "E-Voting Technical Options Report," School of Computing De Montfort University Leicester, available at <http://www.planet-thanet.fsnet.co.uk/government/evoting/tech_1.htm>.

[5587] Id.

[5588] Freedom of Information Act 2000, available at <http://www.cfoi.org.uk/foiact2000.html>. For detailed information on the Act, see the Campaign for Freedom of Information's website <http://www.cfoi.org.uk>.

[5589] <http://www.scotland.gov.uk/consultations/government/dfib-00.asp>.

[5590] Signed May 14, 1981; ratified August 26, 1987; entered into force December 1, 1987.

Convention for the Protection of Human Rights and Fundamental Freedoms.[5591] In November 2001, the UK signed the CoE Convention on Cybercrime but has not ratified it.[5592] The UK is a member of the Organization for Economic Cooperation and Development (OECD) and has adopted the OECD Guidelines on the Protection of Privacy and Transborder Flows of Personal Data.

Territories

The Isle of Man Data Protection Act 2002 came into force in April 2003. It is based on the EU Data Protection Directive. The Office of the Data Protection Supervisor enforces the Act.[5593] The Data Protection (Bailiwick of Guernsey) Law of 2001 was approved in March 2002.[5594] The Isle of Guernsey Data Protection Commissioner enforces the Act.[5595] The EU Article 29 Working Group released an opinion in June 2003 finding that the law is adequate.[5596] In Jersey, a new Data Protection Act was approved in June 2004 and is in the process of being implemented. The Data Protection Registry registers databases and conducts investigations overseeing the Act.[5597]

United States of America

Constitutional Framework

There is no explicit right to privacy in the United States Constitution. The Supreme Court has ruled that there is a limited constitutional right of privacy based on several provisions in the Bill of Rights. This includes a right to privacy from government surveillance into an area where a person has a "reasonable expectation of privacy"[5598] and also in matters relating to marriage, procreation, contraception, sexual activity, family relationships, child rearing and

---

[5591] Signed November 4, 1950; ratified March 8, 1951; entered into force September 3, 1953.

[5592] Signed November 23, 2001.

[5593] Homepage <http://www.gov.im/odps/>.

[5594] The Data Protection (Bailiwick of Guernsey) Law, 2001, available at <http://www.dpcommission.gov.gg/2001%20Law/2001%20Law.htm>.

[5595] Homepage <http://www.dpcommission.gov.gg/>.

[5596] Article 29 Data Protection Working Party, Opinion 5/2003 on the level of protection of personal data in Guernsey (10595/03/EN), June 13, 2003, available at <http://www.europa.eu.int/comm/internal_market/privacy/docs/wpdocs/2003/wp79_en.pdf>.

[5597] Homepage <http://www.dataprotection.gov.je/>.

[5598] Katz v. United States, 386 U.S. 954 (1967).

education.[5599] The Supreme Court has also recognized a right of anonymity[5600] and the right of political groups to prevent disclosure of their members' names to government agencies.[5601] Some states within the country have incorporated explicit privacy protections into their constitutions.[5602] A right to privacy is specifically stated in the constitutions of 10 states.[5603]

The Supreme Court ruled in 1977 that individuals do not have constitutional privacy interests in data transferred to third parties, meaning that specific statutes would have to be enacted to protect data held by others.[5604] Rather than enact general statutory protections for personal data, the United States has taken a sectoral approach to privacy regulation so that records held by third parties, such as consumer marketing profiles or telephone calling records, are generally not protected unless a legislature has enacted a specific law.

The tort of privacy was first adopted in 1905, and all but two of the 50 states recognize a civil right of action for invasion of privacy in their laws.[5605] The four traditionally recognized privacy torts are: intrusion upon an individual's seclusion or private affairs, public disclosure of embarrassing private facts, painting an individual in a "false light" in the public eye, and appropriation of an individual's name or likeness.[5606]

Privacy Case Law

The United States Supreme Court has considered many important privacy cases over the last few years. In January 2000, the Supreme Court heard *Reno v. Condon*, a case addressing the constitutionality of the Drivers Privacy Protection Act (DPPA), a 1994 law that protects drivers' records held by state motor vehicle agencies. In a unanimous decision, the Court found that the information contained in the records was "an article of commerce" and could be regulated by

---

[5599] *See, e.g.*, Griswold v. Connecticut, 381 U.S. 479 (1965); Whalen v. Roe, 429 U.S. 589 (1977); Paul v. Davis, 424 U.S. 714 (1976); Lawrence v. Texas, 539 U.S. 558 (2003).

[5600] McIntyre v. Ohio Elections Commission, 514 U.S. 334 (1995).

[5601] NAACP v. Alabama, 357 U.S. 449 (1958).

[5602] *See, e.g.*, California Constitution, Art. I § I.

[5603] These 10 states are: Alaska, Arizona, California, Florida, Hawaii, Illinois, Louisiana, Montana, South Carolina, and Washington. *See* National Conference of State Legislatures, Privacy Protections in State Constitutions, available at <http://www.ncsl.org/programs/lis/privacy/stateconstpriv03.htm>.

[5604] United States v. Miller, 425 US 435 (1976).

[5605] *See* Lake v. Wal-Mart Stores, Inc., 582 N.W.2d 231 (Minn. 1998), for a review of state adoption of common law privacy torts.

[5606] *See generally* Prosser & Keeton on Torts (5th ed. 1984).

the federal government.[5607] In June 2001, the Supreme Court ruled in the case of *Kyllo v. United States* that the use of a thermal imaging device, without a warrant, to detect heat emanating from a person's residence constituted an illegal search under the Fourth Amendment.[5608] The Fourth Amendment protects individuals from intrusions into areas where there is a "reasonable expectation of privacy."[5609] In November 2000, the Supreme Court held that suspicionless vehicle checkpoints, used to discover and interdict illegal narcotics, violate the Fourth Amendment.[5610] Also, in March 2001, the Supreme Court held that a state hospital cannot perform diagnostic tests to obtain evidence of criminal conduct without the patient's consent; such a test is unreasonable and violates the Fourth Amendment.[5611]

In the 2001 term, the Supreme Court addressed anonymity, searches on buses, and student privacy. In *Watchtower Bible v. Village of Stratton*, the Court invalidated a law that required registration with the government before individuals could engage in door-to-door solicitation. The Court held that a pre-registration requirement violated the First Amendment, which guarantees freedom from government restrictions on free expression, and individuals' right to anonymity.[5612] In *United States v. Drayton*, the Court held that the Fourth Amendment does not require police officers to advise bus passengers of their right not to cooperate and to refuse consent to searches.[5613] Student privacy was diminished in a series of cases involving drug testing, "peer grading" (the practice of allowing a fellow student to score a test), and the right to sue under a federal student privacy law. In *Board of Education v. Earls*, the Court held that random, suspicionless drug testing of students involved in non-athletic extracurricular activities was justified under the "special needs" exception to the Fourth Amendment.[5614] In *Owasso Independent School District v. Falvo*, the Court held that both peer grading and the reporting aloud of peer grades did not violate the Family Educational Rights and Privacy Act of 1974 (FERPA).[5615] In

---

[5607] Reno v. Condon, 528 U.S. 141 (2000).

[5608] Kyllo v. United States, 533 U.S. 27 (2001). The Fourth Amendment states: "The right of the people to be secure in their persons, houses, papers and effects, against unreasonable searches and seizures, shall not be violated, and no Warrants shall issue, but upon probable cause, supported by Oath or affirmation, and particularly describing the place to be searched, and the persons or things to be seized."

[5609] Kyllo v. United States, *supra.*

[5610] City of Indianapolis v. Edmond, 531 U.S. 32 (2000).

[5611] Ferguson v. City of Charlestown, 532 U.S. 67 (2000).

[5612] Watchtower Bible & Tract Soc'y of N.Y. v. Village of Stratton, 536 U.S. 150 (2002).

[5613] United States v. Drayton, 536 U.S. 194 (2002).

[5614] Board of Education v. Earls, 536 U.S. 822 (2002).

[5615] Owasso Independent School District v. Falvo, 534 U.S. 426 (2001).

Gonzaga Univ. v. Doe, the Court held that the FERPA does not give individuals a right to sue for violations of privacy.[5616]

In the 2002 term, the Supreme Court ruled that a "Megan's Law statute," which requires sex offenders to have their pictures and addresses put on the Internet, does not violate the Ex Post Facto clause[5617] of the Constitution.[5618] In a related case, Connecticut Dept. of Public Safety v. Doe, the Court unanimously held that inclusion in a public sex offender registry, without a separate hearing on the offender's risk to the community, does not violate the Due Process Clause of the Constitution.[5619] In a far-reaching opinion in 2003, the Supreme Court ruled in Lawrence v. Texas that a state law that prohibited homosexual sodomy violated the due process rights in the Constitution.[5620] The Court reversed an earlier opinion in which it had upheld sodomy statutes.[5621] The court decision states: "The petitioners are entitled to respect for their private lives. The state cannot demean their existence or control their destiny by making their private sexual conduct a crime..."[5622] The court also cites with approval the European Court of Human Rights and other foreign courts that have affirmed the "rights of homosexual adults to engage in intimate, consensual conduct." The decisions were brought to the attention of the high court in an amicus brief filed by the former UN High Commissioner for Human Rights.[5623]

In the 2003 term, the Supreme Court considered the Privacy Act, a privacy exemption to the Freedom of Information Act, vehicle searches, and the issue of whether police could compel an individual to identify himself in public. In *Doe v. Chao*, the Court ruled that a plaintiff in a Privacy Act suit must demonstrate

---

[5616] Gonzaga Univ. v. Doe, 536 U.S. 273 (2002).

[5617] That clause prohibits the government from applying a revised law that would result in a criminal punishment more severe than that which applied at the time the crime was committed.

[5618] Smith v. Doe, No. 538 U.S. 84 (2003), *available at* <http://www.supremecourtus.gov/opinions/02pdf/01-729.pdf>.

[5619] Connecticut Dept. of Public Safety v. Doe, 539 U.S. 1 (2003), available at <http://www.supremecourtus.gov/opinions/02pdf/01-1231.pdf>.

[5620] Lawrence v. Texas, 539 U.S. 558 (2003), available at <http://www.supremecourtus.gov/opinions/02pdf/01-102.pdf>.

[5621] Bowers v. Hardwick, 478 U.S. 186 (1986).

[5622] "Had those who drew and ratified the Due Process Clauses of the Fifth Amendment or the Fourteenth Amendment known the components of liberty in its manifold possibilities, they might have been more specific. They did not presume to have this insight. They knew times can blind us to certain truths and later generations can see that laws once thought necessary and proper in fact serve only to oppress. As the Constitution endures, persons in every generation can invoke its principles in their own search for greater freedom." Lawrence v. Texas, *supra*.

[5623] Brief amici curiae of Mary Robinson, Amnesty International USA, Human Rights Watch, Interights, the Lawyers Committee for Human Rights, and Minnesota Advocates for Human Rights, available at <http://www.hrw.org/press/2003/07/amicusbrief.pdf>.

actual damages to qualify for the act's minimum statutory award of USD 1,000.[5624] In that case, the Department of Labor identified black lung benefits claimants with their Social Security number and exposed the identifier to public view in violation of the Privacy Act. In *National Archives & Records Administration v. Favish*, the Supreme Court expanded a privacy exemption in the Freedom of Information Act.[5625] That case involved a request for access to pictures of a suicide victim, who happened to be a senior Executive Administration employee. Noting that five separate investigations had been made into the circumstances of the suicide, the Court denied access to the photographs. Although American law generally does not recognize privacy interests after the death of the data subject, the Court held that surviving family members have a right to personal privacy with respect to their close relatives' death-scene images. This right outweighed the public's interest in disclosure. In *United States v. Flores-Montano,* the Court upheld a US Customs search of a gasoline tank at the Mexico-California border, ruling that vehicle searches at US border checkpoints do not require suspicion.[5626] In *Thornton v. United States*, the Court upheld, as a search incident to custodial arrest, the search of the passenger compartment of a vehicle when the suspect was first accosted after exiting the vehicle.[5627] The Court had previously ruled that the Fourth Amendment allowed police to search a passenger compartment, in the interests of evidence preservation and police protection, when the suspect was accosted while still inside the vehicle.[5628] In *Hiibel v. Sixth Judicial District Court*, the Court upheld a state statute that required individuals to identify themselves when requested by a police officer who has "reasonable suspicion" that the individual is involved in wrongdoing.[5629] Such statutes exist in more than 20 US states. The decision is limited in scope because identification requirements must occur within the scope of a "*Terry* Stop*,*" an encounter where a police officer can articulate facts that reasonably indicate that a suspect is involved in criminal activity.[5630] The Court also pointed out that, while the statute requires an individual to reveal his or her name, he or she need not produce an identity document. However, as one of four dissenting Justices noted, a person's name can "provide the key to a broad array of

---

[5624] 540 U.S. 614 (2004), available at <http://www.supremecourtus.gov/opinions/03pdf/02-1377.pdf>.

[5625] 540 U.S. 157 (2004), available at <http://www.supremecourtus.gov/opinions/03pdf/02-954.pdf>.

[5626] 541 U.S. 149 (2004), available at <http://www.supremecourtus.gov/opinions/03pdf/02-1794.pdf>.

[5627] 541 U.S. 615 (2004), available at <http://www.supremecourtus.gov/opinions/03pdf/03-5165.pdf>.

[5628] *See* NY v. Belton, 453 U.S. 454 (1981).

[5629] 542 U.S. 177 (2004).

[5630] Terry v. Ohio, 392 U.S. 1 (1968).

information about the person," particularly when disclosed to officers with access to law enforcement databases.[5631]

In the 2004 term, the Supreme Court ruled in *Illinois v. Caballes* that a canine sniff of an automobile did not violate the driver's constitutionally protected privacy right.[5632] The Court held that. because a canine sniff reveals the location of contraband alone and because one has no legitimate expectation of privacy in contraband under the Fourth Amendment, the measure did not violate a constitutionally cognizable privacy interest.[5633] In *Devenpeck v. Alford,* the Court held that an arrest is justified if there is a legitimate basis, regardless of whether the stated reason for the arrest is meritorious or closely related. In that case, the suspect, who was driving a car with "wigwag" roof lights, tape recorded a conversation with a police officer who had stopped him for suspected impersonation of an officer. The officer then arrested him for violating the state privacy statute. Although the suspect's tape recording was later found not to have violated any state law, the Supreme Court ruled for the state because suspected impersonation of an officer was a legitimate basis for arrest.[5634]

The Privacy Act

The Privacy Act of 1974 protects records held by United States government agencies and requires agencies to apply fair information practices.[5635] Its effectiveness is significantly weakened by administrative interpretations of a provision allowing for disclosure of personal information for a "routine use" compatible with the purpose for which the information was originally collected. Limits on the use of Social Security numbers have also been undercut in recent years because of widespread use of the identifier among governmental agencies[5636] and because the private sector employs the identifier for both identification and authentication purposes.[5637] The act also allows certain agency

---

[5631] 542 U.S. at 196 (Stevens, J., dissenting). *See also* EPIC's Hiibel v. Sixth Judicial District Court of Nevada Web Page <http://www.epic.org/privacy/hiibel/default.html>.

[5632] 543 U.S. 405 (2005), available at <http://www.supremecourtus.gov/opinions/04pdf/03-923.pdf>.

[5633] *Id.*

[5634] 543 U.S. 146 (2004), available at <http://www.supremecourtus.gov/opinions/04pdf/03-710.pdf>.

[5635] Privacy Act, Pub. L. No. 93-579 (1974), codified at 5 USC § 552a, available at <http://www.epic.org/privacy/laws/privacy_act.html>. *See also* EPIC's Privacy Act Web Page <http://www.epic.org/privacy/1974act/>.

[5636] Social Security Numbers: Government Benefits from SSN Use but Could Provide Better Safeguards, Government Accountability Office Report No. GAO-02-352 (May 2002), available at <http://www.gao.gov/new.items/d02352.pdf>.

[5637] Social Security Numbers: Use Is Widespread and Protections Vary, Government Accountability Office Report No. GAO-04-768T (June 15, 2004), available at <http://www.gao.gov/new.items/d04768t.pdf>.

systems of records to be exempt from accuracy and other requirements. In March 2003, the Department of Justice (DOJ) announced that it would exempt the National Crime Information Center (NCIC) from data quality standards in the Privacy Act.[5638] The NCIC contains 39 million criminal records, and is used by more than 80,000 law enforcement agencies. The change was strongly opposed by a broad coalition of organizations and individuals across the United States.[5639] Other databases exempt from certain Privacy Act provisions include the Arrival Departure Information System (ADIS), which stores traveler and arrival and departure information for the United States Visitor and Immigrant Status Indicator Technology program (US-VISIT);[5640] the Central Records System (a comprehensive database encompassing all centralized records of FBI headquarters, field offices, and legal attaché offices);[5641] and the Foreign Terrorist Tracking Task Force's Flight Training Candidates File System.[5642] A 2003 report from the Government Accountability Office (GAO) identified barriers leading to uneven agency compliance with Privacy Act requirements.[5643]

There is no independent privacy oversight agency in the United States. The Office of Management and Budget (OMB) plays a limited role in setting policy for federal agencies under the Privacy Act, but it has not been particularly active or effective in this capacity.[5644] In 1999, a Chief Counselor for Privacy was appointed within the OMB to coordinate federal stances towards privacy. The counselor had only a limited advisory capacity. The Bush Administration has not replaced this privacy officer.

[5638] Privacy Act of 1974, *supra*; Implementation, 68 Fed. Reg. 14140 (Mar. 24, 2003) (to be codified as 28 C.F.R. pt. 16).

[5639] EPIC, Require Accuracy for the NCIC, available at <http://www.epic.org/actions/ncic/>.

[5640] *See* EPIC's United States Visitor and Immigrant Status Indicator Technology (US-VISIT) Web Page <http://www.epic.org/privacy/us-visit/>.

[5641] Central Records System, Department of Justice/Federal Bureau of Investigation <http://foia.fbi.gov/crs552.htm>. For a list of exemptions of governmental records from various provisions of the Privacy Act of 1974, *see* <http://www.washingtonwatchdog.org/documents/cfr/title28/part16.html#16.70>.

[5642] 28 C.F.R. 16.105, available at <http://www.washingtonwatchdog.org/documents/cfr/title28/part16.html#16.105>.

[5643] Privacy Act: OMB Leadership Needed to Improve Agency Compliance, Government Accountability Office Report No. GAO-03-304 (July 2003), available at <http://www.gao.gov>.

[5644] *See* Memorandum M-01-05, from Jacob J. Lew, Director, Office of Management and Budget, to Heads of Executive Departments and Agencies, December 20, 2000, available at <http://www.whitehouse.gov/omb/memoranda/m01-05.html>. This memorandum is the OMB's most recent posted document on personal privacy.

Oversight of Federal Agencies

The Consolidated Appropriations Act of 2005, enacted on December 8, 2004, requires every federal agency to appoint its own privacy officer.[5645] The Electronic (E-)Government Act of 2002, signed by President Bush on December 17, 2002, was passed with the purpose of improving federal technology services and establishes restrictions on government maintenance and use of personal information. The act establishes within the OMB a new agency, the Office of Electronic Government, for administration of the act's provisions. The Federal Information Security Management Act of 2002 requires designation of a senior information security officer by each agency for the purpose of securing all information systems supporting the agency's operations and assets. The Confidential Information Protection and Statistical Efficiency Act of 2002 purports to improve accountability of federal agencies in ensuring confidentiality of personal information provided by the public to the government for statistical purposes.[5646]

Identity Theft

Recently, the Federal Trade Commission (FTC) reported that an estimated 10 million people were victims of identity theft in 2003. The FTC suggested that Congress: extend the Gramm-Leech-Bliley Act Safeguards Rule to companies that are not financial institutions, require customers to be notified in cases of breach of security of private data, adopt laws to restrict the use of Social Security numbers, and enact cross-border fraud legislation to prevent access of databases by offshore third parties.[5647]

The Federal Trade Commission and Consumer Privacy

The Federal Trade Commission (FTC) has oversight and enforcement powers for the laws protecting children's online privacy, consumer credit information, and

---

[5645] Transportation, Treasury, Independent Agencies, and General Government Appropriations Act, § 522, available at <http://frwebgate.access.gpo.gov/cgi-bin/getdoc.cgi?dbname=108_cong_bills&docid=f:h4818enr.pdf>.

[5646] *See* H.R. 2458, E-Government Act of 2002, available at <http://www.regulations.gov/images/e-Gov%20Law.pdf>.

[5647] Prepared Statement of the Federal Trade Commission before the Senate Committee on Commerce, Science, and Transportation, on Data Breaches and Identity Theft, June 16, 2005, available at <http://www.ftc.gov/os/2005/06/050616databreaches.pdf>.

fair trading practices.[5648] The FTC has received thousands of complaints but has issued opinions in only a few cases. The FTC organized a series of workshops[5649] and surveys, which revealed that industry protection of privacy on the Internet is poor. After holding for a long time that the industry should have more time to make self-regulation work, the FTC in June 2000 recommended in a report to the United States Congress that legislation be enacted to protect consumer privacy on the Internet owing to the dismal findings in a survey of online privacy policies.[5650] In October 2001, a new Chairman of the Commission, appointed by President Bush, recommended further study before legislation is passed to protect Internet privacy.[5651] The agency has sought additional powers to pursue cross-border fraud, much of which involves privacy-invasive telemarketing or spam.[5652]

In recent years, the FTC has focused on enforcing existing law in the areas of telemarketing, spam, pretexting, and children's privacy.[5653] In January 2002, the FTC proposed changes to the Telemarketing Sales Rule to tighten use of individuals' account numbers and to create the national Do-Not-Call Registry for individuals who wish to opt-out of telemarketing.[5654] Enrollment began in June 2003, and approximately 86 million numbers have been added to the list.[5655] Of the complaints of Do-Not-Call Registry violations in 2004, 40 percent were the result of identity theft. In the same year, the FTC brought 10 actions for violations of the registry.[5656]

The FTC's actions under federal "unfair and deceptive" practices law essentially have created a "common law" of privacy in the country. Thus, when the agency brings a suit against a company for certain privacy-invasive practices, it can have industry-wide effect. Cases against pharmaceutical giant Eli Lilly,[5657] Microsoft

---

[5648] *See* FTC Privacy Initiatives Web Page <http://www.ftc.gov/privacy/index.html>.

[5649] <http://www.ftc.gov/ftc/workshops.htm>.

[5650] Privacy Online: Fair Information Practices in the Electronic Marketplace: A Federal Trade Commission Report to Congress (May 2000), available at <http://www.ftc.gov/os/2000/05/index.htm#22>.

[5651] Protecting Consumers' Privacy: 2002 and Beyond, Remarks of FTC Chairman Timothy J. Muris, October 2001, available at <http://www.ftc.gov/speeches/muris/privisp1002.htm>.

[5652] FTC's cross-border fraud workshop <http://www.ftc.gov/bcp/workshops/crossborder>.

[5653] *See* FTC Privacy Initiatives <http://www.ftc.gov/privacy/index.html>.

[5654] The Proposed National "Do Not Call" Registry, Amendment to the Telemarketing Sales Rule, January 2002, available at <http://www.ftc.gov/bcp/conline/edcams/donotcall/index.html>.

[5655] "State of the FTC," Deborah Platt Majoras, March 28, 2005, Washington, DC, available at <http://www.ftc.gov/speeches/majoras/050328stateofftc.pdf>.

[5656] *Id.*

[5657] Federal Trade Commission, "Eli Lilly Settles FTC Charges Concerning Security Breach," January 18, 2002 <http://www.ftc.gov/opa/2002/01/elililly.htm>.

Passport,[5658] and American Student List[5659] have improved privacy protections nationwide. The American Student List case, in particular, is likely to change many common industry practices.[5660] That case stands for the proposition that federal law is violated where companies conceal or omit material secondary uses of personal information, a common practice of many private-sector profilers.

However, the FTC continues to allege misrepresentations of the privacy of consumer information by online providers of goods and services. These cases, which have resulted in settlements, include suits against Gateway Learning, which rented personal information of consumers to marketers. The FTC challenged the company's retroactive changing of its privacy policy to allow sharing of this information with third parties.[5661] Petco Animal Supplies, Inc., agreed to a settlement after the FTC alleged that, contrary to privacy protection claims, the merchant failed to take reasonable measures to protect its Web site from hackers.[5662] CartManager International (Vision I Properties, LLC), which supplies shopping-cart software to thousands of Internet merchants, also agreed to a settlement after renting personal information about merchants' customers in violation of the merchants' privacy policies.[5663]

The United States has no comprehensive privacy protection law for the private sector. A patchwork of federal laws covers some specific categories of personal information.[5664] These include financial records,[5665] health information,[5666] credit reports,[5667] video rentals,[5668] cable television,[5669] children's (under age 13)

[5658] Federal Trade Commission, "Microsoft Settles FTC Charges Alleging False Security and Privacy Promises," August 8, 2002 <http://www.ftc.gov/opa/2002/08/microsoft.htm>.

[5659] Federal Trade Commission, "High School Student Survey Companies Settle FTC Charges," October 2, 2002 <http://www.ftc.gov/opa/2002/10/student1r.htm>.

[5660] See Chris J. Hoofnagle, AGs Apply General Consumer Protection Laws to Student Profiling, 6 Consumer Fin. Services L. Rep. 9 (October 9, 2002).

[5661] Federal Trade Commission, "Gateway Learning Settles FTC Privacy Charges," July 7, 2004 <http://www.ftc.gov/opa/2004/07/gateway.htm>.

[5662] Federal Trade Commission, "Petco Settles FTC Charges," November 17, 2004 <http://www.ftc.gov/opa/2004/04/towerrecords.htm>.

[5663] Federal Trade Commission, "Internet Service Provider Settles FTC Privacy Charges," March 10, 2005 <http://www.ftc.gov/opa/2005/03/cartmanager.htm>.

[5664] See EPIC's Financial Privacy Resources Web Page <http://www.epic.org/privacy/financialresources.html>.

[5665] Right to Financial Privacy Act, Pub. L. No. 95-630 (1978); EPIC's Right to Financial Privacy Web Page <http://www.epic.org/privacy/rfpa/>.

[5666] Standards for Privacy of Individually Identifiable Health Information, 45 CFR Parts 160 and 164, promulgated under the Health Insurance Portability and Accountability Act of 1996, Pub. L. No. 104-191; EPIC's Medical Privacy Web Page <http://www.epic.org/privacy/medical/>.

[5667] Fair Credit Reporting Act, Pub. L. No. 91-508 (1970), amended by Pub. L. No. 104-208 (1996), available at <http://www.ftc.gov/os/statutes/fcra.htm>; EPIC's Fair Credit Reporting Act Web Page <http://www.epic.org/privacy/fcra/>.

online activities,[5670] educational records,[5671] motor vehicle registrations,[5672] and telemarketing.[5673]

The end of 1999 brought increased scrutiny of financial privacy. In 1999, the Michigan Attorney General sued several banks for selling information about their customers to marketers, prompting other banks nationwide to admit that they were also selling customer records. The Gramm-Leach-Bliley Act, which formally eliminated traditional ownership barriers between different financial institutions such as banks, securities firms, and insurance companies, set weak protections on financial information that is likely to be shared among merged institutions. These privacy provisions became effective in July 2001. The law allows information sharing amongst affiliates but offers individuals a limited opt-out for information sharing among non-affiliates. Consumer privacy was improved under the law when the FTC determined that the Social Security number qualified as non-public personal information, thus it is subject to the notice and opt-out requirements in certain contexts. The data industry has been unsuccessful in challenging this determination.[5674]

The sole federal law governing information use online is the Children's Online Privacy Protection Act (COPPA), which went into effect in April 2000. This law requires parental consent before information is collected from children under the age of 13.[5675] In April 2005, the FTC requested public comments on the utility of the COPPA Rule, which directs Web site operators that collect information about children to notify parents or obtain parental consent before using or disclosing such information.[5676]

[5668] Video Privacy Protection Act, Pub. L. No. 100-618 (1988); EPIC's Video Privacy Protection Act Web Page <http://www.epic.org/privacy/vppa/>.

[5669] Cable Privacy Protection Act, Pub. L. No. 98-549 (1984), available at <http://www.epic.org/privacy/cable_tv/ctpa.html>.

[5670] Children's Online Privacy Protection Act, Pub. L. No. 105-277 (1998), available at <http://www4.law.cornell.edu/uscode/html/uscode15/usc_sec_15_00006501----000-.html>; EPIC's Children's Online Privacy Protection Act (COPPA) Web Page <http://www.epic.org/privacy/kids/>.

[5671] Family Educational Rights and Privacy Act, Pub. L. No. 93-380 (1974), available at <http://www.epic.org/privacy/education/ferpa.html>; EPIC's Student Privacy Web Page <http://www.epic.org/privacy/student/>.

[5672] Drivers Privacy Protection Act, Pub. L. No. 103-322 (1994), available at <http://www.epic.org/privacy/laws/drivers_privacy_bill.html>; EPIC's Drivers Privacy Protection Act Web Page <http://www.epic.org/privacy/drivers/>.

[5673] Telephone Consumer Protection Act, Pub. L. No. 102-243 (1991); EPIC's Telemarketing Web Page <http://www.epic.org/privacy/telemarketing/>.

[5674] Trans Union v. FTC, No. 01-5202 (D.C. Cir. 2002).

[5675] FTC Privacy Web Page <http://www.ftc.gov/privacy/index.html>; EPIC's Children's Privacy Web Page <http://www.epic.org/privacy/kids>.

[5676] See 70 Fed. Reg. 21,107 (April 22, 2005), Federal Trade Commission, "16 C.F.R. Pt. 312, Children's Online Privacy Protection Rule: Request for Comments," available at <http://www.regulations.gov/fredpdfs/05-

---

In 2003, Congress passed legislation significantly amending the Fair Credit Reporting Act (FCRA) of 1970 and the nation's first spam regulation.[5677] Congress amended the FCRA, passing the Fair and Accurate Credit Transactions Act (FACTA),[5678] because portions of the FCRA statute were expiring that would allow states to pass more stringent privacy protections.[5679] Congress amended the law to protect financial institutions from state privacy regulation but also created new privacy rights. For instance, under regulations that took effect in 2004, individuals may obtain a free credit report from each of the credit bureaus once a year. Credit reporting agencies are required to disclose credit scores, but they may charge a fee for their provision. Individuals will have a new right to opt-out of marketing solicitations that flow from affiliate sharing of personal information. The act also now allows individuals to file fraud alerts, which require credit reporting agencies to inform others that fraud may be present. Identity theft victims also can request transaction records when businesses have extended credit to an impostor in order to try to ascertain the identity of the impostor.

Congress acted with similar motives of preempting more stringent state law in passing the Controlling the Assault of Non-Solicited Pornography and Marketing Act of 2003, known as the "CAN-SPAM" Act.[5680] The act, which became effective January 1, 2004, defines spam as any message whose "primary purpose" is the "commercial advertisement or promotion of a commercial product or service." Spam must include notice that the message is an advertisement or solicitation, an opt-out notice, and a valid postal address of the sender. Address harvesting and dictionary attacks are illegal under the Act, but these practices are considered aggravating offenses, and they cannot serve as the sole basis of prosecution of a spammer. Enforcement of the act is limited to the FTC, state attorneys general, and Internet service providers (ISPs). CAN-SPAM gave the FTC the authority to create a do-not-spam registry, but the agency chose not to, citing impracticability.[5681] Instead, the agency urged the private sector to increase sender authentication in an attempt to reduce "spoofed" spam. In a report to

---

08160.pdf>; EPIC, "In the Matter of COPPA Rule Review 2005, Project No. P054505 [Comments]," June 27, 2005 <http://www.epic.org/privacy/kids/ftc_coppa_62705.html>.

[5677] Fair Credit Reporting Act, Pub. L. No. 91-508 (1970), amended by Pub. L. No. 104-208 (1996), available at <http://www.ftc.gov/os/statutes/fcra.htm>; EPIC's Fair Credit Reporting Act Web Page <http://www.epic.org/privacy/fcra/>.

[5678] Pub. L. No. 108-159 (2003), available at <http://thomas.loc.gov/cgi-bin/bdquery/z?d108:h.r.02622:>.

[5679] See EPIC's Privacy Preemption Web Page <http://www.epic.org/privacy/preemption/>.

[5680] Pub. L. No. 108-187 (2003), available at <http://www.spamlaws.com/pdf/pl108-187.pdf>.

[5681] CAN-SPAM Act of 2003: National Do Not Email Registry: A Federal Trade Commission Report to Congress, June 2004, available at <http://www.ftc.gov/reports/dneregistry/report.pdf>.

Congress in June 2005, the agency recommended against use of the "ADV" (advertising) label in the subject line of commercial e-mail, stating that the measure would have little effect on reducing spam.[5682] In 2004 and early 2005, Florida, Georgia, Indiana, Maryland, Ohio, and Utah passed laws regulating unsolicited or bulk e-mail messages; most other states now have similar statutes.[5683]

Medical Privacy

Protections for medical records were finally introduced in the United States in 2001. On December 20, 2000, the final rules governing the privacy of health records for the Health Insurance Portability and Accountability Act (HIPAA) of 1996 were unveiled; these rules took effect in April 2001. The protection offered by the rules is limited by a large number of exemptions. In addition, a variety of sectoral legislation on the state level may give additional protections to citizens of individual states.[5684]

In April 2003, the first federal regulation protecting individually identifiable health information became effective for enforcement. The Standards for Privacy of Individually Identifiable Health Information, commonly known as the HIPAA Privacy Rule, provide basic protections for individually identifiable health information and give individuals rights with respect to the information about them. The Privacy Rule is permissive in nature because it allows several types of disclosures but requires disclosures only to the individual or his personal representative and to the Secretary of Health and Human Services for the purpose of enforcement. The Privacy Rule allows state laws to remain in place where state law provisions provide greater protection.[5685] State laws deal with health information in areas such as access to medical records, regulation of licenses for medical professionals and organizations, regulations for entitlement programs, mental health records, records related to conditions such as HIV/AIDS, and

---

[5682] Federal Trade Commission, "FTC Issues Report to Congress: Requiring 'ADV' Labeling for Commercial E-Mail Won't Reduce Spam," (press release), June 17, 2005, available at <http://www.ftc.gov/opa/2005/06/adv1.htm>.

[5683] *See* National Council of State Legislatures, Unsolicited Commercial E-Mail Advertisements (Anti-Spam Legislation)
2005 Legislative Activity, Updated May 19, 2005 <http://www.ncsl.org/programs/lis/legislation/spam05.htm>; State Spam Laws Summary <http://www.spamlaws.com/state/summary.shtml>.

[5684] Robert Ellis Smith and Privacy Journal, Compilation of State and Federal Privacy Laws (2002 ed.) <http://www.epic.org/privacy/consumer/states.html>.

[5685] United States Department of Health and Human Services, Office for Civil Rights, Regulation Text (Unofficial Version), "Standards for Privacy of Individually Identifiable Health Information," available at <http://www.hhs.gov/ocr/combinedregtext.pdf>.

---

reproductive rights.[5686] The federal Privacy Rule contains civil penalties for noncompliance and will be enforced by the Office for Civil Rights within the Department of Health and Human Services. The rule also contains criminal penalties for malicious misappropriation and misuse of health information, which are enforced by the DOJ.[5687]

Consumer Information Security Breaches

Several security breaches occurred in private industry in early 2005. Bank of America confirmed in February 2005 that a number of data tapes, containing personal information of bank customers, had been lost in shipment to a backup data center.[5688] In that same month, data warehousing company ChoicePoint announced that it had sold personal data on 145,000 persons to criminals, resulting in some 750 cases of identity theft as of February 2005.[5689] Data broker LexisNexis announced in April 2005 that personal information of 310,000 persons may have been compromised through unauthorized use of passwords for subsidiary Seisint.[5690]

Congress has responded to these breaches with proposed legislation, but no protective laws have thus far been passed. Bills introduced in the US Senate include the Notification of Risk to Personal Data Act,[5691] which would require commercial entities involved in interstate commerce to inform consumers of security breaches exposing their personal data. Bills purporting to limit the use of Social Security numbers have been proposed in the Senate[5692] and the House of Representatives.[5693] A proposed Senate bill for a Privacy Act of 2005[5694]

[5686] *See generally* EPIC's Medical Privacy Web Page <http://www.epic.org/privacy/medical/>.

[5687] *See* United States Department of Health and Human Services, Office of Civil Rights, "Summary of the HIPAA Privacy Rule: HIPAA Compliance Assistance" <http://www.hhs.gov/ocr/privacysummary.pdf>.

[5688] Bank of America, "Bank of America Confirms Lost Data Tapes," (press release), February 25, 2005 <http://www.bankofamerica.com/newsroom/press/press.cfm?PressID=press.20050225.04.htm>.

[5689] Matt Hines, "ChoicePoint Data Theft Widens to 145,000 People," CNET News.com, February 18, 2005 <http://news.com.com/ChoicePoint+data+theft+widens+to+145,000+people/2100-1029_3-5582144.html>; *see also* EPIC's ChoicePoint Web Page <http://www.epic.org/privacy/choicepoint/>.

[5690] LexisNexis, "LexisNexis Concludes Review of Data Search Activity, Identifying Additional Instances of Illegal Data Access," (press release), April 12, 2005 <http://www.lexisnexis.com/about/releases/0789.asp>.

[5691] S. 115, 109th Congress, introduced January 24, 2005, available at <http://frwebgate.access.gpo.gov/cgi-bin/getdoc.cgi?dbname=109_cong_bills&docid=f:s115is.txt.pdf>.

[5692] Social Security Number Misuse Prevention Act, S. 29, 109th Congress, introduced January 24, 2005, available at <http://frwebgate.access.gpo.gov/cgi-bin/getdoc.cgi?dbname=109_cong_bills&docid=f:s29is.txt.pdf>.

[5693] Social Security Number Privacy and Identity Theft Prevention Act; H.R. 1745, 109th Congress, available at <http://thomas.loc.gov/cgi-bin/query/F?c109:44:./temp/~c109IWUVMf:e1751:>.

[5694] S. 116, 109th Congress, introduced January 24, 2005, available at <http://frwebgate.access.gpo.gov/cgi-bin/getdoc.cgi?dbname=109_cong_bills&docid=f:s116is.txt.pdf>.

(modeled on the California statute described below) would regulate the use of data acquired from data brokers, as well as restrict the use of Social Security numbers and records on health, finances, and driver's licenses. Enactment of such federal privacy laws would preempt existing state legislation affording conflicting privacy protection measures.

State legislatures have recently introduced laws requiring notification of consumers after disclosure of financial and other personal data.[5695] Under a California statute effective since July 2003, an entity that stores computerized information must notify California residents of a security breach of unencrypted personal data.[5696] Following California's lead, at least six other state legislatures have passed or are considering statutes requiring residents to be notified of such security breaches,[5697] and similar laws have been proposed in many other states.[5698] Several states are considering legislation allowing credit card holders to "freeze" their accounts to forbid the transfer of their credit card data without their consent; credit card companies would charge a fee for this opt-out service.[5699]

Internet Privacy

Concerns about the adequacy of self-regulation, particularly for Internet-based firms, continue in the United States. In February 2005, EPIC reported the failure of self regulated opt-out systems by industry and recommended that the FTC enforce an Internet user opt-out scheme that would be analogous to the Do-Not-Call telephone registry. By alternately abandoning and renewing its commitment to industry self regulation to ensure consumer protection, the FTC has impeded the US Congress from adopting effective legal safeguards. The agency's approach has also "anesthetized" the public from such issues as the failure of anonymous payment systems, lack of consumer control over the collection and use of personal data, and invasive tracking technologies that monitor users.[5700]

[5695] *See, e.g.,* National Conference of State Legislatures, "2004 Introduced Financial Privacy Information," February 25, 2005 <http://www.ncsl.org/programs/lis/privacy/FinPrivacy2004_Pending.htm>.

[5696] California Civil Code, §§ 1798.29 and 1798.82, *available at* <http://www.privacy.ca.gov/code/cc1798.291798.82.htm>.

[5697] Brian Krebs, "States Keep Watchful Eye on Personal-Data Firms," Washington Post, June 1, 2005, available at <http://www.washingtonpost.com/wp-dyn/content/article/2005/06/01/AR2005060100359.html>.

[5698] Jonathan Krim, "States Scramble to Protect Data," Washington Post, April 9, 2005, available at <http://www.washingtonpost.com/wp-dyn/articles/A38498-2005Apr8.html>.

[5699] *Id.*

[5700] EPIC's Privacy Self Regulation: A Decade of Disappointment Web Page <http://www.epic.org/reports/decadedisappoint.pdf>.

In 2001 and 2002, reports emerged that several profitable companies, including eBay.com, Amazon.com, drkoop.com, and Yahoo.com, either changed users' privacy settings or have changed privacy policies to the detriment of users. In 2000, some companies, including Intel and Microsoft, were discovered to have released products that secretly tracked the activities of Internet users.[5701]

Users filed several lawsuits under the wiretap and computer crime laws. In several cases, TRUSTe, an industry-sponsored self-regulation watchdog group, ruled that the practices did not violate its privacy seal program. Significant controversy arose around online profiling, the practice of advertising companies to track Internet users and compile dossiers on them in order to target banner advertisements. The largest of these advertisers, DoubleClick, ignited widespread public outrage when it began attaching personal information from a marketing firm it purchased to the estimated 100 million previously anonymous profiles it had collected.[5702] The company backed down due to public opposition, a dramatic fall in its stock price and investigations from the FTC and several state attorneys general. In July 2000, the FTC reached an agreement with the Network Advertising Initiative, a group consisting of seven of the largest online advertisers, including DoubleClick, to allow for online profiling and any future merger of such databases to occur with only the opt-out consent.[5703] In January 2001, the FTC dropped its investigation of DoubleClick. However, several private lawsuits were filed against the company. In January 2001, DoubleClick closed its online profiling division, and in May 2002, privacy class actions suits against the company were settled that resulted in little or no benefit to Internet users.[5704] Intel announced in May 2000 that it was dropping the incorporation of unique identifiers in its next-generation computer processors following a consumer boycott.[5705]

In 2004, the year Google went public, the company introduced Gmail, a free e-mail service that scans the content of e-mail messages. The e-mail system matches words from message content with the products and services of Google advertisers and then displays "targeted" advertisements.[5706] This measure, a

---

[5701] *See* Big Brother Inside Campaign <http://www.bigbrotherinside.org>.

[5702] *See* EPIC's DoubleClick Web Page <http://www.epic.org/privacy/doubletrouble/>.

[5703] For a detailed history and critical analysis of this agreement, *see* EPIC and Junkbusters, "Network Advertising Initiative: Principles not Privacy," July 2000 <http://www.epic.org/privacy/internet/NAI_analysis.html>. *See also* Network Advertising Initiative Web Page <http://www.networkadvertising.org/default.asp>.

[5704] "Privacy Advocates Debate Merits of DoubleClick Settlement," Computerworld, May 22, 2002 <http://www.computerworld.com/printthis/2002/0,4814,71382,00.html>.

[5705] *See* <http://www.bigbrotherinside.org>.

[5706] Gmail and Privacy, June 15, 2004, at <http://gmail.google.com/gmail/help/more.html#ads>.

patented process that Google has termed "content extraction," scans the content of e-mail messages of non-subscribers as well as subscribers. Gmail is attractive to subscribers because it offers one gigabyte of storage, thus encouraging subscribers to retain messages. Through this capacity and the company's use of cookies to track users and preserve preferences, Google can use its e-mail program to create detailed records on subscribers.[5707]

The United States Department of Commerce and the European Commission in June 2000 reached an agreement on the Safe Harbor negotiations, allowing US companies to continue to receive personal data from Europe. This measure was taken in response to the European Union Data Protection Directive of 1995, which prohibited the transfer of data from European countries to nations that did not comply with adequate data protection principles. More than 500 companies have joined the Safe Harbor,[5708] which requires organizations to assert compliance with seven principles. These principles include permitting individuals to opt-out from collection of personal data, giving individuals access to their personal data, and ensuring data integrity and security.[5709]

In April 2004, university academicians, at the request of the European Commission, released a study that revealed numerous deficiencies in the implementation of the Safe Harbor program.[5710] Based on the findings, the European Commission reported in October 2004 that a "substantial minority" of the companies on the Safe Harbor list had failed to comply with the principles. Some companies had not placed a visible privacy policy or given consumers control over the sharing of their data with third parties. The European Commission encouraged data protection authorities in the European Union to suspend data flows whenever there is, in the authorities' judgment, a substantial likelihood of a violation of the Safe Harbor Principles. To address deficiencies in the management and enforcement of Safe Harbor, the European Commission asked for greater guidance by the Department of Commerce and more proactive monitoring by the FTC.[5711]

[5707] See EPIC's Gmail Privacy Web Page <http://www.epic.org/privacy/gmail/faq.html>.

[5708] United States Department of Commerce, Safe Harbor List
<http://web.ita.doc.gov/safeharbor/shlist.nsf/webPages/safe+harbor+list>.

[5709] United States Department of Commerce, Safe Harbor Overview, at
<http://www.export.gov/safeharbor/sh_overview.html>.

[5710] See Jan Dhont, María Verónica Pérez Asinari, and Yves Poullet, Safe Harbour Decision Implementation Study, available at <http://europa.eu.int/comm/justice_home/fsj/privacy/docs/studies/safe-harbour-2004_en.pdf>.

[5711] Commission of the European Communities, Staff Working Document: The Implementation of Commission Decision 520/2000/EC on the Adequate Protection of Personal Data Provided by the Safe Harbour Privacy Principles and Related Frequently Asked Questions Issued by the US Department of Commerce,

---

Surveillance of wire, oral, and electronic communications for criminal investigations is governed by the Omnibus Safe Streets and Crime Control Act of 1968 and the Electronic Communications Privacy Act of 1986 ("Title III").[5712] Police are required to obtain a court order based on several legal requirements before capturing the content of a communication. Surveillance for national security purposes is governed by the Foreign Intelligence Surveillance Act of 1978 (FISA), whose requirements are less rigorous than those of the other two statutes, requiring only that the surveillance target be a "foreign power."[5713] In 2004, the so-called Lone Wolf amendment extended FISA's coverage to include any non-United States person who "engages in international terrorism or activities in preparation therefore."[5714] No probable cause to believe in a connection between the surveillance target and any particular nation or group need be shown, nor need the Court find probable cause to believe such a connection exists.[5715] Although the provision is scheduled to "sunset" at the close of 2005, the FBI endorses continuation of the policy.[5716] The number of FISA orders reached an all-time high in 2004, with the secret FISA Court approving 1,754 applications for physical search, electronic surveillance, or both. The Court did not deny, in whole or in part, any application submitted by the federal government in 2004.[5717]

The Foreign Intelligence Surveillance Court of Review (FISCR) convened for its first controversy in 2002 and broadly expanded the DOJ's surveillance authority under FISA. The court held that the DOJ could use looser foreign intelligence standards to conduct criminal investigations in the United States. In doing so, the Court of Review reversed a unanimous lower opinion that revealed a pattern of

---

October 20, 2004, available at <http://europa.eu.int/comm/justice_home/fsj/privacy/docs/adequacy/sec-2004-1323_en.pdf>.

[5712] 18 USC 2510, *et seq.*; 18 USC 2701 *et seq.*, available at
<http://www.law.cornell.edu:80/uscode/18/ch119.html>.

[5713] Foreign Intelligence Surveillance Act of 1978, 50 USC 1801; *see also* Electronic Frontier Foundation, Foreign Intelligence Surveillance Act Frequently Asked Questions (and Answers), at
<http://www.eff.org/Censorship/Terrorism_militias/fisa_faq.html>.

[5714] Congressional Research Service, Intelligence Reform and Terrorism Prevention Act of 2004: "Lone Wolf" Amendment to the Foreign Intelligence Surveillance Act, December 29, 2004, available at
<http://www.fas.org/irp/crs/RS22011.pdf>

[5715] Pub. L. No. 108-458 (2003), § 6001(a).

[5716] Congressional Testimony: Statement of Valerie Caproni, General Counsel, Federal Bureau of Investigation, before the Senate Select Committee on Intelligence, May 24, 2005, available at
<http://www.fbi.gov/congress/congress05/caproni052405.htm>.

[5717] Letter from William E. Moschella, Assistant Attorney General, to J. Dennis Hastert, Speaker, United States House of Representatives, April 1, 2005, available at
<http://www.fas.org/irp/agency/doj/fisa/2004rept.pdf>.

FBI misrepresentations and cast serious doubt on the veracity and accuracy of claims made by the DOJ and the FBI in support of requests for approval of national security and anti-terrorism surveillance.

The lower court found that DOJ and FBI officials had submitted erroneous information in more than 75 applications for search warrants and wiretaps and had improperly shared intelligence information with agents and prosecutors handling criminal cases on at least four occasions.[5718] Because of these problems, the lower court refused to give DOJ the broad new surveillance powers it sought to employ after the September 11, 2001 terrorist attacks. Nevertheless, the Court of Review reversed the earlier decision, and permitted the government to remove the separation that has long existed between officials conducting surveillance on suspected foreign agents and criminal prosecutors investigating crimes.[5719]

The use of electronic surveillance under Title III has more than tripled in the last 10 years. In 2003, 1,442 federal and state wiretaps were completed. About three quarters of the wiretaps were authorized for narcotics investigations. The Administrative Office of the United States Courts reported that state and federal courts authorized an all-time high 1,710 interceptions of wire, oral, and electronic communications in 2004, an increase of 19 percent over the number of interceptions authorized in 2003. The agency also reported that federal officials requested 730 intercept applications in 2004, a 26 percent increase over the number requested in 2003.[5720] Encryption was encountered in two wiretaps terminated in 2004, but the encryption did not prevent law enforcement from accessing either communication. In 2003, one wiretap involved encryption, and law enforcement was able to access the communication.[5721] The question of police decryption methods was raised in the 2001 federal case of *United States v. Scarfo*. In this case, the FBI surreptitiously installed a key logger device on the defendant's computer in order to capture his Pretty Good Privacy encryption passphrase. The defense successfully argued before a federal court in New Jersey that it should be granted access to the details of the key logger technique, in order to determine the legality of the search. The judge directed the government to produce a report "detailing how the key logger device functions" by August 31,

---

[5718] In Re All Matters Submitted to the Foreign Intelligence Surveillance Court, No. Multiple (FISC May 17, 2002), available at <http://www.totse.com/en/law/justice_for_all/166322.html>.

[5719] In Re: Sealed Case No. 02-001 (FISCR November 18, 2002), available at <http://news.findlaw.com/hdocs/docs/terrorism/fisa111802opn.pdf>.

[5720] Administrative Offices of the United States Courts, 2004 Wiretap Report, May 2004, available at <http://www.uscourts.gov/wiretap04/2004WireTap.pdf>.

[5721] Administrative Offices of the United States Courts, 2003 Wiretap Report, May 2003, available at <http://www.uscourts.gov/wiretap03/2003WireTap.pdf>.

2001.[5722] In December 2001, the judge upheld the legality of the key logger device, and ruled that further exposure of its workings "would cause identifiable damage to the national security of the United States."[5723]

In December 2001, the FBI confirmed the existence of a device called "Magic Lantern."[5724] This device would reportedly allow the agency to plant a Trojan horse keystroke logger on a target's computer by sending a computer virus over the Internet, rather than require physical access to the computer, as is now the case. Controversy arose surrounding this announcement, as anti-virus companies argued that they could not leave a hole in their protection software to allow for Magic Lantern's surreptitious placement on computers. Doing so, they argued, would create a conflict of interests. Moreover, if each country's law enforcement agency developed a similar form of virus, each virus would have to be excluded from anti-virus companies' products, translating the purpose of the software, and affecting consumer trust.

The federal wiretap laws were amended in 1994 by the Communications Assistance to Law Enforcement Act (CALEA), which required telephone companies to redesign their equipment to facilitate electronic surveillance.[5725] The Federal Communications Commission (FCC) issued regulations in November 1998 implementing the law.[5726] The regulations include several additional provisions, including a requirement that all mobile phone companies facilitate location tracking of users. Privacy groups challenged the implementation of the law in federal court and telecommunications companies, who argued that the regulations give the government more power than authorized under the law and the Constitution.[5727] In August 2000, the United States Court of Appeals for the District of Columbia Circuit ruled that law enforcement agencies must meet the highest legal standard before using these new surveillance capabilities.

[5722] Selected court documents on the Scarfo case are available at <http://www.epic.org/crypto/scarfo.html>.

[5723] United States v. Nicodemo S. Scarfo, et al., No. 00-404 (NHP) (D. N.J. 2001) (Opinion and Order of December 26, 2001), available at <http://www.epic.org/crypto/scarfo/opinion.html>.

[5724] "'Magic Lantern' Project Exists," Reuters, December 12, 2001.

[5725] Communications Assistance for Law Enforcement Act of 1994, Pub. L 103-411, available at <http://www.epic.org/privacy/wiretap/calea/calea_law.html>.

[5726] Federal Communications Commission, In the Matter of the Communications Assistance for Law Enforcement Act, CC Docket No. 97-213, November 5, 1998, available at <http://www.epic.org/privacy/wiretap/calea/fnprm.html>.

[5727] United States Telecom Association, et al., v. Federal Communications Commission and United States of America, No. 99-1442.

In 2004, the FBI sought greater access to Internet telephony under CALEA, which requires "telecommunications services" to adapt their equipment to allow law enforcement to effectively "wiretap" data and voice transmissions.[5728] Bills proposed but not passed in the House and Senate would have made Voice over Internet Protocol (VoIP) subject to CALEA, thus compelling VoIP providers to design communications in such a way that law enforcement could easily surveil the contents of conversations or routing information.[5729] In September 2004, the FCC issued a Notice of Proposed Rulemaking that tentatively required broadband providers and certain VoIP providers to comply with CALEA but cited non-managed, peer-to-peer VoIP systems and instant-messaging systems as exempt.[5730]

The intelligence agencies have also pushed for more authority and funding to conduct surveillance of Internet communications, arguing that this is necessary to protect the nation's infrastructure from "information warfare." In July 2000, it was revealed that the FBI had developed a system called "Carnivore," which is placed at an ISP's offices and can monitor all traffic about a user including e-mail and browsing.[5731] Earthlink, a major ISP, announced that it refused to install the system in its network.[5732] After the system was discovered, Attorney General Janet Reno promised to conduct a review of its privacy protections.[5733] In the fall of 2000, the DOJ commissioned a team of experts at the Illinois Institute of Technology Research Institute (IITRI) and the Illinois Institute of Technology Chicago-Kent College of Law to undertake an independent review of the Carnivore system. The IITRI group issued its final report on Carnivore in December 2000 and made several recommendations for changes to the

---

[5728] *See* John G. Malcolm, Deputy Assistant Attorney General, Criminal Division, United States Department of Justice, and Patrick W. Kelley, Deputy General Counsel, Federal Bureau of Investigation, Before the Federal Communications Commission, Joint Petition for Expedited Rulemaking, available at <http://www.steptoe.com/publications/FBI_Petition_for_Rulemaking_on_CALEA.pdf>.

[5729] *See* H.R. 4149, VoIP Regulatory Freedom Act of 2004, available *at* <http://www.apcointl.org/about/gov/alerts/hr4129.pdf>; S. 2281, VOIP Regulatory Freedom Act of 2004, available at <http://commerce.senate.gov/pdf/s2281report.pdf>; *see also* ACLU Letter to the Senate Commerce, Science and Transportation Commitee [*sic*] Expressing Concerns about S. 2281, the VOIP Regulatory Freedom Act of 2004, July 21, 2004, available at <http://www.aclu.org/FreeSpeech/FreeSpeech.cfm?ID=16143&c=84#_ftnref14>.

[5730] 69 Fed. Reg. 56976, 56980, (September 23, 2004), available *at* <http://www.askcalea.net/docs/20040923.69fr56976.pdf>.

[5731] Testimony of Robert Corn-Revere, Before the Subcommittee on the Constitution of the Committee on the Judiciary, United States House of Representatives, The Fourth Amendment and the Internet, April 6, 2000, available at <http://www.house.gov/judiciary/corn0406.htm>.

[5732] "EarthLink Says It Refuses to Install FBI's Carnivore Surveillance Device," Wall Street Journal, July 14, 2000.

[5733] "Reno to Double-Check Carnivore's Bite," Reuters, July 13, 2000.

system.[5734] In May 2002, EPIC obtained Freedom of Information Act (FOIA) documents on Carnivore that indicated that the program may have hindered the government's anti-terrorism investigation by over-collecting data in violation of wiretapping laws.[5735] Additional documents obtained in January 2005 revealed that the FBI had not used Carnivore during fiscal years 2002 and 2003, instead using commercially available software in 13 cases of court-ordered Internet surveillance. These documents suggest that Carnivore is no longer needed because Internet service providers are providing information to the government directly.[5736]

The "PATRIOT Act"

The USA PATRIOT Act, which was passed in the wake of the September 11, 2001, attacks, significantly weakened privacy protections in federal wiretapping statutes.[5737] The act extended the "pen register" portions of federal wiretapping law, allowing Carnivore to be used to collect traffic data based solely on a prosecutor's certification that such information was relevant to an ongoing investigation.[5738] The law made computer crimes and terrorism predicate offenses for initiation of a federal wiretap.[5739] The law also authorized national application of a wiretap order, that is, a court in one jurisdiction can issue a warrant that could apply anywhere in the country.[5740] Under the PATRIOT Act, courts can issue roving wiretaps, giving law enforcement the ability to monitor many different devices that a suspect may use.[5741] Although supporters of the PATRIOT Act claimed that a sunset provision in the bill would limit police power, only some of the new surveillance provisions will expire. Also, several states followed suit by passing state legislation that loosens protections against wiretaps.[5742]

[5734] IITRI, Independent Technical Review of the Carnivore System, Final Report, December 8, 2000, available at <http://www.epic.org/privacy/carnivore/carniv_final.pdf>.

[5735] FBI Memo on "FISA Mistakes," available at <http://www.epic.org/privacy/carnivore/fisa.html>.

[5736] EPIC, "EPIC Obtains FBI Reports to Congress on Carnivore," EPIC Alert, Vol. 12.01, January 13, 2005 <http://www.epic.org/alert/EPIC_Alert_12.01.html>.

[5737] H.R. 3162, Uniting and Strengthening America by Providing Appropriate Tools Required to Intercept and Obstruct Terrorism (USA PATRIOT Act of 2001, Pub. L. No. 107-56, available at <http://thomas.loc.gov/cgi-bin/bdquery/z?d107:h.r.03162>.

[5738] Id. at § 216.

[5739] Id. at §201-2.

[5740] Id. at §§216, 220.

[5741] H.R. 3162, supra at § 206.

[5742] National Review of State Surveillance Responses to September 11 Attacks, Constitution Project, April 8, 2002, available at <http://constitutionproject.org/ls/50statesummary.doc>.

After passing the PATRIOT Act, Congress further weakened privacy protections against wiretapping in passing the Cyber Security Enhancement Act (CSEA) in 2002.[5743] CSEA allows communications providers to voluntarily provide government agents with access to the contents of customer communications without consent based on a "good faith" belief that an emergency justifies the release. The same section grants law enforcement the power to install pen register and trap and trace devices without a court order where there is an ongoing attack on a "protected computer." Any computer involved in interstate commerce or communications qualifies as a "protected computer." Further, the law introduces fines and 20-year prison terms for offenders who recklessly cause or attempt to cause serious bodily injury.

In April 2005, the US Attorney General Alberto Gonzales revealed previously classified data on the prevalence of use of the most controversial provisions of the PATRIOT Act since its enactment. Section 206, which allows "roving" surveillance wiretapping in cases of suspected terrorism, had been used 49 times; Section 215, which allows investigators to seek a court order for production of business records, had been used 35 times. In addition to calling for renewal of the 16 USA PATRIOT Act provisions set to expire at the end of 2005, the Attorney General advocated increasing the duration of FISA electronic surveillance and physical search orders and pen register orders of non-US persons under Section 207.[5744]

Congress is now considering not only renewal of the 16 provisions but also the passage of additional provisions that would expand law enforcement powers while reducing accountability. Section 213, the Patriot Reauthorization Act, would permit the FBI to wiretap persons suspected of being national security threats. A second provision would relieve the FBI of the requirement to identify suspected terrorist activity when obtaining special warrants to monitor foreign spies, instead allowing the agency to use the technique to accumulate evidence related to unrelated crimes and thus to justify criminal proceedings against a terrorist suspect. The highly debated proposed administrative subpoena provision would permit the FBI to draft and approve its own subpoenas, without prior approval of a judge or grand jury, to authorize seizure of any tangible item held by a third party. Nor would the FBI be required to show specific facts connecting such items – which could include personal medical, hotel, Internet service

---

[5743] H.R. 3482, The Cyber Security Enhancement Act of 2002, available at <http://thomas.loc.gov/cgi-bin/bdquery/z?d107:h.r.3482>.

[5744] United States Department of Justice, "Attorney General Alberto R. Gonzales Calls on Congress to Renew Vital Provisions of the USA PATRIOT Act," April 5, 2005, available at <http://www.usdoj.gov/opa/pr/2005/April/05_ag_161.htm>.

provider, and bank records – to any terrorist activity.[5745] Yet another provision proposed would enable the FBI to more easily acquire copies of individuals' mail in terrorism cases.

The Senate Select Committee met in secret in June 2005, and failed to reach a consensus on the new provisions. However, the House of Representatives, in the face of a threatened presidential veto, voted for a bill that would prohibit the FBI from searching through library records and bookstore receipts; a similar attempt to limit the FBI's power had failed during the previous term.[5746]

The Department of Homeland Security (DHS), established in 2003 under the Homeland Security Act, combined 22 agencies and was initiated under an estimated USD 38 billion budget.[5747] President Bush requested a budget of USD 41.1 billion for fiscal year 2006, a seven percent increase over the budget for 2005.[5748] This cabinet level agency has been granted increased law enforcement and information sharing powers but more limited open government responsibilities. For instance, the legislation allows the department to share intelligence and grand jury information with state and local authorities but broadly exempts "critical infrastructure information" submitted to the agency from the open government laws.

Limited privacy protections were included in the legislation creating DHS. The legislation created a civil rights officer and a separate privacy officer charged with the responsibility of compliance with the Privacy Act, with formulating privacy impact assessments for rules proposed by the department, and with preparing an annual report to Congress. Other portions of the law prohibit the government from creating a citizen snitch program called the "Terrorism Information Prevention System." The department is statutorily barred from developing a national identification system or card.

[5745] Anita Ramasastry, "Patriot Act Should Be Reigned in," FindLaw/CNN, June 6, 2005, available at <http://edition.cnn.com/2005/LAW/06/01/ramasastry.patriotact2/>.

[5746] Carl Hulse, "House Limits Patriot Act Rules on Library Records," New York Times, June 15, 2005, available at
http://www.nytimes.com/2005/06/16/politics/16patriot.html?ex=1123128000&en=14b1eb69424d2736&ei=5070.

[5747] H.R. 5005, available at <http://www.epic.org/privacy/homeland/homeland_security_act.html>.

[5748] Department of Homeland Security, "Budget in Brief: Fiscal Year 2006," February 7, 2005, available at <http://www.dhs.gov/interweb/assetlibrary/Budget_BIB-FY2006.pdf>.

The 9/11 Commission

Over initial objections from the White House, Congress established the National Commission on Terrorist Attacks Upon the United States (more commonly known as the 9/11 Commission).[5749] The commission was asked to investigate "facts and circumstances relating to the terrorist attacks of September 11, 2001," including those relating to intelligence agencies, law enforcement agencies, diplomacy, immigration issues and border control, the flow of assets to terrorist organizations, commercial aviation, the role of congressional oversight and resource allocation, and other areas determined relevant by the commission.[5750]

The 9/11 Commission, a panel of five Democrats and five Republicans, held 12 public hearings between March 2003 and June 2004 before closing on August 21, 2004. Among the key recommendations of the commission that may affect privacy were the following:

- Improved use of "no-fly" and "automatic selectee" lists should not be delayed while the argument about a successor to CAPPS continues. This screening function should be performed by the Transportation Security Administration (TSA) and should utilize the larger set of watchlists maintained by the federal government. Air carriers should be required to supply the information needed to test and implement this new system.[5751]
- Secure identification should begin in the United States. The federal government should set standards for the issuance of birth certificates and sources of identification, such as driver's licenses. Fraud in identification documents is no longer just a problem of theft. At many entry points to vulnerable facilities, including gates for boarding aircraft, sources of identification are the last opportunity to ensure that people are who they say they are and to check whether they are terrorists.[5752]
- Americans should not be exempt from carrying biometric passports or otherwise enabling their identities to be securely verified when they enter the United States, nor should Canadians or Mexicans. Currently, US persons are exempt from carrying passports when returning from Canada, Mexico, and the Caribbean.[5753]

[5749] Pub. L. No. 107-306, November 27, 2002.

[5750] The 9/11 Commission Report: Final Report of the National Commission on Terrorist Attacks Upon the United States xv (2004) (Preface), New York: W. W. Norton.

[5751] *Id.* at 393.

[5752] *Id.* at 390.

[5753] *Id.* at 388.

Civil liberties organizations expressed caution about the recommendations of the 9/11 Commission. For example, EPIC wrote, "Significant errors have been found in both the no-fly watchlists and the automatic selectee system. This is a particularly serious problem for US persons who travel within the United States. There should be an independent evaluation of how best to operate these screening systems and still safeguard basic rights."[5754] Regarding the development of a system of biometric identification, EPIC further said:

> Some steps should be taken to reduce the risk of fraud and identity theft. Identification documents should be made more secure. However, the integration of secure identity cards with interconnected databases raises substantial privacy risks that will require new legislation and new forms of oversight. Privacy enhancing techniques that minimize the collection and use of personally identifiable information should also be considered. . . . There are significant privacy and civil liberties concerns regarding the use of such devices that must be resolved before the widespread deployment of biometric passports for US citizens. In particular, a system properly designed to ensure the security of the borders should not provide the basis for routine identification within the United States.[5755]

The Commission also recommended certain safeguards to protect privacy and promote government oversight, including:

- As the President determines the guidelines for information sharing among government agencies and by those agencies with the private sector, he should safeguard the privacy of individuals about whom information is shared.[5756]
- At this time of increased and consolidated government authority, there should be a board within the executive branch to oversee adherence to the Commission-recommended guidelines and the commitment the government makes to defend civil liberties.[5757]

Civil liberties organizations, and even one member of the Commission, urged the establishment of an independent oversight board to safeguard civil liberties.[5758]

[5754] EPIC, The 9/11 Commission Report Web Page <http://www.epic.org/privacy/terrorism/911comm.html>.
[5755] Id.
[5756] The 9/11 Commission Report, *supra* at 394.
[5757] Id. at 395.
[5758] Richard Ben-Veniste and Lance Cole, "How to Watch the Watchers," New York Times, September 7, 2004.

Video Surveillance and Face Recognition Technology

Recent years have seen a new trend towards the increased use of video surveillance cameras linked with facial recognition software in public places.[5759] This kind of technology was first used in the United States at the 2001 Super Bowl in Tampa, Florida, to compare the faces of attendees to faces in a database of mug shots. Public usage of the technology then spread to the Ybor City district of Tampa, where the technology encountered much public opposition. In August 2001, the Tampa City Council held a vote on whether they should terminate their contract with Visionics, but they narrowly decided to keep using the software. Later that year, police discontinued use of the system because it produced too many false positive identifications, resulting in wasted police time.[5760] Virginia Beach, Virginia, received funding in 2001 from the state Department of Criminal Justice Services to install a system that can scan and process the facial images of tourists visiting the town. However, reports at three months[5761] and one year[5762] after initiation of the face recognition program in Virginia Beach showed that the technology had produced several false alarms but no arrests. Chicago, Illinois, which in 2004 implemented a major surveillance system funded partly by the DHS, rejected the use of facial recognition technology owing to its inaccuracy.[5763]

Face recognition technology is still not reliable and remains unregulated by US laws. Studies sponsored by the Defense Department have shown the system is right only 54 percent of the time and can be significantly compromised by changes in lighting, weight, hair, sunglasses, subject cooperation, and other factors.[5764] Tests on the face recognition systems in operation at Palm Beach Airport in Florida and at Boston Logan Airport have also shown the technology

---

[5759] Robert O'Harrow, "Matching Faces with Mugshots: Software for Police, Others Stir Privacy Concerns," Washington Post, July 31, 2001, at A1. *See also* EPIC's Face Recognition Web Page <http://www.epic.org/privacy/facerecognition/>.

[5760] ACLU, "Drawing a Blank: The Failure of Facial Recognition Technology in Tampa, Florida," January 3, 2002, available at <http://archive.aclu.org/issues/privacy/drawing_blank.pdf>.

[5761] "Resort Town: Any Familiar Faces?" Wired News, January 13, 2003 <http://wired-vig.wired.com/news/print/0,1294,57189,00.html>.

[5762] Renee Petrina, "The Eyes of the Beholder," Richmond Times-Dispatch, August 11, 2003, at A1.

[5763] *See* Debbie Howlett, "Chicago Plans Advanced Surveillance," USA Today, September 9, 2004, available at <http://www.usatoday.com/news/nation/2004-09-09-chicago-surveillance_x.htm>.

[5764] Declan McCullagh & Robert Zarate, "Scanning Tech a Blurry Picture," Wired News, February 16, 2002, available at <http://www.wired.com/news/print/0,1294,50470,00.html>.

to be ineffective and error-ridden.[5765] State-of-the-art facial recognition technology appears unable to recognize subjects with a high rate of accuracy.[5766]

National Identity Card

On May 11, 2005, President Bush signed into law the Emergency Supplemental Appropriations Act for Defense, the Global War on Terror, and Tsunami Relief, which included the controversial REAL ID Act of 2005.[5767] The Real ID Act's provisions originated in a House bill and were slipped into the USD 82 billion appropriations bill with neither hearings nor committee approval, an act many believe was a deliberate maneuver to avoid Congressional debate. The REAL ID Act is a response to the 9/11 Commission's recommendations to prevent would-be terrorists from obtaining documentation. The law requires all states to comply, by May 2008, with federal standards when issuing driver's licenses. States failing to comply with the national standards would be ineligible to participate in such federally funded programs as veteran's benefits and Social Security – nor would holders of noncompliant driver's licenses be allowed to board airplanes.[5768]

The new driver's licenses issued under the REAL ID Act will contain encoded, machine-readable data, to be determined by the Secretary of the Department of Transportation and the Secretary of the DHS. Applicants for driver's licenses will be required to provide proof of citizenship or immigration status prior to issue of a license; such proof will consist of either a passport or four documents containing a Social Security number, address, and other information. State motor vehicle department employees must then verify the information against federal databases and store the applicant's documentation and digital photograph in the database. Thus, the REAL ID Act creates a de facto national identity card at an

---

[5765] Hiawatha Bray, "'Face Testing' at Logan Is Found Lacking," Boston Globe, July 17, 2002, available at <http://www.boston.com/dailyglobe2/198/metro/_Face_testing_at_Logan_is_found_lacking+.shtml>.

[5766] The federal government has sponsored Face Recognition Vendor Tests, a series of independently administered evaluations of available technology. Ten commercial vendors participated in the 2002 test, the results of which revealed problems in identifying images that were taken outdoors or from a non-frontal angle, as well as difficulty in recognizing subjects who were young, female, or both. (See P. Jonathan Phillips, Patrick Grother, Ross J. Micheals, et al., Face Recognition Vendor Test 2002: Evaluation Report (NISTIR 6965), March 2003, available at <http://www.frvt.org/DLs/FRVT_2002_Evaluation_Report.pdf>.) Because the data set for the 2002 test consisted mostly of images of Mexican subjects – taken from the US Department of State's Mexican non-immigrant visa archive – the effect of race on discernment capability was not assessed. The 2005 test, to be conducted by the National Institute of Standards and Technology (NIST) in the fall, is being sponsored by the DOJ, FBI, DHS, and other federal agencies. (Face Recognition Vendor Test 2005 Web Page <http://www.frvt.org/FRVT2005/default.aspx>.)

[5767] Pub. L. No. 109-13.

[5768] Kim Zetter, "No Real Debate for Real ID," Wired News, May 10, 2005 <http://wired.com/news/privacy/0,1848,67471,00.html?tw=wn_tophead_1>.

estimated cost of up to USD 700 million over the next five years.[5769] In addition to its high monetary cost, the act raises concerns because state motor vehicle department are already a favored target of identity thieves. The law follows several failed proposals to create a national ID card in the wake of the September 11, 2001 terrorist attacks;[5770] however, nothing in the act's provisions would have prevented the September 11, 2001 terrorists from obtaining a driver's license.

Passenger Profiling and Prescreening

The Computer Assisted Passenger Prescreening System II (CAPPS II) aimed to conduct background risk assessments on all air travelers before they fly on commercial airliners. The profiling system will rely on experimental data-mining technology to sift through data from various commercial and government databases, assigning different "risk scores" to passengers. Based on these scores, passengers will either be denied boarding, subjected to a more intrusive physical search, or passed through normal screening. Civil libertarians have noted that CAPPS II may be scaled to other settings in the future, such as train stations, bus stations, or even the entrances of public buildings.[5771] In July 2003, DHS indicated that there would be further revisions to the CAPPS program.[5772] The agency intended to link CAPPS II and US-VISIT (United States Visitor and Immigrant Status Indicator Technology border control program) when both programs were fully operational to ensure that "the processes at both border and airport points of entry and exit are consistent."[5773] In response to a 2004 request by EPIC under the FOIA, the Transportation Security Administration (TSA) failed to produce documents on the agency's use of passenger information under CAPPS II. However, in March 2005, the DHS Office of the Inspector General released a report on the dissemination and use of passenger information stating that during 2003 and 2004, TSA officials had made inaccurate statements about

---

[5769] Id.; see also EPIC's National ID Cards and REAL ID Act Web Page
<http://www.epic.org/privacy/id_cards/>.

[5770] IDs – Not That Easy: Questions about Nationwide Identity Systems (Stephen Y. Kent & Lynette I. Millett, eds., 2002), Committee on Authentication Technologies and Their Privacy Implications, National Research Council, available at <http://www.nap.edu/catalog/10346.html?onpi_topnews_041102>.

[5771] See generally EPIC's Passenger Profiling Web Page
<http://www.epic.org/privacy/airtravel/profiling.html>.

[5772] Robert O'Harrow, "Surveillance Proposal Expanded: CAPPS II Would Look at More Air Passengers," Washington Post, July 31, 2003, at E01, available at <http://www.washingtonpost.com/wp-dyn/articles/A4978-2003Jul30.html>.

[5773] Interim Final Privacy Act Notice, 68 Fed. Reg. 45265 (August 1, 2003).

the transfer of passenger data. The report also stated that passenger data had been improperly disclosed to the public in one instance.[5774]

CAPPS II was abandoned in late 2004, shortly after Delta Airlines refused to provide the government with the passenger data requested. TSA quickly replaced CAPPS II with the passenger-prescreening scheme "Secure Flight," giving the new program a slightly different mandate. Secure Flight is designed to compare passenger names against the "selectee" and "no fly" lists of the Terrorist Screening Database compiled by the Terrorist Screening Center.[5775] Upon creation of Secure Flight, TSA promised to adopt measures for protection of personal data and for redress by passengers who were improperly flagged once the pilot program was completed. In March 2005, the Government Accountability Office (GAO) issued a report questioning the accuracy of Secure Flight passenger data, the efficacy of the program's privacy protections, and the adequacy of measures for redress by passengers.[5776] In June 2005, DHS admitted that under Secure Flight, TSA had stored detailed passenger information[5777] in violation of its own order stating that the agency would not do so.[5778] In July 2005, GAO released another report on Secure Flight, stating that TSA "did not fully disclose to the public its use of personal information in its fall 2004 privacy notices."[5779] Whereas the Secure Flight pilot program is supposed to be limited to data on persons who flew on commercial airlines in June 2004, TSA secretly used about 200,000 variations of the names of 43,000 actual passengers, resulting

---

[5774] *See* United States Department of Homeland Security, Office of the Inspector General, Review of the Transportation Security Administration's Role in the Use and Dissemination of Airline Passenger Data (Redacted) (OIG-05-12), available at <http://www.epic.org/privacy/airtravel/dhsig_03-05.pdf>.

[5775] United States Department of Justice, Transportation Security Administration, Secure Flight Program <http://www.tsa.gov/public/display?theme=5&content=09000519800cf3a7>.

[5776] Government Accountability Office, Aviation Security: Secure Flight Development and Testing Under Way, but Risks Should Be Managed as System is Further Developed (GAO-05-356), March 2005, available at <http://www.epic.org/privacy/airtravel/d05356.pdf>.

[5777] *See* United States Department of Homeland Security, Transportation Security Administration, Notice to Supplement and Amend Existing System of Records and Privacy Impact Assessment, available at <http://www.epic.org/privacy/airtravel/sf_sorn_pia_062205.pdf>; *see generally* EPIC's Secure Flight Web Page <http://www.epic.org/privacy/airtravel/secureflight.html>.

[5778] Leslie Miller, "Gov't Collected Data on Airline Passengers," Associated Press, June 21, 2005, available at <http://www.commondreams.org/headlines05/0621-05.htm>; *see also* United States Department of Homeland Security, Transportation Security Administration, Docket No. TSA-2004-19160, Notice of Final Order for Secure Flight Test Phase; Response to Public Comments on Proposed Order and Secure Flight Test Records, available at <http://a257.g.akamaitech.net/7/257/2422/06jun20041800/edocket.access.gpo.gov/2004/04-25396.htm>.

[5779] Specifically, the report elaborated: "[A] TSA contractor, acting on behalf of the agency, collected more than 100 million commercial data records containing personal information such as name, date of birth, and telephone number without informing the public. As a result of TSA's actions, the public did not receive the full protections of the Privacy Act. *See* Government Accountability Office, Aviation Security: Transportation Security Administration Did Not Fully Disclose Uses of Personal Information during Secure Flight Program Testing in Initial Privacy Notices, but Has Recently Taken Steps to More Fully Inform the Public (GAO-05-864R) (July 22, 2005), available at <http://www.gao.gov/new.items/d05864r.pdf>.

in the collection of information on an estimated 250,000 people who may or may not have flown that month.[5780]

More limited attempts to create national identification systems include "enhanced visa" documents and "trusted traveler" programs. In July 2004, TSA initiated a database for its "Registered Traveler" program.[5781] TSA has since announced that Registered Traveler's database records are exempt from certain provisions of the Privacy Act.[5782] Enrollees in a three-month test period submitted biometric samples (fingerprint and iris scan) and underwent a background check. The value of the program is questionable for travelers, as enrollees were required to submit to normal screening; the card only reduced the likelihood that the travelers would be subject to secondary screening with a metal-detecting wand. The Registered Traveler pilot program was extended to September 2005, and included Boston, Los Angeles, Houston, Minneapolis-St. Paul, and Washington-Reagan airports; enrollment reached the agency's limit of 10,000 volunteers and has closed.[5783]

However, private efforts may lead to a broadening of the federally funded program. Beginning on June 21, 2005, travelers through Orlando International Airport can voluntarily register for the Clear Identity Program, an initiative founded by publishing entrepreneur Steven Brill of Verified Identity Pass, Inc.[5784] Participants submit to a background check and provide a fingerprint, an iris scan, and USD 80 in exchange for an identification card and the opportunity to breeze through security lines. TSA has said it is open to public-private partnerships to expand the Registered Traveler initiative. Such programs raise considerable privacy concerns about the way passenger information will be collected, stored, and used.[5785] EPIC submitted comments on the program, warning that providing an easy route of security clearance could, in practice, ease the way for terrorists while causing inequity in treatment among travelers.[5786]

[5780] Associated Press, "GAO: TSA Data Collection Violated Privacy Act: Agency Says Test Passenger Screening Program Overstepped Restrictions," July 22, 2005, available at <http://www.msnbc.msn.com/id/8672258/>.

[5781] <http://a257.g.akamaitech.net/7/257/2422/14mar20010800/edocket.access.gpo.gov/2004/04-12452.htm>.

[5782] Privacy Act of 1974: Implementation of Exemptions; Registered Traveler Operations Files, Federal Register, to be codified at 49 C.F.R. Pt. 1507, available at <http://thefederalregister.com/d.p/2005-06-08-05-10632>.

[5783] Transportation Security Administration, Registered Traveler <http://www.tsa.gov/public/interapp/editorial/editorial_multi_image_with_table_0207.xml>.

[5784] See Verified Identity Pass, Inc. Web Page <http://www.verifiedidcard.com/>.

[5785] Brian Bergstein, "Orlando Airport First Tester of Quick-Pass Voluntary Biometric ID," TBO.com/AP News, June 3, 2005 <http://ap.tbo.com/ap/florida/MGBUV58UI9E.html>.

[5786] See EPIC, Comments of the Electronic Privacy Information Center in the Matter of Privacy Act Notice Concerning Aviation Security Screening Records, Before the United States Department of Transportation, available at <http://www.epic.org/privacy/airtravel/tsacomments2.24.2003.html>.

In 2002, the government initiated several privacy-invasive programs as a result of the September 11, 2001 attacks. Among these is the United States Visitor and Immigrant Status Indicator Technology program (US-VISIT),[5787] which requires visitors to the country to submit a biometric identifier to the government. When a visitor subject to US-VISIT applies for a visa to travel to the United States, he is fingerprinted and photographed at an overseas US consular office.[5788] This biometric information is then checked against more than 20 interfacing government databases to determine the likelihood that the visitor is a criminal or terrorist.[5789] When the visitor arrives at a US port of entry, he is again fingerprinted and photographed to verify that he is same person who was issued the visa.[5790] The program will eventually be expanded to fingerprint visitors when they exit the US, as well.[5791] In September 2004, US-VISIT was extended to apply to visitors to the United States traveling via air and seaports through the Visa Waiver Program.[5792]

US-VISIT grew out of the National Security Entry-Exit Registration System (NSEERS), a national registry established by the Department of Justice in 2002. NSEERS requires non-immigrant aliens from 25 countries and others who "met a combination of intelligence-based criteria that identified them as a potential security risk."[5793] Although the agency suspended most of the NSEERS requirements in 2003, foreign nationals of Iran, Iraq, Libya, Syria, and Sudan still must register at ports of entry; decisions to compel other foreign nationals to register may be made on the basis of questioning. US-VISIT, once fully implemented, will account for virtually all foreign nationals visiting the United States.[5794] In June 2004, DHS awarded the Smart Border Alliance, led by the consulting firm Accenture, a USD 10 billion contract to design and oversee implementation of radio frequency identification (RFID) technology at border

---

[5787] <http://www.dhs.gov/dhspublic/display?theme=43&content=736>; *see generally* EPIC's US-VISIT Web Page <http://www.epic.org/privacy/us-visit/>.

[5788] *Id.*

[5789] Interim Final Rule and Notice, 69 Fed. Reg. 476 (January 5, 2004).

[5790] Department of Homeland Security, Travel & Transportation: US-VISIT <http://www.dhs.gov/dhspublic/interapp/editorial/editorial_0525.xml> (February 7, 2005).

[5791] *Id.*

[5792] *Id.*

[5793] Department of Homeland Security Web site, US-VISIT FAQs: NSEERS and US-VISIT, at <http://www.dhs.gov/dhspublic/interapp/editorial/editorial_0441.xml>.

[5794] *Id.*

checkpoints under US-VISIT.[5795] By January 5, 2004, the DHS had deployed US-VISIT at 115 airports and 14 major seaports.[5796] US-VISIT is expected to be operational at each of the nation's more than 400 air, land and seaports by the end of 2005.[5797]

A purported goal of US-VISIT is to protect the privacy of visitors to the United States. However, the Government Accountability Office reported in February 2005, that in conducting the legislatively mandated privacy impact assessment for US-VISIT, DHS had failed to address fully the privacy issues in system documentation. The DHS evaluation also failed to comply fully with recommendations of the Office of Management and Budget (OMB) and the National Institute of Standards and Technology (NIST).[5798] Biometric data collected by US-VISIT currently includes digital fingerscans and photographs, the two parameters recommended by NIST. However, the choice of biometric technologies is at the discretion of the United States Secretary of State and the Secretary of Homeland Security.[5799]

Additionally, immigration authorities, in conjunction with several other federal agencies, are implementing the Student and Exchange Visitor Information System (SEVIS).[5800] This program, which is maintained by US Immigration and Customs Enforcement Office of DHS, is an Internet-based system that allows schools to transmit student information to the government for purposes of tracking and monitoring non-immigrant and exchange students. Accessible information includes a student's personally identifiable information, admission at port of entry, academic information, such as changes in program of study, and disciplinary information. Schools are required to transmit such information to the Bureau of Citizenship and Immigration Services (BCIS, formerly the Immigration and Naturalization Service) for the duration of a student's stay in the United States. In accordance with the PATRIOT Act, SEVIS was fully

---

[5795] *See* EPIC's Spotlight on Surveillance: US-VISIT Rolls Out the Unwelcome Mat, July 2005 <http://www.epic.org/privacy/surveillance/spotlight/0705/>; EPIC's US-VISIT Web Page, *supra*.

[5796] Department of Homeland Security, Travel & Transportation: US-VISIT, *supra*; *see also* EPIC's US-VISIT Web Page, *supra*

[5797] *Id.*

[5798] Government Accountability Office, Department of Homeland Security: Some Progress Made, but Many Challenges Remain on US Visitor and Immigrant Status Indicator and Technology Program, Report No. GAO-05-202 (February 2005), available at <http://www.gao.gov/new.items/d05202.pdf>; *see also* Department of Homeland Security Privacy Office Report to Congress, April 2003-June 2004, available at <http://www.dhs.gov/interweb/assetlibrary/privacy_annualrpt_2004_bdy.pdf>.

[5799] Department of Homeland Security Web site, US-VISIT FAQs: Biometrics, at <http://www.dhs.gov/dhspublic/interapp/editorial/editorial_0444.xml>.

[5800] *See* EPIC's Spotlight on Surveillance: SEVIS Database Tracks Every Move of Foreign Students, Visitors, September 2005 <http://www.epic.org/privacy/surveillance/spotlight/0905/>;

implemented by January 1, 2003. A recent Government Accountability Office report showed that problems remain in redressing data errors in student and exchange visitor records and that these errors can take months or even years to correct. Such errors make retention of such students in academic programs difficult.[5801] Of the estimated 15,000 requests for data fixes initiated since the inception of the program through spring 2005, about 6,600 remained unresolved.[5802] In February 2005, the DHS issued a privacy impact statement on SEVIS, wherein the agency reported that data files on students and exchange visitors are archived and retained for the statutory maximum period of 75 years.[5803]

Data Mining

Total Information Awareness (TIA) was one of many post-September 11, 2001 responses to terrorism. TIA is a now-defunct program of the Defense Advanced Research Projects Agency (DARPA); TIA intended to scan ultra-large databases of personal information to detect the "information signature" of terrorists. The program was headed by Admiral John Poindexter and was renamed "Terrorism Information Awareness" to pacify critics.[5804] Congress acted to limit the project in February 2003 by requiring DARPA to submit a detailed report on TIA and later in the year cut funding for Admiral Poindexter's entire Information Awareness Office.

States have pursued information sharing and data mining arrangements. Most notable amongst these systems was the now-defunct MATRIX, or Multi-state Anti-Terrorism Information Exchange.[5805] This prototype database system run by the State of Florida and Seisint, a private company later acquired by LexisNexis, until exhaustion of federal funding on April 15, 2005. Built by a consortium of state law enforcement agencies headed by Florida, MATRIX combined public and private records from multiple databases with data analysis tools and provided

---

[5801] Performance of Foreign Student and Exchange Visitor Information System Continues to Improve, but Issues Remain, Testimony before Congressional Subcommittees, Joint Statement, Randolph C. Hite and Jess T. Ford, Government Accountability Office (March 17, 2005), available at <http://www.gao.gov/new.items/d05440t.pdf>.

[5802] "SEVIS Data Fixes," SEVIS Newsletter (U.S. Immigrations and Customs Enforcement), May 2005, at 3, available at <http://www.ice.gov/graphics/sevis/pdf/SEVISnewsletter.pdf>.

[5803] United States Department of Homeland Security, The Student and Exchange Visitor Information System (SEVIS) Privacy Impact Assessment (February 5, 2005), available at <http://www.ice.gov/graphics/sevis/pdf/privacy_pia_sevis.pdf>.

[5804] See generally EPIC's Terrorism Information Awareness Web Page <http://www.epic.org/privacy/profiling/tia/>.

[5805] <http://www.matrix-at.org/>.

a wealth of personal information in near-real time to law enforcement agents in 13 participating states. Most of the states that had been involved gradually withdrew their participation because of privacy concerns. In April 2005, however, Florida officials called for initiation of a more powerful successor to MATRIX that would include more types of data, such as financial and insurance records.[5806]

Radio Frequency Identification (RFID)

RFID legislation has been proposed, but not yet passed, in at least 11 state legislatures during the past year.[5807] Much of this legislation includes provisions for clear labeling of consumer products bearing RFID tags, a requirement originally proposed for federal legislation drafted by the Consumers Against Supermarket Privacy Invasion and Numbering (CASPIAN), the "RFID Right to Know Act of 2003."[5808] A bill that recently passed in the California senate would prohibit the inclusion of RFIDs that can be read remotely without the person's knowledge in state identity documents, such as driver's licenses, student identification badges, and medical cards.[5809] The bill was created partly in response to parents' outcry when an elementary school in Sutter, California, mandated that each student carry an RFID-equipped identity card that broadcast his or her name, photograph, grade, school name, class year, and student identification number.[5810] Other state efforts to control RFID use have failed, however.

Another California bill, requiring destruction or removal of RFID cards upon checkout at retailers and libraries, was defeated in 2004;[5811] in the same year,

---

[5806] "Florida Planning Son of Matrix," Wired News, April 25, 2005 <http://www.wired.com/news/print/0,1294,67313,00.html>; *see also* Florida Department of Law Enforcement, Request for Information #003: Information Services to Support Domestic Security and Criminal Investigations, available at <http://fcn.state.fl.us/owa_vbspdf/owa/46616_RFI0003_0_0.pdf>.

[5807] *See* National Council of State Legislatures, "2005 Radio Frequency Identification Legislation" <http://www.ncsl.org/programs/lis/privacy/rfid05.htm>.

[5808] This "notice" clause requires any consumer products bearing RFID tags to be conspicuously labeled. CASPIAN, "RFID Right to Know Act of 2003," available at <http://www.nocards.org/rfid/rfidbill.shtml>.

[5809] California Senate Bill 682, available at <http://www.leginfo.ca.gov/pub/bill/sen/sb_0651-0700/sb_682_bill_20050511_amended_sen.html>.

[5810] ACLU, "Bill to Protect Californians' Privacy, Personal Safety, and Financial Security Advances in State Senate" (press release), May 18, 2005 <http://www.aclunc.org/pressrel/050517-rfidbill.html>; *see also* ACLU's Yes on SB 682! Stop RFIDs in California IDs Web Page <http://www.aclunc.org/privacy/technology/yes682/index.html>.

[5811] Claire Swedberg, "California RFID Legislation Rejected," RFID Journal, July 5, 2004 <http://www.rfidjournal.com/article/articleview/1015/1/1/>.

similar bills failed in the Missouri and Utah legislatures.[5812] Bills in the Utah and Missouri legislatures, which failed, and a bill in Maryland, required tags to be labeled only.[5813] A Virginia bill called for a general review of RFID practices and privacy.[5814] A failed Texas bill introduced in 2005 would have prohibited public school districts from using RFID technology to track students.[5815] No RFID legislation is currently being considered in the US at the federal level.

In November 2003, a joint position statement of consumer and privacy groups including EPIC called for a moratorium on the use of RFID tags in individual consumer products until a formal technology assessment be conducted. Further, the statement called for industry use of RFID to abide by Fair Information Practices and stated that certain uses of RFID, such as the tracking of individuals, should be flatly prohibited.[5816]

In May 2005, the Government Accountability Office (GAO) identified 13 federal agencies that were using or planning to use RFID tags, mainly for physical access control and asset-tracking purposes.[5817] GAO reported a general failure to address privacy issues raised by the use of RFID technology.[5818]

The Department of State had planned to introduce the machine-readable "e-Passport," containing an RFID chip in the back cover, for US passport holders by the end of 2005. Privacy advocates and citizens raised concerns[5819] that personal

---

[5812] Alorie Gilbert, "Tracking Tags May Get Congressional Scrutiny, CNET News.com, March 24, 2004 <http://news.com.com/2100-1008_3-5178859.html>.

[5813] Utah House Bill HB 251, available at <http://www.le.state.ut.us/~2004/htmdoc/hbillhtm/hb0251.htm>; Missouri Senate Bill 867, available at <http://www.senate.state.mo.us/04INFO/bills/SB867.htm>; Maryland House Bill 32, available at <http://mlis.state.md.us/2004rs/billfile/HB0032.htm#Exbill>.

[5814] Virginia House Bill 1304, available at <http://leg1.state.va.us/cgi-bin/legp504.exe?041+ful+HB1304>.

[5815] Texas House Bill HB 2953.

[5816] RFID Position Statement of Consumer Privacy and Civil Liberties Organizations," November 20, 2003, available at <http://www.privacyrights.org/ar/RFIDposition.htm>.

[5817] Government Accountability Office, "Information Security: Radio Frequency Identification Technology in the Federal Government," Publication No. GAO-05-551, available at <http://www.gao.gov/new.items/d05551.pdf>.

[5818] "The security of [RFID] tags and databases raises important considerations concerning the confidentiality, integrity, and availability of the data on the tags, in the databases, and in how this information is being protected. Measures to address these security issues, such as compliance with the risk-based framework mandated by FISMA (the Federal Information Security Management Act of 2002) and employing encryption and authentication technologies, can help agencies achieve a stronger security posture. Among the key privacy issues are notifying individuals of the existence or use of the technology; tracking an individual's movements; profiling an individual's habits, tastes or predilections; and allowing for secondary uses of information. While measures to mitigate these issues are under discussion, they remain largely prospective." *Id.*, at 18.

[5819] *See, e.g.*, Letter from Electronic Frontier Foundation, Electronic Privacy Information Center, PrivacyActivism, *et al.* to Office of Passport Policy, United States Department of State, Comments on Department's Proposed Use of Passports Equipped with RFID Technology for US Citizens, April 4, 2005, available at <http://www.epic.org/privacy/rfid/rfid_passports-0405.pdf>.

information—including the passport holder's name, photograph, birth date, and passport number—would be readable from several feet rather than several inches as the State Department had maintained. After test findings revealed that the embedded information could indeed be vulnerable to identity theft, the agency announced in the spring of 2005 that implementation of the electronic passports would be delayed pending resolution of the security issues.[5820]

Privacy advocates also have cautioned that without regulation, RFID use could have significant, negative impact on individual privacy.[5821] At an Federal Trade Commission (FTC) workshop held in June 2004, FTC considered that RFID regulation was premature.[5822] The Federal Communications Commission (FCC) already regulates the use of electromagnetic spectrum in RFID applications. FCC places limits on the power and spectrum allocation of RFID readers, which in turn will limit the read range of a particular tag.[5823] Recently, FCC reduced RF (radio frequency) power restrictions on DHS to improve the effectiveness of scanning shipping containers when they reach US ports.[5824] On October 23, 2004, the Department of Defense (DOD) announced a policy requiring all suppliers to begin using RFID on the "lowest possible piece" of shipments to DOD by January 2005. The announcement cited improvement of data quality, items management, asset visibility, and maintenance of material as reasons for the new policy.[5825] In February 2004, the US Food and Drug Administration (FDA) released a report suggesting that RFID could be instrumental in the fight against counterfeit drugs and help improve patient safety. The report claims it should be feasible to use RFID to track all drugs at the unit level by 2007.[5826] In October 2002, the ruled that the VeriChip, an RFID chip designed to be implanted in the human body, is not a regulated medical device "for security, financial, and personal identification/safety applications," although specific

---

[5820] Sara Kehaulani Goo, "Security Concerns Prompt Passport Redesign," Washington Post, April 30, 2005, available at <http://www.washingtonpost.com/wp-dyn/content/article/2005/04/29/AR2005042901501.html>.

[5821] Federal Trade Commission Workshop, Radio Frequency Identification: Applications and Implications for Consumers, *supra*.

[5822] "FTC Has No Plans to Regulate RFID," RCR Wireless, June 22, 2004, available at <http://rcrnews.com/cgi-bin/news.pl?newsId=18584>.

[5823] *See* Part 15 and other Parts of the Commission's Rules, Notice of Proposed Rulemaking & Order, 66 Fed. Reg. 56793, at para. 21 (2001).

[5824] Kimberly Hill, "FCC Loosens RFID Rule for Homeland Security," CRM Daily, April 16, 2004, available at <http://crm-daily.newsfactor.com/story.xhtml?story_id=23735>.

[5825] United States Department of Defense, "DoD Announces Radio Frequency Identification Policy," October 23, 2004, available at <http://www.dod.mil/releases/2003/nr20031023-0568.html>.

[5826] Food and Drug Administration, "Combating Counterfeit Drugs: A Report of the Food and Drug Administration," February 2004, available at <http://www.fda.gov/oc/initiatives/counterfeit/report02_04.html>.

health applications would be.[5827] In October 2004, FDA allowed the use of the chip to provide easy access to individual medical records.[5828] Airlines are beginning to develop pilot programs to test the use of RFID for luggage tags to enhance security and protect against lost or misdirected bags.[5829]

Recent Developments

In July 2003, the Department of Housing and Urban Development (HUD) announced guidelines for "Homeless Management Information Systems" (HMIS).[5830] HMIS was created to track homeless populations in order to deliver more efficient services. However, the system as proposed by HUD is unnecessarily privacy invasive and requires a homeless person to give his or her name, Social Security number, date of birth, medical information, benefits information, and a history of government services received. A "Client Profile" may also include the name, date of birth, and gender of any child of the data subject. Thus, HMIS enables law enforcement and national security interests to obtain detailed information on homeless individuals with ease. Although persons housed in shelters for victims of domestic violence are already exempted from having to reveal their real names, care workers are concerned that compilation of even limited personal information could endanger their clients.[5831] Such fears have prompted a bill in the US House of Representatives that, if enacted into law, will make victims of domestic violence exempt from the requirement of entry of their personal information into HMIS databases.[5832]

[5827] Nick Farrell, "Chips in Humans Okay, Says FDA," Personal Computer World, October 25, 2002, available at <http://www.pcw.co.uk/News/1136271>.

[5828] *See* EPIC's VeriChip Web Page <http://www.epic.org/privacy/rfid/verichip.html>. *See also* Barnaby J. Feder and Tom Zeller Jr., "Identity Badge Worn under Skin Approved for Use in Health Care," New York Times, October 14, 2004, available at <http://www.nytimes.com/2004/10/14/technology/14implant.html>.

[5829] Jonathan Krim, "Embedding Their Hopes in RFID," E-Commerce Times, June 25, 2004, available at <http://www.ecommercetimes.com/story/34773.html>.

[5830] United States Department of Housing and Urban Development, Homeless Management Information Strategies (HMIS) Web Page <http://www.hud.gov/offices/cpd/homeless/hmis/>; for more information, *see* EPIC's Poverty and Privacy Web Page <http://www.epic.org/privacy/poverty/>.

[5831] *See, e.g.*, National Network to End Domestic Violence, An Advocate's Response to HUD's June 2005 "Domestic Violence Provider Participation in Homeless Management Information Systems (HMIS) Questions & Answers," available at <http://www.ncdsv.org/images/AdvocacyResponseHUD2005.pdf> (accessed August 3, 2005).

[5832] H.R. 2695, 109th Congress, Safe Housing Identification Exception for the Lives of Domestic Violence Victims, available at <http://thomas.loc.gov/cgi-bin/query/z?c109:H.R.2695:>.

Voting Privacy

The Twenty-Sixth Amendment to the United States Constitution grants the right to vote to citizens aged 18 years or older. Application of direct recording electronic (DRE)[5833] paperless voting technology in US public elections addresses some issues of voter privacy while potentially creating others. The greatest privacy benefits of DRE voting machines accrue to those who are visually disabled or have literacy challenges, or to language minorities. Critics of paperless DRE voting technology acknowledge the apparent usability benefits to some voters, but point to a critical vulnerability in their design.[5834] There are also charges that if the restricted space around DRE voting machines were too small this would threaten voter privacy.[5835] DRE voting technology has triggered strong debate between technologists,[5836] election administrators,[5837] voting rights activists, media, and NGOs.

Internet voting in the US is still in its infancy[5838] with only two states, Arizona[5839] and Michigan,[5840] who have attempted some level of public elections using this method. In 2004, the US military sought to undertake for the first time an all Internet voting process for military personal and civilians living abroad.[5841]

Voter registration lists are now the responsibility of state governments.[5842] The Help America Vote Act (HAVA)[5843] requires that voter registrants submit proof of identity by providing a state-issued identity document or the last four digits of

---

[5833] <http://www.epic.org/privacy/voting/crsreport.pdf>.

[5834] NCVI, Hearing Statement to the US Election Assistance Commission, "Use, Security, and Reliability of Electronic Voting Systems," May 5, 2004
<http://www.votingintegrity.org/Testimony/EAC_Hearing5_5_04.html>.

[5835] Annamarie Marcalus, "Mixed Reviews on Voting Electronically," Los Angeles Times, March 6, 2004, at 70, *available at*
<http://pqasb.pqarchiver.com/latimes/572449591.html?did=572449591&FMT=ABS&FMTS=FT&date=Mar+6%2C+2004&author=&desc=LETTERS+TO+THE+TIMES%3B+Mixed+Reviews+on+Voting+Electronically>.

[5836] NVCI Web site <http://www.votingintegrity.org>.

[5837] The National Association of Secretaries of State, Help America Vote Act Web Page
<http://www.nass.org/electioninfo/HAVApage.htm>.

[5838] Richard L. Hasen, "Symposium Internet Voting and Democracy" <http://llr.lls.edu/volumes/v34-issue3/hasenintro.pdf>.

[5839] Scott Thomsen, "Arizona Democrats Make History on Web," Associated Press, March 11, 2000.

[5840] Alexandra R. Moses, "Party Says Just over 46,000 People Voted Online in State Democratic Caucuses," Associated Press, February 7, 2004.

[5841] David Jefferson, Aviel D.Rubin, Barbara Simons, David Wagner, "A Security Analysis of the Secure Electronic Registration and Voting Experiment (SERVE)," available at <http://servesecurityreport.org/>.

[5842] National Committee for Voting Integrity, Web Page on Centralized Voter Registration Databases
<http://www.votingintegrity.org/Issues/CenteralizedData.html>.

[5843] The Help America Vote Act, Pub. L. No. 107-252, *available at* <http://www.fec.gov/hava/law_ext.txt>.

their Social Security number. HAVA also created the US Election Assistance Commission (EAC), which manages the federal government's role in voter registration.[5844] HAVA requires that states create a single statewide-centralized voter registration database that will be used as the official list of qualified voters who may vote in Federal elections. EAC is preparing voluntary guidelines for states to help them in the development of these voter registration systems. Registration forms may include requests for name, current and previous address, home and work telephone numbers, birthplace, social security number,[5845] birth date, race, gender, and party affiliation.[5846] This registration information is made available to the people who manage political campaigns who can use the information to solicit voters for support.[5847]

The Internet is making it much easier to engage in "free speech" in the form of monetary contributions to political causes and candidates.[5848] However, Congress can regulate the volume of this speech.[5849] Contribution of USD 200 or more will expose contributor's personally identifiable information to others.[5850] However, the cumbersome presentation of this personally identifiable information on the Federal Election Commission (FEC) Web page has been greatly enhanced[5851] with data mining technology.[5852] The Federal Election Commission Act of 1971, as amended in 1974, limits political contributions to candidates for federal elective office by individuals or groups.[5853]

The Freedom of Information Act (FOIA) was enacted in 1966 and has been amended several times.[5854] It allows for access to federal government records by any requestor, except those held by the courts or the White House. However,

---

[5844] Help America Vote Act of 2002, available at <http://www.fec.gov/hava/law_ext.txt>.

[5845] Carlos Sanchez, "VA Voters' Social Security Numbers Must Be Private, Appeals Court Rules," Washington Post, March 24, 1993, at C3.

[5846] Kim Zetter, "Mining the Vein of Voter Rolls," Wired News, December 11, 2003 <http://www.wired.com/news/print/0%2C1294%2C61507%2C00.html>.

[5847] Aristotle Industries, US Voter Lists, available at <http://www.aristotle.com/page.asp?page_id=voter_lists&t=67200410>.

[5848] Buckley v. Valeo, 424 U.S. 1, January 30, 1976, No. 75-436, available at <http://www.constitution.org/ussc/424-001.htm>.

[5849] Federal Election Commission Contributions <http://www.fec.gov/pages/brochures/contrib.htm>.

[5850] Federal Election Commission Rules for Contributions <http://herndon1.sdrdc.com/info.html>.

[5851] Leslie Walker, "Political Money, Tracked to Your Door," Washington Post, March 28, 2004, at F07, available at <http://www.washingtonpost.com/wp-dyn/articles/A28770-2004Mar27.html>.

[5852] Fundrace 2004 web site <http://www.fundrace.org/>.

[5853] US Code Title 2, Chapter 14, Subchapter I, Section 441a. – Limitations on contributions and expenditures, available at <http://www4.law.cornell.edu/uscode/2/441a.html>.

[5854] Freedom of Information Act, Pub. L. No. 104-231 (1966), codified at 5 § USC 552, available at <http://www.epic.org/open_gov/foia/us_foia_act.html>; see also Litigation under the Federal Open Government Laws (FOIA) 2004 (Harry A. Hammitt, David L. Sobel, Tiffany A. Stedman, eds., 2004).

there are numerous exceptions, long delays at many agencies, and little oversight unless a requestor files a lawsuit to enforce its rights. It was amended in 1996 by the Electronic Freedom of Information Act to specifically provide access to records in electronic form.[5855] Recently, the Congress enacted a "critical infrastructure information" (CII) exemption to the FOIA for the newly formed Department of Homeland Security. This exemption would shield information voluntarily provided to the government by private entities on security information from the FOIA.[5856] Once disclosed to the government, CII could not be used against the company in civil litigation, and government agents who disclose the information would be subject to criminal penalties and fines. Since the creation of this loophole for the DHS, other agencies have sought similar exemptions from the FOIA. There are also laws in all states on providing access to government records.[5857]

Republic of Uruguay

The Constitutional Framework

The Constitution does not explicitly regulate the right to privacy, however jurists and the national courts unanimously hold that the right to privacy has constitutional standing[5858] in Article 72 of the Constitution,[5859] which provides: "The enumeration of rights, duties, and protections established in the Constitution, does not exclude other rights which are inherent to the human personality or are derived from the republican form of government." This provision permits incorporation with Constitutional standing of any right that, while not explicitly recognized, is inherent to the human person.

[5855] Electronic Freedom of Information Act Amendments of 1996, *available at* <http://www.epic.org/open_gov/efoia.html>.

[5856] Testimony of David L. Sobel, EPIC General Counsel, before the House Committee on Energy and Commerce Subcommittee on Oversight and Investigations, Hearing on Creating the Department of Homeland Security: Consideration of the Administration's Proposal, July 9, 2002, available at <http://www.epic.org/security/infowar/07_02_testimony.html>.

[5857] *See* Tapping Officials' Secrets, Reporters Committee for Freedom of the Press, available at <http://www.reporterscommittee.org/tapping2001/index.cgi>.

[5858] Justino Jiménez de Aréchaga, La Constitución Nacional, Vol. I Fundación de Cultura Universitaria (Montevideo, at 232; José Korseniak, Derecho Constitucional, Vol. II Fundación de Cultura Universitaria (Montevideo), at 87; Martín Risso Ferrand, Derecho Constitucional, Vol. III Ingranusi Ltda. (Montevideo), at 130; Gonzalo Secco, "Bases de Datos y Protección de la Privacidad," VI Congreso Iberoamericano de Derecho e Informática (Montevideo, 1997), at 62.

[5859] Constitution of the Republic of Uruguay, available at <http://www.parlamento.gub.uy/htmlstat/pl/constituciones/const004.htm> (in Spanish).

Regarding the subject of inviolability of correspondence, Article 28[5860] protects individuals' documents and correspondence of any nature (letters, telegraphic or telephone communications) from all sorts of interception, unless those procedures are performed in compliance with applicable laws. When referring to telephone communications, some scholars have interpreted that such rules not only guarantee the inviolability of the content of the conversation, but also the inviolability of the records containing the list of calls made and received by a particular person.[5861]

If the Constitution does not explicitly recognize the right to privacy, obviously it also does not explicitly include *habeas data*. Before Law No. 17.838[5862] was enacted, constitutional scholars had suggested that the *habeas data* be incorporated in Article 72, since that article incorporates the essence of natural law, and hence protects and warrants the inherent rights of men, and the general principles of law derived from human dignity that the Constitution recognizes.[5863] The recent enactment of Law No. 17.838 explicitly incorporates *habeas data* to the Uruguayan legal framework.

Data Protection Framework

The Uruguayan Penal Code[5864] establishes several offences related to the violation of privacy. Article 296 of the Penal Code guarantees the privacy of correspondence, establishing that whoever opens an envelope containing a letter (that is not directed to that person) with the intent of learning about its content is guilty of a felony. Article 298 also punishes the disclosure of information obtained by any means similar to those referred to in Article 296. Article 297 punishes the interception of telephone or telegraphic communications.[5865]

[5860] *Id.* at Article 28: "Papers belonging to individuals, and their correspondence in the form of letters, cables, or any other medium are inviolable, and may be recorded, inspected, or intercepted only in conformity with the laws established for reasons of public interest."

[5861] Hector Gros Espiell, "El Art. 28 de la Constitución y las Comunicaciones Telefónicas," 86 Revista de Admnistración Pública No. 25 (Montevideo, 1999).

[5862] Law No. 17.838 (October 23, 2004), available at <http://www.parlamento.gub.uy/Leyes/Ley17838.htm> (in Spanish).

[5863] Carlos E. Delpiazzo, "Posibles Medios de Protección frente a las Responsabilidades Derivadas de la Gestión de Bases de Datos en el Derecho Uruguayo," 382 Congreso Internacional de Informática y Derecho (Buenos Aires, 1990); Alberto Ramón Real, "Estado de Derecho y Humanismo Personalista," 5 (F.C.U., Montevideo, 1974); Héctor Gros Espiell, "La Dignidad Humana en los Instrumentos Internacionales de Derechos Humanos," 9 Catedra UNESCO de Derechos Humanos (Universidad de la República, Montevideo, 2003); José Aníbal Cagnoni, "La Dignidad Humana. Naturaleza y Alcances," 11 Rev. de Derecho Público (2003, No. 23).

[5864] Penal Code of the Republic of Uruguay, available at <http://www.jasesora.gub.uy/documentos/respuesta/codigo/codigo.doc> (in Spanish).

[5865] *Id.*

Moreover, Articles 300 and 301 increase the maximum penalty when said "information was known by means of fraud and the document was supposed to remain secret by reason of its content or nature." The law also punishes a person who reveals confidential information that has been learned through his job. This provision establishes the obligation to respect professional secrecy. Article 333 of the Penal Code provides the penalty of up to three years' imprisonment for the defamation or slander of any person who can be subject to public scorn. Article 334 provides punishment to any person who by means of speech, gestures, writings, or actions offends the honour of another.

At various times the courts have reviewed disputes in which the right to information conflicts with the right of honor. The courts generally analyze the case and determine: whether the information disseminated concerns events of public interest; whether the description is objective and in accordance with reality; whether it is not aggravating; whether the purpose of providing the information was excessive; or whether the information was published when it was not necessary.[5866]

The Uruguayan Tax Code[5867] and Banking Law No. 15.322,[5868] also regulate privacy and confidentiality in their respective areas. Article 68[5869] of the Tax Code authorizes the Government to require taxpayers and parties in positions of responsibility to produce business records, documents, and correspondence. This documentation is not protected by professional confidentiality, since the taxpayer himself is obligated to produce it. "Business records" are understood to mean the journal and the inventory of assets and liabilities.

The Banking Law establishes the obligation to protect the confidentiality of funds or securities in the checking accounts, deposit accounts, or other accounts belonging to a specific individual or legal entity, and any confidential information received by the bank from its clients. There is some doctrinal discussion about whether secrecy is limited to operations that create liabilities, or also includes operations that create assets. While the financial system has always

---

[5866] *See* Judgment No. 13 from the Civil Court of Appeals, Term 3 from February 27, 1999 of the Civil Court of Appeals, Third Session.

[5867] Tax Code approved by Decree Law No. 14.306, available at <http://www.parlamento.gub.uy/htmlstat/pl/codigos/CodigoTributario/1997/cod_tributario-indice.htm> (in Spanish).

[5868] Decree Law No. 15.322 (September 23, 1982), available at <http://www.parlamento.gub.uy/Leyes/Ley15322.htm> (in Spanish).

[5869] Tax Code, Article 68 "Powers of the Government": "The Government shall have full powers of investigation and inspection. In particular, the Government may require taxpayers and persons in positions of responsibility to produce their own and outside business records, documents, and correspondence, and may require them to appear before the government agency in order to provide information."

been opposed to the expansion of banking secrecy to include asset operations, in practice both types of transactions have always been kept secret.

Act 16.713[5870] protects the confidentiality of employment history and other labor records. The employment history includes information about the length of employment, the benefits and contributions paid by each company reported, and the outcome of inspections. The employee can ask for the correction of inexact information. While there are no regulations that protect information in the contractual stage, some writers have contended that it is unlawful to request information about criminal convictions or data about family status, political beliefs, religious beliefs, or union affiliations.[5871]

Law No. 16.616,[5872] enacted on October 20, 1994, regulates the national statistical system. It establishes that the individual information obtained must be treated with the utmost confidentiality, and that a link should exist between the data requested and the objectives of the statistics or census.[5873]

Finally, Law No. 16.011, which regulates the writ of relief, offers a procedural base to articulate the *habeas data*.[5874] In October 2004, the Parliament approved Law No. 17.838 on the Protection of Personal Data,[5875] also called the DBA. The Law regulates data banks containing commercial information[5876] and establishes the institution of *habeas data*.[5877]

In Uruguay, an individual's access to credit is determined by his credit information. Being aware of this fact, the legislators regulated the handling of

---

[5870] Law No. 16.713 (September 11, 1995), available at
<http://www.parlamento.gub.uy/Leyes/Ley16713.htm> (in Spanish).

[5871] *See* Américo Pla Rodríguez, "Control de Supervisión Tecnológica del Trabajo y Privacidad del Trabajador" in Derecho Informático, Vol. III (Fundación de Cultura Universitaria, Montevideo).

[5872] Law No. 16.616 (October 31, 1994), available at <http://www.parlamento.gub.uy/Leyes/ley16616.htm> (in Spanish).

[5873] Marcelo Bauza, Computer and Personal Data in Uruguay, Derecho Informático, Instituto de Derecho Informático (Fundación de Cultura Universitaria, Montevideo 2004).

[5874] Law 16.011 (December 1, 1988), available at <http://www.parlamento.gub.uy/palacio3/index.htm> (in Spanish).

[5875] Ley de Protección de Datos Personales para Ser Utilizados en Informes Comerciales y Acción de Habeas Data, available at <http://www.clearing.com.uy/clearing/Ley17838.pdf>.

[5876] Report prepared by the Instituto de Derecho Informático and sent to the Dean of the University of the Republic on August 6, 2003, with respect to the bill. It notes: "The bill concerns not all personal data but only 'business' data, and it has two primary objectives: One pertains to protection of personal data for business reporting purposes, and the other regulates the right to information by means of the institution of the Habeas Data action," in Derecho Informático, Vol. IV Fundación de Cultura Universitaria, at 427.

[5877] Initially the bill regulated the processing of any and all personal information, but enough support for this bill could not be mustered. When Senators Alberto Brause and Luis Alberto Heber limited the scope of the bill to personal credit data, the bill passed.

credit information with the intention of facilitating access to credit by establishing clear norms in this area.[5878] In Uruguay commercial reports are a very sensitive issue, considering the small population of the country (approximately 3,000,000 inhabitants). A single bad credit report takes a person out of the formal market for credit. Even though the law only regulates credit reports, its Section II regulates *habeas data* action in such a way as to enable a petitioner to access any information related to him and, if his information is erroneous, inaccurate or discriminatory, enables him to ask for its suppression or rectification. The law also innovates by establishing a data protection authority, which functions under the Ministry of Economy.

The DBA regulates "the recording, storage, distribution, transmission, modification, deletion, and in general, the processing of personal data contained in archives, registers, databases, and other media, whether public or private, designed to provide business reports." This means that any and every method of recording data about individuals or legal entities that are stored for the purpose of providing objective business information is regulated. While the law is vague, parliamentary history allows us to determine the meaning of "objective business information": any information that facilitates evaluation of the ability of individuals to meet their payment obligations.[5879] Possibly this is limited to credit data covering information about operations that create both liabilities and assets.[5880]

In principle, the law provides that individuals who possess data are the owners of the data, and their consent is therefore required for the inclusion of the data in data banks. However, various exceptions establish that certain types of data may be entered without their holder's consent, including, for example, data from public information sources, data collected for the performance of legal assignments or functions, and personal credit data, including data used by companies to meet their own needs.

[5878] *See* Marcelo Bauza, "Iniciativas para la Protección de los Datos Personales de Carácter Comercial," in Derecho Informático, Vol. IV, Fundación de Cultura Universitaria, at 294.

[5879] The Report on the bill sent to the Senate states: "This purpose of protection of personal business data contributes to the goal of ensuring greater transparency of the economy and of parties that grant and receive credit. It is an essential lever and tool for achieving genuine development." In its outline of the grounds for the law, the Report notes that: "Legislation with respect to the objectivity, transparency, and quality of information thus equates with facilitating and democratizing access to credit. The principal purpose is a public-policy purpose, since it promotes protection of the right to private life, transparency of the credit market, and protection of credit, and it facilitates their development by reducing their cost thanks to lower interest rates and indirect contribution to the fight against usury."

[5880] It is clear that the legislator intended to regulate only the processing of data that permits evaluation of an individual's economic solvency. However, the provision concerning data that makes it possible "to furnish objective business information" allows a broader interpretation that could be used by the courts.

The data controller is responsible for ensuring that the data collected is true, appropriate, and impartial. Also, the data entered must not be excessive in view of the purpose for which it was collected and the scope of the consent given by the holder of the data.

The legislation establishes the "right to oblivion" (*derecho al olvido*) insofar as credit data entries must be deleted five years from their recording. If at the end of this period the obligation to the creditor has not been extinguished, the creditor may apply for maintenance of the record for an additional five years.

The DBA also provides that any individual may request access to any information pertaining to him that exists in any data bank, as well as the right to correct erroneous information. Individuals or companies may submit a request for information. If the information is not provided within 20 business days, or its delivery is refused for an unjustifiable reason, the applicant has the right to commence an action for *habeas data*. Deletion is permitted only if the error or the inaccuracy is obvious, or may cause damage to other individuals. The information must then be reviewed and, if appropriate, corrected within 20 business days from the filing of the request for correction. During this period, an entry must be made in the data bank to show that this information is being reviewed. If by the end of the 20-day period the information has not been corrected or deleted, the applicant has the option of starting an action of *habeas data*. Such action is aimed at persuading the court to order access to, or correction of, the information. Such an action can therefore be commenced in two cases: a) when the information has not been provided within the required period; or b) when the errors have not been corrected.

The DBA established that an action for *habeas data* must be treated in the same way as the action for protection of constitutional rights.[5881] The judge must schedule a public hearing within three days after commencing a *habeas data* action.[5882] The DBA designated the Ministry of Economy and Finance as the authority in charge of monitoring compliance with the law.[5883] The Ministry may

---

[5881] Law No. 16011 (December 19, 1988), available at <http://www.parlamento.gub.uy/Leyes/Ley16011.htm>. This law provides that any individual may bring an action for protection of constitutional rights against any act, omission, or deed by the national authorities or by individuals that is manifestly unlawful and which prejudices, or is capable of prejudicing, any of the rights and freedoms implicitly or explicitly established by the laws and regulations.

[5882] The judge may decide not to schedule a public hearing only if the action commenced is manifestly improper.

[5883] To advise the Ministry, a seven-member Consulting Committee was established, with three members representing the Ministry of Economy and Finance (one of whom will serve as Chairperson of the Committee); two representatives of the Ministry of Education and Culture; one representative from the National Chamber of Commerce and Services; and, lastly, one representative from the Business Defence League.

punish violating companies by issuing warnings or assessing fines, or even shutting down the data bank.

Regulations

Decree No. 385/999 approved the adoption of an electronic personnel file for employees of the National Government. This file contains information about the career of each government employee and may include information about the sanctions applied in the performance of his duties. This regulation provides that the files will be available through the website of the National Civil Service Office. This Office is responsible for protecting and maintaining the confidentiality of this information.

Decree No. 396/003 regulates the processing of personal data in public and private healthcare sectors.[5884] This decree provides that all clinical histories should only be used for healthcare; the patient's history should include clear information about the diagnosed or found illnesses and subsequent treatment; that personal data are confidential;, and that patients must have access to their data, not only for correction purposes, but also for other purposes, such as for consulting another doctor for a second opinion, changing healthcare provider, or verifying if malpractice has occurred.

Open Government

Article 694 of Law No. 16.736 establishes the freedom of information at the governmental level and establishes the petitioner's right to amend or rectify erroneous or inaccurate information.[5885]

International Obligations

Uruguay is a signatory of the 1948 Universal Declaration of Human Rights, the 1966 International Covenant on Civil and Political Rights,[5886] and the American

---

[5884] Decree No. 396/003 (September 20, 2003), available at
<http://www.presidencia.gub.uy/decret/2003decret.htm> (in Spanish).

[5885] *See* Carlos E. Delpiazzo, "Automatización de la Actividad Administrativa en el Marco de la Reforma del Estado," 17 Anuario de Derecho Administrativo; *also in* "El Procedimiento Administrativo Electrónico y el Acto Administrativo Automático," 39 A.A.V.V. – "Recopilación de Conferencias y Exposiciones Realizadas" (UTE, Montevideo, 1999); "Marco Legal de la Automatización de la Actividad Administrativa. El Expediente Electrónico en Uruguay," 699 Informática y Derecho (Mérida, 1998); "Enfoque Jurídico de la Automatización de la Actividad Administrativa," 81 Rev. Informática y Derecho (Buenos Aires, 2002).

Convention on Human Rights, which recognizes the right of a person to not be subjected to arbitrary or unlawful interference with his privacy, home or correspondence, nor to unlawful attacks to his honor and reputation.[5887]

Bolivarian Republic of Venezuela

Constitutional Privacy Framework

The Constitution of Venezuela has been written in a manner designed to protect human rights.[5888] The interest of the people guides the constitutional text, in which, according to Articles 28[5889] and 48,[5890] every person has the right to access and manage information on himself, contained in official or private records; to request to the competent court for the update, correction or destruction of any records that are erroneous or unlawfully affect the petitioner's right; and to ensure the secrecy and inviolability of his private communications, regardless of their forms. The Venezuelan legal framework, however, presents inconsistencies with respect to the inclusion of these concepts in other legal instruments. One of these is the Postal Law, in force since 1928, which does not contemplate the inviolability and confidential character of private correspondence.

Articles 60[5891] and 143[5892] of the Constitution refer specifically to data processing and privacy in electronic communications. Every person has the right to know

---

[5886] Signed February 21, 1967; ratified by Law No. 13.751.

[5887] Law No.13751 and Law No. 15.737 (March 8, 1985), available at <http://www.parlamento.gub.uy/palacio3/index.htm> (in Spanish).

[5888] The English version of the Venezuelan Constitution is available at <http://www.vheadline.com/readnews.asp?id=6831>.

[5889] Article 28: "Anyone has the right of access to the information and data concerning him or her or his or her goods which are contained in official or private records, with such exceptions as may be established by law, as well as what use is being made of the same and the purpose thereof, and to petition the court of competent competence for the updating, correction or destruction of any records that are erroneous or unlawfully 'affect the petitioner's right. He or she may, as well, access documents of any nature containing information of interest to communities or group of persons. The foregoing is without prejudice to the confidentiality of sources from which journalist receives information, or law may determine secrecy in other professions."

[5890] Article 48: "The secrecy and inviolability of private communications in all forms are guaranteed. The same may not be interfered with except by order of a competent court, with observance of applicable provisions of law and preserving the secrecy of the private issues unrelated to the pertinent proceedings."

[5891] Article 60: "Every person is entitled to protection of his or her honor, private life, intimacy, self-image, confidentiality and reputation. Law shall restrict the use of electronic information in order to guarantee the personal and family intimacy and honor of citizens and the full exercise of their rights."

[5892] Article 143: "Citizens have the right to be informed by Public Administration, in a timely and truthful manner, of the status of proceedings in which they have a direct interest, and to be apprised of any final decisions adopted in the matter. Likewise, they have access to administrative files and records, without prejudice to the limits acceptable in a democratic society in matters relating to internal and external security, the status of procedures in which he has a direct interest, as long as this does not violates national security or interferes with ongoing law enforcement investigations. Article 60 establishes that every person has the right to his or her honor, private life, intimacy, self-image, confidentiality and reputation.

The Constitution sets out the freedom of expression as a human right, inalienable, free and plural, and without any type of censorship. It also includes a special provision to allow and promote access to means of communication by children and adolescents (Articles 57 and 58). These articles prohibit anonymity, war propaganda messages, as well as those that show religious intolerance. The right to information persists even during "states of exception," during which the right of citizens to "true, opportune and impartial information without censorship" will not be suspended.[5893]

The Constitution also integrates knowledge, communication and creation within the concept of Cultural and Educational Rights (Articles 98, 101, 110 and 124)[5894] in which it considers Internet databases and public libraries to belong to the public interest. The Internet is considered a public service. These articles also reflect an interest in building a legal framework to protect indigenous languages and traditions (*e.g.*, the registration of patents or copyrights concerning indigenous patrimony is prohibited), as well as other folkloric values, authorship and scientific and technological innovations. In the same way, the norms set forth in the Law on Social Responsibility for Radio and TV (the implementation of a section of Article 110) promote the necessity to protect Venezuelan values above foreign values in the programming of mass communications, as well as implement measures ensuring that persons with hearing disabilities will be able to enjoy programming.

---

criminal, investigation and the intimacy of private life, in accordance with law regulating the matter of classification of documents with contents, which are confidential or secret. No censorship of public officials reporting on matters for which they are responsible shall be permitted."

[5893] Article 337: "The President of the Republic, at a meeting of the Cabinet of Ministers, shall have the power to decree states of exception. Expressly defined as such are circumstances of a social, economic, political, natural or ecological nature, which seriously affect the security of the Nation, institutions and citizens, in the face of which the powers available to cope with such events are insufficient. In such case, the guarantees contained in this Constitution may be temporarily restricted, with the exception of those relating to the right to life, prohibition of incommunicative detention or torture, the right to due process, the right to information and other intangible human rights."

[5894] Articles 98, 101, 110 and 124 of the Venezuelan Constitution, available at
<http://www.vheadline.com/readnews.asp?id=6831>.

Freedom of Expression and Mass Communications

One of the most extensive discussions in Venezuelan public opinion has been the consideration, passing and implementation of the Social Responsibility for Radio and TV Law (RESORTE).[5895] In general, this Law establishes protected time slots and programming content containing social responsibility. It also regulates advertising and provides for multiple penalties in case of non-compliance on the part of radio, network and cable television providers.

In spite of the justification of this law as being for the protection of the population, especially concerning the prevention of exposure of children and adolescents to "inappropriate" information, the Interamerican Press Society (*Sociedad Interamericana de Prensa*, or SIP),[5896] Human Rights Watch[5897] and Reporters without Borders[5898] have expressed their concerns about the prior censorship and informational restrictions the RESORTE establishes. The principal elements of the law that the public was sensitive about are the multiple categorizations of content relating to health, sex and violence (Article 6). These categories include the definition of protected time slots, during which the type of information broadcast is restricted.[5899] The concession of space for cultural and educational messages is mandatory, while at the same time war propaganda, incitement to the alteration of the public order or to crime, are prohibited.

RESORTE establishes the creation of a Board of Social Responsibility with 11 members: a General Director of the National Commission of Telecommunications; the ministry or organization that is empowered to direct communications and information; the ministry or organization in charge of education and sports; the National Women's Institute; the National Council on the Rights of Children and Adolescents; a representative of the churches; two representatives of consumers' organizations registered with the National Telecommunications Commission; and an educator representing the Colleges of

---

[5895] Referred to as the "Gag Law" by the opposition parties. See <http://www.cpsr-peru.org/bdatos/venezuela/expresion/> (in Spanish).

[5896] Duro cuestionamiento de la SIP a la Ley de Contenidos de Venezuela, available at <http://www.urru.org/papers/DDHH/LibertadExpresion/20041207_SIP.htm> (in Spanish).

[5897] Humans Rights Watch, Ley de medios coarta libertad de expresión, available at <http://hrw.org/spanish/press/2004/venezuela_ley_de_medios.html> (in Spanish).

[5898] Reporteros sin Fronteras denuncia la aprobación de una ley peligrosa para la libertad de prensa, available at <http://www.rsf.org/article.php3?id_article=11953> (in Spanish).

[5899] For example, between 7 o'clock in the morning and 7 o'clock in the evening, the live transmission of news that might contain elements of violence, health and sex not considered in agreement with the time slot (Article 7), is prohibited, a requirement that service providers have considered beyond their control, and promoting self-censorship.

Social Communication of the National Universities. This action has also been criticized by the opposition and journalism organizations, because it gives too many seats to participants in public (current government) power. This council has decision-making power over concessions, penalties, technical standards and other related aspects.

Statutory Rules Related to Privacy

The main laws that regulate telecommunications, data and privacy are: the Organic Law for Telecommunications; Data Message and Electronic Signature Law; Special Law against Information Crimes; Social Responsibility in Radio and Television Law; and Public Function and Statistics Law, which regulates the national statistics system. In the justification for the Proposal for the Organic Law on the Use of Information Technologies in the State, other laws of particular interest are also mentioned, such as the Public Administration Law, the Financial Administration Law, the Organic Tax Code and the Organic Penal Process Code.

The discussion on the first draft of the project of Law for the Protection of Data and Habeas Data (LPDHD) has stopped. This project intended to guarantee and protect personal data stored in archives, registries, data banks and other data information systems, public or private, and provided data subjects with access, correction and deletion rights.[5900]

In the last few years, the highly polarized political climate in Venezuela has brought about a wide public debate about the relevance and nature of the laws related to electronic media and data protection. In addition to these issues, the Social Responsibility for Radio and TV Law (RESORTE), the Banking Law and the LPDHD have been at the center of these discussions.

The principal objective of the Organic Telecommunications Law, according to its Article 25901, is based upon the defense of previously expressed constitutional principles, which define the right to communication and information, as well as privacy and personal honor, as human rights]. In the same spirit, the Organic Telecommunications Law (LOT) also promotes the implementation of community media. Among other aspects, a third large area of interest of the LOT is the inviolability of personal communications. With respect to service providers, the LOT has created an organization responsible for generating

---

5900 See <http://www.cpsr-peru.org/bdatos/venezuela/privacidad/> (in Spanish)

5901 See <http://www.conatel.gov.ve> (in Spanish).

mechanisms for the protection of consumers and users of services, called the National Commission of Telecommunication. This organization also regulates compliance with the Universal Service Standards, measures adopted in the public interest and for the protection of personal data.[5902]

Decree 1204, the Data Message and Electronic Signature Law[5903] (LSMDFE), is the instrument that recognizes the legal validity of signatures and electronic messages.[5904] Although the mechanism has not yet been implemented, two cases[5905] that refer to this law to validate constitutional protection requested via electronic mail have already been presented to the Supreme Court. The Supreme Court made a progressive interpretation of the Organic Law of Constitutional Protection.[5906] It admitted that, based upon the LSMDFE, telegraphic media, electronic mail and the Internet were media of equal probative value.

Decree 3335, which partially reforms the LSMDFE with the goal of regulating the accreditation of electronic certification service providers,[5907] entered into force on December 14, 2004. The LSMDFE also recognizes foreign electronic certificates.[5908]

[5902] Organic Telecommunications Law, Articles 20 and 50.

[5903] See <http://portal.cnti.ve/cnti_docmgr/sharedfiles/LeyMensajesDatosFirmasElectronica.pdf> (in Spanish).

[5904] Article 8: "Cuando la ley requiera que la información conste por escrito, ese requisito quedará satisfecho con relación a un Mensaje de Datos, si la información que éste contiene es accesible para su ulterior consulta." ("When the law requires that the information be in writing, this requirement will be satisfied by a data message, if the information it contains is accessible for future consultation.")

[5905] The first one is dated July 9, 2000 (<http://www.tsj.gov.ve/decisiones/scon/Abril/523-090401-00-2317%20.htm>); and the second one August 18, 2003 (Boletín Especial TPA: "Competencias del Poder Público," agosto de 2003).

[5906] Article 16: "La acción de amparo es gratuita por excelencia. Para su tramitación no se empleará papel sellado ni estampillas y en caso de urgencia podrá interponerse por vía telegráfica. De ser así, deberá ser ratificada personalmente o mediante apoderado dentro de los tres (3) días siguientes. También procede su ejercicio en forma verbal y, en tal caso, el Juez deberá recogerla en un acta" ("The action of protection is free by definition. Its processing will not require sealed stationary nor tax stamps and, in case of urgency, the intervention may be made by telegraph. In this case, it must be ratified personally or by power of attorney within the following three days. It may also proceed in oral form and, in such a case, the judge should formalize it in an Act").

[5907] José Ovidio Salgueiro A., "Ley sobre Mensajes de Datos y Firmas Electrónicas," February 26, 2005, available at <http://www.cavecome.org.ve/bin_cavecome/main/templates/seccion.asp?tipo=&seccID=4&nivel=2&codigo=109> (in Spanish).

[5908] For an electronic document to be valid, it must fulfill some requirements, according to José Ovidio Salgueiro: "a data message which presents all of the elements of the identification requirement, which is to say, one which has an electronic signature which has generated an electronic certificate that has been provided by a service provider certified and accredited by the Superintendent of Electronic Certification Services (acronym in Spanish SUSCERTE), is one which will have the same validity and probative effectiveness that the law grants to documents signed in autograph form." *Id.*

The Special Law against Information Crimes[5909] regulates crimes against information systems, economic property and patrimony, personal privacy and communications, without including spam. Illegal access to systems, interference, signal interception, unauthorized use, sabotage and damage to systems and data, as well as the creation and introduction of viruses are also considered crimes (Article 8). The law considers as crimes: spying, falsification of documents, fraud and unauthorized use of credit cards, etc. It also covers the violation of personal data and information privacy, whether through damage or the unauthorized destruction of another's data in a computer system. The violation of communication privacy is defined as the access, capture, interception, interference, reproduction, modification, detour or elimination of any data message or transmission signal, or third party's communication, as well as the inappropriate disclosure of personal information. Chapter IV deals with crimes against children and adolescents by criminalizing the publication and diffusion of pornography. The law, however, does not regulate "snuff films"[5910] and does not consider them as sexual practices that degrade and violate a woman's honor (Article 77 of the Constitution; the Law on Violence against Women and Family).

Voting Privacy

The Organic Law on Suffrage and Political Participation was enacted on December 13, 1997.[5911] This law introduced two sweeping changes in the way elections are administered.[5912] First, it calls for the use of electronic voting machines to automate the upcoming elections.[5913] Second, the law curbs the

---

[5909] Available at <http://www.alfa-redi.org>.

[5910] A "snuff film" is a video, sometimes pornographic, that allegedly depicts actual murder, produced for entertainment purposes.

[5911] Available at <http://www.cne.gov.ve/documentos/leyorg.php>.

[5912] Voting is mandatory in Venezuela. Citizens are automatically enrolled in the voter registry (*Registro Electoral*) upon obtaining the official identification card (*cédula de identidad*). The identity card is the only form of identification accepted at polling stations. Without it, a citizen is not allowed to vote. In addition, if a person's name does not appear in the voting center's list of registered voters (*cuaderno de votación*), he will be barred from voting.

[5913] There have been seven elections totally automated and managed by *Indra Systems*, a Spanish firm with extensive experience in Europe and, since 2004, by *Smartmatic*, founded by Venezuelan engineers, under a bid approved by the National Electoral Council (*Consejo Nacional Electoral*, or CNE). The first experience in Venezuela with *Indra* was in the 1998 presidential election when Hugo Chavez won. *Smartmatic* operated the 2004 e-voting election for the presidential revocatory referendum. *See* <http://www.iri.org/pdfs/Venezuelas_LR_Elections_Nov98.rtf>. Principal CNE member, Ezequiel Zamora, declared: "I thought a process as simple as a referendum should be done manually. An untried system is always going to create doubt.".Alexandra Olson "Doubts over Touchscreen Tech Choice for Venezuela Recall," USA Today, July 12, 2004.

---

influence of political parties on the country's electoral institutions.[5914] This law also creates an Electoral Registry. The institution responsible for the compilation of the voter registry is the Electoral Registry Office (*Oficina del Registro Electoral*, or ORE) of the National Electoral Council (*Consejo Nacional Electoral*, or CNE).[5915] For the opposition party, the electoral registry has been at the center of discussions about the accuracy of its information. Another criticism is that the data could be used with different purposes than established by the law, thereby violating the principle of voting secrecy[5916].

In August 2004 and in the following months, the registry of petition signers for the revocatory referendum (*revocatoria del mandato presidencial*, or RPP)[5917] was made available to the public on the Web site of a well-known Member of Parliament belonging to the government party (www.luistascon.com), with the objective that followers of President Chavez could verify whether they had been fraudulently included in that list. For the opposition, this meant that the data of the individuals who signed the petition of the RPP was exposed, with the purpose of mounting a witch hunt against the opposition. This sparked a wide public opinion debate on the loss of voting privacy, which reached a climax with the collection of fingerprints.[5918] To date, the opposition continues to insist on the necessity of reviewing the accuracy of the information of the Electoral Registry, but to no avail.

In August 15, 2004, during the procedure of the RPP, voters were required to present their fingerprints and ID card before being allowed to vote. As a result, it was easy to know if the person voting had or not signed the request of RPP in November 2003 by comparing his ID card with the list of signers.[5919]

The use of electronic voting machines is announced for future elections. These machines would replace the physical notebooks that until now have been used

---

[5914] International Republican Institute, "Venezuela, Legislative and Regional Elections: Assessment Report," November 23, 1998, available at <http://www.iri.org/pdfs/Venezuelas_LR_Elections_Nov98.rtf>.

[5915] The Electoral Registry Office coordinates the compilation of the registry of voters with the National Identification and Immigration Office, the Central Office for Statistics and Data information, Mayors' Offices, Prefectures, State Government Offices, Consulates, the Ministry of Justice, The Ministry of Education, and the Armed Forces (Article 88, Suffrage and Political Participation Law).

[5916] "Fraude a la Democracia. Caso Venezuela" Parts V and VI.

[5917] The revocatory referendum is a right established in Article 72 of the Constitution of Venezuela of 1999 according to which the citizen has the power, by means of voting, to revoke all the positions obtained by popular election. In August 2004, citizens of Venezuela, who live inside and outside the territory, evaluated the management of President Hugo Chávez Frías through a revocatory referendum. *See* Consejo Nacional Electoral, "Boletin electoral: Referendum del 15 de agosto de 2004," September 3, 2004, available at <http://www.cne.gov.ve/referendum_presidencial2004/> (in Spanish).

[5918] Available at <http://www.analitica.com/va/sintesis/nacionales/3860532.asp>.

[5919] See <http://www.sumate.org/democracia-retroceso/eleccionCNEconfiable.asp> (in Spanish).

and that register voters' signature and fingerprints after their vote. These electronic machines do not guarantee the voting secrecy that the Constitution protects,[5920] because the information they collect – the sequence and time of the vote – can be matched with the information contained in voting machines and therefore link votes with voters' identity.[5921]

Regulation of Identification Systems

For the *Coordinadora Democrática*, as well as for *Súmate*, the Electoral Registry is the main source of irregularities in the electoral process, some of which are exemplified by the several inaccuracies that cripple its database, *e.g.*, the number of voters higher than the number of inhabitants in certain regions of the country.[5922] Some governmental initiatives tend to more strongly integrate the electoral and civil registries. For example, on February 2005, the CNE, the Commission of Civil and Electoral Registry (*Comisión del Registro Civil y Electoral*), and the Ministry of Interior and Justice agreed to work together towards the implementation of a system of identification of citizens and on an electoral registry system. The objective is to integrate both the Civil Registry (*Registro Civil*) and the Electoral Registry Database.[5923]

In early 2005, Cuba and Venezuela reached an agreement to improve the Venezuelan identification system in compliance with the Organic Law on Identification. The law aims at using biometric technology to ensure an efficient system of identification by consolidating the digitization and updating of data, as well as by issuing an identification card with a digital fingerprint.[5924]

[5920] Article 63 of the Constitution establishes that the suffrage is a right and that it will be exerted by means of free, universal, direct and secret voting.

[5921] *Súmate*, "The secrete of vote is in danger," available at <http://www.sumate.org/DECIDE.swf> (in Spanish)

[5922] "Fraude a la Democracia. Caso Venezuela" Parts V and VI.

[5923] Consejo Nacional Electoral, "Consejo Nacional Electoral y el Ministerio del Interior y Justicia anunciaron la elaboración de un sistema de identificación y registro de los ciudadanos," February 28, 2005, available at <http://www.cne.gov.ve/noticiaDetallada.php?id=3323> (in Spanish).

[5924] J. Raymond, "Criminalística: ¿Bondades de los sistemas de identificación Cubanos en Venezuela?," March 3, 2005, available at <http://www.tecnoiuris.com/modules.php?name=News&file=article&sid=1074> (in Spanish); see also Delia Da Silva, "Acertadas propuestas de Jesse Chacón en materia de identificación," March 4, 2005, available at <http://www.mij.gov.ve/minpis/Edicion?accion=VerNoticia&idnoticia=855> (in Spanish).

Financial and Credit Information

In November 2001, Decree 1526 of the General Law for Banks and Other Financial Institutions (LGBOIF) was enacted.[5925] The law urges that the security of information systems be maintained in order to reduce or eradicate financial crimes, which affect public deposits, as well as develop better services for their customers in dealing with bank transactions. According to the LGBOIF, other organizations, such as the Ombudsman, the Attorney General, and the Institute for Consumer Defense and Education, should be familiar with depositors' complaints. In September 2004, the Ombudsman requested the annulment of Article 192 of the LGBOIF, stating that it was unconstitutional. In the Ombudsman's opinion, the processing of the personal data contained in the Central Risk Information System (SICRI) allegedly "harms the constitutional rights and the collective and extended (*difusos*) rights of citizens registered in SICRI."[5926]

Private Sector Initiatives

The Venezuelan Chamber of Electronic Commerce (Cavecom-e) and the Chamber of Telecommunications Service Companies (CASETEL) have jointly developed an initiative (Policies for the Proper use of Networks) to research and generate a set of best practices to foster the proper use of networks.[5927] The main objectives of these policies, which were published in October 2003, are to train users in the proper use of networks, identify practical and secure solutions to address the problems of intrusive mass mailings, and try to prevent attacks on networks. The policies consider spam (unsolicited commercial e-mails), malware (adware, spyware, viruses, Trojans), network attacks, and unsolicited opening of ports, open relays or proxies, to be "bad practices."

NGO Advocacy Work

The non-governmental organization (NGO) sector has also participated in identifying problems of access to information, freedom of expression, censorship, voting secrecy and the right to electoral participation. An accusation of

---

[5925] See <http://www.bcv.org.ve/blanksite/c3/leybancos.pdf> (in Spanish).

[5926] Ombudsman, "Defensoría del Pueblo solicitó nulidad del artículo 192 de la Ley General de Bancos y Otras Instituciones Financieras," September, 19, 2004, available at <http://www.defensoria.gov.ve/detalle.asp?sec=200808&id=462&plantilla=1&txt=192> (in Spanish).

[5927] See <http://www.cavecom-e.org.ve/common/noticia/Pol%EDticasdelBuenUsodelasRedes.doc> (in Spanish).

conspiracy and treason was launched against the *Asociación Civil Súmate*[5928] and its directors.

The NGO Venezuelan Education Action Program (PROVEA) has received complaints from more than 70 journalists for acts of aggression and from 60 for censorship, among cases related to the violation of freedom of expression in Venezuela. PROVEA was concerned that the RESORTE Law, which had not yet been published at the time of publication of PROVEA's 2004 report, could be an instrument of censorship.[5929]

Another NGO, Transparency Venezuela (TV), when the Electoral Report[5930] was presented by Venezuela to the Interamerican Convention against Corruption (CICC) in March 2004, declared that it had been difficult to access information that concerned them. However, information should be public for two reasons: 1) state organizations have not assimilated the citizen's right to access information which concerns them, pursuant to the Constitution of 1999, and 2) information systems are outdated and inefficient. Transparency Venezuela sees this situation reflected even in the official report presented before the Committee of Experts of the CICC since the report, lacks data, quantifying studies and statistics, which impede the effective statement of accounts, and a proper factual evaluation in order to reach satisfactory conclusions. They conclude that, as long as the Judicial Branch, the Attorney General's Office (*Ministerio Público*), the Ombudsman and the Public Controller's Office cannot rely on precise statistical data, improvements in the transparency of the administration that affect the country are not likely.

International Obligations

Venezuela ratified the 1948 Universal Declaration of Human Rights,[5931] the 1966 International Covenant on Civil and Political Rights, and the American

---

[5928] *Súmate* is an organization that monitors elections. It launched a campaign called "Voting Secrecy Is in Danger" and coordinated the petition for the presidential recall referendum in 2003 and 2004. The accusation against this NGO states that they received funds from international organizations and used these funds to conspire against the State. According to the *Súmate* Web page, neither the Venezuelan Constitution, nor any of its laws, prohibit the financing of NGOs by international organizations.

[5929] PROVEA, "Situación de los derechos humanos en Venezuela," September 2003-October 2004, at 425-449, available at <http://www.derechos.org.ve>.

[5930] Transparencia Venezuela, "Comentarios con ocasión al Informe presentado por Venezuela a la Convención Interamericana contra la Corrupción en marzo del 2004," July 2004, available at <http://www.miradordemocratico.org.ve/admin/multimedia/imagenes/20041217103003.pdf>.

[5931] United Nations, Universal Declaration of Human Rights, Brief History and Member Nations, available at <http://www.humanrightsandtolerance.org/udhr-members.html>.

Convention on Human Rights on June 23, 1977.[5932] The Convention provides that every person has "the right to have his honor respected and his dignity recognized." Additionally, "no one may be the object of arbitrary or abusive interference with his private life, his family, his home, or his correspondence, or of unlawful attacks on his honor or reputation. And everyone has the right to the protection of the law against such interference or attacks."

[5932] *See* "Convención Americana sobre Derechos Humanos. Pacto de San José de Costa Rica," available at <http://www.oas.org/juridico/spanish/firmas/b-32.html> (in Spanish).

Glossary

ABIN	*Agência Brasileira de Informações* (Brazilian Information Agency)
ABPD	Brazilian Association of Record Producers
ACA	Australian Communications Authority
ACT	Australian Capital Territory
ADA	Americans with Disabilities Act (United States)
AGC	Attorney-General's Chambers of Singapore
AMLC	Anti-Money Laundering Council (Philippines)
AMLO	Anti-Money Laundering Office (Thailand)
APADOR-CH	Association for the Defense of Human Rights in Romania – The Helsinki Committee (Romania)
APCAUCE	Asia Pacific Coalition Against Unsolicited Commercial E-mail
APD	*Agencia de Protección de Datos* (Data Protection Agency, Spain)
APEC	Asia-Pacific Economic Cooperation
API	Advance Passenger Information
APIS	Advanced Passenger Information System
APSIA	Public Sector Information Act (Slovenia)
ASEAN	Association of Southeast Asian Nations
ASIO	Australian Security Intelligence Organization (Australia)

ATCS	Anti-terrorism, Crime and Security Act 2001 (United Kingdom)
BDSG	*Bundesdatenschutzgesetz,* (Federal Data Protection Law, Germany)
BELPIC	Belgian Personal Identity Card
BfD	*Bundesbeauftragter für den Datenschutz* (Federal Data Protection Commissioner, Germany)
BND	Intelligence Service (Germany)
BPO	Business Process Outsourcing
BSA	Broadcasting Standards Authority (New Zealand)
BWIS	*Bundesgesetz über Massnahmen zur Wahrung der inneren Sicherheit* (Switzerland)
CADA	Commission for Access to Administrative Documents (Portugal)
CADA	*Commission d'accès aux documents administratifs* (Commission for Access to Administrative Documents, France)
CALEA	Communications Assistance for Law Enforcement Act (United States)
CAN-SPAM" Act	Controlling the Assault of Non-Solicited Pornography and Marketing Act of 2003 (United States)
CAPPS II	Computer Assisted Passenger Prescreening System (United States)
CBA	Credit Bureau Association (South Africa)

CBP	*College Bescherming Persoonsgegevens* (Data Protection Authority, Netherlands)
CBP	Department of Homeland Security's Bureau of Customs and Border Protection (United States)
CCA	Controller of Certifying Authorities (India)
CCA	Computer Crimes Act (Malaysia)
CCIC	Cyber Crime Investigation Cell (India)
CCRA	Canada Custom's and Revenue Agency
CCT	*Convention collective de travail* (Belgium)
CCTV	Closed Circuit Television
CEPIRS	*Centrales Privadas de Información de Riesgo* (credit reporting agencies in Peru)
CIA	Central Intelligence Agency (United States)
CMA	Communications and Multimedia Act (Malaysia)
CMA	Computer Misuse Act (Singapore)
CNCIS	*Commission nationale de contrôle des interceptions de sécurité* (National Commission for the Control of Security Interceptions, France)
CNDP	*Commission nationale pour la protection des données* (Data Protection Authority, Luxembourg)
CNIL	*Commission nationale de l'informatique et des libertés* (Data Protection Authority, France)
CNPD	*Comissão Nacional de Protecção de Dados* (National Data Protection Commission, Portugal).

CNPD	*Commission nationale pour la protection des données* (National Commission for the Protection of Data, Luxembourg)
CoE	Council of Europe
CONDUSEF	*Comisión Nacional para la Protección y Defensa de los Usuarios de Servicios Financieros* (National Commission for the Protection and Defense of Users of Financial Services, Mexico)
COSATU	Congress of South African Trade Unions
CPA	Consumer Protection Act (Slovenia)
CPNI	Customer Proprietary Network Information
CPR	Computerized Patient Record (France)
CRIA	Canadian Recording Industry Association
CRS	Computerized Reservation System
CSP	Communications Service Provider
CTAG	Counter-Terrorism Action Group
DARPA	Defense Advanced Research Projects Agency (United States)
DAS	Administrative Department of Security (Colombia)
DHS	Department of Homeland Security (United States)
DIB	*Datainspektionen* (Data Inspection Board, Sweden)
DNPDP	*Dirección Nacional de Protección de Datos Personales* (National Directorate for the Protection of Personal Data, Argentina)
DOD	Department of Defense (United States)

DOJ	Department of Justice (United States)
DOT	Department of Transportation (United States)
DPA	Data Protection Authority
DPB	Data Protection Board (Finland)
DPC	Data Protection Commissioner (Ireland)
DPI	Data Protection Inspectorate (Estonia)
DPO	Data Protection Ombudsman (Finland)
DRE	Direct Recording Electronic
DSA	Digital Signatures Act (South Korea)
DSG	*Datenschutzgesetz* (Austria)
DVLA	Driver and Vehicle Licensing Agency (United Kingdom)
DVR	*Datenverarbeitungsregister* (Austria)
EC	European Community
ECHR	European Convention for the Protection of Human Rights and Fundamental Freedoms
ECPA	Electronic Communications Privacy Act (United States)
ECTA	Electronic Communications and Transactions Act (South Africa)
ECtHR	European Court of Human Rights
EDSB	Federal Data Protection Commissioner (Switzerland)
EGAA	Electronic Government Activities Act (Malaysia)

EJPD	Departement of Justice and Police (Switzerland)
EKAM	Single Register Code Number (Greece)
ENUM	Electronic Numbering
EPIC	Electronic Privacy Information Center
EPID	*Einheitlicher Personenidentifikator* (unique ID number, Switzerland)
EPPA	Employee Polygraph Protection Act (United States)
ERP	Electronic Road Pricing (Singapore)
ETA	Electronic Transactions Act (Jordan, Singapore)
ETA	Electronic Transaction Act (Malaysia)
ETSI	European Telecommunication Standardization Institute
EU	European Union
EUROPOL	European Police Office
FAEC	Framework on Electronic Commerce (South Korea)
FATF	Financial Action Task Force
FBI	Federal Bureau of Investigation (United States)
FCC	Federal Communications Commission (United States)
FCRA	Fair Credit Reporting Act (United States)
FDA	Food and Drug Administration (United States)
Fedpol	Federal police (Switzerland)
FERPA	Family Educational Rights and Privacy Act of 1974 (United States)

FINEID	Finnish national ID card
FIPR	Foundation for Information Policy Research (United Kingdom)
FISA	Foreign Intelligence Surveillance Act (United States)
FISCR	Foreign Intelligence Surveillance Court of Review United States)
FLTAIPG	*Ley Federal de Transparencia y Acceso a la Información Pública Gubernamental* (Federal Law of Transparency and Access to Public Governmental Information, Mexico)
FNAEG	*Fichier national automatisé des empreintes génétiques* (National Computerized File of Genetic Data, France)
FOI	Freedom of Information
FOIA	Freedom of Information Act (United States)
FSB	Federal Security Service (Russia)
FTC	Federal Trade Commission (United States)
GAO	General Accounting Office (United States)
Garante	*Garante per la Protezione dei Dati Personali* (Supervisory Authority for Personal Data Protection, Italy)
GCHQ	Government Communications Headquarters (United Kingdom)
GCSB	Government Communications Security Bureau (United Kingdom)
GDS	Global Distribution System

GILC	Global Internet Liberty Campaign
GNP	Grand National Party (South Korea)
GNSO	Generic Names Supporting Organization
GPCL	General Principles of Criminal Law (China)
GPDel	*Geschäftsprüfungsdelegation* (Controlling Delegation of the Federal Parliament, Switzerland)
GPG	GNU Privacy Guard
gTLDs	generic Top Level Domains
GUID	Globally Unique Identifier
HMIS	Homeless Management Information Systems" (United States)
HRC	Human Rights Commission (South Africa)
HUD	Department of Housing and Urban Development (United States)
IATA	International Air Transportation Association
IC	Integrated circuit
ICAC	Independent Commission Against Corruption (Hong Kong)
ICANN	Internet Election for Assigned Names and Numbers
ICAO	International Civil Aviation Organization
ICCPR	International Covenant on Civil and Political Rights
ICESCR	International Covenant on Economic, Social and Cultural Rights

ICPs	Internet Content Providers
ICTs	Information and Communication Technologies
IDA	Info-Communications Development Authority (Singapore)
IDRBT	Institute of Development and Research in Banking Technology (India)
IETF	Internet Engineering Task Force
IFAI	Federal Institute of Access to Public Information (Mexico)
IFG	*Informationsfreiheitsgesetz* (Freedom of Information Act, Germany)
IFJ	International Federation of Journalists
ILETS	International Law Enforcement Telecommunications Seminar
ILO	International Labor Organization
IPRL	Internet Provider Responsibility Law of 2001 (Japan).
ISA	Internal Security Act (Malaysia)
ISO	International Standards Organization
ISP	Internet Service Provider
ITECC	Information Technology and E-Commerce Council
ITU	International Telecommunications Union
JIPDEC	Japan Information Processing Development Center
KGB	*Komitet gosudarstvennoi bezopasnosti* (Committee for State Security, Russia)

KISA	Korea Information Security Agency (South Korea)
LAD	Interior Ministry's Local Administration Department (Thailand)
LAN	Local Area Network
LDH	*Ligue des droits de l'homme* (Human Rights League, France)
LEN	*Loi pour la confiance dans l'économie numérique* (Digital Economy Law, France)
LFTAIPG	Federal Law of Transparency and Access to the Government Public Information (Mexico)
LGT	General Telecommunications Law (Spain)
LIPPI	Law on Information, Informatization and the Protection of Information (Russia)
LOPD	*Ley Orgánica de Protección de Datos* (Data Protection Act, Spain)
LORTAD	*Ley Orgánica de Regulación del Tratamiento Automatizado de los Datos de carácter personal* (Data Protection Act, Spain)
LPD	*Loi fédérale sur la protection des données* (Federal Act of Data Protection of 1992, Switzerland)
LPDUSF	*Ley de Protección y Defensa Al Usuario de Servicios Financieros* (Law for the Protection and Defense of the User of Financial Services, Mexico)
LPDP	Law for the Protection of Personal Data (Argentina)
LPPD	Law for the Protection of Personal Data

LPPDP	Law on the Protection of Personal Data Protection (Poland)
LPPLSI	*Loi sur la société de l'information* (Law on the Information Society, France)
LSI	*Law sur la société de l'information* (Law on the Information Society, France)
LSQ	*Loi sur la Sécurité Quotidienne* (Daily Safety Law, France)
LSSI	Law of Information Society Services and Electronic Commerce (Spain)
MAS	Monetary Authority of Singapore
MATRIX	Multistate Anti-TerRrorism Information exchange (United States)
MCOCA	Maharashtra Control of Organised Crime Act (India)
MDA	Media Development Authority (Singapore)
METI	Ministry of Economy, Trade and Industry (Japan)
MIA	Ministry of Internal Affairs (Ukraine)
MIB	Military Intelligence Bureau (Taiwan)
MIC	Ministry of Information and Communication (South Korea)
MITI	Ministry of International Trade and Industry (Japan)
MMS	Multimedia MeSsaging
MOGAHA	Ministry of Government Administration and Home Affairs (South Korea)

MOJ	Ministry of Justice (Japan)
MPT	Ministry of Posts and Telecommunications (Japan)
MRTDs	Machine-Readable Travel Documents
MSZP	*Magyar Szocialista Párt* (Hungarian Socialist Party, Hungary)
MTS	Mobile Telesystems (Russia)
NAASCOM	National Association of Software and Service Companies (India)
NASA	National Aeronautics and Space Administration (United States)
NATO	North Atlantic Treaty Organization
NCIC	National Crime Information Center (United States)
NCNA	New China News Agency (Hong Kong)
NEIS	National Education Information System (South Korea)
NGO	Non-Governmental Organization
NHRC	National Human Rights Commission (South Korea)
NIA	National Intelligence Agency (South Africa, Thailand)
NIS	National Intelligence Service (South Korea)
NITC	National Information Technology Committee (Thailand)
NITDA	National Information Technology Development Agency (Nigeria)
NPPs	National Privacy Principles (Australia)

NRCC	National Regulatory Commission for Communication (Ukraine)
NSA	National Security Agency (United States)
NSEERS	National Security Entry-Exit Registration System (United States)
NSO	National SIGINT Organization (Netherlands)
NSP	National Security Police (Estonia)
NSS	National Security Service (Bulgaria, Hungary)
NSW	New South Wales
NZSIS	New Zealand Security Intelligence Service
OCC	Office of the Information Commissioner (Canada)
OECD	Organization for Economic Cooperation and Development
OIA	Operational Investigative Act (Ukraine)
OIC	Official Information Commission (Thailand)
OMB	Office of Management and Budget (United States)
ONS	Object Name Service
OPTA	*Onafhankelijke Post en Telecommunicatie Autoriteit* (Independent Post and Telecommunications Authority, Netherlands)
OSCE	Organization for Security and Cooperation in Europe
PAIA	Promotion of Access to Information Act (South Africa)
PASOK	Panhellenic Socialist Movement (Greece)

PCO	Privacy Commissioner's Office (Hong Kong)
PDA	Personal Data Act (Norway, Sweden)
PDPA	Personal Data Protection Act (Bulgaria, Estonia, Finland, Netherlands, Slovenia)
PESEL	Electronic Census System (Poland)
PET	Privacy Enhancing Technology
PGP	Pretty Good Privacy
PIA	Privacy Impact Assessment
PIN	Personal Identification Number
PIPEDA	Personal Information and Electronic Documents Act (Canada)
PISA	Privacy Incorporated Software Agents
PISCES	Personal Identification Security Comparison System (Philippines)
PKI	Public Key Infrastructures
PNR	Passenger Name Record
POT	Norwegian Security Police
POTA	Prevention of Terrorism Act (India)
PPSN	Personal Public Service Number (Ireland)
PRC	People's Republic of China
PRODAT	*Agencia para la Protección de Datos Personales* (Agency for the Protection of Personal Data, Costa Rica)
PSB	The Public Service Broker (Ireland)

PSC	Public Services Card (Ireland)
PUL	*Swedish Personuppgiftslag* (Personal Data Act, Sweden)
RCMP	Royal Canadian Mounted Police
RBI	Royal Bank of India
RFID	Radio Frequency Identification
RIPA	Regulation of Investigatory Powers Act 2000 (United Kingdom)
RRNS	Resident Registry Network System (Japan)
SAHA	South African History Archive
SAR	Special Administrative Region" (Hong Kong)
SARS	Severe Acute Respiratory Syndrome
SBA	Singapore Broadcasting Authority
SBB	Swiss Federal Railway company
SBU	National Security Service (Ukraine)
SDF	Self Defense Forces (Japan)
SDV	National Security Service (Slovenia)
SEVIS	Student and Exchange Visitor Information System (United States)
SFV	*Schweiz. Fussballverband SFV* (Swiss Football Association SFV)
SID	Special Investigation Division (Thailand)
SIGINT	Signals Intelligence

SII	Integrated Informational System (Romania)
SIM	Subscriber Identity Module
SIN	*Servicio de Inteligencia Nacional* (National Intelligence Service, Peru)
SIS	Schengen Information System
SIS	Security Intelligence Service (New Zealand)
SISAA	Slovenian Intelligence and Security Agency Act
SISPA	Slovenian ISP Association
SND	*Strategischer Nachrichtendienst* (Strategic Intelligence Agency, Switzerland)
SORM	System of Operative Investigative Activities (Russia)
SOVA	Slovenian Intelligence and Security Agency
SPPO	Supreme Public Prosecutor's Office (South Korea)
SSU	Secret Service Unit (Ukraine)
StB	Czech Secret Police
STS	*Le Service des Tâches Spéciales*, Agency of Special Services (Switzerland)
TACD	Trans Atlantic Consumer Dialogue
TADA	Terrorists And Disruptive Activities (Prevention) Act (India)
TAS	Telecommunications Authority of Singapore
TEL	Telecommunications Working Group

TFN	Tax File Number
TIA	Total Information Awareness (United States)
TOT	Telephone Organization of Thailand
TRIPs	Trade-Related Aspects of Intellectual Property Rights
TSA	Transportation Security Administration (United States)
TSPs	Telecommunication Service Providers
TWIC	Transportation Worker Identification Credential (United States)
UCE	Unsolicited Commercial E-mail
UK	United Kingdom
UN	United Nations
UNCITRAL	United Nations Commission on International Trade Law
UNESCO	United Nations Education, Scientific, and Cultural Organization
US-VISIT	United States Visitor and Immigrant Status Indicator Technology (United States)
WP29	Article 29 Working Group (European Commission)
WSIS	World Summit on the Information Society

International Privacy Resources

Argentina

Argentinean Data Protection Commissioner
<http://www.jus.gov.ar/minjus/DPDP/docs/English%20version.ppt>.

Argentinean Law Library
<http://www.jus.gov.ar/minjus/links.html>

Habeas Data (Weblog)
<http://dataprotection.blogspot.com/>

Janet Koven Levit, The Constitutionalization of Human Rights in Argentina: Problem or Promise?, 37 Columbia Journal of Transnational Law 281 (1999)

Privacy and Data Protection in Argentina (NGO) available
<http://www.protecciondedatos.com.ar/english.htm>

Australia

Australian Privacy Commissioner
<http://www.privacy.gov.au/>

Australian Privacy Foundation (NGO)
<http://www.privacy.org.au/>

Electronic Frontiers Australia, Online Privacy Issues (NGO)
<http://www.efa.org.au/Issues/Privacy/privacy.html>

Gordon L. Hughes and Margaret Jackson, Hughes on Data Protection in Australia, (The Law Book Co. 2001).

Matthew Kohel, The Privacy Amendment (Private Sector) Bill 2000: The Australian Government's Substandard Attempt To Allay Privacy Concerns And Regulate Internet Privacy In The Private Sector, 27 Brooklyn J. Int'l L. 703 (2002).

Olujoke Akindemowo, *Information Technology Law in Australia*, (LBC Information Services 1999).

Privacy Law and Policy Reporter (NGO)
<http://www.austlii.edu.au/au/journals/PLPR/>

Roger Clarke's Data Surveillance (resource site)
<http://www.anu.edu.au/people/Roger.Clarke/>

Australian IT (online portal)
<http://australianit.news.com.au/>

Austria

Austrian Association for Internet Users (NGO)
<http://www.vibe.at/index_en.html>

Austrian Data Protection Commission
<http://www.dsk.gv.at/indexe.htm>

Austrian Society for Privacy and Data Protection (NGO)
<http://www.argedaten.at/news/news2004.html> (in German)

Kronegger (online privacy resource)
<http://www.kronegger.at/>

Belgium

Association Electronique Libre (NGO)
<http://www.ael.be/>

Commission de la Protection de la vie Privée
<http://www.privacy.fgov.be/> (in French and Dutch)

Droit-Technologie (online portal of legal information: news, legislation, case law, law review articles and theses)
<http://www.droit-technologie.org/>

Research Center for Computer and Law (Centre de Recherche Informatique et Droit)
<http://www.droit.fundp.ac.be/crid/default.en.htm>

Brazil

Andres Guadamuz, Habeas Data: The Latin-American Response to Data Protection
<http://elj.warwick.ac.uk/jilt/00-2/guadamuz.html#fn29>

Brazilian Center of Internet Legal Studies (CBEJI)
<http://www.cbeji.com.br/br/us/index.asp>

Brazilian Information Agency
<http://www.abin.gov.br/abin>

Dorene R. Seidman, Transborder Data Flow: Regulation of the International Information Flow and the Brazilian Example, 1 J.L. & Tech 31 (Spring 1986)

e-Camara, (Brazilian legislature)
<http://www.camara.gov.br/internet/ecamara/> (in Portuguese)

Infocore, Latin America Data Protection Update (industry source)
<http://www.infocoreinc.com/latinamdata.html>

Infolegis (translated Brazilian laws)
<http://www.infolegis.com.br/sumarioing.htm>

Instituto Brasileiro de Peritos em Comércio Eletrônico e Telemática (NGO)
<http://www.ibpbrasil.com.br/news/ileg.htm> (in Portuguese)

Portal Interlegis
<http://www.interlegis.gov.br/processo_legislativo> (in Portuguese)

Renata A. Guidry, The Need for Mercosul Harmonization: Brazil's Consumer Protection Law as the Focal Point, 24 Loy. L.A. Int'l & Comp. L. Rev. 361 (June 2002)

U.S. State Department, Brazil: Country Reports on human Rights
Practices 2003
<http://www.state.gov/g/drl/rls/hrrpt/2003/27888.htm>

Bulgaria

Access to Information Programme (NGO)
<http://www.aip-bg.org/index_eng.htm>

Bulgarian Commission for Personal Data Protection
<http://www.ceecprivacy.org/main.php?s=2&k=bulgaria>

Internet Rights Bulgaria Foundation (NGO)
<http://www.socialrights.org/spip/rubrique1.html>

Canada

Access and Privacy Laws Commissions (government portal)
<http://canada.justice.gc.ca/en/ps/atip/provte.html>

Canadian Internet Policy and Public Interest Clinic
<http://www.cippic.ca/>

Industry Canada—Electronic Commerce Branch (industry source)
<http://e-com.ic.gc.ca/epic/internet/inecic-ceac.nsf/en/home>

Information Commissioner of Canada
<http://www.infocom.gc.ca/>

Lex Informatica (online portal of legal information)
<http://www.lexinformatica.org/>

Privacy Commissioner of Canada
<http://www.privcom.gc.ca>

PrivacyInfo.ca (privacy news, information legislation and decisions)
<http://www.privacyinfo.ca/>

Stephanie Perrin *et al.*, The Personal Information Protection and
Electronic Documents Act: An Annotated Guide (Toronto, 2001).

University of Ottawa Law and Technology Journal
<http://www.commonlaw.uottawa.ca/tech/html/lawjournal.html>

Chile

Consumers International - *Oficina para América Latina y el Caribe*
<http://www.consumidoresint.cl/welcome.asp>

Consumer Organization and Users from Chile (ODECU) (NGO)
<http://www.odecu.cl/detalle.php?tipo=quienes&grupo=73&PHPSESSI
D=3f85bc54a9583e2a0567b34df00fdbb1>

Servicio Nacional de Consumidor (government portal)
<http://www.sernac.cl/> (in Spanish)

Sobre Proteccion De La Vida Privada (Santiago Chamber of Commerce)
<http://www.camaracomercio.cl/html/quienes/privada.htm> (in Spanish)

China

China Information Technology and Law Center (NGO)
<http://www.chinaitlaw.org.hk/index.html>

Colombia

US State Department, Colombia: Country Reports on Human Rights
Practices 2003
<http://www.state.gov/g/drl/rls/hrrpt/2003/27891.htm>

Costa Rica

US State Department, Costa Rica: Country Reports on Human Rights
Practices 2003
<http://www.state.gov/g/drl/rls/hrrpt/2003/27892.htm>

Czech Republic

Charter of Fundamental Rights and Freedoms, 1993
<http://www.psp.cz/cgi-bin/eng/docs/laws/charter.html>

Commission of the European Communities 2003 Regular Report on
Czech Republic's Progress Towards Accession
<http://europa.eu.int/comm/enlargement/report_2003/index.htm>

Commission of the European Communities 2003 Comprehensive
Monitoring Report on the Czech Republic's preparations for membership
<http://europa.eu.int/comm/enlargement/report2003/pdf/summary_paper
2003_full_en.pdf>

Czech News Agency (CTK)
<http://www.ctk.cz/english/index.html>

EU Data Protection Homepage
<http://europa.eu.int/comm/internal_market/privacy/index_en.htm>

Office for Personal Data Protection
<http://www.uoou.cz/>

Prague Post
<http://www.praguepost.cz/>

US State Department Country Reports on Human Rights Practices
<http://www.state.gov/g/drl/rls/hrrpt/>

Denmark

Danish Data Protection Agency
<http://www.datatilsynet.dk/eng/index.html>

Lee E. Bygrave, Data Protection Reform in Scandinavia
<http://folk.uio.no/lee/oldpage/articles/Scandinavia_reform.pdf>

Estonia

Estonian Informatics Centre
<http://www.ria.ee/atp/eng/index.html?id=712>

Estonian National ID Cards
<http://www.id.ee/pages.php/0303>

European Forum Country Update
<http://www.europeanforum.bot-consult.se/cup/estonia/index.htm>

Finland

Data Protection in Working Life, Ministry of Labour, Finland (October 2001)
<http://www.mol.fi/english/working/dataprotection.html>

Electronic Frontier Finland (NGO)
<http://www.effi.org/index.en.html?tmplang=en>

FINLEX (English translations of Finnish acts)
<http://www.finlex.fi/english/laws/index.php>

Finland Legislative Assembly
<http://www.lagtinget.aland.fi/eng/index.htm>

Jorma Kuopus, Data Protection Regulatory System - Data Transmission and Privacy (D. Campbell & J. Fisher, eds., Martinus Nijhoff Publishers 1994).

Peter Blume *et al.*, Nordic Data Protection (DJOF Publishing 2000).

Privacy International, Privacy, Technology, and Europe: A report for Japan's Ministry of Public Management, Home Affairs, Postal, and Telecommunication (March 2003)
<http://is.lse.ac.uk/staff/hosein/pets/japan_pets.pdf>.

France

Juriscom.net (online portal of legal news)
<http://www.juriscom.net>

Legalis.net (online portal of legal news)
<http://www.legalis.net/>

Germany

Brandenburg State Commissioner for Data Protection and Access to
Information
<http://www.lda.brandenburg.de/sixcms/detail.php?template=start_e_lda
&id=97044>

Federal Data Protection Commissioner
<http://www.bfd.bund.de/>

German American Law Journal
http://www.recht.us/amlaw/

Lovells, Data Protection in Germany (2003) (business law firm client
note)
<http://www.lovells.com/germany/ControlServlet/de/publication/pubId/8
45/>

Privireal (online information resource)
<http://www.privireal.org/countries/germany.htm>

Virtual Privacy Office (online portal)
<http://www.datenschutz.de/privo/> (primarily in German)

Greece

Greek Data Protection Act—overview
http://europa.eu.int/ISPO/legal/en/news/9709/chapter6.html>

Hellenic Data Protection Authority
<http://www.dpa.gr/home_eng.htm>

Human Rights Watch, World Report 2002 (New York 2001).

Guatemala

US State Department, Guatemala: Country Reports on Human Rights
Practices 2003
<http://www.state.gov/g/drl/rls/hrrpt/2003/27900.htm>

Hong Kong

Privacy for Personal Data in Hong Kong (industry source)
<http://www.privacy.com.hk/>

Privacy Commissioner for Personal Data
<http://www.pco.org.hk/>

Y.H. Lee, Seminar on Data Protection Technologies for National
Statistical Offices, Country Paper: Hong Kong, China
<http://www.unescap.org/stat/meet/dataprot/dpro-hongkong.asp>

Hungary

Dániel Máté Szabó, Data Protection in Hungary, Hungarian Civil
Liberties Union (Budapest 2003)

Data Protection and Freedom of Information Commissioner
<http://abiweb.obh.hu/dpc/index.htm>

Hungarian Civil Liberties Union (NGO)
<http://www.c3.hu/~hclu/indexuk.htm>

Parliamentary Commissioner's Office of Hungary
<http://www.obh.hu/>

Privireal (online information resource)
<http://www.privireal.org/countries/hungary.htm>

Iceland

Office of Personal Data Protection
<http://www.personuvernd.is/tolvunefnd.nsf/pages/english>

India

Cyberlaw India (online portal)
<http://cyberlaws.net/cyberindia/index1.htm>

Inomy (Indian internet economy news and information)
<http://www.inomy.com/>

Pavan Duggal, Inadequate Data Protection Laws, The Economic Times (March 20, 2004)
http://www1.economictimes.indiatimes.com/articleshow/572297.cms

Ireland

Robert Clark, "Data Protection in Ireland," The Journal of Information, Law and Technology (January 31, 1996)
<http://elj.warwick.ac.uk/jilt/dp/1eire/default.htm>

Data Protection Commissioner
<http://www.dataprivacy.ie/>

Irish Internet Association (industry organization)
<http://www.iia.ie/>

Privireal (online information resource)
<http://www.privireal.org/countries/ireland.htm>

Israel

Boaz Guttman, "The Analyzer: Following the State's Appeal," May 6, 2002, available at <http://www.4law.co.il/206.pdf>

David Banisar, "Israel", Freedom of Information and Access to Government Records Around the World 20, July 2002.

Debbie L. Rabina, Access to Government Information in Israel: Stages in the Continuing Development of a National Information Policy, International Federation of Library Associations and Institutions (August 13, 2000).

Miguel Deutch, Computer Legislation: Israel's New Codified Approach, 14 J. Marshall J. Computer & Info. L. 461 (Spring 1996).

Nahum Bitterman, "The Extent of the Obligation of Secrecy," Israeli Business Law: An Essential Guide, Kluwer Law International, 1996.

Italy

Garante per la Protezione Dei Dati Personali (Data Protection Commissioner)
<http://www.garanteprivacy.it> (in Italian)

Italy's New Data Protection Code, Garante per la Protezione Dei Dati Personali (2004)
<http://www.garanteprivacy.it/garante/doc.jsp?ID=1030925>

eGovernment News – Italy
<http://www.garanteprivacy.it/garante/document?ID=311066>

Electronic Frontiers Italy (NGO)
<http://www.alcei.it/english/default.html>

Privacy.it
<http://www.privacy.it/> (in Italian)

Japan

Big Brother Japan
<http://bigbrotherjapan.info/vote/index.php> (in Japanese)

NaST, Electronic Networks and Privacy
<http://www.jca.apc.org/privacy/> (in Japanese)

Jordan

> US Dept. of State Country Reports on Human Rights Practices
> <http://www.state.gov/g/drl/rls/hrrpt/2003/27930.htm>

Latvia

> CEEC: Data Protection in the Republic of Latvia
> <http://www.ceecprivacy.org/main.php?s=2&k=latvia>
>
> Data State Inspection (Latvian state authority)
> <http://www.dvi.gov.lv/eng/>
>
> Latvian Data Protection Law
> <http://www.privacyexchange.org/legal/nat/omni/latvialaw.html>
>
> Privireal (online information resource)
> http://www.privireal.org/countries/latvia.htm

Lithuania

> CEEC – Lithuania Data Protection Authority
> <http://www.ceecprivacy.org/main.php?s=2&k=lithuania>
>
> Privireal (online information resource)
> <http://www.privireal.org/countries/lithuania.htm>
>
> State Data Protection Inspectorate
> <http://www.ada.lt/en/>
>
> United Nations Economic and Social Council, "Statistical Confidentiality
> and Micro Data," (May 30, 2003)
> <http://www.unece.org/stats/documents/ces/2003/37.e.pdf>

Luxembourg

> Privireal (online information resource)
> <http://www.privireal.org/countries/luxembourg.htm>

Malaysia

US Department of State, Country Reports on Human Rights Practices, Malaysia (2003) <http://www.state.gov/g/drl/rls/hrrpt/2003/27778.htm>.

Malta

Chetcuti Cauchi Advocates (law firm data protection unit) <http://www.cc-advocates.com/data-protection/unit.htm>

Commissioner of Data Protection <http://www.dataprotection.gov.mt/page.asp?p=1374&l=1>

Privireal (online information resource) <http://www.privireal.org/countries/malta.htm>

Mexico

Antonio M. Aveleyra, Communication of Personal Data Messages in Mexico <http://www.thepublicvoice.org/events/buenosaires04/aveleyra-040804.html>

Atlatl (NGO) <http://www.atlatl.com.mx/> (in Spanish)

FIDAC (NGO) <http://www.fidac.org.mx/>

Liberdad de Información (LIMAC) (NGO) <http://www.limac.org.mx/index.php?theme=home>

Tallia Nauman, Mexico's Right-to-Know Movement, Citizen Action in the Americas, No. 4 (February 2003) <http://www.americaspolicy.org/pdf/series/04.rtk.pdf>

Netherlands

Bits of Freedom (NGO)

<http://www.bof.nl/index_uk.html>

Dutch Data Protection Authority
<http://www.cbpweb.nl/en/>

Personal Data Protection Act
<http://home.planet.nl/~privacy1/wbp_en_rev.htm>

The Privacy Page – Dutch Privacy (Related) Law
<http://home.pianet.nl/~privacy1/>

Privacy.pagina.nl (online portal)
<http://privacy.pagina.nl/>

Privireal (online information source)
<http://www.privireal.org/countries/netherlands.htm>

New Zealand

Compilation of the codes of practices issued by Privacy Commissioner,
<http://www.privacy.org.nz/comply/codes.html>

New Zealand Privacy Commissioner
<http://www.privacy.org.nz>

Nigeria

Gamji News
<www.gamji.com>

International Center for Nigerian Law
<http://www.nigeria-law.org/>

Internews Network—Nigeria Nexus (NGO)
<http://www.internews.org/nigeria>

Nigerian Media Rights Agenda (NGO)
<http://www.internews.org/mra/campaigns/campaigns.htm>

Nigerian National Information Technology Development Agency

<http://www.nitda.gov.ng>

US Dept. of State, Country reports on Human Rights Practices, Nigeria (2003) <http://www.state.gov/g/drl/rls/hrrpt/2003/27743.htm

Norway

Fortress Europe Circular Letter (civil liberties and data protection news) <http://www.fecl.org/circular/4305.htm>

Jon Bing, Data Protection in Norway (1996) <http://www.jus.uio.no/iri/forskning/lib/papers/dp_norway/dp_norway.html>

IHF - Human Rights in the OSCE Region: Europe, Central Asia and North America 2003 <http://www.ihf-hr.org/viewbinary/viewdocument.php?doc_id=2261>

Lee A. Bygrave, The body as data? Reflection on the relationship of data privacy law with the human body, (September 2003) <http://www.privacy.vic.gov.au/dir100/priweb.nsf/download/CF51D885BA101AACCA256E050012CBA5/$FILE/Bygrave%20paper.pdf>

Lee A. Bygrave, Data Protection Law: Approaching Its Rationale, Logic and Limits 48 (The Hague: Kluwer Law International, 2002).

Lee A. Bygrave & Ann Helen Aaro, Norway, International Privacy, Publicity and Personality Laws 333 (M. Henry ed., 2001).

Norwegian Data Inspectorate <http://www.datatilsynet.no/>

Per-Kaare Svendsen, The Association for Progressive Communications (APC) European Internet Rights Project, Country Report: Norway (2000) <http://www.apc.org/english/rights/europe/c_rpt/norway.html>

Peru

Andres Guadamuz, Habeas Data: The Latin American Response to Data Protection, The Journal of Information, Law and Technology (June 30, 2000) available at
<http://elj.warwick.ac.uk/jilt/002/guadamuz.html#3.2.3>

Archivo Digital de la Legislación del Perú
<http://www.congreso.gob.pe/ntley/default.asp> (in Spanish)

Habeas Data (data protection weblog)
<http://dataprotection.blogspot.com/>

Privaterra (NGO)
<http://cms.privaterra.org/>

Philippines

Chan Robles Virtual Law Library
<http://www.chanrobles.com/toc.htm>

Christopher Lim, Baker & McKenzie Philippine E-Com Legal Guide (January 2001)
<http://www.bakerinfo.com/apec/philapec_main.htm>

Philippine IT News
<http://itmatters.com.ph/news/>

US Dept. of State Country Report- 2003 Philippines
<http://www.state.gov/g/drl/rls/hrrpt/2003/27786.htm>

Poland

CEEC - Poland Data Protection Authority
<http://www.ceecprivacy.org/main.php?s=2&k=poland>

Inspector General for the Protection of Personal Data
<http://www.giodo.gov.pl/138/j/en/>

Privacy Protection in Data Communication Systems (government produced guide)
<http://techinfo.giodo.gov.pl/index-en.html>

Romania

Association for the Defence of Human Rights in Romania (NGO)
<http://www.apador.org/indexe.htm>

Romanian People's Advocate Institution Ombudsman
<http://www.avp.ro/indexen.html>

Russia

Electronic Commerce in Russia, Clifford Chance Puender
<http://www.russianlaw.net/english/ae04.htm>

Law of the Russian Federation on Information, Informatisation and Information Protection
<http://www.datenschutz-berlin.de/gesetze/internat/fen.htm>

Personal Data Protection in Russia, Gowlings (September 20, 2001)
<http://www.gowlings.com/resources/publications.asp?Pubid=712>

Victor Naumov, Legal Issues in Personal Data Protection on the Russian Internet (February 4, 2004)
<http://www.russianlaw.net/english/ae04.htm>

San Marino

US State Department, San Marino: Country Reports on human Rights Practices 2003
<http://www.state.gov/g/drl/rls/hrrpt/2003/27862.htm>

Singapore

Infocomm Development Authority of Singapore (IDA)
<http://www.ida.gov.sg/idaweb/marketing/index.jsp>

Electronic Engineering Times (industry source)
<http://www.eetasia.com/>

Slovakia

CEEC Privacy (collection of European government data protection information)
<http://www.ceecprivacy.org/main.php?s=2&k=slovakia>

Privireal (online information resource)
<http://www.privireal.org/countries/slovakia.htm>

Slovakian Office for Personal Data Protection
<http://www.dataprotection.gov.sk/buxus/generate_page.php3?page_id=413>

Slovenia

Privireal (online information resource)
<http://www.privireal.org/countries/slovenia.htm>

Slovenian Human Rights Ombudsman
<http://www.varuh-rs.si/cgi/teksti-eng.cgi/Index?vsebina=/cgi/teksti-eng.cgi%3Fpozdrav>

Slovenian Inspectorate for Personal Data Protection
<http://www.gov.si/mp/?vie=content&gr1=OrgVSet&gr2=InPeDaP&gr3=&id=2004030909580277&lang=eng>

South Korea

Korean Information Security Agency
<http://www.kisa.or.kr/english/>

Sri Lanka

Information and Communication Technology Agency of Sri Lanka
<http://www.icta.lk>

e-Sri Lanka (NGO)
<http://www.esrilanka.lk>

Computer Society of Sri Lanka (NGO)
<http://www.cssl.lk>

International Information Technology Conference (NGO)
<http://www.iitc.lk>

Jayawardena K P, Where does the right to privacy end?, Sunday Times (July 18, 2004)

Mahanamahewa P, Internet, e-business and privacy concerns, Sunday Times, (July 20, 2003)

Sweden

Matthias Klang, Country Report—Sweden, APC European Internet Rights Project
<http://europe.rights.apc.org/c_rpt/sweden.html>

Sabin Marcellin, Data Protection in Sweden: review of DAPRO 6.3, NECTAR (February 2, 2000)
<http://www.ejeisa.com/nectar/update/stories/2000020202.htm>

Summary of the New Personal Data Protection Act for Sweden, Privacy Exchange (May 30, 2001)
<http://www.privacyexchange.org/legal/nat/omni/swedensum.html>

Swedish Data Inspection Board
<http://www.datainspektionen.se/in_english/start.shtml>

Switzerland

Association of Cantonal Data Protection Commissioners
<http://www.dsb-cpd.ch> (in German and French)

Data Protection Commissioner of the Canton of Zurich
<http://www.datenschutz.ch>

Directory of compiled Federal laws and regulations (decrees)
<http://www.admin.ch/ch/d/sr/sr.html> (in German, French and Italian)

Directory of decisions of the Swiss Federal Court (*Bundesgericht*)
<http://www.polyreg.ch/##>

Federal Data Protection Commissioner (EDSB)
<http://www.edsb.ch/>

Swiss "Big Brother Awards"
<http://www.bigbrotherawards.ch>

Swiss Federal Government and Administration
<http://www.admin.ch>

Taiwan

Tyeng-Ruey Chuang, Personal Data Protection in Taiwan: Whose Business?
<http://www.iis.sinica.edu.tw/~trc/npq2003.pdf>

Thailand

Office of the Official Information Commission
<http://www.oic.thaigov.go.th/eng/engmain.asp>

Personal Data Protection Law, ICT Laws Project
<http://www.ictlaw.thaigov.net/dp/> (in Thai)

Pravith Mangklatanakul, Baker & McKenzie Philippine E-Com Legal Guide (January 2001) available at
<http://www.bakerinfo.com/apec/thaiapec.htm>

Thailand: Laws and Regulations, Economist Intelligence Unit Business Forum (August 2, 2001) available at
<http://www.ebusinessforum.com/index.asp?layout=rich_story&channelid=6&categoryid=24&doc_id=4165>

Turkey

>Information Society Policy in Turkey
><http://www.policy.hu/akdeniz/>

>Publications of Dr. Yaman Akdeniz
><http://www.cyber-rights.org/yamancv.htm>

Ukraine

>Human Rights in Ukraine (NGO)
><http://www.khpg.org/index.php?r=25>

United Kingdom

>Cyber Rights and Cyber Liberties (NGO)
><http://www.cyber-rights.org/>

>Campaign for Freedom of Information (NGO)
><http://www.cfoi.org.uk/>

>Foundation for Information Policy (NGO)
><http://www.fipr.org/>

>Information Commissioner
><http://www.informationcommissioner.gov.uk/>

>Privacy International (NGO)
><http://www.privacyinternational.org>

>Privacy Laws and Business (NGO)
><http://www.privacylaws.co.uk/>

>Statewatch (NGO)
><http://www.poptel.org.uk/statewatch/>

United States

American Civil Liberties Union (NGO)
<http://www.aclu.org/>

Electronic Privacy Information Center (NGO)
<http://www.epic.org>

Federal Trade Commission Privacy Initiatives
<http://www.ftc.gov/privacy/>

Privacy Journal
<http://www.privacyjournal.net/>

Privacy Rights Clearinghouse (NGO)
<http://www.privacyrights.org/>

Privacy Times
<www.privacytimes.com>

Uruguay

Habeas Data (Weblog)
Habeas Data (Weblog)
<http://dataprotection.blogspot.com/>

US State Department, Country Reports on Human Rights Practices, Uruguay (2003), available at
<http://www.state.gov/g/drl/rls/hrrpt/2003/27922.htm>